connect

McGraw-Hill Connect ™ is a web-based assignment and assessment platform that gives students the means to better connect with their coursework, with their instructors and with the important concepts they will need to know for success now and in the future. With Connect, instructors can deliver assignments, quizzes and tests easily online. Students can practise important skills at their own pace and on their own schedule. With Connect, students also get 24/7 online access to an eBook—an online edition of the text—to aid them in successfully completing their work, wherever and whenever they choose. Now students can access LearnSmart and SmartBook for many McGraw-Hill Products through Connect.

LEARNSMART®

No two students are alike. Why should their learning paths be? LearnSmart uses revolutionary adaptive technology to build a learning experience unique to each student's individual needs. It starts by identifying the topics a student knows and does not know. As the student progresses, LearnSmart adapts and adjusts the content based on his or her individual strengths, weaknesses and confidence, ensuring that every minute spent studying with LearnSmart is the most efficient and productive study time possible.

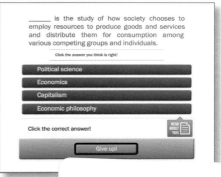

SMARTBOOK™

As the first and only adaptive reading experience, SmartBook is changing the way students read and learn. SmartBook creates a personalized reading experience by highlighting the most important concepts a student needs to learn at that moment in time. As a student engages with SmartBook, the reading experience continuously adapts by highlighting content based on what each student knows and doesn't know. This ensures that he or she is focused on the content needed to close specific knowledge gaps, while it simultaneously promotes long-term learning.

SOCIOLOGY'S GLOBAL VIEW

Sociology: A Brief Introduction explores key sociological issues from the viewpoints of many global cultures. This map serves as a quick guide to a *sample* of passages related to globalization topics.

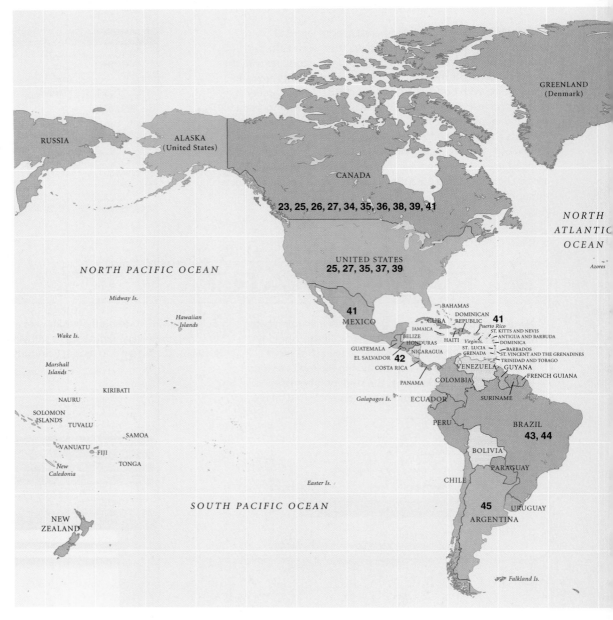

Africa
1. Population structure (Kenya) p. 325
2. Strategies to eradicate poverty (sub-Saharan Africa) p. 132
3. AIDS crisis p. 343
4. Infant mortality (Sierra Leone) p. 330
5. Rites of passage (Congo) p. 79
6. Women in politics (South Africa, Uganda) p. 306

Asia / Oceania
7. Media impact (Bhutan) p. 218
8. Ratio of males to females (China) p. 324

9. Respect for elders (South Korea) p. 79
10. Oligarchy (China) p. 303
11. Capitalism (China) p. 298
12. Working Women (Nepal) p. 302
13. Media censorship (China) p. 207
14. Population policy (China) p. 324
15. Nike and Reebok factories in Indonesia p. 144/145

Central Asia
16. Western media in India p. 77
17. Collapse of communism (U.S.S.R.) p. 297
18. Effects of globalization (India) p. 166

19. Population growth (India) p. 232
20. Microfinancing (India) p. 313
21. Norm violation (India) p. 53
22. Physicians from developing countries (Pakistan/India) p. 330

Europe
23. Childcare policy (Western Europe, Canada) p. 84
24. Prisons (Finland) p. 226
25. Cutbacks in social services (Europe/U.S./Canada) p. 33
26. Cohabitation (Europe/Canada) p. 262
27. Recognition of same-sex partnerships (Europe/U.S./Canada) p. 263

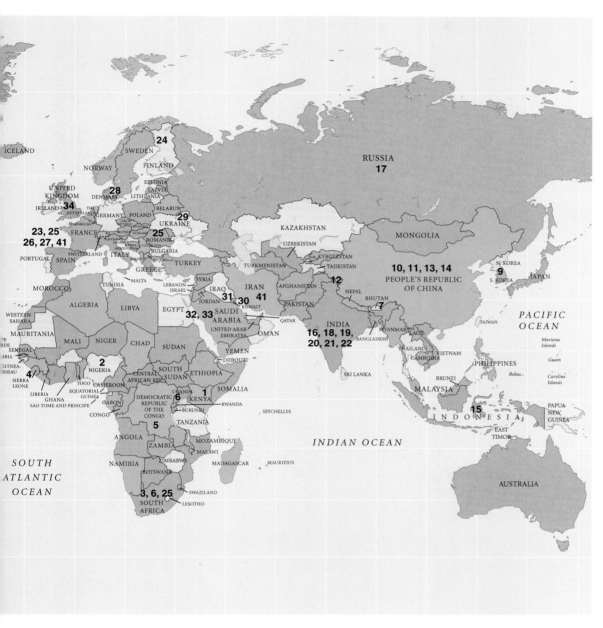

FIFTH
CANADIAN
EDITION

Sociology
A BRIEF INTRODUCTION

Richard T. Schaefer

DePaul University

Bonnie Haaland

Kwantlen Polytechnic University

McGraw-Hill
Ryerson

McGraw-Hill
Ryerson

Sociology: A Brief Introduction
Fifth Canadian Edition

Copyright © 2014, 2011, 2009, 2006, 2001 by McGraw-Hill Ryerson Limited, a Subsidiary of The McGraw-Hill Companies. All rights reserved. No part of this publication may be reproduced or transmitted in any form or by any means, or stored in a data base or retrieval system, without the prior written permission of McGraw-Hill Ryerson Limited, or in the case of photocopying or other reprographic copying, a licence from The Canadian Copyright Licencing Agency (Access Copyright). For an Access Copyright licence, visit www.accesscopyright.ca or call toll free to 1-800-893-5777.

The Internet addresses listed in the text were accurate at the time of publication. The inclusion of a Web site does not indicate an endorsement by the authors or McGraw-Hill Ryerson, and McGraw-Hill Ryerson does not guarantee the accuracy of the information presented at these sites.

ISBN-13: 978-0-07-089105-0
ISBN-10: 0-07-089105-2

1 2 3 4 5 6 7 8 9 TCP 1 9 8 7 6 5 4

Printed and bound in Canada

Care has been taken to trace ownership of copyright material contained in this text; however, the publisher will welcome any information that enables them to rectify any reference or credit for subsequent editions.

Director of Product Management: *Rhondda McNabb*
Senior Product Manager: *Marcia Siekowski*
Marketing Manager: *Stacey Metz*
Product Developer: *Daphne Scriabin*
Senior Product Team Associates: *Stephanie Giles/Marina Seguin*
Photo/Permission Research: *Alison Lloyd Baker*
Supervising Editor: *Graeme Powell*
Copy Editor: *Erin Moore*
Proofreader: *Ashley Rayner*
Production Coordinator: *Tammy Mavroudi*
Cover and Interior Designer: *Dave Murphy, Valid Design*
Cover Image: *Watchtheworld/Shutterstock (RF)*
Page Layout: *Laserwords Private Limited*
Printer: *Transcontinental Printing Group*

Library and Archives Canada Cataloguing in Publication

Schaefer, Richard T. author
    Sociology : a brief introduction / Richard T. Schaefer, DePaul University,
Bonnie Haaland, Kwantlen Polytechnic University. — Fifth Canadian edition.

Includes bibliographical references and indexes.
ISBN 978-0-07-089105-0 (pbk.)

    1. Sociology—Textbooks. I. Haaland, Bonnie, author II. Title.

HM586.S32 2014   301   C2013-906333-1

dedication

To my granddaughter, Tillie, and her parents, Peter and Margaret, for a wonderful life together.

—Richard T. Schaefer

For my new granddaughter Sophie, born August 16, 2013

—Bonnie Haaland

about the authors

Richard T. Schaefer: Professor, DePaul University
BA, Northwestern University
MA, PhD, University of Chicago

Growing up in Chicago at a time when neighbourhoods were going through transitions in ethnic and racial composition, Richard T. Schaefer found himself increasingly intrigued by what was happening, how people were reacting, and how these changes were affecting neighbourhoods and people's jobs. His interest in social issues caused him to gravitate to sociology courses at Northwestern University, where he eventually received a BA in sociology.

"Originally as an undergraduate I thought I would go on to law school and become a lawyer. But after taking a few sociology courses, I found myself wanting to learn more about what sociologists studied, and fascinated by the kinds of questions they raised." This fascination led him to obtain his MA and PhD in sociology from the University of Chicago. Dr. Schaefer's continuing interest in race relations led him to write his master's thesis on the membership of the Ku Klux Klan and his doctoral thesis on racial prejudice and race relations in Great Britain.

Dr. Schaefer went on to become a professor of sociology, and now teaches at DePaul University in Chicago. In 2004 he was named to the Vincent DePaul professorship in recognition of his undergraduate teaching and scholarship. He has taught introductory sociology for over 35 years to students in colleges, adult education programs, nursing programs, and even a maximum-security prison. Dr. Schaefer's love of teaching is apparent in his interaction with his students. "I find myself constantly learning from the students who are in my classes and from reading what they write. Their insights into the material we read or current events that we discuss often become part of future course material and sometimes even find their way into my writing."

Dr. Schaefer is the author of the ninth edition of *Sociology: A Brief Introduction* (McGraw-Hill, 2011), *Sociology in Modules* (McGraw-Hill, 2011), and of the fifth edition of *Sociology Matters* (McGraw-Hill, 2012). He is also the author of *Racial and Ethnic Groups,* now in its thirteenth edition (2012), and *Race and Ethnicity in the United States,* seventh edition, both published by Pearson. Together with William Zellner, he coauthored the ninth edition of *Extraordinary Groups,* published by Worth in 2011. Dr. Schaefer served as the general editor of the three-volume *Encyclopedia of Race, Ethnicity, and Society,* published by Sage in 2008. His articles and book reviews have appeared in many journals, including *American Journal of Sociology; Phylon: A Review of Race and Culture; Contemporary Sociology; Sociology and Social Research; Sociological Quarterly;* and *Teaching Sociology.* He served as president of the Midwest Sociological Society in 1994–1995.

Dr. Schaefer's advice to students is to "look at the material and make connections to your own life and experiences. Sociology will make you a more attentive observer of how people in groups interact and function. It will also make you more aware of people's different needs and interests—and perhaps more ready to work for the common good, while still recognizing the individuality of each person."

Bonnie Haaland: Professor,
Kwantlen Polytechnic University
BA, University of Saskatchewan
MA, University of Western Ontario
PhD, University of Toronto

Over the past 30 years, Dr. Bonnie Haaland has taught sociology to teachers, bankers, and nurses, to new high school graduates, and senior undergraduates at Kwantlen Polytechnic University, the University of Regina, and the University of Western Ontario. Teaching introductory sociology as well as other undergraduate sociology courses, she has instructed classes with as many as 350 students and as few as nine, and has used various modes of instruction. Dr. Haaland was one of the first instructors at the University of Western Ontario to teach courses by using distance education technology, which simultaneously connected clusters of students in smaller cities and towns throughout southwestern Ontario. At Western, she later coordinated a program involving distance education, overseeing the delivery of courses in such fields as chemistry, nursing, psychology, anthropology, and English. During this time, Dr. Haaland was actively involved in research related to distance and continuing education, and presenting papers at conferences, such as the International Congress on Distance Education in Melbourne, Australia.

Dr. Haaland is the author of *Emma Goldman: Sexuality and the Impurity of the State;* a co-author of *Sociology: A Brief Introduction,* First Canadian Edition, Census Update Edition, Second Canadian Edition, Third Canadian Edition, and Fourth Canadian Edition; contributor to the *Canadian Sociology Collection,* Create, McGraw-Hill Ryerson Ltd.: http://create. mcgraw-hill.com/wordpress-mu/canada/; and author of articles published in Canadian and U.S. academic journals. She is the recipient of the Canadian Association for University Continuing Education's Award of Excellence for her article "In Pursuit of Self: The Values of the Post-War Baby Boom Generation and the Implications for Continuing Education."

Bonnie Haaland grew up in Saskatchewan and graduated from the University of Saskatchewan with a BA (with distinction) and a BA (Hons), from the University of Western Ontario with a MA, and from the University of Toronto with a PhD. She currently lives in South Surrey/White Rock, British Columbia.

contents in brief

contents

3 Culture   43

4 Socialization   65

5 Social Interaction, Groups, and Social Structure   89

15 Population, Health, and Communities   317

16 Social Movements, Social Change, and the Environment   347

boxed features

Sociology in the Global Community

research today

social policy sections

dear student

These days, students like you are required to meet ever-increasing and often conflicting demands on both your academic and personal time. Your technological savvy allows you to navigate through social worlds from what seems like a never-ending set of possibilities. In how many ways can your friends contact you? Can you even remember a time, in the past year, when you turned off *all* your tablets, cell phones, laptops, and other communication devices? (Maybe when on an airplane?)

To survive this new age and rise to the challenges it sets for us, we are becoming more and more "connected." Your own social networks, shaped and maintained fundamentally by newer communication technologies, are larger and more wide-reaching than those of other age groups. To be successful, both professionally and personally, you need to learn to connect the dots that represent your networks.

Sociology: A Brief Introduction is your guide. After all, sociology is the study of social worlds. This text offers you the opportunity to learn how to see yourselves as part of a larger entity—a friendship, a university community, a national community, a global community—and to explore diverse and often contradictory interpretations of those relationships.

The ability to draw parallels between the forces shaping your own lives and those shaping a friendship, a university, a nation, or the globe, is the first step in developing your own sociological imagination, and thus, making the connection.

preface

As the years—and even the months—pass, I am struck by how students' lives have changed since I taught my first sociology class in the late 1970s. It seems obvious how connected most students are today; how technologically savvy they appear; how their social networks, shaped and maintained fundamentally by newer communication technologies, are larger and more wide-reaching than those of other age groups. The rapidity of technological change and the diverse—and often conflicting—demands for undergraduates' time and attention are challenges with which students must contend on a daily basis. The dramatic increases in tuition costs and the increased need to hold a job while studying, the need for Internet access and currency in computer skills, the ubiquitous intrusion of the mass media and consumer culture, environmental issues and the building of "green" communities, and the global financial crisis—these are just a few of the concerns that preoccupy students. By implication, of course, my students' challenges, to a large degree, become my challenges. Increasingly, I see my role, and more specifically the role of my discipline, as instrumental in helping undergraduates process and navigate the content of their social worlds. In this way, sociology is a dynamic discipline with great potential to engage learners in their social worlds, not solely as actors but also as observers and interpreters. Sociology offers the opportunity to see ourselves as part of a larger entity—a friendship, a university community, a national community, a global community—and to explore diverse and often contradictory interpretations of those relationships.

To see *sociological imagination* actualized through students' ability to make the connections among the forces shaping their own lives and those shaping a friendship, a university, a nation, or the globe is a challenge and accomplishment for student and instructor alike. *Sociology: A Brief Introduction,* Fifth Canadian Edition, is written with that goal in mind. This text strengthens the foundation laid in the first, second, third and fourth Canadian editions, providing compelling and relevant topics and examples that resonate with students, that are situated in a global context, and that are consistently interpreted through the lens of four theoretical perspectives. Key features of this Fifth Canadian Edition include the following:

- **Thinking About Movies.** Movies that underscore chapter themes are featured at the end of each chapter along with a brief description of the movie.
- **Interior Design.** The interior of the text has been updated to make it easier for students to follow and also to make it more visually appealing.
- **Hot topics of Canadian interest with a strengthened global focus.** The Fifth Canadian Edition covers such topics as; bullying, telecommuting, food banks, family violence and the Occupy Movement.

- **Extensive updates to statistics, research, and visuals.** This edition uses the latest data and reports from Statistics Canada data from the Canadian Council on Learning, Human Resources and Social Development Canada, the International Institute for Democracy and Electoral Assistance, Elections Canada, the Inter-Parliamentary Union, and the United Nations, and the results of polls conducted by such organizations as the Pew Research Center. New research findings have been incorporated, drawing on the work of Canadian researchers whenever possible. In terms of pedagogical features, over 95 percent of the chapter-opening excerpts are new. Furthermore, the photo program has been extensively revised to include current and relevant examples and illustrations for students.
- **Continued focus on providing student applications and fostering the sociological imagination.** Each chapter of *Sociology: A Brief Introduction,* Fifth Canadian Edition, contains Use Your Sociological Imagination critical thinking sections, appropriately positioned, which foster critical thinking about the material covered in the chapter. In addition, as part of the theoretical foundation of this edition, Apply the Theory questions have been retained as well as revised, placed in the popular boxed features, Research Today (previously Research in Action) and Sociology in the Global Community. Think About It captions accompany some figures, encouraging students' critical engagement with sociological data. Updated end-of-chapter Social Policy sections continue to help students forge links between sociological theory and the world around them. Thinking About Movies sections have been updated.
- **Chapter Reorganization** Given the importance of the racialization, gender and social inequality, Chapters 8,9,10 and 11 in the fourth Canadian Edition, these chapters have been moved up to follow Chapter 5, Social Interaction and Social Structure.

The Plan for This Book

Sociology: A Brief Introduction, Fifth Canadian Edition, is divided into 16 chapters that study human behaviour concisely from the perspective of sociologists. The opening chapter ("Understanding Sociology") presents a brief history of the discipline, introduces key Canadian sociologists, and explains the four basic theories and perspectives used in sociology. Chapter 2 ("Sociological Research") describes the major quantitative and qualitative research methods.

The next five chapters focus on key sociological concepts. Chapter 3 ("Culture") illustrates how sociologists study people's behaviour. Chapter 4 ("Socialization") reveals how humans are most distinctively social animals who learn the attitudes and behaviour viewed as appropriate in their particular cultures. We examine "Social Interaction, Groups, and Social Structure" in Chapter 5. The next four chapters consider various aspects of social inequality. Chapter 6 ("Stratification in Canada") introduces us to the presence of social inequality in this country, while Chapter 7("Global Inequality") examines inequality within, between, and among countries and regions of the world. Chapter 8 ("Racial and Ethnic Inequality") and Chapter 9 ("Gender Relations") analyze specific and ubiquitous types of inequality.

"The Mass Media "is now Chapter 10 and Chapter 11, "Deviance and Social Control," examines how people conform and deviate from established norms.

The next three chapters examine the major social institutions of human society. Marriage, family diversity, and divorce are some of the topics discussed in Chapter 12 ("Families and Intimate Relationships"). Other social institutions are considered in Chapter 13 ("Religion and Education") and Chapter 14 ("Politics and the Economy").

The final chapters of the text introduce major themes in our changing world. Chapter 15 helps us understand "Population, Health, and Communities" in Canadian society and around the world. In Chapter 16, we examine the importance of "Social Movements, Social Change, and the Environment" in our lives.

The Fifth Canadian Edition has been fully updated to reflect the most recent developments in sociology both in Canada and around the globe. It provides the most relevant and meaningful applications for students, including the Use Your Sociological Imagination sections, the updated Apply the Theory questions that appear in each boxed feature and Social Policy section, and the new tables that help to sum up the theory discussed. Following is a summary of just some of the content changes in the Fifth Canadian Edition.

Chapter-by-Chapter Changes

Chapter 1: Understanding Sociology
- New Opening excerpt from *What Am I Wearing? A Global Tour to the Countries, Factories, and People making our Clothes*
- Coverage of the aftermath of the Haiti earthquake from a sociological perspective
- New section on French sociologist Pierre Bourdieu
- Expanded section on symbolic interactionism
- Additional perspective on feminist theories
- New Research Today box: "Looking at the Gulf of Mexico Oil Spill from Four Sociological Perspectives"
- New Sociology in the Global Community box: "Your Morning Cup Of Coffee"
- Expanded and updated Thinking About Movies section to include three movies
- Expanded explanation of the use of the sociological imagination throughout the book to include *thinking globally,* the significance and social inequality and thinking across religious lines, as well as those relating to class, gender and race.

Chapter 2: Sociological Research
- New chapter opener *"Hanging out with the wrong crowd".*
- New Research Today box;"Surveying Cell Phone Users"

- New figure on median age of first sex
- Updated material on content analysis
- Greater discussion on ethnography
- New "Think About It" and "Use Your Sociological Imagination"
- Expanded and updated Thinking About Movies section

Chapter 3: Culture
- New chapter opener on Nacirema culture
- Updated material on foreign content by private broadcasters in Canada
- New material and figure on child marriage
- New material on First Nations languages
- New "Think About It" question
- Expanded and updated *"Thinking About Movies"* section

Chapter 4: Socialization
- New chapter opener featuring debate on a "gender free" child.
- New "Research Today" section on on-line socializing
- Updated Sociology in the Global Community box: "Aging Worldwide: Issues and Consequences"
- Updated Social Policy section: "Childcare around the World"
- Updated figure on childcare costs in industrial nations
- Expanded and updated "Thinking About Movies" section to include three movies

Chapter 5: Social Interaction, Groups, and Social Structure
- New chapter opener on the franchising of McDonald's
- New material on virtual worlds
- New Research Today box: "Social Networks and Obesity"
- Updated Social Policy section: "The State of the Unions"
- New figure on labour union membership
- Expanded and updated Thinking About Movies section

Chapter 6: Stratification in Canada (was C8)
- New chapter opener on Toronto's highest paid CEOs
- New material added to interactionist views
- Updated statistics on income of Canadians
- Added material on use of food banks in Canada
- New figure on respect for various professions in Canada
- New "Summing Up" table
- Updated table on the richest Canadians
- Updated Social Policy section "Rethinking Social Assistance in North America and Europe"
- Expanded and updated Thinking About Movies section: *Titanic*

Chapter 7: Global Inequality [was Chapter 9)]
- New Sociology in the Global Community box: "Income Inequality: A Global Perspective."

- New Sociology in the Global Community box;"Stratification in Brazil"
- Updated figure on gross national income per capita
- Updated figure on foreign aid per capita in nine countries
- Updated figure on distribution of wealth in nine nations
- Updated figure on global poverty
- Expanded and updated Thinking About Movies section.

Chapter 8: Racial and Ethnic Inequality (was C10)

- New chapter opener on Prime Minister's apology for residential schools
- Updated Sociology in the Global community box: Cultural Survival in Brazil
- New Sociology in the Global Community box: Cultural Genocide of Aboriginal Peoples
- New figure on Spectrum of Intergroup Relations
- Updated Social Policy section: "Global Immigration"
- New and expanded Thinking About Movies.

Chapter 9: Gender Relations (was C11)

- Updated Sociology in the Global Community box: The Empowerment of Women through Education
- New Research Today box: Gender and the Nyinba
- New section on the Intersection of Racialization, Class and other factors
- New figure on the Matrix of Domination
- New material on the Interactionist Approach
- Updated section on the Status of Women Worldwide
- New figure on Gender Inequality in Housework Worldwide in Selected Countries
- Updated Social Policy section: "Abortion and Sex Selection: The 'New Eugenics'"
- New and Expanded Thinking About Movies section.

Chapter 10: The Mass Media (was C6)

- New table on Canada's fastest rising and most popular internet searches
- New figure "Branding the Globe"
- New figure "Filtering Information: Social Content"
- Added material on cyberbullying
- Expanded section on interactionism
- Updated Sociology in the Global Community box: "Privacy and Censorship in the Digital Village"
- New figure "Media Penetration in Selected Countries"
- Expanded and updated Thinking About Movies section.

Chapter 11 Deviance and Social Control (was C7)

- New chapter opener on stopping violence in British Columbia
- Updated figure on crime in Canadian provinces and territories
- Updated table on cosmetic procedures in Canada and the United States

- Updated Sociology in the Global Community box
- New Research Today box: Binge Drinking on Campus
- Added material on cyberbullying
- Updated internet crime statistics
- Updated Social Policy section
- Updated table on violent crimes in Canada and the relationship to the accused
- New and expanded Thinking About Movies section

Chapter 12: Families and Intimate Relationships

- New chapter opener on honour killings
- New figure on median age of first marriage in selected countries
- New Sociology in the Global Community box: "Family Life Italian Style: Thirty-Something and Living with Mom"
- Updated figure on marriage and divorce rated in Canada
- Updated material on same-sex marriage
- Updated data on family violence in Canada
- Updated Social Policy section on reproductive technology
- New and expanded Thinking About Movies section to include three movies

Chapter 13: Religion and Education

- New chapter opener
- Updated table on religions of the world
- Updated figure on religious participation in selected countries
- New figure on current higher education graduation rates in selected countries
- New Research Today box: Google University
- New and expanded Thinking About Movies section to include three movies

Chapter 14: Politics and the Economy

- New chapter opener on fair trade
- New Sociology in the Global Community box: "Working Women in Nepal"
- Updated Sociology in the Global Community box: Capitalism in China
- Updated figure on women in national legislatures
- New figure on Global Peace Index
- Updated figure on Filtering Information: Political Content
- Updated table on world's largest economies
- New Social Policy section: "Microfinancing"
- Expanded and new Thinking About Movies section

Chapter 15: Population, Health, and Communities

- New chapter opener on the demographic trend, the aging of the world's population
- New Sociology in the Global Community box: Squatter Communities

- New figure on population growth rates in selected countries
- Updated table on estimated time for each successive increase of 1 billion people in world population
- Updated Sociology in the Global Community box: "Population Policy in China"
- Updated statistics
- Updated Social Policy section on HIV/AIDS
- Expanded Thinking About Movies section

Chapter 16: Social Movement, Social Change and the Environment
- Chapter renamed.
- Updated Research Today box: "The Internet's Global Profile"
- New material on the Occupy Movement
- Updated World Consumption Cartogram
- New Sociology in the Global Community box: "Women and New Social Movements in India
- Updated Social Policy section: "Transnationals"
- Updated and expanded Thinking About Movies section to include three movies

Additional Modules on Create

http://create.mcgraw-hill.com/wordpress-mu/canada/

Social Constructionism

Postmodern Theory

Panics and Crazes

Joining Up: Voluntary Associations in Canada

Social Construction of Sex and Sexuality

Gender Identity

Religion and Social Change: An Interactionist View

Political Activism on the Internet

Worker Satisfaction

The Part-Time Workforce

E-Commerce

Physicians, Nurses, and Patients in Canada

Alternatives to Traditional Healthcare in Canada

Population and Migration in Canada

Resistance to Social Change

Environmental Sociology

Stratification by Age

Gender

Acknowledgements from Bonnie Haaland

I am deeply indebted to a number of individuals at McGraw-Hill Ryerson who provided support, encouragement, and technical expertise throughout the development of this project. I wish to express my sincere thanks and appreciation to Daphne Scriabin, Product Developer; Marcia Siekowski, Senior Product Manager; Graeme Powell, Supervising Editor; Erin Moore, Copy Editor; Tammy Mavroudi, Production Co-ordinator.

I would also like to extend sincere thanks to those instructors across Canada whose painstaking reviews helped to inform and strengthen this edition:

Sara Cumming, University of Waterloo

Helene Cummins, University of Western Ontario Brescia College

Stephen Decator, St. Clair College

Deborah Dergousoff, University of Victoria

Shane Dixon, Ryerson University

Nancy Doetzel, Mount Royal University

James Dzisah, Nipissing University

Marissa Fleming, Georgian College

Judith Grant, University of Ontario Institute of Technology

Lynn Hanley, Seneca College

Mervyn Horgan, Acadia University

Chantelle Marlor, University of the Fraser Valley

Daniel Popowich, Mohawk College

Pamela Sugiman, Ryerson University

Amanda Zavitz-Gocan, Fanshawe College

And, finally, to the hundreds of students with whom I shared a classroom over the last number of decades, and to those who might use this book in the future, this work is ultimately for you.

Bonnie Haaland

visual preview

Teaching Students to Think Sociologically

The Fifth Canadian Edition of *Sociology: A Brief Introduction* continues its tradition of teaching students how to think critically about society and their own lives from a wide range of sociological perspectives.

Intriguing Excerpts

Chapter-opening excerpts convey the excitement and relevance of sociological inquiry by means of lively excerpts from the writings of sociologists and others who explore sociological topics. Thirteen are new to this edition, including selections on the highest paid CEOs, the Prime Minister's apology for the residential schools, and stopping violence in British Columbia.

Excerpt Links to Chapters

Chapter overviews provide a bridge between each chapter-opening excerpt and the content of the following chapter.

Use Your Sociological Imagination Sections

Use Your Sociological Imagination sections within each chapter pose questions designed to stimulate students' sociological imagination and help them connect major concepts and issues to their own lives.

Unique Social Policy Sections

The Social Policy sections, highly praised by reviewers of this text, provide a sociological perspective on contemporary social issues, such as microfinancing, rethinking social assistance and the state of the unions. Providing a global view of the issues, these sections are organized around a consistent heading structure and include Apply the Theory questions designed to stimulate critical thinking about the issues being explored.

social policy and the Economy

Microfinancing

The Issue

In India, a very small loan has made a big change in a young mother's life. Not many years ago Siyawati was dependent on what little income her husband could earn as a day labourer. Then a $212 micro-loan allowed her to buy a machine for making candles. Today, Siyawati's cottage venture has expanded into a factory with eight employees, and her monthly income has climbed from $42 to $425. Her increased earnings have allowed her to enroll her children in a good school—the dream of struggling parents in developing countries around the world (Glazer 2010:1).

In some respects it offers a small solution to a big problem. **Microfinancing** is lending small sums of money to the poor so they can work their way out of poverty. Borrowers use the money to start small businesses in the informal economy—to buy yarn to weave into cloth, cows to produce milk, or tools, equipment, and bamboo to make stools. The products they produce are then sold in the local shops. Typically, micro-loans are less than $600, often as little as $20. The recipients are people who ordinarily would not be able to qualify for banking services.

The Setting

Sometimes referred to as "banking the unbanked," microfinancing was the brainchild of Bangladeshi economist Muhammad Yunus (pronounced Iunus). In 1976, in the midst of a devastating famine in Bangladesh, Yunus founded the Grameen (meaning "Village") Bank, which he headed until 2011. The idea came to him when he reached into his pocket to lend money to a group of villagers who had asked him for help. Working through local halls or meeting places, the Grameen Bank has now extended credit to nearly 7 million people. The idea has spread, and has even been underwritten by over a thousand for-profit banks and multinational organizations. According to 2011 estimates, microfinancing is now reaching 91 million people in 100 countries (Microfinance Information Exchange 2011; Yunus 2010).

Although microfinancing has benefited many families, critics charge that some lenders are taking advantage of the poor. Especially in India, the extension of micro-loans to financially questionable projects with little chance for success has left some borrowers in debt. At the other extreme, some lenders have reaped extraordinary profits, both for themselves and for the investment banks they have created.

In some countries, politicians resent microfinancing because it competes with the central government's path to self-sufficiency. In Nicaragua, President Daniel Ortega supports the *movimiento no pago*, or no-pay movement, which encourages borrowers not to repay their debts. So successful has the movement been that one of that nation's leading microfinanciers has been driven out of business.

Sociological Insights

Researchers who draw on the interactionist approach have shown that there is more to microfinancing than money. A study done by microfinance expert Daryl Collins and his colleagues (2009) shows how even with modest assistance, poor people can significantly improve their circumstances through mutual support. Collins asked villagers and slum dwellers in Bangladesh, India, and South Africa to keep diaries of how they spent every penny they earned. He and his team found that most of the poor households they studied did not live hand to mouth, spending everything they earned as soon as they got it. Instead, they used financial tools that were linked to their extended families and informal social networks. They saved money, squeezed it out of creditors whenever possible, ran sophisticated savings clubs, and took advantage of microfinancing whenever it was available. Their tactics suggested new methods of fighting poverty and encouraged the development of broader microfinance programs.

Because an estimated 90 percent of the recipients of microcredit are women, feminist theorists are especially interested in the growth of microfinancing. Women's economic status has

In 2006 Muhammad Yunus, founder of the Grameen Bank, was awarded the Nobel Peace Prize for his work in championing the concept of microfinancing. The small loans his bank makes to the poor, many of them women, have improved the quality of life of countless families.

Politics and the Economy   **313**

Sociology in the Global Community Boxes

The Sociology in the Global Community boxes provide a global perspective on topics such as stratification, marriage and technology use. They also feature Apply the Theory questions.

sociology in the global community

12-1 Family Life, Italian Style: Thirty-Something and Living with Mom

Bamboccioni—adult children who live with their parents—are no longer socially unacceptable in Italy. In fact, they're not even unusual. In December 2009, the Italian government released new data showing that 40 percent of Italian men between ages 30 and 34 live with their parents. So do 20 percent of Italian women in this age bracket. Among those a little older, ages 35 to 39, 17.5 percent of men and 9.3 percent of women live with their parents.

> *About 40 percent of* bamboccioni *live with their parents not because of financial need, but because they enjoy the company.*

This state of affairs is not a recent phenomenon. What is new is that 80 percent of these adult children say they cannot afford to leave their parents' homes. Salaries in Italy are low but rents are high, so these not-so-young adults linger on with mama and papa. As one of them, a 30-year-old biologist, put it, "We are the €1,000-per-month generation—who can afford spending more than €800 for an apartment?"

About 40 percent of *bamboccioni* live with their parents not because of financial need, but because they enjoy the company. Others feel responsible for their aging parents. Among the women ages 35 to 40, more than half feel it is a duty. Sociologist Giampiero dalla Zuanna says their commitment to the family means the elderly in Italy are much more likely to remain in their own homes than those in northern Europe, many of whom must move to retirement communities.

The pattern of adult children staying home with their parents is not unique to Italy. In North America and throughout Europe, young people are feeling the impact of the recent economic downturn. Many are delaying childbearing until their job prospects improve.

One relatively unnoticed factor that is contributing to the trend is parents' greater longevity. Today, more parents survive long enough for their children to become adults, and remain healthy enough to maintain a home for them.

What happens when adult children finally do leave the nest? So close are the ties between parent and child in Italy that services have emerged to support their relationship through the separation in living arrangements. For a small fee, special couriers will pick up Mother's fresh homemade pasta and even homegrown greens and deliver them to her adult children.

Apply the Theory

1. Do you or someone you know live at home with parents? If so, do you see the situation as similar to that of the *bamboccioni*?
2. In Canada, what other factors might contribute to adult children choosing to live with their parents?

Sources: Meichtry 2011; Momigliana 2010; Roberts 2010.

research today

4-1 Impression Management by Students After Exams

When you and fellow classmates get an exam back, you probably react differently depending on the grades that you and they earned. This distinction is part of *impression management*. Researchers have found that students' reactions differ depending on the grades that others received, compared to their own. These encounters can be divided into three categories: those in which all students earned high grades (Ace–Ace encounters); those between Aces and students who received low or failing grades (Ace–Bomber encounters); and those between students who all got low grades (Bomber–Bomber encounters).

Ace–Ace encounters occur in a rather open atmosphere, because there is comfort in sharing a high mark with another high achiever. It is even acceptable to violate the norm of modesty and brag when among other Aces, since as one student admitted, "It's much easier to admit a high mark to someone who has done better than you, or at least as well."

Ace–Bomber encounters are often sensitive. Bombers generally attempt to avoid such exchanges, because "you. . . emerge looking like the dumb one" or "feel like you are lazy or unreliable." When forced into interactions with Aces, Bombers work to appear gracious and congratulatory. For their part, Aces offer sympathy and support to the dissatisfied Bombers and even rationalize their own "lucky" high scores. To help Bombers save face, Aces may emphasize the difficulty and unfairness of the examination.

> *When forced into interactions with Aces, Bombers work to appear gracious and congratulatory.*

Bomber–Bomber encounters tend to be closed, reflecting the group effort to wall off the feared disdain of others. Yet within the safety of these encounters, Bombers openly share their disappointment and engage in expressions of mutual self-pity that they themselves call "pity parties." They devise face-saving excuses for their poor performance, such as "I wasn't feeling well all week" or "I had four exams and two papers due that week."

Of course, grade comparisons are not the only occasion when students engage in impression management. Another study has shown that students' perceptions of how often fellow students work out can also influence their social encounters. In athletic terms, a bomber would be someone who doesn't work out; an ace would be someone who works hard at physical fitness.

Apply the Theory

1. What theoretical perspective would most likely be employed in the study of students' impression management strategies?
2. How do you think some feminist sociologists might approach the study of impression management on the part of their students?

Sources: Albas and Albas 1988, 1996; M. Mack 2003.

Research Today
The Research in Action boxes in the fourth edition have been renamed Research Today. These boxes present sociological findings on relevant topics such as the environment, socializing, gender, and binge drinking. They also feature Apply the Theory questions.

A prospective employer reviews an applicant's qualifications for the job. To present themselves in a positive manner, both interviewer and applicant may resort to *impression management* and *face-work*, two tactics described by the interventionist Erving Goffman.

Again as we discussed in Chapter 1, Mead uses the term *generalized other* to refer to the attitudes, viewpoints, and expectations of society as

::: use your sociological *imagination* :::

How has the *generalized other* influenced the decisions you've made?

www.mcgrawhillconnect.ca

Goffman: Presentation of the Self How do we manage our self? How do we display to others who we are? Erving Goffman, a sociologist associated with the interactionist perspective, suggested that many of our daily activities involve attempts to convey impressions of who we are.

Early in life, the individual learns to slant his or her presentation of the self in order to create distinctive appearances and satisfy particular audiences. Goffman (1959) refers to this altering of the presentation of the self as **impression management**. Box 4-1 provides an everyday example of this concept by describing how students engage in impression management after getting their examination grades.

Demographic Map Program
"Mapping Life Worldwide" maps are featured throughout the text.

figure 10-1 Branding the Globe

MAPPING LIFE WORLDWIDE

Canada
40 Thomson Reuters
63 BlackBerry

Great Britain
32 HSBC
83 BP
84 Smirnoff
98 Burberry

Netherlands
42 Philips
92 Shell

Switzerland
25 Nescafé
58 Nestlé
68 Rolex
72 UBS
77 Cartier

Sweden
21 H&M
28 Ikea

Finland
5 Nokia

South Korea
19 Samsung
69 Hyundai

United States
1 Coca-Cola
2 IBM
3 Microsoft
4 GE
6 McDonald's
7 Google
9 Intel
10 Disney
11 Hewlett-Packard
13 Gillette
14 Cisco
17 Marlboro
20 Apple

Spain
50 Zara

France
16 Louis Vuitton
44 L'Oréal
53 AXA
59 Chanel
60 Danone
76 Hermes
82 Moët & Chandon
91 Lancôme

Germany
12 Mercedes-Benz
15 BMW
27 SAP
47 Siemens
55 Volkswagen
62 Adidas
65 Audi
74 Porsche
81 Allianz
86 Nivea
97 Puma

Italy
41 Gucci
87 Prada
88 Ferrari
89 Georgio Armani

Japan
8 Toyota
18 Honda
29 Sony
33 Canon
39 Nintendo
75 Panasonic
96 Lexus

Note: Map shows the top 100 brands in the world by country of ownership, except for the United States, for which only brands in the top 20 are shown.

Source: Based on Interbrand 2010.

Based on revenue and name recognition, these are the brands that dominate the global marketplace. Just 13 nations account for all the top 100 brands.

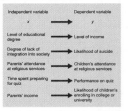

arly studies and information—researchers define the problem under study, clarify possible techniques to be used in collecting data, and eliminate or reduce avoidable mistakes. For our example, we would examine information about salaries for different occupations. We would see if jobs that require more academic training are better rewarded. It would also be appropriate to review other studies on the relationship between education and income.

The review of the literature would soon tell us that many other factors besides level of study's influence on earning potential. For example, we would learn that the children of richer parents are more likely to go to college or university than are those from modest backgrounds, so we might consider the possibility that the same parents may later help their children to secure better-paying jobs.

Formulating the Hypothesis

After reviewing earlier research and drawing on the contributions of sociological theorists, the researchers may then *formulate the hypothesis*. A **hypothesis** is a speculative statement about the relationship between two or more factors known as variables. Income, religion, occupation, and gender can all serve as variables in a study. We can define a **variable** as a measurable trait or characteristic that is subject to change under different conditions.

Researchers who formulate a hypothesis generally must suggest how one aspect of human behaviour influences or affects another. The variable hypothesized to cause or influence another is called the **independent variable**. The second variable is termed the **dependent variable** because its action "depends" on the influence of the independent variable.

Our hypothesis is that the higher one's educational level, the more money one will earn. The independent variable to

28 Chapter 2

Identifying independent and dependent variables is a critical step in clarifying cause-and-effect relationships in society. As shown in Figure 2-2, **causal logic** involves the relationship

figure 2-2 Causal Logic

Independent variable		Dependent variable
x	→	*y*
Level of educational degree	→	Level of income
Degree of lack of integration into society	→	Likelihood of suicide
Parents' attendance at religious services	→	Children's attendance at religious services
Time spent preparing for quiz	→	Performance on quiz
Parents' income	→	Likelihood of children's enrolling in college or university

In *causal logic*, an independent variable (often designated by the symbol *x*) influences a dependent variable (generally designated as *y*); thus, *x* leads to *y*. For example, parents who attend religious services regularly (*x*) are more likely to have children who are regular attendees of religious services (*y*).

Think about It
Identify two or three variables that might "depend" on this independent variable: number of alcoholic drinks ingested.

"Think about It" Caption Feature
The "Think about It" captions, which accompany many of the book's maps, graphs, and tables, encourage students to think critically about information presented in illustrative materials.

table 4-1 Theoretical Approaches to Development of the Self

summing**UP**

Scholar	Key Concepts and Contributions	Main Points of Theory
Sigmund Freud 1856–1939 psychotherapist (Austria)	Psychoanalysis	Self influenced by parents and by inborn drives, such as the drive for sexual gratification
George Herbert Mead 1863–1931 sociologist (U.S.A.)	The self Generalized other	Three distinct stages of development; self develops as children grasp the roles of others in their lives
Charles Horton Cooley 1864–1929 sociologist (U.S.A.)	Looking-glass self	Stages of development not distinct; feelings toward ourselves developed through interaction with others
Jean Piaget 1896–1980 child psychologist (Switzerland)	Cognitive theory of development	Four stages of cognitive development; moral development linked to socialization
Erving Goffman 1922–1982 sociologist (U.S.A.)	Impression management Dramaturgical approach Face-work	Self developed through the impressions we convey to others and to groups

Summing Up Tables recap coverage of the major theoretical perspectives on key topics.

CHAPTER RESOURCES

Summary

2.1 What Is the Scientific Method?
- There are five basic steps in the **scientific method**: defining the problem, reviewing the literature, formulating the hypothesis, selecting the research design and then collecting and analyzing data, and developing the conclusion.
- Whenever researchers want to study abstract concepts, such as intelligence or prejudice, they must develop a workable **operational definition**.
- A **hypothesis** usually states a possible relationship between two or more variables.
- By using a **sample**, sociologists avoid having to test everyone in a population.
- According to the scientific method, research results must possess both **validity** and **reliability**.

2.2 What Are the Major Research Designs?
- Sociologists use four major research designs in their work: **survey** research of a population, utilizing the

interview and the **questionnaire; ethnography** and in-depth interviews, focusing on small groups and communities; **experiment** that tests cause-and-effect relationships; **secondary analysis** or the analysis of existing sources.

2.3 What Are the Ethics of Research?
- The **code of ethics** of the Canadian Sociology and Anthropology Association calls for objectivity and integrity in research, respect for the subject's privacy, and confidentiality.

2.4 How Does Technology Influence Sociological Research?
- Technology today plays an important role in sociological research, whether it is a computer database or information from the Internet.

Critical Thinking Questions

1. Suppose that your sociology instructor has asked you to do a study of the issues facing Canadians today. Which research technique would you find most useful? How would you use that approach to complete your assignment?

2. Do you think you or any sociologist can maintain value neutrality while studying any group of people, such as younger Canadians?

3. Why is it important for sociologists to have a code of ethics?

4. What research method(s) do you think would produce the best results when studying the views and attitudes of the under-30 age group? Why?

End-of-Chapter Resources
Each chapter concludes with a Summary, Critical Thinking Questions, and a Thinking About Movies feature.

THINKING ABOUT MOVIES

Invictus
In post-apartheid South Africa, a rugby team helps Nelson Mandela to build national unity.

The Social Network
This dramatization of the rise of Facebook illustrates the way people connect to one another in the twenty-first century.

Wendy and Lucy
A young woman wanders through life disconnected from social institutions.

Thinking About Movies
This section has been expanded and features movies that underscore chapter themes.

Supplements

 McGraw-Hill Connect™ is a web-based assignment and assessment platform that gives students the means to better connect with their coursework, with their instructors, and with the important concepts that they will need to know for success now and in the future. With Connect, instructors can deliver assignments, quizzes and tests online. Instructors can edit existing questions and author entirely new problems. Track individual student performance – by question, assignment or in relation to the class overall – with detailed grade reports. Integrate grade reports easily with Learning Management Systems (LMS). And much more.

By choosing Connect, instructors are providing their students with a powerful tool for improving academic performance and truly mastering course material. Connect allows students to practice important skills at their own pace and on their own schedule. Importantly, students' assessment results and instructors' feedback are all saved online – so students can continually review their progress and plot their course to success.

Connect also provides 24/7 online access to an eBook – an online edition of the text – to aid them in successfully completing their work, wherever and whenever they choose.

KEY FEATURES

Simple Assignment Management

With Connect, creating assignments is easier than ever, so you can spend more time teaching and less time managing.

- Create and deliver assignments easily with selectable end-of-chapter questions and test bank material to assign online
- Streamline lesson planning, student progress reporting, and assignment grading to make classroom management more efficient than ever
- Go paperless with the eBook and online submission and grading of student assignments

Smart Grading

When it comes to studying, time is precious. Connect helps students learn more efficiently by providing feedback and practice material when they need it, where they need it.

- Automatically score assignments, giving students immediate feedback on their work and side-by-side comparisons with correct answers
- Access and review each response; manually change grades or leave comments for students to review
- Reinforce classroom concepts with practice tests and instant quizzes

Instructor Library

The Connect Instructor Library is your course creation hub. It provides all the critical resources you'll need to build your course, just how you want to teach it.

- Assign eBook readings and draw from a rich collection of textbook-specific assignments
- Access instructor resources, including ready-made PowerPoint presentations and media to use in your lectures
- View assignments and resources created for past sections
- Post your own resources for students to use

eBook

Connect reinvents the textbook learning experience for the modern student. Every Connect subject area is seamlessly integrated with Connect eBooks, which are designed to keep students focused on the concepts key to their success.

- Provide students with a Connect eBook, allowing for anytime, anywhere access to the textbook
- Merge media, animation and assessments with the text's narrative to engage students and improve learning and retention
- Pinpoint and connect key concepts in a snap using the powerful eBook search engine
- Manage notes, highlights and bookmarks in one place for simple, comprehensive review

Instructor Resources

Schaefer *Connect* is a one-stop shop for instructor resources, including:

Instructor's Manual

The Instructor's Manual contains lecture ideas, class discussion topics, essay questions, topics for student research, and lists of audiovisual materials, additional readings, and in-class activities to promote student engagement. A "Thinking About Movies" exercise is also included.

Test Bank in Rich Text Format

The Test Bank features short-answer, multiple-choice, and essay questions. Each question is accompanied by an answer. Multiple-choice questions are categorized by question type.

Computerized Test Bank

This flexible and easy-to-use electronic testing program allows instructors to create tests from book-specific items. It accommodates a wide range of question types, and instructors may add their own questions. Multiple versions of the test can be created and printed.

Microsoft® PowerPoint® Slides

These robust presentations offer high-quality visuals to bring key sociological concepts to life.

LearnSmart Advantage

No two students are alike. Why should their learning paths be? LearnSmart uses revolutionary adaptive technology to build a learning experience unique to each student's individual needs. It starts by identifying the topics a student knows and does not know. As the student progresses, LearnSmart adapts and adjusts the content based on his or her individual strengths, weaknesses and confidence, ensuring that every minute spent studying with LearnSmart is the most efficient and productive study time possible.

SmartBook

SMARTBOOK™

As the first and only adaptive reading experience, SmartBook is changing the way students read and learn. SmartBook creates a personalized reading experience by highlighting the most important concepts a student needs to learn at that moment in time. As a student engages with SmartBook, the reading experience continuously adapts by highlighting content based on what each student knows and doesn't know. This ensures that he or she is focused on the content needed to close specific knowledge gaps, while it simultaneously promotes long-term learning.

Superior Learning Solutions and Support

The McGraw-Hill Ryerson team is ready to help you assess and integrate any of our products, technology, and services into your course for optimal teaching and learning performance. Whether it's helping your students improve their grades, or putting your entire course online, the McGraw-Hill Ryerson team is here to help you do it. Contact your *Learning Solutions Consultant* today to learn how to maximize all of McGraw-Hill Ryerson's resources!

For more information on the latest technology and Learning Solutions offered by McGraw-Hill Ryerson and its partners, please visit us online: **www.mcgrawhill.ca/he/solutions**.

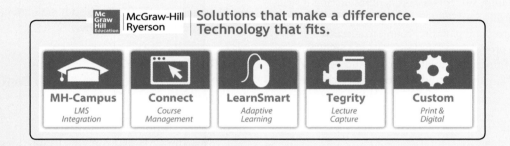

inside

Every day we are influenced by the people with whom we interact.

::: 1

Understanding Sociology

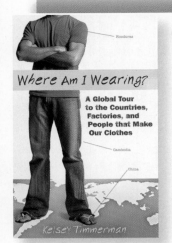

Where Am I Wearing?

A Global Tour to the Countries, Factories, and People that Make Our Clothes

Kelsey Timmerman

> 66 One day while staring at a pile of clothes on the floor, I noticed the tag of my favourite T-shirt: "Made in Honduras."
>
> I read the tag. My mind wandered. A quest was born.
>
> *Where am I wearing?* It seems like a simple question with a simple answer. It's not.
>
> The question inspired the quest that took me around the globe. It cost me a lot of things, not the least of which was my consumer innocence.
>
> Before the quest, I could put on a piece of clothing without reading its tag and thinking about Arifa in Bangladesh or Dewan in China, about their children, their hopes and dreams, and the challenges they face.
>
> *Where am I wearing?* This isn't so much a question related to geography and clothes, but about the people who make our clothes and the texture of their lives. This quest is about the way *we* live and the way *they* live; because when it comes to clothing, others make it, and we have it made. And there's a big, big difference. . . .
>
> Workers flood the narrow alley beside the Delta Apparel Factory in San Pedro Sula, Honduras. They rush to catch one of the many waiting buses at the highway. Merchants hoping to part them from a portion of their daily earnings—$4 to $5—fight for their attention. Vehicles push through the crowd. A minivan knocks over a girl in her mid-20s and then runs over her foot. She curses, is helped to her feet, and limps onto a waiting bus.
>
> The buildings behind the fence are shaded in Bahamian pastels and very well kept. The shrubs have been recently shaped, and the grass trimmed. In the bright Honduran sun, they seem as pleasant as a factory can get.
>
> The lady at Delta Apparel, based in Georgia, U.S., giggled at me on the phone when I told her my plans. She was happy to tell me that their Honduran factory was located in the city of Villanueva just south of San Pedro Sula. She even wished me good luck.
>
> Now that I'm in Honduras, the company doesn't think it's very funny.
>
> *Where am I wearing? This isn't so much a question related to geography and clothes, but about the people who make our clothes and the texture of their lives.*
>
> I stand among the chaos overwhelmed. A thousand sets of eyes stare at me; perhaps they recognize my T-shirt. The irony that this is Tattoo's tropical paradise wore off long ago—somewhere between the confrontation with the big-bellied guards at the factory gate who had guns shoved down their pants like little boys playing cowboy and the conversation with the tight-lipped company representative who failed to reveal much of anything about my T-shirt or the people who assembled it. There was no way I was getting onto the factory floor. All I learned was that eight humans of indiscriminate age and sex stitched my shirt together in less than five minutes—not exactly information that required traveling all the way to Honduras to obtain. 99

(Timmerman 2009:xiii–xiv, 14).

In his book *Where Am I Wearing? A Global Tour to the Countries, Factories, and People that Make Our Clothes,* journalist Kelsey Timmerman recounts his travels to the countries where his jeans, T-shirts, and flip-flops—the uniform of today's young adult—were made. From Honduras to Bangladesh, from Cambodia to the United States, he tracked down the factories and befriended the seamstresses who laboured there. Though owners were reluctant to allow him on the factory floor, they couldn't prevent him from visiting workers' homes and families. Timmerman found that both inside and outside the factory, garment workers lived in what would be considered substandard conditions in rich countries. He argues that global apparel companies should take responsibility for conditions at their suppliers' factories, even if those factories are located halfway around the world (Fairtrade Foundation 2010).

Timmerman's book focuses on an unequal global economy, which is a central topic in sociology. His investigative work, like the work of many other journalists, is informed by sociological research that documents the existence and extent of inequality around the world. Social inequality has a pervasive influence on human interactions and institutions. Certain groups of people control scarce resources, wield power, and receive special treatment.

Although it might be interesting to know how one individual, like Kelsey Timmerman or a foreign factory worker, is affected by social inequality, sociologists consider how entire groups of people are affected by such factors, and how society itself might be altered by them. Sociologists, then, are not concerned with what one individual does or does not do, but with what people do as members of a group or in interaction with one another, and what that means for individuals and for society as a whole. For example, sociologists have considered how, together, university students have taken sociology with them, organizing to confront the sportswear companies that underpay the overseas workers who create their team uniforms and T-shirts proclaiming their school pride (Esbenshade 2008; Silverstein 2010).

Sociology is extremely broad in scope. You will see throughout this book the range of topics sociologists investigate—from suicide to TV viewing habits, from Amish society to global economic patterns, from peer pressure to genetic engineering. Sociologists look at how others influence our behaviour and how major social institutions, like the government, religion, and the economy, affect us.

In this chapter, we will explore the nature of sociology as a field of inquiry and as an exercise of the *sociological imagination*. We'll look at the discipline as a science and consider its relationship to other social sciences. We will evaluate the contributions of pioneering thinkers—Émile Durkheim, Max Weber, Karl Marx, and others—to the development of sociology. Next we will discuss a number of important theoretical perspectives used by sociologists. Finally, we will consider the ways sociology helps us to develop our sociological imagination. ■

::: use your sociological *imagination* :::

Do you think that the labels on your clothes give you any insights into who made the items and under what conditions they were produced?

www.mcgrawhillconnect.ca

What Is Sociology?

Sociology is the systematic study of social behaviour and human groups. It focuses primarily on the influence of social relationships on people's attitudes and behaviour and on how societies are established and change. In this textbook, we deal with such varied topics as families, workplaces, street gangs, business firms, political parties, genetic engineering, schools, religions, and labour unions. Here, we are concerned with love, poverty, conformity, discrimination, illness, technology, and community.

The Sociological Imagination

Have you ever wondered why people in Canada can often be seen walking down the street drinking a cup of coffee, eating a sandwich, or nibbling on a chocolate bar? Or, conversely, why do people sit using chairs and tables to consume a cup of coffee and a snack? You might not question these activities as they may just seem "normal," or "just the ways things are done."

In attempting to understand social behaviour, such as the manner in which food is consumed, sociologists rely on an unusual type of creative thinking. **C. Wright Mills** (1956) described such thinking as the **sociological imagination**—an awareness of the relationship between an individual and the wider society. This awareness allows all of us (not just sociologists) to comprehend the links between our immediate, personal social settings and the remote, impersonal social world that surrounds us and helps to shape us. Kelsey Timmerman certainly used a sociological imagination when he studied foreign garment workers.

A key element in the sociological imagination is the ability to view one's own society as an outsider would, rather than only from the perspective of personal experiences and cultural biases. Consider something as simple as sporting events. On university campuses in Canada students cheer football players. In Bali, Indonesia, dozens of spectators gather around a ring to cheer on roosters trained in cockfighting. In both instances, the spectators debate the merits of their favourites and bet on the outcome of the events. Yet what is considered a normal sporting event in one part of the world is considered unusual and, perhaps illegal, in another part.

The sociological imagination allows us to go beyond personal experiences and observations to understand broader public issues. Divorce, for example, is unquestionably a personal hardship for partners who split apart. However, C. Wright Mills advocated using the sociological imagination to view divorce not as simply an individual's personal problem but rather as a societal concern. Using this perspective, we can see that an increase in the divorce rate actually redefines a major social institution—the family. Today's households frequently include stepparents and half-siblings whose parents have divorced and remarried. Through the complexities of the blended family, this private concern becomes a public issue that affects schools, government agencies, businesses, and religious institutions.

The sociological imagination is an empowering tool. It allows us to look beyond a limited understanding of human behaviour to see the world and its people in a new way and through a broader lens than we might otherwise use. It may be as simple as understanding why a roommate prefers country music to hip-hop, or it may open up a whole different way of understanding other populations in the world. For example, in the aftermath of the terrorist attacks on the United States on September 11, 2001, many Canadians wanted to understand how Muslims throughout the world were being perceived and why. From time to time this textbook will offer you the chance to exercise your sociological imagination in a variety of situations.

::: use your sociological *imagination* :::

What aspects of the social and work environment in a fast-food restaurant would be of particular interest to a sociologist? How would the sociological imagination help in analyzing the topic?

www.mcgrawhillconnect.ca

Sociology and the Social Sciences

Is sociology a science? The term **science** refers to the body of knowledge obtained by methods based on systematic observation. Just like other scientific disciplines, sociology engages in the organized, systematic study of phenomena (in this case, human behaviour) in order to enhance understanding. All scientists, whether studying mushrooms or murderers, attempt to collect precise information through methods of

Are You What You Own?

These photos come from the book *Material World: A Global Family Portrait*. The photographers selected a "statistically average" family in each country they visited and took pictures of that family with all the possessions in the household. Shown here are families in Bhutan, South Africa, Great Britain, and Cuba (Menzel 1994).

Bhutan

Great Britain

South Africa

Cuba

study that are as objective as possible. These researchers rely on careful recording of observations and accumulation of data.

Of course, there is a great difference between sociology and physics, between psychology and astronomy. For this reason, the sciences are commonly divided into natural and social sciences. **Natural science** is the study of the physical features of nature and the ways in which they interact and change. Astronomy, biology, chemistry, geology, and physics are all natural sciences. **Social science** is the study of various aspects of human society.

The social sciences include sociology, anthropology, economics, history, psychology, and political science. The social sciences have a common focus on the social behaviour of people, yet each has a particular orientation. Anthropologists usually study past cultures and pre-industrial societies that continue today, as well as the origins of men and women; this knowledge is used to examine contemporary societies, including industrial societies. Economists explore the ways in which people produce and exchange goods and services, along with money and other resources. Historians are concerned with the peoples and events of the past and their significance for us today. Political scientists study international relations, the workings of government, and the exercise of power and authority. Psychologists investigate personality and individual behaviour. So what does sociology focus on? It emphasizes the influence that society has on people's attitudes and behaviour and the ways in which people shape society. Humans are social animals; therefore, sociologists scientifically examine our social relationships with people. Let's consider how different social scientists would study the impact of the earthquake that hit Port-au-Prince, the capital of Haiti, in 2010. Historians would stress Haiti's past economic exploitation as a colony of France and its resulting poverty today. Economists would discuss ways to rebuild Haiti's economy, perhaps by diversifying it. Environmental ecologists would treat Haiti and its neighbour, the Dominican Republic, as a single ecosystem—the island of Hispaniola. Psychologists would study individual cases of emotional stress caused by the traumatic event. And political scientists would study the short-term prospects for the nation's governance, which might include trustee status under the United Nations.

What approach would sociologists take? They might consider the possibility of reversing Haitians' generation-long migration from the countryside to the capital city, by making life in rural areas more sustainable. They might study the use of new media, such as Twitter, to funnel donations to charities. They might conduct short- and long-term research on the adoption of Haitian orphans by families in rich countries.

Sociologists would take a similar approach to studying episodes of extreme violence. In April 2007, a Virginia Tech student, armed with semi-automatic weapons, killed a total of 32 students and faculty at Virginia's largest university. Observers struggled to describe the events and place them in some social

The earthquake that hit Haiti in January 2010 may have lasted only a few minutes, but the social impact on the small, impoverished island nation will last many years. This "temporary" tent city shelters 375 000 people whose homes were destroyed, and for whom there is still no permanent housing, as of June 2011.

context. These killings were preceded by the killing of a student at Dawson College in Montreal in 2006 and the 1989 massacre of 14 female engineering students at l'Ecole Polytechnique in Montreal. For sociologists in particular, these events raised numerous issues and topics for study, including the media's role in describing the attacks, the presence of violence in our educational institutions, the gun control debate, the difference in gun ownership and use in Canada and the United States, the adequacy of mental health care systems, the status of women in Canada, and the stereotyping and stigmatization of people who suffer from mental illness.

Sociologists put their imaginations to work in a variety of areas—including aging, criminal justice, the family, human ecology, religion, health, and gender. Canadian sociologist Michael Atkinson, for example, has studied why men undergo cosmetic surgery procedures. After interviewing 44 men who had had such procedures done, as well as 12 cosmetic surgeons, Atkinson concluded, "Men are doing it more to maintain a position, to hold on to a sense of power or masculinity. For some women, it's about staying pretty. That's a disempowering image. That's not the same as a guy trying to keep his job" (Schmidt 2004:A8). Throughout this book, the sociological imagination will be used to examine Canada and other societies from the viewpoint of respectful but questioning outsiders.

Sociology and Common Sense

Sociologists focus on the study of human behaviour. We all have experience with human behaviour and at least some knowledge of it. All of us might well have theories about why people get tattoos, for example, or why people become homeless. Our theories and opinions typically come from "common sense"—that is, from our experiences and conversations, from what we read, from what we see on television, and so forth.

In our daily lives, we rely on common sense to get us through many unfamiliar situations. However, this common-sense knowledge, although sometimes accurate, is not always reliable, because it rests on commonly held beliefs rather than on a systematic analysis of facts. It was once considered common sense to accept that Earth was flat—a view rightly questioned by Pythagoras and Aristotle. Incorrect common-sense notions are not just a part of the distant past; they remain with us today.

Common sense, for example, tells us that people panic when faced with natural disasters, such as floods, earthquakes, or ice storms. However, these particular common-sense notions—such as that Earth is flat—are untrue; they are not supported by sociological research. Natural disasters do not generally produce panic. In the aftermath of disasters and even explosions, greater social organization and structure emerge to deal with a community's problems. In Canada, for example, emergency response teams often coordinate public services and even certain services normally performed by the private sector, such as food distribution. Decision making becomes more centralized in times of disaster.

Like other social scientists, sociologists do not accept something as a fact because "everyone knows it." Instead, each piece of information must be tested, recorded, and then analyzed in relation to other data. Sociologists rely on scientific

Do disasters produce panic or an organized, structured response? Common sense might tell us the former, but, in fact, disasters bring out a great deal of structure and organization to deal with their aftermath. Pictured, students evacuate Dawson College in Montreal on September 13, 2006, as police help during a shooting incident at the school.

studies in order to describe and understand a social environment. At times, the findings of sociologists may seem like common sense because they deal with facets of everyday life. The difference is that such findings have been *tested* by researchers. Common sense now tells us that Earth is round. But this particular common-sense notion is based on centuries of scientific work upholding the breakthrough made by Pythagoras and Aristotle.

1.2 What Is Sociological Theory?

Why do people commit suicide? One traditional common-sense answer is that people inherit the desire to kill themselves. Another view is that sunspots drive people to take their own lives. These explanations may not seem especially convincing to contemporary researchers, but they represent beliefs widely held as recently as 1900.

Sociologists are not particularly interested in why any one individual commits suicide; they are more concerned with the social forces that systematically cause some people to take their own lives. In order to undertake this research, sociologists develop a theory that offers a general explanation of suicidal behaviour.

We can think of theories as attempts to explain events, forces, materials, ideas, or behaviour in a comprehensive manner. Within sociology, a **theory** is a template containing definitions and relationships used to organize and understand the social world. A theory may have explanatory power, predictive power, or both. That is, it may help us to see the relationships among seemingly isolated phenomena and to understand how one type of change in an environment leads to others.

The World Health Organization (2010) estimates that almost a million people die from suicide every year. More than a hundred years ago, a sociologist tried to look at suicide data scientifically. **Émile Durkheim** (1951, original edition 1897) looked into suicide data in great detail and developed a highly original theory about the relationship between suicide and social factors. He was primarily concerned not with the personalities of individual suicide victims, but rather with suicide *rates* and how they varied from country to country. As a result, when he looked at the number of reported suicides in France, England, and Denmark in 1869, he also examined the populations of these nations to determine their rates of suicide. He found that whereas England had only 67 reported suicides per million inhabitants, France had 135 per million, and Denmark had 277 per million. The question then became, "Why did Denmark have a comparatively high rate of reported suicides?"

Durkheim went much deeper into his investigation of suicide rates, and the result was his landmark work, *Suicide,* published in 1897. Durkheim refused to automatically accept unproven explanations regarding suicide, including the beliefs that cosmic forces or inherited tendencies caused such deaths. Instead, he focused on such problems as the cohesiveness or lack of cohesiveness of religious, social, and occupational groups.

Durkheim's research suggested that suicide, although a solitary act, is related to group life. Protestants had much higher suicide rates than Catholics did; the unmarried had much higher rates than married people did; soldiers were more likely to take their lives than civilians were. In addition, it appeared that there were higher rates of suicide in times of peace than in times of war and revolution, and in times of economic instability and recession rather than in times of prosperity. Durkheim concluded that the suicide rates of a society reflected the extent to which people were or were not integrated into the group life of the society.

Émile Durkheim, like many other social scientists, developed a theory to explain how individual behaviour can be understood within a social context. He pointed out the influence of groups and societal forces on what had always been viewed as a highly personal act. Clearly, Durkheim offered a more *scientific* explanation for the causes of suicide than that of sunspots or inherited tendencies. His theory has predictive power, since it suggests that suicide rates will rise or fall in conjunction with certain social and economic changes.

Of course, a theory—even the best of theories—is not a final statement about human behaviour. Durkheim's theory of suicide is no exception; sociologists continue to examine factors that contribute to differences in suicide rates around the world and to a particular society's rate of suicide, or differences in rates between and among various groups in a single country. For example, for over a decade, rates of suicide for young people in First Nations communities in Canada have been five or more times greater than the rates for other Canadians (Health Canada 2006). First Nations communities, at the same time, experience marked differences in their rates of suicide among provinces, regions, and even within the same geographic region (Health Canada 2006). "Community wellness" strategies may have the best hope of providing young Aboriginal people with cultural continuity, buffering them somewhat from social changes that may have affected their integration within the community.

::: use your sociological *imagination* :::

If you were Durkheim's successor in his research on suicide, how would you investigate the factors that may explain the suicide rates in Canada today?

1.3 How Did Sociology Develop?

People have always been curious about sociological matters—such as how we get along, what we do, and whom we select as our leaders. Philosophers and religious authorities of ancient and medieval societies made countless observations about human behaviour. They did not test or verify these observations scientifically; nevertheless, these observations often became the foundation for moral codes. Several of the early social philosophers predicted that a systematic study of human

behaviour would one day emerge. Beginning in the nineteenth century, European theorists made pioneering contributions to the development of a science of human behaviour.

Early Thinkers: Comte, Martineau, and Spencer

The nineteenth century was an unsettling time in France. The French monarchy had been deposed in the Revolution of 1789, and Napoleon had subsequently suffered defeat in his effort to conquer Europe. Amid this chaos, philosophers considered how society might be improved. **Auguste Comte** (1798–1857), credited with being the most influential of these philosophers of the early nineteenth century, believed that a theoretical science of society and systematic investigation of behaviour were needed to improve society. He coined the term *sociology* to apply to the science of human behaviour.

Writing in the nineteenth century, Comte feared that the excesses of the French Revolution had permanently impaired France's stability. Yet he hoped that the systematic study of social behaviour would eventually lead to more rational human interactions. In Comte's hierarchy of sciences, sociology was at the top. He called it the "queen" and its practitioners "scientist-priests." This French theorist did not simply give sociology its name; he also presented a rather ambitious challenge to the fledgling discipline.

Scholars were able to learn of Comte's works largely through translations by the English sociologist **Harriet Martineau** (1802–1876). But Martineau was a trailblazer in her own right as a sociologist. She offered insightful observations of the customs and social practices of both her native Britain and North America. Martineau's book *Society in America* (1962, original edition 1837) examines religion, politics, child-rearing, and immigration in the United States. She gave special attention to social class distinctions and to such factors as gender and race.

Martineau's writings emphasized the impact that the economy, law, trade, and population could have on the social problems of contemporary society. She spoke out in favour of the rights of women, the emancipation of slaves, and religious tolerance. In Martineau's view (1896), intellectuals and scholars should not simply offer observations of social conditions; they should act on their convictions in a manner that will benefit society. In line with this view, Martineau conducted research on the nature of female employment and pointed to the need for further investigation of this issue (Deegan 2003; Hill and Hoecker-Drysdale 2001).

Another important contributor to the discipline of sociology was **Herbert Spencer** (1820–1903). A relatively prosperous Victorian Englishman, Spencer (unlike Martineau) did not feel compelled to correct or improve society; instead, he merely hoped to understand it better. Spencer applied the concept of evolution of the species to societies in order to explain how societies change, or evolve, over time. In 1852, in the *Westminster Review,* Spencer's article, "A Theory of Population, Deduced from the General Law of Animal Fertility," presented the evolutionary view of the "survival of the fittest." Charles Darwin, in later editions of *The Origins of the Species,* adopted this last phrase to describe struggle between competing life forms (McIntyre 2006).

Harriet Martineau, an early pioneer of sociology, studied social behaviour both in her native England and in North America, and proposed some of the methods still used by sociologists.

Spencer's approach to societal change was extremely popular in his own lifetime. Unlike Comte, Spencer suggested that societies are bound to change eventually; therefore, no one need be highly critical of present social arrangements or work actively for social change. This position appealed to many influential people in England and North America who had a vested interest in the status quo and were suspicious of thinkers who endorsed change.

Émile Durkheim

Émile Durkheim made many pioneering contributions to sociology, including his important theoretical work on suicide. The son of a rabbi, Durkheim (1858–1917) was educated in France and Germany. He established an impressive academic reputation and was appointed as one of the first professors of sociology in France. Above all, Durkheim will be remembered for his insistence that behaviour must be understood within a larger social context, not just in individualistic terms.

As one example of this emphasis, Durkheim ([1912] 2001) developed a fundamental thesis to help understand all forms of society through intensive study of the Arunta, an Australian tribe. He focused on the functions that religion performed for the Arunta and underscored the role that group life plays in defining what we consider religious. Durkheim concluded that, like other forms of group behaviour, religion reinforces a group's solidarity.

Another of Durkheim's main interests was the consequences of work in modern societies. In his view, the growing division of labour found in industrial societies as workers became much more specialized in their tasks led to what he called *anomie*. **Anomie** refers to the loss of direction that a society feels when social control of individual behaviour has become ineffective. The state of anomie occurs when people

have lost their sense of purpose or direction, often during a time of profound social change. In a period of anomie, people are so confused and unable to cope with the new social environment that they may resort to taking their own lives.

Durkheim was concerned about the dangers that alienation, loneliness, and isolation might pose for modern industrial societies. He shared Comte's belief that sociology should provide direction for social change. As a result, he advocated the creation of new social groups—between the individual's family and the state—which would ideally provide a sense of belonging for members of huge, impersonal societies. Unions would be an example of such a group.

Like many other sociologists, Durkheim did not limit his interests to one aspect of social behaviour. Later in this book, we will consider his thinking on crime and punishment, religion, and the workplace. Few sociologists have had such a dramatic impact on so many different areas within the discipline.

Max Weber

Another important early theorist was **Max Weber** (pronounced "vay-ber"). Born in Germany in 1864, Weber took his early academic training in legal and economic history, but he gradually developed an interest in sociology. Eventually, he became a professor at various German universities. Weber taught his students that they should employ *Verstehen* (pronounced "fehr—SHTEH—ehn"), the German word for "understanding" or "insight," in their intellectual work. He pointed out that we cannot analyze much of our social behaviour by the kinds of objective criteria we use to measure weight or temperature. To fully comprehend behaviour, we must learn the subjective meanings people attach to their actions—how they themselves view and explain their behaviour.

For example, suppose that a sociologist was studying the social ranking of students at a high school. Weber would expect the researcher to employ *Verstehen* to determine the significance of the school's social hierarchy for its members. The researcher might examine the effects of athleticism or grades or social skills or physical appearance in the school. She would seek to learn how students relate to other students of higher or lower status. While investigating these questions, the researcher would take into account people's emotions, thoughts, beliefs, and attitudes (Coser 1977).

We also owe credit to Weber for a key conceptual tool: the ideal type. An **ideal type** is a construct, a made-up model that serves as a measuring rod against which actual cases can be evaluated. In his own works, Weber identified various characteristics of bureaucracy as an ideal type (discussed in detail in Chapter 5). In presenting this model of bureaucracy, Weber was not describing any particular business, nor was he using the term *ideal* in a way that suggested a positive evaluation. Instead, his purpose was to provide a useful standard for measuring just how bureaucratic an actual organization is (Gerth and Mills 1958). Later in this textbook, we use the concept of ideal type to study family, religion, authority, and economic systems and to analyze bureaucracy.

Although their professional careers coincided, Émile Durkheim and Max Weber never met and had little or no impact on each other's ideas. This was certainly not true of the work of **Karl Marx.** Durkheim's thinking about the impact

10   Chapter 1

figure 1-1 Early Social Thinkers

	Émile Durkheim 1858–1917	**Max Weber 1864–1920**	**Karl Marx 1818–1883**
Academic training	Philosophy	Law, economics, history, philosophy	Philosophy, law
Key works	1893—*The Division of Labor in Society* 1897—*Suicide: A Study in Sociology* 1912—*Elementary Forms of Religious Life*	1904–1905—*The Protestant Ethic and the Spirit of Capitalism* 1921—*Economy and Society*	1848—*The Communist Manifesto* 1867—*Das Kapital*

of the division of labour in industrial societies was related to Marx's writings, while Weber's concern for a value-free, objective sociology was a direct response to Marx's deeply held convictions. Thus, it is not surprising that Karl Marx is viewed as a major figure in the development of sociology as well as several other social sciences (see Figure 1-1).

Karl Marx

Karl Marx (1818–1883) shared with Durkheim and Weber a dual interest in abstract philosophical issues and the concrete reality of everyday life. Unlike the others, Marx was so critical of existing institutions that a conventional academic career was impossible, and although he was born and educated in Germany, he spent most of his life in exile.

Marx's personal life was a difficult struggle. When a paper that he had written was suppressed, he fled his native land for France. In Paris, he met **Friedrich Engels** (1820–1895), with whom he formed a lifelong friendship. They lived at a time when European and North American economic life was increasingly being dominated by the factory rather than the farm.

In 1847, Marx and Engels attended the secret meetings in London of an illegal coalition of labour unions known as the Communist League. The following year, they wrote a platform called *The Communist Manifesto*. Here, they argued that the masses of people who had no resources other than their labour (whom they referred to as the *proletariat*) should unite to fight the owners of the means of production (whom they referred to as the *bourgeoisie*) for the overthrow of capitalist societies. In the words of Marx and Engels,

> The history of all hitherto existing society is the history of class struggles. . . . The proletarians have nothing to lose but their chains. They have a world to win. WORKING MEN OF ALL COUNTRIES UNITE! (Feuer 1959:7, 41)

After completing *The Communist Manifesto*, Marx returned to Germany, only to be expelled. He then moved to England, where he continued to write books and essays. Marx lived there in extreme poverty—he pawned most of his possessions, and several of his children died of malnutrition and disease. Marx clearly was an outsider in British society, a fact that may well have affected his view of Western cultures.

In Marx's analysis, society is fundamentally divided between classes, which clash in pursuit of their own class interests. When he examined the industrial societies of his time, such as Germany, England, and the United States, he saw the factory as the centre of conflict between the exploiters (the owners of the means of production) and the exploited (the workers). Marx viewed these relationships in systematic terms; that is, he believed that an entire system of economic, social, and political relationships maintained the power and dominance of the owners over the workers. Consequently, Marx and Engels argued that the working class needed to overthrow the existing class system. Marx's influence on contemporary thinking has been dramatic—his writings inspired those who were later to lead communist revolutions in Russia, China, Cuba, Vietnam, and elsewhere.

Even apart from the political revolutions that his work fostered, Marx's influence on contemporary thinking has been dramatic. Marx emphasized the *group* identifications and associations that influence an individual's place in society. This area of study is the major focus of contemporary sociology. Throughout this textbook, we consider how membership in a particular gender classification, age group, racial or ethnic group, or economic class affects a person's attitudes and behaviour. In an important sense, we can trace this way of understanding society back to the pioneering work of Karl Marx.

Twentieth-Century Developments

Sociology today builds on the firm foundation developed by Émile Durkheim, Max Weber, and Karl Marx. However, the discipline of sociology has certainly not remained stagnant over the last century. Although Europeans have continued to make contributions to the discipline, sociologists from throughout the world have advanced sociological theory and research. Their new insights have helped them to better understand the workings of society.

Today, some of the most exciting developments in sociology are taking place outside of the traditional Eurocentric (meaning "centred on European thought") framework. We now find numerous non-Western developments in sociological theory, such as indigenous or indigenist perspectives. These perspectives highlight the degree to which Western views—through centuries of colonization—define, shape, and name the world (Tuhiwai Smith 2005). Indigenous/indigenist perspectives challenge the domination and control of sociology by Western ideas and methods through the use of decolonizing frameworks.

Charles Horton Cooley (1864–1929) was typical of the sociologists who came to prominence in the early 1900s. Cooley received his graduate training in economics but later became a sociology professor at the University of Michigan. Like other early sociologists, he had become interested in this "new" discipline while pursuing a related area of study.

Cooley shared the desire of Durkheim, Weber, and Marx to learn more about society. But to do so effectively, Cooley preferred to use the sociological perspective to look first at smaller units—intimate, face-to-face groups, such as families, gangs, and friendship networks. He saw these groups as the seedbeds of society in the sense that they shape people's ideals, beliefs, values, and social nature. Cooley's work increased our understanding of groups of relatively small size.

In the early twentieth century, many leading sociologists in the United States saw themselves as social reformers dedicated to systematically studying and then improving what they saw as a corrupt society. They were genuinely concerned about the lives of newcomers to the nation's growing cities, whether these people came from Europe or the rural American south. Early female sociologists, in particular, often took active roles in poor urban areas as leaders of community centres known as *settlement houses*. For example, **Jane Addams** (1860–1935), an active member of the American Sociological Society, co-founded the famous Chicago settlement Hull House. Addams and other pioneering female sociologists commonly combined intellectual inquiry, social service work, and political activism—all with the goal of assisting the underprivileged and creating a more egalitarian society. For example, working with the black journalist and educator Ida B. Wells, Addams successfully prevented the implementation of a racial segregation policy in the Chicago public schools. Addams's efforts to establish a juvenile court system and a women's trade union also reflect the practical focus of her work (Addams 1910). Jane Addams was also known, although to a lesser extent, as an advocate for peace (Allen 2008).

By the middle of the twentieth century, however, the focus of the discipline had shifted. Sociologists for the most

Jane Addams (right) was an early pioneer both in sociology and in the settlement house movement. She was also an activist in the campaign for women's right to vote, as this photograph shows.

part restricted themselves to theorizing and gathering information; the aim of transforming society was left to social workers and others. This shift away from social reform was accompanied by a growing commitment to scientific methods of research and to value-free interpretation of data. Not all sociologists were happy with this emphasis. A new organization, the Society for the Study of Social Problems, was created in 1950 to deal more directly with social inequality and other related problems.

Sociologist **Robert Merton** (1968) made an important contribution to the discipline by successfully combining theory and research. Born in 1910 of Slavic immigrant parents in Philadelphia, Merton's teaching career has been based at Columbia University in New York.

Merton produced a theory that is one of the most frequently cited explanations of deviant behaviour. He noted different ways in which people attempt to achieve success in life. In his view, some may not share the socially agreed-on goal of accumulating material goods or the accepted means of achieving this goal. For example, in Merton's classification scheme, "innovators" are people who accept the goal of pursuing material wealth but use illegal means to do so, including robbery, burglary, and extortion. Merton bases his explanation of crime on individual behaviour—influenced by society's approved goals and means, yet it has wider applications. It helps to account for the high crime rates among the nation's poor, who may see no hope of advancing themselves through traditional roads to success. In Chapter 11, we discuss Merton's theory in greater detail.

Merton also emphasized that sociology should strive to bring together the "macro-level" and "micro-level" approaches to the study of society. **Macrosociology** concentrates on large-scale phenomena or entire civilizations. Thus, Émile Durkheim's cross-cultural study of suicide is an example of macro-level research. More recently, macrosociologists have examined international crime rates (see Chapter 11), the stereotype of Asians as a "model minority" (see Chapter 8), and the population patterns of Islamic countries (see Chapter 15). By contrast, **microsociology** stresses study of small groups and often uses experimental study in laboratories. Sociological research on the micro level has included studies of how divorced men and women, for example, disengage from significant social roles (see Chapter 5); of how conformity can influence the expression of prejudiced attitudes (see Chapter 11); and of how a teacher's expectations can affect a student's academic performance (see Chapter 13).

Pierre Bourdieu   The ideas of the French sociologist **Pierre Bourdieu** (1930–2002) have found a broad following in North America and elsewhere. As a young man, Bourdieu did fieldwork in Algeria during its struggle for independence from France. Today, scholars study Bourdieu's research techniques as well as his conclusions.

Bourdieu wrote about how capital in its many forms sustains individuals and families from one generation to the next. To Bourdieu, *capital* included not just material goods, but cultural and social assets. **Cultural capital** refers to non-economic goods, such as family background and education, which are reflected in a knowledge of language and the arts. Not necessarily book knowledge, cultural capital refers to the kind of education that is valued by the socially elite. Though a knowledge of Chinese cuisine is culture, for example, it is not the prestigious kind of culture that is valued by the elite. In the United States, immigrants—especially those who arrived in large numbers and settled in ethnic enclaves—have generally taken two or three generations to develop the same level of cultural capital enjoyed by more established groups. In comparison, **social capital** refers to the collective benefit of social networks, which are built on reciprocal trust. Much has been written about the importance of family and friendship networks in providing people with an opportunity to advance. In his emphasis on cultural and social capital, Bourdieu's work extends the insights of early social thinkers such as Marx and Weber (Bourdieu and Passerson 1990; Field 2008).

In Canada, the work of sociologists **Harold A. Innis** (1894–1952) and **S.D. Clark** (1910–2003) established a strong foundation for the examination of Canada from a political economy perspective. Innis rejected existing interpretations of Canadian society and theorized about the relationship between the extraction of products, such as fish, timber, wheat, and hydroelectric power, and the development of the Canadian state. Innis's works, such as *A History of the Canadian Pacific Railway* (1923), *The Fur Trade in Canada: An Introduction to Canadian Economic History* (1930), *The Cod Fisheries: The History of an International Economy* (1942), and *Political Economy in the Modern State* (1946), took a historical perspective

on the production of staple goods (e.g., fish, fur, and forest products) in the young Canadian economy, emphasizing the importance of communication and transportation to the development of political and economic systems. Innis's later research at the University of Toronto also included an examination of modern communication theory: *The Bias of Communication* (1951). In addressing the influence of the media on society, Innis made yet another contribution to the development of Canadian sociology.

S.D. Clark studied under Innis at the University of Toronto, completing his PhD in 1938. At that time, Clark began his academic career teaching in the political science department at the University of Toronto, as no department of sociology had yet been formed. Clark's books, such as *The Social Development of Canada* (1942), *Church and Sect in Canada* (1948), and *Movements of Political Protest* (1959), depict the struggle between the hinterlands and the cultural and financial power centres of Canada, which results in regional conflicts, the emergence of new political parties and religions, and social movements. His body of work helped to win increasing respect for sociology as a discipline in Canada, and he is credited with establishing the Department of Sociology at the University of Toronto in 1963.

Later, **John Porter's** *The Vertical Mosaic* (1965) provided a formative examination of social inequality as it relates to race, ethnicity, social class, and gender in Canada. Porter's depiction of Canadian society as a "mosaic" continues to be used in contrast to the U.S. metaphor of the "melting pot." (These concepts will be discussed in more detail in Chapter 3.) Using Canadian census data before 1961, Porter revealed the existence of a hierarchy among ethnic groups in which the charter groups—the French and British—occupied the top socioeconomic positions. The charter groups were followed by other northern Europeans (e.g., Norwegians, Swedes, Dutch, Belgians), who were then followed by southern and Eastern Europeans (e.g., Ukrainians, Hungarians, Italians, Greeks). At the bottom of this socioeconomic hierarchy were visible-minority groups, such as Chinese, blacks, and Aboriginals. Porter referred to groups that were not charter groups as *entrance groups*. These groups typically were assigned to lower-status jobs, according to the stereotypical preferences of the dominant charter groups. According to sociologist Richard Wanner (1998), "*The Vertical Mosaic* set the agenda for several streams of research, including studies of elites and the structure of power, social mobility and the role of education in the occupational attainment process, and immigrant integration and ethnic inequality."

Jim Curtis, who died in 2005, was one of Canada's most prolific and influential sociologists, whose work gained both national and international recognition. He spent his entire career at the University of Waterloo, where he taught since 1970, inspiring and mentoring scores of graduate students who worked under his direction. Curtis is credited with contributing to the founding of an indigenous Canadian sociology, his research spanning an eclectic array of topics such as religion, sport, social inequality, gender, aging, voluntary association activity, social values, and voting. In 2004, he was inducted as a Fellow of the Royal Society of Canada, which is considered the highest academic honour in Canada.

The Royal Society of Canada's citation for Curtis stated, "Among his many contributions is work over several decades comparing Canadian–American values, which has served to challenge the conventional thesis of Canadians being more 'elitist' and less 'achievement oriented' than Americans. This has been the basis for a central debate within sociology and political science. Professor Curtis is author of numerous texts helping to define sociology to students in Canadian terms" (*UW Daily Bulletin* 2004). Those texts include *The Social World: A Canadian Introduction to Sociology* (4th edition, 2005, edited with Lorne Tepperman) and *Social Inequality in Canada: Problems and Policies* (4th edition, 2004, edited with Edward Grabb and Neil Guppy). Jim Curtis was the editor of the *Canadian Review of Sociology and Anthropology* between 1989 and 1992, and in 2000 was recognized by the Canadian Sociology and Anthropology Association for outstanding contribution to the field of sociology. Despite his numerous honours and prestigious recognitions, those who knew Jim Curtis personally—as this author did—were often most impressed by the quality of his character—humble, jolly, hard-working, and compassionate, and guided by the highest standards of integrity.

Contemporary sociology reflects the diverse contributions of earlier theorists. As sociologists approach such topics as divorce, drug addiction, and religious cults, they can draw on the theoretical insights of the discipline's pioneers. A careful reader can hear Comte, Durkheim, Weber, Marx, Cooley, and many others speaking through the pages of current research. Sociology has also broadened beyond the intellectual confines of North America and Europe. Contributions to the discipline now come from sociologists studying and researching human behaviour in other parts of the world. In describing the work of today's sociologists, it is helpful to examine a number of influential theoretical approaches (also known as *perspectives*).

What Are the Major Theoretical Perspectives?

Students studying sociology for the first time may be surprised to learn that sociologists view society in different ways. Some see the world basically as a stable and ongoing entity. They are impressed with the endurance of the family, organized religion, and other social institutions. Some sociologists see society as composed of many groups in conflict, competing for scarce resources. To other sociologists, the most fascinating aspects of the social world are the everyday, routine interactions among individuals that we sometimes take for granted. Others see the world in terms of how gender is socially constructed. These four views, the ones most widely used by sociologists, are the functionalist, conflict, feminist, and interactionist perspectives. They will provide an introductory look at the discipline. One way to think about the theoretical perspectives used by sociologists is to compare them to the wearing of a lens. A sociologist explains the social world according to the assumptions and emphases of his or her theoretical perspective, just as the wearer of a lens sees the world according to the lens's size, shape, colour, and other characteristics.

Functionalist Perspective

Think of society as a living organism in which each part of the organism contributes to its survival. This view is the **functionalist perspective,** which emphasizes the way that parts of a society are structured to maintain its stability.

Let's examine prostitution as an example of the functionalist perspective. Why is it that a practice so widely condemned continues to display such persistence and vitality? Functionalists suggest that prostitution satisfies needs of patrons that may not be readily met through more socially acceptable forms, such as courtship or marriage. The "buyer" receives sex without any responsibility for procreation or sentimental attachment; at the same time, the "seller" makes a living through this exchange.

Such an examination leads us to conclude that prostitution does perform certain functions that society seems to need. However, this is not to suggest that prostitution is a desirable or legitimate form of social behaviour. Functionalists do not make such judgments. Rather, advocates of the functionalist perspective hope to explain how an aspect of society that is so frequently attacked can nevertheless manage to survive (Davis 1937).

The work of James (Jim) Curtis, which examined a broad range of areas (including social inequality, political sociology, and the sociology of sport), contributed to the building of a Canadian sociology.

Talcott Parsons Talcott Parsons (1902–1979), a Harvard University sociologist, was a key figure in the development of functionalist theory. Parsons had been greatly influenced by the work of Émile Durkheim, Max Weber, and other European sociologists. For more than four decades, Parsons dominated sociology in the United States with his advocacy of functionalism. Parsons saw any society as a vast network of connected parts, each of which helps to maintain the system as a whole. His approach, carried forward by German sociologist Niklas Luhmann (1927–1998), holds that if an aspect of social life does not contribute to a society's stability or survival—if it does not serve some identifiably useful function or promote value consensus among members of society—it will not be passed on from one generation to the next (Joas and Knöbl 2009; Knudsen 2010).

Cows (zebu), considered sacred in India, wander freely through this city, respected by all who encounter them. The sanctity of the cow is functional in India, where plowing, milking, and fertilizing are far more important to subsistence farmers than a diet that includes beef.

Let's examine an example of the functionalist perspective. Many North Americans have difficulty understanding the Hindu prohibition against slaughtering cows (specifically, zebu). Cattle browse unhindered through Indian street markets, helping themselves to oranges and mangoes while people bargain for the little food they can afford. What explains this devotion to the cow in the face of human deprivation—a devotion that appears to be dysfunctional?

The simple explanation is that cow worship is highly functional in Indian society, according to economists, agronomists, and social scientists who have studied the matter. Cows perform two essential tasks: plowing the fields and producing milk. If eating their meat were permitted, hungry families might be tempted to slaughter their cows for immediate consumption, leaving themselves without a means of cultivation. Cows also produce dung, which doubles as a fertilizer and a fuel for cooking. Finally, cow meat sustains the neediest group in society, the *Dalit,* or untouchables, who sometimes resort to eating beef in secrecy. If eating beef were socially acceptable, higher-status Indians would no doubt bid up its price, placing it beyond the reach of the hungriest.

Manifest and Latent Functions Your college or university calendar typically states various functions of the institution. It may inform you, for example, that the university intends to offer each student a broad education in classical and contemporary thought, in the humanities, in the sciences, and in the arts. However, it would be quite a surprise to find a calendar that declared, "This university was founded in 1895 to keep people between the ages of 18 and 22 out of the job market, thus reducing unemployment." No postsecondary institution would declare that this is the purpose of postsecondary education. Yet societal institutions serve many functions, some of them quite subtle. Postsecondary education, in fact, *does* delay people's entry into the job market.

Robert Merton (1968) made an important distinction between manifest and latent functions. **Manifest functions** of institutions are open, stated, conscious functions. They involve the intended, recognized consequences of an aspect of society, such as the college or university's role in certifying academic competence and excellence. By contrast, **latent functions** are unconscious or unintended functions and may reflect hidden purposes of an institution. One latent function of colleges and universities is to hold down unemployment. Another is to serve as a meeting ground for people seeking marital partners.

Dysfunctions Functionalists acknowledge that not all parts of a society contribute to its stability all the time. A **dysfunction** refers to an element or a process of society that may actually disrupt a social system or lead to a decrease in stability.

We consider many dysfunctional behaviour patterns, such as homicide, to be undesirable. Yet we should not automatically interpret dysfunctions as negative. The evaluation of a dysfunction depends on a person's own values or, as the saying goes, on "where you sit." For example, the official view in prisons in the United States is that inmate gangs should be eradicated because they are dysfunctional to smooth operations. Yet some guards have actually come to view the presence of prison gangs as functional for their jobs. The danger posed by gangs creates a "threat to security," requiring increased surveillance and special staffing to address the gang problems (Scott 2001).

Conflict Perspective

Where functionalists' emphasis on stability and consensus, conflict sociologists see the social world as being in continual struggle. The **conflict perspective** assumes that social behaviour is best understood in terms of conflict or tension between competing groups. Such conflict and change need not be violent; they can take the form of labour negotiations, gender relations, party politics, competition between religious groups for members, or disputes over the federal budget. Conflict theorists contend that social institutions and practices persist because powerful groups have the ability to maintain control over them. Change has crucial significance, therefore, because it is needed to correct social injustices and inequalities through loosening the grip of the powerful members of society.

Throughout most of the twentieth century, the functionalist perspective had the upper hand in sociology in North America. However, the conflict approach has become increasingly persuasive since the late 1960s. The rise of the feminist and gay rights movements, First Nations land claims, and confrontations at abortion clinics offered support for the conflict approach—the view that our social world is characterized by continual struggle between competing groups. Currently, the discipline of sociology views conflict theory as one way, among many others, to gain insight into a society.

The Marxist View   Karl Marx accepted the evolutionary argument that societies develop along a particular path. However, unlike Comte and Spencer, he did not view each successive stage as an inevitable improvement over the previous one. History, according to Marx, proceeds through a series of stages, each of which exploits a class of people. Ancient society exploited slaves; the estate system of feudalism exploited serfs; modern capitalist society exploits the working class. Ultimately, through a socialist revolution led by the proletariat, human society will move toward the final stage of development: a classless communist society, or "community of free individuals," as Marx described it in *Das Kapital* in 1867 (see Bottomore and Rubel 1956:250).

Karl Marx viewed struggle as inevitable, given the exploitation of workers under capitalism. Marx had an important influence on the development of sociology. His thinking offered insights into such institutions as the economy, the family, religion, and government. The Marxist view of social change is appealing because it does not restrict people to a passive role in responding to inevitable cycles or changes in material culture. Rather, Marxist theory offers a tool for those who want to seize control of the historical process and gain their freedom from injustice. In contrast to functionalists' emphasis on stability, Marx argues that conflict is a normal and desirable aspect of social change. In fact, change must be encouraged as a means of eliminating social inequality (Lauer 1982).

Expanding on Marx's work, sociologists and other social scientists have come to see conflict not merely as a class phenomenon but as a part of everyday life in all societies. Thus, in studying any culture, organization, or social group, sociologists want to know who benefits, who suffers, and who dominates at the expense of others. They are concerned with the conflicts between women and men, parents and children, and urban and rural areas, to name only a few. Conflict theorists are interested in how society's institutions—including the family, government, religion, education, and the media—may help to maintain the privileges of some groups and keep others in a subservient position. Their emphasis on social change and redistribution of resources makes conflict theorists more "radical" and "activist" than functionalists (Dahrendorf 1958).

Feminist Perspectives

Feminist perspectives attempt to explain, understand, and change the ways in which gender socially organizes our public and private lives in such a way as to produce inequality between men and women.

There are as many feminist perspectives as there are social and political philosophies; they run the gamut from liberal feminism to Marxist feminism and from anarchist feminism to eco-feminism. There is no *one* feminist perspective. Feminist perspectives, which can be macro or micro, have been a major contributor to contemporary sociological theory, providing frameworks within which gender inequality can be examined, understood, and changed. The following sections provide a sample of various feminist theories, highlighting the vast diversity among them.

Liberal Feminism   Liberal feminism advocates that women's equality can be obtained through the extension of the principles of equality of opportunity and freedom. Rather than advocating structural change to the capitalist economy or attempting to eliminate patriarchy (the system and practice of male domination in society), liberal feminist approaches assume that extending women's opportunities for education and employment, for example, will result in greater gender equality.

Marxist Feminism   Marxist feminism places the system of capitalism at fault for the oppression of women. Marxist feminists believe that women are not oppressed by sexism or patriarchy, but rather by a system of economic production that is based on unequal gender relations in the capitalist economy (Tong 1989).

Socialist Feminism   Gender relations, according to **socialist feminism,** are shaped by both patriarchy and capitalism. Socialist feminists, unlike Marxist feminists, who believe that the elimination of class distinctions will bring about gender equality, see patriarchy's grip in the home as well as in the public sphere (Luxton 1980).

Radical Feminism   The root of all oppression, according to **radical feminism,** is embedded in patriarchy (Code 1993). Some radical feminists (Firestone 1970) have based their view of women's oppression on reproduction, arguing that women's freedom from reproduction (i.e., through technological developments) will lead to their overall emancipation.

Transnational Feminism   Transnational feminism recognizes that capitalism and systems of political power have severe consequences and oppress women around the world. This form of feminism embraces the multiplicity of cultures, languages, geographies, and experiences that shape the lives of women and highlights the Western/non-Western hierarchy that continues to exist in thought and practice (Grewal 2005; Mohanty 2003).

Critical Race Feminism   Critical race feminism attempts to bring about women's self-definition and naming their reality, free from the oppression of patriarchy and the legacy of colonization of white society. More specifically, "the use of non-traditional writing genres has been the primary strategy for critical race theorists in general and black critical race theorists in particular" (Alexander-Floyd 2010:812).

Despite their differences, according to Patricia Madoo Lengermann and Gillian Niebrugge, contemporary feminist theories ask the following questions:

1. "And what about women?"
2. "Why is all this as it is?"
3. "How can we change and improve the social world so as to make it a more just place for all people?" (2008:451)

Dorothy Smith (1926–) is a Canadian sociologist whose contributions to sociology in general and feminist sociology in particular have been influential worldwide. Smith argues for a sociology that is built on the everyday experiences of women, and she points out how sociology used to ignore these experiences. Smith's groundbreaking work, *The Everyday World as Problematic* (1987), has helped students of sociology see the everyday world from the standpoint of women.

Margrit Eichler (1942–), also a Canadian sociologist, was among the first sociologists in this country to examine the ways in which sexism can influence research in social science (Nelson and Robinson 1999). Eichler examined sexist language and concepts, the androcentric perspective, and sexist methodology and interpretations of results (Eichler 1984:20).

The work of such sociologists as Smith and Eichler addresses the long-standing exclusion of women's standpoint in sociology, as well as sexist biases in the way in which sociological research has been conducted.

Symbolic Interactionist Perspective

Workers interacting on the job, encounters in public places like bus stops and parks, behaviour in small groups—these are all aspects of microsociology that catch the attention of interactionists. Whereas functionalist and conflict theorists both analyze large-scale society-wide patterns of behaviour, the symbolic **interactionist perspective** generalizes about everyday forms of social interaction in order to understand society as a whole. Canadian symbolic interactionist sociologist **Robert Prus,** for example, studies the social world according to how people make sense out of their day-to-day lived experiences (1996). Employing a symbolic interactionist perspective, Prus has studied business, not as a strictly economic activity, but as a social activity based on lived experiences (1989). In the 1990s, for example, the workings of juries became a subject of public scrutiny. Today, given the concern over the cost and availability of gas, interactionists have begun to study a form of commuter behaviour called "slugging." To avoid driving to work, commuters gather at certain preappointed places to seek rides from complete strangers. When a driver pulls into the parking area or vacant lot and announces his destination, the first slug in line who is headed for that destination jumps in. Rules of etiquette have emerged to smooth the social interaction between driver and passenger: neither the driver nor the passenger may eat or smoke; the slug may not adjust the windows or radio or talk on a cellphone. The presence of the slugs, who get a free ride, may allow the driver to use special lanes reserved for high-occupancy vehicles (Slug-Lines.com 2008).

Symbolic interactionism is a sociological framework for viewing human beings as living in a world of meaningful objects. These "objects" may include material things, actions, other people, relationships, and even symbols. Symbolic interactionists see daily life not as static, but rather as constantly changing—changing because people's social relationships, actions, material world, and symbols are constantly being reconstructed and new meanings are given to them. *Social constructionism,* currently a highly popular form of symbolic interactionism, takes the position that what we often assume to be "natural" or possessing innate features is often "constructed" by social forces—forces that vary according to culture, place, and historical period. As human beings, we constantly construct and reconstruct the meanings of what it is to be masculine and feminine, gay and straight, married and single, as well as other aspects of our daily lives. For example, the label of "old maid"—frequently used in the 1940s and early 1950s in Canada—stigmatized single women in their late-20s and beyond as being boring, unattractive, and sexually inactive. Fast forward to the 1990s and 2000s, and think about how the characters are portrayed in the popular television series *Sex and the City*—the single, 30-something woman living in New York City is constructed as being exciting, autonomous, and sexually liberated.

Although functionalist and conflict approaches were initiated in Europe, symbolic interactionism developed first at the University of Chicago in the early 1900s. Interactionism became prominent when the Department of Sociology at the University of Chicago (known as the Chicago School) came to dominate North American sociology during the first four decades of the twentieth century (Marshall 1998). **George Herbert Mead** (1863–1931) is widely regarded as the founder of the interactionist perspective. Mead taught at the University of Chicago from 1893 until his death. His sociological analysis, like that of Charles Horton Cooley, often focused on human interactions within one-to-one situations and small groups. Mead was interested in observing the most minute forms of communication—smiles, frowns, nodding of the head—and in understanding how such individual behaviour was influenced by the larger context of a group or society. Despite his innovative views, Mead only occasionally wrote articles and never a book. He was an extremely popular teacher, and most of his insights have come to us through edited volumes of lectures that his students published after his death. Mead continued Cooley's exploration of symbolic interactionist theory (1934, 1964a), developing a useful model of the process by which the self emerges. According to Mead, this process was defined by three distinct stages, which he called the preparatory stage, the play stage, and the game stage.

Mead is best known for his theory of the self. According to Mead (1964b), the self begins as a privileged, central position in a person's world. Young children picture themselves as the focus of everything around them and find it difficult to consider the perspectives of others. For example, when shown a mountain scene and asked to describe what an observer on the opposite side of the mountain might see (such as a lake or hikers), young children describe only objects visible from their own perspective. As people mature, the self changes and begins to show greater concern about the reactions of others. Parents, friends, teachers, coaches, and co-workers are often among those who play a major role in shaping a person's self. Mead used the term **significant others** to refer to those individuals who are the most important in the development of the self. Many young people, for example, find themselves drawn to the same kind of work as their parents engage in (Schlenker 1985).

Mead uses the term **generalized other** to refer to the attitudes, viewpoints, and expectations of society that a child takes into account. Simply put, this concept suggests that when an individual acts, he or she considers an entire group of people. For example, a child will not act courteously merely to please a particular parent. Rather, the child comes to understand that courtesy is a widespread social value endorsed by parents, teachers, and religious leaders.

Erving Goffman (1922–1982) popularized a particular type of interactionist method known as the **dramaturgical approach.** The dramaturgist compares everyday life to the setting of the theatre and stage. Just as actors project certain images, all of us seek to present particular features of our personalities while we hide other qualities. Thus, in a class, we may feel the need to project a serious image; at a party, we want to look relaxed and friendly.

The Postmodern Critique More recently, sociologists have expanded their thinking to reflect the conditions of postmodern society. A **postmodern society** is a technologically sophisticated society that is preoccupied with consumer goods and media images (Brannigan 1992). Such societies consume goods and information on a mass scale. Postmodern theorists take a global perspective and note the ways that aspects of culture cross national boundaries (Lyotard 1993). For example, residents of Yellowknife may listen to reggae music from Jamaica, eat sushi and other types of Japanese food, and wear clogs from the Netherlands.

Postmodern theorists point to this diversity in their rejection of the notion that the social world can be explained by a single paradigm. The intermingling of cultures and ideologies that characterizes the modern, electronically connected planet has led to a relativist approach. As part of just one of the debates taking place among sociologists, postmodernists reject science as a panacea, arguing that no single theory can accurately explain the causes and consequences of postmodern global society. For example, postmodern theorists suggest that there is no objective way of differentiating true beliefs from false ones, since there is a plurality of claims to truth. As well, postmodern perspectives reject rigid boundaries or distinctions between and among academic disciplines, such as art, philosophy, and sociology, arguing that much can be gained through sharing ideas of many disciplines.

The emphasis of postmodern theorists is on describing emerging cultural forms and patterns of social interaction. Within sociology, the postmodern view offers support for integrating the insights of various theoretical perspectives—functionalism, conflict theory, interactionism, labelling theory, and feminist theories. Some feminist sociologists argue optimistically that, with its indifference to hierarchies and distinctions, postmodernism will discard traditional values of male dominance in favour of gender equality. Yet others

contend that despite new technology, postindustrial and postmodern societies can be expected to experience the problems of inequality that have plagued industrial societies (Ritzer 1995; Sale 1996; Smart 1990; Turner 1990; van Vucht Tijssen 1990).

Contemporary debates in sociological theory may consist of two opposing views: (1) one advocates the presence of a pre-existing social structure (i.e., a "society") in which reality is represented in social institutions and culture; (2) another advocates that reality is socially constructed, locally, on a micro level.

Postmodernism as a sociological approach, for example, focuses on individual action in which reality is socially constructed through a process of negotiated interaction with other individuals. In contrast, sociologists who offer the view that a social structure exists before an individual's entry into the world proceed from a macro rather than a micro perspective; consequently, they focus on how, for example, social institutions, such as the mass media, the education system, and religious organizations, have an impact on individuals. Although the debate may appear to be irreconcilably polarized between the social constructionist view of reality and the idea of a pre-existing social structure, human history may be viewed dialectically—that is, individuals are creators of and, at the same time, creations of their social worlds.

The Sociological Approach

Which perspective should a sociologist use in studying human behaviour? functionalist? conflict? feminist? interactionist?

Sociology makes use of all four perspectives (see Table 1-1), since each offers unique insights into the same issue. Box 1-1 shows how the Gulf of Mexico oil spill might look from the functionalist, conflict, feminist, and interactionist points of view.

No one approach to a particular issue is "correct." In this book, we assume that sociologists can gain the broadest understanding of our society by drawing on all four perspectives in the study of human behaviour and institutions. These perspectives overlap as their interests coincide but can diverge according to the dictates of each approach and of the issue being studied. A sociologist's theoretical orientation influences her approach to a research problem in important ways.

1.5 What Can We Expect from the Use of the Sociological Imagination?

Throughout the book, we will be illustrating the sociological imagination in several different ways—by showing theory in practice and research in action; by thinking globally; by exploring the significance of social inequality; by speaking across race, gender, class, and religious boundaries; and by highlighting social policy throughout the world.

table **1-1** Comparing Major Theoretical Perspectives

	Functionalist	Conflict	Feminist	Interactionist
View of society	Stable, well-integrated	Characterized by tension and struggle between and among groups	Characterized by gender and inequality; causes and solutions vary	Active in influencing and affecting everyday social interaction
Level of analysis emphasized	Macro	Macro	Both macro and micro levels of analysis	Micro-analysis as a way of understanding the larger macro phenomena
Key concepts	Manifest functions Latent functions Dysfunction	Inequality Capitalism Stratification	Standpoint of women Political action Gender inequality Oppression	Symbols Non-verbal communication Face to face
View of the individual	People are socialized to perform societal functions	People are shaped by power, coercion, and authority	Differs according to social class, race, ethnicity, age, sexual orientation, and physical ability	People manipulate symbols and create their social worlds through interaction
View of the social order	Maintained through cooperation and consensus	Maintained through force and coercion	Maintained through standpoints that do not include those of women	Maintained by shared understanding of everyday behavior
View of social change	Predictable, reinforcing	Change takes place all the time and may have positive consequences	Essential in order to bring about equality	Reflected in people's social positions and their communications with others
Example	Public punishments reinforce the social order	Laws reinforce the positions of those in power	Spousal violence, date rape, and economic inequality need to be eliminated	People respect laws or disobey them based on their own past experience
Proponents	Émile Durkheim Talcott Parsons Robert Merton	Karl Marx C. Wright Mills	Dorothy Smith Margrit Eichler	George Herbert Mead Charles Horton Cooley Erving Goffman

Theory in Practice

We will illustrate how the four sociological perspectives—functionalist, conflict, feminist, and interactionist—are helpful in understanding today's issues. Sociologists do not necessarily declare "we are using functionalism," but their research and approaches do tend to draw on one or more theoretical frameworks, as will become clear in the pages that follow.

Research Today

Sociologists actively investigate a variety of issues and social behaviour. We have already seen that such research might involve the meaning of sports. Often, the research has direct applications for improving people's lives, as in the case of increasing the participation of blacks in Canada and the United States in diabetes testing. Throughout the rest of the book, the research done by sociologists and other social scientists that we present will shed light on group behaviour of all types.

Thinking Globally Whatever their theoretical perspective or research techniques, sociologists recognize that social behaviour must be viewed in a global context. **Globalization** is the worldwide integration of government policies, cultures, social movements, and financial markets through trade and the exchange of ideas. Although public discussion of globalization is relatively recent, intellectuals have been pondering both its negative and positive social consequences for a long time. Karl Marx and Friedrich Engels warned in *The Communist Manifesto* (written in 1848) of a world market that would lead to production in distant lands, sweeping away existing working relationships.

Some observers see globalization and its effects as the natural result of advances in communications technology,

research today

1-1 Looking at the Gulf of Mexico Oil Spill from Four Sociological Perspectives

The Gulf of Mexico oil spill, which began on April 20, 2010, dominated the international news for much of that year. Like other disasters, the huge spill had social effects that can be analyzed from the four major sociological perspectives.

Functionalist View

In evaluating the effects of the Gulf Coast oil spill, functionalists would stress society's supportive function. For example:

- Functionalists might expect a revitalization of the environmental movement, as happened in the early 1900s in the United States after the damming of the Hetch Hetchy Valley just outside Yosemite, and later in the 1990s, after massive wildfires swept through the Everglades.
- Functionalists would observe that churches and other charities along the Gulf Coast provided both spiritual and material support to households affected by the spill.
- Functionalists might note full employment in selected occupations, such as the manufacture of containment booms, even when jobs in other industries were scarce.
- Functionalists would not be surprised that because offshore oil drilling is an integral part of the Gulf Coast economy, the governor of Louisiana strongly opposed a moratorium on deep-sea drilling, despite questions about its safety.

Conflict View

Because conflict theorists see the social order in terms of conflict or tension between competing groups, they would emphasize the coercion and exploitation that underlies relations between the oil companies and Gulf Coast communities:

- The oil industry, conflict theorists would note, is a form of big business, in which profits are more important than workers' health and safety.
- Conflict theorists would emphasize the often-overlooked effect of the spill on minority groups living in inland communities, including Vietnamese Americans, Native Americans, and African Americans. These groups, which were living a marginal existence before the spill, endured particularly significant economic setbacks after the spill.
- Conflict theorists would note that although news outlets tend to focus on oil spills that

SWIMMING WATER QUALITY STATUS

HEALTH ADVISORY:

THE PUBLIC IS ADVISED NOT TO SWIM IN THESE WATERS DUE TO THE PRESENCE OF OIL-RELATED CHEMICALS

affect wealthy industrial countries, often the worst spills afflict communities in disadvantaged developing nations, such as Nigeria.

Feminists would note that during times of economic upheaval and dislocation, such as the Gulf Coast oil crisis, women bear a disproportionate share of the burden in their role as caregivers

Feminist View

Feminists would note that during times of economic upheaval and dislocation, such as the Gulf Coast oil crisis, women bear a disproportionate share of the burden in their role as caregivers:

- One family wage earner may leave home to seek work elsewhere; women with children or elderly dependants are left with increased responsibility.
- With time, the physical separation these families experience may turn into marital separation, increasing the rates of single-parent families headed by women.

Interactionist View

Interactionists would examine the Gulf Coast oil spill on the micro level, by focusing on how it shaped personal relations and day-to-day social behaviour:

- Interactionists would note that difficult times often strengthen ties among neighbours and family members.
- At the same time, stressful events can contribute to social breakdowns, including divorce or even suicide—a pattern researchers observed in the aftermath of the Exxon *Valdez* oil spill in 1989.

Despite their differences, functionalists, conflict theorists, feminists, and interactionists would all agree that disasters like the Gulf of Mexico oil spill are a worthy subject for sociological study.

Apply the Theory

1. Which of the four sociological perspectives seems most useful to you in analyzing the Gulf of Mexico oil crisis? Why?
2. For many people, the worldwide economic crisis that began in 2008 had disastrous personal consequences. Use the four sociological perspectives to analyze what happened to you, your family, and your community during the Great Recession.

Sources: Capriccioso 2010; Freudenburg and Gramling 2010; Greenemeier 2010; Jopling and Morse 2010; Liptak 2010; Molotch 1970; Samuels 2010; Wallace 2010.

sociology in the global community

1-2 Your Morning Cup of Coffee

When you drink a cup of coffee, do you give much thought to where the coffee beans came from, or do you think more about the pleasure you get from the popular beverage? Coffee certainly is popular—as an import, it is second only to petroleum, the most traded commodity in the world.

Although the coffee trade has been globalized, the customs of coffee drinking still vary from place to place. Starbucks now has over 17 000 locations worldwide, including over 1200 in Canada and 1000 in Europe. Managers find that in European countries, where the coffeehouse culture originated, 80 percent of their customers sit down to drink their coffee. In the United States, 80 percent of Starbucks' customers leave the store immediately, taking their coffee with them.

Today, the coffee trade relies on the exploitation of cheap labour. Coffee is a labour-intensive crop: there is little that technology can do to ease the coffee picker's burden. The typical coffee picker works in a developing nation near the equator, receiving for a day's wages an amount that matches the price of a single cup of coffee in North America. In the 1940s, advocacy groups began to promote the sale of certified *fair trade coffee,* which gives a living wage to those who harvest the crop, allowing them to become economically self-sufficient. Recently, a similar movement has begun to promote fair trade in the global clothing industry, reported on by Kelsey Timmerman in his book *Where Am I Wearing?*

> *The typical coffee picker works in a developing nation near the equator, receiving for a day's wages an amount that matches the price of a single cup of coffee in North America.*

Ecological activists have drawn attention to what they see as the coffee industry's contribution to the trend toward global warming. The need to make room for more coffee fields, they charge, has encouraged the destruction of rain forests. The same criticism can be aimed at much of the consumption in industrial nations. Of all the products that emerge from developing nations, however, few have as singular a place in many people's daily ritual as that morning cup of joe. The drink in your hand is your tangible link to rural workers in some of the poorest areas of the world.

Apply the Theory

1. Do you enjoy coffee? Would you willingly pay more for a cup of coffee if you knew that the worker who picked the beans would benefit from the higher price?
2. The coffee trade has been blamed for perpetuating social inequality and global warming. Can you think of any positive effects of the coffee trade? Who benefits most from this economic activity?

Sources: Adamy 2008; Fieser 2009; Jaffee 2007; Luttinger and Dicum 2006; E. Marx 2009; Ritzer 2011:218–227.

---

particularly the Internet and satellite transmission of the mass media. Others view it more critically, as a process that allows multinational corporations to expand unchecked. We examine the impact of globalization on our daily lives and on societies throughout the world in Box 1-2 and throughout this book (Fiss and Hirsch 2005).

Speaking Across Race, Gender, Class, and Religious Boundaries

Sociologists include both men and women, people from a variety of socioeconomic backgrounds (some privileged and many not), and individuals from a wealth of ethnic, racial, national, and religious origins. In their work, sociologists seek to draw conclusions that speak to all people—not just the affluent or powerful. This is not always easy. Insights into how a corporation can increase its profits tend to attract more attention and financial support than do, say, the merits of a needle-exchange program for those struggling with addictions in urban centres. More than ever, though, sociology today seeks to better understand the experiences of *all* people. In Box 1-2, we take a look at our consumption of coffee and how it is linked to living standards in producing countries.

Sociologists have noted that the huge tsunami that hit South Asia in 2004 affected men and women differently. When the waves hit, mothers and grandmothers were at home with the children; men were outside working, where they were more likely to become aware of the impending disaster. Moreover, most of the men knew how to swim, a survival skill that women in these traditional societies usually do not learn. As a result, many more men than women survived the catastrophe—about 10 men for every 1 woman. In one Indonesian village typical of the disaster area, 97 of 1300 people survived; only 4 were women. The impact of this gender imbalance will be felt for some time, given women's primary role as caregivers for children and the elderly (BBC News 2005).

The Significance of Social Inequality Who holds power? Who doesn't? Who has prestige? Who lacks it? Perhaps the major theme of analysis in sociology today is **social inequality,** a condition in which members of society have differing amounts of wealth, prestige, or power. For example, the disparity between what coffee bean pickers in developing nations are paid and the price you pay for a cup of coffee underscores global inequality (see Box 1-2). Kelsey Timmerman's research among foreign garment workers uncovered some other aspects of global inequality. The 2011 housing crisis in the Cree community of Attawapiskat, in northern Ontario, drew attention to the long-standing inequalities in living standards between First Nations communities and those in the rest of Canada. And the impact of Hurricane Katrina on residents of the Gulf Coast drew attention to social inequality in the United States. Predictably, the people who were hit the hardest by the massive storm were the poor, who had the greatest difficulty evacuating before the storm and have had the most difficulty recovering from it.

Some sociologists, in seeking to understand the effects of inequality, have made the case for social justice. The African-American sociologist W. E. B. DuBois ([1940] 1968:418) noted that the greatest power in the land is not "thought or ethics, but wealth." As we have seen, the contributions of Karl Marx, and Jane Addams, also stressed this belief in the overarching significance of social inequality, and by extension, social justice. In this book, social inequality will be the central focus of Chapters 6, 7, and 8, and sociologists' work on inequality will be highlighted throughout.

1.6 Social Policy throughout the World

One important way we can use the sociological imagination is to enhance our understanding of current social issues throughout the world. Beginning with Chapter 2, which focuses on research,

each chapter will conclude with a discussion of a contemporary social policy issue. In some cases, we will examine a specific issue facing national governments. For example, government funding of childcare centres will be discussed in Chapter 4, "Socialization"; sexual harassment in Chapter 5, "Social Interaction, Groups, and Social Structure"; and the search for shelters in Chapter 15, "Population, Health, and Communities." These social policy sections will demonstrate how fundamental sociological concepts can enhance our critical-thinking skills and help us to better understand current public policy debates taking place around the world.

Sociologists expect the next quarter-century to be perhaps the most exciting and critical period in the history of the discipline. This is because of a growing recognition—both in Canada and around the world—that current social problems *must* be addressed before their magnitude overwhelms human societies. We can expect sociologists to play an increasing role in the government sector by researching and developing public policy alternatives. It seems only natural for this textbook to focus on the connection between the work of sociologists and the difficult questions confronting the policymakers and people of Canada.

CHAPTER RESOURCES

Summary

::: 1.1 What Is Sociology?

- **Sociology** is the systematic study of social behaviour and human groups.
- The **sociological imagination** is an awareness of the relationship between an individual and the wider society. It is the ability to view our own society as an outsider might, rather than from the perspective of our limited experiences and cultural biases.

::: 1.2 What Is Sociological Theory?

- Sociologists employ theories to examine the relationships between or among observations and data that may seem completely unrelated.

::: 1.3 How Did Sociology Develop?

- Nineteenth-century thinkers who contributed sociological insights included Auguste Comte, a French philosopher; Harriet Martineau, an English sociologist; and Herbert Spencer, an English scholar.
- Other important figures in the development of sociology were Émile Durkheim, who pioneered work on suicide; Max Weber, who taught the need for "insight" in intellectual work; and Karl Marx, who emphasized the importance of the economy and of conflict in society.
- The discipline of sociology is indebted to such twentieth-century sociologists as Charles Horton Cooley, Robert Merton, Harold A. Innis, S.D. Clark, and John Porter.

::: 1.4 What Are the Major Theoretical Perspectives?

- The **functionalist perspective** of sociology emphasizes the way that parts of a society are structured to maintain its stability. Social change should be slow and evolutionary.
- The **conflict perspective** assumes that social behaviour is best understood in terms of conflict or tension between and among competing groups. Social change, spurred by conflict and competition, is viewed as desirable.
- **Feminist perspectives** are varied and diverse; however, they argue that women's inequality is constructed by our society. Feminist perspectives include both micro and macro levels of analysis.
- The **interactionist perspective** is primarily concerned with fundamental or everyday forms of interaction, including symbols and other types of nonverbal communication. Social change is ongoing, as individuals are shaped by society and in turn shape it.

::: 1.5 What Can We Expect from the Use of the Sociological Imagination?

- Sociologists make use of all four perspectives, since each offers unique insights into the same issue.
- In this textbook, we make use of the **sociological imagination** by showing theory in practice and research in action; by speaking across race, gender, class, and national boundaries; and by highlighting aspects of social policy around the world.

Critical Thinking Questions

1. What aspects of the act of drinking coffee might be of particular interest to a sociologist because of his or her "sociological imagination"?

2. What are the manifest and latent functions of the responses to a disaster?

3. How might the interactionist perspective be applied to a place where you have been employed or to an organization you joined?

4. How could the sociological imagination be used to study your consumer purchases?

THINKING ABOUT MOVIES

Brokeback Mountain

In the rural West, two men struggle to reconcile their social roles with their personal identities.

Frozen River

Two working-class women overcome racial prejudice to form an unlikely friendship.

When the Levees Broke

Spike Lee directs this documentary about the devastating social costs of Hurricane Katrina.

inside

Census worker introduces herself to the householder she is about to interview. Note the handheld electronic device she carries to record and transmit data. The census is a survey, one of the many methods sociologists, governments, and businesses use to collect data.

2

Sociological Research

" Long a subterranean topic, the deliberate, nonsuicidal destruction of one's own body tissue emerged from obscurity in the 1990s and began to spread dramatically. . . . Although a range of behaviours may be considered self-injurious, . . . we focus here on . . . self-cutting, burning, branding, scratching, picking at skin or reopening wounds, biting, head banging, hair pulling (trichotillomania), hitting (with a hammer or other object), and bone breaking.

This analysis draws on eighty in-depth interviews conducted in person and on the telephone. Participants ranged in age from 16 to their mid-50s, with more women (65) than men (15), nearly all Caucasian.

In addition, beginning in 2001–2002, we began to explore the Web sites and public postings of self-injurers. We joined several Internet self-injury groups as overt researchers and became active participants in group discussions. Because of the intimate nature of virtual communication . . . , we formed several deep and enduring relationships with people in different friendship circles that lasted for years, and we discussed with people the features of their ordinary lives and rallied around them during their many crises. We worked, with others, on the difficulties of supporting people who were disembodied and distant. Together with them, we learned to discern the seriousness of people's suicidal threats, their claims of abstinence, their presentation of different personas under different pseudonyms in different groups, and the consequences of flame wars. We networked through bulletin boards, MySpace, and the hundreds of self-injury–related Web Usenet support groups.

. . .

Some reported that they hung out with "the wrong crowd" and acted out or were drawn into countercultural groups such as Goths. They were nihilists who delighted in showing off by burning or cutting themselves.

We . . . found a growing number of self-injurers who belonged to alternative youth subcultures. Some reported that they hung out with "the wrong crowd" and acted out or were drawn into countercultural groups such as Goths. They were nihilists who delighted in showing off by burning or cutting themselves. Natalie, a 22-year-old college student, reflected back on her junior high school friends:

Eighth grade was the point at which I really started getting sociable, identifying with this alternative subculture. It wasn't like I hung out with the freaks and the rejects and, like, the outcasts. I definitely was in the subculture of the stoners and the punks, and we hung out on the bridge and I started smoking and doing drugs and, um, at that point I associated with more people who also hurt themselves.

. . .

Some self-injurers rooted their unhappiness in peer social situations. Rachel, a 23-year-old college student with an intact, happy family, blamed her friends for driving her to self-injure:

It happened the first time when my group turned against me for some reason. They alienated me for a week straight, they started rumours about me. I didn't go to any activities that week and I didn't even go to school. I was so sad, it just started. I was crying and so upset and couldn't stop crying, and I just took a coat hanger, and that's how it started.

. . .

Many people continued self-injuring, either continuously or intermittently, into adulthood. Contrary to extant knowledge, roughly two-thirds of the "regulars" we encountered on the Internet were older than 25, and half were older than 35. . . . "

(Adler and Adler 2007:537–538, 540, 541, 544, 545, 547)

This description of the covert practice of self-injury is taken from Patricia Adler and Peter Adler's extensive research on the little-known behaviour and its social underpinnings. Over a six-year period, the Adlers conducted lengthy, emotionally intense interviews with self-injurers, becoming friends with many. They met others in virtual space, through Internet-based support groups and Web postings. "Rather than remaining strictly detached from our subjects, we became involved in their lives, helping them and giving voice to their experiences and beliefs," the Adlers admit (2007:542).

The Adlers' work on self-injury reflects all three major sociological approaches. For self-injurers, who rarely come into contact with others like themselves, the Internet functions as a meeting place, a refuge from their self-imposed social isolation. As conflict theorists would point out, their unconventional behaviour marginalizes them, preventing them from receiving assistance even when they would welcome it. Interactionists would recognize the critical nature of self-injurers' interpersonal contacts, in person and often online. And feminist theorists would look for gender differences in self-injurers' behaviour.

Though many people would like to ignore the phenomenon of self-injury, believing that those who practise it will eventually "grow out of it," the Adlers' research allows us to consider it intelligently and scientifically, within the social context. Self-injurers, the Adlers found, are a diverse group, whose behaviour is carefully planned and considered. Surprisingly, members often begin to injure themselves in the company of others rather than in secret. They have recently begun to coalesce as a subculture (2007:559–560).

Effective sociological research can be quite thought-provoking. It may suggest many new questions that require further study, such as why we make assumptions about people who engage in atypical behaviours like self-injury. In some cases, rather than raising additional questions, a study will simply confirm previous beliefs and findings. Sociological research can also have practical applications. For instance, research results that disconfirm accepted beliefs about marriage and the family may lead to changes in public policy.

This chapter will examine the research process used in conducting sociological studies. How do sociologists go about setting up a research project? How do they ensure that the results of the research are reliable and accurate? Can they carry out their research without violating the rights of those they study?

We will first look at the steps that make up the scientific method used in research. Then we will take a look at various techniques commonly used in sociological research, such as experiments, observations, and surveys. We will pay particular attention to the ethical challenges sociologists face in studying human behaviour, and to the debate raised by Max Weber's call for "value neutrality" in social science research. We will also examine feminist methodology and the role technology plays in research today. Though sociological researchers can focus on any number of subjects, in this chapter we will concentrate on two in particular: the relationship of education to income and the controversial subject of human sexuality. The Social Policy section that closes the chapter considers the difficulties and the challenges in researching human sexuality. ■

What Is the Scientific Method?

Like all of us, sociologists are interested in the central questions of our time. Is the family falling apart? Why is there crime? Is the world failing in its ability to feed the population? Such issues concern most people, whether or not they have academic training. However, unlike the typical citizen, some sociologists have a commitment to the use of the **scientific method** in studying society. The scientific method is a systematic, organized series of steps that ensures maximum objectivity and consistency in researching a problem.

Many of us will never actually conduct scientific research. Why, then, is it important that we understand the scientific method? Because it plays a major role in the workings of our society. Residents of Canada are constantly being bombarded with "facts" or "data." Almost daily, advertisers cite supposedly scientific studies to prove that their products are superior. Such claims may be accurate or exaggerated. We can make better evaluations of such information—and will not be fooled so easily—if we are familiar with the standards of scientific research. These standards are quite stringent and demand as strict adherence as possible.

The scientific method requires precise preparation in developing useful research. Otherwise, the research data collected may not prove accurate. Sociologists and other researchers follow five basic steps in the scientific method: (1) defining the problem, (2) reviewing the literature, (3) formulating the hypothesis, (4) selecting the research design and then collecting and analyzing data, and (5) developing the conclusion (see Figure 2-1). We'll use an actual example to illustrate the workings of the scientific method.

figure 2-1 The Scientific Method

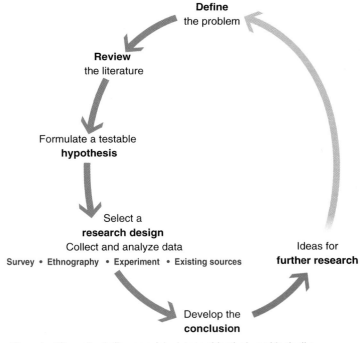

The scientific method allows sociologists to objectively and logically evaluate data they collect. Their findings can prompt further ideas for sociological research.

Defining the Problem

Does it "pay" to go to college or university? Some people make great sacrifices and work hard to get a postsecondary education. Some parents borrow money for their children's tuition. Some students work part-time jobs or even take full-time positions while attending evening or weekend classes. Does it pay off? Are there monetary returns for getting that degree?

The first step in any research project is to state as clearly as possible what you hope to investigate, that is, *define the problem.* In this instance, we are interested in knowing how schooling relates to income. We want to find out the earnings of people with different levels of formal education. An **operational definition** is an explanation of an abstract concept that is specific enough to allow a researcher to assess the concept. For example, a sociologist interested in status might use membership in exclusive social clubs or organized crime as an operational definition of status. Someone studying prejudice might consider a person's unwillingness to hire or work with women or members of minority groups as an operational definition of prejudice. In our example, we need to develop two operational definitions—education and earnings—in order to study whether it pays to get an advanced education. We'll define *education* as the level of study achieved (e.g., college, bachelor's, master's, or doctoral level) and *earnings* as the income a person received two years after graduation.

Initially, we take a functionalist perspective (although we may end up incorporating other approaches). We argue that opportunities for earning power are related to level of schooling and that education prepares students for employment.

Reviewing the Literature

By conducting a *review of the literature*—the relevant scholarly studies and information—researchers define the problem under study, clarify possible techniques to be used in collecting data, and eliminate or reduce avoidable mistakes. For our example, we would examine information about salaries for different occupations. We would see if jobs that require more academic training are better rewarded. It would also be appropriate to review other studies on the relationship between education and income.

The review of the literature would soon tell us that many other factors besides level of study's influence on earning potential. For example, we would learn that the children of richer parents are more likely to go to college or university than are those from modest backgrounds, so we might consider the possibility that the same parents may later help their children to secure better-paying jobs.

Formulating the Hypothesis

After reviewing earlier research and drawing on the contributions of sociological theorists, the researchers may then *formulate the hypothesis.* A **hypothesis** is a speculative statement about the relationship between two or more factors known as variables. Income, religion, occupation, and gender can all serve as variables in a study. We can define a **variable** as a measurable trait or characteristic that is subject to change under different conditions.

Researchers who formulate a hypothesis generally must suggest how one aspect of human behaviour influences or affects another. The variable hypothesized to cause or influence another is called the **independent variable.** The second variable is termed the **dependent variable** because its action "depends" on the influence of the independent variable.

Our hypothesis is that the higher one's educational level, the more money one will earn. The independent variable to

It seems reasonable to assume that university graduates—such as these from Simon Fraser University in B.C.—will earn more than high school graduates. But how would you go about testing this hypothesis?

be measured is the level of education. The variable thought to depend on it—income—must also be measured.

Identifying independent and dependent variables is a critical step in clarifying cause-and-effect relationships in society. As shown in Figure 2-2, **causal logic** involves the relationship

figure 2-2 Causal Logic

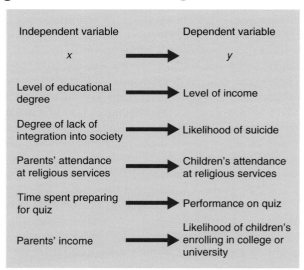

In *causal logic,* an independent variable (often designated by the symbol *x*) influences a dependent variable (generally designated as *y*); thus, *x* leads to *y*. For example, parents who attend religious services regularly (*x*) are more likely to have children who are regular attendees of religious services (*y*).

Think about It
Identify two or three variables that might "depend" on this independent variable: number of alcoholic drinks ingested.

research today

2-1 Surveying Cellphone Users

"Can you hear me now?" This question, familiar to cellphone callers everywhere, could be used to characterize a debate among researchers in sociology. Until recently, calling people on the telephone was a common way for survey takers to reach a broad range of people. Though not everyone owns a telephone—particularly not low-income people—researchers managed to account for that relatively small portion of the population in other ways.

However, the fact that many people now have a cellphone but no landline presents a serious methodological problem to scholars who depend on surveys and public opinion polling. As of 2010, 13 percent of Canadian households could be reached only by cellphone; the proportion has risen from eight percent in 2008 (Statistics Canada 2011d). Among those Canadians between the ages of 18 and 34, the abandonment of landlines has become increasing common with 50 percent of these households using only a cellphone.

Unfortunately, surveying cellphone users has its own problems. In general, cellphone users are more likely than landline users to screen incoming calls or ignore them.

As of 2010, 13 percent of Canadian households could be reached only by cellphone, and the proportion was rising.

And studies show that because cellphone users often take calls while they are involved in other activities, they are much more likely to break off a call midsurvey than someone who is speaking on a landline. Thus, it takes an average of nine calls to a working cellphone number to complete one survey, compared to five calls to a working landline number. Furthermore, federal law requires that calls to cellphones be hand-dialed; the use of automatic dialers, a standard tool of survey firms, is illegal. Survey takers have also found that calling cellphone numbers means they will reach a higher proportion of nonadults than when calling landline numbers. Finally, there are some ethical issues involved in randomly dialing cellphone users, who may be driving a motor vehicle or operating dangerous machinery when they answer.

Researchers are taking steps to stay abreast of technological change. For example, they are making allowances for people who communicate without any kind of telephone, using their personal computers and the Internet. And by drawing on historical data that suggest what kinds of people tend to adopt other wireless technologies, researchers are projecting which people are likely to abandon their landlines in the near future.

Apply the Theory

1. Are you a cellphone–only user? If so, do you generally accept calls from unknown numbers? Aside from underestimating certain health problems and distorting the degree of support for certain politicians, what other problems might result from excluding cellphone–only users from survey research?
2. Apply what you have just learned to the task of surveying Internet users. Which of the problems that arise during telephone surveys might also arise during Internet surveys? Might Internet surveys involve some unique problems?

Sources: Blumberg and Luke 2007; Brown 2009; Harrisinteractive 2008; Keeter and Kennedy 2006; Lavrakas et al. 2007; Statistics Canada 2011d.

---

between a condition or variable and a particular consequence, with one event leading to the other. Under causal logic, being less integrated into society may be directly related to or produce a greater likelihood of suicide. Similarly, the time students spend reviewing material for a quiz may be directly related to or produce a greater likelihood of getting a high score on the quiz.

A **correlation** exists when a change in one variable coincides with a change in the other. Correlations are an indication that causality *may* be present; they do not necessarily indicate causation. For example, data indicate that people who prefer to watch televised news programs are less knowledgeable than those who read newspapers and news magazines. This correlation between people's relative knowledge and their choice of news media seems to make sense, because it agrees with the common belief that television "dumbs down" information. People with poor reading skills are much more likely than others to get their news from television, while those who are educated or skilled turn more often to the print media. Though television viewing is correlated with lower news comprehension, then, it does not *cause* it. Sociologists seek to identify the *causal* link between variables; the suspected causal link is generally described in the hypothesis.

Collecting and Analyzing Data

How do you test a hypothesis to determine whether it is supported or refuted? You need to collect information, using one of the research designs described later in the chapter. The research design guides the researcher in collecting and analyzing data.

Selecting the Sample   In most studies, social scientists must carefully select what is known as a *sample*. A **sample** is a selection from a larger population that is statistically representative of that population. There are many kinds of samples, but the one social scientists most frequently use is the random sample. In a **random sample,** every member of an entire population being studied has the same chance of being selected. Thus, if researchers want to examine the opinions of people listed in a city directory (a book that, unlike the telephone directory, lists all households), they might use a computer to randomly select names from the directory. The results would constitute a random sample. The advantage of using specialized sampling techniques is that sociologists do not need to question everyone in a population (Igo 2007).

It is easy to confuse the careful scientific techniques used in representative sampling with the many *non-scientific* polls that receive much more media attention. For example, Web site viewers are encouraged to register their views on today's headlines or on political contests. Such polls reflect nothing more than the views of those who happened to view the Web site and took the time, perhaps at some cost, to register their opinions. These data do not necessarily reflect (and indeed may distort) the views of the broader population. Not everyone has access to a computer on a regular basis, or the means and/or the inclination to register their opinion. Even when these techniques include answers from tens of thousands of people, their accuracy will be far less than that of a carefully selected representative sample of 1500 respondents.

In our research example, we will use information collected in the 2007 National Graduates Survey (NGS), which was released by Statistics Canada in 2009. The NGS, which began in 1982, asks graduates of Canadian postsecondary institutions questions related to their employment, underemployment, unemployment, career satisfaction, and the extent to which they were successful in obtaining employment since graduation. For the 2007 study, a sample of 60 701 graduates living in Canada and the United States responded to a questionnaire conducted by computer-assisted telephone interviews. The questionnaire was administered two years after graduation.

Ensuring Validity and Reliability The scientific method requires that research results be both valid and reliable. **Validity** refers to the degree to which a measure or scale truly reflects the phenomenon under study. A valid measure of income depends on gathering accurate data. Various studies show that people are reasonably accurate in knowing how much money they earned in the most recent year. If a question is written unclearly, however, the resulting data might not be accurate. For example, respondents to an unclear question about income might report their parents' or spouse's income instead of their own. **Reliability** refers to the extent to which a measure produces consistent results. Some people may not *disclose* accurate information, but most do.

Developing the Conclusion

Scientific studies, including those conducted by sociologists, do not aim to answer all the questions that can be raised about a particular subject. Therefore, the conclusion of a research study represents both an end and a beginning. It terminates a specific phase of the investigation, but it should also generate ideas for future study.

Supporting Hypotheses In our example, we find that the data support our hypothesis: People with more formal education *do* earn more money than others, as Figure 2-3 illustrates. Those with a bachelor's degree earned more than those with a college diploma; those with a master's degree earned more than those with a bachelor's degree. The relationship continues through to the terminal degree—the doctorate.

The relationship is not perfect. Some people with college diplomas earn more than those with bachelor's degrees. The results of the National Graduate Survey showed that 25 percent of college grads earned $44 300 or more per year, while 50 percent of bachelor's graduates earned $45 000 or less (Statistics Canada 2009). Sociologists are interested in both the general pattern that emerges from the data and the exceptions to the pattern.

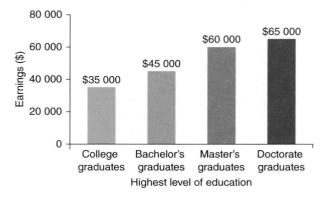

figure **2-3** **Median Annual Earnings* by Level of Education, in 2007**

*For those working full-time
Source: Statistics Canada 2009c.

Sociological studies do not always generate data that support the original hypothesis. In many instances, a hypothesis is refuted, and researchers must reformulate their conclusions. Unexpected results may also lead sociologists to re-examine their methodology and make changes in the research design.

Controlling for Other Factors A **control variable** is a factor held constant to test the relative impact of the independent variable. For example, if researchers wanted to know how adults in Ontario feel about restrictions on smoking in public places, they would probably attempt to use a respondent's smoking behaviour as a control variable. That is, how do smokers versus non-smokers feel about smoking in public places? The researchers would compile separate statistics on how smokers and non-smokers feel about anti-smoking regulations.

> **Think about It**
> What kinds of knowledge and skills do people with a bachelor's degree or higher possess, compared to those with a high school education or less? Why would employers value those kinds of knowledge and skills?

Our study of the influence of education on earnings suggests that not everyone enjoys equal educational opportunities, a disparity that is one of the causes of social inequality. Since education affects a person's income, we may want to call on the conflict perspective to explore this topic further. What impact does a person's "race" or gender have? Is a woman with a university degree likely to earn as much as a man with similar education? Later in the text, we will consider other factors and variables. That is, we will examine the impact that education has on income while controlling for variables such as gender and race.

In Summary: The Scientific Method

Let us briefly summarize the process of the scientific method through a review of the example. We *defined a problem* (the question of whether it pays to achieve higher educational qualifications). We *reviewed the literature* (other studies of the relationship between education and income) and *formulated a hypothesis* (the higher one's level of education, the more money one will earn). We *collected and analyzed the data*, making sure the sample was representative and the data were valid and reliable. Finally, we *developed the conclusion*: The data do support our hypothesis about the influence of education on income. Often, once a study has been completed and released to scholars, policymakers, and the general public, the results precipitate additional research or re-examination of related social and political issues.

What Are the Major Research Designs?

An important aspect of sociological research is deciding *how* to collect the data. A **research design** is a detailed plan or method for obtaining data scientifically. Selection of a research design requires creativity and ingenuity. This choice will directly influence both the cost of the project and the amount of time needed to collect the results of the research. Research designs that sociologists regularly use to generate data include surveys, ethnography, experiments, and use of existing sources.

Surveys

Almost all of us have responded to surveys of one kind or another. We may have been asked what kind of detergent we use, which political candidate we intend to vote for, or what our favourite television program is. A **survey** is a study, generally in the form of an interview or questionnaire, which provides researchers with information about how people think and act. Among Canada's best-known surveys of opinion are those by Ipsos Canada, EKOS, and Environics. As anyone who watches the news during election campaigns knows, polls have become a staple of political life.

When you think of surveys, you may recall seeing many "person on the street" interviews on local television news programs. Although such interviews can be highly entertaining, they are not necessarily an accurate indication of public opinion. First, they reflect the opinions of only those people who happen to be at a certain location. Such a sample can be biased in favour of commuters, middle-class shoppers, or factory workers, depending on which street or area the newspeople select. Second, television interviews tend to attract outgoing people who are willing to appear on the air, while they frighten away others who may feel intimidated by a camera. As we've seen, a survey must utilize precise, representative sampling if it is to genuinely reflect a broad range of the population.

In preparing to conduct a survey, sociologists must not only develop representative samples, but they must also exercise great care in the wording of questions. An effective survey question must be simple and clear enough for people to understand it. It must also be specific enough so that there are no problems in interpreting the results. Open-ended questions ("What do you think of educational programming on television?") must be carefully phrased to solicit the type of information desired. Surveys can be indispensable sources of information, but only if the sampling is done properly and the questions are worded accurately and without bias.

There are two main forms of surveys: the **interview,** in which a researcher obtains information through face-to-face or telephone questioning, and the **questionnaire,** which uses a printed or written form to obtain information from a respondent. Each of these has its own advantages. An interviewer can obtain a high response rate because people find it more difficult to turn down a personal request for an interview than to throw away a written questionnaire. In addition, a skillful interviewer can go beyond written questions and "probe" for a subject's underlying feelings and reasons. However, questionnaires have the advantage of being cheaper, especially in large samples.

Why do people have sex? A straightforward question, but until recently rarely investigated, despite its significance to public health, marital counselling, and criminology. A study published in 2007 involving 2000 undergraduates started with a random sample of 400 students to list all the reasons why they ever had sex. The explanations were diverse, ranging from "I was drunk," to "I wanted to feel closer to God." The researchers then asked another sample of 1500 students to rate the importance of each of the 287 reasons given by the first group. Table 2-1 ranks the results. Nearly every one of the reasons was rated most important by at least some

table 2-1 Top Reasons Why Men and Women Had Sex

Reason	Men	Women
I was attracted to the person	1	1
It feels good	2	3
I wanted to experience the physical pleasure	3	2
It's fun	4	8
I wanted to show my affection to the person	5	4
I was sexually aroused and wanted the release	6	6
I was "horny"	7	7
I wanted to express my love for the person	8	5
I wanted to achieve an orgasm	9	14
I wanted to please my partner	10	11
I realized I was in love	17	9
I was "in the heat of the moment"	13	10

Source: Meston and Buss 2007:506.

respondents. Though there were some gender differences in the replies, there was significant consensus between men and women on the top 10 reasons (Meston and Buss 2007).

Studies have shown that characteristics of the interviewer have an impact on survey data. For example, female interviewers tend to receive more female-centred responses from female subjects than do male researchers, and black interviewers tend to receive more detailed responses about race-related issues from black subjects than do white interviewers. The possible impact of gender and race only indicates again how much care social research requires (Davis and Silver 2003).

The survey is an example of **quantitative research,** which collects and reports data primarily in numerical form. Although quantitative research may make use of large samples, it can't look at a topic in great depth and detail. That is why many researchers prefer to use **qualitative research,** which relies on what is seen in field and naturalistic settings and often focuses on small groups and communities rather than on large groups or whole nations.

While qualitative research cannot answer questions posed in quantitative research—questions such as "how many" and "what are the causes," it can help to reveal how people make, and act upon, decisions in their daily lives:

> Qualitative research is particularly well suited to studying context. It also excels at illuminating *process*, whether this is organizational change or individual decision-making, since it allows us to examine how changes affect daily procedures and interactions. This may lead to us uncovering unintended as well as intended consequences of new arrangements (Barbour 2007:13).

While those sociologists who employ a scientific or positivist methodology, using quantitative data, believe it is important to remove or minimize *bias* from the research agenda, thoughts and feelings—considered by science to be bias—are central elements of qualitative research (Given 2008). The most common form of qualitative research is observation, which will be considered next.

Ethnography

Investigators often collect information or test hypotheses through firsthand studies. **Ethnography** is the study of an entire social setting through extended systematic fieldwork. **Observation,** or direct participation in closely watching a group or organization, is the basic technique of ethnography. However, ethnographic research also includes the collection of historical information and the conduct of in-person interviews. Although ethnography may seem a relatively informal method compared to surveys or experiments, ethnographic researchers are careful to take detailed notes while observing their subjects.

In some cases, the sociologist actually joins a group for a period, to get an accurate sense of how it operates. This approach is called *participant observation*. In Barbara Ehrenreich's widely read book, *Nickel and Dimed: On (Not) Getting By in America*, the author was a participant observer. Disguising herself as a divorced, middle-aged housewife without a college degree, Ehrenreich set out to see what life was like for low-wage workers. Her book chronicles her own and others' experiences trying to make ends meet on a minimum wage (Ehrenreich 2001).

During the 1930s, in a classic example of participant observation research, William F. Whyte moved to a low-income Italian neighbourhood in Boston. For nearly four years he was a member of the social circle of "corner boys" that he describes in *Street Corner Society*. Whyte revealed his identity to these men and joined in their conversations, bowling, and other leisure-time activities. His goal was to gain greater insight into the community that these men had established. As Whyte (1981:303) listened to Doc, the leader of the group, he "learned the answers to questions I would not even have had the sense to ask if I had been getting my information solely on an interviewing basis." Whyte's work was especially valuable, since at the time the academic world had little direct knowledge of the poor, and tended to rely on information from the records of social service agencies, hospitals, and courts (Adler et al. 1992).

The initial challenge that Whyte faced—and that every participant observer encounters—was to gain acceptance into an unfamiliar group. It is no simple matter for a college-trained sociologist to win the trust of a religious cult, a youth gang, a poor Appalachian community, or a circle of skid row residents. It requires a great deal of patience and an accepting, nonthreatening type of personality on the part of the observer.

Ethnographic research poses other complex challenges for the investigator. Sociologists must be able to

Sergeant Britt Damon, a social scientist on the U.S. Army Human Terrain Team, chats with Afghani children during a search operation. The participation of social scientists in the Army program, which some see as a violation of scholarly detachment, has proved controversial.

fully understand what they are observing. In a sense, then, researchers must learn to see the world as the group sees it in order to fully comprehend the events taking place around them. This raises a delicate issue. If the research is to be successful, the observer cannot allow the close associations or even friendships that inevitably develop to influence the subjects' behaviour or the conclusions of the study. Even while working hard to gain acceptance from the group being studied, the participant observer *must* maintain some degree of detachment.

Recently, the issue of detachment became a controversial one for social scientists embedded with the U.S. military in Afghanistan and Iraq. Among other studies, the academicians participated in the creation of the Army's Human Terrain System, a $4-million effort to identify the customs, kinship structures, and internal social conflicts in the two countries. The intention was to provide military leaders with information that would help them to make better decisions. Although the idea of scholars cooperating in any way with soldiers struck many people as inappropriate, others countered that the information they developed would help the military to avoid needless violence and might even facilitate the withdrawal of troops from the region (Glenn 2007; Human Terrain System 2010).

Feminist perspectives in sociology have drawn attention to a shortcoming in ethnographic research as well as other forms of sociological research. For most of the history of sociology, studies were conducted on male subjects or about male-led groups and organizations, and the findings were generalized to all people. For example, for many decades, studies of urban life focused on street corners, neighbourhood taverns, and bowling alleys—places where men typically congregated. Although the insights were valuable, they did not give a true impression of city life because they overlooked the areas where women were likely to gather. Feminist perspectives attempt to redress this bias in the way in which ethnographic research is conducted. Feminist researchers also tend to involve and consult their subjects more than other types of researchers do, and they are more oriented to seeking change, raising consciousness, or trying to affect policy. In addition, feminist research is particularly open to a multidisciplinary approach, such as making use of historical evidence or legal studies as well as feminist theory (Baker 1999; Lofland 1975; Reinharz 1992).

Experiments

When sociologists want to study a possible cause-and-effect relationship, they may conduct experiments. An **experiment** is an artificially created situation that allows the researcher to manipulate variables.

In the classic method of conducting an experiment, two groups of people are selected and matched for similar characteristics, such as age or education. The researchers then assign the subjects to one of two groups: the experimental

Does arresting someone for participating in a riot deter future incidents of violence? Sociological experiments could study this question by making use of control and experimental groups. Above is a burned skeleton of a vehicle following the Vancouver Stanley Cup riot in 2011.

or the control group. The **experimental group** is exposed to an independent variable; the **control group** is not. Thus, if scientists were testing a new type of antibiotic drug, they would administer that drug to an experimental group but not to a control group.

In some experiments, just as in observation research, the presence of a social scientist or other observer may affect the behaviour of people being studied. The recognition of this phenomenon grew out of an experiment conducted during the 1920s and 1930s at the Hawthorne plant of the Western Electric Company. A group of researchers set out to determine how to improve the productivity of workers at the plant. The investigators manipulated such variables as the lighting and working hours to see what impact changes in them had on productivity. To their surprise, they found that *every* step

How do people respond to being observed? Evidently, these employees at the Hawthorne plant enjoyed the attention paid them when researchers observed them at work. No matter what variables were changed, the workers increased their productivity every time, including when the level of lighting was reduced.

they took seemed to increase productivity. Even measures that seemed likely to have the opposite effect, such as reducing the amount of lighting in the plant, led to higher productivity.

Why did the plant's employees work harder even under less favourable conditions? Their behaviour apparently was influenced by the greater attention being paid to them in the course of the research and by the novelty of being subjects in an experiment. Although the carefully constructed study did identify some changes in the workers' behaviour that did not have to do with their being observed, the term **Hawthorne effect** has become synonymous with the placebo or guinea pig effect (Franke and Kaul 1978).

::: use your sociological *imagination* :::

You are a researcher interested in the effect of TV-watching on the grades of school children. How would you go about setting up an experiment to measure this?

Use of Existing Sources

Sociologists do not necessarily have to collect new data in order to conduct research and test hypotheses. The term **secondary analysis** refers to a variety of research techniques that make use of previously collected and publicly accessible information and data. Generally, in conducting secondary analysis, researchers utilize data in ways unintended by the initial collectors of information. For example, census data are compiled for specific uses by the federal government but are also valuable for marketing specialists in locating everything from bicycle stores to nursing homes.

Sociologists consider secondary analysis to be *non-reactive*, since it does not influence people's behaviour. As an example, Émile Durkheim's statistical analysis of suicide neither increased nor decreased human self-destruction. Researchers, then, can avoid the Hawthorne effect by using secondary analysis.

There is one inherent problem, however: the researcher who relies on data collected by someone else may not find exactly what is needed. Social scientists studying family violence can use statistics from police and social service agencies on *reported* cases of spouse abuse and child abuse. But how many cases are not reported? Government bodies have no precise data on *all* cases of abuse.

Many social scientists find it useful to study cultural, economic, and political documents, including newspapers, periodicals, radio and television tapes, the Internet, scripts, diaries, songs, folklore, and legal papers, to name some examples (see Table 2-2). In examining these sources, researchers employ a technique known as **content analysis**, which is the systematic coding and objective recording of data, guided by some rationale.

table 2-2 Existing Sources Used in Sociological Research

Most Frequently Used Sources
Statistics Canada
Polls, such as Ipsos-Reid and Environics
Birth, death, marriage, and divorce statistics
Other Sources
Newspapers and periodicals
Personal journals, diaries, email, and letters
Records and archival material of religious organizations, corporations, and other organizations
Transcripts of radio programs
Videos of motion pictures and television programs
Web pages, blogs, chat rooms
Song lyrics
Scientific records (such as patent applications)
Speeches of public figures (such as politicians)
Votes cast in elections or by elected officials on specific legislative proposals
Attendance records for public events
Videotapes of social protests and rallies
Literature, including folklore

table 2-3 Major Research Designs

Method	Examples	Advantages	Limitations
Survey	Questionnaires Interviews	Yields information about specific issues	Can be expensive and time consuming
Observation	Ethnography	Yields detailed information about specific groups or organizations	Involves months if not years of labour-intensive data collection
Experiment	Deliberate manipulation of people's social behaviour	Yields direct measures of people's behaviour	Ethical limitations on the degree to which subjects' behaviour can be manipulated
Existing sources/ Secondary analysis	Analysis of census or health data Analysis of films or TV commercials	Cost-efficiency	Limited to data collected for some other purpose

Content analysis of popular song lyrics shows that over the last 50 years, female artists such as Lights have used fewer sexually explicit words, while male artists have used more.

Content analysis can be revealing. We might think that in the twenty-first century, blatant favouritism in media representations of men versus women is a thing of the past. However, research suggests otherwise. An analysis of hundreds of characters in children's colouring books shows that males are more likely than females to be shown taking an active role. Gender-stereotyped behaviour dominates, with only 3 percent of males engaged in stereotypically female behaviour, and only 6 percent of females engaged in stereotypically male behaviour (Fitzpatrick and McPherson 2010).

Similarly, despite women's participation in all sports, content analysis of televised sports coverage shows that even when a men's sport is out of season (for example, men's basketball in late summer), it gets more coverage than women's sports in season (for example, women's basketball in July). Furthermore, coverage of female cheerleaders and athletes' wives exceeds coverage of the female athletes who compete in sports (Messner and Cooky 2010).

Table 2-3 summarizes the major research designs, along with their advantages and limitations.

2.3 What Are the Ethics of Research?

A biochemist cannot inject a drug into a human being unless the drug has been thoroughly tested and the subject agrees to the shot. To do otherwise would be both unethical and illegal. Sociologists must also abide by certain specific standards in conducting research—a **code of ethics**.

The professional society of the discipline, the Canadian Sociology and Anthropology Association (CSAA), published a code of ethics in 1994. The following is a short excerpt from the CSAA's *Statement of Professional Ethics*. The complete statement is available online at www.csaa.ca/structure/Code.htm.

Organizing and initiating research

4. Codes of professional ethics arise from the need to protect vulnerable or subordinate populations from harm incurred, knowingly or unknowingly, by the intervention of researchers into their lives and cultures. Sociologists and anthropologists have a responsibility to respect the rights, and be concerned with the welfare, of all the vulnerable and subordinate populations affected by their work. . . .

Protecting people in the research environment

12. Researchers must respect the rights of citizens to privacy, confidentiality and anonymity, and not to be studied. Researchers should make every effort to determine whether those providing information wish to remain anonymous or to receive recognition and then respect their wishes. . . .

Informed consent

15. Researchers must not expose respondents to risk of personal harm. Informed consent must be obtained when the risks of research are greater than the risks of everyday life. . . .

Covert research and deception

20. Subjects should not be deceived if there is any reasonably anticipated risk to the subjects or if the harm cannot be offset or the extent of the harm be reasonably predicted.

On the surface, these and the rest of the basic principles of the CSAA's *Statement of Professional Ethics* probably seem clear-cut. How could they lead to any disagreement or controversy? However, many delicate ethical questions cannot be resolved simply by reading these points. For example, should a sociologist engaged in participant-observation research *always* protect the confidentiality of subjects? What if the subjects are members of a religious cult allegedly engaged in unethical and possibly illegal activities? What if the sociologist is interviewing political activists and is questioned by government authorities about the research?

Most sociological research uses *people* as sources of information—as respondents to survey questions, subjects of observation, or participants in experiments. In all cases, sociologists need to be certain that they are not invading the privacy of their subjects. Generally, they handle this by ensuring anonymity and by guaranteeing the confidentiality of personal information. However, a study by William Zellner raised important questions about the extent to which sociologists can threaten people's right to privacy.

The Right to Know versus the Right to Privacy

A car lies at the bottom of a cliff, its driver dead. Was this an accident or a suicide? Sociologist William Zellner (1978) wanted to learn whether fatal car crashes are sometimes suicides disguised as accidents in order to protect family and friends (and perhaps to collect otherwise unredeemable insurance benefits). These acts of "autocide" are by nature covert. Zellner found that research on automobile accidents in which fatalities occur poses an ethical issue—the right to know against the right to privacy.

In his efforts to assess the frequency of such suicides, Zellner sought to interview the friends, co-workers, and family members of the deceased. He hoped to obtain information that would allow him to ascertain whether the deaths were accidental or deliberate. Zellner told the people approached for interviews that his goal was to contribute to a reduction of future accidents by learning about the emotional characteristics of accident victims. He made no mention of his suspicions of autocide, out of fear that potential respondents would refuse to meet with him.

Zellner eventually concluded that at least 12 percent of all fatal single-occupant crashes are suicides. This information

Are some people who die in single-occupant car crashes actually suicides? One sociological study of possible "autocides" concluded that at least 12 percent of such accident victims had, in fact, committed suicide. But the study also raised some ethical questions concerning the right to know and the right to privacy.

could be valuable for society, particularly since some of the probable suicides actually killed or critically injured innocent bystanders in the process of taking their own lives. Yet the ethical questions still must be faced. Was Zellner's research unethical because he misrepresented the motives of his study and failed to obtain his subjects' informed consent? Or was his deception justified by the social value of his findings?

The answers to these questions are not immediately apparent. Zellner appeared to have admirable motives and took great care in protecting confidentiality. He did not reveal names of suspected suicides to insurance companies, though Zellner did recommend that the insurance industry drop double indemnity (payment of twice the person's life insurance benefits in the event of accidental death) in the future.

Zellner's study raised an additional ethical issue: the possibility of harm to those who were interviewed. Subjects were asked if the deceased had "talked about suicide" and if they had spoken of how "bad or useless" they were. Could these questions have led people to guess the true intentions of the researcher? Perhaps, but according to Zellner, none of the informants voiced such suspicions. More seriously, might the study have caused the bereaved to *suspect* suicide—when before the survey they had accepted the deaths as accidental? Again, there is no evidence to suggest this, but we cannot be sure.

Given our uncertainty about this last question, was the research justified? Was Zellner taking too big a risk in asking the friends and families if the deceased victims had spoken of suicide before their death? Does the right to know outweigh the right to privacy in this type of situation? And who has the right to make such a judgment? In practice, as in Zellner's study, it is the *researcher*, not the subjects of inquiry, who makes the critical ethical decisions. Therefore, sociologists and other investigators bear the responsibility for establishing clear and sensitive boundaries for ethical scientific investigation.

Preserving Confidentiality

Like journalists, sociologists occasionally find themselves subject to questions from law enforcement authorities or to legal threats because of knowledge they have gained in conducting research and maintaining confidentiality. This situation raises profound ethical questions.

In 1994, Russel Ogden was a graduate student at Simon Fraser University (SFU) in British Columbia. In his research, Ogden conducted interviews with people involved in assisted suicide or euthanasia among people with AIDS. A newspaper report about the study came to the attention of the Vancouver coroner, who was already holding an inquest into the death of an "unknown female." Ogden's thesis reported that two research participants had knowledge about her death. The coroner subpoenaed Ogden to identify his sources, but he cited a promise of "absolute confidentiality" and refused to name them. This promise had been authorized by SFU's Research Ethics Board.

The coroner initially found Ogden to be in contempt of court but later accepted a common law argument that the communications between Ogden and his participants were privileged. In doing so, the coroner released Ogden from "any stain or suggestion of contempt." But Ogden's battle in coroner's court was fought without the support of his university. He sued SFU, unsuccessfully, to recover his legal costs. However, the judge condemned SFU for failing to protect academic freedom and urged the university to remedy the situation. Simon Fraser's president responded with a written apology to Ogden, compensation for legal costs and lost wages, and a guarantee that the university would assist "any researchers who find themselves in the position of having to challenge a subpoena" (Lowman and Palys 2000).

This case points to the delicate balance researchers and sponsoring institutions must maintain between the value of research and the confidentiality of the subjects, and the threat of litigation.

Neutrality and Politics in Research

The ethical considerations of sociologists lie not only in the methods they use but also in the way they interpret results. Max Weber ([1904] 1949) recognized that personal values would influence the questions that sociologists select for research. In his view, that was perfectly acceptable, but under no conditions could a researcher allow his or her personal feelings to influence the *interpretation* of data. In Weber's phrase, sociologists must practise **value neutrality** in their research. Weber's use of the concept *Verstehen* is "one of his best-known and most controversial contributions to the methodology of contemporary sociology" (Ritzer 2008:117).

As part of this neutrality, investigators have an ethical obligation to accept research findings even when the data run counter to their own personal views, to theoretically based explanations, or to widely accepted beliefs. For example, Émile Durkheim challenged popular conceptions when he reported that social (rather than supernatural) forces were an important factor in suicide.

Some sociologists believe that neutrality is impossible. At the same time, Weber's insistence on value-free sociology may lead the public to accept sociological conclusions without exploring the biases of the researchers. As we have seen, Weber was quite clear that sociologists may bring values to their subject matter. In his view, however, they must not confuse their own values with the social reality under study.

Let's consider what might happen when researchers bring their own biases to the investigation. A person investigating the impact of intercollegiate sports on alumni contributions, for example, may focus only on the highly visible revenue-generating sports of football and basketball and neglect the so-called minor sports, such as tennis or soccer, which are more likely to involve female athletes. Despite the work of Dorothy Smith and Margrit Eichler, sociologists still need to be reminded that the discipline often fails to adequately consider *all* people's social behaviour.

Theoretical Perspectives and Research Methods

The research methods that researchers choose to employ in their study of social phenomena are informed and guided by the theoretical perspectives they hold. Functionalist thinkers, for example, tend to value neutrality and objectivity, thus leaning toward quantitative methods, such as surveys, experiments, and secondary data analysis. Their focus is on uncovering the truth or the facts about the relationships among specified variables, according to the researchers' interpretation of the data. In response to this approach, conflict thinkers, such as Alvin Gouldner (1970) and others, have suggested that sociologists may use objectivity as a sacred justification for remaining uncritical of the dominant institutions and ruling classes of society. Unlike functionalists, conflict thinkers might employ historical analysis or engage in field research to uncover the hidden economic and political interests of a society. Again, unlike functionalists, conflict thinkers view their research as a basis for action and change.

Such research methods as ethnography and participant observation may be guided by interactionist perspectives, in which the goal of the researcher is to describe the meanings and to understand the definitions that people give to their own situations. As for feminist perspectives, no *single* research method is employed by feminist researchers, just as no *single* feminist theory exists. However, feminist researchers, like

Some feminist theorists see the global trafficking of sex workers as one sign of a close relationship between the industrialized nations and the developing countries that depend on them.

conflict thinkers, are guided by the common desire to bring about action or change through their research.

Feminist sociologist Shulamit Reinharz (1992) has argued that sociological research should not only be inclusive but should also be open to bringing about social change and drawing on relevant research by non-sociologists. Reinharz maintains that research should always analyze whether women's unequal social status has affected the study in any way. For example, a researcher might broaden the study of the impact of family income on education participation to consider the implications of participation according to gender, class, and race. The issue of the importance of value neutrality, which is often emphasized in mainstream or functional sociology, can be contrasted to feminist research, in which researchers integrate their own experiences into the research process. Reinharz contends that feminist researchers may use their own experiences to inform their research questions and to guide the research process; at the same time, however, feminist researchers are discussing the ways in which to "work out the tension between objectivity and subjectivity" (1992:262).

2.4 How Does Technology Influence Sociological Research?

Advances in technology have affected all aspects of life, and sociological research is no exception. The increased speed and capacity of computers enable sociologists to handle larger and larger sets of data. In the recent past, only people with grants or major institutional support could easily work with census data. Now anyone with a desktop computer and modem can access census information to learn more about social behaviour. Moreover, data from other countries concerning crime statistics and health care are sometimes as available as information from Canada.

Researchers usually rely on computers to deal with quantitative data—that is, numerical measures—but electronic technology is also assisting us with qualitative data, such as information obtained in observation research. Numerous software programs, such as Ethnograph and NVivo 7, allow the researcher not only to record observations, as a word processing program does, but also to identify common behavioural patterns or similar concerns expressed in interviews. For example, after observing students in a cafeteria over several weeks and putting your observations into the computer, you could then group all your observations related to certain variables, such as "club" or "study group."

The Internet affords an excellent opportunity to communicate with fellow researchers as well as to locate useful information on social issues posted on Web sites. It would be impossible to calculate all the sociological postings on Internet mailing lists or Web sites. Of course, you need to apply the same critical scrutiny to Internet material that you would use on any resource.

How useful is the Internet for conducting survey research? That's still unclear. It is relatively easy to send out a questionnaire or post one on an electronic bulletin board. This technique is an inexpensive way to reach large numbers of potential respondents and get a quick return of responses. However, there are some obvious dilemmas. How do you protect a respondent's anonymity? Second, how do you define the potential audience? Even if you know to whom you sent the questionnaire, the respondents may forward it on to others. Web-based surveys are still in their early stages. Even so, the initial results are promising.

This new technology is exciting, but there is one basic limitation to the methodology: Internet surveying works only with those who have access to the Internet and are online. For some market researchers, such a limitation is acceptable. For example, if you were interested in the willingness of Internet users to order books or make travel reservations online, limiting the sample population to those already online makes sense. However, if you were surveying the general public about plans to buy a computer in the coming year or about their views on a particular political candidate, your online research would need to be supplemented by more traditional sampling procedures, such as mailed questionnaires.

Sociological research relies on a number of tools—from observation research and use of existing sources of data to the latest computer technologies. We turn now to the Social Policy section, which deals with a research study that used a survey of the general population to learn more about a particular social behaviour—human sexuality.

Carnegie Mellon University's Data Truck lets researchers go where their subjects are—from nightclubs to marathon races. Equipped with the latest technology, the truck allows social scientists to enter the responses to their community surveys into their databases on site. It also gives them access to online social networks in the area, and even lets them videotape street activity.

Social Policy and Sociological Research

Studying Human Sexuality

The Issue

The Kaiser Family Foundation conducts a study of sexual content on U.S. television every two years. The latest report, released in 2005, shows that more than two-thirds of all shows on TV include some sexual content, up from about half of all shows seven years earlier (see Figure 2-4). Media representations of sexual behaviour are important because surveys of teens and young adults tell us that television is a top source of information and ideas about sex for them; it has more influence than school, parents, or peers (Kaiser Foundation 2007). A study on Canadian broadcasting, tabled in the House of Commons in June 2003, demonstrated that the vast majority of English-language programs viewed by Canadians (aged two and older) during prime time are "foreign" (meaning, for the most part, from the United States). Thus, it could be extrapolated that Canadians' exposure to sexual content on television would be roughly equivalent to that of their U.S. neighbours.

In this age of sexually transmitted diseases, it is important to increase our understanding of human sexuality. However, it can be a difficult topic to research because of all the preconceptions, myths, and beliefs that may accompany the subject of sexuality. How can we carry out research of what might be considered a controversial and personal topic?

The Setting

Perhaps the most comprehensive study of sexual behaviour was the famous two-volume Kinsey Report prepared in the 1940s (Kinsey et al. 1948, 1953; see also Igo 2007). Although the Kinsey Report is still widely quoted, the volunteers interviewed for the report were not representative of the adult population. The Kinsey Report revealed the wide range of sexual behaviours among U.S. citizens, including that 70 percent of men in the United States had patronized prostitutes, that 92 percent of men and 58 percent of women had masturbated, and that 60 percent of men had had some form of homosexual experience before adulthood (Nelson and Fleras 1998). Also revealed in the report was the greater tendency for women to be bisexual (having sexual relations with both male and female partners) than exclusively lesbian.

In Canada, statistics on Canadians' sexual behaviour are collected by Statistics Canada, the primary statistical information source of the Canadian government and a major employer of sociologists. The agency's mandate is to collect, analyze, and disseminate statistical information on a broad range of subjects, including employment, health, education, agriculture, and sexual behaviour. Much of the statistical information collected by Statistics Canada

about the sex lives of Canadians comes from the National Public Health Survey, the Canadian Community Health Survey, and the Canadian census. For instance, this research shows about 60 percent of young Canadian females who did not use a condom during their last act of sexual intercourse were sexually active by age 13 (Statistics Canada 2005a). Figure 2-5 below illustrates the median age of first sex in Canada and a number of countries around the world.

Many of the studies that have been done on sexuality in North America over the last decade have included ethnicity as a variable (Meston and Ahrold 2008). Recent studies have revealed, however, that the length of time spent in Canada is a significant factor in influencing some, but not all, sexual attitudes and behaviours of Asian Canadians.

Sociological Insights

The controversy surrounding research on human sexual behaviour raises the issue of value neutrality. And this becomes especially delicate when we consider the relationship of sociology to the government. Canada's federal government has become the major source of funding for sociological research. Yet Max Weber urged that sociology remain an autonomous discipline and not become unduly influenced by any one segment of society. According to his ideal of value neutrality, sociologists

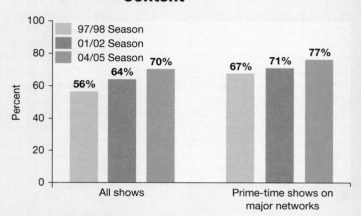

figure **2-4** **Percentage of Television Shows That Contain Sexual Content**

- 97/98 Season
- 01/02 Season
- 04/05 Season

All shows: 56%, 64%, 70%
Prime-time shows on major networks: 67%, 71%, 77%

Source: Kaiser Family Foundation 2005:4.

must remain free to reveal information that is embarrassing to government or, for that matter, is supportive of government institutions. Thus, researchers investigating a prison riot must be ready to examine objectively not only the behaviour of inmates but also the conduct of prison officials before and during the riot.

Conflict theorists and feminists, among others, are critical of some research that claims to be

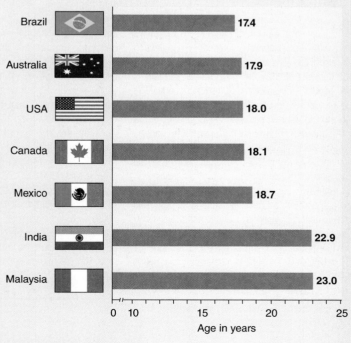

figure **2-5** **Median Age of First Sex**

Country	Age
Brazil	17.4
Australia	17.9
USA	18.0
Canada	18.1
Mexico	18.7
India	22.9
Malaysia	23.0

Age in years

Source: Durex 2007.

objective. In turn, their research is occasionally criticized for not sufficiently addressing Weber's concern for value neutrality. In any case, maintaining objectivity may be difficult if sociologists fear that findings critical of government institutions will jeopardize their chances of obtaining federal support for new research projects.

In the United States, although the American Sociological Association's code of ethics expects sociologists to disclose all funding sources, the code does not address the issue of whether sociologists who accept funding from a particular agency may also accept their perspective on what needs to be studied. Lewis Coser has argued that as sociologists in the United States have increasingly turned from basic sociological research to research with application for government agencies and the private sector, "they have relinquished to a large extent the freedom to choose their own problems, substituting the problems of their clients for those which might have interested them on purely theoretical grounds" (1956:27). Viewed in this light, the importance of government funding for sociological studies raises troubling questions for those who cherish Weber's ideal of value neutrality in research. In the funding of sociological research, the CSAA's code of ethics directly warns its members to guard against the promotion of research that furthers the power of a corporation, a government, or a church over the lives of those being studied. In addition, the code prompts sociologists to be mindful of the implications of their research and the potential for exploitation of particular individuals and groups. As we'll see in the next section, applied sociological research on human sexuality has run into barriers constructed by government funding agencies.

Policy Initiatives

In Canada, there has been willingness to research and openness toward research on such topics as same-sex relationships, condom use among teens, bisexuality, and number of sexual partners, as demonstrated by the vast number and variety of reports published by Statistics Canada. The 2001 Census results, for example, were the first to provide data on same-sex relationships. It is a different story in the United States, where conservative voices in government have made government-sponsored research on the topic of sexual behaviour more difficult.

In 1987, the federal National Institute of Child Health and Human Development sought proposals for a national survey of sexual behaviour. Sociologists responded with various proposals that a review panel of scientists approved for funding. However, in 1991, led by Senator Jesse Helms

and other conservatives, the U.S. Senate voted 66–34 to forbid funding any survey on adult sexual practices. Helms appealed to popular fears by arguing that such surveys of sexual behaviour were intended to "legitimize homosexual lifestyles" and to support "sexual decadence." Two years earlier, a similar debate in Great Britain had led to the denial of government funding for a national sex survey (A. Johnson et al. 1994; Laumann, Gagnon, and Michael 1994a:36).

Despite the vote by the U.S. Senate, sociologists Edward Laumann, John Gagnon, Stuart Michaels, and Robert Michael developed the National Health and Social Life Survey (NHSLS) to better understand the sexual practices of adults in the United States. The researchers raised US$1.6 million of private funding to make their study possible (Laumann et al. 1994a, 1994b).

The researchers made great efforts to ensure privacy during the NHSLS interviews, as well as confidentiality of responses and security in maintaining data files. Perhaps because of this careful effort, the interviewers did not typically experience problems getting responses, even though they were asking people about their sexual behaviour. All interviews were conducted in person, although there was also a confidential form that included questions about such sensitive subjects as family income and masturbation. The researchers used several techniques to test the accuracy of subjects' responses, such as asking redundant questions at different times in different ways during the 90-minute interview. These careful procedures helped establish the validity of the NHSLS findings.

Today, research on human sexuality is not the only target of policymakers. The U.S. Congress began in 1995 considering passage of the Family Privacy Protection Act, which would force all federally funded researchers to obtain written consent from parents before surveying young people on such issues as drug use, antisocial behaviour, and emotional difficulties, as well as sexual behaviour. Researchers around the United States suggest that this legal requirement will make it impossible to survey representative samples of young people. They note that when parents are asked to return consent forms, only about half do so, even though no more than 1 percent to 2 percent actually object to the survey. Moreover, the additional effort required to get all the forms returned raises research costs by 25-fold (Elias 1996; Levine 2001).

Despite the political battles, the authors of the NHSLS believe that their research was important. These researchers argue that using data from their survey allows us to more easily address such public policy issues as AIDS, sexual harassment, rape, welfare reform, sex discrimination, abortion,

Increasingly, researchers who study human sexual behaviour are exploring sexual patterns among the Chinese.

teenage pregnancy, and family planning. Moreover, the research findings help to counter some "common-sense" notions. For instance, contrary to the popular belief that teens have increasing rates of births and abortion, in 2008, U.S. teen birth and abortion rates fell to a 40-year low (Reuters Reporter 2012).

Scholars in China, aware of the NHLS, have begun to collaborate with sociologists in the United States on a similar study in China. The data are now just being analyzed, but responses thus far indicate dramatic differences in the sexual behaviour of people in their 20s, compared to behaviour at the same age by people who are now in their 50s. Younger-generation Chinese are more sexually active and have more partners than their parents did. Partly in response to these preliminary results, the Chinese Ministry of Health has sought U.S. assistance on HIV/AIDS prevention and research (Parish et al. 2007).

Apply the Theory

1. When studying human sexuality, what theoretical perspective(s) would advocate high levels of objectivity and neutrality?
2. Would you be willing to participate in a study related to sexuality if you were asked?
3. For feminist researchers, what might be a major goal or purpose of any study on human sexuality?

CHAPTER RESOURCES

Summary

::: 2.1 What Is the Scientific Method?

- There are five basic steps in the **scientific method**: defining the problem, reviewing the literature, formulating the hypothesis, selecting the research design and then collecting and analyzing data, and developing the conclusion.
- Whenever researchers want to study abstract concepts, such as intelligence or prejudice, they must develop a workable **operational definition**.
- A **hypothesis** usually states a possible relationship between two or more variables.
- By using a **sample**, sociologists avoid having to test everyone in a population.
- According to the scientific method, research results must possess both **validity** and **reliability**.

::: 2.2 What Are the Major Research Designs?

- Sociologists use four major research designs in their work: **survey** research of a population, utilizing the interview and the **questionnaire; ethnography** and in-depth interviews, focusing on small groups and communities; **experiment** that tests cause-and-effect relationships; **secondary analysis** or the analysis of existing sources.

::: 2.3 What Are the Ethics of Research?

- The **code of ethics** of the Canadian Sociology and Anthropology Association calls for objectivity and integrity in research, respect for the subject's privacy, and confidentiality.

::: 2.4 How Does Technology Influence Sociological Research?

- Technology today plays an important role in sociological research, whether it is a computer database or information from the Internet.

Critical Thinking Questions

1. Suppose that your sociology instructor has asked you to do a study of the issues facing Canadians today. Which research technique would you find most useful? How would you use that approach to complete your assignment?

2. Do you think you or any sociologist can maintain value neutrality while studying any group of people, such as younger Canadians?

3. Why is it important for sociologists to have a code of ethics?

4. What research method(s) do you think would produce the best results when studying the views and attitudes of the under-30 age group? Why?

THINKING ABOUT MOVIES

And the Band Played On

In the early years of the AIDS crisis, researchers employ the scientific method to understand how the disease is transmitted.

An Inconvenient Truth

In this documentary about global warming, Al Gore argues that certain social groups are already paying the price for climate change.

Kinsey

A researcher struggles with the ethical challenges of studying human sexual behaviour.

connect **LEARNSMART** **SMARTBOOK**

For more information on the resources available from McGraw-Hill Ryerson, go to **www.mcgrawhill.ca/he/solutions**.

inside

BOXES

Sociology in the Global Community: *Life in the Global Village*

Research Today: *Culture at Walmart*

Social Policy and Culture: *Multiculturalism*

Cultural diversity is celebrated during the Caribana parade in Toronto.

"Nacirema culture is characterized by a highly developed market economy which has evolved in a rich natural habitat. While much of the people's time is devoted to economic pursuits, a large part of the fruits of these labours and a considerable portion of the day are spent in ritual activity. The focus of this activity is the human body, the appearance and health of which loom as a dominant concern in the ethos of the people. While such a concern is certainly not unusual, its ceremonial aspects and associated philosophy are unique.

The fundamental belief underlying the whole system appears to be that the human body is ugly and that its natural tendency is to debility and disease. Incarcerated in such a body, man's only hope is to avert these characteristics through the use of the powerful influences of ritual and ceremony. Every household has one or more shrines devoted to this purpose. The more powerful individuals in the society have several shrines in their houses and, in fact, the opulence of a house is often referred to in terms of the number of such ritual centres it possesses. Most houses are of wattle and daub construction, but the shrine rooms of the more wealthy are walled with stone. Poorer families imitate the rich by applying pottery plaques to their shrine walls.

While each family has at least one such shrine, the rituals associated with it are not family ceremonies but are private and secret. The rites are normally only discussed with children, and then only during the period when they are being initiated into these mysteries. I was able, however, to establish sufficient rapport with the natives to examine these shrines and to have the rituals described to me.

The focal point of the shrine is a box or chest which is built into the wall. In this chest are kept the many charms and magical potions without which no native believes he could live. These preparations are secured from a variety of specialized practitioners. The most powerful of these are the medicine men, whose assistance must be rewarded with substantial gifts. However, the medicine men do not provide the curative potions for their clients, but decide what the ingredients should be and then write them down in an ancient and secret language. This writing is understood only by the medicine men and by the herbalists who, for another gift, provide the required charm.

The focal point of the shrine is a box or chest which is built into the wall. In this chest are kept the many charms and magical potions without which no native believes he could live.

The charm is not disposed of after it has served its purpose, but is placed in the charm-box of the household shrine. As these magical materials are specific for certain ills, and the real or imagined maladies of the people are many, the charm-box is usually full to overflowing. The magical packets are so numerous that people forget what their purposes were and fear to use them again. While the natives are very vague on this point, we can only assume that the idea in retaining all the old magical materials is that their presence in the charm-box, before which the body rituals are conducted, will in some way protect the worshipper."

(Miner 1956:503–504)

In this excerpt from his journal article "Body Ritual among the Nacirema," anthropologist Horace Miner casts his observant eye on the intriguing rituals of an exotic culture. If some aspects of this culture seem familiar to you, however, you are right, for what Miner is describing is actually the culture of the United States ("Nacirema" is "American" spelled backward). Found in Canada and other rich countries as well, the "shrine" Miner writes of is the bathroom; he correctly informs us that in this culture, one measure of wealth is how many bathrooms one's home has. In their bathroom rituals, he goes on, the Nacirema use charms and magical potions (beauty products and prescription drugs) obtained from specialized practitioners (such as hair stylists), herbalists (pharmacists), and medicine men (physicians). Using our sociological imaginations, we could update Miner's description of the Nacirema's charms, written in 1956, by adding tooth whiteners, anti-aging creams, Waterpiks, and hair gel.

When we step back and examine a culture thoughtfully and objectively, whether it is our own culture in disguise or another less familiar to us, we learn something new about society. Take Fiji, an island in the Pacific where a robust, nicely rounded body has always been the ideal for both men and women. This is a society in which "You've gained weight" traditionally has been considered a compliment, and "Your legs are skinny," an insult. Yet a recent study shows that for the first time, eating disorders have been showing up among young people in Fiji. What has happened to change their body image? Since the introduction of cable television in 1995, many Fiji islanders, especially young women, have begun to emulate not their mothers and aunts, but the small-waisted stars of television programs currently airing there, like *Grey's Anatomy* and *Desperate Housewives*. Studying culture in places like Fiji, then, sheds light on our society as well (Becker 2007; Fiji TV 2010)."

The study of culture is basic to sociology. In this chapter, we will examine the meaning of culture and society as well as the development of culture from its roots in the prehistoric human experience to the technological advances of today. The major aspects of culture—including language, norms, sanctions, and values—will be defined and explored. We will see how cultures develop a dominant ideology, and how functionalist, conflict, feminist, and interactionist theorists view culture. The discussion will focus both on general cultural practices found in all societies and on the wide variations that can distinguish one society from another. The social policy section will look at the conflicts in cultural values that underlie current debates about multiculturalism.

::: use your sociological *imagination* :::

How do you think language can be used to separate oneself from others? Can you think of ways in which you use language as a means of connecting with others?

How Do Culture and Society Compare?

Culture is the totality of learned, socially transmitted customs, knowledge, material objects, and behaviour. It includes the ideas, values, customs, and artifacts (for example, iPods, comic books, and birth control devices) of groups of people. Patriotic attachment to the game of ice hockey in Canada is an aspect of culture, as is the widespread passion for the tango in Argentina.

Sometimes, people refer to a particular person as "very cultured" or to a city as having "lots of culture." That use of the term *culture* is different from our use in this book. In sociological terms, *culture* does not refer solely to the fine arts and refined intellectual taste. It consists of all objects and ideas within a society, including ice cream cones, rock music, and slang words. Sociologists consider both a portrait by Rembrandt and a portrait by a billboard painter to be aspects of a culture. A tribe that cultivates soil by hand has just as much of a culture as a people that relies on computer-operated machinery. Each people has a distinctive culture with its own characteristic ways of gathering and preparing food, constructing homes, structuring the family, and promoting standards of right and wrong.

Sharing a similar culture may help to define the group or society to which we belong. A fairly large number of people are said to constitute a **society** when they live in the same territory, are relatively independent of people outside their area, and participate in a culture. Mexico City is more populous than many nations of the world, yet sociologists do not consider it a society in its own right. Rather, it is seen as part of—and dependent on—the larger society of Mexico.

A society is the largest form of human group. It consists of people who share a culture. Members of the society learn a culture and transmit it from one generation to the next. They even preserve their culture through literature, art, video recordings, and other means of expression. If it were not for the social transmission of culture, each generation would have to reinvent television, not to mention the wheel.

Sharing aspects of a common culture may simplify many day-to-day interactions. For example, when you buy an airline ticket, you know you don't have to bring along hundreds of dollars in cash. You can pay with a credit card. When you are part of a society, there are many small, as well as many important, cultural patterns that you take for granted. You assume that theatres will provide seats for the audience, that physicians will not disclose confidential information, and that parents will be careful when crossing the street with young children. All these assumptions reflect the basic values, beliefs, and customs of the culture of Canada.

Language is a critical element of culture that sets humans apart from other species. Members of a society generally share a common language, which facilitates day-to-day exchanges with others. When you ask a hardware store clerk for a flashlight, you don't need to draw a picture of the product. You share the same cultural term for a small, battery-operated, portable light. However, if you were in Britain and needed the same item, you would have to ask for an "electric torch." Of course, even within the same society, a term can have a number of different meanings. In Canada, *grass* signifies both a plant eaten by grazing animals and an intoxicating drug.

How Do Cultures Develop around the World?

We've come a long way from our prehistoric heritage. We can transmit an entire book anywhere in the world via the Internet; we can clone cells; and we can prolong lives through organ transplants. The human species has produced achievements in music, poetry, painting, novels, and films. We can peer into the outermost reaches of the universe, and we can analyze our innermost feelings. In all these ways, we are remarkably different from other species of the animal kingdom.

The process of expanding culture has been under way for thousands of years. The first archaeological evidence of human-like primates places our ancestors back many millions of years. About 700 000 years ago, people built hearths to harness fire. Archaeologists have uncovered tools that date back over 100 000 years. From 35 000 years ago, we have evidence of paintings, jewellery, and statues. By that time, elaborate ceremonies had already been developed for marriages, births, and deaths (Harris 1997; Haviland 1999).

Tracing the development of culture is not easy. Archaeologists cannot "dig up" weddings, laws, or governments, but they are able to locate items that point to the emergence of cultural traditions. Our early ancestors were primates that had characteristics of human beings; they made important advances in the use of tools. Recent studies of chimpanzees in the wild have revealed that they frequently use sticks and other natural objects in ways learned from other members

Navigating cultural differences can be a challenge. During a visit to Tokyo, U.S. President Obama was criticized for his deep bow to Emperor Akihito. And at the 2010 Winter Olympics, Russian ice dancers Domnina and Shabalin were criticized for their interpretation of Aboriginal dress. Favoured to win, they took only third place.

of the group. However, unlike chimpanzees, our ancestors gradually made tools from increasingly durable materials. As a result, the items could be reused and later refined into more effective implements.

Cultural Universals

Despite their differences, all societies have developed certain common practices and beliefs, known as **cultural universals**. Many cultural universals are, in fact, adaptations to meet essential human needs, such as people's need for food, shelter, and clothing. Anthropologist George Murdock (1945:124) compiled a list of cultural universals. Some of these include athletic sports, cooking, funeral ceremonies, medicine, and sexual restrictions.

The cultural practices listed by Murdock may be universal, but the manner in which they are expressed varies from culture to culture. For example, one society may let its members choose their own marriage partners. Another may encourage marriages arranged by the parents.

Not only does the expression of cultural universals vary from one society to another, but it also may change dramatically over time within a society. Each generation, and each year for that matter, most human cultures change and expand.

Innovation

The process of introducing an idea or object that is new to a culture is known as **innovation**. Innovation interests sociologists because of the social consequences that introducing something new can have in any society. There are two forms of innovation: discovery and invention. A **discovery** involves making known or sharing the existence of an aspect of reality. The finding of the DNA molecule and the identification of a new moon of Saturn are both acts of discovery. A significant factor in the process of

discovery is the sharing of new-found knowledge with others. By contrast, an **invention** results when existing cultural items are combined into a form that did not exist before. The bow and arrow, the automobile, and the television are all examples of inventions, as are Protestantism and democracy.

Globalization, Diffusion, and Technology

You don't have to sample gourmet foods to eat "foreign" foods. Breakfast cereal comes originally from Germany, candy from the Netherlands, and chewing gum from Mexico. The United States has also "exported" foods to other lands. Residents of many nations enjoy pizza, which was popularized in the United States. However, in Japan, they add squid; in Australia, it is eaten with pineapple, and in England, people eat kernels of corn with the cheese.

Just as a culture does not always discover or invent its foods, it may also adopt ideas, technology, and customs from other cultures. Sociologists use the term **diffusion** to refer to the process by which a cultural item is spread from group to group or society to society. Diffusion can occur through a variety of means, among them exploration, military conquest, missionary work, the influence of the mass media, tourism, and the Internet (see Box 3-1). In recent decades, international trade and the exchange of ideas have accelerated cultural diffusion. Sociologists use the term *globalization* to refer to the worldwide integration of government policies, cultures, social movements, and financial markets.

Early in human history, culture changed rather slowly through discovery. Then, as the number of discoveries in a culture increased, inventions became possible. The more inventions there were, the more rapidly additional inventions could be created. In addition, as diverse cultures came into contact with one another, they could each take advantage of the other's

sociology in the global community

3-1 Life in the Global Village

Imagine a "borderless world" in which culture, trade, commerce, money, and even people move freely from one place to another. Popular culture is widely shared, whether it is Japanese sushi or U.S. running shoes, and the English speaker who answers questions over the telephone about your credit card account is as likely to be in India or the United States as in Canada. In this world, even the sovereignty of nations is at risk, challenged by political movements and ideologies that span nations.

What caused this great wave of cultural diffusion? First, sociologists take note of advances in communications technology. Satellite TV, cellphones, the Internet, and the like allow information to flow freely across the world, linking global markets. In 2008, this process reached the point where consumers could view videos on handheld devices and surf the Internet on their wireless cellphones, shopping online at Amazon.com, eBay, and other commercial Web sites from cars, airports, and cafeterias. Second, corporations in the industrial nations have become multinational, with both factories and markets in developing countries. Business leaders welcome the

opportunity to sell consumer goods in populous countries such as China. Third, these multinational firms have cooperated with global financial institutions, organizations, and governments to promote free trade—unrestricted or lightly restricted commerce across national borders.

Globalization is not universally welcomed. Many critics see the dominance of "businesses without borders" as benefiting the rich, particularly the very wealthy in industrial countries, at the expense of the poor in less developed nations. They consider globalization to be a successor to the imperialism and colonialism that oppressed poorer nations for centuries.

Another criticism of globalization comes from people who feel overwhelmed by global culture. Embedded in the concept of globalization is the notion of the cultural domination of developing nations by more affluent nations. Simply put, people lose their traditional values and begin to identify with the culture of dominant nations. They may discard or neglect their native language and dress as they attempt to copy the icons of mass-market entertainment and fashion. James Bond movies and Lady Gaga may be

seen as threats to native cultures, if they dominate the media at the expense of local art forms and European fairy tales may be more popular than local traditional stories.

Globalization has its positive side, too. Many developing nations are taking their place in the world of commerce and bringing in much needed income. The communications revolution helps people to stay connected and gives them access to knowledge that can improve living standards and even save lives.

Apply the Theory

1. How are you affected by globalization? Which aspects of globalization do you find advantageous and which objectionable?
2. How would you feel if the customs and traditions you grew up with were replaced by the culture or values of another country? How might you try to protect your culture?

Sources: Dodds 2000; Giddens 1991; Martin et al. 2006; Ritzer 2004; Sernau 2001; Tedeschi 2006.

---

innovations. Thus, when people in Canada read a newspaper, we look at characters invented by the ancient Semites, printed by a process invented in Germany, on a material invented in China (Linton 1936).

Citizens of nations may tend to feel a loss of identity when they are bombarded with culture from outside. Postmodern theorists such as Jean Baudrillard (1983) suggest that reality is simulated through media, cyberspace, and Disney-like theme parks in which the United States is idealized as "heaven." As Stephen M. Fjellman—who studied the worldview of Disney World—suggests, "how nice if they all could be like us—with kids, a dog, and General Electric appliances . . ." (1992:317). We have already mentioned in Chapter 1 that postmodern theorists take a global perspective and note how aspects of culture cross national boundaries, contributing to an intermingling of ideologies and cultures typical of

The fictional Spider-Man first appeared in comic books in the United States in 1962. Since then, the superhero's image and the legends surrounding him have circled the globe through the process of cultural diffusion. In this photograph, taken at a fairground in Iran, a girl enjoys a Spider-Man ride.

an electronically connected planet. People throughout the world decry U.S. cultural exports, from films to language to Bart Simpson. Movies produced in the United States account for 65 percent of the global box office. Magazines as diverse

as *Cosmopolitan* and *Reader's Digest* sell two issues abroad for every one they sell in the United States. *CSI: Crime Scene Investigation* airs in roughly 60 countries. These examples of canned culture all facilitate the diffusion of cultural practices.

figure 3-1 Foreign Content by Private Broadcasters in Canada

Dancing with the Stars became one of the most popular U.S. reality shows in 2011.

Foreign Content by Private Broadcasters in Canada	
$71 million CDN $550 million foreign	**Drama/Comedy**
$68 million CDN $164 million foreign	**Human Interest** (including reality and talk shows)
$22 million CDN $33 million foreign	**Music/Variety**
$5 million CDN $23 million foreign	**Game Shows**

Canadian TV sitcom *Da Kink in My Hair.*

In 2010, private television networks spent $777 million on foreign (primarily U.S.) programming and $681 million on Canadian shows.

Source: Industry Analysis, Policy Development and Research Sector, 2007, Television Statistical and Financial Summaries, 2002–2006, p. 13. Reproduced with the permission of the Minister of Public Works and Government Services Canada, 2007; CRTC 2011.

Many societies try to protect themselves from the invasion of too much culture from other countries, especially the economically dominant United States. Canada's federal government, for example, requires that 35 percent of a radio station's daytime programming be Canadian songs or artists. Among private television networks in Canada in 2006, however, more money was spent on foreign (primarily U.S.) programs than on Canadian programs—12 percent more than the previous year (CRTC 2007; see Figure 3-1). In Brazil, a toy manufacturer has eclipsed Barbie's popularity by designing a doll named Susi that looks more like Brazilian girls. Susi has a slightly smaller chest, much wider thighs, and darker skin than Barbie. Her wardrobe includes the skimpy bikinis favoured on Brazilian beaches as well as a soccer shirt honouring the great Brazilian men's and women's national teams. According to the toy company's marketing director, "we wanted Susi to be more Latin, more voluptuous. We Latins appreciate those attributes."

Technology in its many forms has now increased the speed by which aspects of culture are shared and has broadened the distribution of cultural elements. Sociologist Gerhard Lenski has defined **technology** as "cultural information about how to use the material resources of the environment to satisfy human needs and desires" (Nolan and Lenski 2009:357). Today's technological developments no longer have to await publication in journals with limited circulation. Press conferences, often simultaneously carried on the Internet, now trumpet new developments.

Technology not only accelerates the diffusion of scientific innovations but also transmits culture. The English language and North American culture dominate the Internet and World Wide Web. Such control, or at least dominance, of technology influences the direction of cultural diffusion. For example, Web sites abound with the most superficial aspects of Canadian and U.S. culture but little information about the pressing issues faced by citizens of other nations. People all over the world find it easier to visit electronic chat rooms about *the* latest reality television shows than to learn about their own government's policies on daycare or infant nutrition programs.

Sociologist William F. Ogburn (1922) made a useful distinction between the elements of material and non-material culture. **Material culture** refers to the physical or technological aspects of our daily lives, including food items, houses, factories, and raw materials. **Non-material culture** refers to ways of using material objects and also to customs, beliefs, philosophies, governments, and patterns of communication. Generally, the non-material culture is more resistant to change than the material culture. Consequently, Ogburn introduced the term **culture lag** to refer to the period of maladjustment when the non-material culture is still adapting to new material conditions. For example, in 2010, manufacturers

When a society's non-material culture (its values and laws) does not keep pace with rapid changes in its material culture, people experience an awkward period of maladjustment called *culture lag*. The transition to nuclear power generation that began in the second half of the twentieth century brought widespread protests against the new technology, as well as serious accidents that government officials were poorly prepared to deal with. Tensions over the controversial technology have not run as high in some countries as in others, however. France, where this nuclear power plant is situated, generates 78 percent of all its electricity through nuclear power. The technology is not as controversial there as in the United States and Canada, which generate less than 20 percent of their electricity through nuclear reaction.

introduced electronic cigarettes, battery-powered tubes that turn nicotine-laced liquid into vapour mist. The innovation soon had officials at airlines (which ban smoking) and government regulatory bodies scrambling to respond to the latest technology (Kesmodel and Yadron 2010).

Diffusion can involve a single word, like "cyber," or an entirely new orientation toward living, which may be transmitted through advances in electronic communication. Sociologist George Ritzer (1995) coined the term "McDonaldization of society" to describe how the principles of fast-food restaurants developed in the United States have come to dominate more and more sectors of societies throughout the world. For example, hair salons and medical clinics now take walk-in appointments. In Hong Kong, sex-selection clinics offer a menu of items—from fertility enhancement to methods of increasing the likelihood of producing a child of the desired sex. Religious groups—from evangelical preachers on local stations or Web sites to priests at the Vatican Television Center—use marketing techniques similar to those that sell Happy Meals.

McDonaldization is associated with the melding of cultures, so that we see more and more similarities in cultural expression. In Japan, for example, African entrepreneurs have found a thriving market for hip-hop fashions popularized by teens in the United States. In Austria, the McDonald's organization itself has drawn on the locals' love of coffee, cake, and conversation to inspire the McCafé (Hughlett 2008; Ritzer 2002, 2011).

3.3 What Are the Elements of Culture?

Each culture considers its own distinctive ways of handling basic societal tasks as "natural." But, in fact, methods of education, marital ceremonies, religious doctrines, and other aspects of culture are learned and transmitted through human interactions within specific societies. Parents in India are accustomed to arranging marriages for their children, whereas most parents in Canada leave marital decisions up to their offspring. Lifelong residents of Naples consider it natural to speak Italian, whereas lifelong residents of Buenos Aires feel the same way about Spanish. We'll now take a look at the major aspects of culture that shape the way the members of a society live—language, norms, sanctions, and values.

Language

The English language makes extensive use of words dealing with war. We speak of *conquering* space, *fighting* the *battle* of the bulge, *waging a war* on drugs, making a *killing* on the stock market, and *bombing* an examination; something monumental or great is *the bomb*. An observer from an entirely different and warless culture could gauge the importance that war and the military have had on the English-speaking world simply by recognizing the prominence that militaristic terms have in the language. Words such as *gelding, stallion, mare, piebald,* and *sorrel* have all been used to describe one animal—the horse. Even if we knew little of the period of history in which these words were used, we could conclude from the list of terms that horses were culturally important. The Slavey First

Nations people, who live in the Northwest Territories, have 14 terms to describe ice, including eight for different kinds of solid ice and others for seamed ice, cracked ice, and floating ice. Language reflects the priorities of a culture.

Language is, in fact, the foundation of every culture. **Language** is an abstract system of word meanings and symbols for all aspects of culture. It includes speech, written characters, numerals, symbols, and gestures and expressions of non-verbal communication. Figure 3-2 shows the number of languages spoken in the 10 countries with the highest and the 10 countries with the lowest number of different spoken languages.

Language is not an exclusively human attribute. Although they are incapable of human speech, primates, such as chimpanzees, have been able to use symbols to communicate. However, even at their most advanced level, other animals operate with essentially a fixed set of signs that have fixed meanings. By contrast, humans can manipulate symbols in order to express abstract concepts and rules and to expand human cultures.

Unlike some other elements of culture, language permeates all parts of society. Certain cultural skills, such as cooking or carpentry, can be learned without the use of language through the process of imitation. However, is it possible to transmit complex legal and religious systems to the next generation simply by showing how they are performed? You could put on a black robe and sit behind a bench as a judge does, but would you ever be able to understand legal reasoning without language? People invariably depend on language for the use and transmission of the complex aspects of a culture.

With deliberate past attempts on the part of the Canadian government to eliminate Aboriginal languages, cultural diffusion, and the increased use of dominant languages, efforts have been made to preserve the existing language and culture native to Canada. The Assembly of First Nations (AFN) and Heritage Canada are working together to protect the languages of First Nations groups. Section 35 of the Constitution Act of 1982 protects Aboriginal rights, including language, and the right of enforcement of existing treaties. Despite this legal protection, the First Peoples' Heritage, Language, and Culture Council has designated B.C.'s First Nations languages as ". . . heading toward imminent extinction" (First Peoples' Heritage, Language and Culture Council 2010).

Although many different languages are spoken in Canada, English and French are recognized as the country's official languages.

figure **3-2** Languages of the World: How Many Do You Speak?

MAPPING LIFE WORLDWIDE

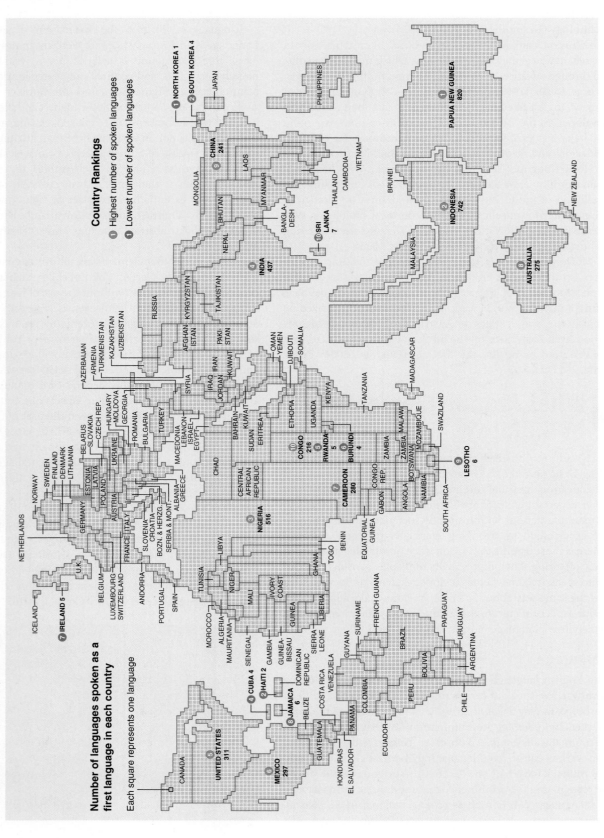

Number of languages spoken as a first language in each country

Each square represents one language

Country Rankings

① Highest number of spoken languages

① Lowest number of spoken languages

Source: From Michael Erard, 2005 "How Linguists and Missionaries Share a Bible of 6,912 Languages," *New York Times* (July 19).

Although language is a cultural universal, striking differences in the use of language are evident around the world. This is the case even when two countries use the same spoken language. For example, an English-speaking person from Canada who is visiting London, England, may be puzzled the first time an English friend says, "I'll ring you up." The friend means, "I'll call you on the telephone." Similarly, the meanings of non-verbal gestures vary from one culture to another. Whereas residents of North America attach positive meanings to the commonly used thumbs-up gesture, the same action carries a vulgar connotation in Australia (Vaughan 2007).

Sapir-Whorf Hypothesis

Language does more than simply describe reality; it also serves to *shape* the reality of a culture. For example, most people in the southern parts of Canada cannot easily make the verbal distinctions about ice that are possible in the Slavey First Nations culture. As a result, they are less likely to notice such differences.

The **Sapir-Whorf hypothesis**, named for two linguists, describes the role of language in interpreting our world. According to Sapir and Whorf, since people can conceptualize the world only through language, language *precedes* thought. Thus, the word symbols and grammar of a language organize the world for us. The Sapir-Whorf hypothesis also holds that language is not a "given." Rather, it is culturally determined and leads to different interpretations of reality by focusing our attention on certain phenomena.

In a literal sense, language may colour how we see the world. Berlin and Kay (1991) have noted that humans possess the physical ability to make millions of colour distinctions, yet languages differ in the number of colours that are recognized. The English language distinguishes between yellow and orange, but some other languages do not. In the Dugum Dani language of New Guinea's West Highlands, there are only two basic colour terms—*modla* for "white" and *mili* for "black." By contrast, there are 11 basic colour terms in English. Russian and Hungarian, though, have 12 colour terms. Russians have terms for light blue and dark blue, while Hungarians have terms for two different shades of red.

Gender-based language can reflect—although in itself it will not determine—the traditional acceptance of men and women in certain occupations. Each time we use such a term as *mailman*, *policeman*, or *fireman*, we are implying (especially to young children) that these occupations can be filled only by males. Yet many women work as *letter carriers, police officers*, and *firefighters*—a fact that is being increasingly recognized and legitimized through the use of such non-sexist language .

Language can also transmit stereotypes related to race. Look up the meanings of the adjective *black* in dictionaries. You will find *dismal, gloomy, forbidding, destitute of moral light or goodness, atrocious, evil, threatening, clouded with anger*. By contrast, dictionaries list *pure* and *innocent* among the meanings of the adjective *white*. Through such patterns of language, our culture reinforces positive associations with the term (and skin colour) *white* and a negative association with *black*. Is it surprising, then, that a list preventing people from working in a profession is called a *blacklist*, while a lie that we think of as somewhat acceptable is called a *white lie*?

Language can shape how we use our senses, how we see, taste, smell, feel, and hear. It also influences the way we think about the people, ideas, and objects around us. Language communicates a culture's most important norms, values, and sanctions to people. That's why the introduction of a new language into a society is such a sensitive issue in many parts of the world.

Non-verbal Communication

If you don't like the way a meeting is going, you might suddenly sit back, fold your arms, and turn down the corners of your mouth. When you see a friend in tears, you may give a quick hug. After winning a big game, you probably high-five your teammates. These are all examples of *non-verbal communication*, the use of gestures, facial expressions, and other visual images to communicate.

We are not born with these expressions. We learn them, just as we learn other forms of language, from people who share our same culture. This statement is as true for the basic expressions of happiness and sadness as it is for more complex emotions, such as shame or distress (Fridlund et al. 1987).

Like other forms of language, non-verbal communication is not the same in all cultures. For example, sociological research done at the micro level documents that people from various cultures differ in the degree to which they touch others during the course of normal social interactions. Even experienced travellers are sometimes caught off guard by these differences. In Saudi Arabia, a middle-aged man may want to hold hands with a partner after closing a business deal. The gesture, which would shock a Canadian businessperson, is considered a compliment in that culture.

A related form of communication is the use of symbols to convey meaning to others. **Symbols** are the gestures, objects, and words that form the basis of human communication. The thumbs-up gesture, a gold star sticker, and the smiley face in an email are all symbols. Often deceptively simple, many symbols are rich in meaning and may not convey the same meaning in all social contexts. Around someone's neck, for example, a cross can symbolize religious reverence; over a grave site, a belief in everlasting life; or set in flames, racial hatred.

Norms

"Wash your hands before dinner." "Thou shalt not kill." "Respect your elders." All societies have ways of encouraging and enforcing what they view as appropriate behaviour while discouraging and punishing what they consider to be improper behaviour. **Norms** are established standards of behaviour maintained by a society.

For a norm to become significant, it must be widely shared and understood. For example, in movie theatres in Canada, we typically expect that people will be quiet while the film is shown. Because of this norm, an usher can tell a member of the audience to stop talking so loudly. Of course, the application of this norm can vary, depending on the particular film and type of audience. People attending a serious art film will be more likely to insist on the norm of silence than those attending a slapstick comedy or horror movie. Norms involving certain activities, such as the online downloading of music, may be murky and their application may also vary.

Types of Norms   Sociologists distinguish between norms in two ways. First, norms are classified as either formal or informal. **Formal norms** generally have been written down and specify strict rules for punishment of violators. In North America, we often formalize norms into laws, which must be very precise in defining proper and improper behaviour. Sociologist Donald Black (1995) has termed **law** to be "governmental social control," establishing laws as formal norms enforced by the state. Laws are just one example of formal norms. The requirements for a college or university major and the rules of a card game are also considered formal norms.

By contrast, **informal norms** are generally understood but they are not precisely recorded. Standards of proper dress are a common example of informal norms. Our society has no specific punishment or sanction for a person who comes to school, say, wearing a monkey suit. Making fun of the non-conforming student is usually the most likely response.

Norms are also classified by their relative importance to society. When classified in this way, they are known as *mores* and *folkways*.

Mores (pronounced "MOR-ays") are norms deemed highly necessary to the welfare of a society, often because they embody the most cherished principles of a people. Each society demands obedience to its mores; violation can lead to severe penalties. Thus, Canada has strong mores against murder and child abuse, which have been institutionalized into formal norms.

Folkways are norms governing everyday behaviour. Folkways play an important role in shaping the daily behaviour of members of a culture. Consider, for example, something as simple as footwear. In Japan, it is a folkway for youngsters to wear flip-flop sandals while learning to walk. A study of Japanese adults has found that, even barefoot, they walk as if wearing flip-flops—braking their thigh muscles and leaning forward as they step. This folkway may even explain why Japan produces so few competitive track and field runners (Stedman 1998).

Society is less likely to formalize folkways than mores, and their violation raises comparatively little concern. For example, walking up a "down" escalator in a department store challenges our standards of appropriate behaviour, but it will not result in a fine or a jail sentence.

In many societies around the world, folkways exist to reinforce patterns of male dominance. Various folkways reveal men's hierarchical position above women within the traditional Buddhist areas of Southeast Asia. In the sleeping cars of trains, women do not sleep in upper berths above men. Hospitals that house men on the first floor do not place women patients on the second floor. Even on clotheslines, folkways dictate male dominance: women's attire is hung lower than that of men (Bulle 1987).

::: use your sociological *imagination* :::

You are a high school principal. What norms would you want to govern the students' behaviour? How might these norms differ from those appropriate for university students?

Acceptance of Norms   People do not follow norms, whether mores or folkways, in all situations. In some cases, they can evade a norm because they know it is weakly enforced. It is illegal for young Canadian teenagers to drink alcoholic beverages, yet drinking by minors is common throughout the nation.

In some instances, behaviour that appears to violate society's norms may actually represent adherence to the norms of a particular group. Teenage drinkers conform to the standards of a peer group at their high school or university. Violating norms of the larger society, many commercially successful hip hop artists and their fans adhere to norms that glorify brutality, the use of firearms, the degradation of women, and the "gangsta" stereotype.

Norms are violated in some instances because one norm conflicts with another. For example, suppose that you live in an apartment building and one night hear the screams of the woman next door, who is being beaten by her husband. If you decide to intervene by ringing their doorbell or calling the police, you are violating the norm of "minding your own business" while, at the same time, following the norm of assisting a victim of violence.

Even when norms do not conflict, there are always exceptions to any norm. The same action, under different circumstances, can cause a person to be viewed either as a hero or as a villain. Secretly taping telephone conversations is normally considered illegal and abhorrent. However, it can be done with a court order to obtain valid evidence for a criminal trial.

Acceptance of norms is subject to change as the political, economic, and social conditions of a culture are transformed. For example, under traditional norms in Canada, a woman was expected to marry, rear children, and remain at home if her husband could support the family without her assistance. However, these norms have changed hugely in recent decades, in part as a result of the contemporary feminist movement (see Chapter 9). As support for traditional norms weakens, people feel free to violate them more frequently and openly and are less likely to be punished for doing so.

Sanctions

Suppose that a hockey coach sends a seventh player onto the ice. Or imagine a business school graduate showing up in shorts for a job interview at a large bank. Or consider a driver who neglects to put any money into a parking meter. These people have violated widely shared and understood norms. So what happens? In each of these situations, the person will receive sanctions if his or her behaviour is detected.

Sanctions are penalties and rewards for conduct concerning a social norm. Note that the concept of *reward* is included in this definition. Conformity to a norm can lead to positive sanctions, such as a pay raise, a medal, a word of gratitude, or a pat on the back. Negative sanctions include fines, threats, imprisonment, and stares of contempt.

Table 3-1 summarizes the relationship between norms and sanctions. As you can see, the sanctions that are associated with formal norms (those written down and codified) tend to be formalized as well. If a hockey coach sends too

When is a kiss more than a kiss? In India, public displays of affection are decidedly not the norm, even among movie stars. When Richard Gere swept actress Shilpa Shetty into his arms at an AIDS awareness event, protests erupted.

table 3-1 Norms and Sanctions

	Sanctions	
Norms	Positive	Negative
Formal	Salary bonus	Demotion
	Testimonial dinner	Firing from a job
	Medal	Jail sentence
	Diploma	Expulsion
Informal	Smile	Frown
	Compliment	Humiliation
	Cheers	Belittling

Values

We each have our own personal set of standards—which may include such things as caring or fitness or success in business—but we also share a general set of objectives as members of a society. Cultural **values** are these collective conceptions of what is considered good, desirable, and proper—or bad, undesirable, and improper—in a culture. They indicate what people in a given culture prefer as well as what they find important and morally right (or wrong). Values may be specific, such as honouring our parents and owning a home, or they may be more general, such as health, love, and democracy. Of course, the members of a society do not uniformly share its values. Angry political debates and billboards promoting conflicting causes tell us that much.

Values influence people's behaviour and serve as criteria for evaluating the actions of others. There is often a direct relationship among the values, norms, and sanctions of a culture. For example, if a culture highly values the institution of marriage, it may have norms (and strict sanctions) that prohibit the act of adultery. If a culture views private property as a basic value, it will probably have stiff laws against theft and vandalism.

many players onto the ice, the team will be called for a two-minute minor penalty. The driver who fails to put money in the parking meter will be given a ticket and expected to pay a fine. But sanctions for violations of informal norms can vary. The business school graduate who comes to the bank interview in shorts will probably lose any chance of getting the job; however, he or she might be so brilliant that the bank officials will overlook the unconventional attire.

Applying sanctions entails first *detecting* violations of norms or obedience to norms. A person cannot be penalized or rewarded unless someone with the power to provide sanctions is aware of the person's actions. Therefore, if none of the referees in the hockey game realizes that there is an extra player on the ice, there will be no penalty. If the police do not check the parking meter, there will be no fine or ticket. Furthermore, there can be *improper* application of sanctions in certain situations. The referee may make an error in counting the number of hockey players and levy an undeserved penalty on one team for too many players on the ice.

The entire fabric of norms and sanctions in a culture reflects that culture's values and priorities. The most cherished values will be most heavily sanctioned; matters regarded as less critical will carry light and informal sanctions.

Girls Not Brides is a global organization with the goal of ending child marriage.

figure 3-3 Percent of Canadian Men and Women Who Prefer to Make Prostitution Illegal, 2010 and 2009

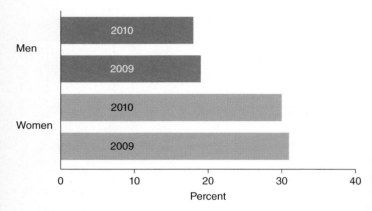

Source: Angus Reid Strategies 2011; adapted by author.

Do you think that there is such a thing as Canadian values? Sociologists disagree about whether or not certain values can be representative as those shared by Canadians. When asked the question "What is it about Canada that gives you the greatest source of pride?" in an Environics Research survey (2007a), a representative sample of 2045 Canadians over the age of 18 gave the following responses (in descending order of frequency):

freedom/democracy
multiculturalism
humanitarianism/kind/caring
peaceful country
beauty of land/geography
quality of life

People's values may differ according to such factors as their age, the period in which they lived, gender, region, ethnic background, and language. For example, a 2011 study by Angus Reid Strategies found that the percentage of Canadian men who would prefer to make prostitution illegal was significantly lower than that of Canadian women. Figure 3-3 shows the difference between Canadian men and women's views on prostitution in 2009 and 2010.

3.4 How Does Culture Relate to the Dominant Ideology?

Functionalist Perspective

Functionalists (see Chapter 1) maintain that stability requires a consensus and the support of society's members; consequently, there are strong central values and common norms. This view of culture became popular in sociology beginning in the 1950s. It was borrowed from British anthropologists who saw cultural traits as all working toward stabilizing a culture. From a functionalist perspective, a cultural trait or practice will persist if it performs functions that society seems to need or it contributes to overall social stability and consensus. This view helps explain why widely condemned social practices, such as prostitution, continue to survive. Both functionalist and conflict theorists agree that culture and society are in harmony with each other, but for different reasons.

Conflict Perspective

Conflict theorists (see Chapter 1) agree that a common culture may exist, but they argue that it serves to maintain the privileges of certain groups. Moreover, while protecting their own self-interests, powerful groups may keep others in a subservient position. The term **dominant ideology** describes the set of cultural beliefs and practices that helps to maintain powerful social, economic, and political interests. This concept was first used by Hungarian Marxist Georg Lukacs (1923) and Italian Marxist Antonio Gramsci (1929). In Karl Marx's view, a capitalist society has a dominant ideology that serves the interests of the ruling class. Box 3-2 illustrates what can happen when a U.S. corporation attempts to export its cultural values to other countries.

From a conflict perspective, the dominant ideology has major social significance. Not only do a society's most powerful groups and institutions control wealth and property, but they also control the means of producing beliefs about reality through religion, education, and the media. For example, if society's message, as communicated by the mass media, is to tell us that we should be consumers, this dominant ideology will help to control us and keep us in a subordinate position (while maximizing the profits of the powerful economic groups).

Neither the functionalist nor the conflict perspective alone can explain all aspects of a culture. Nevertheless, certain cultural practices in our society and others clearly benefit some to the detriment of many. These practices may indeed promote social stability and consensus—but at whose expense?

Feminist Perspectives

Some feminist thinkers would argue that the mass media, acting as mouthpieces for the dominant ideology, contribute to the control and marginalization of women (see Chapter 1). The mass media communicate to their readers, viewers, and listeners the message that women's value in society is based on their sexual attractiveness, their domestic skills, their roles as mothers and wives, their adeptness at staying fit and appearing youthful, and their abilities to provide support and comfort to others (e.g., men, children, the elderly). Some feminist perspectives advocate that the mass media's portrayal of women as powerless, childlike sex objects contributes to cultural norms, beliefs, and values that reinforce and perpetuate patriarchy as a dominant ideology.

Interactionist Perspective

Using the example of consumerism as a dominant ideology found in Canadian culture, an analysis by interactionist (see Chapter 1) thinkers on the topic would differ from those of conflict thinkers and of functional thinkers. Interactionist

research today

3-2 Culture at Walmart

By some measures, Walmart is the largest corporation in the world. By other measures, it is the world's 14th largest economy. Indeed, the Arkansas-based retailer's annual revenue—over one-third of a trillion dollars—surpasses the total value of goods and services produced in many countries, such as Sweden.

Walmart's rise to the status of an economic superpower has not been without criticism. Opponents have criticized its policy of shutting out labour unions, its lack of commitment to elevating women to managerial positions, its slowness to provide adequate health-care benefits, and its negative impact on smaller retailers in the areas where its stores are located. Nonetheless, consumers have embraced Walmart's "everyday low prices." The reaction has not been as positive when the discount giant has tried to enter countries where consumers hold different cultural values (Barbaro 2008).

The company, now located in 15 countries, has not been an unqualified success abroad. In 2006 Walmart pulled out of Germany, due in part to its failure to adjust to the national culture. German shoppers, accustomed to no-nonsense, impersonal service, found Walmart employees' smiling, outgoing style off-putting. The company's "ten-foot attitude"—a salesperson who comes within 10 feet (3 metres) of a customer must look the person in the eye, greet the person, and ask if he or she needs help—simply did not play well there. Food shoppers, used to bagging their own groceries, were turned off by Walmart's practice of allowing clerks to handle their purchases. Furthermore, German employees, who had grown up in a culture that accepts workplace romances, found the company's prohibition against on-the-job relationships bizarre.

Unfortunately, executives did not react quickly enough to the cultural clash. Despite their need for cultural know-how, they passed up the opportunity to install German-speaking managers in key positions. While the company struggled to adjust to unfamiliar cultural standards, fierce competition from German retailers cut into its profits. After an eight-year effort that cost the company one billion dollars, Walmart's executives conceded defeat.

Walmart's withdrawal from Germany was its second exit of the year. Earlier in 2006, the company sold all its facilities in South Korea, where its warehouse-style stores were not appreciated by shoppers accustomed to more elegant surroundings. Today, the successful U.S. retailer is learning not to impose its corporate culture on foreign customers and employees. No longer does the company plan to sell golf clubs in Brazil, where the game is rarely played, or ice skates in Mexico, where skating rinks are hard to find. More important, the corporate giant has begun to study the culture and social patterns of potential customers (Landler and Barbaro 2006; Saporito 2007; Walmart 2010; Zimmerman and Nelson 2006).

Today, rather than risk another mistake abroad, Walmart is considering buying Massmart, a retailer with 288 existing stores in Africa. Time will tell whether the proposed takeover is welcomed, or Walmart is again rejected as the "Beast of Bentonville," as critics in Germany and South Africa called it (Stewart 2010).

Apply the Theory

1. Do you think that Walmart's approach to retailing is in keeping with the cultural values of the communities in your region? Why or why not?
2. Can you think of examples of how Walmart imposes its corporate standards on Canadian customers and employees?

Sources: Barbaro 2008; Landler and Barbaro 2006; Saporito 2007; Walmart 2010; Zimmerman and Nelson 2006.

---

sociologists would examine shopping, or consumer practices, from a micro perspective in order to understand the larger macro phenomenon of consumerism. Interactionists might probe consumers to discover what meaning shopping has for them or what value they attach to the activity. For example, could shopping be viewed as an activity that contributes to the economic and social well-being of Canada? Or is shopping seen as an activity that creates a bond between child and parent as they spend time together at the supermarket selecting groceries? Someone using Goffman's dramaturgical approach (1959, 1963b, 1971) might study particular features of people's personalities that they disclose to fellow shoppers while concealing the same features from the store manager or sales assistant.

What Forms Does Cultural Diversity Take?

Each culture has a unique character. The Inuit people of Canada have little in common with farmers in Southeast Asia. Cultures adapt to meet specific sets of circumstances, such as climate, level of technology, population, and geography. This adaptation to different conditions shows up in differences in all elements of culture, including norms, sanctions, values, and language. Thus, despite the presence of cultural universals, such as courtship and religion, there is still great diversity among the world's many cultures. Moreover, even within a single nation, certain segments of the populace develop cultural patterns that differ from the patterns of the dominant society.

Aspects of Cultural Diversity

Subcultures Residents of a retirement community, workers on an offshore oil rig, rodeo performers, street gangs, goth music fans—all are examples of what sociologists refer to as *subcultures*. A **subculture** is a segment of society that shares a distinctive pattern of mores, folkways, and values that differs from the pattern of the larger society. In a sense, a subculture can be thought of as a culture existing within a larger, dominant culture. The existence of many subcultures is characteristic of complex and diverse societies, such as Canada.

You can get an idea of the impact of subcultures within Canada by considering the variety of seasonal traditions in December. The religious and commercial celebration of the Christmas holiday is an event well entrenched in the dominant culture of our society. However, the Jewish subculture observes Hanukkah, Muslims observe Ramadan (which falls at different times during the year, but at present is occurring during the summer months), and others join in rituals celebrating the winter solstice.

Members of a subculture participate in the dominant culture, while at the same time engaging in unique and distinctive forms of behaviour. Frequently, a subculture will develop an **argot**, or specialized language, that distinguishes it from the wider society, such as the slang used by teen subcultures.

An argot allows insiders, the members of the subculture, to understand words with special meanings. It also establishes patterns of communication that outsiders can't understand. Sociologists associated with the interactionist perspective emphasize that language and symbols offer a powerful way for a subculture to feel cohesive and maintain its identity.

Subcultures develop in a number of ways. Often a subculture emerges because a segment of society faces problems or even privileges unique to its position. Subcultures may be based on common age (teenagers or old people), region (Newfoundlanders), ethnic heritage (Indo-Canadians), occupation (firefighters), or beliefs (environmentalists). Certain subcultures, such as computer hackers, develop because of a shared interest or hobby. In still other subcultures, such as that of prison inmates, members have been excluded from conventional society and are forced to develop alternative ways of living.

Interactionists contend that individuals confer meaning differently: what it means to be a successful surfer living out of a van in Tofino, British Columbia, may be quite different from what it means to be a successful Bay Street lawyer living in Toronto. Feminist perspectives might point to cultural diversity as contributing to the perpetuation of multiple layers and degrees of inequality based on gender, ethnicity, race, and class. The greater the deviation from the norms of the dominant culture, the greater the impact of inequality experienced by various subcultures.

Functionalist and conflict theorists agree that variation exists within a culture. Functionalists view subcultures as variations of particular social environments and as evidence that differences can exist within a common culture. However, conflict theorists suggest that variation often reflects the inequality of social arrangements within a society. A conflict perspective would view the challenge to dominant social norms by Quebec separatists, the feminist movement, and groups representing people with disabilities as a reflection of inequity based on ethnicity, gender, and disability status. Conflict theorists also argue that subcultures sometimes emerge when the dominant society unsuccessfully tries to suppress a practice, such as the use of illegal drugs.

Countercultures   By the end of the 1960s, an extensive subculture had emerged in North America comprising young people turned off by a society they believed was too materialistic and technological. This group primarily included political radicals and "hippies" who had "dropped out" of mainstream social institutions. Hippies rejected societal pressures to accumulate more and more cars, larger and larger homes, and an endless array of material goods. Instead, they expressed a desire to live in a culture based on more humanistic values, such as sharing, love, and coexistence with the environment.

When a subculture conspicuously and deliberately *opposes* certain aspects of the larger culture, it is known as a **counterculture**. Countercultures typically thrive among the young, who have the least investment in the existing culture. In most cases, a 20-year-old can adjust to new cultural standards more easily than can someone who has spent 60 years following the patterns of the dominant culture (Zellner 1995).

An example of a Canadian counterculture is the Front de libération du Québec (FLQ). In 1970, the FLQ opposed the social, economic, political, and educational institutions of the dominant culture of Quebec. Its activities included the murder of a prominent Quebec politician and the kidnapping of a British trade commissioner posted in Quebec. The FLQ produced a manifesto containing all of its demands, which was broadcast through public media.

Culture Shock   Anyone who feels disoriented, uncertain, out of place, or even fearful when immersed in an unfamiliar culture may be experiencing **culture shock**. For example, a resident of Canada

Employees of an international call centre in India socialize after their shift has ended. Call centre employees, whose odd working hours isolate them from others, tend to form tight-knit subcultures.

who visits certain areas in China and wants a local dinner may be stunned to learn that the specialty is scorpion. Similarly, someone from a strict Islamic culture may be shocked on first seeing the comparatively provocative dress styles and open displays of affection that are common in North America and many European cultures. Culture shock can also occur within the larger confines of a person's own culture. For example, a 14-year-old boy from a small town in northern Saskatchewan might feel the effects of culture shock while visiting Toronto for the first time. The speed of the traffic, the level of the street noise, and the intensity and variation of external stimuli may cause him to feel disoriented and uncomfortable within his surroundings.

All of us, to some extent, take for granted the cultural practices of our society. As a result, it can be surprising and even disturbing to realize that other cultures do not follow our way of life. In fact, customs that seem strange to us are considered normal and proper in other cultures, which may in turn see *our* mores and folkways as odd.

::: use your sociological *imagination* :::

You arrive in a developing country as a Canadian International Development Agency (CIDA) volunteer. What aspects of a very different culture do you think would be hardest to adjust to? What might the citizens of that country find shocking about your culture?

Cultural Diversity in Canada If a tourist were to travel across Canada for the first time, he or she would most certainly be struck by the country's diversity—of region, ethnicity, race, and language. Cultural diversity, as the traveller would observe, is greatest in Canada's metropolitan areas, where the largest number of cultural and visible minorities reside. On the basis of his or her observations of cultural diversity, the traveller might conclude that Canada is a "multicultural" society. But what does multiculturalism really mean? Does it simply describe (numerically) the variety of cultures represented in Canada?

Multiculturalism is not only a description of the reality of Canada's cultural makeup—"what is" (Fleras and Kunz 2001)—but, in Canada, it is an explicit policy set out by the federal government. **Multiculturalism** is a policy that promotes cultural and racial diversity and full and equal participation of individuals and communities of all origins as a fundamental characteristic of Canadian identity. The federal Multiculturalism Program of 1997 set three main goals (Communications Canada 2001):

1. *Identity*—fostering a society where people of all backgrounds feel a sense of attachment and belonging to Canada

2. *Civic participation*—developing citizens who are actively involved in their communities and country

3. *Social justice*—building a country that ensures fair and equitable treatment of people of all origins

Multiculturalism can also take the form of an ideology—a set of beliefs, goals, ideals, and attitudes about what multiculturalism *should be*. In embracing multiculturalism as an ideology, Canadians often compare their society's way of expressing cultural diversity with the way it is expressed in the United States (Fleras and Kunz 2001). The analogy of the "mosaic" is commonly used to describe Canada's cultural diversity, where various tiles represent distinct cultural groups that collectively form the whole. In the United States, the "melting pot" analogy represents the model of assimilation, in which U.S. citizens become more like one another, rather than distinct from one another.

Support for the mosaic version of Canada has been declining and shifting toward the melting pot. Across region, age, and education levels, in 1985, 56 percent of Canadians said they preferred the mosaic and 28 percent the melting pot. In 1995, only 44 percent preferred the mosaic, while 40 percent preferred the melting pot (Bibby 1995).

The ideal of multiculturalism in Canada has two desirable outcomes: the survival of ethnic groups and their cultures, and tolerance of this diversity as reflected by an absence of prejudice toward ethnic minorities (Weinfeld 1994). Multiculturalism, however, is not without its critics. Some argue that it is a divisive rather than unifying force in Canada, while others claim that it is only "window dressing," diverting attention from the real problems of ethnic and racial prejudice and discrimination (Nelson and Fleras 1998). The domination of European cultural patterns in Canada—known as **Eurocentrism**—contributes to discrimination and prejudice toward those who are seen as non-European and, thus, the "other."

The American Influence One of the original purposes of multiculturalism was to establish a national uniqueness that would make Canadians distinct from their U.S. counterparts (Bibby 1990). In 1972, Prime Minister Pierre Elliott Trudeau stated that with this policy, "we become less like others; we become less susceptible to cultural, social, or political envelopment by others" (Bibby 1990:49).

The Americanization of Canada (as well as of many other countries) has led to **cultural imperialism**—the influence or imposition of the material or non-material elements of a culture on another culture or cultures. This phenomenon is particularly relevant in the context of the global export of U.S. culture through various forms of that country's mass media. Canadians have been, and continue to be, particularly susceptible to cultural imperialism because of geographic, economic, social, and political ties with the United States. Some organizations, such as the Council of Canadians, have an explicit mandate to protect and preserve Canada's national interests and sovereignty from forces of globalization, in which U.S. cultural imperialism looms large.

A Pew Global Attitudes Project—focusing on the global influence of superpowers—in 2007 surveyed people in 46 countries around the world, including Canada (see Table 3-2). When asked their views of U.S. movies, television, and music, the vast majority of Canadians (73 percent) reported a positive response; Canada was among the

table 3-2 Selected Countries' Views of U.S. Exports, 2007

Positive Views of . . .	U.S. Movies, TV, and Music (%)	U.S. Science and Technology (%)	Spread of U.S. Ideas* (%)
Canada	73	74	22
Peru	50	78	29
Germany	62	65	17
China	42	80	38
Japan	70	81	42
Mali	68	88	45
Turkey	22	37	4
Sweden	77	73	28

*"Good that American customs are spreading here."

Source: Adapted from Pew Global Attitudes Project, 2007a.

top—of 46 countries—in its favourable response to these U.S. pop culture exports. However, in contrast and seeming contradiction, Canadians' views on the statement, "good that American values are spreading here," were considerably lower (22 percent), dropping 13 percent since 2002. Israel, Ethiopia, Ivory Coast, and Nigeria were the only countries outside of the United States where a majority of the population had a favourable view of the spread of U.S. culture (Pew Global Attitudes Project 2007b). The report states, "Despite near universal admiration for U.S. technology and a strong appetite for its culture in most parts of the world, large proportions in most countries think it is bad that American ideas and customs are spreading to their countries" (2007b:5).

Attitudes toward Cultural Diversity

Ethnocentrism Many everyday statements reflect our attitude that our culture is best. We use terms such as *underdeveloped*, *backward*, and *primitive* to refer to other societies. What "we" believe is a religion; what "they" believe is superstition and mythology (Johnson 2000).

It is tempting to evaluate the practices of other cultures on the basis of our own perspectives. Sociologist William Graham Sumner (1906) coined the term **ethnocentrism** to refer to the tendency to assume that our own culture and way of life constitute the norm or are superior to all others. The ethnocentric person sees his or her own group as the centre or defining point of culture and views all other cultures as deviations from what is "normal."

Those westerners who are contemptuous of India's Hindu religion and culture because of its view of cattle as sacred are engaged in ethnocentrism. Another manifestation of ethnocentrism occurs when people in one culture may dismiss as unthinkable the mate-selection or child-rearing practices of another culture.

Conflict theorists point out that ethnocentric value judgments serve to devalue diversity and to deny equal opportunities. The treatment of Aboriginal children in Christian-based residential schools in the middle of the last century is an example of ethnocentrism that conflict theorists might point to in Canadian history. Church authorities were so convinced of the cultural superiority of their own beliefs that they set out to deny Aboriginal children the expression of theirs. Critical race theorists argue that social constructions of the "other" result in differential racialization, which "involves the ways in which the dominant society racializes different minority groups at different times, in response to shifting needs such as the labour market" (Delgado and Stefancic 2001:8). After September 11, 2001, Muslims were racialized, becoming the recipients of racial profiling as they were "constructed" to be a threat to the safety and security of many Western countries. Differential racialization was reasserted after the attempted bombing of an American airline flight to Detroit by an al-Qaeda sympathizer on December 25, 2009.

Functionalists note that ethnocentrism serves to maintain a sense of solidarity by promoting group pride. Canadians' view of their country as peaceful, safe, and relatively free from violence may create a feeling of national solidarity when comparing themselves with their U.S. neighbours.

The importance of the problem of ethnocentrism for students of sociology is particularly relevant. Students must understand that their membership in the social world is not an advantage in the study and practice of sociology.

Cultural Relativism Although ethnocentrism evaluates other cultures by using the familiar culture of the observer as a standard of correct behaviour, **cultural relativism** views people's behaviour from the perspective of their own culture. It places a priority on understanding other cultures, rather than on dismissing them as strange or exotic. Unlike ethnocentrism, cultural relativism employs the kind of value neutrality in scientific study that Max Weber saw as so important.

Cultural relativism stresses that different social contexts give rise to different norms and values. Thus, we must examine such practices as polygamy, bullfighting, and monarchy within the particular contexts of the cultures in which they are found. Although cultural relativism does not suggest that we must unquestionably *accept* every cultural variation, it does require a serious and unbiased effort to evaluate norms, values, and customs in light of their distinctive culture.

figure 3-4 Countries With High Child Marriage Rates

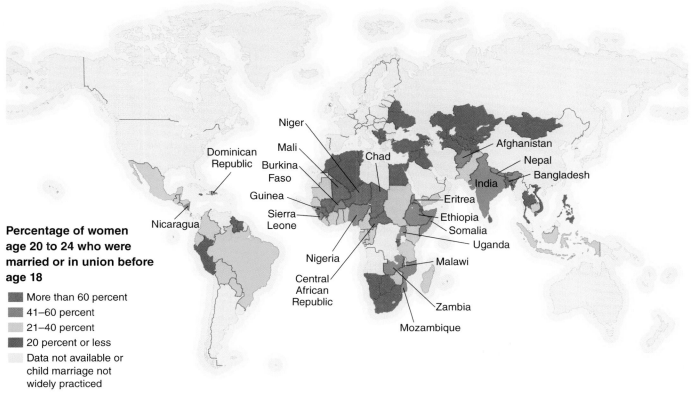

Percentage of women age 20 to 24 who were married or in union before age 18

- More than 60 percent
- 41–60 percent
- 21–40 percent
- 20 percent or less
- Data not available or child marriage not widely practiced

Note: Data are the most recent available, ranging from 1987 to 2006.

Source: UNICEF 2010.

In 21 countries, 40 percent or more of the women under 18 are married.

Think about It

The age of marriage for girls and women varies from country to country and from region to region. What would account for those differences?

Consider the practice of children marrying adults. Most people in North America cannot fathom the idea of a 12-year-old girl marrying. However, in some parts of the world, the majority of women between the ages of 20 and 24 were married before the age of 18 (see Figure 3-4). The custom is illegal in Canada where, generally, the provinces have set the minimum age of marriage to be 18; in West Africa and South Asia the practice of child marriage is common. Should other countries respect such marriages? The apparent answer is no. Fifty-five countries have signed a UN resolution on consent to marry and minimum age of marriage in an attempt to eliminate child marriage and the betrothal of young girls before the age of puberty.

There is an interesting extension of cultural relativism, referred to as *xenocentrism*. **Xenocentrism** is the belief that the products, styles, or ideas of our own society are inferior to those that originate elsewhere (Wilson, Dennis, and Wadsworth 1976). In a sense, it is a reverse ethnocentrism. For example, people in Canada often assume that French wine or Japanese electronic devices are superior to their domestic versions. Are they? Or are people unduly charmed by the lure of goods from exotic places? Such fascination with overseas products can be damaging to competitors in Canada. Conflict theorists are most likely to consider the economic impact of xenocentrism in the developing world. Consumers in developing nations frequently turn their backs on locally produced goods and instead purchase items imported from Europe or North America.

Table 3-3 summarizes the major sociological perspectives on culture. How people view their culture—whether from an ethnocentric point of view or through the lens of cultural relativism—has important consequences in the area of social policy concerned with multiculturalism. We'll take a close look at this issue in the social policy section.

table 3-3 Sociological Perspectives on Culture

	Functionalist Perspective	Conflict Perspective	Feminist Perspective	Interactionist Perspective
Norms	Reinforce societal standards	Reinforce patterns of dominance	Reinforce roles of men and women	Are maintained through face-to-face interaction
Values	Are collective conceptions of what is good	May perpetuate social inequality	May perpetuate men's dominance	Are defined and redefined through social interaction
Culture and society	Culture reflects a society's strong central values	Culture reflects a society's dominant ideology	Culture reflects society's view of men and women	A society's core culture is perpetuated through daily social interactions
Cultural diversity	Subcultures serve the interests of subgroups; ethnocentrism reinforces group solidarity	Countercultures question the dominant social order; ethnocentrism devalues groups	Cultural relativism respects variations in the way men and women are viewed in different societies	Customs and traditions are transmitted through intergroup contact and through the media

Social Policy and Culture

Multiculturalism

The Issue

In 1971, multiculturalism became official government policy in Canada. It was a policy established to promote tolerance for cultural minorities, or in the words of then Prime Minister Pierre Trudeau, to "explore the delights of many cultures." Although the Canadian policy on multiculturalism provides an alternative to the U.S. melting pot approach to cultural diversity, it has generated a great deal of conflict and faced a great deal of opposition (Nelson and Fleras 1998).

Much of the conflict surrounding multiculturalism stems from the variety of meanings or definitions Canadians have for the concept. The term *multiculturalism* can be used to refer to (1) the fact (what is; i.e., the existing complexion of Canadian society); (2) an ideology (what should be); (3) policy (what is proposed); (4) a process (what really happens); (5) a critical discussion (what is being challenged); and (6) a social movement (collective resistance) (Fleras and Elliott 1999). In general, multiculturalism can be defined as a process through which Canadians come to be engaged in their society as different from one another yet equal to one another (Fleras and Kunz 2001).

The Setting

According to Citizenship and Immigration Canada, the government accepts more immigrants, proportional to the size of the country's population, than any other nation in the world. One in every five

residents in Canada was born outside the country. The top five sources for immigration between 2001 and 2006 were countries in Asia and the Middle East (Statistics Canada 2007f). According to the 2006 Census, most foreign-born immigrants who came to Canada between 2001 and 2006 were from China, followed by India, the Philippines, and Pakistan. Overall, multicultural minorities tend to live in Canada's large urban centres, making Toronto, Vancouver, and Montreal the most culturally diverse regions of the country. The majority of all immigrants in Canada settled in one of these three places (Statistics Canada 2012).

From the standpoint of the two major sociological perspectives—conflict theory and structural-functional theory—the implementation of multiculturalism as a social policy has two distinct interpretations. Conflict sociologists view multiculturalism as an attempt to empower minorities to pursue the goals of ethnic identification and equality. It is seen as an attempt to nurture, preserve, and protect different cultural traditions in the midst of domination by one cultural group. Multiculturalism policies also aim to make diversity, and the inevitable struggles that result, an accepted and welcome element of the cultural fabric of Canadian life.

Functional sociologists view culture as something that all Canadians share. It is the common values that unite and integrate us, resulting in a shared sense of identity. Therefore, according to functional thinkers, the more we diversify Canadian culture, the less we share in common;

the more we hyphenate our identities (e.g., Indo-Canadian, Chinese-Canadian, Italian-Canadian, etc.), the less Canadian we actually become. However, both functionalist and conflict theorists have criticized multiculturalism for a number of reasons. Sociologists Augie Fleras and Jean Elliott (1999) argue that criticisms regarding multiculturalism can be classified into four categories:

1. Those claiming that multiculturalism is divisive and serves to weaken Canadian society
2. Those that see multicultural programs and policies as regressive, as a tool to pacify the needs and legitimate claims of the minority cultural groups
3. Those that consider the efforts of multiculturalism to be ornamental or superficial, with much form and little substance
4. Those that consider multiculturalism as a policy impractical in a capitalist society such as Canada, where the principles of individualism, private property, profit, and consumerism prevail

Policy Initiatives

Official multiculturalism in Canada currently is a portfolio in the federal Canadian Heritage Department. According to Fleras and Kunz (2001), policies on multiculturalism have evolved from those in the 1970s, which celebrated Canadians' differences (e.g., cultural sensitivity training programs), through

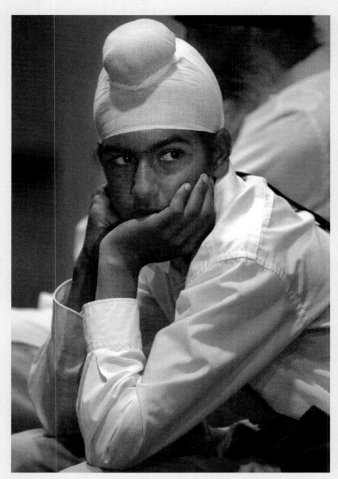

those in the 1980s, which managed diversity through policies on employment equity and race relations, to those of the 1990s, with the objectives of inclusion and integration of cultural minorities. The current policies on multiculturalism encourage the full participation of all cultural groups, based on the goals of social justice. As Fleras and Kunz (2001:16) state, "emphasis is on what we have in common as rights-bearing and equality-seeking individuals rather than on what separates or divides us." Special activities, such as Black History Month and the "Racism: Stop It!" campaign, which focus on the promotion of social justice, have been created by the federal government's multicultural programs.

Fleras and Elliott (1999) state that multiculturalism is not what divides Canada but is rather what unites us, separating us and making us distinct from the United States. They claim that multiculturalism policies focus on institutional barriers for minority groups and therefore attempt to break down the patterns of inequality. A recent study by Jeffery Reitz and Rupa Banerjee from the University of Toronto suggests that the policy of multiculturalism is not working for many people—particularly for newer immigrants and their children who come from East Asia, South Asia, and the Caribbean (Jimenez 2007). These groups face discrimination and marginalization and, thus, are not able to enjoy equal participation in mainstream institutions—this is a setback to the central tenet of multiculturalism. These immigrants often feel excluded and vulnerable, and fearful of racial attacks in Canadian society. Ratna Omidvar, director of a Canadian organization that works with immigrants, says that "good multicultural policy must not only protect our rights to equality, but it must also create real opportunities" (Jimenez 2007).

Apply the Theory

1. What functions do you think the policy of multiculturalism serves? Do you think these functions are manifest or latent?
2. According to the assumptions of conflict thinking, how might the ideology of multiculturalism differ from the reality of living in a multicultural country?

Policies on multiculturalism attempt to preserve, protect, and nurture different cultural traditions in the midst of the domination of one cultural group. This boy sits outside a court hearing to decide whether he has the right to wear his kirpan, a Sikh ceremonial dagger, to school.

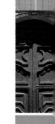

CHAPTER RESOURCES

Summary

::: 3.1 How Do Culture and Society Compare?

- **Culture** is the totality of learned, socially transmitted customs, knowledge, material objects, and behaviour. In this chapter, we examined the basic elements that make up a culture, social practices common to all cultures, and variations that distinguish one culture from another.
- Sharing a similar culture helps to define the group or society to which we belong.

::: 3.2 How Do Cultures Develop around the World?

- **Cultural universals** are general practices found in every culture, including courtship, family, games, language, medicine, religion, and sexual restrictions.
- In recent decades, international trade and the exchange of ideas have accelerated cultural change.
- Sociologists use the term *globalization* to refer to the resulting worldwide integration of government policies, cultures, social movements, and financial markets.

::: 3.3 What Are the Elements of Culture?

- **Language** is an important element of culture, and includes speech, written characters, numerals, symbols, and gestures and other forms of non-verbal communication. Language both describes culture and shapes it for us.
- **Norms** are established standards of behaviour maintained by society. Sociologists distinguish between **formal norms**—those that are written down—and **informal norms**—those that are generally understood.
- **Sanctions** are penalties and rewards for conduct concerning a social norm.

::: 3.4 How Does Culture Relate to the Dominant Ideology?

- The **dominant ideology** of a culture describes the set of cultural beliefs and practices that help to maintain powerful social, economic, and political interests.

- **Subculture** can be thought of as a culture existing within a larger, dominant culture.
- **Counterculture** is a subculture that deliberately opposes aspects of the larger culture.

::: 3.5 What Forms Does Cultural Diversity Take?

- People who measure other cultures by the standard of their own engage in **ethnocentrism**. Using **cultural relativism** allows us to view people from the perspective of *their* culture.
- **Multiculturalism** is a process through which citizens come to be engaged in their society as different from one another, yet equal to one another.

Critical Thinking Questions

1. Who do you think promotes the dominant culture most rigorously?

2. Drawing on the theories and concepts presented in the chapter, apply sociological analysis to one subculture with which you are familiar. Describe the norms, values, argot, and sanctions evident in that subculture.

3. In what ways is the dominant ideology of Canada evident in the nation's literature, music, movies, theatre, television programs, and sporting events?

4. Given your understanding of culture after reading this chapter, in what way do you think the contents of bathrooms, and the activities carried out in them, reflect the culture of a given group?

THINKING ABOUT MOVIES

Smoke Signals
Members of the Coeur d'Alene Aboriginal tribe hold to their own norms and values.

Sugar
A baseball player from the Dominican Republic copes with culture shock after being drafted into the U.S. Major Leagues.

The Wrestler
Through his sport's subculture, a professional wrestler who has passed his prime travels away from the mainstream.

inside

We learn a great deal from those people most important in our lives, such as our family members.

Socialization

"So it's a boy, right?" a neighbour calls out as Kathy Witterick walks by, her four month old baby, Storm, strapped to her chest in a carrier.

Each week the woman asks the same question about the baby with the squishy cheeks and feathery blond hair.

Witterick smiles, opens her arms wide, comments on the sunny spring day and keeps walking.

She's used to it. The neighbours know Witterick and her husband, David Stocker, are raising a genderless baby. But they don't pretend to understand it.

While there's nothing ambiguous about Storm's genitalia, they aren't telling anyone whether their child is a boy or a girl.

The only people who know are Storm's brothers, Jazz 5, and Kio 2, a close family friend and the two midwives who helped deliver the baby in a birthing pool at their Toronto home on New Year's Day.

"When the baby comes out, even the people who love you the most and know you so intimately, the first question they ask is, 'Is it a girl or a boy?'" says Witterick, bouncing Storm, dressed in a red-fleece jumper, on her lap at the kitchen table.

"If you really want to get to know someone, you don't ask what's between their legs," says Stocker.

When Storm was born, the couple sent an email to friends and family. "We've decided not to share Storm's sex for now—a tribute to freedom and choice in place of limitation, a stand up to what the world could become in Storm's lifetime (a more progressive place? . . .)."

The announcement was met with stony silence. Then the deluge of criticisms began. Not just about Storm, but about how they were parenting their other two children.

The grandparents were supportive, but resented explaining the gender-free baby to friends and co-workers. They worried the children would be ridiculed. Friends said they were imposing their political and ideological values on a newborn. Most of all, people said they were setting their kids up for a life of bullying in a world that can be cruel to outsiders.

Witterick and Stocker believe they are giving their children the freedom to choose who they want to be, unconstrained by social norms about males and females. Some say their choice is alienating . . .

Dr. Ken Zucker, considered a world expert on gender identity and head of the gender identity for children at Toronto's Centre for Addiction and Mental Health, calls this a 'social experiment of nurture.' The broader question, he says is how much influence parents have on their kids . . .

When asked what psychological harm, if any, could come from keeping the sex of a child secret, Zucker said: "One will find out."

The couple plan to keep Storm's sex a secret as long as Storm, Kio and Jazz are comfortable with it. In the meantime, philosophy and reality continue to collide.

Out with the kids all day, Witterick doesn't have time or the will to hide in a closet every time she changes Storm's diaper. "If (people) want to peek, that's their journey," she says.

There are questions about which bathroom Storm will use, but that is a couple of years off. Then there is the "tyranny of pronouns" as they call it. They considered referring to Storm as "Z." Witterick now calls the baby she, imagining the "s" in brackets.

For the moment, it feels right.

"Everyone keeps asking us, 'When will this end?'" says Witterick. "And we always turn the question back. Yeah when will this end? When will we live in a world where people can make choices to be whoever they are?"

Canwest News Service, www. star.com, "Parents Keep Child's Gender A Secret," Jayme Poisson, May 2011.

This opening article, featuring the debate over a Toronto family's decision to not to tell people whether their baby was a boy or a girl, highlights the emphasis our society places on this distinction. In their attempt to raise a "gender-free" child, the family stirred up controversy that played out around dinner tables, on blogs, and on television newscasts in many countries around the world.

Sociologists, in general, are interested in the patterns of behaviour and attitudes that emerge throughout the life course, from infancy to old age. These patterns are part of the process of **socialization**, whereby people learn the attitudes, values, and behaviours appropriate for members of a particular culture. Socialization occurs through human interactions. We learn a great deal from those people most important in our lives—immediate family members, friends, and teachers. But we also learn from people we see on the street, on television, on the Internet, and in films and magazines. From a microsociological perspective, socialization helps us to discover how to behave "properly" and what to expect from others if we follow (or challenge) society's norms and values. From a macrosociological perspective, socialization provides for the transmission of a culture from one generation to the next and thereby for the long-term continuance of a society.

Socialization affects the overall cultural practices of a society, and it also shapes our self-image. For example, in North America, a person who is viewed as "too heavy" or "too short" may not conform to the cultural ideal of physical attractiveness. These kinds of unfavourable evaluations can significantly influence a person's self-esteem. In this sense, socialization experiences can help shape our personalities. In everyday speech, the term **personality** is used to refer to a person's typical patterns of attitudes, needs, characteristics, and behaviour.

In this chapter, we will examine the role of socialization in human development. We begin by analyzing the interaction of heredity and environmental factors. We pay particular attention to how people develop perceptions, feelings, and beliefs about themselves. We will also explore important agents of socialization, among them family, schools, peers, and the

media, as well as the lifelong nature of the socialization process. Finally, the social policy section covers the socialization experience of group childcare for infants and toddlers.

::: use your sociological *imagination* :::

What do you think the impact would be on a person who was raised gender-free? Do you think it would be possible?

www.mcgrawhillconnect.ca

What Is the Role of Socialization?

What makes us who we are? Is it the genes we are born with? Or the environment in which we grow up? Researchers have traditionally clashed over the relative importance of biological inheritance and environmental factors in human development—a conflict called the *nature versus nurture* (or *heredity versus environment*) debate. Today, most social scientists have moved beyond this debate, acknowledging instead the interaction of these variables in shaping human development. However, we can better appreciate how heredity and environmental factors interact and influence the socialization process if we first examine situations in which one factor operates almost entirely without the other (Homans 1979).

Environment: The Impact of Isolation

In the 1994 movie *Nell*, Jodie Foster played a young woman hidden from birth by her mother in a backwoods cabin. Raised without normal human contact, Nell crouches like an animal, screams wildly, and speaks or sings in a language all her own. This movie was drawn from the actual account of an emaciated 16-year-old boy who mysteriously appeared in 1828 in the town square of Nuremberg, Germany (Lipson 1994).

The Case of Isabelle Some viewers may have found the story of Nell difficult to believe, but the painful childhood of Isabelle was all too real. For the first six years of her life, Isabelle lived in almost total seclusion in a darkened room. She had little contact with other people, with the exception of her mother, who could neither speak nor hear. Isabelle's mother's parents had been so deeply ashamed of Isabelle's illegitimate birth that they kept her hidden away from the world. Ohio authorities finally discovered the child in 1938, when Isabelle's mother escaped from her parents' home, taking her daughter with her.

When she was discovered at age six, Isabelle could not speak. She could merely make various croaking sounds. Her only communications with her mother were simple gestures. Isabelle had been largely deprived of the typical interactions and socialization experiences of childhood. Since she

had actually seen few people, she initially showed a strong fear of strangers and reacted almost like a wild animal when confronted with an unfamiliar person. As she became accustomed to seeing certain individuals, her reaction changed to one of extreme apathy. At first, it was believed that Isabelle was deaf, but she soon began to react to nearby sounds. On tests of maturity, she scored at the level of an infant rather than a six-year-old.

Specialists developed a systematic training program to help Isabelle adapt to human relationships and socialization. After a few days of training, she made her first attempt to verbalize. Although she started slowly, Isabelle quickly passed through six years of development. In a little over two months, she was speaking in complete sentences. Nine months later, she could identify both words and sentences. Before Isabelle reached the age of nine, she was ready to attend school with other children. By her 14th year, she was in sixth grade, doing well in school, and emotionally well-adjusted.

Yet, without an opportunity to experience socialization in her first six years, Isabelle had been hardly human in the social sense when she was first discovered. Her inability to communicate at the time of her discovery—despite her physical and cognitive potential to learn—and her remarkable progress over the next few years underscore the impact of socialization on human development (Davis 1940, 1947).

Isabelle's experience is important for researchers because it is one of the few cases of children reared in total isolation. Unfortunately, however, there are many cases of children raised in extremely neglectful social circumstances. Recently, attention has focused on infants and young children in orphanages in the formerly communist countries of Eastern Europe. For example, in Romanian orphanages, babies lie in their cribs for 18 or 20 hours a day, curled against their feeding bottles and receiving little adult care. Such minimal attention continues for the first five years of their lives. Many of the Romanian orphans are fearful of human contact and prone to unpredictable antisocial behaviour. This situation came to light as families in North America and Europe began adopting thousands of these children. The adjustment problems for about 20 percent of them were often so dramatic that the adopting families suffered guilty fears of being unfit adoptive parents. Many of them have asked for assistance in dealing with the children. Slowly, efforts are being made to introduce the deprived youngsters to feelings of attachment that they have never experienced before (Groza, Ilena, and Irwin 1999; Talbot 1998).

Increasingly, researchers are emphasizing the importance of early socialization experiences for children who grow up in more normal environments. We know that it is not enough to care for an infant's physical needs; parents must also concern themselves with children's social development. If, for example, children are discouraged from having friends, they will miss out on social interactions with peers that are critical for emotional growth.

::: use your sociological *imagination* :::

What events in your life have had a strong influence on who you are?

Primate Studies Studies of animals raised in isolation also support the importance of socialization in development. Harry Harlow (1971), a researcher at the primate laboratory of the University of Wisconsin, conducted tests with rhesus monkeys that had been raised away from their mothers and away from contact with other monkeys. As was the case with Isabelle, the rhesus monkeys raised in isolation were fearful and easily frightened. They did not mate, and the females who were artificially inseminated became abusive mothers. Apparently, isolation had had a damaging effect on the monkeys.

A creative aspect of Harlow's experimentation was his use of "artificial mothers." In one such experiment, Harlow presented monkeys raised in isolation with two substitute mothers—one cloth-covered replica and one covered with wire that had the ability to offer milk. Monkey after monkey went to the wire mother for the life-giving milk, yet spent much more time clinging to the more mother-like cloth model. In this study, the monkeys valued the artificial mothers that provided a comforting physical sensation (conveyed by the terry cloth) more highly than those that provided food. It appears that the infant monkeys developed greater social attachments from their need for warmth, comfort, and intimacy than from their need for milk.

Although the isolation studies just discussed may seem to suggest that inheritance can be dismissed as a factor in the social development of humans and animals, studies of twins provide insight into a fascinating interplay between hereditary and environmental factors.

The Influence of Heredity

Oskar Stohr and Jack Yufe were identical twins who were separated soon after their birth and raised on different continents in very different cultural settings. Oskar was reared as a strict Catholic by his maternal grandmother in the Sudetenland of the former Czechoslovakia. As a member of the Hitler Youth movement in Nazi Germany, Oskar learned to hate Jews. By contrast, his brother Jack was reared in Trinidad by the twins' Jewish father. Jack joined an Israeli kibbutz (a collective settlement) at age 17 and later served in the Israeli army. But when they were reunited in middle age, some startling similarities emerged:

> Both were wearing wire-rimmed glasses and moustaches, both sported two-pocket shirts with epaulets. They share idiosyncrasies galore: they like spicy foods and sweet liqueurs, are absent-minded, have a habit of falling asleep in front of the television, think it's funny to sneeze in a crowd of strangers, flush the toilet before using it, store rubber bands on their wrists, read magazines from back to front, dip buttered toast in their coffee. (Holden 1980)

The twins also were found to differ in many important respects: as adults, Jack was a workaholic; Oskar enjoyed leisure-time activities. Whereas Oskar was a traditionalist who was domineering toward women, Jack was a political liberal who was much more accepting of feminism. Finally, Jack was extremely proud of being Jewish, while Oskar never mentioned his Jewish heritage (Holden 1987).

Oskar and Jack are prime examples of the interplay of heredity and environment. For a number of years, researchers at the Minnesota Center for Twin and Adoption Research have been studying pairs of identical twins reared apart to determine what similarities, if any, they show in personality traits, behaviour, and intelligence. Thus far, the preliminary results from the available twin studies indicate that both genetic factors and socialization experiences are influential in human development. Certain characteristics, such as temperaments, voice patterns, and nervous habits, appear to be strikingly similar even in twins reared apart, suggesting that these qualities may be linked to hereditary causes. However, identical twins reared apart differ far more in their attitudes, values, types of mates chosen, and even drinking habits; these qualities, it would seem, are influenced by environmental patterns. In examining clusters of personality traits among such twins, the Minnesota studies have found marked similarities in their tendency toward leadership or dominance, but significant differences in their need for intimacy, comfort, and assistance.

Researchers have also been impressed with the similar scores on intelligence tests of twins reared apart in *roughly similar* social settings. Most of the identical twins register scores even closer than those that would be expected if the same person took a test twice. At the same time, however, identical twins brought up in *dramatically different* social environments score quite differently on intelligence tests—a finding that supports the impact of socialization on human development (Joseph 2004; Kronstadt 2008; Minnesota Center for Twin and Family Research 2010).

We need to be cautious when reviewing the studies of twin pairs and other relevant research. Widely broadcast findings have often been based on extremely small samples and preliminary analyses. For example, one study (not involving twin pairs) was frequently cited as confirming genetic links with behaviour. Yet the researchers had to retract their conclusions after they increased the sample and reclassified two of the original cases. After these changes, the initial findings were no longer valid.

Despite the striking physical resemblance between these identical twins, there are undoubtedly many differences between them. Research points to some behavioural similarities between twins, but little beyond the likeness found among non-twin siblings.

Critics add that the studies on twin pairs have not provided satisfactory information concerning the extent to which these separated identical twins may have had contact with each other, even though they were raised apart. Such interactions—especially if they were extensive—could call into question the validity of the twin studies (Horgan 1993; Plomin 1989).

Psychologist Leon Kamin fears that overgeneralizing from the Minnesota Center's twin results—and granting too much importance to the impact of heredity—may lead to blaming the poor and downtrodden for their unfortunate condition. As this debate continues, we can certainly anticipate numerous efforts to replicate the research and clarify the interplay between hereditary and environmental factors in human development.

Sociobiology

Do the *social* traits that human groups display have biological origins? As part of the continuing debate on the relative influences of heredity and the environment, there has been renewed interest in sociobiology in recent years. **Sociobiology** is the systematic study of the biological bases of social behaviour. Sociobiologists basically apply naturalist Charles Darwin's principles of natural selection to the study of social behaviour. They assume that particular forms of behaviour become genetically linked to a species if they contribute to its fitness to survive (van den Berghe 1978). In its extreme form, sociobiology suggests that *all* behaviour is the result of genetic or biological factors and that social interactions play no role in shaping people's conduct.

Sociobiology does not seek to describe individual behaviour on the level of "Why is Fred more aggressive than Jim?" Rather, sociobiologists focus on how human nature is affected by the genetic composition of a *group* of people who share certain characteristics (such as men or women, or members of isolated tribal bands). Many sociologists are highly critical of sociobiologists' tendency to explain, or seemingly justify, human behaviour on the basis of nature and ignore its cultural and social basis.

Some researchers insist that intellectual interest in sociobiology will merely deflect serious study of the more significant factor influencing human behaviour—socialization. Yet Lois Wladis Hoffman (1985), in her presidential address to the Society for the Psychological Study of Social Issues, argued that sociobiology poses a valuable challenge to social scientists to better document their own research. Interactionists, for example, could show how social behaviour is not programmed by human biology but instead adjusts continually to the attitudes and responses of others.

Conflict theorists (like functionalists and interactionists) believe that people's behaviour rather than their genetic structure defines social reality. Conflict theorists fear that the sociobiological approach could be used as an argument against efforts to assist disadvantaged people, such as schoolchildren who are not learning successfully (Harris 1997).

Edward O. Wilson, a zoologist at Harvard University, has argued that there should be parallel studies of human behaviour with a focus on both genetic and social causes. Certainly, most social scientists would agree that there is a biological basis for social behaviour. But there is less support for the most extreme positions taken by certain advocates of sociobiology.

4.2 What Are Some Major Theoretical Perspectives on Socialization?

Social Psychological Perspectives

We all have various perceptions, feelings, and beliefs about who we are and what we are like. How do we come to develop these? Do they change as we age?

We were not born with these understandings. Building on the work of George Herbert Mead (1964b), sociologists recognize that we create our own designation: the self. The **self** is a distinct identity that sets us apart from others. It is not a static phenomenon but continues to develop and change throughout our lives.

Sociologists and psychologists alike have expressed interest in how the individual develops and modifies the sense of self as a result of social interaction. The work of sociologists Charles Horton Cooley and George Herbert Mead, contributors to the development of the interactionist approach (see Chapter 1), has been especially useful in furthering our understanding of these important issues.

Cooley: Looking-Glass Self

In the early 1900s, Charles Horton Cooley advanced the belief that we learn who we are by interacting with others. Our view of ourselves, then, comes not only from direct contemplation of our personal qualities but also from our impressions of how others perceive us. Cooley used the phrase **looking-glass self** to emphasize that the self is the product of our social interactions with other people.

The process of developing a self-identity or self-concept has three phases: First, we imagine how we present ourselves to others—to relatives, friends, even strangers on the street. Second, we imagine how others evaluate us (attractive, intelligent, shy, or strange). Finally, we develop some sort of feeling about ourselves, such as respect or shame, as a result of these impressions (Cooley 1902; Howard 1989).

A subtle but critical aspect of Cooley's looking-glass self is that the self results from an individual's "imagination" of how others view him or her. As a result, we can develop self-identities based on *incorrect* perceptions of how others see us. A student may react strongly to a teacher's criticism and decide (wrongly) that the instructor views the student as stupid. This misperception can easily be converted into a negative self-identity through the following process: (1) *the teacher criticized me,* (2) *the teacher must think that I'm stupid,* (3) *I am stupid.* Yet self-identities are also subject to change. If the student receives an "A" at the end of the course, he or she will probably no longer feel stupid.

Mead: Stages of the Self

As we mentioned in Chapter 1, George Herbert Mead continued Cooley's work in social psychology, developing a useful model of the process by which the self emerges. His model was defined by three distinct stages: the *preparatory stage,* the *play stage,* and the *game stage.*

During the **preparatory stage**, children merely imitate the people around them, especially family members with whom they continually interact. Thus, a small child will bang on a piece of wood while a parent is engaged in carpentry work or will try to throw a ball if an older sibling is doing so nearby.

As they grow older, children become more adept at using symbols to communicate with others. *Symbols* are the gestures, objects, and language that form the basis of human communication. By interacting with relatives and friends, as well as by watching cartoons on television and looking at picture books, children in the preparatory stage begin to understand the use of symbols. Like spoken languages, symbols vary from culture to culture and even between subcultures. Raising an eyebrow may mean astonishment in North America, but in Peru it means "money" or "pay me," while in the Pacific island nation of Tonga it means "yes" or "I agree" (Axtell 1990).

Mead was among the first to analyze the relationship of symbols to socialization. As children develop skill in communicating through symbols, they gradually become more aware of social relationships. As a result, during the **play stage**, the child learns to pretend to be other people. Just as an actor "becomes" a character, a child becomes a doctor, parent, superhero, or ship captain.

Mead, in fact, noted that an important aspect of the play stage is role-playing. **Role-taking** is the process of mentally assuming the perspective of another, thereby enabling the person to respond from that imagined viewpoint. For example, through this process, a young child will gradually learn when it is best to ask a parent for favours. If the parent usually comes home from work in a bad mood, the child will wait until after dinner when the parent is more relaxed and approachable.

In Mead's third stage, the **game stage**, the child of about eight or nine years old no longer just plays roles but begins to consider several actual tasks and relationships simultaneously. At this point in development, children grasp not only their own social positions but also those of others around them—just as in a hockey game the players must understand their own and everyone else's positions. Consider a girl or boy who is part of a scout troop out on a weekend hike in the mountains. The child must understand what he or she is expected to do but also must recognize the responsibilities of other scouts as well as of the leaders. This is the final stage of development under Mead's model; the child can now respond to numerous members of the social environment.

At the game stage, children can take a more sophisticated view of people and the social environment. They now understand what specific occupations and social positions are and no longer equate Mr. Sahota only with the role of "librarian" or Ms. La Haigue only with "principal." It has become clear to the child that Mr. Sahota can be a librarian, a parent, and a marathon runner

Children imitate the people around them, especially family members they continually interact with during the *preparatory stage* described by George Herbert Mead.

research today

4-1 Impression Management by Students After Exams

When you and fellow classmates get an exam back, you probably react differently depending on the grades that you and they earned. This distinction is part of *impression management.* Researchers have found that students' reactions differ depending on the grades that others received, compared to their own. These encounters can be divided into three categories: those in which all students earned high grades (Ace–Ace encounters); those between Aces and students who received low or failing grades (Ace–Bomber encounters); and those between students who all got low grades (Bomber-Bomber encounters).

Ace-Ace encounters occur in a rather open atmosphere, because there is comfort in sharing a high mark with another high achiever. It is even acceptable to violate the norm of modesty and brag when among other Aces, since as one student admitted, "It's much easier to admit a high mark to someone who has done better than you, or at least as well."

Ace–Bomber encounters are often sensitive. Bombers generally attempt to avoid such exchanges, because "you. . . emerge looking like the dumb one" or "feel like you are lazy or unreliable." When forced into interactions with Aces, Bombers work to appear gracious and congratulatory. For their part, Aces offer sympathy and support to the dissatisfied Bombers and even rationalize their own "lucky" high scores. To help Bombers save face, Aces may emphasize the difficulty and unfairness of the examination.

> *When forced into interactions with Aces, Bombers work to appear gracious and congratulatory.*

Bomber–Bomber encounters tend to be closed, reflecting the group effort to wall off the feared disdain of others. Yet within the safety of these encounters, Bombers openly share their disappointment and engage in expressions of mutual self-pity that they themselves call "pity parties." They devise face-saving excuses for their poor performance, such as "I wasn't feeling well all week" or "I had four exams and two papers due that week."

Of course, grade comparisons are not the only occasion when students engage in impression management. Another study has shown that students' perceptions of how often fellow students work out can also influence their social encounters. In athletic terms, a bomber would be someone who doesn't work out; an ace would be someone who works hard at physical fitness.

Apply the Theory

1. What theoretical perspective would most likely be employed in the study of students' impression management strategies?
2. How do you think some feminist sociologists might approach the study of impression management on the part of their students?

Sources: Albas and Albas 1988, 1996; M. Mack 2003.

A prospective employer reviews an applicant's qualifications for the job. To present themselves in a positive manner, both interviewer and applicant may resort to *impression management* and *face-work*, two tactics described by the interventionist Erving Goffman.
Again as we discussed in Chapter 1, Mead uses the term *generalized other* to refer to the attitudes, viewpoints, and expectations of society as a whole that a child takes into account.

at the same time and that Ms. La Haigue is one of many principals in our society. Thus, the child has reached a new level of sophistication in his or her observations of individuals and institutions.

::: use your sociological *imagination* :::

How has the *generalized other* influenced the decisions you've made?

Goffman: Presentation of the Self How do we manage our self? How do we display to others who we are? Erving Goffman, a sociologist associated with the interactionist perspective, suggested that many of our daily activities involve attempts to convey impressions of who we are.

Early in life, the individual learns to slant his or her presentation of the self in order to create distinctive appearances and satisfy particular audiences. Goffman (1959) refers to this altering of the presentation of the self as **impression management**. Box 4-1 provides an everyday example of this concept by describing how students engage in impression management after getting their examination grades.

In examining such everyday social interactions, Goffman makes so many explicit parallels to the theatre that his view has been termed the *dramaturgical approach* (see Chapter 1). According to this perspective, people resemble performers in action. For example, a clerk may try to appear busier than he or she actually is if a supervisor happens to be watching.

A customer in a singles' bar may try to look as if he or she is waiting for a particular person to arrive.

Goffman (1959) has also drawn attention to another aspect of the self: **face-work**. How often do you initiate some kind of face-saving behaviour when you feel embarrassed or rejected? In response to a rejection at the singles' bar, a person may engage in face-work by saying to a friend, "There really isn't an interesting person in this entire crowd." We feel the need to maintain a proper image of the self if we are to continue social interaction.

Goffman's approach is generally regarded as an insightful perspective on everyday life, but it is not without its critics. Writing from a conflict perspective, sociologist Alvin Gouldner (1970) sees Goffman's work as implicitly reaffirming the status quo, including social class inequalities. Using Gouldner's critique, we might ask whether women and members of minority groups are expected to deceive both themselves and others while paying homage to those with power. In considering impression management and other concepts developed by Goffman, sociologists must remember that by describing social reality, a person is not necessarily endorsing its harsh impact on many individuals and groups.

Goffman's work represents a logical progression of the sociological efforts begun by Cooley and Mead on how personality is acquired through socialization and how we manage the presentation of our self to others. Cooley stressed the process by which we come to create a self; Mead focused on how the self develops as we learn to interact with others; Goffman emphasized the ways in which we consciously create images of ourselves for others.

Functionalist Perspectives

Functionalist perspectives stress the importance of consensus, stability, and equilibrium in society; therefore, socialization of society's members is essential to meet these goals (see Chapter 1). Socialization, according to functionalists, serves to ensure that the members of a given society share or buy into the basic values of that society in order to promote consensus or agreement and stability. Without high levels of agreement on the core values of society, functionalists argue that the society will become destabilized and its survival may be threatened.

Since functionalist theorists maintain that a society is analogous to a human body in which the various organs—heart, lungs, kidney, liver, and so on—work as a system to maintain the health or balance of the entire body, so must the parts of society. Such institutions as the family, schools, the state, the mass media, the legal system, and religion must function as an integrated system in which each part contributes to the functioning of the others and to that of the whole society. Here, the function of the socialization of society's members concerning basic values and goals is key, as it provides cohesion and coordination among various institutions, creating equilibrium. For example, Canada's economy, and those of many other countries, is a capitalist one based on the value of competition and individual achievement. For it to function effectively and efficiently, workers must buy in to the value, goal, and means of success as defined by the capitalist economy. Therefore, it becomes imperative, according to functionalists, that the family, for example, socialize its children according to the values of hard work, individual effort, and achievement; this socialization will

ensure the provision of a workforce that is properly primed, ready to meet the challenges of a capitalist economy. Similarly, the education system must socialize its students with these values, as well as with the specific skills and training necessary to meet the demands of the economy.

Overall, functionalist perspectives stress the importance of maintaining the status quo. Socialization, therefore, is viewed as a way to ensure that a society's members share values, beliefs, and goals that contribute to the maintenance of society as a whole.

Conflict Perspectives

Like the functionalist theorists, conflict thinkers agree that the socialization of a society's members by the major institutions (e.g., the economy, the state, and the mass media) contributes to the perpetuation of the status quo. For conflict thinkers, however, this is not viewed as desirable, given the inherent inequalities of the capitalist society.

Since the capitalist society is based on the unequal distribution of power and resources, conflict thinkers advocate that the messages communicated through various forms of socialization will reflect this inequity. Karl Marx, for example, believed that the dominant ideas of a society at any given point in history will be the ideas of the dominant ruling class. Marx argued that the economic base of society (i.e., capitalism) determined the nature of the other institutions, such as the family, the education system, and the mass media, causing them also to reflect the ideas of the ruling class. For example, the mass media has often been considered by conflict thinkers as the mouthpiece of the ruling class, socializing all members of society with values and goals that reflect the economic interests of the ruling class. In this way, socialization serves to ensure that the working classes continue to buy into an economic system based on the dominance and control of the ruling class. According to conflict thinkers Edward Herman and Noam Chomsky (1988), the mass media represent a propaganda model that acts to "manufacture consent" by "generating compliance" on the part of the mass population, which works for and consumes the products produced by the dominant ruling class.

Feminist Perspectives

Given the vast variety of feminist theories and the differences among them, it is not surprising that they do not all stress the importance of socialization as a key element in explaining the condition of women's lives. Some feminist theorists believe that what a society believes to be "masculine" and "feminine" is culturally imposed through systematic socialization of girls and boys, as well as women and men, according to sex. This systematic socialization takes place in the family, among peers, in the school, in the workplace, in religious organizations, and through the mass media. Liberal feminists are one such group of feminist theorists who stress the importance of avoiding this type of socialization in order to achieve equality of the sexes. Liberal feminists, who are sometimes called **equality feminists**, endorse individual freedom and equality of opportunity, which for them takes place in the public or economic sphere, not the private or domestic sphere.

Thus, according to liberal feminists, institutions that socialize children and adults according to a division of labour based on gender deprive girls and women of individual achievement, success, and freedom (as defined by the male-dominated public sphere).

Psychological Approaches

Psychologists have shared the interest of Cooley, Mead, and other sociologists in the development of the self. Early work in psychology, such as that of Sigmund Freud (1856–1939), stressed the role of inborn drives—among them the drive for sexual gratification—in channelling human behaviour. In more recent times, such psychologists as Jean Piaget have emphasized the stages through which human beings progress as the self develops.

Like Charles Horton Cooley and George Herbert Mead, Freud believed that the self is a social product and that aspects of personality are influenced by other people (especially parents). However, unlike Cooley and Mead, he suggested that the self has components that are always fighting with each other. According to Freud, our natural impulsive instincts such as sex and aggression—which he referred to as the *id*—are in constant conflict with societal constraints or the *superego*. The *ego*, according to Freud, is the part of the personality which mediates between the id and the superego. Both the ego and the superego are shaped through the process of socialization: "One of Freud's central theses is that society forces people to suppress basic human impulses such as sex and aggression, so that they must find expression in indirect and often distorted ways" (Collier, Minton, and Reynolds 1991:105).

Research on newborn babies by the Swiss child psychologist Jean Piaget (1896–1980) has underscored the importance of social interactions in developing a sense of self. Piaget found that newborns have no self in the sense of a looking-glass image. Ironically, though, they are quite self-centred; they demand that all attention be directed toward them. Newborns have not yet separated themselves from the universe of which they are a part. For these babies, the phrase "you and me" has no meaning; they understand only "me." However, as they mature, children are gradually socialized into social relationships even within their rather self-centred world.

In his well-known **cognitive theory of development**, Piaget (1954) identifies four stages in the development of children's thought processes. In the first, or **sensorimotor**, stage, young children use their senses to make discoveries. For example, through touching, they discover that their hands are actually a part of themselves. During the second, or **preoperational**, stage, children begin to use words and symbols to distinguish objects and ideas. The milestone in the third, or **concrete operational**, stage is that children engage in more logical thinking. They learn that even when a formless lump of clay is shaped into a snake, it is still the same clay. Finally, in the fourth, or **formal operational**, stage, adolescents are capable of sophisticated abstract thought and can deal with ideas and values in a logical manner.

Piaget has suggested that moral development becomes an important part of socialization as children develop the ability to think more abstractly. When children learn the rules of a game, such as checkers or jacks, they are learning to obey societal norms. Those under eight years old display a basic level of morality: rules are rules, and there is no concept of "extenuating circumstances." However, as they mature, children become capable of greater autonomy and begin to experience moral dilemmas as to what constitutes proper behaviour.

According to Jean Piaget, social interaction is the key to development. As they grow older, children give increasing attention to how other people think and why they act in particular ways. To develop a distinct personality, each of us needs opportunities to interact with others. As we saw earlier, Isabelle was deprived of the chance for normal social interactions, and the consequences were severe (Kitchener 1991).

Table 4-1 shows a summary of the rich literature on the development of the self.

table **4-1 Theoretical Approaches to Development of the Self** summing**UP**

Scholar	Key Concepts and Contributions	Main Points of Theory
Sigmund Freud 1856–1939 psychotherapist (Austria)	Psychoanalysis	Self influenced by parents and by inborn drives, such as the drive for sexual gratification
George Herbert Mead 1863–1931 sociologist (U.S.A.)	The self Generalized other	Three distinct stages of development; self develops as children grasp the roles of others in their lives
Charles Horton Cooley 1864–1929 sociologist (U.S.A.)	Looking-glass self	Stages of development not distinct; feelings toward ourselves developed through interaction with others
Jean Piaget 1896–1980 child psychologist (Switzerland)	Cognitive theory of development	Four stages of cognitive development; moral development linked to socialization
Erving Goffman 1922–1982 sociologist (U.S.A.)	Impression management Dramaturgical approach Face-work	Self developed through the impressions we convey to others and to groups

What Are Some Agents of Socialization?

The continuing and lifelong socialization process involves many different social forces that influence our lives and alter our self-image.

The family is the most important agent of socialization in Canada, especially for children. But we also want to give particular attention in this chapter to five other agents of socialization: the school, the peer group, the mass media, the workplace, and the state. The role of religion in socializing young people into society's norms and values will be explored in Chapter 13.

Family

Children in Amish communities are raised in a highly structured and disciplined manner. But they are not immune to the temptations posed by their peers in the non-Amish world—"rebellious" acts such as dancing, drinking, and riding in cars. Still, Amish families don't get too concerned; they know the strong influence they ultimately exert over their offspring. The same is true for the family in general. It is tempting to say that the peer group or even the media really raise kids these days, especially when the spotlight falls on young people involved in shooting sprees and hate crimes. However, the role of the family in socializing a child cannot be underestimated.

The lifelong process of learning begins shortly after birth. Since newborns can hear, see, smell, taste, and feel heat, cold, and pain, they are constantly orienting themselves to the surrounding world. Human beings, especially family members, constitute an important part of their social environment. People minister to the baby's needs by feeding, cleansing, carrying, and comforting the baby.

The caretakers of a newborn are not concerned with teaching social skills per se. Nevertheless, babies are hardly asocial. An infant enters an organized society, becomes part of a generation, and typically joins a family. Depending on how they are treated, infants can develop strong social attachments and dependency on others.

Most infants go through a relatively formal period of socialization generally called **habit training**. Caregivers impose schedules for eating and sleeping, for terminating breast- or bottle-feeding, and for introducing new foods. In these and other ways, infants can be viewed as objects of socialization. Yet they also function as socializers. Even as the behaviour of a baby is being modified by interactions with people and the environment, the baby is causing others to change their behaviour patterns. He or she converts adults into mothers and fathers, who, in turn, assist the baby in progressing into childhood.

As both Charles Horton Cooley and George Herbert Mead noted, the development of the self is a critical aspect of the early years of life. But how children develop this sense of self can vary from one society to another. For example, many parents in Canada would never think of sending six-year-olds to school unsupervised. But this is the norm in Japan, where parents push their children to commute to school on their own from an early age. In cities like Tokyo, first-graders must learn to negotiate buses, subways, and long walks. To ensure their safety, parents carefully lay out rules: never talk to strangers; check with a station attendant if you get off at the wrong stop; if you miss your stop, stay on to the end of the line, then call; take stairs, not escalators; don't fall asleep. Some parents equip the children with cellphones or code words to use if a stranger approaches them saying their mother has asked the child to go with the stranger.

Family and Gender Socialization Have you ever noticed when parents mention their newborn babies, they may describe their daughters as "pretty," "sweet," or "angelic" and their sons as "tough," "rugged," or "strong"? Although newborn babies look much the same regardless of sex (with one noticeable exception), parents often apply cultural and social assumptions about femininity and masculinity to their children from the moment of birth. With the development of technologies, such as ultrasound and amniocentesis, that can reveal the sex of the fetus, parents may well begin to apply these assumptions before birth. This pattern begins a lifelong process of **gender socialization**—an aspect of socialization through which we learn the attitudes, behaviours, and practices associated with being male or female (called **gender roles**) according to our society and social groups within it.

A young girl displays Razanne, a modestly dressed doll made especially for Muslim children. Because children learn about themselves and their social roles by playing with toys such as dolls, having a doll that represents their own heritage is important to them.

research today

4-2 Online Socializing: A New Agent of Socialization

Membership in the online social networks Facebook, Friendster, and MySpace has grown exponentially in recent years. At first, young adults monopolized these social networks. Indeed, Facebook was created in 2004 as a way for students on a single campus to become acquainted with one another before actually meeting.

Even in the brief history of online networking, sociologists can see social trends. For example, older people are now creating profiles on these sites. As the accompanying figure shows, there is still a clear correlation between age and online profiles: in an Ipsos Reid survey of Canadian social media use, younger people were much more likely than older people to be online. However, the fastest-growing age groups are now those over 30, including those who are much older. As a result, online socializing is becoming much less age-specific—more like socializing in the real world. Moreover, this new agent of socialization can continue to influence people throughout the life course. Twitter is largely the exception to this trend; it is still a very age-specific method of social interaction.

Online networks—especially those that indicate how many "friends" an individual has—can also be seen in terms of social capital. In fact, "friending" is one, if not *the*, main activity on some online sites. Often the number of friends a person socializes with becomes the subject of boasting. By extension, individuals may use these sites to search for "friends" who may prove helpful to them in future endeavours. Becoming aware of new opportunities, either social or economic, through friends is a significant benefit of social capital.

Researchers have looked at the relationship between the display of friends online and the number of real-world friends people socialize with, and have proposed two competing hypotheses. According to the social enhancement hypothesis ("the rich get richer"), those who are popular offline further increase their popularity through online networking sites. According to the social compensation hypothesis ("the poor get richer"), however, social network users try to increase their popularity online to compensate

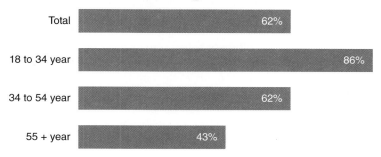

Online Canadians who have a Social Networking Profile

Total	62%
18 to 34 year	86%
34 to 54 year	62%
55 + year	43%

Base: Canadian Internet users (n=80)
Source: Ipsos Canadian Inter@ctive Reid Report, Issue 2, 2011.

for inadequate popularity offline. The social compensation hypothesis, if correct, would be an example of impression management. Research supports elements of both hypotheses; neither hypothesis fully defines the participants in online networking sites.

> *Online networks—especially those that indicate how many "friends" an individual has—can also be seen in terms of social capital.*

Viewed from a societal perspective, socializing online can have both positive and negative functions. For members of some marginalized populations, it is a way to socialize with like-minded people. For example, Muslims in Great Britain connect with friends online to learn how to navigate through a society in which they form a distinct minority. For other people, such as members of the Nazis in Germany and the Mafia in Italy, online networking is a way to proclaim allegiance to socially objectionable organizations. Governments frown on such online organizing, seeing it as dysfunctional, and periodically monitor these sites to see whether any laws have been violated.

Apply the Theory

1. How would an interactionist approach the study of listing "friends" on an online social networking site?
2. According to conflict thinking, how would your "friends list" be linked to your social capital?

Sources: Donadio 2009; Ellison et al. 2007; Facebook 2011; Gentile 2009; Hundley and Ramirez 2008; Ipsos Reid 2011; Lenhart 2009; Miyata and Kobayashi 2008; Zywica and Danowski 2008.

Our society (and various social groups, such as social classes and ethnic groups) produces ideals and expectations about gender roles, reinforcing these ideals and expectations at each stage of the life course. As we will see in Chapter 9, other cultures do not necessarily assign these qualities to each gender in the way that our culture does.

As the primary agents of childhood socialization, parents play a critical role in guiding children into those gender roles deemed appropriate in a society. Other adults, older siblings, the mass media, and religious and educational institutions also have a noticeable impact on a child's socialization into feminine and masculine norms. A culture or subculture may require that one sex or the other take primary responsibility for socialization of children, economic support of the family, or religious or intellectual leadership.

Social class may also play a role in gender socialization. Members of certain social classes may be more or less likely to engage in socialization patterns geared to traditional gender roles. Gender socialization in middle-class homes with career-oriented mothers may be less stereotypical in terms of behaviour expectations of their children. Families of different social classes may exhibit different degrees of conformity to traditional or stereotypical notions of masculinity and femininity and socialize their children accordingly. Daughters, for example, may or may not be expected more than sons to help with domestic chores, such as cooking or attending to the needs of younger siblings.

Some feminists support the view that the socioeconomic situation of a child's family, commingled with that child's gender, sexual orientation, race, and ethnicity, produce non-generalizable experiences in which family contributes to the child's overall situation.

The differential gender roles absorbed in early childhood often help define a child's popularity later on. A qualitative study on norms surrounding beauty and thinness for adolescent girls found that girls who were successful with a peer group were more likely to judge themselves by the appearance norms of the group (Matthews 2000).

Like other elements of culture, socialization patterns are not fixed. The last 40 years, for example, have witnessed a sustained challenge to traditional gender-role socialization in North America, in good part because of the efforts of the feminist movement (see Chapter 9). Nevertheless, despite such changes, children growing up today are hardly free of traditional gender roles.

Interactionists remind us that socialization concerning not only masculinity and femininity but also marriage and parenthood begins in childhood as a part of family life. Children observe their parents as they express affection, deal with finances, quarrel, complain about in-laws, and so forth. This represents an informal process of anticipatory socialization. The child develops a tentative model of what being married and being a parent are like. (We will explore socialization for marriage and parenthood more fully in Chapter 12.)

School

Where did you learn the national anthem? Who taught you about the early Canadian explorers? Where were you first tested on your knowledge of your culture? Like the family, schools have an explicit mandate to socialize people in Canada—and especially children—into the norms and values of the dominant culture.

As conflict theorists Samuel Bowles and Herbert Gintis (1976) have observed, schools foster competition through built-in systems of reward and punishment, such as grades and evaluations by teachers. Consequently, a child who is working intently to learn a new skill can sometimes come to feel stupid and unsuccessful. However, as the self matures, children become capable of increasingly realistic assessments of their intellectual, physical, and social abilities.

Functionalists point out that, as agents of socialization, schools fulfill the function of teaching children the values and customs of the larger society. Conflict theorists agree but add that schools can reinforce the divisive aspects of society, especially those of social class. For example, higher education in Canada is quite costly despite the existence of student-aid programs. Students from affluent backgrounds have an advantage in gaining access to universities and professional training. At the same time, less affluent young people may never receive the preparation that would qualify them for the best-paying and most prestigious jobs. Moreover, conflict sociologists argue that schools tend to socialize students to emulate the dominant values of society, in preparation for them to assume their places as workers in an appropriate social class. According to conflict sociologists, students are socialized by the school system to value hard work and effort, based on the belief that the most deserving students will invariably rise to the top positions. The contrast between the functionalist and conflict views of education will be discussed in more detail in Chapter 13.

In other cultures as well, schools serve socialization functions. Within months of the overthrow of Saddam Hussein in Iraq school textbooks were rewritten to remove the indoctrination on behalf of Hussein and his army, and his Baath Socialist Party (Marr 2003).

School and Gender Socialization In teaching, the values and customs of the larger society invariably seep into the classroom. Educators in Canada are becoming concerned that boys are lagging behind girls in academic achievement, as demonstrated by girls' overrepresentation on the high school honour rolls and lists of scholarship recipients. Patricia Clarke, former president of the B.C. Teachers' Federation, suggests that boys are immersed in a gender-specific culture that undervalues academic achievement and that greater attention needs to be paid to dispelling the myth that "the coolest thing to do is be stupid" (Holmes 2000:11). Pop culture and advertising over the last several years has depicted men in a narrow and stereotypical way—as the Homer Simpson, the incompetent bumbler, the idiot (Krashinsky 2009). A national assessment of teenagers in Canada showed that 26 percent of girls scored in the top level for reading, while only 19 percent of the boys did the same; however, boys and girls scored the same in math and science (*Globe and Mail* 2009). Sixty-four percent of high school dropouts are male, and just 42 percent of university undergraduates are male (*Globe and Mail* 2009). In 2009, the director of the Toronto District School Board announced a proposal of the first all-boy school in Canada's public elementary system. This school is an attempt to close the achievement gap between the genders through creating a learning environment that is specifically geared to boys.

Similar gender gaps in academic performance are being experienced in other countries, such as Britain, where girls are also academically outperforming their male classmates (Galt 1998).

Peer Group

Ask 13-year-olds who matters most in their lives and they are likely to answer "friends." As a child grows older, the family becomes somewhat less important in social development. Instead, peer groups increasingly assume the role of Mead's significant others. Within the peer group, young people associate with others who are approximately their own age and who often enjoy a similar social status (Giordano 2003).

Peer groups can ease the transition to adult responsibilities. At home, parents tend to dominate; at school, the teenager must contend with teachers and administrators. But within the peer group, each member can assert himself or herself in a way that may not be possible elsewhere. Nevertheless, almost all adolescents in our culture remain economically dependent on their parents, and most are emotionally dependent as well.

Teenagers imitate their friends in part because the peer group maintains a meaningful system of rewards and punishments. The group may encourage a young person to follow pursuits that society considers admirable, as in a school club engaged in volunteer work in hospitals and nursing homes. However, the group may encourage someone to violate the culture's norms and values by driving recklessly, shoplifting, engaging in acts of vandalism, taking drugs, or binge drinking.

Peers can be the source of harassment as well as support. This problem has received considerable attention in Japan, where bullying in school is a constant fact of life. Groups of students act together to humiliate, disgrace, or torment a specific student, a practice known in Japan as *ijime*. Most students go along with the bullying out of fear that they might become the target. In some cases, the *ijime* has led to a child's suicide. In 1998, the situation became so desperate that a volunteer association set up a 24-hour telephone hotline in Tokyo just for children. The success of this effort convinced the government to sponsor a nationwide hotline system (Matsushita 1999; Sugimoto 1997).

Peer Group and Gender Socialization   A 2010 study revealed that approximately one in five Canadian students said they had been bullied (CBC 2012a). Bullying may take a variety of forms—cyber-bullying, in which threats or rumours are spread through electronic means; verbal bullying, which may involve harassment and name-calling; physical bullying in the form of attacks; sexual bullying or harassment; and emotional bullying, which may involve isolating, shunning, or excluding other students. Cyber-bullying has been the focus of many anti-bullying efforts after the high profile 2012 suicide of British Columbia high school student Amanda Todd. Amanda Todd's difficulties began when she was in Grade 7 after an unknown man on the Internet asked her to flash her

breasts via Webcam. For years she was bullied online and in the real world, which led her to post a YouTube video, using flash cards, which revealed the harassment she had long endured. Weeks later she committed suicide. Wendy Craig of Queen's University helps run a national anti-bullying coalition and leads a research centre on the issue of bullying. Craig has found that online bullying can be especially hard to deal with because bullies are removed from the human impact of their behaviour (CBC 2012a). For the victim, according to Craig, the bullying is hard to escape since evidence of the bullying can stay online for a long time and they can be harassed whenever they go online (CBC 2012a).

A 2007 Ontario study found that 30 percent of students reported having been bullied since the beginning of the school term; 23 percent reported verbal bullying, 4 percent said that they were primarily physically bullied, and 3 percent reported being victims of theft and vandalism. Twenty-five percent reported that they had bullied other students at school. Overall, 12 percent of Ontario students were generally worried about their safety and were concerned about being harmed or threatened at school (Centre for Addiction and Mental Health 2008). Wendy Craig, along with Debra Pepler of York University, found that girls do more of the verbal and social bullying, while boys' bullying behaviour tends to

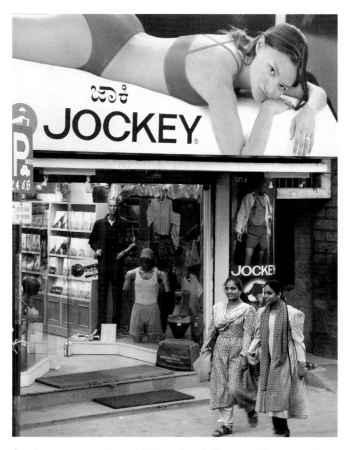

On a busy commercial street in Bangalore, India, pedestrians dressed in traditional garb stroll past a shop and billboard advertising Western fashions. Socialization comes from corporate influences as well as from those who are closest to us, such as family and friends. In today's globalized world, Western media expose children to cultural values their parents and other authorities may not embrace.

be more physical. Girls bullied boys approximately half the time, while boys primarily bullied other boys. Bullies of both sexes tended to be perceived as popular and powerful by their peer groups, while victims were perceived as lacking humour, having a tendency to cry easily, and deserving to be picked on. Pepler and Craig's research also showed that families of bullies tend to be permissive and display more positive attitudes toward aggression and that other students who have not yet been victimized may want to align with bullies to avoid possible bullying in the future.

Gender differences are noteworthy in the social world of adolescents. Males are more likely to spend time in *groups* of males, while females are more likely to interact with a *single* other female. This pattern reflects differences in levels of emotional intimacy; teenage males are less likely to develop strong emotional ties than are females. Instead, males are more inclined to share in group activities.

Mass Media and Technology

In the past 80 years, media innovations—radio, motion pictures, recorded music, television, and the Internet—have become important agents of socialization. Television, and increasingly the Internet, are critical forces in the socialization of children in Canada. In Canada, virtually all households have a least one television set.

These media, however, are not always a negative socializing influence. Television programs and even commercials can introduce young people to unfamiliar lifestyles and cultures. Not only do children in Canada learn about life in "faraway lands," but city children learn about the lives of farm children, and vice versa. The same thing happens in other countries.

Sociologists and other social scientists have begun to consider the impact of technology on socialization. They are particularly interested in the online friendship networks, like Facebook. Does this way of communicating resemble face-to-face interaction, or does it represent a new form of social interaction?

Not just in industrial nations, but in Africa and other developing areas, people have been socialized into relying on new communications technologies. Not long ago, if Zadhe Iyombe wanted to talk to his mother, he had to make an eight-day trip from the capital city of Kinshasa up the Congo River by boat to the rural town where he was born. Now both he and his mother have access to a cellphone, and they send text messages to each other daily. Iyombe and his mother are not atypical. Although cellphones aren't cheap, 1.4 billion owners in developing countries have come to consider them a necessity. Today, there are more cellphones in developing nations than in industrial nations—the first time in history that developing nations have outpaced the developed world in the adoption of a telecommunications technology (Sullivan 2006).

Workplace

Learning to behave appropriately within an occupation is a fundamental aspect of human socialization. It used to be that going to work began with the end of formal schooling, but this is no longer the case in countries such as Canada and the United States.

This young man's day doesn't end when school lets out. Because so many teenagers have jobs after school, the workplace has become another important agent of socialization for that age group.

Some observers feel that the increasing number of teenagers who are working earlier in life and for longer hours are now finding the workplace almost as important an agent of socialization as is school. In fact, a number of educators complain that student time at work is adversely affecting schoolwork. A 2007 study conducted by Statistics Canada showed that Canadian young people, aged 15 to 19, ranked first among 10 industrialized countries—Belgium, United States, Australia, Netherlands, United Kingdom, France, Norway, Germany, and Finland—in terms of hours spent on paid and unpaid work in 2005 (Statistics Canada 2007o). Averaged over a full week (school and non-school days), Canadians aged 15 to 19 performed 7.1 hours of labour per week in 2005.

Socialization in the workplace changes when it involves a more permanent shift from an after-school job to full-time employment. Wilbert Moore (1967:871–880) has divided occupational socialization into four phases. The first phase is **career choice**, which involves selection of academic or vocational training appropriate for the desired job. The second phase, **anticipatory socialization**, may last only a few months or may extend for a period of years. In a sense, young people experience anticipatory socialization throughout childhood and adolescence as they observe their parents at work.

The third phase of occupational socialization—conditioning and commitment—occurs in the work-related role. **Conditioning** consists of reluctantly adjusting to the more unpleasant aspects of one's job. Most people find that the novelty of a new daily schedule quickly wears off and then realize that parts of the work experience are rather tedious. **Commitment** refers to the enthusiastic acceptance of pleasurable duties that comes with recognition of the positive tasks of an occupation.

In Moore's view, if a job proves to be satisfactory, the person will enter a fourth stage of socialization, which Moore calls continuous commitment. At this point, the job becomes an indistinguishable part of the person's self-identity. Violation of proper conduct becomes unthinkable. A person may choose to join professional associations, unions, or other groups that represent the occupation in the larger society.

Occupational socialization can be most intense during the transition from school to job, but it continues through a person's work history. Technological advances may alter the requirements of the position and necessitate some degree of resocialization. Many men and women today change occupations, employers, or places of work many times during their adult years. Therefore, occupational socialization continues throughout a person's years in the labour market (Bialik 2010).

The State

Social scientists have increasingly recognized the importance of the state as an agent of socialization because of its growing impact on the life course. Traditionally, family members have served as the primary caregivers in our culture, but in the twenty-first century, the family's protective function has steadily been transferred to outside agencies, such as hospitals, mental health clinics, and insurance companies. The state runs many of these agencies or licenses and regulates them.

In the past, heads of households and local groups, such as religious organizations, influenced the life course most significantly. However, today national interests are increasingly influencing the individual as a citizen and an economic actor. For example, labour unions and political parties serve as intermediaries between the individual and the state.

The state has had a noteworthy impact on the life course by reinstituting the rites of passage that had disappeared in agricultural societies and in periods of early industrialization. For example, government regulations stipulate the ages at which a person may drive a car, drink alcohol, vote in elections, marry without parental permission, work overtime, and retire. These regulations do not constitute strict rites of passage: most 18-year-olds choose not to vote, and people may choose their age of retirement without reference to government dictates. Still, the state shapes the socialization process by regulating the life course to some degree and by influencing our views of appropriate behaviour at particular ages.

In the social policy section that appears at the end of this chapter, we will see that the state is under pressure to become a provider of childcare, which would give it a new and direct role in the socialization of infants and young children.

4.4 How Does Socialization Occur throughout the Life Course?

The Life Course

Adolescents among the Kota people of the Congo in Africa paint themselves blue, Mexican-American girls go on a daylong religious retreat before dancing the night away, Egyptian mothers step over their seven-day-old infants seven times during the Soboa ceremony, and graduating North American students may throw hats in the air. These are all ways of celebrating **rites of passage**, a means of dramatizing and validating changes in a person's status. The Kota rite marks the passage to adulthood. The colour blue, viewed as the colour of death, symbolizes the death of childhood. Hispanic girls in the United States celebrate reaching womanhood with a *quinceañera* ceremony at age 15. In Miami, Florida, the popularity of the *quinceañera* supports a network of party planners, caterers, dress designers, and the Miss Quinceañera Latina pageant.

These specific ceremonies mark stages of development in the life course. They indicate that the socialization process continues throughout all stages of the human life cycle. Sociologists and other social scientists use the life-course approach in recognition that biological changes mould but do not dictate human behaviour from birth until death.

Within the cultural diversity of Canada, each individual has a "personal biography" that is influenced by events both in the family and in the larger society. Although the completion of religious confirmations, school graduations, marriage, and parenthood can all be regarded as rites of passage in our society, people do not necessarily experience them at the same time. The timing of these events depends on such factors as gender, economic background, region (urban or rural area), and even when a person was born.

Sociologists and other social scientists have moved away from identifying specific life stages that we are all expected to pass through at some point. Indeed, people today are much less likely to follow an "orderly" progression of life events (leaving school, then obtaining their first job, then getting married) than they were in the past. For example, an increasing number of women in Canada are beginning or returning to postsecondary education after marrying and

In Korea, certain birthdays are celebrated as milestones, complete with formal feasts. At a 60th birthday, for example, all the younger family members bow before the fortunate elder one by one, in order of their ages, and offer gifts. Later, they compete with one another in composing poetry and singing songs to mark the occasion. Unfortunately, not all older people are so lucky; in many other cultures, being old is considered next to being dead.

having children. With such changes in mind, researchers are increasingly reluctant to offer sweeping generalizations about stages in the life course.

We encounter some of the most difficult socialization challenges (and rites of passage) in the later years of life. Assessing our accomplishments, coping with declining physical abilities, experiencing retirement, and facing the inevitability of death may lead to painful adjustments. Old age is further complicated by the negative way that many societies view and treat the elderly. The common stereotypes of the elderly as helpless and dependent may well weaken an older person's self-image. However, as we will explore more fully in the next section, many older people continue to lead active, productive, fulfilled lives—whether within the paid labour force or as retirees.

::: use your sociological *imagination* :::

What was the last rite of passage you participated in? Was it formal or informal?

Aging and Society

Aging is one important aspect of socialization—the lifelong process through which an individual learns the cultural norms and values of a particular society. There are no clear-cut definitions for different periods of the aging cycle in Canada. *Old age* has typically been regarded as beginning at 65, which corresponds to the retirement age for many workers, but the concept is an evolving one as Canadians work longer and retire later. With life expectancy being extended, writers are beginning to refer to people in their 60s as the "young old" to distinguish them from those in their 80s and beyond (the "old old").

The particular problems of the elderly have become the focus for a specialized area of research and inquiry known as gerontology. **Gerontology** is the scientific study of the sociological and psychological aspects of aging and the problems of the aged. It originally developed in the 1930s, as an increasing number of social scientists became aware of the plight of the elderly.

Gerontologists rely heavily on sociological principles and theories to explain the impact of aging on the individual and society. They also draw on the disciplines of psychology, anthropology, physical education, counselling, and medicine in their study of the aging process. Two influential views of aging—disengagement theory and activity theory—can be best understood in terms of the sociological perspectives of functionalism and interactionism, respectively. The conflict and feminist perspectives also contribute to our sociological understanding of aging.

Functionalist Approach: Disengagement Theory

Elaine Cumming and William Henry (1961) introduced **disengagement theory** to explain the impact of aging during the life course. This theory, based on a study of elderly people in good health and relatively comfortable economic circumstances, contends that society and the aging individual mutually sever many of their relationships. In keeping with the functionalist perspective, disengagement theory emphasizes that passing social roles on from one generation to another ensures social stability.

According to this theory, the approach of death forces people to drop most of their social roles—including those of worker, volunteer, spouse, hobby enthusiast, and even reader. Younger members of society then take on these functions. The aging person, it is held, withdraws into an increasing state of inactivity while preparing for death. At the same time, society withdraws from the elderly by segregating them residentially (retirement homes and communities), educationally (programs designed solely for senior citizens), and recreationally (senior citizens' social centres). Implicit in disengagement theory is the view that society should *help* older people to withdraw from their accustomed social roles.

Since it was first outlined five decades ago, disengagement theory has generated considerable controversy. Today gerontologists and sociologists are more likely to see the elderly in terms of social connectedness, post-retirement employment, and volunteerism. For their part, producers and retailers of electronic products are likely to see the older population as e-savvy consumers. Since 2008, they note, growth in computer and digital camera sales has been greatest in that market segment. And seniors' complexes have had to make room for residents who want to bowl or play tennis on Nintendo's Wii system (Cornwell et al. 2008; NPD Group 2008).

The Conflict Approach

Conflict theorists have criticized both disengagement theory and activity theory for failing to consider the impact of social structure on patterns of aging. Neither approach, they say, attempts to question why social interaction "must" change or decrease in old age. In addition, these perspectives, in contrast to the conflict perspective, often ignore the impact of social class on the lives of the elderly.

The privileged position of the upper class generally leads to better health and vigour and to a lower likelihood of dependency in old age. Affluence cannot forestall aging indefinitely, but it can soften the economic hardships faced in later years. Although pension plans, retirement packages, and insurance benefits may be developed to assist older people, those whose wealth allows them access to investment funds can generate the greatest income for their later years.

In contrast, working-class jobs often carry greater hazards to health and a greater risk of disability; aging will be particularly difficult for those who suffer job-related injuries or illnesses. Working-class people also depend more heavily on government and private pension programs. During inflationary times, their relatively fixed incomes from these sources barely keep pace with escalating costs of food, housing, utilities, and other necessities (Atchley and Barusch 2004).

Conflict theorists have noted that the transition from agricultural economies to industrialization and capitalism has not always been beneficial for the elderly. As a society's production methods change, the traditionally valued role of older people within the economy tends to erode. Their wisdom is no longer relevant in the new economy.

sociology in the global community

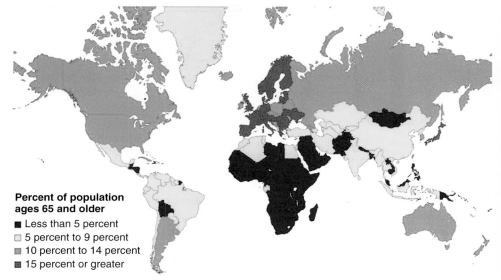

4-3 Aging Worldwide: Issues and Consequences

An electric water kettle is wired so that people in another location can determine if it has been used in the previous 24 hours. This may seem a zany use of modern technology, but it symbolizes a change taking place around the globe—the growing needs of an aging population. The Japanese Welfare Network Ikebukuro Honcho has installed these wired hot pots so that volunteers can monitor whether the elderly have used the devices to prepare their morning tea. An unused pot will trigger personal contact to see if the older person needs help. This technological monitoring system is an indication of the tremendous growth of Japan's elderly population, and particularly significant, the increasing numbers who live *alone*.

Percent of population ages 65 and older

- ■ Less than 5 percent
- □ 5 percent to 9 percent
- ▦ 10 percent to 14 percent
- ■ 15 percent or greater

Sources: Population Reference Bureau, 2007.

Around the world, there are more than 453 million people aged 65 or over, representing about 7 percent of the world's population. By 2050, one in three people will be over 65. In an important sense, the aging of the world's population represents a major success story that unfolded during the latter years of the twentieth century. Through the efforts of both national governments and international agencies, many societies have drastically reduced the incidence of disease and the rate of death. Consequently, these nations—especially the industrialized countries of Europe and North America—now have increasingly higher proportions of older citizens.

The costs of an aging population to Canada will be dramatic, and government officials have already begun to crunch the numbers to identify when the age-specific costs—such as health care, Old Age Security, and government pensions—will sharply rise. Discussions among policymakers are focused on ways to soften the financial blow of an aging Canadian population and include such initiatives as persuading Canadians to have more children, and delaying the age of retirement to 70.

The overall population of Europe is older than that of any other continent. As the proportion of older people in Europe continues to rise, many governments that have long prided themselves on their pension programs have reduced benefits and raised the age at which retired workers can receive benefits.

In most developing countries, people over the age of 60 are likely to be in poorer health than their counterparts in industrialized nations. Yet, few of those countries are in a position to offer extensive financial support to the elderly. Ironically, modernization of the developing world, while bringing with it many social and economic advances, has undercut the traditionally high status of the elderly. In many cultures, the earning power of younger adults now exceeds that of older family members.

Apply the Theory

1. For an older person, how might life in Pakistan differ from life in France?
2. Do you know an elderly person who lives alone? What arrangements have been made (or should be made) for the person's care in case of emergency?

Sources: Hani 1998; Haub 2005; He et al. 2005; Kinsella and Phillips 2005; R. Samuelson 2001; Vieira, 2009.

According to the conflict approach, the treatment of older people in Canada reflects the many divisions in our society. The low status of older people is seen in prejudice and discrimination against them, age segregation, and unfair job practices—none of which is directly addressed by either disengagement or activity theory.

Feminist Approaches   Feminist frameworks view aging in women from a variety of perspectives. However, feminist researchers have frequently challenged two biases in the study of women's aging: (1) an androcentricity in the discussion of the life course (assuming that generalizations on the male life course can be applied to women) and (2) a lack of diversity in identifying the stages and central issues that mark women's lives (Jones, Marsden, and Tepperman 1990). In sociological research in previous decades, women's aging was seen almost exclusively in the context of marriage and family development (Nelson and Robinson 1999). This perspective, to a large degree, implies women's biological determinism; that is, that their life course is largely shaped by reproduction and nurturing of children. Moreover, studies on family life often contain an *ageist* bias: they adopt the perspective of middle-aged adults while regarding the aged as passive members of families (Eichler 2001). This bias also results in a failure to recognize that aging family members, particularly women, not only receive care but also give care to the younger members.

This group of women exercising counteracts the stereotype of older women being passive and physically inactive.

Thus, they are not solely dependent but are interdependent members of the family.

Perhaps most importantly, feminist perspectives have drawn attention to how aging affects women of diverse backgrounds and characteristics. Aging does not manifest itself in all women in a universal, uniform manner, but rather intersects with class, race and ethnicity, and sexual orientation to produce diverse patterns and conditions.

Interactionist Approach: Activity Theory

Often seen as an opposing approach to disengagement theory, **activity theory** argues that the elderly person who remains active and socially involved will be best adjusted. Proponents of this perspective acknowledge that a 70-year-old person may not have the ability or desire to perform the various social roles that he or she had at age 40. Yet they contend that old people have essentially the same need for social interaction as any other group.

The improved health of older people—sometimes overlooked by social scientists—has strengthened the arguments of activity theorists. Illness and chronic disease are no longer quite the scourge of the elderly that they once were. The recent emphasis on fitness, the availability of better medical care, greater control of infectious diseases, and the reduction of fatal strokes and heart attacks have combined to mitigate the traumas of growing old. Accumulating medical research also points to the importance of remaining socially involved. Among those who decline in their mental capacities later in life, deterioration is most rapid in older people who withdraw from social relationships and activities. Fortunately, older people are finding new ways to remain socially engaged, as evidenced by the increasing use of the Internet, especially to keep in touch with family and friends (Clifford 2009b).

Admittedly, many activities open to the elderly may involve unpaid labour, for which younger adults may receive salaries. Such unpaid workers include hospital volunteers (versus aides and orderlies), drivers for charities such as the Red Cross (versus chauffeurs), tutors (as opposed to teachers), and craftspeople for charity bazaars (as opposed to carpenters and dressmakers). However, some companies have recently begun programs to hire retirees for full-time and part-time work.

Disengagement theory suggests that older people find satisfaction in withdrawal from society. Functionally speaking, they conveniently recede into the background and allow the next generation to take over. Proponents of activity theory view such withdrawal as harmful for both the elderly and society; they focus on the potential contributions of older people to the maintenance of society. In their opinion, aging citizens will feel satisfied only when they can be useful and productive in society's terms—primarily by working for wages (Charles and Carstensen 2009; Quadagno 2011).

The four perspectives considered here take different views of the elderly. Functionalists portray them as socially isolated with reduced social roles; conflict theorists regard older people as victimized by social structure, with their social roles relatively unchanged but devalued; feminist perspectives have challenged the androcentricity and biological determinism implicit in many explanations of women's aging; and interactionists see older people as involved in new networks of people in a change of social roles. Feminist perspectives also draw attention to how aging intersects with class, race and ethnicity, and sexual orientation. Table 4-2 summarizes these perspectives.

Ageism

It "knows no one century, nor culture, and is not likely to go away any time soon." This is how physician Robert Butler (1990:178) described prejudice and discrimination against the elderly, which he called **ageism**. Ageism reflects a deep uneasiness among young and middle-aged people about growing old. For many people, old age symbolizes disease, disability, and death; seeing the elderly serves as a reminder that *they* may someday become old and infirm. The notion of ageism was popularized by Maggie Kuhn, a U.S. senior citizen who took up the cause of elder rights after she was forced to retire from her position at the United Presbyterian Church. Kuhn formed the Gray Panthers in 1971, a U.S. organization dedicated to the fight against age discrimination.

With ageism pervasive in North America, it is hardly surprising that older people are barely visible on television and when they are shown they are done so in a negative and stereotypical manner. The social consequences of such images are significant. Research shows that older people who have positive perceptions of aging live an average of 7.5 years longer than those who have negative perceptions (Gardner 2003; Levy et al. 2002; Ramirez 2002).

Feminist perspectives have drawn attention to the social construction of gender as it relates to ageism in North American society. Although men's aging is seen as a sign of wisdom and experience, women's aging is seen as a sign of decline and diminishing status. Standards of beauty in our society are based on women's youth and sexual attractiveness and are often narrowly defined and frequently impossible to achieve. Aging women are, therefore, seen as a departure from our culture's norms of physical beauty and sexual attractiveness. The culture, through messages transmitted by mass media, encourages us to buy the "right" products that will help us to recapture our youth. Thus, a multibillion-dollar beauty industry of cosmetics, fashion, fitness, and cosmetic surgery is flourishing among an aging population in the midst of an anti-aging culture.

table 4-2 Theories of Aging

Sociological Perspective	View of Aging	Social Roles	Portrayal of Elderly
Functionalist	Disengagement	Reduced	Socially isolated
Conflict	Competition	Relatively unchanged	Victimized, organized to confront victimization
Feminist	Challenges androcentric bias and assumptions of homogeneity	Socially constructed, diverse according to class, race and ethnicity, sexual orientation	Caught in a double standard, men gain status and women lose status
Interactionist	Activity	Changed	Involved in new networks

::: use your sociological *imagination* :::

How might women be portrayed by the mass media if society's dominant culture revered age rather than youth?

Anticipatory Socialization and Resocialization

The development of a social self is literally a lifelong transformation that begins in the crib and continues until a person prepares for death. Two types of socialization occur at many points throughout the life course: anticipatory socialization and resocialization.

Anticipatory socialization refers to the processes of socialization in which a person rehearses for future positions, occupations, and social relationships. A culture can function more efficiently and smoothly if members become acquainted with the norms, values, and behaviour associated with a social position before actually assuming that status. Preparation for many aspects of adult life begins with anticipatory socialization during childhood and adolescence and continues throughout our lives as we prepare for new responsibilities.

You can see the process of anticipatory socialization take place when high school students start to consider which post-secondary institutions they may attend. Traditionally, this meant looking at publications received in the mail or making campus visits. However, in this era of new technologies, more and more students are using the Web to begin their educational experience. Institutions are investing more time and money in developing attractive Web sites where students can take virtual campus walks and hear and see clips of everything from a student-based promotion of the university to a sample zoology lecture.

Occasionally, assuming new social and occupational positions or moving to a new region or country requires us to *unlearn* a previous orientation. **Resocialization** refers to the process of discarding former behaviour patterns and accepting new ones as part of a transition in life. Often, resocialization occurs when there is an explicit effort to transform an individual, as happens in therapy groups, prisons, religious conversion settings, and political indoctrination camps. The process of resocialization typically involves considerable stress for the individual, much more so than socialization in general or even anticipatory socialization (Gecas 2004).

Resocialization is particularly effective when it occurs within a total institution. Erving Goffman (1961) coined the term **total institutions** to refer to institutions, such as prisons, the military, mental hospitals, and convents, which regulate all aspects of a person's life under a single authority. Because the total institution is generally cut off from the rest of society, it provides for all the needs of its members. Quite literally, the crew of a merchant vessel at sea becomes part of a total institution. So elaborate are its requirements, and so all-encompassing are its activities, that a total institution often represents a miniature society.

Goffman (1961) has identified four common traits of total institutions:

1. All aspects of life are conducted in the same place and are under the control of a single authority.

2. Any activities within the institution are conducted in the company of others in the same circumstances—for example, novices in a convent or army recruits.

3. The authorities devise rules and schedule activities without consulting the participants.

4. All aspects of life within a total institution are designed to fulfill the purpose of the organization. Thus, all activities in a monastery might be centred on prayer and communion with God (Davies 1989; Rose et al. 1979).

People often lose their individuality within total institutions. For example, a person entering prison may experience the humiliation of a **degradation ceremony** as he or she is stripped of clothing, jewellery, and other personal possessions. Even the person's self is taken away to some extent; the prison inmate loses a name and becomes known to authorities as a number. From this point on, scheduled daily routines allow for little or no personal initiative. The individual becomes secondary and nearly invisible in the overbearing social environment.

In 1934, the world was enthralled by the birth of quintuplets to Olivia and Elzire Dionne in Ontario. In the midst of the Depression, people wanted to hear and see all they could

Prisons are centres of resocialization, where people are placed under pressure to discard old behaviour patterns and accept new ones. These prisoners are learning to use weights to release tension and exert their strength—a socially acceptable method of handling antisocial impulses.

for a worthwhile cause or to flog merchandise. Within their compound, even the Dionne girls' parents and older siblings had to make appointments to see them. A child psychiatrist responsible for their child-rearing ordered they never be spanked—or hugged (to prevent the chance of infection).

After nine years, the quintuplets were reunited with their family. But the legacy of total institutionalization persisted. Sharp divisions and jealousies had developed among the five girls and the other siblings. The parents were caught up in charges of doing too much or too little for all their children. In 1997, the three surviving quintuplets made public a poignant letter to the parents of recently born septuplets in Iowa:

We three would like you to know we feel a natural affinity and tenderness for your children. We hope your children receive more respect than we did. Their fate should be no different from that of other children. Multiple births should not be confused with entertainment, nor should they be an opportunity to sell products. . . .

Our lives have been ruined by the exploitation we suffered at the hands of the government of Ontario, our place of birth. We were displayed as a curiosity three times a day for millions of tourists. . . .

We sincerely hope a lesson will be learned from examining how our lives were forever altered by our childhood experiences. If this letter changes the course of events for these newborns, then perhaps our lives will have served a higher purpose. (Dionne et al. 1997:39)

about these five girls, born generations before fertility drugs made multiple births more common. What seemed like a heart-warming story turned out to be a tragic case of Goffman's total institutionalization. The government of Ontario soon took the quintuplets from their home and set them up in a facility complete with an observation gallery overlooking their playground. Each month, 10 000 tourists paid an entry fee to view the five little "Cinderellas." When the girls left the nine-room compound, it was almost always to raise money

Social Policy and Socialization

Childcare around the World

The Issue

The rise in the number of single-parent families, increased job opportunities for women, and the need for additional family income have all propelled an increasing number of mothers of young children into the paid labour force of Canada. In 2009, 66 percent of women with children 3 years of age and under were in the paid labour force (Statistics Canada 2007m). Who, then, is responsible for children during work hours?

For many preschoolers with employed parents, the solution has become daycare programs. Daycare centres have in many ways become the functional equivalent of the nuclear family, performing some of the nurturing and socialization functions

previously handled only by family members. But how does daycare compare with other forms of childcare? And what is the state's responsibility to ensure high-quality care?

The Setting

Few people in Canada or elsewhere can afford the luxury of having a parent stay at home or of paying for high-quality live-in childcare. For millions of working mothers and fathers, finding the right kind of childcare is a challenge to parenting and to their financial responsibilities.

Researchers have found that high-quality daycare benefits children. The value of preschool

programs was documented in a series of studies conducted in Canada by the Childcare Resource and Research Unit at the University of Toronto. Researchers found no significant differences in infants who had received extensive non-maternal care compared with those who had been cared for solely by their parents. They also reported that more and more infants in Canada are being placed in childcare outside the home and that, overall, the quality of daycare centres is mixed, depending on whether they are non-profit or commercial. It is difficult, therefore, to generalize about childcare. But daycares that are non-profit have been found to be of higher quality than those that are run to make money.

A father dropping off his toddler son at a daycare centre in the morning.

Sociological Insights

Studies that assess the quality of childcare outside the home reflect the micro level of analysis and the interest of interactionists in the impact of face-to-face interaction. These studies also explore macro-level implications for the functioning of social institutions like the family. But some of the issues surrounding daycare have also been of interest to those who take the conflict perspective.

In Canada, high-quality daycare is not equally available to all families. Parents in wealthy neighbourhoods have an easier time finding daycare than do those in poor or working-class communities. Finding affordable childcare is also a problem. Parents in Quebec have more accessible and affordable childcare, as the government currently sponsors a program that costs parents just $7 per day.

Viewed from a conflict perspective, childcare costs are an especially serious burden for lower-income families. The poorest families spend 25 percent of their earnings on preschool childcare, while families who are not poor pay only 6 percent or less of their income for daycare.

Feminists echo the concern of conflict theorists that high-quality childcare has received little government support because it is regarded as a private or personal issue rather than a social one. Nearly all childcare workers are women; many find themselves in low-status, minimum-wage jobs. The average salary of a childcare worker in Canada is among the lowest of all occupational groups, and the job has few fringe benefits. Although parents may complain about childcare costs, the staff members, in effect, subsidize that cost by working for low wages.

Policy Initiatives

Policies regarding childcare outside the home vary throughout the world. As Figure 4-1 shows, the cost of childcare as a proportion of one's income can vary dramatically among the richer countries. Most developing nations do not have the economic base to provide subsidized childcare. Working mothers rely largely on relatives, or they take their children to work. In the comparatively wealthy industrialized countries of Western Europe, government provides childcare as a basic service, at little or no expense to parents.

When policymakers decide that childcare is desirable, they must determine the degree to which taxpayers should subsidize it. Although Canada's rate of female participation in the paid labour force is among the highest of the OECD countries (34 countries including Canada, the U.S. Australia, Britain and many European countries), funding from government for childcare is among the poorest—0.2 percent of gross national product. In Sweden, it is 10 times that rate and in Britain double that rate (OECD 2011). The example of Quebec demonstrates that childcare can be a government priority, provided there is the political will to make it so. Many federal governments in Canada, over the last three decades have made policy promises for a national childcare program; however, none has followed through with this promise. Meanwhile, given that costs and options vary from province to province, from city to city, from rural to rural communities, parents frequently are forced to rely on informal daycare such as friends, neighbours, relatives, and paid babysitters.

There is a long way to go in making quality childcare more affordable and more accessible, not just in Canada, but throughout the world. Government daycare facilities in Mexico have lengthy waiting lists. In China, the country's largest city—Shanghai—has abandoned the one-child policy and is launching a campaign promoting couples to have a second child. One Chinese mother says she would like to have another child but the costs are too great and that she might consider it "if the government was offering some beneficial policies . . . ." (McCabe 2009).

Margrit Eichler, a Canadian feminist and sociologist, proposes a "social responsibility model" for family life, endorsing the establishment and support of public daycare centres (Eichler 1997). Eichler argues that the establishment

figure 4-1 Childcare Costs in Industrial Nations

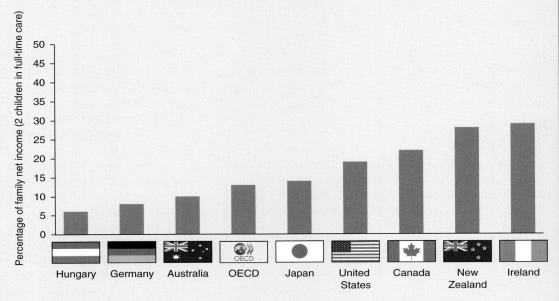

Source: Data collected by the Organisation for Economic Co-operation and Development (OECD), Gender Briefs 2010.

and support of such centres would make good economic sense, generating jobs for daycare workers and enabling mothers to work for pay. In addition, children would benefit from the social setting of the daycare as well as the more individualized setting of the home. Eichler states, "Financing does not have to come from the federal government alone. Part of it can come from municipalities, from employers, and from parents according to the ability to pay" (Eichler 1997:159–160).

A report on childcare released in 2011 by the Organisation for Economic Co-operation and Development (OECD) was critical of the Canadian government's efforts in the area of daycare, indicating that the nation's childcare enrolment of children under age 6 was 40 percent, below OECD standards. Countries such as Denmark have roughly 80 percent enrolment. The OECD stated that "this is a challenge to governments because if parents cannot achieve their desired work/life balance, not only is their welfare lowered but so is development in the country. . .affordability and quality in childcare remains an issue across Canada" (OECD 2011).

Forty percent of all regulated childcare spaces in Canada are currently in Quebec. That province, through large subsidies to childcare providers, currently charges parents only $7 per day. There are now 20 000 subsidized daycare places in the province (with 20 000 more planned), each costing the Quebec government approximately $13 000 and, overall, approximately $1.5 billion (*The Economist* 2009).

France's preschool childcare systems have long been touted as some of the most generous in the world, although it can be difficult to find an available opening. Parents can send their babies to publicly funded nurseries—*crèches*—at the age of three months, and all French cities and towns have this service. There is also a system of qualified nannies—*assistante maternelle*—who are paid to look after young children at home or in the caregiver's home. France regulates the quality of its childcare systems by ensuring that all caregivers meet strict standards of training and education.

Experts in child development view such reports as a vivid reminder of the need for greater government and private-sector support for childcare. A 2007 study by SOMS Surveys suggests that although family matters are of top priority to Canadians, only 29 percent feel their employer cares about their work–life balance (*The Province* 2007). Glenn Thompson, CEO of the Canadian Mental Health Association, states, "Usually, these employees are looking for ways to help a lifestyle that is now encumbered with their senior parents and child care" (*The Province* 2007:A41).

Apply the Theory

1. What importance would liberal feminist thinkers place on the establishment of a national childcare program for Canada? What about radical feminist thinkers?
2. If you were a conflict sociologist, how would you view the establishment of such a program in light of the overall belief in the need to eliminate social inequality?
3. What role do you think a national childcare program might serve in terms of the socialization of Canadian children?

CHAPTER RESOURCES

Summary

::: 4.1 What Is the Role of Socialization?

- **Socialization** is the process whereby people learn the attitudes, values, and actions appropriate for members of a particular culture.
- Socialization affects the overall cultural practices of a society, and it also shapes the images that we hold of ourselves.
- Heredity and environmental factors interact in influencing the socialization process. **Sociobiology** is the systematic study of the biological bases of social behaviour.

::: 4.2 What Are Some Major Theoretical Perspectives on Socialization?

- In the early 1900s, Charles Horton Cooley advanced the belief that we learn who we are by interacting with others, a phenomenon he called the **looking-glass self**.
- George Herbert Mead, best known for his theory of the **self**, proposed that as people mature, their selves begin to reflect their concern about reactions from others—both generalized others and significant others.
- Erving Goffman has shown that many of our daily activities involve attempts to convey distinct impressions of who we are, a process called **impression management**.

::: 4.3 What Are Some Agents of Socialization?

- The major agents in this lifelong process are the family, schools, peer groups, the mass media and technology, the workplace, and the state.

::: 4.4 How Does Socialization Occur throughout the Life Course?

- Sociologists who study socialization throughout the life course are interested in the social factors that influence people throughout their lives, from birth to death.
- The particular problems of the aged have become the focus for a specialized area of research and inquiry known as **gerontology**.
- **Disengagement theory** implicitly suggests that society should help older people withdraw from their accustomed social roles, whereas **activity theory** argues that the elderly person who remains active and socially involved will be best adjusted.
- From a conflict perspective, the low status of older people is reflected in prejudice and discrimination against them in unfair job practices.
- The greying of Canada: An increasing proportion of the population of Canada comprises older people.

Critical Thinking Questions

1. Should social research in such areas as sociobiology be conducted even though many investigators believe that this analysis is potentially detrimental to particular groups of people?

2. Drawing on Erving Goffman's dramaturgical approach, discuss how the following groups engage in impression management: athletes, students, university instructors, parents, physicians, politicians.

3. How would functionalists and conflict theorists differ in their analyses of socialization by the mass media? How would they be similar?

4. Do you think that media socialize the members of our society to be consumers, first and foremost? Why?

THINKING ABOUT MOVIES

The Blind Side

Through football and the help of significant others, a young man's self-identity changes.

Grown Ups

Five childhood friends reunite and come to terms with the aging process.

The Town

A man from Boston struggles against his socialization within a subculture of bank robbers.

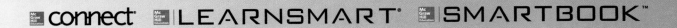

For more information on the resources available from McGraw-Hill Ryerson, go to **www.mcgrawhill.ca/he/solutions**.

inside

People often interpret or define others' actions, such as those of this woman on a street in downtown Toronto.

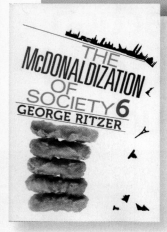

" Ray Kroc (1902–1984), the genius behind the franchising of McDonald's restaurants, was a man with big ideas and grand ambitions. But even Kroc could not have anticipated the astounding impact of his creation. McDonald's is the basis of one of the most influential developments in contemporary society. Its reverberations extend far beyond its point of origin in the United States and in the fast-food business. It has influenced a wide range of undertakings, indeed the way of life, of a significant portion of the world. And having rebounded from some well-publicized economic difficulties, that impact is likely to expand at an accelerating rate in the early twenty-first century.

. . . I devote all this attention to McDonald's . . . because it serves here as the major example of, and the paradigm for, a wide-ranging process I call McDonaldization. . . . McDonaldization has shown every sign of being an inexorable process, sweeping through seemingly impervious institutions (e.g., religion) and regions (European nations such as France) of the world.

Other types of business are increasingly adapting the principles of the fast-food industry to their needs. Said the vice chairman of Toys "R" Us, 'We want to be thought of as a sort of McDonald's of toys.' . . . Other chains with similar ambitions include Gap, Jiffy Lube, AAMCO Transmissions, Midas Muffler & Brake Shops, Great Clips, H&R Block, Pearle Vision, Bally's. . . .

Other nations have developed their own variants on the McDonald's chain. . . . Paris, a city whose love for fine cuisine might lead you to think it would prove immune to fast food, has a large number of fast-food croissanteries; the revered French bread has also been McDonaldized. India has a chain of fast-food restaurants, Nirula's, that sells mutton burgers (about 80% of Indians are Hindus, who eat no beef) as well as local Indian cuisine. Mos Burger is a Japanese chain with 1,373 restaurants that, in addition to the usual fare, sell Teriyaki chicken burgers, rice burgers, and 'Oshiruko with brown rice cake.' . . .

Ray Kroc (1902–1984), the genius behind the franchising of McDonald's restaurants, was a man with big ideas and grand ambitions.

McDonald's is such a powerful model that many businesses have acquired nicknames beginning with Mc. Examples include 'McDentists' and 'McDoctors,' meaning drive-in clinics designed to deal quickly and efficiently with minor dental and medical problems; 'McChild' care centres, meaning childcare centres such as KinderCare; 'McStables,' designating the nationwide race horse–training operation of D. Wayne Lucas; and 'McPaper,' describing the newspaper *USA TODAY.* "

(Ritzer 2011:1, 3, 5, 12)

In this excerpt from *The McDonaldization of Society*, sociologist George Ritzer contemplates the enormous influence of a well-known fast-food organization on modern-day culture and social life. Ritzer defines **McDonaldization** as "the process by which the principles of the fast-food restaurant are coming to dominate more and more sectors of American society as well as of the rest of the world" (Ritzer 2011:1). In his book, he shows how the business principles on which the fast-food industry is founded—efficiency, calculability, predictability, and control—have changed not only the way Americans do business and run their organizations, but the way they live their lives. Despite the runaway success of McDonald's and its imitators, and the advantages these enterprises bring to millions of people around the world (see Box 5-3), Ritzer is critical of their effect on society. The waste and environmental degradation created by billions of disposable containers and the dehumanized work routines of fast-food crews are two of the disadvantages he cites in his critique. Would the modern world be a better one, Ritzer asks, if it were less McDonaldized?

In this chapter, we will study social structure and its effect on our **social interactions**. What determines a person's status in society? How do our social roles affect our social interactions? What is the place of social institutions such as the family, religion, and government in our social structure? How can we better understand and manage large organizations such as multinational corporations? We'll begin by considering how social interactions shape the way we view the world around us. Next, we'll focus on the five basic elements of **social structure**: statuses, social roles, groups, social networks, and social institutions such as the family, religion, and government. We'll see that functionalists, conflict theorists, feminist theorists, and interactionists approach these institutions quite differently. We'll compare our modern social structure with simpler forms, using typologies developed by Émile Durkheim, Ferdinand Tönnies, and Gerhard Lenski. Next, we'll examine how and why formal organizations, such as a corporation, college, or university, came into existence, touching on Max Weber's model of the modern bureaucracy in the process. Finally, we'll discuss recent changes in the workplace. The social policy section at the end of the chapter focuses on the status of organized labour today. ■

How Do We Define and Reconstruct Reality?

When someone in a crowd shoves you, do you automatically push back? Or do you consider the circumstances of the incident and the attitude of the instigator before you react? Chances are you do the latter. According to sociologist Herbert Blumer (1969:79), the distinctive characteristic of social interaction among people is that "human beings interpret or 'define' each other's actions instead of merely reacting to each other's actions." In other words, our response to someone's behaviour is based on the *meaning* we attach to his or her actions. Reality is shaped by our perceptions, evaluations, and definitions.

These meanings typically reflect the norms and values of the dominant culture and our socialization experiences within that culture. As interactionists emphasize, the meanings that we attach to people's behaviour are shaped by our interactions with them and with the larger society. In other words, social reality is literally constructed from our social interactions.

How do we define our social reality? Consider something as simple as how we might regard tattoos. At one time, many Canadians might have considered tattoos weird or kooky. We associated them with fringe counter-cultural groups, such as punk rockers, biker gangs, and skinheads. Among many people, a tattoo elicited an automatic negative response. Now, however, so many people have tattoos—including society's trendsetters and major sports figures—and the ritual of getting a tattoo has become so legitimized, that mainstream culture now regards tattoos differently. At this point, as a result of increased social interaction with ink-adorned people, tattoos look perfectly natural to us in a number of settings.

The ability to define social reality reflects a group's power within a society. In fact, one of the most crucial aspects of the relationship between dominant and subordinate groups is the ability of the dominant or majority group to define a society's values. Sociologist William I. Thomas (1923), an early critic of theories of racial and gender differences, recognized that the "definition of the situation" could mould the thinking and personality of the individual. Writing from an interactionist perspective, Thomas observed that people respond not only to the objective features of a person or situation but also to the *meaning* that person or situation has for them. His statement, and that of co-author Dorothy Thomas, "If men define situations as real, they are real in their consequences" (Thomas and Thomas 1928:572) has become known as the Thomas theorem. For example, in Philip Zimbardo's mock prison experiment, student "guards" and "prisoners" accepted the definition of the situation (including the traditional roles and behaviour associated with being a guard or prisoner) and acted accordingly.

Symbols of status and power, such as this judge's robes, tend to reinforce the position of the dominant groups in society. When such symbols are associated with members of a minority, they challenge prevailing stereotypes, changing what the interactionist William I. Thomas called "the definition of the situation."

As we have seen throughout the last 40 years—through movements to bring about greater rights for members of such groups as women, racialized minorities, the elderly, gays and lesbians, and people with disabilities—an important aspect of the process of social change involves redefining or reconstructing social reality. Members of subordinate groups challenge traditional definitions and begin to perceive and experience reality in a new way. For example, in 1985,

Rick Hansen wheeled around the world to raise money for spinal cord research over 25 years ago and founded the Man in Motion Foundation (now called the Rick Hansen Foundation). Rick represents a proactive attitude among Canadians who have disabilities and are breaking down societal stereotypes.

Rick Hansen began a two-year journey, circling the world in his wheelchair to raise awareness and money for people with spinal cord injuries. After being injured in an automobile accident that left him paralyzed at the age of 15, Hansen became a world-class athlete, winning international wheelchair marathons and world championships, and competing for Canada in the Paralympic Games. Continually breaking down stereotypes of people with disabilities, today, Hansen is the father of three daughters, the president and CEO of the Rick Hansen Foundation, an active environmentalist, and an athlete who enjoys fishing, Pilates, tennis, kayaking, and sit-skiing. In 2009, he continued to break down stereotypes by going bungee-jumping in his wheelchair in Whistler, British Columbia, televised as part of a segment on *The Rick Mercer Report*.

Viewed from a sociological perspective, Rick Hansen was redefining social reality by challenging ways of thinking and terminology that restricted him and other people with disabilities.

5.2 What Are the Elements of Social Structure?

All social interaction takes place within a social structure, including those interactions that redefine social reality. For purposes of study, we can break down any social structure into five elements: *statuses, social roles, groups, social networks*, and *social institutions*. These elements make up social structure just as a foundation, walls, and ceilings make up a building's structure. The elements of social structure are developed through the lifelong process of socialization described in Chapter 4. In addition, human beings create the elements of social structure through a dynamic process involving meaningful interaction (Fleras 2003).

Statuses

We normally think of a person's status as having to do with influence, wealth, and fame. However, sociologists use the term **status** to refer to any of the full range of socially defined positions within a large group or society, from the lowest to the highest. Within our society, a person can occupy the status of CEO, fruit picker, son or daughter, violinist, teenager, resident of Alberta, dental technician, or neighbour. A person can hold a number of statuses at the same time.

Ascribed and Achieved Status Sociologists view some statuses as ascribed and others as achieved (see Figure 5-1). An **ascribed status** is assigned to a person by society without regard for the person's unique talents or characteristics. Generally, the assignment takes place at birth; thus, a person's racial background, gender, and age are all considered ascribed statuses. While people may be born with certain ascribed statuses, these characteristics are significant mainly because of the social meanings they have in a given culture. Conflict theorists are especially interested in ascribed statuses, since they often confer privileges or reflect a person's membership in a subordinate group. The social meanings of race and ethnicity, gender, and age will be analyzed more fully in later chapters.

figure 5-1 Social Statuses

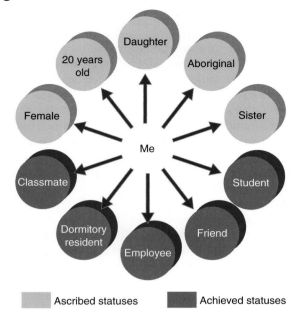

Ascribed statuses   Achieved statuses

Think about It
The young woman in Figure 5-1—"me"—occupies many positions in society, each of which involves distinct statuses. How would you define *your* statuses? Which have the most influence in your life?

In most cases, we can do little to change an ascribed status. But we can attempt to change the traditional constraints associated with such statuses. For example, the Canadian Association of Retired Persons (CARP)—an activist political group founded in 1984 to work for the rights of older people—has tried to modify society's negative and confining stereotypes of seniors. As a result of CARP's work and that of other groups supporting older citizens, the ascribed status of "senior citizen" is no longer as difficult for millions of older people.

An ascribed status does not necessarily have the same social meaning in every society. In a cross-cultural study, sociologist Gary Huang (1988) confirmed the long-held view that respect for the elderly is an important cultural norm in China. In many cases, the adjective *old* is used respectfully: calling someone "old teacher" or "old person" is like calling a judge in North America "your honour." Huang points out that positive age-seniority language distinctions are uncommon in North America; consequently, we view the term *old man* as more of an insult than a celebration of seniority and wisdom. With the large baby boom population in Canada approaching what has been considered—until recently—retirement age, the meanings of *old age, senior citizen*, and *elderly* are being reconstructed; baby boomers are staying active for longer and many plan on working past age 65.

Unlike ascribed statuses, an **achieved status** comes to us largely through our own efforts. Both bank president and prison guard are achieved statuses, as are lawyer, pianist, sorority member, convict, and social worker. We must do something to acquire an achieved status—go to school, learn a skill, establish a friendship, invent a new product. But as we will see in the next section, our ascribed status heavily influences our achieved status. Being male, for example, decreases the likelihood that a person would consider a career in childcare services.

Master Status Each person holds many different and sometimes conflicting statuses; some may connote higher social position and some, lower position. How, then, do others view one's overall social position? According to sociologist Everett Hughes (1945), societies deal with inconsistencies by agreeing that certain statuses are more important than others. A **master status** is a status that dominates others and thereby determines a person's general position in society. For example, Arthur Ashe, who died of AIDS in 1993, had a remarkable career as a tennis star, but at the end of his life, his status as a well-known personality with AIDS may have outweighed his statuses as a retired athlete, author, and political activist. Throughout the world, many people with disabilities find that their status as "disabled" receives undue weight, overshadowing their actual ability to perform successfully in meaningful employment (see Box 5-1).

Our society gives so much importance to race and gender that such labels often dominate our lives. These ascribed statuses frequently influence achieved status. Lee Williams, a long-serving porter for Canadian National Railway, was denied advancement into more senior positions because of racism (Manitoba Human Rights Commission 2004). Williams challenged the lack of opportunity for advancement of black railway workers under the Fair Employment Act and won his case; this allowed him and other black workers to move up the ranks to assume higher achieved status within the corporation. In Canada, ascribed statuses of race and gender can function as master statuses that have an important impact on a person's potential to achieve a desired professional and social status.

Social Roles

What Are Social Roles? Throughout our lives, we acquire what sociologists call social roles. A **social role** is a set of expectations for people who occupy a given social position or status. Thus, in Canada, we expect that cab drivers will know how to get around a city, that receptionists will be reliable in handling phone messages, and that police officers will take action if they see a citizen being threatened. With each distinctive social status—whether ascribed or achieved—come particular role expectations. However, actual performance varies from individual to individual. One secretary may assume extensive administrative responsibilities, while another may focus on clerical duties. Similarly, in Philip Zimbardo's mock prison experiment, some students were brutal and sadistic guards; others were not.

Roles are a significant component of social structure. Viewed from a functionalist perspective, roles contribute to a society's stability by enabling members to anticipate the behaviour of others and to pattern their own actions accordingly. Yet social roles can also be dysfunctional if they restrict people's interactions and relationships. If we view a person *only* as a "police officer" or "supervisor," it will be difficult to relate to him or her as a friend or neighbour.

A person's ascribed status often arises from social or historical circumstances. Above, black descendents of slaves extract sugar from cane on the Caribbean island of Dominica, once a British colony. Below, a prosperous white family in England enjoys sugar with their tea.

Role Conflict Imagine the delicate situation of a woman who has worked for a decade on an assembly line in an electrical plant, and has recently been named supervisor of her unit. How is this woman expected to relate to her long-time friends and co-workers? Should she still go out to lunch with them, as she has done almost daily for years? Is it her responsibility to recommend the firing of an old friend who cannot keep up with the demands of the assembly line?

Role conflict occurs when incompatible expectations arise from two or more social positions held by the same person. Fulfillment of the roles associated with one status may directly violate the roles linked to a second status. In the example just given, the newly promoted supervisor will most likely experience a sharp conflict between her social and occupational roles.

Such role conflicts call for important ethical choices. The new supervisor will have to make a difficult decision about how much allegiance she owes her friend and how much she owes her employers, who have given her supervisory responsibilities.

Another type of role conflict occurs when individuals move into occupations that are not common among people with their ascribed status. Male preschool teachers and female police officers experience this type of role conflict. In the latter case, female officers must strive to reconcile

sociology in the global community

5-1 Disability as a Master Status

When the Canadian Transportation Agency ordered VIA Rail to make the passenger rail cars it had purchased several years ago accessible to people with disabilities, VIA responded by mounting a legal challenge. After a number of lower court decisions, in 2007, the Supreme Court of Canada—guided by the Canadian Charter of Rights and Freedoms—ruled that the rail service must be usable to people with and without disabilities.

Throughout history and around the world, people with disabilities have often been subjected to cruel and inhuman treatment. For example, in the early twentieth century, people with disabilities were frequently viewed as subhuman creatures who were a menace to society. In Alberta, between 1928 and 1972, over 2800 individuals were sterilized because they were deemed to be mentally "unfit." In Japan, more than 16 000 women with disabilities were involuntarily sterilized with government approval from 1945 to 1995. Sweden recently apologized for the same action taken against 62 000 of its citizens in the 1970s.

Such blatantly hostile treatment of people with disabilities generally gave way to a medical model that views people with disabilities as chronic patients. Increasingly, however, those concerned with the rights of people with disabilities have criticized this model as well. In their view, it is the unnecessary and discriminatory barriers present in the environment—both physical and attitudinal—that stand in the way of people with disabilities more than any biological limitations do. Applying a human-rights model, activists emphasize that those with disabilities face widespread prejudice, discrimination, and segregation. For example, some provinces and territories in Canada do not fund basic devices for people with disabilities, such as wheelchairs.

Drawing on the earlier work of Erving Goffman, contemporary sociologists have suggested that society has attached a stigma to many forms of disability and that this stigma leads to prejudicial treatment. People with disabilities frequently observe that other people often see them only as blind, wheelchair-ridden, and so forth, rather than as complex human beings with individual strengths and weaknesses, whose blindness or use of a wheelchair is merely one aspect of their lives. A review of studies of people with disabilities disclosed that most academic research on the subject does not differentiate gender, thereby perpetuating the view that a disability overrides other personal characteristics. Consequently, disability serves as a master status.

Without question, people with disabilities occupy a subordinate position in Canadian society. The first International Day of Persons with Disabilities was declared by the United Nations in 1992, and advocates from around the world continue to lobby for the adoption of an international convention on disability rights. Women and men involved in this movement are working

Would an employee who entered this room see a member of a consulting team or a man in a wheelchair? Disability often functions as a master status.

to challenge negative views of disabled people and to modify the social structure by reshaping laws, institutions, and environments so that people with disabilities can be fully integrated into mainstream society.

Apply the Theory

1. How would interactionist perspectives differ from conflict positions when it comes to the study of disabilities?
2. What emphasis would feminist thinkers be most likely to bring to the study of disabilities?

Sources: Albrecht 2004; Goffman 1963a; Ponczek 1998; Rosenthal 2001; Willett and Deegan 2000.

---

their workplace role in law enforcement with the societal view of a woman's role, which does not embrace many skills needed in police work. And while female police officers encounter sexual harassment, as women do throughout the workforce, they must also contend with the "code of silence," an informal norm that precludes officers from implicating colleagues in wrongdoing (Fletcher 1995; Martin 1994).

::: use your sociological *imagination* :::

If you were a male nurse, what aspects of role conflict might you experience? Now imagine you are a professional boxer and a woman. What conflicting role expectations might that involve? In both cases, how well do you think you would handle role conflict?

Role Strain Role conflict describes the situation of a person dealing with the challenge of occupying two social positions simultaneously. However, even a single position can cause problems. Sociologists use the term **role strain** to describe the difficulty that arises when the same social position imposes conflicting demands and expectations.

A recent study by Sebastien LaRochelle-Cote of Statistics Canada highlights role strain in the context of Canadian families (particularly mothers) with young children. In order to reduce role strain, couples tend to work fewer hours, with women tending to work very few (Proudfoot 2009). Thirty-two-year-old social-service program administrator Emma Willer, who has a husband and two preschool children, is trying to balance her career with the demands of family responsibilities. She says, "We're trying to make a few changes that make things easier, but I'm not sure we're ever going to get there" (Proudfoot 2009:H2).

Role Exit Often, when we think of assuming a social role, we focus on the preparation and anticipatory socialization

Police officers may face role strain when they try to develop positive community relations while maintaining an authoritative position.

at home (like stuffed animals and dolls) are associated with their prior identities. They may remain deeply attached to those objects, but do not want them to be seen as part of their new identities at college. The objects students bring with them symbolize how they now see themselves and how they wish to be perceived—iPods and wall posters, for example, are calculated to say, "This is me."

Groups

In sociological terms, a **group** is any number of people with similar norms, values, and expectations who interact with one another on a regular basis. The members of a women's basketball team, a hospital's business office, a synagogue, or a symphony orchestra constitute a group. However, the residents of a suburb would not be considered a group, since they rarely interact with one another at one time.

Groups play a vital part in a society's social structure. Much of our social interaction takes place within groups and is influenced by their norms and sanctions. Being a teenager or a retired person takes on special meanings when we interact within groups designed for people with that particular status. The

a person undergoes for that role. Such is true if a person is about to become a lawyer, a chef, a spouse, or a parent. Yet, until recently, social scientists have given little attention to the adjustments involved in *leaving* social roles.

Sociologist Helen Rose Fuchs Ebaugh (1988) developed the term **role exit** to describe the process of disengagement from a role that is central to one's self-identity in order to establish a new role and identity. Drawing on interviews with 185 people—among them ex-convicts, divorced men and women, recovering alcoholics, ex-nuns, former doctors, retirees, and transsexuals—Ebaugh (herself a former nun) studied the process of voluntarily exiting from significant social roles.

Ebaugh has offered a four-stage model of role exit. The first stage begins with *doubt*. The person experiences frustration, burnout, or simply unhappiness with an accustomed status and the roles associated with the social position. The second stage involves a *search for alternatives*. A person who is unhappy with his or her career may take a leave of absence; an unhappily married couple may begin what they see as a temporary separation.

The third stage of role exit is the *action stage* or *departure*. Ebaugh found that the vast majority of her respondents could identify a clear turning point that made them feel it was essential to take final action and leave their job, end their marriage, or engage in another type of role exit. Twenty percent of respondents saw their role exit as a gradual, evolutionary process that had no single turning point.

The last stage of role exit involves the *creation of a new identity*. Many of you reading this book participated in a role exit when you made the transition from high school to college or university. You left behind the role of offspring living at home and took on the role of a somewhat independent student living with peers in a dorm or apartment. Sociologist Ira Silver (1996) has studied the central role that material objects play in this transition. The objects students choose to leave

According to sociologist Helen Rose Fuchs Ebaugh, role exit is a four-stage process. Is this transexual in the first or the fourth stage of changing genders?

expectations associated with many social roles, including those accompanying the statuses of brother, sister, and student, become more clearly defined in the context of a group.

Primary and Secondary Groups Charles Horton Cooley (1902) coined the term **primary group** to refer to a small group characterized by intimate, face-to-face association and cooperation. The members of a street gang constitute a primary group; so do members of a family living in the same household, or a group of "sisters" in a college or university sorority.

Primary groups play a pivotal role both in the socialization process (see Chapter 4) and in the development of roles and statuses. Indeed, primary groups can be instrumental in a person's day-to-day existence. When we find ourselves identifying closely with a group, it is probably a primary group.

We also participate in many groups that are not characterized by close bonds of friendship, such as large college or university classes and business associations. The term **secondary group** refers to a formal, impersonal group in which there is little social intimacy or mutual understanding (see Table 5-1). Secondary groups often emerge in the workplace among those who share special understandings about their occupation. The distinction between primary and secondary groups is not always clear-cut, however. Some social clubs may become so large and impersonal that they no longer function as primary groups.

In-Groups and Out-Groups A group can hold special meaning for members because of its relationship to other groups. For example, people in one group sometimes feel antagonistic toward or threatened by another group, especially if that group is perceived as being different either culturally or racially. To identify these "we" and "they" feelings, sociologists use two terms first employed by William Graham Sumner (1906): *in-group* and *out-group*.

An **in-group** can be defined as any group or category to which people feel they belong. Simply put, it comprises everyone who is regarded as "we" or "us." The in-group may be as narrow as a teenage clique or as broad as an entire society. The very existence of an in-group implies that there is an out-group that is viewed as "they" or "them." An **out-group** is a group or category to which people feel they do *not* belong.

table 5-1 Comparison of Primary and Secondary Groups

Primary Group	Secondary Group
Generally small	Usually large
Relatively long period of interaction	Relatively short duration, often temporary
Intimate, face-to-face association	Little social intimacy or mutual understanding
Some emotional depth to relationships	Relationships generally superficial
Cooperative, friendly	More formal and impersonal

::: use your sociological *imagination* :::

Try putting yourself in the shoes of an out-group member. What does your in-group look like from that perspective?

In-group members typically feel distinct and superior, seeing themselves as better than people in the out-group. Proper behaviour for the in-group is simultaneously viewed as unacceptable behaviour for the out-group. This double standard enhances the sense of superiority. Sociologist Robert Merton (1968) described this process as the conversion of "in-group virtues" into "out-group vices." We can see this differential standard operating in worldwide discussions of terrorism. When

A pizza delivery crew is an example of a *secondary group*—a formal, impersonal group in which there is little social intimacy or mutual understanding. While waiting for the next delivery, members of this crew will become well enough acquainted to distinguish those who see the job as temporary from those who view it as permanent. They will learn who looks forward to deliveries in perceived high-risk areas and who does not. They may even spend time together after work, joking or boasting about their exploits on the job, but their friendship typically will not develop beyond that point.

a group or a nation takes aggressive actions, it usually justifies them as necessary, even if civilians are hurt or killed. Opponents are quick to label such actions with the emotion-laden term of *terrorist* and appeal to the world community for condemnation. Yet this same group or nation may retaliate with actions that hurt civilians, which the first group will then condemn.

Conflict between in-groups and out-groups can turn violent on a personal as well as a political level. In 2009, in the metropolitan Vancouver and Fraser Valley regions of British Columbia gang violence spiked, resulting in numerous gun-related deaths. Rival gangs were competing for control of the increasingly scarce resources associated with the illicit drug industry.

In-group members who actively provoke out-group members may have their own problems, including limited time and attention from working parents. Sociologists David Stevenson and Barbara Schneider (1999), who studied 7000 teenagers, found that despite many opportunities for group membership, young people spend an average of three and a half hours alone every day. While youths may claim they want privacy, they also crave attention, and striking out at members of an in-group or out-group, be they the wrong gender, ethnic group, or peer group, seems to be one way to get it.

Reference Groups   Both in-groups and primary groups can dramatically influence the way an individual thinks and behaves. Sociologists call any group that individuals use as a standard for evaluating themselves and their own behaviour a **reference group**. For example, a high school student who aspires to join a social circle of hip-hop music devotees will pattern his or her behaviour after that of the group. The student will begin dressing like these peers, listening to the same music, and hanging out at the same stores and clubs.

Reference groups have two basic purposes: They serve a normative function by setting and enforcing standards of conduct and belief. The high school student who wants the approval of the hip-hop crowd will have to follow the group's dictates, at least to some extent. Reference groups also perform a comparison function by serving as a standard against which people can measure themselves and others. A person will evaluate himself or herself against a reference group when evaluating his/her own circumstances, attitudes, values, and behaviours (Thompson and Hickey 2005).

Reference groups may help the process of anticipatory socialization. For example, a college or university student majoring in finance may read *The Wall Street Journal*, study the annual reports of corporations, and listen to midday stock market news on the radio. Such a student is using financial experts as a reference group to which he or she aspires.

Often, two or more reference groups influence us at the same time. Our family members, neighbours, and co-workers all shape different aspects of our self-evaluation. In addition, reference group attachments change during the life cycle. A corporate executive who quits the rat race at age 45 to become a social worker will find new reference groups to use as standards for evaluation. We shift reference groups as we take on different statuses during our lives.

Coalitions   As groups grow larger, coalitions begin to develop. A **coalition** is a temporary or permanent alliance geared toward a common goal. Coalitions can be broad-based or narrow and can take on many different objectives. Sociologist William Julius Wilson (1999) has described community-based organizations in Texas that include whites and Latinos, both working class and affluent, who have banded together to work for improved sidewalks, better drainage systems, and comprehensive street paving. Out of this type of coalition building, Wilson hopes, will emerge better interracial understanding.

Some coalitions are intentionally short-lived. Short-term coalition building is a key to success in popular "reality" TV programs like *Survivor*. In the first season of *Survivor* (*Borneo*, broadcast in 2000), the four members of the "Tagi alliance" banded together to vote fellow castaways off the island where they were sequestered. The political and business worlds can also foster many temporary coalitions. For example, in 1997, big U.S. tobacco companies joined with anti-smoking groups to draw up a settlement for reimbursing states for tobacco-related medical costs. Soon after the settlement was announced, the coalition members returned to their decades-long fight against each other (Pear 1997).

::: use your sociological *imagination* :::

Describe an experience you have had with coalition building, or one that you have read about—perhaps in politics. Was the coalition effective? What problems did the members need to overcome?

www.mcgrawhillconnect.ca

Can you outwit, outplay, and outlast your competition? Maybe a coalition can help. In *Survivor: Redemption Island*, coalition building continued to be one key to success in the long-running television series.

research today

5-2 Social Networks and Obesity

Over the past two generations, obesity has become a public health problem in the United States. To explain the trend toward excess weight, researchers have focused on Americans' nutritional practices, as well as on their genetic tendencies. Another variable that contributes to obesity, less obvious than diet and heredity, is social networking.

Researchers identified this last variable in the course of a long-term heart health survey, during which they tracked the weight of 12 067 respondents. At the same time, they mapped the social networks that respondents belonged to (see the accompanying figure). Over the three decades since the survey began, they have noted that weight gain in one person is often associated with weight gain in his or her friends, siblings, spouse, and neighbours. In fact, a person's chances of becoming obese increased by 57 percent if a friend became overweight during the same period. This association, they found, was attributable solely to selectivity in the choice of friends—that is, to people of a certain weight seeking out others of roughly the same weight.

Weight gain in one person is often associated with weight gain in his or her friends, siblings, spouse, and neighbours.

This study shows that social networks do influence the way people behave. More important, the results suggest that networking could be exploited to spread positive health behaviours—for example, by recruiting friends to participate

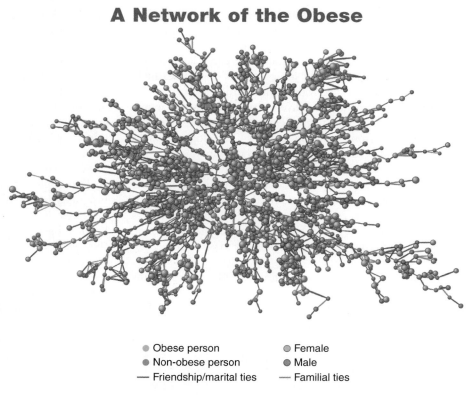

A Network of the Obese

- ● Obese person
- ● Non-obese person
- — Friendship/marital ties
- ● Female
- ● Male
- — Familial ties

Larger circles represent heavier people.

in a person's weight-loss plan. Through a similar approach, health practitioners could include social networking in efforts to control smoking, drinking, and drug abuse.

APPLY THE THEORY

1. Have you ever tried to lose weight, and if so, did your cluster of friends and family help or hinder you? In your experience, do people who are overweight tend to cluster in separate groups from those of normal weight?

2. Besides public health campaigns, what applications can you think of for research on social networking?

Sources: Christakis and Fowler 2007, 2009; Haas et al. 2010.

Social Networks

Groups do not merely serve to define other elements of the social structure, such as roles and statuses; they also link the individual with the larger society. We all belong to a number of different groups, and through our acquaintances make connections with people in different social circles. These connections are known as a **social network**—that is, a series of social relationships that link a person directly to others, and through them indirectly to still more people. Social networks can centre on virtually any activity, from sharing job information to exchanging news and gossip or to sharing sex. Some networks may constrain people by limiting the range of their

interactions, yet networks can also empower people by making vast resources available to them (Watts 2004; see Box 5-2).

Involvement in social networks—commonly known as *networking*—is especially valuable in finding employment. Albert Einstein, who was a poor student, wasn't successful in finding a job until a classmate's father put him in touch with his future employer. These kinds of contacts—even those that are weak and distant—can be crucial in establishing social networks and facilitating the transmission of information.

In the workplace, networking pays off more for men than for women because of the traditional presence of men in leadership positions. One survey of executives found that 63 percent of the men used networking to find new jobs, compared to 41 percent of the women. Thirty-one percent of the women used classified advertisements to find jobs, compared to only 13 percent of the men. Still, women at all levels of the paid labour force are beginning to make effective use of social networks. A study of women who were leaving the welfare rolls to enter the paid workforce found that networking was an effective tool in their search for employment. Informal networking also helped them to locate childcare and better housing—keys to successful employment (Carey and McLean 1997; Henly 1999). For unemployed people, online conversations with friends in the same situation can be an invaluable source of social support (Scherer 2010).

Virtual Worlds

With advances in technology, we can now maintain social networks electronically; we don't need face-to-face contacts. Whether through text-messaging, or social networking sites such as Facebook, a significant amount of networking occurs online. Online network-building companies offer their services free of charge at first. People log in to these sites and create a profile. Rather than remaining anonymous, as they would with an online dating service, users are identified by name and encouraged to list friends—even trusted friends of friends—who can serve as job contacts, offer advice, or simply share interests. One site creates "tribes" of people who share the same characteristic—a religion, hobby, music preference, or postsecondary affiliation (Tedeschi 2004).

Emails, Webcams, and blogs are only the first stage in the creation of alternative forms of social reality. Recently a whole new society, the Second Life® world, has sprung up in virtual space. Web-based and three-dimensional, the Second Life® virtual world included about 18 million networked "players" as of November 2010. Just like real worlds, virtual worlds have become politicized and commercialized. In 2007, Sweden became the first real-world country to place an "embassy" in the Second Life® world.

Sociologist Manuel Castells views these emerging electronic social networks as fundamental to new organizations and the growth of existing businesses and associations. With other scholars, sociologists are now scrambling to understand these environments and their social processes. The Second Life world went public in 2003—a millennium ago in the cyberspace world.

Social Institutions

The mass media, the government, the economy, the family, and the health-care system are all examples of social institutions found in our society. **Social institutions** are organized patterns of beliefs and behaviour centred on basic social needs, such as replacing personnel (the family) and preserving order (the government).

A close look at social institutions gives sociologists insight into the structure of a society. Consider religion, for example. The institution of religion adapts to the segment of society that it serves. Religious work has very different meanings for religious leaders who serve a skid row area and those who serve a suburban middle-class community. Those assigned to a skid row mission will focus on tending to the ill and providing food and shelter. In contrast, religious leaders in affluent suburbs will be occupied with counselling those considering marriage and divorce, arranging youth activities, and overseeing cultural events.

Virtual worlds have just begun to test our imaginations. At the top, a group of avatars interacts in the Second Life® world. On the bottom, in the blockbuster film *Avatar,* the Na'vi people interact in the screen-based virtual world of Pandora.

::: use your sociological *imagination* :::

If you were hearing impaired, what impact might instant messaging, or texting, have on you?

Functionalist View One way to understand social institutions is to see how they fulfill essential functions. Anthropologist David F. Aberle and his colleagues (1950) and sociologists Raymond Mack and Calvin Bradford (1979) have identified five major tasks, or functional prerequisites, that a society or relatively permanent group must accomplish if it is to survive:

1. *Replacing personnel.* Any group or society must replace personnel when they die, leave, or become incapacitated. This task is accomplished through such means as immigration, annexation of neighbouring groups, acquisition of slaves, or biological reproduction. The Shakers, a religious sect that came to North America in 1774, are a conspicuous example of a group that has *failed* to replace personnel. Their religious beliefs commit the Shakers to celibacy; to survive, the group must recruit new members. At first, the Shakers

proved quite successful in attracting new members, reaching a peak of about 6000 people in the United States during the 1840s. As of 2004, however, the only Shaker community left in the United States was a farm in Maine with five members—three men and two women (Sabbathday Lake 2008).

2. *Teaching new recruits.* No group or society can survive if many of its members reject the group's established behaviour and responsibilities. Thus, finding or producing new members is not sufficient; the group or society must also encourage recruits to learn and accept its values and customs. Such learning can take place formally, within schools (where learning is a manifest function), or informally, through interaction in peer groups (where instruction is a latent function).

3. *Producing and distributing goods and services.* Any relatively permanent group or society must provide and distribute desired goods and services to its members. Each society establishes a set of rules for the allocation of financial and other resources. The group must satisfy the needs of most members to some extent, or it will risk the possibility of discontent and ultimately disorder.

4. *Preserving order.* Throughout the world, indigenous and aboriginal peoples have struggled to protect themselves from outside invaders, with varying degrees of success. Failure to preserve order and defend against conquest leads to the death not only of a people, but also of a culture.

5. *Providing and maintaining a sense of purpose.* People must feel motivated to continue as members of a group or society in order to fulfill the first four requirements. After the September 11, 2001, airliner attacks in the United States, memorial services and community gatherings across the nation allowed people to affirm their allegiance to their country and bind up the psychic wounds inflicted by the terrorists. Patriotism, then, assists some people in developing and maintaining a sense of purpose. For others, tribal identities, religious values, or personal moral codes are especially meaningful. Whatever the motivator, in any society there remains one common and critical reality: if an individual does not have a sense of purpose, he or she has little reason to contribute to a society's survival.

Celebrating Remembrance Day may help to encourage patriotism and create a sense of purpose among Canadians.

This list of functional prerequisites does not specify *how* a society and its corresponding social institutions will perform each task. For example, one society may protect itself from external attack by amassing a frightening arsenal of weaponry, while another may make determined efforts to remain neutral in world politics and to promote cooperative relationships with its neighbours. No matter what its particular strategy, any society or relatively permanent group must attempt to satisfy all these functional prerequisites for survival. If it fails on even one condition, the society runs the risk of extinction.

Conflict View Conflict theorists do not agree with the functionalist approach to social institutions. Although proponents of both perspectives agree that social institutions are organized to meet basic social needs, conflict theorists object to the idea that the outcome is necessarily efficient and desirable.

From a conflict perspective, the present organization of social institutions is no accident. Major institutions, such as education, help to maintain the privileges of the most powerful individuals and groups within a society, while contributing to the powerlessness of others. To give one example, public schools in Canada are financed largely through property taxes. This arrangement allows more affluent areas to provide their children with better-equipped schools and better-paid teachers than low-income areas can afford. As a result, children from prosperous communities are better prepared to compete academically than children from impoverished communities. The structure of the nation's educational system permits and even promotes such unequal treatment of schoolchildren.

Conflict theorists argue that social institutions, such as education, have an inherently conservative nature. Without question, it has been difficult to implement educational reforms in Canada that promote equal opportunity—whether these reforms are increased access to English as a second language instruction or the inclusion of more students with disabilities in the classroom. From a functionalist perspective, social change can be dysfunctional, since it often leads to instability. However, from a conflict point of view, one might ask why we should preserve the existing social structure if it is unfair and discriminatory.

Feminist Views Feminist thinkers, such as Patricia Hill Collins (2000), argue that social institutions operate in gendered and racist environments. In schools, offices, and governmental institutions, assumptions about what people can do reflect the sexism and racism of the larger society. For instance, some people may assume that women cannot make tough decisions—even women in the top echelons of corporate management. Others might assume that all Aboriginal students at top universities in Canada represent equity policy admissions. Inequality based on gender, class, race, and ethnicity thrives in such an environment—to which we might add discrimination based on age, physical disability, and sexual orientation. The truth of this assertion can be seen in routine decisions by employers on how to advertise jobs as well as whether to provide fringe benefits, such as childcare and parental leave.

Liberal feminists, or equality feminists, stress these types of benefits as a means of strengthening employment opportunities for women, thus promoting gender equality. Radical feminists, however, believe that a much more fundamental change must occur throughout the various social institutions in order to achieve gender equality: the elimination of patriarchy (the set of social relations that maintains male dominance).

::: use your sociological *imagination* :::

Would social networks be more important to a migrant worker in British Columbia than to someone with political and social clout? Why or why not?

Interactionist View   Social institutions affect our everyday behaviour, whether we are driving down the street or waiting in a long shopping line. Sociologist Mitchell Duneier (1994a, 1994b) studied the social behaviour of the word processors, all women, who work in the service centre of a large Chicago law firm. Duneier was interested in the informal social norms that emerged in this work environment and the rich social network these female employees created.

The Network Center, as it is called, is a single, windowless room in a large office building where the law firm occupies seven floors. It is staffed by two shifts of word processors, who work either from 4:00 P.M. to midnight or from midnight to 8:00 A.M. Each word processor works in a cubicle with just enough room for her keyboard, terminal, printer, and telephone. Work assignments for the word processors are placed in a central basket and then completed according to precise procedures.

At first glance, we might think that these women labour with little social contact, apart from limited breaks and occasional conversations with their supervisor. However, drawing on the interactionist perspective, Duneier learned that despite working in a large office, these women find private moments to talk (often in the halls or outside the washroom) and share a critical view of the law firm's lawyers and day-shift secretaries. Indeed, the word processors routinely suggest that their assignments represent work that the "lazy" secretaries should have completed during the normal workday. Duneier (1994b) tells of one word processor who resented the lawyers' superior attitude and pointedly refused to recognize or speak with any lawyer who would not address her by name.

Interactionist theorists emphasize that our social behaviour is conditioned by the roles and statuses we accept, the groups to which we belong, and the institutions within which we function. For example, the social roles associated with being a judge occur within the larger context of the criminal justice system. The status of "judge" stands in relation to other statuses, such as lawyer, plaintiff, defendant, and witness, as well as to the social institution of government. Although courts and jails have great symbolic importance, the judicial system derives its continued significance from the roles people carry out in social interactions (Berger and Luckmann 1966).

Social institutions affect the way we behave. How might these teens socializing in a mall in South Korea interact differently in school or at home?

5.3 What Does a Global Perspective on Social Structure Look Like?

Modern societies are complex, especially compared to earlier social arrangements. Sociologists Émile Durkheim, Ferdinand Tönnies, and Gerhard Lenski developed ways to contrast modern societies with simpler forms of social structure.

Durkheim's Mechanical and Organic Solidarity

In *Division of Labor* ([1893] 1933), Durkheim argued that social structure depends on the division of labour in a society—in other words, on the manner in which tasks are performed. Thus, a task such as providing food can be carried out almost totally by one individual, or it can be divided among many people. The latter pattern is typical of modern societies, in which the cultivation, processing, distribution, and retailing of a single food item are performed by literally hundreds of people.

In societies in which there is minimal division of labour, a collective consciousness develops that emphasizes group solidarity. Durkheim termed this collective frame of mind **mechanical solidarity**, implying that all individuals perform the same tasks. In this type of society, no one needs to ask, "What do your parents do?" since all are engaged in similar work. Each person prepares food, hunts, makes clothing, builds homes, and so forth. Because people have few options regarding what to do with their lives, there is little concern for individual needs. Instead, the group is the dominating force in society. Both social interaction and negotiation are based on close, intimate, face-to-face social contacts. Since there is little specialization, there are few social roles.

As societies become more technological, they rely on greater division of labour and no individual can go it alone. Dependence on others becomes essential for group survival. In Durkheim's terms, mechanical solidarity is replaced by organic solidarity, a collective consciousness resting on the need a society's members have for one another. Durkheim chose the term organic solidarity because in his view, individuals become interdependent in much the same way as organs of the human body.

Tönnies's *Gemeinschaft* and *Gesellschaft*

Ferdinand Tönnies (1855–1936) was appalled by the rise of an industrial city in his native Germany during the late 1800s. In his view, the city marked a dramatic change from the ideal of a close-knit community, which Tönnies termed a *Gemeinschaft*, to that of an impersonal mass society, known as a *Gesellschaft* (Tönnies [1887] 1988).

The **Gemeinschaft** (pronounced guh-MINE-shoft) is typical of rural life. It is a small community in which people have similar backgrounds and life experiences. Virtually everyone knows one another, and social interactions are intimate and familiar, almost as among kinfolk.

Social control in the *Gemeinschaft* is maintained through informal means such as moral persuasion, gossip, and even gestures. These techniques work effectively because people genuinely care how others feel about them. Social change is relatively limited in the *Gemeinschaft*; the lives of members of one generation may be quite similar to those of their grandparents.

In contrast, the **Gesellschaft** (pronounced guh-ZELL-shoft) is a community that is characteristic of modern urban life. In this community, most people are strangers who feel little in common with other residents. Social control rests on more formal techniques, such as laws and legally defined punishments. Social change is an important aspect of life in the *Gesellschaft*; it can be strikingly evident even within a single generation.

Table 5-2 summarizes the differences between the *Gemeinschaft* and the *Gesellschaft*. Sociologists have used these terms to compare social structures that stress close relationships with those that emphasize less personal ties. It is easy to view the *Gemeinschaft* with nostalgia, as a far better way of life than the rat race of contemporary existence. However, the more intimate relationships of the *Gemeinschaft* come at a price. The prejudice and discrimination found there can be quite confining; ascribed statuses such as family background often outweigh a person's unique talents and achievements. In addition, the *Gemeinschaft* tends to distrust individuals who seek to be creative or just to be different.

Lenski's Sociocultural Evolution Approach

Sociologist Gerhard Lenski (born 1924) takes a very different view of society and social structure. Rather than distinguishing between two opposite types of society, as Tönnies did, Lenski sees human societies as undergoing a process of change characterized by a dominant pattern known as **sociocultural evolution**. This term refers to long-term trends in societies resulting from the interplay of continuity, innovation, and selection (Nolan and Lenski 2009:361).

In Lenski's view, a society's level of technology is critical to the way it is organized. Lenski defines *technology* as "cultural information about the ways in which the material resources of the environment may be used to satisfy human needs and desires" (Nolan and Lenski 2009:361). The available technology does not completely define the form that a particular society and its social structure take. Nevertheless, a low level of technology may limit the degree to which a society can depend on such things as irrigation or complex machinery. As technology advances, Lenski writes, a community changes from a pre-industrial to an industrial and finally a post-industrial society.

table **5-2** **Comparison of the *Gemeinschaft* and *Gesellschaft*** summing**UP**

Gemeinschaft	Gesellschaft
Rural life typifies this form.	Urban life typifies this form.
People share a feeling of community that results from their similar backgrounds and life experiences.	People have little sense of commonality. Their differences appear more striking than their similarities.
Social interactions are intimate and familiar.	Social interactions are likely to be impersonal and task-specific.
People maintain a spirit of cooperation and unity of will.	Self-interest dominates.
Tasks and personal relationships cannot be separated.	The task being performed is paramount; relationships are subordinate.
People place little emphasis on individual privacy.	Privacy is valued.
Informal social control predominates.	Formal social control is evident.
People are not very tolerant of deviance.	People are more tolerant of deviance.
Emphasis is on ascribed statuses.	Emphasis is on achieved statuses.
Social change is relatively limited.	Social change is very evident, even within a generation.

Think about It
How would you classify the communities with which you are familiar? Are they more *Gemeinschaft* or *Gesellschaft*?

Pre-industrial societies still exist in some remote areas. These indigenous people are from the Envira region of the Amazon rain forest, in Brazil.

Pre-industrial Societies   How does a pre-industrial society organize its economy? If we know that, we can categorize the society. The first type of pre-industrial society to emerge in human history was the **hunting-and-gathering society**, in which people simply relied on whatever foods and fibres that were readily available. Technology in such societies is minimal. Organized into groups, people move constantly in search of food. There is little division of labour into specialized tasks.

Hunting-and-gathering societies are composed of small, widely dispersed groups. Each group consists almost entirely of people who are related to one another. As a result, kinship ties are the source of authority and influence, and the social institution of the family takes on a particularly important role. Tönnies would certainly view such societies as examples of the *Gemeinschaft*.

Social differentiation within the hunting-and-gathering society is based on ascribed statuses such as gender, age, and family background. Since resources are scarce, there is relatively little inequality in terms of material goods. By the close of the twentieth century, hunting-and-gathering societies had virtually disappeared (Nolan and Lenski 2009).

Horticultural societies, in which people plant seeds and crops rather than merely subsist on available foods, emerged roughly 10 000 to 12 000 years ago. Members of horticultural societies are much less nomadic than hunters and gatherers. They place greater emphasis on the production of tools and household objects. Yet technology remains limited in these societies, whose members cultivate crops with the aid of digging sticks or hoes (Wilford 1997).

The last stage of pre-industrial development is the **agrarian society**, which emerged about 5000 years ago. As in horticultural societies, members of agrarian societies are engaged primarily in the production of food. However, new technological innovations such as the plow allow farmers to dramatically increase their crop yields. They can cultivate the same fields over generations, allowing the emergence of larger settlements.

The agrarian society continues to rely on the physical power of humans and animals (as opposed to mechanical power). Nevertheless, its social structure has more carefully defined roles than that of horticultural societies. Individuals focus on specialized tasks, such as the repair of fishing nets or blacksmithing.

Table 5-3 summarizes Lenski's three stages of sociocultural evolution, as well as the stages that follow, which are described next.

Industrial Societies   Although the Industrial Revolution did not topple monarchs, it produced changes every bit as significant as those resulting from political revolutions.

table **5-3** Stages of Sociocultural Evolution

Societal Type	First Appearance	Characteristics
Hunting-and-gathering	Beginning of human life	Nomadic; reliance on readily available food and fibres
Horticultural	About 10 000 to 12 000 years ago	More settled; development of agriculture and limited technology
Agrarian	About 5000 years ago	Larger, more stable settlements; improved technology and increased crop yields
Industrial	1760–1950	Reliance on mechanical power and new sources of energy; centralized workplaces; economic interdependence; formal education
Post-industrial	1960s	Reliance on services, especially the processing and control of information; expanded middle class
Postmodern	Latter 1970s	High technology; mass consumption of consumer goods and media images; cross-cultural integration

The Industrial Revolution, which took place largely in England from 1760 to 1830, was a scientific revolution focused on the application of nonanimal (mechanical) sources of power to labour tasks. An **industrial society** is a society that depends on mechanization to produce its goods and services. Industrial societies rely on new inventions that facilitate agricultural and industrial production, and on new sources of energy, such as steam.

As the Industrial Revolution proceeded, a new form of social structure emerged. Many societies underwent an irrevocable shift from an agrarian-oriented economy to an industrial base. No longer did an individual or a family typically make an entire product. Instead, specialization of tasks and manufacturing of goods became increasingly common. Workers, generally men, but also women and even children, left their family homesteads to work in central locations such as factories.

The process of industrialization had distinctive social consequences. Families and communities could not continue to function as self-sufficient units. Individuals, villages, and regions began to exchange goods and services and to become interdependent. As people came to rely on the labour of members of other communities, the family lost its unique position as the source of power and authority. The need for specialized knowledge led to more formalized schooling, and education emerged as a social institution distinct from the family.

Post-industrial and Postmodern Societies When Lenski first proposed the sociocultural evolutionary approach in the 1960s, he paid relatively little attention to how maturing industrialized societies may change with the emergence of even more advanced forms of technology. More recently, he and other sociologists have studied the significant changes in the occupational structure of industrial societies as they shift from manufacturing to service economies. In the 1970s, sociologist Daniel Bell wrote about the technologically advanced **post-industrial society**, whose economic system is engaged primarily in the processing and control of information. The main output of a post-industrial society is services rather than manufactured goods. Jobs in fields such as advertising, public relations, human resources, and computer information systems would be typical of a post-industrial society (Bell 1999).

Bell views the transition from industrial to post-industrial society as a positive development. He sees a general decline in organized working-class groups and a rise in interest groups concerned with national issues such as health, education, and the environment. Bell's outlook is functionalist, because he portrays the post-industrial society as basically consensual. As organizations and interest groups engage in an open and competitive process of decision making, Bell believes, the level of conflict among diverse groups will diminish, thus strengthening social stability.

Conflict theorists take issue with Bell's functionalist analysis of the post-industrial society. For example, Michael Harrington (1980), who alerted North America to the problems of the poor in his book *The Other America*, questioned the significance that Bell attached to the growing class of white-collar workers. Harrington followed in the tradition of Marx by arguing that conflict between social classes will continue in the post-industrial society.

Sociologists have recently gone beyond discussion of the post-industrial society to the model of the postmodern society. As we discussed in Chapter 1, a **postmodern society** is a technologically sophisticated society that is preoccupied with consumer goods and media images and which consumes goods and information on a mass scale. Postmodern theorists take a global perspective, noting the ways in which particular aspects of culture cross national boundaries. For example, George Ritzer proposed a McDonaldization thesis where the principles of the fast-food company—"efficiency, calculability, predictability, control through the substitution of technology for people, and paradoxically, the irrationality of rationality" (e.g., people waiting in long lines, often in cars, for "fast food")—would spread to other sectors and around the world (2007:263).

Durkheim, Tönnies, and Lenski present three distinct visions of society's social structure. While they do differ, each is useful, and this book draws on all three. Lenski's sociocultural evolutionary approach emphasizes a historical perspective. It does not picture

Believe it or not, this photograph was taken in Japan, at Universal Studios theme park in Osaka. In a postmodern society, people consume goods, information, and media images en masse. Universal's park is popularizing U.S. media images abroad, illustrating another characteristic of postmodern societies, globalization.

different types of social structures co-existing within the same society. Consequently, one would not expect a single society to include hunters and gatherers along with a postmodern culture. In contrast, Durkheim's and Tönnies's theories allow for the existence of different types of community—such as a *Gemeinschaft* and a *Gesellschaft*—in the same society. Thus, a rural Manitoba community located 150 kilometres from Winnipeg can be linked to the city by modern information technology. The main difference between these two theories is a matter of emphasis. While Tönnies emphasized the over-riding concern in each type of community—one's own self-interest or the well-being of the larger society—Durkheim emphasized the division (or lack of division) of labour.

The work of these three thinkers reminds us that a major focus of sociology has been to identify changes in social structure and the consequences for human behaviour. At the macro level, we see society shifting to more advanced forms of technology. The social structure becomes increasingly complex, and new social institutions emerge to assume some functions that once were performed by the family. On the micro level, these changes affect the nature of social interactions. Each individual takes on multiple social roles, and people come to rely more on social networks and less on kinship ties. As the social structure becomes more complex, people's relationships become more impersonal, transient, and fragmented.

5.4 How Are Organizations Structured?

Formal Organizations and Bureaucracies

As contemporary societies have shifted to more advanced forms of technology and their social structures have become more complex, our lives have become increasingly dominated by large secondary groups referred to as *formal organizations*. A **formal organization** is a group designed for a special purpose and structured for maximum efficiency. Canada Post, McDonald's, and the Vancouver Symphony are examples of formal organizations. Though organizations vary in their size, specificity of goals, and degree of efficiency, they are all structured to facilitate the management of large-scale operations. They also have a bureaucratic form of organization, which we describe in the next section.

In our society, formal organizations fulfill an enormous variety of personal and societal needs, shaping the lives of every one of us. In fact, formal organizations have become such a dominant force that we must create organizations to supervise other organizations, such as the Ontario Securities Commission (OSC) to regulate brokerage companies. While it sounds much more exciting to say that we live in the "computer age" than to admit that ours is the "age of formal organization," the latter is probably a more accurate description of our times (Azumi and Hage 1972; Etzioni 1964).

Ascribed statuses such as gender can influence how we see ourselves within formal organizations. For example, a study of women lawyers in some of the largest law firms found significant differences in the women's self-images, depending on the relative presence or absence of women in positions of power. In firms in which fewer than 15 percent of partners were women, the female lawyers were likely to believe that "feminine" traits were strongly devalued, and that masculinity was equated with success. As one female lawyer put it, "Let's face it, this is a man's environment, and it's sort of Jock City, especially at my firm." Women in firms where female lawyers were better represented in positions of power had a stronger desire for, and higher expectations of, promotion (Ely 1995:619).

Characteristics of a Bureaucracy

A **bureaucracy** is a component of formal organization that uses rules and hierarchical ranking to achieve efficiency. Rows of desks staffed by seemingly faceless people, endless lines and forms, impossibly complex language, and frustrating encounters with red tape—all these unpleasant images have combined to make *bureaucracy* a dirty word and an easy target in political campaigns. As a result, few people want to identify their occupation as "bureaucrat," despite the fact that all of us perform various bureaucratic tasks. In an industrial society, elements of bureaucracy enter into almost every occupation.

Max Weber ([1913–1922] 1947) first directed researchers to the significance of bureaucratic structure. He developed an *ideal type* of bureaucracy that would reflect the most characteristic aspects of all human organizations. By ideal type, Weber meant a construct or model for evaluating specific cases. In actuality, perfect bureaucracies do not exist; no real-world organization corresponds exactly to Weber's ideal type. Weber proposed that whether the purpose is to run a temple, a corporation, or an army, the ideal bureaucracy displays five basic characteristics. A discussion of those characteristics, as well as the dysfunctions of a bureaucracy, follows.

1. *Division of labour.* Specialized experts perform specific tasks. In your college or university bureaucracy, the admissions officer does not do the job of registrar; the guidance counsellor doesn't see to the maintenance of buildings. By working at a specific task, people are more likely to become highly skilled and carry out a job with maximum efficiency. This emphasis on specialization is so basic a part of our lives that we may not realize it is a fairly recent development in Western culture.

    The downside of division of labour is that the fragmentation of work into smaller and smaller tasks can divide workers and remove any connection they might feel to the overall objective of the bureaucracy. In *The Communist Manifesto* (written in 1848), Karl Marx and Friedrich Engels charged that the capitalist system reduces workers to a mere "appendage of the machine" (Feuer 1989). Such a work arrangement, they wrote, produces extreme **alienation**—a condition of estrangement or dissociation from the surrounding society. According to both Marx and conflict theorists, restricting workers to very small tasks also weakens their job security, since new employees can be easily trained to replace them.

    Although division of labour has certainly enhanced the performance of many complex bureaucracies, in some cases it can lead to **trained incapacity**; that is, workers become so specialized that they develop blind spots and fail to notice obvious problems.

Sometimes, the bureaucratic division of labour can have tragic results. In the wake of the coordinated attacks on the World Trade Center and the Pentagon on September 11, 2001, many wondered aloud how the FBI and CIA could have failed to work together to detect the terrorists' elaborately planned operation. The problem, in part, turned out to be the division of labour between the FBI, which focuses on domestic matters, and the CIA, which operates overseas. Officials at these intelligence-gathering organizations, both of which are huge bureaucracies, are well-known for jealously guarding information from one another. Subsequent investigations revealed that they knew about Osama bin Laden and his al-Qaeda terrorist network in the early 1990s. Unfortunately, five federal U.S. agencies—the CIA, FBI, National Security Agency, Defense Intelligence Agency, and National Reconnaissance Office—failed to share their leads on the network. Although the hijacking of the four commercial airliners used in the massive attacks may not have been preventable, the bureaucratic division of labour definitely hindered efforts to defend against terrorism, undermining U.S. national security.

2. *Hierarchy of authority.* Bureaucracies follow the principle of hierarchy; that is, each position is under the supervision of a higher authority. A president heads a college or university bureaucracy; he or she selects members of the administration, who in turn hire their own staff. In the Roman Catholic Church, the pope is the supreme authority; under him are cardinals, bishops, and so forth.

3. *Written rules and regulations.* What if your sociology professor gave your classmate an "A" for having such a friendly smile? You might think that wasn't fair, that it was against the rules.

   Rules and regulations, as we all know, are an important characteristic of bureaucracies. Ideally, through such procedures, a bureaucracy ensures uniform performance of every task. Thus, your classmate cannot receive an "A" for a nice smile, because the rules guarantee that all students will receive essentially the same treatment.

   Through written rules and regulations, bureaucracies generally offer employees clear standards for an adequate (or exceptional) performance. In addition, procedures provide a valuable sense of continuity in a bureaucracy. Individual workers will come and go, but the structure and past records of the organization give it a life of its own that outlives the services of any one bureaucrat.

   Of course, rules and regulations can overshadow the larger goals of an organization to the point that they become dysfunctional. What if a hospital emergency room physician failed to treat a seriously injured person because he or she failed to present a health-care card? If blindly applied, rules no longer serve as a means to achieving an objective, but instead become important (and perhaps too important) in their own right. Robert Merton (1968) used the term **goal displacement** to refer to overzealous conformity to official regulations.

4. *Impersonality.* Max Weber wrote that in a bureaucracy, work is carried out *sine ira et studio*, "without hatred or passion." Bureaucratic norms dictate that officials perform their duties without giving personal consideration to people as individuals. Although this norm is intended to guarantee equal treatment for each person, it also contributes to the often cold and uncaring feeling associated with modern organizations. Frequently, bureaucratic impersonality produces frustration and disaffection. Today, even small organizations screen callers with electronic menus.

5. *Employment based on technical qualifications.* Within the ideal bureaucracy, hiring is based on technical qualifications rather than on favouritism, and performance is measured against specific standards. Written personnel policies dictate who gets promoted, and people often have a right to appeal if they believe that particular rules have been violated. Such procedures protect bureaucrats against arbitrary dismissal, provide a measure of security, and encourage loyalty to the organization.

   In this sense, the "impersonal" bureaucracy can be considered an improvement over nonbureaucratic organizations. College and university faculty members, for example, are, ideally, hired and promoted according to their professional qualifications, including degrees earned and research published, rather than because of whom they know. Once they are granted tenure, academics' jobs are protected against the whims of officialdom.

   Although any bureaucracy will, ideally, value technical and professional competence, personnel decisions do not always follow that ideal pattern. Dysfunctions within bureaucracy have become well publicized, particularly because of the work of Laurence J. Peter. According to the **Peter Principle**, every employee within a hierarchy tends to rise to his or her level of incompetence (Peter and Hull 1969). This hypothesis, which has not been directly or systematically tested, reflects a possible dysfunctional outcome of advancement on the basis of merit. Talented people receive promotion after promotion, until sadly, some of them finally achieve positions that they cannot handle with their usual competence (Blau and Meyer 1987).

Table 5-4 summarizes the five characteristics of bureaucracy. These characteristics, developed by Max Weber more than 80 years ago, describe an ideal type rather than an actual bureaucracy. Not every formal organization will possess all five of Weber's characteristics. In fact, wide variation exists among actual bureaucratic organizations.

Bureaucracy pervades modern life. Through McDonaldization, bureaucratization has grown unwieldy (see Chapter 3). As Box 5-3 shows, the McDonald's organization provides an excellent illustration of Weber's concept of bureaucracy.

Bureaucratization as a Process Have you ever had to speak to 10 or 12 individuals in a corporation or government agency just to find out which official has jurisdiction over a particular problem? While on the telephone, have you ever been transferred from one department to another until you finally hung up in disgust? Sociologists have used the term **bureaucratization** to refer to the process by which a group, organization, or social movement becomes increasingly bureaucratic.

table 5-4 Characteristics of a Bureaucracy

Characteristic	Positive Consequence	Negative Consequence	
		For the Individual	For the Organization
Division of labour	Produces efficiency in a large-scale corporation	Produces trained incapacity	Produces a narrow perspective
Hierarchy of authority	Clarifies who is in command	Deprives employees of a voice in decision making	Permits concealment of mistakes
Written rules and regulations	Let workers know what is expected of them	Stifle initiative and imagination	Lead to goal displacement
Impersonality	Reduces bias	Contributes to feelings of alienation	Discourages loyalty to company
Employment based on technical qualifications	Discourages favouritism and reduces petty rivalries	Discourages ambition to improve oneself elsewhere	Fosters Peter Principle to operate

Normally, we think of bureaucratization in terms of large organizations. But bureaucratization can also take place within smaller businesses and groups. Sociologist Jennifer Bickham Mendez (1998) studied domestic houseworkers employed by a U.S. franchise. She found that housekeeping tasks were minutely defined, to the point that employees had to follow 22 written steps for cleaning a bathroom. Complaints and special requests went not to the workers, but to an office-based manager.

Oligarchy: Rule by a Few   Conflict theorists have examined the bureaucratization of social movements. The German sociologist Robert Michels (1915) studied socialist parties and labour unions in Europe before World War I and found that such organizations were becoming increasingly bureaucratic. The emerging leaders of the organizations—even some of the most radical—had a vested interest in clinging to power. If they lost their leadership posts, they would have to return to full-time work as manual labourers.

Through his research, Michels originated the idea of the **iron law of oligarchy**—it describes how even a democratic organization will eventually develop into a bureaucracy ruled by a few, which is called an oligarchy. Why do oligarchies emerge? People who achieve leadership roles usually have the skills, knowledge, or charismatic appeal (as Weber noted) to direct, if not control, others. Michels argued that the rank and file of a movement or organization look to leaders for direction and thereby reinforce the process of rule by a few. In addition, members of an oligarchy are strongly motivated to maintain their leadership roles, privileges, and power.

Michels's insights continue to be relevant today. Contemporary labour unions in Canada, the United States, and Western Europe bear little resemblance to those organized spontaneously by exploited workers. Conflict theorists have pointed to the longevity of union leaders, who are not always responsive to the needs and demands of the membership, and seem more concerned with maintaining their own positions and power. (The social policy section at the end of this chapter focuses on the status of labour unions today.)

Bureaucracy and Organizational Culture

How does bureaucratization affect the average individual who works in an organization? The early theorists of formal organizations tended to neglect this question. Max Weber, for example, focused on management personnel within bureaucracies, but had little to say about workers in industry or clerks in government agencies.

According to the **classical theory** of formal organizations, also known as the **scientific management approach**, workers are motivated almost entirely by economic rewards. This theory stresses that only the physical constraints on workers limit their productivity. Therefore, workers may be treated as a resource, much like the machines that began to replace them in the twentieth century. Under the scientific management approach, managerial types attempt to achieve maximum work efficiency through scientific planning, established performance standards, and careful supervision of workers and production. Planning involves efficiency studies but not studies of workers' attitudes or job satisfaction.

Not until workers organized unions—and forced management to recognize that they were not objects—did theorists of formal organizations begin to revise the classical approach. Along with management and administrators, social scientists became aware that informal groups of workers have an important impact on organizations (Perrow 1986). An alternative way of considering bureaucratic dynamics, the **human relations approach**, emphasizes the role of people, communication, and participation in a bureaucracy. This type of analysis reflects the interest of interactionist theorists in small-group behaviour. Unlike planning under the scientific management approach, planning based on the human relations perspective focuses on workers' feelings, frustrations, and emotional need for job satisfaction.

The gradual move away from a sole focus on the physical aspects of getting the job done—and toward the concerns and needs of workers—led advocates of the human relations approach to stress the less formal aspects of bureaucratic structure. Informal groups and social networks within

5-3 McDonald's and the Worldwide Bureaucratization of Society

In his book *The McDonaldization of Society*, sociologist George Ritzer notes the enormous influence of a well-known fast-food organization on modern-day culture and social life. Ritzer defines *McDonaldization* as "the process by which the principles of the fast-food restaurant are coming to dominate more and more sectors of U.S. society as well as of the rest of the world" (Ritzer 2004:1). Through this process, the business principles on which the fast-food industry is founded—efficiency, calculability, predictability, and control—have changed not only the way U.S. citizens do business and run their organizations, but also the way they live their lives. For example, busy families have come to rely on the takeout meals served up by fast-food establishments, and social groups from adolescents to senior citizens now meet at McDonald's.

Max Weber's five characteristics of bureaucracy are apparent in McDonald's restaurants, as well as in the global corporation behind them. Food preparation and order taking reflect a painstaking *division of labour*, implemented by a *hierarchy of authority* that stretches from the food workers up to the shift manager and store operator, and ultimately to the corporate board of directors. Store operators learn the company's *written rules and regulations*, which govern even the amount of ketchup or mustard placed on a hamburger, at Hamburger University (a mandatory training program run by McDonald's). Little bonding occurs between servers and customers, creating a pervasive sense of *impersonality*. Together with McDonald's cookie-cutter architectural designs, this lack of personal character tends to disguise a restaurant's locale—not just the town or city it serves, but often the country or continent as well. Finally, employees are expected to have specific *technical qualifications*, although most of the skills they need to perform their routine tasks can be learned in a brief training period.

The real significance of McDonaldization is that it is not confined to the food-service industry or to coffee outlets like Starbucks. Worldwide, the giant fast-food establishment's brand of predictability, efficiency, and dependence on

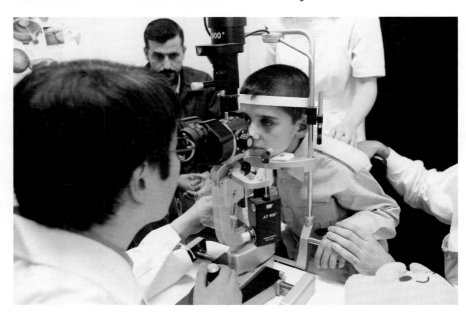

The worldwide success of highly efficient fast-food operations has led to the bureaucratization of many other services including eye care and other forms of medical treatment.

non-human technology have become customary in a number of services, ranging from medical care to wedding planning to education. Even sporting events reflect the influence of this kind of bureaucratization. Around the world, sports stadiums—which are now customarily given forgettable corporate names by sponsors who bid for "naming rights"—are becoming increasingly similar, both physically and in the way they present the sport to spectators. Swipe cards, "sports city" garages and parking lots, and automated ticket sales maximize efficiency. All seats offer spectators an unrestricted view, and a big screen guarantees them access to instant replays. Scores, player statistics, and attendance figures are updated automatically by computer and displayed on an automated scoreboard. Spectator enthusiasm is manufactured through digital displays urging applause or rhythmic chanting. At food counters, refreshments include well-known brands whose customer loyalty has been nourished by advertisers

for decades. And, of course, the merchandising of teams' and even players' names and images is highly controlled.

McDonald's reliance on the five characteristics of bureaucracy is not revolutionary. What is new is the bureaucratization of services and life events that once were highly individualized, at times even spontaneous. More and more, societies around the globe are becoming McDonaldized.

Apply the Theory

1. Do you patronize McDonald's and other fast-food establishments? If so, what features of these restaurants do you appreciate? Do you have any complaints about them?
2. Analyze life at your college or university using Weber's model of bureaucracy. What elements of McDonaldization do you see? Do you wish life were less McDonaldized?

Sources: Ormond 2005; Ritzer 2008, 2011.

---

organizations develop partly as a result of people's ability to create more direct forms of communication than under the formal structure. Charles Page (1946) used the term *bureaucracy's other face* to refer to the unofficial activities and interactions that are such a basic part of daily organizational life.

A series of classic studies illustrates the value of the human relations approach. The Hawthorne studies alerted sociologists to the fact that research subjects may alter their behaviour to match the experimenter's expectations. The major focus of the Hawthorne studies, however, was the role of social factors in workers' productivity. One aspect of the research concerned the switchboard-bank wiring room, where 14 men were making parts of switches for telephone equipment. The researchers discovered that these men were producing far below their physical capabilities. The discovery was especially surprising because the men would have earned more money if they had produced more parts.

What accounted for such an unexpected restriction of output? The men feared that if they produced switch parts at a faster rate, their pay rate might be reduced, or some of them might lose their jobs. As a result, this group of workers had established their own (unofficial) norm for a proper day's work and created informal rules and sanctions to enforce it. Yet management was unaware of these practices and actually believed that the men were working as hard as they could (Roethlisberger and Dickson 1939).

Today, research on formal organizations is following new avenues: first, the recent arrival of women and visible minority group members in a small proportion of high-level management positions; second, the decision-making groups that lie outside the top ranks of leadership in large corporations; third, the loss of fixed boundaries in organizations that have out-sourced key functions; fourth, the role of the Internet and virtual worlds in influencing business and consumer preferences. Though research still embraces Max Weber's insights, then, it has gone well beyond them (Hamm 2007; Kleiner 2003; Scott and Davis 2007).

5.5 How Has the Workplace Changed?

Weber's work on bureaucracy and Michels's thinking on oligarchy are still applicable to the organizational structure and culture of the workplace. But today's factories and offices are undergoing rapid, profound changes unanticipated a century or more ago. Besides the far-reaching impact of technological advances such as computerization, workers must cope with organizational restructuring. In this section, we detail the dramatic changes evident in today's workplace.

Organizational Restructuring

To some extent, individual businesses, community organizations, and government agencies are always changing, if only because of personnel turnover. But since the late twentieth century, formal organizations have been experimenting with new ways of getting the job done, some of which have significantly altered the workplace.

Collective decision making, or the active involvement of employee problem-solving groups in corporate management, first became popular in North America in the 1980s. Management gurus had noted the dazzling success of Japanese automobile and consumer products manufacturers. In studying these companies, they found that problem-solving groups were one key to success. At first, such groups concentrated on small problems at specific points in the production line. But today, these groups often cross departmental and divisional boundaries to attack problems rooted in the bureaucratic division of labour. Thus, they require significant adjustment by employees long used to working in a bureaucracy.

Another innovation in the workplace, called *minimal hierarchy*, replaces the traditional bureaucratic hierarchy of authority with a flatter organizational structure. Minimal hierarchy offers workers greater access to those in authority, giving them an opportunity to voice concerns that might not be heard in a traditional bureaucracy. This new organizational structure is thought to minimize the potential for costly and dangerous bureaucratic oversights.

Finally, organizational *work teams* have become increasingly common, even in smaller organizations. There are two types of work team. *Project teams* address ongoing issues, such as workplace health and safety. *Task forces* pursue non-recurring issues, such as a major building renovation. In both cases, team members are released to some degree from their regular duties in order to contribute to the organization-wide effort (Huff 2007; Scott and Davis 2007).

The common purpose of work teams, minimal hierarchy, and collective decision making is to empower workers. For that reason, these new organizational structures can be exciting for the employees who participate in them. But these innovations rarely touch the vast numbers of workers who perform routine jobs in factories and office buildings. By 2008, it is estimated that roughly 33 percent of the total U.S. non-farm workforce will be part-time or temporary; in Canada, approximately 27 percent of current workers are in part-time or temporary jobs (Canadian Centre for Policy Alternatives [CCPA] 2007). Organizational innovations such as project teams and work teams, no doubt, will have little relevance for part-time and temporary workers who are increasingly being denied their share of the economic pie (CCPA 2007).

The Postmodern Job

Increasingly, in many industrial countries, workers are turning into telecommuters. **Telecommuters** are employees who work full-time or part-time at home rather than in an outside office, and who are linked to their supervisors and colleagues through computer terminals, phone lines, and fax machines. In countries such as Japan and the United States, telecommuting has become part of national policy. In 2007, Japan announced plans to double the number of telecommuters by 2010 (Song 2007). A Statistics Canada report revealed that the number of telecommuters in this country actually dipped slightly in 2005, after increasing steadily from 1991 to 2000. The report conjectured that the use of laptops, BlackBerrys, and mobile phones and the growing proliferation of communication centres may have contributed to this dip, allowing people to work in a variety of locations, in addition to the home (Statistics Canada 2007k). Despite the growing amount of time Canadians spend travelling to and from work and the environmental impact of this travel, the Canadian government has not made telecommuting a national priority.

What are the social implications of a shift toward the virtual office? From an interactionist perspective, the workplace is a major source of friendships; restricting face-to-face social opportunities could destroy the trust that is created by "handshake agreements." Thus, telecommuting may move society further along the continuum from *Gemeinschaft* to

Telecommuters are linked to their supervisors and colleagues through computers, mobile devices, phones, and fax machines.

::: use your sociological *imagination* :::

If your first full-time job after college or university involved telecommuting, what do you think would be the advantages and disadvantages of working out of a home office? Do you think you would be satisfied as a telecommuter? Why or why not?

Gesellschaft. On a more positive note, telecommuting may be the first social change that pulls fathers and mothers back into the home, after years of being pushed out. On the list of Canada's top 100 employers were companies of all sizes that incorporated telecommuting and other flexible options into their workplace culture (Smolkin 2013). The 2013 announcement by Yahoo! CEO Marissa Mayer stating that she would be cancelling telecommuting programs was not typical of the general trend in workplace flexibility in Canada and the U.S. (Smolkin 2013).

Electronic communication in the workplace has generated a lot of heat lately. On the one hand, emailing is a convenient way to push messages around, especially with the copy button. It's democratic, too: lower-level employees are more likely to participate in email discussions than in face-to-face communications, giving organizations the benefit of their experience and views. But email doesn't convey body language, which in face-to-face communication can soften insensitive phrasing and make unpleasant messages (such as a reprimand) easier to take. It also leaves a permanent record, which can be a problem if messages are written thoughtlessly (DiMaggio et al. 2001). Email communication also runs the risk of being sent—unintentionally—to unanticipated recipients, such as in the case of a young Toronto man who, after applying for a government job in 2007, received an email from a lower-level government employee in which he was referred to in a racist manner. When the government worker emailed her colleague, she accidentally copied the message to the young job applicant as well. The premier of Ontario eventually called the young man to apologize on behalf of the provincial government (Diebel 2007).

Electronic communication has contributed significantly to the fragmentation of work. Today, productivity in the workplace is frequently hindered by email, pagers, cellphones, and pop-up windows, as well as face-to-face interruptions and cube drop-ins. In one observational study of office workers, researchers found that employees spent an average of only 11 minutes on any given project before being interrupted. Typically, 25 minutes passed before they returned to their original tasks. While multi-tasking may increase a person's efficiency in some situations, it has become an integral and not necessarily helpful feature of work for many employees (Mark et al. 2005; C. Thompson 2005).

Social Policy and Organizations

The State of the Unions

The Issue

How many people do you know who belong to a labour union? Chances are you can name fewer people than someone could 15 years ago. In 1991, unions represented 35.6 percent of workers in the Canadian economy; in 2011, they represented just 31.2 percent (Statistics Canada 2012). What has happened to diminish the representation for organized labour today? Have unions perhaps outlived their usefulness in a rapidly changing global economy dominated by the service industry? Are there differences between Canada and the United States in terms of legal impediments to union organization? Is Canada more labour-friendly than the United States?

figure 5-2 Labour Union Membership Worldwide

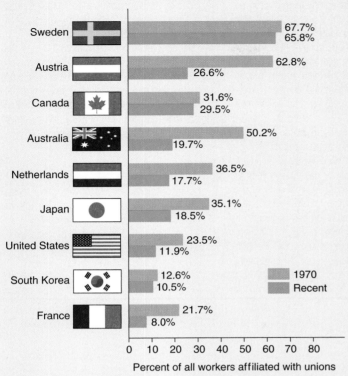

Country	1970	Recent
Sweden	67.7%	65.8%
Austria	62.8%	26.6%
Canada	31.6%	29.5%
Australia	50.2%	19.7%
Netherlands	36.5%	17.7%
Japan	35.1%	18.5%
United States	23.5%	11.9%
South Korea	12.6%	10.5%
France	21.7%	8.0%

Percent of all workers affiliated with unions

Note: Recent data from 2008–2010, except for Sweden and the Netherlands (2007).
Sources: Bureau of Labor Statistics 2011; New Unionism Network 2011; Visser 2006:45.

Think about It
What is the relationship between union membership and public or private sector employment in both Canada and the United States?

The Setting

Labour unions consist of organized workers sharing either the same skill (as in electronics) or the same employer (as in the case of postal employees). Unions began to emerge during the Industrial Revolution in England in the eighteenth century. Groups of workers banded together to extract concessions from employers, as well as to protect their positions. They frequently tried to protect their jobs by limiting entry to their occupation based on gender, race, ethnicity, citizenship, age, and sometimes rather arbitrary measures of skill levels. Generally, we see less of this protection of special interests, but individual labour unions are still often the target of charges of discrimination (as are employers) (Rosenfeld 2010).

The power of labour unions varies widely in different countries. In some, such as Britain and Mexico, unions play a key role in the foundation of governments. In others, such as Japan and Korea, their role in politics is very limited and even their ability to influence the private sector is relatively

weak. Stark differences exist between Canada and the United States in terms of union experiences (see Figure 5-2). Although both countries have much lower rates of unionization in the private sector than in the public sector, Canada's percentages of union membership in both sectors far exceed those in the United States. The United States also exhibits greater disparities between rates of unionization for men and women and between rates for full-time and part-time employees (U.S. Bureau of Labor Statistics 2004). The increase in rates of unionization for women in Canada, which Statistics Canada (2004a) has referred to as a profound transformation in Canadian union membership, has not been duplicated in the United States. Unions in Canada sometimes can have a significant influence on employers and elected officials, but their prominence may vary dramatically by type of industry and even region of the country. In 2011, Quebec was the most highly unionized province, while Alberta was the least.

Few people today would dispute the fact that the Canadian union movement is in transition. What accounts for this transition? Among the reasons offered are the following:

1. *The feminization of the movement.* In 1977, approximately 10 percent of female workers were unionized; by 2011, the number had risen to 32.4 percent (Statistics Canada 2012). According to Statistics Canada (2004a), the growth of women in unions can be attributed to such factors as the growing proportion of women in the paid labour force, their increased representation in the heavily unionized public sector, the rising unionization rate of part-time and temporary workers, and the expansion of unions into female-dominated and non-unionized or less unionized workplaces, such as the service sector.

2. *The rising rate of unionization of the public sector and the falling rate of unionization of*

the private sector. The rate of unionization of the public sector has remained relatively stable for the last 34 years, while the rate for the private sector has fallen from 26 percent to 17 percent.

3. *The waning influence of international unions headquartered outside Canada.* In 1962, unions with headquarters outside the country accounted for two-thirds of union membership in Canada; in 2007, the proportion had fallen to below one-third.

4. *The changing scope of union membership.* The largest inroads in union membership have occurred among women, public administration workers, and community service workers, while losses have been experienced among technical health workers (Statistics Canada 2004a; Statistics Canada 2007n; Statistics Canada 2012). Labour market trends like globalization, the increase of self-employment, and the rise of non-standard work has altered people's relationship with work and weakened their ability to unionize.

Sociological Insights

Both Marxists and functionalists would view unions as a logical response to the emergence of impersonal, large-scale, formal, and often alienating organizations. This view certainly characterized the growth of unions in major manufacturing industries with a sharp division of labour. However, as manufacturing has declined, unions have had to look elsewhere for growth (Statistics Canada 2004a).

Today, labour unions in North America and Europe bear little resemblance to those early unions organized spontaneously by exploited workers. In line with the oligarchic model developed by Robert Michels, unions have become increasingly bureaucratized under a self-serving leadership. Conflict theorists would point out that the longer union leaders are in office, the less responsive they are to the needs and demands of the rank and file and the more concerned they are with maintaining their own positions and power.

Yet research shows that under certain circumstances union leadership can change significantly. Smaller unions are vulnerable to changes in leaders, as are unions whose memberships shift in composition, such as going from being predominantly male to female.

Many union employees encounter role conflict. For example, they agree to provide a needed service and then organize a "strike" to withhold it. This role conflict is especially apparent in the so-called helping occupations: teaching, social work, nursing, law enforcement, and paramedics. These workers may feel torn between carrying out their professional responsibilities and enduring working conditions they find unacceptable.

Sociologists have observed another role conflict: employees who suddenly become "owners" of a business. Take the case of United Airlines (UAL).

Since 1994, the employees have owned the majority of shares of the company. They may have changed the slogan from "fly the friendly skies" to "fly our friendly skies," but tensions still prevail. Union after union within UAL has threatened to strike or has enacted slowdowns, even though the members constitute the major shareholders of the company. Obviously, although everybody agreed to call the workers "owners," the pilots, mechanics, airline attendants, and others did not act like owners, and UAL management did not treat them like owners (Zuckerman 2001).

Policy Initiatives

U.S. law grants workers the right to organize via unions. But that country is unique among industrial democracies in allowing employers to actively oppose their employees' decision to organize. Walmart, the largest employer in the United States—and the largest retailer in the world—is perhaps the most notable example of this (among its employees in the United States, that is). In China, where in 2013 Walmart had over 390 stores in over 150 cities, the story is quite different. Here, Walmart officials announced that if the employees decided to form a union, their wishes would be respected, as long as the union was affiliated with All-China Federation of Trade Unions (Meyerson 2004). This federation is dominated by the Communist Party in China and its unions are headed by members of the company management—hardly a genuine workers' movement (Meyerson 2004).

Within the United States, a major barrier to union growth exists in the 20 states that have so-called right-to-work laws. In these states, workers cannot be *required* to join or pay dues or fees to a union. The very term *right to work* reflects the anti-union view that a worker should not be forced to join a union, even if that union may negotiate on his or her behalf and achieve results that benefit the worker. In contrast to the United States, Canada has fewer legal impediments to union organization.

Labour laws are under the control of the provinces and territories, and some jurisdictions are considered more labour-friendly than others. For example, Quebec, Saskatchewan, and British Columbia will certify a bargaining unit without a vote as soon as the majority of workers in that particular unit have signed a union card (McKenna 2004). In the United States, where union activity is covered by federal law, employers can stall or block a vote on union organization for a significant period of time; once a much-delayed vote takes place, disgruntled workers may have left the company and the drive to unionize may have waned (McKenna 2004).

Apply the Theory

1. If conflict thinker Karl Marx were alive today, how do you think he would view the role of unions in contemporary Canadian society?
2. How do you view the relevance of unions as a means of promoting gender equality?

CHAPTER RESOURCES

Summary

::: 5.1 How Do We Define and Reconstruct Reality?

- Through **social structure**, a society is organized into predictable relationships based on **social interactions**.
- People interact based on the meaning that situations or others' behaviour have for them. The ability to define reality reflects a group's power in society.

::: 5.2 What Are the Elements of Social Structure?

- An **ascribed status** is generally assigned to a person at birth, whereas an **achieved status** is attained largely through one's own effort. Some ascribed statuses, such as race and gender, can function as a **master status** that affects one's potential to achieve a certain professional or social status.
- With each distinctive status—whether ascribed or achieved—comes a particular **social role**: a set of expectations for people who occupy that status.
- Much of our social behaviour takes place in a **group**. When we find ourselves identifying closely with a group, it is probably a **primary group**. A **secondary group** is more formal and impersonal.
- People tend to see the world in terms of an **in-group** and an **out-group**, a perception often fostered by the very group that they belong to or identify with.

- A **reference group** sets and enforces standards of conduct and serves as a source of comparison for people's evaluations of themselves and others.
- Groups serve as links to a **social network** and its vast resources.
- **Social institutions** are organized patterns of beliefs and behaviour centred on the provision of basic social needs as well as the production and reproduction of social relations. The mass media, the government, the economy, the family, and the health-care system are all examples of social institutions.
- Conflict theorists charge that social institutions help to maintain the privileges of the powerful while contributing to the powerlessness of others.
- Interactionist theorists stress that our social behaviour is conditioned by the roles and statuses we accept, the groups to which we belong, and the institutions within which we function.

::: 5.3 What Does a Global Perspective on Social Structure Look Like?

- Émile Durkheim thought that social structure depends on the division of labour in a society. According to Durkheim, societies with minimal division of labour have a collective consciousness called **mechanical solidarity**; those with greater division of labour show an interdependence called **organic solidarity**.

- Ferdinand Tönnies distinguished the close-knit community of *Gemeinschaft* from the impersonal mass society known as *Gesellschaft*.
- Gerhard Lenski thinks that a society's social structure changes as its culture and technology become more sophisticated, a process he calls **sociocultural evolution**.

::: 5.4 How Are Organizations Structured?

- As a society becomes more complex, a large **formal organization** becomes more powerful and pervasive.
- Max Weber argued that in its ideal form, every **bureaucracy** has five basic characteristics: division

of labour, hierarchical authority, written rules and regulations, impersonality, and employment based on technical qualifications. Carefully constructed bureaucratic policies can be undermined or redefined by an organization's informal structure, however.

::: 5.5 How Has the Workplace Changed?

- Organizational restructuring and new technologies have transformed the workplace through innovations such as *collective decision making, minimal hierarchy, work teams,* and *telecommuting*. At the same time, major shifts in the economy have reduced the power of **labour unions**.

Critical Thinking Questions

1. People in certain professions seem particularly susceptible to role conflict. For example, journalists commonly experience role conflict when covering natural disasters, crimes, and other distressing situations. Should they offer assistance to the needy or cover breaking news? Select two other professions and discuss the role conflicts people in them might experience.

2. The functionalist, conflict, feminist, and interactionist perspectives can all be used in analyzing social institutions. What are the strengths and weaknesses in each perspective's analysis of those institutions?

3. Are primary groups, secondary groups, in-groups, out-groups, and reference groups likely to be found within a formal organization? What functions do these groups serve for a formal organization? What dysfunction might occur as a result of their presence?

4. Max Weber identified five basic characteristics of bureaucracy. Select an actual organization familiar to you (for example, your college or university, a workplace, a religious institution, or civic association you belong to) and apply Weber's analysis to that organization. To what degree does it correspond to Weber's ideal type of bureaucracy?

THINKING ABOUT MOVIES

Invictus

In post-apartheid South Africa, a rugby team helps Nelson Mandela to build national unity.

The Social Network

This dramatization of the rise of Facebook illustrates the way people connect to one another in the twenty-first century.

Wendy and Lucy

A young woman wanders through life disconnected from social institutions.

inside

A young man panhandling for change contrasting great wealth, modest means, and deep poverty in society.

" January 3, 2012

TORONTO—The highest paid 100 CEOs on Canada's TSX Index had reason to cheer the New Year: By noon January 3, they had already pocketed $44 366—what it takes the average wage earner an entire year to make.

The Canadian Centre for Policy Alternatives' (CCPA) annual look at CEO compensation reveals Canada's Elite 100 CEOs pocketed an average $8.38 million in 2010—a 27 percent increase over the average $6.6 million they took in 2009.

In contrast, after taking inflation into account, the average worker's weekly earnings are lower now than they were during the worst of the 2008–2009 recession.

'The average of Canada's CEO Elite 100 makes 189 times more than Canadians earning the average wage,' says the report's author, economist Hugh Mackenzie.

'If you think that's normal, it's not. In 1998, the highest paid 100 Canadian CEOs earned 105 times more than the average wage, itself likely more than double the figure for a decade earlier.'

Among the report's findings:

Canada's Elite 100 CEOs are among the country's richest 0.01 percent, a privileged group of 2460 tax filers whose minimum income was $1.85 million in 2007. Their incomes soar above the average income of $404 500 (2007) required to enter the richest 1 percent club.

The lowest paid of Canada's CEO Elite 100 pocketed $3.9 million in 2010.

All but one of Canada's highest paid 100 CEOs on the TSX Index is male.

'The conclusion from these data is inescapable,' says Mackenzie. 'Soaring executive pay plays a significant role in driving the growth in income inequality in Canada.'

'The gap between Canada's CEO Elite 100 and the rest of us is growing at a fast and steady pace, with no signs of letting up.' "

(Canadian Centre for Policy Alternatives 2012)

This report by the Canadian Centre for Policy Alternatives draws attention to the gap between the rich and the rest of the population in Canada, focusing on how executive pay plays a large role in the growth of income inequality.

Ever since people first began to speculate about the nature of human society, their attention has been drawn to the differences between individuals and groups within any society. The term **social inequality** describes a condition in which members of a society have different amounts of wealth, prestige, or power. Some degree of social inequality characterizes every society.

When a system of social inequality is based on a hierarchy of groups, sociologists refer to it as **stratification**: a structured ranking of entire groups of people that perpetuates unequal economic rewards and power in a society. These unequal rewards are evident not only in the distribution of wealth and income but also in the distressing mortality rates of impoverished communities. Stratification involves the ways in which one generation passes on social inequalities to the next, thereby producing groups of people arranged in rank order from low to high.

Stratification is a crucial subject of sociological investigation because of its pervasive influence on human interactions and institutions. It inevitably results in social inequality because certain groups of people stand higher in social rankings, control scarce resources, wield power, and receive special treatment. As we will see in this chapter, the consequences of stratification are evident in the unequal distribution of wealth and income within industrial societies. The term **income** refers to salaries and wages. By contrast, **wealth** encompasses all of a person's material assets, including land, stocks, and other types of property.

Do you think that social inequality is an inevitable part of any society? How do you think government policy affects the life chances of the working poor? How are wealth and income distributed, and how much opportunity does the average worker have to move up the social ladder? What economic and political conditions explain the divide between rich nations and poor? In this chapter, we focus on the unequal distribution of socially valued rewards, and its consequences. We will examine three general systems of stratification, paying particular attention to the theories of Karl Marx and Max Weber, as well as to functionalist, conflict, feminists, and interactionist theories. We see how sociologists define social class and examine the consequences of stratification for people's wealth and income, health, and educational opportunities. And we confront the question of social mobility, both upward and downward, focusing on stratification in Canada. Finally, in the social policy section, we address the issue of welfare reform in both North America and Europe. ∎

::: use your sociological *imagination* :::

What are the possible consequences of having a significant gap between the rich and the working poor who earn minimum wage?

www.mcgrawhillconnect.ca

Think about It

What determines how much or how little a person will receive for the work he or she contributes to society?

What Is Stratification?

Systems of Stratification

Look at the three general systems of stratification examined here—slavery, castes, and social classes—as ideal types useful for purposes of analysis. Any stratification system may include elements of more than one type.

To understand these systems better, it may be helpful to review the distinction between achieved status and ascribed status, described in Chapter 5. Ascribed status is a social position "assigned" to a person without regard for that person's unique characteristics or talents. By contrast, achieved status is a social position attained by a person largely through his or her own effort. The two are closely linked. A nation's most affluent families generally inherit wealth and status, while many members of racial and ethnic minorities inherit disadvantaged status. Age and gender, as well, are ascribed statuses that influence a person's wealth and social position.

Slavery   The most extreme form of legalized social inequality for individuals or groups is **slavery**. What distinguishes this oppressive system of stratification is that enslaved individuals are *owned* by other people. They treat these human beings as property, just as if they were household pets or appliances.

Slavery has varied in the way it has been practised. In ancient Greece, most slaves were captives of war and piracy. Although succeeding generations could inherit slave status, it was not necessarily permanent. A person's status might change depending on which city-state happened to triumph in a military conflict. In effect, all citizens had the potential of becoming slaves or of being granted freedom, depending on the circumstances of history. By contrast, in the United States, Canada, the Caribbean, and Latin America, where slavery was an ascribed status, racial and legal barriers prevented the freeing of slaves. As Box 6-1 shows, millions of people around the world still live as slaves.

Castes   Castes are hereditary systems of rank, usually religiously dictated, that tend to be fixed and immobile. The caste system is generally associated with Hinduism in India and other countries. In India, there are four major castes, called *varnas*. A fifth category, referred to as *untouchables*, is considered to be so lowly and unclean as to have no place within this system of stratification. There are also many minor castes. Caste membership is an ascribed status (at birth, children automatically assume the same position as their parents). Each caste is quite sharply defined, and members are expected to marry within that caste.

Caste membership generally determines a person's occupation or role as a religious functionary. An example of a lower caste in India is the Dons, whose main work is the undesirable job of cremating bodies. The caste system promotes a remarkable degree of differentiation. Thus, the single caste of chauffeurs has been split into two separate subcastes: drivers of luxury cars have a higher status than drivers of economy cars.

In recent decades, industrialization and urbanization have taken their toll on India's rigid caste system. Many villagers have moved to urban areas where their low-caste status is unknown. Schools, hospitals, factories, and public transportation facilitate contacts between different castes that were previously avoided at all costs. In addition, the government has tried to reform the caste system. India's constitution, adopted in 1950, includes a provision abolishing discrimination against untouchables, who had traditionally been excluded from temples, schools, and most forms of employment. Yet, the caste system prevails, and its impact is now evident in electoral politics, as various political parties compete for the support of frustrated untouchable voters who constitute one-third of India's electorate. For the first time, in the 1990s and early 2000s, India had someone from an untouchable background serving in the symbolic but high-status position of president. Meanwhile, however, dozens of low-caste people continue to be killed for overstepping their lowly status in life (Dugger 1999; Schmetzer 1999).

Social Classes   A **class system** is a social ranking based primarily on economic position in which achieved characteristics can influence social mobility. In contrast to slavery and caste systems, the boundaries between classes are imprecisely defined, and people can move from one stratum, or level, of society to another. Even so, class systems maintain stable stratification hierarchies and patterns of class divisions, and they, too, are marked by unequal distribution of wealth and power.

Income inequality is a basic characteristic of a class system. In 2010, the median after-tax income for a family of two or more in Canada was $65 400 (Statistics Canada 2011). This figure does nothing to convey the income disparities in our society. In 2009, Canadian families in the top 20 percent of income accounted for 40 percent of total after-tax family income, while families in the bottom 20 percent earned 7 percent of total after-tax family income (Statistics Canada 2011b). In 2011 the top 100 richest Canadian individuals/families included Vancouver entrepreneur Jimmy Pattison, Jeff Skoll of eBay, and Galen Weston, Sr., of George Weston Ltd., which controls the Loblaw supermarket chain (Canadian Business Online 2011). Table 6-1 shows the ranking of Canada's richest families—all of which are led by white males—and reveals the fortunes of each. In stark contrast to this wealth, roughly 3 million people in Canada lived in situations of low income in 2009 (Statistics Canada 2011b).

The people with the highest incomes, generally those heading private companies, earn well above even affluent wage earners. In 2011, Canada's 100 highest-paid CEOs were paid more in one day than most Canadian workers made in one year, and 189 times more than the average worker (Canadian Centre for Policy Alternatives 2012; see Figure 6-1). The compensation CEOs receive is not necessarily linked to conventional measures of success. For example, as the U.S. economy worsened in 2008, CEOs of failing financial and automotive companies continued to receive the highest compensations among wage earners.

Statistics reflecting personal wealth or *net worth* (assets minus debts) demonstrate an enormous gap between the richest 20 percent and the poorest 20 percent of Canadian families. In 2005, for example, the poorest 20 percent of Canadian families had an average net worth of –$2400 (meaning that

sociology in the global community

6-1 Slavery in the Twenty-First Century

Around the world, at least 27 million people were still enslaved at the beginning of the twenty-first century. And yet the 1948 Universal Declaration of Human Rights, which is supposedly binding on all members of the United Nations, holds that "no one shall be held in slavery or servitude; slavery and the slave trade shall be prohibited in all their forms" (Masland 1992:30, 32).

Canada considers any person a slave who is unable to withdraw his or her labour voluntarily from an employer. In many parts of the world, bonded labourers are imprisoned in virtual life-time employment as they struggle to repay small debts. In other places, human beings are owned outright.

The Swiss-based human rights group Christian Solidarity International has focused world-wide attention on the plight of slaves in the African nation of Sudan. The organization solicits funds and uses them to buy slaves their freedom—at about $50 a slave.

In Ivory Coast, where 43 percent of the world's cocoa beans are produced, child slavery is used to produce and harvest crops. These children are beaten and forced to do hard labour—up to 100 hours per week (Sierra Club of Canada 2003).

Although contemporary slavery may be most obvious in developing countries, it also afflicts the industrialized nations of the West. Throughout Europe, guest workers and maids are employed by masters who hold their passports, subject them to degrading working conditions, and threaten them with deportation if they protest. Similar tactics are used to essentially imprison young women from Eastern Europe and Asia who have been brought (through deceptive promises) to work in the sex industries of Canada, the United States, Belgium, France, Germany, Greece, the Netherlands, and Switzerland.

Within Canada and other developed countries, illegal immigrants are forced to labour for years under terrible conditions, either to pay off debts or to avoid being turned over to immigration authorities. According to RCMP reports, at least 800 workers are trafficked in Canada each year (Brazao 2008). Trafficking of children—used for cheap labour or for sexual exploitation—is now a global problem, with an estimated 1.2 million children being trafficked every year (UNICEF 2009).

Apply the Theory

1. According to conflict theorists, why are many bonded labourers around the world in the position of slaves?
2. What explanations might some feminist sociologists have for the varying incidence rates of forced sex work from one country to another?

Sources: Brazao 2008; Fisher 1999; France 2000; Jacobs 2001; Masland 1992; Richard 2000.

---

they owed more than they owned), while the richest 20 percent had an average net worth of $1 264 200 (Statistics Canada 2006i). What is most distressing about this disparity is that the poorest 20 percent control 0.1 percent of the total wealth of Canadian families, while the richest 20 percent control 69 percent of the total wealth.

Both of these groups, at opposite ends of the nation's economic hierarchy, reflect the importance of ascribed status and achieved status. Ascribed statuses, such as race, gender, and class, clearly influence a person's wealth and social position. And sociologist Richard Jenkins (1991) has researched how the ascribed status of having a disability marginalizes people in society. People with disabilities are particularly vulnerable to unemployment, are often poorly paid, and in many cases are on the lower rung of occupational ladders. Regardless of their actual performance on the job, people

table 6-1 Canada's Richest Families/Persons, 2011

Family/Person (Organization)	Net Worth (billions of CDN$)
1. Thomson family (Thomson Reuters, Woodbridge Co. Ltd.)	21.34
2. Galen Weston (George Weston Ltd., Loblaws Cos. Ltd.)	8
3. Irving family (Irving Oil Ltd., J.D. Irving Ltd.)	7.8
4. Rogers family (Rogers Communications Inc.)	5.94
5. Jimmy Pattison (Jim Pattison Group)	5.73
6. Saputo family	4.34
7. Paul Desmarais (Power Corp.)	4.27
8. Jeff Skoll (eBay Inc.)	3.75
9. Fred and Ron Mannix (Mancal Group)	3.44
10. Barry Sherman (Apotex Group of Cos.)	3.31

Source: Canadian Business Online October 2011, http://www.canadianbusiness.com/rankings/rich100/2011. Adapted by author.

figure 6-1 Canada's Top-Paid CEOs and the Rest of Us

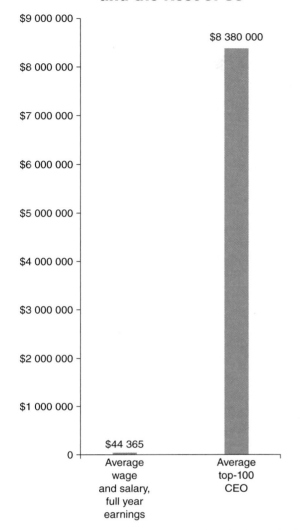

Source: From "A Soft Landing: Recession and Canada's 100 Highest Paid CEOs" by Hugh Mackenzie, Canadian Centre for Policy Alternatives 2012.

Think about It
Why are CEOs "worth" so much more than other workers?

with disabilities are stigmatized as not "earning their keep." Such are the effects of ascribed status.

Social class is one of the independent or explanatory variables most frequently used by social scientists to shed light on social issues. In later chapters, we will analyze the relationships among social class and divorce patterns (Chapter 12), religious behaviour (Chapter 13), and formal schooling (Chapter 13), as well as other relationships in which social class is a variable.

Theoretical Perspectives on Social Stratification

Must some members of society receive greater rewards than others? Do people need to feel socially and economically superior to others? Can social life be organized without structured inequality? These questions have been debated for centuries, especially among political activists. Utopian socialists, religious minorities, and members of recent countercultures have all attempted to establish communities that, to some extent or another, would abolish inequality in social relationships.

Social science research has found that inequality exists in all societies—even the simplest. For example, when anthropologist Gunnar Landtman ([1938] 1968) studied the Kiwai Papuans of New Guinea, he initially noticed little differentiation among them. Every man in the village did the same work and lived in similar housing. However, on closer inspection, Landtman observed that certain Papuans—the men who were warriors, harpooners, and sorcerers—were described as "a little more high" than others. By contrast, villagers who were female, unemployed, or unmarried were considered "down a little bit" and were barred from owning land.

Stratification is universal in that all societies maintain some form of social inequality among members. Depending on its values, a society may assign people to distinctive ranks based on their religious knowledge, skill in hunting, beauty, trading expertise, or ability to provide health care. But why has such inequality developed in human societies? And how much differentiation among people, if any, is actually essential?

Functionalist and conflict sociologists offer contrasting explanations for the existence and necessity of social stratification. Functionalists maintain that a differential system of rewards and punishments is necessary for the efficient operation of society. Conflict theorists argue that competition for scarce resources results in significant political, economic, and social inequality. Some feminist sociologists argue that gender and its interconnections with race, age, class, and disability come together to produce various levels of inequality in society. Interactionist sociologists focus their attention on the interactions among individuals that serve to create and maintain social inequality.

Functionalist View

Would people go to school for many years to become physicians if they could make as much money and gain as much respect working as street cleaners? Functionalists say no, which is partly why they believe that a stratified society is universal.

In the view of Kingsley Davis and Wilbert Moore, society must distribute its members among a variety of social positions (1945). It must not only make sure that these positions are filled but also see that they are staffed by people with the appropriate talents and abilities. Rewards, including money and prestige, are based on the importance of a position and the relative scarcity of qualified personnel. Yet this assessment often devalues work performed by certain segments of society, such as women's work as homemakers or other occupations traditionally filled by women, or low-status work in fast-food outlets.

Davis and Moore argue that stratification is universal and that social inequality is necessary so that people will be motivated to fill functionally important positions (1945). But, critics say, unequal rewards are not the only means of encouraging people to fill critical positions and occupations. Personal pleasure, intrinsic satisfaction, and value orientations

This family's expensive lifestyle and acquisitions underscore the unequal distribution of wealth and power in Canada.

also motivate people to enter particular careers. Functionalists agree but note that society must use some type of reward to motivate people to enter unpleasant or dangerous jobs and jobs that require a long training period. This response does not justify stratification systems in which status is largely inherited, such as slave or caste societies. Similarly, it is difficult to explain the high salaries our society offers to professional athletes or entertainers on the basis of how critical these jobs are to the survival of society (Collins 1975; Kerbo 2000; Tumin 1953, 1985).

Even if stratification is inevitable, the functionalist explanation for differential rewards does not explain the wide disparity between the rich and the poor. Critics of the functionalist approach point out that the richest 10 percent of households account for 20 percent of the nation's income in Sweden, 25 percent in France, 28 percent in Canada, and 31 percent in the United States. In their view, the level of income inequality found in contemporary industrial societies cannot be defended—even though these societies have a legitimate need to fill certain key occupations (World Bank 2002:74–76).

Conflict View

Karl Marx's View of Stratification   Sociologist Leonard Beeghley aptly noted that "Karl Marx was both a revolutionary and a social scientist" (1978:1). Marx was concerned with stratification in all types of human societies, beginning with primitive agricultural tribes and continuing into feudalism. But his main focus was on the effects of economic inequality on all aspects of life in nineteenth-century Europe. The plight of the working class made him feel that it was imperative to strive for changes in the class structure of society.

In Marx's view, social relations during any period of history depend on who controls the primary mode of economic production, such as land or factories. Differential access to scarce resources shapes the relationships among groups. Thus, under the feudal estate system, most production was agricultural, and the land was owned by the nobility. Peasants had little choice but to work according to terms dictated by those who owned the land.

Using this type of analysis, Marx examined social relations within **capitalism**—an economic system in which the means of production are largely in private hands and the main incentive for economic activity is the accumulation of profits (Rosenberg 1991). Marx focused on the two classes that began to emerge as the feudal estate system declined—the bourgeoisie and the proletariat. The **bourgeoisie**, or capitalist class, owns the means of production, such as factories and machinery, whereas the **proletariat** is the working class. In capitalist societies, the members of the bourgeoisie maximize profit in competition with other firms. In the process, they exploit workers, who must exchange their labour for subsistence wages. In Marx's view, members of each class share a distinctive culture. He was most interested in the culture of the proletariat, but he also examined the ideology of the bourgeoisie, through which it justifies its dominance over workers.

A miner peers into the dark in a coal mine. Karl Marx would identify coal miners as members of the proletariat, or working class. Even today, miners are poorly compensated for the considerable dangers they face. Such exploitation of the working class is a core principle of Marxist theory.

According to Marx, exploitation of the proletariat will inevitably lead to the destruction of the capitalist system because the workers will revolt. But, first, the working class must develop **class consciousness**—a subjective awareness of common vested interests and the need for collective political action to bring about social change. Workers must often overcome what Marx termed **false consciousness**, or an attitude held by members of a class that does not accurately reflect its objective position. A worker with false consciousness may adopt an individualistic viewpoint toward capitalist exploitation ("I am being exploited by my boss"). By contrast, the class-conscious worker realizes that all workers are being exploited by the bourgeoisie and have a common stake in revolution (Vanneman and Cannon 1987).

For Karl Marx, class consciousness is part of a collective process whereby the proletariat comes to identify the bourgeoisie as the source of its oppression. Revolutionary leaders will guide the working class in its class struggle. Ultimately, the proletariat will overthrow the rule of the bourgeoisie and the government (which Marx saw as representing the interests of capitalists) and will eliminate private ownership of the means of production. In his utopian view, classes and oppression will cease to exist in the post-revolutionary workers' state.

How accurate were Marx's predictions? He failed to anticipate the emergence of labour unions, whose power in collective bargaining weakens the stranglehold that capitalists maintain over workers. Moreover, as contemporary conflict theorists note, he did not foresee the extent to which political liberties and relative prosperity could contribute to "false consciousness." Many people have come to view themselves as individuals striving for improvement within "free" societies with substantial mobility—rather than as downtrodden members of social classes facing a collective fate. Finally, Marx did not predict that communist party rule would be established and later overthrown in the former Soviet Union and throughout Eastern Europe. Still, the Marxist approach to the study of class is useful in stressing the importance of stratification as a determinant of social behaviour and the fundamental separation in many societies between two distinct groups, the rich and the poor.

The writings of Karl Marx are at the heart of conflict theory. Marx viewed history as a continuous struggle between the oppressors and the oppressed that would ultimately culminate in an egalitarian, classless society. In terms of stratification, he argued that the dominant class under capitalism manipulated the economic and political systems in order to maintain control over the exploited proletariat. Marx did not believe that stratification was inevitable, but he did see inequality and oppression as inherent in capitalism (Wright et al. 1982).

The Views of Ralf Dahrendorf

Like Marx, contemporary conflict theorists believe that human beings are prone to conflict over such scarce resources as wealth, status, and power. However, where Marx focused primarily on class conflict, more recent theorists have extended this analysis to include conflicts based on gender, race, age, and other dimensions. British sociologist Ralf Dahrendorf is one of the most influential contributors to the conflict approach.

As the reality television series *Ice Road Truckers* suggests, long-haul truck drivers take pride in their low-prestige job. According to the conflict perspective, the cultural beliefs that form a society's dominant ideology, such as the popular image of the truck driver as hero, help the wealthy to maintain their power and control at the expense of the lower classes.

Dahrendorf modified Marx's analysis of capitalist society to apply to *modern* capitalist societies (1959). For Dahrendorf, social classes are groups of people who share common interests resulting from their authority relationships. In identifying the most powerful groups in society, he includes not only the bourgeoisie—the owners of the means of production—but also the managers of industry, legislators, the judiciary, heads of the government bureaucracy, and others. In that respect, Dahrendorf has merged Marx's emphasis on class conflict with Weber's recognition that power is an important element of stratification (Cuff et al. 1990).

Conflict theorists, including Dahrendorf, contend that the powerful of today, like the bourgeoisie of Marx's time, want society to run smoothly so that they can enjoy their privileged positions. Because the status quo suits those with wealth, status, and power, they have a clear interest in preventing, minimizing, or controlling societal conflict.

Max Weber's View of Stratification

Unlike Karl Marx, Max Weber insisted that no single characteristic (such as class) totally defines a person's position within the stratification system. Instead, writing in 1916, he identified three distinct components of stratification: class, status, and power (Gerth and Mills 1958).

Weber used the term **class** to refer to people who have a similar level of wealth and income. For example, certain workers in Canada try to support their families through minimum-wage jobs. According to Weber's definition, these wage earners constitute a class because they share the same economic position and fate. Although Weber agreed with Marx on the importance of this economic dimension of stratification, he argued that the actions of individuals and groups could not be understood solely in economic terms.

Weber used the term **status group** to refer to people who rank the same in prestige or lifestyle. An individual gains status through membership in a desirable group, such as the medical profession. But status is not the same as economic class standing. In our culture, a successful pickpocket may be in the same income class as a university professor. Yet, the thief is widely regarded as a member of a low-status group, whereas the professor holds high status.

For Weber, the third major component of stratification reflects a political dimension. **Power** is the ability to exercise our will over others. In Canada, power stems from membership in particularly influential groups, such as corporate boards of directors, government bodies, and interest groups. Conflict theorists generally agree that two major sources of power—big business and government—are closely interrelated (see Chapter 14).

In Weber's view, then, each of us has not one rank in society but three. Our position in a stratification system reflects some combination of class, status, and power. Each factor influences the other two, and in fact the rankings on these three dimensions often tend to coincide. Pierre Trudeau came from a wealthy family, attended exclusive schools, graduated from elite universities, such as Harvard and the Sorbonne, and went on to become prime minister of Canada. Like Trudeau, many people from affluent backgrounds achieve impressive status and power.

At the same time, these dimensions of stratification may operate somewhat independently in determining a person's position. Jean Chrétien had a small legal practice in Shawinigan, Quebec, but he used a political power base to work his way up into federal politics to eventually become prime minister. A widely published poet may achieve high status while earning a relatively modest income. Successful professional athletes have little power but enjoy a relatively high position in terms of class and status. To understand the workings of a culture more fully, sociologists must carefully evaluate the ways in which that culture distributes its most valued rewards, including wealth and income, status, and power (Duberman 1976; Gerth and Mills 1958).

One way for the powerful to maintain the status quo is to define and disseminate the society's dominant ideology. The term *dominant ideology* describes a set of cultural beliefs and practices that helps to maintain powerful social, economic, and political interests. For Karl Marx, the dominant ideology in a capitalist society serves the interests of the ruling class. From a conflict perspective, the social significance of the dominant ideology is that not only do a society's most powerful groups and institutions control wealth and property, but, even more important, they also control the means of producing beliefs about reality through religion, education, and the media (Abercrombie, Hill, and Turner 1980, 1990; Robertson 1988).

The powerful, such as leaders of government, also use limited social reforms to buy off the oppressed and reduce the danger of challenges to their dominance. For example, minimum wage laws and unemployment compensation unquestionably give some valuable assistance to needy men and women. Yet these reforms also serve to pacify those who might otherwise rebel. Of course, in the view of conflict theorists, such manoeuvres can never entirely eliminate conflict, since workers will continue to demand equality, and the powerful will not give up their control of society.

Conflict theorists see stratification as a major source of societal tension and conflict. They do not agree with Davis and Moore (1945) that stratification is functional for a society or that it serves as a source of stability. Rather, conflict sociologists argue that stratification will inevitably lead to instability and social change (Collins 1975; Coser 1977).

Feminist Views

As we described earlier, feminist sociological perspectives comprise a diverse group of viewpoints. A central belief, however, unites the various feminist perspectives: gender inequality is pervasive and women are the subordinated and dominated sex. Feminist thinkers, however, differ greatly in their views on the root causes of gender inequality; on how gender inequality manifests itself in homes, workplaces, and political arenas; and on how to address this inequality. Radical feminists, for example, place great emphasis on patriarchy—as a form of social organization and ideology. In 1971, radical feminist Kate Millet wrote:

> Our society . . . is a patriarchy. The fact is evident at once if one recalls that the military, industry, technology, universities, science, political offices, finances—in short, every avenue of power within our society, including the coercive force of the police, is entirely in male hands. (1971:25)

In effect, radical feminists maintain that gender stratification is systemic, permeating society and creating a culture in which male values and priorities prevail. Since women are excluded from this culture, they stand to be controlled and oppressed by it.

Liberal feminists, in contrast, recognize the inequality that women face but believe that it could be addressed by providing women with greater access to the public sphere and by making that sphere (i.e., workplaces) more "female friendly."

Liberal feminists, then, believe less in a systemic pattern of gender inequality and more in the necessity of approaches that would provide women with greater access to employment opportunities, upward mobility, and, eventually, economic equality.

Interactionist View

Although functionalist, conflict, and some feminist perspectives tend to use a macrosociological approach to examine social inequality, interactionist thinkers tend to be more micro in their orientation. They are interested in the "person-to-person" (Naiman 2004:19) ways in which social stratification is maintained, perhaps in the forms of interpersonal and non-verbal communication.

Interactionists might consider the symbolic meaning that people attach to their purchases. The theorist Thorstein Veblen (1857–1929) noted that those at the top of the social hierarchy typically convert part of their wealth into *conspicuous consumption*, purchasing more cars than they can drive and building houses with more rooms than they can possibly occupy. Or they may engage in *conspicuous leisure*, jetting to a remote destination and staying just long enough to have dinner or view the sunset over some historic site (Veblen [1899] 1964).

Erving Goffman (1967) theorized on the activity of *deference*, a symbolic act that conveys appreciation from one person to another. The pattern of showing deference, in which one person is the giver and the other is the recipient, often is symbolic of the unequal power relations between the two and, thus, serves to maintain and perpetuate social inequality. For example, would an employee be more likely than an

Buying an Andy Warhol painting for over $20 million is an example of Thorstein Velben's concept of conspicuous consumption, a spending pattern common to those at the very top of the social ladder.

employer to open a door for the other? To call the other "Ms." or "Mr." rather than by a first name? To let the other lead in the conversation and not be prone to interrupt?

Judith Rollins's study (1985) of the person-to-person interactions between domestic workers and their employers, based on interviews and participant observation, showed the patterns of deference displayed between white female employers and primarily women who were members of a visible minority. Rollins found that touching (or the absence thereof), calling the domestic workers "girls" regardless of their age, and keeping certain spatial distances were all rituals of deference that served to maintain the social class inequality between the two women.

Anti-colonial Views Anti-colonial views of stratification reject the notion that social inequality can be reduced to one element, such as class. Colonialism, as further discussed in Chapter 7, simply means rule by outsiders which includes political, social, economic, and cultural domination. Class reductionism—attributing all forms of oppression and inequality to class, while ignoring or minimizing factors such as race, colonialism, gender, and sexuality—is rejected by anti-colonial thinkers such as Albert Memmi in his work, *The Colonizer and the Colonized*:

> To observe the life of the colonizer and the colonized is to discover rapidly that the daily humiliations of the colonized, his objective subjugation, are not merely economic. Even the poorest colonizer thought himself to be—and actually was—superior to the colonized. This too was part of colonial privilege. The Marxist discovery of the importance of the economy in all oppressive relationships is not the point. This relationship has other characteristics which I believe I have discovered in the colonial relationship. (Memmi 1965:xii)

Aboriginal people of Canada, for example, continue to experience powerlessness and poverty as a result of a legacy of colonization (Green 2003). In 2011 the world's attention was drawn to the living conditions of Canada's Aboriginal people, specifically the First Nation of Attawapiskat. Here people were living in construction trailers and shacks with no bathrooms and running water. Food in the community is very expensive, particularly fresh produce. Humanitarian aid packages of food and water were flown in by the Red Cross and other agencies as some opposition politicians attempted to keep the focus on the condition of this First Nation community (and others) by referring to it as "Canada's Third World."

To reduce the unequal conditions experienced by Aboriginal people to simply a matter of "class" would be a totally inadequate explanation of their socioeconomic position in Canada today. As Matthew Coon Come, former national chief of the Assembly of First Nations, stated:

> . . . Without adequate access to lands, resources, and without the jurisdictions required to benefit meaningfully and sustainably from them . . . no number of apologies, policies, token programs, or symbolic healing funds are going to remedy this fundamental socio-economic fact. (cited in Barnsley 1999:1)

Table 6-2 summarizes and compares the four major perspectives on social stratification.

Lenski's Viewpoint Let's return to a question posed earlier—Is stratification universal?—and consider the sociological response. Some form of differentiation is found in every culture. Sociologist Gerhard Lenski, in his sociocultural evolution approach, described how economic systems change as their level of technology becomes more complex, beginning with hunting and gathering and culminating eventually with industrial society. In subsistence-based, hunting-and-gathering societies, people focus on survival. Although some inequality and differentiation are evident, a stratification system based on social class does not emerge because there is no real wealth to be claimed.

table 6-2 Sociological Perspectives on Social Stratification summingUP

	Functionalist	Conflict	Feminist	Interactionist
Purpose of social stratification	Facilitates filling of social positions	Facilitates exploitation	Maintains and perpetuates male domination	Influences people's lifestyles
Attitude toward social inequality	Necessary to some extent	Excessive and growing	Change is necessary in order to achieve gender equality	Influences intergroup relations
Analysis of the wealthy	Talented and skilled, creating opportunities for others	Use the dominant ideology to further their own interests	Wealth is greatly associated with gender	Exhibit conspicuous consumption and conspicuous leisure

As a society advances in technology, it becomes capable of producing a considerable surplus of goods. The emergence of surplus resources greatly expands the possibilities for inequality in status, influence, and power and allows a well-defined, rigid social class system to develop. To minimize strikes, slowdowns, and industrial sabotage, the elite may share a portion of the economic surplus with the lower classes, but not enough to reduce their own power and privilege.

As Lenski argued, the allocation of surplus goods and services controlled by those with wealth, status, and power reinforces the social inequality that accompanies stratification systems. Although this reward system may once have served the overall purposes of society, as functionalists contend, the same cannot be said for the large disparities separating the haves from the have-nots in current societies. In contemporary industrial society, the degree of social and economic inequality far exceeds what is needed to provide for goods and services (Lenski 1966; Nolan and Lenski 2009).

6.2 How Are Stratification and Social Class Related?

Measuring Social Class

We continually assess how wealthy people are by looking at the cars they drive, the houses they live in, the clothes they wear, and so on. Yet, it is not so easy to locate an individual within our social hierarchies as it would be in slavery or caste systems of stratification. To determine someone's class position, sociologists generally rely on the objective method.

Objective Method The **objective method** of measuring social class views class largely as a statistical category. Researchers assign individuals to social classes on the basis of criteria such as occupation, education, income, and residence. The key to the objective method is that the *researcher*, rather than the person being classified, identifies an individual's class position.

The first step in using this method is to decide what indicators or causal factors will be measured objectively, whether wealth, income, education, or occupation. The prestige ranking of occupations has proven to be a useful indicator of a person's class position. For one thing, it is much easier

to determine accurately than income or wealth. The term **prestige** refers to the respect and admiration that an occupation holds in a society. "My daughter, the physicist" connotes something very different from "my daughter, the waitress." Prestige is independent of the particular individual who occupies a job, a characteristic that distinguishes it from esteem. **Esteem** refers to the reputation that a specific person has earned within an occupation. Therefore, one can say that the position of prime minister of Canada has high prestige, even though it has been occupied by people with varying degrees of esteem. A hairdresser may have the esteem of his clients, but he lacks the prestige of a corporation president.

Table 6-3 ranks the prestige as measured by the amount of respect for various occupations in Canada.

table 6-3 Prestige Rankings of Occupations, 2009

Occupation	Score*	Occupation	Score*
Nurse	97	Psychiatrist	72
Farmer	95	Auto mechanic	71
Doctor	94	Priest/minister	65
Scientist	94	Athlete	65
Veterinarian	91	Actor	60
Teacher	89	Building contractor	60
Engineer	88	Journalist	58
Military officer	87	Business executive	48
Dentist	86	Lawyer	48
Architect	83	Banker	47
Judge	77	Politician	30
Accountant	74	Car salesperson	23

*Percentage of Canadians who had a "great deal" and "fair amount" of respect for selected professions.
Source: Angus Reid Strategies 2009; adapted by author.

Gender and Occupational Prestige For many years, studies of social class tended to neglect the occupations and incomes of *women* as determinants of social rank. In an exhaustive study of 589 occupations, sociologists Mary Powers and Joan Holmberg (1978) examined the impact of women's participation in the paid labour force on occupational status. Since women tend to dominate the relatively low-paying occupations, such as bookkeepers and childcare workers, their participation in the workforce leads to a general upgrading of the status of most male-dominated occupations. More recent research conducted in both the United States and Europe has assessed the occupations of husbands *and* wives in determining the class positions of families (Sørensen 1994). With more than half of all married women now working outside the home (see Chapter 9), this approach seems long overdue, but it also raises some questions. For example, how is class or status to be judged in dual-career families—by the occupation regarded as having greater prestige, the average, or some other combination of the two occupations?

Sociologists—and, in particular, feminist sociologists in Great Britain—are drawing on new approaches in assessing women's social class standing. One approach is to focus on the individual (rather than the family or household) as the basis of categorizing a woman's class position. Thus, a woman would be classified based on her own occupational status rather than that of her spouse (O'Donnell 1992).

Another feminist effort to measure the contribution of women to the economy reflects a more clearly political agenda. International Women Count Network, a global grassroots feminist organization, has sought to give a monetary value to women's unpaid work. Besides providing symbolic recognition of women's role in labour, this value would also be used to calculate pension programs and benefits that are based on wages received. In 1995, the United Nations placed an $11 trillion price tag on unpaid labour by women, largely in childcare, housework, and agriculture. Whatever the figure today, the continued undercounting of many workers' contributions to a family and to an entire economy means virtually all measures of stratification are in need of reform (United Nations Development Programme 1995; Wages for Housework Campaign 1999).

Multiple Measures Another complication in measuring social class is that advances in statistical methods and computer technology have multiplied the factors used to define class under the objective method. No longer are sociologists limited to annual income and education in evaluating a person's class position. Today, studies use as criteria the value of homes, sources of income, assets, years in present occupations, neighbourhoods, and considerations regarding dual careers. Adding these variables will not necessarily paint a different picture of class differentiation in Canada, but it does allow sociologists to measure class in a more complex and multi-dimensional way. Whatever the technique used to measure class, the sociologist is interested in real and often dramatic differences in power, privilege, and opportunity in a society. The study of stratification is a study of inequality. Nowhere is this more evident than in the distribution of wealth and income. As Figure 6-2 illustrates, in Canada, there is greater inequality in wealth than in income.

figure **6-2** Comparison of Family Income (2009) and Wealth (2005) in Canada

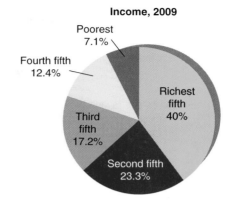

Income, 2009

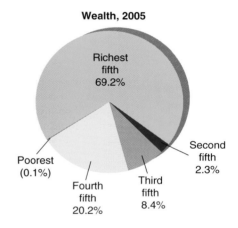

Wealth, 2005

Note: Data do not add to 100 percent due to rounding.
Sources: Statistics Canada 2006i; Statistics Canada 2011b.

Wealth and Income

Wealth in Canada is much more unevenly distributed than is income. As Figure 6-2 shows, in 2005, the richest fifth of the population held 69 percent of the nation's wealth. Researchers have also found dramatic disparities in wealth between families headed by a single parent (particularly a mother) and those headed by two parents, between those headed by Aboriginal parents and by non-Aboriginal parents, and between those headed by parents who have a mental disability and by those who do not (Wolff 2002).

By all measures, income in Canada is distributed unevenly. Nobel Prize–winning economist Paul Samuelson has described the situation in the following words: "If we made an income pyramid out of building blocks, with each layer portraying $500 of income, the peak would be far higher than Mount Everest, but most people would be within a few feet of the ground" (Samuelson and Nordhaus 2010:386).

The recent "Occupy" movement focused attention on the growing level of inequality in Canada, asking the question "Who are the one percent?" The one percent at the top of the pyramid, to which Samuelson refers, is controlling more and more of the country's total income. In the 1970s, 8 percent of

Canada's total income was concentrated in the hands of 1 percent of the population; by 2006, 14 percent of Canada's total income was controlled by 1 percent of the population (Fortin et al. 2012). Unions, which have historically bargained for fair wages for workers, are losing ground due to factors such as globalization and technological advancement. In 2010 union membership in Canada had declined to 31.5 percent of the population, down from 37.6 percent in the 1970s.

> ### Think about It
> In addition to generous raises and favourable government policies, what else might have accounted for the sharp rise in income for the richest 1 percent of Canadians?

Survey data show that more than 50 percent of Canadians (as opposed to 38 percent of U.S. citizens) believe that government should take steps to reduce the income disparity between the rich and the poor. By contrast, 80 percent of people in Italy, 66 percent in Germany, and 65 percent in Great Britain support governmental efforts to reduce income inequality. It is not surprising, then, that many European countries, particularly in Scandinavia, provide more extensive "safety nets" to assist and protect the disadvantaged. By contrast, the strong cultural value placed on individualism in the United States leads to greater possibilities for both economic success and failure (Lipset 1996).

Poverty

According to the 2009 *Report Card on Child and Family Poverty in Canada* (Campaign 2000 2009), approximately one out of every 10 children in Canada lives below the low-income cut-offs established by the federal government. Despite the federal government's goal (established over two decades ago) of eradicating child poverty by 2000, the report noted that Canada still has far to go. In this section, we'll consider just how we define *poverty* and who is included in that category.

Studying Poverty The efforts of sociologists and other social scientists to better understand poverty are complicated by the difficulty of defining it. This problem is evident even in government programs that conceive of poverty in either absolute or relative terms. **Absolute poverty** refers to a minimum level of subsistence that no family should be expected to live below. Government policies concerning minimum wages, labour market barriers for excluded groups, housing standards, or school lunch programs for the poor imply a need to bring citizens up to some predetermined level of existence.

Although Canada's federal government does not have an official poverty line, it does have what is called a LICO (low-income cut-off), which is calculated for families of different sizes, and for individuals, living in different communities of varying size, from rural to urban. For example, a family of three living in a city of over 500 000 people, would have a LICO of $34 646 (see Table 6-4). If a family spends 20 percent more than the average family does on the essentials (e.g., clothing, food, shelter), it falls below the LICO. As of 2010, a family spending more than 63 percent of its gross income on the necessities of clothing, food, and shelter would fall below the LICO. Figure 6-3 shows poverty rates in Canada and in other countries. Canada's poverty rate, although higher than those in Norway, Finland, and Sweden, is significantly lower than that of the United States.

table 6-4 Low Income Cut-Offs Before Tax, 2006

Size of family unit	Community size				
	Rural areas outside CMA or CA[1]	Census Agglomeration (CA)		Census Metropolitan Area (CMA)	
		Less than 30 000 inhabitants [2]	Between 30 000 and 99 999 inhabitants	Between 100 000 and 499 999 inhabitants	500 000 inhabitants or more
2010	Current dollars				
1 person	15 583	17 729	19 375	19 496	22 637
2 persons	19 400	22 070	24 120	24 269	28 182
3 persons	23 849	27 132	29 652	29 836	34 646
4 persons	28 957	32 943	36 003	36 226	42 065
5 persons	32 842	37 363	40 833	41 086	47 710
6 persons	37 041	42 140	46 054	46 339	53 808
7 or more persons	41 240	46 916	51 274	51 591	59 907

1. Can include some small population centres.
2. Includes population centres with less than 10 000 inhabitants.

Source: Statistics Canada 2011b www.statcan.gc.ca accessed August 20, 2012.

figure **6-3** Poverty in Selected Industrial Countries.

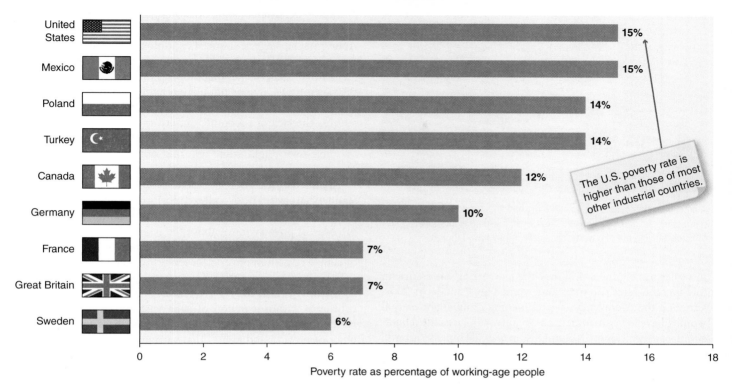

United States 15%
Mexico 15%
Poland 14%
Turkey 14%
Canada 12%
Germany 10%
France 7%
Great Britain 7%
Sweden 6%

The U.S. poverty rate is higher than those of most other industrial countries.

Poverty rate as percentage of working-age people

Note: Data are averages for mid-2000s, as reported in 2009. Poverty threshold is 50 percent of a nation's median household income.

Source: Organisation for Economic Co-operation and Development 2009.

If anything, this cross-national comparison understates the extent of poverty in the United States, since U.S. residents are likely to pay more for housing, health care, childcare, and education than residents of other countries, where such expenses are often subsidized.

By contrast, **relative poverty** is a floating standard of deprivation by which people at the bottom of a society, whatever their lifestyles, are judged to be disadvantaged *in comparison with the nation as a whole.* Therefore, even if the poor of the 2000s are better off in absolute terms than the poor of the 1930s or 1960s, they are still seen as deserving special assistance.

Campaign 2000 is an organization made up of more than 90 national, provincial or territorial, and community groups focused on the goal of eliminating child and family poverty in Canada. In its 2009 report (Campaign 2000 2009), it revealed the following:

- One in four children from First Nations communities grows up in poverty.
- Forty percent of low-income children live in families where at least one parent works full-year, full-time.
- Rates of child and family poverty (LICO before tax) are in the double-digits in most provinces.
- For every dollar the poorest 10 percent of families had in 2007, the richest 10 percent of families had almost 12 times more.

In 2012, half of the households receiving food from food banks in Canada were families with children. The number of Canadians turning to food banks reached an all-time high in 2012—882 000 people including 339 000 (38 percent) children (HungerCount 2012). One in five households using food banks has income from recent or current employment (HungerCount 2012). Katherine Schmidt, Executive Director of Food Banks Canada, states:

> It is shocking that, in a country as prosperous as Canada, hundreds of thousands of children rely on food banks to have enough to eat each month . . .Though food banks do what they can to fill the need, too many kids are still going to school on empty stomachs. (CNW Canada Newswire 2012)

Who Are the Poor? Not only does the category of the poor defy any simple definition, but it also counters the common stereotypes about "poor people." One such stereotype is that the vast majority of the poor are able to work but will not. Yet, as revealed in the report by Campaign 2000, many poor adults do work full-year, full-time outside the home. Sociological researchers call this group the **working poor**. A working poor individual is one who works a minimum number of hours a year and whose family income falls below the LICO. In 2009, 4.5% of Canadian workers were in this category (Statistics Canada 2011b).

The majority of lone-parent families are headed by women and, in 2009, 21.5 percent of single mothers lived in poverty (Statistics Canada 2011b). Canadian women's wages remain unequal to those of Canadian men, and many women in Canadian workplaces still hold jobs in female-dominated

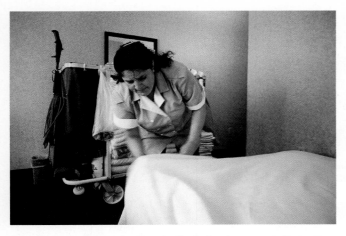

A hotel housekeeper hurries to make the bed and move on to the next room to be cleaned. At low wage rates, even full-time workers have difficulty staying out of poverty, especially if they have families.

In Canada, this class is often associated with such factors as race, ethnicity, age, disability, and geographic region. For example, persistently and disproportionately represented in the so-called underclass of Canadian society are those of Aboriginal heritage. The social condition of Canada's Aboriginal people will be explored in greater detail in Chapter 8.

Conflict theorists, among others, have expressed alarm at the portion of Canada's population living on this lower rung of the stratification hierarchy and at society's reluctance to address the lack of economic opportunities for these people. Often, portraits of the underclass seem to "blame the victims" for their own plight while ignoring other factors that push people into poverty.

Analyses of the poor in general reveal that they are not a static social class. The overall composition of the poor changes continually, because some individuals and families near the top edge of poverty move above the poverty level after a year or two while others slip below it. Still, hundreds of thousands of people remain in poverty for many years at a time.

job ghettos. Figure 6-4 shows the narrowing difference in low-income rates for men and women in Canada in 2009, although the overall rate (for all income groups) shows that women have lower incomes. This reality, known as the *feminization of poverty*, is evident not just in Canada but also around the world. Some feminist thinkers trace the lower income levels among women to such factors as affordable and reliable childcare, and sex discrimination in the labour market, while others attribute it to more deep-rooted systemic factors (see Chapter 9).

As Figure 6-5 illustrates, in 2009, Aboriginal people, people with disabilities, recent immigrants, unattached people, and lone parents (mainly women) were more likely to experience low income.

Sociologist William Julius Wilson (1980, 1987, 1989, 1996) and other social scientists have used the term **underclass** to describe the long-term poor who lack training and skills.

Explaining Poverty Why is it that pervasive poverty continues within a nation of such vast wealth? Sociologist Herbert Gans has applied functionalist analysis to the existence of poverty and argues that various segments of society actually *benefit* from the existence of the poor (1995). Gans has identified a number of social, economic, and political functions that the poor perform for society:

- The presence of poor people means that society's dirty work—physically dirty or dangerous, dead-end and underpaid, undignified and menial jobs—will be performed at low cost.

- Poverty creates jobs for occupations and professions that service the poor. It creates both legal employment (public health experts, welfare caseworkers) and illegal jobs (drug dealers, numbers runners).

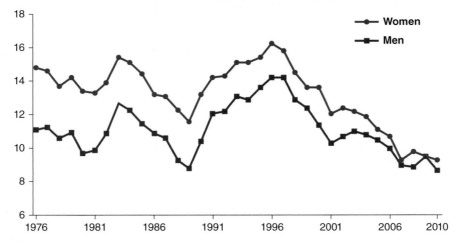

figure **6-4** **Low-Income Rate by Gender, Canada, 1976–2010 (percent of population)**

Note: Based on after-tax LICOs.
Source: Statistics Canada, Persons in Low Income Families, Annual (CANSIM Table 202-0802), Ottawa: Statistics Canada, 2012e.

figure 6-5 Low-Income Rates among Individuals Aged 18–64 Years Old, Various Groups 2009

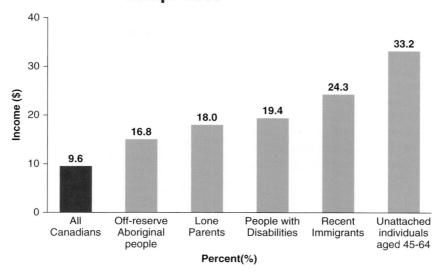

Source: Statistics Canada calculations based on Statistics Canada, Survey of Labour and Income Economics, Ottawa: Statistics Canada, 2011b.

- The identification and punishment of the poor as deviants upholds the legitimacy of conventional social norms and mainstream values regarding hard work, thrift, and honesty.

- Within a relatively hierarchical society, the existence of poor people guarantees the higher status of the more affluent. As psychologist William Ryan has noted, affluent people may justify inequality (and gain a measure of satisfaction) by "blaming the victims" of poverty for their disadvantaged condition (1976).

- Because of their lack of political power, the poor often absorb the costs of social change. Under the policy of deinstitutionalization, people with mental illnesses released from long-term hospitals have been "dumped" primarily into low-income communities and neighbourhoods. Similarly, halfway houses for rehabilitated drug abusers are often rejected by more affluent communities and end up in poorer neighbourhoods.

In Gans's view, then, poverty and the poor actually satisfy positive functions for many non-poor groups in society.

Life Chances

Max Weber saw class as closely related to people's **life chances**—that is, their opportunities to provide themselves with material goods, positive living conditions, and favourable life experiences (Gerth and Mills 1958). Life chances are reflected in such measures as housing, education, and health. Occupying a higher position in a society improves your life chances and brings greater access to social rewards. By contrast, people in the lower social classes are forced to devote a larger proportion of their limited resources to the necessities of life.

Class position also affects health in important ways. In fact, class is increasingly being viewed as an important predictor of health. The affluent avail themselves of improved health services while such advances bypass poor people. The chances of a child's dying during the first year of life are much higher in poor families than among the middle class. This higher infant mortality rate results in part from the inadequate nutrition received by low-income expectant mothers. Even when they survive infancy, the poor are more likely than the affluent to suffer from serious, chronic illnesses, such as arthritis, bronchitis, diabetes, and heart disease.

All these factors contribute to differences in the death rates of the poor and the affluent. Studies drawing on health data in Canada document the impact of class (as well as race) on mortality. Ill health among the poor only serves to increase the likelihood that the poor will remain impoverished (Link and Phelan 1995).

Some people have hoped that the Internet revolution would help level the playing field by making information and markets uniformly available. Unfortunately, however, not everyone is able to get onto the "information highway," and so yet another aspect of social inequality has emerged—the *digital divide* (see Chapter 10). People who are poor, who have less education, who are members of minority groups, or who live in rural communities are not getting connected at home or at work. For example, in 2007, 73 percent of Canadians aged 16 and over used the Internet for personal reasons. However, about 84 percent of these who used the Internet for personal reasons had some postsecondary education, compared to 58 percent with less education (Statistics Canada 2008). As more-educated people continue to buy high-speed Internet connections, they will be able to take advantage of even more sophisticated interactive services, and the digital divide will grow larger.

Wealth, status, and power may not ensure happiness, but they certainly provide additional ways of coping with problems and disappointments. For this reason, the opportunity for advancement—for social mobility—is of special significance to those who are at the bottom of society looking up. These people want the rewards and privileges that are granted to high-ranking members of a society.

The social policy section that closes this chapter focuses on the Canadian welfare system, a government program that serves many women and men who are trapped in poverty. The aim of welfare reform has been to encourage these people to find jobs and become self-supporting. We'll also see how other governments have approached welfare reform, and what the results have been.

::: use your sociological *imagination* :::

Imagine a society in which there are no social classes—no differences in people's wealth, income, and life chances. What would such a society be like? Would it be stable, or would its social structure change over time?

www.mcgrawhillconnect.ca

6.9 Does Social Mobility Exist?

Jimmy Pattison, a self-made billionaire and international businessman, grew up in impoverished circumstances in Luseland, Saskatchewan. He began his business career by selling used cars. Today, he is one of the wealthiest individuals in Canada and sole owner of one of the largest companies in Canada. The rise of a child from a poor background to a position of great prestige, power, and financial reward is an example of social mobility. The term **social mobility** refers to movement of individuals or groups from one position of a society's stratification system to another. But how significant—how frequent, how dramatic—is mobility in such a class society as Canada?

Open versus Closed Stratification Systems

Sociologists use the terms open stratification system and closed stratification system to indicate the amount of social mobility in a society. An **open system** implies that the position of each individual is influenced by the person's achieved status. At the other extreme of social mobility is the **closed system**, which allows little or no possibility of moving up. The slavery and caste systems of stratification are examples of closed systems. In such societies, social placement is based on ascribed statuses, such as race or family background, which cannot be changed.

Types of Social Mobility

A medical doctor who becomes a scientist moves from one social position to another of the same rank. Sociologists call this kind of movement **horizontal mobility**. However, if a journalist were to become a medical doctor, he or she would experience **vertical mobility**, the movement from one social position to another of a different rank. Vertical mobility can also involve moving downward in a society's stratification system, as would be the case if the doctor became a journalist. Pitirim Sorokin was the first sociologist to distinguish between horizontal and vertical mobility ([1927] 1959). Most sociological analysis, however, focuses on vertical rather than horizontal mobility.

One way of examining vertical social mobility is to contrast intergenerational and intragenerational mobility. **Intergenerational mobility** involves changes in the social position of children relative to their parents. Thus, a plumber whose father was a physician provides an example of downward intergenerational mobility. A film star whose parents were both factory workers illustrates upward intergenerational mobility.

Intragenerational mobility involves changes in social position within a person's adult life. A woman who enters the paid labour force as a teacher's aide and eventually becomes superintendent of the school district experiences upward intragenerational mobility. A man who becomes a taxicab driver after his accounting firm goes bankrupt undergoes downward intragenerational mobility.

Social Mobility in Canada

The belief in upward mobility is an important value in our society. Does this mean that Canada is indeed the land of opportunity? This can only be the case if such ascriptive characteristics as race, gender, and family background have ceased to be significant in determining someone's future prospects. We can see the impact of these factors in the occupational structure.

Occupational Mobility "You are three times more likely as a young man to move from rags to rags than rags to riches. And moving from riches to riches is the most likely of all." These are the words of the authors of a major Canadian study on the occupational mobility of 400 000 men between the ages of 16 and 19 (Corak and Heisz 1996). The authors concluded that although there is limited upward mobility in the middle ranges of the Canadian occupational hierarchy, the richest and poorest individuals tend to reproduce the income level of their fathers. This study is consistent with other studies of intragenerational mobility in Canada, which found that the majority of Canadians experienced no occupational mobility in their working lives (Creese, Guppy, and Meissner 1991). In Canada, achievement is not simply based on hard work and merit; ascribed characteristics, such as race, gender, and ethnicity, are significant in their influence on a person's chances for both intergenerational and intragenerational occupational mobility.

The Impact of Education Education plays a critical role in social mobility. The impact of advanced education on adult status is clearly evident in Canada, as documented in statistics showing the relationship between the highest level of educational achievement and income and wealth in adulthood. Generally, the higher a person's level of educational achievement, the higher his or her level of income and wealth (expressed as net worth). For example, in 2007, people with master's degrees working full-time made a median income of $60 000, while those holding bachelor's degrees working full-time made a median income of $45 000. The earning gap between those with a bachelor's level and master's level was 33 percent (Statistics Canada 2009c).

Although educational achievement is linked to social mobility, the stark reality is that the chance of achieving an education continues to be associated with family background. In 2002, 53 percent of Canadian 18- to 24-year-olds whose family income was less than $43 000 had never taken postsecondary education, while 83 percent of those in the same age group whose family income was $80 000 or more had taken postsecondary education (CAUT 2007). With the increased costs of tuition and other expenses associated with a postsecondary education, students who attend university are increasingly likely to have parents from the higher socio-economic groups.

The Impact of Racialization Racialization, class, and gender are intertwined in such a way as to produce diverse chances for both intergenerational mobility and intragenerational mobility. Canadian women who are racialized persons earn less than other Canadian women who are not. They also earn less than men, whether the men are racialized persons or not. For example, in 2005, racialized women earned roughly $5000 a year less than non-racialized women, roughly $9000 less than racialized men, and roughly $22 000 less than non-racialized men (Statistics Canada 2008). The glaring absence of racialized persons from corporate boardrooms, political office, and other positions of power and influence reflects a systemic pattern of inequality. As Joseph Mensah (2002:129) states in his book on blacks in Canada, "the unabashed racial discrimination in the job market impacts Blacks more than any other form of bigotry."

The Impact of Gender Studies of mobility, even more than those of class, have traditionally ignored the significance of gender, but some research findings are now available that explore the relationship between gender and mobility.

Women's employment opportunities are much more limited than men's (as we will see in Chapter 9). Moreover, according to recent research, women whose skills far exceed the jobs offered them are more likely than men to withdraw entirely from the paid labour force. This withdrawal violates an assumption common to traditional mobility studies: that most people will aspire to upward mobility and seek to make the most of their opportunities.

In contrast to men, women's jobs are heavily concentrated in the sales and service areas. But the modest salary ranges and few prospects for advancement in many of these positions limit the possibility of upward mobility. Self-employment as shopkeepers, entrepreneurs, independent professionals, and the like—an important road to upward mobility for men—is difficult for women, who find it harder to secure the necessary financing. Although sons often follow in the footsteps of their fathers, women are less likely to move into their fathers' positions. Consequently, gender remains an important factor in shaping social mobility within Canada. Women in Canada (and in other parts of the world) are especially more likely to be trapped in poverty and less able to rise out of their low-income status (Campaign 2000 2009).

So far we have focused on stratification and social mobility within Canada. In the next chapter, we broaden our focus to consider stratification from a global perspective. In Box 6-2, we provide a look at global inequality.

Christine Magee, president and co-founder of Sleep Country Canada, is one of the few women in Canada who have risen towards the top of the corporate hierarchy. Despite the implementation of employment-equity policies, occupational barriers still limit women's social mobility.

sociology in the global community

6-2 Poverty and Global Inequality

Rustica Banda is a midwife who delivers 10 to 13 babies a day at a community hospital near Lilongwe in Malawi, in sub-Saharan Africa. In 2008, two-thirds of all people infected with human immunodeficiency virus/acquired immune deficiency syndrome (HIV/AIDS) lived in sub-Saharan Africa. In addition, more than half of those infected globally, and three-fourths of those infected who lived in that part of Africa, were women, contributing to what has been called the "feminization of HIV/AIDS." Because of a lack of state funding to local hospitals for wages and basic medical supplies, such as plastic gloves, Rustica Banda and others like her work for low wages in unsafe and dangerous conditions to care for patients, some of whom have HIV/AIDS. Banda attributes the poverty in her country to global economic interconnectedness—more specifically, to debts with other countries. In 2003, owing more than 1.5 times its annual income, Malawi was one of the most heavily indebted countries in the world. In 2003, the country spent more than twice its funding for health care in servicing its debt. In this context, Rustica Banda describes the conditions in her life:

> I have five children to support, as well as five orphaned grandchildren. There is a great staff shortage here in Mitunda. At any one time, there are only two nurses on duty. . . . The pregnant woman must buy her own things for labour; a plastic sheet to put on the bed to protect her from the blood of other patients. . . . I have to use my bare hands when collecting blood, even when I don't know the HIV status of the patient. . . . The government says it does not have money for salaries or to buy enough equipment to run the hospital. It has too many debts with other countries. I call on the state of Malawi to consider its nurses and our salaries; we should not be running away from the government hospitals. I also ask the G8 to cancel Malawi's debt.

Make Poverty History, an alliance of charities, religious organizations, trade unions, anti-poverty groups, rock stars, and celebrities, mobilized to promote global awareness (e.g., Live 8) and to apply pressure on the G8 leaders (that is, leaders of the richest countries: Canada, the United States, Great Britain, Italy, Germany, France, Russia, and Japan) when they met in Scotland in 2005 for the G8 Summit. Make Poverty History called for governments and international decision makers to change policies regarding three inextricably connected areas—trade, debt, and aid—as they relate to the dealings between the world's richest and poorest countries. Falling short of some anti-poverty and AIDS activist groups' expectations, the G8 leaders did, however, agree to the following:

- to increase aid by US$25 billion annually to Africa by 2010
- to provide universal access to AIDS treatment by 2010
- to establish efforts to save 600 000 lives lost to malaria by 2015
- to train 20 000 additional peacekeepers for an African union peace force
- to call for trade talks to eliminate agricultural subsidies, which would help African products find markets

At the G8 summit held in Ontario in 2010, the leaders of the world's richest countries met with leaders from seven African countries to discuss the Canadian government's proposal of increasing support for maternal and child health in poor countries. The group of leaders also reviewed the US$18 billion shortfall in reaching what was pledged—at the 2005 G8 Summit—to fight poverty in Africa. For the first time, the G8 published a report on what each country has pledged and how close each has come to meeting its commitments of the past.

Apply the Theory

1. Have you ever been involved in a fundraising or awareness-raising campaign in your community or university to fight poverty in Africa?
2. Do you think that Canada is doing enough in its efforts to close the gap between the rich and the poor countries of the world?

Sources: Clark 2005; *Guardian Unlimited* 2005; UNAIDS 2010.

Social Policy and Stratification

Rethinking Social Assistance in North America and Europe

The Issue

- After five years of living on social assistance in Saskatchewan, a single mother of three is a success story. The 28-year-old has landed a job at a storage company and moved up to a $12-an-hour customer service position. However, another single mother employed in a nearby hotel for $8 per hour worries about being edged back into unemployment by the stiff competition for low-wage jobs.
- Hélène Desegrais, a single mother in Paris, France, waited for four months to obtain a place in government-subsidized daycare for her daughter. Now she can seek a full-time job, but she is concerned about government threats to curtail such services to keep taxes down (Simons 1997).
- Marcia Missouri of Worcester, Massachusetts, tacks up a handwritten advertisement in the public housing project in which she lives to say that she is available to clean yards and braid hair for a few extra dollars. The sign lists a friend's phone number; she doesn't have a phone of her own (Vobejda and Havenmann 1997).

These are the faces of people living on the edge—often women with children seeking to make a go of it amid changing social policies. Governments in all parts of the world are searching for the right approach to social assistance: How much subsidy should they provide? How much responsibility should fall on the shoulders of the poor?

The Setting

By the 1990s, there was intense debate in Canada over the issue of welfare. Welfare programs were costly, and there was widespread concern (however unfounded) that welfare payments discouraged recipients from seeking jobs. On the one hand, there were declarations to "end poverty as we know it" (Pear 1996:20); on the other, neoconservative forces in Canada voiced concern about government spending.

According to a Canadian report by the National Council of Welfare (2010), it is now more difficult to get welfare than during the economic downturn in the early 1990s. Most provinces now force people in need to have little savings in order to qualify for welfare. Welfare rates fall below the poverty line; in 2009 monthly welfare rates in Ontario were $576 for a single person and $1500 for a single parent.

Countries vary widely in their commitment to social service programs. But some industrialized nations devote higher proportions of their expenditures to housing, social security, welfare, health care, and unemployment compensation than Canada does. Data available in 2004 indicated that

in Great Britain, 82 percent of health expenditures were paid for by the government; in Spain and Canada, 71 percent; but in the United States, only 44 percent (World Bank 2004:88–90).

Sociological Insights

Many sociologists tend to view the debate over welfare throughout industrialized nations from a conflict perspective: the "haves" in positions of policymaking listen to the interests of other "haves," while the cries of the "have-nots" are drowned out. Critics of so-called welfare reform believe that Canada's economic problems are unfairly being blamed on welfare spending and the poor. From a conflict perspective, this backlash against welfare recipients reflects deep fears and hostility toward the country's poor and dispossessed. Sylvia Bashevkin, in her book *Welfare Hot Buttons: Women, Work, and Social Policy Reform*, examines welfare reform in three countries—Canada, the United States, and the United Kingdom—over the last two decades (2002). She discovered similarities in the consequences of welfare reform in these three countries. In each, there was a decline in caseloads, an increase in the rates of employment of single mothers, and a backlash against poor women and welfare-reliant mothers. In Canada, single-parent households—overwhelmingly headed by women, disproportionately poor and, thus, more likely to require welfare assistance—make up an unprecedented one in four families (Statistics Canada 2007m). Bashevkin argues that we are moving toward a "duty state" where citizens are viewed as having a responsibility and obligation to the state, based on a market exchange.

Those critical of the backlash note that "welfare scapegoating" conveniently ignores the lucrative government handouts that go to *affluent* individuals and families. British Columbia's government, for example, has reduced income taxes for all residents, including the wealthy, while at the same time reducing or eliminating government services and programs that most benefit the poor. A 2009 study by the Canadian Centre for Policy Alternatives concluded that "Canadians depend to a significant extent on public services such as education, health care, child care, public pensions, employment insurance and family benefits for their standard of living" (2009:3). Making the argument that tax cuts that result in fewer public services are socially harmful, the study concluded that most Canadians are "getting a quiet bargain by investing in taxes that produce enormous public benefits" (2009:3).

Those who take a conflict perspective also urge policymakers and the general public to look closely at *corporate welfare*—the tax breaks, direct payments, and grants that governments make to

For nations like Sweden, which have comparatively little income disparity, programs aimed at alleviating disparity are not as necessary as they are in the United States and Canada.

corporations—rather than to focus on the comparatively small allowances being given to mothers on social assistance and their children. Any suggestion to curtail such corporate welfare brings a strong response from special-interest groups that are much more powerful than any coalition on behalf of the poor. One example of corporate welfare was the bailouts of large financial corporations in the United States and automobile companies in both the United States and Canada during the economic recession of 2008–2009. While many executives were able to hold on to their jobs, many lower-paid employees were laid off. In Canada from October 2008 to October 2009, those receiving regular employment insurance benefits increased by 55.5 percent. Particularly hard hit were young Canadians (those under 25 years old), whose rate of benefit increase was 77.5 percent (Statistics Canada 2010b).

Policy Initiatives

Governments like to highlight success stories. It is true that some people who previously depended on tax dollars are now working and paying taxes themselves. But it is much too soon to say whether or not welfare reform will be successful. The new jobs that were generated by the booming economy of the late 1990s and early 2000s may be an unrealistic test of the system. Prospects for the chronically jobless—those people who are hard to train or who have drug or alcohol dependency, physical disabilities, or childcare needs—remain a challenge.

In the United States, fewer people are on welfare since the enactment of the welfare reform law in 1996. By June 2007, fewer than 1.7 million families were on welfare, down 65 percent from the high of 5.4 million in 1994. While the welfare rolls have declined, the number of Americans who receive Medicaid and food stamps increased 50 percent since 2000 (Cherlin 2008b; Haskins 2006; Health and Human Services 2007; Wolf 2006).

European governments have encountered some of the same citizen demands as those that occur in North America: keep taxes low, even if it means reducing services to the poor. However, nations in Eastern and Central Europe have faced a special challenge since the fall of communism. The governments in those nations had traditionally provided an impressive array of social services, but they differed from capitalist systems in several important respects. First, the communist system was premised on full employment, so there was no need to provide employment insurance or social services focused on older people and those with disabilities. Second, subsidies, such as those for housing and even utilities, played an important role. With new competition from the West and tight budgets, some

of these countries are beginning to realize that universal coverage is no longer affordable and must be replaced with targeted programs. Even Sweden, despite its long history of social welfare programs, is feeling the pinch. Still, only modest cutbacks have been made in European social service programs, leaving them much more generous than those in Canada and the United States (Petrásöva 2006).

Both in North America and Europe, people are beginning to turn to private means to support themselves. For instance, they are investing money for their later years rather than depending on government social security programs. But that solution works only if you have a job and can save money. Increasing proportions of people are seeing the gap growing between themselves and the

affluent with fewer government programs aimed at assisting them. Solutions are frequently left to the private sector, while government policy initiatives at the national level all but disappear.

Apply the Theory

1. What might be the focus of some feminist sociologists as they study the changes in welfare reform in Canada and elsewhere?
2. How would you explain the trend of the decreasing number of Canadians receiving social assistance?
3. Have you or has anyone you know applied for social assistance? If so, what caused you or them to do so?

CHAPTER RESOURCES

Summary

::: 6.1 What Is Stratification?

- **Stratification** is the structured ranking of entire groups of people in a society, which leads to the perpetuation of **social inequality**. Stratification is manifested in all cultures through systems of stratification, which include **slavery, castes,** and social **class**.
- Karl Marx saw that differences in access to the means of production created social, economic, and political inequality and distinct classes of owners and labourers.
- Max Weber identified three analytically distinct components of stratification: **class, status group,** and **power**.
- Functionalists argue that stratification is necessary to motivate people to fill society's important

positions; conflict theorists see stratification as a major source of societal tension and conflict.

::: 6.2 How Are Stratification and Social Class Related?

- One measure of social class is occupational **prestige**. A consequence of social class in Canada is that both **wealth** and **income** are distributed unevenly.
- The category of the "poor" defies any simple definition, and counters common stereotypes about "poor people." The long-term poor, who lack training and skills, form an **underclass**.
- Functionalists find that the poor satisfy positive functions for many of the non-poor in capitalist societies.

- A person's **life chances**— opportunities for obtaining material goods, positive living conditions, and favourable life experiences—are related to social class. Occupying a high social position improves a person's life chances.

::: 6.3 Does Social Mobility Exist?

- **Social mobility** is more likely to be found in an **open system** that emphasizes achieved status than in a **closed system** that focuses on ascribed characteristics.
- Race, gender, and class intersect to produce compounded chances for social mobility.

Critical Thinking Questions

1. How would functional thinkers explain the growing gap between the rich and the poor in Canada? What about among nations?
2. Sociological study of stratification generally is conducted at the macro level and draws most heavily on the functionalist and conflict perspectives. How might sociologists use the interactionist perspective to examine social class inequalities within a university?

3. Imagine you have the opportunity to do research on changing patterns of social mobility in a developing nation from a feminist perspective. What specific question would you want to investigate, and how would you go about it?
4. Why do you think companies like Nike and Walmart do not produce products in their own country?

THINKING ABOUT MOVIES

Titanic
This film illustrates Weber's concept of life chances.

The Fighter
Two working-class brothers strive for upward mobility in the world of professional boxing.

Pursuit of Happyness
A homeless man struggles to make a life for his son.

inside

BOXES

In Trinidad, Bolivia, open drains threaten children's health. Bolivia is a highly stratified society in which a significant portion of the population lives in poverty.

136

7 Global Inequality

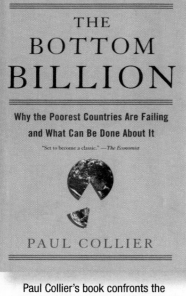

THE BOTTOM BILLION

Why the Poorest Countries Are Failing and What Can Be Done About It

"Set to become a classic." —*The Economist*

PAUL COLLIER

Paul Collier's book confronts the causes and conditions of the world's poorest people and what can be done to alleviate poverty.

> The third world has shrunk. For forty years the development challenge has been a rich world of one billion people facing a poor world of five billion people . . . . By 2015, however, it will be apparent that this way of conceptualizing development has become outdated. Most of the five billion, about 80 percent, live in countries that are indeed developing, often at amazing speed. The real challenge of development is that there is a group of countries at the bottom that are falling behind, and often falling apart.

The countries at the bottom coexist with the twenty-first century, but their reality is the fourteenth century: civil war, plague, ignorance. They are concentrated in Africa and Central Asia, with a scattering elsewhere. Even during the 1990s, in retrospect the golden decade between the end of the Cold War and 9/11, incomes in this group declined by 5 percent. We must learn to turn the familiar numbers upside down: a total of five billion people who are already prosperous, or at least are on track to be so, and one billion who are stuck at the bottom.

This problem matters, and not just to the billion people who are living and dying in fourteenth-century conditions. It matters to us. The twenty-first-century world of material comfort, global travel, and economic interdependence will become increasingly vulnerable to these large islands of chaos. And it matters now. As the bottom billion diverges from an increasingly sophisticated world economy, integration will become harder, not easier.

And yet it is a problem denied, both by development *biz* and by development *buzz*. Development biz is run by the aid agencies and the companies that get the contracts for their projects. They will fight this thesis with the tenacity of bureaucracies endangered, because they like things the way they are. A definition of development that encompasses five billion people gives them license to be everywhere, or more honestly, everywhere but the bottom billion. At the bottom, conditions are rather rough. Every development agency has difficulty getting its staff to serve in Chad and Laos; the glamour postings are for countries such as Brazil and China. The World Bank has large offices in every major middle-income country but not a single person resident in the Central African Republic. . . .

. . .

What of the governments of the countries at the bottom? The prevailing conditions bring out extremes. Leaders are sometimes psychopaths who have shot their way to power, sometimes crooks who have bought it, and sometimes brave people who, against the odds, are trying to build a better future. Even the appearance of modern government in these states is sometimes a façade . . . the government of Somalia continued to be officially "represented" in the international arena for years after Somalia ceased to have a functioning government in the country itself. So don't expect the governments of the bottom billion to unite in formulating a practical agenda.

(Collier 2007:3–5)

How can poverty be alleviated—not just poverty in a household or a neighbourhood, but poverty among hundreds of millions of the world's poorest people? For most of his adult life, Paul Collier, an economist at Oxford University, has pondered this question. In this excerpt from his book *The Bottom Billion: Why the Poorest Countries Are Failing and What Can Be Done About It*, Collier outlines the magnitude of the challenge. He thinks that the answer lies in avoiding the pitfalls that developing countries may fall into: depletion of their natural resources, ineffective government, prolonged internal conflict, protracted wars, and insufficient economic development.

What economic and political conditions explain the divide between rich nations and poor? Within developing nations, how are wealth and income distributed, and how much opportunity does the average worker have to move up the social ladder? How do race and gender affect social mobility in these countries? In this chapter, we focus on global inequality, beginning with the global divide. We consider the impact of colonialism and neo-colonialism, globalization, the rise of multinational corporations, grinding poverty, and the trend toward modernization. Then, we focus on stratification within nations, in terms of the distribution of wealth and income and social mobility. The chapter closes with a social policy section on universal human rights.

::: use your sociological *imagination* :::

Have you ever considered some actions that might reduce the inequality between rich and poor nations?

People's needs and desires differ dramatically depending on where they live. On the left, eager customers endure crowded lines at a Toronto mall during a Boxing Day sale. On the right, residents of Ethiopia line up to receive water.

7-1 What Is the Global Divide?

In some parts of the world, the people who have dedicated their lives to fighting starvation refer to what they call "coping mechanisms"—ways in which the desperately poor attempt to control their hunger. Eritrean women will strap flat stones to their stomachs to lessen their hunger pangs. In Mozambique, people eat the grasshoppers that have destroyed their crops, calling them "flying shrimp." Though dirt eating is considered a pathological condition (called *geophagy*) among the well-fed, the world's poor eat dirt to add minerals and taste, and to provide immunological support to their diet. And in many countries, mothers have been known to boil stones in water, to convince their hungry children that supper is almost ready. As they hover over the pot, these women hope that their malnourished children will fall asleep (McNeil 2004).

Around the world, inequality is a significant determinant of human behaviour, opening doors of opportunity to some and closing them to others. Indeed, disparities in life chances are so extreme that in some places, the poorest of the poor may not be aware of them. Western media images may have circled the globe, but in extremely depressed rural areas, those at the bottom of society are not likely to see them. A few centuries ago, such vast divides in global wealth did not exist. Except for a very few rulers and landowners, everyone in the world was poor. In much of Europe, life was as difficult as it was in Asia or South America. This was true until the Industrial Revolution and rising agricultural productivity produced explosive economic growth. The resulting rise in living standards was not evenly distributed across the world.

Figure 7-1 compares the industrial nations of the world to the developing nations. Using total population as a yardstick, we see that the developing countries have more than their fair share of rural population, as well as of total births, disease, and childhood deaths. At the same time, the industrial nations of

figure 7-1 Fundamental Global Inequality

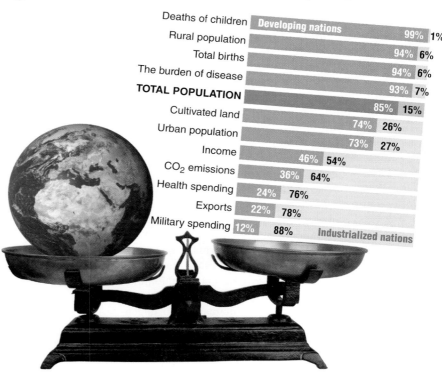

	Developing nations	Industrialized nations
Deaths of children	99%	1%
Rural population	94%	6%
Total births	94%	6%
The burden of disease	94%	6%
TOTAL POPULATION	93%	7%
Cultivated land	85%	15%
Urban population	74%	26%
Income	73%	27%
CO_2 emissions	46%	54%
Health spending	36%	64%
Exports	24%	76%
Military spending	22%	78%
	12%	88%

Note: In this comparison, industrial nations include Canada and the United States, Japan, and countries of Western Europe and Australasia. Developing nations include countries of Africa, Asia (except for Japan), Latin America, Eastern Europe, the Caribbean, and the Pacific.

Source: Adapted from Sutcliffe 2002:18.

Think about It
What is the relationship among health spending, disease, and deaths of children? Among CO_2 emissions, income, and exports?

the world, with a much smaller share of total population, have significantly more income and exports than the developing nations. Industrial nations also spend more on health and the military than other nations, and they emit more carbon dioxide (CO_2) (Sachs 2005a; Sutcliffe 2002).

7-2 What Forms Does Global Inequality Take?

The divide between industrial and developing nations is sharp, but sociologists recognize a continuum of nations, from the richest of the rich to the poorest of the poor. For example, in 2004, the average value of goods and services produced per citizen (or per capita gross national income) in the industrialized countries of the United States, Japan, Switzerland, Belgium, and Norway was more than US$30 000. In at least 12 poorer countries, the value was just $900 or less. But most countries fell somewhere between those extremes, as Figure 7-2 shows.

Still, the contrasts are stark. Three forces discussed here are particularly responsible for the domination of the world marketplace by a few nations: the legacy of colonialism, the advent of multinational corporations, and modernization.

The Legacy of Colonialism

Colonialism occurs when a foreign power maintains political, social, economic, and cultural domination over a people for an extended period. Central to colonialism are values, beliefs, and ideas of inferiority/superiority regarding race and white superiority. In simple terms, colonialism is rule by outsiders. The long reign of the British Empire over much of North America, parts of Africa, and India is an example of colonial domination. The same can be said of French rule over Algeria, Tunisia, and other parts of North Africa. Relations between the colonial nation and colonized people are similar to those between the dominant capitalist class and the proletariat, as described by Karl Marx.

By the 1980s, colonialism had largely disappeared from the world. Most of the nations that were colonies before World War I had achieved political independence and established their own governments. However, for many of these countries, the transition to genuine self-rule was not yet complete. Colonial domination had established patterns of economic exploitation that continued even after nationhood was achieved—in part because former colonies were unable to develop their own industry and technology. Their dependence on more industrialized nations, including their former colonial masters, for managerial and technical expertise, investment capital, and manufactured goods kept former colonies in a subservient position. Such continuing dependence and foreign domination are referred to as **neo-colonialism**.

The economic and political consequences of colonialism and neo-colonialism are readily apparent. Drawing on the conflict perspective, sociologist Immanuel Wallerstein views the global economic system as being divided between nations that control wealth and nations from which resources are taken (1974, 1979a, 2000). Through his **world systems analysis**, Wallerstein has described the unequal economic and political relationships in which certain industrialized nations (among them the United States, Japan, and Germany) and their global corporations dominate the core of this system (see Figure 7-3). At the *semi-periphery* of the system are countries with marginal economic status, such as Israel, Ireland, and South Korea. Wallerstein suggests that the poor developing countries of Asia, Africa, and Latin America are on the *periphery* of the world economic system. The key to Wallerstein's analysis is the exploitative relationship of *core* nations toward *non-core* nations. Core nations and their corporations control and exploit non-core nations' economies. Unlike other nations, the core nations are relatively independent of outside control (Chase-Dunn and Grimes 1995).

The division between core and periphery nations is significant and remarkably stable. A study by the International Monetary Fund (IMF) found little change over the course of the *last 100 years* for the 42 economies that were studied (2000). The only changes were Japan's movement up into the group of core nations and China's movement down toward the margins of the semi-periphery nations. Yet Immanuel Wallerstein (2000) speculates that the world system as we currently understand it may soon undergo unpredictable changes. The world is becoming increasingly urbanized, a trend that is gradually eliminating the large pools of low-cost workers in rural areas. In the future, core nations will have to find other ways to reduce their labour costs. The exhaustion of land and water resources through clear-cutting and pollution is also driving up the costs of production.

Wallerstein's world systems analysis is the most widely used version of **dependency theory**. According to this theory, even as developing countries make economic advances, they remain weak and subservient to core nations and corporations in an increasingly intertwined global economy. This interdependency allows industrialized nations to continue to exploit developing countries for their own gain. In a sense, dependency theory applies the conflict perspective on a global scale.

In the view of world systems analysis and dependency theory, a growing share of the human and natural resources of developing countries is being redistributed to the core industrialized nations. This redistribution happens in part because developing countries owe huge sums of money to industrialized nations as a result of foreign aid, loans, and trade deficits. The global debt crisis has intensified the Third World dependency begun under colonialism, neo-colonialism, and multinational investment. International financial institutions are pressuring indebted countries to take severe measures to meet their interest payments. The result is that developing nations may be forced to devalue their currencies, freeze workers' wages, increase privatization of industry, and reduce government services and employment.

Closely related to these problems is *globalization*, the worldwide integration of government policies, cultures, social movements, and financial markets through trade and the exchange of ideas. Because world financial markets transcend governance by conventional nation states, international organizations such as the World Bank and the IMF have emerged as major players in the global economy. The function of these institutions, which are heavily funded and influenced by core nations, is to encourage economic trade and development and to ensure the smooth operation of international financial

figure **7-2** Gross National Income per Capita

MAPPING LIFE WORLDWIDE

GNI per capita in 2010

Below $3,100

$3,100–$7,995

$8,000–$19,100

Over $19,200

No available data

Note: Country sizes and incomes based on 2010 estimates. Includes only those countries with 3 million or more people.

Sources: Haub 2010; Weeks 2012.

This stylized map reflects the relative population sizes of the world's nations. The colour for each country shows the gross national income (the total value of goods and services produced by the nation in a given year) per capita.

figure 7-3 World Systems Analysis at the Beginning of the Twenty-First Century

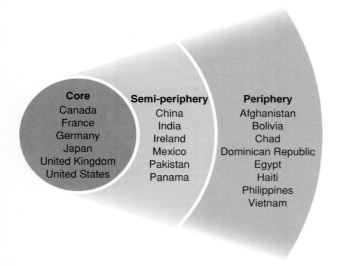

Core	Semi-periphery	Periphery
Canada	China	Afghanistan
France	India	Bolivia
Germany	Ireland	Chad
Japan	Mexico	Dominican Republic
United Kingdom	Pakistan	Egypt
United States	Panama	Haiti
		Philippines
		Vietnam

Note: Figure shows only a partial listing of countries.

markets. As such, they are seen as promoters of globalization and defenders primarily of the interests of core nations. Critics call attention to a variety of issues, including violations of workers' rights, the destruction of the environment, the loss of cultural identity, and discrimination against minority groups in periphery nations (Box 7-1).

Some observers see globalization and its effects as the natural result of advances in communications technology, particularly the Internet and satellite transmission of the mass media. Others view it more critically, as a process that allows multinational corporations to expand unchecked, as we will see in the next section.

Modernization

Around the world, millions of people are witnessing a revolutionary transformation of their day-to-day life. Contemporary social scientists use the term **modernization** to describe the far-reaching process by which periphery nations move from traditional or less developed institutions to those characteristic of more developed societies.

Wendell Bell, whose definition of modernization we are using, notes that modern societies tend to be urban, literate, and industrial (1981). These societies have sophisticated transportation and media systems. Their families tend to be organized within the nuclear family unit rather than the extended-family model (see Chapter 12). Thus, members of societies that undergo modernization must shift their allegiance from traditional sources of authority, such as parents, elders, and priests, to newer authorities, such as government officials.

Many sociologists are quick to note that terms such as *modernization* and even *development* contain an ethnocentric bias. The unstated assumption behind these terms is that "they" (people living in developing countries) are struggling to become more like "us" (in the core industrialized nations). Viewed from a conflict perspective, these terms perpetuate the dominant ideology of capitalist societies.

The term *modernization* also suggests positive change. Yet, change—if it comes at all—often comes slowly; and when it does, it tends to serve the affluent segments of industrial nations. This truism seems to apply to the spread of the latest electronic technologies to the developing world.

A similar criticism has been made of **modernization theory**, a functionalist approach that proposes that modernization and development will gradually improve the lives of people in developing nations. According to this theory, even though countries develop at uneven rates, the development of peripheral countries will be assisted by innovations transferred from the industrialized world. Critics of modernization theory, including dependency theorists, counter that any such technology transfer only increases the dominance of core nations over developing countries and facilitates further exploitation. (Table 7-1 summarizes the three major approaches to global inequality.)

::: use your sociological *imagination* :::

You are travelling through a developing country. What evidence do you see of neo-colonialism and globalization?

table 7-1 Three Approaches to Global Inequality: Sociological Approach, Perspective, and Explanation

Sociological Approach	Sociological Perspective	Sociological Explanation
World systems analysis	Functionalist and conflict	Unequal economic and political relationships maintain sharp divisions among nations.
Dependency theory	Conflict	Industrial nations exploit developing countries through colonialism and multinational corporations.
Modernization theory	Functionalist	Developing countries are moving away from traditional cultures and toward the cultures of industrialized nations.

sociology in the global community

7-1 Income Inequality: A Global Perspective

Just how do incomes compare across the globe? Within nations? Sociologists Roberto Korzeniewicz and Timothy Moran faced these questions head-on and obtained some dramatic answers.

To simplify the task of comparing incomes across billions of people, the two researchers divided residents of each country into 10 deciles, or groups of 10 percent, based on per capita incomes. Then they ranked each set of deciles from the highest (Decile 10) to the lowest (Decile 1). Finally, they did the same for the world as a whole, dividing the world's population into deciles based on income.

Korzeniewicz and Moran found that in Norway and Switzerland, members of Decile 10 made slightly more income than members of the same decile in Denmark, Canada, and Germany. Outside Europe and North America, however, inequality became more apparent, both between and within nations. In the United States, members of Decile 4—that is, those people with incomes in the bottom 31 to 40 percent—fell within the top decile for the world as a whole. In the United States (or Germany or France, for that matter), members of Decile 4 were better off than members of Decile 10 in Brazil, Malaysia, Poland, and Russia.

You might think you would rather be in the richest decile in Poland than the seventh richest decile in the United States. However, in Poland an engineer or doctor may earn a salary equivalent to a factory worker's salary in the United States. Although the Polish professor may enjoy a relatively high status, he or she may not be able to afford to own a home or to go away on vacation. Similarly, the average income of a food service worker in Decile 2 in the United States may exceed the earnings of a middle-class worker in China, Romania, or Mexico. From the perspective of a U.S. resident, income inequality within the nation may be sharp, but from a global perspective it is not nearly as dramatic as income inequality in a world where hundreds of millions of people struggle just to survive.

The American Pet Products Manufacturers Association estimates the average annual expenditure on a dog in the United States at around $1400—a figure comparable to human incomes in nations like Paraguay and Egypt.

The degree of global inequality becomes even more apparent if we compare the resources consumed by dogs in the United States to the incomes of people around the world. The American Pet Products Manufacturers Association estimates the average annual expenditure on a dog in the United States at around $1400—a figure comparable to human incomes in nations like Paraguay and Egypt. U.S. dogs, in fact, are better off than 40 percent of the world's people. Their health care expenditures alone exceed those of 80 percent of the world's humans.

Apply the Theory

1. Does your family have a pet? If so, how much money do you think you spend on your pet every year? How does that figure compare to the average annual income in China or India?
2. By itself, do you think Korzeniewicz and Moran's income-based measure is a sufficient indicator of global inequality? If not, what other kinds of information would you want to consider?

Sources: Korzeniewicz and Moran 2009; Therborn 2010.

Multinational Corporations

Worldwide, corporate giants play a key role in neo-colonialism. The term **multinational corporation** refers to any commercial organization that is headquartered in one country but does business throughout the world. Such private trade and lending relationships are not new; merchants have conducted business abroad for hundreds of years, trading gems, spices, garments, and other goods. However, today's multinational giants are not merely buying and selling overseas; they are also *producing* goods all over the world (Wallerstein 1974).

Moreover, today's "global factories" (factories throughout the developing world that are run by multinational corporations) may now have the "global office" alongside them. Multinationals based in core countries are beginning to establish reservation services and centres for processing data and insurance claims in the periphery nations. As service industries become a more important part of the international marketplace, many companies are concluding that the low costs of overseas operations more than offset the expense of transmitting information around the world.

Do not underestimate the size of these global corporations. As Figure 7-4 shows, the total revenues of multinational businesses are on a par with the total value of goods and services exchanged in *entire nations*. Foreign sales represent an important source of profit for multinational corporations—these sales encourage them to expand into other countries (in many cases, the developing nations). The economy of the United States is heavily dependent on foreign commerce, much of which is conducted by multinationals. Over one-quarter of all commerce in the United States has to do with either the export of goods to foreign countries or the import of goods from abroad (U.S. Trade Representative 2007).

Functionalist View Functionalists believe that multinational corporations can actually help the developing nations of the world. They bring jobs and industry to areas where subsistence agriculture once served as the only means of survival. Multinationals also promote rapid development through the diffusion of inventions and innovations from industrial nations. Viewed from a functionalist perspective, the combination of skilled technology and management provided by multinationals and the relatively cheap labour available in developing nations is ideal for a global enterprise. Multinationals can take maximum advantage of technology while reducing costs and boosting profits.

In a factory in China, workers assemble toys for export to the United States. The pitfalls of globalization were brought home—literally—to U.S. consumers in 2007, when U.S. companies were forced to recall toys manufactured in China because they were finished with lead-based paint.

figure 7-4 Multinational Corporations Compared to Nations

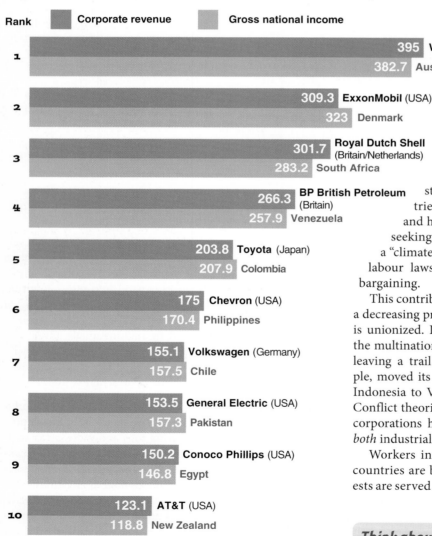

Rank | Corporate revenue | Gross national income

Rank		
1	395 **Walmart** (USA)	
	382.7 Austria	
2	309.3 **ExxonMobil** (USA)	
	323 Denmark	
3	301.7 **Royal Dutch Shell** (Britain/Netherlands)	
	283.2 South Africa	
4	266.3 **BP British Petroleum** (Britain)	
	257.9 Venezuela	
5	203.8 **Toyota** (Japan)	
	207.9 Colombia	
6	175 **Chevron** (USA)	
	170.4 Philippines	
7	155.1 **Volkswagen** (Germany)	
	157.5 Chile	
8	153.5 **General Electric** (USA)	
	157.3 Pakistan	
9	150.2 **Conoco Phillips** (USA)	
	146.8 Egypt	
10	123.1 **AT&T** (USA)	
	118.8 **New Zealand**	

Sources: Rankings prepared by author. Revenue from corporate quarterly report statements (Q2 2009 through Q2 2010). GNI from World Bank 2010:32–34.

Through their international ties, multinational corporations also make the nations of the world more interdependent. These ties may prevent certain disputes from reaching the point of serious conflict. A country cannot afford to sever diplomatic relations or engage in warfare with a nation that is the headquarters for its main business suppliers or a key outlet for its exports.

Conflict View Conflict theorists challenge this favourable evaluation of the impact of multinational corporations. They emphasize that multinationals exploit local workers to maximize profits. Starbucks—the international coffee retailer based in Seattle, Washington—gets much of its coffee from farms in Ethiopia. A recent documentary, entitled *Black Gold*, documented the dismal working conditions of the Ethiopian coffee workers (Kornell 2007).

The pool of cheap labour in the developing world prompts multinationals to move factories out of core countries. An added bonus for the multinationals is that the developing world discourages strong trade unions. In industrialized countries, organized labour insists on decent wages and humane working conditions, but governments seeking to attract or keep multinationals may develop a "climate for investment" that includes repressive anti-labour laws that restrict union activity and collective bargaining.

This contributes to a process of de-unionization, in which a decreasing proportion of a region or country's labour force is unionized. If labour's demands become too threatening, the multinational firm will simply move its plant elsewhere, leaving a trail of unemployment behind. Nike, for example, moved its factories from the United States to Korea to Indonesia to Vietnam in search of the lowest labour costs. Conflict theorists conclude that on the whole, multinational corporations have a negative social impact on workers in *both* industrialized and developing nations.

Workers in Canada, the United States, and other core countries are beginning to recognize that their own interests are served by helping to organize workers in developing

Think about It
What happens to society when corporations grow richer than countries and spill across international borders?

figure 7-5 Poverty Worldwide

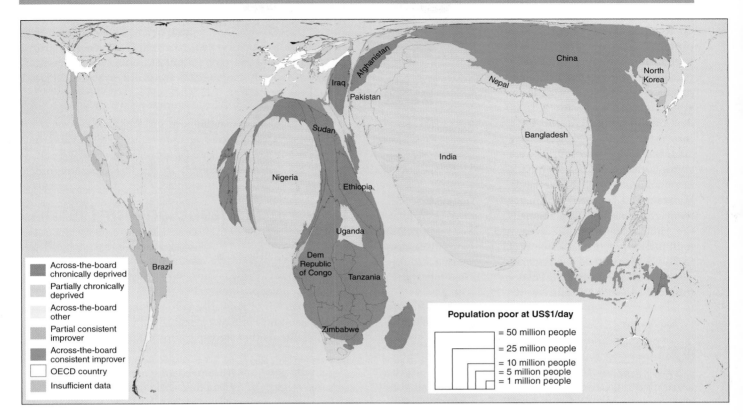

Population poor at US$1/day

	= 50 million people
	= 25 million people
	= 10 million people
	= 5 million people
	= 1 million people

Legend:
- Across-the-board chronically deprived
- Partially chronically deprived
- Across-the-board other
- Partial consistent improver
- Across-the-board consistent improver
- OECD country
- Insufficient data

Sources: Chronic Poverty Research Centre 2009.

The scale of this map is based on the number of people in each region who are chronically poor. The colours represent the income levels of those who are poorest. In OECD countries—those that belong to the Organisation for Economic Co-Operation and Development (white)—chronic poverty is not a nationwide issue.

> ### Think about It
> To what degree does the map in Figure 7-5 minimize those countries you have studied or might want to visit? To what degree does it emphasize parts of the world about which you know very little?

nations. As long as multinationals can exploit cheap labour abroad, they will be in a strong position to reduce wages and benefits in industrialized countries. With this in mind, in the 1990s, labour unions, religious organizations, campus groups, and other activists mounted public campaigns to pressure companies such as Nike, Starbucks, Reebok, The Gap, and Walmart to improve wages and working conditions in their overseas operations (Global Alliance for Workers and Communities 2003; Gonzalez 2003; Thottam 2005).

Several sociologists who have surveyed the effects of foreign investment by multinationals conclude that although it may initially contribute to a host nation's wealth, it eventually increases economic inequality within developing nations. This conclusion holds true for both income and ownership of land. The upper and middle classes benefit most from economic expansion, whereas the lower classes

are less likely to benefit. As conflict theorists point out, multinationals invest in limited economic sectors and restricted regions of a nation. Although certain sectors of the host nation's economy expand, such as hotels and expensive restaurants, their very expansion appears to retard growth in agriculture and other economic sectors. Moreover, multinational corporations often buy out or force out local entrepreneurs and companies, thereby increasing economic and cultural dependence (Chase-Dunn and Grimes 1995; Kerbo 2003; Wallerstein 1979b).

Worldwide Poverty

What would a map of the world look like if we drew it to a scale that reflects the number of *poor* people in each country instead of the number of people, as in Figure 7-2? As Figure 7-5 shows, when we focus on the poverty level rather than the population, the world looks quite different. Note the huge areas of poverty in Africa and Asia, and the comparatively small areas of affluence in industrialized North America and Europe. Poverty is a worldwide problem that blights the lives of billions of people.

In 2000, the United Nations launched the Millennium Project, whose objective is to eliminate extreme poverty worldwide by the year 2015 (see Box 7-2). While 15 years may seem a long time, the challenge is great. Today, almost 3 billion people subsist on $2 a day or less. To accomplish the project's goal, planners estimate that industrial nations must set aside 0.7 percent of their **gross national product**—the value of a nation's goods and services—for aid to developing nations. At the time the Millennium Project was launched, only five countries were giving at that target rate: Denmark, Luxembourg, the Netherlands, Norway, and Sweden. To match their contribution proportionally, the United States would need to multiply its present aid level by 45 (Sachs 2005a). Figure 7-6 illustrates foreign aid to developing nations from eight wealthy nations.

figure **7-6** Foreign Aid per Capita in Nine Countries

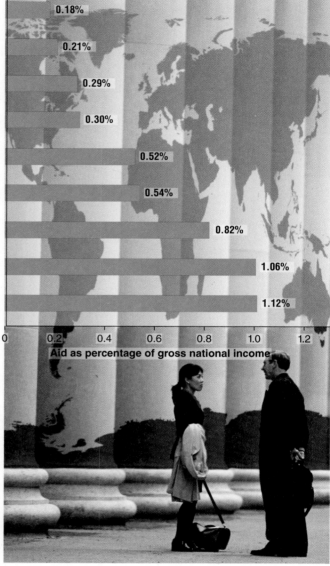

Total aid in $ millions

Country	Total aid in $ millions	Aid as percentage of gross national income
Japan	9.5	0.18%
USA	28.8	0.21%
Australia	2.8	0.29%
Canada	4.0	0.30%
Great Britain	11.5	0.52%
Ireland	1.0	0.54%
Netherlands	6.4	0.82%
Norway	4.1	1.06%
Sweden	4.5	1.12%

Note: Actual net development assistance in 2009.

Source: Organisation for Economic Co-operation and Development 2011:2.

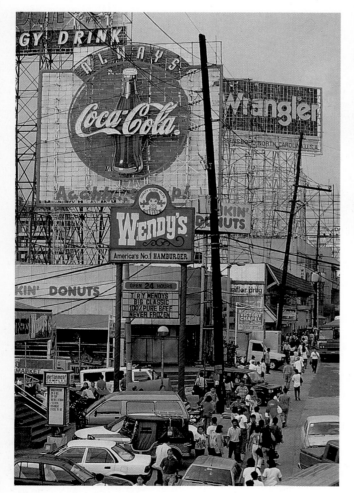

The influence of multinational corporations abroad can be seen in this street scene from Manila, capital of the Philippines.

Privileged people in industrialized nations tend to assume that the world's poor lack significant assets. Yet, again and again, observers from these countries have been startled to discover how far even a small amount of capital can go. Numerous micro-finance programs, which involve relatively small grants or loans, have encouraged marginalized people to invest not in livestock, which may die, or jewellery, which may be stolen, but in technological improvements such as small cooking stoves. In Indonesia, for example, some 60 000 micro-loans have enabled families who once cooked their food in a pit to purchase stoves. Improvements such as this not only enable people to cook more food at a more consistent

sociology in the global community

7-2 Cutting Poverty Worldwide

The goal of the United Nations Millennium Project is to cut the world's poverty level in half by 2015. The project has eight objectives:

1. *Eradicate extreme poverty and hunger.* Poverty rates are falling in many parts of the globe, particularly in Asia. But in sub-Saharan Africa, where the poor are hard-pressed, millions more have sunk deeper into poverty. In 2001, more than 1 billion people worldwide were living on less than US$1 a day. These people suffer from chronic hunger. In 2006, an estimated 100 million of the world's children were malnourished—a statistic that has negative implications for their countries' economic progress.

2. *Achieve universal primary education.* While many parts of the developing world are approaching universal school enrollment, in sub-Saharan Africa, less than two-thirds of all children are enrolled in primary school.

3. *Promote gender equality and empower women.* The gender gap in primary school enrollment that has characterized the developing world for so long is slowly closing. However, women still lack equal representation at the highest levels of government. Worldwide, they hold only about 16 percent of all parliamentary seats. Numerous research studies have shown that advances in women's education and governance are critical to improved health and economic development.

4. *Reduce child mortality.* Death rates among children under age five are dropping, but not nearly fast enough. About 59 of every 1000 children die in the first year of life in developing nations, compared to just three of every 1000 in developed nations. Sadly, evidence indicates that progress toward reducing child mortality has slowed in recent decades.

5. *Improve maternal health.* Each year, more than half a million women die during pregnancy or childbirth. Progress has been made in reducing maternal death rates in some developing regions, but not in countries where the risk of giving birth is highest.

6. *Combat HIV/AIDS, malaria, and other diseases.* AIDS has become the leading cause of premature death in sub-Saharan Africa, where two-thirds of the world's AIDS patients reside. Worldwide, the disease is the fourth most frequent killer. Though new drug treatments can prolong life, there is still no cure for this scourge. Moreover, each year, malaria and tuberculosis kill almost as many people as AIDS, severely draining the labour pool in many countries.

7. *Ensure environmental sustainability.* While most countries have publicly committed themselves to the principles of sustainable development (development that can be maintained across generations), sufficient progress has not been made toward reversing the loss of the world's environmental resources through rampant clear-cutting of forests and other forms of environmental destruction. Even so, many developing countries lack the infrastructure needed to support public health. Though access to safe drinking water has increased, half the developing world lacks toilets and other forms of basic sanitation.

8. *Develop a global partnership for development.* The United Nations Millennium Declaration seeks a global social compact in which developing countries pledge to do more to ensure their own development, while developed countries support them through aid, debt relief, and improved trade opportunities. However, despite the much publicized G8 summit (a meeting of the heads of state of the eight major economies) in Gleneagles, Scotland, in 2005 and the accompanying Live 8 global concerts, the developed nations have fallen far short of the targets they set themselves. The G8 summit in Ontario in 2010 resulted in a commitment to publicize the target shortfalls of each country.

Apply the Theory

1. As a conflict thinker, do you think the Millennium Project's objectives are realistic, given the enormity of the obstacles that must be overcome? Why do you think the project's founders gave themselves only 15 years to accomplish their goal?

2. How are the project's eight objectives related to one another? Could some of the objectives be reached successfully without addressing the others? If you were a government planner with the resources to address just one objective, which would you pick, and why?

Sources: Haub 2005; Katel 2005; Sachs 2005a; United Nations 2005; Weisbrot et al. 2005; World Bank 2006.

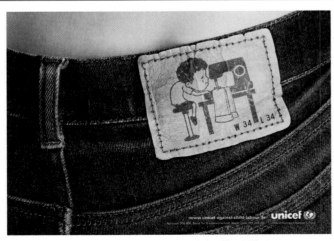

Where am I wearing? This UNICEF poster reminds affluent Western consumers that the brand-name jeans they wear may be produced by exploited workers in developing countries. In sweatshops throughout the developing world, nonunion garment workers—some of them children—labour long hours for what we would consider extremely low wages—even if for the workers in those semi-periphery countries, those wages are relatively high.

temperature—they can also become the basis of small-scale home businesses (*The Economist* 2007).

When we see all the Coca-Cola and IBM signs going up in developing countries, it is easy to assume that globalization and economic change are effecting cultural change. But that is not always the case, researchers note. Distinctive cultural traditions, such as a particular religious orientation or a nationalistic identity, often persist, and can soften the impact of modernization on a developing nation. Some contemporary sociologists emphasize that both industrialized and developing countries are "modern." Researchers increasingly view modernization as movement along a series of social indicators—among them degree of urbanization, energy use, literacy, political democracy, and use of birth control. Clearly, some of these are subjective indicators; even in industrialized nations, not everyone would agree that wider use of birth control represents an example of progress.

Current modernization studies generally take a convergence perspective. Using the indicators we just noted, researchers focus on how societies are moving closer together, despite traditional differences. From a conflict perspective, the modernization of developing countries often perpetuates their dependence on and continued exploitation by more industrialized nations. Conflict theorists view such continuing dependence on foreign powers as an example of contemporary neo-colonialism.

7.3 How Does Stratification within Nations Compare?

At the same time that the gap between rich and poor nations is widening, so, too, is the gap between rich and poor citizens *within* nations. As we discussed earlier, stratification in developing nations is closely related to their relatively weak and dependent position in the global economy. Local elites work hand in hand with multinational corporations and prosper from such alliances. At the same time, the economic system creates and perpetuates the exploitation of industrial and agricultural workers. That's why foreign investment in developing countries tends to increase economic inequality. As Box 7-3 makes clear, inequality within a society is also evident in Latin America's most populous nation, Brazil.

Distribution of Wealth and Income

Global inequality is staggering. Worldwide, the richest 2 percent of adults own more than half the world's household wealth. In at least 24 nations around the world, the most affluent 10 percent of the population receives at least 40 percent of all income. The list includes the African nation of Namibia (the leader, at 65 percent of all income), as well as Colombia, Mexico, Nigeria, and South Africa. Figure 7-7 compares the distribution of income in selected industrialized and developing nations (World Bank 2010:94–96).

To varying degrees, based on the intersection of factors such as race, class, age, disability, sexuality, and nationality, women in developing countries may find life especially difficult. Karuna Chanana Ahmed, an anthropologist from India who has studied women in developing nations, calls women the most exploited of oppressed people (2001). Beginning at birth, women may face sexual discrimination. They may be fed less than male children, denied educational opportunities, and hospitalized only when they are critically ill. As is the case in industrialized countries, inside or outside the home, women's work is frequently devalued. When economies fail, as they did during the global financial crisis of 2008, women are the first to be laid off from their work (Memecan 2010).

Only one-third of Pakistan's sexually segregated schools are for women, and one-third of those schools have no buildings. In Kenya and Tanzania, it is illegal for a woman to own a house. In Saudi Arabia, women were prohibited from driving until 2008, when the Saudi Shura Council recommended that they be allowed to drive a vehicle (with a number of stipulations such as obtaining the permission of a male relative) (Assyrian International News Agency 2008). We explore women's status throughout the world more fully in Chapter 9.

Social Mobility

Mobility in Industrial Nations Studies of intergenerational mobility in industrialized nations have found the following patterns:

1. Substantial similarities exist in the ways that parents' positions in stratification systems are transmitted to their children.
2. As in Canada, mobility opportunities in other nations have been influenced by structural factors, such as labour market changes that lead to the rise or decline of an occupational group within the social hierarchy.
3. Immigration continues to be a significant factor in shaping a society's level of intergenerational mobility.

Cross-national studies suggest that intergenerational mobility has been increasing in the past 50 years in most but not all countries. In particular, they noted a common pattern of movement away from agriculture-based occupations. However, they are quick to point out that growth in mobility does not bring growth in equality. Indeed, despite the evidence of steady upward mobility, their studies show that the gap between the rich and the poor has grown. Over the past 20 years, poverty levels of the 30 largest industrial economies have remained relatively constant (Organisation for Economic Co-operation and Development 2008).

Mobility in Developing Nations Mobility patterns in industrialized countries are usually associated with intergenerational and intragenerational mobility. However, in developing nations, macro-level social and economic changes often overshadow micro-level movement from one occupation to another. For example, there is typically a substantial wage differential between rural and urban areas, which leads to high levels of migration to the cities. Yet the urban industrial sectors of developing countries generally cannot provide sufficient employment for all those seeking work.

In large developing nations, the most socially significant mobility is the movement out of poverty. This type of mobility is difficult to measure and confirm, however, because economic trends can differ from one area of a country to another. For instance, China's rapid income growth has been accompanied by a growing disparity in income between urban and rural areas, and among different regions. Similarly, in India during the 1990s, poverty declined in urban areas but may have remained static at best in rural areas. Around the world, social mobility is also dramatically influenced by catastrophes such as crop failure and warfare.

Gender Differences and Mobility Only relatively recently have researchers begun to investigate the impact of gender on the mobility patterns of developing nations. Many aspects of the development process—such as the rural-to-urban migration just described—may result in the modification or abandonment of traditional cultural practices and even marital systems. The effects on women's social standing and

sociology in the global community

7-3 Stratification in Brazil

Brazil conjures up exotic images: dazzling beaches, tropical foliage, colourful *Carnival* in Rio de Janeiro. Deep, grinding poverty and persistent inequality may not spring to mind, yet they are as much a part of South America's largest nation and economy as the expensive tourist resorts. Brazil has been described as three nations in one: a rich country with a population the size of Canada's; a poor country with a population equal to Mexico's; and a third nation of indigents—totally impoverished people with no income at all—whose population equals Argentina's.

> *As in the United States, Brazil's social inequality is compounded by racial distinctions that originated in slavery.*

Not until 1988 did Brazil's government begin to consider a redistribution of wealth or land to remedy these inequities. The resulting program did not get under way until 2003. Since then, the gap between rich and poor has narrowed only a bit.

As in the United States, Brazil's social inequality is compounded by racial distinctions that originated in slavery. However, race is not socially constructed as it is in the United States. In Brazil, unlike the United States, dark skin colour has never been a measure of innate inferiority.

Still, Brazil is no racial paradise. Rather, it is a multitiered racist society, one whose government has acknowledged the existence of racism. A country that once prided itself on its freedom from racial intolerance, Brazil has now outlawed discrimination against people of colour. Opinion is divided over the effectiveness of the legislation.

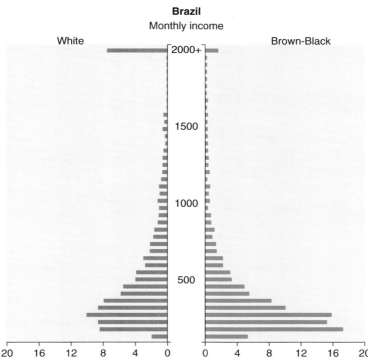

Income by Race, Brazil and the United States

Brazil
Monthly income

White — Brown-Black

2000+ / 1500 / 1000 / 500

Percent
20 16 12 8 4 0 0 4 8 12 16 20

United States
Monthly income

White — Black

4000+ / 3000 / 2000 / 1000

Percent
20 16 12 8 4 0 0 4 8 12 16 20

Source: Government agencies, as reported in Telles 2004:108.

Today, the Brazilian economy shows a significant degree of racially related income disparity. As the accompanying figure shows, people of colour are clustered disproportionately on the lowest levels of the income pyramid. To remedy this entrenched inequality, Brazil's government has instituted a quota-based affirmative action program that ensures access to higher education for people of colour. Because of the lack of clear-cut racial categories in Brazil—Brazilians recognize many different colour gradients—charges of reverse racism and complaints about inexplicable classifications have been common. As in the United States, finding solutions to the twin problems of racism and inequality is a challenge.

Apply the Theory

1. Look at the bottom of each of the accompanying graphs. Which income distribution, Brazil's or the United States', appears to be more unequal? Now look at the top of each graph. Which income distribution appears to be more unequal? What aspect of these graphs do you find most striking?

2. Race-based college admissions quotas have been the subject of hot debate in the United States. Why do you think they have been accepted as law in Brazilian society?

Sources: Ash 2007; Daniel 2006; Dzidzienyo 1987; Fiola 2008; Margolis 2009; Santos 2006; SustainAbility 2006; Telles 2004.

figure 7-7 Distribution of Income in Nine Nations

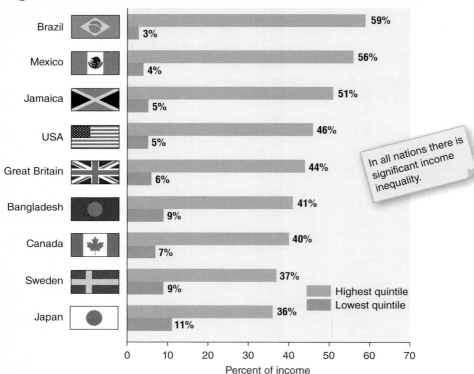

Brazil: 59% (Highest quintile), 3% (Lowest quintile)
Mexico: 56%, 4%
Jamaica: 51%, 5%
USA: 46%, 5%
Great Britain: 44%, 6%
Bangladesh: 41%, 9%
Canada: 40%, 7%
Sweden: 37%, 9%
Japan: 36%, 11%

In all nations there is significant income inequality.

Highest quintile
Lowest quintile

Percent of income

Note: Data are considered comparable although based on statistics covering 1993 to 2008.

Source: World Bank 2010:94–96.

and negotiated more than 2000 peace pacts among community members. They have also run in elections, campaigned against social problems, and organized residents to work together for the common good (United Nations Development Programme 2000:87).

Studies of the distribution of wealth and income within various countries, together with cross-cultural research on mobility, consistently reveal stratification based on class, gender, and other factors within a wide range of societies. Clearly, a worldwide view of stratification must include not only the sharp contrast between wealthy and impoverished nations but also the layers of hierarchy *within* industrialized societies and developing countries.

mobility are not necessarily positive. As a country develops and becomes more urban, women's vital role in food production deteriorates, jeopardizing both their autonomy and their material well-being. Moreover, the movement of families to the cities weakens women's ties to relatives who can provide food, financial assistance, and social support (Lawson 2008).

In the Philippines, however, women have moved to the forefront of the indigenous peoples' struggle to protect their ancestral land from exploitation by outsiders. Having established their right to its rich minerals and forests, members of indigenous groups had begun to feud among themselves over the way in which the land's resources should be developed. Aided by the United Nations Partners in Development Programme, women volunteers established the Pan-Cordillera Women's Network for Peace and Development—a coalition of women's groups dedicated to resolving local disputes. The women mapped boundaries, prepared development plans,

In developing countries, people who hope to rise out of poverty often move from the country to the city, where employment prospects are better. The jobs available in industrialized urban areas offer perhaps the best means of upward mobility. This woman works in an electronics factory in Kuala Lumpur, Malaysia.

::: use your sociological *imagination* :::

Imagine a day when the border between Canada and the United States is completely open. What would the two countries' economies be like? What would their societies be like?

Social Policy and Global Inequality

Universal Human Rights

The Issue

Poised on the third millennium, the world seemed capable of mighty feats, ranging from explorations of distant solar systems to the refinement of tiny genes within human cells. At the same time, though, came constant reminders of how quickly people and their fundamental human rights could be trampled.

Human rights are universal moral rights possessed by all people because they are human. The most important elaboration of human rights appears in the Universal Declaration of Human Rights, adopted by the United Nations in 1948. This declaration prohibits slavery, torture, and degrading punishment; grants everyone the right to a nationality and its culture; affirms freedom of religion and the right to vote; proclaims the right to seek asylum in other countries to escape persecution; and prohibits arbitrary interference with one's privacy and the arbitrary taking of a person's property. It also emphasizes that mothers and children are entitled to special care and assistance.

What steps, if any, can the world community take to ensure the protection of these rights? Is it even possible to agree on what those rights are?

The Setting

The 1990s brought the term *ethnic cleansing* into the world's vocabulary. In the former Yugoslavia, Serbian paramilitary groups attempted to "cleanse" Muslims from parts of Bosnia-Herzegovina, and ethnic Albanians from the province of Kosovo. In both of these regions, hundreds of thousands of people were killed in fighting, while many others were uprooted from their homes. Moreover, reports surfaced of substantial numbers of rapes of Muslim, Croatian, and Kosovar women by Serbian soldiers. In 1996, a United Nations tribunal indicted eight Bosnian Serb military and police officers for rape, thus marking the first time that sexual assault was treated as a war crime under international law (Power 2002). In 2007, the highest U.N. court ruled that Serbia failed to use its influence to prevent the genocide of Bosnian Muslims and punish those who carried out the killings; the court, however, ruled that Serbia—as a nation—did not commit genocide in the 1992–1995 war (*International Herald Tribune Europe* 2007).

In the wake of the terrorist attacks in the United States on September 11, 2001, increased security and surveillance at U.S. airports and border crossings caused some observers to wonder whether human rights were not being jeopardized at home. At the same time, thousands of non-citizens of Arab and South Asian descent were questioned for no other reason than their ethnic and religious

backgrounds. In the case of the Syrian-born Canadian Maher Arar, the consequences were much graver. While travelling home to Canada through the United States in 2002, Arar was detained and shipped to Syria where he was tortured and imprisoned for almost a year. The Canadian government cooperated with the U.S. authorities in supplying information—which it attempted to keep secret—leading to Arar's detainment. In 2006, an inquiry determined that Arar was an innocent citizen; shortly after, the Canadian government made an official apology and paid Arar $10.9 million in compensation plus legal fees. The United States government has made no such apology. Other North Americans have been placed in custody, sometimes without access to legal assistance. As the so-called war on terror moved overseas, human-rights concerns escalated. In 2005, the United Nations' secretary-general, Kofi Annan, criticized the United States and Britain for equating people who were speaking out against the presence of foreign troops in Afghanistan and Iraq with terrorists. For the foreseeable future, it seems, the United States and other Western countries will walk a delicate tightrope between human rights and the need to take national security measures (Parker 2004; Steele 2005).

Sociological Insights

By its very name, the Universal Declaration of Human Rights emphasizes that such rights should be universal. Even so, cultural relativism encourages understanding and respect for the distinctive norms, values, and customs of each culture. In some situations, conflicts arise between human rights standards and local social practices that rest on alternative views of human dignity. For example, is India's caste system an inherent violation of human rights? What about the many cultures of the world that view the subordinate status of women as an essential element in their traditions? Should human rights be interpreted differently in various world locations?

In 2007, Canada's federal government reiterated its support of the United Nations Convention on the Elimination of All Forms of Discrimination against Women. Currently, the principle of gender equality is systematically integrated into Canada's development programs in countries around the world. The human-rights watchdog Amnesty International states, however, that Canada must also be mindful of domestic human-rights concerns, asserting that "there is no corner of the planet where women are safe from the threat or reality of violence. In the home, at work, on the street, in the midst of war, violence stalks women everywhere from Sudan to Colombia, India to Russia,

Iran to Canada" (Amnesty International Canada 2005:2). In the late 1990s, certain Asian and African nations were reviving arguments about cultural relativism in an attempt to block sanctions by the United Nations Human Rights Commission. For example, female genital mutilation, a practice that is common in more than 30 countries around the world, has been condemned in Western nations as a human-rights abuse. This controversial practice often involves removal of the clitoris, in the belief that its excision will inhibit a young woman's sex drive, making her chaste and, thus, more desirable to her future husband. Though some countries have passed laws against the practice, these laws have largely gone unenforced. Immigrants from countries where genital mutilation is common often insist that their daughters undergo the procedure so they'll be protected from Western cultural norms that allow premarital sex. In this context, how does one define human rights (*Religious Tolerance* 2005)?

It is not often that a nation makes a bold statement related solely to human rights. Policymakers, including those in Canada and the United States, more frequently look at human-rights issues from an economic perspective. Functionalists would point out how much more quickly we become embroiled in "human-rights" concerns when oil is at stake, as in the Middle East, or when military alliances come into play, as in Europe. Governments ratify human-rights laws but resist independent efforts to enforce them within their own borders (Hafner-Burton and Tsutsui 2005).

Because international human rights can be highly contextual, they may also be difficult to enforce within the formal requirements of a country's legal process. Despite the apparent torture exposed in digital camera shots from Iraq and Afghanistan, for example, numerous investigations by the British and U.S. military have been inconclusive. Either because of the tenets of military necessity in wartime or because of an inability to locate the victims, many apparent violations have gone unpunished (Klug 2005).

Policy Initiatives

Human-rights issues come wrapped up in international diplomacy. For that reason, many national policymakers hesitate to interfere in human-rights issues, especially if they conflict with what are regarded as more pressing national concerns. Stepping up to fill the gap are international organizations such as the United Nations and non-governmental organizations (NGOs) like Médecins sans Frontières (Doctors without Borders) and Amnesty International. Most initiatives come from these international bodies.

Médecins sans Frontières, the world's largest independent emergency medical-aid organization, won the 1999 Nobel Peace Prize for its work in countries worldwide. Founded in 1971 and based in Paris, the organization has 5000 doctors and nurses working in 80 countries. "Our intention is to highlight current upheavals, to bear witness to foreign tragedies and reflect on the principles of humanitarian aid," explains Dr. Rony Brauman, the organization's former president (Spielmann 1992:12).

In recent years, awareness has been growing of lesbian and gay rights as an aspect of universal human rights. In 1994, Amnesty International published a pioneering report in which it acknowledged that "[lesbians and gay men] in many parts of the world live in constant fear of government persecution" (1994:2). The report examined abuses in Brazil, Greece, Mexico, Iran, the United States, and other countries, including cases of torture, imprisonment, and extrajudicial execution. Later in 1994, the U.S. government issued an order that would allow lesbians and gay men to seek political asylum in the United States if they could prove they had suffered government persecution in their home countries solely because of their sexual orientation (Johnston 1994).

A Chechen boy who witnessed his father's killing stands outside a refugee camp in Russia, where he and his brother are receiving mental health care from Médecins sans Frontières. Civilian assassinations are one of the many violations of human rights that typically occur during wartime.

Ethnic cleansing in the former Yugoslavia, human-rights violations in Iraq and Afghanistan, increased surveillance in the name of counter-terrorism, violence against women inside and outside the family, governmental torture of lesbians and gay men—all these are vivid reminders that social inequality today can have life-and-death consequences. Universal human rights remain an ideal, not a reality.

Apply the Theory

1. Why do definitions of *human rights* vary?
2. How might conflict and functionalist thinkers differ in their view of human-rights violations in time of war?
3. How might feminist thinkers assess Canada's respect for human rights, both at home and abroad?

CHAPTER RESOURCES

Summary

::: 7.1 What Is the Global Divide?

- Worldwide, stratification can be seen both in the gap between rich and poor nations and in the inequality within countries. In this chapter, we examined the global divide and stratification within the world economic system; the impact of globalization, **modernization**, and the **multinational corporation** on developing countries; and the distribution of wealth and income in various nations.
- Developing nations account for most of the world's population and most of its births, but they also bear the burden of most of its poverty, disease, and childhood deaths.

::: 7.2 What Forms Does Global Inequality Take?

- Former colonized nations are kept in a subservient position, subject to foreign domination, through the process of **neo-colonialism**.

- Drawing on the conflict perspective, sociologist Immanuel Wallerstein views the global economic system as one divided between nations that control wealth (core nations) and those from which capital is taken (periphery nations).
- According to **dependency theory**, even as developing countries make economic advances, they remain weak and subservient to core nations and corporations in an increasingly integrated global economy.
- Globalization is a controversial trend that critics blame for contributing to the cultural domination of periphery nations by core nations.
- A **multinational corporation** brings jobs and industry to developing nations, but it also tends to exploit workers in order to maximize profits.
- Poverty is a worldwide problem that blights the lives of billions of people. In 2000, the United Nations launched the Millennium Project. Its goal is to eliminate extreme poverty worldwide by 2015.

- Many sociologists are quick to note that terms such as *modernization* and even *development* contain an ethnocentric bias.
- According to **modernization theory**, development in periphery countries will be assisted by innovations transferred from the industrialized world.

::: 7.3 How Does Stratification within Nations Compare?
- The gap between rich and poor nations is widening, as is the gap between rich and poor citizens *within* nations.

Critical Thinking Questions

1. How have multinational corporations and the trend toward globalization affected you, your family, and your community? List both the pros and the cons. Have the benefits outweighed the drawbacks?

2. Imagine that you have the opportunity to spend a year in Mexico studying inequality in that nation. How would you draw on specific research designs (surveys, observation, experiments, existing sources) to better understand and document stratification in Mexico?

3. How active should the Canadian government be in addressing violations of human rights in other countries? At what point, if any, does concern for human rights turn into ethnocentrism through failure to respect the distinctive norms, values, and customs of another culture?

THINKING ABOUT MOVIES

The End of Poverty?

This documentary asks whether we can close the gap between rich and poor nations by redistributing the world's wealth.

Hotel Rwanda

A hotel becomes a safe haven from the Rwandan genocide.

Slumdog Millionaire

Authorities question a young man's victory on India's version of *Who Wants to Be a Millionaire?* because of his low socioeconomic status.

inside

First Nations protest.

8

Racial and Ethnic Inequality

"Prime Minister Harper offers full apology on behalf of Canadians for the Indian Residential Schools system.

June 11, 2008 Ottawa, Ontario

The treatment of children in Indian Residential Schools is a sad chapter in our history.

For more than a century, Indian Residential Schools separated over 150 000 Aboriginal children from their families and communities. In the 1870s, the federal government, partly in order to meet its obligation to educate Aboriginal children, began to play a role in the development and administration of these schools. Two primary objectives of the Residential Schools system were to remove and isolate children from the influence of their homes, families, traditions, and cultures, and to assimilate them into the dominant culture. These objectives were based on the assumption that Aboriginal cultures and spiritual beliefs were inferior and unequal. Indeed, some sought, as it was infamously said, "to kill the Indian in the child." Today, we recognize that this policy of assimilation was wrong, has caused great harm, and has no place in our country.

One hundred and thirty-two federally supported schools were located in every province and territory, except Newfoundland, New Brunswick, and Prince Edward Island. Most schools were operated as "joint ventures" with Anglican, Catholic, Presbyterian, or United Churches. The Government of Canada built an educational system in which very young children were often forcibly removed from their homes, often taken far from their communities. Many were inadequately fed, clothed, and housed. All were deprived of the care and nurturing of their parents, grandparents, and communities. First Nations, Inuit, and Métis languages and cultural practices were prohibited in these schools. Tragically, some of these children died while attending residential schools and others never returned home.

The government now recognizes that the consequences of the Indian Residential Schools policy were profoundly negative and that this policy has had a lasting and damaging impact on Aboriginal culture, heritage, and language. While some former students have spoken positively about their experiences at residential schools, these stories are far overshadowed by tragic accounts of the emotional, physical, and sexual abuse and neglect of helpless children, and their separation from powerless families and communities.

The legacy of Indian Residential Schools has contributed to social problems that continue to exist in many communities today.

It has taken extraordinary courage for the thousands of survivors that have come forward to speak publicly about the abuse they suffered. It is a testament to their resilience as individuals and to the strength of their cultures. Regrettably, many former students are not with us today and died never having received a full apology from the Government of Canada.

The government recognizes that the absence of an apology has been an impediment to healing and reconciliation. Therefore, on behalf of the Government of Canada and all Canadians, I stand before you, in this Chamber so central to our life as a country, to apologize to Aboriginal peoples for Canada's role in the Indian Residential Schools system.

To the approximately 80 000 living former students, and all family members and communities, the Government of Canada now recognizes that it was wrong to forcibly remove children from their homes and we apologize for having done this. We now recognize that it was wrong to separate children from rich and vibrant cultures and traditions that it created a void in many lives and communities, and we apologize for having done this. We now recognize that, in separating children from their families, we undermined the ability of many to adequately parent their own children and sowed the seeds for generations to follow, and we apologize for having done this. We now recognize that, far too often, these institutions gave rise to abuse or neglect and were inadequately controlled, and we apologize for failing to protect you. Not only did you suffer these abuses as children, but as you became parents, you were powerless to protect your own children from suffering the same experience, and for this we are sorry.

The burden of this experience has been on your shoulders for far too long. The burden is properly ours as a Government, and as a country. There is no place in Canada for the attitudes that inspired the Indian Residential Schools system to ever prevail again. You have been working on recovering from this experience for a long time and in a very real sense, we are now joining you on this journey. The Government of Canada sincerely apologizes and asks the forgiveness of the Aboriginal peoples of this country for failing them so profoundly.

Nous le regrettons
We are sorry

Nimitataynan
Niminchinowesamin
Mamiattugut

In moving towards healing, reconciliation and resolution of the sad legacy of Indian Residential Schools, implementation of the Indian Residential Schools Settlement Agreement began on September 19, 2007. Years of work by survivors, communities, and Aboriginal organizations culminated in an agreement that gives us a new beginning and an opportunity to move forward together in partnership.

A cornerstone of the Settlement Agreement is the Indian Residential Schools Truth and Reconciliation Commission. This Commission presents a unique opportunity to educate all Canadians on the Indian Residential Schools system. It will be a positive step in forging a new relationship between Aboriginal peoples and other Canadians, a relationship based on the knowledge of our shared history, a respect for each other, and a desire to move forward together with a renewed understanding that strong families, strong communities, and vibrant cultures and traditions will contribute to a stronger Canada for all of us."

Prime Minister Harper offers full apology on behalf of Canadians for the Indian Residential Schools system, http://www.pm.gc.ca/eng/media.asp?id=2149 Office of the Prime Minister, 2008 Reproduced with the permission of the Minister of Public Works and Government Services Canada, 2013

Despite the often glowing view of ethnic diversity in Canada, patterns of inequality exist and persist, whereby some groups—most notably the Aboriginal peoples of this country—have been and continue to be systematically subjugated by the dominant groups, resulting in grave social problems such as poverty and lack of adequate housing. This apology, made by the Prime Minister of Canada on behalf of the Canadian government, signifies the recognition of the government's role in attempting to strip Aboriginal children of their cultural heritage through the development and administration of the Indian Residential Schools system.

Today, thousands of people who are members of racial and ethnic minorities continue to experience the often bitter contrast between the Canadian ideals of diversity and equality and the grim realities of poverty, prejudice, and discrimination. Class, gender, and the social definitions of race and ethnicity intersect to produce systems of inequality, not only in this country but throughout the world. High incomes, a good command of French or English, and hard-earned professional credentials do not always override racial and ethnic stereotypes or protect those who fit them from the sting of racism.

What is prejudice, and how is it institutionalized in the form of discrimination? In what ways have race and ethnicity affected the experience of immigrants from other countries? What are the fastest-growing minority groups in Canada today? In this chapter, we focus on the meaning of race and ethnicity. We begin by identifying the basic characteristics of a minority group and distinguishing between racial groups and ethnic groups. Then we examine the dynamics of prejudice and discrimination. After considering the functionalist, conflict, feminist, and interactionist perspectives on race and ethnicity, we look at patterns of intergroup relations, particularly in Canada. Finally, in the social policy section, we explore issues related to immigration worldwide. ■

What Are Minority, Racial, and Ethnic Groups?

Categories of people can often be thought of as "racial" and ethnic groups. The term **racial group** describes a category that is set apart and treated differently from others because of perceived physical differences. White, black, and Asian Canadians are all perceived to be racial groups in Canada. It is the culture of a particular society, however, that constructs and attaches social significance to these perceived differences, as we will see later. Unlike racialized groups, an **ethnic group** is set apart from others primarily because of its national origin or distinctive cultural patterns. In Canada, Italian Canadians, Jewish people, and Polish Canadians are all categorized as ethnic groups (even though Jewishness isn't, by definition, an ethnicity). Both types of groups are considered to be minority groups by sociologists, as the next section shows.

Minority Groups

A numerical minority is any group that makes up less than half of some larger population. The population of Canada includes thousands of numerical minorities, including television actors, green-eyed people, tax lawyers, and snowboarders. However, these numerical minorities are not considered to be minorities in the sociological sense; in fact, the number of people in a group does not necessarily determine its status as a social minority (or a dominant group). When sociologists define a minority group, they are primarily concerned with the economic and political power, or powerlessness, of that group. A **minority group** is a subordinate group whose members have significantly less control or power over their own lives than the members of a dominant or majority group have over their own.

In Canada, the term **visible minority** is used to refer to those Canadians who are non-white or are identified as being physically different from white Canadians of European descent, who compose the dominant group. Visible minorities, according to the official government definition, include such groups as South Asians, Japanese, Arabs, Latin Americans, and Chinese. Aboriginal people form a distinct and unique minority group in Canada; but for government and statistical purposes, they are not categorized as a minority group. Aboriginal peoples, however, have been and continue to be treated as a visible minority group, experiencing generations of systemic brutalization by whites of European descent—most notably via the Residential Schools system. The cruel treatment that Aboriginal peoples have received from the dominant ethnic groups will be explained more fully later in this chapter.

Sociologists have identified five basic properties of a minority group—unequal treatment, physical or cultural traits, ascribed status, solidarity, and in-group marriage (Wagley and Harris 1958):

1. Members of a minority group experience unequal treatment as compared with members of a dominant group. For example, the management of an apartment complex may refuse to rent to blacks, Asians, or Jews. Social inequality may be created or maintained by prejudice, discrimination, segregation, or even extermination.

2. Members of a minority group share physical or cultural characteristics that distinguish them from the dominant group. Each society arbitrarily decides which characteristics are most important in defining the groups.

3. Membership in a minority group (or in a dominant group, for that matter) is not voluntary; people are born into the group. Thus, race and ethnicity are considered *ascribed* statuses.

4. Minority group members have a strong sense of group solidarity. William Graham Sumner, writing in 1906, noted that people make distinctions between members of their own group (the in-group) and everyone else (the out-group). When a group is the object of long-term prejudice and discrimination, the feeling of "us versus them" can and often does become extremely intense.

5. Members of a minority generally marry others from the same group. A member of a dominant group is often unwilling to marry into a supposedly inferior minority. In addition, the minority group's sense of solidarity encourages marriages within the group and discourages marriages to outsiders.

Race

As explained earlier, the term *racial group* refers to those minorities (and the corresponding dominant groups) set apart from others by what are perceived to be obvious physical differences. But what is an "obvious" physical difference? Each society determines which differences are important while ignoring other characteristics that could serve as a basis for social differentiation. In Canada, we see differences in both skin colour and hair colour. Yet people learn informally that differences in skin colour have a dramatic social and political meaning, while differences in hair colour do not.

When observing skin colour, people in Canada tend to lump others rather casually into such categories as "black," "brown," "white," and "Asian." More subtle differences in skin colour often go unnoticed. However, this is not the case in some other societies. Many nations of Central America and South America have colour gradients distinguishing people on a continuum from light to dark skin colour. Brazil has approximately 40 colour groupings, while in other countries people may be described as "Mestizo Hondurans," "Mulatto Colombians," or "African Panamanians." What people see as obvious differences, then, are subject to each society's social definitions.

Three groups make up the largest visible minorities in Canada: those who identified themselves in the 2006 Census as South Asian, Chinese, and black. Figure 8-1 provides information about where the vast majority of immigrants settle—Montreal, Toronto, and Vancouver. A high and growing number of immigrants to those cities are members of visible minority groups.

Biological Significance of Race Viewed from a biological perspective, the term *race* would refer to a genetically isolated group with distinctive gene frequencies. But it

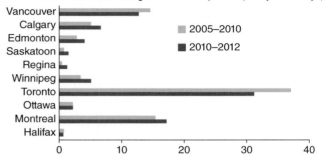

figure 8-1 Share of Immigrants in Canada: Montreal, Toronto and Vancouver 2002, 2006, 2011

% of Canada's immigrants in each period (mid yr. to mid yr.)

Source: *Excerpt from Altus Group Housing Report, January 2013.*

is impossible to scientifically define or identify such a group. Contrary to popular belief, there are no "pure races." Nor are there physical traits—whether skin colour or baldness—that can be used to describe one group to the exclusion of all others. If scientists examine a smear of human blood under a microscope, they cannot tell whether it came from a Chinese, Aboriginal, or black Canadian. There is, in fact, more genetic variation *within* races than across them.

Migration, exploration, and invasion have led to the mixing of genetic material from people around the world. Research indicates that the percentage of North American blacks with white ancestry ranges from 20 percent to as much as 75 percent. Such statistics challenge the view that we can accurately categorize, for example, "black" and "white." Therefore, the belief that we are able to neatly categorize individuals according to race is a myth.

Some people would like to find biological explanations to help social scientists understand why certain peoples of the world have come to dominate others (see the discussion of sociobiology in Chapter 4). Given the absence of pure racial groups, there can be no satisfactory biological answers for such social and political questions.

What Is the Social Construction of Race? In the southern part of the United States, it was known as the "one-drop rule." If a person had even a single drop of "black blood," that person was defined and viewed as black, even if he or she *appeared* to be white. Clearly, race had social significance in that region, enough so that white legislators established official standards about who was "black" and who was "white."

The one-drop rule was a vivid example of **racialization**—the social processes by which people come to define a group as a "race" based in part on physical characteristics, but also on historical, cultural, and economic factors.

According to the 2006 Census, approximately 13 million or 40 percent of Canadians reported having multiple ethnic origins. With rates of intermarriage increasing in Canada,

Children who have one black parent are categorized as "black," even though they may appear to be "white." This is an example of how race is socially constructed.

Ethnicity

An ethnic group, unlike a racial group, is set apart from others because of its national origin or distinctive cultural patterns. Among the ethnic groups in Canada are people with a French-speaking background, which includes people from Tracadie, New Brunswick; Paris, France; Coderre, Saskatchewan; and Quebec City, Quebec. Other ethnic groups in Canada include Japanese, Irish, Italian, and Norwegian Canadians. Although these groupings are convenient, they serve to obscure differences *within* these ethnic categories as well as to overlook the mixed ancestry of so many ethnic people in Canada.

The Canadian census, however, does address this problem, to some extent, by providing Canadians with the option of giving single or multiple responses to the question of ethnic origin (see Table 8-1). For example, the 2006 Census reported that 231 110 Canadians identified themselves as being of Jamaican origin, with 134 320 declaring this as their sole response and 96 785 declaring this as one of multiple responses.

so, too, is the multiplicity of backgrounds. In 2006, over 5 million Canadians—more than 16 percent—defined themselves as members of a visible minority group.

A dominant or majority group has the power not only to define itself legally but also to define a society's values. Sociologist William I. Thomas (1923), an early critic of theories of racial and gender differences, saw that the "definition of the situation" could mould the personality of the individual. To put it another way, Thomas, writing from the interactionist perspective, observed that people respond not only to the objective features of a situation or person but also to the *meaning* that situation or person has for them. Thus, we can create false images or stereotypes that become real in their consequences. **Stereotypes** are unreliable generalizations about all members of a group that do not recognize individual differences within the group.

In the last 30 years, critics have pointed out the power of the mass media to perpetuate false racial and ethnic stereotypes. Television is a prime example: Almost all the leading dramatic roles are cast as whites, even in urban-based programs. Blacks tend to be featured mainly in crime-based dramas.

The distinction between racial and ethnic minorities is not always clear-cut. Many members of racial minorities, such as Asian Canadians, may have significant cultural differences from other groups. At the same time, certain ethnic minorities, such as Indo-Canadians, may have physical differences that are perceived to set them apart from other residents of Canada.

Despite categorization problems, sociologists continue to feel that the distinction between racial groups and ethnic groups is socially significant. In most societies, including Canada, physical differences tend to be more visible than ethnic differences. Partly as a result of this fact, racialized stratification is more resistant to change than is stratification along ethnic lines. Members of an ethnic minority sometimes can become, over time, indistinguishable from the majority—although this process may take generations and may never include all members of the group. By contrast, members of a racialized minority find it much more difficult to blend in with the larger society and to gain acceptance from the majority. Michael Ornstein, of York University in Toronto, found, after studying the ethno-racial groups of Toronto from 1971 to 2001, that poverty is highly racialized. In his 2006 report, Ornstein found that the economic gap between European and non-European groups has been increasing over the past 30 years; he states that "as the population from non-European groups in Canada has increased from about four percent in 1971 to about 40 percent in 2001, the racialization of poverty has increased" (York University 2006).

::: use your sociological *imagination* :::

Count the various ethnicities portrayed in Canadian television programming between the hours of 8 and 11 p.m. Using a TV remote control, how quickly do you think you could find a television show in which all the characters share your own background? What about a show in which all the characters share a different background from your own—how quickly could you find one of those?

table 8-1 Population by Selected Ethnic Origins, Canada, 2006 Census

Ethnic Origins	Total Responses	Single Responses	Multiple Responses
Total Population	31 241 030	18 319 580	12 921 445
Canadian	10 066 290	5 748 725	4 317 570
English	6 570 015	1 367 125	5 202 890
French	4 941 210	1 230 535	3 710 675
Scottish	4 719 850	568 515	4 151 340
Irish	4 354 155	491 030	3 863 125
German	3 179 425	670 640	2 508 785
Italian	1 445 335	741 045	704 285
Chinese	1 346 510	1 135 365	211 145
North American Indian	1 253 615	512 150	741 470
Ukrainian	1 209 085	300 590	908 495
Dutch (Netherlands)	1 035 965	303 400	732 560
Polish	984 565	269 375	715 190
East Indian	962 665	780 175	182 495
Russian	500 600	98 245	402 355
Welsh	440 965	27 115	413 855
Filipino	436 190	321 390	114 800
Norwegian	432 515	44 790	387 725
Portuguese	410 850	262 230	148 625
Métis	409 065	77 295	331 770
Swedish	334 765	28 445	306 325
Spanish	325 730	67 475	258 255
American	316 350	28 785	287 565
Hungarian (Magyar)	315 510	88 685	226 820
Jewish	315 120	134 045	181 070
Greek	242 685	145 250	97 435
Jamaican	231 110	134 320	96 785
Danish	200 035	33 770	166 265
Austrian	194 255	27 060	167 195
Romanian	192 170	79 650	112 515
Vietnamese	180 125	136 445	43 685
Belgian	168 910	33 670	135 240
Lebanese	165 150	103 855	61 295
Québécois	146 585	96 835	49 750
Korean	146 550	137 790	8 755
Swiss	137 775	25 180	112 800
Finnish	131 040	30 195	100 850
Pakistani	124 730	89 605	35 125

Source: Statistics Canada 2008c.

What Are Prejudice and Discrimination?

In recent years, university campuses across North America have been the scene of bias-related incidents. Student-run newspapers and radio stations have ridiculed racial and ethnic minorities; threatening literature has been stuffed under the doors of minority students; graffiti endorsing the views of white supremacist organizations, such as the Ku Klux Klan, has been scrawled on university walls. In some cases, there have even been violent clashes between groups of white and black students (Bunzel 1992; Schaefer 2004).

In April 2004, the United Talmud Torahs elementary school—a Jewish school in Montreal—was firebombed, destroying the school's library and adjoining offices and classrooms. The attack on the school was accompanied by a rash of anti-Semitic actions around the world. Since then, Jewish schools in Canada have spent millions of dollars implementing tighter security measures in an attempt to ensure the safety of their students and staff.

Prejudice

Prejudice is a negative attitude toward an entire category of people, often an ethnic or a racial minority. If you resent your roommate because he or she is sloppy, you are not necessarily guilty of prejudice. However, if you immediately stereotype your roommate on the basis of such characteristics as race, ethnicity, or religion, that is a form of prejudice. Prejudice tends to perpetuate false definitions of individuals and groups.

Sometimes, prejudice can result from ethnocentrism—the tendency to assume that your own culture and way of life represent the norm or are superior to all others.

Ethnocentric people judge other cultures by the standards of their own group, which leads quite easily to prejudice against cultures viewed as inferior.

One important and widespread form of prejudice is **racism**, the belief that one group is supreme and all others are innately inferior. When racism prevails in a society, members of minority groups generally experience prejudice, discrimination, and exploitation.

The activity level of organized hate groups appears to be increasing, both in reality and in virtual reality. Although only a few hundred such groups may exist, thousands of Web sites advocate racial hatred on the Internet. The technology of the Internet has allowed race-hate groups to expand far beyond their regional bases to reach millions (Marriott 2004).

Discriminatory Behaviour

Prejudice often leads to **discrimination**, the denial of opportunities and equal rights to individuals and groups based on some type of arbitrary bias. For example, perhaps a white corporate chief executive officer (CEO) with a prejudice against Indo-Canadians has to fill an executive position. The most qualified candidate for the job is of Indian descent. If the CEO refuses to hire this candidate and instead selects a less-qualified white person, he or she is engaging in an act of racial discrimination.

Prejudiced *attitudes* should not be equated with discriminatory *behaviour*. Although the two are generally related, they are not identical, and either condition can be present without the other. A prejudiced person does not always act on his or her biases. The white CEO, for example, might choose—despite his or her attitude—to hire the Indo-Canadian. This would be prejudice without discrimination. However, a white corporate CEO with a completely respectful view of Indo-Canadians might refuse to hire someone of Indian descent for executive posts out of fear that biased clients would take their business elsewhere. In this case, the CEO's action would constitute discrimination without prejudice.

Discrimination persists even for the most educated and qualified minority group members from the best family backgrounds. Despite their talents and experiences, they sometimes encounter attitudinal or organizational bias that prevents them from reaching their full potential. The term **glass ceiling** refers to an invisible barrier that blocks the promotion of a qualified individual in a work environment because of the individual's gender, race, or ethnicity (Schaefer 2006; Yamagata et al. 1997).

Glass ceilings continue to block women and minority-group men from top management positions in government, education, politics, and business. Even in *Fortune* magazine's 2002 listing of the most diversified corporations, white men held more than 80 percent of both the board of directors' seats and of the top 50 paid positions in companies. The existence of this glass ceiling results principally from the fears and prejudices of many middle- and upper-level white male managers, who believe that the inclusion of women and minority group men in management circles will threaten their own prospects for advancement (Hickman 2002).

The Privileges of the Dominant

One aspect of discrimination that is often overlooked is the privilege dominant groups enjoy at the expense of others. For instance, there is often a tendency to focus more on the difficulty many women have in getting ahead at work, juggling paid and unpaid work at home, than on the ease with which many men avoid domestic work and manage to make their way in the world. Similarly, there may be more of a focus on discrimination against racial and ethnic minorities than on the advantages that the dominant groups enjoy. Indeed, most white people rarely think about their "whiteness," taking their status for granted. But sociologists and other social scientists are becoming increasingly interested in what it means to be "white," as white privilege is the other side of the proverbial coin of racial discrimination.

The feminist scholar Peggy McIntosh became interested in white privilege after noticing that most men would not acknowledge that there were privileges attached to being male—even if they would agree that being female had its disadvantages (1988). McIntosh wondered if white people suffer from a similar blind spot regarding their own racial privilege. Intrigued, McIntosh began to list all the ways in which she benefited from her whiteness. She soon realized that the list of unspoken advantages was long and significant.

Black customers have different experiences from white customers. They are more likely than whites to have their cheques or credit cards refused, and they are more likely to be viewed with suspicion by security guards.

evaluate her in racial terms. When she appeared in public, she didn't need to worry that her clothing or behaviour might reflect poorly on white people. If she was recognized for an achievement, it was seen as her achievement, not that of an entire race. And no one ever assumed that the personal opinions she voiced should be those of all white people. Because Peggy McIntosh blended in with the people around her, she wasn't always onstage.

These are not all the privileges white people take for granted in North American life. White job seekers enjoy tremendous advantages over non-whites who face discrimination when it comes to employment opportunities (Ornstein 2006; Pager and Quillian 2005).

McIntosh found that as a white person, she rarely needed to step out of her comfort zone, no matter where she went. If she wished to, she could spend most of her time with people of her own race. She could find a good place to live in a pleasant neighbourhood, buy the foods she liked to eat from almost any grocery store, and get her hair styled in almost any salon. She could attend a public meeting without feeling that she did not belong, that she was different from everyone else.

McIntosh discovered, too, that her skin colour opened doors for her. She could cash cheques and use credit cards without suspicion, and browse through stores without being shadowed by security guards. She could be seated without difficulty in a restaurant. If McIntosh asked to see the manager of an establishment, she could assume he or she would be of her own race. If she needed help from a doctor or a lawyer, she could get it. It became evident that McIntosh's whiteness made her job of parenting easier. She did not need to worry about protecting her children from people who didn't like them. She could be sure that their textbooks would show pictures of people who looked like them, and that their history texts would describe white people's achievements. McIntosh knew that the television programs they watched would include white characters.

Finally, McIntosh had to admit that others did not constantly

Institutional Discrimination

Discrimination is practised not only by individuals in one-to-one encounters but also by institutions in their daily operations. Social scientists are particularly concerned with the ways in which structural factors, such as employment, housing, health care, and government operations, maintain the social significance of race and ethnicity. **Institutional discrimination** refers to the denial of opportunities and equal rights to individuals and groups that result from the normal operations of a society. This kind of discrimination consistently affects certain racial and ethnic groups more than others.

White people are accustomed to seeing other white people in professional positions and jobs with authority and prestige. Whiteness *does* have its privileges.

The following are examples of institutional discrimination:

- rules requiring that only English be spoken at a place of work, even when it is not a business necessity to restrict the use of other languages
- preferences shown by law schools and medical schools in the admission of children of wealthy and influential alumni, nearly all of whom are not members of minorities
- restrictive employment-leave policies, coupled with prohibitions on part-time work, that make it difficult for the heads of single-parent families (most of whom are women) to obtain and keep jobs

Racial or ethnic profiling, which is the use of the social construct of "race" as a consideration in suspect profiling in law enforcement and national security practices, is a form of institutional discrimination. A study released in 2005 and conducted by University of Toronto criminologist Scott Wortley using Kingston, Ontario, police statistics found that young black men and Aboriginal men had a greater chance of being stopped by the police than did members of other groups. More specifically, the study showed that a black man was 3.7 times more likely to be stopped by police than was a white man (CBC 2005).

Even the world of computers reflects a kind of discrimination—perhaps we could call this technological discrimination. As the Internet and computer technology spread globally, access to this technology is crucial in determining who moves ahead and who stays behind in our hard-wired society. In Canada, a disproportionate number of those with postsecondary education and higher income are from white ethnic and non-Aboriginal groups. Similarly, a disproportionately high number of Aboriginal people are from lower-income and lower-education groups. As of 2003, Canadians with postsecondary education and higher income levels were at the forefront of Internet use in the home (Statistics Canada 2004b). The significance of differential access to the Internet may only increase as better-paying jobs, and even information itself, become increasingly tied to computer access and literacy.

::: use your sociological *imagination* :::

Suddenly, you don't have access to a desktop computer—not at home, at school, or even at work. How will your life change?

For more than 20 years, employment-equity programs have been instituted in an attempt to make the workforce more diverse and to overcome discrimination. **Employment equity** comprises positive efforts to recruit historically disadvantaged groups for jobs, promotions, and educational opportunities. Some people, however, resent these programs, arguing that advancing one group's cause merely shifts the discrimination to another group. Critics argue that by giving priority to visible minorities in school

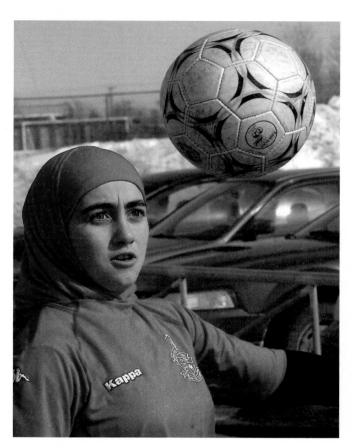

Asmahan Mansour, a member of Ottawa's under-12 girls' soccer team, was ejected from a game in Laval, Quebec, after she refused to remove her hijab. The Quebec Soccer Federation defended the action, citing that wearing the hijab broke a safety rule of Fédération Internationale de Football Association (FIFA), soccer's international governing organization. In 2012, FIFA reversed its decision and now allows players to wear hijabs that have been approved for safety.

admissions, for example, more qualified white ethnic group candidates may be overlooked.

Discriminatory practices continue to pervade nearly all areas of life in Canada today. In part, this is because various individuals and groups actually *benefit* from racial and ethnic discrimination in terms of money, status, and influence. Discrimination permits members of the majority to enhance their wealth, power, and prestige at the expense of others. Less-qualified people get jobs and promotions simply because they are members of the dominant group. Such individuals and groups will not surrender these advantages easily. We'll take a closer look at this functionalist analysis, as well as the conflict, feminist, and interactionist perspectives.

How Are Race and Ethnicity Studied?

Relations among dominant and ethnic minority groups lend themselves to analysis from the four major perspectives of sociology. From the macro level, functionalists observe that racism toward ethnic minorities serves positive functions for dominant groups, whereas conflict theorists see the economic structure as a central factor in the exploitation of minorities. The feminist perspective looks at both micro-level and macro-level issues. The micro-level analysis of interactionist researchers stresses the manner in which everyday contact between people from different ethnic minorities contributes to tolerance or leads to hostility.

Functionalist Perspective

What possible use could racism have for society? Functionalist theorists, while agreeing that racism is hardly to be admired, point out that it indeed serves positive functions for those practising discrimination.

Anthropologist Manning Nash has identified three functions of racist beliefs for the dominant group (1962):

1. Racist views provide a moral justification for maintaining an unequal society that routinely deprives a minority of its rights and privileges. Slavery has been justified, for example, by those who believed that Africans were physically and spiritually subhuman and devoid of souls (Hoebel 1949).

2. Racist beliefs discourage the subordinate minority from attempting to question its lowly status, which would be to question the very foundations of society.

3. Racial myths suggest that any major societal change (such as an end to discrimination) would only bring greater poverty to the minority and lower the majority's standard of living. As a result, Nash suggests, racial prejudice grows when a society's value system (for example, one underlying a colonial empire or a regime perpetuating slavery) is being threatened.

Although racism may serve the interests of the powerful, such unequal treatment can also be dysfunctional to a society and even to its dominant group. Sociologist Arnold Rose has outlined four dysfunctions associated with racism (1951):

1. A society that practises discrimination fails to use the resources of all individuals. Discrimination limits the search for talent and leadership to the dominant group.

2. Discrimination aggravates social problems, such as poverty, delinquency, and crime, and places the financial burden to alleviate these problems on the dominant group.

3. Society must invest a good deal of time and money to defend its barriers to full participation of all members.

4. Racial prejudice and discrimination often undercut goodwill and friendly diplomatic relations between nations.

Conflict Perspective

Conflict theorists would certainly agree with Arnold Rose that racial prejudice and discrimination have many harmful consequences for society. Sociologists such as Oliver Cox (1948), Robert Blauner (1972), and Herbert M. Hunter (2000) have used **exploitation theory** (or Marxist class theory) to explain the basis of racial subordination. As we saw in Chapter 6, Karl Marx viewed the exploitation of the lower class as a basic part of the capitalist economic system. From a Marxist point of view, racism keeps minority group members in low-paying jobs, thereby supplying the capitalist

ruling class with a pool of cheap labour. Moreover, by forcing racial minorities to accept low wages, capitalists can restrict the wages of *all* members of the proletariat. Workers from the dominant group who demand higher wages can always be replaced by minorities who have no choice but to accept low-paying jobs.

The conflict view of race relations seems persuasive in a number of instances. In the late nineteenth century, the Canadian government encouraged thousands of Chinese workers to come to Canada, without their families, to build the Canadian Pacific Railway. These men faced dangerous working and living conditions, and many died before the railway was completed in 1885. After the railway's completion, when their labour was no longer needed, the government attempted to force the workers to return to China. To discourage future immigration from China, the Canadian government imposed what was called a head tax on every Chinese immigrant.

However, the exploitation theory is too limited to explain prejudice in its many forms. Not all minority groups have been economically exploited to the same extent. In addition, some groups, such as the Jews, have been victimized by prejudice for other than economic reasons. Still, as Gordon Allport concludes, the exploitation theory correctly "points a sure finger at one of the factors involved in prejudice . . . rationalized self-interest of the upper classes" (1979:210).

Feminist Perspectives

Given the great diversity of feminist perspectives, it is perhaps not surprising to discover differences among these theories in their treatment of race. Some feminist perspectives have taken white, middle-class, heterosexual women's experiences to be the norm, while ignoring "the specificity of black, native, and other ethnic and cultural experiences" (Elliot and Mandell 1998:14). Although such perspectives as radical feminism treat women as a uniform, undifferentiated group whose major source of oppression is sexism, other perspectives have strenuously challenged this point of view (Brand 1993; Grant 1993). Such perspectives as anti-racist and critical-race feminism point out that gender is not the sole source of oppression; gender, race, and other sources of oppression intersect to produce multiple degrees of inequality. Anti-racist feminists argue that all people are racialized, gendered, and differently constructed—they do not participate on an equal footing in social interactions, and unequal power relations permeate all social institutions. According to Enakshi Dua, anti-racist feminism "attempts to integrate the way race and gender function together in structuring inequality" (1999:9). Like anti-racist feminism, critical-race feminism examines the interconnection of race or racism and other forms of oppression, with gender, emphasizing the social difference and multiplicity within feminism (Hua 2003). Unlike white, middle-class women, immigrant women, visible minority women, and Aboriginal women, for example, experience the compounded effects of inequality associated with their race and class as well as their gender. As introduced in Chapter 1, transnational feminism recognizes the roles that capitalism and systems of political power play in perpetuating gender inequality within and among regions of the world (e.g., Western and non-Western, developed and developing, rich and poor). According to the United Nations Development Fund for Women (UNIFEM, from the French *Fonds de développement des Nations unies pour la femme*), "Women bear the burden of the world's poverty," representing 70 percent of the world's poor. The wealth of the richer nations depends to a great extent on the poverty of the poorer nations, the poorest citizens of whom are women. According to UNIFEM, women constitute 60 to 80 percent of the manufacturing workforce in the developing world. These women often work for low pay in factories run by multinational corporations that produce apparel and consumer goods for the richer countries.

Interactionist Perspective

An Aboriginal woman is transferred from a job on an assembly line to a similar position working next to a white man. At first, the white man is patronizing, assuming that she must be incompetent. She is cold and resentful; even when she needs assistance, she refuses to admit it. After a week, the growing tension between the two leads to a bitter quarrel. Yet, over time, each slowly comes to appreciate the other's strengths and talents. A year after they begin working together, these two workers become respectful friends.

This is an example of what interactionists call the *contact hypothesis* in action. The **contact hypothesis** states that interracial contact between people of equal status in cooperative circumstances will cause them to become less prejudiced and to abandon previous stereotypes. People begin to see one another as individuals and discard the broad generalizations characteristic of stereotyping. Note the factors of *equal status* and *cooperative circumstances*. In the example just given, if the two workers had been competing for one vacancy as a supervisor, the racial hostility between them might have worsened (Allport 1979; Schaefer 2004; Sigelman et al. 1996).

As visible minorities slowly gain access to better-paying and more responsible jobs in Canada, the contact hypothesis may take on even greater significance. The trend in our society is toward increasing contact between individuals from dominant and subordinate groups. This may be one way of eliminating—or at least reducing—racial and ethnic stereotyping and prejudice. Another may be the establishment of interracial coalitions, an idea suggested by sociologist William Julius Wilson (1999). To work, such coalitions would obviously need to be built on an equal role for all members.

Table 8-2 summarizes the four major sociological perspectives on race. No matter what explanation is given, the racialization of non-dominant groups has powerful consequences in the form of prejudice and discrimination.

8.4 What Are Some Patterns of Intergroup Relations?

Racial and ethnic groups can relate to one another in a wide variety of ways, ranging from friendships and intermarriages to the killing of those from particular minority groups, from behaviours that require mutual approval to behaviours imposed by the dominant group.

Conflict sociologists emphasize the ways in which dominant groups exercise their political, social, economic, and

table 8.2 Sociological Perspectives on Race

Perspective	Emphasis
Functionalist	The dominant majority benefits from the subordination of racial minorities.
Conflict	Vested interests perpetuate racial inequality through economic exploitation.
Feminist	Race, class, and gender intersect to produce multiple levels of inequality.
Interactionist	Cooperative interracial contacts can reduce hostility.

summing**UP**

cultural domination over other groups. Historically, dominant groups—primarily white—have subjugated less powerful groups whom they perceived to be different; they constructed these groups as the "other." This subjugation, as we discussed in the previous chapter on global stratification, can take the form of colonialism, and, more recently, neo-colonialism. Thus, as conflict and some feminist sociologists have pointed out, "otherized" groups have historically been exploited, oppressed, and controlled by dominant groups through such systems as colonialism, globalized labour exploitation, slavery, and genocide (Hua 2003).

Genocide is the deliberate, systematic killing of an entire people or nation. For example, the killing of a million Armenians by Turkish authorities beginning in 1915 was genocide. *Genocide* is most commonly used as a descriptor for Nazi Germany's extermination of 6 million European Jews, as well as gays, lesbians, and the Romani people, during World War II. The term is also appropriate in describing the U.S. government's policies toward Native Americans in the nineteenth century. During the Seven Years' War (1756–1763), germ warfare decimated the North American Aboriginal population. Blankets contaminated with smallpox were distributed to Aboriginal groups that were allied with France (Harrison and Friesen 2004). In a recent example of genocide, in Rwanda in 1994, an estimated 800 000 Tutsis were slaughtered by Hutus in 100 days.

The *expulsion* of a people is another extreme means of acting out racial or ethnic prejudice. In 1979, Vietnam expelled nearly a million ethnic Chinese, partly as a result of centuries of hostility between Vietnam and neighbouring China. In a more recent example of expulsion, Sudan's government began a campaign of "ethnic cleansing" in its Darfur region. According to the global human rights watchdog Human Rights Watch, the conflict has been mischaracterized and oversimplified as a clash between "Arab" and "non-Arab" African people; rather, "the ways in which both rebel groups and the Sudanese government have manipulated ethnic tensions have served to polarize much of the Darfur population along ethnic lines" (Human Rights Watch 2007:1). Many deaths have occurred and approximately 2.4 million people (including 200 000 refugees) have been displaced since 2003 (Human Rights Watch 2007). Genocide and expulsion are arguably the most extreme examples of hostile inter-group relations. Other patterns of intergroup relations that are explored by sociologists are assimilation, segregation, and multiculturalism. Each pattern defines the dominant group's actions and the responses of various minority groups. Inter-group relations are rarely restricted to just one of the three patterns, although invariably one does tend to dominate. Therefore, think of these patterns primarily as ideal types.

Assimilation

Many Hindus in India complain about Indian citizens who copy the traditions and customs of the British. In Australia, Aborigines who have become part of the dominant society refuse to acknowledge their darker-skinned grandparents on the street. In Canada, some Poles, Ukrainians, and Jews, among others, have changed their ethnic-sounding family names to surnames that are typically found among British and Northern European families.

Assimilation is the process by which a person forsakes his or her own cultural tradition to become part of a different culture. Generally, it is practised by a minority group member who wants to conform to the standards of the dominant group. Assimilation can be described as an ideology in which $A + B + C \rightarrow A$. The majority A dominates in such a way that members of minorities B and C imitate A and attempt to become indistinguishable from the dominant group (Newman 1973).

Assimilation can strike at the very roots of a person's identity. Alphonso D'Abruzzo, for example, changed his name to Alan Alda (following the lead of his actor father, Robert Alda). Legendary Canadian rock singer Geddy Lee was born Gary Lee Weinrib, and British actor Joyce Frankenberg changed her name to Jane Seymour. Name changes, switches in religious affiliation, and dropping of native languages can obscure a person's roots and heritage. However, assimilation does not necessarily bring acceptance for the minority group individual. A Chinese Canadian may speak English fluently, achieve high educational standards, and become a well-respected professional or business person and *still* be seen as different. Some Canadians may reject him or her as a business associate, neighbour, or marriage partner, simply because he or she is seen as different.

::: use your sociological *imagination* :::

You have immigrated to another country with a very different culture. How are you treated?

Segregation

Separate schools, separate seating sections on buses and in restaurants, separate washrooms, even separate drinking fountains—these were all part of the lives of African Americans in the American South when segregation ruled in the first half of the twentieth century. **Segregation** is the physical separation of two groups of people in terms of residence, workplace,

French police remove a member of the Roma minority who is resisting deportation to his home country. The expulsion of certain racial or ethnic groups is an extreme result of prejudice.

and social events. Generally, a dominant group imposes it on a minority group. Segregation is rarely complete, however. Intergroup contact inevitably occurs, even in the most segregated societies.

From 1948 (when it received its independence) to 1990, the Republic of South Africa severely restricted the movement of blacks and other non-whites by means of a wide-ranging system of segregation known as **apartheid**. Apartheid even included the creation of homelands where blacks were expected to live. However, decades of local resistance to apartheid, combined with international pressure, led to marked political changes in the 1990s. In 1994, a prominent black activist, Nelson Mandela, was elected as South Africa's president. This was the first election in which blacks (the majority of the nation's population) were allowed to vote. Mandela had spent almost 28 years in South African prisons for his anti-apartheid activities. His election was widely viewed as the final blow to South Africa's oppressive apartheid policy.

The most blatant form of segregation in Canada is that of the reserve system established by the federal government for Aboriginal peoples. Although Aboriginal peoples do have a choice as to where they live, they do not receive the same privileges off reserves as they would on them. Effectively, reserves segregate Aboriginal peoples by placing their schools, housing, recreational facilities, and medical services in remote areas, separate from the larger community. This segregation creates centres of "shiftlessness and inertia," where Aboriginal peoples are transformed into a "great family of wards, dependent on government for direction and assistance" (Harrison and Friesen 2004:187).

Some forms of segregation can be voluntary and, thus, may be referred to as **self-segregation**. An example of self-segregation is the residential segregation found in Canada's major cities, such as Montreal, Toronto, and Vancouver where residents in Chinese-, Jewish-, and Indo-Canadian neighbourhoods remain residentially separated from other ethnic groups. The recent approval, in 2008, by the Toronto District School Board allowing the creation of Canada's first black-focused public school was considered to be segregation by

sociology in the global community

8-1 Cultural Survival in Brazil

When the first Portuguese ships landed on the coast of what we now know as Brazil, more than 2 million people inhabited the vast, mineral-rich land. The natives lived in small, isolated settlements, spoke a variety of languages, and embraced many different cultural traditions.

Today, over five centuries later, Brazil's population has grown to more than 180 million. According to the 2013 Brazilian Census, 896 917 Brazilians are indigenous peoples. Over 230 different indigenous groups—making up 0.47 percent of the country's population—have survived, living a life tied closely to the land and the rivers, just as their ancestors did. But over the past two generations, their numbers have dwindled as booms in mining, logging, oil drilling, and agriculture have encroached on their land and their settlements.

Many indigenous groups were once nomads, moving from one hunting or fishing ground to another. Now they are hemmed in on the reservations the government confined them to,

surrounded by huge farms or ranches whose owners deny their right to live off the land. State officials may insist that laws restrict the development of indigenous lands, but indigenous peoples tell a different story. In Mato Grosso, a heavily forested state near the Amazon River, loggers have been clear-cutting the land at a rate that alarms the Bororo, an indigenous group that has lived in the area for centuries. According to one elder, the Bororo are now confined to six small reservations of about 1290 square kilometres—much less than the area officially granted them in the nineteenth century.

In the face of dwindling resources, indigenous groups like the Bororo struggle to maintain their culture. Though the tribe still observes the traditional initiation rites for adolescent boys, members are finding it difficult to continue their hunting and fishing rituals, given the scarcity of game and fish in the area. Pesticides in the run-off from nearby farms have poisoned the water

they fish and bathe in, threatening both their health and their culture's survival.

The Internet has become crucial in the fight for survival of many indigenous groups. In 2011 the Ashaninka people used a solar-powered computer to inform outsiders of the invasion of their land by Peruvian woodcutters. They also addressed the chief of the Supreme Court in 2013, in the form of an online petition, seeking reparation for the lumbering activities (Earth Peoples 2013).

Apply the Theory

1. Compare the frontier in Brazil today to the American West in the 1800s. What similarities do you see?
2. What does society lose when indigenous cultures die?

Sources: Brazier and Hamed 2007; Chu 2005; Earth Peoples 2013.

---

opponents of the plan. Those in support of the move, which features a curriculum and teaching that focuses on black culture and history, believe that it will help to keep black students in school longer (CBC 2008b).

Box 8-1 discusses the cultural survival of indigenous peoples in Brazil, segregated on reserves.

Multiculturalism

In 1969, Canada's federal government adopted an official policy of bilingualism in response to the rise of nationalism in Quebec (Harrison and Friesen 2004). But in 1971, the government adopted a policy of multiculturalism in recognition of the growing number of Canadians who were from ethnic backgrounds other than British or French. The multiculturalism

policy was, and still is, an attempt to establish a larger framework within which to respond to Canadian ethnic and racial diversity.

The meaning of multiculturalism in Canada goes beyond simply describing what is (or the obvious): that Canada is a country comprising people from many diverse ethnic and racial origins. *Multiculturalism,* officially, is a policy that attempts to promote ethnic and racial diversity in all aspects of Canadian life, and to establish diversity as a fundamental characteristic of the Canadian identity. The policy of multiculturalism, however, is not without its critics, who assert that it is simply window dressing that diverts attention from the economic and political inequalities that persist among various ethnic groups (e.g., between members of visible minorities and members of other minorities). Figure 8-2 presents the spectrum of typical intergroup relations.

figure 8-2 Spectrum of Intergroup Relations

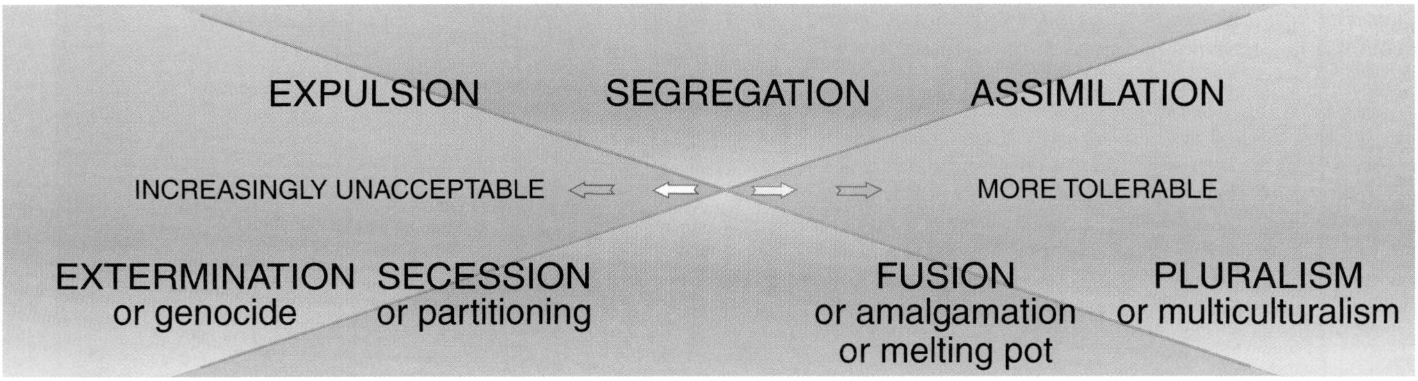

EXPULSION	SEGREGATION	ASSIMILATION
INCREASINGLY UNACCEPTABLE ⇐ ⇐ ⇒ ⇒		MORE TOLERABLE
EXTERMINATION SECESSION		FUSION PLURALISM
or genocide or partitioning		or amalgamation or multiculturalism
		or melting pot

What Are Some Groups that Make Up Canada's Multi-Ethnic Character?

Few societies have a more diverse population than Canada; the nation is truly a multiracial, multi-ethnic society. Of course, this has not always been the case. The population of what is now Canada has changed dramatically since the arrival of French settlers in the 1600s. Immigration has largely been responsible for shaping the racial and ethnic makeup of our present-day society.

Canada's diversity is evident from the statistical profile presented in Table 8-1. That diversity, particularly with regard to visible minority status, has been increasing dramatically in recent years. Between the early 1960s and the 2006 Census, there has been a marked shift away from Europe and toward Asia as the source of the majority of immigrants to Canada (Statistics Canada 2007n).

Ethnic Groups

The 2006 Census revealed the 10 top ethnic origins to be, in descending order, Canadian, English, French, Scottish, Irish, German, Italian, Chinese, North American Indian, and Ukrainian. We will now explore some of the groups that make up Canada's multi-ethnic character.

Aboriginal Peoples The history of Aboriginal groups in Canada is one, first and foremost, of colonialism, the effects of which continue to be felt by Aboriginal peoples today. The historical legacy of oppression is one many Native peoples still cope with daily, as they continue to be marginalized and struggle against various forms of racism. They have endured years of overt attempts on the part of the dominant culture to eradicate their Aboriginal identities (Box 8-2).

The Indian Act of 1876 granted the federal government the power to control most aspects of Aboriginal life, denying First Nations peoples the right to vote or to buy land. This pivotal piece of legislation transformed Aboriginals from self-governing, autonomous peoples to externally regulated, controlled, and, thus, dependent ones. Ten years before the Indian Act, after breaking treaty after treaty to make way for European settlement, Canada's government decided that particular parcels of land would be used for reserves. Yet, as Lee Maracle argues in her 1996 book *I Am Woman: A Native Perspective on Sociology and Feminism*, Native peoples in Canada, despite decades of colonization, have not had their culture "stolen":

> We have not "lost our culture" or had it "stolen." Much of the information that was available to us through our education process has been expropriated and consigned to deadwood leaves in libraries. The essence of Native culture still lives on in the hearts, minds, and spirits of our folk. Some of us have forsaken our culture in the interests of becoming integrated. This is not the same thing as losing something. The expropriation of the accumulated knowledge of Native peoples is one legacy of

colonization. Decolonization will require the repatriation and rematriation of the knowledge by Native peoples themselves. (Maracle 1996:92)

Over 160 years ago, Egerton Ryerson, chief superintendent of education for Upper Canada, set out to "civilize" Aboriginal children through, as a federal government report published in 1847 described it, a "weaning from the habits and feelings of their ancestors and the acquirement of the language, arts and customs of civilized life." Residential schools established in the mid-nineteenth century, with mandatory attendance beginning in 1920, were run as a partnership between the federal government and the major churches. Thousands of Native children were excised from their families and communities to be "whitened" and "educated" in the ways of European culture.

Many of these children endured conditions of neglect, isolation, and emotional, physical, and sexual abuse. As many have argued, they were also the victims of a cultural genocide. The final report of the Royal Commission on Aboriginal Peoples, issued in 1996, stated that "the schools were . . . part of the contagion of colonialization. In their direct attack of language, beliefs and spirituality, the schools had been a particularly virulent strain of that epidemic of empire, sapping children's bodies and beings" (Wilson 2000). The last residential schools closed in the mid-1980s; however, the now-adult survivors continue to struggle with the traumatic effects of their experiences as children in these schools.

British Columbia psychiatrist and professor Charles Brasfield, who runs a practice focusing on the needs of Aboriginal peoples, suggests that "residential school syndrome" might be a diagnostic term appropriately applied to survivors of the Residential Schools system (2001:80). In his practice, Brasfield treats Aboriginal peoples who are trying to overcome nightmares, flashbacks, relationship problems, sleeping difficulties, and anger-management issues, all of which are rooted in their experiences in the residential schools. Not having good parenting role models while in the schools, many now lack parenting skills. Often, Brasfield sees his Aboriginal clients struggling to deal with alcohol or drug abuse.

Attawapiskat First Nation community

sociology in the global community

8-2 Cultural Genocide of Aboriginal Peoples

Usually, the term *genocide* refers to the deliberate, systematic killing of an entire people or nation. However, social scientists have long recognized another form of genocide, called *cultural genocide*, in which a nation's culture is eliminated even though the people live on.

Cultural genocide refers to the systematic destruction of a group's culture. Social scientists have used the term to describe one nation's efforts to suppress another nation's language. Japan's attempt to eliminate the Korean people's language, history, and even names during its occupation of Korea in the early twentieth century is one example. However, the term also applies to government efforts to eliminate indigenous peoples' traditions. Canada, Australia, New Zealand, and the United States illustrate this second form of cultural genocide.

In Canada, Aboriginal children were taken from their homes and placed in schools far from their families. The Residential Schools system, established in the 1870s had as its expressed purpose to "kill the Indian in the child." All cultural practices and languages of First Nations, Inuit, and Métis were prohibited and children were severely punished for any "transgressions."

The degree of emotional and physical abuse was severe; some children died. Today, in Canada, approximately 80 000 former students of the Indian Residential Schools system are left with a legacy of this trauma.

In the United States, government officials encouraged white families to "adopt" indigenous children and raise them in the dominant culture. Agents of the U.S. government took American Indian children from their parents' homes and sent them to be raised in families far from their native culture. Sometimes the children were removed with their parents' permission, but often they were taken against their parents' will. Government officials assumed that the supposed benefit of familiarizing the children with the dominant culture would outweigh and ultimately excuse the personal and cultural losses the children experienced.

In Australia, as in Canada and the United States, the dominant group's view of Aboriginal peoples as inferior became the basis for an effort to stamp out their culture. From 1910 to 1970, thousands of Aboriginal children were forcibly removed from their families so they could be raised by whites and impressed into the

dominant culture. Between 10 to 30 percent of all Aboriginal children were affected by this program. Not until 2008, as was the case in Canada, did the Australian government finally apologize to Aboriginals for "the Stolen Generations."

Apply the Theory

1. Can you imagine being taken from your parents' home by a government agent and moved to a different family with a different culture? How would you react?
2. What continues to be the long-term consequences of Indian Residential Schools system?

Sources: Cantzler 2008; National Indian Child Welfare Association 2010; Schaefer 2012.

In November 2005, the federal government announced plans to distribute a $2 billion compensation package to survivors of Aboriginal residential schools and, by 2008, more than $1.3 billion worth of claims had been paid. Approximately 86 000 former students are eligible to receive a $10 000 basic payment and $3000 for every year spent in a residential school. In addition, compensation will be offered for claims of sexual and physical abuse, and loss of language and culture. The Aboriginal Healing Foundation will receive five years of funding ($125 million), $60 million will be available for a truth and reconciliation process, and $10 million will be spent to commemorate what happened in the schools. In return, the recipients give up the right to sue the federal government and the churches that ran the schools, except in cases of sexual and serious physical abuse. As seen in the opener of this chapter, an official apology on the part of the federal government for the abuses suffered by students of residential schools was issued by Prime Minister Stephen Harper in June 2008.

In addition to, and interrelated with, the effects of the residential schools' legacy, Aboriginal peoples have higher rates of poverty, suicide, tuberculosis, infant mortality, and incarceration than the non-Aboriginal population (Statistics

Canada 2003a). Aboriginal peoples also have lower rates of education and employment than non-Aboriginals, as well as shorter life expectancies.

In 2006, the number of people who identified themselves as Aboriginal passed the 1 million mark (Statistics Canada 2008c). Between 1996 and 2006, the Aboriginal population increased 45 percent, while the non-Aboriginal population grew by 8 percent over the same period (Statistics Canada 2008c).

Despite more than a century of colonial oppression, Aboriginal peoples have made strides toward regaining self-determination and autonomy. For example, the 1999 ratification of a treaty with the Nisga'a of northern British Columbia established a precedent for Aboriginal land claims and political autonomy. Figure 8-3 shows an overview of the First Nations peoples of British Columbia.

Asian Canadians Peter Li, author of *Chinese in Canada* (1988), argues that Asian, and Chinese in particular, is a racial distinctiveness and cultural inferiority articulated in the ideology and practice of Canada, while the normative order upholding Europeans as the desirable race is well entrenched (Li 2003). The social significance of race is also evident in public discourse, economic relations, and the arts and media

figure 8-3 First Nations Peoples of British Columbia

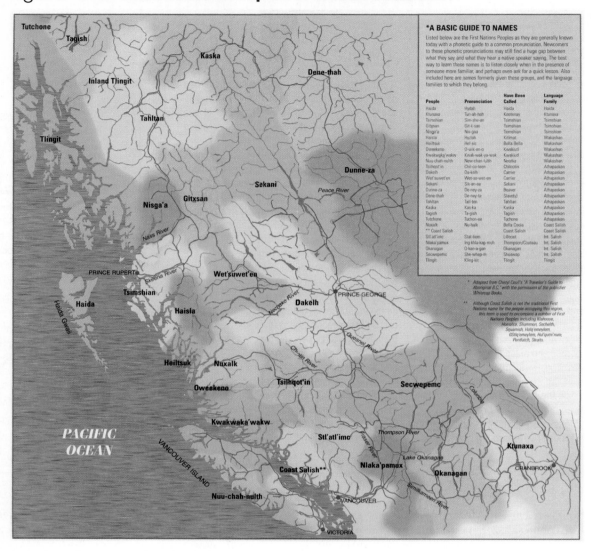

(Fleras and Kunz 2001; Li 2003). Canadians are fed a steady diet of mainstream media images in which Asians are portrayed as a homogeneous group, defined on the basis of a single racialized identity:

> We make up more than one half of the world's population, yet in spite of our numbers and contributions to the world, our images and perspectives are seldom seen. Our histories and our cultures are obscured, overlooked, buried or tokenized in a world dominated by Western classism. Our voices are seldom heard, our stories are left untold and our realities are seldom represented by those who control the means and resources to name and shape a picture of reality. (Park 1997)

These images are translated through the mainstream media into "us and them" scenarios (Fleras and Kunz 2001:131–132). For example, Asian Canadians are often portrayed in films as

- being foreigners who cannot be assimilated
- having no power or influence when playing leading roles
- having restricted features or mannerisms that are comical or sinister
- playing supporting roles even in the contexts that are unmistakably Asian
- having a negative or non-existent sexuality (for men)
- having regressive speech patterns that compound low intellectual capabilities
- having suicidal impulses in defence of honour, name, or country
- being overachievers but emotionally bankrupt

Given a normative social order in which Europeans were seen as desirable, the histories of Asian Canadians are ones in which institutional racism was entrenched in the social, political, and economic life of Canada. Chinese immigrants, who, for example, first came to Canada in the late 1850s to work in the mines, establish small businesses, and provide necessary labour for the building of the national railway, were

A Chinese head tax receipt, issued by the Canadian Immigration Branch, Vancouver, August 2, 1918.

viewed as a threatening and potentially dangerous "other" and treated accordingly. The Canadian government actively recruited Chinese labourers to complete the most dangerous phases of work on the Canadian Pacific Railway, paying them a fraction of the wages paid to white workers (Creese et al. 1991; Lampkin 1985). Institutional racism, as carried out by Canada's federal government, became more pronounced in 1885 with an act to restrict and regulate Chinese immigration to Canada. With this act began the imposition of a head tax of $50 in 1885, $100 in 1901, and $500 in 1904—a year's wages (Finkel et al. 1993)—to be paid by every Chinese immigrant entering Canada.

Institutional racism toward Chinese immigrants became even more wide-ranging in 1923, with the passing of the Chinese Exclusion Act, which, among other restrictions, barred the families of men working in Canada from joining them, resulting in years of separation of family members. Despite a history of institutional racism and current self-reported experiences of discrimination, Chinese Canadians are now among the best-educated groups in Canada, many having attained middle-class status, frequently as professionals (Derouin 2004; Nguyen 1982; Reitz 1980).

Other Asian groups have also endured various forms of racism, including institutional racism. In 1907, a Vancouver-bound ship carrying more than 1000 Japanese immigrants and some Sikh immigrants was met by a racist mob of workers protesting their arrival on the grounds that they were a threat to the job security of white workers. This anti-Asian riot, organized by the Asiatic Exclusion League, also targeted Asian-run businesses in downtown Vancouver. Vandals smashed windows and destroyed signs. Many years later, in 1941, Japanese Canadians faced a major attack of institutional racism by the Canadian government. The government rounded up Japanese Canadians who lived within 160 kilometres of the Pacific Coast for reasons of "national security," regardless of whether or not they supported Japan's involvement in World

War II. Japanese Canadians were placed in internment camps in the interior of British Columbia and on sugar beet farms in Alberta and Manitoba (David Suzuki, the Canadian environmentalist and television host/producer, spent part of his childhood with his family in an internment camp in British Columbia). Between 1943 and 1946, the federal government sold all the property and possessions of the internees, and new Japanese immigrants were barred from entering Canada until 1967, when a new immigration policy was introduced based on a point system. In 1988, the federal government offered an apology and compensation to Japanese Canadians for the racist treatment they had received during the internment. In 2006, the federal government formally apologized to Chinese Canadians for both the head tax and other government measures to bar Chinese immigration between 1923 and 1947.

Institutional racism is also entrenched in the history of Indo-Canadians, with the case of the *Komagata Maru*—a ship carrying 376 passengers from India to Canada in 1914—being perhaps the most notable example. The ship remained anchored just off the Vancouver coast for two months, while debates based on racist ideologies on the part of the government and the public ensued. During this time, passengers and crew were left without adequate supplies of food and water and without proper medical care. Conditions on board deteriorated rapidly. Eventually, based on the view that the Indian passengers constituted the category of "other," and thus warranted racist treatment, the Canadian government did not allow the ship to dock, forcing it to return to India.

In 1939, the Supreme Court of Canada ruled that discrimination based on race was legally enforceable (Henry et al. 1995). This ruling remained in place until the multiculturalism policy of 1971 was enacted, which brought about the modification of rules of engagement and entitlement for the "containment" of ethnicity (Fleras and Kunz 2001). Today, Asian Canadians, who tend to settle in Montreal, Toronto, and Vancouver, are the fastest-growing segment of new immigrants to Canada. The diverse groups found within this category are often stereotyped as "model" or ideal minority groups, as many members tend to succeed, educationally and economically, even while enduring various forms of racism.

The success of many of the members of these visible minorities, particularly the Chinese, may be used to bolster the position of those who argue that all it takes to get ahead in Canada is hard work and effort (as discussed when we examined the functionalist view in Chapter 6). The implication of this view is that if some members of visible minorities do succeed, those who do not must suffer from personal inadequacies. However, in their review of the vertical mosaic thesis, Lian and Matthews concluded that "similar educational qualifications carried different economic values in the Canadian labour market for individuals of different 'racial' origins

In 1914, passengers who arrived in Vancouver on the *Komagata Maru* were forced to turn back to India after a two-month standoff. Most of the passengers were Sikhs, and the remaining were Muslims and Hindus. Discriminatory laws at the time made it difficult for Asian immigrants to come to Canada.

which individuals or groups are denied social opportunities, economic rewards and other privileges as a result of their 'racial designation'" (2003:1).

Given that *race* is a value-laden term, racial markers have provided the basis on which to distinguish the "desirable" from the "undesirable," "us" from "them" (Li 2003). The normative social order of Canada has favoured Europeans, positioning them as "us," institutionalizing their interests and cultural values and thus providing them greater power to set the norms of society. Initial immigrant policies were racist in orientation, intending to encourage assimilation, and had an exclusionary result (Fleras and Elliott 2003). "Preferred" groups were from Northern and Western Europe and, later, in response to the settlement needs of Western Canada, groups from Eastern and Southern Europe that, although lower in preferred ranking, were also deemed acceptable. These groups faced limited or no entry restrictions, while other groups, such as Jews and Mediterranean populations, "otherized" on the basis of perceived racial differences, required special permits for entry.

and that a 'coloured mosaic' now exists, in which educational achievement at any level fails to protect persons of visible minority background from being disadvantaged in terms of income they receive" (1998:475–476).

The disadvantage of having a visible minority background affects those born outside the country as well as others who are native Canadians (Pendakur and Pendakur 2002). A 2004 study showed that one-third of members of visible minorities in Canada—more than a million people—reported having been discriminated against or treated unfairly because of their ethnicity, culture, race, skin colour, language, accent, or religion (Derouin 2004). Asian Canadians reported lower levels of discrimination than members of the visible minority category did overall, with Chinese Canadians reporting marginally lower rates of discrimination than members of the Asian category did overall (see Figure 8-4).

It is imperative to keep in mind the ways in which certain categories, such as gender and age, intersect with a visible-minority background, diversifying and compounding the degrees of discrimination experienced by many Canadians.

White Ethnic Groups Unlike minority groups whose identities have been racialized, those of both dominant and minority white ethnic groups have not. As a result of their "invisibility," they experience a greater chance of social inclusion and, in the case of white minorities, a lesser chance of social exclusion through racism, discrimination, and exploitation after the initial adaptation period (Fleras and Elliott 1992). As Peter Li argues, "social inclusion of 'racial' groups that have been historically marginalized implies the use of 'race' as grounds to signify the value of people. In contrast, racial exclusion involves constructing social boundaries based on phenotypic features [physical appearance], by

figure 8-4 Percentage of Canadians Who Agree that Discrimination against Visible Minorities Is a Problem in Canada

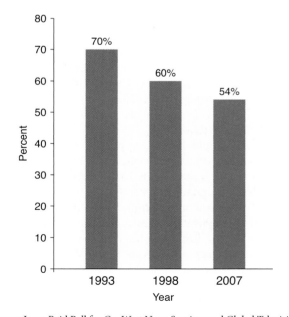

Source: Ipsos Reid Poll for CanWest News Services and Global Television 2007.

John Porter's landmark study *The Vertical Mosaic* (1965) used the concept of *charter groups* to represent the French and English, the so-called founding groups of Canadian society. Porter's work documented the imbalances in the distribution of power, wealth, and resources, showing that the British and French were more positively rewarded and evaluated than were newly arrived immigrants (Fleras and Elliott 1992; Kazemipur 2002). Porter's thesis study, as discussed in earlier chapters, in which various ethnic groups were hierarchically arranged such that European groups held higher socioeconomic positions than non-European groups, has been re-examined in more contemporary contexts. These studies show that whites are advantaged over non-whites in relation to occupational status and earnings (Geschwender 1994; Lautard and Guppy 1999; Lautard and Loree 1984; Li 1988). Even when such factors as demographic features are controlled for, substantial income disparities persist between Canadians of European origin and those of visible-minority groups (Beach and Worswick 1993; Boyd 1984, 1992;

Li 1992, 2000; Pendakur and Pendakur 1998). Studies conducted since the release of *The Vertical Mosaic*, which included the impact of the major influx of immigrants from non-European countries, have "resulted in an increase in the salience of race at the expense of ethnicity . . . as the 1960s' reforms in Canadian immigration policy have raised the number of visible minority immigrants, and along with it the potential to racial discrimination" (Kazemipur 2002).

Members of white ethnic groups, who continue to hold the bulk of economic and political power in Canada (federal and provincial or territorial), have co-opted Canada's ethnic and racial diversity for trade, investment, and commercial purposes. For example, in her article "Multiculturalism, or the United Colours of Capitalism?" Katharyne Mitchell argues that Canada's multicultural character has been used by Canadian power-holders to attract transnational elites to Canada, by selling an ideology of racial harmony that may provide reassurance for nervous investors (Fleras and Kunz 2001).

Social Policy and Race and Ethnicity

Global Immigration

The Issue

Worldwide, there are an estimated 191 million immigrants, with the last 50 years seeing almost a doubling of immigration (UNFPA 2006). As Figure 8-5 shows, immigration has had a significant effect on virtually every country of the world because it has become either a source of migrants or an entry point of immigrants. The increasing numbers of migrants raise questions for the recipient countries, the majority of which are developed. Who should be allowed in? Should immigration be expanded? At what point should it be curtailed?

The Setting

The migration of people is not uniform across time or space. At certain times, wars or famines may precipitate large movements of people either temporarily or permanently. Temporary dislocations occur when people wait until it is safe to return to their home areas. However, more and more migrants who cannot make adequate livings in their home nations are making permanent moves to developed nations. The major migration streams flow into North America, the oil-rich areas of the Middle East, and the industrial economies of Western Europe and Asia. Currently, seven of the

world's wealthiest nations (including Canada, Germany, France, the United Kingdom, and the United States) shelter about one-third of the world's migrant population, but less than one-fifth of the total world population. As long as there are disparities in job opportunities among countries, there is little reason to expect this international migration trend to end.

Countries, such as Canada, that have long been a destination for immigrants have a history of policies to determine who has preference to enter. Often, clear racial and ethnic biases are built into these policies. Until the 1960s, Canadian immigration policy favoured immigrants from Northern Europe and Britain. Immigrants who were members of visible minority groups were explicitly excluded and discriminated against, as Canadian politicians and policymakers believed that they were not a "good fit" for Canadian society. The first hundred years of post-Confederation immigration were essentially about European migration to Canada. Not all Europeans, however, were treated equally or looked on favourably by Canadian immigration policy. The British and Northern Europeans were preferred over Eastern and Southern Europeans, the latter being recruited only if there were not sufficient numbers of eligible British and Northern Europeans.

Since the late 1960s, policies in Canada have encouraged immigration of people from non-European nations. This change has significantly altered the pattern of immigrants' country of birth. Previously, Europeans dominated; but for the last 20 years, immigrants have come primarily from Asia.

People from Asia and the Middle East made up 58.3 percent of immigrants to Canada between 2001 and 2006 (Statistics Canada 2007d). In 2010, the top three countries of origin of immigrants to Canada were Philippines, India, and China. The impact that immigration has on Canada, however, is not experienced equally by all Canadians; it has a much larger impact, for the most part, on those living in larger urban centres. More specifically, immigrants arriving in Canada between 2001 and 2006 tended to settle in Toronto, Montreal, and Vancouver and their suburbs (Statistics Canada 2007d). These three cities are also among the cities in the world with the largest foreign-born populations (see Figure 8-6).

Sociological Insights

Immigration can provide many valuable functions. For the destination society, it alleviates

figure 8-5 World Immigration since 1500

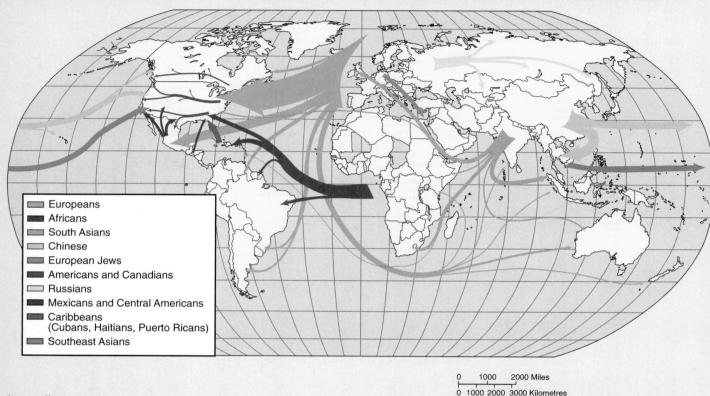

Europeans
Africans
South Asians
Chinese
European Jews
Americans and Canadians
Russians
Mexicans and Central Americans
Caribbeans
(Cubans, Haitians, Puerto Ricans)
Southeast Asians

| 0 | 1000 | 2000 Miles |
| 0 | 1000 2000 | 3000 Kilometres |

Source: Allen 2008.

labour shortages, such as in the areas of health care, business, and technology in Canada. For the sending nation, migration can relieve economies unable to support large numbers of people. Often overlooked is the large amount of money that immigrants send back to their home nations. For example, worldwide, immigrants from Portugal alone send more than US$4 billion annually back to their home country (World Bank 1995).

Immigration can be dysfunctional as well. Although studies generally show that immigration has a positive impact on the receiving nation's economy, areas experiencing high concentrations of immigrants may find it difficult to meet short-term social service needs. Critics of the way in which Canada's federal government is handling immigration say that although the country may be creating a few vibrantly multicultural urban centres, the government is also fostering cities that lack the services to deal with this growth and diversity. When migrants with skills or educational potential leave developing countries, it can be dysfunctional for those nations. No amount of money sent back home can make up for the loss of valuable human resources from poor nations (Martin and Midgley 1999).

Conflict theorists note how much of the debate over immigration is phrased in economic terms. But this debate is intensified when the arrivals are of different racial and ethnic background from the host population. For example, Europeans often refer to "foreigners," but the term does not necessarily mean one of foreign birth. In Germany, "foreigners" refers to people of non-German ancestry, even if they were born in Germany; it does not refer to people of German ancestry born in another country who may choose to come to their "mother country." Fear and dislike of "new" ethnic groups may divide countries throughout the world (Saunders 2012). In Canada, fear or dislike of high levels of immigration is not as evident as that experienced in other countries.

Policy Initiatives

The long border with Mexico provides ample opportunity for illegal immigration into the United States. Throughout the 1980s, there was a perception among some observers that the United States had lost control of its borders. Feeling public pressure for immigration control, the U.S. Congress ended a decade of debate by approving the Immigration Reform and Control Act of 1986. The Act marked a historic change in immigration policy. For the first time, hiring of illegal aliens was outlawed, and employers caught violating the law became subject to fines and even prison sentences. Just as significant a change was the extension of amnesty

and legal status to many illegal immigrants already living in the United States. Over two decades later, however, the 1986 immigration law appears to have had mixed results. Substantial numbers of illegal immigrants continue to enter the United States each year, with an estimated 11 million present in March 2005 (Passel 2006).

Of particular concern for Canadian policymakers is the distribution or dispersion of immigrants. The fact that the vast majority of newcomers to Canada have settled in large metropolitan regions has created a problem of "two solitudes— overtaxed megalopolises and waning small towns" (Jimenez and Lunman 2004:A5). In the large centres, pressure is placed on public housing, English-language courses, support services for immigrants, public transportation, and the cities' infrastructures in general. Policymakers and politicians at all levels of government are currently devising strategies to deal with these challenges.

Throughout the world, globalization has had an overwhelming impact on immigration patterns. Overseas, the European Union (EU) agreement of 1997 gave the EU's governing commission authority to propose a continent-wide policy on immigration. European Union policy allows residents of one EU country to live and work in another member state—an arrangement that is expected to become more complicated when nations such as

figure 8-6 Foreign Born as a Percentage of Metropolitan Population, 2006

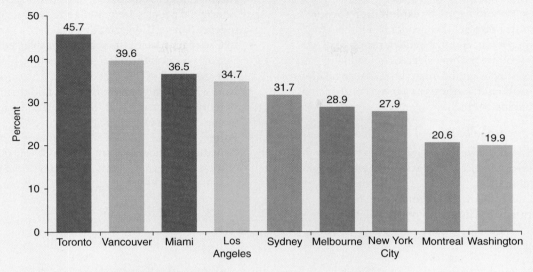

Note: The data from the United States is from 2005.

Sources: Statistics Canada, 2006d; Australian Bureau of Statistics, 2006 Census; U. S. Census Bureau, 2006 American Community Survey.

Turkey become members of the EU. In many EU countries, immigrants from Turkey's predominantly Muslim population are not welcome, no matter how pressing the local economy's need for labour (Denny 2004).

The intense debate over immigration reflects deep value conflicts in the cultures of many developed nations. One strand of the debate, for example, emphasizes egalitarian principles and a desire to be inclusive. At the same time, however, another strand is based on hostility to potential immigrants and refugees, reflecting not only racial, ethnic, and religious prejudice but also a desire to maintain the dominant culture of the in-group by keeping out those viewed as outsiders.

Apply the Theory

1. Did you or your parents or grandparents immigrate to Canada? If so, when? Where did your family come from, and why? Did you or they face discrimination?

2. Do you live, work, or study with recent immigrants to Canada? If so, are they well accepted in your community, or do they face prejudice and discrimination?

3. In your opinion, is there a backlash against immigrants in Canada?

4. In your view, does the functionalist perspective on race and ethnicity provide a realistic interpretation of unequal access to opportunity in Canada?

CHAPTER RESOURCES

Summary

::: 8.1 What Are Minority, Racial, and Ethnic Groups?

- A **racial group** is socially constructed through a process of racialization, based on perceived physical differences, whereas an **ethnic group** is set apart primarily because of national origin or distinctive cultural patterns.
- When sociologists define a **minority group**, they are primarily concerned with the economic and political power, or powerlessness, of the group.
- There is no biological basis for the concept of "race," and there are no physical traits that can be used to describe one racial group to the exclusion of all others.

- The meaning that people give to the physical differences between certain groups gives social significance to race and ethnicity, leading to **stereotypes**.

::: 8.2 What Are Prejudice and Discrimination?

- **Prejudice** often leads to **discrimination**, but the two are not identical; and each can be present without the other.
- **Institutional discrimination** results when the structural components of a society create or foster differential treatment of groups.

:::8.3 How Are Race and Ethnicity Studied?

- Functionalists point out that discrimination is both functional and dysfunctional in society. Conflict theorists explain racial subordination by **exploitation theory**.
- Some feminists point out that gender is not the sole source of oppression, and that gender, race, and class intersect to produce multiple degrees of inequality.
- Interactionists focus on the micro level of race relations, posing the **contact hypothesis** as a means of reducing prejudice and discrimination.

:::8.4 What Are Some Patterns of Intergroup Relations?

- Three patterns describe typical intergroup relations in North America and elsewhere: **assimilation, segregation**, and multiculturalism.
- In Canada, the ideal pattern of intergroup relations is multiculturalism. There is an ongoing debate over whether the ideal is, in fact, the reality of life for most minority Canadians.

:::8.5 What Are Some Groups that Make Up Canada's Multi-Ethnic Character?

- After a century and a half of degradation, Canada's Aboriginal peoples are poised to reclaim their status as an independent, self-determining people.
- In Canadian society, the socially constructed category of "Asian" obscures the differences among various groups that are placed in this broad category.
- Non-white immigrants commonly find themselves stereotyped, portrayed as the "other," and marginalized by mainstream Canadian society.
- Porter's "vertical mosaic" is as accurate a portrayal of Canadian multiculturalism today as it was in 1965; however, *race* is now more salient than *ethnicity*.

Critical Thinking Questions

1. How is institutional discrimination even more powerful than individual discrimination? How would functionalists, conflict theorists, feminists, and interactionists examine institutional discrimination?

2. Do you think that multiculturalism in Canada is real or an ideal? Can you think of ways in which it might serve to mask the disparities between various ethnic and racial groups?

3. What place do you see Canada's Aboriginal peoples occupying in the twenty-first century? Do you think Aboriginal peoples will become more integrated into mainstream culture, or will they distance themselves from it by re-establishing their traditional communities?

THINKING ABOUT MOVIES

Amreeka

A Palestinian family that has immigrated to the United States struggles with judgments against their ethnicity.

Crash

The lives of multiple characters collide, revealing layers of prejudice directed at a wide range of racialized groups and ethnicities.

Pride

In the 1970s, an African American swim team battles racial prejudice in the United States.

inside

Around the world, most occupations are dominated by either men or women. Men still predominate in military organizations, although women occupy many roles. Pictured here is Kirsty Moore, a female pilot with the RAF acrobatic display team the Red Arrows of Great Britain.

Difference of opinion exists in Canada and elsewhere on whether Muslim women should be permitted to cover their faces in public.

"Middle Eastern garments designed to cover a woman's face are 'medieval' and 'misogynist' symbols of extremism with no basis in Islam, said a Canadian Muslim lobby group as it urged Ottawa to ban the burka and the niqab.

The Muslim Canadian Congress [in October 2009] called on the federal government to prohibit the two garments in order to prevent women from covering their faces in public—a practice the group said has no place in a society that supports gender equality.

'To cover your face is to conceal your identity,' congress spokeswoman Farzana Hassan said in a telephone interview, describing the issue as a matter of public safety, since concealing one's identity is a common practice for criminals.

The tradition of Muslim women covering their faces in public is a tradition rooted more in Middle Eastern culture than in the Islamic faith, Ms. Hassan added.

There is nothing in any of the primary Islamic religious texts, including the Koran, that requires women to cover their faces, she said—not even in the ultra-conservative tenets of Sharia law.

Considering the fact that women are in fact forbidden from wearing burkas in the grand mosque in Mecca, Islam's holiest site, it hardly makes sense that the practice should be permitted in Canada, she said.

'If a government claims to uphold equality between men and women, there is no reason for them to support a practice that marginalizes women.'

The proposed ban would include the burka, an iconic head-to-toe gown with a mesh-like panel over the face that allows the wearer to see and to breathe, as well as the niqab—a veil that leaves only the eyes exposed.

Ms. Hassan said the ban would not extend to the hijab, a traditional headscarf that does not cover the face.

The proposed ban comes on the heels of reports that Sheikh Mohamed Tantawi, dean of Egypt's al-Azhar university and the country's highest Muslim authority, is poised to issue a fatwa, or religious edict, against the garments.

Media reports [earlier] said Sheikh Tantawi described the face coverings as 'a custom that has nothing to do with the Islamic faith.'

Mohamed Elmasry, former president of the Canadian Islamic Congress, said he agrees the tradition has its roots in cultural customs rather than religious teachings, but that the issue is irrelevant in Canada where the practice is not widespread.

Mr. Elmasry disputed suggestions that the garments pose a security threat, saying only a minority of Muslim women living in Canada feel the need to conceal their features in public.

He said he believes those women should have the freedom to decide whether they wish to cover their faces, and that a ban would limit freedom of expression.

'People feel it's part of their identity, people feel it's part of their culture,' Mr. Elmasry said.

'It's not for you and me to decide.'"

("Muslim group moves to ban burka; Canadian lobbyists say garments are 'medieval' and 'misogynist'" Toronto - The Canadian Press Last updated on Wednesday, Oct. 07, 2009 08:47PM . Used with permission of the Globe and Mail.)

In this article, the issue of Muslim women covering their faces with garments known as "burkas" and "niqabs" is discussed. The Muslim Canadian Congress has called for the government to prevent women form wearing such garments in public places, stating that the practice "has no place in a society that supports gender equality." Others support the view that, although the wearing of these garments has nothing to do with the Islamic faith, women in Canada should have the freedom to decide if they wish to cover their faces.

Expectations related to physical appearance are one example of how cultural norms may lead to differentiation based on gender. Such differentiation is evident in virtually every human society about which we have information. We saw in Chapters 7 and 8 that most societies establish hierarchies based on social class, race, and ethnicity. In this chapter, we examine the ways in which societies stratify their members on the basis of gender, in relation to social class, race, and ethnicity. We also see that increases in educational participation among women have not resulted in the elimination of the long-standing economic disparity between men and women in Canada.

We begin by looking at how various cultures, including our own, assign women and men to particular social roles. Then we consider sociological explanations for gender stratification. Next, we focus on the diverse experiences of women as an oppressed majority, and analyze the social, economic, and political aspects of women's subordinate position in society. Here, we also examine the emergence of the feminist movement, its goals, and its contradictions. Finally, the social policy section provides a discussion about the links among abortion, new reproductive technology, and women's reproductive choices. ∎

::: use your sociological *imagination* :::

Have you ever had a conversation with a Muslim woman at your university about the wearing of a burka or niqab? What meanings could be attached to the wearing of these garments?

How Is Gender Socially Constructed?

How many air passengers do you think feel a start when the captain's voice from the cockpit belongs to a woman? Consciously or unconsciously, many assume that flying a commercial plane is a *man's* job. Gendered practices and organization are an integral part of our social world; so much so that we may take them for granted and only take notice when they deviate from conventional behaviour and expectations.

Although a few people begin life with an unclear sex identity, the overwhelming majority begin with a definite sex and quickly receive societal messages about how to behave. Thus, the term **sex** is a biological category. Many societies have established distinctions between "female" and "male" that are not "natural" but are cultural and social. This is what is meant by *gender*. When we use the term **gender**, we are "using a shorthand term which encodes a crucial point: that our basic social identities as men and women are socially constructed rather than based on fixed biological characteristics" (Young 1988:98).

In studying gender, sociologists are interested in the gender-role socialization that leads women and men to behave differently. In Chapter 4, *gender roles* were defined as expectations regarding the proper behaviour, attitudes, and activities of men and women. The application of traditional gender roles leads to many forms of differentiation between women and men. Both sexes are physically capable of learning to cook and sew, yet most Western societies determine that women should perform these tasks. Both men and women are capable of learning to weld and fly airplanes, but these functions are generally assigned to men.

Gender roles are evident not only in our work and behaviour but also in how we react to others. We are constantly "doing gender" without realizing it. If a father sits in the doctor's office with his son in the middle of a workday, he will probably receive approving glances from the receptionist and from other patients. "Isn't he a wonderful father?" runs through their minds. But if the boy's mother leaves *her* job and sits with the son in the doctor's office, she will not receive such silent applause.

We socially construct our behaviour so that male–female differences are either created or exaggerated. For example, men and women come in a variety of heights, sizes, and ages. Yet norms related to appropriate occupations for men and women—such as male firefighters and female preschool teachers—continue to be perpetuated. As well, traditional norms regarding marriage and even casual dating tell us that in heterosexual couples, the man should be older, taller, and wiser than the woman. As we will see throughout this chapter, such social norms help to reinforce and legitimize patterns of male dominance.

In recent decades, women have increasingly entered occupations and professions previously dominated by men. Yet our society still focuses on "masculine" and "feminine" qualities as if men and women must be evaluated in these terms. Clearly, we continue to "do gender," and this social construction of

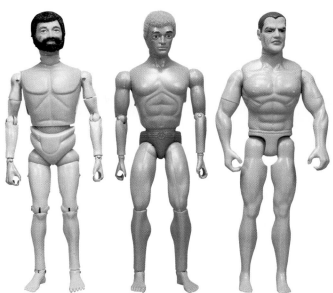

In our society, men and women receive different messages about the ideal body image. For women, the Miss America pageant promotes a very slim, statuesque physique. For men, "action figures" like the G.I. Joe doll promote an exaggerated muscularity typical of professional wrestlers (Angier 1998; Byrd-Bredbenner and Murray 2003).

gender continues to define significantly different expectations for females and males in North America (Lorber 1994; Rosenbaum 1996; West and Zimmerman 1987).

Gender Roles in North America

Gender-Role Socialization   Male babies get blue blankets, while female babies get pink ones. Boys are expected to play with trucks, blocks, and toy soldiers; girls are given dolls and kitchen goods. Boys must be masculine—active, aggressive, tough, daring, and dominant—whereas girls must be feminine—soft, emotional, sweet, and submissive. These traditional gender-role patterns have been influential in the socialization of children in North America.

An important element in traditional views of proper "masculine" and "feminine" behaviour is fear of homosexuality. **Homophobia** is a fear of and prejudice against homosexuality. Homophobia contributes significantly to rigid gender-role socialization, since many people stereotypically associate male homosexuality with femininity and lesbianism with masculinity. Consequently, men and women who deviate from traditional expectations about gender roles are often presumed to be gay. Despite the advances made by the gay rights movement, the continuing stigma attached to homosexuality in our culture places pressure on all males (whether gay or not) to exhibit only narrow masculine behaviour and on all females (whether lesbian or not) to exhibit only narrow feminine behaviour (Seidman 1994; see also Lehne 1995).

It is adults, of course, who play a critical role in guiding children into those gender roles deemed appropriate in a society. Parents are normally the first and most crucial agents of socialization. But other adults, older siblings, the mass media, and religious and educational institutions also exert an important influence on gender-role socialization in Canada and elsewhere.

It is not hard to test how rigid gender-role socialization can be. Just try transgressing some gender norms—say, by smoking a cigar in public if you are female or carrying a purse if you are male. That was exactly the assignment given to a group of sociology students. Professors asked the students to behave in ways that they thought violated norms of how a man or woman should act. The students had no trouble coming up with gender norm "transgressions" (see Table 9-1), and they

table 9-1 An Experiment of Gender Norm Violations by University Students

Norm Violations by Women	Norm Violations by Men
Send men flowers	Wear fingernail polish
Spit in public	Needlepoint in public
Use men's bathroom	Throw Tupperware party
Buy jock strap	Cry in public
Buy/chew tobacco	Have pedicure
Talk knowledgably about cars	Apply to babysit
Open doors for men	Shave body hair

Sociology students were asked to behave in ways that might be regarded as violating gender norms. This is a sample of their actual choices over a seven-year period. Do you agree that these actions test the boundaries of conventional behaviour?
Source: Nielsen et al. 2000:287.

kept careful notes on how others reacted to their behaviour, ranging from amusement to disgust (Nielsen, Walden, and Kunkel 2000).

Gender-Role Socialization and Social Class The 2000 movie *Billy Elliot* portrays the life of a young boy growing up in a British mining town and the gender socialization he undergoes. His father and older brother, both coal miners on strike, discover that Billy is secretly attending ballet classes rather than the boxing lessons he pretended to be taking. Billy's behaviour causes his father great concern and displeasure. He sees his son's dancing as a lack of conformity to gender-role expectations. Billy's father actively discourages him from pursuing his love of dance, until he comes to the realization that Billy possesses great talent. At that point, even though his son is defying cultural norms and community standards of appropriate male behaviour, the father begins to support and encourage Billy in his dream to become a professional dancer.

Research shows that patterns of gender socialization are not homogeneous, but rather vary according to the social class to which a person belongs. Working-class parents tend to be more concerned with their children's outward conformity to society's norms and roles (Kohn, Slomeznsky, and Schoenbach 1986). Middle-class parents, in contrast, tend to be more concerned with their children's motivation for certain behaviours and focus on developing such qualities as self-expression and self-control (Langman 1987). Upper-middle-class families are most likely to support more egalitarian gender relations and thus socialize their children accordingly (Langman 1987; Lips 1993). Children who are raised by middle-class, career-oriented mothers tend to hold more egalitarian attitudes relating to men's and women's roles (Tuck, Rolfe, and Adair 1994).

Women's Gender Roles How does a girl come to develop a feminine self-image whereas a boy develops one that is masculine? In part, they do so by identifying with females and males in their families and neighbourhoods and in the media. If a young girl regularly sees female characters on television working as defence lawyers and judges, she may believe that she herself can become a lawyer and then a judge. And it will not hurt if women that she knows—her mother, sister, parents' friends, or neighbours—are lawyers. By contrast, if this young girl sees women portrayed in the media only as models, nurses, and secretaries, her identification and self-image will be quite different. Even if she does become a professional, she may secretly regret falling short of the media stereotype—a shapely, sexy young woman in a bathing suit (Wolf 1991).

Television is far from being alone in stereotyping women. Studies of children's books published in North America in the 1940s, 1950s, and 1960s found that females were significantly underrepresented in central roles and illustrations. Virtually all female characters were portrayed as helpless, passive, incompetent, and in need of a strong male caretaker. By the 1980s, there was somewhat less stereotyping in children's books, with some female characters shown to be active. An example of this change is seen in the 1980 children's book *The Paper Bag Princess*, by Canadian writer Robert Munsch, where the female character is the active one who takes control of her life. Nevertheless, boys were still shown engaged in active play three times as often as girls (Kortenhaus and Demarest 1993). Females tended to be shown mostly in traditional roles, such as mother, grandmother, or volunteer, even though they also held non-traditional roles, such as working professional (Etaugh 2003).

Social research on gender roles reveals some persistent differences between men and women in North America and Europe. Women experience a mandate to both marry and be a mother. Often, marriage is viewed as the true entry into adulthood. And women are expected not only to become mothers but to *want* to be mothers. Obviously, men play a role in these events, but the events do not appear to be as critical in identifying the life course for a man. Society defines men's roles by economic success. Although women may achieve recognition in the labour force, it is not as important to their identity as it is for men (Doyle and Paludi 1998; Russo 1976).

Traditional gender roles have most severely restricted females. Throughout this chapter, we will see how women have been confined to subordinate roles within the political and economic institutions of Canada and elsewhere. Yet, it is also true that gender roles have restricted males.

Men's Gender Roles

> During the game I always played the outfield. Right field. Far right field. And there I would stand in the hot sun wishing I was anyplace else in the world. (Fager et al. 1971)

This is the childhood recollection of a man who, as a boy, disliked sports, dreaded gym classes, and had particular problems with baseball. Obviously, he did not conform to the socially constructed male gender role and no doubt paid the price for it.

Men's roles are socially constructed in much the same way as women's roles are. Family, peers, and the media all influence how a boy or a man comes to view his appropriate role in society. Robert Brannon (1976) and James Doyle (1995) have identified five aspects of the male gender role:

- anti-feminine element—show no "sissy stuff," including any expression of openness or vulnerability
- success element—prove their masculinity at work and sports
- aggressive element—use force in dealing with others
- sexual element—initiate and control all sexual relations
- self-reliant element—stay cool and unflappable

No systematic research has established all these elements as common aspects among boys and men, but specific studies have confirmed individual elements.

Being anti-feminine is basic to men's gender roles. Males who do not conform to the socially constructed gender role face constant criticism and even humiliation both from children when they are boys and from adults as men. It can be agonizing to be treated as a "chicken" or a "sissy"—particularly if such remarks come from a father or brothers. At the same time, boys who successfully adapt to cultural standards of masculinity may grow up to be inexpressive men who cannot share their feelings with others. They remain forceful and tough—but as a result they are also closed and isolated and, in some instances, more prone to suicide, stemming from untreated depression (Powell 2013). Head of a suicide prevention charity in the U.K., Jane Powell states; "We believe that if we are to combat suicide we have to ensure that all men are aware of the symptoms of depression and feel able to access help without being seen as less of a man for doing so . . . We need to challenge the idea that a 'strong and silent' man is desirable and challenge the notion that men talking, showing emotion and being 'sensitive' is weak" (Powell 2013). In his film *Tough Guise*, Jackson Katz presents the case of societal violence being a product of socialized maleness.

In the past four decades, inspired in good part by the contemporary feminist movement (examined later in the chapter), increasing numbers of men in North America have criticized the restrictive aspects of the traditional male gender role. Some men have taken strong public positions in support of women's struggle for full equality and have even organized voluntary associations, such as the White Ribbon Campaign (WRC), founded in Canada in 1991 to end men's violence against women. Nevertheless, traditional male gender roles remain well entrenched as an influential element of many cultures. Susan D. Somach, author of the 2011 report "The Other Side of the Gender Equation: Gender Issues for Men in the Europe and Eursasia Region," states ". . . men and boys everywhere have struggles of their own based on the gender box in which society tries [too often successfully] to put them. Together, we can be partners in addressing the gender issues faced by women and by men, by girls and by boys—and in seeking true gender equality that will benefit all of us" (2011:vi).

Cross-Cultural Perspective

To what extent do actual biological differences between the sexes contribute to the cultural differences associated with gender? This question brings us back to the debate over "nature versus nurture." In assessing the alleged and real differences between men and women, it is useful to examine cross-cultural data.

The research of anthropologist Margaret Mead points to the importance of cultural conditioning—as opposed to biology—in defining the social roles of males and females. In *Sex and Temperament* (1963, original edition 1935; 1973), Mead describes typical behaviours of each sex in three different cultures in New Guinea:

> In one [the Arapesh], both men and women act as we expect women to act—in a mild parental responsive way; in the second [the Mundugumor], both act as we expect men to act—in a fierce initiating fashion; and in the third [the Tchambuli], the men act according to our stereotypes for women—are catty, wear curls, and go shopping—while the women are energetic, managerial, unadorned partners. (Preface to 1950 ed.)

If biology determined all differences between the sexes, then cross-cultural differences, such as those described by Mead, would not exist. Her findings confirm the influential role of culture and socialization in gender-role differentiation.

Gender roles serve to discourage men from entering certain low-paying female-dominated occupations, such as childcare. Only about 5 percent of daycare workers are male.

How Are Gender Relations Explained?

Cross-cultural studies indicate that societies dominated by men are much more common than those in which women play the decisive role. Sociologists have turned to all the major theoretical perspectives to understand how and why these social distinctions are established. Each approach focuses on culture, rather than biology, as the primary determinant of gender differences. Yet, in other respects, there are wide disagreements among advocates of these sociological perspectives. Box 9-1 discusses the role of education in the empowerment of women.

There appears to be no innate or biological reason to designate completely different gender roles for men and women.

In any society, gender stratification requires not only individual socialization into traditional gender roles within the family, but also the promotion and support of these traditional roles by other social institutions, such as religion, mass media, government, and education. For example, the United Arab Emirates (UAE) has launched a program involving workshops, lectures, and television programs geared towards young women in order to raise awareness about femininity and the "proper" way to dress. This initiative comes in the wake of young women in high school and university who began to wear short hair, baggy pants, and gym shoes, and were thus considered to be "too manly" by cultural standards (*The Economist* 2010a). However, even with all major institutions socializing the young into conventional gender roles, every society has women and men who resist and successfully oppose these stereotypes: women who become political leaders, men who care for children, and so forth. It seems clear that differences between the sexes are not dictated by biology. Indeed, the maintenance of traditional gender roles requires constant social controls—and these controls are not always effective.

The Functionalist View

Functionalists maintain that gender differentiation has contributed to overall social stability. Sociologists Talcott Parsons

Women often have difficulty entering what is considered to be men's sports; however, gender roles vary considerably from one country to another. The photo above shows the Canadian Women's Olympic Soccer team celebrating their bronze medal in 2012. The photo below shows the female judo Olympic competitor from Saudi Arabia. In 2012 in London, the countries of Brunei, Qatar, and Saudi Arabia sent female athletes to the Olympics for the first time.

::: use your sociological *imagination* :::

How would your life and the lives of your family and friends be different if you lived in a society that was not gendered?

sociology in the global community

9-1 The Empowerment of Women through Education

International declarations and targets to achieve certain rights for women include the education of girls and women as a key priority. For example, the UN Women's Conference in Cairo in 1990, the UN Social Summit in Copenhagen in 1995, the UN Conference in Beijing in 1995, and the UN Millennium Summit in 2000 all made declarations to close the gender gap in primary and secondary education by 2005. All four international conferences set a target date of 2015 for the provision of universal primary education in all countries. Many of these declarations may not be achieved by the stated target date; however, they are often used as benchmarks for the overall social and economic development of a country. As well, the declarations may be used by women's groups of various countries to lobby for the achievement of these goals locally.

Globally, great disparities exist among the young women of the world: in 2009, approximately one-fifth of the world's population was illiterate, and the majority were poor women from sub-Saharan Africa, Asia, and Latin America. Although sociocultural, gender-based barriers to education and literacy are factors that have been associated with the disempowerment of girls and women, educating girls and women has profound empowering benefits for them as individuals:

- It improves their health as well as that of their children.
- It decreases their fertility.

- It increases their productivity.
- It enhances their ability to make informed decisions.
- It increases their status and power within the family.
- It increases their opportunity to take on leadership roles in the community.
- It decreases their chances, and their children's chances, of living in poverty.

These benefits are inextricably connected to those of the community as a whole. Many countries, recognizing the key role of education in their social and economic development, are addressing the issue of girls' and women's education through integrated socioeconomic, cultural, and institutional approaches, in order to improve the educational participation of girls and women. In Benin, for example, school fees for girls are being eliminated in public primary schools in the rural areas, and a media campaign to sensitize parents on issues related to gender and education has been implemented. UNICEF's *State of the World's Children 2007* report states that even though women's education is linked to children's survival and development, almost one out of every five girls in developing countries won't complete primary education. The UNICEF report—subtitled *Women and Children: The Double Dividend of Gender Equality*—suggested seven initiatives to promote gender equality, one of which was to abolish school fees and to

encourage investment in girls' education by parents and communities.

A 2011 World Bank study emphasized that there is a correlation between gross domestic product per capita and gender equality stating: "Gender equality is smart economics." Increasing girls' school enrollment is linked to faster rates of economic development, higher productivity, and improved outcomes for children (Grant 2011). The World Bank's chief economist stated: "Blocking women and girls from getting the skills and earnings to succeed in a globalized world is not only wrong, but also economically harmful" (Lin in Grant 2011).

Apply the Theory

1. Why is the education of girls and women such a powerful force in changing the social and economic conditions of a community as a whole?
2. In what way does the empowerment of women through education relate to class and race?
3. How might conflict sociologists explain the global disparities in girls' and women's access to education?

Sources: CAF America 2009; Grant 2011; UNESCO 2002; UNICEF 2006; van der Gaag 2004.

---

and Robert Bales argued that to function most effectively, the family requires adults who will specialize in particular roles (1955). They viewed the traditional arrangement of gender roles as arising out of this need to establish a division of labour between marital partners.

Parsons and Bales contended that women take the expressive, emotionally supportive role and men the instrumental, practical role, with the two complementing each other. **Instrumentality** refers to emphasis on tasks, and a focus on more distant goals, as well as a concern for the external relationship between the family and other social institutions. **Expressiveness** denotes concern for the maintenance of harmony and the internal emotional affairs of the family. According to this theory, women's interest in expressive goals frees men for instrumental tasks, and vice versa. Women become "anchored" in the family as wives, mothers, and household managers; men are anchored in the occupational world outside the home. Of course, Parsons and Bales offered this framework in the 1950s, when many more women were full-time homemakers than is true today. These theorists did not explicitly endorse traditional gender roles, but they implied that dividing tasks between spouses was functional for the family unit.

Given the typical socialization of women and men in North America, the functionalist view is initially persuasive. However, it would lead us to expect girls and women with no interest in children to become babysitters and mothers. Similarly, males who love spending time with children might be "programmed" into careers in the business world. Such differentiation might harm the individual who does not fit into prescribed roles while also depriving society of the contributions of many talented people who are confined by gender stereotyping. Moreover, the functionalist approach does not convincingly explain why men should be categorically assigned to the instrumental role and women to the expressive role.

The Conflict Response

Viewed from a conflict perspective, this functionalist approach masks underlying power relations between men and women. Parsons and Bales never explicitly presented the expressive and instrumental tasks as unequally valued by society, yet this inequality is quite evident. Although social institutions may pay lip service to women's expressive skills, it is men's instrumental skills that are most highly rewarded—whether in terms of money or prestige. Consequently, according to feminists and conflict theorists, any division of labour by gender into instrumental and expressive tasks is far from neutral in its impact on women.

Conflict theorists contend that the relationship between females and males has traditionally been one of unequal power and ownership of resources, with men in a dominant position over women. Men may originally have become powerful in pre-industrial times because their size, physical strength, and freedom from childbearing duties allowed them to dominate women physically. In contemporary societies, such considerations are not as important, yet cultural beliefs about the sexes are long established, as anthropologist Margaret Mead and feminist sociologist Helen Mayer Hacker (1951, 1974) both stressed. Such beliefs support a social structure that places males in controlling positions.

Thus, conflict theorists see gender inequality as the systematic subjugation of women. If we use an analogy to Marx's analysis of class conflict in capitalist societies, we can say that males are like the bourgeoisie, or capitalists; they control most of the society's wealth, prestige, and power. Females are like the proletarians, or workers; they can acquire valuable resources only by following the dictates of their "bosses." Men's work is uniformly valued, while women's work (whether unpaid labour in the home or wage labour) is devalued.

Both functionalist and conflict theorists acknowledge that it is not possible to change gender roles drastically without dramatic revisions in a culture's social structure. Functionalists perceive potential for social disorder, or at least unknown social consequences, if all aspects of traditional gender stratification are disturbed. Yet, for conflict theorists, no social structure is ultimately desirable if it is maintained by oppressing a majority of its citizens. These theorists argue that gender inequality may be functional for men—who hold power and privilege.

Feminist Perspectives

As we have noted in earlier chapters, feminist perspectives encompass a wide-ranging and diverse group of theories focusing on gender inequality, its causes, and its remedies. Feminist perspectives, however, despite their diversity, share the belief that women have been subordinated, undervalued, underrepresented, and excluded in male-dominated societies, which in practical terms means most of the world. As varied as political philosophies, feminist perspectives include post-modern feminism, global feminism, liberal feminism, Marxist feminism, socialist feminism, anti-racist feminism, cultural feminism, eco-feminism, and radical feminism, to name a few. We discussed some of these streams in the first chapter. To briefly recap these theories, liberal feminism advocates that women's equality can be attained through minor adjustments to key institutions, creating greater opportunities for women's advancement in the public sphere. Marxist feminism places capitalism, with its private ownership of resources and unequal class relations, at fault for the oppression of women. Socialist feminism, in contrast, is based on the belief that the inextricably connected systems of capitalism and patriarchy are responsible for women's subjugation. Radical feminists see the root of women's oppression as being embedded in

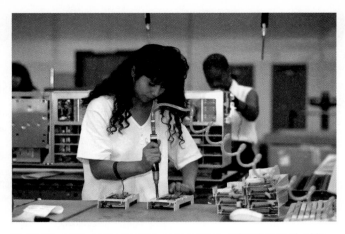

Conflict theorists emphasize that men's work is uniformly valued, while women's work (whether unpaid labour in the home or wage labour) is devalued. This woman is assembling computer parts in a factory.

the patriarchy that exists in all societies, whether they are capitalist, communist, or socialist.

Ongoing developments and debates in feminist theory are producing theories of global feminism, which acknowledge and pay attention to differences in power, material resources, geographies, and histories (i.e., colonialism) and reject the use of the Western World as the normative standard (Weedon 1999).

Although it might appear that there has been an explosion in the growth of feminist perspectives since the mid-1960s, the critique of women's position in society and culture goes back to some of the earliest works that have influenced sociology. Among the most important are Mary Wollstonecraft's *A Vindication of the Rights of Women* (originally published in 1792), John Stuart Mill's *The Subjection of Women* (originally published in 1869), and Friedrich Engels's *The Origin of Private Property, the Family, and the State* (originally published in 1884).

Engels, a close associate of Karl Marx, argued that women's subjugation coincided with the rise of private property during industrialization. Only when people moved beyond an agrarian economy could males "enjoy" the luxury of leisure and withhold rewards and privileges from women. Drawing on the work of Marx and Engels, some contemporary feminist theorists view women's subordination as part of the overall exploitation and injustice that they see as inherent in capitalist societies. Some radical feminist theorists, however, view the oppression of women as inevitable in *all* male-dominated societies, whether they be labelled "capitalist," "socialist," or "communist" (Feuer 1959; Tuchman 1992).

Feminist sociologists are more likely to embrace a political action agenda. Also, some feminist perspectives argue that the very discussion of women and society has been distorted by the exclusion of women from academic thought, including sociology. Perhaps one of the best examples of this exclusion of women from academic sociology is that of the U.S. sociologist Jane Addams (1860–1935). Although Addams made significant contributions to sociology through her work on women and the family, urban settlements, and working-class immigrants, she was viewed by mainstream sociology as an outsider and not as a legitimate member of academia. At the time, her efforts, while valued as humanitarian, were seen as unrelated to the research and conclusions being reached in academic circles, which, of course, were male academic circles (Andersen 1997; Howard 1999).

For most of the history of sociology, studies were conducted on male subjects or about male-led groups and organizations, and the findings were generalized to all people. For example, over many decades, studies of urban life focused on street corners, neighbourhood taverns, and bowling alleys—places where men typically congregated. Although the insights were valuable, they did not give a full impression of city life because they overlooked the areas where women were likely to gather (Lofland 1975).

Since men and women have had different life experiences, the issues they approach are different, and even when they have similar concerns, they approach them from different perspectives. For example, women who enter politics today typically do so for different reasons than men do. Men often embark on a political career to make business contacts or build on them, a natural extension of their livelihood; women generally become involved because they want to help. This difference in interests is relevant to the likelihood of their future success. The areas in which women achieve political recognition revolve around such social issues as daycare, the environment, education, and child protection—areas that do not attract a lot of big donors. Men focus on tax policies, business regulation, and trade agreements—issues that excite big donors. Sometimes, women do become concerned with these issues but then they must constantly reassure voters that they are still concerned about "family issues." Male politicians who occasionally focus on family issues, however, are seen as enlightened and ready to govern (G. Collins 1998).

Feminist theorists emphasize that male dominance in Canada and the world goes far beyond the economic sphere. In fact, although on the surface economic inequality may appear to be separate from gender inequality, it is actually inextricably related to spousal abuse, sexual harassment, and sexual assault. Violence toward women by men is a major component of many interrelated experiences that contribute to women's inequality in Canada and elsewhere.

Gender inequality is embedded in the various institutions of Canadian society—the family, the workplace, the state, the mass media, the religious organizations—and thus produces a systemic pattern of discrimination. This systemic pattern of discrimination on the basis of gender does not work alone but rather is interconnected with race, class, sexual orientation, and disability to produce multiple layers of inequality and discrimination. Feminists who emphasize the intersection of many factors point to the diversity of women's lives and situations, maintaining that gender alone cannot fully explain how Canadian women experience inequality.

Intersections with Racialization, Class, and Other Social Factors

Contemporary feminists recognize the differential treatment of some women not only because of their gender, but also because of the intersection of racialization, ethnicity, and socioeconomic status. Simply put, whites dominate non-white

figure 9-1 Matrix of Domination

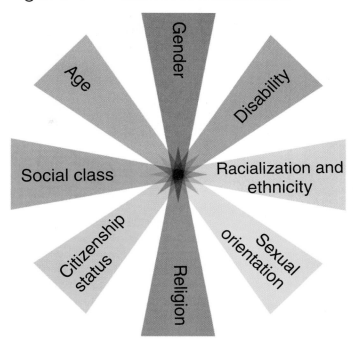

The matrix of domination illustrates how several social factors, including gender, social class, and racialization and ethnicity, can converge to create a cumulative impact on a person's social standing.
Source: Developed by author.

women because they are non-white; men dominate them because they are women; and the affluent dominate them because they are poor. Feminist theorist Patricia Hill Collins (2000) has termed the convergence of social forces that contributes to the subordinate status of these low-status women the **matrix of domination** (Figure 9-1).

Gender, racialization, and social class are not the only sources of oppression in Canada and elsewhere, though they profoundly affect women and people of colour. Other forms of categorization and stigmatization that might be included in the matrix are sexual orientation, religion, disability, and age. If we apply the matrix to the world as a whole, we might add citizenship status or perceived colonial or neocolonial status to the list (Winant 2006).

The matrix of domination highlights the confluence of these factors with gender discrimination, which we must include to fully understand the plight of women of colour.

::: use your sociological *imagination* :::

Which elements of the matrix of domination privilege you? Which place you at a disadvantage?

The Interactionist Approach

While functionalists and conflict theorists who study gender stratification typically focus on macro-level social forces and institutions, interactionist researchers tend to examine gender

table 9-2 Sociological Perspectives on Gender

Theoretical Perspective	Emphasis
Functionalist	Gender differentiation contributes to social stability
Conflict	Gender inequality is rooted in the female–male power relationship
Feminist	Women's subjugation is integral to society and social structure
Interactionist	Gender distinctions and "doing gender" are reflected in people's everyday behaviour

stratification on the micro level of everyday behaviour. The key to this approach is the way gender is socially constructed in everyday interactions. We "do gender" by reinforcing traditionally masculine and feminine actions. For example, a man "does masculinity" by opening a door for his girlfriend; she "does femininity" by consenting to his assistance. Obviously, the social construction of gender goes beyond these relatively trivial rituals. Interactionists recognize, too, that people can challenge traditional gender roles. A female golfer who uses the men's tees and a man who actively arranges a birthday luncheon at work are redoing gender.

One continuing subject of investigation is the role of gender in cross-sex conversations (sometimes referred to as "cross-talk"), specifically the idea that men interrupt women more than women interrupt men. Interestingly, empirical research does not clearly support this assertion. True, people in positions of authority or status—who are much more likely to be male than female—dominate interpersonal conversations. That does not necessarily mean that women per se cannot be heard, however. Future research results may deemphasize the clichéd advice that women must speak up and focus instead on the situational structures that cast men in dominant positions (Cameron 2007; Hyde 2005; Tannen 1990).

Table 9-2 summarizes the major sociological perspectives on gender.

9.3 How Can Women Be an "Oppressed Majority"?

Many people—both male and female—find it difficult to conceive of women as a subordinate group in Canada. Yet, take a look at the political structure of Canada: Women remain underrepresented with four of the provincial or territorial premiers in Canada being female in 2012. Although the past decades have brought many firsts for women in Canadian public life—Beverly McLachlin as the first woman to serve as chief justice of the Supreme Court of Canada (2000), Catherine Callbeck of Prince Edward Island as the first female to be elected premier (1993), Kim Campbell as first woman to serve as Canada's prime minister (1993)—women remain underrepresented in both federal and provincial/territorial politics. In 2011, women made up approximately 24.7 percent of those elected to the federal House of Commons, while women, as a group, made up approximately 51 percent of the Canadian population.

This lack of women in the highest decision-making positions is evidence of their relative powerlessness in Canada. In Chapter 8, we identified five basic properties that define a minority or subordinate group. If we apply this model to the situation of women in Canada, we find that a numerical majority group fits our definition of a *subordinate minority* (Dworkin 1982; Hochschild 1973):

1. Women experience unequal treatment. In 2005 in Canada, women working on a full-time, full-year basis had average earnings that constituted 76 percent of what their male counterparts made (Statistics Canada 2008).

2. Women, despite their diversity, share physical and cultural characteristics that distinguish them from the dominant group (men).

3. Membership in this subordinate group is involuntary.

4. Through the rise of contemporary feminism, women are developing a greater sense of group solidarity, as we will see later in the chapter.

5. Many women feel that their subordinate status is most irrevocably defined within the institution of marriage. Even when women are employed outside the home, they are still largely responsible for the care of their homes and families (TD Bank 2007e).

Visible-minority women in Canada not only earned less than both visible- and non–visible-minority men but also earned less than other women. In 2005, female visible-minority workers aged 15 years and over earned an average of approximately $5000 less than non–visible-minority women. As Table 9-3 illustrates, these women, in turn, earned less than both visible-minority men and non–visible-minority men (Statistics Canada 2008).

The majority of women employed continue to work in occupations in which women have traditionally been concentrated—nursing and other health-related occupations, sales and service, clerical and administrative positions, and teaching (Statistics Canada 2006e).

Moreover, women are increasingly dominating the ranks of the impoverished, leading to what has been called the *feminization of poverty*. In Canada, a large number of women will face poverty in their senior years due to low CPP (Canada Pension Plan) and OAS (Old Age Security) pension benefits; newly arrived immigrant women are particularly vulnerable to poverty, as their contributions to CPP may be lower.

This photo of world leaders taken at the 2011 summit in Paris shows that power remains inextricably related to gender.

Globally, women and girls make up a disproportionate number of the world's poor. The United Nations Population Fund's *State of World Population Report 2009* stated that women and girls the world over are still being denied access to health care and education. In Canada, women make up a disproportionate number of those with low incomes; in 2003, 31 percent of unattached women 16 and over had a low income (Statistics Canada 2006e).

Sexism and Sex Discrimination

Just as visible minorities in Canada are victimized by racism, women suffer from the sexism of our society. **Sexism** is the ideology that one sex is superior to the other. The term is generally used to refer to male prejudice and discrimination against women. In Chapter 8, we noted that visible minorities can suffer from both individual acts of racism and institutional discrimination. *Institutional discrimination* was defined as the denial of opportunities and equal rights to individuals or groups that results from the normal operations of a society. In the same sense, women suffer both from individual acts of sexism (such as sexist remarks and acts of violence) and from institutional sexism.

It is not simply that particular men in Canada and elsewhere are biased in their treatment of women. All the major institutions of our society—including the government, armed forces, large corporations, the media, universities, and the medical establishment—are controlled by men. These institutions, in their "normal," day-to-day operations, often discriminate against women and perpetuate sexism. For example, if the central office of a nationwide bank sets a policy that single women are a bad risk for loans—regardless of their income and investments—the institution will discriminate against women as a group. It will do so even at bank branches in which loan officers hold no personal biases concerning women but are merely "following orders." We will examine institutional discrimination against women within the educational system in Chapter 13.

Our society is run by male-dominated institutions, yet with the power that flows to men comes responsibility and stress. Men have higher reported rates of certain types of mental illness, shorter life spans, and greater likelihood of death from heart attack or strokes (see Chapter 15). The pressure on some men to succeed—and then to remain on top in a competitive world of work—can be especially intense. This is not to suggest that gender stratification may be as damaging to men as it is to women. But it is clear that the relative power and privilege men (white men in particular) enjoy are no guarantee of well-being.

The Status of Women Worldwide

Inequality is a theme that figures large when we examine the global status of women.

A detailed overview of the status of the world's women, issued by the United Nations, noted that women and men live in two different worlds. In too many nations women are denied equal pay, sexually harassed at work, or dismissed

table **9-3** **Average Employment Earnings for Visible-Minority Women Compared with Non–Visible-Minority Women, Visible-Minority Men, and Non–Visible-Minority Men, 2005**

Category	Earnings ($)
Women from visible minorities	23 369
Women not from visible minorities	28 410
Men from visible minorities	32 442
Men not from visible minorities	45 611

Note: Figures are for paid workers, 15 years and over, 2005.
Source: Statistics Canada 2008.

from their jobs because they are pregnant. These abuses happen even in places where such treatment is prohibited by law. Women who assert their rights are routinely ignored or even punished for their protests. To achieve gender equality, the report concludes, society must hold the powerful accountable to women (United Nations Development Fund for Women 2009).

This critique applies to Western as well as non-Western countries. Although Westerners tend to view some societies—for example, Muslim countries—as being particularly harsh toward women, that perception is actually an overgeneralization. Muslim countries are exceedingly varied and complex and do not often fit the stereotypes created by the Western media.

Regardless of culture, however, women generally suffer from second-class status. It is estimated that women grow half the world's food, but they rarely own land. They constitute one-third of the world's paid labour force, but are generally found in the lowest-paying jobs. Single-parent households headed by women, which appear to be on the rise in many nations, are typically found in the poorest sections of the population. The feminization of poverty has become a global phenomenon. As in Canada, women around the world are underrepresented politically.

Despite these challenges, women are not responding passively. They are mobilizing, individually and collectively. Given the significant underrepresentation of women in government offices and national legislatures, however, the task is difficult, as we shall see in Chapter 14.

Not surprisingly, there is a link between the wealth of industrialized nations and the poverty of women in developing countries. Viewed from a conflict perspective or through the lens of Immanuel Wallerstein's world systems analysis, the economies of developing nations are controlled and exploited by industrialized countries and multinational corporations based in those countries. Much of the exploited labour in developing nations, especially in the nonindustrial sector, is performed by women. Women workers typically toil long hours for low pay, but contribute significantly to their families' incomes (Chubb et al. 2008).

In industrialized countries, women's unequal status can be seen in the division of housework, as well as in the jobs they hold and the pay they earn. Sociologist Jan Paul Heisig analyzed gender inequality among the rich (the top decile in income) and the poor (the bottom decile) in 33 industrialized countries. Typically, poor men did more housework than rich men, but as Figure 9-2 shows, rich or poor, men did much less housework than women.

figure 9-2 Gender Inequality in Housework in Selected Countries

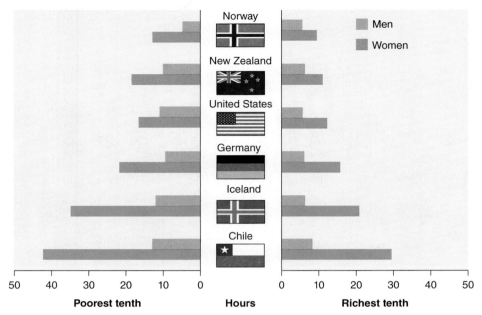

Note: Housework includes laundry, grocery shopping, dinner preparation, and care for sick family members. Around the world, rich or poor, women do much more housework than men.

Source: Adapted from Heisig 2011:84.

Think about It
How does Canada compare to a number of other industrialized countries in terms of gender inequality?

Women in the Paid Workforce in Canada

One of the most significant social changes witnessed in Canada over the past half-century has been the movement of women into the paid workforce. Even though the majority of Canadian women now work for pay outside the home, most continue to experience gendered patterns of inequality relating to pay, working conditions, and opportunities for advancement.

A Statistical Overview No longer is the adult woman associated solely with the role of caregiver. Instead, millions of women—married and single, with and without children—are working in the labour force (see Figures 9-3 and 9-4). In 2011, 57.9 percent of all women in Canada aged 15 and over had jobs in the paid labour force, up from 42 percent in 1976. A majority of women are now members of the paid labour force, not full-time caregivers. The vast majority of employed women in Canada return to the paid labour force after giving birth. In 2011, 66.8 percent of all women with children under age 3 were employed, compared to 27.6 percent in 1976 (Statistics Canada 2012).

Yet women entering the job market find their options restricted in important ways. Particularly damaging is occupational segregation, or confinement to sex-typed "women's

figure 9-3 Employment Rate for Women

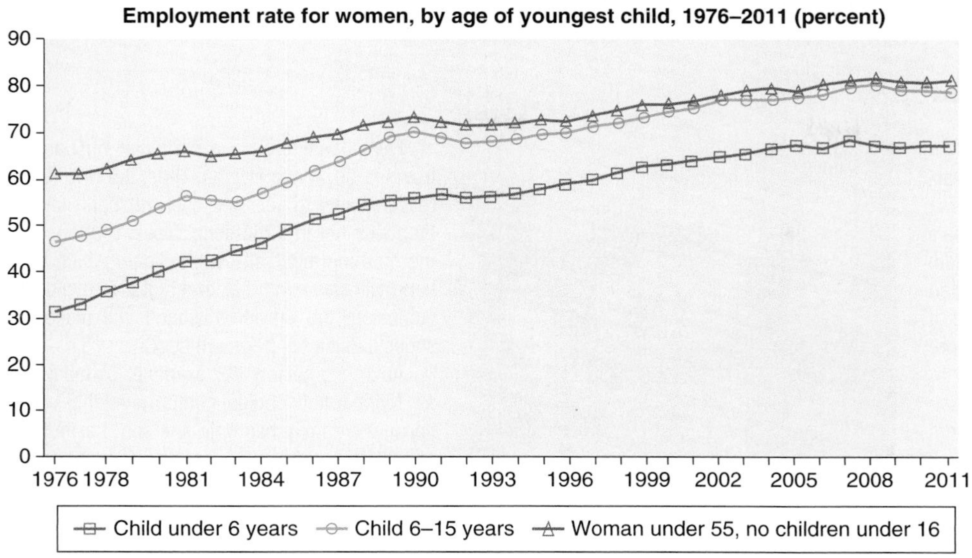

Employment rate for women, by age of youngest child, 1976–2011 (percent)

Legend: Child under 6 years ; Child 6–15 years ; Woman under 55, no children under 16

Source: Statistics Canada 2012.

Women from all groups, particularly those from visible minorities or those from older age groups, are at increased risk of encountering discrimination that prevents them from reaching their full potential. As we saw in Chapter 8, the term *glass ceiling* refers to an invisible barrier that blocks the promotion of a qualified individual in a work environment because of the individual's gender, race, or ethnicity. A study of boards of directors in Canada found that only 12 percent of the seats on these boards were held by women (TD Bank 2007).

One response to the glass ceiling and other gender biases in the workplace is to start your own business and work for yourself. This route to success, traditionally jobs" (see Box 9-2 on how the Nyinba culture devalues the social worth of women). For example, in 2009, women accounted for 80 percent of all health-related jobs and 57.5 percent of all sales and service jobs. Entering such sex-typed occupations places women in "service" roles that parallel the traditional gender-role expectations of housewives "serving" their husbands and children.

Women are underrepresented in many occupations historically defined as "men's jobs," which often carry much greater financial rewards and prestige than women's jobs. For example, in 2009, women accounted for slightly over one-half of the paid labour force in Canada. Yet they constituted only 40 percent of managerial occupations; 25 percent of those employed in natural and applied science and related occupations; and 7.4 percent in trades, transport, and equipment operation (see Table 9-4).

taken by men from immigrant and racial minority groups, has become more common among women as they have increasingly sought paid employment outside the home. Female entrepreneurs constitute a rapidly growing employment category in Canada. According to a report by TD Economics, the cumulative growth since 1987 of women's self-employment in the fields of finance, insurance, and real estate as well as professional, scientific and technical services is twice that of males (2007). Between 2001 and 2011 the number of self-employed women grew by 23 percent (Statistics Canada 2012c).

The workplace patterns described here have one crucial result: Women earn much less money than men in Canada's paid labour force. In 2005, the average earnings of full-time female workers were about 76 percent of those for full-time male workers. Women in Canada are more likely to

figure 9-4 Employment of Women with Children under Age 16, by Family Status, 1976–2006

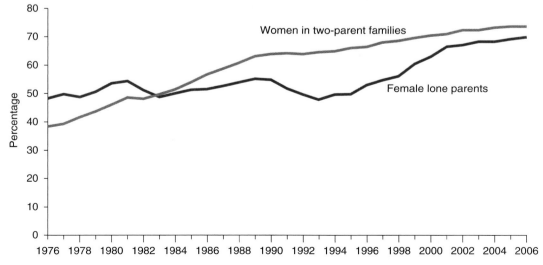

Source: Statistics Canada 2007m.

sociology in the global community

9-2 Gender and The Nyinba

The Nyinba culture of Nepal and Tibet is an agrarian society located in the remote valleys of the Himalaya Mountains, more than 9000 feet above sea level. Despite the Nyinba's isolation, they have been closely studied. Scholars from around the world have travelled to the Himalayas to observe this people, one of the few remaining cultures on earth to where one woman takes more than one husband at the same time.

In the physically challenging environment of the Himalayas, this practice seems to work well. Because the land and climate make it difficult to sustain crops, farming is labour-intensive: many Nyinba labourers must work the fields to support a single family. Thus, a typical marriage involving three brothers and one wife provides the necessary adult male labourers, yet minimizes the number of offspring—a necessity in a place where the food supply is limited.

While an outsider might suppose that Nyinba women dominate their families, in fact authority and inheritance rest on the husband or son. The birth of a son is celebrated; the birth of a

A Nyinba family threshing buckwheat in the field. At left is the wife; in the centre, one of her five husbands (with raised mallet); at right, her mother-in-law.

daughter, regardless of who might be the father, brings disappointment. Paternity appears to be a nonissue in this culture, since households are shared by brothers from the same family. The literal head of the household is the oldest brother, who typically chooses a wife from outside his extended family.

Favouritism toward a particular husband is frowned on by the Nyinba. Thus, it is the wife's responsibility to see that each husband shares time with her in a rotational fashion. Often, over the morning meal, she will indicate which husband will sleep with her that night. To avoid any confusion, the chosen husband will place his shoes outside her bedroom door.

As in any society (for example, Canada), not all Nyinba households conform to the social norm. If a family has only one son, he must of necessity marry monogamously—an unfortunate outcome in this society. If a wife is unable to have children, a second wife, typically her sister or cousin, may be welcomed into the marriage.

Apply the Theory

1. Why would the birth of a daughter be considered disappointing in the Nyinba culture?
2. What might be some other ways for a society to handle the physical constraints of life in a mountainous terrain?

Sources: Levine 1988; Stockard 2002; Zeitzen 2008.

table 9-4 Percentage Distribution of Males and Females Aged 25 to 64 Across Major Occupational Groups

	Male	Female
	Percentage	
Occupations Unique to Primary Industry	4	1
Trades, Transport and Equipment Operators and Related Occupations	27	2
Occupations Unique to Processing, Manufacturing and Utilities	7	3
Occupations in Art, Culture, Recreation and Sport	3	3
Natural and Applied Sciences and Related Occupations	12	4
Management Occupations	12	8
Health Occupations	3	12
Occupations in Social Science, Education, Government Service and Religion	6	15
Sales and Service Occupations	17	23
Business, Finance and Administrative Occupations	10	29

Source: Statistics Canada 2012c.

hold contract or temporary positions, giving them less pay and job security; 57 percent of contract workers are female (Statistics Canada 2005e). Given these data, it is hardly surprising to learn that many women are living in poverty, particularly when they must function as heads of households. In the discussion of poverty in Chapter 6, we noted that female heads of households and their children accounted for most of the nation's poor people living in families. Yet, not all women are in equal danger of experiencing poverty. Aboriginal women as well as women who are members of visible minorities suffer from double jeopardy or multiple jeopardies. **Double jeopardy** refers to the discrimination that women experience as a result of the compounded effects of gender and race and ethnicity, while **multiple jeopardies** refers to the compounded effects of gender, race and ethnicity, class, age, or physical disability. Aboriginal women are more likely to live in poverty, to experience family violence, to be unemployed, to experience poor health, to be paid lower wages, to possess lower levels of education, and even to live shorter lives than non-Aboriginal women. Aboriginal women hold multiple memberships in disadvantaged categories and experience multiple forms of discrimination, all at the same time. Nelson and Robinson (1999:261) explain in this way:

> Women possessing multiple memberships in disadvantaged categories are in jeopardy of experiencing double, triple, or more forms of discrimination simultaneously. Since multiple jeopardies are difficult to disentangle, it is almost impossible to isolate which disadvantaged status has been accorded primary discrimination.

Social Consequences of Women's Employment

"What a circus we women perform every day of our lives. It puts a trapeze artist to shame." These words by the writer Anne Morrow Lindbergh (1955) attest to the lives of women today who try to juggle their work and family lives.

The consequence of this "role complexity" for women is to feel more time-stressed and to experience greater work–life conflict, which occurs when participation in one part of life (e.g., paid work) makes it difficult to fulfill responsibilities in another part (e.g., family) (Statistics Canada 2006e). Canadian research on "role overload"—having too much to do and too little time to do it—suggests that mothers in the paid labour force experience much greater high role overload than do fathers in the paid labour force (Duxbury and Higgins 2001). Fathers' time spent in caring for children has, however, increased between 1996 and 2006; still, mothers continue to be the ones who spend more time caring for children under 15 years of age (see Figure 9-5).

This situation has many social consequences. For one thing, it puts pressure on childcare facilities and on public financing of daycare and even on the fast-food industry, which provides many of the meals that women used to prepare during the day. For another, it raises questions about what responsibility male wage earners have in the household.

Who does the housework when women become wage earners? Studies indicate that there continues to be a clear gender gap in the performance of housework, although the

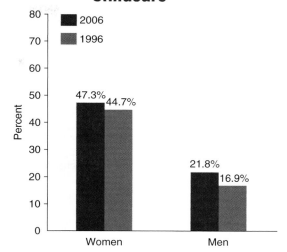

figure **9-5** **Percentage of Women and Men Spending at Least 30 Hours a Week in Unpaid Childcare**

Note: At least one child was under 15 years of age.

Source: Statistics Canada 2009.

Think about It

How might the percentages in Figure 9-5 be related to growing rates of depression and anxiety among working women?

---

differences are narrowing (Statistics Canada 2006e). Joanna Hemm, a 34-year-old banquet server from Ottawa, expressed the reality of women's unpaid labour as follows:

> Men have their jobs. . . . When they come home they feel the need to unwind. They don't regard housework or cooking or cleaning as something that needs to be stuck to. (Freeze 2001)

Sociologist Arlie Hochschild has used the phrase "second shift" to describe the double burden—work outside the home followed by childcare and housework—that many women

For some women, the workday never seems to end. Women who undertake most of the childcare and housework in addition to working outside the home have a double burden, known as a "second shift."

figure 9-6 Reasons to Choose Work at Another [Law] Firm, by Gender

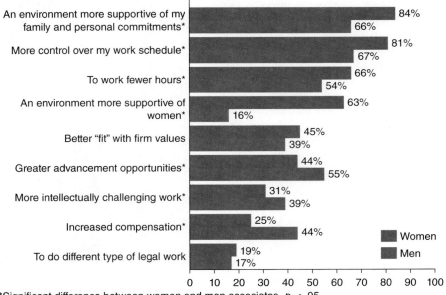

*Significant difference between women and men associates, $p < .05$

Source: The Neilsen Company 2011.

face and few men share equitably (1989, 1990, 2005). On the basis of interviews with and observations of 52 couples over an eight-year period, Hochschild reports that the wives (and not their husbands) drive home from the office while planning domestic schedules and play dates for children—and then begin their second shift. Drawing on national studies, she concludes that women spend 15 fewer hours in leisure activities each week than their husbands do. In a year, these women work an extra month of 24-hour days because of the second shift; over a dozen years, they work an extra year of 24-hour days. Hochschild found that the married couples she studied were fraying at the edges, and so were their careers and their marriages. Juggling so many roles means that more things can go wrong for women, which contributes to stress. A recent poll of 381 Canadian government workers found that heavy family responsibilities had a profound impact on their paid jobs (Luciw 2007).

With such reports in mind, many academics, policy analysts, and organizational experts have advocated greater governmental and corporate support for childcare, more flexible family-leave policies, and other reforms designed to ease the burden on families (Moen and Roehling 2005).

Most studies of gender, childcare, and housework focus on the time actually spent by women and men performing these duties. However, sociologist Susan Walzer was interested in whether there are gender differences in the amount of time that parents spend *thinking* about the care of their children (1996). Drawing on interviews with 25 couples, Walzer found that mothers are much more involved than fathers in the invisible mental labour associated with taking care of a baby. For example, while involved in work outside the home, mothers are more likely to think about their babies and to feel guilty if they

become so consumed with the demands of their jobs that they *fail* to think about their babies.

The very idea of what constitutes "work" in our society, whether it is done by men or women, at home or in the public sphere, is shaped by a "male-work role model" (Pleck and Corfman 1979). This model assumes that work will be full-time, continuous from graduation to retirement, that all other roles will be subordinate, and that a man's self-actualization will be based on this role. Implicit in this model is the assumption of paid work and stereotypical masculinity (Nelson and Robinson 2002). Since Canadian women, on average, engage in greater amounts of mental and physical labour in the care of their families and households, they run a greater risk of not having their labour considered as work.

The greater amounts of time women put into caring for their children, and to a lesser degree into housework, takes a special toll on women who are pursuing careers. In a 2005 survey published in the *Harvard Business Review*, about 40 percent of women indicated that they had voluntarily left work for months or years, compared to only 24 percent of men. As Figure 9-6 shows, Canadian women lawyers' major reason to choose another employer would be to find an environment more supportive of family and personal commitments, with 84 percent of the women respondents giving this reason as opposed to 66 percent of their male counterparts (Catalyst 2005).

Women: The Emergence of Feminism in Canada

Social movements involve the organized attempts of masses of people to bring about social change through their collective action. The women's movement, or feminist movement, is one such movement by which women and men have attempted to change their society—not only for the betterment of women but also for the betterment of society as a whole. Often, however, those in the movement have been white, middle-class women who fought for their own vision of social or moral reform—a vision that might improve the welfare of some women (depending on their race, ethnicity, and class) but not necessarily all. From the mid-nineteenth century to the mid-twentieth century, women's movements emerged in 32 countries worldwide (Nelson and Robinson 1999).

In Canada, the first wave of feminism beginning in the mid-nineteenth century had three faces—moral reform (or maternal feminism), liberalism, and socialism (Banks 1981). It concentrated largely on female suffrage and efforts to expand educational and employment opportunities for girls and women. Nellie McClung, perhaps Canada's foremost "maternal feminist," believed women were the "guardians of the race" and that it was therefore their responsibility to "lift high the standard of morality" (Adamson, Briskin, and McPhail 1998:31). During the 1920s, McClung and four fellow suffragettes—Irene Parlby, Henrietta Muir Edwards, Louise McKinney, and Emily Murphy—petitioned the Supreme Court of Canada to declare that women could become members of the Senate. The "Famous Five," as they were later known, appealed the negative decision of the Supreme Court of Canada to the British Privy Council. In 1929, the Privy Council declared that women were "persons" in the eyes of the law, making them eligible for appointment to the Senate. The "Persons case" marked a significant achievement for Canadian women.

The Famous Five were willing to fight for equality of some women; however, they were also willing to exclude others from their cause. Emily Murphy, Nellie McClung, and Louise McKinney were supporters of the eugenics movement, which espoused the desirability of certain races, ethnic groups, and classes. Emily Murphy, for example, spoke out against "aliens of colour," targeting the "black and yellow" races and advocating "whites-only" immigration and citizenship policies. The progress of the women's movement has affected Canadian women unevenly, depending on their race, ethnicity, and class.

Although women in Canada were granted the right to vote in federal elections in 1918 (Manitoba, Saskatchewan, Alberta, British Columbia, and Ontario had granted the provincial vote to women shortly before 1918), until 1960, Aboriginal women and men were entitled to vote only if they gave up their Indian status (Mossman 1994). It is worth noting that although Clare Brett Martin, in 1897, was the first woman to become a lawyer in the Commonwealth, "it was not until 1946 that the first Asian Canadian woman graduated from law school in Ontario" (Nelson and Robinson 1999:493).

The second wave of feminism emerged in Canada in the 1960s, coinciding with the rise of feminist consciousness in the United States. The second wave of the movement in Canada focused on two areas of concern: (1) that women were treated differently and discriminated against (at home as well as in the paid workplace) and (2) that women's unique qualities were undervalued (arguing for the recognition of these qualities) (Black 1993). This wave saw

Nellie McClung was one of a group of Canadian women's rights activists who later became known as the Famous Five. Although the Famous Five were concerned about the social injustice encountered by some Canadian women, their concerns excluded injustices because of ethnicity, race, and class.

the huge growth of feminist perspectives in the social sciences, where feminist scholars challenged mainstream or "malestream" sociology's treatment of gender as it relates to studying crime, deviance, morality, aging, politics, and so on.

During this period, feminism began to become entrenched in institutions. Although essentially a grassroots movement, governments and international agencies around the world began to address some of the movement's concerns. In 1967, the Canadian government established the Royal Commission on the Status of Women, and the United Nations declared 1975–1985 the decade for women.

The third wave of feminism of the 1990s shifted focus away from common sources of oppression for women to multiple sources, acknowledging that what might be a source of oppression for some woman may not be for others. Today, there are movements on behalf of women in most countries of the world; however, the disparities of advantage and disadvantage remain great among the world's girls and women, not only between them and their male counterparts but also between females in developing and developed countries.

Social Policy and Gender Relations

Abortion and Sex Selection: The "New Eugenics"

The Issue

Today in Canada, a woman's decision to have an abortion is usually made in consultation with her doctor based on factors related to her overall health and well-being. However, as new reproductive and genetic technologies, referred to collectively as "reprogenetics" (McTeer 1999), emerge in our society and around the world, the twinning of abortion and reprogenetics presents new ethical and moral considerations. The most controversial of these is what some sociologists are calling "the new eugenics"—a new movement to promote the reproduction of those with particular characteristics, while attempting to limit or control the reproduction of those with other, less desirable traits. Thus, with new reproductive and genetic technologies, abortion has the potential to become no longer a choice a woman makes simply on the basis of her health and well-being, but an instrument of social control over what "type" (e.g., sex) of person is to be reproduced.

The Setting

Canada's first Criminal Code, established in 1892, made "procuring or performing an abortion a crime punishable by life imprisonment" (McTeer 1999:32). In 1968, amendments to the Criminal Code made abortion legal under certain conditions. The conditions included the approval of a special committee and that the abortion take place in an accredited hospital. However, hospitals and provincial or territorial governments were not required to establish the committee and many did not, thus making abortion inaccessible to many women in Canada, particularly those in non-urban areas. In 1988, the law on abortion was changed again; today, it is a decision "left to the pregnant woman alone, and usually made in consultation with her doctor" (McTeer 1999:33).

In 2006, 91 310 abortions were performed in Canada—roughly 40 percent were performed on women 24 years of age and under (Statistics Canada 2009). Race, class, and age differences are apparent as they relate to the incidence of abortion in Canada (Calliste 2001). For example, Aboriginal women in Canada were subjected to forced sterilization as a tactic of genocide, thus a policy of abortion on demand did not reflect their needs.

In the late 1980s, the Canadian government called for the establishment of a royal commission investigating new reproductive technologies. These technologies and procedures included assisted reproduction, such as artificial insemination (AI), in vitro fertilization (IVF), and direct ovum and sperm transfer (DOST); surrogacy (one woman carrying a pregnancy to term for another); and prenatal diagnosis (PND), which can include identification of the sex of the fetus. With the emergence of those technologies, the question becomes, "How can we as a society protect those who might be exploited or mistreated (e.g., surrogates, IVF-created human embryos, female fetuses) while still safeguarding women's reproductive rights relating to abortion and contraception?" (McTeer 1999).

In 1996, the Canadian government introduced Bill C-47, a legislative attempt to ban practices such as commercial surrogacy and sex selection for reasons other than those related to the health of the fetus (i.e., sex-linked hereditary diseases). Bill C-47, which set out to ban 13 different reproductive technological practices, died on the Order Paper when the 1997 federal election was called.

Sociological Insights

Sociologists see gender and social class as largely defining the issues surrounding abortion. The intense conflict over reproductive rights reflects broad differences over women's position in society. Sociologist Kristin Luker has offered a detailed study of activists in the pro-choice and pro-life movements (1984). Luker interviewed 212 activists, overwhelmingly women, who spent at least five hours a week working for one of these movements. According to Luker, each group has a consistent, coherent view of the world. Feminists involved in defending abortion rights typically believe that men and women are essentially similar: they support women's full participation in work outside the home and oppose all forms of sex discrimination. By contrast, most pro-life activists believe that men and women are fundamentally different. In their view, men are best suited for the public world of work, whereas women are best suited for the demanding and crucial task of rearing children. These activists are troubled by women's growing participation in work outside the home, which they view as destructive to the family and ultimately to society as a whole. The pro-life, or anti-abortion, activists see abortion as an act that denies nurturance and therefore diminishes the family, since the family is viewed as the major source of nurturance in society. Thus, these activists hold a view similar to that of functionalism, which connects the family to particular functions.

Feminist perspectives on abortion and reproductive technology have been led by the radical feminist vanguard, later to be joined by liberal and socialist perspectives (Nelson and Robinson 1999). The hope that technology would offer women escape from the "tyranny of their reproduction biology" (Firestone 1970) is now being tempered by the possible negative impact that technology could have on women's lives. Thus, radical feminist perspectives are now joined by many other forms of feminism in defining abortion, reproductive rights, and reproductive technologies as feminist issues (Nelson and Robinson 1999).

Policy Initiatives

The policies of the United States are intertwined with those of developing nations. From the 1980s through January 2009, members of Congress who opposed abortion successfully blocked foreign aid to countries that might use the funds to encourage abortion. Yet developing nations generally have the most restrictive abortion laws. As Figure 9-7 shows, it is primarily in Africa, Latin America, and parts of Asia that women are not allowed to terminate a pregnancy on request. As might be expected, illegal abortions are most common in those nations. An estimated quarter of the world's women live in countries where abortion is illegal or is permitted only if a woman's life is in jeopardy. Indeed, the rate of abortions in countries with legal restrictions on the procedure matches the rate in countries that permit it. Hence, 40 percent of abortions worldwide—about 16 million procedures each year—are performed illegally (Baker 2009; Guttmacher Institute 2008).

In 2009, Prime Minister Stephen Harper announced that maternal and child health in the developing world would be a policy priority for the meeting of the G8 (the world's richest nations) to be held in Canada in the summer of 2010. The Liberal opposition leader, Michael Ignatieff—noting the stance on reproductive rights taken by the former Bush administration—stated: "We don't want us to go that way. We want to make sure that women have access to all contraceptive methods available to control their fertility" (Taber 2010).

Globally, countries' responses to new reproductive and genetic technologies vary in terms of the guidelines and legislation set in place to regulate their use. For example, Australia, Austria, Brazil, the Czech Republic, Denmark, Egypt, France, Germany, Hungary, Israel, Mexico, the Netherlands, Norway, Saudi Arabia, Singapore, South Africa, Spain, Sweden, Taiwan, Turkey, and the United Kingdom have some form of legislation to deal with how these technologies can be used. Other countries, such as Argentina, Egypt, Finland, Italy, Poland, Japan, South Korea, Switzerland, and the United States, have guidelines rather than legislation for the use of assisted reproductive technologies. Since the failure of Bill C-47 to become law, Canada's federal government has established a voluntary moratorium on certain reproductive

figure 9-7 The Global Divide on Abortion

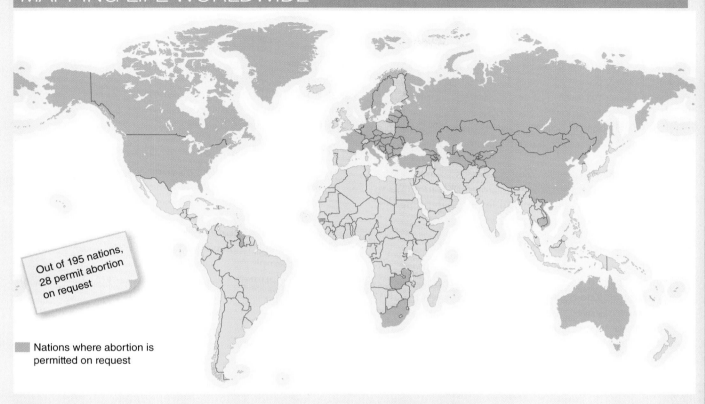

Out of 195 nations, 28 permit abortion on request

Nations where abortion is permitted on request

Note: Data current as of November 2007.

Source: Developed by the author based on United Nations Population Division 2007.

and genetic practices. Greece, India, Jordan, and Portugal are among the countries that have neither legislation nor guidelines.

In India, and other countries where cultural preferences for male offspring remain strong, the coupling of prenatal diagnosis techniques, such as ultrasound and amniocentesis, which identify the sex of the fetus, and the use of abortion, can result in the birth of fewer female children. Although these Western-based prenatal diagnosis technologies can be used to identify and abort fetuses with genetic abnormalities, they also open the door to sex selection for cultural or social reasons. Saraswati Raju, a professor of gender and demography at Jawaharlal Nehru University in New Delhi, states that the fate of the female infant in India has been getting worse in recent decades (Lakshimi 2001). The most recent Indian census showed that the percentage of girls under age six has dropped since the previous census. Although the Indian government has banned the use of sex-selection tests and doctors' associations have discouraged their use, the tests persist and the government is unable to stop the practice. Despite widespread

societal efforts to improve the status of girls and women in Indian society, a baby girl is viewed as a liability and a strong cultural preference for male children persists.

A recent report by UNICEF notes that "birth histories and census data reveal an unusually high proportion of male births and male children under [age] five in Asia, especially India and China, suggesting sex-selection through abortion and infanticide in the world's two most populous countries" (CBC 2006c).

In 2012 the interim editor of the *Canadian Medical Association Journal*, Rajendra Kale, has called for a ban disclosing the sex of the fetus until 30 weeks, based on research that suggests that many immigrants from countries which highly value male children are aborting female fetuses (Friesen 2012). Dr Kale stated that: "There's no way this should happen in Canada. This is discrimination against women at its worst" (Kale in Friesen 2012).

According to Maureen McTeer, a former member of the Royal Commission on New Reproductive Technologies, sex selection violates our notions

of equality as enshrined in the Canadian Charter of Rights and Freedoms and in our human-rights laws. In addition, she argues, allowing sex-selection practices at home would detract from Canada's international commitment to eliminate discrimination against women.

Apply the Theory

1. According to conflict thinkers, who is most vulnerable to exploitation through the use of new reproductive and genetic technologies?
2. How might some feminist perspectives weigh the individual's right to reproduce against the society's need to regulate the use of these new technologies?
3. How might interactionist sociologists approach the study of reproductive or genetic technology for the purpose of selecting the sex of their offspring?

CHAPTER RESOURCES

Summary

::: 9.1 How Is Gender Socially Constructed?

- Like race, gender is an ascribed status that is socially constructed, providing a basis for social differentiation.
- The social construction of gender defines significantly different expectations for females and males.
- This social construction produces gender roles, which are revealed in our work and behaviour and in how we react to others.
- Females are restricted by gender roles, as are males.
- The research of anthropologist Margaret Mead points to the importance of cultural conditioning in defining the social roles of males and females.

::: 9.2 How Are Gender Relations Explained?

- Functionalists maintain that sex differentiation contributes to overall social stability, whereas conflict theorists contend that the relationship between females and males has been one of unequal power, with men in a dominant position over women. This dominance also shows up in everyday interactions.

- Feminist perspectives are diverse and vary in their explanation of the sources of women's inequality; they all agree, however, about the importance of social change, which would lead to greater equality.
- Interactionists study gender relations as reflections of everyday behaviour.

::: 9.3 How Can Women Be an "Oppressed Majority"?

- Although numerically a majority, in many respects, women fit the definition of a subordinate minority group, within Canada and in most parts of the world.
- Women around the world experience **sexism** and institutional discrimination.
- Even though women have taken on more and more hours of paid employment outside the home, they continue to bear the primary responsibility for the care of their homes and families.

Critical Thinking Questions

1. Sociologist Barbara Bovee Polk suggests that women are oppressed because they constitute an alternative subculture that deviates from the prevailing masculine value system (1974). Does it seem valid to view women as an "alternative subculture"? In what ways do women support and deviate from the prevailing masculine value system evident in Canada?

2. In what ways is the social position of white women in Canada similar to that of Asian-Canadian women, black women, or Aboriginal women? In what ways is a woman's social position markedly different, given her racial and ethnic status?

3. In what ways do you think your behaviour, values, educational choices, or career plans have been influenced by gender socialization? Can you think of ways in which the social class of your family has influenced your gender socialization?

4. How might interactionist sociologists approach the emerging trend of more men engaging in cosmetic surgery?

THINKING ABOUT MOVIES

Billy Elliot

Facing discrimination from many of his peers and family, a working-class boy from England fights against traditional gender-role expectations.

La Mission

A man redefines his masculinity after he learns that his son is gay.

North Country

A woman who works in an iron mine fights against sexual harassment.

inside

Mass media are an integral part of modern culture. Transmission takes all forms as indicated in this photo.

200

swatch® bijoux

Times Square
72nd & Columbus
NoHo
SoHo
1.800.8SWATCH
www.swatch.com

The Mass Media

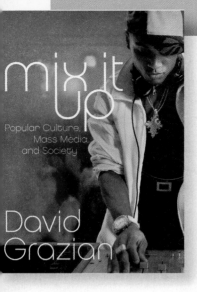

mix it
up

Popular Culture,
Mass Media,
and Society

David
Grazian

"

Over forty years ago communications theorist Marshall McLuhan (1967) developed a path-breaking idea—media not only pass along messages from sender to receiver but actively reshape how we process information, knowledge, and text. . . .

. . . For instance, about $60 billion is illegally gambled in Internet poker games each year, a pursuit that draws in an estimated 1.6 million U.S. college students. . . . In 2005 Lehigh University sophomore class president Greg Hogan, Jr., lost $7500 playing online poker, and out of desperation, in December of that year he held up a Wachovia bank for $2871 in cash. With no casino dealers, card shuffling, or friendly table partners to distract him, Hogan found the seamless, fast-paced action of digital poker 'paralyzing' and 'narcotic,' a familiar sensation among addicts, men and women alike. According to M. Schwartz (2006), 'Many, like Lauren Patrizi, a 21-year-old senior at Loyola University in Chicago, have had weeks when they're playing poker during most of their waking hours. Rarely leaving their rooms, they take their laptops with them to bed, fall asleep each night in the middle of a hand and think, talk and dream nothing but poker.'

According to cultural anthropologist Natasha Dow Schull (2005, p. 73), digital technologies succeed in creating what consumers call the *zone*, a dissociated subjective state marked by a suspension of normative parameters—monetary, bodily, temporal, and spatial. Gambling sites rely on cashless transactions (performed with credit and debit card numbers) in which financial stakes are transformed into pixilated 'chips' that no longer seem like real money. Unlike dorm-lounge poker games in which classmates eventually get tired, punch-drunk, or else lose their shirts, online casinos never close, but consistently and relentlessly maintain a steady rhythm of play that keeps addicts glued to their screens alone for hours, nights, and weeks on end. With only computer keys to depress, players never drop their cards; moreover, gambling software allows gamers to bet multiple hands simultaneously, further increasing the hypnotic speed and tempo with which one gains and (more often) loses.

With no casino dealers, card shuffling, or friendly table partners to distract him, Hogan found the seamless, fast-paced action of digital poker "paralyzing" and "narcotic," a familiar sensation among addicts, men and women alike.

How else do goings-on within the virtual world impact our everyday lives offline? Certainly, the ease with which information flows online among otherwise discrete interpersonal networks has obvious consequences for how we maintain control over our reputations and identities. . . . Since anyone with an Internet connection can post intimate photographs, juicy gossip, or vicious rumours on the Web for a potential worldwide audience of billions, personal reputations can easily be maligned within hours. In 2003 Kelley D. Parker, a partner at the elite New York law firm of Paul, Weiss, Rifkind, Wharton and Garrison, allegedly ordered a paralegal to conduct research on nearby sushi restaurants after eating some bad takeout. The underling wrote up a three-page memo replete with interview quotes, footnotes, and exhibitions, and the scanned document later appeared on the Web site Gawker for her colleagues to mock. . . . While it was never determined whether the infamous 'sushi memo' was a hoax or a prank, it presumably hardly matters to Ms. Parker, whose reputation has been forever marred by the online posting.

Of course, rumours of bad behaviour among celebrities likely travel faster online than any other kind of hearsay. Web sites like Gawker, The Smoking Gun, TMZ, and YouTube are veritable clearinghouses for such gossip, as actor Christian Bale learned after he cursed out the director of photography on the movie set of *Terminator: Salvation* in 2008 for nearly four minutes, and a full-length audio recording of his tantrum resurfaced on YouTube the following year. (Bale has since apologized for the outburst, but notably did so only after its public airing.) The Web site Bitter Waitress provides an ongoing list of celebrity (as well as civilian) diners who have stingily tipped less than 15 percent of their check: famous cheapskates shamed by the site include actresses Lindsay Lohan and Helena Bonham Carter, former Miami Dolphins quarterback Dan Marino, rock singer David Lee Roth, and reality TV figure Dog the Bounty Hunter. In March 2009, People for the Ethical Treatment of Animals (or PETA) published an online list of celebrities who unabashedly wear fur, including Madonna, Maggie Gyllenhaal, Kanye West, Elizabeth Hurley, Kate Moss, Demi Moore, Ashton Kutcher, Mary J. Blige, and Mary-Kate and Ashley Olsen.

"

(Grazian 2010:197, 200, 203; see also Glater 2003; Schull 2005; Schwartz 2006)

In this excerpt from *Mix It Up: Popular Culture, Mass Media, and Society*, sociologist David Grazian describes how today's mass media are actively reshaping the way we process information, as Marshall McLuhan predicted they would in 1967. Playing poker and video games online, Grazian writes,

is a qualitatively different experience from playing them in person. He also discusses the social consequences of the instant dissemination of information through the mass media, from the embarrassment of an attorney who assigned a paralegal to research a lunch locale to the humiliation of an actor whose four-minute tantrum went viral on YouTube. In this age, thanks to digital recording, anyone can become a global personality for any reason, at any time.

We have come a long way from the 1950s, when rabbit-ear antennas sat atop black-and-white television sets. Both television and the Net are forms of **mass media**, a term that refers to the print and electronic means of communication that carry messages to widespread audiences. Print media include newspapers, magazines, and books; electronic media include radio, satellite radio, television, motion pictures, and the Internet. Advertising, which falls into both categories, is also a form of mass media.

The social impact of the mass media is obvious. Consider a few examples: In the 1950s, *TV dinners* were invented to accommodate the millions of "couch potatoes" who couldn't bear to miss their favourite television programs. Today, screen time encompasses not just television viewing but also playing video games and surfing the Internet. Candidates for political office rely on their media consultants to project a winning image both in print and in the electronic media. World leaders use all forms of media for political advantage, whether to gain territory or to bid on hosting an Olympic games. In parts of Africa and Asia, AIDS education projects owe much of their success to media campaigns. And during the 2003 invasion of Iraq, both the British and U.S. governments allowed journalists to be embedded with frontline troops as a means of "telling their story."

Few aspects of society are as central as the mass media. Through the media, we expand our understanding of people and events beyond what we experience in person. The media inform us about different cultures and lifestyles and about the latest forms of technology. For sociologists, the key questions are how the mass media affect our social institutions and how they influence our social behaviour.

The social impact of the mass media has become so huge, in fact, that scholars have begun to speak of *cultural convergence*. The term **cultural convergence** refers to the flow of content across multiple media, and the accompanying migration of media audiences. As you watch a television program, for example, you wonder what the star of the show is doing at the moment, and turn to the Internet. Later, while texting your best friend, you tell her what you learned, accompanied by a Google Earth map showing the celebrity's location. Using Photoshop, you may even include the star's image next to your own, post the photo on your Facebook page, and then tweet your friends (send them a mini-blog) to create a caption. Media convergence is not orchestrated by the media, sophisticated though they may be. You initiate it, using techniques you likely learned by interacting with others, either face-to-face or through the media (Jenkins 2006).

Why are the media so influential? Who benefits from media influence and why? How do we maintain cultural and ethical standards in the face of negative media images? In this chapter, we consider the ways sociology helps us to answer these questions. First, we will look at how proponents of the various sociological perspectives view the media. Then we will examine just who makes up the media's audience, as well as how the media operate, especially in their global reach. In the social policy section at the end of the chapter, we consider people's right to privacy in a digital age. ■

::: use your sociological *imagination* :::

Can you think of any institutions of society that are not affected by the mass media?

10.1 What Are the Theoretical Perspectives on the Mass Media?

Over the past decade, new technologies have made new forms of mass media available to households around the world. These new technologies have changed people's viewing and listening habits. Canadians spend a lot of time with the media, more and more of it on the Internet. Canadians have to a great extent moved away from broadcast TV and toward cable outlets (CRTC 2007). The Internet is increasingly popular among Canadians, while the popularity of traditional television and radio is declining (CRTC 2007). Consumers have moved away from television and toward digital images downloaded to their computers and portable devices. Increasingly, they learn not just about the famous but about ordinary people by viewing personal Web sites or pages on Facebook or MySpace. Adam Finkelstein of Instructional Multimedia Services at McGill University states, "It's not as if TV is disappearing; it's just that the Internet is really consuming it" (CTV 2007). A 2007 study by the Canadian Radio-television and Telecommunications Commission (CRTC) found that a growing number of Canadians are listening to radio and watching television online and are using cellphones, MP3 players, BlackBerrys, or other electronic devices to access the Internet. What do these changes in people's viewing and listening habits signify? In the following sections, we'll examine the impact of the mass media and changes in their usage patterns from the four major sociological perspectives (Nelson 2004).

Functionalist View

One obvious function of the mass media is to entertain. Except for clearly identified news or educational programming, we often think the explicit purpose of the mass media is to occupy our leisure time—from newspaper comics and crossword puzzles to the latest music releases on the Internet. While that is true, the media have other important functions. They also socialize us, enforce social norms, confer status, and promote consumption. An important dysfunction of the mass media is that they may act as a narcotic, desensitizing us to distressing events (Lazarsfeld and Merton 1948; Wright 1986).

Agent of Socialization The media increase social cohesion by presenting a common, more or less standardized view of culture through mass communication. Sociologist Robert Park (1922) studied how newspapers helped immigrants adjust to their environment by changing their customary habits and teaching them the opinions of people in their new home country. Unquestionably, the mass media play a significant role in providing a collective experience for members of society. Think about how the mass media bring together members of a community or even a nation by broadcasting important events (such as press conferences, parades, state funerals, and the Olympics) and by covering large disasters.

Which media sources do consumers turn to for the news? When the space shuttle *Atlantis* was launched into orbit on November 16, 2009, it was NASA's first "tweetup." The space agency invited 100 "Twitters" to "tweet" about the lift-off, spreading the news to thousands of cellphones and computers.

Today, the news media have moved further online. Afghans of all political persuasions now connect with the Muslim community overseas to gain both social and financial support. In the realm of popular culture, a spontaneous global sharing of reactions to Michael Jackson's sudden death in 2009 crashed the Web sites for Google, the *Los Angeles Times*, TMZ celebrity news, Perez Hilton's blog, and Twitter (Rawlinson and Hunt 2009; Shane 2010).

Some are concerned about the media's socialization function, however. For instance, many people worry about the effect of using television as a babysitter and the impact of violent programming on viewer behaviour. Some people adopt a blame-the-media mentality, holding the media accountable for anything that goes wrong, especially with young people. Yet the media also have positive effects on young people. For young and even not-so-young adults, for example, a new sort of tribalism is emerging online, in which communities develop around common interests or shared identities (Adams and Smith 2008).

Enforcer of Social Norms The media often reaffirm proper behaviour by showing what happens to people who act in a way that violates societal expectations. These messages are conveyed when the bad guy gets clobbered in cartoons or is thrown in jail on *CSI*. Yet the media also sometimes glorify disapproved behaviour, whether it is physical violence, disrespect to a teacher, or drug use.

The media play a critical role in human sexuality. Many people object to the widespread availability of pornography on the Web; others are concerned about the way sexual predators use chat rooms to take advantage of children. Yet innovative uses of new media may also have positive consequences. On Valentine's Day 2007, New York City introduced the official "NYC Condom" on Facebook, in an attempt to make safer sex a social norm. Not only has New York's Department of Health and Mental Hygiene given away millions of condoms, but thousands of *e-condoms*, as they are called, have been distributed to Facebook users.

Programs have also been created to persuade teens not to send nude images of themselves to selected friends. Such images often go viral (that is, spread across the Internet) and may be used to harass teens and their parents. To define normative behaviour regarding these images, one organization has launched a "That's not cool" campaign, complete with stalker messages that can be emailed to those who misuse such images. The widespread dissemination of compromising images that were meant to be shared only among close friends is just one aspect of the new social phenomenon called *cyberbullying* (Chan 2009; Clifford 2009a; Gentile 2009).

Conferral of Status The mass media confer status on people, organizations, and public issues. Whether it is an issue such as homelessness or a celebrity such as Justin Bieber, the mainstream media can, and do, single out one story from thousands of others and make that story become significant. *People* magazine has featured the late Princess Diana on its cover more than anyone else. The magazine was not responsible for making Diana into a worldwide celebrity, but all the media outlets collectively created a notoriety that Princess Victoria of Sweden, for one, did not enjoy.

Another way the media confer celebrity status on individuals is by publishing information about what figures receive the most frequent Internet searches. Some newspapers and Web sites carry regularly updated lists of the most heavily researched individuals and topics of the week. The means may have changed since the first issue of *Time* magazine hit the stands in 1923, but the media still confer status—often electronically. Table 10-1 shows the fastest-rising searches on Google by Canadians in 2011, illustrating the status of various topics and people.

Promotion of Consumption Twenty thousand commercials a year—that is the number the average child in the United States watches on television, according to the American Academy of Pediatrics. Young people cannot escape commercial messages. They show up on high school scoreboards, at rock concerts, and as banners on Web pages. They are even embedded in motion pictures (remember Budweiser in *The Departed*?). Such *product placement* is nothing new. In the 1951 movie *The African Queen*, an ad for Gordon's Gin was prominently displayed aboard the boat carrying Katharine Hepburn and Humphrey Bogart. But commercial promotion has become far more common today. *American Idol* alone features over 4600 product appearances each season. Moreover, advertisers are attempting to develop brand or logo loyalty among younger and younger customers (Buckingham 2007; Rodman 2011:395).

table 10-1 Canada's Fastest-Rising Internet Searches on Google, 2011
Fastest Rising
1. www.census2011.gc.ca
2. Skyrim
3. Canada Post Strike
4. Rebecca Black
5. Ryan Dunn
6. Japan earthquake
7. Game of Thrones
8. Jack Layton
9. Royal wedding
10. Google Plus

Source: Google Canada Zeitgeist 2011.

Think about It
Do you think lists like the one in Table 10-1 capture of the spirit of the times? Why? Why not?

Media advertising has several clear functions: it supports the economy, provides information about products, and underwrites the cost of media. In some cases, advertising becomes part of the entertainment industry, with the Super Bowl being the best example.

Yet, related to these functions are *dysfunctions*. Media advertising contributes to a consumer culture that creates "needs" and raises unrealistic expectations of what is required to be happy or satisfied. Moreover, because the media depend heavily on advertising revenue, advertisers can influence media content (Carey and Gelles 2010; Neilsen Company 2009).

Using advertising to develop a brand name with global appeal is an especially powerful way to encourage consumption. An analysis of the 100 most successful brands worldwide, each of which derives at least a third of its earnings from outside the home country, shows that 51 of them originated in the United States; 49 others come from 12 different countries (see Figure 10-1).

Dysfunction: The Narcotizing Effect As we have just noted, the mainstream media perform a *dysfunction*. Sociologists Paul Lazarsfeld and Robert Merton (1948) created the term **narcotizing dysfunction** to refer to the phenomenon in which the media provide such massive amounts of coverage that the audience becomes numb and fails to act on the information, regardless of how compelling the issue. Interested citizens may take in the information but make no decision or take no action.

Product placement ("brand casting") is an increasingly important source of revenue for motion picture studios. The movie *New Moon* (2009), which was geared toward teens, featured many brands, including Coca-Cola and Apple. But the real winner was Burger King, which integrated its entire marketing strategy with the film's release (Brandchannel.com 2010).

Consider how often the media initiate a great outpouring of philanthropic support in response to natural disasters or family crises. Then what happens? Research shows that as time passes, viewer fatigue sets in. The mass media audience becomes numb, desensitized to the suffering, and may even conclude that a solution to the crisis has been found (Moeller 1999).

The media's narcotizing dysfunction was identified nearly 70 years ago, when just a few homes had television—well before the proliferation of electronic media. At that time, the dysfunction went largely unnoticed; but, today, commentators often point out the ill effects of addiction to television or the Internet, especially among young people. Issues such as cyberbullying, global wars, and HIV/AIDS apparently are such overwhelming topics that some in the audience may feel they have acted—or at the very least learned all they need to know—simply by watching the news.

::: use your sociological *imagination* :::

You are a news junkie. Where do you gather your facts or information—from newspapers, radio, tabloids, magazines, TV newscasts, blogs, or the Internet? Explain your choice of medium.

figure **10-1** Branding the Globe

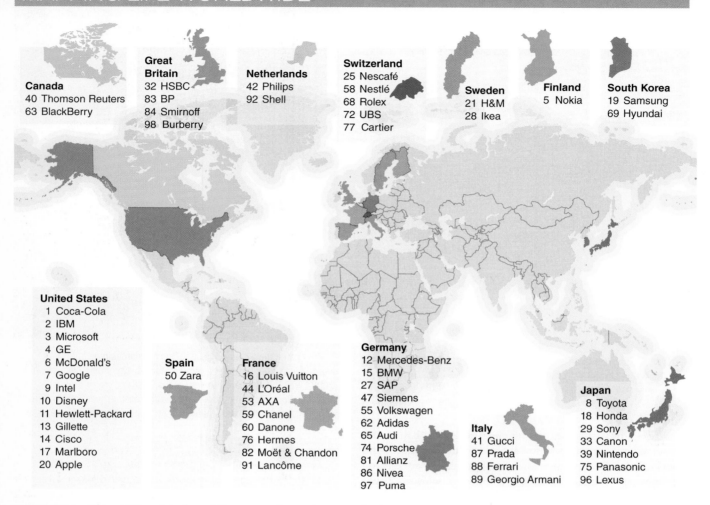

Canada
40 Thomson Reuters
63 BlackBerry

Great Britain
32 HSBC
83 BP
84 Smirnoff
98 Burberry

Netherlands
42 Philips
92 Shell

Switzerland
25 Nescafé
58 Nestlé
68 Rolex
72 UBS
77 Cartier

Sweden
21 H&M
28 Ikea

Finland
5 Nokia

South Korea
19 Samsung
69 Hyundai

United States
1 Coca-Cola
2 IBM
3 Microsoft
4 GE
6 McDonald's
7 Google
9 Intel
10 Disney
11 Hewlett-Packard
13 Gillette
14 Cisco
17 Marlboro
20 Apple

Spain
50 Zara

France
16 Louis Vuitton
44 L'Oréal
53 AXA
59 Chanel
60 Danone
76 Hermes
82 Moët & Chandon
91 Lancôme

Germany
12 Mercedes-Benz
15 BMW
27 SAP
47 Siemens
55 Volkswagen
62 Adidas
65 Audi
74 Porsche
81 Allianz
86 Nivea
97 Puma

Italy
41 Gucci
87 Prada
88 Ferrari
89 Georgio Armani

Japan
8 Toyota
18 Honda
29 Sony
33 Canon
39 Nintendo
75 Panasonic
96 Lexus

Note: Map shows the top 100 brands in the world by country of ownership, except for the United States, for which only brands in the top 20 are shown.

Source: Based on Interbrand 2010.

Based on revenue and name recognition, these are the brands that dominate the global marketplace. Just 13 nations account for all the top 100 brands.

Conflict View

Conflict theorists emphasize that the media reflect, and even exacerbate, many of the divisions in our society and world, including those based on gender, race, ethnicity, and social class. They point in particular to the media's ability to decide what is transmitted through a process called *gatekeeping*.

Gatekeeping What story appears on page one of the morning newspaper? Which motion picture plays on three screens rather than just one at the local cineplex? What movie isn't released at all or can't get onto theatre screens? Behind these decisions are powerful figures—publishers, editors, film executives, and other media moguls.

The mass media constitute a form of big business in which profits are generally more important than the quality of the programming. Within the mass media, a relatively small number of people control what eventually reaches the audience

through a process known as **gatekeeping**. This term describes how material must travel through a series of checkpoints (or gates) before reaching the public. Thus, a select few decide what images to bring to a broad audience, particularly in countries such as Canada where media mergers have taken place. In many countries, the government plays a gatekeeping role. A study done for the World Bank found that in 97 countries, 60 percent of the top 5 TV stations and 72 percent of the largest radio stations are government-owned (World Bank 2001:183).

Gatekeeping prevails in all kinds of media. As sociologist C. Wright Mills ([1956] 2000b) observed, the real power of the media is that they can control what is being presented. In the recording industry, gatekeepers may reject a popular local band because it competes with a group already on their label. Even if a band lands a recording deal, radio programmers may reject the music because it does not fit the station's "sound." Television programmers may keep a pilot for a new TV series

figure 10-2 Filtering Information: Social Content

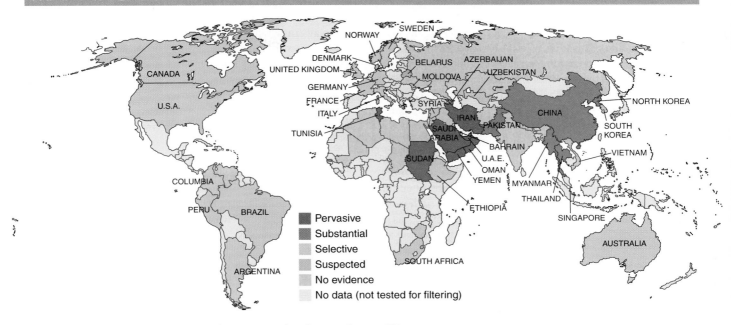

Pervasive
Substantial
Selective
Suspected
No evidence
No data (not tested for filtering)

Note: "No evidence" sections, shown in grey, do not necessarily indicate an absence of filtering.

Source: OpenNet Initiative 2008; see also Faris and Villeneuve 2008.

This map highlights nations that restrict public access to the Internet or filter its content, including material related to sexuality, gambling, illegal drugs, and alcohol, as well as other socially sensitive or offensive topics.

off the air because they believe it does not appeal to the target audience (which is sometimes determined by advertising sponsors). Similar decisions are made by gatekeepers in the publishing industry (Hanson 2005). Lost in all of this is the quality of the product itself.

Gatekeeping is not as dominant in at least one form of mass media: the Internet. You can send virtually any message to an electronic bulletin board, and create a Web page or a blog to advance any argument, including one that insists the earth is flat. The Internet is a means of quickly disseminating information (or misinformation) without going through any significant gatekeeping process. The lack of a gatekeeping process—which has led to cases of cyberbullying or online harassment—became the concern of federal and provincial government leaders in 2013 after the suicide of 17-year-old Rehtaeh Parsons from Nova Scotia. Parsons was 15 when she was allegedly sexually assaulted by a group of boys. Photos of the alleged assault were posted online, which led to years of inescapable online harassment and bullying of Parsons. Government leaders came together in April of 2013 to begin a process for creating provisions in the Criminal Code to address this type of online activity, acknowledging that the law has lagged behind the rapid pace of technological change.

In an entirely different context, in 2011, online criticism fueled dissent in Arab countries like Egypt, Tunisia, Libya, and Bahrain. To encourage the opposition, activists posted cellphone videos of the protests on the Internet. Even in China, where the government limits or bans access to Google, Facebook, and Twitter, media-savvy Chinese have created local networks to share their dissatisfaction with the government (MacLeod 2010; Preston and Stelter 2011).

Nevertheless, the Internet is not totally without restrictions. In many nations, laws regulate content on topics such as gambling, pornography, and even politics. Popular Internet service providers will terminate accounts for offensive behaviour. In the fallout of 9/11, the Web auctioneer eBay did not allow people to sell parts of the World Trade Center via its online auction. As of 2008, 21 countries placed significant controls on Internet content (see Figure 10-2). For example, China routinely blocks search engines like Google and Alta-Vista from accessing the names of groups or individuals critical of the government (French 2004; World Bank 2001:187). And when anti-government protests escalated in Myanmar (Burma) in 2007, the government blocked video and photographs of the demonstrations—and the government response—from being posted on the Internet (Diebert et al. 2008; Mydans 2007; OpenNet Initiative 2008).

Critics of the content of mass media argue that the gatekeeping process reflects a desire to maximize profits. Why else, they argue, would movie star Julia Roberts, rather than Afghanistan's leader Hamid Karzai, make the cover of *Time* magazine? Later in this chapter, we consider the role that corporate structure plays in the makeup and delivery of mass media content. The gatekeeping process also receives criticism because much content that sees the light of day does not reflect the diversity of the audience.

Media Monitoring In the past, the term **media monitoring** has been used to refer to interest groups' monitoring of media content. Recently, however, use of the term has expanded to include monitoring of individuals' media usage and choices without their knowledge. New technologies related to video on demand, downloading of audio/video clips, and satellite programming have created records of individual viewing and listening preferences. In 2006, Google opposed U.S. government efforts to obtain company records of users' Web-browsing activities. At the same time, members of the general public expressed concern both that companies such as Google were maintaining such records and that government agencies were interested in them.

What are the practical and ethical limits of media monitoring? In daily life, parents often oversee their children's online activities and scan the blogs they read—which are, of course, available for anyone to see. Many parents may see such monitoring of children's media use and communications as an appropriate part of adult supervision. Yet, their snooping sets an example for their children, who may use the technique for their own ends. Some media analysts have noted a growing trend among adolescents: the use of new media to learn not-so-public information about their parents (Delaney 2005).

Dominant Ideology: Constructing Reality Conflict theorists argue that the mass media maintain the privileges of certain groups. Moreover, while protecting their own interests, powerful groups may limit the media's representation of others. Karl Marx saw economic determinism as shaping the way in which media are viewed. The economic base of a capitalist society, founded on class distinction and exploitation, determines the nature of the other institutions, such as the family, the education system, the legal system, and, more applicably, the media. The media are used to ensure that the economy—based on exploitative class relations—is maintained and that profits for the ruling class will grow.

Marxist theorists see advertising as a key ingredient in the maintenance of advanced capitalism, as consumers are "created" in order to maximize the economic power of the ruling class. The Italian Marxist Antonio Gramsci (1891–1937) took Marx's idea of economic determinism further to include the ways in which the ruling classes convince the oppressed groups to consent to their oppression. According to Gramsci, the term **hegemony** refers to a situation where the powerful groups are able to convince the less powerful to accept the way that the powerful group acts or sees the world as "normal" or "common sense." This helps to maintain the social, economic, and political interests of the dominant classes. For example, the mainstream media transmit messages that virtually define what we regard as the real world, even though those images frequently vary from what the larger society experiences. Today, television is dominated by reality shows, which are particularly popular among younger viewers. Box 10-1 shows how the diverse audience for these shows is reflected in the programs themselves.

Mass media decision makers are overwhelmingly white, male, and wealthy. It may come as no surprise, then, that many types of mainstream media tend to ignore the lives and ambitions of subordinate groups, among them working-class people of colour, gays and lesbians, people with disabilities, overweight people, and older people. Worse, media content may create false images or stereotypes of these groups that then become accepted as accurate portrayals of reality. *Stereotypes* are unreliable generalizations about all members of a group that do not recognize individual differences within the group. Such are the depictions of Aboriginal peoples disseminated through Hollywood movies. The Canadian documentary *Reel Injun* (2009), directed by Cree filmmaker Neil Diamond who grew up on the Waskaganish First Nation in western Quebec, is an examination of popular images of North American Aboriginal peoples. In his documentary, Diamond traces the history of stereotypes of Aboriginals created by Hollywood films, which have affected how non-Aboriginals perceive Aboriginals as well as how Aboriginals perceive themselves. *Reel Injun* exposes how Hollywood found that there was a market for portraying Aboriginal peoples as "savages."

Television content is a prime example of this tendency to ignore reality. How many overweight TV characters can you name? Even though in real life, one out of every four women is obese (15 or more kilograms over a healthy body weight), only three out of 100 TV characters are portrayed as obese. Heavy-set television characters have fewer romances, talk less about sex, eat more often, and are more frequently the object of ridicule than their thinner counterparts (Hellmich 2001).

In the days following the 2010 earthquake in Haiti, foreign governments monitored social media sites to identify potential locations for rescue missions and supply deliveries.

research today

10-1 Diversity in Reality Television

The underrepresentation of racial and ethnic minorities in the television industry is well documented. Not only are minorities less likely than whites to play recurring roles, they are also underrepresented among key decision makers, such as directors, producers, and casting agents.

The new media phenomenon of reality TV may be an exception to this rule. Reality, or unscripted, television dominated prime-time television during the first decade of the 21st century. Popular with consumers and relatively inexpensive to produce, it soon became a staple on both broadcast and cable networks. Shows featured ordinary people or C-list celebrities confronting various challenges.

Although these series have been criticized on artistic grounds, they do present a diverse cast of characters. Content analysis shows that as a group, reality programs accurately represent the diversity of the general population. As such, they offer a new and significant exception to television programming that is otherwise dominated by white actors and actresses. One show, *America's Got Talent*, even has a minority host, African American Nick Cannon.

Reality shows do not necessarily promote racial and ethnic enlightenment. Instead, the broad collection of players often seems to fuel friction and build racial, social class, or sexual tension, based on either explicit or implicit issues. Far from being a multicultural paradise, reality TV is a low-wage segment of the industry in which the stars, unlike the actors in scripted dramas, receive little to no compensation. Perhaps not much has changed after all.

The colour line remains in place in one segment of the reality genre, shows that promote romantic partnerships. For the first 17 seasons (through 2009), *The Bachelor* and *The*

A rare sight on prime-time television: people of colour playing leading roles. Reality shows such as *America's Next Top Model* are one of the few categories in network TV that whites do not dominate.

Bachelorette featured an all-white dating gallery. Like scripted TV, these shows are likely to remain white-only. Of the nearly 70 scripted pilot projects under development by the four major networks in 2009, just four featured a minority person in a starring role.

> *Far from being a multicultural paradise, reality TV is a low-wage segment of the industry in which the stars, unlike the actors in scripted dramas, receive little to no compensation.*

Apply the Theory

1. Do you watch reality TV? If so, what do you like about the shows? Have you noted any tension or conflict based on race, social class, or gender? What about friendship and support that cross those lines—have you seen it?
2. What does the popularity of reality TV shows tell us about a culture and society?

Sources: Belton 2009; Braxton 2009; Grazian 2010:129; NAACP 2008; Wyatt 2009.

Racialized minority groups are stereotyped in television shows. Almost all leading roles are cast to be white, as media racism persists in filtering images through a "Eurocentric prism of whiteness" (Fleras 2003:284). The misrepresentation, stereotyping, ignoring, caricaturing, trivializing, and ridiculing of racialized minorities leads one to ask the question, "Is the Canadian mainstream media racist or is there media racism in Canada?" (Fleras 2003). Canadian sociologist Augie Fleras asserts that, while it is difficult to prove Canada has racist media, one can look at evidence showing how racism has been institutionalized through organizational characteristics such as codified procedures that openly discriminate against minorities and argue convincingly that Canada does suffer from media racism. In Fleras's words, "Media racism exists in the foundational principles that govern media values, agendas, and priorities, [which] continue to be rooted in the primacy of whiteness as the standard by which others are judged" (2003:283).

Despite the popularity of Hollywood entertainment, media that are produced abroad for local consumption also do well. The animated series *Freej* features Muslim grandmothers who stumble on a cursed book while tackling their culture's wedding traditions. Produced in Dubai, the United Arab Emirates, for adult viewers, the series was launched in 2006.

Dominant Ideology: Whose Culture? In the United States, on the popular television contest *The Apprentice*, the dreaded dismissal line is "You're fired." In Finland, on *Dilli* (The Deal), it's "*Olet vapautettu*" ("You're free to leave"); in Germany, on *Big Boss*, it's "*Sie haben frei*" ("You're off"). Although people throughout the world decry American exports, from films to language to Bart Simpson, U.S. media models and popular culture are still widely imitated. Sociologist and cultural commentator Todd Gitlin describes U.S. pop culture as something that "people love, and love to hate" (2002:177; Wentz and Atkinson 2005).

This love–hate relationship is so enduring that the U.S. media have come to rely on overseas markets for major revenue streams. However, it is risky to overstress U.S. media domination. Canadian-made sitcoms *Little Mosque on the Prairie* and *Corner Gas* are cases in point. As of 2012 *Little Mosque on the Prairie* aired in 80 countries around the world, including the 2012 purchase of the U.S. broadcasting rights to the series, including cable and syndication. *Corner Gas*, as of 2008, aired in 26 countries and scored a distribution deal in the U.S. in 2007. *Survivor, Who Wants to Be a Millionaire, Big Brother*, and *Iron Chef*—immensely popular TV programs in the United States—came from Sweden, Britain, the Netherlands, and Japan, respectively. Even *American Idol* originated in Britain as *Pop Idol*, featuring Simon Cowell. And the steamy telenovelas of Mexico and other Spanish-speaking countries owe very little of their origin to the soap operas on U.S. television. Unlike motion pictures, television is gradually moving away from U.S. domination and is now more likely to be locally produced. By 2003, all the top 50 British TV shows were locally produced. *Medium* may appear on television in London, but it is shown late at night. Even U.S.-owned TV ventures such as Disney, MTV, and CNN had dramatically increased their locally produced programming overseas. Still, *CSI: NY* was on top in France, where only sports programs had a higher rating (Bielby and Harrington 2008; Colucci 2008; *The Economist* 2003).

In fact, some motion pictures have brought in more monies abroad than at home. Through early 2006, for example, *Titanic* had earned a record-breaking US$600 million in the United States and another US$1.2 billion from overseas box offices.

Nations that feel a loss of identity may try to defend against the cultural invasion from foreign countries, especially the economically dominant United States. Many developing nations have long argued for a greatly improved two-way flow of news and information between industrialized nations and developing nations. They complain that news from the developing world is scant, and what news there is reflects unfavourably on the developing nations. For example, what do you know about South America? Many people in North America will mention the topics that dominate the news from that continent: revolution and drugs. Most know little else about South America.

In 2006, Al Jazeera expanded its programming to include an all-English channel; since then its following has grown. Israel's top cable company, for example, dropped CNN and added AJE to its lineup.

To remedy this imbalance, a resolution to monitor the news and content that cross the borders of developing nations was passed by the United Nations Educational, Scientific, and Cultural Organization (UNESCO) in the 1980s. The United States disagreed with the proposal, which became one factor in the U.S. decision to withdraw from UNESCO in the mid-1980s. In 2005, the United States opposed another UNESCO plan, meant to reduce the diminishment of cultural differences. Hailed as an important step toward protecting threatened cultures, particularly the media markets in developing nations, the measure passed the UN's General Assembly by a vote of 148–2. The United States, one of the two dissenters, objected that the measure's wording was vague (Dominick 2005:455; Riding 2005).

Feminist Views

Many feminists share the view of conflict theorists that the mass media stereotype and misrepresent social reality. According to these views, the media powerfully influence how we look at women and men, communicating unrealistic, stereotypical, and limiting images of the sexes. Here are three problems feminists believe arise from media coverage (Wood 1994):

1. Women are underrepresented, which suggests that men are the cultural standard and women are insignificant.

2. Men and women are portrayed in ways that reflect and perpetuate stereotypical views of gender. Women, for example, are often shown in peril, needing to be rescued by a male—rarely the reverse.

3. Depictions of male–female relationships emphasize traditional sex roles and normalize violence against women.

Educators and social scientists have long noted the stereotypical portrayal of women and men in the mass media. Women are often shown as being shallow and obsessed with beauty. They are more likely than men to be presented unclothed, in danger, or even physically victimized. Responding to the way advertising and the entertainment media objectify and even dehumanize women, Jean Kilbourne argues in her writings and film documentaries that "we [women] are the product." Feminist Vivian Gornick asserts that the portrayal of women in the media reflects "innumerable small murders of the mind and spirit [that] take place daily" (1979:ix; Cortese 1999; Goffman 1979; Kilbourne 2000a, 2000b).

A continuing, troubling issue for some feminists—particularly radical feminists—is pornography. Pornography frequently presents women as objects and attempts to normalize sexual violence by men toward women. Some feminists would argue that this type of objectification and imagery represents an implicit endorsement of violence against women and is a clear example of the unrelenting grip of patriarchal social structure and culture. According to radical feminist Leisbet van Zoonen, pornography is "a form of sexual violence against women, simultaneously a source and product of a deeply misogynistic society" (1994:19). The industry that creates sexually explicit adult images for videos, DVDs, and the Internet is largely unregulated, putting its own performers at risk. A 2002 health survey of triple-X, as the porn industry refers to itself, found that 40 percent of performers had at least one sexually transmitted disease, compared to 0.1 percent of the general population. The career span of these women and men is short, usually about 18 months, but the profits for the industry are continuous and enormous (Huffstutter 2003).

As in other areas of sociology, feminist researchers caution against assuming that what holds true for men's media use is true for everyone. Researchers, for example, have studied the different ways that women and men approach the Internet. Though men are only slightly more likely than women ever to have used the Internet, they are much more likely to use it daily. According to a 2005 study, about a third of men use the Internet every day, compared to a quarter of women. Not surprisingly, men account for 91 percent of the players in online sports fantasy leagues. But perhaps more socially significant is that women are more likely than men to maintain friendship networks through email (Boase et al. 2006; Fallows 2006; Rainie 2005).

Unlike feminist perspectives that point to necessary social action to change the media's portrayal of women, post-feminist views are those that individualize women's concerns, *discouraging* a radical change to social institutions, including the mass media. In her book *Postfeminist News: Political Women in Media Culture*, Mary Douglas Vavrus argues that the ways in which women are portrayed in the mass media, and news programs in particular, promote a post-feminist view. Regrettably, these media accounts, according to Vavrus, encourage women's focus on private consumer lifestyles and middle-class aspirations while discouraging public life and political aspirations (2002).

Interactionist View

Interactionists are especially interested in shared understandings of everyday behaviour. These scholars examine the media on the micro level to see how they shape day-to-day social behaviour. Increasingly, researchers point to the mass media as the source of major daily activity; some argue that television serves virtually as a primary group for many individuals who share TV viewing time together. Other mass media participation is not necessarily face to face. For example, we usually listen to music or read the newspaper online as a solitary activity, although it is possible to share it with others (Cerulo et al. 1992; Waite 2000).

Interactionists note, too, that friendship networks can emerge from shared viewing habits or from recollection of a cherished television series from the past. Family members and friends often gather for parties centred on the broadcasting of popular events such as the Super Bowl or the Academy Awards. And, as we've seen, television often serves as a "babysitter" or "playmate" for children and even infants.

The power of the mass media encourages political leaders and entertainment figures to carefully manipulate their images through public appearances called photo opportunities (or photo ops). By embracing symbols (posing with celebrities or in front of prestigious landmarks), participants in these staged events attempt to convey self-serving definitions of social reality (M. Weinstein and D. Weinstein 2002).

The mass media, and television in particular, have the ability to influence the social construction of what it means to be gay, straight, old, young, working class, disabled, single,

British, Russian, Aboriginal, male, female, and so forth. Our shared understanding of the meaning of social phenomena—delivered to us through the mass media—is shaped through what we hear, read, and see. Currently, men are being portrayed in popular culture, including advertising, as incompetent, goofy, lazy, messy, stupid, and domestically inept. Whether it is Tim Hortons, Glade, Johnson & Johnson, Dairy Queen, or Canadian Tire, similar stereotypes are being propagated by advertisers and delivered by television. Paul Nathanson of McGill University, who studies the way in which men are socially constructed in popular culture, states, "We are creating a society in which thuggish, piggish men are the dominant images" (Krashinsky 2009). Deborah Adams, a senior executive of a Canadian marketing company agrees with Professor Nathanson's assessment. She states, "They're applying that same formula every time you see an ad. . . . It's not just advertising, it's in pop culture, depicting men in a narrow, stereotypical view" (Krashinsky 2009). Is it possible that young boys and adolescents are getting this message and considering it "cool" to be stupid? As mentioned in Chapter 3, some school officials think so.

The rise of the Internet has facilitated new forms of communication and social interaction, often referred to as "the new media." Grandparents can now keep up with their grandchildren via email. Gay and lesbian teens have online resources for support and information. People can find their life partners through computer dating services or search for children to adopt. Social-networking sites, such as Facebook, particularly popular among younger people, provide the opportunity to exchange information and to maintain and expand social contacts. As Figure 10-3 shows, throughout the world, the Internet is casting an increasingly wider net over social interactions.

Some troubling issues have been raised about day-to-day life on the Internet. What, if anything, should be done about extremist groups who use cyberspace to exchange messages of hatred? What, if anything, should be done about the issue of sexual "expression" on the Internet? How can children be protected from sexual predators and cyberbullies? Should "hot chat" and X-rated film clips be censored? Or should expression be completely free?

figure **10-3 The Internet Explosion**

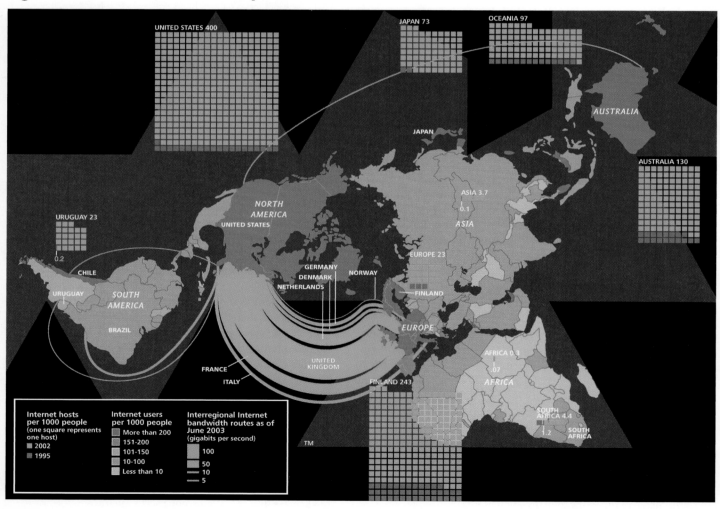

Source: National Geographic 2005:21 and the Buckminster Fuller Institute[TM].

In little more than a decade, the World Wide Web has exploded, touching 600 million users in every single country on the earth. Still, a **digital divide**, measured in the form of relative bandwidth, separates rich countries from poor ones.

figure 10-4 Who's on the Internet?

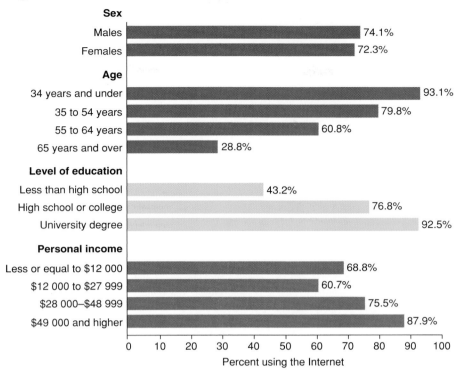

Source: Statistics Canada 2008, CANSIM Table 358-0124, adapted by author.

Though the Internet has created a new platform for extremists and pornographers, it has also given people greater control over what they see and hear. That is, the Internet allows people to manage their media exposure so as to avoid sounds, images, and ideas they do not enjoy or endorse. The legal scholar Cass Sunstein (2002) has referred to this personalized approach to news information gathering as *egocasting*. Other media commentators have observed the shift away from the dominance of *broadcasting* to what has become referred to as *narrowcasting*. One possible social consequence of this trend may be a less tolerant society. If we read, see, and hear only what we know and agree with, we may become much less prepared to meet with people from different backgrounds or converse with those who express new viewpoints.

Finally, while many people in Canada and elsewhere embrace the Internet, we should mention here that not everyone has equal access to it. The same people, by and large, who experience poor health, enjoy few job opportunities, and have been generally marginalized by society are left off the information highway. Figure 10-4 breaks down Internet usage by gender, age, income, and education. Note the large disparities in usage between those with high and low incomes, the younger and the older, and between those with more or less education. Though educators and politicians have touted the potential benefits to the disadvantaged, Internet usage may be reinforcing existing inequality. Box 10-2 places the topic of unequal Internet access in a global context.

The interactionist perspective helps us to understand one important aspect of the entire mass media system: the audience. How do we actively participate in media events? How do we construct with others the meaning of media messages?

We will explore these questions in the section that follows. (Table 10-2 summarizes the various sociological perspectives on all media, and Box 10-3 looks at television from those four perspectives.)

table 10-2 Sociological Perspectives on the Mass Media

Theoretical Perspective	Emphasis
Functionalist	Socialization
	Enforcement of social norms
	Conferral of status
	Promotion of consumption
	Narcotizing effect (dysfunction)
Conflict	Gatekeeping
	Media monitoring
	Construction of reality
Feminist	Underrepresentation of women
	Misrepresentation of women
Interactionist	Impact on social behavior
	Source of friendship networks

summing**UP**

10-2 The Global Disconnect

Bogdan Ghirda, a Romanian, is paid 50 cents an hour to participate in multiplayer Internet games like City of Heroes and Star Wars. He is sitting in for someone in an industrialized country who does not want to spend days ascending to the highest levels of competition in order to compete with players who are already "well armed." This arrangement is not unusual. U.S.-based services can earn hundreds of dollars for recruiting someone in a less developed country, like Ghirda, to represent a single player in an affluent industrial country.

Meanwhile, villagers in Arumugam, India, are beginning to benefit from their new Knowledge Centre. The facility, funded by a nonprofit organization, contains five computers that offer Internet access—an amenity unknown until now to thousands of villagers.

These two situations illustrate the technological disconnect between the developing and industrial nations. Around the world, developing nations lag far behind industrial nations in their access to and use of new technologies. The World Economic Forum's Networked Readiness Index (NRI), a ranking of 139 nations, shows the relative preparedness of individuals, businesses, and governments to benefit from information technologies. As the accompanying table shows, the haves of the world—countries like Singapore, the United States, and Denmark—are network ready; the have-nots—countries like Zimbabwe, Chad, and Nepal—are not.

For developing nations, the consequences of the global disconnect are far more serious than an inability to surf the Net. Thanks to the Internet, multinational organizations can now function as a single global unit, responding instantly in real time, 24 hours a day. This new capability has fostered the emergence of what sociologist Manuel Castells calls a "global economy." But if large numbers of people—indeed, entire nations—are disconnected from the new **global economy,** their economic growth will remain slow and the well-being of their people will remain retarded. Those citizens who are educated and skilled will immigrate to other labour markets, deepening the impoverishment of nations on the periphery.

> *For developing nations, the consequences of the global disconnect are far more serious than an inability to surf the Net.*

Apply the Theory

1. For nations on the periphery, what are some of the social and economic consequences of the global disconnect?

Networked Readiness Index

1. Switzerland	130. Nepal
2. Sweden	131. Mozambique
3. Singapore	132. Mali
4. United States	133. Timor-Leste
5. Germany	134. Burkina Faso
6. Japan	135. Mauritania
7. Finland	136. Zimbabwe
8. Netherlands	137. Burundi
9. Denmark	138. Angola
10. Canada	139. Chad

2. What factors might complicate efforts to remedy the global disconnect in developing nations?

Sources: Castells 2010; Dutta and Mia 2010; *The Economist* 2005; Lim 2007; T. Thompson 2005; World Economic Forum 2010.

Who Are the Media's Audiences?

The mass media are distinguished from other social institutions by the necessary presence of an audience. It can be an identifiable, finite group, such as an audience at a jazz club or a Broadway musical, or a much larger and undefined group, such as MuchMusic viewers or readers of the same issue of *The Globe and Mail*. The audience may be a secondary group gathered in a large auditorium or a primary group, such as a family watching the latest *Harry Potter* video at home.

We can look at the audience from the level of both *microsociology* and *macrosociology*. At the micro level, we might consider how audience members, interacting among themselves, respond to the media, or in the case of live performances, actually influence the performers. At the macro level, we might examine broader societal consequences of the media's influence, such as the widespread early childhood education delivered through programming like *Sesame Street*.

Even if an audience is spread out over a wide geographic area and members don't know one another, it is still distinctive in terms of age, gender, income, political allegiance, education, and ethnicity. The audience for a ballet, for example, would differ substantially from the audience for country music.

::: use your sociological *imagination* :::

Think about the last time you were part of an audience. How similar or different from yourself were the other audience members? What might account for whatever similarities or differences you noticed?

The Segmented (or Niche) Audience

Increasingly, the media are marketing themselves to a *particular* audience (sometimes referred to as **narrowcasting**). Once a media outlet, such as a radio station or a magazine, has identified its audience, it targets that group—such a group can be

research today

10-3 Looking at Television from Four Sociological Perspectives

Television to most of us is that box sitting on the shelf or hanging on the wall that diverts us, occasionally entertains us, and sometimes puts us to sleep. But sociologists look much more deeply at the medium. Here is what they find using the four sociological perspectives:

Functionalist View

In examining any aspect of society, including television, functionalists emphasize the contribution it makes to overall social stability. Functionalists regard television as a powerful force in communicating the common values of our society and in promoting an overall feeling of unity and social solidarity:

- Television vividly presents important national and international news. On a local level, television communicates vital information on everything from storm warnings and school closings to the locations of emergency shelters.
- Television programs transmit valuable learning skills (*Curious George*) and factual information (CBC's *The National*).
- Television "brings together" members of a community or even a nation by broadcasting important events and ceremonies (press conferences, parades, and state funerals) and through coverage of tragedies, such as the shocking murder of four RCMP officers in 2005.
- Television contributes to economic stability and prosperity by promoting and advertising services and (through shopping channels) serving as a direct marketplace for products.

Conflict View

Conflict theorists argue that the social order is based on coercion and exploitation. They emphasize that television reflects and even exacerbates many of the divisions of our society and world, including those based on gender, race, ethnicity, and social class:

- Television is a form of big business in which profits are more important than the quality of the product (programming).
- Television's network executives are overwhelmingly white, male, and prosperous; by contrast, television programs tend to ignore the lives and ambitions of subordinate groups, among them working-class people, visible minorities, Aboriginal peoples, gays and lesbians, people with disabilities, and older people.
- Television distorts the electoral process in politics, as candidates with the most money (often backed by powerful lobbying groups) buy TV commercial time and saturate the air with negative attack ads.
- By exporting *Modern Family*, *Mad Men*, and other programs around the world, U.S. television undermines the distinctive traditions and art forms of other societies and encourages their cultural and economic dependence on the United States.

Feminist Views

Feminist theorists believe that gender is constructed by society; thus, television plays a major role not only in reflecting society's ideas about gender but also in constructing its own images:

- Television reinforces gender inequality through its portrayal of women as subordinate and powerless and men as dominant and powerful.
- Television objectifies women through its portrayal of women as objects to be admired for their physical appearance and sexual attractiveness.
- Television creates the false impression that most women are the same—young, white, middle-class, slim, and heterosexual.

Interactionist View

In studying the social order, interactionists are especially interested in shared understandings of everyday behaviour. Consequently, interactionists examine television on the micro level by focusing on how day-to-day social behaviour is shaped by television:

- Neglectful parents use television as a "baby-sitter" or "playmate" for many children, often over long periods of time.
- Friendship networks can emerge from shared viewing habits or from recollections of an old, cherished TV series. Family members and friends often gather for parties centred on the broadcasting of popular events, such as a Stanley Cup playoff game, the Academy Awards, or even "reality" series like *Canadian Idol*.
- The frequent appearance of violence in the news and in entertainment programming creates feelings of fear and may actually make interpersonal relations more charged or aggressive.
- The power of television encourages political leaders and even entertainment figures to carefully manipulate symbols (by publicly posing with celebrities or in front of prestigious landmarks) and to attempt to convey self-serving definitions of social reality.

Despite their differences, feminist theorists, functionalists, conflict theorists, and interactionists would agree that there is much more to television than simply "entertainment." They would also agree that television and other popular forms of culture are worthy subjects for serious study by sociologists.

Apply the Theory

1. What functions does television serve? What might be some dysfunctions?
2. If you were a television network executive, which perspective would influence your choice of programs? Why?

---

called a **niche audience** or a **segmented audience**. To some degree, this specialization is driven by advertising. Media specialists have sharpened their ability, through survey research, to identify particular target audiences. As a result, Nike would be much more likely to promote a new line of golf clubs on the Golf Channel, for example, than on an episode of *SpongeBob SquarePants*. The many more choices that the growing Internet and satellite/digital broadcast channels offer audiences also foster specialization. Members of these audiences are more likely to *expect* content geared to their own interests.

In 2010, hip-hop artist UnK's "2 Step" was one of the most frequently downloaded cellphone ringtones. Because today's media provide multiple services, music fans can use the Internet to access recorded music and listen to it on their cellphones.

Marketing research has developed to the point that those who are interested can estimate the size of the audience for a particular performer. In fact, computer programs have been written to simulate not just specific audiences, but the connections among them. The specialized targeting of audiences has led many scholars to increasingly question the "mass" in mass media.

Audience Behaviour

Sociologists have long researched how audiences interact with one another and how they share information after a media event. The role of audience members as opinion leaders particularly intrigues social researchers. An **opinion leader** is someone who influences the opinions and decisions of others through day-to-day personal contact and communication. For example, a movie or theatre critic functions as an opinion leader. Sociologist Paul Lazarsfeld and his colleagues (1948) pioneered the study of opinion leaders in their research on political voting behaviour in the 1940s. They found that opinion leaders encourage their relatives, friends, and co-workers to think positively about a particular candidate, perhaps pushing them to listen to the politician's speeches or read the campaign literature.

Today, film critics often attribute the success of low-budget independent films to word of mouth. This is another way of saying that the mass media influence opinion leaders, who in turn influence others. The audience, then, can be seen not as a group of passive people but as a dynamic collective of active consumers who are often inspired to interact with others after a media event (Croteau and Hoynes 2003; Wright 1986).

10.3 What Does the Media Industry Look Like?

Who owns the media production and distribution process? The answer is an ever-shrinking group of very large corporations. As we will see in the following section, two social consequences of this trend are a reduction in the number of truly independent information outlets and an increase in corporate opportunities for cross-promotion.

Media Concentration

The United States is the major global exporter of media products and programs, and, as noted in Chapter 3, the influence of U.S. media on Canadian culture remains substantial. A few multinational corporations now dominate the publishing, broadcasting, and film industries, though they may be hard to identify, since global conglomerates manage many different subsidiary companies as brands. The Walt Disney Company alone owns 16 television channels that reach 140 countries. Disney (which includes ABC, ESPN, and Pixar, among many others) is a global media giant. Other conglomerates include AOL Time Warner (CNN, *Time* magazine, and HBO); Rupert Murdoch's News Corporation of Australia (Fox Network Television, book publisher HarperCollins, numerous newspapers and magazines, and 20th Century Fox); Sony of Japan (Columbia Pictures, IMAX, CBS Records, and Columbia Records); and Viacom (Paramount, MTV, CBS, UPN, Black Entertainment Television, Simon and Schuster, and Blockbuster). This concentration of media giants fosters considerable cross-promotion. For example, the release of the Warner Brothers film *The Matrix Reloaded* in 2003 was heavily promoted by both CNN and *Time* magazine. In fact, *Time* managed to devote its cover to the film's release in the midst of the war in Iraq.

Similar concerns have been raised about the situation in countries such as China, Cuba, Iraq, and North Korea, where various ruling parties own and control the media. The difference, which is considerable, is that in the United States the gatekeeping process is in the hands of private individuals, who desire to maximize profits. In the other countries, such as Canada, the same process is sometimes carried out by private business people but can also be done by political leaders and senior bureaucrats, who are mandated to strengthen Canada's cultural integrity.

As mentioned in Chapter 3, Canada has historically been concerned about cultural diffusion and U.S. cultural imperialism as they relate to Canadian cultural sovereignty. The establishment of the Canadian Broadcasting Corporation (CBC), which is publicly owned, could be viewed as an attempt to protect and preserve Canada's national cultural interests. Today, many still see the CBC as having an essential role in buffering Canadians from the forces—to some, the absorption—of globalization (i.e., Americanization). Canadians have been, and continue to be, particularly susceptible to U.S. cultural imperialism because of geographic, economic, social, and political ties with the United States. According to the independent organization Media Awareness Network, "Canada has long been the largest importer of American television programming. This is due to its geographic proximity to the U.S., as well as an inability to produce profitable programming for a small domestic market" (Media Awareness Network 2008:1). In 1968, the federal government set up the Canadian Radio-television and Telecommunications Commission (CRTC) to regulate media broadcasting in Canada. The job of the CRTC is to oversee the restrictions on foreign ownership of broadcast outlets, ensure adequate amounts of Canadian content, and provide a vision of broadcasting as a means of strengthening Canada's cultural, social, and economic structures (CBC 2006a). As a result of the CRTC mandate, for example, 35 percent of a radio station's programming in the daytime must be Canadian.

Media concentration on a global level is not the only concern of government regulators. Media concentration—on a national level—has long been a concern for regulators and many Canadians alike. The ownership of Canadian mass media outlets tends to be concentrated in the hands of a few companies that may own not only newspapers, but television and radio stations as well. For example, CTVglobemedia (CTVgm) is one of Canada's largest media conglomerates, owning multiple sectors of media (cross media ownership). The company owns the CTV television network, newspapers such as *The Globe and Mail*, and 27 conventional television stations across Canada; and it has interests in 35 specialty channels, including TSN (The Sports Network) and MuchMusic. CTVgm also owns CHUM Radio, which operates 35 radio stations across Canada. Another example of media concentration is that of Quebecor Media, which owns eight daily newspapers and 200 other local and community newspapers, as well as Videotron and its French-language TV network,

and Canoe.com. Also, until October 2009, CanWest Global Communications owned 11 of Canada's biggest daily newspapers, including the *National Post, The Gazette* in Montreal, and the *Ottawa Citizen*. Currently, the company is being restructured, which has led to the sell-off of 10 of Canada's daily newspapers.

Many people who see media concentration as a threat to a diversity of views are concerned about media ownership in Vancouver, where both major daily newspapers—*The Vancouver Sun* and *The Province*—were, up until 2009, owned by CanWest Global. In 2008, the CRTC announced policies to curb the concentration of media ownership, which included restrictions limiting one person or entity from (1) controlling two types of media (a local radio station, a local television station, or a local newspaper) in the same market; and (2) controlling more than 45 percent of the total television audience as a result of a merger or acquisition (CBC 2008a).

We should note one significant exception to the centralization and concentration of the media: the Internet. Research shows that more and more people, especially those under age 35, are receiving their media content—whether it be watching television, listening to radio, or reading online news reports—through the Internet. A 2007 CRTC report noted that in 2006, about 48 percent of Canadians with Internet access went online for up to 10 hours per week, while 52 percent of Canadians aged 18–24 went online for more than 10 hours per week (CRTC 2007). Currently, the World Wide Web is accessible through independent outlets to millions of producers of media content. Obviously, the producer must be technologically proficient and must have access to a computer, but compared to other media outlets, the Internet is readily available for aspiring content producers. Media conglomerates, well aware of the Internet's potential, have adapted to the new landscape and have been delivering their material via the Web for some time now. Still, for now, the Internet allows the individual to become a media entrepreneur with a potential audience of millions (Gamson and Latteier 2004; Schwartz 2004).

The Media's Global Reach

Has the rise of the electronic media created a "global village"? Canadian communications theorist Marshall McLuhan predicted it would more than 40 years ago. McLuhan envisioned the global village as an electronically interconnected world where people would experience mass culture as if they were all in the same hometown. This interconnectedness, however, would have a dark side, as it would exclude many people whose values were not those of the dominant ones being put forth by a particular medium. According to McLuhan, the mass media could potentially have the effect of creating a "Big Brother" society, where one voice prevailed (McLuhan 1962). Today, physical distance is no longer a barrier, and instant messaging is possible across the world. The mass media have indeed created a global village. Not all countries are equally connected, as Figure 10-5 shows; but the progress has been staggering, considering that voice transmission was just beginning a little over a century ago (McLuhan 1964; McLuhan and Fiore 1967).

Cultural critic Todd Gitlin considers "global torrent" a more apt metaphor for the media's reach than "global village."

figure 10-5 Media Penetration in Selected Countries

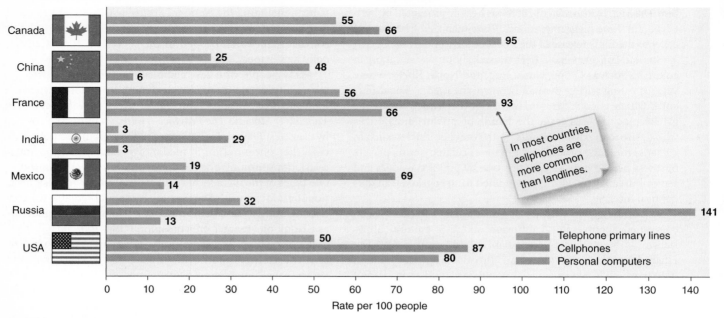

Canada — 55, 66, 95
China — 25, 48, 6
France — 56, 93, 66
India — 3, 29, 3
Mexico — 19, 69, 14
Russia — 32, 141, 13
USA — 50, 87, 80

In most countries, cellphones are more common than landlines.

Telephone primary lines
Cellphones
Personal computers

Rate per 100 people

Note: Personal computer data for 2006, released in 2009; for 2008, released in 2011.

Sources: Bureau of the Census 2009:Table 1345; 2010a:Table 1392.

Think about It
What is the economic and political significance of media penetration?

New technologies can create new social norms. In Gurupá, Brazil, television watching became a community social activity when three new TV owners agreed to share their sets with the community of 3000.

The media permeate all aspects of everyday life. Take advertising, for example. Consumer goods are marketed vigorously worldwide, from advertisements on airport baggage carriers to imprints on sandy beaches.

The key to creating a truly global network that reaches directly into workplaces, schools, and homes is the Internet. Although much of the online global transmission today is limited to print and pictures, the potential to send audio and video via the Internet will increasingly reach into every part of the world. Social interaction will then truly take place on a global scale.

The Internet has also facilitated other forms of communication. Reference materials and data banks can now be made accessible across national boundaries. Information related to international finance, marketing, trade, and manufacturing is literally just a keystroke away. We have seen the emergence of truly world news outlets and the promotion of a world music that is not clearly identifiable with any single culture. Even the most future-oriented thinker would find the growth in the reach of the mass media in post-industrial and postmodern societies remarkable (Castells 2000, 2001; Croteau and Hoynes 2003, 2006).

The lack of one national home for the various forms of mass media raises a potential dilemma for media consumers. People worry that unhealthy influences and even crime pervade today's electronic global village, and that few if any controls prevent them. For example, the leaders of Bhutan worry about the impact of newly introduced television programming on their culture and their people. Similarly, in industrial countries, including Canada, officials are concerned about everything from online pornography to the menace posed by hackers. In the social policy section that follows, we'll discuss the use of media and right to privacy.

Social Policy and the Mass Media

The Right to Privacy

In 2010, humans added 1.2 zettabytes of digital information to the world's already huge data library. A zettabyte equals 1 trillion gigabytes—a quantity which, if placed on DVDs, would require a stack of disks stretching to the moon and back. By 2020, the size of this imaginary DVD tower will triple, quadruple, or even quintuple (Acohido 2010).

Within this mound of data lies personal information about people's finances, health, and individual tastes. In the postmodern digital age, do people have a right to keep that kind of information private? If so, can they expect others to respect that right?

Looking at the Issue

Although much of the sweeping change that accompanied the transition to digital media has benefited society, scholars have noted some negative effects. In particular, recent advances in computer technology have made it increasingly easy for business firms, government agencies, and even criminals to retrieve and store information about private individuals. In public places, at work, and on the Internet, surveillance devices track our every move, whether it is a keystroke or an ATM withdrawal. The information they accumulate includes everything from our buying habits to our Web-surfing patterns.

As these technologies increase the power to monitor our behaviour, they raise fears of their misuse for criminal or even undemocratic purposes. In short, they threaten not just our privacy, but our freedom from crime and censorship as well. Some obvious violations of privacy, such as identity theft—the misuse of credit card and Social Insurance numbers to masquerade as another person—have been well documented. Other violations involve online surveillance of dissident political groups by authoritarian regimes and the unauthorized release of classified government documents. In 2010, WikiLeaks released thousands of classified U.S. foreign policy documents on its Web site, causing some people to condemn the action as treasonous and others to praise it as a blow against government censorship (O'Harrow Jr. 2005).

Other privacy violations are subtler, and not strictly illegal. For example, many commercial Web sites use "cookies" and tracking technology to monitor visitors' Web surfing. Using that information, marketers can estimate a visitor's age, gender, and postal code, and from that data, the person's income. They can then select advertisements that will appeal specifically to that person. So depending on who we are, or at least appear to be, one of us might see ads about weight-loss products and another, ads about travel to exotic locations.

Our society's growing dependence on electronic transactions has greatly increased concerns about our privacy.

Is this approach to online marketing just effective advertising, or is it an invasion of privacy? Because the information that marketers gather in this way can be tied to other devices a person uses, such as a cellphone or computer, some critics see online tracking as a form of fingerprinting (Angwin 2010; Angwin and Valentino-DeVries 2010).

Applying Sociology

From a sociological point of view, the complex issues of privacy and censorship can be considered illustrations of culture lag. As usual, the material culture (technology) is changing faster than the nonmaterial culture (norms for controlling the use of technology). Too often, the result is an anything-goes approach to the use of new technologies.

Sociologists' views on the use and abuse of new technologies differ depending on their theoretical perspective. Functionalists take a generally positive view of the Internet, pointing to its manifest function of facilitating communication. From their perspective, the Internet performs the latent function of empowering people with few resources—from hate groups to special-interest organizations—to communicate with the masses.

In contrast, conflict theorists stress the danger that the most powerful groups in a society will use technology to violate the privacy of the less powerful.

Initiating Policy

To protect the privacy and personal information of Canadians in the digital landscape, the federal government implemented the Personal Information Protection and Electronic Documents Act (PIPEDA) in 2004. PIPEDA sets out 10 key principles that organizations must follow when collecting, using, and disclosing Canadians' personal information. Central to the law are the following provisions:

- Organizations must seek the consent of individuals before collecting, using, or disclosing their personal information.
- Organizations must protect personal information with security safeguards according to the sensitivity of the information.
- Individuals may access personal information about themselves and have it corrected if necessary.
- The purposes for which the information is collected must be identified by the organization at the time of its collection.

PIPEDA provides a consistent set of provisions to protect Canadians' personal information and privacy, regardless of what province or territory they live in. It also allows Canadian companies to seamlessly do business with the European Union (EU), which has implemented legislation called the European Union Data Protection Directive.

Canada also has a privacy commissioner, whose responsibility it is to monitor and protect the privacy of Canadians. Just weeks after the official launch of Google Street View (a 360-degree online mapping service of streets in major cities) in Canada on October 7, 2009, the commissioner expressed concern that Google was not doing enough to protect the privacy of Canadians by ensuring that faces were blurred in the images. Google responded by stating that it is committed to work on the efficacy of its blurring technology (Schmidt 2009). Meanwhile, also in 2009, Switzerland launched a lawsuit against Google surrounding the issue of the protection of privacy on Google Street View.

If anything, however, many people seem to be less vigilant about maintaining their privacy today than they were before the information age. Young people who have grown up browsing the Internet seem to accept the existence of the "cookies" and "spyware" they may pick up while surfing. They have become accustomed to adult surveillance of their conversation in electronic chat rooms. And many see no risk in providing personal information about themselves to strangers they meet online. Little wonder that some university professors find their students do not appreciate the political significance of their right to privacy (Turkle 2004, 2011).

Compared to online tracking, most people seem more worried about government surveillance and crimes like identity theft. Although online piracy is a real threat, in the long run, online tracking and other questionable forms of surveillance may pose a greater threat to society. As Nicholas Carr (2010:W2), former editor of the *Harvard Business Review*, has noted, "The continuing erosion of personal privacy. . . may lead us as a society to devalue the concept of privacy, to see it as outdated and unimportant. . . merely as a barrier to efficient shopping and socializing." From the point of view of many technology companies, however, abandoning the right to privacy is only realistic. As Sun Microsystems CEO Scott McNealy remarked in 1999, "You have no privacy. Get over it" (Carr 2010:W2).

Apply the Theory

1. How would you react if you discovered that the government was monitoring your use of the mass media?
2. If your safety were in jeopardy, would you be willing to sacrifice your privacy?
3. Which do you consider the greatest threat to society: government censorship, cybercrime, or Internet surveillance? Explain.

CHAPTER RESOURCES

Summary

::: **10.1** What Are the Theoretical Perspectives on the Mass Media?

- The **mass media** are print and electronic instruments of communication that carry messages to often-widespread audiences. They pervade all social institutions, from entertainment to education to politics.
- From the functionalist perspective, the media entertain, socialize, enforce social norms, confer status, and promote consumption. They can be dysfunctional to the extent that they desensitize us to serious events and issues (the **narcotizing dysfunction**).
- Conflict theorists think the media reflect and even deepen the divisions in society through **gatekeeping**, or control over which material reaches the public; **media monitoring**, the covert observation of people's media usage and choices; imposed **hegemony**, which is the process of creating acceptance of the views of the ruling class so that they are seen as "normal" by the exploited classes; and support of dominant ideology, which defines reality and overwhelms local cultures.
- Some feminist theorists point out that media images of the sexes communicate unrealistic, stereotypical, limiting, and sometimes violent perceptions of women.
- Interactionists examine the media on the micro level to see how they shape day-to-day social behaviour. Interactionists have studied shared TV viewing and staged public appearances intended to convey self-serving definitions of reality.

::: **10.2** Who Are the Media's Audiences?

- The mass media require the presence of an audience—whether it is small and well defined or large and amorphous. With the ever-increasing number of media outlets come more and more targeting of a **segmented audience** (or a **niche audience**).
- Social researchers have studied the role of **opinion leader** in influencing audiences.

::: **10.3** What Does the Media Industry Look Like?

- The media industry is becoming more and more concentrated, creating media conglomerates. This concentration raises concerns about how innovative and independent the media can be. In some countries, governments own and control the media.
- The Internet is the one significant exception to the trend toward centralization, allowing millions of people to produce their own media content.
- The media have a global reach thanks to new communications technologies, especially the Internet. Some people are concerned that the media's global reach will spread unhealthy influences to other cultures. Also of concern is the **digital divide** between developing and developed countries.

Critical Thinking Questions

1. What kind of audience is targeted by the producers of televised professional wrestling? By the creators of an animated film? By a rap group? What factors determine who makes up a particular audience?

2. Trace the production process for a new television situation comedy (sitcom). Who do you imagine are the gatekeepers in the process?

3. Use the functionalist, conflict, feminist, and interactionist perspectives to assess the effects of global TV programming on developing countries.

THINKING ABOUT MOVIES

Pirate Radio

In the 1960s, an independent English radio station broadcasts from international waters, threatening the British Broadcasting Corporation's monopoly.

Talk to Me

In Washington, D.C., an R&B station struggles to keep its radio audience during the massive social change that followed the civil rights movement.

We Live in Public

This documentary traces the rise and fall of an Internet entrepreneur.

connect   LEARNSMART   SMARTBOOK

For more information on the resources available from McGraw-Hill Ryerson, go to **www.mcgrawhill.ca/he/solutions**.

221

inside

Occupy Movement Protesters

Deviance and Social Control

" Gang Violence being Fuelled by Prohibition on Pot: Report
Vancouver Sun October 27, 2011

A new coalition of B.C. health, academic, and law enforcement experts is calling for the legalization and regulation of marijuana, saying existing laws only drive the billion-dollar industry underground and fuel gang violence.

Stop the Violence B.C., which consists of dozens of police officials, doctors, university professors, legal experts, and more, released a report today titled Breaking the Silence, which aims to show that marijuana prohibition, while well intentioned, has been ineffective and, in fact, has adverse effects.

'There's a huge problem that nobody, particularly political and other leaders in B.C., is talking about, and that is the link between cannabis prohibition and organized crime,' said Dr. Evan Wood, a coalition member and director of urban health research initiative at the B.C. Centre for Excellence in HIV/AIDS.

'The gang warfare that's playing out on our streets is a natural consequence of cannabis prohibition.'

The report points out marijuana is locally produced in large quantities, unlike cocaine or heroin, which must be imported. The report also cites a 2009 Health Canada survey that estimated there to be 'well over 430 000 cannabis users' in B.C., while the number of heroin and cocaine users is only a fraction of the size. This accounts for the high-profit margins for marijuana in B.C., and explains why prohibition 'has made such a key financial contribution to the growth of organized crime in this province,' the report notes.

An Angus Reid poll commissioned by the coalition found: 87 percent of British Columbians polled attribute gang violence to battles over profits from the illegal marijuana trade; 69 percent think arresting marijuana producers and sellers is ineffective and B.C. would be better off taxing and regulating marijuana; 75 percent reject the notion that possession of marijuana should lead to a criminal record; only 12 percent support keeping current marijuana laws in place.

The online poll, conducted September 7 to 9, surveyed 800 B.C. adults who are Angus Reid Forum panellists.

While legalizing and promoting the use of marijuana also would lead to social harms, legalizing and handling it under a strict regulatory framework would reduce them significantly, the report found.

Jodie Emery, outspoken marijuana advocate and wife of Canada's jailed 'Prince of Pot' Marc Emery, has long called for legalization to reduce social harm. 'When you consider at least half of all Canadians want it to be legal, but only about 10 percent use marijuana regularly, [you see] it's not that all the pot smokers want it legal so they can get high,' Emery said. 'It's a huge number of people who say their money is being wasted, police resources are being wasted, and people's lives are being destroyed.' **"**

(CanWest Mediaworks Publications. 2011. "Gang Violence Being Fuelled by Prohibition on Pot: Report." Andrea Woo. October 27. © CanWest MediaWorks Publications Inc.)

This article by Andrea Woo in the *Vancouver Sun* discusses the views of health, academic, and law enforcement experts in British Columbia who have formed the group "Stop the Violence B.C." The group takes the position that the prohibition of the use of marijuana has resulted in violence on the streets of the province—violence related to gang warfare. The report found that the social harms caused by marijuana could be reduced significantly if the substance was legalized and handled under a regulatory framework (CanWest Mediaworks Publications 2011).

What behaviours should be considered deviant may not always be obvious. Take the issue of gang violence. On the one hand, we can view it as *deviant*, violating the criminal laws of the country; but on the other hand, it can be seen as *conforming* to local "laws" of the various gang cultures. In Canada, people are socialized to have mixed feelings about both conforming and non-conforming behaviour. The term *conformity* can conjure up images of mindless imitation of a peer group—whether a group of teenagers with pierced tongues or a group of business executives dressed in similar grey suits. Yet, the same term can also suggest that an individual is cooperative or a "team player." What about those who do not conform? They may be respected as individualists, leaders, or creative thinkers who break new ground. Or they may be labelled as "troublemakers" and "weirdos" (Aronson 1999).

In this chapter, we examine the relationships among conformity, deviance, and social control. We begin by distinguishing between conformity and obedience and then look at two experiments regarding conforming behaviour and obedience to authority. The informal and formal mechanisms used by societies to encourage conformity and discourage deviance are analyzed. We give particular attention to the legal order and how it reflects underlying social values.

In the second part of the chapter, we focus on theoretical explanations for deviance, including the functionalist approach employed by Émile Durkheim and Robert Merton; the interactionist-based theories; labelling theory, which draws on both the interactionist and the conflict perspectives; conflict theory; and feminist theories.

In the third part of the chapter, we examine crime, a specific type of deviant behaviour. As a form of deviance subject to official, written norms, crime has been a special concern of policymakers and the public in general. We will look at various types of crime found in Canada, the ways crime is measured, and international crime rates. Finally, in the social policy section, we consider the use of illicit drugs in Canada.

What Is Social Control?

As we saw in Chapter 3, each culture, subculture, and group has distinctive norms governing what it deems appropriate behaviour. Laws, dress codes, bylaws of organizations, course requirements, and rules of sports and games all express social norms.

How does a society bring about acceptance of basic norms? The term **social control** refers to the techniques and strategies for preventing deviant human behaviour in any society. Social control occurs at all levels of society. In the family, we are socialized to obey our parents simply because they are our parents. Peer groups introduce us to informal norms, such as dress codes, that govern the behaviour of members. Universities establish standards they expect of their students. In bureaucratic organizations, workers encounter a formal system of rules and regulations. Finally, the government of every society legislates and enforces social norms.

Most of us respect and accept basic social norms and assume that others will do the same. Even without thinking, we obey the instructions of police officers, follow the day-to-day rules at our jobs, and move to the rear of elevators when people enter. Such behaviour reflects an effective process of socialization to the dominant standards of a culture. At the same time, we are well aware that individuals, groups, and institutions *expect* us to act "properly." If we fail to do so, we may face punishment through informal *sanctions*, such as fear and ridicule, or formal sanctions, such as jail sentences or fines. The impediment to effective social control is that people often receive competing messages about how to behave. Although the state or government may clearly define acceptable behaviour, friends or fellow employees may encourage quite different behaviour patterns. For example, consider a behaviour that is officially discouraged but nevertheless engaged in by some young people: living on the streets. As of 2007, it was estimated that approximately 300 000 people in Canada were homeless (Laird 2007).

Functionalists contend that people must respect social norms if any group or society is to survive. In their view, societies literally could not function if massive numbers of people defied standards of appropriate conduct. By contrast, conflict theorists maintain that "successful functioning" of a society will consistently benefit the powerful and work to the disadvantage of other groups. They point out, for example, that widespread resistance to social norms was necessary to overturn the institution of slavery.

Conformity and Obedience

Techniques for social control operate on both the group level and the societal level. People whom we regard as our peers or as our equals influence us to act in particular ways; the same is true of people who hold authority over us or occupy awe-inspiring positions. Stanley Milgram made a useful distinction between these two important levels of social control (1975).

Milgram defined **conformity** as going along with peers—individuals of our own status, who have no special right to direct our behaviour. By contrast, **obedience** is defined as compliance with higher authorities in a hierarchical structure. Thus, a recruit entering military service will typically conform to the habits and language of other recruits and will obey the orders of superior officers. Students will conform to the drinking behaviour of their peers and will obey the requests of campus security officers.

The Asch conformity experiments (which became known as the "Asch Paradigm"), conducted by Solomon Asch in the 1950s, demonstrated the power of conformity in groups. In these experiments (1951, 1955), Asch found that students were likely to conform to other students' answers, even though they knew they were incorrect. In other words, the students conformed by providing answers that were—to themselves—obviously wrong, thus allowing group pressure to distort their judgment.

Conformity to Prejudice We often think of conformity in terms of rather harmless situations, such as members of an expensive health club who all work out in elaborate and costly sportswear. But researchers have found that people may conform to the attitudes and behaviour of their peers even when such conformity means expressing intolerance toward others.

Fletcher Blanchard, Teri Lilly, and Leigh Ann Vaughn (1991) conducted an experiment at a U.S. university and found that statements people overhear others make influence their own expressions of opinion on the issue of racism. A student employed by the researchers approached 72 white students as each was walking across the campus to get responses for an opinion poll she said she was conducting for a class. At the same time, a second white student—actually another working with the researchers—was stopped and asked to participate in the survey. Both students were then asked how their university should respond to anonymous racist notes that were sent to four black students. The student employed by the

In Finland (left), a young man relaxes in his prison cell, which resembles a college dorm room. In the United States (right), prisoners at a super-maximum-security prison watch television in cages that prevent them from making physical contact with guards or other prisoners. The rate of imprisonment in Finland is less than one-half that of England and one-fourth that of the United States.

researchers always answered first. In some cases, she condemned the notes; in others, she justified them.

Blanchard and his colleagues (1991:102–103) conclude that "hearing at least one other person express strongly anti-racist opinions produced dramatically more strongly anti-racist public reactions to racism than hearing others express equivocal opinions or opinions more accepting of racism." A second experiment demonstrated that when the student working on behalf of the researchers expressed sentiments justifying racism, subjects were much *less* likely to express anti-racist opinions than were those who heard no one else offer opinions. In these experiments, social control (through the process of conformity) influenced people's attitudes, or at least the expression of those attitudes. In the next section, we will see that social control (through the process of obedience) can alter people's behaviour.

Obedience to Authority

If ordered to do so, would you comply with an experimenter's instruction to give people increasingly painful electric shocks? Most people would say no; yet, the research of social psychologist Stanley Milgram (1963, 1975) suggests that most of us *will* obey such orders. In Milgram's words, "Behaviour that is unthinkable in an individual . . . acting on his own may be executed without hesitation when carried out under orders" (1975:xi).

Milgram placed advertisements in New Haven, Connecticut, newspapers to recruit subjects for what was announced as a learning experiment at Yale University. Participants included postal clerks, engineers, high school teachers, and labourers. They were told that the purpose of the research was to investigate the effects of punishment on learning. The experimenter, dressed in a grey technician's coat, explained that in each testing, one subject would be randomly selected as the "learner" while another would function as the "teacher." However, this lottery was rigged so that the "real" subject would always be the teacher while an associate of Milgram's served as the learner.

At this point, the learner's hand was strapped to an electric apparatus. The teacher was taken to an electronic "shock generator" with 30 lever switches. Each switch was labelled with graduated voltage designations from 15 to 450 volts. Before beginning the experiment, subjects were given sample shocks of 45 volts to convince them of the authenticity of the experiment.

The experimenter instructed the teacher to apply shocks of increasing voltage each time the learner gave an incorrect answer on a memory test. Teachers were told that "although the shocks can be extremely painful, they cause no permanent tissue damage." In reality, the learner did not receive any shocks.

The learner deliberately gave incorrect answers and acted out a prearranged script. For example, at 150 volts, the learner would cry out, "Experimenter, get me out of here! I won't be in the experiment any more!" At 270 volts, the learner would scream in agony. When the shock reached 350 volts, the learner would fall silent. If the teacher wanted to stop the experiment, the experimenter would insist that the teacher continue, using such statements as "The experiment requires that you continue" and "You have no other choice; you *must* go on" (Milgram 1975:19–23).

The results of this unusual experiment stunned and dismayed Milgram and other social scientists. A sample of psychiatrists had predicted that virtually all subjects would refuse to shock innocent victims. In their view, only a "pathological fringe" of less than 2 percent of the population would continue administering shocks up to the maximum level. Yet almost two-thirds of participants fell into the category of "obedient subjects."

Why did these subjects obey? Why were they willing to inflict seemingly painful shocks on innocent victims who had never done them any harm? There is no evidence that these subjects were unusually sadistic; few seemed to enjoy administering the shocks. Instead, in Milgram's view, the key to obedience was the experimenter's social role as a "scientist" and "seeker of knowledge."

Milgram pointed out that in the modern industrial world, we are accustomed to submitting to impersonal authority figures whose status is indicated by a title (professor, lieutenant, doctor) or by a uniform (the technician's coat). The authority is viewed as larger and more important than the individual; consequently, the obedient individual shifts responsibility for

In one of Stanley Milgram's experiments, a supposed victim received an electric shock when his hand rested on a shock plate. At the 150-volt level, the victim would demand to be released and would refuse to place his hand on the shock plate. The experimenter would then order the actual subject to force the victim's hand onto the plate, as shown in the photo. Though 40 percent of the true subjects stopped complying with Milgram at this point, 60 percent did force the victim's hand onto the shock plate, despite the victim's pretended agony.

his or her behaviour to the authority figure. Milgram's subjects frequently stated, "If it were up to me, I would not have administered shocks." They saw themselves as merely doing their duty (Milgram 1975).

From an interactionist perspective, one important aspect of Milgram's findings is the fact that subjects in follow-up studies were less likely to inflict the supposed shocks as they were moved physically closer to their victims. Moreover, interactionists emphasize the effect of incrementally administering additional dosages of 15 volts. In effect, the experimenter negotiated with the teacher and convinced the teacher to continue inflicting higher levels of punishment. It is doubtful that anywhere near the two-thirds rate of obedience would have been reached had the experimenter told the teachers to administer 450 volts immediately to the learners (Allen 1978; Katovich 1987).

Milgram launched his experimental study of obedience to better understand the involvement of Germans in the annihilation of 6 million Jews and millions of other people during World War II. In an interview conducted long after the publication of his study, Milgram suggested that "if a system of death camps were set up in the United States of the sort we had seen in Nazi Germany, one would be able to find sufficient personnel for those camps in any medium-sized American town" (CBS News 1979:7–8).

Informal and Formal Social Control

The sanctions used to encourage conformity and obedience— and to discourage violation of social norms—are carried out through informal and formal social control. As the term implies, people use **informal social control** casually to enforce norms. Examples of informal social control include smiles, laughter, a raised eyebrow, and ridicule.

In Canada, the United States, and many other cultures, one common and yet controversial example of informal social control is parental use of corporal punishment. Adults often view spanking, slapping, or kicking children as a proper and necessary means of maintaining authority. Child development specialists counter that corporal punishment is inappropriate because it teaches children to solve problems through violence. They warn that slapping and spanking can escalate into more serious forms of abuse. Yet, despite the fact that pediatric experts now believe that physical forms of discipline are undesirable and encourage their patients to use non-physical means of discipline (Tidmarsh 2000), approximately 70 percent of Canadian parents have used physical punishment (Durrant and Rose-Krasnor 1995). In 1999, the Canadian Foundation for Youth and the Law challenged the constitutionality of section 43 of the Criminal Code of Canada, which allows parents to use reasonable force in disciplining their children. Section 43 was upheld.

Sometimes, informal methods of social control are not adequate to enforce conforming or obedient behaviour. In those cases, **formal social control** is carried out by authorized agents, such as police officers, physicians, school administrators, employers, military officers, and managers of movie theatres. It can serve as a last resort when socialization and informal sanctions do not bring about desired behaviour. In Canada, of those who end up in a penitentiary or prison, a disproportionately high number are Aboriginal peoples, who account for 23 percent of federal correctional institutions' populations while making up only 4 percent of Canada's population (Ljunggren 2013).

Societies vary in deciding which behaviours will be subjected to formal social control and how severe the sanctions will be. In Singapore, chewing gum is prohibited, feeding birds can lead to fines of up to US$640, and there is even a US$95 fine for failing to flush the toilet (see Box 11-1). Singapore deals with serious crimes especially severely. The death penalty is mandatory for murder, drug trafficking, and crimes committed with firearms (recently, a Canadian arrested for drug trafficking in Singapore came very close to being executed). Japan has created a special prison for reckless drivers. While some are imprisoned for vehicular homicide, others serve prison time for drunken driving and fleeing the scene of an accident (Elliott 1994).

Another controversial example of formal social control is the use of surveillance techniques. In 1992, police in Great Britain began to install closed-circuit television systems on "high streets" (the primary shopping and business areas of local communities) in an effort to reduce street crime. Within two years, 300 British towns had installed or made plans to install such surveillance cameras, and the use of public surveillance had spread to North America. Supporters of surveillance believe that it makes the public feel more secure. Moreover, it can be cheaper to install and maintain cameras than to put more police officers on street patrol. For critics, however, the use of surveillance cameras brings to mind the

sociology in the global community

11-1 Singapore: A Nation of Campaigns

"Males with Long Hair Will Be Attended to Last!" "Throwing Litter from Apartments Can Kill!" "No Spitting!" These are some of the posters sponsored by the Singapore government in its effort to enforce social norms in this small nation of some 4 million people living in a totally urbanized area in Southeast Asia.

Although Singapore is governed by a democratically elected Parliament, one party has dominated the government since the country's independence in 1965. And it has not hesitated to use its authority to launch a number of campaigns to shape the social behaviour of its citizens. In most cases, these campaigns are directed against "disagreeable" behaviour: littering, spitting, chewing gum, failing to flush public toilets, teenage smoking, and the like. Courtesy is a major concern, with elaborate "Courtesy Month" celebrations scheduled to both entertain and educate the populace.

Some campaigns take on serious issues and are backed by legislation. For example, in the 1970s, Singapore's government asked its citizens to "Please Stop at Two" in family planning; tax and schooling benefits rewarded those who complied. However, this campaign was so successful that in the 1980s, the government began a "Have Three or More If You Can Afford To" campaign. In 2012, with an increasing number of young Singapore citizens remaining single and childless, the government rebranded Singapore's National Day as "National Night," explicitly urging people to go home and "make babies." Government-sponsored programs such as speed dating have been established to help younger people find a mate; government officials act as "dating advisors" (Allemang 2012).

In another attempt at social control, the government launched a "Speak Mandarin" campaign to encourage the multi-ethnic, multilingual population to accept Mandarin as the dialect of choice.

For the most part, Singaporeans cheerfully accept their government's admonitions and encouragement. They see the results of being clean and courteous: Singapore is a better place to live. Corporations also go along with the government and even help to sponsor some of the campaigns. As one corporate sponsor noted, "If [people] see Singapore as a clean country, they will view companies here as clean." Political scientist Michael Haas refers to this compliance as "the Singapore puzzle": citizens of Singapore accept strict social control dictates in exchange for continuing prosperity and technological leadership in the world.

Apply the Theory

1. How would a functionalist thinker view an administration-sponsored campaign at your educational institution against drinking? What would be some latent functions of such a campaign?
2. According to conflict thinkers, why would these social-control campaigns work in Singapore?

Sources: Allemang 2012; Dorai 1998; Haas 1999; Haub and Cornelius 2000; Instituto del Tercer Mundo 1999.

::: use your sociological *imagination* :::

If you were a participant in Milgram's research on conformity, how far do you think you would go in carrying out orders? Do you see any ethical problem with the experimenter's manipulation of the control subjects?

grim, futuristic world presented by Britain's own George Orwell in his dystopian novel *1984* (1949). In the world of *1984,* an all-seeing "Big Brother" represents an authoritarian government that watches people's every move and takes immediate action against anyone who questions the oppressive regime (Halbfinger 1998; Uttley 1993).

Law and Society

Some norms are so important to a society they are formalized into laws controlling people's behaviour. *Law* may be defined as governmental social control (Black 1995). Some laws, such as the prohibition against murder, are directed at all members of society. Others, such as fishing and hunting regulations, primarily affect particular categories of people. Still others govern the behaviour of social institutions (corporate law and laws regarding the taxing of non-profit enterprises).

Sociologists have become increasingly interested in the creation of laws as a social process. Laws are created in response to perceived needs for formal social control. Sociologists have sought to explain how and why such perceptions arise. In their view, law is not merely a static body of rules handed down from generation to generation. Rather, it reflects continually changing standards of what is right and wrong, of how violations are to be determined, and of what sanctions are to be applied.

Sociologists representing varying theoretical perspectives agree that the legal order reflects underlying social values. Therefore, the creation of criminal law can be a most controversial matter. Should it be against the law to employ illegal immigrants in a factory (see Chapter 8), to have an abortion (see Chapter 9), or to smoke on a sidewalk? Such issues have been bitterly debated because they require a choice among competing values. Not surprisingly, laws that are unpopular—such as the Canadian law requiring the registration of firearms—become difficult to enforce owing to lack of consensus supporting the norms.

Socialization is actually the primary source of conforming and obedient behaviour, including obedience to law. Generally, it is not external pressure from a peer group or authority figure that makes us go along with social norms. Rather, we have internalized such norms as valid and desirable and are committed to observing them. In a profound sense, we want to see ourselves (and to be seen) as loyal, cooperative,

In Singapore, a custodian removes a bit of litter from an otherwise spotless floor. Strict social controls prevail in the city-state, where the careless disposal of a cigarette butt or candy wrapper carries a $200 fine.

of appearance and body image place a huge strain on people—especially on women and girls—based on how they look. Author Naomi Wolf has used the term *the beauty myth* to refer to an exaggerated ideal of beauty, beyond the reach of all but a few females, which has unfortunate consequences (1991). In order to shed their "deviant" image and conform to (unrealistic) societal norms, many women and girls become consumed with adjusting their appearances. For example, in a *People* magazine "health" feature, a young actress stated that she would always know it was time to eat when she passed out on the set. When females carry adherence to the beauty myth to an extreme, they may develop eating disorders or undertake costly and unnecessary cosmetic surgery procedures. Yet, what is deviant in our culture may be celebrated in another. In Nigeria, for example, being fat is a mark of beauty. Part of the coming-of-age ritual calls for young girls to spend months in a "fattening room." Among Nigerians, being thin at this point in the life course is deviant (Simmons 1998).

Deviance involves the violation of group norms, which may or may not be formalized into law. It is a comprehensive concept that includes not only criminal behaviour but also many actions not subject to prosecution. The public official who takes a bribe has defied social norms, but so has the high school student who refuses to sit in an assigned seat or cuts class. Of course, deviation from norms is not

responsible, and respectful of others. In Canada and other societies around the world, people are socialized both to want to belong and to fear being viewed as different or deviant.

Control theory suggests that our connection to members of society leads us to systematically conform to society's norms. According to sociologist Travis Hirschi and other control theorists, we are bonded to our family members, friends, and peers in a way that leads us to follow the mores and folkways of our society while giving little conscious thought to whether we will be sanctioned if we fail to conform (1969). Socialization develops our self-control so well that we don't need further pressure to obey social norms. Although control theory does not effectively explain the rationale for every conforming act, it nevertheless reminds us that although the media may focus on crime and disorder, most members of nearly all societies conform to and obey basic norms (Gottfredson and Hirschi 1990; Hirschi 1969).

11.2 What Is Deviance?

Defining Deviance

For sociologists, the term deviance does not mean perversion or depravity. **Deviance** is behaviour that violates the standards of conduct or expectations of a group or society (Wickman 1991:85). In Canada, alcoholics, compulsive gamblers, and people with mental illnesses would all be classified as deviants. Being late for class is categorized as a deviant act; the same is true of dressing too casually for a formal wedding. On the basis of the sociological definition, deviance is universal, as we are all deviant from time to time. Each of us violates common social norms in certain situations.

Is being overweight an example of deviance? In North America and many other cultures, unrealistic standards

Because deviance is socially constructed, it is subject to different social interpretations over time and across cultures. Clothing and behaviour that appear deviant to some may be acceptable—even admired—in other cultures. Even within the same culture, not everyone may share the same idea of proper behaviour. Here, Muslim women swim at the beach in the Middle East.

always negative, let alone criminal. A member of an exclusive social club who speaks out against its traditional policy of excluding women and Jews from admittance is deviating from the club's norms. So is a police officer who becomes a whistle-blower on corruption or brutality within the department.

Standards of deviance vary from one group (or subculture) to another. In Canada, it is generally considered acceptable to sing along at a folk or rock concert, but not at the opera. Just as deviance is defined by place, so, too, is it relative to time. For instance, drinking alcohol at 6:00 P.M. is a common practice in our society, but engaging in the same behaviour at breakfast is viewed as a deviant act and as symptomatic of a drinking problem.

From a sociological perspective, deviance is viewed according to normative standards. It is subject to social definitions within a particular society; in most instances, those individuals and groups with the greatest status and power define what is acceptable and what is deviant. For example, despite serious medical warnings about the dangers of tobacco as far back as 30 years ago, cigarette smoking continued to be accepted—in good part because of the power of tobacco farmers and cigarette manufacturers. It was only after a long campaign led by public health and anti-cancer activists that cigarette smoking became more of a deviant activity. Today, many local laws limit where people can smoke.

Although deviance can include relatively minor day-to-day decisions about our personal behaviour, in some cases, it can become part of a person's identity. This process is called *stigmatization*, as we will now see.

Deviance and Social Stigma

There are many ways a person can acquire a deviant identity. Because of physical or behavioural characteristics, some people are unwillingly cast in negative social roles. Once they have been assigned a deviant role, they have trouble presenting a positive image to others and may even experience lowered self-esteem. Whole groups of people—for instance, "short people" or "redheads"—may be labelled in this way (Heckert and Best 1997). The interactionist Erving Goffman (see Chapters 1 and 4) introduced the term **stigma** to sociological theory to describe the labels society uses to devalue members of certain social groups (Goffman 1963a).

Prevailing expectations about beauty and body shape may prevent people who are regarded as ugly or obese from advancing as rapidly as their abilities permit. Both obese and anorexic people are assumed to be weak in character, slaves to their appetites or to media images. Because they do not conform to the beauty myth, they may be viewed as "disfigured" or "strange" in appearance, bearers of what Goffman calls a "spoiled identity." However, what constitutes disfigurement is a matter of interpretation. Of the more than 1 million cosmetic procedures done every year in Canada and the United States, many are performed on women who would be objectively defined as having a normal appearance. And although feminist sociologists have accurately noted that the beauty myth makes many women feel uncomfortable with themselves, many men, too, lack confidence in their appearance. The number of males who choose to undergo cosmetic

Deviant or normal? Television personality and recording artist Heidi Montag shocked fans in 2010 by revealing that she had undergone 10 plastic surgery procedures in a single day. Montag had already undergone breast augmentation, collagen lip injections, and rhinoplasty. Would you consider her behaviour deviant?

procedures has risen sharply in recent years; in 2010, men accounted for 13 percent of such surgeries, up 8 percentage points from 2000 (American Society of Plastic Surgeons 2007b; 2011).

The American Board of Plastic Surgery, made up of doctors from both Canada and the United States, tracks the statistics on the number of cosmetic surgeries performed in both countries (see Table 11-1). Between 1998 and 2010, the total number has almost doubled.

Often, people are stigmatized for deviant behaviours they may no longer engage in. The labels "compulsive gambler," "ex-convict," "recovering alcoholic," and "ex–mental patient" can stick with a person for life. Goffman draws a useful distinction between a prestige symbol that draws attention to a positive aspect of a person's identity, such as a wedding band or a badge, and a stigma symbol that discredits or debases a person's identity, such as a conviction for child molestation (1963a). Although stigma symbols may not always be obvious, they can become a matter of public knowledge. Some communities, for instance, publish the names and addresses, and in some instances even the pictures, of convicted sex offenders on the Web.

A person need not be guilty of a crime to be stigmatized. Homeless people often have trouble getting a job because employers are wary of applicants who cannot give a home address. Moreover, hiding homelessness is difficult, since

table 11-1 Selected Cosmetic Procedures in Canada and the United States

	1998	2004	2006	2010
Liposuction	172 079	324 891	302 789	203 106
Breast augmentation	132 378	264 041	329 396	212 500
Facelift	70 947	114 279	104 055	112 955
Nose reshaping	55 953	305 475	307 258	252 261
Tummy tuck	46 597	107 019	146 240	116 352
Breast lift	31 525	75 805	103 788	89 931
Male breast reduction	9 023	13 963	19 881	18 280
Buttock lift	1 246	3 496	3 710	3 289

Sources: Adapted from the American Society of Plastic Surgeons 2002, 2005, 2007a, 2011.

agencies generally use the telephone to contact applicants about job openings. If a homeless person has access to a telephone at a shelter, the staff generally answer the phone by announcing the name of the institution—a sure way to discourage prospective employers.

Although some types of deviance will stigmatize a person, other types do not carry a significant penalty. Some good examples of socially tolerated forms of deviance can be found in the world of high technology.

Deviance and Technology Technological innovations can redefine social interactions and the standards of behaviour related to them. Since the Internet was first made available to the general public, norms or regulations governing its use have lagged behind the technology. Because online activity offers a high degree of anonymity, uncivil behaviour—posting damaging images or messages—has quickly become common. Most notable are the cases of online harassment/cyberbullying that culminated in the suicides of two teenage girls from opposite sides of the country—Rehtaeh Parsons of Nova Scotia in 2013 and Amanda Todd of British Columbia in 2012. After the death of Rehtaeh Parsons, federal and provincial government officials acknowledged that provisions in the Criminal Code of Canada have not kept up with how quickly technology is changing and pledged to bring forward measures to address these deficiencies. The prime minister stated that "something that is a crime is a crime if it happens on the Internet as well" (CBC 2013).

The sheer length of time people spend using the Internet may soon be an indication of deviance. Some psychiatrists and psychologists are now deciding whether or not Internet addiction may eventually be labelled a new disorder and, thus, a new form of deviant behaviour. Dr. Kimberly Young of the University of Pittsburgh has studied Internet addiction in the United States, placing it in the same category as pathological gambling and compulsive shopping. She found addicted users

spent an average of 38 hours per week online, compared with 8 hours per week for non-addicts (Dalfen 2000). In 2008 Canadians spent an average of roughly 12.5 hours per week on online activities (CRTC 2008).

Other uses of technology are criminal, though not all participants see it that way. The pirating of software, motion pictures, and CDs has become a big business. At conventions and swap meets, pirated copies of movies and CDs are sold openly. Some of the products are obviously counterfeit, but many come in sophisticated packaging, complete with warranty cards. When vendors are willing to talk, they say they merely want to be compensated for their time and the cost of materials, or that the software they have copied is in the public domain.

Though most of these black market activities are clearly illegal, many consumers and small-time pirates are proud of their behaviour. They may even think themselves smart for figuring out a way to avoid the "unfair" prices charged by "big corporations." Few people see the pirating of a new software program or a first-run movie as a threat to the public good, as they would embezzlements from a bank. Similarly, most businesspeople who "borrow" software from another department, even though they lack a site licence, do not think they are doing anything wrong. No social stigma attaches to their illegal behaviour.

Deviance, then, is a complex concept. Sometimes, it is trivial; sometimes, profoundly harmful. Sometimes, it is accepted by society and sometimes soundly rejected. What accounts for deviant behaviour and people's reaction to it? In the next section, we will examine four theoretical explanations for deviance.

Explaining Deviance

Why do people violate social norms? We have seen that deviant acts are subject to both informal and formal sanctions of social control. The non-conforming or disobedient person may face disapproval, loss of friends, fines, or even imprisonment. Why, then, does deviance occur?

Early explanations for deviance identified supernatural causes or genetic factors (such as "bad blood" or evolutionary throwbacks to primitive ancestors). By the 1800s, there were substantial research efforts to identify biological factors that lead to deviance and especially to criminal activity. Although such research was discredited in the twentieth century, contemporary studies, primarily by biochemists, have sought to isolate genetic factors leading to a likelihood of certain personality traits. Although criminality (much less deviance) is hardly a personality characteristic, researchers have focused on traits that might lead to crime, such as aggression. Of course, aggression can also lead to success in the corporate world, professional sports, or other areas of life.

The contemporary study of possible biological roots of criminality is but one aspect of the larger sociobiology debate. In general, sociologists reject any emphasis on genetic roots of crime and deviance. The limitations of current knowledge, the possibility of reinforcing racist and sexist assumptions, and the disturbing implications for rehabilitation of criminals have led sociologists to largely draw on other approaches to explain deviance (Sagarin and Sanchez 1988).

Functionalist Perspective

According to functionalists, deviance is a common part of human existence, with positive (as well as negative) consequences for social stability. Deviance helps to define the limits of proper behaviour. Children who see one parent scold the other for belching at the dinner table learn about approved conduct. The same is true of the driver who receives a speeding ticket, the department store cashier who is fired for yelling at a customer, and the university student who is penalized for handing in essays weeks overdue.

Durkheim's Legacy Émile Durkheim investigated a range of social facts that illuminated different forms of social solidarity within societies (1964, original edition 1895). In Durkheim's view, the punishments established within a culture (including both formal and informal mechanisms of social control) help to define acceptable behaviour and, thus, contribute to stability. If improper acts were not committed and then sanctioned, people might stretch their standards of what constitutes appropriate conduct.

Kai Erikson illustrated this boundary-maintenance function of deviance in his study of the Puritans of seventeenth-century New England (1966). By today's standards, the Puritans placed tremendous emphasis on conventional morals. Their persecution of Quakers and execution of women as witches represented continuing attempts to define and redefine the boundaries of their community. In effect, their changing social norms created "crime waves," as people whose behaviour was previously acceptable suddenly faced punishment for being deviant (Abrahamson 1978; Davis 1975).

Durkheim also introduced the term *anomie* into sociological literature (1951, original edition 1897). Anomie is a state of normlessness that typically occurs during a period of profound social change and disorder, such as during an economic collapse. People may become more aggressive or depressed, and this may result in higher rates of violent crime and suicide. Since there is much less agreement on what constitutes proper behaviour during times of revolution, sudden prosperity, or economic depression, conformity and obedience become less significant as social forces. It also becomes much more difficult to state exactly what constitutes deviance.

Merton's Theory of Deviance

What do a mugger and a teacher have in common? Each is "working" to obtain money that can then be exchanged for desired goods. As this example illustrates, behaviour that violates accepted norms (such as mugging) may be performed with the same basic objectives in mind as those of people who pursue more conventional lifestyles.

Using this analysis, sociologist Robert Merton adapted Durkheim's notion of anomie to explain why people accept or reject the goals of a society, the socially approved means of fulfilling their aspirations, or both (1968). Merton maintained that one important cultural goal in capitalist societies is success, measured largely in terms of money. In addition to providing this goal for people, our society offers specific instructions on how to pursue success—go to school, work hard, do not quit, take advantage of opportunities, and so forth.

What happens to individuals in a society with a heavy emphasis on wealth as a basic symbol of success? Merton reasoned that people adapt in certain ways, either by conforming to or by deviating from such cultural expectations. Consequently, he developed the **anomie theory of deviance**, which posits five basic forms of adaptation (see Table 11-2).

Conformity to social norms, the most common adaptation in Merton's typology, is the opposite of deviance. It involves acceptance of both the overall societal goal ("become affluent") and the approved means ("work hard"). In Merton's view, there must be some consensus regarding accepted cultural goals and legitimate means for attaining them. Without such consensus, societies could exist only as collectives of people—rather than as unified cultures—and might function in continual chaos.

Of course, in a society such as ours, conformity is not universal. For example, the means for realizing objectives are not equally distributed. People in the lower social classes often identify with the same goals as those of more powerful and affluent citizens yet lack equal access to high-quality education and training for skilled work. Even within a society, institutionalized means for realizing objectives vary. For example, a Statistics Canada report found that in 1997, access to legalized gambling varied across provinces and territories. Lotteries were legal in all provinces and territories, government casinos were legal in approximately half of the provinces, and VLTs (video lottery terminals) were legal in most provinces (Marshall 1999).

The other four types of behaviour represented in Table 11-2 all involve some departure from conformity. The "innovator" accepts the goals of a society but pursues them through means regarded as improper. For example, Harry King, a professional thief who specialized in safecracking for 40 years,

table **11-2** Modes of Individual Adaptation

Mode	Institutionalized Means (Hard Work)	Societal Goal (Acquisition of Wealth)
Non-deviant		
Conformity	+	+
Deviant		
Innovation	−	+
Ritualism	+	−
Retreatism	−	−
Rebellion	±	±

Note: + indicates acceptance; − indicates rejection; ± indicates replacement with new means and goals.
Source: Merton 1968:1940.

gave a lecture to a sociology class and was asked if he had minded spending time in prison. King responded:

> I didn't exactly like it. But it was one of the necessary things about the life I had chosen. Do you like to come here and teach this class? I bet if the students had their wishes they'd be somewhere else, maybe out stealing, instead of sitting in this dumpy room. But they do it because it gets them something they want. The same with me. If I had to go to prison from time to time, well, that was the price you pay. (Chambliss 1972:x)

Harry King saw his criminal lifestyle as an adaptation to the goal of material success or "getting something you want." Denied the chance to achieve success through socially approved means, some individuals (like King) turn to illegitimate paths of upward mobility.

In Merton's typology, the "ritualist" has abandoned the goal of material success and become compulsively committed to the institutional means. Work becomes simply a way of life rather than a means to the goal of success, as in the case of bureaucratic officials who blindly apply rules and regulations without remembering the larger goals of an organization. Certainly, this would be true of a welfare caseworker who refuses to assist a homeless family because their last apartment was in another district.

The "retreatist," as described by Merton, has basically withdrawn (or "retreated") from both the goals *and* the means of a society. In Canada, drug addicts and residents of skid row are typically portrayed as retreatists. There is also growing concern that adolescents addicted to alcohol will become retreatists at an early age.

The final adaptation identified by Merton reflects people's attempts to create a *new* social structure. The "rebel" feels alienated from dominant means and goals and may seek a dramatically different social order. Members of revolutionary political organizations, such as the Irish Republican Army (IRA) or right-wing militia groups, can be categorized as rebels according to Merton's model.

Merton has stressed that he was not attempting to describe five types of individuals. Rather, he offered a typology to explain the actions that people *usually* take. Thus, leaders of organized crime syndicates will be categorized as innovators, since they do not pursue success through socially approved means. Yet they may also attend church and send their children to medical school. Conversely, "respectable" people may occasionally cheat on their taxes or violate traffic laws. According to Merton, the same person will move back and forth from one mode of adaptation to another, depending on the demands of a particular situation.

Merton's theory, though popular, has had relatively few applications. Little effort has been made to determine to what extent all acts of deviance can be accounted for by his five modes. Moreover, although Merton's theory is useful in examining certain types of behaviour, such as illegal gambling by disadvantaged people functioning as innovators, his formulation fails to explain key differences in rates. Why, for example, do some disadvantaged groups have lower rates of reported crime than others? Why is criminal activity not viewed as a viable alternative by many people in adverse circumstances?

Merton's theory of deviance does not answer such questions easily (Cloward 1959; Hartjen 1978).

Still, Merton has made a key contribution to the sociological understanding of deviance by pointing out that deviants (such as innovators and ritualists) share a great deal with conforming people. The convicted felon may hold many of the same aspirations as people with no criminal background. Therefore, we can understand deviance as socially created behaviour, rather than as the result of momentary pathological impulses.

Interactionist Perspective

The functionalist approach to deviance explains why rule violation continues to exist in societies despite pressures to conform and obey. However, functionalists do not indicate how a given person comes to commit a deviant act or why on some occasions crimes do or do not occur. The emphasis on everyday behaviour that is the focus of the interactionist perspective is reflected in two explanations of crime: cultural transmission and routine activities theory.

Cultural Transmission White teenagers in the suburbs and cities attempt to achieve fame within a subculture of "taggers." These young people "tag" (spray graffiti on) poles, utility boxes, bridges, and highway signs. Although law-enforcement officials prefer to view them as "visual terrorists," the taggers gain respect from their peers by being "up the most" on prominent walls and billboards and by displaying the flashiest styles. Even parents may tolerate or endorse such deviant behaviour by declaring, "At least my kid's not shooting people. He's still alive" (Wooden 1995:124).

These teenagers demonstrate that humans *learn* how to behave in social situations—whether properly or improperly. There is no natural, innate manner in which people interact with one another. These simple ideas are not disputed today, but this was not the case when sociologist Edwin Sutherland (1883–1950) first advanced the argument that an individual undergoes the same basic socialization process whether learning conforming or deviant acts.

Sutherland's ideas have been the dominating force in criminology. He drew on the **cultural transmission** school, which emphasizes that a person learns criminal behaviour through interactions with others. Such learning includes not only techniques of lawbreaking (for example, how to break into a car quickly and quietly) but also the motives, drives, and rationalizations of criminals. We can also use the cultural transmission approach to explain the behaviour of people who engage in habitual—and ultimately life-threatening—use of alcohol or drugs.

Sutherland maintained that through interactions with a primary group and significant others, people acquire definitions of proper and improper behaviour. He used the term **differential association** to describe the process through which exposure to attitudes *favourable* to criminal acts leads to violation of rules. Research suggests that this view of differential association also applies to such non-criminal deviant acts as sitting down during the singing of the national anthem or lying to a friend (Jackson, Tittle, and Burke 1986).

Under cover of darkness, drag racers await the start signal on a deserted street. Sutherland's concepts of differential association and cultural transmission would both apply to the practice of drag racing on city streets.

To what extent will a given person engage in activity regarded as proper or improper? For each individual, it will depend on the frequency, duration, and importance of two types of social interaction experiences—those that endorse deviant behaviour and those that promote acceptance of social norms. People are more likely to engage in norm-defying behaviour if they are part of a group or subculture that stresses deviant values, such as a street gang.

Sutherland offers the example of a boy who is sociable, outgoing, and athletic, and who lives in an area with a high rate of delinquency. The youth is very likely to come into contact with peers who commit acts of vandalism, fail to attend school, and so forth, and may come to adopt such behaviour. However, an introverted boy living in the same neighbourhood may stay away from his peers and avoid delinquency. In another community, an outgoing and athletic boy may join a baseball team or a scout troop because of his interactions with peers. Thus, Sutherland views learning improper behaviour as the result of the types of groups to which a person belongs and the kinds of friendships that person has with others (Sutherland and Cressey 1978).

According to its critics, however, the cultural transmission approach may explain the deviant behaviour of juvenile delinquents or graffiti artists, but it fails to explain the conduct of the first-time impulsive shoplifter or the impoverished person who steals out of necessity.

Routine Activities Theory

Another more recent interactionist explanation considers the requisite conditions for a crime or deviant act to occur: there must be at the same time and in the same place a perpetrator, and a victim and/or an object of property. **Routine activities theory** contends that criminal victimization is increased when motivated offenders and suitable targets converge. It goes without saying that you cannot have car theft without automobiles, but the greater availability of more valuable automobiles to potential thieves

heightens the likelihood that such a crime will occur. Campus and airport parking lots, where vehicles may be left in isolated locations for long periods, represent a new target for crime unknown just a generation ago. Routine activity of this nature can occur even in the home. For example, adults may save money by buying 24-packs of beer, but buying in bulk also allows juveniles to siphon off contents without attracting attention to their "crime." The theory derives its name of *routine* from the fact that the elements of a criminal or deviant act come together in normal, legal, and routine activities.

Advocates of this theory see it as a powerful explanation for the rise in crime during the past 50 years. Routine activity has changed to make crime more likely. Homes left vacant during the day or during long vacations are more accessible as targets of crime. The greater presence of consumer goods that are highly portable, such as video equipment and computers, also makes crime more likely (Cohen and Felson 1979; Felson 1998).

Perhaps what is most compelling about this theory is that it broadens our effort to understand crime and deviance. Rather than focus just on the criminal, routine activities theory also brings into the picture the behaviour of the victim. However, we need to resist the temptation to *expect* the higher victimization of some groups, such as racial and ethnic minorities, much less to consider it their own fault (Akers 1997).

Labelling Theory

The Saints and Roughnecks were two groups of high school males who were continually engaged in excessive drinking, reckless driving, truancy, petty theft, and vandalism. There the similarity ended. None of the Saints was ever arrested, but every Roughneck was frequently in trouble with police and townspeople. Why the disparity in their treatment? On the basis of his observational research in their high school, sociologist William Chambliss concluded that social class played an important role in the varying fortunes of the two groups (1973).

The Saints effectively produced a façade of respectability. They came from "good families," were active in school organizations, expressed the intention of attending university, and received good grades. People generally viewed their delinquent acts as a few isolated cases of "sowing wild oats." By contrast, the Roughnecks had no such aura of respectability. They drove around town in beat-up cars, were generally unsuccessful in school, and were viewed with suspicion no matter what they did.

We can understand such discrepancies by using an approach to deviance known as **labelling theory**. Unlike Sutherland's work, labelling theory does not focus on why some individuals come to commit deviant acts. Instead, it attempts to explain why certain people (such as the Roughnecks) are *viewed* as deviants, delinquents, "bad kids," "losers," and criminals, while others whose behaviour is similar (such

research today

11-2 Binge Drinking on Campus

University and college students die each year of unintentional alcohol-related injuries. A survey of Canadian campuses in 2004 by the Centre for Addiction and Mental Health found that 32 percent of undergraduates drink at a dangerous level (CBC 2008). Similarly, a study, published by the Harvard School of Public Health, found that 44 percent of American postsecondary students indulge in binge drinking (defined as at least five drinks in a row for men and four in a row for women). These numbers represent an increase from 1990s data, despite efforts on many campuses across the nation to educate students about the risks of binge drinking.

The problem is not confined to North America—Britain, Europe, Russia, and South Africa all report regular "drink till you drop" alcoholic consumption among young people. According to a study that compared data from 22 countries, however, college students in the United States have the highest rate of drinking

and driving. Nor does binge drinking begin in college or university. A Canadian Association for Mental Health study found that 19 percent of high school students engaged in drinking at a hazardous level (CBC 2008).

Binge drinking on campus presents a difficult social problem. On the one hand, it can be regarded as *deviant*, violating the standards of conduct expected of those in an academic setting. In fact, Harvard researchers consider binge drinking the most serious public health hazard facing colleges and universities. On the other hand, binge drinking represents *conformity* to the peer culture. Most students seem to take an "everybody does it—no big deal" attitude toward the behaviour.

Some colleges and universities are taking steps to make binge drinking a bit less "normal" by means of *social control*—banning kegs, encouraging liquor retailers not to sell in high volume to students, and expelling students after

a certain number of alcohol-related infractions. In 2008 Queen's University in Kingston, Ontario announced it was cancelling homecoming celebrations for the next two years. This decision came after an unofficial street party, which coincided with the 2008 homecoming celebration, got out of hand resulting in a high number of charges, arrests, and injuries (CBC 2008).

Apply the Theory

1. Why do you think most college or university students regard binge drinking as a normal rather than a deviant behaviour?

2. Which do you think would be more effective in stopping binge drinking on your campus, informal or formal social control?

Sources: Bernstein 2007; CBC 2008; Centers for Disease Control and Prevention 2010; Miller et al. 2007; National Center on Addiction and Substance Abuse at Columbia University 2007; Outside the Classroom 2009; Wechsler et al. 2002, 2004.

---

as the Saints) are not seen in such harsh terms. Reflecting the contribution of interactionist theorists, labelling theory emphasizes how a person comes to be labelled as deviant or to accept that label. Sociologist Howard Becker (1963:9; 1964), who popularized this approach, summed it up with this statement: "Deviant behavior is behavior that people so label." In Box 11-2, we examine binge drinking among university and college students, who receive conflicting messages about the acceptability of the behaviour from sources of social control.

Labelling theory is also called the **societal-reaction approach**, reminding us that it is the *response* to an act and not the behaviour itself that determines deviance. For example, studies have shown that some school personnel and therapists expand educational programs designed for students who have learning disabilities to include those with behavioural problems. Consequently, a "troublemaker" can be improperly labelled as having a learning disability and vice versa.

A study by three British psychologists underscores the implications of using different labels to describe people with learning difficulties or disabilities. A total of 111 subjects completed a questionnaire designed to assess attitudes toward three labelled groups: "mentally subnormal adults," "mentally handicapped adults," and "people with learning difficulties." The researchers found that subjects reacted more positively to the label "people with learning difficulties" than to the other labels. Subjects view "people with learning difficulties" as more competent and as deserving of more rights than

"mentally handicapped" or "mentally subnormal" individuals (Eayrs, Ellis, and Jones 1993).

Traditionally, research on deviance has focused on people who violate social norms. In contrast, labelling theory focuses on police, probation officers, psychiatrists, judges, teachers, employers, school officials, and other regulators of social control. These agents, it is argued, play a significant role in creating the deviant identity by designating certain people (and not others) as "deviant." An important aspect of labelling theory is the recognition that some individuals or groups have the power to *define* labels and apply them to others. This view recalls the conflict perspective's emphasis on the social significance of power.

In recent years, the practice of *racial* or *ethnic profiling*, in which people are identified as criminal suspects purely on the basis of their race or ethnicity, has come under public scrutiny. Studies conducted in the United States confirm the public's suspicions that in some jurisdictions, police officers are much more likely to stop black males than white males for routine traffic violations. In Canada, the United States, and many European countries, the events of September 11, 2001, have caused civil rights activists to raise concerns about the use of racial profiling in safety and security policies and practices.

The labelling approach does not fully explain why certain people accept a label and others are able to reject it. In fact, this perspective may exaggerate the ease with which societal judgments can alter our self-image. Labelling theorists do suggest, however, that how much power a person has relative to others is important in determining that person's ability to resist an undesirable label. Competing approaches (including that of Sutherland) fail to explain why some deviants continue to be viewed as conformists rather than as violators of rules. According to Howard Becker, labelling theory was not conceived as the *sole* explanation for deviance (1973); its proponents merely hoped to focus more attention on the undeniably important actions of those people officially in charge of defining deviance (Davis 1975; compare with Cullen and Cullen 1978).

The popularity of labelling theory is reflected in the emergence of a related perspective, called social constructionism. According to the **social constructionist perspective**, deviance is the product of the culture we live in. Social constructionists focus specifically on the decision-making process that creates the deviant identity. They point out that "missing children," "deadbeat dads," "spree killers," and "date rapists" have always been with us but at times have become the major social concern of the moment because of intensive media coverage (Liska and Messner 1999; Wright, Gronfein, and Owens 2000).

::: use your sociological *imagination* :::

You are a teacher. What kinds of labels freely used in educational circles might be attached to your students?

Demonstrators protest against the policies of the Canadian government.

Conflict Perspective

For many years, a husband who forced his wife to have sexual intercourse—without her consent and against her will—was not legally considered to have committed rape. The laws defined rape as pertaining only to sexual relations between people not married to each other. These laws reflected the overwhelmingly male composition of government and legal decision makers. Conflict theorists would not be surprised by this. They point out that people with power protect their own interests and define deviance to suit their own needs. It wasn't until 1983 in Canada that rape laws were broadened to sexual assault laws and it became a criminal act for a man to rape his wife.

Feminist legal scholar Catherine MacKinnon argues that male sexual behaviour represents "dominance eroticized," in that male sexuality is linked to dominance and power (1987). Edwin Schur expands on this view of male sexuality, stating that "forced sex is the ultimate indicator and preserver of male dominance" (1983:148). Canadian laws have historically sanctioned the abuse of women within marriage, based on the assumption of male control and ownership of his family (Johnson 1996). According to Statistics Canada (2009), female victims of spousal abuse are more likely to be subjected to sexual assault and more severe forms of violence, such as beating and choking, than are male victims.

Sociologist Richard Quinney is a leading proponent of the view that the criminal justice system serves the interests of the powerful (1974, 1979, 1980). Crime, according to Quinney, is a definition of conduct created by authorized agents of social control—such as legislators and law enforcement officers—in a politically organized society (1970). He and other conflict theorists argued that lawmaking is often an attempt by the powerful to coerce others into their own morality (see also Spitzer 1975).

This helps to explain why our society has laws against gambling, drug usage, and prostitution, many of which are violated on a massive scale. (We examine these "victimless crimes" later in the chapter.) According to the conflict school, criminal law does not represent a consistent application of societal values but instead reflects competing values and interests.

Conflict theorists contend that the entire criminal justice system of Canada treats suspects differently on the basis of their racial, ethnic, or social class background. The case of Donald Marshall, an Aboriginal man from Nova Scotia who was wrongfully convicted of murder, and who served years in prison for a crime he did not commit, is one of the most illustrative examples of the bias against Aboriginal persons in Canadian legal history.

Today, Aboriginal men have the highest rate of over-representation in prisons of any group in Canada. Quinney argues that, through such differential applications of social control, the criminal justice system helps to keep the poor and oppressed in their deprived position (1974). In his view, disadvantaged individuals and groups who represent a threat to those with power become the primary targets of criminal law. He maintains the real criminals in poor neighbourhoods are not the people arrested for vandalism and theft but rather absentee landlords and exploitative store owners. Even if we do not accept this challenging argument, we cannot ignore the role of the powerful in creating a social structure that perpetuates suffering.

The perspective advanced by labelling and conflict theorists forms quite a contrast to the functionalist approach to deviance. Functionalists view standards of deviant behaviour as merely reflecting cultural norms, whereas conflict and labelling theorists point out that the most powerful groups in a society can shape laws and standards and determine who is (or is not) prosecuted as a criminal. Thus, the label "deviant" is rarely applied to the corporate executive whose decisions lead to large-scale environmental pollution. In the opinion of conflict theorists, agents of social control and powerful groups can generally impose their own self-serving definitions of deviance on the general public.

Feminist Perspectives

Although feminist theories of deviance are diverse, most tend to challenge other mainstream theories on the grounds that women's experiences have not been included and that gender-based perspectives have not been employed. Feminist theories of deviance are generally eager to understand the gendered nature of institutions, such as the criminal justice system, and the inequities in the system that lead to differential treatment of men and women.

Many feminist perspectives contend that courts, prisons, law-enforcement agencies, welfare agencies, and families alike are organized on the basis of gender as well as power, class, race, and sexuality (Elliot and Mandell 1998). Of concern are ways in which such factors as gender, sexuality, class, and race intersect to produce patterns of and responses to deviant behaviour. As well, these perspectives in general hold the view that since gender relations are not "natural," but rather are produced by social, cultural, and historical conditions, gendered patterns of deviance will reflect these conditions. For example, the social acceptability of smoking for women (and the labelling of some women smokers as deviants) has been shaped by history, class, and sexuality. From the 1800s to the 1920s in North America, smoking by women was associated with prostitution and lesbianism. Women who smoked were labelled "sluts," "whores," and "sinners," and were considered "fallen women" (Greaves 1996:18).

As previously mentioned, feminist perspectives are varied. For example, liberal feminist perspectives tend to view women's rates of crime and deviance as a reflection of the degree to which they participate in all areas of social life—sports, politics, business, education, and so on. Because women are confronted with obstacles in their climb to the top corporate positions, they are limited in their opportunities to engage in particular deviant acts, such as corporate crime.

In contrast, radical feminist perspectives see patriarchy (the set of social relations that maintains male control) as the key to understanding female crime and deviance. Patriarchy, according to radical feminist analysis, puts men in control of women's bodies and minds and sets in place oppressive social institutions, such as the family and the law, in order to maintain control. Sexual offences for women, therefore, are more common, since men control the institutions that regulate activities such as prostitution. This imbalance of power results in a higher rate of arrest and conviction for the female prostitute than for the male customer. In the aftermath of the Pickton trial (Robert "Willie" Pickton was sentenced in 2007 for the murders of six missing women who worked in the sex-trade in the downtown eastside of Vancouver) and as police continue to search for other missing women, in 2009, three Canadian prostitutes launched a challenge to the existing prostitution laws to the Ontario Supreme court. The women argue that that laws exacerbate the risks of an already dangerous profession; they want the courts to "strike down prohibitions against living off the avails of prostitution, communication with potential clients and setting up of brothels" (Makin 2009:A4). The three women will make their case that the present laws infringe on their Charter right to life, liberty, and security of their person (Makin 2009).

We have seen that over the past century, sociologists have taken many different approaches in studying deviance, arousing some controversy in the process. Table 11-3 summarizes the various theoretical approaches to this topic.

What Is Crime?

Crime is a violation of criminal law for which some governmental authority applies formal penalties. It represents a deviation from formal social norms administered by the state. Laws divide crimes into various categories, depending on the severity of the offence, the age of the offender, the potential punishment that can be levied, and the court that holds jurisdiction over the case.

Crimes tend to affect some groups more than others; for example, their impact can be gender-specific and age-specific. In Canada, of all the victims of crimes against the person, women and girls make up the vast majority of victims of dating violence. In 2010, over three times the number of girls and women were victims of such violence as compared to boys and men (Statistics Canada 2012).

Types of Crime

Rather than relying solely on legal categories, sociologists classify crimes in terms of how they are committed and how society views the offences. In this section, we will examine four types of crime as differentiated by sociologists: professional crime, organized crime, white-collar crime, and so-called victimless crimes.

Professional Crime Although the adage "crime doesn't pay" is familiar, many people do make a career of illegal activities. A **professional criminal** is a person who pursues crime

table 11-3 Sociological Perspectives on Deviance

summingUP

Approach	Perspective	Proponents	Emphasis
Anomie	Functionalist	Émile Durkheim Robert Merton	Adaptation to societal norms
Cultural transmission/ Differential association	Interactionist	Edwin Sutherland	Patterns learned through others
Routine activities	Interactionist	Marcus Felson	Impact of the social environment
Labelling/Social constructionist	Interactionist	Howard Becker	Societal response to acts
Conflict	Conflict	Richard Quinney	Dominance by authorized agents Discretionary justice
Feminist	Feminist/Conflict	Freda Adler Meda Chesney-Lind	Role of gender Women as victims and perpetrators

as a day-to-day occupation, developing skilled techniques and enjoying a certain degree of status among other criminals. Some professional criminals specialize in burglary, safe-cracking, hijacking of cargo, pick-pocketing, and shoplifting. Such people have acquired skills that reduce the likelihood of arrest, conviction, and imprisonment. As a result, they may have long careers in their chosen "professions."

Edwin Sutherland offered pioneering insights into the behaviour of professional criminals by publishing an annotated account written by a professional thief (1937). Unlike the person who engages in crime only once or twice, professional thieves make a business of stealing. They devote their entire working time to planning and executing crimes and sometimes travel across the nation to pursue their "professional duties." Like people in regular occupations, professional thieves consult with their colleagues concerning the demands of work, thus becoming part of a subculture of similarly occupied individuals. They exchange information on possible places to burglarize, on outlets for unloading stolen goods, and on ways of securing bail bonds if arrested.

Organized Crime   For our purposes, we will consider **organized crime** to be the work of a group that regulates relations among various criminal enterprises involved in the smuggling and sale of drugs, prostitution, gambling, and other illegal activities. In Canada, gangs are increasingly involved in organized crime, as "gang imperialism" (Taylor 1990) promotes linkages between gangs for the purpose of financial gain (Astwood Strategy Corporation 2003). Organized crime dominates the world of illegal business just as large corporations dominate the conventional business world. It allocates territory, sets prices for goods and services, and acts as an arbitrator in internal disputes.

Organized crime is a secret, conspiratorial activity that generally evades law enforcement. Organized crime takes over legitimate businesses, gains influence over labour unions, corrupts public officials, intimidates witnesses in criminal trials, and even "taxes" merchants in exchange for "protection" (National Advisory Commission on Criminal Justice 1976). An example of the intimidation tactics used by organized crime is the gunning down of Montreal crime reporter

Michel Auger in 2000. Auger specialized in stories on Quebec organized crime and biker gangs. Auger was shot five times, but recovered. Although it has not yet been proven that biker gangs were responsible for the execution-style attack, it came a day after his paper, *Le Journal*, printed one of his articles on biker-related murders.

There has always been a global element in organized crime. But law-enforcement officials and policymakers have acknowledged the emergence of a new form of organized crime that takes advantage of advances in electronic communications. *Transnational* organized crime includes drug and arms smuggling, money laundering, and trafficking in illegal immigrants and stolen goods such as automobiles (Office of Justice Programs 1999).

White-Collar and Technology-Based Crime   Income tax evasion, stock manipulation, consumer fraud, bribery and extraction of "kickbacks," embezzlement, and misrepresentation in advertising—these are all examples of **white-collar crime**: illegal acts committed in the course of business activities, often by affluent, "respectable" people. Perhaps one of the most notable examples of white-collar crime would be that of Canadian-born businessman Conrad Black—a member of the British House of Lords and a high-profile newspaper baron—who, in 2007, was found guilty on several criminal charges stemming from his many business ventures. Edwin Sutherland (1949, 1983) likened white-collar crime to organized crime because it is often perpetrated through occupational roles (Friedrichs 1998).

A new type of white-collar crime has emerged in recent decades: computer crime. The use of such high technology allows people to carry out embezzlement or electronic fraud without leaving a trace, or to gain access to a company's inventory without leaving home. An adept programmer can gain access to a firm's computer by telephone and then copy valuable files. In Canada, between 1998 and 2003, identity-theft reports grew by 500 percent, while the RCMP estimates the impact of such theft to be approximately $500 million a year (El Akkad 2009). In 2009, several business groups urged the federal government to pass a bill to create new Criminal Code offences related to identity theft.

Sutherland (1940) coined the phrase *white-collar crime* in 1939 to refer to acts by individuals, but the term has been broadened more recently to include offences by organizations as well. *Organizational crime* is an offence committed with the approval and encouragement of a company to advance its own interests (Coleman 1985). Corporations, for example, may engage in anti-competitive behaviour, acts that lead to environmental pollution, tax fraud, stock fraud and manipulation, the production of unsafe goods, bribery and corruption, and worker health-and-safety violations (Simpson 1993).

Given the economic and social costs of white-collar crime, you might expect the criminal justice system to take this problem quite seriously. Yet, research done in the United States shows that white-collar offenders are more likely to receive fines than prison sentences. In federal courts—where most white-collar cases end up—probation is granted to 40 percent of those who have violated anti-trust laws, 61 percent of those convicted of fraud, and 70 percent of convicted embezzlers (Gest 1985). Amitai Etzioni's study (1985, 1990) found that in 43 percent of the incidents, either no penalty was imposed or the company was required merely to cease engaging in the illegal practice and to return any funds gained through illegal means (for a different view, see Manson 1986).

Moreover, conviction for such illegal acts does not generally harm a person's reputation and career aspirations nearly as much as conviction for street crime would. Apparently, being labelled a "white-collar criminal" does not carry the stigma of the label "felon convicted of a violent crime." Conflict theorists are not surprised by such differential labelling and treatment. They argue that the criminal justice system largely disregards the white-collar crimes of the affluent, while focusing on crimes known as "street crimes" often committed by the poor. Street crimes include such activities as assault, arson, robbery, and breaking and entering. If an offender holds a position of status and influence, his or her crime is treated as less serious, and the sanction is much more lenient than for those with less status and influence (Maguire 1988).

::: use your sociological *imagination* :::

As a newspaper editor, how might you treat stories on corporate crime differently from those on violent crimes?

Victimless Crimes White-collar or street crimes endanger people's economic or personal well-being against their will (or without their direct knowledge). By contrast, sociologists use the term **victimless crime** to describe the willing exchange among adults of widely desired, but illegal, goods and services (Schur 1965, 1985).

Although the term *victimless crime* is widely used, many people object to the notion that there is no victim when such offences take place. Excessive drinking, compulsive gambling, and illegal drug use contribute to an enormous amount of personal and property damage. And feminist sociologists contend that the so-called victimless crime of prostitution, as

well as the more disturbing aspects of pornography, reinforce the misconception that women are "toys" who can be treated as objects rather than as people (Flavin 1998; Jolin 1994).

Nonetheless, some activists are working to decriminalize many of these illegal practices. Supporters of decriminalization are troubled by the attempt to legislate a moral code of behaviour for adults. In their view, it is impossible to prevent prostitution, gambling, and other so-called victimless crimes.

The controversy over decriminalization reminds us of the important insights of labelling and conflict theories presented earlier. Underlying this debate are two interesting questions: Who has the power to define gambling, prostitution, and public drunkenness as "crimes"? And who has the power to label such behaviours as "victimless"? It is generally the government and, in some cases, the police and the courts.

Again, we can see that criminal law is not simply a universal standard of behaviour agreed on by all members of society. Rather, it reflects the struggle among competing individuals and groups to gain governmental support for their particular moral and social values. For example, such organizations as Mothers Against Drunk Driving (MADD) and Students Against Drunk Driving (SADD) have had success over the years in modifying public attitudes toward drunkenness. Rather than being viewed as a victimless crime, drunkenness is increasingly being associated with the potential dangers of driving while under the influence of alcohol. As a result, the mass media are giving greater (and more critical) attention to people who are guilty of drunk driving, and many provincial and territorial governments have instituted more severe fines and jail terms for a wide variety of alcohol-related offences.

Crime Statistics

Crime statistics are not as accurate as social scientists would like. However, since they deal with an issue of grave concern to people in many countries, they are frequently cited as if they were completely reliable. Such data do serve as an indicator of police activity, as well as an approximate indication of the level of certain types of crimes. Yet it would be a mistake to interpret these data as an exact representation of the incidence of crime.

Public opinion polls reveal that Canadians believe the crime rate is increasing in this country, despite the release of statistics that indicate the national crime rate in 2010 hit its lowest point since the early 1970s (Statistics Canada 2012). In 2010 the volume and severity of police-reported crime decreased from the previous by 5 percent and 6 percent respectively (Statistics Canada 2012).

In 2010, the volume and severity of crime fell or remained stable in every jurisdiction in Canada except Newfoundland, the Northwest Territories, and Nunavut. In Nova Scotia, the crime rate rose slightly; however, the severity of crimes remained stable. Within Canada, however, vast regional differences exist in rates of crime. As Figure 11-1 illustrates, Saskatchewan, continuing a trend since 1998, had the highest crime severity index among the provinces. As can be seen, crime severity and volume are greater in the west of Canada than in the east.

figure 11-1 Police-reported Crime Severity Indexes, by Province and Territory, 2010

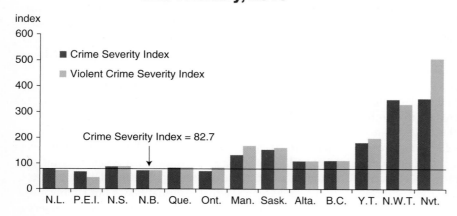

Source: Statistics Canada 2012.

Canada's crime rates are significantly lower than those of the United States, particularly for violent crimes, such as homicide, for which the U.S. rate is more than three times greater than Canada's. Research has shown, however, that Canadian and U.S. rates converge in the area of spousal assault, showing that "Canadian men are just as, if not more, likely to beat their spouses as American men" (DeKeseredy and Schwartz 1998:vii).

Despite the fact that women in Canada are most likely to be assaulted, not only by men they know but also by men who might actually like them, and that the assault is most likely to take place in a private location, they fear "stranger danger" (DeKeseredy and Schwartz 1998; Statistics Canada 2009). Table 11-4 shows the percent of violent crimes by sex and relationship to the accused, reported to a subset of police services.

Think about It
Do you think that women's feelings of safety on campus contribute to their overall assessment of the quality of their university?

Sociologists have several ways of measuring crime. Historically, they have relied on official statistics, but underreporting has always been a problem with such measures. Because members of racial and ethnic minority groups have not always trusted law-enforcement agencies, they have often refrained from contacting the police. Feminist sociologists and others have noted that many women do not report sexual assault or spousal abuse out of fear that officials will regard the crime as the women's fault. Partly because of the deficiencies of official statistics, **victimization surveys** question ordinary people, not police officers, to learn how much crime occurs.

Unfortunately, like other crime data, victimization surveys have particular limitations. They require first that victims understand what has happened to them and then that victims disclose such information to interviewers. Fraud, income tax evasion, and blackmail are examples of crimes that are unlikely to be reported in victimization studies. Even though victimization surveys have their limitations, they can be helpful in augmenting police statistics. For example, both police statistics and victimization surveys report that, although the majority of violent-crime offenders tend to be males, victims are equally likely to be male or female (Johnson 1996).

International Crime Rates If it is difficult to develop reliable crime data in Canada, it is even trickier to make useful cross-national comparisons. Nevertheless, with some care, we can offer preliminary conclusions about how crime rates differ around the world.

Canada's homicide rate is roughly one-third of that of the U.S but more than four times of that of Japan (Statistics Canada 2012). However, some types of property crimes are lower in the US than Canada. For example, in 2006, rates of vehicle theft were 22% higher in Canada than the U.S. (Effgen 2010).

Why are rates of violent crime so much higher in the United States? Although there is no simple answer to this question, sociologist Elliot Currie has suggested a reason could be that U.S. society places greater emphasis on individual economic achievement than do other societies (1985, 1998). At the same time, many observers have noted that the culture of the United States has long tolerated, if not condoned, many forms of violence. When coupled with high rates of handgun ownership, sharp disparities between poor and affluent citizens, significant unemployment, and substantial alcohol and drug abuse, all these factors combine to produce a climate conducive to crime.

There are, however, disturbing increases in violent crime evident in other Western societies. For example, crime in Russia has skyrocketed since the overthrow of Communist Party rule (with its strict controls on guns and criminals) in 1991. Whereas there were fewer than 260 homicides in Moscow in 1978 and again in 1988, there are now more than 1000 homicides per year. Organized crime has filled a power vacuum in Russia (as well as a number of other former Eastern Bloc countries) since the end of communism; one result is that gangland shootouts and premeditated "contract hits" have become more common. Some prominent reformist politicians have been targeted as well. Russia is the only nation in the world that incarcerates a higher proportion of its citizens than the United States. Russia imprisons 580 per 100 000 of its adults on a typical day compared with 550 in the United States, 150 in Canada, fewer than 100 in Mexico or Britain, and only 16 in Greece (Currie 1998; Shinkai and Zvekic 1999).

Transnational Crime More and more, scholars and police officials are turning their attention to **transnational crime**, or crime that occurs across multiple national borders. In the past, international crime was often limited to the

table 11-4 Victims of Police-reported Violent Crime, by Sex of Victim and Relationship of the Accused to the Victim, Canada 2010

Relationship of Accused to Victim	Total (%)	Sex of Victim	
		Female (%)	Male (%)
Total family	**25**	**34**	**16**
Total spouse	12	19	3
Current spouse (includes legally married and common-law)	8	13	2
Ex-spouse (includes separated and divorced)	4	6	1
Other immediate or extended family	13	14	11
Parent	4	5	4
Child	2	3	2
Sibling	3	3	2
Extended family	3	4	3
Total friends/acquaintances	**38**	**40**	**35**
Boyfriend/girlfriend	6	10	2
Ex-boyfriend/girlfriend	4	6	1
Close friend	3	3	3
Casual acquaintance	19	17	22
Business relationship	4	3	5
Criminal relationship	1	0	1
Authority figure	1	1	1
Stranger	**23**	**14**	**32**
Unknown	**17**	**15**	**19**

Notes: Percentages may not total 100% due to rounding. Excludes incidents where the sex and/or age of the victim was unknown. Current spouse and ex-spouse categories include victims aged 15 to 98.
Source: Statistics Canada 2010d. Adapted by author.

clandestine shipment of goods across the border between two countries. But increasingly, crime is no more restricted by such borders than is legal commerce. Rather than concentrating on specific countries, international crime now spans the globe, leading us to the following question: How is crime exported as a function of globalization?

Historically, probably the most dreaded example of transnational crime has been the enslavement and trafficking of Africans. At first, governments did not regard slavery as a crime, but merely regulated it as they would the trade in goods, placing human life on the same level of importance as objects. In the twentieth century, transnational crime grew to embrace trafficking in endangered species, drugs, and stolen art and antiquities.

Transnational crime is not exclusive of some of the other types of crime we have discussed. For example, organized criminal networks are increasingly global. Technology definitely facilitates their illegal activities, such as trafficking in child pornography. Beginning in the 1990s, the United Nations began to categorize transnational crimes; Table 11-5 lists some of the more common types.

Bilateral cooperation in the pursuit of border criminals such as smugglers has been common for many years. The first global effort to control international crime began with the establishment of the International Criminal Police Organization (Interpol), a cooperative network of European police forces founded to stem the movement of political revolutionaries across borders. While such efforts to fight transnational crime may seem lofty—an activity with which any

table 11-5 Types of Transnational Crime

Bankruptcy and insurance fraud
Computer crime (treating computers as both a tool and a target of crime)
Corruption and bribery of public officials
Environment crime
Hijacking of airplanes ("skyjacking")
Illegal drug trade
Illegal money transfers ("money laundering")
Illegal sales of firearms and ammunition
Infiltration of legal businesses
Networking of criminal organizations
Sea piracy
Terrorism
Theft of art and cultural objects
Trafficking in body parts (includes illegal organ transplants)
Trafficking in human beings (includes sex trade)

Source: Compiled by the author based on Mueller 2001 and United Nations Office on Drugs and Crime 2005.

government should cooperate—they are complicated by sensitive legal and security issues. Most nations that have signed protocols issued by the United Nations, including the United States, have expressed concern over potential encroachments on their national judicial systems, as well as concern over their national security. Thus, they have been reluctant to share certain types of intelligence data. The 9/11 attacks increased both the interest in combating transnational crime and sensitivity to the risks of sharing intelligence data (Deflem 2005; Felson and Kalaitzidis 2005).

Social Policy and Social Control

Illicit Drug Use in Canada

The Issue

Vancouver's municipal government spends more money per capita in dealing with illicit drugs than any other city in Canada (Bula 2000). In 2000, then mayor of Vancouver Philip Owen claimed that although Vancouver's drug problem is so well known and has been highlighted in many media reports, it does not mean that other big cities are not struggling with the same concerns. Owen stated, "Everyone has a drug problem, all the big-city mayors have talked about this. Every single one is looking for solutions. But nobody is prepared to stand up to the plate" (Bula 2000). In response to this problem, Vancouver authorities devised a drug strategy and harm-reduction plan. According to the former mayor, this is an "international crisis," and cities such as Yokohama, Japan, and Seattle, Washington, have asked for a copy of Vancouver's drug strategy (Bula 2000).

The Setting

National surveys have shown that in Canada, people living in British Columbia were most likely to report the personal use of illicit substances (Nelson and Fleras 1995). The drug "problem" is particularly apparent in Vancouver's downtown eastside, an area that is the poorest in all of Canada and that houses people who have some of the most severe social, economic, and health problems in the country. The death rate in the downtown eastside is high because of the growing incidence of hepatitis C and HIV, acquired through intravenous-injection drug use. Activities such as youth prostitution and panhandling become the means through which addicts can sustain their addiction.

Sociological Insights

Functionalists view alienation and anomie to be the cause of many forms of addiction, including alcohol and drug addiction (Nelson and Fleras 1995). The activities of addicts, according to functionalist theorists, have functional consequences for society.

For example, they demonstrate the boundaries of so-called "rule-breaking behaviour," and they create social agreement and cohesion regarding unacceptable behaviours.

Conflict theorists, in contrast, ask the questions "Who benefits?" and "Why is it that some drug users receive the label 'addict,' while other users do not?" Conflict thinkers argue that the state and its various agencies, such as prisons, police, and rehabilitation programs, serve to benefit from such labels because they create employment for correction officers, police officers, social workers, and counsellors. They also address the reasons why society does not label those addicted to prescription drugs and "legal" drugs, such as tobacco, in the same manner as it labels and scapegoats those addicted to such drugs as cocaine and heroin.

Feminist approaches to addiction are as diverse as feminist theories themselves. Some argue that for women, addiction grows out of their overall status of subordination in society; in other words, women's powerlessness leads to various forms of self-destructive escapes, such as drug use (Lundy 1991). Other feminist theories argue that the concept of gender and the various related roles and behaviours deny both men and women full expression of their own humanity; addiction becomes a metaphor for the gender stereotypes in our society (Nelson and Fleras 1995).

Interactionist approaches frame drug addiction in the context of continual action on the part of the drug addict and reaction on the part of those around her or him. They stress the process through which the person is identified as an "addict" and the impact that this label has on the person's sense of self. Goffman's dramaturgical approach is an example of this process of individual action and social reaction, in which the individual plays many roles, as would an actor. The drug addict, for example, may play one role in dealing with the police (for example, presenting himself or herself as someone trying to get "clean") while presenting a different image to peers.

Policy Initiatives

Vancouver's drug strategy and harm-reduction plan is the first of its kind in North America. It shifts the focus away from drug use as a criminal activity and toward drug use as a health-and-safety issue; under the plan, users would receive treatment rather than jail terms and special treatment beds would be allocated to young users.

The drug strategy and harm-reduction plan, similar to those implemented in many European cities, is based on a four-pillar approach:

1. *Enforcement.* This pillar includes a pilot drug-treatment court that would weigh various options of treatment, an increase in the police drug and organized-crime squads to target larger dealers, and the creation of a "drug action team" that would respond to neighbourhood drug issues.
2. *Harm reduction.* This notion encompasses the creation of an overdose-death prevention campaign, the provision of short-term shelter and housing for drug users on the street, and the establishment of street-drug testing.
3. *Treatment.* The treatment element of the plan would provide treatment beds for young people outside the downtown eastside; special treatment for women who are pregnant and/or have children; needle exchanges in primary health-care clinics, hospitals, and pharmacies; pilot day centres for addicts; and different kinds of housing for users and those trying to go clean.
4. *Prevention.* This pillar of the plan would give communities and neighbourhoods more power to combat drug abuse and to develop a pilot citywide school curriculum on drugs and drug abuse.

As part of its harm-reduction strategy, in 2003, Vancouver opened its first safe-injection site (INSITE)—a facility where people with addictions can safely inject drugs in a clean, sterile environment rather than on the streets with needles that may be dirty. This site is the first of its kind in North America and, as a consequence, the whole world has been watching. In 2004, the International Narcotics Board (INB)—an independent United Nations organization—criticized the Vancouver safe-injection site, claiming that it violated international drug treatises. Then-mayor of Vancouver Larry Campbell dismissed the INB's criticisms, stating that, because of its overwhelming U.S. funding, the INB simply reflects the U.S. policy on the "war on drugs," which does not embrace the principle or practice of harm reduction. However, according to Colin Mangham, director of research for the Drug Prevention Network of Canada, the principle of harm reduction, as represented by INSITE, has overpowered the other three pillars of Vancouver's drug strategy to become the foundation of drug policy. Mangham states that drug policy has become so politicized, based upon an ideology of harm reduction, that the failures or deficiencies of INSITE are rarely discussed. For example, he notes that only a small percentage of intravenous drug users frequent INSITE for even a majority of their injections and, thus, a major problem of this harm-reduction approach is its inability to control a free-moving population of drug users (Mangham 2007).

In 2008, the federal Conservative government wanted to shut down INSITE, which resulted in a court challenge. The 2011 unanimous decision of the Supreme Court of Canada ruled that not allowing the clinic to remain open would be a violation of the Charter of Rights and Freedoms (CBC 2011). The Chief Justice of the court stated in the ruling that: "INSITE saves lives. Its benefits have been proven. There has been no discernible negative impact on the safety and health objectives of Canada during its eight years of operation" (CBC 2011).

International health experts and observers have commented that facilities such as INSITE should be expanded to other communities in Canada where there is a need.

Apply the Theory

1. How might conflict sociologists explain why certain drugs, and the individuals who use them, have been treated so differently?
2. According to functionalist perspectives, what functions might drug or alcohol addiction have in society?

CHAPTER RESOURCES

Summary

::: 11.1 What Is Social Control?

- **Conformity** and **deviance** are two ways in which people respond to real or imagined pressures from others. In this chapter, we examined the relationship among conformity, deviance, and mechanisms of social control.
- **Social control** involves the mechanisms used by society to bring about conformity to social norms.
- Stanley Milgram defined **conformity** as going along with our peers; **obedience** is defined as compliance with higher authorities in a hierarchical structure.
- Some norms are so important to a society, that they are formalized into laws. Socialization is a primary source of conforming and obedient behaviour, including obedience to law.

::: 11.2 What Is Deviance?

- **Deviance** is behaviour that violates any social norm. Some forms of deviance carry a negative social **stigma**, while other forms are more or less acceptable.
- From a functionalist point of view, deviance and its consequences help to define the limits of proper behaviour.
- Interactionists maintain that we learn criminal behaviour from interactions with others—an approach called **cultural transmission**. They also stress that for crime

to occur, there has to be a convergence of motivated offenders and suitable targets of crime; this approach is known as **routine activities theory**.
- The theory of **differential association** holds that deviance results from exposure to attitudes favourable to criminal acts.
- **Labelling theory** is based upon the recognition that some people are viewed as deviant while others engaged in the same behaviour are not.
- The conflict perspective views laws and punishments as reflecting the interests of the powerful.
- Feminist perspectives on deviance are varied. Often, they emphasize that crimes involving women are defined and treated differently.

::: 11.3 What Is Crime?

- **Crime** represents a deviation from formal social norms administered by the state.
- Sociologists differentiate among professional crime, **organized crime, white-collar crime, victimless crime**, and **transnational crime**.
- Crime statistics are among the least reliable social data, partly because so many crimes are not reported to law-enforcement agencies.

Critical Thinking Questions

1. What mechanisms of formal and informal social control are evident in your university or college classes and in day-to-day life and social interactions at your school?

2. What approach to deviance do you find most persuasive, that of functionalists, conflict theorists, interactionists, labelling theorists, or feminist theorists? Why is this approach more convincing than the others? What are the main weaknesses of each approach?

3. Rates of violent crime are lower in Canada, Western Europe, Australia, and New Zealand than in the United States. Draw on as many of the theories discussed in the chapter as possible to explain why Canada is a comparatively less violent society than the United States.

4. Why do you think a computer hacker might be viewed differently from a person who commits a break-and-enter or steals something from a department store?

THINKING ABOUT MOVIES

American Gypsy

This documentary sheds light on the Romani, a minority group whose members are often stereotyped as criminals.

Hurt Locker

During the Iraq War, a U.S. Army sergeant who uses unortho-dox methods assumes command of a bomb squad.

Temple Grandin

An autistic woman fights for animal rights.

inside

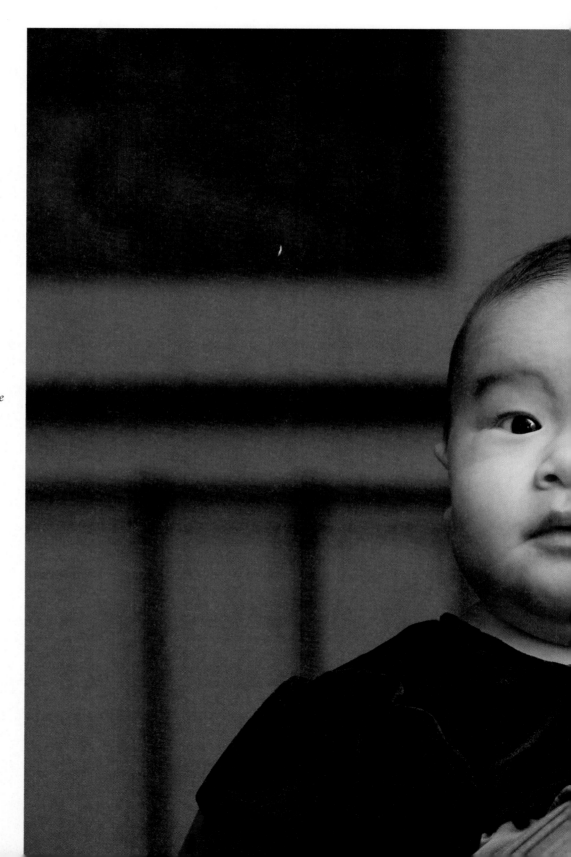

Mother with her son

" KINGSTON, Ont.—After a dizzying parade of nearly 50 witnesses in 25 days, jurors in the Shafia honour killing trial heard one final prosecution witness Monday—an academic who testified that in some cultures, family honour is considered more important than human life.

"A rumour could cause the killing of a young woman," testified Shahrzad Mojab, a native of Iran who is a professor at the University of Toronto. The judge accepted her as an expert on honour killings and related issues of culture, religion, patriarchy, and violence in Middle Eastern and South Asian societies and in immigrant diasporas in western nations.

Mojab has been studying these issues for more than 15 years, edited a book on honour killing, has written dozens of research papers, and has attended dozens of conferences and seminars. She has provided advice to the United Nations and, last year, she explained the concept of honour killing at a conference of Toronto Police homicide investigators.

Prosecutors allege that Montreal businessman Mohammad Shafia, 58, his wife Tooba Mohammad Yahya, 41, and their son Hamed, 20, killed four family members in an honour killing. Each of them has pleaded not guilty to four counts of first-degree murder.

Sisters Zainab Shafia, 19, Sahar, 17, Geeti, 13, and Rona Amir Mohammad, 52, were found dead inside a submerged car discovered at the bottom of a shallow canal in Kingston on June 30, 2009. Mohammad was Shafia's first wife, whom he married in his native Afghanistan before the family moved to Canada in 2007.

Prosecutors allege that the murders were orchestrated because the teenage sisters dressed provocatively, took boyfriends, disobeyed their father and, in the case of Zainab, ran away from home to be with a young man of her choosing. Jurors heard that Rona Mohammad complained of abuse and wanted a divorce.

Mojab was not asked to comment on the facts of the Shafia case. She explained the concept of honour killing and the motivations of perpetrators.

"The shedding of the blood is a way of purifying the name of the family . . . and restoration of the honour of the family," Mojab told the seven women and five men on the jury.

She said that in traditional, patriarchal families, the chastity, virginity, and obedience of girls and women is vital to the maintenance of family honour. Men, who have power in the families, control women's bodies and have exclusive access to them. If a woman dresses immodestly or consorts with other men, or is believed to have done those things, she may be perceived to have shamed the patriarch and may be marked for death.

"There are cases that female members of the family and, in particular mothers, participate by different means in the . . . planning or (are) directly involved in the act of the killing," Mojab testified.

She said the conspiracy among family members is a characteristic that distinguishes honour killings from domestic violence. She said honour killing is an ancient cultural practice among Muslims, Jews, Hindus, and Christians.

"It doesn't have any direct connection with religion at all," she said, characterizing it as a means for men to maintain the gender inequality which affords them a privileged position in families and society.

Mojab said that in many cases she has studied, perpetrators who murder their children claim that they loved them but say that their deaths were necessary because they restored the honour of the family and the honour of the child who transgressed.

"It is (considered) part of the continuum of love and care," Mojab testified.

She said some immigrants don't shed these strict views when they move to new countries. Instead, they "freeze" their concept of their home culture at the moment in time when they left their native country and resist integration in a new home by clinging to old beliefs.

Defence lawyer Peter Kemp, who represents Shafia, asked Mojab if the shame of a family would not be purified if an honour killer denied committing the murder.

"That's often the initial reaction," she replied. "But then there are many cases that, even after the father is imprisoned, they acknowledge that the act that was committed was to purify the name of the family."

In answer to another question, Mojab said an honour killing would still be considered to have cleansed the family's shame, even if the death was disguised as an accident.

The trial was adjourned until Thursday, when it is expected that Mohammad Shafia will testify as the defence begins presenting evidence.

Jurors were told the case is likely to extend into January. "

(Used with the permission of Postmedia News)

The opening article by Rob Tripp of the *National Post* discusses the phenomenon of "honour killings" where female family members are killed by male family members—as well as by their mothers—in order to restore the "honour" of the family and to purify the family name. This was the case of the Shafias in Ontario where four female family members were killed in 2009 because they were perceived to have disgraced the family name.

Families are often thought to be sources of support, comfort, and security; however, they also may be sources of violence, danger, and abuse, particularly for girls and women.

In this chapter, we address the subject of family and intimate relationships in Canada as well as in other parts of the world. As we will see, family patterns differ from one culture to another and within the same culture. A **family** can be defined as a set of people related by blood, marriage (or some other agreed-on relationship), or adoption who share the primary responsibility for reproduction and caring for members of society. A Census family, as defined by Statistics Canada during the 2006 census, includes married couples with or without children of either/both spouses; common-law couples with or without children of either/both partners; and lone parents of any marital status with at least one child living in the same dwelling. The children, who may be biological children, stepchildren, or adopted children, live in the same dwelling as the parents. Also included in the definition of a census family are grandchildren living with their grandparents without their parent(s). With the 2005 passage of Bill C-38, the Civil Marriage Act, gays and lesbians can now be afforded spousal status, as their civil unions are legal in all Canadian jurisdictions.

The diverse forms of families found in Canada are underscored by social factors, such as the ethical complexities of modern reproductive technologies and new legal dynamics of same-sex marriage. New laws, new technologies, and new child-rearing patterns have all combined to create diverse forms of family life. Today, for example, more women are essential contributors to their families through their paid work, whether married or as single parents. Blended families—the result of divorces and remarriages—are almost the norm. Many Canadians are seeking intimate relationships and having children outside marriage, particularly in Quebec, whether it be in same-sex or opposite-sex cohabiting arrangements.

In this chapter, we see that families are universal—found in every culture—however varied in their organization. We will look at families and intimate relationships from the functionalist, conflict, feminist, and interactionist points of view, and at the variations in marital patterns and family life, including different family forms of child-rearing. We pay particular attention to the increasing number of people in dual-income or single-parent families, the decline in the adult population that is married, and the legalization of same-sex marriage in Canada. We examine divorce in Canada and consider diversity patterns, including cohabitation, remaining single, lesbian and gay relationships, and marriage without children. In the social policy section, we look at controversial issues surrounding the use of reproductive technology. ■

 ## What Are Families?

Among Tibetans, a woman may be simultaneously married to more than one man, usually brothers. This system allows sons to share the limited amount of good land. Among the Betsileo of Madagascar, a man has multiple wives, each one living in a different village where he cultivates his rice. Wherever he has the best rice field, that wife is considered his first or senior wife. Among the Yanomani of Brazil and Venezuela, it is considered proper to have sexual relations with your opposite-sex cousins if they are the children of your mother's brother or your father's sister. But if your opposite-sex cousins are the children of your mother's sister or your father's brother, the same practice is considered to be incest (Haviland et al. 2008; Kottak 2011).

As these examples illustrate, there are many variations in families from culture to culture. Yet families as a social institution are present in all cultures. Moreover, certain general principles concerning their composition, kinship patterns, and authority patterns are universal.

Composition of Families

If we were to take our information on what a family is from what we see on television, we might come up with some very strange scenarios. The media don't always help us get a realistic view of the family. Moreover, many people still think of the family in very narrow terms—as a heterosexual married couple and their unmarried children living together, like the families in old television sitcoms such as *The Cosby Show*, *Family Ties*, and *Growing Pains*. However, this is but one type of family, what sociologists refer to as a **nuclear family.** The term nuclear family is well chosen, since this type of family serves as the nucleus, or core, upon which larger family groups

There are variations in families from culture to culture; however, families as a social institution are present in all cultures.

figure 12-1 Distribution of Census Families, 2001 and 2006

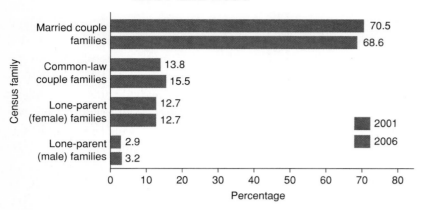

Source: Statistics Canada 2007d.

Think about It
In 10 years what changes would you expect to see in Figure 12-1's percentages?

are built. Some people in Canada may see the nuclear family as the preferred family arrangement. Yet the 2006 Census revealed that for the first time ever there were more couples without children than with children (Statistics Canada 2007d).

The proportion of households in Canada comprising married heterosexual couples with children at home has decreased steadily over the past 30 years, and this trend is expected to continue. At the same time, there have been increases in the number of single-parent households (see Figure 12-1). Similar trends are evident in other industrialized nations, including the United States, Great Britain, and Japan.

A family in which relatives—such as grandparents, aunts, or uncles—live in the same home as parents and their children is known as an **extended family.** Although not common, such living arrangements do exist in Canada. The structure of the extended family offers certain advantages over that of the nuclear family. Crises, such as death, divorce, and illness, put less strain on family members, since there are more people who can provide assistance and emotional support. In addition, the extended family constitutes a larger economic unit than the nuclear family. If the family is engaged in a common enterprise—a farm or a small business—the additional family members may represent the difference between prosperity and failure.

In considering these differing family types, we have limited ourselves to the form of marriage that is characteristic of Canada—monogamy. The term **monogamy** describes a form of marriage in which two people are married only to each other. Some observers, noting the rate of divorce in Canada, have suggested that "serial monogamy" is a more accurate description of marriage as it exists in this part of the world. Under **serial monogamy,** a person may have several spouses in his or her life but only one spouse at a time.

Some cultures allow an individual to have several spouses simultaneously. This form of marriage is known as **polygamy.** In fact, most societies throughout the world, past and present, have preferred polygamy to monogamy. Anthropologist

George Murdock sampled 565 societies and found that more than 80 percent had some type of polygamy as their preferred form (1949, 1957). Although polygamy steadily declined through most of the twentieth century, in at least five countries in Africa, 20 percent of men are still in polygamous marriages (Population Reference Bureau 1996).

There are two basic types of polygamy. According to Murdock, the most common— endorsed by the majority of cultures he sampled— was **polygyny.** Polygyny refers to the marriage of a man to more than one woman at the same time. The various wives are often sisters, who are expected to hold similar values and who have already had experience sharing a household. In polygynous societies, relatively few men actually have multiple spouses. Most individuals live in typical monogamous families; having multiple wives is viewed as a mark of status.

The other principal variation of polygamy is **polyandry,** under which a woman can have more than one husband at the same time. This is the case in the culture of the Todas of southern India, as well as the Nyinba of Nepal and Tibet. Polyandry, however, tends to be exceedingly rare in the world today. It has been accepted by some extremely poor societies that practise female infanticide (the killing of baby girls) and thus have a relatively small number of women. Like many other societies, polyandrous cultures devalue the social worth of women.

Kinship Patterns: To Whom Are We Related?

Many of us can trace our roots by looking at a family tree or listening to elderly family members tell us about their lives— and about the lives of ancestors who died long before we were even born. Yet, a person's lineage is more than simply a personal history; it also reflects societal patterns that govern descent. In every culture, children encounter relatives to whom they are expected to show an emotional attachment. The state of being related to others is called **kinship.** Kinship is culturally learned and is not totally determined by biological or marital ties. For example, adoption creates a kinship tie that is legally acknowledged and socially accepted.

The family and the kin group are not necessarily the same. Although the family is a household unit, kin do not always live together or function as a collective body on a daily basis. Kin groups include aunts, uncles, cousins, in-laws, and so forth. In a society such as Canada, the kinship group may come together only rarely, as for a wedding or funeral. However, kinship ties frequently create obligations and responsibilities. We may feel compelled to assist our kin and feel free to call on relatives for many types of aid, including loans and babysitting.

How do we identify kinship groups? The principle of descent assigns people to kinship groups according to their relationship to an individual's mother or father. There are three primary ways of determining descent. Generally in Canada, people follow the system of **bilateral descent,** which means that both sides of a person's family are regarded as

sociology in the global community

12-1 Family Life, Italian Style: Thirty-Something and Living with Mom

Bamboccioni—adult children who live with their parents—are no longer socially unacceptable in Italy. In fact, they're not even unusual. In December 2009, the Italian government released new data showing that 40 percent of Italian men between ages 30 and 34 live with their parents. So do 20 percent of Italian women in this age bracket. Among those a little older, ages 35 to 39, 17.5 percent of men and 9.3 percent of women live with their parents.

> *About 40 percent of* bamboccioni *live with their parents not because of financial need, but because they enjoy the company.*

This state of affairs is not a recent phenomenon. What is new is that 80 percent of these adult children say they cannot afford to leave their parents' homes. Salaries in Italy are low but rents are high, so these not-so-young adults linger on with mama and papa. As one of them, a 30-year-old biologist, put it, "We are the €1,000-per-month generation—who can afford spending more than €800 for an apartment?"

About 40 percent of *bamboccioni* live with their parents not because of financial need, but because they enjoy the company. Others feel responsible for their aging parents. Among the women ages 35 to 40, more than half feel it is a duty. Sociologist Giampiero dalla Zuanna says their commitment to the family means the elderly in Italy are much more likely to remain in their own homes than those in northern Europe, many of whom must move to retirement communities.

The pattern of adult children staying home with their parents is not unique to Italy. In North America and throughout Europe, young people are feeling the impact of the recent economic downturn. Many are delaying childbearing until their job prospects improve.

One relatively unnoticed factor that is contributing to the trend is parents' greater longevity. Today, more parents survive long enough for their children to become adults, and remain healthy enough to maintain a home for them.

What happens when adult children finally do leave the nest? So close are the ties between parent and child in Italy that services have emerged to support their relationship through the separation in living arrangements. For a small fee, special couriers will pick up Mother's fresh homemade pasta and even homegrown greens and deliver them to her adult children.

Apply the Theory

1. Do you or someone you know live at home with parents? If so, do you see the situation as similar to that of the *bamboccioni*?
2. In Canada, what other factors might contribute to adult children choosing to live with their parents?

Sources: Meichtry 2011; Momigliana 2010; Roberts 2010.

---

equally important. For example, no higher value is given to the brothers of a father than to the brothers of a mother.

Most societies—according to George Murdock, 64 percent—give preference to one side of the family or the other in tracing descent. **Patrilineal descent** (from the Latin *pater*, "father") indicates that only the father's relatives are important in terms of property, inheritance, and emotional ties. Conversely, in societies that favour **matrilineal descent** (from the Latin *mater*, "mother"), only the mother's relatives are significant.

New forms of reproductive technology (discussed in the chapter-ending social policy section) will force a new way of looking at kinship. Today, a combination of biological and social processes can "create" a family member, requiring that more distinctions be made about who is related to whom (Cussins 1998).

Authority Patterns: Who Rules?

Imagine that you have recently married and must begin to make decisions about the future of your new family. You and your spouse face many questions. Where will you live? How will you furnish your home? Who will do the cooking, the shopping, and the cleaning? Whose friends will be invited to dinner? Each time a decision must be made, an issue is raised: Who has the power to make the decision? In simple terms, who rules the family? The conflict perspective examines these questions in the context of gender stratification, in which men hold dominant positions over women in capitalist societies in general and in opposite-sex families in particular.

Societies vary in the way that power within the family is distributed. If a society expects males to dominate in all

Although spouses in an egalitarian family may not share all their decisions, they regard themselves as equals. This pattern of authority is becoming more common in North America.

Functionalist View

There are six paramount functions performed by the family, first outlined more than 65 years ago by sociologist William F. Ogburn (Ogburn and Tibbits 1934):

1. *Reproduction.* For a society to maintain itself, it must replace dying members. In this sense, the family contributes to human survival through its function of reproduction.

2. *Protection.* Unlike the young of other animal species, human infants need constant care and economic security. The extremely long period of dependency for children places special demands on older family members. In all cultures, it is the family that assumes ultimate responsibility for the protection and upbringing of children.

family decision making, it is termed a **patriarchy.** Frequently, in patriarchal societies, such as Iran, the eldest male wields the greatest power, although wives are expected to be treated with respect and kindness. A woman's status in Iran is typically defined by her relationship to a male relative, usually as a wife or daughter. In many patriarchal societies, a woman finds it more difficult to obtain a divorce than a man does (Farr 1999). By contrast, in a **matriarchy,** women have greater authority than men. Matriarchies, which are very uncommon, emerged among some of Canada's Aboriginal tribal societies and in nations in which men were absent for long periods of time for warfare or food gathering.

A third type of authority pattern, the **egalitarian family,** is one in which spouses are regarded as equals. This does not mean, however, that each decision is shared in such families. Wives may hold authority in some spheres, husbands in others. Many sociologists believe the egalitarian family has begun to replace the patriarchal family as the social norm in Canada.

12.2 How Do Sociologists Study Families?

Do we really need families? A century ago, Friedrich Engels, a colleague of Karl Marx's, described the family as the ultimate source of social inequality because of its role in the transfer of power, property, and privilege (1884). More recently, conflict theorists have argued that the family contributes to societal injustice, denies opportunities to women that are extended to men, and limits freedom in sexual expression and selection of a mate. By contrast, the functionalist perspective focuses on the ways in which the family gratifies the needs of its members and contributes to the stability of society. The interactionist view considers more intimate, face-to-face relationships.

3. *Socialization.* Parents and other kin monitor a child's behaviour and transmit the norms, values, and language of a culture to the child (see Chapters 3 and 4).

4. *Regulation of sexual behaviour.* Sexual norms are subject to change over time (for instance, changes in customs for dating) and across cultures (Islamic Saudi Arabia compared with more permissive Denmark). However, whatever the time period or cultural values in a society, standards of sexual behaviour are most clearly defined within the family circle. The structure of society influences these standards. In male-dominated societies, for example, formal and informal norms generally permit men to express and enjoy their sexual desires more freely than women may.

5. *Affection and companionship.* Ideally, the family provides members with warm and intimate relationships and helps them feel satisfied and secure. Of course, a family member may find such rewards outside the family—from peers, in school, at work—and may perceive the home as an unpleasant place. Nevertheless, unlike other institutions, the family is obligated to serve the emotional needs of its members. We *expect* our relatives to understand us, to care for us, and to be there for us when we need them.

6. *Provision of social status.* We inherit a social position because of the "family background" and reputation of our parents and siblings. The family unit presents the newborn child with an ascribed status of race and ethnicity that helps to determine his or her place within a society's stratification system. Moreover, family resources affect children's ability to pursue certain opportunities, such as higher education and specialized lessons.

The family has traditionally fulfilled a number of other functions, such as providing religious training, education, and recreational outlets. Ogburn argued that other social institutions have gradually assumed many of these functions. Although the family once played a major role in religious life, this function has largely shifted to churches, synagogues, and other religious organizations. Similarly, education once took place at the family fireside; now it is the responsibility of professionals working in schools and universities. Even the family's traditional recreational function has been transferred to outside groups, such as soccer leagues, dance lessons, and Internet chat rooms.

Conflict View

Conflict theorists view the family not as a contributor to social stability, but as a reflection of the inequality in wealth and power found within the larger society. Feminist theorists and conflict theorists note that the family has traditionally legitimized and perpetuated male dominance. Throughout most of human history—and in a very wide range of societies—husbands have exercised overwhelming power and authority within the family. Not until the first wave of contemporary feminism in North America in the mid-nineteenth century was there a substantial challenge to the historic status of wives and children as the legal property of husbands.

Although the egalitarian family has become a more common pattern in North America in recent decades—owing in good part to the activism of feminists beginning in the late 1960s and early 1970s—male dominance within the family has hardly disappeared. Sociologists have found that women are significantly more likely to leave their jobs when their husbands find better employment opportunities, than men are when their wives receive desirable job offers (Bielby and Bielby 1992). And, unfortunately, many husbands reinforce their power and control over wives and children through acts of domestic violence. (Box 12-2, found later in this chapter, considers cross-cultural findings about violence within the home.)

Conflict theorists also view the family as an economic unit that contributes to societal injustice. The family is the basis for transferring power, property, and privilege from one generation to the next. North America is widely viewed as a "land of opportunity," yet social mobility is restricted in important ways. Children "inherit" the privileged or less-than-privileged social and economic status of their parents (and, in some cases, of earlier generations as well). As conflict theorists point out, the social class of their parents significantly influences children's socialization experiences and the protection they receive. This means that the socioeconomic status of a child's family will have a marked influence on his or her nutrition, health care, housing, educational opportunities, and, in many respects, life chances as an adult. For that reason, conflict theorists argue that the family helps to maintain inequality.

Feminist Views

No single theory fully represents how feminism conceptualizes families. Feminist perspectives do, however, share certain assumptions in their study of families. Some of these assumptions include a rejection of the belief in the family's "naturalness" (Luxton 2001). Feminist theorists argue that families are socially constructed institutions and, thus, vary according to time and place. Families are not seen as "monolithic" or the same, but rather as diverse, flexible, and changeable. Although feminists' views on the family agree that women have a position of inequality and discrimination in the family, they argue that these, too, vary according to class, race, and ethnicity. The functional view of family is challenged by feminist theorists, who raise the question "For whom and for whose interests is the family functional?"

Canadian feminist theorist Margrit Eichler argues that the ways in which sociologists study the family often contain biases (2001). These include a *monolithic bias*, which is a tendency to assume "the family" is uniform rather than diverse; a *conservative bias*, which treats recent changes in the family as fleeting and ignores or treats as rare some of the uglier aspects of family life (e.g., family violence); an *ageist bias*, which regards children and the aged only as passive members of families; a *sexist bias*, which is exhibited in such patterns as double standards and gender insensitivity; a *microstructural bias*, which overemphasizes micro-level variables and neglects macro-level variables; a *racist bias*, which explicitly or implicitly assumes the superiority of the family form of the dominant group and ignores race and racism when relevant; and a *heterosexist bias*, which either ignores same-sex families or treats them as problematic and deviant.

Interactionist View

Interactionists focus on the micro level of family and other intimate relationships. They are interested in how individuals interact with one another, whether they are gay, lesbian,

Interactionists are particularly interested in the ways in which parents relate to each other and to their children. The close and loving relationship illustrated here is one of the foundations of a strong family.

Families and Intimate Relationships **253**

or heterosexual couples, and so on. For example, interactionists have looked at the nature of family interactions and relationship quality (e.g., interparental conflict, parenting stress, love between parents and for their children), and have found that those factors, rather than the parents' sexual orientation, strongly predict children's behavioural adjustment (Chan, Rayboy, and Patterson 1998).

Another interactionist study might examine the role of the stepparent. The increased number of single parents who remarry has sparked an interest in those who are helping to raise their partner's children. Although children likely do not dream about one day becoming a stepmom or stepdad, this is hardly an unusual occurrence today.

Table 12-1 summarizes the four major theoretical perspectives on the family.

What Are the Diverse Patterns of Marriage and Families?

Historically, the most consistent aspect of family life in this country has been the high rate of heterosexual marriage. However, for the first time, according to the 2006 Census, married people were the minority—51.5 percent of the adult population were not married in 2006. "Not married" in this context can mean never married, living in common-law relationships, divorced, separated, or widowed (Statistics Canada 2007i). Of those heterosexuals who separate or divorce, more men than women will go on to remarry or enter common-law relationships (Statistics Canada 2007i).

Here, we will examine various aspects of love, marriage, and parenthood in Canada, and we will contrast them with cross-cultural examples. In Western societies, romance and mate selection are often viewed as strictly a matter of individual preference. Yet, sociological analysis tells us that social institutions and distinctive cultural norms and values also play an important role.

table 12-1 Sociological Perspectives Families

Theoretical Perspective	Emphasis
Functionalist	The family as a contributor to social stability Roles of family members
Conflict	The family as a perpetuator of inequality Transmission of poverty or wealth across generations
Feminist	Families as a gendered institution Female-headed households
Interactionist	Relationships among family members

Courtship and Mate Selection

"My rugby mates would roll over in their graves," says Tom Buckley of his online courtship and subsequent marriage to Terri Muir. But Tom and Terri are hardly alone these days in turning to the Internet for matchmaking services. By the end of 1999, more than 2500 Web sites were helping people find mates. You could choose from oneandonly.com, 2ofakind.com, or cupidnet.com, among others. One service alone claimed 2 million subscribers. Tom and Terri carried on their romance via email for a year before they met face to face. According to Tom, "email made it easier to communicate because neither one of us was the type to walk up to someone in the gym or a bar and say, 'You're the fuel to my fire'" (Morris 1999:D1).

Internet romance is only the latest of many courtship practices. In the central Asian nation of Uzbekistan and many other traditional cultures, courtship is defined largely through the interaction of two sets of parents. They arrange spouses for their children. Typically, a young Uzbekistani woman is socialized to eagerly anticipate her marriage to a man whom she will have met only once—when he is presented to her family at the time of the final inspection of her dowry. In Canada, by contrast, courtship is conducted primarily by individuals who may have a romantic interest in each other. In Western culture, courtship often requires these individuals to rely heavily on intricate games, gestures, and signals. Courtship is influenced by the norms and values of the larger society.

One unmistakable pattern in mate selection is that the process appears to be taking longer today than in the past. A variety of factors, including concerns about financial security and personal independence, has contributed to this delay in marriage. Most people are now well into their 20s before they marry, both in Canada and in other countries (see Figure 12-2).

Take our choice of a mate. Why are we drawn to a particular person in the first place? To what extent are these judgments shaped by the society around us?

Aspects of Mate Selection Many societies have explicit or unstated rules that define potential mates as acceptable or unacceptable. These norms can be distinguished in terms of endogamy and exogamy. **Endogamy** (from the Greek *endon*, "within") specifies the groups within which a spouse must be found and prohibits marriage with others. For example, in Canada, many people are expected to marry within their own racial, ethnic, or religious group and are strongly discouraged or even prohibited from marrying outside the group. Endogamy is intended to reinforce the cohesiveness of the group by suggesting to the young that they should marry someone "of our own kind."

By contrast, **exogamy** (from the Greek *exo*, "outside") requires mate selection outside certain groups, usually outside the family or certain kinfolk. The **incest taboo**, a social norm common to virtually all societies, prohibits sexual relationships between certain culturally specified relatives. For people in Canada, this taboo means that Canadians must marry outside the nuclear family. We cannot marry our siblings; however, we are able to marry our first cousins.

Endogamous restrictions may be seen as preferences for one group over another. In the United States, such preferences

figure 12-2 Median Age at First Marriage in Eight Countries

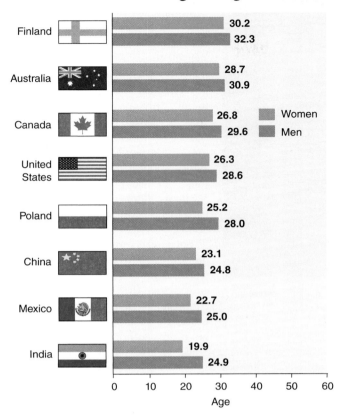

Country	Women	Men
Finland	30.2	32.3
Australia	28.7	30.9
Canada	26.8	29.6
United States	26.3	28.6
Poland	25.2	28.0
China	23.1	24.8
Mexico	22.7	25.0
India	19.9	24.9

Source: United Nations Statistics Division 2008.

Think about It
Why do people marry earlier in India than in Finland?

are most obvious in racial barriers. Until the 1960s, some American states outlawed interracial marriages. This practice was challenged by Richard Loving (a white man) and Mildred Jeter Loving (a part-black, part-Aboriginal woman), who married in 1958. Eventually, in 1967, the U.S. Supreme Court ruled that it was unconstitutional to prohibit marriage solely on the basis of race. The decision struck down statutes in Virginia and 16 other American states.

In Canada, there is evidence to suggest that people are more likely to marry someone outside of their own ethnic group the longer they reside in Canada. Northern, Western, and Eastern European ethnic groups are the most likely to marry outside their own ethnic group, while Asians, Africans, and Latin Americans are the least likely. Despite the effort the federal government expends promoting the ideology and policies of multiculturalism, Canadian families are coming to resemble one another more and more through increased intermarriage among various ethnic groups. Between 2001 and 2006 the number of mixed ethnocultural unions grew by 33 percent, five times more quickly than the average for all couples. In Canada, approximately 340 000 children are growing up in mixed ethnocultural unions (Milan et al. 2010). Increasing numbers of exogamous unions force a society to reconsider

its definitions of race and ethnicity. In Chapter 8, we noted that race is socially constructed in Canada and around the world. As increasing proportions of children in Canada come from backgrounds of more than one race or ethnicity, single ethnic and racial identifiers become less relevant. The Canadian census allows individuals to report two or more ethnicities as well as to respond to an "Other" category for race—this last category is aimed at those whose racial background does not fall neatly into one category (Howell et al. 2001).

The Love Relationship Whatever the social construction of "love," most people would agree it is a complicated one. Nancy Netting, a professor of sociology at the University of British Columbia–Okanagan, has conducted three surveys, in 1980, 1990, and 2000. Netting's most recent data reveals some interesting trends: She found that students are having a great deal less casual sex. In 1980, 67 percent of men and 34 percent of women at her postsecondary institution described their sexual encounters as being a one-night stand or with a stranger. In 2000, the percentages had dropped to 14 and 8 respectively. "Back then, more people were saying, 'I don't love you but you seem like a nice person so why not get together,' " says Netting. "Now, people really weigh in their minds whether this is someone to take a chance on. They're trying to find the person they can love" (Intini 2007).

In North America, love is socially constructed as important in the courtship process. Living in their own home may make the affectional bond between two people especially important. The couple may be expected to develop its own emotional ties, free of the demands of other household members for affection. Sociologist William Goode observed that opposite-sex spouses in a nuclear family have to rely heavily on each other for the companionship and support that might be provided by other relatives in an extended-family situation (1959).

Given this social construction of love, parents in North America tend to value it highly as a rationale for marriage, and they encourage their children to develop intimate relationships based on heterosexual love and affection. In addition, songs, films, books, magazines, television shows, and even cartoons and comic books reinforce the theme of heterosexual love. At the same time, our society may expect parents and peers to help a person confine his or her search for a mate to "socially acceptable" members of the opposite sex.

The social construction of love-and-marriage, as witnessed in North America, is by no means a cultural universal. In fact, in many cultures (both today and in the past), love and marriage are unconnected and are sometimes at odds with each other.

Many of the world's cultures give priority in mate selection to factors other than romantic feelings. In societies with **arranged marriages**, often engineered by parents or religious authorities, economic considerations play a significant role. The newly married couple is expected to develop a feeling of love *after* the legal union is formalized, if at all.

Within Canada, some subcultures carry on the arranged marriage practices of their native cultures. Young people among the Sikhs and Hindus who have immigrated from India, and among Islamic Muslims and Hasidic Jews, allow their parents or designated matchmakers to find spouses

When some children of immigrants to Canada want a mate, they may bow to their parents' wishes and select an arranged marriage.

within their ethnic community. As one young Sikh declared, "I will definitely marry who my parents wish. They know me better than I know myself" (R. Segall 1998:48). This practice of arranged marriage may be gradually changing, however, because of the influence of the larger society's cultural practices. Young people who have emigrated without their families often turn to the Internet to find partners who share their background and goals. For example, matrimonial ads for the Indian community run on such Web sites as SuitableMatch.com and Indolink.com. One Hasidic Jewish woman noted that the system of arranged marriages "isn't perfect, and it doesn't work for everyone, but this is the system we know and trust, the way we couple, and the way we learn to love. So it works for most of us" (R. Segall 1998:53).

::: use your sociological *imagination* :::

Your parents or a matchmaker will arrange a marriage for you. What kind of mate will they select? Will your chances of having a successful marriage be better or worse than if you had selected your own mate?

Social Class Differences Various studies have documented the differences in family organization among social classes in North America. The upper-class emphasis is on lineage and maintenance of family position. If you are in the upper class, you are not simply a member of a nuclear family; rather, you are a member of a larger family tradition. As a result, upper-class families are quite concerned about what they see as "proper training" for children.

Lower-class families do not often have the luxury of worrying about the "family name"; they must first struggle to pay their bills and survive the crises often associated with life in poverty. Such families are more likely to have only one parent in the home, creating special challenges in childcare and financial needs. Children in lower-class families typically assume adult responsibilities—including marriage and parenthood—at an earlier age than children of affluent homes. In part, this is because they may lack the money needed to remain in school.

Social-class differences in family life are less striking than they once were. In the past, family specialists agreed that there were pronounced contrasts in child-rearing practices. Lower-class families were found to be more authoritarian in rearing children and more inclined to use physical punishment. Middle-class families were more permissive and restrained in punishing their children. However, these differences may have narrowed as more and more families from all social classes have turned to the same books, magazines, and even television talk shows for advice on rearing children (M. Kohn 1970; Luster, Rhoades, and Haas 1989).

Among the poor, women often play a significant role in the economic support of the family. According to the 2006 Census, the median household income for single-parent families—80 percent being headed by women—was less than half that for two-parent families (Fenlon and Agrell 2007).

Many racial and ethnic groups appear to have distinctive family characteristics. However, racial and class factors are often closely related. In examining family life among racial and ethnic minorities, keep in mind that certain patterns may result from class as well as cultural factors.

Racial and Ethnic Differences The ways in which race, ethnicity, gender, and class intersect contributes to the diversity of Canadian families. The subordinate status of racial and ethnic minorities and Canada's Aboriginal peoples has profound effects on the family life of these groups.

Aboriginal peoples are a heterogeneous group with different histories, geographies, languages, economies, and cultures. Their families, which often include those who are kin as well as those who come together in a common community purpose, have been fundamentally disrupted by hundreds of years of European domination. For example, the First Nations peoples of the Montagnais-Naskapi of the eastern Labrador peninsula underwent major changes in family structure and gender relations as they moved to trapping, introduced by Europeans, and away from traditional hunting and fishing.

The division of labour between the sexes became more specialized and families began to get smaller, approaching the size of a nuclear family (Leacock 2001).

Aboriginal families have been devalued and undermined by the Canadian government and religious institutions. In the past, children were sent away from their homes to residential schools, where they were punished for speaking their own language and expressing their own culture. There, they were often subjected to sexual and physical abuse at the hands of those who ran the schools—people who were assigned to be their guardians.

In the 1960s, many Aboriginal children were put up for adoption and taken in, most often, by white families in Canada and the United States, rather than by those from within their own band (Eichler 1997). Today, after years of cultural oppression under government control, problems of domestic abuse, youth suicide, and substance abuse plague Aboriginal families.

Research carried out in Nova Scotia and Ontario of opposite-sex couples demonstrates the links among race, class, and gender and their impact on black families (Calliste 2001). Significantly more black families than non-black families were headed by women; these women-headed black families earned approximately half of the income of their married counterparts, who in turn earned less than non-black families headed by married couples. The study concludes that the high rate of teenage pregnancy and the feminization of poverty need to be addressed by black community groups and government in the form of education, employment equity, sex education, and parenting sessions (Calliste 2001:417). Some similarities exist between Canadian and U.S. black families because race, class, and gender intersect to produce inequality for families in both countries.

Child-Rearing Patterns in Family Life

Caring for children is a universal function of the family, yet the ways in which different societies assign this function to family members can vary significantly. Within Canada, child-rearing patterns are varied. We'll look here at parenthood and grandparenthood, adoption, dual-income families, single-parent families, and stepfamilies. (See Figure 12-3 for proportions of children aged 14 and under living with married parents, common-law parents, and lone parents.)

Parenthood and Grandparenthood

The socialization of children is essential to the maintenance of any culture. Consequently, parenthood is one of the most important (and most demanding) social roles in North America. Sociologist Alice Rossi (1968, 1984) has identified four factors that complicate the transition to parenthood and the role of socialization. First, there

is little anticipatory socialization for the social role of caregiver. The normal school curriculum gives scant attention to the subjects most relevant to successful family life—such as childcare and home maintenance. Second, only limited learning occurs during the period of pregnancy itself. Third, the transition to parenthood is quite abrupt. Unlike adolescence, it is not prolonged; unlike socialization for work, you cannot gradually take on the duties of caregiving. Finally, in Rossi's view, our society lacks clear and helpful guidelines for successful parenthood. There is little consensus on how parents can produce happy and well-adjusted offspring—or even on what it means to be "well adjusted." For these reasons, socialization for parenthood involves difficult challenges for most men and women in North America.

One recent development in family life in Canada has been the extension of parenthood, as adult children continue to (or return to) live at home. The 2006 Census revealed that 44 percent of adult children in their 20s lived in their parents' home, up 12 percent from 1986 (Statistics Canada 2007d). In some instances, financial constraints are at the heart of these living arrangements, particularly in the country's large urban centres. Although rents and real estate prices skyrocketed, salaries for younger workers did not keep pace, and many found themselves unable to afford their own homes. Moreover, with many marriages now ending in divorce—most commonly in the first seven years of marriage—divorced sons and daughters are returning to live with their parents, sometimes with their own children. Sociologist Monica Boyd at the University of Toronto states, "It has become normal" for parents to foster this living arrangement as a way of successfully launching their children (Andreatta 2007).

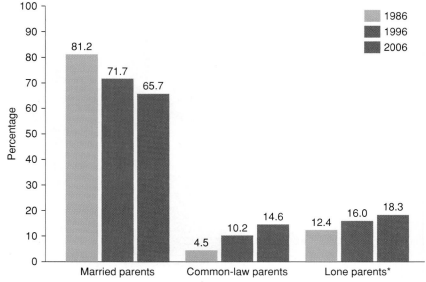

figure **12-3 Distribution of Children Aged 14 and Under by Family Structure**

*Historical comparisons for census families, particularly lone-parent families, must be interpreted with caution due to conceptual changes in 2001.

Source: Statistics Canada, 2007d.

As life expectancy increases in North America, more and more parents are becoming grandparents and even great-grandparents. After interviewing many grandparents, sociologists Andrew Cherlin and Frank Furstenberg, Jr., identified three principal styles of grandparenting (1992):

1. More than half (55 percent) of grandparents surveyed functioned as "specialists in recreational caregiving." They enriched their grandchildren's lives through recreational outings and other special activities.
2. More than one-fourth (29 percent) carried on a "ritualistic" (primarily symbolic) relationship with their grandchildren. In some instances, this was because the grandparents lived far away from their grandchildren and could see them only occasionally.
3. About one-sixth (16 percent) of grandparents surveyed were actively involved in everyday routine care of their grandchildren and exercised substantial authority over them.

In Canada, more than 55 000 grandparents are raising their grandchildren on their own (Vallas 2005).

Adoption   In a legal sense, **adoption** is a "process that allows for the transfer of the legal rights, responsibilities, and privileges of parenthood" to a new legal parent or parents (Cole 1985:638). In many cases, these rights are transferred from a biological parent or parents (often called birth parents) to an adoptive parent or parents.

Viewed from a functionalist perspective, government has a strong interest in encouraging adoption. Policymakers, in fact, have both a humanitarian and a financial stake in the process. In theory, adoption offers a stable family environment for children who otherwise might not receive satisfactory care. Moreover, government data show that unwed mothers who keep their babies tend to be of lower socioeconomic status and often require public assistance to support their children.

Government can lower its social welfare expenses if children are transferred to economically self-sufficient families. From a conflict perspective, however, such financial considerations raise the ugly spectre of adoption as a means whereby affluent (often infertile) couples "buy" the children of the poor (Bachrach 1986). For decades during the last century, Aboriginal children were adopted into white families in Canada and the United States; this practice has since been identified as a form of cultural genocide and has "fallen into disrepute" (Baker 2007).

With greater access to contraception and legal abortion, the rate of unplanned births to young women has declined since the 1950s, and the availability of Canadian infants has decreased. As well, more and more single mothers have been keeping their babies and supporting them through earnings or social assistance. In addition, the goals of family preservation in the Canadian child welfare system, and Canadians' current preference to adopt infants and younger children, will make the case for international adoption (most likely from developing countries) more compelling (Baker 2001). This supports the conflict view that the wealthier, more powerful countries have control over the poorer, less powerful countries. In this case, it involves the "purchase" of children.

Dual-Income Families   The idea of a family consisting of a wage-earning male spouse and a female spouse who stays at home has largely given way to the dual-income household. In Canada, dual-income families make up 63 percent of all households (TD Bank 2007). Why has there been such a rise in the number of dual-income families? A major factor is economic need. Manitoba Agriculture and Food, in 2004, estimated the costs of raising a child from birth to age 18 to be $166 762. Raising children in urban centres, where the bulk of the Canadian population resides, is expensive; housing costs over the past decade have increased dramatically in many cities across Canada. Other factors contributing to the rise of the dual-income model include the nation's declining birth rate (see Chapter 15), the increase in the proportion of women with postsecondary educations, the shift in the economy of North America from manufacturing to service industries, and the impact of the feminist movement in influencing societal attitudes.

Single-Parent Families   In recent decades, the stigma attached to "unwed mothers" and other single parents has significantly diminished. **Single-parent families**, in which there is only one parent to care for the children, can hardly be viewed as a rarity in Canada. In 2006, approximately 26 percent of families were run by a lone parent (up from 11 percent in 1981); the overwhelming

A father and husband reads to his family via Skype. For employment reasons he lives in a distant city.

majority of these families were female-headed. Variation and diversity exists among single-parent families. For example, according to Statistics Canada, almost half of black families were headed by a single parent, compared with 18 percent of other families (Canadian Press 2007). The interaction of race, class, and gender is evident in patterns of black family structure (Calliste 2001).

Although marital dissolution is the major cause of the increase in lone-parent families, never-married lone parents are growing in number. Never-married lone parents constituted 29.5 percent of all lone parents in Canada in 2006, while in 1951, they made up 1.5 percent of the total number of single parents (Statistics Canada 2007i).

The lives of single parents and their children are not necessarily more difficult than life in other types of families. It is as inaccurate to assume that a single-parent family is necessarily "deprived" as it is to assume that a two-parent family is always secure and happy. Nevertheless, life in a single-parent family can be extremely stressful, in both economic and emotional terms. Economic inequality and poverty are striking characteristics of lone-parent families. When compared with two-parent families, female-led (particularly those who are younger) lone-parent families are the most vulnerable to poverty, a fact that contributes to the phenomenon known as the "feminization of poverty."

A family headed by a single mother faces especially difficult problems if the mother is a teenager. Drawing on two decades of social science research, sociologist Kristin Luker observes:

> The short answer to why teenagers get pregnant and especially to why they continue those pregnancies is that a fairly substantial number of them just don't believe what adults tell them, be it about sex, contraception, marriage, or babies. They don't believe in adult conventional wisdom. (1996:11)

Why might low-income teenage women want to have children and face the obvious financial difficulties of motherhood? Viewed from an interactionist perspective, these young women tend to have low self-esteem and limited options; a child may provide a sense of motivation and purpose for a teenager whose economic worth in our society is limited at best. Given the barriers that many young women face because of their gender, race, ethnicity, and class, many teenagers may believe that they have little to lose and much to gain by having a child.

Countries belonging to the Organisation for Economic Co-operation and Development (OECD; i.e., developed nations) have experienced an increase in lone-parent families since the early 1970s, with the greatest increase occurring in the United States (Baker 2001). However, poverty rates for these families vary among industrialized countries, depending on the availability of social welfare programs, the rates of male and female unemployment, government disincentives to work while receiving social assistance, and the availability of special employment training programs and childcare.

Despite the current concern over the increase in the number of lone-parent families, this family type has existed for more than 100 years in Canada. In 1901, the ratio of lone-parent to two-parent families was only slightly lower than today's ratio. A major interdisciplinary study carried out at the University of Victoria, based on 1901 Census data, concluded that the family has always been a variable and flexible institution. With unsanctioned or non-formalized divorce being more common in the past than is generally known, "there was much more volatility and shifting of marital status than anyone was prepared to admit at the state level" (Gram 2001).

Blended Families   For a couple or individual who separates or divorces and then goes on to form a second or third relationship, a **blended family** may be the result.

Blended families are an exceedingly complex form of family organization. Here is how one 13-year-old boy described his family:

> Tim and Janet are my stepbrother and sister. Josh is my stepdad. Carin and Don are my real parents, who are divorced. And Don married Anna and together they had Ethan and Ellen, my half-sister and brother. And Carin married Josh and had little Alice, my half-sister. (Bernstein 1988)

The exact nature of these blended families has social significance for adults and children alike. Certainly, resocialization is required when an adult becomes a stepparent or a child becomes a stepchild and stepsibling. Moreover, an important

When nine-year-old Blake Brunson shows up for a basketball game, so do his eight grandparents—the result of his parents' remarriage.

distinction must be made between first-time stepfamilies and households where there have been repeated divorces, breakups, or changes in custodial arrangements.

In evaluating the rise of blended families, some observers have assumed that children would benefit from remarriage because they'd be gaining a second custodial parent and, potentially, have greater economic security. However, after reviewing many studies on stepfamilies, sociologist Andrew Cherlin concluded that "children whose parents have remarried do not have higher levels of well-being than children in lone-parent families" (2009:5) Stepparents can play valuable and unique roles in their stepchildren's lives, but their involvement does not guarantee an improvement. In fact, standards may decline. Some studies found that children raised in families with stepmothers are likely to have less health-care attention, education, and money spent on their nutrition than are children raised by biological mothers. The measures are also negative for children raised by a stepfather, but only half as negative as in the case of stepmothers. It may be that the stepmother recedes from the stepchild/stepchildren in an effort to avoid seeming too intrusive, or relies mistakenly on the biological father to carry out these parental duties (Schmeeckle 2007; Schmeeckle et al. 2006).

Family Violence in Canada The family is often portrayed through the mass media and other institutions as a source of comfort, security, and safety, as a place to which its members retreat to escape the rough and tumble of the public world of work and school. This social construction of the family as a "haven in a heartless world" (Lasch 1977) often obscures the reality that many members of families face; that is, the family can be a source of conflict and, possibly, danger. Sociologists Gelles and Straus point out that "you are more likely to be physically assaulted, beaten, and killed in your own home at the hands of a loved one than anyplace else, or by anyone else in society" (1988:18). There are various types of family violence, including violence against women, violence against children, sibling violence, and violence against elders (DeKeseredy 2005).

In 2010, 48 656 cases of spousal violence—violence against legally married, common-law, separated, and divorced partners—were reported to police, representing 12 percent of all violent crime reported to the police (Statistics Canada 2012). The majority of victims of spousal violence are female; in 2010 women accounted for approximately 81 percent of the victims. Statistics Canada's definition of violent crime includes violations causing death, attempted murder, sexual assaults, assaults, robbery, criminal harassment, uttering threats and other violations involving violence or the threat of violence. Women experience the more serious forms of spousal violence and are more likely to state that their spouse had been drinking before and during the time of the violent incident. Between 1998 and 2007, the overall decline in spousal assault against women in Canada may have been due to such factors as availability of shelters for abused women, increased reporting to police by victims of abuse, mandatory arrest policies for men who assault their wives, growth in the number of treatment programs for violent men, changes in the economic and social status of women that allow them to more easily leave violent relationships, and changes in society's attitudes recognizing assault of female spouses as a crime.

Contrary to a commonly held assumption that spousal violence ends after the breakdown of a marriage, violence continues and often occurs for the first time after the couple separates. In 2004 in Canada, "half of the women who reported experiencing spousal assault by a past partner indicated that the violence occurred after the couple separated, and in one-third of post-separation assaults, the violence became more severe or actually began after the separation" (Statistics Canada 2006a:38). Male "proprietariness" or sexual jealousy has often been used to explain patterns of male violence toward female ex-partners, particularly in acts of killing (Gartner, Dawson, and Crawford 2001).

Spousal homicide—the ultimate form of spousal violence—carries the greatest risk for women during marital separation. "Women killed by their spouses during marital separation also outnumber women in similar situations in the general population: 26 percent of female spousal homicide victims were separated compared with just 4 percent of women in the population" (Statistics Canada 2006a:38).

Canadian children and youth who die from homicide are most likely to be killed by family members (Statistics Canada 2009). In 2007, family members were responsible for 41 percent of homicides of children and youth recorded by police in Canada. The majority of cases of family violence toward children involved physical or sexual assault; a parent was identified as the abuser in roughly 6 out of every 10 incidents and male family members were responsible for the majority of the assaults (Statistics Canada 2009).

Family violence may also be committed against older members of the family, such as grandparents, although the rate of family violence against seniors is much lower than that for other age groups in the family. In these cases—as in other age groups—women are more likely to be the victims; spouses and adult children are most often the perpetrators. In 2007 in Canada, family members aged 25 to 34 had rates of violent victimization eight times greater than that of seniors (Statistics Canada 2009).

Box 12-2 presents a discussion of family violence in the global community.

Divorce

"Do you promise to love, honour, and cherish . . . until death do you part?" Every year, people of all social classes, racial and ethnic groups, and, now, sexual orientations make this legally binding agreement. Yet, a number of these promises end in divorce. According to Statistics Canada, in 2008, the crude divorce rate was 211 for every 100 000 people in the population (2011). Roughly one in three marriages ends in divorce within a 30-year period.

Statistical Trends in Divorce Just how common is divorce? Surprisingly, this is not a simple question; divorce statistics are difficult to interpret.

The media frequently report that one out of every three opposite-sex marriages ends in divorce. And in 2004 the first same-sex legal divorce occurred in Canada. Figures can be

sociology in the global community

12-2 Family Violence

The phone rings two or three dozen times a day at the Friend of the Family Hotline in San Salvador, the capital city of El Salvador. Each time the staff receives a report of family violence, a crisis team is immediately dispatched to the caller's home. Caseworkers provide comfort to victims, as well as accumulate evidence for use in the attacker's prosecution. In the first three years of its existence, Friend of the Family handled more than 28 000 cases of domestic violence.

Spousal abuse and other forms of family violence are not confined to El Salvador. Drawing on studies conducted throughout the world, we can make the following generalizations:

- Women are most at risk of violence from the men they know.
- Violence against women occurs in all socioeconomic groups.
- Family violence is at least as dangerous as assaults committed by strangers.
- Though women sometimes exhibit violent behaviour toward men, the majority of violent acts that cause injury are perpetrated by men

against women. Violence against men frequently goes unreported since male gender roles and domestic violence are incongruous in many cultures.

- Violence within intimate relationships tends to escalate over time.
- Emotional and psychological abuse can be at least as debilitating as physical abuse.
- Use of alcohol exacerbates family violence but does not cause it.

Using the conflict and feminist models, researchers have found that in relationships in which the inequality between men and women is great, the likelihood of assault on wives increases dramatically. This discovery suggests that much of the violence between intimates, even when sexual in nature, is about power rather than sex.

The family can be a dangerous place for women, children, and the elderly. In 2010, 55 percent of all police-reported violent crime was committed against females by spouses, ex-spouses, other immediate and extended family members (i.e., child), current/former dating

partners, or other intimate partners (Statistics Canada 2012). Between April 1, 2007, and March 31, 2008, 62 000 women and 38 000 children were admitted to 569 shelters across Canada, making up the vast majority of those shelter admittees (Statistics Canada 2009); between 1978 and 2007, women experienced spousal homicide rates four to five times greater than that of men (Statistics Canada 2009).

Apply the Theory

1. Do you know of a family that has experienced family violence? Did the victim(s) seek outside help, and, if so, was it effective?
2. Why might the degree of equality in a relationship correlate to the likelihood of family violence? How might conflict theorists explain this finding?

Sources: American Bar Association 1999; Gelles and Cornell 1990; Heise, Ellsberg, and Gottemuelle 1999; Rennison and Welchans 2000; Spindel, Levy, and Connor 2000; Statistics Canada 2009; Statistics Canada 2012; Valdez 1999; Wilson 2000.

---

misleading, since many marriages last for decades. They are based on a comparison of all divorces that occur in a single year (regardless of when the couples were married) against the number of new marriages in the same year.

Heterosexual divorce in Canada, and many other countries, began to increase in the late 1960s but then started to level off and even decline since the late 1980s and has remained relatively stable since 1999 (Statistics Canada 2005i, 2011). This is partly due to the aging of the baby boomer population and the corresponding decline in the proportion of people of marriageable age (see Figure 12-4).

Doug Norris, of the research firm Environics, notes, in his analysis of the 2006 Census, that after separations and divorces Canadian women tend not to form unions again. Norris states, "When those relationships break up, women tend, for whatever reason, not to get into a second relationship. They live on their own, or perhaps as single parents, but they're not forming a couple. They are not remarrying, not going into a common law union to nearly the extent that males do, and that gap widens with age" (Fenlon and Agrell 2007).

Some people regard remarriage as an endorsement of the institution of marriage, but it does lead to the new challenges of a remarriage kin network comprising current and prior marital relationships. This network can be particularly complex if children are involved or if an ex-spouse remarries.

Factors Associated with Divorce

Perhaps the most important factor in the increase in heterosexual divorce throughout the twentieth century and into the twenty-first century has been the greater social *acceptance* of divorce. It's no longer considered necessary to endure an unhappy marriage. Most importantly, various religious denominations have relaxed their attitudes toward divorce, and many religious leaders no longer treat it as negatively.

A few other factors deserve mention:

- No-fault divorce provisions, allowing a couple to end their marriage without fault on either side (such as specifying adultery), accounted for an initial surge in the divorce rate after they were introduced in 1985, although they appear to have had little effect beyond that.
- Divorce has become a more practical option in newly formed families, since they now tend to have fewer children than in the past.
- A general increase in family incomes, coupled with the availability of free legal aid for some poor people, has meant that more couples can afford the cost of divorce proceedings.
- As society provides greater opportunities for women, more and more women are becoming less dependent on their spouses—both economically and emotionally. They may then feel more able to leave if the marriage seems hopeless.

figure **12-4** **Marriage and Divorce Rates in Canada, 1967–2008**

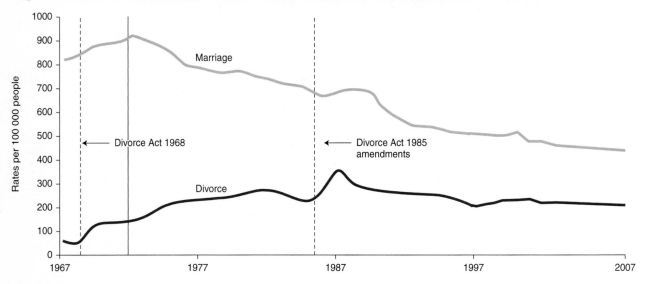

Sources: Baker 2001:218; Statistics Canada 1997, 2003o, 2003p, 2004h, 2004i, 2005i, 2007i, 2011.

Impact of Divorce on Children   According to Statistics Canada, nearly one in two divorces in Canada involves dependent children (2005d). For some of these children, divorce signals the welcome end to being witness to a very dysfunctional relationship. A study that tracked 6332 children both before and after their parents' divorce found that their behaviour did not suffer from the marital breakup. Other researchers have found greater unhappiness for children living in homes with marital conflict than among children whose parents are divorced. Still, it would be simplistic to assume that children are automatically better off following the breakup of their parents' marriage. The interests of the parents do not necessarily serve children well (Zi 2007).

Other studies in Canada, the United States, and Britain have shown that some of the alleged negative effects of heterosexual divorce actually resulted from conditions (such as poverty) that existed *before* the parental separation. A study on divorce and the mental health of children in Canada concluded that, although children whose parents divorced had higher levels of depression and antisocial behaviour, these behaviours were associated with their parents reporting lower levels of marital satisfaction, and higher levels of depression and family dysfunction. The study found that the same characteristics associated with parental divorce—before it happened—were also associated with children's depression and antisocial behaviour (Statistics Canada 2005). Moreover, if divorce does not lower children's access to resources and does not increase stress, its impact on children may be neutral or even positive.

::: use your sociological *imagination* :::

In a society that maximizes the welfare of all family members, how easy should it be for couples to divorce? How easy should it be to get married? Remarried?

Cohabitation

One of the most dramatic trends of recent years in Canada has been the tremendous increase in the number of opposite-sex couples who choose to live together without marrying, engaging in what is commonly called **cohabitation.**

In 2006, 15.5 percent of all Canadian couples were cohabiting, up from 7.2 percent in 1986. Since 2001, common-law relationships have increased by 19 percent, five times faster than the growth in the number of married couples (Statistics Canada 2007d).

In much of Europe, cohabitation is so common that the general sentiment seems to be "love, yes; marriage, maybe." In Iceland, 62 percent of all children are born to single mothers; in France, Britain, and Norway, the proportion is roughly 40 percent. Government policies in these countries make few legal distinctions between married and unmarried couples or households (Lyall 2002).

In Canada, Quebec stands out from the rest of the country in its rates of marriage and cohabitation. The 2006 Census found that 35 percent of couples in Quebec are in common-law relationships, making up 44.4 percent of the country's total number (Statistics Canada 2007d). Quebec residents are increasingly turning away from traditional institutions, such as church and state, in the establishment of their families. More people there than in any other jurisdiction live in common-law relationships; in 2006, the ratio was approximately one in every three couples.

Census figures have documented increases in cohabitation among older people in Canada, with huge increases among those 40 and over; the number of Canadians between 60 and 64 living common-law rose 77 percent between 2001 and 2006 (Statistics Canada 2007d). Older couples may choose cohabitation rather than marriage for many reasons: because of religious differences, to preserve the full pension benefits they receive as single people, out of fear of commitment, to avoid upsetting children from previous marriages, because one partner or both are not legally divorced, or because one or both have lived through a spouse's illness and death and do not want to experience that again. But some older couples simply see no need for marriage and report being happy living together as they are.

Zheng Wu, professor of sociology at the University of Victoria and expert in the area of cohabitation, states, "More people are substituting cohabitation for marriage and really treat it as marriage. . . . [Common] law has become a protected social institution" (Agrell 2007).

Remaining Single

Looking at TV programs today, you would be justified in thinking most households are composed of singles. Although this is not the case, it is true that more and more people in Canada are postponing entry into first marriages. In 1973, the average age of first marriage in Canada was approximately 25 years for men and 23 years for women; by 2003, the average age at first marriage was approximately 30 years and 28 years for men and women respectively, constituting an average increase for both sexes of five years (Statistics Canada 2007i). Partly because of the postponement of marriage and the increase in common-law relationships, married Canadians are now in the minority (Statistics Canada 2007i).

The trend toward maintaining a single lifestyle for a longer period of time is related to the growing economic independence of young people. This is especially significant for women. Freed from financial needs, women don't necessarily have to marry to enjoy a satisfying life.

There are many reasons why a person may choose not to marry. Singleness is an attractive option for those who do not want to limit their sexual intimacy to one life partner. Also, some men and women do not want to become highly dependent on any one person—and do not want anyone depending heavily on them. In a society that values individuality and self-fulfillment, the single lifestyle can offer certain freedoms that married couples may not enjoy.

Remaining single represents a clear departure from societal expectations of the dominant culture; indeed, it has been likened to "being single on Noah's Ark." A single adult must confront the inaccurate view that he or she is always lonely, is a workaholic, and is immature. These stereotypes help support the traditional assumption in North America and most other societies that to be truly happy and fulfilled, a person must get married and raise a family. To help counter these societal expectations, singles have formed numerous support groups, such as the Alternatives to Marriage Project (www.unmarried.org).

Lesbian and Gay Relationships

We were both raised in middle-class families, where the expectation was we would go to college, we would become educated, we'd get a nice white-collar job, we'd move up and own a nice house in the suburbs. And that's exactly what we've done. (*The New York Times* 1998:B2)

In 2005, Bill C-38 was passed by Canada's federal government, making same-sex marriage legal in all jurisdictions. Here, a same-sex wedding is taking place.

Sound like a heterosexual couple? The "we" described here is a gay couple.

The lives of lesbians and gay men vary greatly. Some live in long-term, monogamous relationships, legal or common-law. Some couples live with adopted children or children from former heterosexual marriages. The 2006 Census in Canada counted 25 345 same-sex couples, up 32 percent from 2001. Same-sex couples make up 0.6 percent of all couples and live primarily in Canada's three largest cities—Vancouver, Toronto, and Montreal (Fenlon and Agrell 2007).

In 2005, Bill C-38 was passed by the federal government, making same-sex civil marriage legal in *all* jurisdictions in Canada. In 2006, for the first time, the Canadian census allowed individuals to indicate if they were in a same-sex marriage; 7465 couples indicated that they were (Fenlon and Agrell 2007). Canada was the third country in the world to legalize same-sex marriage, following the Netherlands (2000) and Belgium (2003). Shortly after Canada's passage of Bill C-38 in 2005, Spain's government announced the legalization of same-sex marriage. Other countries later followed suit—South Africa in 2006, Norway and Sweden in 2009, Iceland, Argentina, and Portugal in 2010, Denmark in 2012, Uruguay, New Zealand, Great Britain, and France in 2013. In April 2013, Russian President Vladimir Putin warned that his country is considering a ban of adoption of Russian children for countries that allow same-same marriage (Parfitt 2013).

In Canada, the debate over the legalization of same-sex marriage played out over such concerns as rights (e.g., in the federal Department of Justice), human dignity and concern over the perpetuation of prejudicial attitudes (e.g., in the United Church of Canada), consequences for freedom of religion and conscience (e.g., in the Canadian Conference of Bishops), and the concern of being "overinclusive" (e.g., by the attorney general of Alberta).

Marriage without Children

According to the 2006 Census, for the first time in Canada, there were more families without children (42.7 percent) than with children (41.4 percent). Twenty years ago, more than half of Canadian couples had children, defined as offspring under 25 (Grewal 2007). Anne Milan, an analyst with Statistics Canada, attributes the trend to an aging population and to more women postponing or foregoing parenthood (Grewal 2007). Rates of childlessness began to increase for women born after 1941. These women entered young adulthood at a time when options were expanding for women in the form of advanced education and job opportunities. As well, this time in history witnessed the second wave of feminism, when ideas such as those expressed by Betty Friedan in *The Feminine Mystique* (1963) challenged conventional views about full-time motherhood and caregiving. Despite changing attitudes and the expansion of educational and employment options for women born after this date, women today continue to shoulder more responsibility for housework and child care at home than men. This reality contributes to the trend of women postponing marriage or never marrying, and postponing childbearing or remaining child-free.

Childlessness within opposite-sex marriage has generally been viewed as a problem that can be solved through such means as adoption and artificial insemination. More and more couples today, however, choose not to have children and regard themselves as child-free, not childless. They do not believe that having children automatically follows from marriage, nor do they feel that reproduction is the duty of all married couples. Child-free opposite-sex couples have formed support groups (with names like "No Kidding") and set up support Web sites (Terry 2000).

Economic considerations have contributed to this shift in attitudes; having children has become very expensive. Aware of the financial pressures, some couples are having fewer children and at a later age, and others are weighing the advantages of a child-free marriage. Alexis Victor who, with her partner, lives in an area of Toronto with one of the highest rates of childlessness, states, "There aren't close-knit communities anymore where you can raise well-adjusted, balanced children. The world's population is way too high, it needs to be balanced. We're both very busy" (Grewal 2007). Her partner, Gardiner Cranston, asks, "Why would you want to have kids in this city? . . . There's nothing for kids to enjoy. . . . You need at least $600 000 to buy a decent house" (Grewal 2007).

Meanwhile, some childless couples—both same-sex and opposite-sex—who desperately want children, may be willing to try any means necessary to get pregnant. The social policy section that follows explores the controversy surrounding recent advances in reproductive technology.

::: use your sociological *imagination* :::

What would happen to our society if more married couples decided not to have children? How would society change if cohabitation or singlehood became the norm?

www.mcgrawhillconnect.ca

Social Policy and the Family

Reproductive Technology

The Issue

The 1997 feature film *Gattaca* tells the story of a future in which genetic engineering enhances people's genes. Those who are not "enhanced" in the womb—principally, those whose parents could not afford the treatments—suffer discrimination and social hurdles throughout their lives. To borrow a line from the movie, "Your genes are your résumé."

Far-fetched? Perhaps, but today we are commonly witnessing aspects of reproductive technology that were regarded as so much science fiction just a generation ago. In April 2007, it was revealed that a Quebec woman had frozen her eggs so that her seven-year-old daughter, who was infertile

because of a genetic disorder, could use them in the future (CBC 2007c). "Test-tube" babies, frozen embryos, surrogate mothers, sperm and egg donation, and cloning of human cells are raising questions about the ethics of creating and shaping human life. How will these technologies change the nature of families and the definitions we have of motherhood and fatherhood? To what extent should social policy encourage or discourage innovative reproductive technology?

The Setting

In an effort to overcome infertility, many couples turn to a recent reproductive advance known as

in vitro fertilization (IVF). In this technique, an egg and a sperm are combined in a laboratory dish. If the egg is fertilized, the resulting embryo (the so-called test-tube baby) is transferred into a woman's uterus. The fertilized egg could be transferred into the uterus of the woman from whom it was harvested or of a woman who has not donated the egg but who plays the role of surrogate (i.e., substitute). A surrogate mother carries the pregnancy to term and then transfers the child to the social mother. After this occurs, depending on the agreement between the social mother and the surrogate mother, the child may or may not be a part of the surrogate mother's life.

These possibilities, and many more, make the definition and attending responsibilities of motherhood complicated and somewhat murky. How should motherhood be defined—as providing gestation, as providing care for the child, as providing the egg, or all or some combination of these?

Sociological Insights

Replacing personnel is a functional prerequisite that the family as a social institution performs. Obviously, advances in reproductive technology allow childless couples to fulfill their personal and societal goals. The new technology also presents opportunities not previously considered. A small but growing number of same-sex couples are using donated sperm or eggs to have genetically related children and fulfill their desire to have children and a family (Bruni 1998).

As we have mentioned, sometimes it is difficult to define relationships. For example, in 1995, a U.S. couple, John and Luanne Buzzanca, hired a married woman to carry a child to term for them—a child conceived of the sperm and egg of anonymous, unrelated donors. One month before the birth, John filed for divorce and claimed he had no parental responsibilities, including child support. Eventually, the court ruled that the baby girl had no legal parents; she is temporarily living with Luanne, who may seek to adopt the baby. Although this is an unusual case, it suggests the type of functional confusion that can arise in trying to establish kinship ties (Weiss 1998).

Feminist sociologist Margrit Eichler has developed a typology of motherhood in this age of new reproductive technology. She states that there can be up to 25 types of mothers, considering that mothers can now be "partial Reproductive Technology biological mothers—genetic but not gestational, or gestational but not genetic" (Eichler 1997:80). Her list of possible types of mothers include (1) genetic and gestational but not social mothers (mothers who have given up their child); (2) genetic, non-gestational, and non-social mothers (those who provide an egg); (3) non-genetic, but gestational, social, exclusive, full mothers (those who receive an egg); (4) a dead mother whose egg has been fertilized (mother number 1), implanted in a carrier (mother number 2), and transferred to a third woman (mother number 3).

Eichler adds that new reproductive technologies have had a far less dramatic impact on fatherhood, the most noticeable change coming in the form of what she calls "postmortem biological fathers" (Eichler 1997:72). This term refers to fatherhood that occurs after a man's death, when his sperm is harvested and used to impregnate a woman.

In the future depicted in *Gattaca,* the poor are at a disadvantage because they are not able to genetically control their lives. The conflict perspective would note that in the world today, the technologies available are often accessible only to the most affluent. In addition, a report by the 1993 Royal Commission on New Reproductive Technologies warned that these technologies could potentially be used for commercial purposes (e.g., surrogacy), making women of lower classes vulnerable to exploitation. Thus, today in Canada, there is a voluntary ban on some technologies that could be used commercially and that would enable those with resources to "buy" a reproductive service and those with perhaps few resources to "sell" the services in demand. Ontario Health Minister, Deb Matthews, says that "the unregulated landscape of the industry is a problem" (CBC 2012b).

Interactionists observe that the quest for information and social support connected with reproductive technology has created new social networks. Like other special-interest groups, couples with infertility problems band together to share information, offer support to one another, and demand better treatment. They develop social networks—sometimes through voluntary associations or Internet support groups—where they share information about new medical techniques, insurance plans, and the merits of particular physicians and hospitals. One Internet self-help group, Mothers of Supertwins, offers supportive services for mothers but also lobbies for improved counselling at infertility clinics to better prepare couples for the demands of many babies at one time.

Policy Initiatives

In Japan, some infertile couples have caused a controversy by using eggs or sperm donated by siblings for in vitro fertilization. This violates an ethical (though not legal) ban on "extramarital fertilization," the use of genetic material from anyone other than a spouse for conception. Although opinion is divided on this issue, most Japanese agree that there should be government guidelines on reproductive technology. Many nations, such as Canada, Britain, and Australia, bar payments to egg donors—this results in there being very few donors in these countries. Even more countries limit how many times a man can donate sperm. In Canada, payment for both eggs and sperm is illegal. Because the United States has no such restrictions, infertile foreigners with enough money to afford the

costs involved view the United States as a land of opportunity (CBC 2012b).

In 2004, Canada enacted legislation (Bill C-13) to regulate assisted human reproduction and, in 2006, established the Assisted Human Reproduction Agency of Canada. This agency was created to oversee and regulate assisted human reproduction in Canada, making sure that standards are followed and laws are enforced. Under Bill C-18, the following are some of the practices that were not allowed:

- Cloning of people
- Selecting sex
- Making changes to human DNA
- Buying or selling embryos, sperm, eggs, or other human reproduction material

The following are some of the practices that are allowed:

- Using surrogate mothers
- Donating sperm, eggs, and other reproductive material
- Using human embryos and stem cells in research (CBC 2007c)

In 2010, the Supreme Court of Canada struck down the federal government's attempt to regulate assisted reproductive technology, leaving it to the individual provinces to oversee (Abraham 2012). One of the restrictions the Supreme Court left in place was sex selection; however, embryo screening for other characteristics is possible. Embryo scanning can test for various medical conditions as well as to allow for the possibility for parents to choose what they regard as the most "desirable" embryo—a "designer baby" in effect (Abraham 2012).

Apply the Theory

1. How might functional thinkers view the changing definitions of motherhood and fatherhood?
2. What concerns might some feminist thinkers raise over recent innovations in the area of reproductive technology?

CHAPTER RESOURCES

Summary

::: 12.1 What Are Families?

- There are many variations in families from culture to culture and within the same culture.
- The structure of the **extended family** can offer certain advantages over that of the **nuclear family**.
- All cultures determine kinship in one of these ways—by descent from both parents or **bilateral descent**, from the father or **patrilineal descent**, or from the mother or **matrilineal descent**.
- Sociologists do not agree on whether the **egalitarian family** has replaced the patriarchal family as the social norm in Canada.

::: 12.2 How Do Sociologists Study Families?

- Functionalist sociologists have identified six basic functions of the family: reproduction, protection, socialization, regulation of sexual behaviour, companionship, and the provision of social status.
- Conflict theorists argue that the family contributes to societal injustice and denies opportunities to women that are extended to men.
- Feminist views on the family are diverse yet hold the common assumption that families are socially constructed.
- Interactionists focus on the micro level—on how individuals interact in the family.

::: 12.3 What Are the Diverse Patterns of Marriage and Families?

- In Canada, there is considerable variation in family life associated with sexual orientation, social class, race, and ethnic differences.
- Currently, the majority of all couples in Canada have both partners active in the paid labour force.
- Among the factors that contribute to the current divorce rate among couples in Canada are the greater social acceptance of divorce and the liberalization of divorce laws.
- More and more people are living together without marrying, thereby engaging in what is called **cohabitation**. People are also staying single longer or deciding not to have children within marriage.
- In 2005, Canada passed Bill C-38, the Civil Marriage Act, which legalized same-sex civil marriages.
- Reproductive technology has advanced to such an extent that ethical questions have arisen about the creation and shaping of human life and, thus, the formation of families.

Critical Thinking Questions

1. Recent political discussions have focused on the definition of *family*. Should some governments promote the model of family that includes both same-sex and opposite-sex couples? Are there ways in which family might be defined other than on the basis of sexual orientation? If so, name them.

2. In an increasing proportion of couples in Canada, both partners work outside the home. What are the advantages and disadvantages of the dual-income model for women, for men, for children, and for society as a whole?

3. Given the current rate of divorce in Canada, is it more appropriate to view divorce as dysfunctional or as a normal part of our marriage system? What are the implications of viewing divorce as normal rather than as dysfunctional?

4. What might be the focus of interactionist sociologists in their study of biological and non-biological parents' relationships with their children?

THINKING ABOUT MOVIES

Blue Valentine

A marriage unravels under personal and social pressure.

Goodbye Solo

In this moving drama about the role of family in people's lives, two quite different men form an unlikely pair.

The Kids Are Alright

A family copes when the children's birth father, a sperm donor, tries to become part of their lives.

inside

Religion is expressed in a variety of social settings. At this Christian rock festival, fans pray in response to the music.

Religion and Education

> There are many types of religious toys: stuffed torahs; Moses, David, and Jesus and the Tomb action figures; Noah's ark collections; and Resurrection Eggs, which supplement a young child's Easter book. "Lead your kids on a fun, faith-filled Easter egg hunt this year—one that teaches them about Jesus' death and resurrection! Each egg carton is filled with a dozen colorful plastic eggs. Pop them open and find miniature symbols of the Easter story inside." One of the dozen plastic eggs contains a crown of thorns, another is empty, representing the disappearance of the body of Jesus from the tomb, and pointing to his resurrection. Muslim toys include a mosque building set, mosque jewelry cases, and a prayer practice chart. Jewish toys include dreidels, wooden Shabbat sets, toy *sukkahs,* and a Plush Plagues Bag that includes "all 10 Plagues!"
>
> Religious dolls are part of this wonderland of sacred fun. There are plush and plastic talking Bible dolls, pumped-up Christian action figures, dolls designed to support a Jewish girl's religious identity and conform to religious requirements, Goddess dolls designed for affluent young feminists, talking Muslim dolls that teach Arabic phrases, and "anti-Barbies"—Muslim dolls deliberately designed to compete with Barbie for the hearts and minds of young girls. There are plush Buddha and Siva dolls, and cuddly Jesus and Esther dolls as well.
>
> Numerous card games and puzzles teach a variety of languages, including Hebrew, Arabic, and Punjabi. The Christian Book Distributors Web site not only offers religiously themed educational materials, they also offer nonreligious toys that appeal to parents with religious consciences who may be looking for nonviolent toys, such as a food groups toy with hand-painted pieces in four wooden crates, a pizza party game with different toppings, and a car towing game.
>
> Not all religious toys are meant for the edification of the young. Many religious games and toys are satirical or simply products meant to be amusing enough to sell in an era where we are oversatiated with things, and any cultural phenomenon is fair game for marketing purposes. These items amuse or appall us, depending on how clever or offensive the item is, and for whom it is intended. . . .
>
> Games and toys not only transmit cultural values but reflect them as well. . . . Games and religion have a long and complex history—they were used for divination and gambling, for this-worldly satire, and in the afterlife. Games were objects and methods used to interpret divine powers and influence supernatural forces. These religious and magical functions reflect the presence and movement of the sacred in the material world, indicators of a complex whole rather than a dualism where sacred and ordinary occupy separate realms.

(Bado-Fralick and Norris 2010:7–8, 29–30)

In this excerpt from *Toying with God: The World of Religious Games and Dolls,* religious studies scholars Nikki Bado-Fralick and Rebecca Sachs Norris consider how religiously themed toys and games reflect both popular and religious culture. Depending on their purpose and design, the authors note, as well as on the social context in which they are used, these dolls and board games can either reinforce or undermine organized religion. Their impact on the children who play with them parallels the broader influence of religion on society. Despite the much-publicized decline of organized religion over the past century, even a casual observer can see that religion still permeates our social environment. As a result, nonbelievers are influenced by believers, whether they want to be or not. Similarly, believers are influenced by nonbelievers and by those of different faiths, despite any attempts they may make to screen out other points of view.

Religion, however, does play a major role in many people's lives, and religious practices of some sort are evident in every society. That makes religion a cultural universal, along with other general practices found in every culture, such as dancing, food preparation, the family, and personal names. At present, an estimated 4 billion people belong to the world's many religious faiths (see Figure 13-1).

When religion's influence on other social institutions in a society diminishes, the process of **secularization** is said to be underway. During this process, religion will survive in the private sphere of individual and family life; it may even thrive on a personal level. But, at the same time, other social institutions—such as the economy, politics, and education—maintain their own sets of norms independent of religious guidance (Stark and Iannaccone 1992).

Education, like religion, is a cultural universal. As such, it is an important aspect of socialization—the lifelong process of learning the attitudes, values, and behaviour considered appropriate to members of a particular culture, as we saw in Chapter 4. When learning is explicit and formalized—when some people consciously teach, while others adopt the role of learner—the process of socialization is called **education**.

figure **13-1** Religions of the World

MAPPING LIFE WORLDWIDE

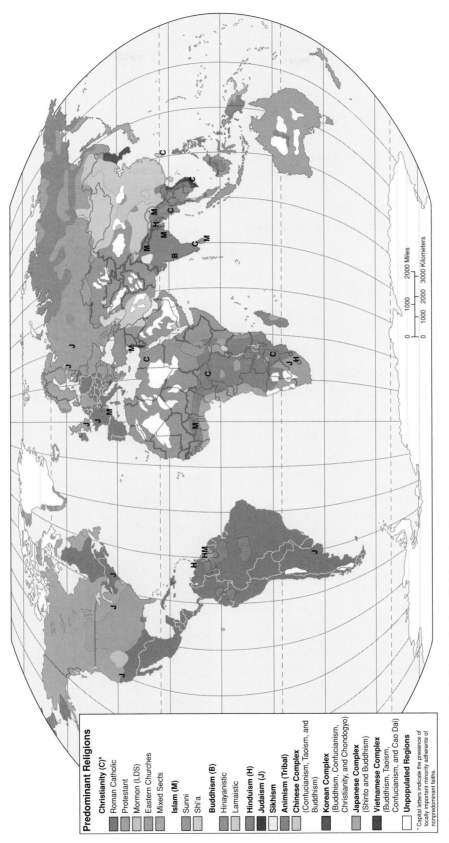

Predominant Religions

Christianity (C)*
- Roman Catholic
- Protestant
- Mormon (LDS)
- Eastern Churches
- Mixed Sects

Islam (M)
- Sunni
- Shi'a

Buddhism (B)
- Hinayanistic
- Lamaistic

Hinduism (H)

Judaism (J)

Sikhism

Animism (Tribal)

Chinese Complex
(Confucianism, Taoism, and Buddhism)

Korean Complex
(Buddhism, Confucianism, Christianity, and Chondogyo)

Japanese Complex
(Shinto and Buddhism)

Vietnamese Complex
(Buddhism, Taoism, Confucianism, and Cao Dai)

□ **Unpopulated Regions**

* Capital letters indicate the presence of locally important minority adherents of nonpredominant faiths.

0 1000 2000 Miles
0 1000 2000 3000 Kilometers

Religious adherence is one of the defining social characteristics of a culture.

Source: Allen 2008:11.

In this chapter, we first look at religion as it has emerged in modern industrial societies. We begin with a brief overview of the approaches that Émile Durkheim first introduced and those that later sociologists have used in studying religion. We explore religion's role in societal integration, social support, social change, and social control. We examine three important dimensions of religious behaviour—belief, ritual, and experience—as well as the basic forms of religious organization. We pay particular attention to the emergence of new religious movements.

In the second part of this chapter, we focus on the formal systems of education that characterize modern industrial societies, beginning with a discussion of four theoretical perspectives on education: functionalist, conflict, feminist, and interactionist. As we will see, education can both perpetuate the status quo and foster social change.

An examination of schools as formal organizations—as bureaucracies and subcultures of teachers and students—follows. Two types of education that are becoming more common in North America today—adult education and home-schooling—merit special mention. We close the chapter with a social policy discussion of the controversy over religion in public schools. ■

www.mcgrawhillconnect.ca

::: use your sociological *imagination* :::

What evidence do you see of different religions in the area surrounding your college or university? What about on campus?

What Is Durkheim's Sociological Approach to Religion?

If a group believes that it is being directed by a "vision from God," sociologists will not attempt to prove or disprove this revelation. Instead, they will assess the effects of the religious experience on the group. What sociologists are interested in is the social impact of religion on individuals and institutions (McGuire 1981:12).

Émile Durkheim was perhaps the first sociologist to recognize the critical importance of religion in human societies. He saw its appeal for the individual, but—more importantly—he stressed the social impact of religion. In Durkheim's view, religion is a collective act and includes many forms of behaviour in which people interact with others. As in his work on suicide, Durkheim was not as interested in the personalities of religious believers as he was in understanding religious behaviour within a social context.

Durkheim defined **religion** as a "unified system of beliefs and practices relative to sacred things." In his view, religion involves a set of beliefs and practices that are uniquely the property of religion—as opposed to other social institutions and ways of thinking. Durkheim argued that religious faiths distinguish between certain events that transcend the ordinary and the everyday world (1947, original edition 1912). He referred to these realms as the *sacred* and the *profane*.

The **sacred** encompasses elements beyond everyday life that inspire awe, respect, and even fear. People become a part of the sacred realm only by completing some ritual, such as prayer or sacrifice. Believers have faith in the sacred; this faith allows them to accept what they cannot understand. By contrast, the **profane** includes the ordinary and commonplace. It can get confusing, however, because the same object can be either sacred or profane depending on how it is viewed. A normal dining room table is profane, but it becomes sacred to Christians if it bears the elements of communion.

A candelabra becomes sacred for Jews when it is a menorah. For Confucians and Taoists, incense sticks are not mere decorative items; they are highly valued offerings to the gods in religious ceremonies marking new and full moons.

Following the direction established by Durkheim almost a century ago, contemporary sociologists view religions in two different ways: First, they study the norms and values of religious faiths through examination of their substantive

A Hindu holy man prays at the sacred Ganges River in India. Hindus hold many aspects of life sacred, and emphasize the importance of being good in this life in order to advance in the next.

religious beliefs. For example, it is possible to compare the degree to which Christian faiths literally interpret the Bible, or Muslim groups follow the Qur'an (or Koran), the sacred book of Islam. Second, sociologists examine religions in terms of the social functions they fulfill, such as providing social support or reinforcing the social norms. By exploring both the beliefs and the functions of religion, we can better understand its impact on the individual, groups, and society as a whole.

13.2 What Are the Major World Religions?

Worldwide, tremendous diversity exists in religious beliefs and practices. Overall, roughly 89 percent of the world's population adheres to some religion; only about 10 percent is non-religious. This level of adherence changes over time, and also varies by country and age group. In Canada in 2006, those who were non-religious accounted for 17.5, up from 12.3 in 1991 (Statistics Canada 2010).

Christianity is the largest single religion in the world; the second largest is Islam (see Table 13-1). Although global news events often suggest an inherent conflict between Christians and Muslims, the two religions are similar in many ways. Both are monotheistic (based on a single deity); both include a belief in prophets, an afterlife, and a judgment day. In fact, Islam recognizes Jesus as a prophet, though not the son of God. Both faiths impose a moral code on believers, which varies from fairly rigid proscriptions for fundamentalists to relatively relaxed guidelines for liberals.

The followers of Islam, called Muslims, believe that Islam's holy scriptures were received from Allah (God) by the prophet Mohammad nearly 1400 years ago. They see Mohammad as the last in a long line of prophets, preceded by Adam, Abraham, Moses, and Jesus. Islam is more communal in its expression than Christianity, particularly than the latter's more individualistic Protestant denominations.

Consequently, in countries that are predominantly Muslim, the separation of religion and the state is not considered necessary or even desirable. In fact, Muslim governments often reinforce Islamic practices through their laws. Muslims do vary sharply in their interpretation of several traditions, some of which—such as the wearing of veils by women (see Box 13-1)—are more cultural than religious in origin.

Like Christianity and Islam, Judaism is monotheistic. Jews believe that God's true nature is revealed in the Torah, which Christians know as the first five books of the Old Testament. According to these scriptures, God formed a covenant, or pact, with Abraham and Sarah, the ancestors of the tribes of Israel. Even today, Jews believe, this covenant holds them accountable to God's will. If they follow both the letter and spirit of the Torah, a long-awaited Messiah will one day bring paradise to earth. Although Judaism has a relatively small following compared to other major faiths, it forms the historical foundation for both Christianity and Islam. That is why Jews revere many of the same sacred Middle Eastern sites as Christians and Muslims.

Two other major religions developed in a different part of the world—India. The earlier one, Hinduism, originated circa 1500 B.C. Hinduism differs from Judaism, Christianity, and Islam in that it embraces a number of gods and minor gods, although most worshippers are devoted primarily to a single deity, such as Shiva or Vishnu. Hinduism is also distinguished by a belief in reincarnation, or the perpetual rebirth of the soul after death. Unlike Judaism, Christianity, and Islam, which are based largely on sacred texts, Hindu beliefs have been preserved mostly through oral tradition.

A second religion, Buddhism, developed in the sixth century B.C. as a reaction against Hinduism. This faith is founded on the teachings of Siddhartha Gautama (later called Buddha, or "the enlightened one"). Through meditation, followers of Buddhism strive to overcome selfish cravings for physical or material pleasures, with the goal of reaching a state of enlightenment, or nirvana. Buddhists created the first monastic orders, which are thought to be the models for monastic orders in other religions, including Christianity. Though Buddhism emerged in India, its followers were eventually driven out of that country by the Hindus. Buddhists are now found primarily in other parts of Asia. (Contemporary adherents of Buddhism in India are relatively recent converts.)

table 13-1 Major World Religions

Faith	Current Following, in Millions (and Percentage of World Population)	Primary Location of Followers Today	Founder (and Approximate Birth Date)	Important Texts (and Holy Sites)
Buddhism	463 (6.7%)	Southeast Asia, Mongolia, Tibet	Gautama Siddhartha (563 B.C.)	Triptaka (areas in Nepal)
Christianity	2,281 (33.0%)	Europe, North America, South America	Jesus (6 B.C.)	Bible (Jerusalem, Rome)
Hinduism	935 (13.7%)	India, Indian communities overseas	No specific founder (1500 B.C.)	Sruti and Smrti texts (seven sacred cities, including Vavansi)
Islam	1,553 (22.5%)	Middle East, Central Asia, North Africa, Indonesia	Mohammad (A.D. 570)	Qur'an, or Koran (Mecca, Medina, Jerusalem)
Judaism	15 (0.2%)	Israel, United States, France, Russia	Abraham (2000 B.C.)	Torah, Talmud (Jerusalem)

Sources: Author, based on Britannica Online 2011; Swatos 1998.

sociology in the global community

13-1 The Head Scarf and the Veil: Complex Symbols

The wearing of a veil or head scarf by women is common to many but not all Middle Eastern societies.

However, Muslim women are not alone in their observance of certain standards for dress. All Muslims, men and women alike, are expected to cover themselves and avoid revealing clothes designed to accentuate the body's contours or emphasize its physical beauty. The Qur'an (or Koran) does permit Muslims to wear revealing garments in private, with their families or with members of the same sex.

The prophet Muhammad recommended that women cover all of their bodies except for the face, hands, and feet. The Qur'an adds that a woman's head-covering should fall over the upper chest and neck. A variety of women's outergarments comply with these guidelines for modest attire; collectively, they are referred to as the *hijab*. Face veils, or *niqabs,* are dictated by cultural tradition, however—not by Islam.

For some, the veil represents a rejection of the beauty myth, which is so prevalent in Western societies. By covering themselves almost completely, Muslim women assure themselves and their families that their physical appearance will not play a role in their contacts outside the family.

In the twentieth century, the veil was politicized by modernization movements that pitted Western cultural values against traditional Islamic values. In Turkey, for instance, in the early twentieth century, government officials attempted to subordinate traditional ethnic and religious influences to their nationalistic goals. Though women weren't forbidden to wear the veil, they were not allowed to veil themselves in public places like schools. Not surprisingly, many Muslims resented these forced social changes.

In Canada today, Muslim women select from an array of traditional garments, including a long, loose tailored coat and a loose black overgarment that is worn with a scarf or perhaps a face veil. However, they may also choose to wear an overblouse and a long skirt or loose pants, which they can buy at local clothing stores.

Researchers have identified three perspectives on the *hijab* among Muslim women in Canada and other non-Islamic countries. Younger, better-educated women who support wearing the *hijab* in public draw on Western ideas of individual rights, arguing in favour of veiling as a form of personal expression. In contrast, older, less well-educated women who support the *hijab* do so without referring to Western ideology; they cannot see why veiling should be an issue. A third group of women, of all ages and educational backgrounds, opposes the *hijab*.

In some non-Muslim countries, notably France, officials have banned the *hijab* or the head scarf in public schools and services. In Quebec, there is broad consensus opposing the wearing of the niqab when accessing public services: "veils provoke vivid memories of Catholic domination, when priests ordered women to stay out of the workplace and politics" (Perreaux 2010).

The head scarf—an expression of modesty, a woman's right as an individual, or a sign of oppression?

Apply the Theory

1. Consider life in a society in which women wear veils. Can you see any advantages, from the woman's point of view? From the man's?

2. Do you find the Western emphasis on physical beauty oppressive? If so, in what ways?

Sources: al-Jadda 2006; Haeri 2004; Killian 2003; Perreaux 2010; Scott 2007; Selod 2008.

Although the differences among religions are striking, they are exceeded by variations within faiths. Consider the differences within Christianity, from relatively liberal denominations such as Presbyterians or the United Church of Canada to the more conservative Mormons and Greek Orthodox Catholics. Similar divisions exist within Hinduism, Islam, and the other world religions (Barrett et al. 2006; Swatos 1998).

What Role Does Religion Play?

Since religion is a cultural universal, it is not surprising that it plays a basic role in human societies. In sociological terms, these include both manifest and latent functions. Among its *manifest* (open and stated) functions, religion defines the spiritual world and gives meaning to the divine. Religion provides an explanation for events that seem difficult to understand, such as what happens after death.

The *latent* functions of religion are unintended, covert, or hidden. Even though the manifest function of church services is to offer a forum for religious worship, they might at the same time fulfill a latent function as a meeting ground for unmarried members.

Functionalists and conflict theorists both evaluate religion's impact as a social institution on human societies. We'll consider a functionalist view of religion's role in integrating society, in social support, and in promoting social change, and then look at religion as a means of social control from the conflict perspective. Note that, for the most part, religion's impact is best understood from a macro-level viewpoint, oriented toward the larger society. The social support function is an exception: it is best viewed on the micro level, directed toward the individual.

The Integrative Function of Religion

Émile Durkheim viewed religion as an integrative power in human society—a perspective reflected in functionalist thought today. Durkheim sought to answer a perplexing question: "How can human societies be held together when they are generally composed of individuals and social groups with diverse interests and aspirations?" In his view, religious bonds often transcend these personal and divisive forces. Durkheim acknowledged that religion is not the only integrative force—nationalism or patriotism may serve the same end.

How does religion provide this "societal glue"? Religion, whether it be Buddhism, Islam, Christianity, or Judaism, offers people meaning and purpose for their lives. It gives them certain ultimate values and ends to hold in common. Although subjective and not always fully accepted, these values and ends help a society to function as an integrated social system. For example, funerals, weddings, bar mitzvahs and bat mitzvahs, and confirmations serve to integrate people into larger communities by providing shared beliefs and values about the ultimate questions of life.

The integrative power of religion can be seen in the role that churches, synagogues, temples, and mosques have traditionally played and continue to play for immigrant groups in Canada. For example, Roman Catholic immigrants may settle near a parish church that offers services in their native language, such as Polish or Portuguese. Similarly, Korean immigrants may join a Presbyterian church with many Korean-Canadian members and with religious practices like those of churches in Korea. Like other religious organizations, these Roman Catholic and Presbyterian churches help to integrate immigrants into their new homeland.

In some instances, religious loyalties are *dysfunctional;* they contribute to tension and even to conflict between groups or nations. During World War II, the German Nazis attempted to exterminate the Jewish people; approximately 6 million European Jews were killed. In modern times, nations such as Lebanon (Muslims versus Christians), Israel (Jews versus Muslims, as well as Orthodox versus secular Jews), Northern Ireland (Roman Catholics versus Protestants), and India (Hindus versus Muslims and, more recently, Sikhs) have been torn by clashes that are in large part based on religion.

Religious conflict (though on a less violent level) is evident in Canada as well. Christian fundamentalists in many communities battle against their liberal counterparts for control of the secular culture. The battlefield is an array of familiar social issues, among them multiculturalism, abortion, sex education in schools, and gay and lesbian rights.

Religion and Social Support

Most of us find it difficult to accept the stressful events of life—the death of a loved one, serious injury, bankruptcy, divorce, and so forth. This is especially true when something "senseless" happens. How, for example, can family and friends come to terms with the death of a talented university student, not even 20 years old, from a terminal disease?

Through its emphasis on the divine and the supernatural, religion allows us to "do something" about the calamities we face. In some faiths, adherents can offer sacrifices or pray to a deity in the belief that such acts will change their earthly condition. At a more basic level, religion encourages us to view our personal misfortunes as relatively unimportant in the broader perspective of human history—or even as part of an undisclosed divine purpose. Friends and relatives of the deceased university student may see this death as being "God's will" and as having some ultimate benefit that we cannot understand now. This perspective may be much more comforting than the terrifying feeling that any of us can die senselessly at any moment—and that there is no divine "answer" as to why one person lives a long and full life, while another dies tragically at a relatively early age.

Religion and Social Change

The Weberian Thesis When someone seems driven to work and succeed, we often attribute the "Protestant work ethic" to that person. The term comes from the writings of Max Weber, who carefully examined the connection between religious allegiance and capitalist development. His findings appeared in his pioneering work *The Protestant Ethic and the Spirit of Capitalis*m ([1904] 2011).

Weber noted that in European nations with both Protestant and Catholic citizens, an overwhelming number of business leaders, owners of capital, and skilled workers were Protestant. In his view, this was no mere coincidence. Weber pointed out that the followers of John Calvin (1509–1564), a leader of the Protestant Reformation, emphasized the disciplined work ethic, worldly concerns, and rational orientation to life that have become known as the **Protestant ethic.** One byproduct of the Protestant ethic was a drive to accumulate savings that could be used for future investment. This "spirit of capitalism," to use Weber's phrase, contrasted with the moderate work hours, leisurely work habits, and lack of ambition that he saw as typical of the times.

Few books on the sociology of religion have aroused as much commentary and criticism as Weber's work. It has been hailed as one of the most important theoretical works in the field and as an excellent example of macro-level analysis. Like Durkheim, Weber demonstrated that religion is not solely a matter of intimate personal beliefs. He stressed that the collective nature of religion has social consequences for society as a whole.

Weber provides a convincing description of the origins of European capitalism. But this economic system has subsequently been adopted by non-Calvinists in many parts of the world. Apparently, the "spirit of capitalism" has become a generalized cultural trait rather than a specific religious tenet (Greeley 1989).

Conflict theorists caution that Weber's theory—even if it is accepted—should not be regarded as an analysis of mature capitalism as reflected in the rise of multinational corporations that cross national boundaries. Marxists would disagree with Weber not on the origins of capitalism but on its future. Unlike Marx, Weber believed that capitalism could endure indefinitely as an economic system. He added, however, that the decline of religion as an overriding force in society opened the way for workers to express their discontent more vocally (Collins 1980).

Liberation Theology Sometimes, the clergy can be found in the forefront of social change. Many religious activists, especially in the Roman Catholic Church in Latin America, support **liberation theology**—the use of a church in a political effort to eliminate poverty, discrimination, and other forms of injustice evident in a secular society. Advocates of this religious movement sometimes sympathize with Marxism. Many believe that radical change, rather than economic development in itself, is the only acceptable solution to the desperation of the masses in impoverished developing countries.

Liberation theology may be seen by some as dysfunctional, however. Some Roman Catholics have come to believe that by focusing on political and governmental injustice, the clergy are no longer addressing their personal and spiritual needs. Partly as a result of such disenchantment, some Catholics in Latin America, for example, are converting to mainstream Protestant faiths or to Mormonism.

::: use your sociological *imagination* :::

The social support that religious groups provide is suddenly withdrawn from your community. How will your life or the lives of others change? What will happen if some religious groups stop pushing for social change?

Religion and Social Control: A Conflict View

Liberation theology is a relatively recent phenomenon and marks a break with the traditional role of churches. It was this traditional role that Karl Marx opposed. In his view, religion *impeded* social change by encouraging oppressed people to focus on other-worldly concerns rather than on their immediate poverty or exploitation. Marx described religion as "opium of the masses," particularly harmful to oppressed peoples. He felt that religion was widely used to "drug" less fortunate people into submission by offering a consolation for their harsh daily lives: the hope of salvation in an ideal afterlife. For example, Aboriginal children housed in residential schools in Canada were forbidden to practise their own forms of spirituality and were forced to adopt Christianity. These children were taught that obedience would lead to salvation and eternal happiness in the hereafter. Viewed from a conflict perspective, Christianity may be an attempt to pacify certain oppressed groups and blunt the rage that often fuels rebellion.

Marx acknowledged that religion plays an important role in propping up the existing social structure. The values of religion, as already noted, reinforce other social institutions and the social order as a whole. From Marx's perspective, however, religion's promotion of stability within society only helps to perpetuate patterns of social inequality. According to Marx, the dominant religion reinforces the interests of those in power.

Consider, for example, India's traditional caste system. It defined the social structure of that society, at least among the Hindu majority. The caste system was almost certainly the creation of the priesthood, but it also served the interests of

India's political rulers by granting a certain religious legitimacy to social inequality.

Contemporary Christianity, like the Hindu faith, reinforces traditional patterns of behaviour that call for the subordination of the less powerful. Like Marx, conflict theorists argue that to whatever extent religion actually influences social behaviour, it reinforces existing patterns of dominance and inequality.

From a Marxist perspective, religion functions as an "agent of depoliticization" (Wilson 1973). In simpler terms, religion keeps people from seeing their lives and societal conditions in political terms—for example, by obscuring the overriding significance of conflicting economic interests. Marxists suggest that by inducing a "false consciousness" among the disadvantaged, religion lessens the possibility of collective political action that can end capitalist oppression and transform society.

Feminist Perspectives on Religion

Feminist thinkers draw attention to the reality that the positions of women in religious organizations tend to be ones of subjugation. Assumptions about gender often place women in subservient positions, both within many religious faiths and in the private sphere. In fact, as they do in the corporate world, women find it difficult to achieve leadership positions within many religious faiths. For example, 37 percent of Anglican active clergy are female (Sison 2012). Among Canadian Aboriginals, however, women have traditionally been granted roles of spiritual leadership.

Female spiritual leaders are more likely to serve in subsidiary roles and to wait longer for desirable assignments. Although women may play a significant role as volunteers in religious communities, men are more likely to make the major theological and financial judgments for nationwide spiritual organizations. Feminist perspectives on religion and female spirituality recognize the diversity of women's spiritual expression and reveal the ways in which religious systems are "gendered," reflecting dominant political and cultural assumptions (Stuckey 1998). These perspectives run the gamut from those suggesting that religions revise their messages and interpretations, to those unequivocally rejecting religious traditions as "irremediably sexist" (Stuckey 1998:269).

Table 13-2 summarizes the major sociological perspectives on religion.

13.4 What Are the Components of Religion?

All religions have certain elements in common, yet these elements are expressed in the distinctive manner of each faith. The patterns of religious behaviour, like other patterns of social behaviour, are of great interest to sociologists, since they underscore the relationship between religion and society.

Religious beliefs, rituals, and experience all help to define what is sacred and to differentiate the sacred from the profane. Let us now examine these three dimensions of religious behaviour.

table 13-2 Sociological Perspectives on Religion

Theoretical Perspective	Emphasis
Functionalist	Religion as a source of social integration and unification Religion as a source of social support for individuals
Conflict	Religion as a potential obstacle to structural social change Religion as a potential source of structural social change (through liberation theology)
Feminist	Religious systems as gendered, reflecting dominant political and cultural assumptions
Interactionist	Individual religious expression through belief, ritual, and experience (see the next section of this chapter)

Belief

Some people believe in life after death, in supreme beings with unlimited powers, and/or in supernatural forces. The strength of belief in God varies dramatically worldwide. **Religious beliefs** are statements to which members of a particular religion adhere. These views can vary dramatically from religion to religion.

The Christian and Jewish story of Adam and Eve—an account of creation—found in Genesis, the first book of the Old Testament and the Torah, is an example of a religious belief. Some people in Canada strongly adhere to this biblical explanation of creation. These people, known as *creationists,* are worried by the secularization of society and oppose teaching that directly or indirectly questions biblical scripture.

Pilgrims on *hajj* to the Grand Mosque in Mecca, Saudi Arabia. Islam requires all Muslims who are able to undertake this religious ritual at least once in a lifetime.

::: use your sociological *imagination* :::

Canada and the United States are similar in many ways. Why would religious participation in the United States be greater than that in Canada?

Ritual

Religious rituals are practices required or expected of members of a faith. Rituals usually honour the divine power (or powers) worshipped by believers; they also remind adherents of their religious duties and responsibilities. Rituals and beliefs can be interdependent; rituals generally involve the affirmation of beliefs, as in a public or private statement confessing a sin (Roberts 1995). Like any social institution, religion develops distinctive normative patterns to structure people's behaviour. Moreover, there are sanctions attached to religious rituals, whether rewards (bat mitzvah gifts) or penalties (expulsion from a religious institution for violation of norms).

In North America, rituals may be very simple, such as saying grace at a meal or observing a moment of silence to commemorate someone's death. Yet, certain rituals, such as the process of canonizing a saint, are quite elaborate. Most religious rituals in our culture focus on services conducted at houses of worship. Attendance at a service, silent and spoken prayers, and singing of spiritual hymns and chants are common forms of ritual behaviour that generally take place in group settings. From an interactionist perspective, these rituals serve as important face-to-face encounters in which people reinforce their religious beliefs and their commitment to faith.

For Muslims, a very important ritual is the *hajj,* a pilgrimage to the Grand Mosque in Mecca, Saudi Arabia. Every

figure 13-2 Religious Participation in Selected Countries

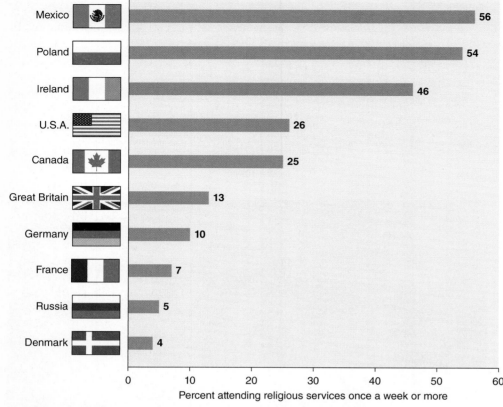

Country	Percent
Mexico	56
Poland	54
Ireland	46
U.S.A.	26
Canada	25
Great Britain	13
Germany	10
France	7
Russia	5
Denmark	4

Percent attending religious services once a week or more

Note: Data are for 2006, except for Canada and Mexico, which are for 2004.

Source: Tom W. Smith 2009:28, 60, 72.

::: use your sociological *imagination* :::

Choose a religious tradition other than your own. How would your religious beliefs, rituals, and experience differ if you had been raised in that tradition?

www.mcgrawhillconnect.ca

Muslim who is physically and financially able is expected to make this trip at least once. Each year, 2 million pilgrims go to Mecca during the week-long period indicated by the Islamic lunar calendar. Muslims from all over the world make the *hajj*, including those in Canada, where many tours are arranged to facilitate this ritual.

In recent decades, participation in religious ritual has tended to hold steady or decline in most countries. Figure 13-2 shows the change in religious participation in selected countries from 1981 to 2001.

Experience

In the sociological study of religion, the term **religious experience** refers to the feeling or perception of being in direct contact with the ultimate reality, such as a divine being, or of being overcome with religious emotion. A religious experience may be rather slight, such as the feeling of exaltation a person receives from hearing a choir sing Handel's "Hallelujah Chorus." But many religious experiences are more profound,

such as a Muslim's experience on a *hajj*. In his autobiography, the late U.S. black activist Malcolm X wrote of his *hajj* and how deeply moved he was by the way that Muslims in Mecca came together across lines of race and colour. For Malcolm X, the colour blindness of the Muslim world "proved to me the power of the One God" (1964:338).

Still another profound religious experience is being "born again"—that is, at a turning point in one's life, making a personal commitment to Jesus. According to a 2010 national survey, 42 percent of people in the United States claimed that they had a born-again Christian experience at some time in their lives. An earlier survey found that Baptists (75 percent) were the most likely to report such experiences; by contrast, only 21 percent of Catholics and 24 percent of Episcopalians stated that they had been born again. The collective nature of religion, as emphasized by Durkheim, is evident in these statistics. The beliefs and rituals of a particular faith can create an atmosphere either friendly or hostile to this type of religious experience. Thus, a Baptist would be encouraged to come forward and share such experiences with others, whereas an Episcopalian who claimed to have been born again would receive much less interest (Gallup 2011; Gallup Opinion Index 1978).

13.5 What Are the Forms of Religious Organization?

The collective nature of religion has led to many forms of religious association. In modern societies, religion has become increasingly formalized. Specific structures, such as churches and synagogues, are constructed for religious worship; individuals are trained for occupational roles within various fields. These developments make it possible to distinguish clearly between the sacred and secular parts of life—a distinction that could not be made in earlier societies in which religion was largely a family activity carried out in the home.

Sociologists find it useful to distinguish among four basic forms of organization: the ecclesia, the denomination, the sect, and the new religious movement or cult. We can see differences among these types of organizations in such factors as size, power, degree of commitment expected from members, and historical ties to other faiths.

Ecclesiae

An **ecclesia** (plural, *ecclesiae*) is a religious organization that claims to include most or all of the members of a society and is recognized as the national or official religion. Since virtually everyone belongs to the faith, membership is by birth rather than conscious decision. Examples of ecclesiae include the Lutheran church in Sweden, the Catholic Church in Spain, Islam in Saudi Arabia, and Buddhism in Thailand. However, there can be significant differences even within the category of ecclesia. In Saudi Arabia's Islamic regime, leaders of the ecclesia hold vast power over actions of the state. By contrast, the Lutheran church in contemporary Sweden has no such power over the Riksdag (Parliament) or the prime minister.

Generally, ecclesiae are conservative in that they do not challenge the leaders of a secular government. In a society with an ecclesia, the political and religious institutions often act in harmony and mutually reinforce each other's power over their relative spheres of influence. Within the modern world, ecclesiae tend to be declining in power.

Denominations

A **denomination** is a large, organized religion not officially linked with the state or government. Like an ecclesia, it tends to have an explicit set of beliefs, a defined system of authority, and a generally respected position in society. Denominations claim as members large segments of a population. Generally, children accept the denomination of their parents and give little thought to membership in other faiths. Denominations also resemble ecclesiae in that generally few demands are made on members. However, there is a critical difference between these two forms of religious organization. Although the denomination is considered respectable and is not viewed as a challenge to the secular government, it lacks the official recognition and power held by an ecclesia (Doress and Porter 1977).

Although a projected 43 percent of all Canadians were Roman Catholic in 2006 (a question on religion is asked only once every 10 years and, therefore, was not asked in the 2006 Census), this country is marked by great religious diversity. With the exception of Aboriginal peoples, we are a country of immigrants, and Canadian religious diversity (see Table 13-3) reflects patterns of immigration and population change.

Protestantism follows Catholicism in popularity and is practised by a projected 27.6 percent of the population in Canada. From 1991 to 2006, the projected percentage of Muslims in Canada tripled (Statistics Canada 2010). The percentage of Jews has remained the same, while the percentage of people declaring no religious affiliation rose from 12.3 percent in 1991 to a projected 17.5 percent in 2006; at the same time, the percentage of those belonging to Protestant denominations dropped from 34.9 in 1991 to a projected 27.6 percent in 2006. A significant increase in affiliation was reported in the category "Christian, not included elsewhere," which includes Christian fundamentalist denominations.

Statistics Canada projects that if immigration continues to come from non-European countries, by 2031, 32 percent of the population would be non-Christian. Fewer than 66 percent of Canadians would have a Christian religion in 2031, compared to 97 percent in 1981. The shift away from the dominance of Christian religions reflects the overall pattern of growing ethnocultural diversity in the Canadian population (Statistics Canada 2010).

Sects

A **sect** can be defined as a relatively small religious group that has broken away from some other religious organization to renew what it considers the original vision of the faith. Many sects, such as that led by Martin Luther during the Reformation, claim to be the "true church" because they seek to cleanse the established faith of what they regard as extraneous beliefs and rituals (Stark and Bainbridge 1985). Max Weber termed the sect a "believer's church," because affiliation is based on conscious acceptance of a specific religious dogma (1958b:114, original edition 1916).

Sects are fundamentally at odds with society and do not seek to become established national religions. Unlike ecclesiae and denominations, sects require intensive commitments and demonstrations of belief by members. Partly owing to their "outsider" status in society, sects frequently exhibit a higher degree of religious fervour and loyalty than more established religious groups do. Recruitment focuses mainly on adults, and acceptance comes through conversion.

Sects also exist in the Islamic faith. See Box 13-2 for a discussion of Islamic sects in Canada.

table 13-3 Major Religious Denominations, Canada, 1991, 2001, and 2006

	2006 (%)	2001 (%)	1991[1] (%)
Roman Catholic	42.5	43.2	45.2
Protestant	27.6	29.2	34.9
Christian Orthodox	1.7	1.6	1.4
Christian, not included elsewhere[2]	3.0	2.6	1.3
Muslim	2.7	2.0	0.9
Jewish	1.1	1.1	1.2
Buddhist	1.1	1.0	0.6
Hindu	1.2	1.0	0.6
Sikh	1.2	0.9	0.5
No religion	17.5	16.2	12.3

[1]For comparability purposes, 1991 data are presented according to 2001 boundaries.
[2]Includes persons who report "Christian," as well as those who report "Apostolic," "Born-again Christian," and "Evangelical."
Note: A question on religion is asked only once every 10 years and, therefore, was not asked in the 2006 Census; 2006 percentages are projected.
Sources: Statistics Canada 2003j, 2010.

research today

13-2 Islam in Canada

The growing presence of Islam in Canada may, perhaps, lead to a better understanding of the significant diversity within Islam. Throughout the world, including in Canada, Muslims are divided into a variety of sects—the two major sects are Sunni and Shia (or Shiite). These divisions sometimes result in antagonism, just as rivalries between denominations of other faiths can cause friction. Yet, the Islamic faith is expressed in many different ways, even among Sunnis or Shia. To speak of Muslims as either Sunni or Shia would be like speaking of Christians as either Roman Catholic or Baptist.

The great majority of Muslims in Canada are Sunni Muslims—literally, those who follow the *Sunnah,* or way of the prophet. Compared to other Muslims, Sunnis tend to be moderate in their religious orthodoxy. The Shia, who come primarily from Iraq and Iran, are the second largest group. Shia Muslims are more attentive to guidance from accepted Islamic scholars than are Sunnis. In sufficient numbers, these two Muslim groups will choose to worship separately, even if they must cross ethnic or linguistic lines to do so. That certainly is the case in Canadian cities with large and varied Muslim communities.

In 2010 Canada was home to roughly 940 000 Muslim Canadians, 2.8 percent of the total population of Canada (Pew Research Center 2011). By 2030, the number of Muslims in Canada is expected to nearly triple to 2.7 million or 6.6 percent of the total Canadian population. Jack Jedwab, executive director of the Association for Canadian Studies compiled 2008 data comparing Canadian opinion towards Muslims and Jews to those of the U.S. and selected other countries. Jedwab points out that Canada is between the U.S. and Britain, Germany, and Spain in its favourable opinion towards Muslims (see Table 13-4).

Here, Muslim girls are playing basketball without compromising culturally appropriate norms.

A 2007 Environics poll revealed that a majority of Muslim Canadians—53 percent—responded that they would like to see Islamic sharia law adopted for divorce and family disputes, while 86 percent do not believe governments should ban the wearing of headscarves by Muslim women in public places (including public schools). Haideh Moghissi, a sociologist at York University in Toronto, asserts that these concerns should probably be seen more as a "'political gesture than a religious one' by those who have felt their community 'bearing the brunt of this suspicion and fear' since the September 11, 2001, attacks."

On many college and university campuses in Canada, administrators have responded constructively to the growing numbers of Muslim students by hiring imams (prayer leaders) to minister to their needs, dedicating space for daily prayer, and providing for Muslim dietary restrictions. However, the wearing of the niqab (a veil covering the mouth and nose) has not been "accommodated" in some Quebec college language courses, where it was decided that the instructor needed to see the student's mouth in order to provide effective instruction.

Apply the Theory

1. Is there a mosque in your community or a Muslim congregation on your campus? If so, are the members primarily Sunni or Shia?

2. Should communities be allowed to block the construction of mosques or dictate their appearance? What about a church or temple?

Sources: Ba-Yunus and Kone 2004; Belt 2002; CBC 2007a; Environics Research Group 2007b; Institute for Social Policy and Understanding 2004; King 2004; Leonard 2003; McCloud 1995; Paik 2001; Perreaux 2010; Pew Global Attitudes Project 2006; Pew Research Center 2011; Smith 2001.

table 13-4 Percentage Who Hold Favourable Opinions Towards Muslims in Canada and Selected Countries, 2008

Percentage of "favourable" opinions towards Muslims	Canada	Great Britain	Germany	France	Spain	U.S.
	50	63	40	62	33	56

Source: Jedwab 2008.

New Religious Movements or Cults

In 1997, 38 members of the Heaven's Gate cult were found dead in Southern California after a mass suicide timed to occur with the appearance of the Hale-Bopp comet. They believed the comet hid a spaceship on which they could ride once they had broken free of their "bodily containers."

Partly as a result of the notoriety generated by such groups, the popular media have stigmatized the word *cult* by associating cults with the occult and the use of intense and forceful conversion techniques. The stereotyping of cults as uniformly bizarre and unethical has led sociologists to abandon the term and refer to a cult instead as a *new religious movement* (NRM). Although some NRMs, like the Branch Davidians, exhibit strange behaviour, many do not. They attract new members just like any other religion and often follow teachings similar to established Christian denominations but with less ritual.

It is difficult to distinguish sects from cults. A **new religious movement (NRM)** or **cult** is a generally small, secretive religious group that represents either a new religion or a major innovation of an existing faith. An example would be the Church of Scientology, to which a number of Hollywood actors belong. To its members, Scientology is an NRM; to its critics, it is a cult. NRMs are similar to sects in that they tend to be small and are often viewed as less respectable than more established religions.

However, unlike sects, NRMs normally do not result from schisms or breaks with established ecclesiae or denominations. Some cults, such as those focused on UFO sightings, may be totally unrelated to the existing faiths in a culture. Even when a cult does accept certain fundamental tenets of a dominant faith—such as belief in Jesus as divine or Mohammad as a messenger of God—it will offer new revelations or new insights to justify its claim to be a more advanced religion (Stark and Bainbridge 1979, 1985).

Like sects, NRMs may undergo transformation over time into other types of religious organizations. An example is the Christian Science Church, which began as a new religious movement under the leadership of Mary Baker Eddy. Today, this church exhibits the characteristics of a denomination. New religious movements may be in the early stages of what may develop into a denomination, or they may just as easily fade away through loss of members or weak leadership (Schaefer and Zellner 2007).

Comparing Forms of Religious Organization

How can we determine whether a particular religious group falls into the sociological category of ecclesia, denomination, sect, or NRM? As we have seen, these types of religious organizations have somewhat different relationships to society. Ecclesiae are recognized as national churches; denominations, although not officially approved by the state, are generally widely respected. By contrast, sects as well as NRMs are much more likely to be at odds with the larger culture.

Still, ecclesiae, denominations, and sects are best viewed as ideal types along a continuum rather than as mutually exclusive categories. Table 13-5 summarizes some of the primary characteristics of these ideal types. Since Canada has no ecclesiae, sociologists studying this country's religions have naturally focused on denominations and sects. These religious forms have been pictured on either end of a continuum, with denominations being accommodating to the secular world and sects making a protest against established religions. Although new religious movements have also been included in Table 13-5, they lie outside the continuum, because they generally define themselves as a new view of life rather than in terms of existing religious faiths.

table 13-5 Characteristics of Ecclesiae, Denominations, Sects, and New Religious Movements

Characteristic	Ecclesia	Denomination	Sect	New Religious Movement (or Cult)
Size	Very large	Large	Small	Small
Wealth	Extensive	Extensive	Limited	Variable
Religious services	Formal, little participation	Formal, little participation	Informal, emotional	Variable
Doctrines	Specific, but interpretation may be tolerated	Specific, but interpretation may be tolerated	Specific, purity of doctrine emphasized	Innovative, path-breaking
Clergy	Well-trained, full-time	Well-trained, full-time	Trained to some degree	Unspecialized
Membership	By virtue of being a member of society	By acceptance of doctrine	By acceptance of doctrine	By an emotional commitment
Relationship to the state	Recognized, closely aligned	Tolerated	Not encouraged	Ignored or challenged

Source: Adapted from G. Vernon 1962; see also Chalfant et al. 1994.

Advances in electronic communications have led to still another form of religious organization: the electronic church. Facilitated by cable television and satellite transmissions, *televangelists* direct their messages to more people—especially in the United States—than are served by all but the largest denominations. The Internet has given the electronic church another dimension: the religious blogosphere. According to a 2005 survey, roughly 1 million religious blogs (or Web logs) have been established in the United States alone, primarily to address people's views about religion or their personal spiritual experiences (D. Cohen 2005). Even the virtual world of *Second Life* has a rich spiritual landscape, with functioning congregations of Buddhist, Jewish, Muslim, and Christian avatars (Kiper 2008; MacDonald 2007; Simon 2007).

We turn now to another major social institution in every society: education. Education prepares citizens for the various roles demanded by other institutions, including religion. Education and religion sometimes get intertwined, as we will see in this chapter's social policy section about the role of religion in the schools.

13.6 What Are Some Sociological Perspectives on Education?

Education is a massive industry in Canada as well as a major agent of socialization. In the last few decades, increasing numbers of people have obtained a high school diploma and postsecondary education. (Figure 13-3 shows where Canada ranks among other developed nations.) According to Statistics Canada, university enrollment increased 13.9 percent between 2002–03 and 2007–08 (Statistics Canada 2010).

Globally, enrollments in educational institutions have been increasing; however, vast regional and national differences exist in this overall trend. For example, in less developed regions, although progress has been made, only 79 percent of boys and 66 percent of girls finished primary education in 2002 (UNICEF 2005). These numbers mask the fact that most girls in less developed countries receive less education than boys do, and in some of the world's poorest countries, fewer than half of young women receive the basic seven years of schooling (UNICEF 2005). According to the United Nations Population Fund's *State of World Population Report 2000,* girls and women throughout the world are still routinely denied access to education. As a result, the United Nations Children's Fund reported in 2004 only 42 percent of women in the least-developed countries can read, compared with 62 percent of men (UNICEF 2004). The functionalist, conflict, feminist, and interactionist perspectives offer distinctive ways of examining education as a social institution.

Functionalist View

Like other social institutions, education has both manifest (open, stated) and latent (hidden) functions. The most basic *manifest* function of education is the transmission of knowledge. Schools teach students such things as how to read, how to speak foreign languages, and how to repair automobiles. Education has another important manifest function: it bestows status. Because many people believe this function is performed inequitably, we will consider this later, in the section on the conflict view of education.

In addition to these manifest functions, education performs a number of *latent* functions: it transmits culture, promotes social and political integration, maintains social control, and serves as an agent of change.

figure **13-3** **Current Higher Education Graduation Rates (BA/BSc), Selected Countries**

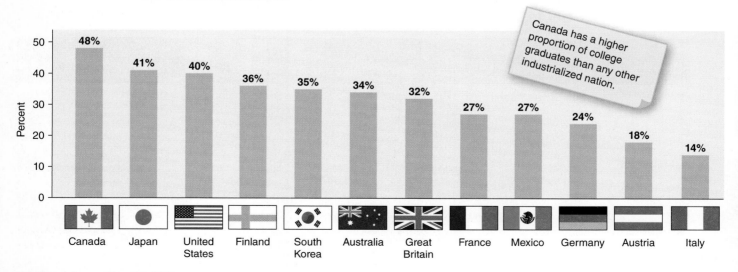

Note: For adults ages 25 to 64 in 2007.

Source: Bureau of the Census 2010:Table 1371.

research today

13-3 Google University

From comic books, television, and fast-paced video games to educational films and online college courses, technological innovations in communication have been seen as both a threat to culture and a boon to education. Like these new media, the search engine called Google has been greeted with both praise and scorn. Founded by two students at Stanford University in 1998, Google handled some 65 percent of all Internet searches in the United States in early 2011. Its familiar multicoloured logo stands for one of the most trusted brands in the world (see Figure 10-1 in Chapter 10).

Using Google or some other search engine, a researcher can now retrieve facts, viewpoints, images, and sounds within minutes. Just a few years ago, that task would have taken days. As Nicholas Carr (2008b:56), former editor of the *Harvard Business Review*, notes, "Once I was a scuba diver in the sea of words. Now I zip along the surface like a guy on a Jet Ski." Yet some critics of search engines charge that placing more and more of the world's knowledge just a mouse click away has made students lazy. Quick access to information, they point out, does not necessarily encourage concentration, let alone contemplation.

The availability of information online may also be changing the way people read. Educators worry that habitual skimming of the computer screen may carry over to students' print reading. Some have found that younger readers, faced with anything of length online, such as a short PDF file, simply ignore it. In response, researchers have begun to study whether those who read online in preference to books and other printed media still read sentence by sentence, as they were taught to do in school.

Other scholars are not disturbed by potential changes in what and how people read. They note that true literacy is not merely the ability to read to the end of an article or book, but to find the information you need amid a flood of sources—not all of them trustworthy—and use it correctly and responsibly. In other words, literacy includes critical thinking.

Ultimately, education is more than just collecting, organizing, and comprehending information. Accessing information and arguments regarding political and social issues is a form of civic engagement. Thus, the search feature on a Web page becomes a portal to a virtual town square. Perhaps that is why today's students are not only spending more time online than yesterday's students, but also doing more volunteer work.

Well before the advent of the Internet, much less Google, sociologist Daniel Bell (1973) wrote that *intellectual technologies* tend to institutionalize new approaches to the gathering and dissemination of information. Like the invention of the printing press, Google's advent is changing not just the university, but the universe of learning.

Apply the Theory

1. Do you prefer to do your reading online or in a magazine, newspaper, or book? Has the availability of online information changed the way that you read the written word?
2. Have you participated in any social or political causes or volunteered your time while on campus? If so, did you use the Internet to organize or disseminate information about your activities?

Sources: Bauerlein 2008; Brabazon 2007; Carr 2008a, 2008b; Maestretti 2009; Search Engine Watch 2011; Vaidhyanathan 2008; Workman 2008.

Transmitting Culture   As a social institution, education performs a conservative function—transmitting the dominant culture. Schooling exposes each generation of young people to the existing beliefs, norms, and values of their culture. In many societies, students are taught respect for social control and reverence for established institutions, such as religion, the family, and government.

Sometimes, nations need to reassess the ways in which they transmit culture to students. Recently, the Chinese government revised the nation's history curriculum. Students are now taught that the Chinese Communist Party played a central role in defeating Japan in World War II. No mention is made of the estimated 30 million Chinese who died from the famine because of party founder Mao Zedong's disastrous Great Leap Forward (1958–1962), a failed effort to transform China's agrarian economy into an industrial powerhouse.

Today, the Internet offers a new and potentially revolutionary way of transmitting culture. Box 13-3 discusses the educational impact of Google and other search engines.

At all levels of the education system in Canada, controversy surrounds the exclusion from the curriculum of authors and historical figures who do not represent the dominant culture.

Critics charge that standard academic curricula have failed to represent the important contributions of immigrants, Aboriginal peoples, women, and visible minorities to history, literature, and other fields of study. Several underlying questions are raised by this debate and are still to be resolved: Which ideas and values are essential for instruction? Which cultural beliefs should be taught by the schools and postsecondary institutions of Canada?

Promoting Social and Political Integration   Many prestigious universities require their first-year students to live together on campus in order to foster a sense of community. Education serves the latent function of promoting social and political integration by transforming a population comprising diverse ethnic and religious groups into a society whose members share—to some extent—a common identity. Schools have historically played an important role in socializing the children of immigrants into the norms, values, and beliefs of the dominant culture. From a functionalist perspective, the common identity and social integration fostered by education contribute to societal stability and consensus (Touraine 1974).

Although the school Harry Potter attends in the film *Harry Potter and the Deathly Hallows: Part 2* is fictitious, like real schools, it transmits a socially sanctioned culture to students.

bureaucratic organization. As a social institution, education reflects the interests of the family and in turn prepares young people for their participation in yet another social institution: the economy. Students are being trained for what is ahead, whether it be the assembly line or a physician's office. In effect, then, schools serve as a transitional agent of social control—between parents and employers in the life cycle of most individuals (Bowles and Gintis 1976; Cole 1988).

Schools direct and even restrict students' aspirations in a manner that reflects societal values and prejudices. School administrators may allocate funds for athletic programs while giving much less support to music, art, and dance. Teachers and guidance counsellors may encourage male students to pursue careers in the sciences but may steer equally talented female students into careers as early childhood educators. Such socialization into traditional gender roles can be viewed as a form of social control.

In Canada, perhaps the most egregious example of an attempt to promote social integration through education is that of residential schools for First Nations children. Residential schools were established by the Canadian government and operated by the Roman Catholic, Anglican, United, and Presbyterian churches for the purpose of assimilating Aboriginal children into the dominant culture. Operating widely until the middle decades of the twentieth century, with the last ones closing in the 1980s, these schools had as their express purpose the goal of cultural assimilation. Aboriginal children were taken from their homes and forced to speak languages other than their own. In residential schools, they learned the values and norms of the dominant European groups and at the same time learned that their own culture was inferior and thus needed to be replaced. In this process of promoting conformity to the dominant culture, many Aboriginal children were emotionally, physically, and sexually abused by those operating the residential schools. Today, many First Nations adults are enduring difficult lives because of their traumatizing experiences as children in these schools.

Maintaining Social Control

In performing the manifest function of imparting knowledge, schools go far beyond teaching such skills as reading, writing, and mathematics. Like other social institutions, such as the family and religion, education prepares young people to lead productive and orderly lives as adults by introducing them to the norms, values, and sanctions of the larger society.

Through the exercise of social control, schools teach students various skills and values essential to their future positions within the labour force. They learn punctuality, discipline, scheduling, and responsible work habits, as well as how to negotiate their way through the complexities of a

Serving as an Agent of Change

So far, we have focused on conservative functions of education—on its role in transmitting the existing culture, promoting social and political integration, and maintaining social control. Yet education can also stimulate or bring about desired social change. Sex education classes were introduced in public schools in response to higher rates of sexual activity among teens. Special "girls only" science and mathematics classes were created in response to female graduates' low participation rates in such fields as science, technology, and engineering. Anti-racism programs in schools were created in response to the prevalence of racism in schools and society in general.

Education also promotes social change by serving as a meeting ground where distinctive beliefs and traditions can be shared. In 2008, there were more than 130 000 international students at Canadian universities. Cross-cultural exchanges between these visitors and citizens of Canada ultimately broaden the perspective of both the hosts and their guests. The same is certainly true when students from Canada attend schools in Europe, Latin America, Africa, or Asia.

Numerous sociological studies have revealed that increased numbers of years of formal schooling are associated with openness to new ideas and more liberal social and political viewpoints. Sociologist Robin Williams points out that better educated people tend to have greater access to information, more diverse opinions, and the ability to make subtle distinctions in analysis. Formal education stresses both the importance of qualifying statements (in place of broad generalizations) and the need to be skeptical of (rather than simply accept) established truths and practices. As we saw in Chapter 2, the scientific method relies on *testing* hypotheses and reflects the questioning spirit that characterizes modern education (Williams et al. 1964).

Conflict View

The functionalist perspective portrays contemporary education as basically benign. For example, it argues that schools rationally sort and select students for future high-status positions, thereby meeting society's need for talented and expert personnel. In contrast, the conflict perspective views education as an instrument of elite domination. Conflict theorists point out the sharp inequalities that exist in educational opportunities available to different socioeconomic and ethnic groups. Schools convince subordinate groups of their inferiority, reinforce existing social class inequality, and discourage alternative and more democratic visions of society.

Criticizing the functionalist view, conflict theorists argue that the educational system socializes students into values dictated by the powerful, that schools stifle individualism and creativity in the name of maintaining order, and that the level of change promoted by education is relatively insignificant. From a conflict perspective, the inhibiting effects of education are particularly apparent in the "hidden curriculum" as well as in the differential way in which status is bestowed.

The Hidden Curriculum Schools are highly bureaucratic organizations. Many teachers rely on the rules and regulations of schools to maintain order. Unfortunately, the need for control and discipline can take precedence over the learning process. Teachers may focus on obedience to the rules as an end in itself. If this occurs, students and teachers alike become victims of what Philip Jackson has called the "hidden curriculum."

The term **hidden curriculum** refers to standards of behaviour that are deemed proper by society and are taught subtly in schools. According to this curriculum, children must not speak until the teacher calls on them and must regulate their activities according to the clock or bells. In addition, they are expected to concentrate on their own work rather than assist other students who learn more slowly. A hidden curriculum is evident in schools around the world.

In a classroom overly focused on obedience, value is placed on pleasing the teacher and remaining quiet rather than on creative thought and academic learning. Habitual obedience to authority may result in the type of distressing behaviour documented by Stanley Milgram in his classic obedience studies.

Bestowal of Status Both functionalist and conflict theorists agree that education performs the important function of bestowing status. As we noted earlier, an increasing proportion of people in Canada are obtaining high school diplomas; postsecondary certificates, diplomas, and degrees;

Angela Wilson, left, and Donna Harrow celebrate after Toronto public school trustees, on January 29, 2008, vote 11–9 to open an alternative Afrocentric school, in an effort to help curb the dropout rate of black students in the Greater Toronto Area.

and advanced professional degrees. From a functionalist perspective, this widening bestowal of status is beneficial not only to particular recipients but also to society as a whole. In the view of Kingsley Davis and Wilbert Moore, society must distribute its members among a variety of social positions (1945). Education can contribute to this process by sorting people into appropriate levels and courses of study that will prepare them for appropriate positions in the labour force.

Conflict sociologists are far more critical of the *differential* way education bestows status. They stress that schools sort pupils according to social class background. Although the educational system helps certain poor children to move into middle-class professional positions, it denies most disadvantaged children the same educational opportunities afforded children of the affluent. In this way, schools tend to preserve social class inequalities in each new generation.

Research suggests that Canadian students whose parents earn at least $75 000 are more likely to engage in university studies compared to students whose family income is not as great (Canadian Council of Learning 2009).

Even a single school can reinforce class differences by putting students in tracks. The term **tracking** refers to the practice of placing students in specific curriculum groups on the basis of test scores and other criteria. Tracking begins very early in the classroom, often in reading groups during grade 1. The practice can reinforce the disadvantages that children from less affluent families may face if they haven't been exposed to reading materials, computers, and other forms of educational stimulation during their early childhood years. To ignore this connection between tracking and students' ethnicity and social class is to fundamentally misunderstand how schools perpetuate the existing social structure.

Conflict theorists hold that the educational inequalities resulting from tracking are designed to meet the needs of modern capitalist societies. Samuel Bowles and Herbert Gintis argue that capitalism requires a skilled, disciplined labour force and that the educational system of the United States is structured with this objective in mind (1976). Citing numerous studies, they offer support for what they call the **correspondence principle**. According to this approach, schools promote the values expected of individuals in each social class and perpetuate social class divisions from one generation to the next. Thus, working-class children, assumed to be destined for subordinate positions, are more likely to be placed in high school vocational and general tracks, which emphasize close supervision and compliance with authority. In contrast, young people from more affluent families are largely directed to university preparatory tracks, which stress leadership and decision-making skills—the skills they are expected to need as adults.

Feminist Views

In her 1928 book *A Room of One's Own,* Virginia Woolf advocated the value of educational reform so that the female student could "live and write her poetry" (Woolf 1977:123). She contended that even if someone had to struggle in "poverty and obscurity" to bring about educational reform on behalf of girls and women, it was worthwhile. Although feminist perspectives on education are diverse, today, many share the view that educational institutions must attempt to prevent gendered patterns of inequality found in the larger society from being perpetuated in the classroom.

In the twentieth century feminist perspectives on education raised a wide range of concerns stemming from the historical exclusion of girls and women in education and the persistent "chilly climate" that many females experience in educational institutions that treat them as outsiders. Some perspectives have articulated the need to understand how the social construction of gender plays a role in the educational experiences of students from elementary school to university, and how these experiences are connected to such factors as race, class, and age (Mandell 1998). The hidden curriculum of the school system contributed to gender socialization through the use of language that is not gender-inclusive, curricula that are androcentric, and role models of male principals and female elementary school teachers that reinforce traditional patterns of male dominance and authority.

Since the 1970s, Canadian universities and colleges have been developing women's studies programs that provide feminist frameworks for research, teaching, and educational reform. Despite the fact that today women outnumber men in enrollment in universities in Canada and have made significant inroads into what were previously male-dominated faculties (e.g., medicine and law), public school teachers are still primarily female and the highest ranks at universities are disproportionately filled by men.

Interactionist View

In George Bernard Shaw's play *Pygmalion,* later adapted into the hit Broadway musical *My Fair Lady,* flower girl Eliza Doolittle is transformed into a "lady" by Professor Henry Higgins. He changes her manner of speech and teaches her the etiquette of "high society." When she is introduced into society as an aristocrat, she is readily accepted. People treat her as a "lady," and she responds as one.

The labelling approach suggests that if we treat people in particular ways, they may fulfill our expectations. Children labelled as "troublemakers" come to view themselves as delinquents. A dominant group's stereotyping of racial minorities may limit their opportunities to break away from expected roles.

Can this labelling process operate in the classroom? Because of their focus on micro-level classroom dynamics, interactionist researchers have been particularly interested in this question. Howard Becker studied public schools in low-income and more affluent areas of Chicago (1952). He noticed that administrators expected less of students from poor neighbourhoods, and he wondered if teachers were accepting this view. Subsequently, in *Pygmalion in the Classroom,* psychologist Robert Rosenthal, school principal Lenore Jacobson, and Elisha Babad documented what they referred to as a **teacher-expectancy effect**—the impact that a teacher's expectations about a student's performance may have on the student's actual achievements (1968). This appears to be especially true in lower grades, through grade 3 (Brint 1998).

In Tokyo, a mother escorts her daughter to an admissions interview at a highly competitive private cram school. Some Japanese families enroll children as young as 2 in cram schools to better prepare them for such exams.

table 13-6 Sociological Perspectives on Education

Theoretical Perspective	Emphasis
Functionalist	Transmission of the dominant culture Integration of society Promotion of social norms, values, and sanctions Promotion of desirable social change
Conflict	Domination by the elite through unequal access to schooling Hidden curriculum Bestowal of status
Feminist	Educational systems exhibit and reproduce gendered patterns of inequality
Interactionist	Teacher-expectancy effect

In the first experiment, children in a San Francisco elementary school were given a verbal and reasoning pretest. Rosenthal and Jacobson then *randomly* selected 20 percent of the sample and designated them as "spurters"—children of whom teachers could expect superior performance. The teachers then treated these children as superior students in the classroom. On a later verbal and reasoning test, the spurters were found to score significantly higher than before. Moreover, teachers evaluated them as more interesting, more curious, and better adjusted than their classmates. These results were striking. Apparently, teachers' perceptions that these students were exceptional led to noticeable improvements in performance.

Studies have revealed that teachers wait longer for an answer from a student believed to be a high achiever and are more likely to give such children a second chance. In one experiment, teachers' expectations were even shown to have an impact on students' athletic achievements. Teachers obtained better athletic performance—as measured in the number of sit-ups or push-ups performed—from those students of whom they *expected* higher numbers. Despite the controversial nature of these findings, some researchers continue to document the existence of the teacher-expectancy effect. Interactionists emphasize that ability alone may be less predictive of academic success than one might think (Babad and Taylor 1992; Brint 1998; R. Rosenthal and Jacobsen 1992:247–262).

Table 13-6 summarizes the four major sociological perspectives on education.

What Makes Schools Formal Organizations?

In many respects, today's schools, when viewed as an example of a formal organization, are similar to factories, hospitals, and business firms. Like these organizations, schools do not operate autonomously; they are influenced by the market of potential students. This is especially true of private schools. Currently, approximately 8 percent of students in Canada attend private schools. The parallels between schools and other types of formal organizations will become more apparent as we examine teaching as an occupational role and the student subculture.

Teachers: Employees and Instructors

Whether they serve as instructors of preschoolers or graduate students, teachers are employees of formal organizations with bureaucratic structures. There is an inherent conflict in serving as a professional within a bureaucracy. The organization follows the principles of hierarchy and expects adherence to its rules, but professionalism demands the individual responsibility of the practitioner. This conflict is very real for teachers, who experience all the positive and negative consequences of working in bureaucracies.

A teacher undergoes many perplexing stresses every day. Although teachers' academic assignments have become more specialized, the demands on their time remain diverse and contradictory. There are conflicts inherent in serving as an instructor, a disciplinarian, and an employee of a school district at the same time. For university professors, different types of role strain arise. Although formally employed as teachers, they are also expected to work on committees and are encouraged to conduct scholarly research. In many universities, security of position (tenure) is based primarily on the publication of original scholarship. As a result, instructors must fulfill goals that compete for time.

University professors rarely have to take on the role of disciplinarian, but this task has become a major focus of schoolteachers' work in such countries as Canada and the United States. Order is needed to establish an environment in which students can learn effectively. Some observers believe that schools have been the scene of increasingly violent misbehaviour in recent years, although these concerns may be overblown.

Canada is becoming an increasingly "schooled society" (Guppy and Davies 1998), which will contribute to the employment prospects of students wanting to become teachers. The Canadian Council on Learning (CCL) states that between 1971 and 2001 the percentage of "knowledge workers" almost doubled, with the highest level of knowledge intensity in the fields of health and education (2005). As well, the demographic composition of teachers is changing, reflecting the aging population; a greater number of retiring teachers will need to be replaced in the near future. This trend is also occurring in the United States where, because of teacher shortages in some regions, school boards are advertising for and recruiting teachers from Canada.

The status of any job reflects several factors, including the level of education required, the financial compensation, and the respect given the occupation within society. The teaching profession is feeling pressure in all three of these areas. First, the amount of formal schooling required for teaching remains high, and now the public has begun to call for new competency examinations for teachers. Second, statistics demonstrate that teachers' salaries are significantly lower than those of many professionals and skilled workers. Wages differ by field of study; graduates of education and social science, who are disproportionately female, earn less, for example, than graduates of computer science and engineering, who are disproportionately male (Statistics Canada 2006b). Finally, as we have seen, the overall prestige of the teaching profession has declined in the last two decades. Many teachers have become disappointed and frustrated and have left the educational world for careers in other professions. Many are simply "burned out" by the severe demands, limited rewards, and general sense of alienation that they experience on the job.

Despite efforts to establish positive relationships among students and between teachers and students, many young people view their schools as impersonal institutions.

The Student Subculture

An important latent function of education relates directly to student life: Schools provide for students' social and recreational needs. Education helps toddlers and young children develop interpersonal skills that are essential during adolescence and adulthood. During high school and the years of postsecondary education, students may meet future partners and may establish lifelong friendships.

When people observe high schools and postsecondary institutions from the outside, students appear to constitute a cohesive, uniform group. However, the student subculture is actually much more complex and diverse. High school cliques and social groups may crop up based on ethnicity, social class, physical attractiveness, placement in courses, athletic ability, and leadership roles in the school and community. In his classic community study of "Elmtown," August Hollingshead found some 259 distinct cliques in a single high school (1975). These cliques, whose average size was five people, were centred on the school itself, on recreational activities, and on religious and community groups.

Adult Education

Picture a college or university student. Most likely, you will imagine a 19- or 20-year-old. This reflects the belief that education is something experienced and completed during the first two or three decades of life and rarely supplemented after that. However, many postsecondary institutions have witnessed a dramatic increase in the number of mature students pursuing higher education.

In 2008, students who were 25–34 years of age had a rate of participation in adult education of 50 percent. Those who had less than secondary school completion had a rate of participation of 18 percent in adult education, while those who had postsecondary education had a rate of 54 percent (Statistics Canada 2010). Obviously, sociological models of the postsecondary subculture will have to be revised in light of the trends in adult education.

One explanation for the adult education boom is that society is changing rapidly in an age of technological innovation and a growing knowledge-based economy. Business firms have come to accept the view of education as lifelong and may encourage (or require) employees to learn job-related skills. Thus, administrative assistants are sent to special schools to be trained to use the latest computer software. Realtors attend classes to learn about alternative forms of financing for homebuyers. In occupation after occupation, long-time workers and professionals are going back to school to adapt to the new demands of their jobs. About 14 percent of Canadian workers participated in adult education between 1993 and 2001; on average, those who participated in adult education and who obtained a postsecondary certificate made significant gains in wages and earnings (Statistics Canada 2006b). Taking a conflict perspective, Canadian sociologist David Livingstone argues that, despite Canadians' growing technological proficiency and growing levels of training and education, employers are failing to fully utilize their skills, thus contributing to *underemployment* (1999).

According to a 2008 report released by the Canadian Council on Learning (CCL), Canada's weakest link in education is lifelong learning. Unlike many other developed countries, Canada has not developed a lifelong learning strategy. According to the report, "Ongoing learning can influence income, job satisfaction, political participation and health and well-being. It also enhances Canada's economic productivity and competitiveness" (*The Gazette* 2008).

Home-Schooling

When most people think of school, they think of bricks and mortar, and the teachers, administrators, and other employees who staff school buildings. But for an increasing number of students in Canada and the United States, home is the classroom and a parent is the teacher. Estimates of the number of children being home-schooled in Canada vary and difficult to obtain since many home-schools are not registered.

In the past, families that taught their children at home lived in isolated environments or held strict religious views at odds with the secular environment of public schools. But today, home-schooling is attracting a broader range of families not necessarily tied to organized religion. Poor academic quality, threat of school strikes, peer pressure, and school violence are motivating many parents to teach their children at home. In addition, the growing presence of computers in the home and the availability of online educational resources have motivated some parents to educate their children themselves.

Although supporters of home-schooling feel that children can do just as well or better in home-schools as in public schools, critics counter that because home-schooled children are isolated from the larger community, they lose an important chance to improve their socialization skills. But proponents of home-schooling claim their children benefit from contact with others besides their own age group. They also see home-schools as a good alternative for children who suffer from attention deficit disorder (ADD) and learning disorders.

Quality control is an issue in home-schooling. Although home-schooling is legal in Canada, provincial and territorial governments require that parents register their children. In Alberta, where home-schooling is particularly popular, estimates point to a high number of unregistered children—children the government cannot monitor in terms of curricular and academic achievement. Many of these children are from families where the motivating factor to home-school is religion; these families believe that the secular school system does not reflect their values, particularly those concerning abortion, homosexuality, and evolution.

In 1988, the Supreme Court of Canada ruled that the Alberta government had a "compelling interest" in ensuring that the children of that province be properly educated (Mitchell 1999). This would mean making sure that home-schooled children followed a government-approved curriculum and that they were tested annually according to provincial standards. Despite the court ruling, many Christian parents continue to believe that the government should not be in the business of monitoring their children's education and that the values of secular education are not those to which they want their children exposed.

Home-schooling works, particularly for those who have made a commitment to it (Calhoun 2000; Matthews 1999; Paulson 2000). Home-schooling allows parents to integrate religion into their children's studies if they choose, but controversy brews when public schools do so, as you will see in the following social policy section.

Social Policy and Religion

Religion in Public Schools

The Issue

Should public schools be allowed to sponsor organized prayers in the classroom? Should the Lord's Prayer be part of the agenda at weekly school assemblies? How about reading Bible verses? Or just a collective moment of silence? Can public school athletes offer up a group prayer in a team huddle? Should students be able to initiate voluntary prayers at school events? Should a school be allowed to post the Ten Commandments in a hallway? Each of these situations has been an object of great dissension among those who see a role for prayer in public schools and those who want to maintain a strict separation of church and state.

Another area of controversy centres on the teaching of theories about the origin of humans and of the universe. Mainstream scientific thinking theorizes that humans evolved over billions of years from one-celled organisms and that the

universe came into being 15 billion years ago as a result of a "big bang." But these theories are challenged by people who hold to the Biblical account of the creation of humans and the universe some 10 000 years ago—a viewpoint known as **creationism.** Creationists want their theory taught in the schools as the only one or, at the very least, as an alternative to the theory of evolution.

Who has the right to decide these issues? And what is considered the "right" decision? Religion in the public schools constitutes one of the thorniest issues in Canadian public policy today.

The Setting

In Canada, the Charter of Rights and Freedoms provides for freedom of religion. The Charter, along with the Canadian Constitution, protects the rights and privileges held by denominational schools at

the time of Confederation in 1867. This has meant that in addition to the public school system, some provinces and territories fund Catholic school education, while Quebec, where the majority of schools are Catholic, funds Protestant education. In 1999, a government-mandated task force in Quebec recommended that the Catholic and Protestant status for public schools be abolished and replaced with "secular" public schools. In the case of non-denominational or so-called secular schools, where explicit religious affiliation is not established, the issue of religious content in the form of prayers and Bible readings has become a contentious one.

Quebec is not the only province to experience these tensions in the secular schools. In 1999, Saskatchewan became the fourth province in Canada to oppose prayer in public schools. In 1993, a complaint by nine Saskatoon parents launched a challenge against the 100-year-old tradition of encouraging public school teachers to say the Lord's Prayer in classrooms and at assemblies. The Saskatchewan Act, part of the provincial constitution, permitted prayer and Bible readings in the public schools. The group of nine Saskatoon parents, which included Muslims, Jews, Unitarians, and atheists, complained that this practice violated the Saskatchewan Human Rights Code. More specifically, they argued, it violated their children's (and other children's) right to freedom of conscience. They claimed that students were being denied the right to enjoy an education without discrimination because of creed or religion. As a result, in 1999, a board of inquiry ruled that it was discriminatory to require recitation of the Lord's Prayer in Saskatoon classrooms and assemblies.

Sociological Insights

Supporters of school prayer and of creationism feel that strict court rulings force too great a separation between what Émile Durkheim called the *sacred* and the *profane*. They insist that use of non-denominational prayer can in no way lead to the establishment of an ecclesia in Canada. Moreover, they believe that school prayer—and the teaching of creationism—can provide the spiritual guidance and socialization that many children today do not receive from parents or regular church attendance. Many communities also believe that schools should transmit the dominant culture of Canada by encouraging prayer.

A 1998 General Social Survey stated that 55 percent of adults in the United States disapproved of a Supreme Court ruling against the required reading of the Lord's Prayer or Bible verses in public schools. A national survey in 1999 showed that 68 percent of the public favoured teaching creationism along with evolution in public schools, and 40 percent favoured teaching *only* creationism. These numbers still hold up in 2009. No other Western society has such a large body of opinion supporting views that depart so much from contemporary scientific understanding. Perhaps this is a reflection of a deep-rooted and enduring strain of religious fundamentalism in the United States and the fact that religious belief in general is stronger there than in Canada and in other Western societies (Davis and Smith 1999; Johnson 1999; Lewis 1999).

Opponents of school prayer argue that a religious majority in a community might impose religious viewpoints specific to its faith, at the expense of religious minorities. Viewed from a conflict perspective, organized school prayer could reinforce the religious beliefs, rituals, and interests of the powerful; it could also violate the rights of the powerless, increase religious dissension, and threaten the multiculturalism of Canada. These critics question whether school prayer can remain truly voluntary. Drawing on the interactionist perspective and small-group research, they suggest that children will face enormous social pressure to conform to the beliefs and practices of a religious majority.

Policy Initiatives

A more recent case involving the Saskatoon Board of Education provides a good example of how in some communities policymakers are trying to find a compromise between those who want prayer in schools and those who do not. In 2001, two years after the Lord's Prayer was removed from the daily routine of public schools, the Saskatoon Public School Board considered a Christian education program for children of religious parents. Modelled after the Logos Christian Education program already in place in Edmonton public schools, Christian students would have received instruction in a separate classroom with a religious environment. Opposition to the proposal was raised by those who felt that the Logos program would have divided students along religious lines and undermined the basis of the public school system.

In 2006, the issue resurfaced in Manitoba, where the Public Schools Act allowed a petition from parents of at least 60 students (or 75 percent of that school's student population) to be voted on by the school board, for the approval of religious exercises during the school year. School trustee Gary Nelson, who voted against the motion, stated:

> What some, but not all, schools . . . had been doing when those petitions were received and approved by the board, was to broadcast the Lord's Prayer over the public address. Unfortunately, in so doing, the school was also providing the "religious exercise" to all of its students including those children whose parents did not request the Lord's Prayer. . . . The only real way for a school to comply with the Act, and the practice of most schools when they receive a petition, is also problematic. That is to segregate the children by either removing those children whose parents petitioned for prayer from the class; or to remove the children who were not named in the petition from the class. I am sure you can understand the problems that can occur when children are singled out: bullying, teasing, and ridicule often are the result. (Nelson 2006)

The activism of religious fundamentalists in the nation's public school system raises a more general question: Whose ideas and values deserve a hearing in classrooms? Critics see this campaign as one step toward sectarian religious control of public education. They worry that at some point in the future, teachers may not be able to use books or make statements that conflict with fundamentalist interpretations of the Bible. For advocates of a liberal education who are deeply committed to intellectual (and religious) diversity, this is a genuinely frightening prospect. Recently the Alberta Human Rights Commission refused to consider a complaint by parents of a small community in that province, in regard to the complete lack of secular education available to their children. The community's only schools were Catholic, requiring students to study religion every day. Some parents were forced to move to other communities in order to ensure their children's access to secular education (National Post 2012).

University of Toronto education professor Ben Levin states, "I don't think issues on religion and language will ever be resolved in Canada; they're deeply contentious issues" (Wilson 2007).

Apply the Theory

1. Do you think promoting religious observance is a legitimate function of the social institution of education?
2. Do you agree with a conflict view on the issue of organized school prayer?
3. Are there functions served by Christian fundamentalists and their allies attempting to reshape public education in Canada?

CHAPTER RESOURCES

Summary

::: **13.1** What Is Durkheim's Sociological Approach to Religion?

- Émile Durkheim stressed the social impact of religion and attempted to understand individual religious behaviour within the context of the larger society.

::: **13.2** What Are the Major World Religions?

- Eighty-five percent of the world's population adheres to some form of religion. Tremendous diversity exists in religious beliefs and practices, which may be heavily influenced by culture.

::: 13.3 What Role Does Religion Play?

- According to functionalists, religion serves the functions of integrating people in a diverse society and providing social support in time of need.
- Max Weber saw a connection between religious allegiance and capitalistic behaviour through a religious orientation known as the **Protestant ethic**.
- **Liberation theology** uses the church in a political effort to alleviate poverty and social injustice.
- From a Marxist point of view, religion serves to reinforce the social control of those in power. It lessens the possibility of collective political action that can end capitalist oppression and transform society.

::: 13.4 What Are the Components of Religion?

- Religious components include **religious beliefs, religious rituals**, and **religious experience**.

::: 13.5 What Are the Forms of Religious Organization?

- Sociologists have identified four basic types of religious organization: the **ecclesia**, the **denomination**, the **sect**, and the **new religious movement (NRM)** or **cult**.

- Advances in communication have led to a new type of church organization: the electronic church.

::: 13.6 What Are Some Sociological Perspectives on Education?

- According to functionalist thinkers, transmission of knowledge and bestowal of status are manifest functions of **education**. Among its latent functions are transmitting culture, promoting social and political integration, maintaining social control, and serving as an agent of social change.
- In the view of conflict theorists, education serves as an instrument of elite domination through the **hidden curriculum** and by bestowing status unequally.
- According to interactionist sociologists, the **teacher-expectancy effect** can sometimes have an impact on a student's actual achievements.

::: 13.7 What Makes Schools Formal Organizations?

- Most schools in Canada today are organized on the basis of Weber's model of bureaucracy.

Critical Thinking Questions

1. From a conflict point of view, explain how religion could be used to bring about social change.
2. Why is it so difficult for women to become leaders of religious organizations?
3. What are the functions and dysfunctions of tracking in schools? Viewed from an interactionist perspective, how would the tracking of high school students influence the interactions between students and teachers? In what ways might tracking have positive and negative impacts on the self-concepts of various students?
4. Why are some religions granted greater social approval or higher status than others?

THINKING ABOUT MOVIES

Freedom Writers
A teacher attempts to defuse conflict among her students.

Trembling Before G-D
This documentary explores the tension between religious belief and sexual orientation.

Monsieur Ibrahim
In this film, which draws comparisons between Islam and Judaism, a Muslim grocer befriends a Jewish boy.

connect **LEARNSMART** **SMARTBOOK**

For more information on the resources available from McGraw-Hill Ryerson, go to **www.mcgrawhill.ca/he/solutions**.

inside

Fresh produce tempts shoppers at an outdoor market. In any society, the exchange of goods and services depends on the interaction of people.

Politics and the Economy

THE FAIR TRADE REVOLUTION

EDITED BY
JOHN BOWES
FOREWORD BY
MARY ROBINSON

" It is rare in life to have a moment of personal epiphany. Mine came in the millennium year when, at the Co-op, we had just introduced the UK's first own brand Fairtrade product: a chocolate bar with its key ingredient sourced from Ghana. We had supported the concept of fair trade right from the beginning but, although always empathetic to the ethical agenda, my interest was primarily commercial; the intention was to develop responsible retailing, a holistic approach to this agenda, as a modern day reflection of cooperative values and a vehicle for differentiating the business from its competitors. But in concert with the chocolate initiative a BBC crew visited Kuapa Kokoo in Ghana and their 14-minute film changed my view of the world. At the end of their report they unwrapped a chocolate bar, which was starting to melt in the heat, and gave some to a young woman and her daughter. As they tasted the product their eyes lit up and their faces were transformed into bright smiles and the young woman said 'oh, it's so sweet, so sweet'. This lady had spent her whole life toiling in the fields for a pittance and had never tasted the product of her own labours; she had no concept of what it was about chocolate that made it so important and appealing to the people living thousands of miles away in the northern hemisphere. In one sense the film captured a joyous experience but in another it was extraordinarily sad. I felt a catch in my throat and knew I was hooked for the rest of my life.

. . .

It has been estimated that fair trade may, currently, be benefiting more than 7 million people in the developing world. This is an impressive achievement but set in the context of the sheer scale of world poverty it still represents only a relatively small contribution towards addressing an enormous problem.

The United States of America is the largest consumer market on Earth. No other country on the planet could do more to address the climate problem and establish a fairer trading system.

It is estimated that 1.4 billion people, one fifth of the world's population, are trying to survive at or below the World Bank's official poverty line of just $1.25 a day. And 2.6 billion people, about 40 per cent of humanity, are living on less than $2 a day.

These astonishing numbers are so large that it is difficult to fully comprehend them. They reflect the appalling collective failure of human society. And the scale of the failure becomes even more dramatic when we consider *disparities* in world income. The poorest 40 per cent account for just 5 per cent of global income whilst the richest 20 per cent take three quarters of the pot. The truth is that fair trade is still very much in its infancy. Those who are committed to making a real difference in the developing world will recognise that we are not at the end of a process, or anywhere near the end, but really only at the very beginning. If we strip away all of the commercial spin, and occasional wishful thinking, we might be left with the uncomfortable conclusion that, far from capitalising on a consumer movement, we have perhaps not yet recognised its full potential and have so far failed to put mechanisms into place to ensure that its momentum can be fully realised.

. . .

The United States of America is the largest consumer market on Earth. No other country on the planet could do more to address the climate problem and establish a fairer trading system. While fair trade has experienced strong growth in the States, which in absolute terms is the largest single market for fair trade products, overall market penetration is low. Yet, if we are to have a true revolution in trading practices it is difficult to see how it can be achieved without the US fully on board. This represents the greatest single challenge for fair trade campaigners. . . . "

(Bowes 2011:ix, 2–3, 231–232)

John Bowes, editor of this excerpt from *The Fair Trade Revolution,* once served as a top executive in a British grocery chain. In the process, he became acutely aware of the low wages paid to those who harvest the food sold in grocery stores. To address their plight, he helped to originate a movement called **fair trade**, in which consumers in industrialized countries voluntarily pay above-market prices for certain foods so that the workers who plant, pick, and pack the crops can receive higher wages. Supporters of fair trade often seek to subsidize export crops grown in developing countries, such as coffee, bananas, and chocolate (Stark 2011).

While acknowledging Bowes's point of view, sociologists also try to see foreign agricultural laborers and farm owners from the perspective of their own cultures—an approach called *cultural relativism* (see Chapter 3). That is, besides comparing farm work in developing countries to similar work in industrial nations, sociologists would compare it to the other jobs available to foreign workers. For example, sweatshops certainly aren't the sort of places where people in industrial countries would want to work, but from the foreign worker's perspective, they may be preferable to a farm in an isolated rural area or a lower-paying job with a local employer. In sum, foreign workers and producers face a different *economic system* from the one in industrial nations, so their attitudes and the choices they make may differ from our own.

The term **economic system** refers to the social institution through which goods and services are produced, distributed, and consumed. As with social institutions such as the family, religion, and government, the economic system shapes other aspects of the social order and is in turn influenced by them. Throughout this textbook, you have been reminded of the economy's impact on social behaviour—for example, on individual and group behaviour in factories and offices. You have studied the work of Karl Marx and Friedrich Engels, who emphasized that a society's economic system can promote social inequality. And you have learned that foreign investment in developing countries can intensify inequality among residents.

By **political system,** sociologists mean the social institution that is founded on a recognized set of procedures for implementing and achieving society's goals, such as the allocation of valued resources. Like religion and the family, the political system is a cultural universal: It is found in every society. In Canada, the political system holds the ultimate responsibility for addressing the social policy issues examined in this book: childcare, the AIDS crisis, welfare reform, and so forth.

It is hard to imagine two social institutions more intertwined than government and the economy. Besides serving as the largest employer in the nation, government at all levels regulates commerce and entry into many occupations. At the same time, the economy generates the revenue to support government services. In this chapter, we present a combined analysis of government and the economy. How does the power elite maintain its power? Is war necessary in settling international disputes? How have the trends toward deindustrialization and the outsourcing of service jobs affected our economy? We begin the chapter with a macro-level analysis of two ideal types of economic systems: capitalism and socialism. This theoretical discussion is followed by a case study of China's decision to allow capitalist entrepreneurial activity within its socialist economy. Next, we examine some general theories of power and authority, with the four major types of government in which that power and authority is exerted. We see how politics works, with particular attention to citizens' participation and the changing role of women. We look at two models of power in Canada, the elite and the pluralist models. Then, we touch briefly on war, peace, and terrorism, followed by a look at ways in which economies are changing in response to globalization. The chapter closes with a social policy section on microfinancing. ■

::: use your sociological *imagination* :::

Do you see additional ways that Canadians could be made more aware of the unfair practices of food production and consumption?

What Forms Do Economic Systems Take?

The sociocultural evolution approach developed by Gerhard Lenski categorizes pre-industrial society according to the way in which the economy is organized. The principal types of pre-industrial society, as you recall, are hunting-and-gathering societies, horticultural societies, and agrarian societies.

As we noted in Chapter 5, with the Industrial Revolution, a new form of social structure emerged: the *industrial society,* a society that depends on mechanization to produce its goods and services.

Two basic types of economic systems distinguish contemporary industrial societies: capitalism and socialism. As described in the following sections, capitalism and socialism serve as ideal types of economic system. No nation precisely fits either model. Instead, the economy of each individual state represents a mixture of capitalism and socialism, although one type or the other is generally more useful in describing a society's economic structure.

Capitalism

In pre-industrial societies, land functioned as the source of virtually all wealth. The Industrial Revolution changed all that. It required that certain individuals and institutions be willing to take substantial risks in order to finance new inventions, machinery, and business enterprises. Eventually, bankers, industrialists, and other holders of large sums of money replaced landowners as the most powerful economic force. These people invested their funds in the hope of realizing even greater profits, and thereby became owners of property and business firms.

The transition to private ownership of business was accompanied by the emergence of the capitalist economic system. *Capitalism* is an economic system in which the means of production are held largely in private hands and the main incentive for economic activity is the accumulation of profits. In practice, capitalist systems vary in the degree to which the government regulates private ownership and economic activity.

Immediately following the Industrial Revolution, the prevailing form of capitalism was what is termed **laissez-faire** ("let them do"). Under the principle of laissez-faire, as expounded and endorsed by British economist Adam Smith (1723–1790), people could compete freely, with minimal government intervention in the economy. Business retained the right to regulate itself and operated essentially without fear of government interference (Smelser 1963).

Two centuries later, capitalism has taken on a somewhat different form. Private ownership and maximization of profits still remain the most significant characteristics of capitalist economic systems. However, in contrast to the era of laissez-faire, capitalism today features government regulation of economic relations. Without restrictions, business firms can mislead consumers, endanger workers' safety, and even defraud the companies' investors—all in the pursuit of greater profits. That is why the government of a capitalist nation often monitors prices, sets safety and environmental standards for industries, protects the rights of consumers, and regulates collective bargaining between labour unions and management. Yet, under capitalism as an ideal type, government rarely takes over ownership of an entire industry.

Contemporary capitalism also differs from laissez-faire in another important respect: capitalism tolerates monopolistic practices. A **monopoly** exists when a single business firm controls the market. Domination of an industry allows the firm to effectively control a commodity by dictating pricing, quality standards, and availability. Buyers have little choice but to yield to the firm's decisions; there is no other place to purchase the product or service. Monopolistic practices violate the ideal of free competition cherished by Adam Smith and other supporters of laissez-faire capitalism.

Some capitalistic nations, such as Canada, restrict monopolies through federal legislation. Such laws prevent any business from taking over so much of the competition in an industry that it controls the market. The federal government allows monopolies to exist only in certain exceptional cases, such as the utility and transportation industries. Even then, regulatory agencies scrutinize these officially approved monopolies to protect the public. The protracted legal

battle in the United States between the Justice Department and Microsoft, owner of the dominant operating system for personal computers, illustrates the uneasy relationship between governments and private monopolies in capitalistic countries.

Conflict theorists point out that although *pure* monopolies are not a basic element of the economy in countries such as Canada and the United States, competition is much more restricted than one might expect in a free enterprise system. In numerous industries, a few companies largely dominate the field and keep new enterprises from entering the marketplace.

As we have seen in earlier chapters, globalization and the rise of multinational corporations have spread the capitalistic pursuit of profits around the world. Especially in developing countries, governments are not always prepared to deal with the sudden influx of foreign capital and its effects on their economies. One particularly striking example of how unfettered capitalism can harm developing nations is found in the Democratic Republic of Congo (formerly Zaire). The Congo has significant deposits of the metal columbite-tantalite—*coltan,* for short—which is used in the production of electronic circuit boards. Until the market for cellphones, pagers, and laptop computers heated up, high-tech companies got much of their coltan from Australia. But at the height of consumer demand, they turned to miners in the Congo to increase their supply.

Predictably, the escalating price of the metal—as much as $400 a kilogram at one point, or more than three times the average Congolese worker's yearly wages—attracted undesirable attention. Soon, the neighbouring countries of Rwanda, Uganda, and Burundi, at war with one another and desperate for resources to finance the conflict, were raiding the Congo's national parks, slashing and burning to expose the coltan underneath the forest floor. Indirectly, the sudden increase in the demand for coltan was financing war and the rape of the environment. Many manufacturers have since cut off their sources in the Congo in an effort to avoid abetting the destruction. But their action has only penalized legitimate miners in the impoverished country (Austin 2002; Delawala 2002).

A worker mines for coltan with sweat and a stick. The sudden increase in demand for the metal by U.S. computer manufacturers caused incursions into the Congo by neighbouring countries hungry for capital to finance a war. Too often, globalization can have unintended consequences for a nation's economy and social welfare.

For more than a century, the board game of Monopoly has entertained millions of people around the world. In the game, players strive to dominate the fictitious economy, gleefully bankrupting other players. Ironically, Monopoly was actually developed to demonstrate the weaknesses of capitalist economies, such as excessive rents and the tendency for money to accumulate in the hands of a few.

Socialism

Socialist theory was refined in the writings of Karl Marx and Friedrich Engels. These European radicals were disturbed by the exploitation of the working class that emerged during the Industrial Revolution. In their view, capitalism forced large numbers of people to exchange their labour for low wages. The owners of an industry profit from the labour of workers primarily because they pay workers less than the value of the goods produced.

As an ideal type, a socialist economic system attempts to eliminate such economic exploitation. Under **socialism**, the means of production and distribution in a society are collectively rather than privately owned. The basic objective of the economic system is to meet people's needs rather than to maximize profits. Socialists reject the laissez-faire philosophy that free competition benefits the general public. Instead, they believe that the central government, acting as the representative of the people, should make basic economic decisions. Therefore, government ownership of all major industries—including steel production, automobile manufacturing, and agriculture—is a primary feature of socialism as an ideal type.

In practice, socialist economic systems vary in the extent to which they tolerate private ownership. For example, in Britain, a nation with some aspects of both a socialist and a capitalist economy, passenger airline service is concentrated in British Airways, a government-owned corporation. Yet private airlines are allowed to compete with it.

Socialist countries typically offer government-financed medical care and other services to *all* citizens. In theory, the collective wealth of the people is used to provide health care, housing, education, and other key services to each individual and family.

Canada—also a mixture of socialist and capitalist elements—has a system of universal health care that is funded by taxpayer dollars and which, when it was established, was derogatorily declared as "socialist" by its opponents. (See Chapter 15 for a detailed account of the health-care system in Canada.)

Marx believed that socialist states would eventually "wither away" and evolve into *communist* societies. As an ideal type, **communism** refers to an economic system under which all property is communally owned and no social distinctions are made on the basis of people's ability to produce. In recent decades, the Soviet Union, the People's Republic of China, Vietnam, Cuba, and nations in Eastern Europe were popularly thought of as examples of communist economic systems. However, this usage represents an incorrect application of a term with sensitive political connotations. All nations known as communist in the twentieth century actually fell far short of the ideal type.

By the early 1990s, Communist parties were no longer ruling the nations of Eastern Europe. The first major challenge to Communist rule came in 1980, when Poland's Solidarity movement—led by Lech Walesa and backed by many workers—questioned the injustices of that society. Though martial law forced Solidarity underground, the movement eventually negotiated the end of Communist Party rule, in 1989. Over the next two years, Communist parties were overthrown by popular uprisings in the Soviet Union and throughout the Eastern Bloc. The former Soviet Union, Czechoslovakia, and Yugoslavia were subdivided to accommodate ethnic, linguistic, and religious differences.

As of 2010, China, Cuba, and Vietnam remained socialist societies ruled by Communist parties. Even in those countries, however, capitalism had begun to make inroads. In China, fully 25 percent of the country's production originated in the private business sector. (See Box 14-1 for a fuller discussion.)

As we have seen, capitalism and socialism serve as ideal types of economic systems. In reality, the economy of each industrial society—including Canada, the United States, the European Union, and Japan—contains certain elements of both capitalism and socialism (see Table 14-1). Whatever the differences—whether a society more closely fits the ideal type of capitalism or socialism—all industrial societies rely chiefly on mechanization in the production of goods and services.

The Informal Economy

In many countries, one aspect of the economy defies description as either capitalist or socialist. In the **informal economy** (also known as the **underground economy**), transfers of money, goods, or services take place but are not reported to the government. Examples of the informal economy include trading services with someone—say, a haircut for a computer lesson; selling goods on the street; and engaging in illegal transactions, such as gambling or drug deals. Participants in this type of economy avoid taxes and government regulations.

table 14-1 Characteristics of the Three Major Economic Systems

Economic System	Characteristics	Contemporary Examples
Capitalism	Private ownership of the means of production Accumulation of profits the main incentive	Canada, Mexico, United States
Socialism	Collective ownership of the means of production Meeting people's needs the basic objective	Germany, Russia, Sweden
Communism	Communal ownership of all property No social distinctions made on basis of people's ability to produce	Cuba, North Korea, Vietnam

Note: Countries listed in column 3 are typical of one of the three economic systems, but not perfectly so. In practice, the economies of most countries include a mix of elements from the three major systems.

sociology in the global community

14-1 Capitalism in China

Today's China is not the China of past generations; it is expected to become the world's largest economy by 2020. (Figure 14-1 shows the world's largest economies over the past 20 years.) In this country where the Communist party once dominated people's lives, few now bother to follow party proceedings. Instead, after a decade of rapid economic growth, most Chinese are more interested in acquiring the latest consumer goods. Ironically, it was party officials' decision to transform China's economy by opening it up to capitalism that reduced the once-omnipotent institution's influence.

The Road to Capitalism

When the communists assumed leadership of China in 1949, they cast themselves as the champions of workers and peasants and the enemies of those who exploited workers, namely landlords and capitalists. Profit making was outlawed, and those who engaged in it were arrested. By the 1960s, China's economy was dominated by huge state-controlled enterprises, such as factories. Even private farms were transformed into community-owned organizations. Peasants essentially worked for the government, receiving payment in goods based on their contribution to the collective good. In addition, they could receive a small plot of land on which to produce food for their families or for exchange with others. But while the centralization of production for the benefit of all seemed to make sense ideologically, it did not work well economically.

In the 1980s, the government eased restrictions on private enterprise somewhat, permitting small businesses with no more than seven employees. But business owners could not hold policymaking positions in the party, at any level. Late in the decade, party leaders began to make market-oriented reforms, revising the nation's legal structure to promote private business. For the first time, private entrepreneurs were allowed to compete with some state-controlled businesses. By the mid-1990s, impressed with the results of the experiment, party officials had begun to hand some ailing state-controlled businesses over to private entrepreneurs, in hopes they could be turned around (Bell 2008).

The Chinese Economy Today

Today, the entrepreneurs who weathered government harassment during the Communist party's early years are among the nation's wealthiest capitalists. Some even hold positions on government advisory boards. The growing free-market economy they spawned has brought significant inequality to Chinese workers, however, especially between urban and rural workers. Though the move toward market-driven development has been slowing, questions are still being raised about the accumulation of wealth by a few (Sicular et al. 2006).

Chinese capitalists have had to compete with multinational corporations, which can operate more easily in China now, thanks to government

figure **14-1 Largest Economies**

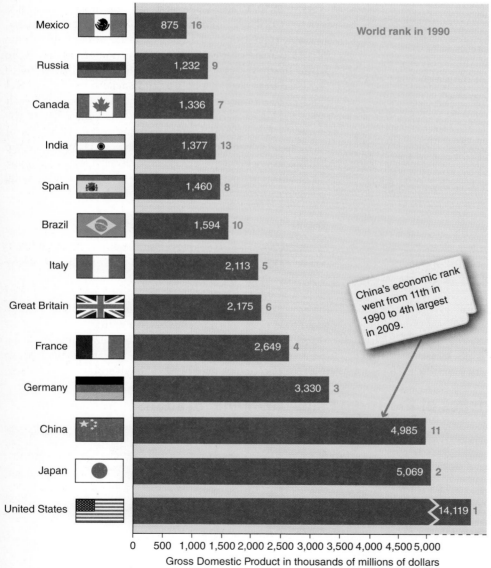

World rank in 1990

	GDP	Rank
Mexico	875	16
Russia	1,232	9
Canada	1,336	7
India	1,377	13
Spain	1,460	8
Brazil	1,594	10
Italy	2,113	5
Great Britain	2,175	6
France	2,649	4
Germany	3,330	3
China	4,985	11
Japan	5,069	2
United States	14,119	1

China's economic rank went from 11th in 1990 to 4th largest in 2009.

Gross Domestic Product in thousands of millions of dollars

Note: 2009 data standardized in terms of estimated purchasing power parity to eliminate differences in buying power.

Sources: World Bank 2007:194–196; 2011.

For better or worse, the expansion of capitalism in China has linked U.S. businesses to that expanding economy.

economic reforms. General Motors (GM) first became interested in China in 1992, hoping to use the nation's low-cost labour to manufacture cars for overseas markets. But more and more, foreign-owned enterprises like GM are selling to the Chinese market. By 2009 the Chinese were buying more automobiles than people were in the United States (Miles 2009).

Chinese Workers in the New Economy

For Chinese workers, the loosening of state control over the economy has meant a rise in occupational mobility, which was severely limited in the early days of Communist party rule. The new markets created by private entrepreneurs are allowing ambitious workers to advance their careers by changing jobs or even cities. On the other hand, many middle-aged urban workers have lost their jobs to rural migrants seeking higher wages. Moreover, the privately owned factories that churn out lawn chairs and power tools for multinational corporations

offer limited opportunities and very long hours. Wages average just below $400 a month for a six-day workweek. As low as wages are in China, they are still double what workers earn in Indonesia, the Philippines, and Vietnam, where multinationals are now establishing factories (*The Economist* 2010b).

Serious social problems have accompanied China's massive economic growth. Because safety is not a priority in many businesses, workers suffer from high injury rates. Harsh working conditions contribute to rapid turnover in the labour force. There is no pension system in China, so retirees must struggle to find other ways to support themselves. Pollution is common in urban areas, and environmental problems are extraordinary (Barboza 2008; French 2008).

For the average worker, party membership is less important now than in the past. Instead, managerial skill and experience are much in demand. Hong Kong sociologist Xiaowei Zang (2002) surveyed 900 workers in a key industrial city and found that party members still had an

advantage in government and state-owned companies, where they earned higher salaries than other workers. But in private businesses, seniority and either managerial or entrepreneurial experience were what counted. As might be expected, being male and well educated also helped.

Women have been slower to advance in the workplace than men. Traditionally, Chinese women have been relegated to subservient roles in the patriarchal family structure. Communist party rule has allowed them to make significant gains in employment, income, and education, although not as quickly as promised. For rural women in China, the growth of a market economy has meant a choice between working in a factory or on a farm. Still, despite recent economic changes, emerging research shows that Chinese women receive lower wages than men who work in the same job sectors (Wang and Cai 2006).

With the growth of a middle class and increased education, many Chinese are seeking the same opportunities as their Western counterparts. The struggle has been particularly visible in the Chinese people's desire for open, unrestricted access to the World Wide Web. In most countries of the world, a Web search for images of Tiananmen Square will call up photos of the 1989 crackdown on student protesters, in which soldiers in tanks attacked unarmed students. But on the other side of what has been dubbed the Great Firewall of China, the same search yields only photos of visiting diplomats—including those from the United States—posing in the square (Deibert et al. 2008).

Apply the Theory

1. What research topics might be relevant to feminist sociologists studying the Chinese economy today?
2. What might conflict thinkers stress in studying the economic changes currently occurring in China?

Sources: Barboza 2008; Bell 2008; Deibert et al. 2008; *The Economist* 2010d; French 2008; Kahn 2003d, 2006; Miles 2009; Sicular et al. 2006; Wang and Cai 2006.

Functionalists contend that bureaucratic regulations sometimes contribute to the rise of an informal economy. In the developing world, governments often set up burdensome business regulations that overworked bureaucrats must administer. When requests for licences and permits pile up, delaying business projects, legitimate entrepreneurs find they need to "go underground" to get anything done. Despite its apparent efficiency, this type of informal economy is dysfunctional for a country's overall political and economic well-being. Since informal firms typically operate in remote locations to avoid detection, they cannot easily

expand when they become profitable. And given the limited protection for their property and contractual rights, participants in the informal economy are less likely than others to save and invest their income. Box 14-2 explains how the informal economy operates in Nepal.

Whatever functions an informal economy may serve, it is in some respects dysfunctional for workers. Working conditions in these illegal businesses are often unsafe or dangerous, and the jobs rarely provide any benefits to those who become ill or cannot continue to work. Perhaps more significant, the longer a worker remains in the informal economy, the less likely that person is to make the transition to the regular economy. No matter how efficient or productive a worker, prospective employers expect to see experience in the formal economy on a job application. Experience as a successful street vendor or self-employed house-cleaner does not carry much weight with interviewers (Venkatesh 2008).

::: use your sociological *imagination* :::

Some of your relatives are working full-time in the informal economy—for example, babysitting, lawn-cutting, house-cleaning—and are earning all their income that way. What will be the consequences for them in terms of job security and health care? Will you try to persuade them to seek formal employment, regardless of how much money they are making?

14.2 How Do Forms of Power and Authority Differ?

In any society, someone or some group—whether a tribal chief, a dictator, or a parliament—makes important decisions about how to use resources and how to allocate goods. Another cultural universal, then, is the exercise of power and authority. Inevitably, the struggle for power and authority involves **politics**, which political scientist Harold Lasswell tersely defined as "who gets what, when, and how" (1936). In their study of politics and government, sociologists are concerned with social interactions among individuals and groups and their impact on the larger political and economic order.

Power

Power lies at the heart of a political system. According to Max Weber, *power* is the ability to exercise one's will over others. To put it another way, whoever can control the behaviour of others is exercising power. Power relations can involve large organizations, small groups, or even people in an intimate association.

Because Weber developed his conceptualization of power in the early 1900s, he focused primarily on the nation-state and its sphere of influence. Today, scholars recognize that the trend toward globalization has brought new opportunities, and with them new concentrations of power. Power is now exercised on a global as well as a national stage, as countries and multinational corporations compete to control access to resources and manage the distribution of capital.

There are three basic sources of power within any political system: force, influence, and authority. **Force** is the actual or threatened use of coercion to impose one's will on others. When leaders imprison or even execute political dissidents, they are applying force; so, too, are terrorists when they seize or bomb an embassy or assassinate a political leader.

In the twenty-first century, force has taken on new meaning as nations clamp down on the use of the Internet to oppose the central government or assert freedom of expression, human rights, and minority or religious views. As of 2008, 18 nations had placed political controls on Internet content (see Figure 14-2). Censorship of online content is just as much a use of force as closing down a newspaper or arresting dissidents (Deibert et al. 2008; OpenNet Initiative 2008; Zittrain and Palfrey 2008).

Influence, on the other hand, refers to the exercise of power through a process of persuasion. A citizen may change his or her view of a political leadership candidate because of a newspaper editorial, the character assessment given by the candidate's ex-colleague, or a stirring speech by a political activist at a convention rally. In each case, sociologists would view such efforts to persuade people as examples of influence. Now, let's take a look at the third source of power, *authority*.

Types of Authority

The term **authority** refers to institutionalized power that is recognized by the people over whom it is exercised. Sociologists commonly use the term in connection with those who hold legitimate power through elected or publicly acknowledged positions. A person's authority is often limited. Thus, a referee has the authority to decide whether a penalty should be called during a hockey game, but has no authority over the price of tickets to the game.

Max Weber ([1913] 1947) developed a classification system for authority that has become one of the most useful and frequently cited contributions of early sociology ([1913] 1947). He identified three ideal types of authority: traditional, rational-legal, and charismatic. Weber did not insist that only one type applies to a given society or organization. All can be present, but their relative importance will vary. Sociologists have found Weber's typology valuable in understanding different manifestations of legitimate power within a society.

Traditional Authority Until the middle of the last century, Japan was ruled by a revered emperor whose absolute power was passed down from generation to generation. In a political system based on **traditional authority**, legitimate power is conferred by custom and accepted practice. A king or queen is accepted as ruler of a nation simply by virtue of inheriting the crown; a tribal chief rules because that is the accepted practice. The ruler may be loved or hated, competent or destructive; in terms of legitimacy, that does not matter. For the traditional leader, authority rests in custom, not in personal characteristics, technical competence, or even written law. People accept the ruler's authority because that is how things have always been done. Traditional authority is absolute when the ruler has the ability to determine laws and policies.

Rational-Legal Authority The Constitution Acts of 1867 and 1982 give our government the authority to make and enforce laws and policies. Power made legitimate by law is known as **rational-legal authority**. Leaders derive their rational-legal authority from the written rules and regulations of political systems, such as a constitution. Generally, in societies based on rational-legal authority, leaders are thought to have specific areas of competence and authority but are not thought to be endowed with divine inspiration, as in certain societies with traditional forms of authority.

figure **14-2** Filtering Information: Political Content

MAPPING LIFE WORLDWIDE

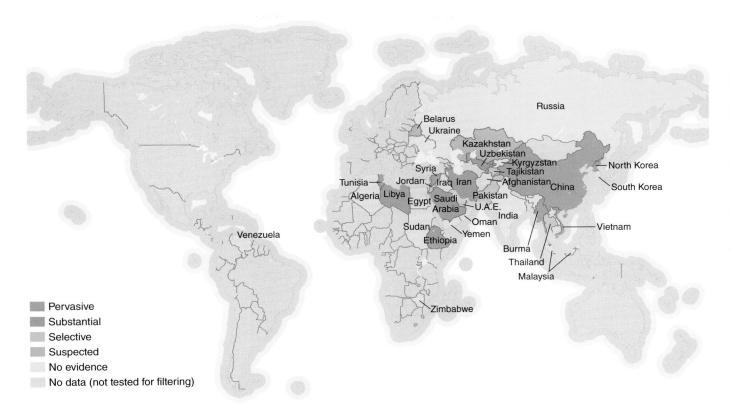

- Pervasive
- Substantial
- Selective
- Suspected
- No evidence
- No data (not tested for filtering)

Note: "No data" (see the gray portions of the map) does not necessarily indicate an absence of filtering.

Sources: OpenNet Initiative 2011; see also Deibert et al. 2008; Faris and Villeneuve 2008.

This map highlights nations that filter or restrict content that expresses views in opposition to those of the current government, or is related to human rights, freedom of expression, minority rights, and religious movements.

Charismatic Authority Joan of Arc was a simple peasant girl in medieval France, yet she was able to rally the French people and lead them into major battles against English invaders. How was this possible? As Weber observed, power can be legitimized by the charisma of an individual. The term **charismatic authority** refers to power made legitimate by a leader's exceptional personal or emotional appeal to his or her followers.

Charisma lets a person lead or inspire without relying on set rules or traditions. In fact, charismatic authority is derived more from the beliefs of followers than from the actual qualities of leaders. So long as people *perceive* a leader as having qualities that set him or her apart from ordinary citizens, that leader's authority will remain secure and often unquestioned.

Unlike traditional rulers, charismatic leaders often become well known by breaking with established institutions and advocating dramatic changes in the social structure and the economic system. Their strong hold over their followers makes it easier to build protest movements that challenge the dominant norms and values of a society. Thus, charismatic leaders such as Joan of Arc, Gandhi, and Martin Luther King, Jr., all

used their power to press for changes in accepted social behaviour. But so did Adolf Hitler, whose charismatic appeal turned people toward violent and destructive ends in Nazi Germany.

Observing from an interactionist perspective, sociologist Carl Couch points out that the growth of the electronic media has facilitated the development of charismatic authority (1996). During the 1930s and 1940s, the heads of state of the United States, Great Britain, and Germany all used radio to issue direct appeals to citizens. Now, television and the Internet allow leaders to "visit" people's homes and communicate with them. In both Taiwan and South Korea in 1996, troubled political leaders facing re-election campaigns spoke frequently to national audiences and exaggerated military threats from neighbouring China and North Korea, respectively.

As we noted earlier, Weber used traditional, rational-legal, and charismatic authority as ideal types. In reality, particular leaders and political systems combine elements of two or more of these forms. Pierre Trudeau, arguably one of the most remarkable prime ministers in Canadian history, wielded power through the rational-legal and charismatic forms of authority.

14-2 Working Women in Nepal

Nepal, a small and mountainous Asian country of about 28 million people, has a per capita gross domestic product (GDP) of just $1120 per year. (The comparable figure in the United States is $45 850.) However, gross domestic product seriously understates the true production level in Nepal, for several reasons. Among the most important is that many Nepalese women work in the informal economy, whose activities are not included in the GDP.

Because women's work is undervalued in this traditional society, it is also underreported and underestimated. Official figures state that women account for 27 percent of GDP and form 40 percent of the labour force. But Nepalese women are responsible for 60 percent of additional nonmarket production—that is, work done in the informal economy—and 93 percent of the housework (see the accompanying figure).

> *Because women's work is undervalued in this traditional society, it is also underreported and underestimated.*

Most female workers cultivate corn, rice, and wheat on the family farm, where they spend hours on labour-intensive tasks such as fetching water and feeding livestock. Because much of the food they raise is consumed at home, however, it is considered to be nonmarket production. At home, women concentrate on food processing and preparation, caregiving, and other household tasks, such as clothes making. Childbearing and rearing and elder care are particularly crucial activities. Yet none of these chores are considered part of GDP; instead, they are dismissed as "women's work," both by economists and by the women themselves.

Gender Contributions to GDP and Household Maintenance in Nepal

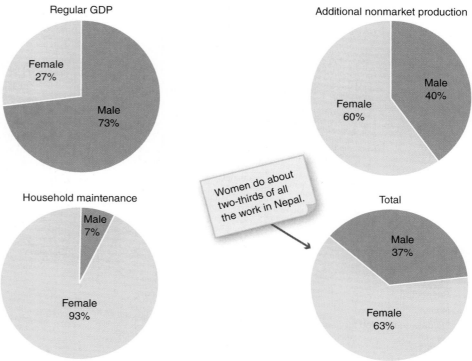

Source: Survey by M. Acharya as cited in Mahbub ul Haq Human Development Centre 2000:54.

The figures on housework and nonmarket production in Nepal come from an independent economic study. To compile them, researchers had to adapt the conventional accounting system by adding a special account dedicated to household maintenance activities. When they did so, women's "invisible work" suddenly became visible and valuable. Not just in Nepal, but in every country, economists need to expand their definitions of work and the labour force to account for the tremendous contributions women make to the world economy.

Apply the Theory

1. In your family, is "women's work" taken for granted? Have you ever tried to figure out what it would cost your family to pay for all the unpaid work women do?

2. Why is recognizing women's work important? How might life for both men and women change if the true economic value of women's work were recognized?

Sources: Acharya 2000; Haub 2010; Mahbub ul Haq Human Development Centre 2000:54–57.

::: use your sociological *imagination* :::

What would our government be like if it were founded on traditional rather than rational-legal authority? What difference would it make to the average citizen?

14.3 What Are the Various Types of Government?

Each society establishes a political system through which it is governed. In modern industrial nations, these formal systems of government make a significant number of critical political decisions. We will survey five basic types of government here: monarchy, oligarchy, dictatorship, totalitarianism, and democracy.

The emotional appeal that former prime minister Pierre Trudeau had to many Canadians was an example of charismatic authority.

Monarchy

A **monarchy** is a form of government headed by a single member of a royal family, usually a king, queen, or some other hereditary ruler. In earlier times, many monarchs claimed that God had granted them a divine right to rule. Typically, they governed on the basis of traditional forms of authority, sometimes accompanied by the use of force. By the beginning of the twenty-first century, however, monarchs held genuine governmental power in only a few nations, such as Monaco. Most monarchs now have little practical power; they serve primarily ceremonial purposes.

Oligarchy

An **oligarchy** is a form of government in which a few individuals rule. An old method of governing that flourished in ancient Greece and Egypt, oligarchy now often takes the form of military rule. In developing nations in Africa, Asia, and Latin America, small factions of military officers will forcibly seize power, either from legally elected regimes or from other military cliques.

Strictly speaking, the term *oligarchy* is reserved for governments that are run by a few selected individuals. However, the People's Republic of China can be classified as an oligarchy if we stretch the meaning of the term. In China, power rests in the hands of a large but exclusive ruling *group*—the Communist party. In a similar vein, drawing on conflict theory, one might argue that many industrialized nations of the West should be considered oligarchies (rather than democracies), since only a powerful few—leaders of big business, government, and the military—actually rule. Later in this chapter, we examine the "elite model" of political systems in greater detail.

Dictatorship and Totalitarianism

A **dictatorship** is a government in which one person has nearly total power to make and enforce laws. Dictators rule primarily through the use of coercion, which often includes torture and executions. Typically, they *seize* power rather than being freely elected (as in a democracy) or inheriting power (as in a monarchy). Some dictators are quite charismatic and manage to achieve a degree of popularity, though their supporters' enthusiasm is almost certainly tinged with fear. Other dictators are bitterly hated by the people over whom they rule.

Frequently, dictators develop such overwhelming control over people's lives that their governments are called *totalitarian*. (Monarchies and oligarchies may also achieve this type of dominance.) **Totalitarianism** involves virtually complete government control and surveillance over all aspects of a society's social and political life. Germany during Hitler's reign, the former Soviet Union, and North Korea today are classified as totalitarian states.

Political scientists Carl Friedrich and Zbigniew Brzezinski have identified the traits that are typical of totalitarian states (1965:22). They include the widespread use of ideological propaganda and state control of the media and the economy.

Democracy

In a literal sense, **democracy** means government by the people. The word *democracy* originated in two Greek roots—*demos*, meaning "the populace" or "the common people," and *kratia*, meaning "rule." Of course, in large nations such as Canada, government by the people is impractical at the national level. Canadians cannot vote on every important issue that comes before their elected representatives. Consequently, popular rule is generally maintained through **representative democracy**, a form of government in which certain individuals are selected to speak for the people.

North Korea has a totalitarian government whose leadership attempts to control all aspects of people's lives. This billboard, a blatant example of government propaganda, portrays the country's ruthless leader as a benevolent father figure.

Canada is commonly classified as a *representative democracy*, since the elected members to the federal parliament and provincial legislatures make our laws. However, critics have questioned how *representative* our democracy really is. Do Parliament and the provincial legislatures genuinely represent the masses? Are the people of Canada legitimately self-governing, or has our government become a forum for powerful elites? We explore these issues in the remainder of the chapter.

14.4 How Does Political Participation Manifest Itself in Canada?

Citizens of Canada take for granted many aspects of their political system. They are accustomed to living in a nation with a Charter of Rights and Freedoms, an elected prime minister, provincial or territorial and local governments distinct from the federal government, and so forth. Yet each society has its own ways of governing itself and making decisions. Just as Canadian residents expect candidates from numerous political parties to compete for public office, residents of Cuba and the People's Republic of China are accustomed to one-party rule. In this section, we examine several aspects of political participation within Canada.

Participation and Apathy

In theory, a representative democracy will function most effectively and fairly if an informed and active electorate communicates its views to government leaders. Unfortunately, that is hardly the case in Canada. Many citizens are familiar with the basics of the political process, but decreasing numbers of Canadians identify with a political party (Mendelsohn 2002), and only a small minority (often members of the higher social classes) actually participate in political organizations. Very few Canadians belong to a political party.

In the 1980s, it became clear that many people in Canada were beginning to be turned off by political parties, politicians, and big government. The most dramatic indication of this growing alienation came from voting statistics. Today, voters appear to be less enthusiastic than ever about elections. In 2008, voter turnout for the federal election—at 59 percent—was the lowest since Confederation in 1867 (CBC 2008c).

While a few nations still command high voter turnout, it is increasingly common to hear national leaders in other countries complain of voter apathy. Despite lower rates of voter turnout in the recent past, Canada, from 1945 to 2005, has had a higher rate of turnout than the United States (see Figure 14-3). In 2008, however, voter turnout for the U.S. presidential election, in which Barack Obama was elected, was 70 percent. This was greater than the voter turnout in the 2008 and 2011 federal elections in Canada.

In the end, political participation on the part of citizens makes government accountable to the voters. If participation declines, government operates with less of a sense of accountability to society. This issue is most serious for the least powerful individuals and groups in society. In Canada, for over

Citizens participating in the Occupy movement camped out in Vancouver in 2011 drew attention to the growing inequality in Canada.

a decade, voter turnout has been particularly low among members of younger age groups. In 2000, approximately 25 percent of eligible voters in the 18–24 age group voted in that year's federal election. A 2007 study by Elections Canada surveyed non-voters in the 2000 federal election and found that younger Canadians were much more likely not to vote because they were "just not interested"; 59 percent of 18- to 20-year-olds as opposed to 34 percent of 58- to 67-year-olds gave this response (Elections Canada 2007). In 2011, the percentage of young voters was roughly the same as it was for the 2008 election—just under 40 percent—while the overall voter turnout for the 2011 general election was 61.4 percent.

Women in Politics

Women continue to be dramatically underrepresented in the halls of government. As we mentioned in Chapter 11, most women in Canada (with the notable exception of Aboriginal women) were granted the right to vote in federal elections in 1918. It wasn't until 1929, however, that women in Canada were considered "persons" under the law, making them eligible for appointment to the Canadian Senate.

Sexism has been the most serious barrier to women interested in holding office. Female candidates continue to attempt to overcome the prejudices of both men and other women regarding women's fitness for leadership. Although Canada has had one female prime minister, Kim Campbell in 1993, her tenure was short-lived and she did not obtain her position through a federal election. Campbell earned the top job by winning her party's leadership race to succeed the retiring prime minister, Brian Mulroney. In 2011, approximately 24.7 percent of members of the House of Commons were female—this despite the fact that women make up 51 percent of the Canadian population. The proportion of women in the federal parliament has remained relatively unchanged over the last decade. There are, however, four female provincial or territorial premiers in Canada today. Moreover, women may encounter prejudice, discrimination, and abuse *after* they are elected.

Female politicians may be enjoying more electoral success now than in the past, but there is evidence that the media cover women in politics differently from their male counterparts.

figure 14-3 Voter Turnout Worldwide

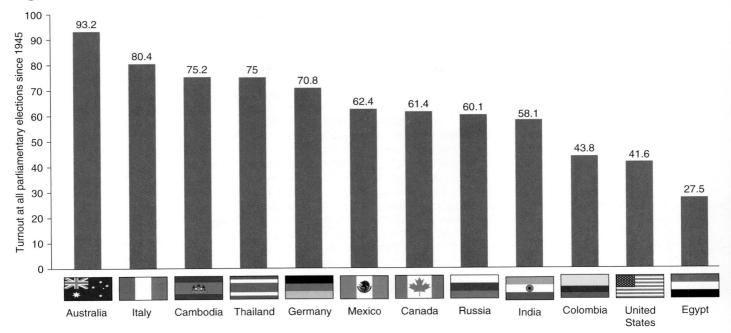

Note: Based on turnout in recent elections for seats in national congress or parliament.

Source: International Institute for Democracy and Electoral Assistance 2011.

A content analysis of newspaper coverage showed that reporters wrote more often about a female candidate's personal life, appearance, or personality than a male candidate's, and less often about her political positions and voting record (Wicks and Lang-Dion 2008).

Although the proportion of women in legislatures has increased in Canada and many other nations, women account for over half the members of the national legislature in just one country—the African Republic of Rwanda has 56.3 percent of its legislative seats held by women. Overall, Canada in 2012 ranked 43rd among 189 nations in the proportion of women serving as national legislators (Inter-Parliamentary Union 2012). To remedy this imbalance, many countries—including the world's largest democracy, India—have reserved a minimum number of legislative seats for women. (Figure 14-4 shows the representation of women in selected national legislatures; Box 14-3 discusses the issue of gender quotas in politics.)

A gender gap becomes apparent when we examine the relationship between gender and politics. In the 2011 Canadian

figure 14-4 Women in National Legislatures, Selected Countries, 2009

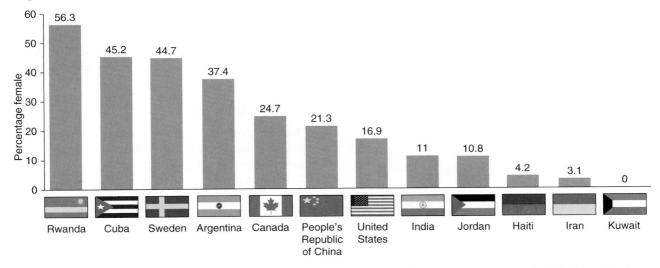

Notes: Data are for lower legislative houses only, as of June 30, 2012; data on upper houses, such as the Canadian Senate or the U.K. House of Lords, are not included.

Sources: Inter-Parliamentary Union 2009 (IPU), 2012, Women in National Parliaments, www.ipu.org/wmn-e/classif.htm. Used by permission.

sociology in the global community

14-3 Gender Quotas at the Ballot Box

Worldwide, women are underrepresented in government. In national legislatures, they make up only 19.6 percent of the total membership—far below their share of the world's population in 2012.

To remedy this situation, many countries have adopted quotas for female representatives. In some, the government sets aside a certain proportion of seats for women, usually from 10 to 30 percent. In others, political parties have decided that 20 to 40 percent of their candidates should be women. Roughly half of all countries now have some kind of female quota system.

In sheer numbers, India has seen the biggest gains in female representation. After a third of all village council seats were set aside for women, almost a million Indian women won election to local office. In South Africa, another country with quotas, women now hold 44.5 percent or more of the seats in both houses of parliament. As previously mentioned, in Canada, where there are no quotas, 24.7 percent of the seats in the federal parliament are held by women. In Norway,

where all parties must have 50 percent women on their party lists, 39.6 percent of all seats are filled by women.

In Africa, quotas have been particularly popular in countries where women contributed to independence movements. South African women fought hard against apartheid and received constitutional guarantees against discrimination in return. Ugandan women fought in the National Resistance Army in the 1980s, earning new respect—and new political power—from men. Women now comprise almost 35 percent of Uganda's parliament and form a minimum required percentage of all elected bodies in that country.

With support from President Yoweri Museveni (under whom a woman, Wandira Kazibwe, was elected vice president in 1994 and is now serving a second term), Ugandan women have used their new-found power to enact new privileges for themselves. Married women can now share property ownership with their husbands,

and widows can retain property after their husbands' death. Women legislators have also increased educational opportunities for girls in an effort to reduce the harsh poverty in their country. In President Museveni's opinion, the presence of women in government has helped to stabilize politics in Uganda. And in a country where women produce much of the wealth, he notes, they deserve to be empowered.

Apply the Theory

1. How might a conflict thinker explain why Canada has so few women in government compared to some other nations?
2. What interpretation might a functionalist sociologist give to the low rates of female representation in elected politics?

Sources: Center for American Women and Politics 2006; Hanes 2005; Inter-Parliamentary Union 2012; Simmons and Wright 2000; Vasagar 2005; Wax 2005.

---

federal election 451 female candidates ran for elected office—and 76 were elected—representing the New Democratic Party (NDP), followed by (in descending order as to number elected), the Conservative Party, the Liberal Party, the Green Party, and the Bloc Québécois. Of the four major political parties (Liberal, Conservative, NDP, and Bloc Québécois), the NDP had the largest percentage of women elected as members of Parliament in 2012.

A gender gap has also emerged in relation to voting patterns in Canada. Between 1993 and 2000, Canadian men tended to support more conservative, right-wing political parties, while Canadian women did not. Research suggests that gender differences in values and beliefs have contributed to corresponding gender differences in terms of party support (Gidengil et al. 2003). In 2006, Canadian women were less likely to support the Conservative Party due to its programs, policies, and proposals on social programs (Gidengil et al. 2006).

::: use your sociological *imagination* :::

Imagine a world in which women, not men, held the majority of elective offices. What kind of world would it be?

14.5 What Are the Various Models of Power in Canada?

Who really holds power in Canada? Do "the people" genuinely run the country through our elected representatives? Or is it true that behind the scenes a small elite controls both the government and, to a lesser extent, the economic system? In exploring these critical questions, social scientists have developed views on nations' power structures: the power elite and the pluralist models.

Power Elite Models

Karl Marx believed that nineteenth-century representative democracy was essentially a sham. He argued that industrial societies were dominated by relatively small numbers of people who owned factories and controlled natural resources. In Marx's view, government officials and military leaders were essentially servants of this capitalist class and followed their wishes. Therefore, any key decisions made by politicians inevitably reflected the interests of the dominant bourgeoisie. Like others who see the world as holding an **elite model** of power relations, Marx believed that society is ruled by a small group of individuals who share a common set of political and economic interests.

Mills's Model Sociologist C. Wright Mills took this model a step further in his pioneering work *The Power Elite* ([1956] 2000b). Mills described a small group of military, industrial, and government leaders who controlled the fate of a country—the **power elite**. Power rested in the hands of a few, both inside and outside government.

A pyramid illustrates the power structure of Mills's model (see the left-hand visual in Figure 14-5). At the top are the corporate rich, leaders of the executive branch of government, and heads of the military (whom Mills called the "warlords"). Directly below are local opinion leaders, members of the legislative branch of government, and leaders of special-interest groups. Mills contended that these individuals and groups would usually follow the wishes of the dominant power elite. At the bottom of the pyramid are the unorganized, exploited masses.

The power elite model is, in many respects, similar to the work of Karl Marx. The most striking difference is that Mills believed that the economically powerful coordinate their manoeuvres with the military and political establishments to serve their common interests. Yet, reminiscent of Marx, Mills argued that the corporate rich were perhaps the most powerful element of the power elite (first among "equals"). And the powerless masses at the bottom of Mills's model certainly bring to mind Marx's portrait of the oppressed workers of the world, who have "nothing to lose but their chains."

A fundamental element in Mills's thesis is that the power elite not only includes relatively few members but also operates as a self-conscious, cohesive unit. Although not necessarily diabolical or ruthless, the elite comprises similar types of people who interact regularly with one another and have essentially the same political and economic interests. Mills's power elite is not a conspiracy, but rather a community of interest and sentiment among a small number of influential people (Hacker 1964).

Admittedly, Mills failed to clarify when the elite opposes protests and when it tolerates them; he also did not provide detailed case studies that would substantiate the interrelationships among members of the power elite. Nevertheless, his challenging theories forced scholars to look more critically at the democratic political systems of Canada and the United States. In Canada, Fox and Ornstein revealed the existence of expensive networks linking corporations with the federal cabinet, Senate, and bureaucracy; they also showed the growth of these links over the last three decades of the period they examined (1986).

In commenting on the scandals that have rocked major financial outfits and corporations such as Freddie Mac, Fannie Mae, Enron, and Arthur Andersen over the last several years, observers in the United States have noted that members of the business elite are closely linked to these events as well. In a study of the members of the boards of directors of Fortune 1000 corporations, researchers found that each director can reach *every* other board of directors in just 3.7 steps. That is, by consulting acquaintances of acquaintances, each director can quickly reach someone who sits on each of the other 999 boards. Furthermore, the face-to-face contact directors regularly have in their board meetings makes them a highly cohesive elite. Finally, the corporate elite is not only wealthy, powerful, and cohesive, but also overwhelmingly white and male (Davis 2003, 2004; Kentor and Jang 2004; Mizruchi 1996; Strauss 2002).

Domhoff's Model Over the last three decades, sociologist G. William Domhoff, co-author with Richard L. Zweigenhaft of *Diversity in the Power Elite*, has agreed with Mills that a powerful elite runs the developed world (2006). He finds that it is still largely white, male, and upper class. But Domhoff stresses the role played both by elites of the corporate community and by the leaders of policy-formation organizations,

figure **14-5** Power Elite Models

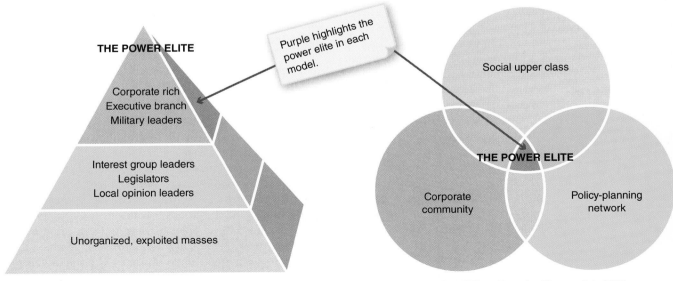

a. C. Wright Mills's model, 1956

b. G. William Domhoff's model, 2010

Sources: Left, author based on C.W. Mills [1956] 2000b; right, Domhoff 2010:116.

such as chambers of commerce and labour unions. Many of the people in both groups are also members of the social upper class.

While these groups overlap, as shown by the right-hand visual in Figure 14-5, they do not necessarily agree on specific policies. Domhoff notes that in the electoral arena, in the United States, two different coalitions have exercised influence. A corporate–conservative coalition has played a large role in both of the major political parties in the United States, generating support for particular candidates through direct-mail appeals. A liberal–labour coalition in the United States is based in unions, local environmental organizations, a segment of the minority group community, liberal churches, and the university and arts communities (Zweigenhaft and Domhoff 2006).

Pluralist Model

Several social scientists insist that power in capitalist countries, such as Canada, is shared more widely than the elite models indicate. In their view, a pluralist model more accurately describes the nation's political system. According to the **pluralist model**, many competing groups within the community have access to government, so that no single group is dominant.

The pluralist model suggests that a variety of groups play a significant role in decision making. Typically, pluralists make use of intensive case studies or community studies based on observation research. One of the most famous—an investigation of decision making in New Haven, Connecticut—was reported by Robert Dahl (1961). Dahl found that although the number of people involved in any important decision was rather small, community power was nonetheless diffuse. Few political actors exercised decision-making power on all issues. One individual or group might be influential in a battle over urban renewal, but have little impact on educational policy.

The pluralist model, however, has not escaped serious questioning. Domhoff re-examined Dahl's study of decision making and argued that Dahl and other pluralists had failed to trace how local elites who were prominent in decision making belonged to a larger national ruling class (1978, 2006). In addition, studies of community power, such as can be found in Dahl's work, examine decision making only on issues that become part of the political agenda. They fail to address the potential power of elites to keep certain matters entirely out of the realm of government debate.

Many sociologists and political scientists have criticized the pluralist model for failing to account for the exclusion of disadvantaged groups (the poor, women, Aboriginal peoples) from the political process. The pluralist claim that diverse and conflicting groups have access to government, with no single group being dominant, is seriously flawed. For example, members of Parliament in Canada do not reflect the characteristics of the Canadian population in terms of race, ethnicity, gender, education, or class (Dyck 2006).

In the United States, drawing on her studies of Chicago politics, Dianne Pinderhughes points out that the residential and occupational segregation of blacks and their long political disenfranchisement violates the logic of pluralism—which

would hold that such a substantial minority should always have been influential in community decision making (1987). This critique applies to many cities across the United States, where other large racial and ethnic minorities, among them Asian Americans, Puerto Ricans, and Mexican Americans, are relatively powerless.

Historically, pluralists have stressed ways in which large numbers of people can participate in or influence governmental decision making. New communications technologies like the Internet and other digitized messaging devices are increasing the opportunity to be heard, not just in countries such as Canada and the United States but also in developing countries the world over. One common point of the elite and pluralist perspectives stands out, however: In Canada's political system, power is unequally distributed. All citizens may be equal in theory, yet those who are high in the nation's power structure are "more equal." New communications technology may or may not change that distribution of power, but any change, if it happens, will take time.

14.6 How Do Sociologists Conceptualize War and Peace?

Perhaps the ultimate test of power, no matter what a nation's power structures, involves broaching the decision to go to war. Because the rank and file of the military is generally drawn from the lower classes—the least powerful groups in society—such a decision has life-and-death consequences for people far removed from the centre of power. In the long run, if the general population is not convinced that war is necessary, military action is unlikely to succeed. Thus, war is a risky way in which to address conflict between countries. In this section we contrast war and peace as ways of addressing societal conflict, and more recently, the threat of terrorism.

Conflict is a central aspect of social relations. Too often, it becomes ongoing and violent, engulfing innocent bystanders as well as intentional participants. Sociologists Theodore Caplow and Louis Hicks have defined **war** as conflict between organizations that possess trained combat forces equipped with deadly weapons (2002:3). This meaning is broader than the legal definition, which typically requires a formal declaration of hostilities.

War

Sociologists approach war in three different ways: There are those who take a global view to study how and why two or more nations become engaged in military conflict; those who take a nation-state view to stress the interaction of internal political, socioeconomic, and cultural forces; and those who take a micro-level view to focus on the social impact of war on individuals and the groups they belong to (Kiser 1992).

From a micro-level point of view, war can bring out the worst as well as the best in people. In 2004, graphic images of the abuse of Iraqi prisoners of war by U.S. soldiers at Iraq's Abu Ghraib prison shocked the world. For social scientists, the deterioration of the guards' behaviour brought to mind Philip Zimbardo's mock prison experiment, conducted in 1971.

Though the results of the experiment, which we highlighted in Chapter 5, have been applied primarily to civilian correctional facilities, Zimbardo's study was actually funded by the Office of Naval Research. In July 2004, the U.S. military began using a documentary film about the experiment to train military interrogators to avoid mistreatment of prisoners (Zarembo 2004; Zimbardo 2004).

Peace

Sociologists have considered **peace** both as the absence of war and as a proactive effort to develop cooperative relations among nations. While we focus here on international relations, it is worth noting that in the 1990s, 90 percent of the world's armed conflicts occurred *within*, rather than between, states. Often, outside powers became involved in these internal conflicts, either as supporters of particular factions or in an attempt to broker a peace accord. In 28 countries where such conflicts occurred—none of which would be considered core nations in world systems analysis—at least 10 000 people died (Kriesberg 1992; Smith 1999).

Sociologists and other social scientists who draw on sociological theory and research have tried to identify conditions that deter war. One of their findings is that international trade may act as a deterrent to armed conflict. As countries exchange goods, people, and then cultures, they become more integrated and less likely to threaten each other's security. Viewed from this perspective, not just trade but immigration and foreign exchange programs have a beneficial effect on international relations.

Another means of fostering peace is the activity of international charities and activist groups called non-governmental organizations (NGOs). The Red Cross, Doctors Without Borders, and Amnesty International donate their services wherever they are needed, without regard to nationality. In the last decade or so, these global organizations have been expanding in number, size, and scope. By sharing news of local conditions and clarifying local issues, they often prevent conflicts from escalating into violence and war. Some NGOs have initiated ceasefires, reached settlements, and even ended warfare between former adversaries.

Finally, many analysts stress that nations cannot maintain their security by threatening violence. Peace, they contend, can best be maintained by developing strong mutual security agreements between potential adversaries (Etzioni 1965; Shostak 2002).

Terrorism

After the terrorist attacks of September 11, 2001, governments worldwide have renewed their efforts to fight terrorism. Figure 14-6 shows the global reach of terrorism.

A representative of the International Red Crescent Society delivers an aid parcel in the southern Iraqi town of Safwan. The Red Crescent provides emergency aid to victims of war and disaster in Muslim communities. Such nongovernmental organizations (NGOs) help to bind countries together, promoting peaceful relations.

Acts of terror, whether perpetrated by nation-states, a few, or many people, can be a powerful political force. Formally defined, **terrorism** is the use or threat of violence against random or symbolic targets in pursuit of political aims. For terrorists, the end justifies the means. They believe the status quo is oppressive, and desperate measures are essential to end the suffering of the deprived. Convinced that working through formal political processes will not affect the desired political change, terrorists insist that illegal actions—often directed against innocent people—are needed. Ultimately, they hope to intimidate others and thereby secure their position or bring about a new political order.

An essential aspect of contemporary terrorism involves use of the media. Terrorists may wish to keep secret their individual identities, but they want their political messages and goals to receive as much publicity as possible. Drawing on Erving Goffman's dramaturgical approach, sociologist Alfred McClung Lee has likened terrorism to the theatre, where certain scenes are played out in predictable fashion. Whether through calls to the media, anonymous manifestos, or other means, terrorists typically admit responsibility for and defend their violent acts.

14.7 How Are Economies Changing?

As advocates of the power elite model point out, the trend in capitalist societies has been toward concentration of ownership by giant corporations, especially transnational ones. The nature of national economies is changing in important ways, in part because each nation's economy is increasingly intertwined with and dependent on the global economy.

figure **14-6** **The Global Reach of Terrorism**

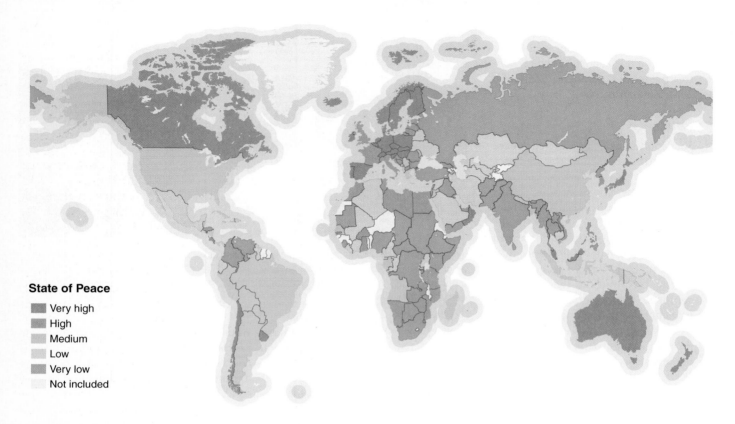

State of Peace

- Very high
- High
- Medium
- Low
- Very low
- Not included

Source: Institute for Economics and Peace 2010.

In the following sections, we examine the economy and the nature of work from four theoretical perspectives: conflict, functionalist, feminist, and interactionist. We also examine two developments in the global economy that have interested sociologists: the changing face of the workforce and deindustrialization. As these trends show, any change in the economy inevitably has social and political implications and soon becomes a concern of policymakers.

Conflict View

Conflict theorists view the economy as the central institution of a society and as the institution that defines the character of the entire society and, correspondingly, the quality of people's lives. In 1887, Karl Marx laid the foundation for the conflict perspective in his critique of capitalism. According to Marx's framework of economic determinism, the economy was the base of society, determining the character of all other institutions: the family, religion, the education system, the legal system, and the mass media. In capitalist societies, according to Marx, the economy is based on a division of classes: those who own the means of production (i.e., the factories and the workplaces), called the *bourgeoisie*, and those who work for the owners of the means of production, the *proletariat*. These classes are in conflict with each other, as the owning class

exploits the workers to maximize profits. The nature of work, therefore, in capitalist societies is one in which workers experience great inequality, exploitation, and alienation. Work, for Marx, was central to human happiness and fulfillment; however, the conditions inherent in the capitalist economy denied workers the actualization of this basic human desire. In Marx's view, the alienation of the proletariat from the product that was being produced, from the way in which it was produced, from themselves, and from their fellow workers was rooted in the nature of the capitalist economy.

Today, conflict thinkers still maintain the view that the interests of the dominant economic class and the working class are opposed and, for the most part, incompatible. Conflict theorist Richard Edwards has called the workplace in capitalist economies "contested terrain" in which struggle and competition between these two groups is inevitable (1979).

Functionalist View

Although conflict thinkers see the capitalist economy as the basis for inequality, and, thus, as an institution requiring radical change, functionalist thinkers view the economy in an uncritical fashion. The economy, for functionalists, is an integral part of the whole society in which the various institutions (family, religion, education, and so on) contribute to the functioning of that society through their interdependence and interrelationships. Functionalists believe that the economy, with workplaces containing diverse jobs and occupations, serves to provide order and regulation.

Functional sociologists Kingsley Davis and Wilbur Moore, in their classic argument on the function of social stratification, maintain that an economy based on inequality, such as the capitalist economy, ensures that the best people reach the top positions of the workplace (1945). Critics of this view, such as Melvin Tumin, maintain that those who are disadvantaged because of ascribed characteristics, such as class, race, and gender, may, in fact, be the "best," but because of the barriers they face in hiring and employment practices (e.g., the glass ceiling), they rarely make it to the top positions in the economy (1953). Today, when we examine who makes it to the highest positions of the Canadian economy, clearly, the economy is more "functionally" beneficial to some Canadians than to others.

Feminist Views

Although feminist perspectives are diverse, many point to the economy as a source of gender inequality. As with conflict thinkers, Marxist feminists, for example, maintain that the principle of private ownership, central to capitalist economies, creates massive inequalities between those who own and those who work. Marxist feminists believe that at the heart of gender inequality is the fact that it is men who own the means of production and women who are used as a reserve of surplus labour—labour to be included or excluded at the whim of the owning class. Marxist feminists believe, therefore, that the root of women's opposition lies in the nature of the capitalist economy, where women's work in the paid workforce constitutes exploited labour and work done in the home goes unpaid.

In contrast to the Marxist feminists' view, socialist feminists maintain that because the capitalist economy and patriarchy are inextricably connected, both must be eliminated to bring about gender equality. For example, socialist feminists state that the economy could change from being privately owned to being publicly owned; however, this would not ensure the elimination of patriarchal values, beliefs, and norms, which perpetuate sexism.

Liberal feminism, which tends to be moderate in its recommendations for change, suggests how the economy could be tweaked, rather than overhauled, to provide women with greater access to jobs and economic power.

Interactionist View

Interactionist sociologists examine the meaning that people give to work and the economy. Using this theoretical perspective allows us to see not only what work means to people but also why they work, why they choose to retire, how they view being unemployed, and how they view work relative to other aspects of their lives. Do people work only because they need money to feed and house themselves and their families? Or do they also work for intrinsic reasons, such as self-fulfillment and a sense of identity? Sociologist Robert Wuthnow found that although people said that the most important reason for working was for the money, when asked what they preferred

about their jobs, 48 percent said "a feeling of accomplishment" (1996). Work also may provide people with a social network, a feeling of engagement in the larger society, or a sense of attachment to a community.

The Changing Face of the Canadian Workforce

The workforce in Canada is constantly changing. During World War II, when men were mobilized to fight abroad, women entered the workforce in large numbers. During the postwar years, however, many women retreated to the household, where domesticity and family life took primacy over paid employment. During the 1970s, a trend began that proved to be one of the most significant forces of social change in the latter half of the twentieth century—the changing role of women in Canadian society. Of particular significance—as we've outlined in previous chapters—is the growing number of women in the paid workforce with children under six years of age. These women thus have an accompanying need for quality childcare. In 2011, 57.9 percent of all women 15 years of age and over were part of the paid workforce; this percentage is up from 42 percent in 1976 (Human Resources and Skills Development Canada 2012; Statistics Canada 2007m, 2009). Figure 14-7 shows the increases in the percentage of women in the workforce. In addition, the federal government's Employment Equity Act of 1986 established the existence of four target groups: women, people of Aboriginal descent, people with disabilities, and members of visible minorities. It was the government's plan to increase the representation of these groups in the Canadian workforce.

Although predictions are not always reliable, sociologists and labour specialists foresee a workforce increasingly comprising women and members of racial and ethnic minorities. In 1960, there were twice as many men in the paid labour force as women. Today, women constitute slightly less than half of all Canadians in the paid labour force. It's likely that by 2015, the total numbers of male and female workers will be equal.

The Canadian employment landscape increasingly reflects the diversity of the population as ethnic and visible minority immigrants enter the labour force. All immigrants, however, do not face the same treatment when entering the Canadian workforce. Visible-minority immigrants experience greater inequality in income and employment than do those immigrants whose identities are not racialized. The "double jeopardy" of being a member of a visible minority and female compounds the effects of inequality in the workforce, resulting in lower incomes and fewer employment opportunities. The impact of this changing labour force is not merely statistical. A more diverse workforce means that relationships among workers are more likely to cross gender, racial, and ethnic lines. Interactionists note that people will find themselves supervising and being supervised by people very different from them.

Deindustrialization

What happens when a company decides it is more profitable to move its operations out of an established community to

figure 14-7 Employment of Canadian Women Aged 15 and Over, 1976–2011

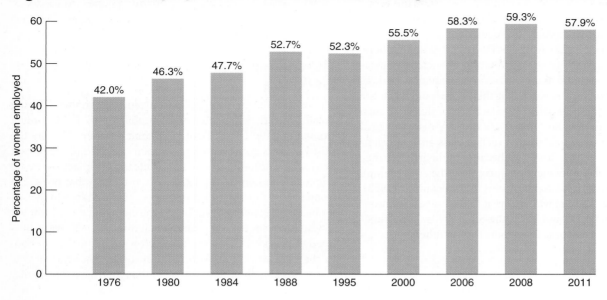

Sources: Adapted by the author from Human Resources and Skills Development Canada 2012; Statistics Canada 2007m, 2009.

another part of the country or out of the country altogether? People lose jobs; stores lose customers; the local government's tax base declines and it cuts services. This devastating process has occurred again and again in the past decade or so.

The term **deindustrialization** refers to the systematic, widespread withdrawal of investment in basic aspects of productivity, such as factories and plants. Giant corporations that deindustrialize are not necessarily refusing to invest in new economic opportunities. Rather, the targets and locations of investment change, and the need for permanent or standard labour decreases as technology continues to automate production. First, there may be a relocation of plants from central cities to the suburbs. The next step may be relocation from suburban areas to jurisdictions where labour laws place more restrictions on unions. Finally, a corporation may simply relocate *outside* Canada to a country, such as Mexico, with a lower rate of prevailing wages. General Motors, for example, decided to build a multi-billion-dollar plant in Spain rather than in Kansas City (Bluestone and Harrison 1982; Rifkin 1995).

Although deindustrialization may involve relocation, in some instances, it takes the form of corporate restructuring as companies seek to reduce costs in the face of growing worldwide competition. When such restructuring occurs, the impact on the bureaucratic hierarchy of formal organizations can be significant. A large corporation may choose to sell off or entirely abandon less productive divisions and eliminate layers of management viewed as unnecessary. Wages and salaries may be frozen and fringe benefits cut—all in the name of "restructuring." Increasing reliance on automation also spells the end of work as we have known it.

The term **downsizing** was introduced in 1987 to refer to reductions in a company's workforce. Downsizing contributed to the elimination of 60 percent of the workforce in British Columbia's sawmills between 1979 and 1998.

Viewed from a conflict perspective, the unprecedented attention given to downsizing in the mid-1990s reflected the continuing importance of social class in Canada. Conflict theorists note that job loss, affecting factory workers in particular, has long been a feature of deindustrialization. But when large numbers of middle-class managers and other white-collar employees with substantial incomes began to be laid off, suddenly there was great concern in the media over downsizing. The social policy section that follows highlights the positive impact that microfinancing has on the lower classes in developing nations.

The social costs of deindustrialization and downsizing cannot be minimized. Layoffs in auto plants in Ontario have led to substantial unemployment in various communities; this can have a devastating impact on both the micro and macro levels. On the micro level, the unemployed person and

The closing of a manufacturing plant is difficult for a community, as well as for workers and their families.

his or her family must adjust to a loss of spending power. Both marital happiness and family cohesion may suffer as a result. Although many dismissed workers eventually re-enter the paid labour force, they often must accept less desirable positions with lower salaries and fewer benefits. Unemployment and underemployment are tied into many of the social problems discussed throughout this book, among them the need for childcare, the controversy over welfare, and immigration issues.

On the societal, or macro, level, the impact on a community of a plant closing can be as difficult as it is for an individual worker and his or her family. As we noted earlier, the community will experience a significant loss of tax revenues. It then becomes more difficult to support police and fire protection, schools, parks, and other public services. Moreover, rising unemployment in a community leads to a reduced demand for goods and services. Sales by retail firms and other businesses fall off, and this can lead to further layoffs.

social policy and the Economy

Microfinancing

The Issue

In India, a very small loan has made a big change in a young mother's life. Not many years ago Siyawati was dependent on what little income her husband could earn as a day labourer. Then a $212 micro-loan allowed her to buy a machine for making candles. Today, Siyawati's cottage venture has expanded into a factory with eight employees, and her monthly income has climbed from $42 to $425. Her increased earnings have allowed her to enroll her children in a good school—the dream of struggling parents in developing countries around the world (Glazer 2010:1).

In some respects it offers a small solution to a big problem. **Microfinancing** is lending small sums of money to the poor so they can work their way out of poverty. Borrowers use the money to start small businesses in the informal economy—to buy yarn to weave into cloth, cows to produce milk, or tools, equipment, and bamboo to make stools. The products they produce are then sold in the local shops. Typically, micro-loans are less than $600, often as little as $20. The recipients are people who ordinarily would not be able to qualify for banking services.

The Setting

Sometimes referred to as "banking the unbanked," microfinancing was the brainchild of Bangladeshi economist Muhammad Yunus (pronounced Iunus). In 1976, in the midst of a devastating famine in Bangladesh, Yunus founded the Grameen (meaning "Village") Bank, which he headed until 2011. The idea came to him when he reached into his pocket to lend money to a group of villagers who had asked him for help. Working through local halls or meeting places, the Grameen Bank has now extended credit to nearly 7 million people. The idea has spread, and has even been underwritten by over a thousand for-profit banks and

multinational organizations. According to 2011 estimates, microfinancing is now reaching 91 million people in 100 countries (Microfinance Information Exchange 2011; Yunus 2010).

Although microfinancing has benefited many families, critics charge that some lenders are taking advantage of the poor. Especially in India, the extension of micro-loans to financially questionable projects with little chance for success has left some borrowers in debt. At the other extreme, some lenders have reaped extraordinary profits, both for themselves and for the investment banks they have created.

In some countries, politicians resent microfinancing because it competes with the central government's path to self-sufficiency. In Nicaragua, President Daniel Ortega supports the *movimento no pago*, or no-pay movement, which encourages borrowers not to repay their debts. So successful has the movement been that one of that nation's leading microfinanciers has been driven out of business.

Sociological Insights

Researchers who draw on the interactionist approach have shown that there is more to microfinancing than money. A study done by microfinance expert Daryl Collins and his colleagues (2009) shows how even with modest assistance, poor people can significantly improve their circumstances

In 2006 Muhammad Yunus, founder of the Grameen Bank, was awarded the Nobel Peace Prize for his work in championing the concept of microfinancing. The small loans his bank makes to the poor, many of them women, have improved the quality of life of countless families.

through mutual support. Collins asked villagers and slum dwellers in Bangladesh, India, and South Africa to keep diaries of how they spent every penny they earned. He and his team found that most of the poor households they studied did not live hand to mouth, spending everything they earned as soon as they got it. Instead, they used financial tools that were linked to their extended families and informal social networks. They saved money, squeezed it out of creditors whenever possible, ran sophisticated savings clubs, and took advantage of microfinancing whenever it was available. Their tactics suggested new methods of fighting poverty and encouraged the development of broader microfinance programs.

Because an estimated 90 percent of the recipients of microcredit are women, feminist theorists are especially interested in the growth of microfinancing. Women's economic status has been found to be critical to the well-being of their children, and the key to a healthy household environment. In developing countries, where women often are not treated as well as men, being entrusted with credit is particularly empowering to them. Research indicates that women recipients are more likely than men to participate in networks and collective action groups, perhaps because they must overcome resistance to women as economic decision makers (Karides 2010; Sanyal 2009).

Drawing on world systems analysis (see Chapter 7), sociologist Marina Karides (2010) contrasts microfinancing with the Western model of economic development, in which multinational corporations based in core countries take advantage of the low wages and natural resources in periphery and semi-periphery countries. The low-wage workers employed by the multinationals rarely escape subsistence living, while the vast majority of people in core nations enjoy a comparatively high standard of living. Microfinanciers hope that in contrast, the cottage industries they help to establish will contribute to the local economies in developing countries, and ultimately to the well-being of those societies, rather than merely serve the economic interests of core nations.

Some critics complain that the creation of small home-based industries reduces the demand for formal employment opportunities. Supporters of microenterprise counter that much time has passed without a significant change in job growth. Microfinancing, they claim, is the best way to create sustainable market opportunities for the poor in developing nations, even if those opportunities are much less attractive than those available in core nations.

Policy Initiatives

Even supporters of microfinancing acknowledge the need to reduce overlending and monitor the success of small loans in helping borrowers to escape poverty. Some indicators suggest that many borrowers do not achieve self-sufficiency. If that is true, lenders should increase their oversight and attempt to identify best practices—that is, those types of assistance that are most effective in helping the poor. Less than a decade ago, microfinancing was hailed as the single best solution to world poverty. With modifications, it should continue to reduce hardship and suffering among the poor (Bajaj 2011a, 2011b; Glazer 2010).

Lenders also need to work with political leaders, and vice versa, to ensure that they do not regard one another as competitors for political support from the poor. Some government leaders have gone so far as to charge lenders with profiteering at the expense of the poor, and to take extraordinary measures for the protection of borrowers. In 2010, officials of one state in India required all loans to be approved by the government, and their eventual repayment to be made in person before a public official. To the degree that profiteering is truly a problem, some type of remedy, whether

At a workshop in Mumbai, India, Sharda Bhandare cuts the pieces for a pair of gloves from a towel. Micro-loans make such small businesses possible, and help them to become self-sustaining.

through legislation or self-monitoring, may need to be introduced. Given the cultural, political, and legal differences among nations where microfinanciers operate, the development of this type of government policy will be a major undertaking.

Apply the Theory

1. Do you think microfinancing might be useful in Canada? If so, how and under what conditions?
2. Using sociological concepts, explain why some politicians might resent microfinancing programs.
3. What obstacles might prevent poor people, either in Canada or elsewhere, from improving their lives through microfinancing? Might the government have a role to play in removing those obstacles?

CHAPTER RESOURCES

Summary

::: **14.1** What Forms Do Economic Systems Take?
- Although systems of *capitalism* vary in the degree to which the government regulates private ownership and economic activity, they all emphasize the profit motive and private ownership.
- Socialist economic systems, in contrast, aim to eliminate economic exploitation and meet people's needs.

::: **14.2** How Do Forms of Power and Authority Differ?
- There are three basic sources of *power* within any political system: **force, influence**, and **authority**.

- Max Weber identified three ideal types of authority: **traditional authority, rational-legal authority**, and **charismatic authority**.

::: **14.3** What Are the Various Types of Government?
- There are five basic types of government: **monarchy, oligarchy, dictatorship, totalitarianism**, and **democracy**.

::: **14.4** How Does Political Participation Manifest Itself in Canada?

- Political participation may make government accountable to its citizens, but voters display varying degrees of apathy, both in Canada and in other countries.
- Women are still underrepresented in politics, but are becoming more successful at winning election to public office.

::: **14.5** What Are the Various Models of Power in Canada?

- Advocates of the **elite model** of the Canadian power structure see the nation as being ruled by a small group of individuals—a **power elite**—who share common political and economic interests, whereas advocates of a **pluralist model** believe that power ought to be shared more widely among conflicting groups.

::: **14.6** How Do Sociologists Conceptualize War and Peace?

- Sociologists approach **war** in three different ways: There are those who take a global view, those who take a nation-state view, and those who take a micro-level focus. Sociologists have considered **peace** both as the absence of war and the proactive effort to develop cooperative relations among nations.

::: **14.7** How Are Economies Changing?

- The nature of the Canadian economy and those around the world is changing. Sociologists are especially interested in the changing face of the workforce and the effects of **deindustrialization**.

Critical Thinking Questions

1. How are the decision makers of Canada different from those whose lives are being affected by their decisions?
2. Who really holds power at the college or university you attend? Describe the distribution of power at your school, drawing on the elite and pluralist models where relevant.
3. Do you vote during provincial/territorial or federal elections? If not, why not? What do you think the implications of growing political apathy might be?
4. If you had the power to change the way in which electoral politics work, how would you increase the diversity of those elected to represent Canadians?
5. Why do you think there are age-related patterns in voter turnout?
6. How are changes in the global economy affecting the economic well-being of Canada?

THINKING ABOUT MOVIES

The Company Men
Corporate downsizing forces a white-collar worker to enter a blue-collar profession.

Inside Job
This documentary explores the near collapse of the global financial industry in 2008.

Up in the Air
The tables are about to turn on a corporate downsizing expert who makes his living by laying people off.

inside

BOXES

Sociology in the Global Community: *Population Policy in China*

Sociology in the Global Community: *Squatter Settlements*

Social Policy and Health: *The AIDS Crisis*

These generations together emphasize the sandwich generation looking after aging parents and growing children.

::: **15** Population, Health, and Communities

TED C. FISHMAN

SHOCK
OF GRAY

The aging of the world's
population and how it pits
young against old, child
against parent, worker against
boss, company against rival,
and nation against nation

"Now in her eighties, my mother still dances at her grandsons' Led Zeppelin tribute concerts, swims Lake Michigan when the water is brisk, hikes among penguins in Patagonia, and dons cross-country skis as soon as the snow is deep enough. My late father, in contrast, was at the peak of his professional and creative success in his early sixties, but a barrage of ailments hit him hard at sixty-three. He began a cruel fifteen-year decline that left him blind, immobile, slow of speech, and utterly dependent. That he never lost his wit or kindness or his ability to hold on to the joys of life was, to me, heroic.

My parents' different experiences neatly represent what is happening to millions of Americans and to vast portions of the globe's population. The world is going gray. Getting not just older but *old*. Sometime after sixty, it seems to happen to everyone: life-altering events cascade one after another. In some combination, family nests are emptied; jobs end or change; spouses, friends, and kin grow gravely ill or die; bodies and minds decline; one's status and power in the family and in social circles inverts; money draws down; and, as remaining years grow fewer, relationships with time and eternity shift.

And yet new worlds can open up, too. Time can expand, social circles grow bigger, new passions take root. Freed from the relentless demands of family and work, older people may experience a sweet rejuvenation. People whom one might expect to be decrepit and infirm are, well, dancing at Led Zeppelin tribute concerts; or even performing in them.

Meanwhile, although the world well understands how young people shape social life and business, it is just now beginning to see how the arrival of a historically enormous older population will affect all of us. Many old people, like my mother, will be healthy and vibrant, but many others, like my father, will need extraordinary resources to make it from one day to the next. The aging of the globe is having profound economic, political, cultural, and familial effects that are only going to intensify. Some of these changes will be welcome and others will not. Certain people will benefit and others will be harmed. Money and power are at stake, of course, as well as the well-being of millions of older people who have worked and loved and given themselves to all that life offers. But the well-being of the globe's young is also at stake, because it is they who need resources also required by the old, and because in the end, it is largely the young who, as family members, friends, and citizens traveling the continuum of an aging world, will eventually care for the old. And in time their older selves.

The aging of the globe is having profound economic, political, cultural, and familial effects that are only going to intensify.

The signs of the shift, large and small, are everywhere, if we only will see them. Consider:

In a room full of telephones and flat-panel displays, where staff is on hand twenty-four hours a day, calls begin to pick up around 9:00 a.m. That's when the more than 6 million elderly customers of Philips Lifeline tend to begin their daily routines. The service allows its clients to alert the company if anything threatens them. The morning is rife with dangers. The average age of a customer is eighty-two, but thousands of centenarians use the service, too. The large majority are women, a predictable reality in an older group. The mornings see millions of Lifeline clients head to the showers, step out on slippery tiles, and then make their way to the kitchen, where fire, knives, tall cabinets, area rugs, and wood flooring are mortal threats. If customers slip and fall, or a sleeve catches fire, or if they are overcome with anxiety and fear as the day begins, devices around their necks or on their wrists let them send signals, sometimes automatically, to the Lifeline call center. By mid-morning on a beautiful fall day, Lifeline has handled nearly seven hundred thousand *calls*."

(Fishman 2010:1–2)

Journalist Ted C. Fishman, author of this opening excerpt, is known for his reporting on global trade and finance. During the course of his work, he became aware of a powerful demographic trend, the aging of the world's population. In his book *Shock of Gray*, Fishman confronts the consequences of the rise in the proportion of elderly, not only for elders themselves and their families, but for entire societies and economies. He predicts a growing conflict between young and old, developed and developing nations, over limited resources.

It has been predicted that half of Canadians born in 2007 will live to 104 years of age, and the study predicts that people will be employed for a longer portion of their lives, spreading their income over a greater age span.

Communities are deeply affected by topics such as health and population patterns, which are covered in this chapter. We will explore communities of all sorts, from rural towns to inner-city neighbourhoods and the suburbs that surround them. In sociological terms, a **community** may be defined as a spatial or political unit of social organization that gives people a sense of belonging. The sense of belonging can be based on shared residence on the globe, in a particular city or neighbourhood, or on a common identity, such as that of homeless people or gays and lesbians. Whatever the members have in common, communities give people the feeling that they are part of something larger than themselves.

Population patterns determine which communities will grow and prosper and which will wither and die. Population patterns can also promote or undermine the health of those who live in communities. How is the world's population changing, and what effect will it have on our communities? Throughout the world, why have large communities grown at the expense of small villages? How do a population's health and well-being vary from one community to another and from one part of the world to another?

In this chapter, we try to answer these questions by taking a sociological overview of the world's population and its effects on our communities and health. We begin with Thomas Robert Malthus's analysis of population trends and Karl Marx's critical response. Brief overviews of population and fertility patterns follow, with particular emphasis on the current problem of overpopulation. Next, we trace the development of communities

from pre-industrial cities to the birth of the modern megalopolis. We consider two different views of urbanization, one stressing its functions and the other its dysfunctions. And we compare three very different types of communities: the city, the suburb, and the rural area. Finally, we see how functionalists, conflict theorists, interactionists, and feminist theorists study health issues. We discover that the distribution of disease in a population varies with social class, race and ethnicity, gender, and age. In the social policy section that closes the chapter, we explore the most pressing health problem in the world today: the AIDS crisis. ■

What Is Demography?

The study of population issues engages the attention of both natural and social scientists. The biologist explores the nature of reproduction and casts light on factors that affect **fertility**, the level of reproduction among women of child-bearing age. The medical pathologist examines and analyzes trends in the causes of death. Geographers, historians, and psychologists also have distinctive contributions to make to our understanding of population. Sociologists, more than these other researchers, focus on the *social* factors that influence population rates and trends.

In their study of population issues, sociologists are keenly aware that various elements of population—such as fertility and **mortality** (the amount of death)—are profoundly affected by the norms, values, and social patterns of a society. Fertility is influenced by people's age of entry into sexual unions and by their use of contraception—both of which, in turn, reflect the social and religious values that guide a particular culture. Mortality is shaped by a nation's level of nutrition, acceptance of immunization, and provisions for sanitation, as well as its general commitment to health care and health education. Migration from one country to another can depend on marital and kinship ties, the relative degree of tolerance of diversity in various societies, and people's evaluations of employment opportunities.

Demography is the scientific study of population. It draws on several components of population, including size, composition, and territorial distribution, to understand the social consequences of population. Demographers study geographical variations and historical trends in their effort to develop population forecasts. They also analyze the structure of a population—the age, gender,

race, and ethnicity of its members. A key figure in this type of analysis was Thomas Robert Malthus.

Malthus's Thesis and Marx's Response

The Reverend Thomas Robert Malthus (1766–1834) was educated at Cambridge University in Britain and spent his life teaching history and political economy. He strongly criticized two major institutions of his time—the church and slavery—yet his most significant legacy for contemporary scholars is his still-controversial *Essays on the Principle of Population*, published in 1798.

Essentially, Malthus held that the world's population was growing more rapidly than the available food supply. Malthus argued that the food supply increases in an arithmetic progression (1, 2, 3, 4, and so on), whereas the population expands by a geometric progression (1, 2, 4, 8, and so on). According to his analysis, the gap between the food supply and the population will continue to grow over time. Even though the food supply will increase, it will not increase nearly enough to meet the needs of an expanding world population.

Malthus advocated population control to close the gap between the rising population and the food supply, yet he explicitly denounced artificial means of birth control because they were not sanctioned by religion. For Malthus, the appropriate way to control population was to postpone marriage. He argued that couples must take responsibility for the number of children they choose to bear; without such restraint, the world would face widespread hunger, poverty, and misery (Malthus, Huxley, and Osborn 1960, original edition 1824; Petersen 1979). Today, Malthus's ideas have spawned a legacy of population policies that facilitate racial inequality, class exploitation, and gender subordination (Kuumba 1999).

Karl Marx strongly criticized Malthus's views on population. Marx pointed to the nature of economic relations in Europe's industrial societies as the central problem. He could not accept the Malthusian notion that a rising world population, rather than capitalism, was the cause of social ills. In Marx's opinion, there was no special relationship between world population figures and the supply of resources (including food). If society were well ordered, increases in population should lead to greater wealth, not to hunger and misery.

Of course, Marx did not believe that capitalism operated under these ideal conditions. He maintained that capitalism devoted its resources to the financing of buildings and tools rather than to more equitable distribution of food, housing, and other necessities of life. Marx's work is important to the study of population because he linked overpopulation to the unequal distribution of resources—a topic that will be taken up again later in this chapter. His concern with the writings of Malthus also testifies to the importance of population in political and economic affairs.

The insights of Malthus and Marx regarding population issues have come together in what is termed the *neo-Malthusian view*. Best exemplified by the work of Paul Ehrlich (1968; Ehrlich and Ehrlich 1990), author of *The Population Bomb*, neo-Malthusians agree with Malthus that world population growth is outstripping natural resources. However, in contrast to the British theorist, they insist that birth-control measures are needed to regulate population increases. Neo-Malthusians have a Marxist flavour in their condemnation of developed nations that, despite their low birth rates, consume a disproportionately large share of world resources. Although rather pessimistic about the future, these theorists do see a way forward and stress that birth control and sensible use of resources are essential responses to rising world population (Tierney 1990; Weeks 2002; for a critique, see Commoner 1971).

Studying Population Today

The relative balance of births and deaths is no less important today than it was during the lifetime of Malthus and Marx. The suffering that Malthus spoke of is certainly a reality for many people of the world who are hungry and poor. Malnutrition remains the largest contributing factor to illness and death among children in the developing countries. Almost 18 percent of these children will die before age five—a rate more than 11 times higher than in developed nations. Warfare and large-scale migration intensify problems of population and food supply. For example, strife in Bosnia, Iraq, and Sudan caused very uneven distribution of food supplies, leading to regional concerns about malnutrition and even starvation. Combating world hunger may require reducing human births, dramatically increasing the world's food supply, or perhaps both at the same time. The study of population-related issues, then, seems to be essential.

In Canada and most other countries, the census is the primary mechanism for collecting population information. A **census** is an enumeration or counting of a population. The Constitution Act of Canada requires that a full census be held every 10 years to determine the breakdown of ridings by province/territory represented in the House of Commons. The five-year census, which is mandated by Statistics Canada, provides the basis for government policies and decision making for social programs, such as housing, health care, daycare, and federal–provincial/territorial transfer payments. The questions asked on the census reflect changing social and political patterns and reveal the dynamic nature of Canadian society. Table 15-1 shows some of the milestones of the Canadian census that demonstrate changing values and attitudes on such matters as unpaid work, common-law and same-sex partnerships, and fertility of those who have mental illnesses. As well, the study of our population is supplemented by vital statistics;

table 15-1 Selected Milestones in the History of the Census in Canada

1921:	The population questions no longer include those on "insanity and idiocy" and fertility.
1931:	Questions are added to gauge the extent and severity of unemployment, and to analyze its causes.
1956:	The first five-year national census is conducted. It is introduced to monitor the rapid economic growth and urbanization that took place during the postwar years.
1971:	The majority of respondents now complete the census questionnaire themselves, a process called *self-enumeration*. Under the new Statistics Act, it becomes a statutory requirement to hold censuses of population and of agriculture every five years.
1986:	The Census of Population contains a question on disability, which is also used to establish a sample of respondents for the first post-censal survey on activity limitation. Also for the first time, the Census of Agriculture asks a question on computer use for farm management.
1991:	For the first time, the census asks a question on common-law relationships.
1996:	A question on unpaid work is included in the census.
2001:	The definition of *common-law* is expanded to include both opposite-sex and same-sex partners. Also, the Census of Agriculture asks about production of certified organic products.
2006:	A question on where individuals received their highest level of education is included.
2010:	Canada's federal government scraps the long-form census in favour of a voluntary household survey.

Sources: Adapted from CBC.ca 2010; Flanders 2001:4; Statistics Canada 2006d.

these records of births, deaths, marriages, and divorces are gathered through a registration system maintained by governments. In addition, Statistics Canada provides up-to-date information based on surveys of such topics as educational trends, the status of women, children, racial and ethnic minorities, agricultural crops, medical care, and time spent on leisure and recreational activities, to name only a few.

In administering a nationwide census and conducting other types of research, demographers employ many of the skills and techniques described in Chapter 2, including questionnaires, interviews, and sampling. The precision of population projections depends on the accuracy of a series of estimates that demographers must make. First, they must determine past population trends and establish a base population as of the date at which the forecast began. Next, birth rates and death rates must be established, along with estimates of future fluctuations. In making projections for a nation's population trends, demographers must consider migration as well, since a significant number of individuals may enter and leave a country.

Elements of Demography

Demographers communicate population facts with a language derived from the basic elements of human life—birth and death. The **birth rate** (or, more specifically, the *crude birth rate*) is the number of live births per 1000 population in a given year. In 2009, for example, there were an estimated 10.28 live births per 1000 people in Canada. The birth rate provides information on the actual reproductive patterns of a society.

One way demography can project future growth in a society is to make use of the **total fertility rate (TFR)**. The TFR is the average number of children born alive to any woman, assuming that she conforms to current fertility rates. The TFR estimated for Canada in 2009 was 1.58 live births per woman, as compared with nearly 8 births per woman in a developing country, such as Niger.

Mortality, like fertility, is measured in several different ways. The **death rate** (also known as the *crude death rate*) is the number of deaths per 1000 population in a given year. In 2009, Canada had an estimated death rate of 7.74 per 1000 population. The **infant mortality rate** is the number of deaths of infants under one year of age per 1000 live births in a given year. This particular measure serves as an important indicator of a society's level of health care; it reflects prenatal nutrition, delivery procedures, and infant screening measures. The infant mortality rate also functions as a useful indicator of future population growth, since those infants who survive to adulthood will contribute to further population increases.

Nations vary widely in the rate of death of newborn children. In 2009, the estimated infant mortality rate for Canada was 4.69 deaths per 1000 live births, whereas for the world as a whole it was an estimated 44.13 deaths per 1000 live births. At the same time, some nations have lower rates of infant mortality than Canada, including Switzerland, Japan, and Sweden.

A general measure of health used by demographers is **life expectancy**, the median number of years a person can be expected to live under current mortality conditions. Usually the figure is reported as life expectancy at birth. At present, Japan reports a life expectancy at birth of 82 years, slightly higher than Canada's figure of 81.23 years. By contrast, life expectancy at birth is less than 45 years in several developing nations.

The **growth rate** of a society is the difference between births and deaths, plus the difference between immigrants (those who enter a country to establish permanent residence) and emigrants (those who leave a country permanently) per 1000 population. For the world as a whole, the growth rate is simply the difference between births and deaths per 1000 population, since worldwide immigration and emigration must of necessity be equal. In 2010, Canada had an estimated growth rate of 0.4 percent, compared with an estimated 2 percent for the entire world (see Figure 15-1).

15.2 What Are the Patterns of World Population?

One important aspect of demographic work involves study of the history of population. But how is this possible? After all, official national censuses were relatively rare before 1850. Researchers interested in early population must turn to

figure **15-1** **Population Growth Rate in Selected Countries**

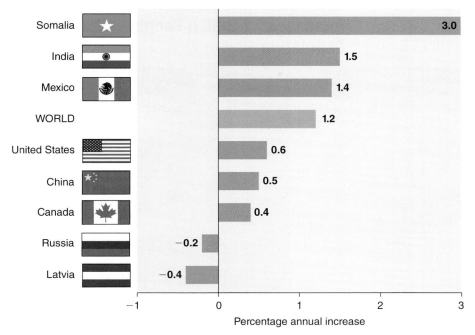

Percentage annual increase

Source: Haub 2010.

archaeological remains of settlements, burial sites, baptismal and tax records, and oral history sources.

On October 13, 1999, in a maternity clinic in Sarajevo, Bosnia-Herzegovina, Helac Fatina gave birth to a son, who has been designated as the 6 billionth person on this planet. Yet, until modern times, there were relatively few humans living in the world. One estimate placed the world population of a million years ago at only 125 000 people. As Table 15-2 indicates, the population has exploded in the past 200 years and continues to accelerate rapidly (Bureau of the Census 2011; Kunzig 2011).

Demographic Transition

The phenomenal growth of the world population in recent times can be accounted for by changing patterns of births and deaths. Beginning in the late eighteenth century—and continuing until the middle of the twentieth century—there was a gradual reduction in death rates in Northern and Western Europe. People were able to live longer because of advances in food production, sanitation, nutrition, and public health care. Although death rates fell, birth rates remained high; as a result, there was unprecedented population growth during this period of European history. However, by the late nineteenth century, the birth rates of many European countries began to decline, and the rate of population growth also decreased (Bender and Smith 1997).

The changes in birth rates and death rates in nineteenth-century Europe serve as an example of *demographic transition*. Demographers use this term to describe an observed pattern in changing vital statistics. Specifically, **demographic transition** is the change from high birth rates and death rates to relatively low birth rates and death rates. This concept, which was introduced in the 1920s, is now widely used in the study of population trends.

As illustrated in Figure 15-2, demographic transition is typically viewed as a three-stage process:

1. *Pre-transition stage:* high birth rates and death rates with little population growth
2. *Transition stage:* declining death rates, primarily the result of reductions in infant deaths, along with high to medium fertility—resulting in significant population growth
3. *Post-transition stage:* low birth rates and death rates with little population growth

Demographic transition should be regarded not as a "law of population growth" but rather as a generalization of the population history of industrial nations. This concept helps us understand the growth problems faced by the world in the 1990s. About two-thirds of the world's nations have yet to pass fully through the second stage of demographic transition. Even if such nations make dramatic advances in fertility control, their populations will nevertheless increase greatly because of the large base of people already at prime childbearing age.

The pattern of demographic transition varies from nation to nation. One particularly useful distinction is the contrast between the transition now occurring in developing nations—which include roughly two-thirds of the world's population—and that which occurred over almost a century in more industrialized countries. Demographic transition in developing nations has involved a rapid decline in death rates without adjustments in birth rates.

Specifically, in the post–World War II period, the death rates of developing nations began a sharp decline. This revolution in "death control" was triggered by antibiotics, immunization, insecticides (such as DDT, used to strike at malaria-bearing mosquitoes), and largely successful campaigns against such fatal diseases as smallpox. Substantial medical and public health technology was imported almost overnight from more developed nations. As a result, the drop in death rates that had taken a century to happen in Europe was telescoped into two decades in many developing countries.

Birth rates had time to adjust. Cultural beliefs about the proper size of families could not possibly change as quickly as the falling death rates. For centuries, couples had given birth to as many as eight or more children, knowing that perhaps only two or three would survive to adulthood. Families were more willing to accept technological advances that prolonged life than to abandon fertility patterns that reflected centuries of tradition and religious training. The result over time was a huge increase in the global population.

table 15-2 Estimated Time for Each Successive Increase of 1 Billion People in World Population

Population Level	Time Taken to Reach New Population Level	Year of Attainment
First billion	Human history before 1800	1804
Second billion	123 years	1927
Third billion	32 years	1959
Fourth billion	15 years	1974
Fifth billion	13 years	1987
Sixth billion	12 years	1999
Seventh billion	12 years	2011
Eighth billion	13 years	2024
Ninth billion	21 years	2045

Sources: Bureau of the Census 2011; Kunzig 2011:40.

The Population Explosion

Apart from war, rapid population growth has been perhaps the dominant international social problem of the past 40 years. Often,

figure **15-2** Demographic Transition

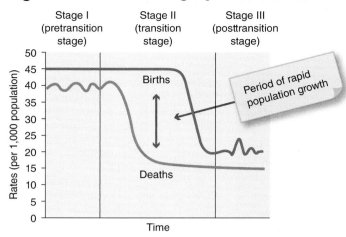

Demographers use the concept of *demographic transition* to describe changes in birth rates and death rates during stages of a nation's development. This graph shows the pattern that took place in developed nations. In the first stage, both birth rates and death rates were high, so that there was little population growth. In the second stage, the birth rate remained high while the death rate declined sharply, which led to rapid population growth. By the last stage, which many developing countries have yet to enter, the birth rate also declined and there was again little population growth.

this issue is referred to in emotional terms as the "population bomb" or the "population explosion." Such striking language is not surprising, given the staggering increases in world population during the twentieth century.

By the middle 1970s, demographers had observed a slight decline in the growth rate of many developing nations (Kent and Haub 2005). These countries were still experiencing population increases, yet their *rates* of increase had declined as death rates could not go much lower and birth rates began to fall. It appears that family planning efforts have been instrumental in this demographic change. Beginning in the 1960s, governments in certain developing nations sponsored or supported campaigns to encourage family planning. For example, in good part as the result of government-sponsored birth control campaigns, Thailand's total fertility rate fell from 6.1 births per woman in 1970 to 1.65 in 2009. And China's strict one-child policy resulted in some serious social consequences (see Box 15-1).

Through the efforts of many governments (among them Canada's) and private agencies (such as Planned Parenthood), the fertility rates of many developing countries have declined. However, some critics, reflecting a conflict perspective, have questioned why Canada and other industrialized nations are so enthusiastic about population control in the developing world. In line with Marx's response to Malthus, they argue that large families and even population growth are not the causes of hunger and misery. Rather, the unjust economic domination by the developed countries of the world results in an unequal distribution of world resources and in widespread poverty in exploited developing nations.

Even if family-planning efforts are successful in reducing fertility rates, the momentum toward a growing world

population is well established. The developing nations face the prospect of continued population growth, since a substantial proportion of their population is approaching childbearing years. This is evident in Figure 15-3, comparing the population structures of Canada and Kenya.

A **population pyramid** or population structure is a special type of bar chart that distributes the population by gender and age; it is generally used to illustrate the population structure of a society. As Figure 15-3 shows, a substantial portion of the population of Kenya consists of children under the age of 15, whose child-bearing years are still to come. Thus, the built-in momentum for population growth is much greater in Kenya (and in many developing countries in other parts of the world) than in Western Europe or Canada.

Consider also India, which, in 2000, surpassed 1 billion in population. At some point between the years 2040 and 2050, India's population will surpass China's. The substantial momentum for growth built into India's age structure means that the nation will face a staggering increase in population in the coming decades—even if its birth rate declines sharply (Population Reference Bureau 2004).

Throughout the world, population patterns vary widely. As this scene suggests, Eastern Europe has been losing population as the birth rate falls and young people immigrate to other countries. In Africa, by contrast, the population is growing. Over the next four decades, Somalia is expected to double in population.

sociology in the global community

15-1 Population Policy in China

This billboard, photographed in China, promotes the government's policy of allowing only one child per family. For several decades, the People's Republic of China has been struggling with a population explosion that threatens to outstrip the nation's ability to provide for all its citizens.

In a residential district in Shanghai, a member of the local family-planning committee knocks on the door of a childless couple. Why, she inquires, have they not started a family?

Such a question would have been unthinkable in 1979, when family-planning officials, in an attempt to avoid a looming population explosion, began resorting to sterilization to enforce the government rule of one child per family. Since then, the government has granted some limited exceptions to the one-child policy. For example, in 2008 officials allowed parents

As a result of the rising sex ratio, Chinese officials have begun to worry about a future with too few women.

who had lost a child in an earthquake to have another child.

Chinese families are beset, too, by the unforeseen results of their attempts to circumvent the one-child policy. In the past, in an effort to ensure that their one child would be a male

capable of perpetuating the family line, many couples chose to abort female fetuses, or quietly allowed female infants to die of neglect. As a result, in 2011, among children ages one to four, China's sex ratio (the ratio of males to females) was about 120 to 100—well above the normal rate at birth of 105 to 100.

As a result of the rising sex ratio, Chinese officials have begun to worry about a future with too few women. In about 20 to 25 years, they expect, almost one-fifth of the baby boys now being born will be unable to find brides. In an attempt to reverse the situation, the government is paying the parents of daughters to speak with other parents and persuade them to raise girls.

Another legacy of the one-child policy is a shortage of caretakers for the elderly. Coupled with improvements in longevity, the generation-long decline in births has greatly increased the ratio of dependent elders to able-bodied children. The migration of young adults to other parts of China has further compromised the care of the elderly. To compound the crisis, barely one in four of China's elders receives any pension at all. No other country in the world faces the prospect of caring for such a large population of seniors with so little social support.

Apply the Theory

1. Does any government, no matter how overpopulated a country is, have a right to sterilize people who do not voluntarily limit the size of their families? Why or why not?
2. What do you think has been the most dramatic consequence of the one-child policy?

Sources: *The Economist* 2011; Greenhalgh 2008; Page 2011; Wang 2011; Wang and Yong 2011.

Population growth is not a problem in all nations. Its effects, however, as feminist thinkers have pointed out, are undoubtedly gendered. A handful of countries are even adopting policies that *encourage* growth. Some of these countries include Russia, France, and Japan, where total fertility rates have fallen sharply. Nevertheless, a global perspective underscores the serious consequences that could result from overall continued population growth.

A tragic new factor has emerged in the last three decades that will restrict worldwide population growth: the spread of HIV/AIDS. Currently, about 33 million people around the world are infected with HIV and the AIDS and 25 million

have died since the early 1980s. Sub-Saharan Africa is the hardest-hit region of the world; the majority of those infected are women, mainly between the ages of 15 and 49. Women are disproportionately affected because of such factors as sexual violence, less access to education, and lack of power to refuse sexual contact or insist on condom use (UNAIDS 2007). As a result of the increasing number of the disease's implications for women, the reality of the "feminization of AIDS" has been acknowledged by academics, politicians, and journalists alike. The social policy section at the end of this chapter considers the AIDS crisis and the devastating effects on African communities.

figure 15-3 Population Structure of Canada and Kenya, 2007 (estimated)

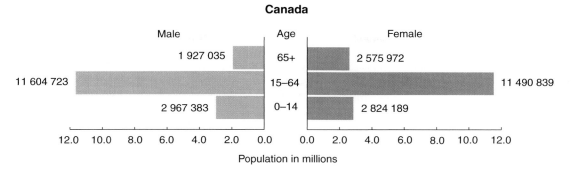

Canada

Male	Age	Female
1 927 035	65+	2 575 972
11 604 723	15–64	11 490 839
2 967 383	0–14	2 824 189

Population in millions

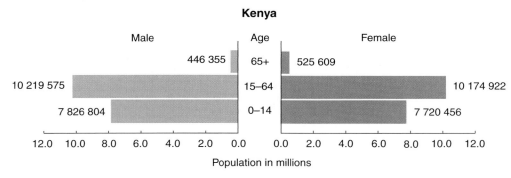

Kenya

Male	Age	Female
446 355	65+	525 609
10 219 575	15–64	10 174 922
7 826 804	0–14	7 720 456

Population in millions

Source: Central Intelligence Agency 2007.

What Are the Fertility Patterns in Canada?

During the past half century, Canada and other industrial nations have passed through two different patterns of population growth—the first marked by high fertility and rapid growth (stage II in the theory of demographic transition), the second marked by declining fertility and little growth (stage III). Sociologists are keenly aware of the social impact of these fertility patterns.

The Baby Boom

The most recent period of high fertility in Canada has often been referred to as the *baby boom*. The return of soldiers after World War II, high wages, and general prosperity during the postwar period encouraged many married couples to have children and purchase homes. In addition, several sociologists—as well as feminist author Betty Friedan (1963)—have noted that there were pervasive pressures on women during the 1950s to marry and become mothers and homemakers (Bouvier 1980).

The dramatic increase in births between 1946 and 1966 produced an age cohort in Canada that made up approximately one-third of the population. By the end of the boom in 1966, the age structure reflected a young, dependent population with a high percentage of Canadians under 15 years of age. As the baby boomers have aged, society has responded to their needs in education, recreation, consumer preferences,

housing, and so on. Now, a significant challenge to society is to meet the needs of aging baby boomers as they begin to require greater medical attention at a time when health-care resources are severely strained.

::: use your sociological *imagination* :::

The country you are living in is so heavily populated that basic resources, such as food, water, and living space, are running short. What will you do? How will you respond to the crisis if you are a government social planner? A politician?

www.mcgrawhillconnect.ca

Stable Population Growth

Although the total fertility rate of Canada has remained low in the past two decades, the nation continues to grow in size because of two factors: the momentum built into our age structure by the postwar population boom and immigration. In 2009, Canada's fertility rate was 1.58 children per woman, below the 2.1 children needed to sustain the population. Despite low levels of fertility, Canada's population grew 5.4 percent between 2001 and 2006. This growth of population represented, in part, a demographic "echo" of the baby boom generation, many of whom are now parents (with some even inching closer to the traditional retirement age of 65). Because of the upsurge of births beginning in the late 1940s—in 1956, the fertility rate in Canada was four children per woman—there were, between 2001 and 2006, more people in their child-bearing years than in older age groups (where most deaths occur). Most of the growth, however, was due to international migration to Canada (Weeks 2007).

In the 1980s and early 1990s, some analysts projected that there would be relatively low fertility levels and moderate net migration over the coming decades. As a result, it seemed possible that Canada might reach **zero population growth (ZPG)** in the near future. Zero population growth is the state of a population in which the number of births plus immigrants equals the number of deaths plus emigrants. In the recent past, although some nations have achieved ZPG, it has been relatively short-lived. Yet, today, projections of population change between 2010 and 2050 indicate 28 countries showing a decline in population (Haub 2010).

What would a Canadian society with stable population growth be like? In demographic terms, it would be quite different from the Canada we live in today. There would be relatively equal numbers of people in each age group, and the median age of the population would be higher.

By 2026, the percentage of Canadians age 65 and older will increase to 21.2 percent from 13.2 percent in 2006 (Canadian Press 2007). Based on this projection, the population pyramid of Canada would look more like a rectangle. There would also be a much larger proportion of older people, especially age 75 and over. They would place a greater demand on the nation's social-service programs and health-care institutions.

On a positive note, the economy would be less volatile under ZPG, since the number of entrants into the paid labour force would remain stable. Zero population growth would also lead to changes in family life. With fertility rates declining, women would devote fewer years to child-rearing and to the social roles of motherhood; the proportion of married women entering the labour force would continue to rise (McFalls 2007; Weeks 2008).

Canada's actual rate of population growth between 2001 and 2006 was the highest of all the G8 industrialized countries. As you can see, population growth owes much to the age structure of a given region or country.

An Aging Canadian Population

As an index of aging, the United Nations uses the proportion of individuals 65 years of age and older to classify a population as "young," "mature," or "aged." A population is "young" if its proportion of older adults is under 4 percent; it is considered "mature" if its proportion of those 65 years of age and older is between 4 and 8 percent; and it is considered "aged" if this age group makes up 8 percent or more. Canada became an "aged" population according to census data by 1971, when 8.1 percent of Canadians were 65 years of age and older. By 2011, 14.8 percent of the population were 65 years of age and older, following a steady increase of the proportion of this group in the total population (Statistics Canada 2012). According to population projections, the numbers of seniors in Canada could double in the next 25 years (Statistics Canada 2007j).

National averages of aging, however, mask great diversity within Canada as it relates to such factors as region, gender, race, and ethnicity. There is a vast variation among regions in the percentage of the older age group, resulting in some regions being classified as "aged" populations while others are considered "young." According to the 2011 Census, the Atlantic provinces, British Columbia, and Quebec, for example, had the highest percentage of seniors, while Alberta had the lowest (Statistics Canada 2012). Although Canada's overall population is aging, regional responses in the form of specialized housing, health care, caregiving services, and other social services may vary.

Gender differences sharply punctuate overall rates of aging in Canadian society. The proportion of older women in Canada has been increasing steadily since 1961. Given women's greater life expectancy, they constitute a disproportionate number of the aged. Because of women's lower average incomes and overall financial security, they are more likely to experience poverty than their male counterparts. The feminization of poverty, then, is accentuated by an aging population of which women make up a disproportionately high number. Although some may view their greater life expectancy as a positive gain, for many women, particularly immigrants, women of colour, Aboriginal women, and those of lower social class, living longer means an even greater chance of living in poverty. Aboriginal men and women are more likely to suffer from poor health and have lower life expectancies because of the prevailing conditions of poverty in their lives. This situation will be discussed in more detail in the upcoming sections on health.

15.4 What Is Social Epidemiology?

Social epidemiology is the study of the distribution of disease, impairment, and general health status across a population. In the preamble to its 1946 constitution, the World Health Organization (WHO) defined **health** as a "state of complete physical, mental, and social well-being, and not merely the absence of disease and infirmity" (Leavell and Clark 1965:14). Epidemiology initially concentrated on the scientific study of epidemics (and, more largely, pandemics), focusing on how they started and spread. Contemporary social epidemiology is much broader in scope, concerned not only with epidemics but also with non-epidemic diseases, injuries, drug addiction and alcoholism, suicide, and mental illness. Epidemiology draws on the work of a wide variety of scientists and researchers, among them physicians, sociologists, public health officials, biologists, veterinarians, demographers, anthropologists, psychologists, and meteorologists.

Researchers in social epidemiology commonly use two concepts: incidence and prevalence. **Incidence** refers to the number of *new* cases of a specific disorder occurring within a given population during a stated period of time, usually a year. For example, the incidence of HIV in Canada in 2008 was 2518 cases. By contrast, **prevalence** refers to the total number of cases of a specific disorder that exist at a given time. The prevalence of HIV in Canada in 2008 was about 65 000 cases (Public Health Agency of Canada 2010).

When incidence figures are presented as rates, or as the number of reports per 100 000 people, it is called the **morbidity rate.** (The term **mortality rate**, you will recall, refers to the incidence of *death* in a given population.) Sociologists find morbidity rates useful because they reveal that a specific disease occurs more frequently among one segment of a population than another. As we will see, social class, race, ethnicity, gender, and age can all affect a population's morbidity rates.

Social Class

Social class is clearly associated with differences in morbidity and mortality rates. Studies in Canada and other countries have consistently shown that people in the lower classes have higher rates of mortality and disability. Health Canada has identified 12 determinants of health, which include income and social status, employment, education, gender, and culture (see Table 15-3).

Although available data do suggest the relationship between health and social class, they mask the vast diversity within Canada. For example, because social class, racialization, and gender intersect, First Nations living on reserves have a rate of diabetes three to five times higher than other Canadians (Public Health Agency of Canada 2011).

Numerous studies document the impact of social class on health. An examination of data from 11 countries in North America and Europe found strong associations between household income and health, and between household income and life expectancy, when comparing families of similar size. Researchers from the Harvard School of Public Health found that higher overall mortality rates—as well as higher incidence of infant mortality and deaths from coronary heart disease, cancer, and homicide—were associated with lower incomes.

Why is class linked to health? Crowded living conditions, substandard housing, poor diet, and stress all contribute to the ill health of many low-income people in Canada. In certain instances, limited education and literacy may lead to a lack of awareness of measures necessary to maintain good health.

table 15-3 Twelve Determinants of Health Identified by Health Canada

- Income and social status
- Employment and working conditions
- Education
- Social environments
- Physical environments
- Healthy child development
- Personal health practices and coping skills
- Health services
- Social support networks
- Biology and genetic endowment
- Gender
- Culture

Source: Health Canada 2002.

Another factor in the link between class and health is evident at the workplace: the occupations of people in the working and lower classes of Canada tend to be more dangerous than those of more affluent citizens. Miners, for example, must face the possibility of injury or death from explosions and cave-ins; they are also likely to develop respiratory diseases, such as black lung. Workers in textile mills may contract a variety of illnesses caused by exposure to toxic substances, including one disease commonly known as brown lung disease, while a particular worry for construction workers has been asbestos poisoning.

In the view of Karl Marx and other contemporary conflict theorists, capitalist societies, such as Canada, would be seen as caring more about maximizing profits than about the health and safety of industrial workers. As a result, government agencies do not take forceful action to regulate conditions in the workplace, and workers suffer many preventable, job-related injuries and illnesses.

Research also shows that the lower classes are more vulnerable to environmental pollution than the affluent; this is the case not only where the lower classes work but also where they live (Moffatt 1995).

Sociologists Link and Phelan maintain that socioeconomic status is "a fundamental cause of disease" since it is linked to access to resources "that can be used to avoid risks or minimize the consequences of disease once it occurs . . . resources that include money, knowledge, power, prestige and kinds of interpersonal resources embodied in the concepts of social support and social network" (Link and Phelan 1995:87).

Racialization and Ethnicity

Health profiles of many racialized and ethnic minorities reflect the social inequality evident in Canada. The most glaring examples of the relationship between race and ethnicity and health can be found within Canada's Aboriginal communities. The health of Aboriginal peoples reflects patterns of exclusion, past and present, that have limited and continue to limit their access to many of the social determinants of health—such determinants as income, employment, education, and literacy. Aboriginal peoples not only experience a lack of material resources but also face limited opportunities, isolation, discrimination, and racism.

Aboriginal peoples "sustain a disproportionate share of the burden of physical disease and mental illness" (MacMillan, Offord, and Dingle 1996:1569). Many Aboriginal populations have an increased risk of death from alcoholism, homicide, suicide, and pneumonia; overall death rates for both men and women are higher among the Aboriginal population than their counterparts in the wider Canadian population (Health Canada 2006). Rates of tuberculosis in First Nations communities are 31 times greater than in non-Aboriginal communities, and the most susceptible are the Inuit (Curry 2010). Aboriginal communities have identified such problems as substance abuse, unemployment, suicide, and family violence as concerns affecting their members' health. The health of Aboriginal peoples as well as that of other disadvantaged ethnic and racialized minorities is interwoven with the conditions of poverty and marginalization.

Gender

A large body of research indicates that, in comparison with men, women experience a higher prevalence of many illnesses, though they tend to live longer. Females born between 2007 and 2009 have a life expectancy of 83 years; males born at the same time are expected to live for about 79 years. The difference in life expectancy between Canadian men and women has been attributed to such factors as risk-taking behaviour (e.g., drinking and dangerous driving on the part of males); levels of danger associated with male-dominated occupations (e.g., mining and construction); and women's tendency to use health-care services more often and at earlier stages of their illness. The difference in life expectancy between men and women decreased to a gap of 4 years from a gap of 7.4 years in 1979 (Statistics Canada 2012). The narrowing of the gap has been partially attributed to deaths due to cardiovascular disease, which was previously thought to be a "man's" disease. Cardiovascular disease is now the leading cause of death for both men and women with rates dramatically increasing for particular groups of women (Kirkey 2012) Many predict that the narrowing of the gender gap in life expectancy will continue in the twenty-first century because of women's changing roles and their exposure to stress, because there are fewer men in dangerous jobs, because men are becoming more attentive to their health, and because of the general aging of the population (Weeks 2010).

Studies suggest that the genuine differences in morbidity between women and men may be less pronounced than the data show. Researchers argue that women are much more likely than men to seek treatment, to be diagnosed as having a disease, and thus to have their illnesses reflected in the data examined by epidemiologists.

From a conflict perspective, women have been particularly vulnerable to the medicalization of society, with everything from birth to beauty treated in an increasingly medical context. Such medicalization may contribute to women's higher morbidity rates as compared with those of men. Ironically, although women have been especially affected by medicalization, women have been underrepresented in clinical studies. Female physicians and researchers charge that sexism is at the heart of such research practices and insist that there is a desperate need for studies with female subjects (Center for Disease Control and Prevention 2011b).

Moreover, many feminist researchers state the need for greater investigation into the health effects of discrimination as a function of gender, racialization, sexual orientation, or disability, as well as how these variables interact to produce varying levels of health and disease. They argue that since gender is not a uniform category, research approaches are needed that will lead to a better understanding of the "dynamics of diversity" among and within the various groups of Canadian women (Vissandjee 2001:3).

Research on the relationship between culture and gender as they relate to health reveals that immigrant women's experiences differ from those that are depicted to be the Canadian "norm" (Repper et al. 1996). Certain immigrant women, for example, are less likely to participate in cancer-screening programs (e.g., mammograms and pap smears), while others with concerns arising from female genital mutilation are reluctant to consult health-care providers (Vissandjee 2001).

Despite renewed attention to women's health, recent studies confirm that women still are sometimes neglected by the medical establishment. A study published in the *Canadian Medical Association Journal* in 2007 found that seriously ill women—particularly those who are older—are about one-third less likely to be treated in an intensive care unit (ICU) than male patients with comparable conditions; women, as a result, are more likely to die of a critical illness (Picard 2007).

Age

Health is the overriding concern of the elderly. Most older people in Canada report having at least one chronic illness, but only some of these conditions are potentially life-threatening or require medical care. At the same time, health problems can affect the quality of life of older people in important ways. Arthritis and visual or hearing impairments can interfere with the performance of everyday tasks.

As the Canadian population ages, led by the baby boom generation to which roughly one-third of all Canadians belong, our society will experience a greater prevalence of particular types of diseases. The Vancouver Brain Research Centre predicts that in 2020 brain diseases, such as Alzheimer's and Parkinson's, to which older people are more prone, will be the leading cause of death and disability among Canadians (Fong 2001). In Canada in 2008, 480 600 Canadians or 1.5 percent of the population had Alzheimer's disease or related dementia. Since the likelihood of contracting these diseases increases with age, by 2038 that number is expected to increase to 1 125 200 or 2.8 percent of the Canadian population (Alzheimer's Society of Canada 2010). The incidence of diseases related to vision (e.g., glaucoma and macular degeneration) is currently on the increase and will continue to rise as the baby boomers make their way into the senior years; the same is true of stroke. Overall, these afflictions will surpass heart disease and cancer, which currently are the leading causes of death and disability. Gender is of particular importance in the study of health and aging, since women on average live longer lives. Living longer means older women are at increased risk of disease, and thus greater life expectancy can actually be viewed as a threat to women's health.

Social support is a key factor related to the health of both older men and women. In older women, research reveals that depression is more strongly related to social support than to physical health (Albarracin, Fishbein, and Goldstein de Muchinik 1997). Older people tend to visit doctors more frequently and require hospitalization more often than do their younger counterparts. Given the demographic shift toward an older population accentuated by baby boomers, it is obvious that the disproportionate use of the health-care system in Canada by older people is a critical factor in all discussions about the cost of health care and possible reforms of the health-care system.

Sexual Orientation

Since heterosexuality is assumed to be the norm in Canadian society, there is a lack of attention paid to gays and lesbians in health research (Weber 1998). There does, however, tend to be more research carried out on gay men than on lesbians (Lynch and Ferri 1997). Lesbians, then, face the combined effects of sexism and sexual orientation as they relate to health research and provision of health care. Research on health is conducted using mainly white, middle-class women, which results in a lack of knowledge about the health of bisexual women, older lesbians, lesbians of colour, and lesbians from rural areas (Hart 1995).

The assumption of diversity is, however, being integrated into some health-care systems, such as the Vancouver–Richmond Health Board, which represents the needs of lesbian, gay, bisexual, and transgender patients, as well as other groups who traditionally have not been adequately served by the health-care system. As well, there have been concerns expressed over the curricula of Canadian medical schools regarding gay, lesbian, and bisexual issues. Medical schools are being prompted to ensure that the doctors they graduate are competently trained to care for *all* Canadians.

In sum, to achieve the goal of 100 percent access and zero health disparities, public health officials must overcome inequities that are rooted not just in age but in social class, race and ethnicity, gender, and sexual orientation. If that were not enough, they must also deal with a geographical disparity in health-care resources. Dramatic differences in the availability of physicians, hospitals, and nursing homes also exist between urban and rural areas within the same province or territory. In the next section, we will look at the sociological perspectives on health and illness, some of which address these inequities in health care.

15.5 What Are the Sociological Perspectives on Health and Illness?

From a sociological point of view, social factors contribute to the evaluation of a person as "healthy" or "sick." People define themselves as healthy or sick on the basis of criteria established by each individual, relatives, friends, co-workers, and medical practitioners. Because health is relative, we can view it in a social context and consider how it varies in different situations or cultures.

Why is it that you may consider yourself sick or well when others do not agree? Who controls definitions of health and illness in our society, and for what ends? What are the consequences of viewing yourself (or being viewed) as ill or disabled? Drawing on four sociological perspectives—functionalism, conflict theory, feminist theories, and interactionism—we can gain greater insight into the social context shaping definitions of health and treatment of illness.

An Overview

As you know, the sociological approaches should not be regarded as mutually exclusive. In the study of health-related issues, they share certain common themes. First, any person's health or illness is more than an organic condition, since it is subject to the interpretation of others.

Owing to the impact of culture, family and friends, and the medical profession, health and illness are not purely biological occurrences but are sociological occurrences as well. Second, since members of a society (especially industrial societies) share the same health-delivery system, health is a group and societal concern. Although health may be defined as the complete well-being of an individual, it is also the result of his or her social environment. As we will see, such factors as a person's social class, race and ethnicity, gender, and age can influence the likelihood of contracting a particular disease (Cockerham 1998).

Functionalist Approach

Illness entails at least a temporary disruption in a person's social interactions both at work and at home. Consequently, from a functionalist perspective, "being sick" must be controlled so that not too many people are released from their societal responsibilities at any one time. Functionalists contend that an overly broad definition of illness would disrupt the workings of a society. "Sickness" requires a person to take on a social role, even if temporarily. The **sick role** refers to societal expectations about the attitudes and behaviour of a person viewed as being ill. Sociologist Talcott Parsons, well known for his contributions to functionalist theory (see Chapter 1), has outlined the behaviour required of people considered "sick" (1951, 1972, 1975). They are exempted from their normal, day-to-day responsibilities and generally are not blamed for their condition. Yet, they are obligated to try to get well, and this may include seeking competent professional care. Attempting to get well is particularly important in the world's developing countries. Modern, automated industrial societies can absorb a greater degree of illness or disability than can horticultural or agrarian societies in which the availability of workers is far more critical (Conrad 2009).

According to Parsons's theory, physicians function as "gatekeepers" for the sick role, either verifying a patient's condition as "illness" or designating the patient as "recovered." The ill person becomes dependent on the doctor because the latter can control valued rewards (not only treatment of illness but also excused absences from work and school). Parsons suggests that the doctor–patient relationship is somewhat like that between parent and child. Like a parent, the physician helps the patient to return to society as a full and functioning adult (Weitz 2007).

The concept of sick role is not without criticism. First, patients' judgments regarding their own state of health may be related to their gender, age, social class, and ethnic group. For example, younger people may fail to detect warning signs of a dangerous illness while the elderly may focus too much on the slightest physical malady. Second, the sick role may be more applicable to people experiencing short-term illnesses than to those with recurring, long-term illnesses. Finally, even simple factors, such as whether a person is employed or not, seem to affect willingness to assume the sick role—as does the impact of socialization into a particular occupation or activity. For example, beginning in childhood, athletes learn to define certain ailments as "sports injuries" and therefore do not regard themselves as sick. Nonetheless, sociologists continue to rely on Parsons's model for functionalist analysis of the relationship between illness and societal expectations for the sick (Curry 1993).

Conflict Approach

Functionalists seek to explain how health-care systems meet the needs of society as well as those of individual patients and medical practitioners, but conflict theorists take issue with this view. They express concern that the profession of medicine has assumed a pre-eminence that extends well beyond whether to excuse a student from school or an employee from work. Sociologist Eliot Freidson has likened the position of medicine today to that of state religions yesterday—it has an officially approved monopoly on the right to define health and illness and to treat illness (1970:5). Conflict theorists use the term **medicalization of society** to refer to the growing role of medicine as a major institution of social control (Conrad 2007; McKinlay and McKinlay 1977; Zola 1972, 1983).

Social control involves techniques and strategies for regulating behaviour in order to enforce the distinctive norms and values of a culture. Typically, we think of informal social control as occurring within families and peer groups, and formal social control as carried out by authorized agents, such as police officers, judges, school administrators, and employers. However, viewed from a conflict perspective, medicine is not simply a "healing profession"; it is a regulating mechanism as well.

How does medicine manifest its social control? First, it has greatly expanded its domain of expertise in recent decades. Physicians have become much more involved in examining a wide range of issues, among them sexuality (including homosexuality), old age, anxiety, obesity, child development, alcoholism, and drug addiction. Society tolerates such expansion of the boundaries of medicine because we hope that these experts can bring new "miracle cures" to complex human problems, as they have to the control of certain infectious diseases. The social significance of medicalization is that once a problem is viewed using a *medical model*—once medical experts become influential in proposing and assessing relevant public policies—it becomes more difficult for "others" to join the discussion and exert influence on decision making. It also becomes more difficult to view these issues as being shaped by social, cultural, or psychological factors, rather than simply by physical or medical factors (Caplan 1989; Conrad 2007).

Second, medicine serves as an agent of social control by retaining absolute jurisdiction over many health-care procedures. Public health officials have even attempted to guard their jurisdiction by placing such health-care professionals as chiropractors and nurse-midwives outside the realm of acceptable medicine. Despite the fact that midwives first brought professionalism to child delivery, they have been portrayed as having invaded the "legitimate" field of obstetrics in North America. Nurse-midwives have sought licensing as a way to achieve professional respectability, but physicians continue to exert power to ensure that midwifery remains a subordinate occupation (Scharnberg 2007).

The medicalization of society is but one concern of conflict theorists as they assess the workings of health-care institutions. As we have seen throughout this book, when analyzing any issue, conflict theorists seek to determine who benefits, who suffers, and who dominates at the expense of others. Viewed from a conflict perspective, there are glaring inequities in health-care delivery within Canada. For example, northern and rural areas tend to be underserved because medical services concentrate where people are numerous or wealthy.

Similarly, from a global perspective, there are obvious inequities in health-care delivery. In 2008, Canada had 19.5 physicians per 10 000 people, while African nations had fewer than 1 per 10 000. This situation is only worsened by the "brain drain"—the immigration to industrialized nations of skilled workers, professionals, and technicians who are desperately needed by their home countries. As part of this brain drain, physicians and other health-care professionals have come to developed countries from developing countries such as India, Pakistan, and various African states. Conflict theorists view such emigration out of the developing world as yet another way in which the world's core industrialized nations enhance their quality of life at the expense of developing countries.

In another example of global inequities in health care, multinational corporations based in industrialized countries have reaped significant profits by "dumping" unapproved drugs on unsuspecting consumers in the developing world. In some cases, fraudulent capsules and tablets are manufactured and marketed as established products in developing countries. These "medications" contain useless ingredients or perhaps one-tenth of the needed dosage of a genuine medication. Even when the drugs dumped on developing countries are legitimate, the information available to physicians and patients is less likely to include warnings of side effects or health hazards and more likely to include undocumented testimonials than in industrialized nations (Silverman, Lydecker, and Lee 1990).

Conflict theorists emphasize that inequities in health-care resources have clear life-and-death consequences. For example, in 2007, the infant mortality rate in Sierra Leone was estimated to be 158 infant deaths per 1000 live births. By contrast, Japan's infant mortality rate was only 2.8 deaths per 1000 live births and Sweden's was 3.1. From a conflict perspective, the dramatic differences in infant mortality rates around the world reflect, at least in part, unequal distribution of health-care resources based on the wealth or poverty of various communities and nations.

In 2007, the United States had a rate of 6.5 infant deaths per 1000 live births (although it is estimated that the rate in some poor, inner-city neighbourhoods in that country exceeds 30 deaths per 1000 live births). Despite the wealth of the United States, at least 22 nations have lower infant mortality rates, among them Canada, Iceland, and Japan. Conflict theorists point out that, unlike the United States, Canada and these other countries offer some form of government-supported health care for all citizens, which typically leads to greater availability and better use of prenatal care than is the case in the United States.

Feminist Approaches

Many feminist approaches to health and illness have pointed to a historical pattern of concentrating on women's reproductive potential, overshadowing a diversity of concerns related to health and illness. Early research on women focused on their roles as mothers and wives as they related to women's

The growing concern about obesity among the young has focused attention on their eating habits and their need for exercise.

mental health, while comparable studies on men focused more on their physical health and job conditions. This bias still can be found in the research literature, even though most women now work in the paid labour force.

Other feminist perspectives point out the need to recognize that patterns of women's health and illness are as diverse as Canadian women themselves and that this diversity (e.g., poor women, immigrants, refugees, women of colour, lesbians, disabled women) must not be masked by talking about "women" as a universal category. Feminist sociologists argue:

> Women are often discussed as a single group defined chiefly by their biological sex, members of an abstract universal (and implicitly white) category. In reality, we are a mixed lot, our gender roles and options shaped by history, culture and deep divisions across class and colour lines. . . . Traditionally, women as a group are defined by this reproductive potential. Usually ignored are the many ways that gender as a social reality gets into the body and transforms our biology. (Krieger and Fee 1994:18)

Sociological investigations of women's health must, many feminist theorists argue, shift the focus from reproduction potential and roles as mothers and wives to women's health and illness, to reflect the diversity of Canadian women.

Interactionist Approach

In examining health, illness, and medicine as a social institution, interactionists generally focus on micro-level study of the roles played by health-care professionals and patients. They emphasize that the patient should not always be viewed as passive, but instead as an actor who often shows a powerful intent to see the physician (Alonzo 1989; Zola 1983).

Sometimes, patients play an active role in health care by *failing* to follow a physician's advice. For example, some patients stop taking medications long before they should, some take an incorrect dosage on purpose, and others never even fill their prescriptions. Such non-compliance results in part from the prevalence of self-medication in our society; many people are accustomed to self-diagnosis and self-treatment. Conversely, patients' active involvement in their own health care can sometimes have very *positive* consequences. Some patients read books about preventive health-care techniques, attempt to maintain healthful and nutritious diets, carefully monitor any side effects of medication, and adjust dosage based on such perceived side effects.

Labelling theorists suggest that the designation "healthy" or "ill" generally involves social definition by others. Just as police officers, judges, and other regulators of social control have the power to define certain people as criminals, health-care professionals (especially physicians) have the power to define certain people as "sick."

An example from history illustrates the labelling of women by the medical profession as fragile and possessing a limited source of energy. During the early years of the last century, women who expended energy pursuing intellectual activities (such as advanced education) were perceived to be endangering their womanhood. The medical establishment viewed the female body as a closed system of energy in which use of the brain would leave less energy to be used in other parts, such as the reproductive system. Women's brains and ovaries, according to doctors of the time, competed for the same supply of energy. Women who spent too much energy in intellectual pursuits were labelled "unhealthy" and unwomanly:

> A young woman . . . who consumed her vital force in intellectual activities was necessarily diverting these energies from the achievement of true womanhood. She would become weak and nervous, perhaps sterile . . . capable of bearing only sickly and neurotic children. . . . The brain and ovary could not develop at the same time. (Smith-Rosenberg and Rosenberg 1974:340)

Patriarchal views of women's health during this period even went so far as to suggest that male semen had a therapeutic and soothing effect on the female reproductive organs (Smith-Rosenberg 1986).

By the late 1980s, the power of a label—"person with AIDS"—had become quite evident. This label often functions as a master status that overshadows all other aspects of a person's life. Once someone is told that he or she has tested positive for HIV, the virus associated with AIDS, that person is forced to confront immediate and difficult questions: "Should I tell my family members, my sexual partner(s), my friends, my co-workers, my employer? How will these people respond?" People's intense fear of this disease has led to prejudice and discrimination—even social ostracism—against those who have (or are suspected of having) AIDS.

Consequently, a person who has AIDS must deal with not only the serious medical consequences of the disease but also with the distressing social consequences associated with the label.

According to labelling theorists, we can view a variety of life experiences as illnesses or not. Recently, premenstrual syndrome, post-traumatic disorders, and hyperactivity have been labelled as medically recognized disorders. Following the 1991 Gulf War against Iraq, more than 21 000 U.S. soldiers and other personnel reported a variety of symptoms ranging from fatigue and rashes to respiratory disorders. These symptoms have come to be called the Gulf War Syndrome (or illness); in 2008, the U.S. government officially recognized a clear link between the combat situation and subsequent symptoms (Rutten 2008).

Probably the most noteworthy recent medical example of labelling is the case of homosexuality. For years, psychiatrists classified being gay or lesbian as a mental disorder subject to treatment. This official sanction by the psychiatry profession became an early target of the growing gay and lesbian rights movement in North America. In 1974, members of the American Psychiatric Association voted to drop homosexuality from the standard manual on mental disorders (Adam 1995; Charmaz and Paterniti 1999; Monteiro 1998).

Interactionist perspectives attempt to illuminate the social meaning of illness, as well as how these meanings affect a person's self-concept and relationships with others. For example, in the case of someone suffering from a mental illness, such as depression, interactionist approaches might shed light on the social stigma of the illness. In addition, these approaches might focus on how the stigma of the illness affects the individual's interpersonal relationships with family, friends, and co-workers. The interactionist perspective has been especially helpful in unravelling cultural differences that affect health care in a multicultural society, such as that of Canada. For example, regular exercise is not part of the culture of some ethnic groups; attitudes on diet, smoking, drinking, and body image, as well as fatalistic views of illness, may be culturally specific (Buchanan 2008; S. Levine 2006). Cultural sensitivity is necessary at all levels of health-care delivery in order to effectively treat a diverse patient population where many face language barriers, racism, social isolation, and inequality. Determining the different cultural meanings that individuals might attach to a doctor's report, a referral to a medical specialist, or a health survey are examples of how interactionists might approach the study of health and illness.

The four sociological perspectives on health and illness are summarized, and their key proponents listed, in Table 15-4.

15.6 What Is the Health-Care Situation in Canada?

In 1947, Swift Current, Saskatchewan, became the first region in North America to embrace a public hospital insurance program, in which all of its citizens were provided access to hospital services without direct payment. The following year, Premier Tommy Douglas introduced a program for all of Saskatchewan, based largely on the Swift Current model. Ten years later, the federal government followed suit by introducing the first national hospital insurance plan in North America. In 1962, Saskatchewan was again at the forefront of public health care when it introduced North America's first medicare program, which would cover doctors' fees incurred outside hospitals. The program sparked the highly profiled Saskatchewan doctors' strike, which saw many physicians threatening to leave the province if this perceived threat to "free enterprise" in medical care went through. Critics of the medicare plan accused the government of "communist" and "socialist" tendencies, and of attempting to destroy the private relationship between physicians and patients.

The doctors' strike, which lasted three weeks, became the focus of media attention not only in Canada but also in the United States. The American Medical Association supported the dissenting Saskatchewan doctors in their attempt to resist the public administration of medical care and to preserve "free enterprise."

In 1968, the public administration of medical care became national policy, after the provinces and territories moved to implement their own insurance plans for in-hospital care. Justice Emmett Hall, after carrying out a review of the Canadian health-care system in 1979, reported it to be among the best in the world. He did, however, warn that the system was being weakened by extra billing by doctors and that user fees were creating a "two-tiered" system. These unresolved issues still pose a threat to the principles of accessibility, universality, and public administration, which are cornerstones of Canadian medicare.

table 15-4 Sociological Perspectives on Health and Illness summingUP

	Functionalist	Conflict	Feminist	Interactionist
Major emphasis	Control of the number of people who are considered sick	Overmedicalization Gross inequities in health care	Need to recognize patterns of women's health and illness as diverse and not uniform	Doctor–patient relationship Interaction of medical staff
Controlling factors	Physician as gatekeeper	Medical profession Social inequalities	Medical profession	Medical profession
Proponents	Talcott Parsons	Paul Starr Thomas Szasz Irving Zola	Dorothy Smith	Doug Maynard

The Role of Government in Health Care in Canada

In 1984, the federal government's Canada Health Act became the basis for the administration of our health-care system, known as *medicare*. The Health Act set out to ensure (in theory) that all Canadians receive access to hospital and doctors' services on the basis of need, not on the ability to pay. It also sets the conditions and criteria under which the provinces and territories receive transfer payments—payments that are then used to finance health-care services in their respective jurisdictions. The principles of the Canada Health Act are as follows (Health Canada 2001):

1. *Public administration:* Health care in a province or territory must be carried out by public institutions on a non-profit basis.

2. *Comprehensiveness:* All services carried out by hospitals and doctors and deemed to be medically necessary must be insured.

3. *Universality:* All residents of a province or territory are entitled to uniform health coverage.

4. *Portability:* Health coverage must be maintained when a person moves or travels across provinces and territories or outside Canada.

5. *Accessibility:* Reasonable access to necessary medical services should be available to all Canadians.

In many respects the principles of public administration, comprehensiveness, universality, portability, and accessibility represent Max Weber's ideal types; that is, they act as abstract measuring rods against which we are able to compare our perceptions of reality. For example, most Canadians would be able to give an example of how our health-care system today may not measure up to at least one of these principles. Whether the concern is waiting lists for surgery, access to specialists in remote locations, the growth of private, fee-for-service clinics, long waits in hospital emergency wards, waiting lists for specialized tests (such as MRIs), the closing of rural hospitals the reduction of beds in urban hospitals, or the shortage of nurses nationwide, Canadians consider the delivery of health-care services a concern of major priority. Canadians living in northern or rural areas or outside major metropolitan areas, immigrants, those with low incomes, Aboriginal persons, and people with disabilities represent some of the groups vulnerable to the so-called crisis in the Canadian health-care system.

15.7 How Have Communities Changed?

As we noted at the outset of this chapter, a community is a spatial or political unit of social organization that gives people a sense of belonging. The nature of community has changed greatly over the course of history—from early hunting-and-gathering societies to highly modernized post-industrial cities, as we will now see.

For most of human history, people used very basic tools and knowledge to survive. They satisfied their need for an adequate food supply through hunting, foraging for fruits or vegetables, fishing, and herding. In comparison with later industrial societies, early civilizations were much more dependent on the reproductive cycle of the physical environment and much less able to alter that environment to their advantage. The emergence of horticultural societies, in which people actually cultivated food rather than merely gathering fruits and vegetables, led to many dramatic changes in human social organization.

It was no longer necessary to move from place to place in search of food. Because people had to remain in specific locations to cultivate crops, more stable and enduring communities began to develop. As agricultural techniques became more and more sophisticated, a cooperative division of labour involving both family members and others developed. It gradually became possible for people to produce more food than they actually needed for themselves. They could then provide food, perhaps as part of an exchange, to others who might be involved in non-agricultural labour. This transition from subsistence to surplus represented a critical step in the emergence of cities.

Eventually, people produced enough goods to cover both their own needs and those of people not engaged in agricultural tasks. Initially, the surplus was limited to agricultural products, but it gradually evolved to include all types of goods and services. Residents of a city came to rely on community members who provided craft products and means of transportation, gathered information, and so forth (Nolan and Lenski 2009).

With these social changes came an even more elaborate division of labour, as well as a greater opportunity for differential rewards and privileges. As long as everyone was engaged in the same tasks, stratification was limited to such factors as gender, age, and perhaps the ability to perform the task (a skillful hunter could win unusual respect from the community). However, the surplus allowed for expansion of goods and services, leading to greater differentiation, a hierarchy of occupations, and social inequality. Therefore, surplus was a precondition not only for the establishment of cities but also for the division of members of a community into social classes (see Chapter 6). The ability to produce goods for other communities marked a fundamental shift in human social organization.

Pre-industrial Cities

It is estimated that, beginning about 10 000 BCE, permanent settlements free from dependence on crop cultivation emerged. Yet, by today's standards of population, these early communities would barely qualify as cities. The **pre-industrial city**, as it is termed, generally had only a few thousand people living within its borders and was characterized by a relatively closed class system and limited mobility. Status in these early cities was usually based on ascribed characteristics, such as family background; and education was limited to members of the elite. All the residents relied on perhaps 100 000 farmers and their own part-time farming to provide them with the needed agricultural surplus. The Mesopotamian city of Ur had a population of about 10 000 and was limited to roughly 90 hectares (220 acres) of land, including the canals, the temple, and the harbour.

Why were these early cities so small and relatively few in number? Several key factors restricted urbanization:

- *Reliance on animal power (from both humans and beasts of burden) as a source of energy for economic production.* This limited people's ability to make use of and alter the physical environment.

- *Modest levels of surplus produced by the agricultural sector.* Between 50 and 90 farmers may have been required to support one city resident (Davis [1949] 1995).

- *Problems in transportation and storage of food and other goods.* Even an excellent crop could easily be lost as a result of such difficulties.

- *Hardships of migration to the city.* For many peasants, migration was both physically and economically impossible. A few weeks of travel was out of the question without more sophisticated techniques of food storage.

- *Dangers of city life.* Concentrating a society's population in a small area left it open to attack from outsiders, as well as more susceptible to extreme damage from plagues and fires.

A sophisticated social organization is also an essential precondition for urban existence. Specialized social roles bring people together in new ways through the exchange of goods and services. A well-developed social organization ensures that these relationships are clearly defined and generally acceptable to all parties.

Table 15-5 summarizes the contrasts between pre-industrial and industrial cities as outlined by Sjoberg. Admittedly, Sjoberg's view of city life is an ideal type, since inequality did not vanish with the emergence of urban communities.

Industrial and Post-industrial Cities

Imagine how life could change by harnessing the energy of air, water, and other natural resources to power society's tasks.

Advances in agricultural technology led to dramatic changes in community life, but so did the process of industrialization. The Industrial Revolution, which began in the middle of the eighteenth century, focused on the application of non-animal sources of power to labour tasks. Industrialization had a wide range of effects on people's lifestyles as well as on the structure of communities. Emerging urban settlements became centres not only of industry but also of banking, finance, and industrial management.

The factory system that developed during the Industrial Revolution led to a much more refined division of labour than was evident in pre-industrial cities. The many new occupations that were created produced a complex set of relationships among workers. Thus, the **industrial city** was not merely more populous than its pre-industrial predecessors; it was also based on very different principles of social organization.

In comparison with pre-industrial cities, industrial cities have a more open class system and more mobility. After initiatives in industrial cities by women's-rights groups, labour unions, and other political activists, formal education gradually became available to many children from poor and working-class families. Although ascribed characteristics, such as gender, race, and ethnicity, remained important, a talented or skilled individual had a greater opportunity to better his or her social position. In these and other respects, the industrial city is genuinely a "different world" from the pre-industrial urban community.

In the latter part of the twentieth century, a new type of urban community emerged. The **postindustrial city** is a city in which global finance and the electronic flow of information dominate the economy. Production is decentralized and often takes place outside urban centres, but control is centralized in multinational corporations whose influence transcends urban

table **15-5 Comparing Types of Cities**

Pre-industrial Cities (through eighteenth century)	Industrial Cities (eighteenth through mid-twentieth century)	Post-industrial Cities (beginning late twentieth century)
Closed class system—pervasive influence of social class at birth	Open class system—mobility based on achieved characteristics	Wealth based on ability to obtain and use information
Economic realm controlled by guilds and a few families	Relatively open competition	Corporate power dominates
Beginnings of division of labour in creation of goods	Elaborate specialization in manufacturing of goods	Sense of place fades, transitional networks emerge
Pervasive influence of religion on social norms	Influence of religion limited to certain areas as society becomes more secularized	Religion becomes more fragmented; greater openness to new religious faiths
Little standardization of prices, weights, and measures	Standardization enforced by custom and law	Conflicting views of prevailing standards
Population largely illiterate; communication by word of mouth	Emergence of communication through posters, bulletins, and newspapers	Emergence of extended electronic networks
Schools limited to elites and designed to perpetuate their privileged status	Formal schooling open to the masses and viewed as a means of advancing the social order	Professional, scientific, and technical personnel are increasingly important

Sources: Based on Phillips 1996:132–135; Sjoberg 1960:323–328.

and even national boundaries. Social change is a constant feature of the post-industrial city. Economic restructuring and spatial change seem to occur each decade, if not more frequently. In the post-industrial world, cities are forced into increasing competition for economic opportunities, which deepens the plight of the urban poor (Phillips 1996; Smith and Timberlake 1993).

::: use your sociological *imagination* :::

What would the ideal city of the future look like? Describe its architecture, public transportation, neighbourhoods, schools, and workplaces. What kinds of people would live and work there?

15.8 What Is Urbanization, and What Are Its Consequences?

The 2011 Census showed that 81 percent of Canadians live in urban centres, compared with 78.5 percent in 1996. Over one half of Canada's population is concentrated in four broad urban areas: southern Ontario, Montreal and environs, the lower mainland of British Columbia and southern Vancouver Island, and the Calgary–Edmonton corridor.

Urbanization can be seen throughout the rest of the world, too. In 1900, only 10 percent of the world's people lived in urban areas; by 2000, that proportion had risen to around 50 percent. By the year 2025, the number of city dwellers could reach 5 billion (Koolhaas et al. 2001:3). During the nineteenth and twentieth centuries, rapid urbanization occurred primarily in Europe and North America. But since World War II, the population of cities in developing countries has exploded: see Figure 15-4 (Koolhaas et al. 2001:3).

Some metropolitan areas have spread so far that they have connected with other urban centres. Such a densely populated area, containing two or more cities and their suburbs, has become known as a **megalopolis**. An example is the so-called Golden Horseshoe region of Southern Ontario, which encompasses such communities as Hamilton, Burlington, and the Greater Toronto Area. Even when it is divided into autonomous political jurisdictions, the megalopolis can be viewed as a single economic entity. The megalopolis is also evident in Great Britain, Germany, Italy, Egypt, India, Japan, and China.

Functionalist View: Urban Ecology

Human ecology is concerned with the relationships between people and their environment. Human ecologists have long been interested in how the physical environment shapes people's lives (e.g., rivers can serve as a barrier to residential expansion) and also how people influence the surrounding environment (air conditioning has accelerated the growth of major metropolitan areas in the American Southwest). **Urban ecology** focuses on such relationships as they emerge in urban areas. Although the urban ecological approach examines social change in cities, it is nevertheless functionalist in its orientation because it emphasizes that different elements in urban areas contribute to stability.

figure **15-4** **Global Urbanization, 2015 (projected)**

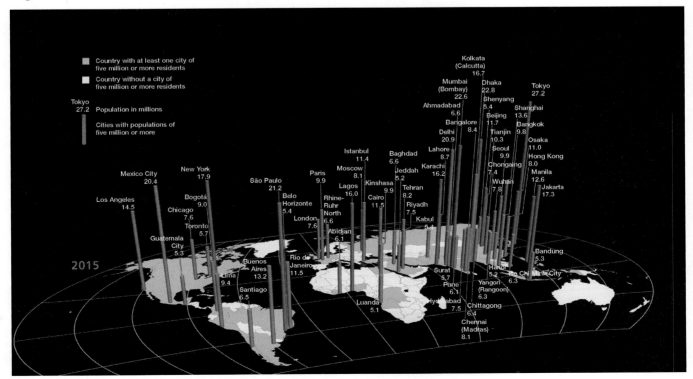

Source: National Geographic 2005:104–105.

Early urban ecologists, such as Robert Park (1916, 1936) and Ernest Burgess (1925), concentrated on city life but drew on the approaches used by ecologists who studied plant and animal communities. With few exceptions, urban ecologists trace their work back to the **concentric-zone theory** devised in the 1920s by Burgess (see the left-hand visual in Figure 15-5). Using Chicago as an example, Burgess proposed a theory for describing land use in industrial cities. At the centre, or nucleus, of such a city is the central business district. Large department stores, hotels, theatres, and financial institutions occupy this highly valued land. Surrounding this urban centre are succeeding zones that contain other types of land use and that illustrate the growth of the urban area over time.

Note that the creation of zones is a *social* process, not the result of nature alone. Families and business firms compete for the most valuable land; those possessing the most wealth and power are generally the winners. The concentric-zone theory proposed by Burgess also represented a dynamic model of urban growth. As urban growth proceeded, each zone would move even farther from the central business district.

Because of its functionalist orientation and its emphasis on stability, the concentric-zone theory tended to understate or ignore certain tensions apparent in metropolitan areas. For example, the growing use by the affluent of land in a city's peripheral areas was uncritically approved, while the arrival of visible minorities in white neighbourhoods has been described by some sociologists in such terms as "invasion" and "succession." Moreover, the urban ecological perspective gave little thought to gender inequities, such as the establishment of men's private golf clubs and softball leagues in city parks without any programs for women's sports. Consequently, the urban ecological approach has been criticized for its failure to address issues of gender, race, and class.

By the middle of the twentieth century, urban populations had spilled beyond the traditional city limits. No longer could urban ecologists focus exclusively on growth in the central city, for large numbers of urban residents were abandoning the cities to live in suburban areas. As a response to the emergence of more than one focal point in some metropolitan areas, Chauncy D. Harris and Edward Ullman (1945) presented the **multiple-nuclei theory** (see the right-hand visual in Figure 15-5). In their view, not all urban growth radiates outward from a central business district. Instead, a metropolitan area may have many centres of development, each of which reflects a particular urban need or activity. Thus, a city may have a financial district, a manufacturing zone, a waterfront area, an entertainment centre, and so forth. Certain types of business firms and certain types of housing will naturally cluster around each distinctive nucleus (Squires 2002).

The rise of suburban shopping malls is a vivid example of the phenomenon of multiple nuclei within metropolitan areas. Initially, all major retailing in cities was located in the central business district. Each residential neighbourhood had its own grocers, bakers, and butchers, but people travelled to the centre of the city to make major purchases at department stores. However, as major metropolitan areas expanded and the suburbs became more populous, an increasing number of people began to shop nearer their homes. Today, the suburban mall is a significant retailing and social centre for communities across Canada.

In a refinement of multiple-nuclei theory, contemporary urban ecologists have begun to study what journalist Joel Garreau (1991) has called "edge cities." These communities,

figure **15-5 Comparison of Ecological Theories of Urban Growth**

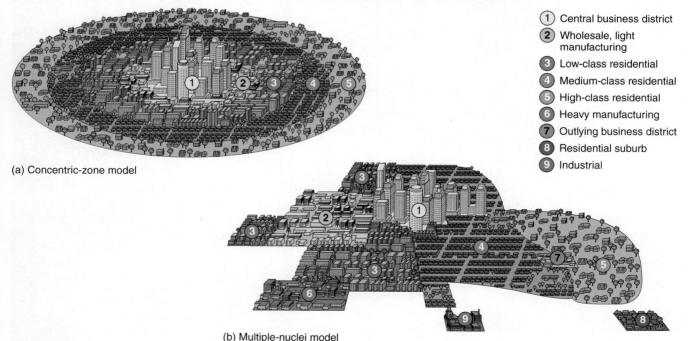

1 Central business district
2 Wholesale, light manufacturing
3 Low-class residential
4 Medium-class residential
5 High-class residential
6 Heavy manufacturing
7 Outlying business district
8 Residential suburb
9 Industrial

(a) Concentric-zone model

(b) Multiple-nuclei model

Source: C. Harris and Ullmann 1945:13.

which have grown up on the outskirts of major metropolitan areas, are economic and social centres with identities of their own. By any standard of measurement—height of buildings, amount of office space, presence of medical facilities, presence of leisure-time facilities, or, of course, population—edge cities qualify as independent cities rather than as large suburbs.

Whether they include edge cities or multiple nuclei, more and more metropolitan areas are characterized by spread-out development and unchecked growth. A David Suzuki Foundation report, entitled *Understanding Sprawl,* argues that, in some parts of Canada, urban sprawl is the largest creator of greenhouse gas emissions, as it segregates houses from stores and workplaces, forcing residents to rely on cars to get around (Gurin 2003). Large corporations are capitalizing on this so-called sprawl by building stores and services that depend on the use of the automobile. The former CEO of Starbucks, Orin Smith, recently stated that the suburbs and small towns in the United States would be the focus of growth for the coffee juggernaut; allowing people to stay in their cars by increasingly using drive-throughs—another huge source of pollution—is one of the company's goals. Smith states:

> We know from our studies that the reason our most frequent users—and as well our most infrequent users—don't use us more is because there are not enough of us and we're not convenient enough. . . . [North] Americans don't want to walk, so if you have to go more than two blocks, they don't go. (*The Vancouver Sun* 2004b)

Conflict View: New Urban Sociology

Contemporary sociologists point out that metropolitan growth is not governed by waterways and rail lines, as a purely ecological interpretation might suggest. From a conflict perspective, communities are human creations that reflect people's needs, choices, and decisions—but some people have more influence over these decisions than others do. Drawing on conflict theory, an approach that has come to be called the **new urban sociology** considers the interplay of local, national, and worldwide forces and their effect on local space, with special emphasis on the impact of global economic activity (Gottdiener and Hutchison 2006).

New urban sociologists note that ecological approaches typically have avoided examining the social forces, largely economic in nature, that have guided urban growth. For example, central business districts may be upgraded or abandoned, depending on whether urban policymakers grant substantial tax exemptions to developers. The suburban boom in the post–World War II era was fuelled by highway construction and federal housing policies that channelled investment capital into the construction of single-family homes rather than affordable rental housing in cities. Similarly, although some observers suggest that the growth of Sunbelt cities in the United States is due to a "good business climate," new urban sociologists counter that this term is actually a euphemism for hefty state and local government subsidies and anti-labour policies intended to attract manufacturers (Gottdiener and Feagin 1988; Smith 1988).

The new urban sociology draws generally on the conflict perspective and more specifically on sociologist Immanuel Wallerstein's world systems analysis. Wallerstein argues that certain industrialized nations (among them, the United States, Japan, and Germany) hold a dominant position at the *core* of the global economic system. At the same time, the poor developing countries of Asia, Africa, and Latin America are on the *periphery* of the global economy, where they are controlled and exploited by core industrialized nations. Through the use of world systems analysis, new urban sociologists consider urbanization from a global perspective. They view cities not as independent and autonomous entities but rather as the outcome of decision-making processes directed or influenced by a society's dominant classes and by core industrialized nations. New urban sociologists note that the rapidly growing cities of the world's developing countries were shaped first by colonialism and then by a global economy controlled by core nations and multinational corporations (Gottdiener and Feagin 1988; Smith 1995). The outcome has not been beneficial to the poorest, as Box 15-2 shows.

The urban ecologists of the 1920s and 1930s were aware of the role that the larger economy played in urbanization, but their theories emphasized the impact of local rather than national or global forces. By contrast, through a broad, global emphasis on social inequality and conflict, new urban sociologists are interested in such topics as the existence of an underclass, the power of multinational corporations, deindustrialization, homelessness, and residential segregation.

Developers, builders, and investment bankers are not especially interested in urban growth when it means providing housing for middle- or low-income people. This lack of interest contributes to the problem of homelessness. These urban elites counter that the nation's housing shortage and the plight of the homeless are not the fault of the elites—and insist that they do not have the capital needed to construct and support such housing. But affluent people *are* interested in growth and *can* somehow find capital to build new shopping centres, office towers, and professional sports facilities.

Why, then, can't they provide the capital for affordable housing? ask new urban sociologists. Part of the answer is that developers, bankers, and other powerful real estate interests view housing in quite a different manner from tenants and most homeowners. For a tenant, an apartment is shelter, housing, a home. But for developers and investors—many of them large (and sometimes multinational) corporations—an apartment is simply a housing investment. These financiers and owners are primarily concerned with maximizing profit, not with solving social problems (Feagin 1983; Gottdiener and Hutchison 2000).

As we have seen throughout this textbook, in studying such varied issues as deviance and race and ethnicity, no single theoretical approach necessarily offers sociologists the only valuable perspective. As is shown in Table 15-6, urban ecology and new urban sociology offer significantly different ways of viewing urbanization that enrich our understanding of this complex phenomenon

Feminist Views

Feminist perspectives outlining the ways in which gender intersects with the conditions of city life have long been absent from the sociological literature. Studies on urban

15-2 Squatter Settlements

Bariadas, favelas, bustees, kampungs, and *bidonvilles:* The terms vary depending on the nation and language, but the meaning is the same—"squatter settlements." In **squatter settlements,** areas occupied by the very poor on the fringe of cities, housing is constructed by the settlers themselves from discarded material, including crates from loading docks and loose lumber from building projects. While the term *squatter settlement* has wide use, many observers prefer to use a less pejorative term, such as *autonomous settlements.*

This type of settlement is typical of cities in the world's developing nations. In such countries, new housing has not kept pace with the combined urban population growth resulting from births and migration from rural areas. Squatter settlements also swell when city dwellers are forced out of housing by astronomical jumps in rent. By definition, squatters living on vacant land are trespassers and can be legally evicted. However, given the large number of poor people who live in such settlements, governments generally look the other way.

Obviously, squatters live in substandard housing, yet that is only one of the many problems they face. Residents do not receive most public services, since their presence cannot be legally recognized. Police and fire protection, paved streets, and sanitary sewers are virtually nonexistent. In some countries, squatters may have trouble voting or enrolling their children in public schools.

Despite such conditions, squatter settlements are not always as bleak as they may appear from the outside. You can often find a well-developed social organization there, rather than a disorganized collection of people. Typically, a thriving

Even Mongolia has squatter communities. Nomadic herders created this shantytown near Mongolia's capital, Ulan Bator, home to one-quarter of the nation's population.

"informal economy" develops: residents establish small, home-based businesses such as grocery stores, jewellery shops, and the like. Local churches, men's clubs, and women's clubs are often established in specific neighbourhoods within settlements.

> *Squatter settlements are not always as bleak as they may appear from the outside.*

Squatter settlements remind us that theoretical models that were developed in the United States may not apply directly to other cultures. The various ecological models of urban growth, for example, would not explain a metropolitan expansion that locates the poorest people on the urban fringes. Furthermore, solutions that are logical in a highly industrialized nation may not be relevant to developing nations. In developing nations, rather than focusing on large-scale solutions to urban problems, planners must think in terms of providing basic amenities, such as water or electrical power for the ever-expanding squatter settlements.

Apply the Theory

1. Do you know of any squatters in your community? If so, describe them and the place where they live.
2. Given the number of homeless people in Canada, why aren't there more squatters?

Sources: Neuwirth 2004; Perlman 2010; Yap 1998.

table 15-6 Comparing Approaches to Urbanization

	Urban Ecology	New Urban Sociology
Theoretical Perspective	Functionalist	Conflict
Primary Focus	Relationship of urban areas to their spatial setting and physical environment	Relationship of urban areas to global, national, and local forces
Key Source of Change	Technological innovations, such as new methods of transportation	Economic competition and monopolization of power
Initiator of Actions	Individuals, neighbourhoods, communities	Real estate developers, banks and other financial institutions, multinational corporations
Allied Disciplines	Geography, architecture	Political science, economics

Though the African country of Kenya is mostly rural, Nairobi, a city with almost a million residents, is a modern urban area with international business connections. According to world systems analysis, the cities of developing nations exist on the periphery of the global economy, controlled and exploited by the more powerful industrialized nations.

being based on primary relationships (i.e., face to face, personal, and ongoing) to secondary relationships (i.e., detached, impersonal, and fragmented). Although people in urban areas, according to Wirth, gain greater autonomy, independence, and freedom from community norms and sanctions, they also lose the sense of intimacy, connection, and support that accompany primary forms of interaction.

Urban life is noteworthy for its diversity, so it would be a serious mistake to see all city residents as being alike. Sociologist Herbert J. Gans has distinguished among five types of people found in cities (1991):

1. *Cosmopolites*. These residents remain in cities to take advantage of unique cultural and intellectual benefits. Writers, artists, and scholars fall into this category.

life have generally neglected the impact of industrialization and urbanization on the lives of women—women in the private sphere caring for their children, and those, as has increasingly been the case, also employed in workplaces in urban areas. Recently, urban studies have highlighted the ways in which patriarchy underpins how social life is organized, both in private and in public spheres or urban centres (Markusen 2013).

As is consistent with the research in Chapter 9 on female students' feelings of safety on Canadian university campuses, safety is a major concern for women living in urban centres. In 2004, Statistics Canada revealed that 58 percent of women worried about their safety waiting for or using public transportation alone after dark (twice the proportion of male night-time users). Women, in contrast to men, were almost three times as likely to be afraid to walk in their neighbourhoods after dark (Statistics Canada 2005j).

Interactionist View

Sociologist Louis Wirth argued that a relatively large and permanent settlement leads to distinctive patterns of behaviour, which he called **urbanism** (1928, 1938). He identified three critical factors contributing to urbanism: the size of the population, the population density, and the heterogeneity (variety) of the population. A frequent result of urbanism, according to Wirth, is that we become insensitive to events around us and restrict our attention to the primary groups to which we are emotionally attached.

Wirth suggested that urbanization brings with it a way of life resulting from such factors as the spatial segregation of people according to class, race and ethnicity, and occupation. In this way of life, human interaction changes from

2. *Unmarried and child-free people.* Such people choose to live in cities because of the active nightlife and varied recreational opportunities.

3. *Ethnic villagers.* These urban residents prefer to live in their own tight-knit communities. Typically, immigrant groups isolate themselves in such neighbourhoods to avoid resentment from well-established urban dwellers.

4. *The deprived.* Very poor people and families have little choice but to live in low-rent, and often run-down, urban neighbourhoods.

5. *The trapped.* Some city residents want to leave urban centres but cannot because of their limited economic resources and prospects. Gans includes the "downward mobiles" in this category—people who once held higher social positions but who are forced to live in less prestigious neighbourhoods owing to the loss of a job, death of a wage earner, or old age. Both elderly individuals living alone and families may feel "trapped" in part because they resent changes in their communities. Their desire to live elsewhere may reflect their uneasiness with unfamiliar immigrant groups who have become their neighbours.

These categories remind us that the city represents a choice (even a dream) for certain people and a nightmare for others. Gans's work underscores the importance of neighbourhoods in contemporary urban life. Ernest Burgess, in his study of life in Chicago in the 1920s, paid special attention to the ethnic neighbourhoods of that city. Many decades after Burgess conducted his study, residents in such districts as Chinatown or Greektown in many large urban centres continue to feel attached to their own ethnic communities rather than to the larger unit of a city. Even outside ethnic enclaves, a special sense of belonging can take hold in a neighbourhood.

The term *defended neighbourhood* is one which is used to refer to people's definitions of their community boundaries. Neighbourhoods acquire unique identities because residents view them as geographically separate—and socially different—from adjacent areas. The **defended neighbourhood**, in effect, becomes a sentimental union of similar people. Neighbourhood phone directories, community newspapers, school and parish boundaries, and business advertisements all serve to define an area and distinguish it from nearby communities.

15.9 What Are Some Types of Communities?

Communities vary substantially in the degree to which their members feel connected and share a common identity. Ferdinand Tönnies used the term *Gemeinschaft* to describe a close-knit community in which social interaction among people is intimate and familiar ([1887] 1988). It is the kind of place where people in a coffee shop will stop talking when anyone enters, because they are sure to know whoever walks through the door. A shopper at the small grocery store in this town would expect to know every employee and probably every other customer as well. By contrast, the ideal type of *Gesellschaft* describes modern urban life, in which people feel little in common with others. Their social relationships often are a result of interactions focused on immediate tasks, such as purchasing a product. Contemporary city life in Canada generally resembles a *Gesellschaft*.

The following sections will examine different types of communities found in Canada, focusing on the distinctive characteristics and problems of central cities, suburbs, and rural communities.

Central Cities

In terms of land mass, Canada is the second-largest nation in the world. Yet, more than two-thirds of the population is located near the U.S. border on land that comprises a mere fraction of the nation's total geographical area. As we have mentioned, more than half of Canada's population is heavily concentrated in four urban regions or **central cities.** Even those who live outside central cities, such as residents of suburban and rural communities, find that urban centres heavily influence their lifestyles.

Urban Dwellers Many urban residents are the descendants of European immigrants—Irish, Italians, Jews, Poles, and others—who came to Canada in the nineteenth and early twentieth centuries. With a "vertical mosaic" firmly entrenched in Canada, the cities socialized newcomers to the norms, values, and language of their new homeland and gave them unequal opportunity to work their way up the economic ladder. In addition, a substantial number of Canadians of European descent came to the cities from rural farming areas in the period following World War II.

Cities in Canada are the destinations of immigrants from around the world, particularly those from China, India, the

Philippines, and Hong Kong. Yet, unlike those who came to this country 100 years ago, current immigrants are arriving at a time of high housing costs in the larger cities. This makes it more difficult for them to find decent housing.

With the increase of immigration to centres other than Toronto and Vancouver, such as Calgary and Regina, "multiculturalism is spreading to second tier cities as well as small towns in the form of ethnic institutions and services. . . There is a need for reasonable accommodation of ethnic needs in urban planning [in Canada]" (Qadeer 2009).

Issues Facing Cities People and neighbourhoods vary greatly within any city in Canada. Yet all residents of a central city—regardless of social class, racial, and ethnic differences—face certain common problems. Crime, air pollution, noise, crumbling infrastructures, congested roads and freeways, inadequate public transportation—these unpleasant realities and many more are an increasing feature of contemporary urban life. Municipal governments of large metropolitan cities, such as Toronto, have long been lobbying the federal and provincial governments to increase the amount of revenue that is transferred to the cities. City governments argue that the provincial and federal governments ought to carry more of the burden for the cost of upgrading roads and bridges, repairing crumbling sewers, and refurbishing and expanding public transportation systems.

A critical problem for the cities is mass transportation. In 1951, there were five people for every registered vehicle in Canada; by the mid-1980s, there were two people for every registered vehicle and that number has remained steady (Statistics Canada 2006f). By 2010, in some provinces, such as Newfoundland and Labrador, the number of vehicles outnumbered the number of people (CBC News 2012c). Canada has the fifth highest rate of car ownership per capita in the world. Growing traffic congestion in metropolitan areas has led many cities to recognize a need for safe, efficient, and inexpensive mass transit systems. However, the federal government has traditionally given much more assistance to highway programs than to public transit. Conflict theorists note that such a bias favours the relatively affluent (automobile owners) as well as corporations such as auto manufacturers, tire makers, and oil companies. Meanwhile, low-income residents of metropolitan

Large cities in Canada, such as Toronto (shown here), are becoming increasingly diverse due to international migration.

To alleviate gridlock, officials in London, England, charge vehicles about $15 a day to enter designated congestion zones. At least initially, significant traffic reductions resulted, leading city planners around the world to consider adopting the idea.

areas, who are much less likely to own cars than are members of the middle and upper classes, face higher fares on public transit along with deteriorating service.

Suburbs

The term *suburb* was derived from the Latin *sub urbe,* meaning "under the city." Until recent times, most suburbs were just that—tiny communities totally dependent on urban centres for jobs, recreation, and even water.

Today, the term **suburb** defies any simple definition. The term generally refers to any community near a large city or any territory within a metropolitan area that is not included in the central city. Large cities and the suburbs that surround them make up a metropolitan area in which people live in one part of the area and work or go to school in another (e.g., living in Delta, British Columbia, and working in Vancouver). In the 2011 Census, Statistics Canada considered Census Metropolitan Areas (CMAs) to be urban, suburban, and rural areas of more than 100 000 people that are socially and economically integrated.

Three social factors differentiate suburbs from cities. First, suburbs are generally less dense than cities; in the newest suburbs, there are often no more than four dwellings on a hectare of land. Second, the suburbs consist almost exclusively of private space. Private ornamental lawns replace common park areas for the most part. Third, suburbs have more exacting building design codes than cities, and these codes have become increasingly precise in the last decade. Although the suburbs may be diverse in population, such design standards give the impression of uniformity.

It can also be difficult to distinguish between suburbs and rural areas. Certain criteria generally define suburbs: Most people work at urban (as opposed to rural) jobs, and local governments provide services, such as water supply, sewage disposal, and fire protection. In rural areas, these services are less common, and a greater proportion of residents are employed in farming and related activities.

Suburban Expansion Whatever the precise definition of a suburb, it is clear that suburbs have expanded. In fact, suburbanization was the most dramatic demographic trend in Canada throughout the twentieth century. Suburban areas grew at first along railroad lines, then at the terminal points of streetcar tracks, and, by the 1950s, along the nation's growing systems of freeways and expressways. The suburban boom has been especially evident since World War II.

According to University of Toronto demographer David Foot, increased urbanization was arguably the most controversial finding of the 2001 Census. However, he believes that the real trend was suburbanization, not urbanization (Foot 2002). For example, the City of Toronto has grown by 4 percent since 1996, while the Greater Toronto Area's growth was twice that number. Foot notes that similar patterns occurred in Edmonton, Montreal, Calgary, and Vancouver. Foot contends that during the 1980s and 1990s, the baby boom generation moved to the suburbs to raise their children (what he refers to as the "echo boom"). When considering whether such a trend will continue, Foot looks at the issue this way: "Migration to these urban clusters from the rest of the country will, undoubtedly, continue to contribute to this suburban growth. And most aging boomers will not immediately sell their suburban homes because they are hoping that their future grandchildren will come and visit" (Foot 2002: A17). Numbers from the 2006 Census show that the trend of suburbanization has continued. Between 2001 and 2006, the percentage growth of suburban residents was greater than that of the core city itself (Weeks 2007).

Suburbanization was the most dramatic demographic trend in Canada throughout the twentieth century. The exacting building design codes often give the impression of uniformity.

Population, Health, and Communities **341**

Diversity in the Suburbs In Canada, race and ethnicity remain the most important factors distinguishing cities from suburbs. Nevertheless, the common assumption that suburbia includes only prosperous whites is far from correct. In the last 20 years, we have witnessed the diversification of suburbs in terms of race and ethnicity. For example, by 2006, more than 45 percent of the people living in the Vancouver suburb of Richmond were Chinese; Richmond also has a significant South Asian population. Like the rest of the nation, members of racial and ethnic minorities are becoming suburban dwellers (Statistics Canada 2008).

The term *ethnoburbia* was coined by geographer Wei Li. Ethnoburbia refers to the growing trend toward **ethnoburbs**— suburbs that are multiethnic, multicultural, multiracial, multilingual, and often multinational and contain a wide variety of income groups whose members are white-collar and well educated. The ethnoburb serves not only as an ethnic residential suburb but also as a community centre and place of business (Li 2008). In the United States, a study of suburban residential patterns in 11 metropolitan areas found that Asian Americans and Hispanics tend to reside in equivalent socioeconomic areas with whites—that is, affluent Hispanics live alongside affluent whites, poor Asians near poor whites, and so on. However, the case for African Americans is quite distinct. Suburban blacks live in poorer suburbs than whites do, even after taking into account differences in individuals' income, education, and home ownership.

Again, in contrast to prevailing stereotypes, the suburbs include a significant number of low-income people from diverse backgrounds, including both visible-minority and non–visible-minority groups. Poverty is not conventionally associated with the suburbs, partly because the suburban poor tend to be scattered among more affluent people. In some instances, suburban communities intentionally hide social problems, such as homelessness, so they can maintain a "respectable image."

Rural Communities

As we have seen, the people of Canada live mainly in urban centres; according to the 2011 Census, this includes 81 percent of Canadians. As is true of the suburbs, it would be a mistake to view rural communities as fitting into one set image. Grain farms, potash towns, cattle ranches, and gas stations along the Trans-Canada Highway are all part of the rural landscape of Canada.

The historic stereotype of the farmer is a white male. Yet women have long played a significant role in agriculture, both in Canada and throughout the world. Women participate actively in agriculture—on large and small farms, and in profitable and failing family businesses. Farming women are almost always married and generally have families. In Canada, in 2006 the percentage of farms operated by women was 27.8 percent, up slightly from the 2001 Census (Statistics Canada 2009). Segregation by gender is typical of farm labour: men

are more likely to be engaged in fieldwork, while women are more likely to serve their farms as accountants, personnel and equipment managers, and purchasing agents.

The 2011 Census showed that a disproportionately high number of self-employed Canadians live in rural areas and small towns, outside the commuting distances to larger cities (Statistics Canada 2012) Agriculture made up the largest sector of self-employed Canadians living in rural communities (Statistics Canada 2012).

In 2004, the federal government appointed a Canada research chair in the new rural economy. The appointee studies the linkages between technological change and economic growth in rural areas. The focus of this research on rural life includes an examination of how information and knowledge-intensive technologies play a role in the sustainability of rural areas in Canada.

In smaller communities, the construction of oversized malls (known as *power centres*) that usually contain large businesses, such as Walmart, Home Depot, or Costco, can create problems. Although many residents welcome the new employment opportunities and the convenience of one-stop shopping, local merchants see their long-time family businesses endangered by formidable 200 000-square-foot competitors with national reputations. Even when such big-box discount stores provide a short-term boost to a local economy (and they do not always do so), they can undermine a town's sense of community and identity.

Rural communities that do survive may feel threatened by provincial and territorial governments that, in the name of fiscal responsibility, have cut such services as health care, education, legal and court services, and various other social programs in rural areas. Many rural residents must now travel to larger urban areas to seek medical treatment or counselling or to attend court hearings.

On a more positive note, advances in electronic communication have allowed some people in Canada to work wherever they want. For those who are concerned about quality-of-life issues (e.g., clean environment, affordable housing, community cohesion, lack of congestion), working at home in a rural area that has access to the latest high-tech services is the perfect arrangement. No matter where people make their homes—whether in the city, the suburbs, or a rural village— economic and technological change will have an impact on their quality of life.

::: use your sociological *imagination* :::

You have fast-forwarded to a future in which there are no central cities—just sprawling suburbs and isolated rural communities. What are the economic and social effects of the disappearance of the downtown area?

Social Policy and Health

The AIDS Crisis

The Issue

In his novel *The Plague,* Albert Camus (1948:34) wrote, "There have been as many plagues as wars in history, yet always plagues and wars take people equally by surprise." Regarded by many as the distinctive plague of the modern era, AIDS certainly caught major social institutions—particularly the government, the health-care system, and the economy—by surprise when it was first noticed by medical practitioners in the early 1980s. It has since spread around the world. While encouraging new therapies have been developed to treat AIDS, there is currently no way to eradicate the disease by medical means. Therefore, it is essential to protect people by reducing the transmission of the fatal virus. But how is that to be done, and whose responsibility is it? What is the role of social institutions in preventing the spread of AIDS?

The Setting

AIDS is the acronym for *acquired immune deficiency syndrome.* Rather than being a distinct disease, AIDS is actually a predisposition to disease that is caused by a virus, the human immunodeficiency virus (HIV). The virus gradually destroys the body's immune system, leaving the carrier vulnerable to infections such as pneumonia that those with healthy immune systems can generally resist. Transmission of the virus from one person to another appears to require either intimate sexual contact or exchange of blood or bodily fluids (whether from contaminated hypodermic needles or syringes, transfusions of infected blood, or transmission from an infected mother to her child before or during birth).

The first cases of AIDS in Canada were reported in 1982. While the numbers of new cases and deaths have recently shown some evidence of decline, an estimated 65 000 people in Canada were living with AIDS or HIV by the end of 2008 (Public Health Agency of Canada 2010). Aboriginal peoples, particularly Aboriginal women, are over-represented in the AIDS epidemic in Canada. Worldwide, AIDS is stabilizing, with an estimated 33.3 million people infected (see Figure 15-6). The disease is not evenly distributed; those areas least equipped to deal with it—the developing nations of sub-Saharan Africa—face the greatest challenge (Centers for Disease Control and Prevention 2011a).

Sociological Insights

Dramatic crises like the AIDS pandemic are likely to bring about certain transformations in a society's social structure. From a functionalist perspective, if established social institutions cannot meet a crucial need, new social networks are likely to emerge

figure 15-6 People Living With HIV

MAPPING LIFE WORLDWIDE

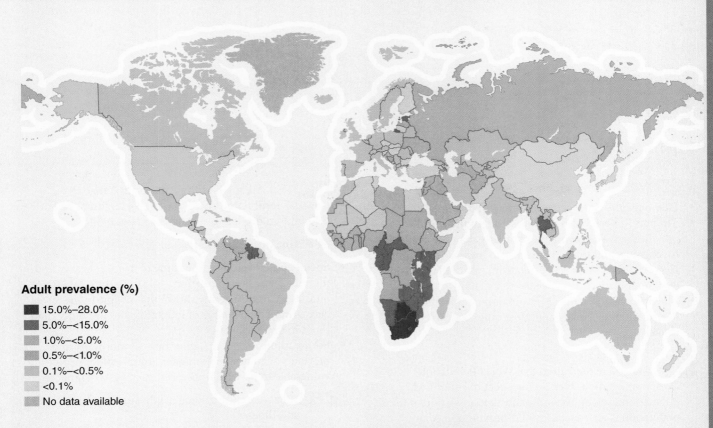

Adult prevalence (%)

- 15.0%–28.0%
- 5.0%–<15.0%
- 1.0%–<5.0%
- 0.5%–<1.0%
- 0.1%–<0.5%
- <0.1%
- No data available

Note: Data for the 33.3 million people (estimated range, 31.4–35.8 million) living with HIV at the end of 2009.

Source: UNAIDS 2010:23.

to perform that function. In the case of AIDS, self-help groups—especially in the gay communities of major cities—have organized to care for the sick, educate the healthy, and lobby for more responsive public policies.

The label "person with AIDS" or "HIV-positive" often functions as a master status. People who have AIDS or are infected with the HIV virus face a powerful dual stigma. Not only are they associated with a lethal and contagious disease, but they also have to contend with a disease that disproportionately afflicts already stigmatized groups, such as gay males and intravenous drug users. This link to stigmatized groups delayed recognition of the severity of the AIDS pandemic. The media took little interest in the disease until it seemed to be spreading beyond the gay community.

Viewed from a conflict perspective, policymakers were slow to respond to the AIDS crisis because those in high-risk groups—gay men and IV drug users—were comparatively powerless. Furthermore, studies show that some racialized and ethnic groups are diagnosed later and are slower to get treatment. New programs have been launched to address this disparity in treatment (Glanton 2007).

On the micro level of social interaction, observers once forecast that AIDS would lead to a more conservative sexual climate in which people would be much more cautious about becoming involved with new partners. Yet it appears that many sexually active people have not heeded precautions about so-called safe sex. Data from studies conducted in the early 1990s indicated a growing complacency about AIDS, even among those who were most vulnerable (Bernstein 2004).

Policy Initiatives

AIDS has struck all societies, but not all nations can respond in the same manner. Studies done in North America show that, today, people with HIV or AIDS who receive appropriate medical treatment are living longer than they did in the past. This advance may put additional pressure on policymakers to address the issues raised by the spread of AIDS.

In some nations, cultural practices may prevent people from dealing realistically with the AIDS epidemic. They may not be likely to take the necessary preventive measures, including open discussion of sexuality and drug use. Prevention has shown signs of working among target groups, such as drug users, pregnant women, and gay men, but preventive initiatives are few and far between in developing nations.

Despite an increase in the availability of AIDS drugs in non-industrial countries, concern remains about the equity in the global fight against HIV/AIDS. In 2007 activists criticized pharmaceutical companies for delaying the delivery of new AIDS medicines to countries like Thailand, because of suspicion that those nations were planning to produce their own generic versions. Officials in the affected countries responded that the corporations' efforts to lower drug prices in their countries were insufficient (Japsen 2007).

The high cost of drug-treatment programs has generated intensive worldwide pressure on the major pharmaceutical companies to lower the prices to patients in developing nations, especially in sub-Saharan Africa. Bowing to this pressure, several of the companies agreed to make the combination therapies available at cost. As a result, the accessibility of HIV treatment has increased steadily, though it has hardly become universal. By the beginning of 2008, only 11 percent of mothers who needed therapy to prevent transmission of the virus to their babies were receiving it (R. Wolf 2008).

Apply the Theory

1. What perspective might feminist sociologists bring to the discussion on the global crisis of HIV/AIDS?
2. From a conflict perspective, what groups would be less likely to receive experimental treatments for HIV/AIDS? Why?
3. If you were an interactionist sociologist who wanted to understand why some people knowingly ignore the dangers of AIDS, how would you go about studying the problem?

CHAPTER RESOURCES

Summary

::: **15.1** What Is Demography?
- **Demography** is the scientific study of population.
- Thomas Robert Malthus suggested that the world's population was growing more rapidly than the available food supply and that this gap would increase over time. However, Karl Marx saw capitalism, rather than a rising world population, as the cause of social ills.
- The primary mechanism for obtaining population information in Canada and most other countries is the **census**.

::: **15.2** What Are the Patterns of World Population?
- Developing nations face the prospect of continued population growth because a substantial portion of their population is approaching child-bearing age. Many developed nations have begun to stabilize their population growth.

::: **15.3** What Are the Fertility Patterns in Canada?
- Canada's fertility rate in 2006 was 1.54 children, below the 2.1 children needed to sustain the population.

::: **15.4** What Is Social Epidemiology?
- **Social epidemiology** is the study of disease, health, and disability, across a population.
- Studies have consistently shown that people in the lower classes have higher rates of **mortality** and disability than those in upper classes.
- Ethnic minorities have higher rates of morbidity and mortality than do the dominant groups. Older people are vulnerable to particular diseases, such as Alzheimer's.

::: **15.5** What Are the Sociological Perspectives on Health and Illness?
- The functionalist perspective on health and illness sees physicians as "gatekeepers" for the **sick role**, either

verifying a person's condition as "ill" or designating the person as "recovered."

- Conflict theorists use the term **medicalization of society** to refer to medicine's growing role as a major institution of social control. Feminist theorists look at the ways in which the institution of medicine is gendered.

::: 15.6 What Is the Health-Care Situation in Canada?
- Canada's health-care system, as set out in the Canada Health Act, is based on the principles of public administration, comprehensiveness, universality, portability, and accessibility.

::: 15.7 How Have Communities Changed?
- Stable communities emerged when humans became farmers and their surplus production allowed others to inhabit pre-industrial cities.
- Mechanization of production brought about the **industrial city**, characterized by a large population and domination

of factories. Globalization and technology have led to the emergence of the **post-industrial city**, where corporate offices are dominant rather than factories.

::: 15.8 What Is Urbanization, and What Are Its Consequences?
- **Urban ecology** is a functionalist view of urbanization that focuses on how the different elements of the urban area are interrelated and contribute to stability.
- **New urban sociology** is a conflict view of urbanization, which considers the interplay of a community's political and economic interests as well as the impact of the global economy on communities. This view draws on Immanuel Wallerstein's *world-systems analysis* (see Chapter 7 for a discussion of this term).

::: 15.9 What Are Some Types of Communities?
- Types of communities include central cities, suburbs, and rural communities.

Critical Thinking Questions

1. Some European nations are now experiencing population declines. Their death rates are low and their birth rates are even lower than in stage III of the demographic transition model. Does this pattern suggest that there is now a fourth stage in the demographic transition? Even more important, what are the implications of negative population growth for an industrialized nation in the twenty-first century?

2. How would you characterize the relationship between you and your doctor? How does the dimension of power play into that relationship?

3. How has your home community changed over the years you have lived there? Have there been significant changes in the community's economic base? Have the community's social problems intensified or lessened over time? What are the community's future prospects?

THINKING ABOUT MOVIES

Sicko

Made by the controversial documentary filmmaker Michael Moore, *Sicko* tells the story of the U.S. health-care system. With comparisons to the health-care systems in countries like France and Canada, Moore builds the case for drastic change in the U.S. health-care system.

Dark Days

This documentary tells the story of a community of homeless people who live underground near a railroad station.

Winter's Bone

In an economically disadvantaged part of rural America, a young woman uses community ties to search for her father.

connect **LEARNSMART** **SMARTBOOK**

For more information on the resources available from McGraw-Hill Ryerson, go to **www.mcgrawhill.ca/he/solutions**.

inside

Sometimes a low-tech solution can be more helpful than a high-tech invention. In Nepal, Bhutanese refugees use solar cookers, a low-tech adaptation of traditional cooking methods. This simple device, which heats food without firewood, addresses a critical need for fuel in many parts of the world.

> "If you pull out your smart phone and click the button that says 'locate me' on your Google or Yahoo! map application, you will see a small dot appear in the middle of your screen.
>
> That's you!
>
> If you start walking down the street in any direction, the whole screen will move right along with you, no matter where you go. This is a dramatic change from the print-on-paper world, where maps and locations are based around places and landmarks, not on you or your location. People don't go to the store and say, 'Oh, excuse me, can I buy a map of me?' They go to the store and ask for a map of New York, or Amsterdam, or the subway system. You and I aren't anywhere to be seen on these maps. The maps are locations that we fit into.
>
> But today's digital world has changed that. Kevin Slavin, a creator of location-based services and games and the cofounder of the gaming company Area/Code, put this succinctly at a technology conference last year: 'We are always in the center of the map.'
>
> Though Slavin was talking about location-based games and Google maps, the center of the map, it turns out, is actually much bigger than a dot on the screen. It's a very powerful place to be.
>
> Being in the center—instead of somewhere off to the side or off the page altogether—changes everything. It changes your conception of space, time, and location. It changes your sense of place and community. It changes the way you view the information, news, and data coming in over your computer and your phone. And it changes your role in a transaction, empowering you to decide quite specifically what content to buy and how to buy and use it rather than simply accepting the traditional material that companies have packaged on your behalf.
>
> Now you are the starting point. Now the digital world follows you, not the other way around.
>
> . . .
>
> I got my own hard lesson in this new Me! Now! world when some friends stopped by our house with their teenage cousin Lauren. As I started making coffee for our guests, Lauren asked if she could use my laptop to 'check the news.' I handed it over.
>
> I was curious about which news sites she was going to, so I asked her, expecting to hear something like CNN or NYTimes, or maybe TMZ, the Hollywood gossip site. With a sincere face she looked up at me and said, 'Facebook.' Then she turned back to the computer and continued reading.
>
> *Being in the center—instead of somewhere off to the side or off the page altogether—changes everything. It changes your conception of space, time, and location. It changes your sense of place and community.*
>
> 'I thought you were going to read the news,' I said.
> 'This is my news,' she replied.
> To Lauren and many in her age group, news is not defined by newspapers, or broadcast television stations, or even bloggers or renegades. Instead, news is what is relevant to the individual. . . ."

(Bilton 2011:161–162, 164–165)

In this excerpt from *I Live in the Future & Here's How It Works: Why Your World, Work, and Brain Are Being Creatively Disrupted*, technology writer Nick Bilton suggests that, increasingly, new communications technologies are allowing us to centre our communities, as well as our news and entertainment, on ourselves. So besides the global community—a virtual community knit together by new information technologies—we are creating a multitude of personal communities, each revolving around a single individual. How will this self-centred approach to information gathering change what we know (or do not know) about our society and other societies? More important, will our society change? The answers to these questions rest with each of us.

Social change often does follow the introduction of a new technology, in this case the computer. **Social change** has been defined as significant alteration over time in behaviour patterns and culture (Moore 1967). But what constitutes a "significant" alteration? Certainly, the dramatic rise in formal education documented in Chapter 13 represents a change that has had profound social consequences. Other social changes that have had long-term and important consequences include the emergence of slavery as a system of stratification (see Chapter 6), the Industrial Revolution (Chapters 5 and 15), the increased participation of women in the paid labour force in Canada and other industrialized countries (Chapter 9), and the worldwide population explosion (Chapter 15). In many instances, the social movements that we cover in this chapter have played an important role in promoting social change.

How does social change happen? Is the process unpredictable, or can we make certain generalizations about it? Has globalization contributed to social change? And how has our environment been affected by social change? In this chapter, we examine the process of social change, with special emphasis on the impact of globalization and the effects on our environment. We begin with social movements—collective efforts to bring about deliberate social change. Then, we turn to the unanticipated social change that occurs when innovations such as new technologies sweep through society. Efforts to explain long-term social change have led to the development of theories of change; we consider the evolutionary, functionalist, conflict, feminist, and interactionist approaches to change. We see how vested interests attempt to block changes that they see as threatening. We see, too, that the process of globalization means that these social changes often happen on a global scale. And we look at what social change has done to our environment. Finally, in the social policy section, we discuss a controversial effect of global social change, the creation of **transnationals**—immigrants with an allegiance to more than one nation. ■

What Are Social Movements?

Although such factors as physical environment, population, technology, and social inequality serve as sources of change, it is the collective effort of individuals organized in social movements that ultimately leads to change. Sociologists use the term **social movement** to refer to an organized collective activity to bring about or resist fundamental change in an existing group or society (Benford 1992). Herbert Blumer recognized the special importance of social movements when he defined them as "collective enterprises to establish a new order of life" (1955:19).

In many nations, including Canada, social movements have had a dramatic impact on the course of history and the evolution of the social structure. Consider the actions of environmentalists, feminists, anti-globalization protesters, and anti-poverty activists. Members of each social movement stepped outside traditional channels for bringing about social change, yet had a noticeable influence on public policy. In Eastern Europe, equally dramatic collective efforts helped to topple Communist party regimes in a largely peaceful manner, in nations that many observers had thought were "immune" to such social change (Ramet 1991).

Though social movements imply the existence of conflict, we can also analyze their activities from a functionalist perspective. Even when they are unsuccessful, social movements contribute to the formation of public opinion. Initially, people thought the ideas of Margaret Sanger and other early advocates of birth control were radical, yet contraceptives are now widely available in North America. Moreover, functionalists view social movements as training grounds for leaders of the political establishment. Former heads of state such as Cuba's Fidel Castro and South Africa's Nelson Mandela came to power after serving as leaders of revolutionary movements.

Occupy Vancouver protesters gather at the Vancouver Art Gallery on September 17, 2012.

Poland's Lech Walesa, Russia's Boris Yeltsin, and the Czech playwright Vaclav Havel all led protest movements against Communist party rule and later became leaders of their countries' governments.

Because social movements know no borders, even nationalistic movements like those led by Castro and Walesa are deeply influenced by global events. Increasingly, social movements are taking on an international dimension from the

Occupy Wall Street protesters march through the streets of New York's financial district on the one year anniversary of the Occupy Wall Street movement on September 17, 2012.

start. Global enterprises, in particular, lend themselves to targeting through international mobilization, whether they are corporations like McDonald's, events such as the Olympics, or governmental bodies like the World Trade Organization (WTO). Global activism is not new, however; it is generally held that it began with the writing of Karl Marx, who sought to mobilize oppressed peoples in other industrialized countries. Today, activist networking is facilitated by the Internet and by relatively cheap travel costs. Participation in transnational activism is much wider now than in the past, and passions are quicker to ignite (Della Porta and Tarrow 2005; Tarrow 2005). In 2011, the Occupy Movement became an international phenomenon focusing upon economic, political, and social inequality. Occupy Wall Street, inspired by the Canadian anti-consumerist group Adbusters, spread to Occupy protests in 82 countries including 20 cities in Canada. Advancing the slogan "We are the 99%," the protests focused on issues related to growing inequality specific to various countries and the

Two members of People for the Ethical Treatment of Animals (PETA) protest against the killing of animals for fur coats. Social movements like PETA seek public attention for the positions they espouse.

increasing wealth of the top 1 percent. In Canada, the top 1 percent is 83 percent male and has an average income of $450 000. According to the Canadian Centre for Policy Alternatives, the average CEO makes 189 times more than the average Canadian wage and the economic disparity between the 1 percent and the 99 percent is widening (Canadian Centre for Policy Alternatives 2012).

How and why do social movements emerge? Obviously, people are often discontented with the way things are. But what causes them to organize at a particular moment in a collective effort to effect change? Sociologists rely on two explanations for why people mobilize: the relative deprivation and resource mobilization approaches.

Relative Deprivation Approach

Those members of a society who feel most frustrated and disgruntled by social and economic conditions are not necessarily the worst off in an objective sense. Social scientists have long recognized that what is most significant is the way in which people *perceive* their situation. As Karl Marx pointed out, although the misery of the workers was important to their perception of their oppressed state, so was their position *in relation to* the capitalist ruling class (Marx and Engels [1847] 1955).

The term **relative deprivation** is defined as the conscious feeling of a negative discrepancy between legitimate expectations and present actualities (Wilson 1973). In other words, things aren't as good as you hoped they would be. Such a state may be characterized by scarcity rather than a complete lack of necessities (as we saw in the distinction between absolute and relative poverty in Chapter 6). A relatively deprived person is dissatisfied because he or she feels downtrodden relative to some appropriate reference group. Thus, blue-collar workers who live in apartments, though hardly at the bottom of the economic ladder, may nevertheless feel deprived in comparison to corporate managers and professionals who live in lavish homes in exclusive suburbs.

In addition to the feeling of relative deprivation, two other elements must be present before discontent will be channelled into a social movement. People must feel that they have a *right* to their goals, that they deserve better than what they have. For example, the struggle against European colonialism in Africa intensified when growing numbers of Africans decided that it was legitimate for them to have political and economic independence. At the same time, the disadvantaged group must perceive that its goals cannot be attained through conventional means. This belief may or may not be correct. Whichever is the case, the group will not mobilize into a social movement unless there is a shared perception that members can end their relative deprivation only through collective action (Morrison 1971).

Critics of this approach have noted that people don't need to feel deprived to be moved to act. In addition, this approach fails to explain why certain feelings of deprivation are transformed into social movements, whereas in other similar situations, no collective effort is made to reshape society. Consequently, in recent years, sociologists have paid increasing attention to the forces needed to bring about the emergence of social movements (Pastor and Ortiz 2009; Ramos and Standbridge 2012).

Resource Mobilization Approach

It takes more than desire to start a social movement. It helps to have money, political influence, access to the media, and personnel. The term **resource mobilization** refers to the ways in which a social movement utilizes such resources. The success of a movement for change will depend in good part on what resources it has and how effectively it mobilizes them (see also Gamson 1989; Staggenborg 1989a, 1989b). Sociologist Anthony Oberschall has argued that to sustain social protest or resistance, there must be an "organizational base and continuity of leadership" (1973:199). As people become part of a social movement, norms develop to guide their behaviour. Members of the movement may be expected to attend regular meetings of organizations, pay dues, recruit new adherents, and boycott "enemy" products or speakers. An emerging social movement may give rise to special language or new words for familiar terms. Social movements have been responsible for such new terms of self-reference as *blacks, African Canadians,* and *African Americans* (used to replace *Negroes*); *senior citizens* (used to replace *old folks*); *gays* (used to replace *homosexuals*); and *people with disabilities* (used to replace *the handicapped*).

Leadership is a central factor in the mobilization of the discontented into social movements. Often, a movement will be led by a charismatic figure, such as Nelson Mandela or Dr. Martin Luther King Jr. As Max Weber described it in 1904, *charisma* is that quality of an individual that sets him or her apart from ordinary people. Of course, charisma can fade abruptly, which helps to account for the fragility of certain social movements (Morris 2000).

Yet many social movements do persist over long periods because their leadership is well organized and ongoing. Ironically, as Robert Michels noted, political movements that are fighting for social change eventually take on some of the aspects of the bureaucracy that they were organized to protest (1915). Leaders tend to dominate the decision-making process without directly consulting followers. The bureaucratization of social movements is not inevitable, however. Recent movements—such as the Occupy Movement—that advocate major structural change in society and embrace mass action tended not to be hierarchical or bureaucratic (OccupyWallSt.org 2012).

Why do certain individuals join a social movement while others who are in similar situations do not? Some of them are recruited to join. Karl Marx recognized the importance of recruitment when he called on workers to become aware of their oppressed status and to develop a class consciousness. Like theorists of the resource-mobilization approach, Marx held that a social movement (specifically, the revolt of the proletariat) would require leaders to sharpen the awareness of the oppressed. They would need to help workers to overcome feelings of *false consciousness*, or attitudes that do not reflect workers' objective position, in order to organize a revolutionary movement. Similarly, one of the challenges faced by feminists of the late 1960s and early 1970s in North America was to convince women that they were being deprived of their rights and of socially valued resources. As we mentioned in an earlier discussion on the feminist movement in Canada (see Chapter 9), white, middle-class women have often fought for their vision of social or moral reform, which did not necessarily serve the interests of all women.

Gender and Social Movements

Sociologists point out that gender is an important element in understanding social movements. In male-dominated societies, such as Canada, many women—particularly those who are older, disabled, and/or members of a visible minority—may find it more difficult than men to assume leadership positions in social movement organizations. While women often serve disproportionately as volunteers in these movements, their work is not always recognized, nor are their voices as easily heard as men's. Moreover, gender bias causes the real extent of women's influence to be overlooked. Traditional examination of the socio-political system tends to focus on such male-dominated corridors of power as legislatures and corporate boardrooms, to the neglect of the socially constructed female-dominated domains such as households, community-based groups, and faith-based networks. But efforts to influence family conditions, child-rearing, relationships between parents and schools, and spiritual values are clearly significant to a culture and society (Ferree and Merrill 2000; Noonan 1995).

Scholars of social movements now realize that gender can affect even the way we view organized efforts to bring about or resist change. For example, an emphasis on using rationality and cold logic to achieve goals helps to obscure the importance of passion and emotion in successful social movements. It would be difficult to find any movement—from labour battles to voting rights to animal rights—in which passion was not part of its activities. Yet calls for a more serious study of the role of emotion are frequently seen as applying only to the women's movement, because emotion continues to be characterized as stereotypically feminine (Ferree and Merrill 2000; Taylor 1995).

New Social Movements

Beginning in the late 1960s, European social scientists observed a change in both the composition and the targets of emerging social movements. Previously, traditional social movements had focused on economic issues, often led by labour unions or by people who shared the same occupation. However, many social movements that have become active in recent decades—including the contemporary women's movement, the peace movement, and the environmental movement—do not have the social class roots typical of the labour protests in Canada, the United States, and Europe over the past century (Tilly 1993, 2004).

The term **new social movement** refers to organized collective activities that address values and social identities, as well as improvements in the quality of life. These movements may be involved in developing collective identities. Many have complex agendas that go beyond a single issue; some cross national boundaries. Educated, middle-class people are significantly represented in some of these new social movements, such as the anti-globalization movement. Box 16-1 describes some new social movements in India.

New social movements generally do not view government as their ally in the struggle for a better society. While they typically do not seek to overthrow the government, they may criticize, protest, or harass public officials. Researchers have

sociology in the global community

16-1 Women and New Social Movements in India

In the more than 60 years since India gained its independence from Great Britain, a variety of new social movements has emerged. These grassroots efforts deal primarily with women's rights, discrimination against the *Dalits* (untouchables), environmental issues, and farming problems. Although they tend to be most visible in the media when their demonstrations occur in cities, most of these movements are based in India's vast rural areas, where about 71 percent of the nation's 1.2 billion people live.

Sociologists and other scholars have emphasized the central role that women play in starting these movements and creating social networks with activists in neighbouring villages and adjacent states. Sometimes these movements connect to form nationwide networks through the assistance of the Women's Development Program (WDP). Founded by UNICEF in 1984, the WDP helps women to improve their quality of life, freeing them from dependence on slow and cumbersome government bureaucracies.

> *The initial goal of the movement was to provide drought relief for villagers, but the deeper goal was to empower rural areas.*

One notable social movement occurred in the Indian textile industry. In the mid-1980s, 5000 striking textile workers came home from Mumbai to mobilize support in their rural villages and gather food for strikers in the city. As the strike wore on, some remained in their villages and sought employment on government drought-relief projects. However, there weren't enough jobs for rural residents, much less for these new migrants from Mumbai.

This experience became the origin of a new social movement in rural India. With unemployment threatening an expanded population in rural areas, activists formed what came to be called the *Shoshit, Shetkari, Kashtakari, Kamgar, Mukti Sangharsh (SSKKMS),* which means "exploited peasants, toilers, workers liberation struggle." The initial goal of the movement was to provide drought relief for villagers, but the deeper goal was to empower rural areas.

The SSKKMS was unusual compared to other social movements in India: about half its participants and many of its leaders were women. This was no accident, for the movement also sought to address gender inequities. Some men have joined the women of the SSKKMS in their political activism, using direct-action tactics such as roadblocks.

Women have also marched on government offices to demand that at least a third of the seats in Parliament and the state assemblies be reserved for them. And they have begun to improve their families' lot through microfinance programs (see Chapter 14). Clearly, Indian women's traditional role of maintaining their households' health and nutrition is critical to their families' survival. Thus, their leadership in seeking improved living conditions is winning them new respect in India's patriarchal society. From the environment to the voting booth, from untouchables' rights to workers' rights, women's social movements are an increasingly common feature of Indian politics.

Apply the Theory

1. Why do you think so many of India's women participate in new social movements? Describe their goals.
2. What would happen if "powerless" people in the United States formed a similar social movement? Would it succeed? Why or why not?

Sources: Bystydzienski and Sekhon 1999; Daley-Harris 2002; Desai 1996; Haub 2010; Ray 1999; Sengupta 2009; Subramaniam 2006; Working Women's Forum 2010.

---

found that members of new social movements show little inclination to accept established authority, even scientific or technical authority. This characteristic is especially evident in the environmental and anti–nuclear power movements, whose activists present their own experts to counter those of government or big business (Garner 1996; Polletta and Jasper 2001; A. Scott 1990). In Canada, for example, Earth Day was one of the original green movements in the country. Activists protested against large companies that caused environmental damage and encouraged other Canadians to be more mindful of how they dispose of household garbage. In 2008, millions of Canadians turned off their lights during Earth Hour. Nearly two decades after its initial launch, Earth Day Canada now has garnered numerous corporate sponsors, a move that has offended many unions and social justice organizations (Welsh 2008).

The environmental movement is one of many new movements with a worldwide focus. In their efforts to reduce air and water pollution, curtail global warming, and protect endangered animal species, environmental activists have realized that strong regulatory measures within a single country are not sufficient. Similarly, labour union leaders and human-rights advocates cannot adequately address exploitative sweatshop conditions in a developing country if a multinational corporation can simply move the factory to another country, where workers earn even less. Whereas traditional views of social movements tended to emphasize resource mobilization on a local level, new social movement theory offers a broader, global perspective on social and political activism. Table 16-1 summarizes the sociological approaches that have contributed to social movement theory. Each has added to our understanding of the development of social movements.

::: use your sociological *imagination* :::

Try to imagine a society without any social movements. Under what conditions could such a society exist? Would you want to live in it?

16.2 How Can Social Change Be Explained?

We have defined social change as significant alteration over time in behaviour patterns and culture. Social change can occur so slowly as to be almost undetectable to those it affects, but it can also happen with breathtaking rapidity.

Explanations of social change are clearly a challenge in the diverse and complex world we inhabit today. Nevertheless, theorists from several disciplines have sought to analyze social change. In some instances, they have examined historical events to arrive at a better understanding of contemporary changes. We will review five theoretical approaches to change—evolutionary, functionalist, conflict, feminist, and interactionist theories—and then we will take a look at resistance to change.

Evolutionary Theory

The pioneering work of Charles Darwin (1809–1882) in biological evolution contributed to nineteenth-century theories of social change. Darwin's approach stresses a continuing progression of successive life forms. For example, human beings

came at a later stage of evolution than reptiles and represent a more complex form of life. Social theorists seeking an analogy to this biological model originated **evolutionary theory**, in which society is viewed as moving in a definite direction. Early evolutionary theorists generally agreed that society was progressing inevitably to a higher state. As might be expected, they concluded—in ethnocentric fashion—that their own behaviour and culture were more advanced than those of earlier civilizations.

August Comte (1798–1857), a founder of sociology, was an evolutionary theorist of change. He saw human societies as moving forward in their thinking, from mythology to the scientific method. Similarly, Émile Durkheim ([1893] 1933) maintained that society progressed from simple to more complex forms of social organization.

Today, evolutionary theory influences sociologists in a variety of ways. For example, it has encouraged sociobiologists to investigate the behavioural links between humans and other animals (Maryanski 2004). Many sociologists, as we previously mentioned in Chapter 1, are critical of evolutionary theory on the grounds that it attempts to provide justification for class differentiation and domination of the powerful over the powerless.

Functionalist Theory

Because functionalist sociologists focus on what *maintains* a system, not on what changes it, they might seem to offer little to the study of social change. Yet, as the work of sociologist Talcott Parsons demonstrates, functionalists have made a distinctive contribution to this area of sociological investigation.

Parsons (1902–1979), a leading proponent of functionalist theory, viewed society as being in a natural state of equilibrium. By "equilibrium," he meant that society tends toward a state of stability or balance. Parsons would view even prolonged labour strikes or civilian riots as temporary disruptions in the status quo rather than as significant alterations in social structure. Therefore, according to his **equilibrium model**, as changes occur in one part of society, adjustments must be made in other parts. If not, society's equilibrium will be threatened and strains will occur.

Reflecting the evolutionary approach, Parsons maintained that four processes of social change are inevitable (1966). The first, *differentiation*, refers to the increasing complexity of social organization. The transition from "medicine man" to physician, nurse, and pharmacist is an illustration of differentiation in the field of health. This process is accompanied by *adaptive upgrading*, by which social institutions become more specialized in their purposes. The division of physicians

table **16-1** Contributions to Social Movement Theory

Approach	Emphasis
Relative deprivation approach	Social movements are especially likely to arise when rising expectations are frustrated.
Resource mobilization approach	The success of social movements depends on which resources are available and how effectively they are used.
New social movement theory	Social movements arise when people are motivated by value issues and social identity questions.

into obstetricians, internists, surgeons, and so forth is an example of adaptive upgrading.

The third process Parsons identified is the *inclusion* of groups that were previously excluded because of their gender, race, ethnicity, or social class. Medical schools have practised inclusion by admitting increasing numbers of women and visible minorities. Lastly, Parsons contends that societies experience *value generalization*, the development of new values that tolerate and legitimate a greater range of activities. The acceptance of preventive and alternative medicine is an example of value generalization: society has broadened its view of health care. All four processes identified by Parsons stress consensus—societal agreement on the nature of social organization and values (Johnson 1975; Wallace and Wolf 1980).

On the outskirts of Buenos Aires, Argentina, a shantytown forms a stark contrast to the gleaming skyscrapers in the wealthy downtown area. Marxists and conflict theorists see social change as a way of overcoming the kind of social inequality evident in this photograph.

Though Parsons's approach explicitly incorporates the evolutionary notion of continuing progress, the dominant theme in his model is stability. Society may change, but it remains stable through new forms of integration. For example, in place of the kinship ties that provided social cohesion in the past, people develop laws, judicial processes, and new values and belief systems.

Functionalists assume that social institutions would not persist unless they continued to contribute to society. This assumption leads them to conclude that drastically altering institutions will threaten societal equilibrium. Critics note that the functionalist approach virtually disregards the use of coercion by the powerful to maintain the illusion of a stable, well-integrated society (Gouldner 1960).

Conflict Theory

The functionalist perspective minimizes the importance of change. It emphasizes the persistence of social life, and sees change as reform, allowing for the maintenance of society's equilibrium. In contrast, conflict theorists contend that social institutions and practices persist because powerful groups have the ability to maintain the status quo. Change—possibly in the form of revolution—has crucial significance, since it is needed to correct social injustices and inequalities.

Karl Marx accepted the evolutionary argument that societies develop along a particular path. However, unlike Auguste Comte and Herbert Spencer, Marx did not view each successive stage as an inevitable improvement over the previous one. History, according to Marx, proceeds through a series of stages, each of which exploits a class of people. Ancient society exploited slaves; the estate system of feudalism exploited serfs; modern capitalist society exploits the working class. Ultimately, through a socialist revolution led by the proletariat,

human society will move toward the final stage of development: a classless communist society, or "community of free individuals," as Marx described it in 1867 in *Das Kapital* (see Bottomore and Rubel 1956:250).

As we have seen, Marx had an important influence on the development of sociology. His thinking offered insights into such institutions as the economy, the family, religion, and government. The Marxist view of social change is appealing because it does not restrict people to a passive role in responding to inevitable cycles or changes in material culture. Instead, Marxist theory offers a tool for those who wish to seize control of the historical process and gain their freedom from injustice. In contrast to functionalists' emphasis on stability, Marx argues that conflict is a normal and desirable aspect of social change. In fact, change must be encouraged as a means of eliminating social inequality (Lauer 1982).

One conflict theorist, Ralf Dahrendorf, has noted that the contrast between the functionalist perspective's emphasis on stability and the conflict perspective's focus on change reflects the contradictory nature of society (1958). Human societies are stable and long-lasting, yet they also experience serious conflict. Dahrendorf found that the functionalist and the conflict approaches were ultimately compatible, despite their many points of disagreement. Indeed, Parsons spoke of new functions that result from social change, and Marx recognized the need for change so that societies could function more equitably.

Feminist Theories

Unlike other sociological perspectives, social change is the hallmark of feminist perspectives. Feminist sociologists, diverse as they are, share a desire to deepen their understanding of society in order to change the world; it is their desire to make it more just and humane (Lengermann and Niebrugge-Brantley 1998). Confronting social injustice in order to promote change for those groups in society who are disadvantaged by their "social location"—their class, race, ethnicity, sexual preference, age, or global location—is a key feature of feminist perspectives. As feminist sociologist Patricia Hill Collins explains, change is sought for "people differently placed in specific political, social, and historic contexts characterized by injustice" (1998:xiv).

Increasingly, feminist perspectives advance the view that acknowledging women's differences must be paramount in guiding the direction of social change. The interests of white, middle-class women, for example, must not be assumed to represent the interests of all women. Social change must be inclusive of the interests of women of diverse backgrounds. As feminist theorists Rosemary Hennessy and Chrys Ingraham ask, "What are the consequences of this way of thinking for transforming the inequities in women's lives?" and "How is this way of explaining the world going to improve life for all women?" (Lengermann and Niebrugge-Brantley 1998:445).

Interactionist Theory

The symbolic interactionist perspective sees people as active agents or actors and the social world as being active, so constant adjustment and change occur through social interaction. People give meaning to events as they interpret their own "social reality." Movements for social change, therefore, are not the results of external or objective factors, but rather a social construction based on the meaning or interpretation the participants give to their actions. As Herbert Blumer notes, and as mentioned in Chapter 15:

> Human beings interpret or "define" each other's actions instead of merely reacting to each other's actions. Their response is not made directly to the actions of one another but instead is based on the meaning which they attach to such actions. Thus, human interaction is mediated by the use of symbols, by interpretation, or by ascertaining the meaning of one another's actions. (1969:180)

More recent theories, founded on the principles of symbolic interactionism, are based on the assumption that social movements involve participants, opponents, and bystanders engaged in a process that is interactive, symbolically defined, and negotiated (Buechler 2000). Using the work of Erving Goffman—who suggested that our interpretation of events depends on the way we "frame" them—theories, such as that of Steven M. Buechler, articulate the relationship between this framing and social movement theory:

> In the context of social movements, framing refers to the interactive, collective ways that movement actors assign meaning to their activities in the conduct of social movement activism. The concept of framing is designed for discussing the social construction of grievances as a fluid and variable process of social interaction. (2000:41)

Social movements may modify or recreate their frames to advance their goals. An example would be an environmental group whose frame was global deforestation but who reframes it to air quality and the health effects on children (e.g., increasing rates of childhood asthma).

Table 16-2 summarizes the differences among the five major theories of social change.

16-3 What Forms Does Resistance to Social Change Take?

Efforts to promote social change are likely to meet with resistance. In the midst of rapid scientific and technological innovations, many people are frightened by the demands of an ever-changing society. Moreover, certain individuals and groups have a stake in maintaining the existing state of affairs. Social economist Thorstein Veblen (1857–1929) coined the term **vested interests** to refer to those people or groups who will suffer in the event of social change. For example, in the United States, the American Medical Association (AMA) has taken strong stands against national health insurance and the professionalization of midwifery. National health insurance could lead to limits on physicians' income, and a rise in the status of midwives could threaten the pre-eminent position of doctors as deliverers of babies. In general, those with a disproportionate share of society's wealth, status, and power, such as members of the American Medical Association, have a vested interest in preserving the status quo (Starr 1982; Veblen 1919).

Economic and Cultural Factors

Economic factors play an important role in resistance to social change. For example, it can be expensive for manufacturers to meet high standards for the safety of products and workers, and for the protection of the environment. Conflict theorists argue that in a capitalist economic system, many firms are not willing to pay the price of meeting strict safety and environmental standards. They may resist social change by cutting corners or by pressuring the government to ease regulations. Communities, too, protect their vested interests, often in the name of "protecting property values." The abbreviation *NIMBY* stands for "not in my backyard," a cry often heard when homeowners protest the arrival of nearby landfills, prisons, nuclear power facilities, big-box malls, and even bike trails and group

table 16-2 Sociological Perspectives on Social Change

Evolutionary	Social change moves society in a definite direction, frequently from simple to more complex.
Functionalist	Social change must contribute to society's stability. Modest adjustments or reforms must be made to accommodate social change.
Conflict	Fundamental social change is necessary to correct social injustices and inequalities.
Feminist	Social change is necessary to bring about equality for women.
Interactionist	Constant adjustment and change occur through social interaction.

homes for people with developmental disabilities. The targeted community may not challenge the need for the facility, but may simply insist that it be located elsewhere. The NIMBY attitude has become so common that it is almost impossible for policymakers to find acceptable locations for facilities such as hazardous waste dumps (Jasper 1997).

Like economic factors, cultural factors frequently shape resistance to change. William F. Ogburn distinguished between material and non-material aspects of culture (1922). *Material culture* includes inventions, artifacts, and technology; *non-material culture* encompasses ideas, norms, communications, and social organization. Ogburn pointed out that one cannot devise methods for controlling and using new technology before the introduction of a technique. Thus, non-material culture typically must respond to changes in material culture. Ogburn introduced the term *culture lag* to refer to the period of maladjustment when the non-material culture is still struggling to adapt to new material conditions. One example is the Internet—its rapid uncontrolled growth raises questions about whether to regulate it, and if so, how much.

In certain cases, changes in material culture can strain the relationships between social institutions. For example, new means of birth control have been developed in recent decades. Large families are no longer economically necessary, nor are they commonly endorsed by social norms. But certain religious faiths, among them Roman Catholicism, continue to oppose "unnatural" methods of limiting family size, such as contraception and abortion. This issue represents a lag between aspects of material culture (technology) and non-material culture (religious beliefs). Conflicts may also emerge between religion and other social institutions, such as government and the educational system, over the dissemination of birth control and family-planning information (Riley et al. 1994a, 1994b).

Resistance to Technology

Technological innovations are examples of changes in material culture that often provoke resistance. The Industrial Revolution, which took place largely in England during the period 1760 to 1830, was a scientific revolution focused on the application of non-animal sources of power to labour tasks. As this enormous change proceeded, societies came to rely on new inventions that facilitated agricultural and industrial production, and on new sources of energy such as steam. In some industries, the introduction of power-driven machinery reduced the need for factory workers and made it easier for factory owners to cut wages.

Strong resistance to the Industrial Revolution emerged in some countries. In England, beginning in 1811, masked craft workers took extreme measures: They mounted night-time raids on factories and destroyed some of the new machinery. The government hunted these rebels, known as **Luddites**, and ultimately banished or hanged them. In a similar effort in France, angry workers threw their wooden shoes (*sabots*) into factory machinery to destroy it, giving rise to the term *sabotage*. While the resistance efforts of the Luddites and the French workers were short-lived and unsuccessful, they have come to symbolize resistance to technology.

Are we now in the midst of a second industrial revolution, with a contemporary group of Luddites engaged in resisting? Many sociologists believe that we are living in a *post-industrial society*. It is difficult to pinpoint exactly when this era began. Generally, it is viewed as having begun in the 1950s, when for the first time the majority of workers in industrial societies became involved in services rather than in the actual manufacture of goods (Bell 1999; Fiala 1992).

Just as the Luddites resisted the Industrial Revolution, people in many countries have resisted post-industrial technological changes. The term *neo-Luddites* refers to those who are wary of technological innovations, and who question the incessant expansion of industrialization, the increasing destruction of the natural and agrarian world, and the "throw-it-away" mentality of contemporary capitalism, with its resulting pollution of the environment. Neo-Luddites insist that whatever the presumed benefits of industrial and post-industrial technology, such technology has distinctive social costs, and may represent a danger to the future of both the human species and our planet (Bauerlein 1996; Rifkin 1995; Sale 1996; Snyder 1996).

16.4 How Does Globalization Affect Global Social Change?

We are at a truly dramatic time in history to consider global social change. Maureen Hallinan, in her 1997 presidential address to the American Sociological Association, asked those present to consider just a few of the recent political events: the collapse of communism; terrorism in various parts of the world, including the United States; major regime changes and severe economic disruptions in Africa, the Middle East, and Eastern Europe; the spread of AIDS; and the computer revolution. Just a few months after her remarks came the first verification of the cloning of a complex animal, Dolly the sheep.

In this era of massive social, political, and economic change on a global scale, is it possible to predict change? Some technological changes seem obvious, but the collapse of communist governments in the former Soviet Union and Eastern Europe in the early 1990s took people by surprise. Yet, prior to the Soviet collapse, sociologist Randall Collins, a conflict theorist, had observed a crucial sequence of events that most observers had missed (1986, 1995).

In seminars as far back as 1980, and in a book published in 1986, Collins had argued that Soviet expansionism had resulted in an overextension of resources, including disproportionate spending on military forces. Such an overextension will strain a regime's stability. Moreover, geopolitical theory suggests that nations in the middle of a geographic region, such as the Soviet Union, tend to fragment into smaller units over time. Collins predicted that the coincidence of social crises on several frontiers would precipitate the collapse of the Soviet Union.

And that is just what happened. In 1979, the success of the Iranian Revolution had led to an upsurge of Islamic fundamentalism in nearby Afghanistan, as well as in Soviet

In 2010, protesters in London disguised themselves as characters in the movie *Avatar* to draw attention to the plight of an indigenous tribe in India. The Dongria Kondh people's way of life, they charged, was threatened by a multinational corporation's plan to construct a mine on their land. The Indian government blocked the project, agreeing with protesters that it would have violated the tribe's rights.

republics with substantial Muslim populations. At the same time, resistance to Communist party rule was growing both throughout Eastern Europe and within the Soviet Union itself. Collins had predicted that the rise of a dissident form of communism within the Soviet Union would likely facilitate the breakdown of the regime. Beginning in the late 1980s, Soviet leader Mikhail Gorbachev chose not to use military power and other types of repression to crush dissidents in Eastern Europe. Instead, he offered plans for democratization and social reform of Soviet society, and seemed willing to reshape the Soviet Union into a loose federation of somewhat autonomous states. But in 1991, six republics on the western periphery declared their independence, and within months, the entire Soviet Union had formally disintegrated into Russia and a number of other independent nations.

In her 1997 address, Hallinan cautioned that we need to move beyond the restrictive models of social change—the linear view of evolutionary theory and the assumptions about equilibrium in functionalist theory. She and other sociologists have looked to the "chaos theory" advanced by mathematicians to understand erratic events as a part of change. Hallinan noted that upheavals and major chaotic shifts do occur, and that sociologists must learn to predict their occurrence, as Collins did with the Soviet Union. For example, imagine the dramatic non-linear social change that will result from major innovations in communications and biotechnology—topics we will discuss next.

Computer Technology

The last decade witnessed an explosion of computer technology around the world. Its effects were particularly noteworthy with regard to the Internet, the world's largest computer network. In 2010 the Internet reached 1.8 billion users, compared to just 50 million in 1996. Box 16-2 sketches the worldwide access to and use of the Internet.

The Internet evolved from a computer system built in 1962 by the U.S. Defense Department to enable scholars and military researchers to continue their government work even if part of the nation's communications system were destroyed by a nuclear attack. Until fairly recently, it was difficult to gain access to the Internet without holding a position at a university or a government research laboratory. Today, however, virtually anyone can reach the Internet with a phone line, a computer, and a modem. People buy and sell cars, trade stocks, auction off items, research new medical remedies, vote, and track down long-lost friends online—to mention just a few of the thousands of possibilities.

Unfortunately, not everyone can get onto the information highway, especially not the less affluent. Moreover, this pattern of inequality is global. The core nations that Immanuel Wallerstein described in his world systems analysis have a virtual monopoly on information technology; the peripheral nations of Asia, Africa, and Latin America depend on the core nations both for technology and for the information it provides. For example, North America, Europe, and a few industrialized nations in other regions possess almost all the world's *Internet hosts*—computers that are connected directly to the worldwide network.

What is the solution to this global disconnect between the haves and the have-nots? Some people have suggested giving everyone a computer—or at least, everyone who can't afford one.

Privacy and Censorship in a Global Village

New technologies like the personal computer and the Internet have brought about sweeping social change. While much of that change has been beneficial, there have been some negative effects. Recent advances in computer technology have made it increasingly easy for business firms, government agencies, and even criminals to retrieve and store information about everything from our buying habits to our Web-surfing patterns. In public places, at work, and on the Internet, surveillance devices now track our every move, be it a keystroke or an ATM withdrawal. At the same time that these innovations have increased others' power to monitor our behaviour, they have raised fears that they might be misused for criminal or undemocratic purposes. In short, new technologies threaten not just our privacy, but our freedom from crime and censorship (Rheingold 2003).

research today

The old notion of an Internet dominated by English-only content is passé. In fact, usage patterns are changing so fast, generalizing about global use of the Internet requires careful research and phrasing.

For example, Figure A, Internet Users by World Region, shows an Internet that is dominated by users in Asia and Europe, two relatively populous continents. However, Figure B, Internet Penetration by World Region, shows a dramatically different picture, one in which the *proportion* of people in each region who access the Internet is highest in North America and Australia. That is, numerically, most Internet users live in Asia and Europe, but the likelihood of a person being an Internet user is greatest in North America and Australia. Figure B shows dramatically low Internet use in Africa, where only 10.9 percent of residents access the global network.

The old notion of an Internet accessed primarily in the United States and dominated by English-only content is passé.

Though English is still the primary language of Internet users, as Figure C shows, use of the Chinese language has become much more common. Chinese usage on the Internet increased 1277 percent between 2000 and 2010, compared to 281 percent for English. Interestingly, 82 percent of all Japanese speakers use the Internet, compared to 42 percent of all English speakers, though in absolute terms, speakers of Japanese are a significantly smaller group.

figure A Internet Users by World Region

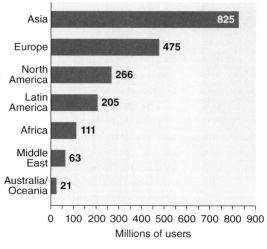

figure B Internet Penetration by World Region

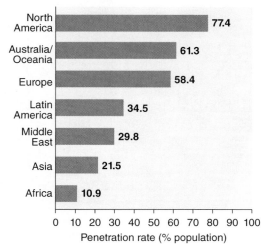

figure C Internet's Top 10 Languages

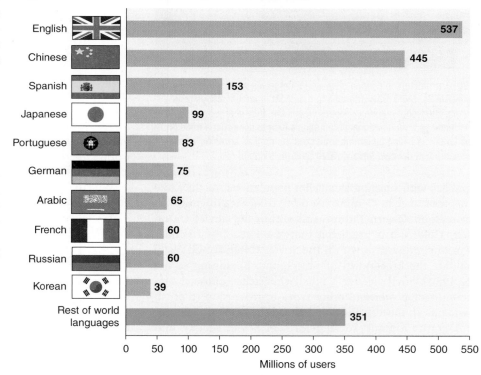

Apply the Theory

1. In surfing the Web, how often do you encounter a Web site that is written in a language you do not read or speak? Do you think that experience will become increasingly common in the future?

2. Why do you think the use of Chinese on the Internet has increased so dramatically in just a decade? What kind of information would you expect to find in Chinese? Who would use it?

Source: All data taken from Internet World Stats 2011 as of April 25, 2011.

In recent years, concern about the criminal misuse of personal information has been underscored by the theft of customer information from some huge databases. In 2007, for example, hackers stole customer information from the computer systems of the parent company of Winners and Home Sense, affecting 2 million Canadian credit card accounts. Unfortunately, technologies that facilitate the sharing of information have also created new types of crime.

From a sociological point of view, the complex issues of privacy and censorship can be considered illustrations of culture lag. As usual, the material culture (technology) is changing faster than the non-material culture (norms for controlling the use of technology). Too often, the result is an anything-goes approach to the use of new technologies.

Legislation regarding the surveillance of electronic communications has not always upheld citizens' right to privacy. In 1986 in the United States, for example, the federal government passed the Electronic Communications Privacy Act, which outlawed the surveillance of telephone calls except with the permission of both the U.S. attorney general and a federal judge. Telegrams, faxes, and email did not receive the same degree of protection, however (Eckenwiler 1995). In 2001, one month after the terrorist attacks of September 11, Congress passed the Patriot Act, which relaxed existing legal checks on surveillance by law-enforcement officers. Federal agencies are now freer to gather data electronically, including credit card receipts and banking records.

Sociologists' views on the use and abuse of new technologies differ depending on their theoretical perspective. Functionalists take a generally positive view of the Internet, pointing to its manifest function of facilitating communication. From their perspective, the Internet performs the latent function of empowering those with few resources—from hate groups to special interest organizations—to communicate with the masses. Conflict theorists, in contrast, stress the danger that the most powerful groups in a society will use technology to violate the privacy of the less powerful. Indeed, officials in the People's Republic of China have attempted to censor online discussion groups and Web postings that are critical of the government (see Chapter 14).

Biotechnology and the Gene Pool

Another field in which technological advances have spurred global social change is biotechnology. Sex selection of fetuses, genetically engineered organisms, cloning of sheep and cows—these have been among the significant yet controversial scientific advances in the field of biotechnology in recent years. George Ritzer's concept of McDonaldization applies to the entire area of biotechnology. Just as the fast-food concept has permeated society, no phase of life now seems exempt from therapeutic or medical intervention. In fact, sociologists view many aspects of biotechnology as an extension of the recent trend toward the medicalization of society, which we discussed in Chapter 15. Through genetic manipulation, the medical profession is expanding its turf still further (Clarke et al. 2003; Human Genome Project 2010).

Today's biotechnology holds itself out as totally beneficial to human beings, but it is in constant need of monitoring. As we will see, biotechnological advances have raised many difficult ethical and political questions, among them the desirability of tinkering with the gene pool, which could alter our environment in unexpected and unwanted ways.

One startling biotechnological advance is the possibility of altering human behaviour through genetic engineering. Fish and plant genes have already been mixed to create frost-resistant potato and tomato crops. Human genes have been implanted in pigs to provide human-like kidneys for organ transplants (Schmitz 1999).

One of the latest developments in genetic engineering is gene therapy. Geneticists working with mouse fetuses have managed to disable genes that carry an undesirable trait and replace them with genes carrying a desirable trait. Such advances raise staggering possibilities for altering animal and human life forms.

The debate on genetic engineering escalated in 1997 when scientists in Scotland announced that they had cloned a sheep (the aforementioned Dolly). After many unsuccessful attempts, they had finally been able to replace the genetic material of a sheep's egg with DNA from an adult sheep, creating a lamb that was a clone of the adult. The very next year, Japanese researchers successfully cloned cows. These developments raised the possibility that in the near future, scientists would be able to clone human beings.

William F. Ogburn probably could not have anticipated such scientific developments when he wrote of culture lag 75 years earlier. However, the successful cloning of sheep and cows illustrates again how quickly material culture can change, and how non-material culture moves more slowly in absorbing such changes.

While cloning grabs the headlines, controversy has been growing concerning genetically modified (GM) food. The idea behind the technology is to increase food production and make agriculture more economical. Critics use the term *Frankenfood* (as in "Frankenstein") to refer to everything from breakfast cereals made from genetically engineered grains to "fresh" GM tomatoes. Members of the anti-biotech movement object to tampering with nature; they are concerned about the possible health effects of GM food. Supporters of genetically modified food include not just biotech companies, but those who see the technology as a way to help feed the burgeoning populations of Africa and Asia (Petersen 2009; World Health Organization 2009). The vast majority of the roughly 14 million farmers benefiting from genetically modified crop technology live in the poor countries of the world (*The Economist* 2010b).

Another form of biotechnology with a potentially wide-ranging impact is the Human Genome Project. This effort involves teams of scientists around the world in sequencing and mapping all 30 000 to 40 000 human genes in existence, collectively known as the **human genome**. Supporters say that the resulting knowledge could revolutionize doctors' ability to treat and even prevent disease. But sociologists worry about the ethical implications of such research.

16.5 What Impact Does Social Change Have on the Environment?

Sociologists and others may debate the potential impact of biotechnology, but technological change has already had serious environmental consequences. We can see signs of despoliation almost everywhere: Our air, our water, and our land are being polluted, whether we live in Kitchener, Ontario, or Lagos, Nigeria. In some parts of the United States, each summer brings power failures or brownouts to sweltering cities as the voracious consumption of electricity exceeds the supply. In some parts of Canada, summer has become a time of frequent smog alerts, warning the elderly and those who suffer from respiratory conditions to remain indoors.

In recent years, public attention has turned to global warming, manifested in the shrinking of the polar ice caps and the increasing ferociousness of tropical storms as they cross warmer-than-normal ocean waters. Human activities have contributed to the documented warming of the planet over the last half century, through the altered chemical composition of the atmosphere and the buildup of greenhouse gases such as carbon dioxide, methane, and nitrous oxide. While environmental problems may be easy to identify scientifically, however, devising socially and politically acceptable solutions is much more difficult. In the following sections, we will survey some identifiable environmental problems and see what sociologists have to say about them (Easterbrook 2006; Gore 2006).

Environmental Problems: An Overview

In recent decades, the world has witnessed serious environmental disasters. In 1986, for example, a series of explosions set off a catastrophic nuclear reactor accident at Chernobyl, a part of Ukraine (in what was then the Soviet Union). Thousands of people died, and some 400 000 residents had to be evacuated. For nearly 31 kilometres in any direction, the area became uninhabitable. High levels of radiation were found as far as 48 kilometres from the reactor site, and radioactivity levels climbed well above normal even in Sweden and Japan. According to one estimate, the Chernobyl accident and the resulting nuclear fallout may ultimately result in 100 000 cases of cancer worldwide (Chernobyl Forum 2005).

Much more common than nuclear power plant disasters are oil spills in the ocean or coastal waters, typically from supertankers. The heavier types of crude or fuel oil, such as that carried by the *Exxon Valdez* in 1989, can contaminate the shoreline for years following a spill, even after a massive cleanup. Globally, oil spills occur regularly. In 2013, a pipeline carrying Canadian heavy crude from Illinois to the Texas Gulf coast, ruptured in Arkansas, spilling more than 10 000 barrels (or 1.59 million litres) of oil.

While reactor accidents, oil spills, and other environmental disasters understandably grab the headlines, it is the silent, day-to-day deterioration of the environment that ultimately poses a devastating threat to humanity. Examining all our environmental problems in detail would be impossible, but four broad areas of concern stand out: air pollution, water pollution, global warming, and the impact of globalization.

Air Pollution Worldwide, more than 1 billion people are exposed to potentially health-damaging levels of air pollution. Unfortunately, in cities around the world, residents have come to accept smog and polluted air as normal. Urban air pollution is caused primarily by emissions from automobiles and secondarily by emissions from electric power plants and heavy industries. Smog not only limits visibility—it can also lead to health problems as uncomfortable as eye irritation and as deadly as lung cancer. Such problems are especially severe in developing countries. The World Health Organization has estimated that, globally, 1.3 million deaths *per year* are caused from urban outdoor air pollution (World Health Organization 2013).

People are capable of changing their behaviour, but they are also unwilling to make such changes permanent. During the 1984 Olympics in Los Angeles, residents were asked to carpool and stagger their work hours to relieve traffic congestion and improve the quality of the air athletes would breathe. These changes resulted in a remarkable 12 percent drop in ozone levels. But when the Olympians left, people reverted to their normal behaviour and the ozone levels climbed back up. Similarly, at the 2008 Olympics, China took drastic action to ensure that Beijing's high levels of air pollution did not mar the games. For a two-month period, all construction work in the city ceased, polluting factories and power plants closed down, and roads were swept and sprayed with water several times a day. But this temporary solution was hardly a solution to China's ongoing pollution problems (*The Economist* 2008b).

Water Pollution Around the world, water pollution is a growing concern. Oceans, lakes, rivers, and streams are becoming increasingly polluted as a result of waste dumping, fuel leaks from shipping, and occasional oil spills. In North America, dumping of waste materials by industries and local governments has polluted streams, rivers, and lakes. Accidents contribute to the contamination of soil and water. For example, in July 2007, in the Vancouver suburb of Burnaby, a construction crew accidentally ruptured a major crude oil pipeline, causing the spewing of oil over homes and gardens and the environmental contamination of soil and water. Consequently, many bodies of water have become unsafe for drinking, fishing, and swimming.

Less dramatic than large-scale accidents or disasters, but more common in many parts of the world, are problems with the basic water supply. Worldwide, over 1.1 billion people lack safe and adequate drinking water, and 2.6 billion have no acceptable means of sanitation—a problem that further threatens the quality of water supplies. The health costs of unsafe water are enormous (United Nations Development Programme 2006).

Global Warming Based on complex computer models, scientists have made hundreds of projections of global warming. The term *global warming* refers to the significant rise in the earth's surface temperatures that occurs when industrial gases like carbon dioxide turn the planet's atmosphere into a virtual greenhouse. Even one additional degree of warmth in the globe's surface temperature can increase the likelihood of wildfires, cause shrinkage of rivers and lakes, lead to expansion of deserts, and cause torrential downpours, including typhoons and hurricanes.

Although scientific concern over global warming has heated up, climate change remains low on policymakers' list of priorities in Canada as well as the United States. The Kyoto Protocol was intended to reduce global warming and climate change, but to date only 169 countries have signed the protocol. Although Canada signed the protocol, it has failed to meet its targets for the reduction of greenhouse gases, and emissions have actually increased. The present government under Prime Minister Stephen Harper has abandoned the Kyoto targets, calling for a "made in Canada" approach to climate change. The United States, which produces approximately one-quarter of the world's carbon dioxide, failed to ratify the protocol.

In writing about the global environment, activists often assert, "We're all in this together." Though we *are* all in it together, the reality is that globally, the most vulnerable countries tend to be the poorest. Developing nations are more likely than others to have economies that are built on limited resources or a small number of crops vulnerable to drought, flood, and fluctuations in worldwide demand (Revkin 2007).

We can view global warming from the point of view of world systems analysis. Historically, core nations have been the major emitters of greenhouse gases. Today, manufacturing has moved to semi-periphery and periphery nations, where greenhouse gas emissions are escalating. Ironically, many of the forces that are now calling for a reduction in the human activity that contributes to global warming are located in core nations, which have contributed disproportionately to the problem. We want our hamburgers, but we decry the destruction of the rain forests to create grazing land for cattle. We want inexpensive clothes and toys, but we condemn developing countries for depending on coal-fired power plants, which are expected to increase 46 percent by 2030. The challenge of global warming, then, is closely tied to global inequality (M. Jenkins 2008; J. Roberts et al. 2003).

The Impact of Globalization Globalization can be both good and bad for the environment. On the negative side, it can create a race to the bottom, as polluting companies relocate to countries with less stringent environmental standards.

In a makeshift recycling centre, a woman in China uses a hammer to open an old cathode ray tube. She wants the copper that is inside, but in the process she will release several kilograms of lead into the soil and groundwater. Scientists have found alarmingly high levels of toxic heavy metals in the rivers that flow by such rural recycling operations.

Similarly, globalization allows multinationals to reap the resources of developing countries for short-term profit. From Mexico to China, the industrialization that often accompanies globalization has increased pollution of all types.

Yet globalization can have a positive impact, as well. As barriers to the international movement of goods, services, and people fall, multinational corporations have an incentive to carefully consider the cost of natural resources. Overusing or wasting resources makes little sense, especially when they are in danger of depletion (Kwong 2005).

One reflection of the interplay between globalization and the environment is the emergence of so-called *environmental refugees*. Europe in particular is beginning to see an influx of such immigrants from developing nations. According to a European Union report, global warming can be viewed as a "threat multiplier" that exacerbates prolonged droughts and a shortage of arable land, and along with them, poverty, poor health, and poor living conditions. Viewed through the lens of world systems analysis, periphery countries may become overburdened by environmental problems, precipitating migrations to industrial nations or conflicts that cause mass displacements of their populations. "Europe must expect substantially increased migratory pressure" from these environmental refugees, the report concludes (Traynor 2008).

What are the causes of this global environmental crisis? Some observers, such as Paul Ehrlich and Anne Ehrlich, see the pressure of world population growth as the central factor in environmental deterioration. They argue that population control is essential in preventing widespread starvation and environmental decay. Barry Commoner, a biologist, counters that the primary cause of environmental ills is the increasing use of technological innovations that are destructive to the environment—among them plastics, detergents, synthetic fibres, pesticides, herbicides, and chemical fertilizers. Conflict theorists see the despoliation of the environment through the lens of world systems analysis (Commoner 1971, 1990, 2007; Ehrlich 1968; Ehrlich and Ehrlich 1990; Ehrlich and Ellison 2002).

Conflict View of Environmental Issues

In Chapter 7, we drew on world systems analysis to show how a growing share of the human and natural resources of developing countries is being redistributed to the core industrialized nations. This process only intensifies the destruction of natural resources in poorer regions of the world. From a conflict perspective, less affluent nations are being forced to exploit their mineral deposits, forests, and fisheries in order to meet their debt obligations. The poor turn to the only means of survival available to them: They plow mountain slopes, burn plots in tropical forests, and overgraze grasslands (Livernash and Rodenburg 1998).

Brazil exemplifies this interplay between economic troubles and environmental destruction. Each year, more than 2.3 million hectares of forest are cleared for crops and livestock. The elimination of the rain forest affects worldwide weather patterns, heightening the gradual warming of the earth. These socioeconomic patterns, with their harmful environmental consequences, are evident not only in Latin America but in many regions of Africa and Asia. Conflict theorists are well aware of the environmental implications of land use policies in the developing world, but they contend that focusing on developing countries is ethnocentric. Who, they ask, is more to blame for environmental deterioration: the poverty-stricken and "food-hungry" populations of the world or the "energy-hungry" industrialized nations? These theorists point out that the industrialized nations of North America and Europe account for only 12 percent of the world's population but are responsible for 60 percent of worldwide consumption and, thus, a disproportionately large ecological footprint (see Figure 16-1 for the 2006 World Consumption Cartogram). The money their residents spend on ocean cruises each year could provide clean drinking water for everyone on the planet. Ice cream expenditures in Europe alone could be used to immunize every child in the world. Thus, conflict theorists charge, the most serious threat to the environment comes from the global consumer class (G. Gardner et al. 2004).

Allan Schnaiberg further refines this analysis by criticizing the focus on affluent consumers as the cause of environmental troubles (1994). In his view, a capitalist system creates a "treadmill of production" because of its inherent need to build ever-expanding profits. This treadmill necessitates creating an increasing demand for products, obtaining natural resources at minimal cost, and manufacturing products as quickly and cheaply as possible—no matter what the long-term environmental consequences.

Environmental Justice

Deline, Northwest Territories, is an Aboriginal community of about 800 people. A uranium mine near the town used many local people to work as labourers without providing necessary safety measures. As a result, the town—now dubbed "A Village of Widows"—has one of the highest cancer rates in Canada. The workers (mostly men) were not the only ones exposed to the hazards of uranium mining; their families were also unknowingly exposed to hazardous waste landfills and dumps, which contaminated their food sources and water.

Observations like this one have given rise to **environmental justice**, a legal strategy based on claims that ethnic minorities are subjected disproportionately to environmental hazards. The approach has had some success. In 1998, a U.S. chemical company called Shintech dropped plans to build a plastics plant in a poor black community in Mississippi after opponents filed a civil rights complaint with the Environmental Protection Agency (EPA) in the United States. EPA administrator Carol Browner praised the company's decision: "The principles applied to achieve this solution should be incorporated into any blueprint for dealing with environmental justice issues in communities across the nation" (Associated Press 1998:18).

Following reports from the EPA and other organizations documenting the discriminatory location of hazardous waste sites, then U.S. president Bill Clinton issued an executive order in 1994 that requires all federal agencies to ensure that low-income and minority communities have access to better information about

Increasingly, people from developed countries are turning to ecotourism as an environmentally friendly way to see the world. The new trend bridges the interests of environmentalists and business people, especially in developing countries.

figure **16-1** World Consumption Cartogram, 2005

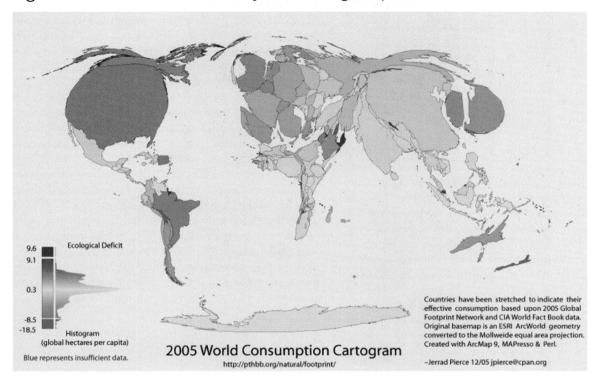

Ecological Deficit

9.6
9.1

0.3

-8.5
-18.5

Histogram
(global hectares per capita)

Blue represents insufficient data.

Countries have been stretched to indicate their effective consumption based upon 2005 Global Footprint Network and CIA World Fact Book data. Original basemap is an ESRI ArcWorld geometry converted to the Mollweide equal area projection. Created with ArcMap 9, MAPresso & Perl.

2005 World Consumption Cartogram
http://pthbb.org/natural/footprint/

–Jerrad Pierce 12/05 jpierce@cpan.org

Source: Pierce 2007.

their environment, and an opportunity to participate in shaping government policies that affect their health. Initial efforts to implement the policy have aroused widespread opposition because of the delays it imposes in establishing new industrial sites. Some observers question the wisdom of an order that slows economic development in areas that are in dire need of employment opportunities. Others point out that such businesses employ few unskilled or less skilled workers, and only make the environment less livable (Stretesky 2006; D. Taylor 2000).

Meanwhile, the poor and oppressed continue to bear the brunt of environmental pollution. In the 1990s, the U.S. government, unable to find a disposal site for spent nuclear fuel, turned to tribal reservations. Agents eventually persuaded a tiny band of Goshute Indians in Skull Valley, Utah, to accept more than 44 000 barrels of the hot, highly radioactive substance, which will remain dangerous for an estimated 10 000 years. The government is currently attempting to implement the plan despite opposition from surrounding towns and cities, whose residents object to the movement of the material through their communities. This is not the first time the U.S. government has prevailed upon the impoverished tribe to accept environmentally objectionable installations. The military's nerve gas storage facility resides on or near the reservation, along with the Intermountain Power Project, which generates coal-fired electrical power for consumers in California (Eureka County 2006; Skull Valley Band Goshute 2006).

As is evident from this discussion, much of the literature on environmental justice is based on U.S. studies and cases (Bryant and Mohai 1992; Bullard 1990; Hofrichter 1993). In 2001, however, Alice Nabalamba published a Canadian study using 1996 Census data in which she investigated the links among socioeconomic status, visible-minority group status, and the location of pollution sources in Toronto, Hamilton, and the Niagara region. Nabalamba's findings suggest that poorer people are more likely than the general population to live in neighbourhoods near sources of pollution and industrial land use. Nabalamba predicts that future use of land for industrial discharges, waste treatment, disposal, storage, and so on, will continue to affect those Canadians of lower socioeconomic status—those who have, obviously, less political clout to fight back (2001).

A Ugandan farmer checks the price of coffee beans on his cellphone.

Feminist View: Eco-feminism

None of the various feminist perspectives addresses the links between gender and the environment as directly as eco-feminism does. Eco-feminism forges an alliance between the environmental movement and the feminist movement, between ecology and feminist principles. Central to the core tenets of eco-feminism is the belief that, historically, men have dominated and exploited both nature and women. Androcentric thinking, rooted in principles of dualism and hierarchy, has justified activities that have led to men's domination over nature and women. Eco-feminists reject this way of thinking and acting and the harm that it has caused the environment. Instead, they argue that women inherently have a closer, more intimate, and less exploitive connection to nature. Women's relationships with nature, eco-feminists contend, are not ones of domination, control, and exploitive self-interest but rather of protection and nurturance. Critics of eco-feminism suggest that arguing that women have inherent qualities of nurturance reduces their position to a form of biological determinism. Biological determinism has long been used as a justification for the separation, exclusion, and oppression of women, because their differences, in an androcentric world, have been interpreted as inferiorities.

Interactionist View

The symbolic interactionist perspective focuses on the meaning or symbolic significance that people attribute to one another's actions. Through social interaction, "human beings interpret or 'define' each other's actions instead of merely reacting to each other's actions" (Blumer 1969:79). Symbolic interactionism, therefore, may concentrate on the meaning we give to one another's actions as they relate to environmental practices. For example, your neighbour's use of a blue box for recycling might be interpreted as a sign that he or she is a good citizen, with the blue box as a symbol of concern for the environmental sustainability of the local community, or simply as an opportunity to meet or chat with other neighbours as they place their blue boxes at the roadside to be picked up. The interactionist perspective encompasses the phenomenon of social constructionism, in which individuals continually construct and reconstruct their meaning of environmental practices. Sociologists Clay Schoenfeld, Robert Meir, and Robert Griffin (1979) studied how environmental issues become the concerns of everyday citizens and how concern for an environmental issue one year (e.g., child labour or deforestation) may be supplanted by a different environmental concern the next year (e.g., public transportation or genetically modified foods). The meaning we give to human interaction is continually reconstructed; thus, different environmental issues may emerge as being of a higher profile than others are.

::: use your sociological *imagination* :::

Your community is designated as a site for the burial of toxic waste. How would you react? Would you organize a protest? Or would you make sure the authorities carry the project out safely? How can such sites be chosen fairly?

www.mcgrawhillconnect.ca

social policy and Globalization

Transnationals

The Issue

Around the world, new communications technologies—cellphones, the World Wide Web—have definitely hastened the process of globalization. Yet without human capital, these innovations would not have spurred the huge increase in global trade and development that occurred over the last several decades. Who are the people behind the trend toward globalization? Often, they are people who see a business opportunity abroad and strike out on their own to take advantage of it. In the process, many of them become migrants.

To facilitate trade and investment with other countries, migrants often exploit their social connections and their familiarity with their home language and culture. In Southeast Asia, for example, Chinese migrants dominate the trade with China; in Africa, Indian migrants dominate. Some migrants invest directly in their home countries to get the manufactured goods they sell abroad. Opportunities abound, and those with capital and good business skills can become quite wealthy (Guest 2011).

The millions of migrant labourers who leave home in search of a better life also play a role in the global economy, filling jobs where there are shortages in the labour market. Although they do not become wealthy working as landscapers or short-order cooks, they consider themselves better off than they were in the old country. Unfortunately, citizens of the host countries often react negatively to the migrants' arrival, worrying that they will take jobs away from the native-born.

The Setting

As of 2011, 192 million people, or about 3 percent of the world's population, were international migrants. That is more than double the number in 1970. The rest of the world's population were "stayers"—that is, people who continued to live in the countries where they were born (International Organization for Migration 2011).

Figure 16-2 shows the worldwide movement of workers with and without the legal right to immigrate. Several areas, such as the European Union, have instituted international agreements that

figure 16-2 Labour Migration

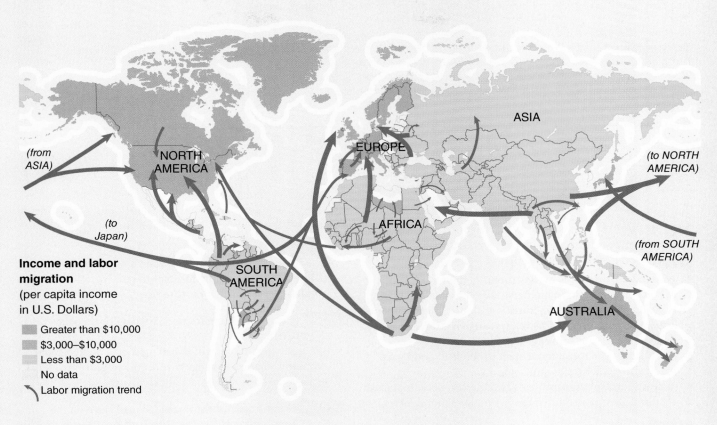

Income and labor migration
(per capita income in U.S. Dollars)

- Greater than $10,000
- $3,000–$10,000
- Less than $3,000
- No data
- Labor migration trend

Source: National Geographic 2005:16.

provide for the free movement of labourers. But in most other parts of the world, immigration restrictions give foreign workers only temporary status. Despite such legal restrictions, the labour market has become an increasingly global one. Just as globalization has integrated government policies, cultures, social movements, and financial markets, it has unified what were once discrete national labour markets. So today, for example, immigrants from at least eight different countries work in one small Middle Eastern state, Dubai.

Globalization has changed the immigrant experience as well as the labour market. In generations past, immigrants read foreign language newspapers to keep in touch with events in their home countries. Today, the Internet gives them immediate access to their countries and kinfolk. In this global framework, immigrants are less likely than they were in the past to think of themselves as residents of just one country. *Transnationals* are immigrants who sustain multiple social relationships that link their societies of origin with their societies of settlement (P. Levitt and Jaworsky 2007).

Sociological Insights

As with other issues, sociologists differ in their opinion of transnationals, depending on their theoretical

perspective. Functionalists see the free flow of immigrants, even when it is legally restricted, as one way for economies to maximize their use of human labour. Given the law of supply and demand, they note, countries with too few workers will inevitably attract labourers, while those with too many will become unattractive to residents.

Conflict theorists charge that globalization and international migration have increased the economic gulf between developed and developing nations. Today, residents of North America, Europe, and Japan consume 32 times more resources than the billions of people who live in developing countries. Through tourism and the global reach of the mass media, people in the poorer countries have become aware of the affluent lifestyle common in developed nations—and of course, many of them now aspire to it (Diamond 2003).

Interactionists are interested in the day-to-day relationships transnationals have with the people around them, from those of their country of origin to those of the host country and fellow workers from other countries. These scholars are studying transnationals' involvement in local ethnic organizations, to see whether their membership facilitates or retards their integration into the

host society. They have discovered that members of global social networks provide one another with mutual support and trust. Just as interesting is the question of how migrants see themselves—how they see their own identities as well as those of their children. In effect, transnationals negotiate their identities, depending on which social network they belong to at the moment. Some sociologists note that while being a transnational can be exhilarating, it can also isolate a person, even in a city of millions. Others worry that transnationals may become so cosmopolitan that they will lose touch with their national identities (Calhoun 2003; Evergeti and Zontini 2006; Plüss 2005; Portes et al. 2008; Rajan and Sharma 2006; Tilly 2007).

Policy Initiatives

Although connecting to two societies can be an enriching experience, transnationals face continuing adjustment problems in their new home countries. Immigrant labourers often face difficult living and working conditions. Some sending countries, such as Indonesia and the Philippines, have created national agencies to ensure the protection of their workers abroad. Their objective is ambitious, given that funding for the agencies is limited, and diplomatic and legal challenges complicate their task (United Nations Development Programme 2009:102–104).

Another unresolved transnational issue is voter eligibility. Not all nations allow dual citizenship; even those countries that do may not allow absent nationals to vote. The United States and Great Britain are rather liberal in this regard, permitting dual citizenship and allowing émigrés to continue to vote. Mexico, in contrast, has been reluctant to allow citizens who have emigrated to vote. Mexican politicians worry that the large number of Mexicans who live abroad (especially those in the United States) might vote differently from local voters, causing different outcomes (P. Levitt and Jaworsky 2007; Sellers 2004).

Finally, the controversial issue of illegal immigration has yet to be settled, perhaps because of culture lag. That is, both public attitudes and government policies (nonmaterial culture) have not kept pace with, much less adjusted to, the increasing ease of migration around the globe (material culture). Though globalization has created a global labour market—one that many countries depend on, legal or illegal—the general public's attitude toward illegal immigrants remains hostile, especially in the United States.

Apply the Theory

1. According to conflict thinkers, what role does globalization play in relation to the gulf between developing and developed countries?
2. Suppose you are an interactionist thinker. What topic of research might you construct relating to transnationals?

CHAPTER RESOURCES

Summary

::: 16.1 What Are Social Movements?

- A **social movement** is more structured than other forms of collective behaviour and persists over longer periods.
- A group will not mobilize into a social movement without a shared perception that its **relative deprivation** can be ended only through collective action.
- The success of a social movement depends in good part on effective resource mobilization.
- A **new social movement** tends to focus on more than just economic issues, and often crosses national boundaries.

::: 16.2 How Can Social Change Be Explained?

- Early advocates of the **evolutionary theory** of social change believed that society was progressing inevitably toward a higher state.
- Talcott Parsons, a leading advocate of functionalist theory, viewed society as being in a natural state of equilibrium or balance.
- Conflict theorists as well as feminist theorists see change as having crucial significance, since it is needed to correct social injustices and inequalities.

::: 16.3 What Forms Does Resistance to Social Change Take?

- In general, those with a disproportionate share of society's wealth, status, and power have a **vested interest** in preserving the status quo, and will resist change.

- The period of maladjustment when a non-material culture is still struggling to adapt to new material conditions is known as **culture lag**.

::: 16.4 How Does Globalization Affect Global Social Change?

- We are living in a time of sweeping social, political, and economic change—change that occurs not just on a local or national basis, but on a global scale.

::: 16.5 What Impact Does Social Change Have on the Environment?

- Advances in biotechnology have raised difficult ethical questions about genetic engineering and the sex selection of fetuses.
- Air pollution, water pollution, global warming and the impact of globalization are four major areas of environmental concern. Though globalization can contribute to environmental woes, it can also have beneficial effects.
- Conflict theorists charge that the most serious threat to the environment comes from Western industrialized nations.

Critical Thinking Questions

1. Select one social movement that is currently working for change in Canada. Analyze that movement, drawing on the concepts of relative deprivation, resource mobilization, and false consciousness.
2. In the last few years, we have witnessed phenomenal growth in the use of cellphones around the world. Analyze this form of material culture in terms of culture lag. Consider usage, government regulation, and privacy issues.
3. Imagine that you have been asked to study the issue of air pollution in the largest city in your province or territory. How might you draw on surveys, observation research, experiments, and existing sources to study the issue?

THINKING ABOUT MOVIES

Afghan Star

This documentary presents the Afghan version of *American Idol*.

Babies

This cross-cultural comparison explores the lives of several real-life babies from different parts of the world.

Up the Yangtze

A ship cruises the Yangtze River, revealing the dramatic changes occurring in China today.

glossary

Absolute poverty A standard of poverty based on a minimum level of subsistence below which families should not be expected to live. (p. 126)

Achieved status A social position that a person attains largely through his or her own efforts. (p. 92)

Activity theory An interactionist theory of aging that argues that elderly people who remain active and socially involved will be best adjusted. (p. 82)

Adoption A process that allows for the transfer of the legal rights, responsibilities, and privileges of parenthood to a new legal parent or parents. (p. 258)

Ageism Prejudice and discrimination against the elderly. (p. 82)

Agrarian society The most technologically advanced form of pre-industrial society. Members are engaged primarily in the production of food, but increase their crop yields through technological innovations such as the plow. (p. 103)

Alienation A condition of estrangement or dissociation from the surrounding society. (p. 105)

Anomie The loss of direction felt in a society when social control of individual behaviour has become ineffective. (p. 10)

Anomie theory of deviance Robert Merton's theory that explains deviance as an adaptation either of socially prescribed goals or of the norms governing their attainment, or both. (p. 232)

Anticipatory socialization Processes of socialization in which a person "rehearses" for future positions, occupations, and social relationships. (p. 78)

Apartheid The former policy of the South African government designed to maintain the separation of blacks and other non-whites from the dominant whites. (p. 166)

Argot Specialized language used by members of a group or subculture. (p. 56)

Arranged marriages Marriages engineered by parents or religious authorities, in which economic considerations play a significant role. (p. 255)

Ascribed status A social position assigned to a person by society without regard for the person's unique talents or characteristics. (p. 92)

Assimilation The process by which a person forsakes his or her own cultural tradition to become part of a different culture. (p. 166)

Authority Institutionalized power that is recognized by the people over whom it is exercised. (p. 300)

Bilateral descent A kinship system in which both sides of a person's family are regarded as equally important. (p. 250)

Birth rate The number of live births per 1000 population in a given year. Also known as the *crude birth rate*. (p. 321)

Blended family The result when a couple or individual who separates or divorces and then goes on to form a new relationship, when children are involved (p. 259)

Bourgeoisie Karl Marx's term for the capitalist class, comprising the owners of the means of production. (p. 120)

Bureaucracy A component of formal organization that uses rules and hierarchical ranking to achieve efficiency. (p. 105)

Bureaucratization The process by which a group, organization, or social movement becomes increasingly bureaucratic. (p. 106)

Capitalism An economic system in which the means of production are largely in private hands and the main incentive for economic activity is the accumulation of profits. (p. 120)

Career choice The first phase of occupational socialization. (p. 78)

Castes Hereditary systems of rank, usually religiously dictated, that tend to be fixed and immobile. (p. 117)

Causal logic The relationship between a condition or variable and a particular consequence, with one event leading to the other. (p. 28)

Census An enumeration, or counting, of a population. (p. 320)

Central cities Large urban areas where population is concentrated. (p. 340)

Charismatic authority Power made legitimate by a leader's exceptional personal or emotional appeal to his or her followers. (p. 301)

Class A group of people who have a similar level of wealth and income. (p. 122)

Class consciousness In Karl Marx's view, a subjective awareness held by members of a class regarding their common vested interests and need for collective political action to bring about social change. (p. 120)

Class system A social ranking based primarily on economic position in which achieved characteristics can influence social mobility. (p. 117)

Classical theory An approach to the study of formal organizations that views workers as being motivated almost entirely by economic rewards. (p. 107)

Closed system A social system in which there is little or no possibility of individual mobility. (p. 130)

Coalition A temporary or permanent alliance geared toward a common goal. (p. 97)

Code of ethics The standards of acceptable behaviour developed by and for members of a profession. (p. 35)

Cognitive theory of development Jean Piaget's theory explaining how children's thought progresses through four stages. (p. 73)

Cohabitation The practice of living together as a couple without marrying. (p. 262)

Colonialism The maintenance of political, social, economic, and cultural dominance over a people by a foreign power for an extended period. (p. 140)

Commitment Part of the third phase of occupational socialization, it involves a worker enthusiastically accepting the pleasurable duties; this acceptance comes with the recognition by the person of the positive tasks of an occupation. (p. 78)

Communism As an ideal type, an economic system under which all property is communally owned and no social distinctions are made on the basis of people's ability to produce. (p. 297)

Community A spatial or political unit of social organization that gives people a sense of belonging. (p. 318)

Concentric-zone theory A theory for describing land use in industrial cities, where the centre (or nucleus) of a city is the central business district. (p. 336)

Concrete operational The third stage in Piaget's theory of cognitive development. (p. 73)

Conditioning Part of the third phase of occupational socialization, it involves a worker reluctantly adjusting to the more unpleasant aspects of a job. (p. 78)

Conflict perspective A sociological approach that assumes that social behaviour is best understood in terms of conflict or tension between competing groups. (p. 15)

Conformity Going along with peers, individuals of a person's own status who have no special right to direct that person's behaviour. (p. 225)

Contact hypothesis An interactionist perspective that states that interracial contact between people of equal status in cooperative circumstances will reduce prejudice. (p. 165)

Content analysis The systematic coding and objective recording of data, guided by some rationale. (p. 34)

Control group Subjects in an experiment who are not introduced to the independent variable by the researcher. (p. 33)

Control theory A view of conformity and deviance that suggests our connection to members of society leads us to systematically conform to society's norms. (p. 229)

Control variable A factor held constant to test the relative impact of an independent variable. (p. 30)

Correlation A relationship between two variables whereby a change in one coincides with a change in the other. (p. 29)

Correspondence principle The tendency of schools to promote the values expected of individuals in each social class and to prepare students for the types of jobs typically held by members of their class. (p. 286)

Counterculture A subculture that deliberately opposes certain aspects of the larger culture. (p. 56)

Creationism A literal interpretation of the Bible regarding the creation of humanity and the universe, used to argue that evolution should not be presented as established scientific fact. (p. 289)

Crime A violation of criminal law for which some governmental authority applies formal penalties. (p. 237)

Cult A generally small, often secretive religious group that represents either a new religion or a major innovation of an existing faith. (p. 281)

Cultural capital Noneconomic goods, such as family background and education, which are reflected in a knowledge of language and the arts. (p. 13)

Cultural convergence The flow of content across multiple media, and the accompanying migration of media audiences. (p. 203)

Cultural imperialism The influence or imposition of the material or non-material elements of a culture on another culture or cultures. (p. 57)

Cultural relativism The viewing of people's behaviour from the perspective of their own culture. (p. 58)

Cultural transmission A school of criminology which argues that criminal behaviour is learned through social interactions. (p. 233)

Cultural universals General practices found in every culture. (p. 46)

Culture The totality of learned, socially transmitted customs, knowledge, material objects, and behaviour. (p. 45)

Culture lag Ogburn's term for a period of maladjustment during which the non-material culture is still adapting to new material conditions. (p. 48)

Culture shock The feeling of surprise and disorientation that is experienced when people witness cultural practices different from their own. (p. 56)

Death rate The number of deaths per 1000 population in a given year. Also known as the *crude death rate*. (p. 321)

Defended neighbourhood A sentimental union of similar people, where inhabitants apply their own definitions of community boundaries. (p. 340)

Degradation ceremony An aspect of the socialization process within total institutions, in which people are subjected to humiliating rituals. (p. 83)

Deindustrialization The systematic, widespread withdrawal of investment in basic aspects of productivity, such as factories and plants. (p. 312)

Democracy In a literal sense, government by the people. (p. 303)

Demographic transition A term used to describe the change from high birth rates and death rates to relatively low birth rates and death rates. (p. 322)

Demography The scientific study of population. (p. 319)

Denomination A large, organized religion not officially linked with the state or government. (p. 279)

Dependency theory An approach which contends that industrialized nations continue to exploit developing countries for their own gain. (p. 140)

Dependent variable The variable in a causal relationship that is subject to the influence of another variable. (p. 28)

Deviance Behaviour that violates the standards of conduct or expectations of a group or society. (p. 229)

Dictatorship A government in which one person has nearly total power to make and enforce laws. (p. 303)

Differential association A theory of deviance proposed by Edwin Sutherland that holds that violation of rules results from exposure to attitudes favourable to criminal acts. (p. 233)

Diffusion The process by which a cultural item is spread from group to group or society to society. (p. 46)

Digital divide The gap between developing and developed countries, in computer and Internet use as well as in factors such as age, gender, income, and education. (p. 220)

Discovery The process of making known or sharing the existence of an aspect of reality. (p. 46)

Discrimination The process of denying opportunities and equal rights to individuals and groups because of prejudice or for other arbitrary reasons. (p. 161)

Disengagement theory A functionalist theory of aging that contends that society and the aging individual mutually sever many of their relationships. (p. 80)

Dominant ideology A set of cultural beliefs and practices that helps to maintain powerful social, economic, and political interests. (p. 54)

Double jeopardy Discrimination that women experience as a result of the compounded effects of gender and race and ethnicity. (p. 193)

Downsizing Reductions taken in a company's workforce as part of deindustrialization. (p. 312)

Dramaturgical approach A view of social interaction that examines people as if they were theatrical performers. (p. 18)

Dysfunction An element or a process of society that may disrupt a social system or lead to a decrease in stability. (p. 15)

Ecclesia A religious organization that claims to include most or all of the members of a society and is recognized as the national or official religion. (p. 279)

Economic system The social institution through which goods and services are produced, distributed, and consumed. (p. 295)

Education A formal process of learning in which some people consciously teach while others adopt the social role of learner. (p. 270)

Egalitarian family An authority pattern in which the adult members of the family are regarded as equals. (p. 250)

Elite model A view of society as being ruled by a small group of individuals who share a common set of political and economic interests. (p. 306)

Employment equity A federal act that attempts to eliminate barriers faced in the area of employment. (p. 163)

Endogamy The restriction of mate selection to people within the same group. (p. 254)

Environmental justice A legal strategy based on claims that racial minorities are subjected disproportionately to environmental hazards. (p. 362)

Equality feminists Another term for liberal feminists, who endorse individual freedom and equality of opportunity in the public and economic spheres. (p. 72)

Equilibrium model Talcott Parsons's functionalist view of society as tending toward a state of stability or balance. (p. 353)

Esteem The reputation that a particular individual has earned within an occupation. (p. 124)

Ethnic group A group that is set apart from others because of its national origin or distinctive cultural patterns. (p. 157)

Ethnoburbs Suburbs that are ethnically diverse. (p. 342)

Ethnocentrism The tendency to assume that our own culture and way of life represent the norm or are superior to all others. (p. 58)

Ethnography The study of an entire social setting through extended, systematic observation. (p. 32)

Eurocentrism The dominance of European cultural patterns that contribute to the view of non-European people and cultural patterns as being "other." (p. 57)

Evolutionary theory A theory of social change that holds that society is moving in a definite direction. (p. 353)

Exogamy The requirement that people select mates outside certain groups. (p. 254)

Experiment An artificially created situation that allows the researcher to manipulate variables. (p. 33)

Experimental group Subjects in an experiment who are exposed to an independent variable introduced by a researcher. (p. 33)

Exploitation theory A Marxist theory that views racial subordination, such as that in Canada, as a manifestation of the class system inherent in capitalism. (p. 164)

Expressiveness The concern for maintenance of harmony and the internal emotional affairs of the family. (p. 185)

Extended family A family in which relatives—such as grandparents, aunts, or uncles—live in the same home as parents and their children. (p. 250)

Face-work The efforts of people to maintain the proper image and avoid embarrassment in public. (p. 72)

Fair trade A movement in which consumers in industrialized countries voluntarily pay above-market prices for certain foods so that the workers who plant, pick, and pack the crops can receive higher wages. (p. 294)

False consciousness A term used by Karl Marx to describe an attitude held by members of a class that does not accurately reflect their objective position. (p. 120)

Family A set of people related by blood, marriage (or some other agreed-on relationship), or adoption, who share the responsibility for reproducing and caring for members of society. (p. 248)

Feminist perspectives Sociological approaches that attempt to explain, understand, and change the ways in which gender socially organizes our public and private lives in such a way as to produce inequality between men and women. (p. 16)

Fertility The amount of reproduction among women of child-bearing age. (p. 319)

Folkways Norms governing everyday social behaviour whose violation raises comparatively little concern. (p. 52)

Force The actual or threatened use of coercion to impose one's will on others. (p. 300)

Formal norms Norms that generally have been written down and that specify strict rules for punishment of violators. (p. 52)

Formal operational The fourth stage in Piaget's theory of cognitive development. (p. 73)

Formal organization A group designed for a special purpose and structured for maximum efficiency. (p. 105)

Formal social control Social control carried out by authorized agents, such as police officers, judges, school administrators, and employers. (p. 227)

Functionalist perspective A sociological approach that emphasizes the way that parts of a society are structured to maintain its stability. (p. 14)

Game stage In interactionist theory, the third stage of Mead's three-stage model for the emergence of self. (p. 70)

Gatekeeping The process by which a relatively small number of people in the media industry control what material eventually reaches the audience. (p. 206)

Gemeinschaft A close-knit community, often found in rural areas, in which strong personal bonds unite members. (p. 102)

Gender Culturally and socially constructed identity as a man or a woman. (p. 181)

Gender roles Expectations regarding the proper behaviour, attitudes, and activities of males and females. (p. 74)

Gender socialization An aspect of socialization through which we learn the attitudes, behaviours, and practices associated with being male and female according to our society and social groups within it. (p. 74)

Generalized other A term used by George Herbert Mead to refer to the attitudes, viewpoints, and expectations of society as a whole that a child takes into account in his or her behaviour. (p. 18)

Genocide The deliberate, systematic killing of an entire people or nation. (p. 165)

Gerontology The scientific study of the sociological and psychological aspects of aging and the problems of the aged. (p. 80)

Gesellschaft A community, often urban, that is large and impersonal, with little commitment to the group or consensus on values. (p. 102)

Glass ceiling An invisible barrier that blocks the promotion of a qualified individual in a work environment because of the individual's gender, race, or ethnicity. (p. 161)

Global economy The economy of the world when people have the capacity to work as a single unit in real time. (p. 214)

Globalization The worldwide integration of government policies, cultures, social movements, and financial markets through trade and the exchange of ideas. (p. 19)

Goal displacement Overzealous conformity to official regulations of a bureaucracy. (p. 106)

Gross national product (GNP) The value of a nation's goods and services. (p. 145)

Group Any number of people with similar norms, values, and expectations who interact with one another on a regular basis. (p. 95)

Growth rate The difference between births and deaths, plus the differences between immigrants and emigrants, per 1000 population. (p. 321)

Habit training A relatively formal period of infant socialization, during which caregivers impose routines on the infant. (p. 74)

Hawthorne effect The unintended influence that observers or experimenters can have on their subjects. (p. 34)

Health As defined by the World Health Organization, a "state of complete physical, mental, and social well-being, and not merely the absence of disease and infirmity." (p. 326)

Hegemony The process through which the views of the ruling class are accepted and seen as "normal" by the exploited classes. (p. 208)

Hidden curriculum Standards of behaviour that are deemed proper by society and are taught subtly in schools. (p. 285)

Homophobia Fear of and prejudice against homosexuality. (p. 182)

Horizontal mobility The movement of an individual from one social position to another of the same rank. (p. 130)

Horticultural society A pre-industrial society in which people plant seeds and crops rather than merely subsisting on available foods. (p. 103)

Human ecology   A field of study concerned with the relationships between people and their environment. (p. 335)

Human genome   The 30 000 to 40 000 human genes in existence. (p. 360)

Human relations approach   An approach to the study of formal organizations that emphasizes the role of people, communication, and participation in a bureaucracy and tends to focus on the informal structure of the organization. (p. 107)

Human rights   Universal moral rights possessed by all people because they are human. (p. 151)

Hunting-and-gathering society   A pre-industrial society in which people rely on whatever foods and fibres are readily available in order to survive. (p. 103)

Hypothesis   A speculative statement about the relationship between two or more variables. (p. 28)

Ideal type   A construct or model that serves as a measuring rod against which actual cases can be evaluated. (p. 10)

Impression management   The altering of the presentation of the self to create distinctive appearances and satisfy particular audiences. (p. 71)

Incest taboo   The prohibition of sexual relationships between certain culturally specified relatives. (p. 254)

Incidence   The number of *new* cases of a specific disorder occurring within a given population during a stated period. (p. 326)

Income   Salaries and wages. (p. 116)

Independent variable   The variable in a causal relationship that causes or influences a change in a second variable. (p. 28)

Industrial city   The city that emerged following the Industrial Revolution; a centre of banking, finance, and industrialization, with a more open class system. (p. 334)

Industrial society   A society that depends on mechanization to produce its goods and services. (pp. 104)

Infant mortality rate   The number of deaths of infants under one year of age per 1000 live births in a given year. (p. 321)

Influence   The exercise of power through a process of persuasion. (p. 300)

Informal economy   Transfers of money, goods, or services that are not reported to the government. (p. 297)

Informal norms   Norms that generally are understood but are not precisely recorded. (p. 52)

Informal social control   Social control carried out casually by ordinary people through such means as laughter, smiles, and ridicule. (p. 227)

In-group   Any group or category to which people feel they belong. (p. 96)

Innovation   The process of introducing new elements into a culture through either discovery or invention. (p. 46)

Institutional discrimination   The denial of opportunities and equal rights to individuals and groups that results from the normal operations of a society. (p. 162)

Instrumentality   The emphasis on tasks, along with a focus on more distant goals and a concern for the external relationship between the family and other social institutions. (p. 185)

Interactionist perspective   A sociological approach that generalizes about fundamental or everyday forms of social interaction. (p. 17)

Intergenerational mobility   Changes in the social position of children relative to their parents. (p. 130)

Interview   A face-to-face or telephone questioning of a respondent to obtain desired information. (p. 31)

Intragenerational mobility   Changes in a person's social position within his or her adult life. (p. 130)

Invention   The combination of existing cultural items into a form that did not previously exist. (p. 46)

Iron law of oligarchy   A principle of organizational life under which even a democratic organization will eventually develop into a bureaucracy ruled by a few individuals. (p. 107)

Kinship   The state of being related to others. (p. 250)

Labelling theory   An approach to deviance that attempts to explain why certain people are viewed as deviants while others engaging in the same behaviour are not. (p. 234)

Labour unions   Organized workers who share either the same skill or the same employer. (p. 111)

Laissez-faire   A form of capitalism under which people compete freely, with minimal government intervention in the economy. (p. 295)

Language   An abstract system of word meanings and symbols for all aspects of culture. It also includes gestures and other non-verbal communication. (p. 49)

Latent functions   Unconscious or unintended functions; hidden purposes. (p. 15)

Law   Governmental social control. (p. 52)

Liberal feminism   The stream of feminism asserting that women's equality can be obtained through the extension of the principles of equality of opportunity and freedom. (p. 15)

Liberation theology   Use of a church, primarily Roman Catholicism, in a political effort to eliminate poverty, discrimination, and other forms of injustice evident in a secular society. (p. 276)

Life chances   People's opportunities to provide themselves with material goods, positive living conditions, and favourable life experiences. (p. 129)

Life expectancy   The median number of years a person can be expected to live under current mortality conditions. (p. 321)

Looking-glass self   A concept that emphasizes the self as the product of our social interactions with others. (p. 70)

Luddites   Rebellious craft workers in nineteenth-century England who destroyed new factory machinery as part of their resistance to the Industrial Revolution. (p. 356)

Macrosociology   Sociological investigation that concentrates on large-scale phenomena or entire civilizations. (p. 13)

Manifest functions   Open, stated, and conscious functions. (p. 15)

Marxist feminism   The stream of feminist sociological approaches that place the system of capitalism at fault for the oppression of women and hold that women are not oppressed by sexism or patriarchy, but rather by a system of economic production that is based on unequal gender relations in the capitalist economy. (p. 15)

Mass media   Print and electronic means of communication that carry messages to widespread audiences. (p. 203)

Master status   A status that dominates others and thereby determines a person's general position in society. (p. 93)

Material culture   The physical or technological aspects of our daily lives. (p. 48)

Matriarchy   A society in which women dominate in family decision making. (p. 250)

Matrilineal descent   A kinship system that favours the relatives of the mother. (p. 250)

Matrix of domination   The cumulative impact of oppression because of race and ethnicity, gender, and social class, as well as religion, sexual orientation, disability, age, and citizenship status. (p. 187)

McDonaldization   The process by which the principles of the fast-food restaurant have come to dominate more and more sectors of U.S. society as well as of the rest of the world. (p. 90)

Mechanical solidarity   A collective consciousness that emphasizes group solidarity, characteristic of societies with minimal division of labour. (p. 101)

Media monitoring   The monitoring of media content by interest groups, as well as the monitoring of individuals' media usage and choices. (p. 208)

Medicalization of society   The growing role of medicine as a major institution of social control. (p. 330)

Megalopolis   A densely populated area, containing two or more cities and their suburbs. (p. 335)

Microfinancing   Lending small sums of money to the poor so they can work their way out of poverty. (p. 313)

Microsociology   Sociological investigation that stresses study of small groups and often uses laboratory experimental studies. (p. 10)

Minority group   A subordinate group whose members have significantly less control or power over their own lives than the members of a dominant or majority group have over theirs. (p. 157)

Modernization   The far-reaching process by which periphery nations move from traditional or less developed institutions to those characteristic of more developed societies. (p. 142)

Modernization theory   A functionalist approach that proposes that modernization and development will gradually improve the lives of people in developing nations. (p. 142)

Monarchy   A form of government headed by a single member of a royal family, usually a king, queen, or count some other hereditary ruler. (p. 303)

Monogamy   A form of marriage in which one woman and one man are married only to each other. (p. 250)

Monopoly   Control of a market by a single business firm. (p. 295)

Morbidity rate   The incidence of diseases in a given population. (p. 326)

Mores   Norms deemed highly necessary to the welfare of a society. (p. 52)

Mortality   Number of deaths. (p. 319)

Mortality rate   The incidence of death in a given population. (p. 326)

Multiculturalism   A policy that promotes cultural and racial diversity and full and equal participation of individuals and communities of all origins as a fundamental characteristic of Canadian identity. (p. 57)

Multinational corporation   A commercial organization that is headquartered in one country but does business throughout the world. (p. 143)

Multiple jeopardies   Compounded effects of gender, race and ethnicity, class, age, or physical disability. (p. 193)

Multiple-nuclei theory   A response to the emergence of more than one focal point in some metropolitan areas. In this view, a metropolitan area may have many centres of development, each of which reflects a particular urban need or activity. (p. 336)

N

Narcotizing dysfunction   The phenomenon in which the media provide such massive amounts of coverage that the audience becomes numb and fails to act on the information, regardless of how compelling the issue. (p. 205)

Narrowcasting   Marketing of the media to a particular audience. (p. 214)

Natural science   The study of the physical features of nature and the ways in which they interact and change. (p. 07)

Neo-colonialism   Continuing dependence of former colonies on more industrialized foreign countries, including those that are former colonial masters. (p. 140)

New religious movement (NRM)   A generally small, often secretive religious group that represents either a new religion or a major innovation of an existing faith. (p. 281)

New social movement   An organized collective activity that addresses values and social identities, as well as improvements in the quality of life. (p. 351)

New urban sociology   Field of sociology that considers the interplay of local, national, and worldwide forces and their effect on local space, with special emphasis on the impact of global economic activity. (p. 337)

Niche audience   A particular audience to which the media market themselves. (p. 215)

Non-material culture   Cultural adjustments to material conditions, such as customs, beliefs, patterns of communication, and ways of using material objects. (p. 48)

Norms   Established standards of behaviour maintained by a society. (p. 51)

Nuclear family   A married couple and their unmarried children living together. (p. 249)

O

Obedience   Compliance with higher authorities in a hierarchical structure. (p. 225)

Objective method   A technique for measuring social class that assigns individuals to classes on the basis of such criteria as occupation, education, income, and place of residence. (p. 124)

Observation   A research technique in which an investigator collects information through direct participation or by closely watching a group or community. (p. 32)

Oligarchy   A form of government in which a few individuals rule. (p. 303)

Open system   A social system in which the position of each individual is influenced by his or her achieved status. (p. 130)

Operational definition   An explanation of an abstract concept that is specific enough to allow a researcher to assess the concept. (p. 28)

Opinion leader   Someone who influences the opinions and decisions of others through day-to-day personal contact and communication (e.g., a film or theatre critic). (p. 216)

Organic solidarity   A collective consciousness that rests on mutual interdependence, characteristic of societies with a complex division of labour. (p. 102)

Organized crime   The work of a group that regulates relations among various criminal enterprises involved in the smuggling and sale of drugs, prostitution, gambling, and other illegal activities. (p. 238)

Out-group   A group or category to which people feel they do not belong. (p. 96)

P

Patriarchy   A society in which men dominate in family decision making. (p. 250)

Patrilineal descent   A kinship system that favours the relatives of the father. (p. 250)

Peace   The absence of war; or a proactive effort to develop cooperative relations among nations. (p. 309)

Personality   In everyday speech, a person's typical patterns of attitudes, needs, characteristics, and behaviour. (p. 67)

Peter Principle   A principle of organizational life according to which every employee within a hierarchy tends to rise to his or her level of incompetence. (p. 106)

Play stage   In interactionist theory, the second stage of Mead's three-stage model for the emergence of self. (p. 70)

Pluralist model   A view of society in which many competing groups within the community have access to government, so that no single group is dominant. (p. 308)

Political system   The social institution that is founded on a recognized set of procedures for implementing and achieving society's goals. (p. 295)

Politics   In Harold Lasswell's words, "who gets what, when, and how." (p. 300)

Polyandry   A form of polygamy in which a woman can have more than one husband at the same time. (p. 250)

Polygamy   A form of marriage in which an individual can have several husbands or wives simultaneously. (p. 250)

Polygyny   A form of polygamy in which a husband can have several wives at the same time. (p. 250)

Population pyramid   A special type of bar chart that shows the distribution of population by gender and age. (p. 323)

Post-industrial city   A city in which global finance and the electronic flow of information dominate the economy. (p. 334)

Post-industrial society   A society whose economic system is engaged primarily in the processing and control of information. (p. 104)

Postmodern society   A technologically sophisticated society that is preoccupied with consumer goods and media images. (p. 18)

Power   The ability of people to exercise their will over others. (p. 122)

Power elite   A small group of individuals who share a common set of political and economic interests. (p. 307)

Pre-industrial city   An old city that had a few thousand people living within its borders and was also characterized by a relatively closed class system and limited mobility. (p. 333)

Prejudice   A negative attitude toward an entire category of people, such as a racial or an ethnic minority. (p. 161)

Preoperational   The second stage in Piaget's theory of cognitive development. (p. 73)

Preparatory stage   In interactionist theory, the first stage of Mead's three-stage model for the emergence of self. (p. 70)

Prestige   The respect and admiration that an occupation holds in a society. (p. 124)

Prevalence   The total number of cases of a specific disorder that exist at a given time. (p. 326)

Primary group   A small group characterized by intimate, face-to-face association and cooperation. (p. 96)

Profane   The ordinary and commonplace elements of life, as distinguished from the sacred. (p. 272)

Professional criminal   A person who pursues crime as a day-to-day occupation, developing skilled techniques and enjoying a certain degree of status among other criminals. (p. 237)

Proletariat   Karl Marx's term for the working class in a capitalist society. (p. 120)

Protestant ethic   Max Weber's term for the disciplined work ethic, worldly concerns, and rational orientation to life emphasized by John Calvin and his followers. (p. 275)

Qualitative research   Research that relies on what is seen in field or naturalistic settings more than on statistical data. (p. 32)

Quantitative research   Research that collects and reports data primarily in numerical form. (p. 32)

Questionnaire   A printed or written form used to obtain desired information from a respondent. (p. 31)

Racial group   A group that is set apart and treated differently from others because of perceived physical attributes. (p. 157)

Racial or ethnic profiling   The use of a social construct of race as a consideration in suspect profiling in law enforcement and national security practices. (p. 163)

Racialization   The social processes by which people come to define a group as a "race," based in part on physical characteristics, but also on historical, cultural, and economic factors. (p. 158)

Racism   The belief that one race is supreme and all others are innately inferior. (p. 161)

Radical feminism   The stream of feminism maintaining that the root of all oppression of women is embedded in patriarchy. (p. 16)

Random sample   A sample for which every member of the entire population has the same chance of being selected. (p. 29)

Rational-legal authority   Power made legitimate by law. (p. 300)

Reference group   Any group that individuals use as a standard for evaluating themselves and their own behaviour. (p. 97)

Relative deprivation   The conscious feeling of a negative discrepancy between legitimate expectations and present actualities. (p. 350)

Relative poverty   A floating standard of deprivation by which people at the bottom of a society, whatever their lifestyles, are judged to be disadvantaged in comparison with the nation as a whole. (p. 127)

Reliability   The extent to which a measure provides consistent results. (p. 30)

Religion   A unified system of beliefs and practices relative to sacred things. (p. 272)

Religious beliefs   Statements to which members of a particular religion adhere. (p. 277)

Religious experience   The feeling or perception of being in direct contact with the ultimate reality, such as a divine being, or of being overcome with religious emotion. (p. 278)

Religious rituals   Practices required or expected of members of a faith. (p. 277)

Representative democracy   A form of government in which certain individuals are selected to speak for the people. (p. 303)

Research design   A detailed plan or method for obtaining data scientifically. (p. 31)

Resocialization   The process of discarding former behaviour patterns and accepting new ones as part of a transition in life. (p. 83)

Resource mobilization   The ways in which a social movement utilizes such resources as money, political influence, access to the media, and personnel. (p. 351)

Rites of passage   Rituals marking the symbolic transition from one social position to another. (p. 79)

Role conflict   The situation that occurs when incompatible expectations arise from two or more social positions held by the same person. (p. 93)

Role exit   The process of disengagement from a role that is central to one's self-identity in order to establish a new role and identity. (p. 95)

Role strain   The difficulty that arises when the same social position imposes conflicting demands and expectations. (p. 94)

Role-taking   The process of mentally assuming the perspective of another, thereby enabling a person to respond from that imagined viewpoint. (p. 70)

Routine activities theory   The notion that criminal victimization increases when there is a convergence of motivated offenders and suitable targets. (p. 234)

S

Sacred   Elements beyond everyday life that inspire awe, respect, and even fear. (p. 272)

Sample   A selection from a larger population that is statistically representative of that population. (p. 29)

Sanctions   Penalties and rewards for conduct concerning a social norm. (p. 52)

Sapir-Whorf hypothesis   A hypothesis concerning the role of language in shaping cultures. It holds that language is culturally determined and serves to influence our mode of thought. (p. 51)

Science   The body of knowledge obtained by methods based on systematic observation. (p. 5)

Scientific management approach   Another name for the classical theory of formal organizations. (p. 107)

Scientific method   A systematic, organized series of steps that ensures maximum objectivity and consistency in researching a problem. (p. 27)

Secondary analysis   A variety of research techniques that make use of previously existing and publicly accessible information and data. (p. 34)

Secondary group   A formal, impersonal group in which there is little social intimacy or mutual understanding. (p. 96)

Sect   A relatively small religious group that has broken away from another religious organization to renew what it views as the original vision of the faith. (p. 279)

Secularization   The process through which religion's influence on other social institutions diminishes. (p. 270)

Segmented audience   A particular audience to which the media market themselves. (p. 215)

Segregation   The act of physically separating two groups; often imposed on a minority group by a dominant group. (p. 166)

Self   A distinct identity that sets us apart from others. (p. 69)

Self-segregation   The situation that arises when members of a minority deliberately develop residential, economic, or social network structures that are separate from those of the majority population. (p. 166)

Sensorimotor   The first stage in Piaget's theory of cognitive development. (p. 73)

Serial monogamy   A life choice in which a person can have several spouses in his or her lifetime but only one spouse at a time. (p. 250)

Sex   Biological category that distinguishes between female and male. (p. 181)

Sexism   The ideology that one sex is superior to the other. (p. 189)

Sick role   Societal expectations about the attitudes and behaviour of a person viewed as being ill. (p. 329)

Significant others   A term used by George Herbert Mead to refer to those individuals who are most important in the development of the self, such as parents, friends, and teachers. (p. 18)

Single-parent families   Families in which there is only one parent to care for the children. Also known as lone-parent families. (p. 258)

Slavery   A system of enforced servitude in which people are legally owned by others and in which enslaved status is transferred from parents to children. (p. 117)

Social capital   The collective benefit of social networks, which are built on reciprocal trust. (p. 13)

Social change   Significant alteration over time in behaviour patterns and culture, including norms and values. (p. 348)

Social constructionist perspective   An approach to deviance that emphasizes the role of culture in the creation of the deviant identity. (p. 236)

Social control   The techniques and strategies for preventing deviant human behaviour in any society. (p. 225)

Social epidemiology   The study of the distribution of disease, impairment, and general health status across a population. (p. 326)

Social inequality   A condition in which members of a society have different amounts of wealth, prestige, or power. (p. 21)

Social institutions   Organized patterns of beliefs and behaviour centred on basic social needs. (p. 99)

Social interactions   The ways in which people respond to one another. (p. 90)

Social mobility   Movement of individuals or groups from one position of a society's stratification system to another. (p. 130)

Social movement   An organized collective activity to bring about or resist fundamental change in an existing group or society. (p. 349)

Social network   A series of social relationships that link a person directly to others, and through them indirectly to still more people. (p. 98)

Social role   A set of expectations for people who occupy a given social position or status. (p. 93)

Social science   The study of various aspects of human society. (p. 7)

Social structure   The way in which a society is organized into predictable relationships. (p. 90)

Socialism   An economic system under which the means of production and distribution are collectively owned. (p. 297)

Socialist feminism   The stream of feminism that maintains that gender relations are shaped by both patriarchy and capitalism, and thus equality for women implies that both the system of capitalism and the ideology of patriarchy must be challenged and eliminated. (p. 16)

Socialization   The process whereby people learn the attitudes, values, and behaviours appropriate for members of a particular culture. (p. 66)

Societal-reaction approach   Another name for *labelling theory.* (p. 235)

Society   A fairly large number of people who live in the same territory, are relatively independent of people outside it, and participate in a common culture. (p. 45)

Sociobiology   The systematic study of biological bases of social behaviour. (p. 69)

Sociocultural evolution   Long-term trends in societies resulting from the interplay of continuity, innovation, and selection. (p. 102)

Sociological imagination   An awareness of the relationship between an individual and the wider society. (p. 05)

Sociology   The systematic study of social behaviour and human groups. (p. 05)

Squatter settlements   Areas occupied by the very poor on the fringe of a city, in which housing is constructed by the settlers themselves from discarded material. (p. 338)

Status   A term used by sociologists to refer to any of the full range of socially defined positions within a large group or society. (p. 92)

Status group   People who have the same prestige or lifestyle, independent of their class positions. (p. 122)

Stereotypes   Unreliable generalizations about all members of a group that do not recognize individual differences within the group. (p. 159)

Stigma   A label used to devalue members of deviant social groups. (p. 230)

Stratification   A structured ranking of entire groups of people that perpetuates unequal economic rewards and power in a society. (p. 116)

Subculture   A segment of society that shares a distinctive pattern of mores, folkways, and values that differs from the pattern of the larger society. (p. 55)

Suburb   A term that generally refers to any community near a large city or any territory within a metropolitan area that is not included in the central city. (p. 341)

Survey A study, generally in the form of interviews or questionnaires, that provides researchers with information concerning how people think and act. (p. 31)

Symbols The gestures, objects, and language that form the basis of human communication. (p. 51)

Teacher-expectancy effect The impact that a teacher's expectations about a student's performance may have on the student's actual achievements. (p. 286)

Technology Information about how to use the material resources of the environment to satisfy human needs and desires. (p. 48)

Telecommuters Employees who work full-time or part-time at home rather than in an outside office, and who are linked to supervisors and colleagues through computer terminals, phone lines, and fax machines. (p. 109)

Terrorism The use or threat of violence against random or symbolic targets in pursuit of political aims. (p. 309)

Theory A template through which to organize a way to view the world. (p. 08)

Total fertility rate (TFR) The average number of children born alive to a woman, assuming that she conforms to current fertility rates. (p. 321)

Total institutions Institutions that regulate all aspects of a person's life under a single authority, such as prisons, the military, mental hospitals, and convents. (p. 83)

Totalitarianism Virtually complete government control and surveillance over all aspects of a society's social and political life. (p. 303)

Tracking The practice of placing students in specific curriculum groups on the basis of test scores and other criteria. (p. 285)

Traditional authority Legitimate power conferred by custom and accepted practice. (p. 300)

Trained incapacity The tendency of workers in a bureaucracy to become so specialized that they develop blind spots and fail to notice obvious problems. (p. 105)

Transnationals Immigrants with an allegiance to more than one nation. (p. 349)

Transnational crime Crime that occurs across multiple national borders. (p. 240)

Transnational feminism The stream of feminism that recognizes that capitalism and systems of political power have severe consequences and oppress women around the world. This form of feminism embraces the multiplicity of cultures, languages, geographies, and experiences that shape the lives of women and highlights the Western/non-Western hierarchy that continues to exist in thought and practice. (p. 16)

Underclass People who are poor for the long term and who lack training and skills. (p. 128)

Underground economy Transfers of money, goods, or services that are not reported to the government. (p. 297)

Urban ecology A field of study that focuses on various relationships as they emerge in urban areas; it emphasizes that different elements in urban areas contribute to stability. (p. 335)

Urbanism Louis Wirth's term for a distinctive pattern of behaviour emanating from a relatively large and permanently settled community. (p. 339)

Validity The degree to which a scale or measure truly reflects the phenomenon under study. (p. 30)

Value neutrality Objectivity of sociologists in the interpretation of data. (p. 37)

Values Collective conceptions of what is considered good, desirable, and proper—or bad, undesirable, and improper—in a culture. (p. 53)

Variable A measurable trait or characteristic that is subject to change under different conditions. (p. 28)

Verstehen The German word for "understanding" or "insight"; used to stress the need for sociologists to take into account people's emotions, thoughts, beliefs, and attitudes. (p. 10)

Vertical mobility The movement of a person from one social position to another of a different rank. (p. 130)

Vested interests Those people or groups who will suffer in the event of social change, and who have a stake in maintaining the status quo. (p. 355)

Victimization surveys Questionnaires or interviews used to determine whether people have been victims of crime. (p. 240)

Victimless crime A term used by sociologists to describe the willing exchange among adults of widely desired, but illegal, goods and services. (p. 239)

Visible minority Canadians who are non-white or are identified as being physically different from white Canadians of European descent. (p. 157)

War Conflict between organizations that possess trained combat forces equipped with deadly weapons. (p. 308)

Wealth An inclusive term encompassing all of a person's material assets, including land and other types of property. (p. 308)

White-collar crime Crimes committed by usually affluent individuals or corporations in the course of their daily business activities. (p. 238)

Working poor People who work a certain number of hours a year but whose family income still falls below the low-income cut-off (LICO). (p. 127)

World systems analysis A view of the global economic system as one divided among certain industrialized nations that control wealth and developing countries that are controlled and exploited. (p. 140)

Xenocentrism The belief that the products, styles, or ideas of our own society are inferior to those that originate elsewhere. (p. 59)

Zero population growth (ZPG) The state of a population with a growth rate of zero, achieved when the number of births plus immigrants is equal to the number of deaths plus emigrants. (p. 326)

references

Abercrombie, Nicholas, Bryan S. Turner, and Stephen Hill, eds. 1990. *Dominant Ideologies.* Cambridge, MA: Unwin Hyman.

——, Stephen Hill, and Bryan S. Turner. 1980. *The Dominant Ideology Thesis.* London: George Allen and Unwin.

Aberle, David F., A. K. Cohen, A. K. Davis, M. J. Leng, Jr., and F. N. Sutton. 1950. "The Functional Prerequisites of a Society." *Ethics* 60 (January): 100–111.

Abraham, Carolyn. 2012. "Unnatural Selection: Is Evolving Reproductive Technology Ushering in a New Age of Eugenics?" *The Globe and Mail,* January 7.

Abrahamson, Mark. 1978. *Functionalism.* Englewood Cliffs, NJ: Prentice Hall.

Acharya, Meena. 2000. *Labor Market Developments and Poverty: With Focus on Economic Opportunities for Women.* Kathmandu, Nepal: Tanka Prasad Acharya Foundation/FES.

Acohido, Byron. 2010. "Tech-Savvy Put Explosion to Work." *USA Today,* November 17, pp. B1, B2.

Adam, Barry D. 1995. *The Rise of a Gay and Lesbian Movement,* rev. ed. New York: Twayne.

Adams, Tyrene L., and Stephen A. Smith. 2008 *Electronic Tribes: The Virtual Worlds of Geeks, Gamas, Shamans, and Scammers.* Austin: University of Texas Press.

Adamson, Nancy, Linda Briskin, and Margaret McPhail. 1998. *Feminist Organizing for Change: The Contemporary Women's Movement in Canada.* Toronto: Oxford University Press.

Addams, Jane. 1910. *Twenty Years at Hull-House.* New York: Macmillan.

——. 1930. *The Second Twenty Years at Hull-House.* New York: Macmillan.

Adamy, Janet. 2008. "Starbucks Plans to License 150 Stores in Europe." *New York Times,* June 12, p. B3.

Adler, Patricia A., Peter Adler, and John M. Johnson. 1992. "Street Corner Society Revisited: New Questions about Old Issues." *Journal of Contemporary Ethnography* 21(April): 3–10.

Adler, Patricia A., and Peter Adler. 2007. "The Demedicalization of Self-Injury: From Psychopathology to Sociological Deviance." *Journal of Contemporary Ethnography* 36 (October): 537–570.

Agrell, Siri. 2007. "Then They Won't Get Married. . .," *Globe and Mail,* September 13, p. L1.

Akers, Ronald L. 1997. *Criminological Theories: Introduction and Evaluation,* 2nd ed. Los Angeles, CA: Roxbury Publishing Co.

Albarracin, Dolores, Martin Fishbein, and Eva Goldstein de Muchinik. 1997. "Seeking Social Support in Old Age as a Reasoned Action: Structural and Volitional Determinants in a Middle-Aged Sample of Argentinean Women." *Journal of Applied Social Psychology* 27: 463–476.

Albas, Daniel, and Cheryl Albas. 1988. "Aces and Bombers: The Post-exam Impression Management Strategies of Students." *Symbolic Interaction* 11 (Fall): 289–302.

——. 1996. "Aces and Bombers: The Post-exam Impression management Strategies of Students." *Symbolic Interaction* 11(2).

Albrecht, Gary L. 2004. "Disability: Sociological Perspectives." Pp. 3710–3713 in *International Encyclopedia of the Social and Behavioral Sciences,* edited by Neil J. Smelser and Paul B. Baltes. New York: Elsevier.

Alexander-Floyd, N. G. 2010. "Critical Race Black Feminism: A 'Jurisprudence of Resistance' and the Transformation of the Academy." *Signs: Journal of Women in Culture & Society* 35(4): 810–820.

al-Jadda, Souheila. 2006. "A Veil Doesn't Mean Oppressed." *USA Today,* June 22, p. 13A.

Allemang, John. 2012. "Civic Booty Duty: Should the State have a Place in Our Bedrooms" *The Globe and Mail,* August 11.

Allen, Bem P. 1978. *Social Behavior: Fact and Falsehood.* Chicago: Nelson-Hall.

Allen, John L. 2008. *Student Atlas of World Politics* 8th ed. New York: McGraw-Hill.

Allport, Gordon W. 1979. *The Nature of Prejudice,* 25th anniversary ed. Reading, MA: Addison-Wesley.

Alonzo, Angelo A. 1989. "Health and Illness and the Definition of the Situation: An Interactionist Perspective." Presented at the annual meeting of the Society for the Study of Social Problems, Berkeley, CA.

Altus Group Housing Report. 2013. Altus Group Economic Consulting. January.

Alzheimer's Society of Canada. 2010. "The Impact of Dementia on Canadian Society." *Alzheimer Society,* 2010.

American Bar Association. 1999. "Commission on Domestic Violence." Accessed July 20, 1999 (www.abanet.org/domviol/stats.html).

American Society of Plastic Surgeons. 2002. "National Clearinghouse of Plastic Surgery Statistics." Accessed February 1, 2002 (www. plasticsurgery.org/mediactr/stats_ncs.htm).

——. 2005. "National Plastic Surgery Statistics: Cosmetic and Reconstructive Procedure Trends." Accessed October 23, 2005 (www.plasticsurgery.org/public_education/2004Statistics.cfm).

——. 2007a. "2000/2005/2006 National Plastic Surgery Statistics: Cosmetic and Reconstructive Procedure Trends." Arlington Heights, IL: American Society of Plastic Surgeons.

——. 2007b. "2006 Gender Quick Facts: Cosmetic Plastic Surgery." Arlington Heights, IL: American Society of Plastic Surgeons.

——. 2011. "Men Fuel Rebound in Cosmetic Surgery." March 21.

Amnesty International. 1994. *Breaking the Silence: Human Rights Violations Based on Sexual Orientation.* New York: Amnesty International.

Amnesty International Canada. 2005. *Human Rights in Canada: Overview.* Ottawa.

Andersen, Margaret. 1997. *Thinking about Women: Sociological Perspectives on Sex and Gender,* 4th ed. Boston: Allyn and Bacon.

Andreatta, David. 2007. "First Your Kids Won't Leave. . . " *Globe and Mail,* September 13. Accessed August 13, 2007 (www.theglobeand-mail.com/servlet/story/RTGAM.20070913.wlslackers13/BNStory/. . .).

Angier, Natalie. 1998. "Drugs, Sports, Body Image and G.I. Joe." *New York Times,* December 22, pp. D1, D3.

Angus Reid Strategies. 2009. "Special Report-Three Country Survey."

——. 2011. "Canadians Remain Divided on How to Deal with Prostitution." June 30.

Angwin, Julia. 2010. "The Web's New Gold Mine: Your Secrets." *Wall Street Journal,* July 31, pp. W1, W2.

——, and Jennifer Valentino-DeVries. 2010. "Race Is On to 'Fingerprint' Phones, PCs," *Wall Street Journal,* December 1, pp. A1, A15.

Aronson, Elliot. 1999. *The Social Animal,* 8th ed. New York: Worth.

Asch, Solomon. 1951. Effects of group pressure upon the modification and distortion of judgement. In H. Guetzkow (ed.) *Groups, Leadership, and Men.* Pittsburgh, PA: Carnegie Press.

——. 1955. Opinions and social pressure. *Scientific American, 193,* 31–35.

Ash, Timothy Garton. 2007. "Welcome to a Mixed-Up World." *The Globe and Mail,* July 14, p. A19.

Associated Press. 1998. "Environmental Test Case Averted." *Christian Science Monitor,* September 21, p. 18.

Astwood Strategy Corporation. 2003. *Results of the 2002 Canadian Police Survey on Youth Gangs.* Ottawa: Public Safety and Emergency Preparedness Canada.

Atchley, Robert C, and Amanda S. Barusch. 2004. *Social Forces and Agency: An Introduction to Social Gerontology,* 10th ed. Belmont, CA: Thomson.

Austin, April. 2002. "Cellphones and Strife in Congo." *Christian Science Monitor,* December 5, p. 11.

Australian Bureau of Statistics. 2006. 2006 Census.

Axtell, Roger E. 1990. *Do's and Taboos around the World,* 2nd ed. New York: John Wiley and Sons.

Azumi, Koya, and Jerald Hage. 1972. *Organizational Systems.* Lexington, MA: Health

Babad, Elisha Y., and P.J. Taylor. 1992. "Transparency of Teacher Expectancies across Language, Cultural Boundaries." *Journal of Educational Research* 86: 120–125.

Bachrach, Christine A. 1986. "Adoption Plans, Adopted Children, and Adoptive Mothers." *Journal of Marriage and the Family* 48 (May): 243–253.

Bado-Fralick, Nikki, and Rebecca Sachs Norris. 2010. *Toying with God: The World of Religious Games and Dolls.* Waco, TX: Baylor University Press.

Bajaj, Vikas. 2011a. "15 Years in Microcredit Has Suffered a Black Eye." *New York Times,* January 6, p. B3.

———. 2011b. "Luster Dims for a Public Microlender." *New York Times,* May 11, pp. 1, 4.

Baker, Maureen. 2001. "The Future of Family Life." pp. 285–302 in *Families: Changing Trends in Canada,* 4th ed., edited by Maureen Baker. Toronto: McGraw-Hill Ryerson.

———. 2007. *Choices and Constraints in Family Life.* Don Mills, ON: Oxford University Press.

Baker, Peter. 2009. "Obama Reverses Rules on U.S. Abortion Aid." *New York Times,* January 24.

Baker, Therese L. 1999. *Doing Social Research,* 3rd ed. New York: McGraw-Hill Ryerson.

Banks, Olive. 1981. *Faces of Feminism: A Study of Feminism as a Social Movement.* Oxford: Martin Robertson.

Barbaro, M. 2008. "Wal-Mart Says Most Workers Have Health Plan." *New York Times,* January 22.

Barbour, Rosaline S. 2007. *Introducing Qualitative Research: A Student's Guide to the Craft of Doing Qualitative Research.* London: SAGE Publications.

Barboza, David. 2008. "Reform Stalls in Chinese Factories." *New York Times,* January 5, pp. B1, B6.

Barnsley, Paul. 1999. "Cree Chief Slams Gathering Strength." *Windspeaker,* January 1.

Barrett, David B., Todd M. Johnson, and Peter F. Crossing. 2006. "The 2005 Annual Megacensus of Religions." Pp. 282–283 in 2006 *Book Year.* Chicago: Encyclopedia Britannica

Bashevkin, Sylvia B. 2002. *Welfare Hot Buttons.* Toronto: University of Toronto Press.

Baudrillard, Jean 1983. *Simulations.* New York: Semiotexte.

Bauerlein, Mark. 2008. "Online Literacy Is a Lesser Kind." *Chronicle of Higher Education,* September 19, pp. B10–B11.

Bauerlein, Monika. 1996. "The Luddites Are Back." *Utne Reader* (March–April), pp. 24, 26.

Ba-Yunus, Ilyas, and Kassim Kone. 2004. "Muslim Americans: A Demographic Report." Pp. 299–322 in *Muslims in the American Public Square,* edited by Zahid H. Bukhari et al. Walnut Creek, CA: Alta Mira Press.

BBC News. 2005. "Indonesian Village Report: January 12, 2005." Accessed January 19 (www.theworld.org).

Beach, Charles M., and Christopher Worswick. 1993. "Is There a Double-Negative Effect on the Earnings of Immigrant Women?" *Canadian Public Policy* 19(1): 36–53.

Becker, Anne E. 2007. "Facets of Acculturation and Their Diverse Relations to Body Shape Concerns in Fiji." *International Journal of Eating Disorders* 40 (1): 42–50.

Becker, Howard S. 1963. *The Outsiders: Studies in the Sociology of Deviance.* New York: Free Press.

———. 1973. *The Outsiders: Studies in the Sociology of Deviance,* rev. ed. New York: Free Press.

Beeghley, Leonard. 1978. *Social Stratification in America: A Critical Analysis of Theory and Research.* Santa Monica, CA: Goodyear Publishing.

Bell, Daniel. 1999. *The Coming of Post-industrial Society: A Venture in Social Forecasting,* with a new foreword. New York: Basic Books.

———. 2008. *China's New Confucianism: Politics and Everyday Life in a Changing Society.* Princeton, NJ: Princeton University Press.

Belt, Don. 2002. "The World of Islam." *National Geographic* (January): 26–85.

Belton, Danielle C. 2009. "Blacks in Space." *American Prospect* (June): 47–49.

Bender, William, and Margaret Smith. 1997. "Population, Food, and Nutrition." *Population Bulletin* 51 (February).

Benford, Robert D. 1992. "Social Movements." pp. 1880–1887 in *Encyclopedia of Sociology,* Vol. 4, Edgar F. Borgatta and Marie L. Borgatta, eds. New York: Macmillan.

Berger, Peter, and Thomas Luckmann. 1966. *The Social Construction of Reality.* New York: Doubleday.

Berlin, Brent, and Paul Kay. 1991. *Basic Color Terms: Their Universality and Evolution.* Berkeley, CA: University of California Press.

Bernstein, Anne C. 1988. "Unraveling the Tangles: Children's Understanding of Stepfamily Kinship." pp. 83–111 in *Relative Strangers: Studies of Step-Family Processes,* W. R. Beer, ed. Totowa, NJ: Rowman & Littlefield.

Bernstein, Elizabeth. 2007. "Colleges Move Boldly on Student Drinking." *Wall Street Journal,* December 6, pp. D1, D2.

Bernstein, Sharon. 2004. "Under the Radar, HIV Worsens." *Los Angeles Times,* October 16, pp. A1, A12.

Bialik, Carol. 2010. "Seven Careers in a Lifetime? Think Twice, Researchers Say." *Wall Street Journal,* September 4, p. A6.

Bibby, Reginald W. 1990. *Mosaic Madness.* Toronto: Stoddart.

———. 1995. *The Bibby Report: Social Trends Canadian Style.* Toronto: Stoddart.

Bielby, Denise D., and C. Lee Harrington. 2008. *Global TV: Exporting Television and Culture in the World Market.* New York: New York University Press.

Bielby, William T., and Denise D. Bielby. 1992. "I Will Follow Him: Family Ties, Gender-Role Beliefs, and Reluctance to Relocate for a Better Job." *American Journal of Sociology* 97 (March): 1241–1267.

Bilton, Nick. 2011. *I Live in the Future and Here's How It Works.* New York: Crown Business.

Black, Donald. 1995. "The Epistemology of Pure Sociology." *Law and Social Inquiry* 20 (Summer): 829–870.

Blanchard, Fletcher A., Teri Lilly, and Leigh Ann Vaughn. 1991. "Reducing the Expression of Racial Prejudice." *Psychological Science* 2 (March): 101–105.

Blau, Peter M., and Marshall W. Meyer. 1987. *Bureaucracy in Modern Society,* 3rd ed. New York: Random House.

Blauner, Robert. 1972. *Racial Oppression in America.* New York: Harper and Row.

Bluestone, Barry, and Bennett Harrison. 1982. *The Deindustrialization of America.* New York: Basic Books.

Blumberg, Stephen J., and Julian V. Luke. 2007. "Coverage Bias in Traditional Telephone Surveys of Low-Income and Young Adults." *Public Opinion Quarterly* 71 (5): 734–749.

Blumer, Herbert. 1955. "Collective Behavior." pp. 165–198 in *Principles of Sociology,* 2nd ed., Alfred McClung Lee, ed. New York: Barnes and Noble.

———. 1969. *Symbolic Interactionism: Perspective and Method.* Englewood Cliffs, NJ: Prentice Hall.

Boase, Jeffery, John B. Horrigan, Barry Wellman, and Lee Rainie. 2006. *The Strength of Internet Ties.* Washington, DC: Pew Internet and American Life Project.

Bottomore, Tom, and Maximilien Rubel, eds. 1956. *Karl Marx: Selected Writings in Sociology and Social Philosophy.* New York: McGraw-Hill Ryerson.

Bourdieu, Pierre, and Jean-Claude Passerson. 1990. *Reproduction in Education, Society and Culture,* 2nd ed. London. Sage. Originally published as *La reproduction.*

Bouvier, Leon F. 1980. "America's Baby Boom Generation: The Fateful Bulge." *Population Bulletin* 35 (April).

Bowes, John. 2011. *The Fair Trade Revolution.* London: Pluto Press.

Bowles, Samuel, and Herbert Gintis. 1976. *Schooling in Capitalist America: Educational Reforms and the Contradictions of Economic Life.* New York: Basic Books.

Boyd, Monica. 1984. "At a Disadvantage: The Occupational Attainments of Foreign-Born Women in Canada." *International Migration Review* 18(4): 1091–1119.

———. 1992. "Gender, Visible Minority, and Immigrant Earnings Inequality: Reassessing Employment Equity Premise." pp. 279–321 in *Deconstructing a Nation: Immigration, Multiculturalism and Racism in '90s Canada,* Vic Satzewch, ed. Halifax: Fernwood Publishing.

Brabazon, Tara. 2007. *The University of Google: Education in the (post) Information Age.* Burlingaton, VT: Ashgate.

Brandchannel.com. 2010. "2009 Movie Lust." Accessed February 7 (www.brandchannel.com/brandcameo_films. asp?movie_year_az52009#movie_list).

Brand, Dionne. 1993. "A Working Paper on Black Women in Toronto: Gender, Race, and Class." pp. 220–241 in *Returning the Gaze: Essays on Racism, Feminism and Politics,* Himani Bannerji, ed. Toronto: Sister Vision Press.

Brannigan, Augustine. 1992. "Postmodernism." pp. 1522–1525 in *Encyclopedia of Sociology,* Vol. 3, Edgar F. Borgatta and Marie L. Borgatta, eds. New York: Macmillan.

Brannon, Robert. 1976. "Ideology, Myth, and Reality: Sex Equality in Israel." *Sex Roles: A Journal of Research* 6: 403–419.

Brasfield, Charles R. 2001. "Residential School Syndrome." *BC Medical Journal* 43(2): 78–81.

Braxton, Gregory. 2009. "'Reality Television' in More Ways than One." *Los Angeles Times,* February 17, pp. A1, A15.

Brazao, Dale. 2008. "Exploited Workers Canada's 'Slave Trade'." *Toronto Star,* August 30.

Brazier, Chris, and Amir Hamed, eds. 2007. *The World Guide,* 11th ed. Oxford, UK: New Internationalist.

Brint, Steven. 1998. *Schools and Societies.* Thousand Oaks, CA: Pine Forge Press.

Britannica Online. 2011. "Worldwide Adherents of All Religions by Six Continental Areas. Mid-2010." Accessed March 28.

Brown, David. 2009. "Doing a Number on Surveys." *Washington Post National Weekly Edition* 26 (January 19):,37.

Bryant, Bunyan, and Paul Mohai, eds. 1992. *Race and the Incidence of Environmental Hazards.* Boulder, CO: Westview Press.

Buchanan, Joy. 2008. "Medicine Meets a Culture Gap." *USA Today,* February 14, p. 9D.

Buckingham, David. 2007. "Selling Childhood? Children and Consumer Culture." *Journal of Children and Media* 1 (1): 15–24.

Buechler, Steven M. 2000. *Social Movements in Advanced Capitalism: The Political Economy and Cultural Construction of Social Activism.* New York: Oxford University Press.

Bula, Francis. 2000. "This Is an International Crisis." *Vancouver Sun,* November 21, pp. A1, A6.

Bullard, Robert. 1990. *Dumping in Dixie: Race, Class, and Environmental Quality.* Boulder, CO: Westview Press.

Bulle, Wolfgang F. 1987. *Crossing Cultures? Southeast Asian Mainland.* Atlanta: Centers for Disease Control.

Bunzel, John H. 1992. *Race Relations on Campus: Stanford Students Speak.* Stanford, CA: Portable Stanford.

Bureau of the Census. 2009. *Statistical Abstract of the United States 2010.* Washington, DC: U.S. Government Printing Office.

———. 2010. *Statistical Abstract of the United States 2011.* Washington, DC: U.S. Government Printing Office.

———. 2011a. International Data Base (IDB). Accessible at http://www.census.gov/ipc/www/idb/informationGateway.php.

Bureau of Labor Statistics. 2004. "Current Labor Statistics." Accessed January 28 (www.bls.gov/opub/mlr/mlrhome.htm).

———. 2011b. "Union Members—2010." News Release, January 21. Accessible at http://www.bls.gov/news.release/pdf/union2.pdf.

Burgess, Ernest W. 1925. "The Growth of the City." pp. 47–62 in *The City,* Robert E. Park, Ernest W. Burgess, and Roderick D. McKenzie, eds. Chicago: University of Chicago Press.

Butler, Robert N. 1990. "A Disease Called Ageism." *Journal of American Geriatrics Society* 38 (February): 178–180.

Byrd-Bredbenner, Carol, and Jessica Murray. 2003. "Comparison of the Anthropometric Measurements of Idealized Female Body Images in Media Directed to Men, Women, and Mixed Gender Audiences." *Topics in Clinical Nutrition* 18 (2): 117–129.

Bystydzienski, Jill M., and Joti Sekhon. 1999. *Democratization and Women's Grassroots Movements.* Bloomington: Indiana University Press.

C

CAF America 2009. "Global Literacy." Accessed on May 11, 2010. (www.cafamerica.org/dnn/Portals/O/Issue%20Brief/CAF_globalliteracy2.pdf).

Calhoun, Craig. 2003. "Belonging in the Cosmopolitan Imaginary." *Ethnicities* 3 (December): 531–553.

Calhoun, David B. 2000. "Learning at Home." p. 193 in *Yearbook of the Encyclopedia Britannica 2000.* Chicago: Encyclopedia Britannica.

Calliste, Agnes. 2001. "Black Families in Canada: Exploring the Interconnections of Race, Class and Gender." pp. 401–419 in *Family Patterns, Gender Relations,* Bonnie J. Fox, ed. Toronto: Oxford University Press.

Cameron, Deborah. 2007. *The Myth of Mars and Venus.* Oxford: Oxford University Press.

Campaign 2000. 2009. "2009 Report Card on Child and Family Poverty in Canada." Accessed January 19, 2010 (www.campaign2000.ca/reportcards.html).

Camus, Albert. 1948. *The Plague.* New York: Random House.

Canada Newswire. 2012. "Food Bank Use on the Rise in Canada: Report." Jessica Hume. October 30.

Canadian Association of University Teachers (CAUT). 2007. *CAUT Almanac of Post-Secondary Education in Canada.* Ottawa.

Canadian Broadcasting Corporation (CBC) News. 2004. "Minorities Missing on Canadian TV." July 15. Accessed March 8, 2007 (www.cbc.ca/arts/story/2004/07/15/minorityreport040715.html).

———. 2004. "Voter Turnout Lowest Since Confederation." June 30. Accessed October 26, 2007 (www.cbc.ca/canada/story/2004/06/29/turnout040629.html).

———. 2005. "Police Stop More Blacks, Ont. Study Finds." Accessed May 27, 2005 (www.cbc.ca/story/canada/national/2005/05/26/race050526.html).

———. 2006a. "Guardian of the Airwaves." April 7. Accessed January 24, 2008 (www.cbc.ca/news/background/crtc/).

———. 2006b. "Indepth: Summit of the Americas: NAFTA." March 30. Accessed June 25, 2007 (www.cbc.ca/news/background/summito-famericas/nafta.html).

———. 2006c. "Gender Inequality Deals Blow to Mothers and Children: UNICEF." December 11. Accessed December 11, 2006 (www.cbc.ca/world/story/2006/12/11/unicef-report.html).

———. 2007. "Homelessness 'Chronic' in Canada: Study." June 26. Accessed March 28, 2008 (www.cbc.ca/canada/story/2007/06/26/shelter.html).

———. 2007a. "Residential School Payout a 'Symbolic' Apology: Fontaine." September 19. Accessed September 19, 2007 (www.cbc.ca/canada/story/2007/09/19/residential–schools.html).

———. 2007b. "Vacation Nations: How Canada Compares to Other G8 Countries." Accessed September 19, 2007 (www.cbc.ca/news/interac-tives/map-vacation-days).

———. 2007c. "Glad to be Canadian, Muslims Say." February 13. Accessed April 21, 2008 (www.cbc.ca/canada/story/2007/02/12/mus-lim-poll.html).

———. 2007d. "Regulating 'Assisted Human Reproduction.'" April 23. Accessed April 24, 2007 (www.cbc.ca/news/background/genetics_reproduction/rgtech.html).

———. 2008. "Student Binge Drinking: A Problem Well Past the Tipping Point." November 19.

———. 2008a. "CRTC imposes cross-media own-ership restrictions." January 15. Accessed December 7, 2008 (www.cbc.ca/money/story/2008/01/15crtc.html).

———. 2008b. "Toronto Trustees Vote in Favour of Black-Focused Schools." January 29. Accessed April 16, 2008 (www.cbc.ca/canada/toronto/story/2008/01/29/tto-schools.html).

———. 2008c. "Voter turnout drops to record low." October 15. Accessed October 27, 2008 (www.cbc.ca/news/canadavotes/story/2008/10/15/voter-turnout.html).

———. 2010. "The Long and Short of the Census Over Time." July 26.

———. 2011. "Vancouver's INSITE Drug Injection Clinic Will Stay Open." September 30.

———. 2012. "Half of Canadians Report being Bullied as Youth." February 15.

———. 2012a. "Pregnant Woman Who Bought U.S. Donor Egg Speaks Out." April 25.

———. 2012b. "Vehicles Outnumber People in Newfoundland and Labrador." January 18.

———. 2013. "Rehtaeh Parson's Family has Heartfelt Talk with Harper." April 23.

Canadian Business Online. 2011. http://list.canadi-anbusiness.com/rankings/rich100/2011.

Canadian Centre for Policy Alternatives. 2007. "No New Year's Hangover for Top CEOs." Press Release, January 2. Accessed September 2, 2007 (www.policyalternatives.ca/News/2007/01/PressRelease1523/index.cfm?pa=F4FB3E9D).

———. 2012. "A Soft Landing: Recession and Canada's 100 Highest Paid CEOs." Hugh Mackenzie. January.

———. 2012a. "CEOs vs. the 99%: No Contest When It Comes to Pay." January 3.

Canadian Council on Learning. 2005. "Canada's High School Dropout Rates Are Falling." Accessed October 1, 2007 (www.ccl-cca.ca/CCL/Reports/LessonsInLeaning/LiL-16Dec2005.htm).

———. 2009. "Post-secondary Education in Canada: Who Is Missing Out?" April 1.

Canadian Press. 2007. "Number of Single–Parent Families Rising: Census." September 12. Accessed September 12, 2007 (www.cbc.ca/can-ada/story/2007/09/12/census-families.html).

Canadian Radio-television and Telecommunications Commission (CRTC). 2007. *Broadcasting Policy Monitoring Report 2006.* Ottawa.

———. 2008. "Media Technology Monitor Survey 2005." *Report 2006.* Ottawa.

Cantzler, Julia Miller. 2008. "Indian, Child Welfare Act of 1978." pp. 714–716, vol. 2, in *Encyclopedia of Race, Ethnicity, and Society,* edited by Richard T. Schaefer. Thousand Oaks, CA: Sage.

CanWest MediaWorks Publications. 2011. "Gang Violence being Fuelled by Prohibition on Pot: Report." Andrea Woo. October 27.

Caplan, Ronald L. 1989. "The Commodification of American Health Care." *Social Science and Medicine* 28(11): 1139–1148.

Caplow, Theodore, and Louis Hicks. 2002. *Systems of War and Peace,* 2nd ed. Lanham, MD: University Press of America.

Capriccioso, Rob. 2010. "Obama Mentions Tribes as Part of Oil Spill Restoration; Chief Testifies on Mess." *Indian Country Today,* June 23, pp. 1, 2.

Carey, Anne R., and Elys A. McLean. 1997. "Heard It through the Grapevine?" *USA Today,* September 15, p. B1.

———. 2000. *The Information Age: Economy, Society and Culture* (3 vols.), 2nd ed. Oxford, UK: Blackwell.

Carey, Anne R., and Karl Gelles. 2010. "What Viewers Enjoy Most about Watching the Super Bowl on TV." *USA Today,* February 5, p. A1; *Gallup Poll* (May): 3.

Carr, Nicholas. 2008a. *The Big Switch: Rewiring the World: From Edison to Google.* New York: Norton.

———. 2008b. "Is Google Making Us Stoopid?" *Atlantic* (July/August): 56–58, 60, 62–63.

———. 2010. "Tracking Is an Assault on Liberty, with Real Dangers." *Wall Street Journal,* August 7, pp. W1, W2.

Castells, Manuel. 2010. *The Rise of the Network Society,* 2nd ed. With a new preface. Malden, MA: Wiley-Blackwell.

Catalyst. 2005. *Beyond a Reasonable Doubt: Building a Business Case for Flexibility.* The Catalyst series on flexibility in Canadian law firms. Toronto: Catalyst Canada.

CBS News. 1979. Transcript of *60 Minutes* segment, "I Was Only Following Orders." March 31, pp. 2–8.

Center for American Women and Politics. 2006. *Fact Sheet: Women in the U.S. Congress 2006 and Statewide Elective Women 2006.* Rutgers, NJ: CAWP.

Centers for Disease Control and Prevention. 2010. "Binge Drinking among High School Students and Adults—United States, 2009." Washington, DC: CDC. Accessible at http://www.cdc.gov/mmwr/preview/mmwrhtml/mm5939a4.htm?s_cid5mm5939a4_w.

———. 2011a. *HIV in the United States.* Accessed May 24 (www.cdc.gov).

———. 2011b. *Health Disparities and Inequalities Report—United States, 2011.*

Central Intelligence Agency (CIA). 2007. *The World Fact Book.* Washington DC: Central Intelligence Agency.

Centre for Addiction and Mental Health. 2008. *2007 Ontario Student Drug Use and Health Survey, Mental Health and Well-Being Report.* Toronto.

Cerulo, Karen A., Janet M. Ruane, and Mary Chagko. 1992. "Technological Ties that Bind: Media Generated Primary Groups." *Communication Research* 19: 109–129.

Chalfant, H. Paul, Robert E. Beckley, and C. Eddie Palmer. 1994. *Religion in Contemporary Society,* 3rd ed. Itasca, IL: F.E. Peacock.

Chambliss, William. 1972. "Introduction." pp. ix–xi in *Box Man,* by Henry King. New York: Harper and Row.

———. 1973. "The Saints and the Roughnecks." *Society* 11 (November–December): 24–31.

Chan, R. W., B. Rayboy, and C. J. Patterson. 1998. "Psychological Adjustment among Children Conceived via Donor Insemination by Lesbian and Heterosexual Mothers." *Child Development* 69: 443–457.

Chan, Sewell. 2009. "City Unveils Facebook Page to Encourage Condom Use." *New York Times,* February 12, p. A32.

Charles, Susan T., and Laura L. Carstensen. 2009. "Social and Emotional Aging." *Annual Review of Psychology* 61: 383–409.

Charmaz, Kathy, and Debora A. Paterniti, eds. 1999. *Health, Illness, and Healing: Society, Social Context, and Self.* Los Angeles, CA: Roxbury.

Chase-Dunn, Christopher, and Peter Grimes. 1995. "World-Systems Analysis." pp. 387–417 in *Annual Review of Sociology,* 1995, John Hagan, ed. Palo Alto, CA: Annual Reviews.

Cherlin, Andrew J. 1999. *Public and Private Families: An Introduction,* 2nd ed. New York: McGraw-Hill Ryerson.

———. 2008. "Can the Left Learn the Lessons of Welfare Reform?" *Contemporary Sociology* 37 (March): 101–104.

———. 2009. *The Marriage-Go-Round: The State of Marriage and the Family in America Today.* New York: Knopf.

———, and Frank Furstenberg. 1992. *The New American Grandparent: A Place in the Family, A Life Apart.* Cambridge, MA: Harvard University Press.

Chernobyl Forum. 2005. *Chernobyl's Legacy: Health, Environmental and Socio-economic Impacts and Recommendations to the Governments of Belarus, the Russian Federation and Ukraine.* Geneva, Switzerland: International Atomic Energy Agency.

Christakis, Nicholas A., and James H. Fowler. 2007. "The Spread of Obesity in a Large Social Network over 32 Years." *New England Journal of Medicine* 357 (July 26): 370–379.

———. 2009. *Connected: The Amazing Power of Social Networks and How They Shape Our Lives.* New York: Harper.

Chu, Henry. 2005. "Tractors Crush Heart of a Nation." *Los Angeles Times,* July 10, p. A9.

Chubb, Catherine, Simone Melis, Louisa Potter, and Raymond Storry. 2008. *The Global Gender Pay Gap.* London: Incomes Data Services.

Clark, Campbell. 2005. "G8 Boosts Africa Aid by $25-Billion." *The Globe and Mail,* July 9. Accessed July 9, 2005 (www.theglobeandmail.com).

Clarke, Adele E., Janet K. Shim, Laura Maro, Jennifer Ruth Fusket, and Jennifer R. Fishman. 2003. "Bio Medicalization: Techno-scientific Transformations of Health, Illness, and U.S. Biomedicine." *American Sociological Review* 68 (April): 161–194.

Clifford, Stephanie. 2009a. "Teaching Teenagers about Harassment." *New York Times,* January 27, p. B1.

———. 2009b. "Online 'A Reason to Keep on Going.'" *New York Times,* June 2, pp. D5–D6.

Cloward, Richard A. 1959. "Illegitimate Means, Anomie, and Deviant Behavior." *American Sociological Review* 24 (April): 164–176.

Cockerham, William C. 1998. *Medical Sociology,* 7th ed. Upper Saddle River, NJ: Prentice Hall.

Code, Lorraine. 1993. "Feminist Theory." pp. 19–57 in *Changing Patterns: Women in Canada,* 2nd ed., Sandra Burt, Lorraine Code, and Lindsay Dorney, eds. Toronto: McClelland & Stewart.

Cohen, Lawrence E., and Marcus Felson. 1979. "Social Change and Crime Rate Trends: A Routine Activities Approach." *American Sociological Review* 44: 588–608.

Cole, Elizabeth S. 1985. "Adoption, History, Policy, and Program." pp. 638–666 in *A Handbook of Child Welfare,* John Laird and Ann Hartman, eds. New York: Free Press.

Cole, Mike. 1988. *Bowles and Gintis Revisited: Correspondence and Contradiction in Educational Theory.* Philadelphia: Falmer.

Coleman, James William. 1985. *The Criminal Elite: Sociology of White Collar Crime.* New York: St. Martin's Press.

Collier, Gary, Henry L. Minton, and Graham Reynolds. 1991. *Currents of Thought in American Social Psychology.* New York: Oxford University Press.

Collier, Paul. 2007. *The Bottom Billion.* Oxford: Oxford University Press.

Collins, Daryl, Jonathan Morduch, Stuart Rutherford, and Orlanda Ruthgen. 2009. *Portfolios of the Poor: How the World's Poor Live on $2 a Day.* Princeton, NJ: Princeton University Press.

Collins, Gail. 1998. "Why the Women Are Fading Away." *New York Times,* October 25, pp. 54–55.

Collins, Patricia Hill. 2000. *Black Feminist Thought: Knowledge, Consciousness, and the Politics of Empowerment,* rev. 10th anniv. 2nd ed. New York: Routledge.

Collins, Randall. 1975. *Conflict Sociology: Toward an Explanatory Sociology.* New York: Academic.

———. 1980. "Weber's Last Theory of Capitalism: A Systematization." *American Sociological Review* 45 (December): 925–942.

———. 1986. *Weberian Sociological Theory.* New York: Cambridge University Press.

———. 1995. "Prediction in Macrosociology: The Case of the Soviet Collapse." *American Journal of Sociology* 100 (May): 1552–1593.

Colucci, Jim. 2008. "All the World's a Screen." *Watch!* (June): 50–53.

Commoner, Barry. 1971. *The Closing Circle.* New York: Knopf.

———. 1990. *Making Peace with the Planet.* New York: Pantheon.

———. 2007. "At 90, an Environmentalist from the 70's Still Has Hope." *New York Times,* June 19, p. D2.

Communications Canada. 2001. "Facts on Canada." Accessed April 11, 2001 (www.info-can.gc.ca/facts/multi_e.html).

Conrad, Peter, ed. 2005. *The Sociology of Health and Illness: Cultural Perspectives,* 7th ed. New York: Worth.

———. 2007. *The Medicalization of Society: On the Transformation of Human Conditions into Treatable Disorders.* Baltimore, MD: John Hopkins University

———. 2009. *The Sociology of Health and Illness: Cultural Perspectives,* 8th ed. New York: Worth.

Cooley, Charles H. 1902. *Human Nature and the Social Order.* New York: Scribner.

Corak, Miles, and Andrew Heisz. 1996. *The Intergenerational Income Mobility of Canadian*

Men. Analytical Studies Branch no. 89. Ottawa: Statistics Canada.

Cornwell, Benjamin, Edward O. Laumann, and L. Phip Schumm. 2008. "The Social Connectedness of Older Adults: A National Profile." *American Sociological Review* 73 (April): 185–203.

Cortese, Anthony J. 1999. *Provocateur: Images of Women and Minorities in Advertising.* Lanham, MD: Rowman & Littlefield.

Coser, Lewis A. 1956. *The Functions of Social Conflict.* New York: Free Press.

———. 1977. *Masters of Sociological Thought: Ideas in Historical and Social Context,* 2nd ed. New York: Harcourt, Brace and Jovanovich.

Couch, Carl. 1996. *Information Technologies and Social Orders.* David R. Maines and Shing-Ling Chien, eds. and intro. New York: Aldine de Gruyter.

Cox, Oliver C. 1948. *Caste, Class and Race: A Study in Social Dynamics.* Detroit: Wayne State University Press.

Creese, Gillian, Neil Guppy, and Martin Meissner. 1991. *Ups and Downs on the Ladder of Success: Social Mobility in Canada.* Ottawa: Statistics Canada.

Croteau, David, and William Hoynes. 2003. *Media/Society: Industries, Images, and Audiences,* 3rd ed. Thousand Oaks, CA: Pine Forge.

Cuff, E. C., W. W. Sharrock, and D. W. Francis, eds. 1990. *Perspectives in Sociology,* 3rd ed. Boston: Unwin Hyman.

Cullen, Francis T., Jr., and John B. Cullen. 1978. *Toward a Paradigm of Labeling Theory,* ser. 58. Lincoln: University of Nebraska Studies.

Cumming, Elaine, and William E. Henry. 1961. *Growing Old: The Process of Disengagement.* New York: Basic Books.

Currie, Elliot. 1985. *Confronting Crime: An American Challenge.* New York: Pantheon.

———. 1998. *Crime and Punishment in America.* New York: Metropolitan Books.

Curry, Bill. 2010. "Aboriginals in Canada Face 'Third World'-Level Risk of Tuberculosis." *The Globe and Mail,* March 10. Accessed March 10, 2010 (www.theglobeandmail.com/news/national/aboriginals-in-canada-face-third-world-level-risk-of-tuberculosis/article1496790/).

Curry, Timothy Jon. 1993. "A Little Pain Never Hurt Anyone: Athletic Career Socialization and the Normalization of Sports Injury." *Symbolic Interaction* 26 (Fall): 273–290.

Cussins, Choris M. 1998. In *Cyborg Babies: From Techno-Sex to Techno-Tots,* Robbie Davis-Floyd and Joseph Dumit, eds. New York: Routledge.

D

Dahl, Robert A. 1961. *Who Governs?* New Haven, CT: Yale University Press.

Dahrendorf, Ralf. 1958. "Toward a Theory of Social Conflict." *Journal of Conflict Resolution* 2 (June): 170–183.

———. 1959. *Class and Class Conflict in Industrial Sociology.* Stanford, CA: Stanford University Press.

Daley-Harris, Sam, ed. 2002. *Pathways out of Poverty: Innovations in Microfinance for the Poorest Families.* Bloomfield, CT: Komarian Press.

Dalfen, Ariel K. 2000. "Cyberaddicts in Cyberspace? Internet Addiction Disorder." *Wellness Options* (Winter): 38–39.

Daniel, G. Reginald. 2006. *Race and Multiraciality in Brazil and the United States: Converging Paths?* University Park: Pennsylvania State University Press.

Davies, Christie. 1989. "Goffman's Concept of the Total Institution: Criticisms and Revisions." *Human Studies* 12 (June): 77–95.

Davis, Darren W., and Brian D. Silver. 2003. "Stereotype Threat and Race of Interviewer Knowledge." *American Journal of Political Science* 47 (January): 33–45.

Davis, Gerald. 2003. America's Corporate Banks Are Separated by Just Four Handshakes. Accessed March 7 (www.bus.umich.edu/research/davis.html).

———. 2004. "American Cronyism: How Executive Networks Inflated the Corporate Bubble." *Contexts* (Summer): 34–40.

Davis, James Allan, and Tom W. Smith. 1999. *General Social Surveys, 1972–1998.* Storrs, CT: The Roper Center.

Davis, Kingsley. 1937. "The Sociology of Prostitution." *American Sociological Review* 2 (October): 744–755.

———. 1940. "Extreme Social Isolation of a Child." *American Journal of Sociology* 45 (January): 554–565.

———. 1947. "A Final Note on a Case of Extreme Isolation." *American Journal of Sociology* 52 (March): 432–437.

———. [1949] 1995. *Human Society,* reprint. New York: Macmillan.

———, and Wilbert E. Moore. 1945. "Some Principles of Stratification." *American Sociological Review* 10 (April): 242–249.

Davis, Nanette J. 1975. *Sociological Constructions of Deviance: Perspectives and Issues in the Field.* Dubuque, IA: Wm. C. Brown.

Deegan, Mary Jo, ed. 2003. "Textbooks, the History of Sociology, and the Sociological Stock of Knowledge." *Sociological Theory* 21 (November): 298–305.

Deflem, Mathieu. 2005. "'Wild Beasts Without Nationality': The Uncertain Origins of Interpol, 1898–1910." pp. 275–285 in *Handbook of Transnational Crime and Justice,* edited by Philip Rerchel. Thousand Oaks, CA: Sage.

Deibert, Ronald J., John Palfrey, Rafal Rohozinski, and Jonathan Zittrain. 2008. *Access Denied: The Practice and Policy of Global Internet Filtering.* Cambridge, MA: MIT Press.

DeKeseredy, Walter S. 2005. "Patterns of Family Violence." pp. 229–257 in *Families: Changing Trends in Canada,* 5th ed., Maureen Baker, ed. Toronto: McGraw-Hill Ryerson.

———, and Martin D. Schwartz. 1998. *Woman Abuse on Campus: Results from the Canadian National Survey.* Thousand Oaks, CA: Sage Publications.

Delaney, Kevin J. 2005. "Big Mother Is Watching." *Wall Street Journal,* November 26, pp. A1, A6.

Delawala, Imtyaz. 2002. "What Is Coltran?" January 21, 2002 (www.abcnews.com).

Delgado, Richard, and Jean Stefancic 2001. *Critical Race Theory: An Introduction.* New York: New York University Press.

Della Porta, Donatella, and Sidney Tarrow, eds. 2005. *Transnational Protest and Global Activism.* Lanham, MD: Rowman & Littlefield.

Denny, Charlotte. 2004. "Migration Myths Hold No Fears." *Guardian Weekly* (February 26): 12.

Derouin, Jodey Michael. 2004. "Asians and Multiculturalism in Canada's Three Major Cities: Some Evidence from the Ethnic Diversity Survey." pp. 58–62 in *Our Diverse Cities,* number 1, Caroline Andrew, ed. Ottawa: Metropolis Project.

Desai, Manisha. 1996. "If Peasants Build Their Own Dams, What Would the State Have Left to Do?" pp. 209–224, vol. 19, in *Research in Social Movements, Conflicts and Change,* edited by Michael Dobkowski and Isidor Wallimann. Greenwich, CT: JAI Press.

Diamond, Jared. 2003. "Globalization, Then." *Los Angeles Times,* September 14, pp. M1, M3.

Diebel, Linda. 2007. "McGuinty Apologizes for 'Ghetto Dude' Email." *Toronto Star,* July 23. Accessed October 16, 2008 (www.thestar.com/News/Ontario/article/238744).

DiMaggio, Paul, Eszter Hargittai, W. Russell Neuman, and John P. Robinson. 2001. "Social Implications of the Internet." pp. 307–336 in *Annual Review of Sociology, 2001,* edited by Karen S. Cook and John Hogan. Palo Alto, CA: Annual Reviews.

Dionne, Annette, Cecile Dionne, and Yvonne Dionne. 1997. "Letter." *Time,* December 1, p. 39.

Dodds, Klaus. 2000. *Geopolitics in a Changing World.* Harlow, England: Pearson Education.

Domhoff, G. William. 1978. *Who Really Rules? New Haven and Community Power Reexamined.* New Brunswick, NJ: Transaction.

———. 2006. *Who Rules America?* 5th ed. New York: McGraw-Hill.

———. 2010. *Who Rules America?* 6th ed. New York: McGraw-Hill.

Dominick, Joseph R. 2005. *The Dynamics of Mass Communication: Media in the Digital Age,* 8th ed. New York: McGraw-Hill Ryerson.

Donadio, Rachel. 2009. "Facebook 'Fans' of the Mafia May Be More, Authorities Say." *New York Times,* January 20, pp. A1, A8.

Dorai, Frances. 1998. *Insight Guide: Singapore.* Singapore: Insight Media, APA Publications.

Doress, Irwin, and Jack Nusan Porter. 1977. *Kids in Cults: Why They Join, Why They Stay, Why They Leave.* Brookline, MA: Reconciliation Associates.

Doyle, James A. 1995. *The Male Experience,* 3rd ed. Dubuque, IA: Brown & Benchmark.

———, and Michele A. Paludi. 1998. *Sex and Gender: The Human Experience,* 4th ed. New York: McGraw-Hill Ryerson.

Dua, Enakshi. 1999. "Introduction: Canadian Anti-racist Feminist Thought: Scratching the Surface of Racism." pp. 7–31 in *Scratching the Surface: Canadian Anti-racist Feminist Thought,* Enakshi Dua and Angela Robertson, eds. Toronto: Women's Press.

Duberman, Lucille. 1976. *Social Inequality: Class and Caste in America.* Philadelphia: Lippincott.

DuBois, W. E. B. [1940] 1968. *Dusk of Dawn.* New York: Harcourt, Brace. Reprint. New York: Schocken Books.

Dugger, Celia W. 1999. "Massacres of Low-Born Touch off a Crisis in India." *New York Times,* March 15, p. A3.

Duneier, Mitchell. 1994a. "On the Job, but Behind the Scenes." *Chicago Tribune,* December 26, pp. 1, 24.

———. 1994b. "Battling for Control." *Chicago Tribune,* December 28, pp. 1, 8.

Durex. 2007. "The Face of Global Sex 2007—First Sex: An Opportunity of a Lifetime." Accessible at http://www.durexnetwork.org/SiteCollectionDocuments/Research%20%20Face%20of%20Global%20Sex%202007.pdf.

Durkheim, Émile. [1893] 1933. *Division of Labor in Society,* reprint. George Simpson, transl. New York: Free Press.

———. [1895] 1964. *The Rules of Sociological Method,* reprint. Sarah A. Solovay and John H. Mueller, transl. New York: Free Press.

———. [1897] 1951. *Suicide,* reprint. John A. Spaulding and George Simpson, transl. New York: Free Press.

———. [1912] 1947. *The Elementary Forms of the Religious Life,* reprint. Glencoe, IL: Free Press.

Durrant, Joan E., and Linda Rose-Krasnor. 1995. *Corporal Punishment Research Review and Policy Development.* Ottawa: Ontario Health Canada and Department of Justice Canada.

Dutta, Soumitra, and Irene Mia. 2010. *The Global Information Technology Report 2009–2010.* Geneva: World Economic Forum and INSEAD. Accessible at http://networkedreadiness.com/gitr/main/fullreport/index.html.

Duxbury, Linda, and Chris Higgins. 2001. "Work-Life Balance in Canada: Making the Case for Change." Asia Pacific Research. Accessed May 27, 2008 (www.asiapacificresearch.ca/caprn/cjsp_project/duxbury_final.pdf).

Dworkin, Rosalind J. 1982. "A Woman's Report: Numbers Are Not Enough." pp. 375–400 in *The Minority Report,* Anthony Dworkin and Rosalind Dworkin, eds. New York: Holt Rinehart & Winston.

Dzidzienyo, Anani. 1987. "Brazil." In *International Handbook on Race and Race Relations,* Jay A. Sigler, ed. New York: Greenwood Press.

E

Earth Peoples. 2013. www.earthpeoples.com.

Easterbrook, Gregg. 2006. "Case Closed: The Debate about Global Warning Is Over." Working paper. Washington, DC: Brookings Institution.

Eayrs, Caroline B., Nick Ellis, and Robert S. P. Jones. 1993. "Which Label? An Investigation into the Effects of Terminology on Public Perceptions of and Attitudes toward People with Learning Difficulties." *Disability, Handicap, and Society* 8(2): 111–127.

Ebaugh, Helen Rose Fuchs. 1988. *Becoming an Ex: The Process of Role Exit.* Chicago: University of Chicago Press.

Eckenwiler, Mark. 1995. "In the Eyes of the Law." *Internet World* (August): 74, 76–77.

The Economist. 2003. "The One Where Pooh Goes to Sweden." (April 5): 59.

———. 2005. "Behind the Digital Divide." (March 2): 22–25.

———. 2007. "Half-Measures on Poverty." (July 7): 27.

———. 2008. "A Ravenous Dragon: A Special Report on China's Quest for Resources." (March 15): 1–22.

———. 2009. "The Cradle's Costly Revenge." (January 10): 34.

———. 2010. "Cross about Cross-Dressing." (January 30): 59.

———. 2010a. "Taking Root: The Spread of GM Crops." (February 27): 70–72.

———. 2010b. "Plus One Country." (September 4): 46.

———. 2011. "China's Population: The Most Surprising Demographic Crisis." (May 7): 43–44.

Edwards, Richard. 1979. *Contested Terrain: The Transformation of the Workplace in America.* New York: Basic Books.

Effgen, Christopher. 2010. "U.S. Crime Rates 1960–2006." Disastercenter.com. June 30.

Ehrenreich, Barbara. 2001. *Nickel and Dimed: On (Not)Getting By in America.* New York: Metropolitan.

Ehrlich, Paul R. 1968. *The Population Bomb.* New York: Ballantine.

———, and Anne H. Ehrlich. 1990. *The Population Explosion.* New York: Simon and Schuster.

———, and Katherine Ellison. 2002. "A Looming Threat We Won't Face." *Los Angeles Times,* January 20, p. M6.

Eichler, Margrit. 1984. "Sexism in Research and Its Policy Implications." pp. 17–39 in *Taking Sex into Account: The Policy Implications of Sexist Research,* J. McCells Vickers, ed. Ottawa: Carleton University Press.

———. 1997. *Family Shifts: Families, Policies, and Gender Equality.* Toronto: Oxford University Press.

———. 2001. "Biases in Family Literature." pp. 51–66 in *Families: Changing Trends in Canada,* 4th ed. Maureen Baker, ed. Toronto: McGraw-Hill Ryerson.

El Akkad, Dareen. 2009. "Identity Theft a Fast-Growing Offence." *The Globe and Mail,* June 28. Accessed June 29, 2009 (www.theglobeandmail.com/news/technology/identity-theft-a-fast-growing-offence/a. . .).

Elections Canada. 2007. *Voter Turnout at Federal Elections and Referendums, 1867–2006.*

Elias, Marilyn. 1996. "Researchers Fight Child Consent Bill." *USA Today,* January 2, p. A1.

Elliot, Patricia, and Nancy Mandell. 1998. "Feminist Theories." pp. 2–25 in *Feminist Issues: Race, Class, and Sexuality,* 2nd ed. Nancy Mandell, ed. Scarborough, ON: Allyn and Bacon.

Elliott, Michael. 1994. "Crime and Punishment." *Newsweek* 123 (April 18): 18–22.

Ellison, Nicole, Charles Stein Field, and Cliff Lampe. 2007. "The Benefits of Facebook 'Friends': Exploring the Relationship between College Students' Use of Online Social Networks and Social Capital." *Journal of Computer-Mediated Communication* 12 (4): 1143–1168.

Ely, Robin J. 1995. "The Power of Demography: Women's Social Construction of Gender Identity at Work." *Academy of Management Journal* 38(3): 589–634.

Environics Research Group. 2007a. "Basis of Pride in Being Canadian, 2006." *Focus Canada.* Toronto: Environics.

———. 2007b. *Environics Survey of Muslims in Canada.* Toronto: Environics.

Erikson, Kai. 1966. *Wayward Puritans: A Study in the Sociology of Deviance.* New York: John Wiley and Sons.

Esbenshade, Jill. 2008. "Giving Up Against the Global Economy: New Developments in the Anti-Sweatshops Movement." *Critical Sociology* 34 (3): 453–470.

Etaugh, Claire. 2003. "Witches, Mothers and Others: Females in Children's Books." *Hilltopics* (Winter): 10–13.

Etzioni, Amitai. 1964. *Modern Organization.* Englewood Cliffs, NJ: Prentice Hall.

———. 1965. *Political Unification.* New York: Holt, Rinehart, and Winston.

———. 1985. "Shady Corporate Practices." *New York Times,* November 15, p. A35.

———. 1990. "Going Soft on Corporate Crime." *Washington Post,* April 1, p. C3.

Eureka CountyYucca Mountain Information Office. 2006. "EPA Hears Testimony on Proposed Radiation Rule." *Nuclear Waste Office Newsletter* 11 (Winter).

Evergeti, Venetia, and Elisabetta Zontini. 2006. "Introduction: Some Critical Reflections on Social Capital, Migration and Transnational Families." *Ethnic and Racial Studies* 29 (November): 1025–1039.

F

Facebook. 2011. Statistics. Accessed January 21 (www.facebook.com/press/info.php?statistics).

Fager, Marty, Mike Bradley, Lonnie Danchik, and Tom Wodetski. 1971. *Unbecoming Men.* Washington, NJ: Times Change.

Fairtrade Foundation. 2010. "Retail Products." Accessed Jan. 5 (www.fairtrade.org.uk/products/retail_products/default.aspx).

Fallows, Deborah. 2006. *Pew Internet Project Data.* Washington, DC: Pew Internet and American Life Project.

Faris, Robert, and Nart Villeneuve. 2008. "Measuring Global Internet Filtering." pp. 5–56 in *Access Denied: The Practice and Policy of Global Internet Filtering,* Ronald Deibert, John Palfrey, Rafal Rohozinski, and Jonathan Zittrain, eds. Cambridge, MA: MIT Press.

Farr, Grant M. 1999. *Modern Iran.* New York: McGraw-Hill Ryerson.

Feagin, Joe R. 1983. *The Urban Real Estate Game: Playing Monopoly with Real Money.* Englewood Cliffs, NJ: Prentice Hall.

Felson, David, and Akis Kalaitzidis. 2005. "A Historical Overview of Transnational Crime." pp. 3–19 in *Handbook of Transnational Crime and Justice,* Philip Reichel, ed. Thousand Oaks, CA: Sage.

Felson, Marcus. 1998. *Crime and Everyday Life: Insights and Implications for Society,* 2nd ed. Thousand Oaks, CA: Pine Forge Press.

Fenlon, Brodie, and Siri Agrell. 2007. "Canada's Changing Family." *The Globe and Mail,* September 12. Accessed September 13, 2007 (www.theglobeandmail.com/servlet/story/RTGAM.20070912.wcensusrelease0912/BNStory/National).

Ferree, Myra Marx, and David A. Merrill. 2000. "Hot Movements, Cold Cognition: Thinking about Social Movements in Gendered Frames." *Contemporary Society* 29 (May): 454–462.

Feuer, Lewis, ed. 1959. *Marx and Engels: Basic Writings on Politics and Philosophy.* Garden City, NY: Anchor Books.

———. 1989. *Marx and Engels: Basic Writings on Politics and Philosophy.* New York: Anchor Books.

Fiala, Robert. 1992. "Postindustrial Society." pp. 1512–1522 in *Encyclopedia of Sociology,* vol. 3. Edgar F. Borgatta and Marie L. Borgatta, eds. New York: Macmillan.

Field, John. 2008. *Social Capital,* 2nd ed. London: Routledge.

Fieser, Ezra. 2009. "What Price for Good Coffee?" *Time,* October 5, pp. 61–62.

Fiji TV. 2010. Home Page. Accessed January 17 (www.fijitv.com.fj).

Finkel, Alvin, and Margaret Conrad, with Veronica Stong-Boag. 1993. *History of the Canadian Peoples: 1867 to Present.* Toronto: Copp Clark Pitman.

Fiola, Jan. 2008. "Brazil." pp. 200–204, vol. 2, in *Encyclopedia of Race, Ethnicity, and Society,* edited by Richard T. Schaefer. Thousand Oaks, CA: Sage.

Firestone, Shulamith. 1970. *The Dialectic of Sex: The Case for Feminist Revolution.* New York: Bantam.

First Peoples' Heritage. 2010. Language and Culture Council (www.fpcc.ca).

Fisher, Ian. 1999. "Selling Sudan's Slaves into Freedom." *New York Times,* April 25, p. A6.

Fishman, Ted C. 2010. *Shock of Gray.* New York: Scribner.

Fitzpatrick, Maureen J., and Barbara J. McPherson. 2010. "Coloring within the Lines: Gender Stereotypes in Contemporary Coloring Books." *Sex Roles* 62: 127–137.

Fjellman, Stephen. 1992. *Vinyl Leaves: Walt Disney, eds World and America.* Boulder CO: Westview Press.

Flanders, John. 2001. "Getting Ready for the 2001 Census." *Canadian Social Trends* (Spring). Statistics Canada. Catalogue No. 11-008. Ottawa: Minister of Industry.

Flavin, Jeanne. 1998. "Razing the Wall: A Feminist Critique of Sentencing Theory, Research, and Policy." pp. 145–164 in *Cutting the Edge,* Jeffrey Ross, ed. Westport, CT: Praeger.

Fleras, Augie. 2003. *Mass Communication in Canada.* Scarborough, ON: Nelson.

———, and Jean Leonard Elliott. 1992. *The Nations Within: Aboriginal–State Relations in Canada, the United States, and New Zealand.* Toronto: Oxford University Press.

———, and Jean Leonard Elliott. 1999. *Unequal Relations: An Introduction to Race, Ethnic and Aboriginal Dynamics.* Scarborough, ON: Prentice Hall.

———, and Jean Leonard Elliott. 2003. *Unequal Relations: An Introduction to Race, Ethnic, and Aboriginal Dynamics in Canada,* 4th ed. Don Mills, ON: Prentice Hall.

———, and Jean Lock Kunz. 2001. *Media and Minorities: Representing Diversity in Multicultural Canada.* Scarborough, ON: Thomson Educational Publishing.

Fletcher, Connie. 1995. "On the Line: Women Cops Speak Out." *Chicago Tribune Magazine,* February 19, pp. 14–19.

Fong, Petti. 2001. "Brain Diseases 'Loom as Next Big Health Threat.'" *Vancouver Sun,* March 20, p. A3.

Foot, David K. 2002. "Boomers Blow Up Census." *The Globe and Mail,* March 21, A17.

Fortin, Nicole et al. 2012. "Canadian Inequality: Recent Developments and Policy Options."

University of British Columbia: Department of Economics, May.

France, David. 2000. "Slavery's New Face." *Newsweek,* December 18, pp. 61–65.

Franke, Richard Herbert, and James D. Kaul. 1978. "The Hawthorne Experiments: First Statistical Interpretation." *American Sociological Review* 43 (October): 623–643.

Freeze, Colin. 2001. "Women Outwork Men by Two Weeks Every Year." *The Globe and Mail,* March 13, p. A1.

Freidson, Eliot. 1970. *Profession of Medicine.* New York: Dodd, Mead.

French, Howard W. 2004. "Despite an Act of Clemency, China Has Its Eye on the Web." *New York Times,* June 27, p. 6.

———. 2008. "Lines of Grinding Poverty, Untouched by China's Boom." *New York Times,* January 13, p. 4.

Freudenburg, William, and Robert Gramling. 2010. *Blowout in the Gulf: The BP Oil Spill Disaster and the Future of Energy in America.* Cambridge: MIT Press.

Fridlund, Alan J., Paul Erkman, and Harriet Oster. 1987. "Facial Expressions of Emotion; Review of Literature 1970–1983." pp. 143–224 in *Nonverbal Behavior and Communication,* 2nd ed., Aron W. Seigman and Stanley Feldsteineds. Hillsdale, NJ: Erlbaum.

Friedan, Betty. 1963. *The Feminine Mystique.* New York: W.W. Norton.

Friedrich, Carl J., and Zbigniew Brzezinski. 1965. *Totalitarian Dictatorship and Autocracy,* 2nd ed. Cambridge, MA: Harvard University Press.

Friedrichs, David O. 1998. "New Directions in Critical Criminology and White Collar Crime." pp. 77–91 in *Cutting the Edge,* Jeffrey Ross, ed. Westport, CT: Praeger.

Friesen, Joe. 2012. "A Medical Provocateur Loses His Bully Pulpit." *The Globe and Mail,* January 20.

G

Gallup Opinion Index. 1978. "Religion in America, 1977–1978." 145 (January).

Gallup. 2011. *Religion.* Accessed March 27 (www.gallup.com).

Galt, Virginia. 1998. "Where the Boys Aren't: At the Top of the Class." *The Globe and Mail,* February 26, p. A6.

Gamson, Josh. 1989. "Silence, Death, and the Invisible Enemy: AIDS Activism and Social Movement 'Newness.'" *Social Problems* 36 (October): 351–367.

———, and Pearl Latteier. 2004. "Do Media Monsters Devour Diversity?" *Contexts* (Summer): 26–32.

Gans, Herbert J. 1991. *People, Plans, and Policies: Essays on Poverty, Racism, and Other National Urban Problems.* New York: Columbia University Press and Russell Sage Foundation.

———. 1995. *The War against the Poor: The Underclass and Antipoverty Policy.* New York: Basic Books.

Gardner, Gary, Erik Assadourian, and Radhika Sarin. 2004. "The State of Consumption Today." pp. 3–21 in *State of the World 2004,* Brian Halweil and Lisa Mastny, eds. New York: W.W. Norton.

Gardner, Marilyn. 2003. "This View of Seniors Just Doesn't 'Ad' Up." *Christian Science Monitor,* January 15, p. 15.

Garner, Roberta. 1996. *Contemporary Movements and Ideologies.* New York: McGraw-Hill Ryerson.

Garreau, Joel. 1991. *Edge City: Life on the New Frontier.* New York: Doubleday.

Gartner, Rosemary, Myrna Dawson, and Maria Crawford. 2001. "Confronting Violence in Women's Lives." pp. 473–490 in *Family Patterns, Gender Relations,* Bonnie J. Fox, ed. Toronto: Oxford University Press.

The Gazette. 2008. "Embrace Lifelong Learning, Canada Told." *The Gazette,* August 1. Accessed March 29, 2010 (www.canada.com/montrealgazette/news/story.html?id = 584fd693-382f-4c5f-85fa-2fa. . .).

Gecas, Viktor. 2004. "Socialization, Sociology of." pp. 14525–14530 in *International Encyclopedia of the Social and Behavioral Sciences,* Neil J. Smelser and Paul B. Baltes, ed. Cambridge, MA: Elsevier.

Gelles, Richard J., and Claire Pedrick Cornell. 1990. *Intimate Violence in Families,* 2nd ed. Newbury Park, CA: Sage.

———, and Murray A. Straus. 1988. *Intimate Violence: The Causes and Consequences of Abuse in the American Family.* New York: Simon and Schuster.

Gentile, Carmen. 2009. "Student Fights Record of 'Cyberbullying.'" *New York Times,* February 8, p. 20.

Gerth, H. H., and C. Wright Mills. 1958. *From Max Weber: Essays in Sociology.* New York: Galaxy.

Geschwender, James A. 1994. "Married Women's Waged Labour and Racial/Ethnic Stratification in Canada." *Canadian Ethnic Studies* 26(3): 53–73.

Gest, Ted. 1985. "Are White-Collar Crooks Getting off Too Easy?" *U.S. News & World Report,* July 1, p. 43.

Giddens, Anthony. 1991. *Modernity and Self-Identity: Self and Society in the Late Modern Age.* Cambridge, UK: Polity.

Gidengil, Elizabeth, Matt Hennigar, Andre Blais, Richard Nadeau and Neil Nevitte. 2003. "The Gender Gap in Support for the New Right: The Case of Canada." Paper prepared for the conference "Populisms in North America, South America, and Europe: Comparative and Historical," Bogliasco Italy, January.

———, André Blais, Joanna Everitt, Patrick Fournier, and Neil Nevitte. 2006. "Back to the Future? Making Sense of the 2004 Canadian Election Outside Quebec." *Canadian Journal of Political Science* 39: 1–25.

Giordano, Peggy C. 2003. "Relationships in Adolescence." pp. 257–281 in *Annual Review of Sociology, 2003,* Karen S. Cook and John Hagan, eds. Palo Alto, CA: Annual Reviews.

Gitlin, Todd. 2002. *Media Unlimited: How the Torrent of Images and Sounds Overwhelms Our Lives.* New York: Henry Holt and Company.

Given, Lisa M. 2008. *The Sage Encyclopedia of Qualitative Research Methods.* Sage Publications Inc.

Glanton, Dahleen. 2007. "Law AIDS Awareness Adds to Crisis." *Chicago Tribune,* February 7, p. 3.

Glater, Jonathan D. 2003. "Legal Research? Get Me Sushi with Footnotes." *New York Times,* October 22, p. A1.

Glazer, Susan. 2010. "Evaluating Microfinance." *LQ Global Research* 4 (April).

———. 2007. "Anthropologists in a War Zone: Scholars Debate Their Role." *Chronicle of Higher Education* 54 (September 30): A1, A10–A12.

Global Alliance for Workers and Communities. 2003. *About Us.* Accessed April 28 (www.theglobalalliance.org).

The Globe and Mail. 2009a. "Hey Kids, Start Planning for Your 100th Birthday." *The Globe and Mail,* October 2. Accessed October 2, 2009. (www.theglobeandmail.com/news/national/hey-kids-start-planning-for-your-100th-birthday/. . .).

———. 2009b. "Muslim Group Moves to Ban Burka." *The Globe and Mail,* October 7. Accessed October 7, 2009 (www.theglobeandmail.com/news/national/muslim-group-moves-to-ban-burka/article. . .).

Goffman, Erving. 1959. *The Presentation of Self in Everyday Life.* New York: Doubleday.

———. 1961. *Asylums: Essays on the Social Situation of Mental Patients and Other Inmates.* Garden City, NY: Doubleday.

———. 1963. *Stigma: Notes on Management of Spoiled Identity.* Englewood Cliffs, NJ: Prentice Hall.

———. 1963a. *Behavior in Public Places.* New York: Free Press.

———. 1971. *Relations in Public.* New York: Basic Books.

———. 1979. *Gender Advertisements.* New York: Harper and Row.

Gonzalez, David. 2003. "Latin Sweatshops Pressed by U.S. Campus Power." *New York Times,* April 4, p. A3.

Goode, William J. 1959. "The Theoretical Importance of Love." *American Sociological Review* 24 (February): 38–47.

———. 2011. "Canada's Zeitgeiast page 2010."

Gore, Al. 2006. *An Inconvenient Truth: The Planetary Emergency of Global Warming and What We Can Do About It.* New York: Rodale Books.

Gornick, Vivian. 1979. "Introduction" to *Gender Advertisements.* Cambridge, MA: Harvard University Press.

Gottdiener, Mark, and Joe R. Feagin. 1988. "The Paradigm Shift in Urban Sociology." *Urban Affairs Quarterly* 24 (December): 163–187.

———, and Ray Hutchison. 2000. *The New Urban Sociology,* 2nd ed. New York: McGraw-Hill Ryerson.

———, and Ray Hutchison. 2006. *The New Urban Sociology,* 3rd ed. Boulder, CO: Westview.

Gottfredson, Michael, and Travis Hirschi. 1990. *A General Theory of Crime.* Palo Alto, CA: Stanford University Press.

Gouldner, Alvin. 1960. "The Norm of Reciprocity." *American Sociological Review* 25 (April): 161–177.

———. 1970. *The Coming Crisis of Western Sociology.* New York: Basic Books.

Gram, Karen. 2001. "Hard Times in the Good Ol' Days." *Vancouver Sun,* May 5, p. A21.

Gramsci, Antonio. 1929. *Selections from the Prison Notebooks.* Quintin Hoare and Geoffrey Nowell-Smith, eds., and intro. London: Lawrence and Wishort.

Grant, Judith. 1993. *Fundamental Feminism: Contesting the Core Concepts of Feminist Theory.* New York and London: Routledge.

Grant, Tavia. 2011. "'Gender Equality is Smart Economics,' World Bank Says." *The Globe and Mail,* September 20.

Grazian, David. 2010. *Mix It Up: Popular Culture, Mass Media, and Society.* New York: Norton.

Greaves, Lorraine. 1996. *Smoke Screen: Women's Smoking and Social Control.* Halifax: Fernwood Publishing.

Greeley, Andrew M. 1989. "Protestant and Catholic: Is the Analogical Imagination Extinct?" *American Sociological Review* 54 (August): 485–502.

Green, Joyce. 2003. "Decolonizing in the Age of Globalization." *Canadian Dimension* (March/April): 3–5.

Greenemeier, Larry. 2010. "Gulf Spillover: Will BP's Deepwater Disaster Change the Oil Industry?" *Scientific American* (June 7). Accessible at http://www.scientificamerican.com/article.cfm?id5molotch-deepwater-environmental-sociology.

Greenhalgh, Susan. 2008. *Just One Child: Science and Policy in Deng's China.* Berkeley: University of California Press.

Grewal, Inderpal. 2005. *Transnational America: Feminisms, Diasporas, Neoliberalisms.* Durham: Duke University Press.

Grewal, San. 2007. "Childless Families on the Rise." *Toronto Star,* September 13. Accessed September 24, 2007 (www.thestar.com/News/article/256083).

Groza, Victor, Daniela F. Ileana, and Ivor Irwin. 1999. *A Peacock or a Crow: Stories, Interviews, and Commentaries on Romanian Adoptions.* Euclid, OH: Williams Custom Publishing.

Guardian Unlimited. 2005. "Eight Women, One Voice." Accessed July 9, 2005 (www.guardian.co.uk/africa8).

Guest, Robert. 2011. "Tribes Still Matter." *The Economist* (January 22): 17–18.

Guppy, Neil, and Scott Davies. 1998. *Education in Canada: Recent Trends and Future Challenges.* Ottawa: Statistics Canada.

Gurin, David. 2003. *Understanding Sprawl.* Vancouver: David Suzuki Foundation.

Guttmacher Institute. 2008. *Facts on Induced Abortion Worldwide.* New York: Guttmacher.

H

Haas, Michael, ed. 1999. *The Singapore Puzzle.* Westport, CT: Praeger.

Haas, Steven A., David R. Schaefer, and Olga Kornienko. 2010. "Health and the Structure of Adolescent Social Networks." *Journal of Health and Social Behavior* 5 (4):424–439.

Hacker, Helen Mayer. 1951. "Women as a Minority Group." *Social Forces* 30 (October): 60–69.

Hacker, Helen Mayer. 1974. "Women as a Minority Group, Twenty Years Later." pp. 124–134 in *Who Discriminates against Women?* Florence Denmark, ed. Beverly Hills, CA: Sage.

Haeri, Shaykh Fadhilalla. 2004. *The Thoughtful Guide to Islam.* Alresford, UK: O Books.

Hafner-Burton, Emilie M., and Kiyoteru Tsutsui. 2005. "Human Rights in a Globalizing World: The Paradox of Empty Promises." *American Journal of Sociology* 110 (March): 1373–1411.

Halbfinger, David M. 1998. "As Surveillance Cameras Peer, Some Wonder If They Also Pry." *New York Times,* February 22, p. A1.

Hamm, Steve. 2007. "Children of the Web." *BusinessWeek,* July 2, pp. 50–56, 58.

Hanes, Stephanie. 2005. "Woman Quota Changes Dynamics of Lesotho Vote." *USA Today,* June 10, p. 12A.

Hani, Yoko. 1998. "Hot Pots Wired to Help the Elderly." *Japan Times Weekly International Edition,* April 13, p. 16.

Hanson, Ralph E. 2005. *Mass Communication: Living in a Media World.* New York: McGraw-Hill Ryerson.

Harlow, Harry F. 1971. *Learning to Love.* New York: Ballantine.

Harrington, Michael. 1980. "The New Class and the Left." pp. 123–138 in *The New Class,* B. Bruce-Briggs, ed. New Brunswick, NJ: Transaction.

Harris, Chauncy D., and Edward Ullman. 1945. "The Nature of Cities." *Annals of the American Academy of Political and Social Science* 242 (November): 7–17.

Harris, Marvin. 1997. *Culture, People, Nature: An Introduction to General Anthropology,* 7th ed. New York: Longman.

Harrisinteractive. 2008. "Cell Phone Usage Continues to Increase." Accessed January 13 (www.harrisinteractive.com).

Harrison, Trevor W., and John W. Friesen. 2004. *Canadian Society in the Twenty-First Century.* Don Mills, ON: Prentice Hall.

Hart, Stacey. 1995. "(Re)searching Lesbian Health Care: Methodological Considerations for Future Directions." Accessed April 18, 2002 (www.usc.edu/isd/archives/queerfrontiers/queer/papers/hart.html).

Hartjen, Clayton A. 1978. *Crime and Criminalization,* 2nd ed. New York: Praeger.

Haskins, Ron. 2006. "Welfare Reform, 10 Years Later." *Poverty Research Insights* (Fall). 2001. *World Population Data Sheet.* Washington, DC: Population Reference Bureau.

Haub, Carl. 2005. *World Population Data Sheet 2005.* Washington, DC: Population Reference Bureau.

———. 2007. *World Population Data Sheet 2007.* Washington, DC: Population Reference Bureau.

———. 2010. 2010 World Population Data Sheet. Washington, DC: Population Reference Bureau.

———, and Diana Cornelius. 2000. *2000 World Population Data Sheet.* Washington, DC: Population Reference Bureau.

Haviland, William A. 1999. *Cultural Anthropology (Case Studies in Cultural Anthropology),* 9th ed. Fort Worth, TX: Harcourt Brace.

———, Harald E. L. Prins, Dana Walrath, and Bunny McBride. 2008. *Cultural Anthropology—The Human Challenge,* 12th ed. Belmont, CA: Wadsworth.

Health Canada. 2001. *Canada Health Act Annual Report, 1999–2000.* Ottawa: Queen's Printers.

———. 2002. "Women's Health Strategy." Ottawa: Health Canada, Women's Health Bureau. Accessed April 4, 2002 (www.hcsc.gc.ca/english/women/womenstrat.htm).

———. 2006. "Aboriginal Health." Accessed October 16, 2007 (www.hc-sc.gc.ca/ahc-asc/media/nr-cp/2006/2006_118bk1_e.html).

Heckert, Druann, and Amy Best. 1997. "Ugly Duckling to Swan: Labeling Theory and the Stigmatization of Red Hair." *Symbolic Interaction* 20(4): 365–384.

Heise, Lori, M. Ellseberg, and M. Gottemuelle. 1999. "Ending Violence against Women." *Population Reports,* ser. L, no. 11. Baltimore: Johns Hopkins University School of Public Health.

Heisig, Jan Paul. 2011. "Who Does More Housework: Rich or Poor? A Comparison of 33 Countries." *American Sociological Review* 76 (1): 74–99.

Hellmich, Nanci. 2001. "TV's Reality: No Vast American Waistlines." *USA Today,* October 8, p. 7D.

Henly, Julia R. 1999. "Challenges to Finding and Keeping Jobs in the Low-Skilled Labor Market." *Poverty Research News* 3 (No. 1): 3–5.

Henry, Francis, C. Tator, W. Mattis, and T. Reese. 1995. *The Colour of Democracy: Racism in Canadian Society.* Toronto: Harcourt Brace.

Herman, Edward S., and Noam Chomsky. 1988. *Manufacturing Consent: The Political Economy of the Mass Media.* New York: Pantheon Books.

Hickman, Jonathan. 2002. "America's 50 Best Corporations for Minorities." *Fortune,* July 8, pp. 110–120.

Hill, Michael R., and Susan Hoecker-Drysdale, eds. 2001. *Harriet Martineau: Theoretical and Methodological Perspectives.* New York: Routledge.

Hirschi, Travis. 1969. *Causes of Delinquency.* Berkeley, CA: University of California Press.

Hochschild, Arlie Russell. 1973. "A Review of Sex Role Research." *American Journal of Sociology* 78 (January): 1011–1029.

———. 1990. "The Second Shift: Employed Women Are Putting in Another Day of Work at Home." *Utne Reader* 38 (March–April): 66–73.

———. 2005. *The Commercialization of Intimate Life: Notes from Home and Work.* Berkeley: University of California Press.

Hoebel, E. Adamson. 1949. *Man in the Primitive World: An Introduction to Anthropology.* New York: McGraw-Hill Ryerson.

Hoffman, Lois Wladis. 1985. "The Changing Genetics/Socialization Balance." *Journal of Social Issues* 41 (Spring): 127–148.

Hofrichter, Richard, ed. 1993. *Toxic Struggles: The Theory and Practice of Environmental Justice.* Philadelphia: New Society.

———. 1987. "The Genetics of Personality." *Science* 257(August 7): 598–601.

Hollingshead, August B. 1975. *Elmtown's Youth and Elmtown Revisited.* New York: John Wiley and Sons.

Holmes, Tracy. 2000. "Performance Anxiety." *Peace Arch News,* February 2, p. 11.

Homans, George C. 1979. "Nature versus Nurture: A False Dichotomy." *Contemporary Sociology* 8 (May): 345–348.

Horgan, John. 1993. "Eugenics Revisited." *Scientific American* 268 (June): 122–128, 130–133.

Howard, Judith A. 1999. "Border Crossings between Women's Studies and Sociology." *Contemporary Sociology* 28 (September): 525–528.

Howard, Michael C. 1989. *Contemporary Cultural Anthropology,* 3rd ed. Glenview, IL: Scott Foresman.

Howell, Nancy, Patricia Albanese, and Kwaku Obusu-Mensah. 2001. "Ethnic Families." pp. 116–142 in *Families: Changing Trends in Canada,* 4th ed. Maureen Baker, ed. Toronto: McGraw-Hill Ryerson.

Hua, Anh. 2003. "Critical Race Feminism." Presented at the Canadian Critical Race Conference 2003: Pedagogy and Practice. University of British Columbia, Vancouver, May 2–4.

Huang, Gary. 1988. "Daily Addressing Ritual: A Cross-Cultural Study." Presented at the annual meeting of the American Sociological Association, Atlanta.

Huff, Charlotte. 2007. "Survival of the Fittest." *American Way,* May 1, pp. 30–35.

Huffstutter, P. J. 2003. "See No Evil." *Los Angeles Times,* January 12, pp. 12–15, 43–45.

Hughes, Everett. 1945. "Dilemmas and Contradictions of Status." *American Journal of Sociology* 50 (March): 353–359.

Hughlett, Mike. 2008. "Sitting Pretty." *Chicago Tribune,* September 14, sec. 5, pp. 1, 7.

Human Genome Project. 2010. "Human Genome Project Information." Accessed April 21 (www.ornl.gov/sci/techresources/human_genome/home.shtml).

Human Resources and Skills Development Canada. 2012. "Canada's Labour Minister Meets with Key Stakeholders to Discuss Issues Related to Women in the Workforce." Canada News Centre, August 1.

Human Rights Watch. 2007. "Darfur 2007: Chaos by Design: Peacekeeping Challenges for AMIS and UNAMID." 19: 15. Accessed January 9, 2008 (http://hrw.org/reports/2007/sudan0907).

Human Terrain System. 2010. "Welcome to the HTS Home Page." Accessed January 6, 2011 (http://humanterrainsystem.army.mil).

Hundley, Tom, and Margaret Ramirez. 2008. "Young Muslims Put Faith in Facebook." *Chicago Tribune,* February 10, p. 12.

HungerCount. 2012. Food Banks Canada (www.foodbankscanada.ca).

Hunter, Herbert, ed. 2000. *The Sociology of Oliver C. Cox: New Perspectives: Research in Race and Ethnic Relations,* vol. II. Stanford, CT: JAI Press.

Hyde, Janet Shibley. 2005. "The Gender Similarities Hypothesis." *American Psychologist* 60 (6): 581–592.

Igo, Sarah E. 2007. *The Average American: Surveys, Citizens, and the Making of a Mass Public.* Cambridge, MA: Harvard University Press.

Institute for Economics and Peace. 2010. "Global Peace Index." Accessible June 29 (www.vision-ofhumanity.org/gpi/results/world-map.php).

Institute for Social Policy and Understanding. 2004. *The USA PATRIOT Act: Impact on the Arabs and Muslim American Community.* Clinton Township, MI: ISPU.

Instituto del Tercer Mundo. 1999. *The World Guide 1999/2000.* Oxford, UK: New International Publications.

Interbrand. 2010. "Best Global Brands: 2009 Rankings." Accessible at www.interband.com/best_global_brands.aspx.

International Herald Tribune Europe. 2007. "Serbia Failed to Prevent Genocide, UN Court Rules." February 26. Accessed August 25, 2007 (www.int.com/articles/2007/02/26/news/serb.php).

International Institute for Democracy and Electoral Assistance. 2011. "Voter Turnout Database—Custom Query." Accessed April 11 (http://www.idea.int/vt/viewdata.cfm#).

International Organization for Migration. 2011. "Facts and Figures." Accessed April 25 (www.iom.int/jahia/jahia/about/migration/lang/en).

Internet World Stats. 2011. "Usage and Population Statistics" and "Internet World Users by Language." Updated on April 25, 2011. Accessed April 25 (www.internetworldstats.com).

Inter-Parliamentary Union. 2009. *Women in National Parliaments,* December 31. Accessed February 8, 2010 (www.ipu.org/wmn-e/classif.htm).

———. 2012. *Women in National Parliaments.* March 31. Accessed April 23 (www.ipu.org).

Intini, John. 2007. "When It Comes to Love, Sex Hurts." *Maclean's,* March 23. Accessed April 17, 2008 (www.macleans.ca/article.jsp?content520070323_161000_7800).

Ipsos Reid. 2007. "Majority (54%) Agree Discrimination against Visible Minorities A Problem in Canada." Ipsos Reid poll for Canwest News Service and Global Television, Sunday June 17, 2007.

———. 2011. "Canada's Love Affair with Online Social Networking Continues." July 14.

J

Jackson, Elton F., Charles R. Tittle, and Mary Jean Burke. 1986. "Offense-Specific Models of the Differential Association Process." *Social Problems* 33 (April): 335–356.

Jacobs, Charles A. 2001. "Slavery in the 21st Century." pp. 310–311 in *Britannica Book of the Year, 2001.* Chicago: Encyclopedia Britannica.

Jaffee, Daniel. 2007. *Brewing Justice: Fair Trade Coffee, Sustainability, and Survival.* Berkeley: University of California Press.

Japsen, Bruce. 2007. "AIDS activists Call for Boycott of Abbott Products." Reuters, April 27.

Jasper, James M. 1997. *The Art of Moral Protest: Culture, Biography, and Creativity in Social Movements.* Chicago: University of Chicago Press.

Jenkins, Matt. 2008. "A Really Inconvenient Truth." *Miller-McCure* 1 (March–April): 38–41.

Jenkins, Richard. 1991. "Disability and Social Stratification." *British Journal of Sociology* 42 (December): 557–580.

Jimenez, Marina. 2007. "How Canadian Are You? Visible-Minority Immigrants and Their Children Identify Less and Less with the Country, Report Says." *The Globe and Mail,* January 12, p. A1.

———, and Kim Lunmann. 2004. "Canada's Biggest Cities See Influx of New Immigrants." *The Globe and Mail,* August 19, p. A5.

Joas, Hans, and Wolfgang Knöbl. 2009. *Social Theory: Twenty Introductory Lectures.* Cambridge: Cambridge University Press.

Johnson, Allan G. 2000. *The Blackwell Dictionary of Sociology.* Oxford, UK: Blackwell Publishing.

Johnson, Anne M., Jane Wadsworth, Kaye Wellings, and Julie Field. 1994. *Sexual Attitudes and Lifestyles.* Oxford, UK: Blackwell Scientific.

Johnson, Benton. 1975. *Functionalism in Modern Sociology: Understanding Talcott Parsons.* Morristown, NJ: General Learning.

Johnson, George. 1999. "It's a Fact: Faith and Theory Collide over Evolution." *New York Times,* August 15, pp. 1, 12.

Johnson, Holly. 1996. *Dangerous Domains: Violence against Women in Canada.* Scarborough, ON: Nelson Canada.

Johnston, David Cay. 1994. "Ruling Backs Homosexuals on Asylum." *New York Times,* June 12, pp. D1, D6.

Jolin, Annette. 1994. "On the Backs of Working Prostitutes: Feminist Theory and Prostitution Policy." *Crime and Delinquency* 40 (No. 2): 69–83.

Jones, Charles, Lorna Marsden, and Lorne Tepperman. 1990. *Lives of Their Own: The Individualization of Women's Lives.* Toronto: Oxford University Press.

Jopling, John, and Reilly Morse. 2010. "The BP Oil Disaster and Its Disproportionate Impacts on Minorities and Communities of Color." *Focus* 36 (October–November): 12–14.

Joseph, Jay. 2004. *The Gene Illusion: Genetic Research in Psychiatry and Psychology under the Microscope.* New York: Algora Books.

K

Kahn, Joseph. 2003. "Made in China, Bought in China." *New York Times,* January 5, sec. 3, pp. 1, 10.

Kaiser Family Foundation. 2007. "Parents Say They're Getting Control of Their Children's Exposure to Sex and Violence in the Media— Even Online." Accessed January 2, 2008 (www.kff.org/entmedia/entmedia061907nr.cfm).

Karides, Marina. 2010. "Theorizing the Rise of Microenterprise Development in Caribbean Context." *Journal of World-Systems Research* 16 (2): 192–216.

Katel, Peter. 2005. "Ending Poverty." *CQ Researcher* 15 (September 9): 733–760.

Katovich, Michael A. 1987. Correspondence. June 1.

Kazemipur, Abdie. 2002. "The Intersection of Socio-Economic Status and Race/Ethnicity/Official Language/Religion." Prepared for the Intersections of Diversity Seminar, Draft, March 8.

Keeter, Scott, and Courtney Kennedy. 2006. "The Cell Phone Challenge to Survey Research." Washington, DC: Pew Research Center.

Kent, Mary M., and Carl Haub. 2005. "Global Demographic Divide." *Population Bulletin* 60 (December).

Kentor, Jeffrey, and Yong Suk Jang. 2004. "Yes, There Is a (Growing) Transnational Business Community." *International Sociology* 19 (September): 355–368.

Kerbo, Harold R. 2003. *Social Stratification and Inequality: Class Conflict in Historical, Comparative, and Global Perspective,* 5th ed. New York: McGraw-Hill Ryerson.

Kesmodel, David, and Danny Yadron. 2010. "E-Cigarettes Spark New Smoking War." *Wall Street Journal,* August 25, pp. A1, A12.

Kilbourne, Jean. 2000a. *Can't Buy My Love: How Advertising Changes the Way We Think and Feel.* New York: Touchstone Books, Simon and Schuster.

———. 2000b. *Killing Us Softly 3.* Videorecording. Northampton, MA: Media Education Foundation (Cambridge Documentary Films).

Killian, Caitlin. 2003. "The Other Side of the Veil: North Africa Women in France Respond to the Headscarf Affair." *Gender and Society* (August 17): 576–590.

King, Peter H. 2004. "Their Spiritual Thirst Found a Desert Spring." *Los Angeles Times,* August 4, pp. A1, A10, A11.

Kinsella, Kevin, and David R. Phillips. 2005. "Global Aging: The Challenge of Success." *Population Bulletin* 60 (March).

Kinsey, Alfred C, Wardell B. Pomeroy, and Clyde E. Martin. 1948. *Sexual Behavior in the Human Male.* Philadelphia: Saunders.

Kiper, Dmitry. 2008. "GodTube.com Puts Christian Worship Online." *Christian Science Monitor,* February 6.

Kirkey, Sharon. 2012. "High-powered Women See Heightened Risk of Heart Attack." *The Vancouver Sun,* July 18.

Kiser, Edgar. 1992. "War." pp. 2243–2247 in *Encyclopedia of Sociology,* Edgar F. Borgatta and Marie L. Borgatta, eds. New York: Macmillan.

Kitchener, Richard F. 1991. "Jean Piaget: The Unknown Sociologist." *British Journal of Sociology* 42 (September): 421–442.

Kleiner, Art. 2003. "Are You In with the In Crowd?" *Harvard Business Review* 81 (July): 86–92.

Klug, Heinz. 2005. "Transnational Human Rights: Exploring the Persistence and Globalization of Human Rights." pp. 85–103 in *Annual Review of Law and Social Sciences.* Palo Alto, CA: Annual Reviews.

Knudsen, Morten. 2010. "Surprised by Method— Functional Method and System Theory." *Forum: Qualitative Social Research* 11 (September): article 12.

Kohn, Melvin L. 1970. "The Effects of Social Class on Parental Values and Practices." pp. 45–68 in *The American Family: Dying or Developing,* David Reiss and H. A. Hoffman, eds. New York: Plenum.

———, Kazimierz M. Slomeznsky, and Carrie Schoenbach. 1986. "Social Stratification and the Transmission of Values in the Family: A Cross-National Assessment." *Sociological Forum* 1, 1: 73–102.

Koolhaas, Rem, et al. 2001. *Mutations.* Barcelona, Spain: Actar.

Kornell, Sam. 2007. "The Pros and Cons of Fair-Trade Coffee." *The Santa Barbara Independent,* April 5. Accessed April 9, 2008 (www.organic-consumers.org/articles/article_4738.cfm).

Kortenhaus, Carol M., and Jack Demarest. 1993. "Gender Role Sterotyping in Children's Literature: An Update." *Sex Roles: A Journal of Research* 28(3–4): 219–232.

Korzeniewicz, Roberto Patricio, and Timothy Patrick Moran. 2009. *Unveiling Inequality: A World Historical Perspective.* New York: Russell Sage Foundation.

Kottak, Conrad. 2011. *Anthropology: Appreciating Human Diversity,* 14th ed. New York: McGraw-Hill.

Krashinsky, Susan, 2009. "Why Men in Ads Are Dumb, Goofy, or Completely Inept." *The Globe and Mail,* August 7. Accessed August 7, 2009 (http://license.icopyright.net/user/view-FreeUse.act?fuid5NDQwNTU5Ng%3D%3D).

Krieger, Nancy, and Elizabeth Fee. 1994. "Man-Made Medicine and Women's Health." pp. 11–29 in *Women's Health Politics and Power: Essays on Sex/Gender, Medicine and Public Health,* Elizabeth Fee and Nancy Krieger, eds. Amityville, NY: Baywood Publications.

Kriesberg, Louis. 1992. "Peace." pp. 1432–1436 in *Encyclopedia of Sociology,* Edgar F. Borgatta and Marie L. Borgatta, eds. New York: Macmillan.

Kronstadt, Jessica. 2008. "Genetics and Economic Mobility." Washington, DC: Economic Mobility Project. Also accessible at www.economicmobility.org/reports_and_research/literature_reviews?id50004.

Kunzig, Robert. 2011. "Seven Billion." *National Geographic* (January): 40–69.

Kuumba, M. Bahati. 1999. "A Cross-Cultural Race/Class/Gender Critique of Contemporary Population Policy: The Impact of Globalization." *Sociological Forum* 14(3): 447–463.

Kwong, Jo. 2005. "Globalization's Effects on the Environment." *Society* 42 (January/February): 21–28.

L

Laird, Gordon. 2007. *The True Cost of Homelessness.* Chumir Foundation.

Lakshimi, Rama. 2001. "Gender Prejudice in India Still against Daughters." *The Globe and Mail,* April 4, p. A10.

Lampkin, Lorna. 1985. *Visible Minorities in Canada.* Research paper for the Abella Royal Commission on Equality in Employment. Ottawa: Ministry of Supply and Services.

Landler, Mark, and Michael Barbaro. 2006. "No, Not Always." *New York Times,* August 2, pp. C1, C4.

Landtman, Gunnar. [1938] 1968. *The Origin of Inequality of the Social Class.* New York: Greenwood (original edition 1938, Chicago: University of Chicago Press).

Langman, L. 1987. "Social Stratification." pp. 211–249 in *Handbook of Marriage and the Family.* Marvin B. Sussman and Suzanne K. Steinmetz, eds. New York: Plenum.

Lasch, Christopher. 1977. *Haven in a Heartless World: The Family Besieged.* New York: Basic Books.

Lasswell, Harold D. 1936. *Politics: Who Gets What, When, How.* New York: McGraw-Hill Ryerson.

Lauer, Robert H. 1982. *Perspectives on Social Change,* 3rd ed. Boston: Allyn and Bacon.

Laumann, Edward O., John H. Gagnon, and Robert T. Michael. 1994. "A Political History of the National Sex Survey of Adults." *Family Planning Perspectives* 26 (February): 34–38.

Lautard, Hugh E., and Donald J. Loree. 1984. "Ethnic Stratification in Canada, 1931–1971." *Canadian Journal of Sociology* 9: 333–343.

———, and Neil Guppy. 1999. "Revisiting the Vertical Mosaic: Occupational Stratification among Canadian Ethnic Groups." pp. 219–252 in *Race and Ethnic Relations in Canada,*

2nd ed., Peter S. Li, ed. Toronto: Oxford University Press.

Lavrakas, Paul J., Charles D. Shuttles, Charlotte Steel, and Howard Fienberg. 2007. "The State of Surveying Cell Phone Numbers in the United States: 2007 and Beyond." *Public Opinion Quarterly* 71 (5): 840–854.

Lawson, Sandra. 2008. *Girls Count.* New York: Goldman Sachs.

Lazarsfeld, Paul, and Robert K. Merton. 1948. "Mass Communication, Popular Taste, and Organized Social Action." pp. 95–118 in *The Communication of Ideas,* Lymon Bryson, ed. New York: Harper and Brothers.

Leacock, Eleanor. 2001. "Women in an Egalitarian Society: The Montagnais-Naskapi of Canada." pp. 55–66 in *Family Patterns, Gender Relations,* 2nd ed., Bonnie J. Fox, ed. Toronto: Oxford University Press.

Leavell, Hugh R., and E. Gurney Clark. 1965. *Preventive Medicine for the Doctor in His Community: An Epidemiologic Approach,* 3rd ed. New York: McGraw-Hill Ryerson.

Lehne, Gregory K. 1995. "Homophobia among Men: Supporting and Defining the Male Role." pp. 325–336 in *Men's Lives,* Michael S. Kimmel and Michael S. Messner, eds. Boston: Allyn and Bacon.

Lengermann, Patricia Madoo, and Jill Niebrugge-Brantley. 1998. *The Women Founders: Sociology and Social Theory, 1830–1930.* Boston: McGraw-Hill Ryerson.

———, and Jill Niebrugge-Brantley. 2008. "Contemporary Feminist Theory." pp. 436–486 in *Sociological Theory,* 7th ed., George Ritzer, ed. New York: McGraw-Hill Ryerson.

Lenhart, Amanda. 2009. "Pew Internet Project Data Memo: Adults and Social Network Websites." Accessible at www.pewinternet.org/PPF/r/272/report_display.asp.

Lenski, Gerhard. 1966. *Power and Privilege: A Theory of Social Stratification.* New York: McGraw-Hill Ryerson.

Leonard, Koren Isakser. 2003. *Muslims in the United States: The State of Research.* New York: Russell Sage Foundation.

Levine, Felice. 2001. "Deja Vu All over Again—The Third Amendment." *Footnotes* 29 (May/June).

Levine, Nancy. 1988. *The Dynamics of Polyandry: Kinship, Domesticity, and Population on the Tibetan Border.* Chicago: University of Chicago Press.

Levine, Susa. 2006. "Culturally Sensitive Medicine." *Washington Post National Weekly Edition* 23 (March 26), p. 31.

Levitt, Peggy, and B. Nadya Jaworsky. 2007. "Transnational Migration Studies: Past Developments and Future Trends." *Annual Review of Sociology* 33: 129–156.

Levy, Becca R., Martin D. Slade, Suzanne R. Kunkel, and Stanislav V. Kasl. 2002. "Longevity Increased by Positive Self-Perceptions of Aging." *Journal of Personality and Social Psychology* 83 (2): 261–270.

Lewis, Anthony. 1999. "Abroad at Home: Something Rich and Strange," *New York Times,* October 12.

Li, Peter S. 1988. *Ethnic Inequality in a Class Society.* Toronto: Wall and Thompson.

———. 1992. "Race and Gender as Bases of Class Fractions and Their Effects on Earnings."

Canadian Review of Sociology and Anthropology 29(4): 488–510.

———. 2000. "Earning Disparities between Immigrants and Native-Born Canadians." *Canadian Review of Sociology and Anthropology* 37(3).

———. 2003. "Social Inclusion of Visible Minorities and Newcomers: The Articulation of 'Race' and 'Racial' Difference in Canadian Society." Presented at the Conference on Social Inclusion, Ottawa, March 27–28.

Li, Wei. 2008. *Ethnoburb: The New Ethnic Community in Urban America.* University of Hawaii Press.

Lian, Jason Z., and David Ralph Matthews. 1998. "Does the Vertical Mosaic Still Exist? Ethnicity and Income in Canada, 1991." *Canadian Review of Sociology and Anthropology* 35(4): 461–481.

Lim, Louisa. 2007. "Digital Culture: China's 'Gold Farmers' Play a Grim Game." May 14, 2007 broadcast on NPR. Accessible at www.npr.org.

Lindbergh, Anne Morrow. 1955. *Gift from the Sea.* Reprint. New York: Pantheon.

Link, Bruce G., and Jo Phelan. 1995. "Social Conditions as Fundamental Causes of Disease." *Journal of Health and Social Behaviour* (Extra Issue): 80–94.

Linton, Ralph. 1936. *The Study of Man: An Introduction.* New York: Appleton-Century.

Lips, Hilary M. 1993. *Sex and Gender: An Introduction,* 2nd ed. Mountain View, CA: Mayfield.

Lipset, Seymour Martin. 1996. *American Exceptionalism: A Double-Edged Sword.* New York: Norton.

Lipson, Karen. 1994. "'Nell' Not Alone in the Wilds." *Los Angeles Times,* December 19, F1, F6.

Liptak, Adam. 2010. "Study Finds Questioning of Nominees to Be Useful." *New York Times,* June 28, pp. A10, A11.

Liska, Allen E., and Steven F. Messner. 1999. *Perspectives on Crime and Deviance,* 3rd ed. Upper Saddle River, NJ: Prentice Hall.

Livernash, Robert, and Eric Rodenburg. 1998. "Population Change, Resources, and the Environment." *Population Bulletin* 53 (March).

Ljunggren, David. 2013. "Alarming Number of Aboriginals in Canada's Prisons." Reuters, March 7.

Lofland, Lyn H. 1975. "The 'Thereness' of Women: A Selective Review of Urban Sociology." pp. 144–170 in *Another Voice,* M. Millman and R. M. Kanter, eds. New York: Anchor/Doubleday.

Lorber, Judith. 1994. *Paradoxes of Gender.* New Haven, CT: Yale University Press.

Lowman, John, and Ted Palys. 2000. "Ethics and Institutional Conflict of Interest: The Research Confidentiality Controversy at Simon Fraser University." *Sociological Practice: A Journal of Clinical and Applied Sociology* 2(4): 245–264.

Luciw, Roma. 2007. "Overworked Before You Get to the Office? You'll Pay for It." *Globe and Mail,* April 10. Accessed April 10, 2007 (www.theglobeandmail.com/servlet/story/RTGAM.20070410.wworkersfamilty0410).

Lukacs, Georg. 1923. *History and Class Consciousness.* London: Merlin.

———. 1996. *Dubious Conceptions: The Politics of Teenage Pregnancy.* Cambridge, MA: Harvard University Press.

Lundy, Colleen. 1991. "Women and Alcohol: Moving Beyond Disease Theory." pp. 57–73 in

Health Futures: Alcohol and Drugs, Douglas J. McCready, ed. Waterloo: Interdisciplinary Research Committee, Wilfred Laurier University.

Luster, Tom, Kelly Rhoades, and Bruce Haas. 1989. "The Relation between Parental Values and Parenting Behavior: A Test of the Kohn Hypothesis." *Journal of Marriage and the Family* 51(February): 139–147.

Luttinger, Nina, and Gregory Dicum. 2006. *The Coffee Book: Anatomy of an Industry from Crop to the Last Drop.* Revised and updated. New York: New Press.

Luxton, Meg. 1980. *More Than a Labour of Love: Three Generations of Women's Work in the Home.* Toronto: Women's Press.

———. 2001. "Husbands and Wives." pp. 176–198 in *Family Patterns, Gender Relations,* 2nd ed., Bonnie J. Fox, ed. Toronto: Oxford University Press.

Lyall, Sarah. 2002. "For Europeans, Love, Yes; Marriage, Maybe." *New York Times,* March 24, pp. 1–8.

Lynch, Margaret, and Richard Ferri. 1997. "Health Needs of Lesbian Women and Gay Men." *Clinicians Reviews* 7(1): 85–88, 91–92, 95, 98–102, 105–107, 108–115, 117–118.

Lyotard, Jean François. 1993. *The Postmodern Explained: Correspondence, 1982–1985.* Minneapolis: University of Minnesota Press.

M

MacLeod, Calum. 2010. "Chinese Use Internet to Show Dissent." *USA Today,* December 29, p. 31.

MacDonald, G. Jeffrey. 2007. "Go in Search of a Church by Way of the Web." *USA Today,* October 17, p. 8D.

Mack, Raymond W., and Calvin P. Bradford. 1979. *Transforming America: Patterns of Social Change,* 2nd ed. New York: Random House.

MacKinnon, Catharine A. 1987. *Feminism Unmodified: Discourses on Life and Law.* Cambridge, MA: Harvard University Press.

MacMillan, Angus B., David R. Offord, and Jennifer L. Dingle. 1996. "Aboriginal Health." *Canadian Medical Association Journal* 155(11): 1569–78.

Maestretti, Danielle. 2009. "Information Overload." *Utne Reader* (July–August): 22–23.

Mahbub ul Haq Human Development Centre. 2000. *Human Development in South Asia 2000.* Oxford, UK: Oxford University Press for Mahbub ul Haq Human Development Centre.

Makin 2009. "Changing How the World's Oldest Profession Is Policed." *The Globe and Mail,* October 6.

Malcolm X, with Alex Haley. 1964. *The Autobiography of Malcolm X.* New York: Grove.

Malthus, Thomas Robert, Julian Huxley, and Frederick Osborn. [1824] 1960. *Three Essays on Population.* Reprint. New York: New American Library.

Mandell, nancy, ed. 1998. *Feminist Issues,* 2nd ed. Scarborough, ON: Prentice Hall, Allyn and Bacon.

Mangham, Colin. 2007. "A Critique of Canada's INSITE Injection Site and its Parent Philosophy: Implications and Recommendations for Policy." *Journal of Global Drug Policy and Practice* 1(2).

Manitoba Human Rights Commission. 2004. "The Fighting Spirit of Lee Williams." *Connections* 4(2): 1–2.

Manson, Donald A. 1986. *Tracking Offenders: White-Collar Crime.* Bureau of Justice Statistics Special Report. Washington, DC: United States Government Printing Office.

Maracle, Lee. 1996. *I Am a Woman: A Native Perspective on Sociological Feminism.* Vancouver: Press Gang Publishers.

Margolis, Mac. 2009. "The Land of Less Contrast: How Brazil Reined in Inequality." *Newsweek,* November 28.

Mark, Gloria, Victor M. Gonzalez, and Justin Harris. 2005. "No Task Left Behind? Examining the Nature of Fragmented Work." Paper presented at CHI 2005, Portland, Oregon.

Markusen, Ann. 2013. "Fuxxy Concepts, Proxy Data." *GIA Reader* 24(1).

Marr, Phebe. 2003. "Civics 101, Taught by Saddam Hussein: First, Join the Paramilitary." *New York Times,* April 20.

Marriott, Michel. 2004. "The Color of Mayhem, in a Wave of Urban Games." *New York Times,* August 12.

Marshall, Gordon. 1998. *Dictionary of Sociology.* Oxford: Oxford University Press.

Marshall, Kathleen. 1999. *The Gambling Industry: Raising the Stakes.* Ottawa: Minister of Industry.

Martin, Dominique, Jean-Luc Metzger, and Philippe Pierre. 2006. "The Sociology of Globalization: Theoretical and Methodological Reflections." *International Sociology* 21 (July): 499–521.

Martin, Philip, and Elizabeth Midgley. 1999. "Immigrants to the United States." *Population Bulletin* 54 (June): 1–42.

Martin, Susan E. 1994. "Outsider within the Station House: The Impact of Race and Gender on Black Women Politics." *Social Problems* 41 (August): 383–400.

Martineau, Harriet. [1837] 1962. *Society in America.* Reprint edited, abridged, with an introductory essay by Seymour Martin Lipset. Garden City, NY: Doubleday.

Marx, Earl. 2009. "How Will Fair Fare?" *Christian Science Monitor,* April 19, pp. 30–31.

Marx, Karl. [1844] 1964. "Contribution to the Critique of Hegel's Philosophy of Right." In *On Religion,* Karl Marx and Friedrich Engels. New York: Schocker Books.

Marx, Karl, and Friedrich Engels. [1847] 1955. *Selected Work in Two Volumes.* Reprint. Moscow: Foreign Languages Publishing House.

Maryanski, Alexandra R. 2004. "Evaluation Theory." pp. 257–263 in *Encyclopedia of Social Theory,* George Ritzer, ed. Thousand Oaks, CA: Sage.

Masland, Tom. 1992. "Slavery." *Newsweek,* May 4, pp. 30–32, 37–39.

Matsushita, Yoshiko. 1999. "Japanese Kids Call for a Sympathetic Ear." *Christian Science Monitor,* January 20, p. 15.

Matthews, Beverly. 2000. "The Body Beautiful: Adolescent Girls and Images of Beauty." pp. 208–219 in *New Perspectives on Deviance: The Construction of Deviance in Everyday Life,* Lori G. Beaman, ed. Scarborough, ON: Prentice Hall.

Matthews, Jay. 1999. "A Home Run for Home Schooling." *Washington Post National Weekly Edition,* March 29, p. 34.

McCabe 2009. "Shanghai Parents Urged to Add Siblings." *The Leaderpost.* Accessed August 1, 2009 (www.leaderpost.com/story_print.html?id=1825723&sponsor=).

McCloud, Aminah Beverly. 1995. *African American Islam.* New York: Routledge.

McFalls, Joseph A., Jr. 2007. *Population: A Lively Introduction,* 5th ed. Washington, DC: Population Reference Bureau.

McGuire, Meredith B. 1981. *Religion: The Social Context.* Belmont, CA: Wadsworth.

McIntosh, Peggy. 1988. "White Privilege and Male Privilege: A Personal Account of Coming to See Correspondence through Work and Women's Studies." Working Paper No. 189, Wellesley College Center for Research on Women, Wellesley, MA.

McIntyre. Lisa J. 2006. *The Practical Skeptic.* New York: McGraw-Hill Ryerson.

McKenna, Barrie. 2004. "Unions Starting to Make Inroads at Wal-Mart." *The Globe and Mail,* August 23, pp. B1, B12.

McKinlay, John B., and Sonja M. McKinlay. 1977. "The Questionable Contribution of Medical Measures to the Decline of Mortality in the United States in the Twentieth Century." *Milbank Memorial Fund Quarterly* 55 (Summer): 405–428.

McLuhan, Marshall. 1962. *The Gutenberg Galaxy: The Making of Typographic Man.* Toronto: University of Toronto Press.

———. 1964. *Understanding Media: The Extensions of Man.* New York: New American Library.

———, and Quentin Fiore. 1967. *The Medium Is the Message: An Inventory of Effects.* New York: Bantam Books.

McNeil, Donald G., Jr. 2004. "When Real Food Isn't an Option." *New York Times,* September 3, pp. A1, A5.

McTeer, Maureen A. 1999. *Tough Choices: Living and Dying in the 21st Century.* Toronto: Irwin Law.

Mead, George H. 1934. *Mind, Self and Society,* Charles W. Morris, ed. Chicago: University of Chicago Press.

———. 1964a. *On Social Psychology,* Anselm Strauss, ed. Chicago: University of Chicago Press.

———. 1964b. "The Genesis of the Self and Social Control." pp. 267–293 in *Selected Writings: George Herbert Mead,* Andrew J. Reck, ed. Indianapolis: Bobbs-Merrill.

Mead, Margaret. [1935] 1950. *Sex and Temperament in Three Primitive Societies.* Reprint, New York: Morrow.

———. [1935] 1963. *Sex and Temperament in Three Primitive Societies.* Reprint, New York: Morrow.

———.1973. "Does the World Belong to Men—Or to Women?" *Redbook,* October, pp. 46–52.

Media Awareness Network. 2008. "Government and Industry Responses to Media and Violence." Accessed January 23, 2008 (www.media-awareness.ca/english/issues/violence/govt_industry_responses.cfm).

Meichtry, Stacy. 2011. "Italian Mammas Put Meals on Wheels, Say 'Mangia!' to Faraway Offspring." *Wall Street Journal,* March 31, pp. A1, A14.

Memecan, Nursuna. 2010. "Women and the Economic and Financial Crisis." Committee on Equal Opportunities for Women and Men, Report. Parliamentary Assembly, Council of Europe.

Memmi, Albert. 1965. *The Colonizer and the Colonized.* New York: Orion Press.

Mendelsohn, Matthew. 2002. *Canadian Public Opinion on Representative Democracy.* Ottawa: Canadian Centre for Management Development.

Mendez, Jennifer Bickham. 1998. "Of Mops and Maids: Contradictions and Continuities in Bureaucratized Domestic Work." *Social Problems* 45 (February): 114–135.

Mensah, Joseph. 2002. *Black Canadians: History, Experiences, Social Conditions.* Halifax: Fernwood.

Menzel, Peter. 1994. *Material World: A Global Family Portrait.* University of California Press.

Merton, Robert K. 1968. *Social Theory and Social Structure.* New York: Free Press.

Messner, Michael A, and Cheryl Cooky. 2010. *Gender in Televised Sports: News and Highlights Shows, 1989–2009.* Los Angeles: Center for Feminist Research, University of Southern California.

Meston, Cindy M., and David M. Buss. 2007. "Why Humanoids Have Sex." *Archives of Sexual Behavior* 36 (August).

———, and Tierney Ahrold. 2008. "Ethnic, Gender, and Acculturation Influences on Sexual Behaviors." *Archives of Sexual Behavior.* Springer Science + Business Media.

Meyerson, Harold. 2004. "Wal-Mart Loves Unions (in China)." *Washington Post,* December 1, p. A25.

Michels, Robert. 1915. *Political Parties* Reprint Glencoe, IL: Free Press.

Microfinance Information Exchange. 2011. "MIX Market." Accessed May 24 (www.themix.org).

Milan, Anne, Hélène Maheux, and Tina Chui. "A Portrait of Couples in Mixed Unions." Canadian Social Trends, No. 89. April 20.

Miles, James. 2009. "A Wary Repeat: A Special Report on China and America." *The Economist* (October 24): 1–16.

Milgram, Stanley. 1963. "Behavioral Study of Obedience." *Journal of Abnormal and Social Psychology* 67 (October): 371–378.

———. 1975. *Obedience to Authority: An Experimental View.* New York: Harper and Row.

Miller, Jacqueline W., Timothy S. Naimi, Robert D. Brewer, and Sherry Everett Jones. 2007. "Binge Drinking and Associated Health Risk Behaviors among High School Students." *Pediatrics* 119 (January): 76–85.

Millet, Kate. 1971. *Sexual Politics.* New York: Avon Books.

Mills, C. Wright. 1956. *The Power Elite.* New York: Oxford University Press.

———. [1956] 2000. *The Power Elite.* A New Edition. Afterword by Alan Wolfe. New York: Oxford University Press.

Miner, Horace. 1956. "Body Ritual among the Nacirema." *American Anthropologist* 58 (June): 503–507.

Minnesota Center for Twin and Family Research. 2010. "Research at the MCTFR." Accessed January 24 (http://mctfr.psych.umn.edu/research/).

Mitchell, Alanna. 1999. "Home Schooling Goes AWOL." *The Globe and Mail,* February 2, pp. A1, A6.

Miyata, Kakuko, and Tetsuro Kobayashi. 2008. "Causal Relationship between Internet Use and Social Capital in Japan." *Asian Journal of Social Psychology* 11: 42–52.

Mizruchi, Mark S. 1996. "What Do Interlocks Do? An Analysis, Critique, and Assessment of Research on Interlocking Directorates." pp. 271–298 in *Annual Review of Sociology, 1996,* John Hagan and Karen Cook, ed. Palo Alto, CA: Annual Reviews.

Moeller, Susan D. 1999. *Compassion Fatigue.* London: Routledge.

Moen, Phyllis, and Patricia Roehling. 2005. *The Career Mystique: Cracks in the American Dream.* Lanham, MD: Rowman and Littlefield.

Moffatt, Susan. 1995. "Minorities Found More Likely to Live Near Toxic Sites." *Los Angeles Times,* August 30, pp. B1, B3.

Mohanty, Chandra T. 2003. *Feminism Without Borders: Decolonizing Theory, Practicing Solidarity.* Durham, NC: Duke University Press.

Molotch, Harvey. 1970. "Oil in Santa Barbara and Power in America." *Sociological Inquiry* 40 (Winter): 131–144.

Momigliana, Anna. 2010. "Italy: Over 30 and Still Living with Mom." *Christian Science Monitor,* January 27. Accessible at www.csmonitor.com/layout/set/print/content/view/print/275435.

Monteiro, Lois A. 1998. "Ill-Defined Illnesses and Medically Unexplained Symptoms Syndrome." *Footnotes* 26 (February): 3, 6.

Moore, Wilbert E. 1967. *Order and Change: Essays in Comparative Sociology.* New York: John Wiley and Sons.

Morris, Aldon. 2000. "Reflections on Social Movement Theory: Criticisms and Proposals." *Contemporary Sociology* 29 (May): 445–454.

Morris, Bonnie Rothman. 1999. "You've Got Romance! Seeking Love on Line." *New York Times,* August 26, p. D1.

Morrison, Denton E. 1971. "Some Notes toward Theory on Relative Deprivation, Social Movements, and Social Change." *American Behavioral Scientist* 14 (May–June): 675–690.

Mossman, M. J. 1994. "Running Hard to Stand Still: The Paradox of Family Law Reform." *Dalhousie Law Journal* 17(5).

Mueller, G.O. 2001. "Transnational Crime: Definitions and Concepts." pp. 13–21 in *Combating Transnational Crime: Concepts, Activities, and Responses,* P. Williams and D. Vlassis, eds. London: Franklin Cass.

Murdock, George P. 1945. "The Common Denominator of Cultures." pp. 123–142 in *The Science of Man in the World Crisis,* Ralph Linton, ed. New York: Columbia University Press.

———. 1949. *Social Structure.* New York: Macmillan.

———. 1957. "World Ethnographic Sample." *American Anthropologist* 59 (August): 664–687.

Mydans, Seth. 2007. "Monks Are Silenced, and for Now, the Web Is, Too." *New York Times,* October 4, pp. A1, A15.

N

NAACP. 2008. *Out of Focus—Out of Sync Take 4.* Baltimore: NAACP.

Nabalamba, Alice. 2001. *Locating Risk: A Multivariate Analysis of the Spatial and Socio-demographic Characteristics of Pollution.*

Unpublished Ph.D. dissertation, University of Waterloo, Ontario.

Naiman, Joanne. 2004. *How Societies Work: Class Power and Change in the Canadian Context,* 3rd ed. Scarborough, ON: Nelson.

Nash, Manning. 1962. "Race and the Ideology of Race." *Current Anthropology* 3 (June): 285–288.

National Advisory Commission on Criminal Justice. 1976. *Organized Crime.* Washington, DC: U.S. Government Printing Office.

National Center on Addiction and Substance Abuse at Columbia University. 2007. *Wasting the Best and the Brightest: Substance Abuse at America's Colleges and Universities.* New York: NCASA at Columbia University.

National Council of Welfare. 2010. "Canadian Welfare System Outdated." December 13.

National Geographic. 2005. *Atlas of the World,* 8th ed. Washington DC: National Geographic.

National Indian Child Welfare Association. 2010. "ICWA Online Training Course." Accessed January 15 (www.nicwa.org/ica_course).

National Post. 2012. "Alberta Refuses to Give Parents Freedom from Religion in Schools." Justin Trottier. February 15.

Neilsen Company. 2009. "Global Online Consumer Survey." March–April.

———. 2011. "A Study of Women Around the World." June.

Nelson, Adie, and Augie Fleras. 1998. *Social Problems in Canada: Conditions and Consequences,* 2nd ed. Scarborough, ON: Prentice Hall.

———, and Barrie W. Robinson. 1999. *Gender in Canada.* Scarborough, ON: Prentice Hall.

Nelson, Emily. 2004. "Goodbye, 'Friends'; Hello, New Reality." *Wall Street Journal,* February 9, pp. B6, B10.

Nelson, Gary. 2006. "Manitoba School Trustee Favours Tolerance." *Humanist Association of Manitoba.* Accessed October 2, 2007 (www.mb.humanists.ca/manitoba_school_trustee.html).

Neuwirth, Robert. 2004. *Shadow Cities: A Billion Squatters, a New Urban World.* New York: Routledge.

New Unionism Network. 2011. "State of the Unions." Accessed February 10 (http://www.newunionism.net/State_of_the_Unions.htm).

New York Times. 1998. "2 Gay Men Fight Town Hall for a Family Pool Pass Discount." July 14, p. B2.

Newman, William M. 1973. *American Pluralism: A Study of Minority Groups and Social Theory.* New York: Harper and Row.

Nguyen, S. D. 1982. "The Psycho-social Adjustment and Mental Health Needs of Southeast Asian Refugees." *Psychiatric Journal of the University of Ottawa* 7(1): 6–34.

Nielsen, Joyce McCarl, Glenda Walden, and Charlotte A. Kunkel. 2000. "Gendered Heteronormativity: Empirical Illustrations in Everyday Life." *Sociological Quarterly* 41(2): 283–296.

———, and Gerhard Lenski. 2006. *Human Societies: An Introduction to Macrosociology.* 10th ed. Boulder, CO: Paradigm.

Nolan, Patrick, and Gerhard Lenski. 2009. *Human Societies: An Introduction to Macrosociology,* 11th ed. Boulder, CO: Paradigm.

Noonan, Rita K. 1995. "Women against the State: Political Opportunities and Collective Action

Frames in Chile's Transition to Democracy." *Sociological Forum* 10: 81–111.

NPD Group. 2008. "Wired Baby Boomers Going Digital, Visiting Social Networks and Watching Videos on the Web." Accessed March 18 (www.npd.com/press/releases/press_080909.html).

O

Oberschall, Anthony. 1973. *Social Conflict and Social Movements.* Englewood Cliffs, NJ: Prentice Hall.

Occupy WallStreet.org. 2012.

O'Donnell, Mike. 1992. *A New Introduction to Sociology.* Walton-on-Thames, United Kingdom: Thomas Nelson and Sons.

Office of Justice Programs. 1999. "Transnational Organized Crime." *NCJRS* Catalog 49 (November/December): 21.

Ogburn, William F. 1922. *Social Change with Respect to Culture and Original Nature.* New York: Huebsch (reprinted 1966, New York: Dell).

———, and Clark Tibbits. 1934. "The Family and Its Functions." pp. 661–708 in *Recent Social Trends in the United States,* Research Committee on Social Trends, ed. New York: McGraw-Hill.

O'Harrow, Jr., Robert. 2005. "Mining Personal Data." *Washington Post National Weekly Edition,* February 6, pp. 8–10.

OpenNet Initiative. 2008. Home Page. Accessed January 12 (http://opennet.net).

———. 2011. Home Page. Accessed April 11 (http://opennet.net).

Organisation for Economic Co-operation and Development. 2008. *Growing Unequal? Income Distribution and Poverty in OECD Countries.* Geneva: OECD.

———. 2009. *OECD Factbook.* Paris: OECD. Accessed February 20, 2010 (http://titania.sourceoecd.org/pdf/factbook2009/302009011e-12-02-02.pdf).

———. 2010. *Gender Briefs.* March (www.oecd.org/els/social).

———. 2011. *Statistics on Resource Flows to Developing Countries.* Geneva: OECD. Accessible at http://www.oecd.org/dataoecd/53/43/47137659.pdf.

Ormond, James. 2005. "The McDonaldization of Football." Accessed January 23, 2006 (http://courses.essex.ac.uk/sc/sc111).

Ornstein, M. 2006. *Ethno-Racial Groups in Toronto, 1971–2000: A Demographic and Socio-Economic Profile.* Toronto, ON: Institute for Social Research, York University.

Outside the Classroom. 2009. "College Students Spend More Time Drinking than Studying." Accessed March 11 (www.outsidetheclassroom.com).

P

Page, Charles H. 1946. "Bureaucracy's Other Face." *Social Forces* 25 (October): 89–94.

Page, Jeremy. 2011. "China's One-Child Plan Faces New Fire." *New York Times,* April 29, pp. A1, A12.

Pager, Devah, and Lincoln Quillian. 2005. "Walking the Talk? What Employers Say Versus What They Do." *American Sociological Review* 70 (June): 355–380.

Paik, Nancy. 2001. *One Nation: Islam in America.* Accessed March 15 (www.channelonenews.com/special/islam/media.html).

Parfitt, Tom. 2013. "Putin Threatens to Change Russia's Adoption Laws over Gay Marriage." *The Telegraph,* April 26.

Parish, William, Edward Lavmann, and Sanyu Mojola. 2007. "Sexual Behavior in China: Trends and Comparisons." *Population of Development Review* 33 (December): 729–756.

Park, Robert E. 1916. "The City: Suggestions for the Investigation of Human Behavior in the Urban Environment." *American Journal of Sociology* 20 (March): 577–612.

———. 1922. *The Immigrant Press and Its Control.* New York: Harper.

———. 1936. "Succession, an Ecological Concept." *American Sociological Review* 1 (April): 171–179.

Park, Steve. 1997. "In the Spirit of Jerry Maguire, I Submit This to the Hollywood Community." *Social Culture. Korean newsgroups* 48: 17. Accessed August 17, 2005 (www.dpg.devry.edu/akim/sck/ho1.html).

Parker, Alison. 2004. "Inalienable Rights: Can Human-Rights Law Help to End U.S. Mistreatment of Noncitizens?" *American Prospect* (October): A11–A13.

Parsons, Talcott. 1951. *The Social System.* New York: Free Press.

———. 1966. *Societies: Evolutionary and Comparative Perspectives.* Englewood Cliffs, NJ: Prentice Hall.

———. 1972. "Definitions of Health and Illness in the Light of American Values and Social Structure." pp. 166–187 in *Patients, Physicians and Illness,* Gartley Jaco, ed. New York: Free Press.

———. 1975. "The Sick Role and the Role of the Physician Reconsidered." *Milbank Medical Fund Quarterly, Health and Society* 53 (Summer): 257–278.

Passel, Jeffrey S. 2006. *The Size and Characteristics of the Unauthorized Migrant Population in the U.S. Estimates Based on the March 2005 Current Population Survey.* Washington: Pew Hispanic Center.

Pastor, Manuel, and Rhonda Ortiz. 2009. "Making Change: How Social Movements Work and How to Support Them." Los Angeles: USC Program for Environmental and Regional Equity.

Paulson, Amanda. 2000. "Where the School Is Home." *Christian Science Monitor,* October 10, pp. 18–21.

Pear, Robert. 1996. "Clinton Endorses the Most Radical of Welfare Trials." *New York Times,* May 19, pp. 1, 20.

———. 1997. "Now, the Archenemies Need Each Other." *New York Times,* June 22, pp. 1, 4.

Pendakur, Krishna, and Ravi Pendakur. 1998. "The Colour of Money: Earnings Differentials across Ethnic Groups in Canada." *Canadian Journal of Economics* 31(3): 518–548.

Perlman, Janice. 2010. *Favela: Four Decades of Living on the Edge in Rio de Janeiro.* London: Oxford University Press.

Perreaux, Les. 2010. "Asked to Remove Niqab, Quebec Woman Lodges Human-Rights Complaint." *The Globe and Mail,* March 2,

2010. Accessed March 17, 2010 (http://license.icopyright.net/user/viewFreeUse.act?fuid5NzU0Njc4Mw%3D%3D).

———. 2010a. "Quebec's View on Niqab Creates Fault Line." *The Globe and Mail,* March 19. Accessed March 20, 2010 (www.theglobeandmail.com/news/national/quebec/quebecs-view-on-niqab-creates-fa. . .).

Perrow, Charles. 1986. *Complex Organizations,* 3rd ed. New York: Random House.

Petersen, John L. 2009. "How 'Wild Cards' May Reshape Our Future." *Futurist* (May–June): 19–20.

Petersen, William. 1979. *Malthus.* Cambridge, MA: Harvard University Press.

Petrásová, Alexandra. 2006. *Social Protection in the European Union.* Brussels: European Union.

Pew Global Attitudes Project. 2006. *Muslims in Europe: Economic Worries Top Concerns About Religious and Cultural Identity.* Report. Washington, DC: Pew Global Attitudes Project.

———. 2007a. *Selected Countries' Views of American Exports: 2007.* Washington, DC: Pew Global Attitudes Project.

———. 2007b. *Global Unease With Major World Powers.* Report. Washington, DC: Pew Global Attitudes Project.

Pew Research Centre. 2011. "The Future of the Global Muslim Population." January.

Phillips, E. Barbara. 1996. *City Lights: Urban–Suburban Life in the Global Society.* New York: Oxford University Press.

Piaget, Jean. 1954. *The Construction of Reality in the Child.* Translated by Margaret Cook. New York: Basic Books.

Picard, André. 2007. "Sex and Age Affect Access to Critical Care." *The Globe and Mail,* November 15. Accessed November 15, 2007 (www.theglobeandmail.com/servlet/story/RTGAM. 20071115.wlwomen15/BNStory/specialScienceandHealth).

Pierce, Jerrad. 2005. 2003 World Consumption Cartogram. Accessed September 23, 2010 (http://pthbb.org/natural/footprint/img/cartogram.png).

Pleck, J. H., and E. Corfman. 1979. "Married Men: Work and Family." *Families Today: A Research Sampler on Families and Children* 1: 387–411.

Plomin, Robert. 1989. "Determinants of Behavior." *American Psychologist* 44 (February): 105–111.

Plüss, Caroline. 2005. "Constructing Globalized Ethnicity." *International Sociology* 20 (June): 201–224.

Polletta, Francesca, and James M. Jasper. 2001. "Collective Identity and Social Movements." pp. 283–305 in *Annual Review of Sociology, 2001,* Karen S. Cook and Leslie Hogan, eds. Palo Alto, CA: Annual Review of Sociology.

Ponczek, Ed. 1998. "Are Hiring Practices Sensitive to Persons with Disabilities?" *Footnotes* 26(3): 5.

Population Reference Bureau. 1996. "Speaking Graphically." *Population Today* 24 (June/July).

———. 2004. *Population Handbook.* Washington, DC: Population Reference Bureau.

———. 2007. "2007 World Population Data Sheet." Washington, DC: Population Reference Bureau. (www.prb.org/pdf07/07WPDS_Eng.pdf).

Porter, John. 1965. *The Vertical Mosaic: An Analysis of Social Class and Power in Canada.* Toronto: University of Toronto Press.

Portes, Alejandro, Cristina Escobar, and Renelinda Arana. 2008. "Bridging the Gap:

Transnational and Ethnic Organizations in the Political Incorporation of Immigrants in the United States." *Ethnic and Racial Studies* 31 (September 6): 1056–1090.

PostMedia News. 2009. "Honour Killing Trial." Postmedia News (http://news.nationalpost.com/2011/12/05/honour-killing-trial-sometimes-purifying-the-name-of-the-family-trumps-human-life-expert-tells-shafia-trial/).

Powell, Jane. 2013. "Suicide is a Gender Issue That Can No Longer be Ignored." *The Guardian,* January 23.

Power, Samantha. 2002. *A Problem from Hell: America and the Age of Genocide.* New York: Perennial.

Powers, Mary G., and Joan J. Holmberg. 1978. "Occupational Status Scores: Changes Introduced by the Inclusion of Women." *Demography* 15 (May): 183–204.

Preston, Jennifer, and Brian Stelter. 2011. "Cellphone Cameras Become World's Eyes and Ears on Protests across the Middle East." *New York Times,* February 19, p. A7.

Proudfoot, Shannon. 2009. "Having Children Changes Work Patterns." *National Post,* August 29, p. H2.

The Province (Vancouver). 2007. "74% of Us Want to Put Family First." May 6, p. A41.

Prus, Robert. 1989. *Pursuing Customers: An Ethnography of Marketing Activities.* Newbury Park, California: Sage.

———. 1996. *Symbolic Interaction and Ethnographic Research: Intersubjectivity and the Study of Human Lived Experience.* Albany, NY: State University of New York Press.

Public Health Agency of Canada. 2010. "HIV/AIDS Epi Updates." July.

———. 2011. "Diabetes in Canada: Facts and Figures from a Public Health Perspective."

Q

Qadeer, Mohammad. 2013. "What Is this Thing Called Multicultural Planning?" *The Bridge* 2(9).

Quadagno, Jill. 2008. *Aging and the Life Course: An Introduction to Social Gerontology,* 4th ed. New York: McGraw-Hill.

Quinney, Richard. 1970. *The Social Reality of Crime.* Boston: Little, Brown.

———. 1974. *Criminal Justice in America.* Boston: Little, Brown.

———. 1979. *Criminology,* 2nd ed. Boston: Little, Brown.

———. 1980. *Class, State and Crime,* 2nd ed. New York: Longman.

R

Rainie, Lee. 2005. *Sports Fantasy Leagues Online.* Washington, DC: Pew Internet and American Life Project.

Rajan, Gita, and Shailja Sharma. 2006. *New Cosmopolitanisms: South Asians in the U.S.* Stanford, CA: Stanford University Press.

Ramet, Sabrina. 1991. *Social Currents in Eastern Europe: The Source and Meaning of the Great Transformation.* Durham, NC: Duke University Press.

Ramirez, Eddy. 2002. "Ageism in the Media Is Seen as Harmful to Health of the Elderly." *Los Angeles Times,* September 5, p. A20.

Ramos, Howard, and Karen Standbridge. 2012. *Seeing Politics Differently: A Brief Introduction to Political Sociology.* Don Mills, ON: Oxford University Press.

Rawlinson, Linnie, and Nick Hunt. 2009. "Jackson Dies, Almost Takes Internet with Him." Accessed July 1 (www.cnn.com/2009/TECH/06/26/michael.jackson.internet/).

Ray, Raka. 1999. *Fields of Protest: Women's Movement in India.* Minneapolis: University of Minnesota Press.

Reinharz, Shulamit. 1992. *Feminist Methods in Social Research.* New York: Oxford University Press.

Reitz, Jeffrey. 1980. *The Survival of Ethnic Groups.* Toronto: McClelland and Stewart.

Religious Tolerance. 2005. "Female Genital Mutilation (FGM): Informational Materials." Accessed March 15 (www.religioustolerance.org).

Rennison, Callie Marie, and Sarah Welchans. 2000. *Intimate Partner Violence.* Washington, DC: United States Government Printing Office.

Repper, J., R. Perkins, S. Owen, D. Deighton, and J. Robinson. 1996. "Evaluating Services for Women with Serious and Ongoing Mental Health Problems: Developing an Appropriate Research Method." *Journal of Psychiatric and Mental Health Nursing* 3: 39–46.

Reuters Reporter. 2012. "Teen Pregnancy and Abortion Rates in U.S. Plummet to 40-year Low." February 8.

Revkin, Andrew C. 2007. "Wealth and Poverty, Drought and Flood: Report from Four Fronts in the War on Warming." *New York Times,* April 3, pp. D4–D5.

Rheingold, Howard. 2003. *Smart Mobs: The Next Social Revolution.* Cambridge, MA: Perseus.

Richard, Amy O'Neill. 2000. *International Trafficking in Women to the United States: A Contemporary Manifestation of Slavery and Organized Crime.* Washington, DC: Center for the Study of Intelligence, CIA.

Riding, Alan. 2005. "Unesco Adopts New Plan Against Cultural Invasion." *New York Times,* October 21, p. B3.

Rifkin, Jeremy. 1995. *The End of Work: The Decline of the Global Labor Force and the Dawn of the Post-Market Era.* New York: Tarcher/Putnam.

Riley, Matilda White, Robert L. Kahn, and Anne Foner. 1994a. *Age and Structural Lag.* New York: Wiley Inter-Science.

———, Robert L. Kahn, and Anne Foner, in association with Karin A. Mock. 1994b. "Introduction: The Mismatch between People and Structures." pp. 1–36 in *Age and Structural Lag,* Matilda White Riley, Robert L. Kahn, and Ann Foner, eds. New York: Wiley Inter-Science.

Ritzer, George. 1995. *The McDonaldization of Society.* Thousand Oaks, CA: Pine Forge Press.

———. 2002. *McDonaldization: The Reader.* Thousand Oaks, CA: Pine Forge Press.

———. 2004. *The Globalization of Nothing.* Thousand Oaks, CA: Pine Forge Press.

———. 2007. *Sociological Theory,* 7th ed. New York: McGraw-Hill.

———. 2008. *The McDonaldization of Society 5.* Thousand Oaks, CA: Sage.

———. 2011. *McDonaldization of Society 6.* Thousand Oaks, CA: Sage.

Roberts, J. Timmons, Peter E. Grines, and Jodie L. Ma'nale. 2003. "Social Roots of Global Environmental Change: A World-Systems Analysis of Carbon Dioxide Emissions." *Journal of World-Systems Research* 9 (Summer): 277–315.

Roberts, Keith A. 1995. *Religion in Sociological Perspective,* 3rd ed. Belmont, CA: Wadsworth.

Roberts, Sam. 2010. "Extended Family Households Are on the Rise, Census Finds." *New York Times,* March 19.

Rodman, George. 2011. *Mass Media in a Changing World,* 3rd ed. New York: McGraw-Hill.

Roethlisberger, Fritz J., and W. J. Dickson. 1939. *Management and the Worker.* Cambridge, MA: Harvard University Press.

Rollins, Judith. 1985. *Between Women: Domestics and Their Employers.* Philadelphia: Temple University Press.

Rose, Arnold. 1951. *The Roots of Prejudice.* Paris: UNESCO.

Rose, Peter I., Myron Glazer, and Penina Migdal Glazer. 1979. "In Controlled Environments: Four Cases of Intense Resocialization." pp. 320–338 in *Socialization and the Life Cycle,* Peter I. Rose, ed. New York: St. Martin's Press.

Rosenbaum, Lynn. 1996. "Gynocentric Feminism: An Affirmation of Women's Values and Experiences Leading Us toward Radical Social Change." *SSSP Newsletter* 27(1): 4–7.

Rosenberg, Douglas H. 1991. "Capitalism." pp. 33–34 in *Encyclopedic Dictionary of Sociology,* 4th ed., Dushkin Publishing Group, ed. Guilford, CT: Dushkin.

Rosenfeld, Jake. 2010. "Little Labor." *Pathways* (Summer): 4–6.

Rosenthal, Elizabeth. 2001. "College Entrance in China: 'No' to the Handicapped." *New York Times,* May 23, p. A3.

Rosenthal, Robert, Elisha Y. Babad, and Lenore Jacobson. 1968. *Pygmalion in the Classroom: Teacher Expectation and Pupils' Intellectual Development.* New York: Holt.

———, and Lenore Jacobson. 1992. *Pygmalion in the Classroom: Teacher Expectations and Pupils' Intellectual Development.* Newly expanded edition. Bancy Felin, UK: Crown House.

Russo, Nancy Felipe. 1976. "The Motherhood Mandate." *Journal of Social Issues* 32: 143–153.

Rutten, Tim. 2008. "A grateful nation needs to do more." *Los Angeles Times,* November 19. Accessed November 20, 2008 (www.latimes.com/news/opinion/sunday/laoe-rutten19-2008nov19,1,5385587.colu. . .).

Ryan, William. 1976. *Blaming the Victim,* rev. ed. New York: Random House.

S

Sabbathday Lake. 2008. Interview by author with Sabbathday Lake Shaker Village. January 8.

Sachs, Jeffrey D. 2005a. *The End of Poverty: Economic Possibilities for Our Time.* New York: Penguin.

———. 2005b. "Can Extreme Poverty Be Eliminated?" 56–65.

Sagarin, Edward, and Jose Sanchez. 1988. "Ideology and Deviance: The Case of the Debate over the Biological Factor." *Deviant Behavior* 9(1): 87–99.

Sale, Kirkpatrick. 1996. *Rebels against the Future: The Luddites and Their War on the Industrial Revolution* (with a new preface by the author). Reading, MA: Addison-Wesley.

Samuels, Robert. 2010. "A Suicide Reminds Gulf Coast of Oil Spill." *Miami Herald,* June 28. Accessible at http://www.mcclatchydc.com/2010/06/28/96665/a-suicide-reminds-gulf-coast-of.html.

Samuelson, Paul A., and William D. Nordhaus. 2010. *Economics.* 19th ed. New York: McGraw-Hill.

Samuelson, R. 2001. "The Specter of Global Aging." *Washington Post National Weekly Edition,* March 11, p. 27.

Santos, José Alcides Figueiredo. 2006. "Class Effects on Racial Inequality in Brazil." *Dados* 2: 1–35.

Sanyal, Paromita. 2009. "From Credit to Collective Action: The Role of Microfinance in Promoting Women's Social Capital and Normative Influence." *American Sociological Review* 74 (August): 529–550.

Saporito, Bill. 2007. "Restoring Wal-Mart." *Time* 170 (November 12): pp. 46–48, 50, 52.

Saunders, Doug. 2012. "Germany's Season of Angst: Why a Prosperous Nation is Turning on Itself." *The Globe and Mail, European,* August 24.

Schaefer, Richard T. 2004. *Racial and Ethnic Relations,* 9th ed. Upper Saddle River, NJ: Prentice Hall.

———. 2006. *Racial and Ethnic Relations,* 10th ed. Upper Saddle River, NJ: Prentice Hall.

———. 2012. *Racial and Ethnic Groups,* 13th ed. Upper Saddle River, NJ: Pearson.

———, and William W. Zellner. 2007. *Extraordinary Groups,* 8th ed. New York: Worth.

Scharnberg, Kirsten. 2007. "Black Market for Midwives Defies Bans." *Chicago Tribune,* November 25, pp. 1, 10.

Scherer, Ron. 2010b. "For Jobless, Online Friends Can Be Lifelines." *Christian Science Monitor,* March 25, p. 21.

Schlenker, Barry R., ed. 1985. *The Self and Social Life.* New York: McGraw-Hill Ryerson.

Schmeeckle, Maria. 2007. "Gender Dynamics in Stepfamilies: Adult Stepchildren's Views." *Journal of Marriage and Family* 69 (February): 174–189.

———, Roseann Giarrusso, Du Feng, and Vern L. Bengtson. 2006. "What Makes Someone Family? Adult Children's Perceptions of Current and Former Stepparents." *Journal of Marriage and Family* 68 (August): 595–610.

Schmetzer, Uli. 1999. "Modern India Remains Shackled to Caste System." *Chicago Tribune,* December 25, p. 23.

Schmidt, Sarah. 2004. "Older Men Kick Tradition, Opt for Cosmetic Surgeries." *Vancouver Sun,* October 29, p. A8.

———. 2009. "Privacy Not Protected on Google Street View, MPs Told." *Canwest News Service,* October 29. Accessed November 15, 2009 (www.leaderpost.com/story_print.html?id=2133506&sponsor=).

Schmitz, Sonja. 1999. "Promiscuity, Pollination, and Genes." *Synthesis/Regeneration* 18 (Winter

1999). Accessed November 25, 2008 (www. greens.org/s-r/18/18-13.html).

Schnaiberg, Allan. 1994. *Environment and Society: The Enduring Conflict.* New York: St. Martin's.

Schoenfeld, A. Clay, Robert F. Meier, and Robert J. Griffin. 1979. "Constructing a Social Problem: The Press and the Environment." *Social Problems* 27: 38–61.

Schull, Natasha Dow. 2005. "Digital Gambling: The Coincidence of Desire and Design." *Annals of the American Academy of Political and Social Science* 597 (1): 65–81.

———. 1983. *Labeling Women Deviant: Gender, Stigma and Social Control.* Philadelphia: Temple University Press.

Schwartz, John. 2004. "Leisure Pursuits of Today's Young Man." *New York Times,* March 29.

Schwartz, Mattathias. 2006. "The Hold-'Em Holdup." *New York Times Magazine,* June 11.

Scott, Alan. 1990. *Ideology and the New Social Movements.* London: Unwin Hyman.

Scott, Gregory. 2001. "Broken Windows behind Bars: Eradicating Prison Gangs through Ecological Hardening and Symbolic Cleansing." *Corrections Management Quarterly* 5 (Winter): 23–36.

Scott, Joan Wallach. 2007. "Veiled Politics." *Chronicle of Higher Education* 54 (November 23): B10–B11.

Scott, W. Richard, and Gerald F. Davis. 2007. *Organizations and Organizing: Rational, Natural and Open Systems Perspectives.* New York: Pearson.

Search Engine Watch. 2011. "comScore: Bing Grows for Sixth Straight Year." March 16. Accessible at http://searchenginewatch. com/3642400.

Segall, Rebecca. 1998. "Sikh and Ye Shall Find." *Village Voice* 43 (December 15): 46–48, 53.

Seidman, Steven. 1994. "Heterosexism in America: Prejudice against Gay Men and Lesbians." pp. 578–593 in *Introduction to Social Problems,* Craig Calhoun and George Ritzer, eds. New York: McGraw-Hill Ryerson.

Sellers, Frances Stead. 2004. "Voter Globalization." *Washington Post National Weekly Edition,* November 29, p. 22.

Selod, Saher Farooq. 2008. "Veil." pp. 1359–1360, vol. 3, in *Encyclopedia of Race, Ethnicity, and Society,* Richard T. Schaefer, ed. Thousand Oaks, CA: Sage.

Sernau, Scott. 2001. *Worlds Apart: Social Inequalities in a New Century.* Thousand Oaks, CA: Pine Forge Press.

Sengupta, Somini. 2009. "An Empire for Poor Working Women, Guided by a Gandhian Approach." *New York Times,* March 7, p. A6.

Shane, Scott. 2010. "Wars Fought and Wars Googled." *New York Times,* June 27, pp. PWK1–5.

Shinkai, Hiroguki, and Ugljesa Zvekic. 1999. "Punishment." pp. 89–120 in *Global Report on Crime and Justice,* Graeme Newman, ed. New York: Oxford University Press.

Shostak, Arthur B. 2002. "Clinical Sociology and the Art of Peace Promotion: Earning a World Without War." pp. 325–345 in *Using Sociology: An Introduction from the Applied and Clinical Perspectives,* Roger A. Straus, ed. Lanham, MD: Rowman and Littlefield.

Sicular, Terry, Ximing Yue, Bjorn Gustafsson, and Shi Li. 2006. "The Urban-Rural Income Gap and Inequality in China." Research Paper No. 2006/135, United Nations University—World Institute for Development Economic Research.

Silver, Ira. 1996. "Role Transitions, Objects, and Identity." *Symbolic Interaction* 19(1): 1–20.

Silverman, H., M. Lydecker, and P.R. Lee. 1990. "The Drug Swindlers." *International Journal of Health Services* 20: 561–572.

Silverstein, Ken. 2010. "Shopping for Sweat: The Human Cost of a Two-Dollar T-shirt." *Harpers* 320 (January): 36–44.

Simmons, Ann M. 1998. "Where Fat Is a Mark of Beauty." *Los Angeles Times,* September 30, pp. A1, A12.

———, and Robin Wright. 2000. "Gender Quota Puts Uganda in Role of Rights Pioneer." *Los Angeles Times,* February 23, p. A1.

Simon, Stephanie. 2007. "It's Easter; Shall We Gather at the Desktops?" *Los Angeles Times,* April 8, p. A13.

Simons, Marlise. 1997. "Child Care Sacred as France Cuts Back the Welfare State." *New York Times,* December 31, pp. A1, A6.

Simpson, Sally. 1993. "Corporate Crime." pp. 236–256 in *Introduction to Social Problems,* Craig Calhoun and George Ritzer, eds. New York: McGraw-Hill Ryerson.

Sison, Marites. 2012. "Get Ready to Be 'Turned Inside Out', says noted Theologian."*Anglican Journal,* November 21.

Sjoberg, Gideon. 1960. *The Preindustrial City: Past and Present.* Glencoe, IL: Free Press.

Skull Valley Band Goshutes. 2006. Homepage. Accessed May 2 (www.skullvalleygoshutes.org).

Slug-Lines.com. 2008. "A Unique Commuter Solution." Accessed January 9, 2009 (www.slug-lines.com).

Smart, Barry. 1990. "Modernity, Postmodernity, and the Present." pp. 14–30 in *Theories of Modernity and Postmodernity,* Bryan S. Turner, ed. Newbury Park, CA: Sage.

Smelser, Neil. 1963. *The Sociology of Economic Life.* Englewood Cliffs, NJ: Prentice Hall.

Smith, Dan. 1999. *The State of the World Atlas,* 6th ed. London: Penguin.

Smith, David A. 1995. "The New Urban Sociology Meets the Old: Rereading Some Classical Human Ecology." *Urban Affairs Review* 20 (January): 432–457.

———, and Michael Timberlake. 1993. "World Cities: A Political Economy/Global Network Approach." pp. 181–207 in *Urban Sociology in Transition,* Ray Hutchison, ed. Greenwich, CT: JAI Press.

Smith, Michael Peter. 1988. *City, State, and Market.* New York: Basil Blackwell.

Smith, Tom W. 2001. *Estimating the Muslim Population in the United States.* New York: American Jewish Committee.

———. 2009. *Religious Change around the World.* Chicago: NORC/University of Chicago.

Smith-Rosenberg, Carroll. 1986. *Disorderly Conduct: Visions of Gender in America.* Toronto: Oxford University Press.

———, and Charles Rosenberg. 1974. "The Female Animal: Medical and Biological Views of Woman and Her Role in Nineteenth-Century America." *Journal of American History* 60 (March): 332–356.

Smolkin, Sheryl. 2013. "Telecommuting, Other Flexible Work Options Alive and Well." *Toronto Star,* March 17.

Snyder, Thomas D. 1996. *Digest of Education Statistics 1996.* Washington, DC: United States Government Printing Office.

Somach, Susan D. 2011. "The Other Side of the Gender Equation: Gender Issues for Men in the Europe and Eurasia Region." *USAID,* July 15.

Song, Vivian. 2007. "Home, Sweet Home." *CNews,* June 10. Accessed July 21, 2007 (http://cnews. canoe.ca/cnews/science/2007/06/10/4249814-sun.html).

Sørensen, Annemette. 1994. "Women, Family and Class." pp. 27–47 in *Annual Review of Sociology, 1994,* Annemette Sørensen, ed. Palo Alto, CA: Annual Reviews.

Spielmann, Peter James. 1992. "11 Population Groups on 'Endangered' List." *Chicago Sun-Times,* November 23, p. 12.

Spindel, Cheywa, Elisa Levy, and Melissa Connor. 2000. *With an End in Sight.* New York: United Nations Development Fund for Women.

Spitzer, Steven. 1975. "Toward a Marxian Theory of Deviance." *Social Problems* 22 (June): 641–651.

Squires, Gregory D., ed. 2002. *Urban Sprawl: Causes, Consequences and Policy Responses.* Washington: Urban Institute.

Stark, Andrew. 2011. "The Price of Moral Purity." *Wall Street Journal,* February 4.

Stark, Rodney, and Laurence R. Iannaccone. 1992. "Sociology of Religion." pp. 2029–2037 in *Encyclopedia of Sociology.* Vol. 4, Edgar F. Borgatta and Marie L. Borgatta, eds. New York: Macmillan.

———, and William Sims Bainbridge. 1979. "Of Churches, Sects, and Cults: Preliminary Concepts for a Theory of Religious Movements." *Journal for the Scientific Study of Religion* 18 (June): 117–131.

———, and William Sims Bainbridge. 1985. *The Future of Religion.* Berkeley, CA: University of California Press.

Starr, Paul. 1982. *The Social Transformation of American Medicine.* New York: Basic Books.

Statistics Canada. 2003a. *Aboriginal Peoples of Canada. 2001 Census (Analysis Series).* Accessed September 15, 2003 (www12.statcan. ca/english/census01/products/analytic/companion/abor/contents.cfm). Catalogue No. 96F003XIE2001007.

———. 2003b. "Religions in Canada," *2001 Census* (Analysis Series). Catalogue No. 96F0030XIE2001015. Accessed November 27, 2005 (www12.statcan.ca/english/census01/Products/Analytic/companion/rel/canada.cfm).

———. 2004a. "Study: The Union Movement in Transition." *The Daily,* August 31. Accessed November 4, 2004 (www.statcan.ca/Daily/English/040831/d040831b.htm).

———. 2004a. "E-commerce: Household Shopping on the Internet." *The Daily,* September 23. Accessed September 23, 2004 (www.stat.ca/Daily/English/040923/d040923a.htm).

———. 2005. "Study: Divorce and the Mental Health of Children, 2005." *The Daily,* December 13. Accessed October 2, 2010 (http://statcan.gc.ca/daily-quotidien/051213/dq051213c-eng.htm).

———. 2005a. *Health Reports* 16(3). Catalogue No. 82-003-XIE2004003.

———. 2005b. "Divorce and the Mental Health of Children." *The Daily,* December 13. Accessed

September 24, 2007 (www.statcan.ca/Daily/English/051213/d051213c.htm).

———. 2005c. "Divorces, 2003." Catalogue No. 84F0213XPB.

———. 2005d. "General Social Survey: Victimization." *The Daily,* July 7. Accessed April 24, 2008 (www.statcan.ca/Daily/English/050707/d050707b.htm).

———. 2006a. "Measuring Violence against Women: Statistical Trends 2006." Catalogue No. 85-570-XIE.

———. 2006b. "Study: Adult Education and Its Impact on Earnings." *The Daily,* March 24. Accessed October 2, 2007 (www.statcan.ca/Daily/English/060324/d060324a.htm).

———. 2006d. "The Wealth of Canadians: An Overview of the Results of the Survey of Financial Security: 2005." Minister of Industry, Catalogue No. 13F0026MIE.

———. 2006e. "What's New in the 2006 Census Questionnaire?" Accessed October 14, 2007 (www12.statcan.ca/english/census06/info/new/whatsnew.cfm).

———. 2006f. *Women in Canada,* 5th ed. 2006 cat. No. 89-503-XIE. Accessed October 12, 2007 (www.statcan.ca/Daily/English/060307/d060307a.htm).

———. 2007. *Family Portrait: Continuity and Change in Canadian Families and Households in 2006.* Catalogue No. 97-553-XWE200601. Accessed January 8, 2008 (www12.statcan.ca/english/census06/analysis/famhouse/charts/chart13.htm).

———. 2007a. "Marriages." *The Daily,* January 17. Accessed September 17, 2007 (www.statcan.ca/Daily/English/070117/d070117a.htm).

———. 2007b. *Portrait of the Canadian Population in 2006, by Age and Sex, 2006 Census.* Catalogue No. 97-551-XWE2006001. Accessed October 15, 2007 (www.statcan.ca/bsolc/enlglish/bsolc?catno=.97-551-XWE2006001).

———. 2007c. "Study, Service Offshoring and Employment." *The Daily,* May 22. Accessed October 26, 2007 (www.statcan.ca/Daily/English/070522/d070522b.htm).

———. 2007d. *Women in Canada: Work Chapter Updates: 2006.* Catalogue No. 89F0133XWE. Accessed March 17, 2008 (www.statcan.ca/bsolc/enlglish/bsolc?catno=89F0133XWE).

———. 2007e. *World: Place of Birth of Recent Immigrants to Canada, Census 2006.* Produced by Geography Division.

———. 2007f. *The Busy Lives of Teens. Perspectives on Labour and Income.* May 23, 2007. Statistics Canada Catalogue number 75-001-XIE.

———. 2008a. Ethnocultural Portrait of Canada Highlights, 2006 Census. Catalogue No. 97-562-WE2006002.

———. 2009. *Income in Canada 2009.* Cat No. 75-202-X.

———. 2009a. "Induced Abortions." *The Daily,* August 24. Accessed February 8, 2010 (www.statcan.gc.ca/stcsr/query.html?qt=abortions&GO%21=Search&col=alle&ht=0&...).

———. 2009b. *Labour Force Historical Review 2008* (Table Cd1T01an). Ottawa, Statistics Canada, 2009. Cat. No. 71F0004XCB.

———. 2009c. "Projections of the Diversity of the Canadian Population." March 9, 2010. Catalogue No. 91-551-XWE.

———. 2009d. *Snapshot of Canadian Agriculture.* 2006 Census of Agriculture.

———. 2009e. "Study: Family Violence and Shelters for Abused Women 2007." *The Daily,* October 15. Accessed October 28, 2009 (www.statcan.gc.ca/daily-quotidien/091015/dq091015b-eng.htm).

———. 2009f. "University Degrees, Diplomas and Certificates Awarded." *The Daily.* Monday July 13, 2009.

———. 2010. "Education: Indicators in Canada." September 6.

———. 2010a. "Employment Insurance Beneficiaries Receiving Regular Benefits by Age, Sex, And Province and Territory (Monthly)" *Employment Insurance Statistics,* October 2009. Accessed May 5, 2010 (www40.statcan.gc.ca/101/cst01/labor02a-eng.htm).

———. 2010b. *The Ethnocultural Diversity of the Canadian Population.* Catalogue No. 91-551-X.

———. 2010c. "Police-Reported Crime Statistics in Canada." July 20.

———. 2011. "Divorces and Crude Divorce Rate."

———. 2011a. "Income in Canada: Catalogue No. 75-202-XWE.

———. 2011b. "Marriage by Type."

———. 2011c. "Residential Telephone Service Survey." No. 4426.

———. 2012. "Canadian Population 2011, Age and Sex."

———. 2012a. "Family Violence in Canada: A Statistical Profile." May 22.

———. 2012b. "Labour Force Survey." No. 3701. May.

———. 2012c. "Labour Force Statistical Review 2010." Catalogue No. 71F0004XVB.

———. 2012d. "Persons in Low-Income Families." Annual.

———. 2012e. "Rural and Small Town Canada Analysis Bulletin." July 12.

———. 2012f. "2011 Census: Population and Dwelling Counts." *The Daily,* February 8.

Stedman, Nancy. 1998. "Learning to Put the Best Shoe Forward." *New York Times,* October 27.

Steele, Jonathan. 2005. "Annan Attacks Britain and U.S. over Erosion of Human Rights." *Guardian Weekly,* March 16, p. 1.

Stevenson, David, and Barbara L. Schneider. 1999. *The Ambitious Generation: America's Teenagers, Motivated but Directionless.* New Haven, CT: Yale University Press.

Stockard, Janice E. 2002. *Marriage in Culture.* Belmont, CA: Thomson Wadsworth.

Strauss, Gary. 2002. "'Good Old Boys' Network Still Rules Corporate Boards." *USA Today,* November 1, pp. B1, B2.

Stretesky, Paul B. 2006. "Corporate Self-Policing and the Environment." *Criminology* 44(3): 671

Stuckey, Johanna H. 1998. "Women and Religion: Female Spirituality, Feminist Theology, and Feminist Goddess Worship." In *Feminist Issues: Race, Class, and Sexuality,* 2nd ed., Nancy Mandell, ed. Scarborough, ON: Prentice Hall.

Subramaniam, Mangala. 2006. *The Power of Women's Organization: Gender, Caste, and Class in India.* Lanham, MD: Lexington Books.

Sugimoto, Yoshio. 1997. *An Introduction to Japanese Society.* Cambridge, UK: Cambridge University Press.

Sullivan, Kevin. 2006. "Bridging the Digital Divide." *Washington Post National Weekly Edition* 25 (July 17): 11–12.

Sumner, William G. 1906. *Folkways.* New York: Ginn.

Sunstein, Cass. 2002. *Republic.com.* Rutgers, NJ: Princeton University Press.

Surk, Barbara. 2007. "MTV Flag Planted on Arab Airwaves." *Chicago Tribune,* November 19, p. 16.

SustainAbility. 2006. *Brazil—Country of Diversities and Inequalities.* London: SustainAbility.

Sutcliffe, Bob. 2002. *100 Ways of Seeing an Unequal World.* London: Zed Books.

Sutherland, Edwin H. 1937. *The Professional Thief.* Chicago: University of Chicago Press.

———. 1940. "White-Collar Criminality." *American Sociological Review* 5 (February): 1–11.

———. 1949. *White Collar Crime.* New York: Dryden.

———. 1983. *White Collar Crime: The Uncut Version.* New Haven, CT: Yale University Press.

———, and Donald R. Cressey. 1978. *Principles of Criminology,* 10th ed. Philadelphia: Lippincott.

Swatos, William H., Jr., ed. 1998. *Encyclopedia of Religion and Society.* Lanham, MD: Alta Mira.

T

Taber, Jane. 2010. "Will Michael Ignatieff's Abortion Gambit Work?" *The Globe and Mail,* February 6. Accessed February 7, 2009 (www.theglobeandmail.com/blogs/bureau-blog/will-michael-ignatieffs-abortion-gambi...).

Talbot, Margaret. 1998. "Attachment Theory: The Ultimate Experiment." *New York Times Magazine,* May 24, pp. 4–30, 38, 46, 50, 54.

Tannen, Deborah. 1990. *You Just Don't Understand: Women and Men in Conversation.* New York: Ballantine.

Tarrow, Sidney. 2005. *The New Transnational Activism.* Boulder, CO: Rowman and Littlefield.

Taylor, Carl S. 1990. "Gang Imperialism." In *Gangs in America,* C. Ronald Huff, ed. London: Sage Publications.

Taylor, Dorceta E. 2000. "The Rise of the Environmental Justice Paradigm." *American Behavioral Scientist* 43 (January): 508–580.

Taylor, Verta. 1995. "Watching for Vibes: Bringing Emotions into the Study of Feminist Organizations." pp. 223–233 in *Feminist Organizations: Harvest of the New Women's Movement,* Myra Marx Ferree and Patricia Yancy Martin, eds. Philadelphia: Temple University Press.

TD Bank Financial Group. 2007. "Markets Are a Woman's Best Friend." TD Economics Special Report, September 25, 2007.

Tedeschi, Bob. 2004. "Social Networks: Will Users Pay to Get Friends?" *New York Times,* February 9, pp. C1, C3.

———. 2006. "Those Born to Shop Can Now Use Cellphones." *New York Times,* January 2.

Telles, Edward E. 2004. *Race in America: The Significance of Skin Color in Brazil.* Princeton, NJ: Princeton University Press.

Terry, Sara. 2000. "Whose Family? The Revolt of the Child-Free." *Christian Science Monitor,* August 29, pp. 1, 4.

Therborn, Göran. 2010. Review of "Unveiling Inequality." *Contemporary Sociology* 39 (5): 585–586.

Thomas, W.I., and Thomas, Dorothy. 1928. *The Child in America: Behavior Problems and Programs.* New York: Knopf.

Thomas, William I. 1923. *The Unadjusted Girl.* Boston: Little, Brown.

Thompson, Clive. 2005. "Meet the Life Hackers." *New York Times Magazine,* October 16, pp. 40–45.

Thompson, Tony. 2005. "Romanians Are Being Paid to Play Computer Games for Westerners." *Guardian Weekly,* March 25, p. 17.

Thompson, William, and Joseph Hickey. 2005. *Society in Focus.* Boston: Pearson.

Thottam, Jyoti. 2005. "Social Security: Going Private: Lessons from Overseas." *Time,* February 7.

Tidmarsh, Lee. 2000. "If I Shouldn't Spank, What Should I Do? Behaviour Techniques for Disciplining Children." *Canadian Family Physician* 46: 1119–1123.

Tierney, John. 1990. "Betting the Planet." *New York Times Magazine,* December 2, pp. 52–53, 71, 74, 76, 78, 80–81.

Tilly, Charles. 1993. *Popular Contention in Great Britain, 1758–1834.* Cambridge, MA: Harvard University Press.

———. 2004. *Social Movements, 1768–2004.* Boulder, CO: Paradigm.

———. 2007. "Trust Networks in Transnational Migration." *Sociological Forum* 22 (March): 3–24.

Timmerman, Kelsey. 2009. *Where Am I Wearing?* Hoboken NJ: Wiley.

Tong, Rosemary. 1989. *Feminist Theory: A Comprehensive Introduction.* Boulder, CO: Westview.

Tönnies, Ferdinand. [1887] 1988. *Community and Society.* Rutgers, NJ: Transaction.

Touraine, Alain. 1974. *The Academic System in American Society.* New York: McGraw-Hill Ryerson.

Traynor, Ian. 2008. "Europe Expects a Flood of Climate Refugees." *The Guardian Weekly,* March 14, pp. 1–2.

Tuchman, Gaye. 1992. "Feminist Theory." pp. 695–704 in *Encyclopedia of Sociology.* Vol. 2, Edgar F. Borgatta and Marie L. Borgatta, eds. New York: Macmillan.

Tuck, Bryan, Jan Rolfe, and Vivienne Adair. 1994. "Adolescents' Attitudes toward Gender Roles within Work and Its Relationship to Gender, Personality Type and Parental Occupations." *Sex Roles: A Journal of Research* 31(9–10): 547–558.

Tuhiwai Smith, Linda. 2005. *Decolonizing Methodologies: Research and Indigenous Peoples.* New York: Zed Books.

Tumin, Melvin M. 1953. "Some Principles of Stratification: A Critical Analysis." *American Sociological Review* 18 (August): 387–394.

Turkle, Sherry. 2004. "How Computers Change the Way We Think." *Chronicle of Higher Education* 50 (January 30): B26–B28.

———. 2011. *Alone Together: Why We Expect More from Technology and Less from Each Other.* New York: Basic Books.

———. 1985. *Social Stratification,* 2nd ed. Englewood Cliffs, NJ: Prentice Hall.

Turner, Bryan S., ed. 1990. *Theories of Modernity and Postmodernity.* Newbury Park, CA: Sage.

UNAIDS. 2007. *AIDS Epidemic Update December 2007.* Geneva: Author.

UNAIDS. 2010. *Global Report: UNAIDS Report on the Global AIDS Epidemic 2010.* Geneva: UNAIDS.

UNESCO. 2002. *Education for All, 2002.* Paris, France: UNESCO.

United Nations. 2005. *The Millennium Development Goals Report.* Washington, DC: United Nations.

United Nations Children's Fund (UNICEF). 2004. *Report: The State of the World's Children, 2004.* New York: UNICEF.

———. 2005. *Report: Child Poverty in the Rich Countries, 2005.* New York: UNICEF.

———. 2006. *The State of the World's Children, 2007: The Double Dividend of Gender Equality.* New York: UNICEF.

———. 2010. "Child Marriage." Accessed January 15 (www.unicef.org/progressfprchildren/2007n6/index_41848.htm?q5printme).

United Nations Development Fund for Women. 2009. *Who Answers to Women?* New York: UNIFEM.

United Nations Development Programme. 1995. *Human Development Report 1995.* New York: Oxford University Press.

———. 2006. *Human Development Report 2006.* New York: UNDP.

———. 2009. *Overcoming Barriers: Human Mobility and Development.* New York: Palgrave Macmillan.

United Nations Office on Drugs and Crime. 2005. "The United Nations Convention Against Transnational Organized Crime and Its Protocols." Accessed March 18, 2005 (www.unodc.org).

United Nations Population Fund (UNFPA). 2006. *State of World Population 2006.* New York: UNFPA.

U.S. Census Bureau. 2006. "American Community Survey."

Uttley, Alison. 1993. "Who's Looking at You, Kid?" *Times Higher Education Supplement* 30 (April 30): 48.

UW Daily Bulletin. 2004. "Sociology Professor Made a Fellow of the Royal Society of Canada." *Faculty of Arts News Items: University of Waterloo,* November 23. Accessed November 10, 2009. (http://arts.uwaterloo.ca/arts/ugrad/arts_news/curtis_j.html).

Vaidhyanathan, Siva. 2008. "Generational Myth: Not All Young People Are Tech-Savvy." *Chronicle of Higher Education,* September 19, pp. B7–B9.

Valdez, Enrique. 1999. "Using Hotlines to Deal with Domestic Violence: El Salvador." pp. 139–142 in *Too Close to Home,* Andrew R. Morrison and Maria Loreto Biehl, eds. Washington, DC: Inter-American Development Bank.

Vallas, Mary. 2005. "When Grandkids Don't Leave." *National Post,* October 8, p. A1.

van den Berghe, Pierre. 1978. *Race and Racism: A Comparative Perspective,* 2nd ed. New York: John Wiley and Sons.

van der Gaag, Nikki. 2004. *The No-Nonsense Guide to Women's Rights.* Toronto: New International Publications.

van Vucht Tijssen, Lieteke. 1990. "Women between Modernity and Postmodernity." pp. 147–163 in *Theories of Modernity and Postmodernity,* Bryan S. Turner, ed. London: Sage.

Vancouver Sun. 2004. "Not Enough Starbucks in the World, CEO Says." October 15, p. H4.

Vanneman, Reeve, and Lynn Weber Cannon. 1987. *The American Perception of Class.* Philadelphia: Temple University Press.

Vasagar, Jeeran. 2005. "'At Last Rwanda Is Known for Something Positive.'" *Guardian Weekly,* July 22, p. 18.

Vaughan, R. M. 2007. "Cairo's Man Show." *Utne Reader* (March–April): 94–95.

Vavrus, Mary D. 2002. *Postfeminist News: Political Women in Media Culture.* New York: State University of New York Press.

Veblen, Thorstein. [1899] 1964. *Theory of the Leisure Class.* New York: Macmillan. New York: Penguin.

———. 1919. *The Vested Interests and the State of the Industrial Arts.* New York: Huebsch.

Venkatesh, Sudhir Alladi. 2008. *Gang Leader for a Day: A Rogue Sociologist Takes to the Streets.* New York: Penguin Press.

Vieira, Paul. 2009. "Retirement Age Needs to Be 70: Think-tank." *The Vancouver Sun,* July 2. Accessed July 2, 2009 (www.vancouversun.com/story_print.html?id=1753221&sponsor=).

Vissandjee, Bilkis. 2001. "The Consequences of Cultural Diversity." *The Canadian Women's Health Network* 4(2): 3–4.

Visser, Jelle. 2006. "Union Membership Statistics in 24 Countries." *Monthly Labor Review* (January): 38–49.

Vobejda, Barbara, and Judith Havenmann. 1997. "Experts Say Side Income Could Hamper Reforms." *Washington Post,* November 3, p. A1.

Wages for Housework Campaign. 1999. *Wages for Housework Campaign.* Circular. Los Angeles.

Wagley, Charles, and Marvin Harris. 1958. *Minorities in the New World: Six Case Studies.* New York: Columbia University Press.

Waite, Linda. 2000. "The Family as a Social Organization: Key Ideas for the Twentieth Century." *Contemporary Sociology* 29 (May): 463–469.

Wallace, Nicole. 2010. "Gifts for Oil Spill Total $4 Million, but More Is Needed." *The Chronicle of Philanthropy* 24 (14): 1.

Wallace, Ruth A., and Alison Wolf. 1980. *Contemporary Sociological Theory.* Englewood Cliffs, NJ: Prentice Hall.

Wallerstein, Immanuel. 1974. *The Modern World System.* New York: Academic Press.

———. 1979. *Capitalist World Economy.* Cambridge, UK: Cambridge University Press.

———. 2000. *The Essential Wallerstein.* New York: The New Press.

Walmart. 2010. "The Ten-foot Attitude." Accessed January 17 (www.wal-martchina.com/english/walmart/rule/10.htm).

Walzer, Susan. 1996. "Thinking about the Baby: Gender and Divisions of Infant Care." *Social Problems* 43 (May): 219–234.

Wang, Feng. 2011. "The Future of a Demographic Overachiever: Long-Term Implications of the Demographic Transition in China." *Population and Development Review* 37 (Suppl.): 173–190.

———, and Cai Yong. 2011. "China's One-Child Policy at 39." May 31. Washington, DC: Brooking Institution.

Wang, Meiyan, and Fand Cai. 2006. *Gender Wage Differentials in China's Urban Labor Market.* Research Paper No. 2006/141. United Nations University World Institute for Development Economics Research

Watts, Duncan J. 2004. "The 'New' Science of Networks." pp. 243–270 in *Annual Review of Sociology, 2004,* Karen S. Cook and John Hagan, eds. Palo Alto, CA: Annual Reviews.

Wax, Emily. 2005. "Where Woman Rule." *Washington Post National Weekly Edition* July 18, p. 18.

Weber, Martha L. 1998. "She Stands Alone: A Review of the Recent Literature on Women and Social Support." *Prairie Women's Health Centre of Excellence.* Winnipeg: Prairie Women's Health Centre of Excellence.

Weber, Max. [1904] 1949. *Methodology of the Social Sciences.* Edward A. Shils and Henry A. Finch, transl. Glencoe, IL: Free Press.

———. [1904] 2011. *The Protestant Ethic and the Spirit of Capitalism.* Stephen Kalberg, transl. Oxford University Press.

———. [1913–1922] 1947. *The Theory of Social and Economic Organization.* Translated by A. Henderson and T. Parsons. New York: Free Press.

———. [1916] 1958b. *The Religion of India: The Sociology of Hinduism and Buddhism.* New York: Free Press.

Wechsler, Henry, J. E. Lee, M. Kuo, M. Seibring, T. F. Nelson, and H. Lee. 2002. "Trends in College Binge Drinking during a Period of Increased Prevention Efforts: Findings from Four Harvard School of Public Health College Alcohol Surveys: 1993–2001." *Journal of American College Health* 50 (5): 203–217.

———, Mark Seibring, I-Chao Liu, and Marilyn Ahl. 2004. "Colleges Respond to Student Binge Drinking: Reducing Student Demand or Limiting Access." *Journal of American College Health* 52 (4): 159–168.

Weedon, Chris. 1999. *Feminism, Theory and the Politics of Difference.* Oxford, UK: Blackwell Publishers.

Weeks, Carly. 2007. "Canada's Growth Outpaces Rest of G-8." *Vancouver Sun,* March 14, p. A5.

Weeks, John R. 2002. *Population: An Introduction to Concepts and Issues,* 8th ed. Belmont, CA: Wadsworth.

———. 2008. *Population: An Introduction to Concepts and Issues,* 10th ed. Belmont, CA: Wadsworth.

———. 2012. *Population: An Introduction to Concepts and Issues,* 11th ed. Belmont, CA: Cengage.

Weisbrot, Mark, Dean Baker, and David Rusnick. 2005. *The Scorecard on Development: 25 Years of Diminished Progress.* Washington, DC: Center for Economic and Policy Research.

Weiss, Rick. 1998. "Beyond Test-Tube Babies." *Washington Post National Weekly Edition,* February 16, pp. 6–7.

Weitz, Rose. 2007. *The Sociology of Health, Illness, and Heath Care,* 4th ed. Belmont, CA: Thomson.

Welsh, Moira. 2008. "Is Earth Day Still Relevant 18 Years On?" *Toronto Star,* April 22. Accessed April 24, 2008 (www.thestar.com/article/416854).

Wentz, Laurel, and Claire Atkinson. 2005. "'Apprentice' Translators Hope for Hits All Over Globe." *Advertising Age,* February 14, pp. 3, 73.

West, Candace, and Don H. Zimmerman. 1987. "Doing Gender." *Gender and Society* 1 (June): 125–151.

Whyte, William Foote. 1981. *Street Corner Society: Social Structure of an Italian Slum,* 3rd ed. Chicago: University of Chicago Press.

Wickman, Peter M. 1991. "Deviance." pp. 85–87 in *Encyclopedic Dictionary of Sociology,* 4th ed. Guilford, CT: Dushkin.

Wicks, Ann, and Raylene Lang-Dion. 2008. "Women in Politics: Still Searching for An Equal Voice." *Canadian Parliamentary Review.* Spring.

Wilford, John Noble. 1997. "New Clues Show Where People Made the Great Leap to Agriculture." *New York Times,* November 18, pp. B9, B12.

Willett, Jeffrey G., and Mary Jo Deegan. 2000. "Liminality and Disability: The Symbolic Rite of Passage of Individuals with Disabilities." Presented at the annual meeting of the American Sociological Association, Washington, DC.

Williams, Robin M. (in collaboration with John P. Dean and Edward A. Suchman). 1964. *Strangers Next Door: Ethnic Relations in American Communities.* Englewood Cliffs, NJ: Prentice Hall.

Wilson, David. 2000. "Residential Schools: Bearing History's Burden." *The United Church Observer.* Accessed August 16, 2005 (www.ucobserver.org/archives/nov00_cvst-part1.htm).

Wilson, Jennifer. 2007. "Faith-Based Schools." CBC News online, September 17. Accessed October 1, 2007 (www.cbc.ca/ontariovotes2007/features/features-faith.html).

Wilson, John. 1973. *Introduction to Social Movements.* New York: Basic Books.

Wilson, Jolin J. 2000. *Children as Victims.* Washington, DC: United States Government Printing Office.

Wilson, Warner, Larry Dennis, and Allen P. Wadsworth, Jr. 1976. "Authoritarianism Left and Right." *Bulletin of the Psychonomic Society* 7 (March): 271–274.

Wilson, William Julius. 1980. *The Declining Significance of Race: Blacks and Changing American Institutions,* 2nd ed. Chicago: University of Chicago Press.

———. 1987. *The Truly Disadvantaged: The Inner City, the Underclass and Public Policy.* Chicago: University of Chicago Press.

———, ed. 1989. *The Ghetto Underclass: Social Science Perspectives.* Newbury Park, CA: Sage.

———. 1996. *When Work Disappears: The World of the New Urban Poor.* New York: Knopf.

———. 1999. "Towards a Just and Livable City: The Issues of Race and Class." *Address at the Social Science Centennial Conference, April 23.* Chicago, IL: DePaul University.

Winant, Howard B. 2006. "Race and Racism: Towards a Global Future." *Ethnic and Racial Studies* 29 (September): 986–1003.

Wirth, Louis. 1928. *The Ghetto.* Chicago: University of Chicago Press.

———. 1938. "Urbanism as a Way of Life." *American Journal of Sociology* 44 (July): 1–24.

Wolf, Naomi. 1991. *The Beauty Myth: How Images of Beauty Are Used against Women.* New York: Anchor Books.

Wolf, Richard. 2006. "How Welfare Reform Changed America." *USA Today,* July 18, pp. 1A, 6A.

Wolfe, Richard. 2008. "New Week, Bush's Agenda Is Africa." *USA Today,* February 15, p. 6A.

Wolff, Edward N. 2002. *Top Heavy.* Updated ed. New York: New Press.

Woo, Andrea. 2011. *Vancouver Sun,* October 27.

Wood, Julia T. 1994. *Gendered Lives: Communication, Gender and Culture.* Belmont, CA: Wadsworth.

Wooden, Wayne. 1995. *Renegade Kids, Suburban Outlaws: From Youth Culture to Delinquency.* Belmont, CA: Wadsworth.

Woolf, Virginia. 1977. *A Room of One's Own.* San Diego, CA: Harvest/HBJ.

Working Women's Forum. 2010. Home Page. Accessed April 28 (www.workingwomensforum.org).

Workman, Thomas A. 2008. "The Real Impact of Virtual Worlds." *Chronicle of Higher Education,* September 19, pp. B12–B13.

World Bank. 1995. *World Development Report, 1994: Workers in an Integrating World.* New York: Oxford University Press.

———. 2001. *World Development Report 2002: Building Instructions for Markets.* New York: Oxford University Press.

———. 2002. *World Development Indicators, 2002.* Washington, DC: World Bank.

———. 2004. *World Development Report 2005. A Better Investment Climate for Everyone.* Washington, DC: World Bank.

———. 2006. *Repositioning Nutrition as Central to Development: A Strategy for Large-Scale Action.* Washington, DC: World Bank.

———. 2010. *World Development Indicators 2010.* Washington, DC: World Bank.

World Economic Forum. 2010. "The Global Competitiveness Report 2010–2011." Geneva: WEF. Accessible at http://www.weforum.org/en/initiatives/gcp/Global%20Competitiveness%20Report/index.htm.

World Health Organization. 2009. "Biotechnology (GM Foods)." Accessed May 11 (www.who.int/foodsafety/biotech/en/).

———. 2013. "Database: Outdoor Air Pollution in Cities." Public Health and Environment.

Wright, Charles R. 1986. *Mass Communication: A Sociological Perspective,* 3rd ed. New York: Random House.

Wright, Eric R., William P. Gronfein, and Timothy J. Owens. 2000. "Deinstitutionalization, Social Rejection, and the Self-Esteem of Former Mental Patients." *Journal of Health and Social Behavior* (March).

Wright, Erik Olin, David Hachen, Cynthia Costello, and Joy Sprague. 1982. "The American Class Structure." *American Sociological Review* 47 (December): 709–726.

Wuthnow, Robert. 1996. *Poor Richard's Principle: Recovering the American Dream through the Moral Dimension of Work, Business, and Money.* Princeton, NJ: Princeton University Press.

Wyatt, Edward. 2009. "No Smooth Ride on TV Networks' Road to Diversity." *New York Times,* March 18, pp. 1, 5.

Y

Yamagata, Hisashi, Kuang S. Yeh, Shelby Stewman, and Hiroko Dodge. 1997. "Sex Segregation and Glass Ceilings: A Comparative Statistics Model of Women's Career Opportunities in the Federal Government over a Quarter Century." *American Journal of Sociology* 103 (November): 566–632.

Yap, Kioe Sheng. 1998. "Squatter Settlements." pp. 554–556 in *The Encyclopedia of Housing,* Willem van Vliet, ed. Thousand Oaks, CA: Sage.

York University. 2006. "Toronto Poverty Is Highly Racialized: York University Census Study." Media Release. Accessed January 2, 2008 (www.yorku.ca/mediar/archive/Release.asp).

Young, K. 1988. "The Social Relations of Gender." In *Gender in Caribbean Development,* P. Mohammed and C. Shepard, eds. Mona, Jamaica: Women and Development Studies Group.

Yunus, Muhammad. 2010. *Building Social Business.* New York: Perseus.

Z

Zarembo, Alan. 2004. "A Theater of Inquiry and Evil." *Los Angeles Times,* July 15, pp. A1, A24, A25.

Zeitzen, Miriam Koktvedgaard. 2008. *Polygamy: A Cross-Cultural Analysis.* Oxford, UK: Berg.

Zellner, William M. 1978. "Vehicular Suicide: In Search of Incidence." Unpublished M.A. thesis. Western Illinois University, Macomb.

———. 1995. *Counter Cultures: A Sociological Analysis.* New York: St. Martin's Press.

Zi, Jui-Chung Allen. 2007. *The Kids Are OK: Divorce and Children's Behavior Problems.* Santa Monica, CA: RAND.

Zimbardo, Philip G. 2004. "Power Turns Good Soldiers into 'Bad Apples.'" *Boston Globe,* May 9.

Zimmerman, Ann, and Emily Nelson. 2006. "With Profits Elusive, Wal-Mart to Exit Germany." *Wall Street Journal* (July 29): A1, A6.

Zittrain, Jonathan, and John Palfrey. 2008. "Reluctant Gatekeepers: Corporate Ethics on a Filtered Internet." pp. 103–122 in *Access Denied,* Ronald Deibert, John Palfrey, Rafal Rohozinski, and Jonathan Zittrain, eds. Cambridge, MA: The MIT Press.

Zola, Irving K. 1972. "Medicine as an Institution of Social Control." *Sociological Review* 20 (November): 487–504.

Zuckerman, Laurence. 2001. "Divided, An Airline Stumbles." *New York Times,* March 14, pp. C1, C6.

Zweigenhaft, Richard L., and G. William Domhoff. 2006. *Diversity in the Power Elite: How It Happened, Why It Matters,* 2nd ed. New York: Rowman and Littlefield.

Zywica, Jolene, and James Danowski. 2008. "The Faces of Facebookers: Investigating Social Enhancement and Social Compensation Hypotheses; Predicting Facebook and Offline Popularity from Sociability and Self-Esteem, and Mapping the Meanings of Popularity with Semantic Networks." *Journal of Computer-Mediated Communication* 14: 1–34.

acknowledgements

Chapter 1

page 4: Quotation from Kelsey Timmerman. 2009. *Where Am I Wearing? A Global Tour to the Countries, Factories and People that Make Our Clothes.* © 2009. Reproduced with permission of John Wiley & Sons, Inc.

Chapter 2

page 26 Quotation from Patricia A. Adler and Peter Adler. 2007. "The Demedicalization of Self-Injury: From Psychopathology to Sociological Deviance," *Journal of Contemporary Ethnography* 36, Issue 5, (October 2007):537–570. Copyright © 2007. Reprinted by permission of SAGE Publications.

page 39 Figure 2-4: From Henry J. Kaiser Family Foundation. February 2005. Executive Summary of Sex on TV 4:4; A Biennial Report of the Kaiser Family Foundation (#7399). This information was reprinted with permission from the Henry J. Kaiser Family Foundation. The Kaiser Family Foundation, based in Menlo Park, California, is a nonprofit, private operating foundation focusing on the major healthcare issues facing the nation and is not associated with Kaiser Permanente or Kaiser Industries.

Chapter 3

page 44: Quotation from Horace Miner. 1956. "Body Ritual among the Nacirema." *American Anthropologist,* vol. 58 (3), 1956: pp. 503–504. © 1956 American Anthropological Association.

page 54 Figure 3-4: Angus Reid Strategies, 2009, adapted by author.

page 58 Table 3-2: Adapted from Pew Global Attitudes Project, 2007a.

page 59 Figure 3-1 adapted in part from "The State of the World's Children 2009," UNICEF, and in part from "Progress for Children: A World Fit for Children Statistical Review," Number 6, December 2007, UNICEF global databases, UNICEF, NY.

Chapter 4

page 68 Quotation: Canwest News Service, www. star.com, "Parents Keep Child's Gender A Secret," Jayme Poisson, May 2011.

page 71 Box 4-1: Quotation from Daniel Albas and Cheryl Albas. 1988. "Aces and Bombers: The Post-Exam Impression Management Strategies of Students." *Symbolic Interaction* Copyright 1988 by University of California Press—Journals. Reproduced by permission of the University of California Press—Journals via Copyright Clearance Center.

page 81 Figure: From Population Reference Bureau 2007. 2007 World Population Data Sheet. www.prb.org/pdf07/07/WPDS_eng.pdf. Reprinted by permission.

page 85 Figure 4-1: Data collected by the Organisation for Economic Co-operation and Development (OECD). Gender Brief 2010.

Chapter 5

page 90 Quotation from George Ritzer. 2010. *The McDonaldization of Society 6.* Copyright © 2010 by Sage Publications, Inc. Books. Reproduced with permission of Pine Forge Press, a Division of Sage Publications, Inc. via Copyright Clearance Center.

page 99 Screen shot from Second Life. Second Life® is a trademark of Linden Research, Inc. Certain materials have been reproduced with the permission of Linden Research, Inc.

page 111 Figure 5-2: Bureau of Labor Statistics 2011; New Unionism Network 2011; Visser 2006:45.

Chapter 6

page 116 Quotation from Canadian Centre for Policy Alternatives 2012.

page 118 Table 6-1: Canadian Business Online October 2011, http://www. canadianbusiness.com/rankings/rich100/2011. Adapted by author.

page 119 Figure 6-1: From "A Soft Landing: Recession and Canada's 100 Highest Paid CEOs" by Hugh Mackenzie, Canadian Centre for Policy Alternatives 2012.

page 124 Table 6-3: Angus Reid Strategies 2009; adapted by author.

page 125 Figure 6-2: Statistics Canada 2006i; Statistics Canada 2011b.

page 127 Figure 6-3: Organisation for Economic Co-operation and Development 2009.

page 128 Figure 6-4: Statistics Canada, Persons in Low Income Families, Annual (CANSIM Table 202-0802), Ottawa: Statistics Canada, 2012e.

page 129 Figure 6-5: Statistics Canada calculations based on Statistics Canada, Survey of Labour and Income Economics, Ottawa: Statistics Canada, 2011b.

Chapter 7

page 138 Quotation from Paul Collier. 2007. *The Bottom Billion: Why the Poorest Countries Are Failing and What Can Be Done About It.* © 2007 Paul Collier. Used with permission of Oxford University Press, UK.

page 139 Figure 7-1: adapted from Bob Sutcliffe. 2002. *100 Ways of Seeing an Unequal World,* Fig 1, p. 18. London: Zed Books. Reprinted by permission.

page 141 Figure 7-2: Figure adapted in part from John R. Weeks. 2012. *Population* 11e. © 2012 Wadsworth, a part of Cengage Learning Inc. Reproduced by permission of www.cengage.com/permissions. And adapted in part from Carl Haub. 2010. *2010 World Population Data Sheet.* Used by permission of Population Reference Bureau.

page 144 Figure 7-4 adapted from World Development Indicators 2010 by the World Bank 2010. Copyright 2010. Used by permission of the International Bank for Reconstruction and Development/World Bank via Copyright Clearance Center.

page 145 Figure 7-5: From the Chronic Poverty Research Center 2009, administered by the Institute for Development Policy and Management, School of Environment and Development, University of Manchester, UK. Used by permission.

page 146 Figure 7-6: OECD Statistics on Resource Flows to Developing Countries (Feb 2011), Table 1, p. 2. www.oecd.org/dataoecd/53/43/47137659.pdf.

page 149 Figure adapted from Edward Telles. 2004:108. *Race in Another America: The Significance of Skin Color.* Princeton University Press. Reprinted by permission of Princeton University Press.

page 150 Figure 7-7 World Bank. 2010. W*orld Development Indicators 2010.* Copyright 2010. Used by permission of the International Bank for Reconstruction and Development/World Bank via Copyright Clearance Center.

Chapter 8

page 156 Quotation: Prime Minister Harper offers full apology on behalf of Canadians for the Indian Residential Schools system, http://www.pm.gc.ca/eng/media.asp?id=2149 Office of the Prime Minister, 2008 Reproduced with the permission of the Minister of Public Works and Government Services Canada, 2013

page 170 Figure 8-2: Copyright © Province of British Columbia. All rights reserved. Reprinted with permission of the Province of British Columbia. www.ipp.gov.bc.ca.

page 172 Figure 8-4: Ipsos Reid Poll for Can West News Service and Global Television, 2007.

page 174 Figure 8-5: J. From John L. Allen, 2008. *Student Atlas of World Politics,* Eighth Edition. Copyright © 2008 by The McGraw-Hill Companies. Reproduced by permission of McGraw-Hill Contemporary Learning Series.

page 175 Figure 8-6: Statistics Canada, 2006d; Australian Bureau of Statistics, 2006 Census; U. S. Census Bureau, 2006 American Community Survey.

Chapter 9

page 180 Quotation: "Muslim group moves to ban burka. Canadian lobbyists say garments are 'medieval' and 'misogynist,'" Toronto— The Canadian Press Last updated on Wednesday, Oct. 07, 2009 08:47PM . Used with permission of the Globe and Mail.

page 182 Table 9-1: from Joyce McCarl Nielsen, et al. 2000. "Gendered Heteronormativity: Empirical Illustrations in Everyday Life," *Sociological Quarterly* 41 (no. 2):287. © 2000. Blackwell Publishing. Reprinted by permission.

page 189 Table 9-3: Adapted from Statistics Canada publication, "Women in Canada: Work Chapter Updates, 2006," Table 11, Catalogue No. 89F0133XIE, Release date: April 20, 2008.

page 190 Figure 9-2: Adapted from Makiko Fuwa 2004. "Macro-level Gender Inequality and the Division of Household Labor in 22 Countries." *American Sociological Review* 69: December 2004, Table 2, page 757. Used by permission of the American Sociological Association and the author.

page 191 Figure 9-3: Adapted from Statistics Canada publication, "Women in Canada: Work Chapter Updates, 2006," Table 6, Catalogue No. 89F0133XIE, Release date: 2012.

page 191 Figure 9-4: Adapted from Statistics Canada publication, "Women in Canada: Work Chapter Updates, 2006," Table 11, Catalogue No. 89F0133XIE, Release date: April 20, 2007.

page 192 Table 9-4: Statistics Canada, Labour Force Survey 2012.

page 193 Figure 9-5: Statistics Canada 2009.

page 194 Figure 9-6 The Neilsen Company, 2011. The Women of the World Study.

Chapter 10

page 202 Quotation from David Grazian. 2010. *Mix It Up: Popular Culture, Mass Media, and Society.* Copyright © 2010 by W. W. Norton & Company, Inc. Used by permission of W. W. Norton & Company, Inc.

page 205 Table 10-1: Google Canada Zeitgeist 2011.

page 206 Figure 10-1: Based on Interbrand 2010.

page 207 Figure 10-2: Adapted from Open Net Initiative 2008. Copyright © The Open Net Initiative 2008. All Rights Reserved. See also Faris and Villeneuve 2008.

page 212 Figure 10-3: National Geographic 2005: 21 and the Buckminster Fuller Institute.

page 213 Figure 10-4: Adapted from Statistics Canada, Characteristics of individuals using the internet. CANSIM Table 358-0124 adapted by author.

page 214 Networked Readiness Index taken from World Economic Forum. 2010. *The Global Competitiveness Report 2010–2011.* World Economic Forum, Switzerland. Copyright © 2010 by the World Economic Forum.

Chapter 11

page 224 Quotation from CanWest Mediaworks Publications. 2011. "Gang Violence Being Fuelled by Prohibition on Pot: Report." Andrea Woo. October 27. © CanWest MediaWorks Publications Inc.)

page 231 Table 11-1: Adapted from the American Society of Plastic Surgeons 2002, 2005, 2007a, 2011.

page 232 Table 11-2: Adapted with permission of The Free Press, copyright renewed 1985 by Robert K. Merton.

page 240 Figure 11-1: Statistics Canada 2012.

page 241 Table 11-4: Statistics Canada 2010.

Chapter 12

page 248 Quotation: "Honour Killing Trial" Kingston, Ont. Postmedia News Source:

http://news.nationalpost.com/2011/12/05/honour-killing-trial-sometimes-purifying-the-name-of-the-family-trumps-hu. Used with the permission of Postmedia News.

page 250 Figure 12-1: Adapted from Statistics Canada publication, "Family portrait: Continuity and change in Canadian families and households in 2006: National portrait: Census families," Catalogue No. 97-553-XWE2006001, http://www12.statcan.ca/english/census06/analysis/famhouse/cenfam1.cfm.

page 255 Figure 12-2: United Nations Statistics Division 2008.

page 257 Figure 12-3: Adapted from Statistics Canada publication, "Family Portrait: Continuity and Change in Canadian Families and Households in 2006, 2006 Census," Catalogue No. 97-553-XWE2006001, http://www12.statcan.ca/english/census06/analysis/famhouse/charts/chart13.htm.

page 262 Figure 12-4: Baker 2001:218; Statistics Canada 1997, 2003o, 2003p, 2004h, 2004i, 2005i, 2007i, 2011.

Chapter 13

page 270 Quotation from Nikki Bado-Fralick and Rebecca Sachs Norris. 2010. *Toying with God: The World of Religious Games and Dolls,* pp. 7–8, 29–30. © 2010. Reprinted by permission of Baylor University Press.

page 271 Figure 13-1: From John L. Allen, 2008. *Student Atlas of World Politics,* Eighth Edition. Copyright © 2008 by The McGraw-Hill Companies. Reproduced by permission of McGraw-Hill Contemporary Learning Series.

page 278 Figure 13-2: Tom W. Smith 2009: 28, 60, 72.

page 279 Table 13-3: Adapted from Statistics Canada publication, "2001 Census: Analysis Series, Religions in Canada," Catalogue No. 96F0030XIE2001015, May 13, 2003, http://www12.statcan.ca/english/census01/products/analytic/companion/rel/contents.cfm.

page 282 Figure 13-3: Bureau of the Census 2010a: T 1371.

Chapter 14

Page 294 Quotation from John Bowes (ed.). 2011. *The Fair Trade Revolution,* pp. ix, 2–3, 231–232, Pluto Press. Reprinted by permission of Pluto Press.

Page 299 Cartoon by Mike Thompson, Detroit Free Press.

Page 307 Figure 14-5 (left): author based on C.W. Mills (1956) 2000b; (right) From G. William Domhoff. 2009. *Who Rules America,* Sixth Edition: 116. © 2009 by The McGraw-Hill Companies, Inc. Reproduced by permission of the publisher.

Page 310 Figure 14-6: 2010 Global Peace Index, Institute for Economics and Peace.

Chapter 15

page 318 Quotation from Fishman, Ted C. 2010a. Shock of Gray. New York: Scribner.

page 320 Table 15-1: Adapted from Statistics Canada publication, Canadian Social Trends, Catalogue No. 11-008, No. 60, Spring 2001, p. 4, http://www.statcan.ca/bsolc/english/bsolc?catno=11-008-X.; cbc.ca 2010.

page 321 Figure 15-1: Haub, Carl. 2004. World Population Data Sheet, 2004. Washington, DC: Population Reference Bureau.

page 325 Figure 15-3: Central Intelligence Agency 2007.

page 335 Figure 15-4: Figure 15-4: Adapted from *National Geographic Atlas of the World,* Eighth Edition. National Geographic Society, 2005. NG Maps/National Geographic Image Collection. Used by permission.

page 336 Figure 15-5: From Chauncy Harris and Edward Ullmann. 1945. "The Nature of Cities," *Annals of the American Academy of Political and Social Science,* 242 (November):13. Reprinted by permission of the American Academy of Political and Social Science, Philadelphia.

page 343 Figure 15-6: From UNAIDS 2010. Adapted from p. 23 of "UNAIDS, AIDS Epidemic Update." Reprinted by permission from UNAIDS, Geneva, Switzerland.

Chapter 16

page 348 Quotation from Nick Bilton. 2010. *I Live in the Future & Here's How It Works: Why Your World, Work, and Brain are Being Creatively Disrupted.* Copyright © 2010 by Nick Bilton. Used by permission of Crown Business, a division of Random House, Inc.

page 363 Figure 16-1: Jerrad Pierce 12/05. 2005 World Consumption Cartogram.

page 365 Figure 16-2: Adapted from *National Geographic Atlas of the World,* Eighth Edition. National Geographic Society, 2005. NG Maps/National Geographic Image Collection. Used by permission.

photo credits

Chapter 1: Chapter opener: Jiawangkun / Dreamstime.com; p. 4: Digital Vision/Getty Images; p. 6: Top left: © Peter Menzel/Menzel Photography; p. 6: Top right: © Peter Menzel/Menzel Photography; p. 6: Bottom left: © David Reed; p. 6: Bottom right: © Peter Menzel/Menzel Photography; p. 7: AP Images/ Micheal Laughlin; p. 8: CP Photo/Peter McCabe; p. 10: © Spencer Arnold/Getty Images; p. 11: Left: Bibliothèque Nationale de France; p. 11: Centre: The Granger Collection; p. 11: Right: Archivo Iconografico, S.A./Corbis; p. 12: ©Seven Settlements Data Base of Photos/ University of Illinois Chicago; p. 14: By permission of Penny Curtis; p. 15: © Earl and Nazima Kowall/ Corbis; p. 20: © Dave Martin/ AP Images; p. 21: ©John Foxx/Imagestate Media/Imagestate.

Chapter 2: Chapter opener: © US Census Bureau; p. 26: © Scott Camazine/PhotoTake; p. 28: Sampete/Dreamstime.com; p. 32: © Department of Defense photo by Staff Sgt. Michael L. Casteel, US Army; p. 33: Top: The Canadian Press Images/Vancouver Sun/Steve Bosch; p. 33: Bottom: Courtesy of AT&T Archives and History Center, Warren, NJ; p. 36: The Canadian Press/Christian Lapid; p. 36: Royalty Free/Corbis; p. 37: © Lorena Ros/Panos Pictures; p. 38: Carnegie Mellon University; p. 40: © Aksakalko / Dreamstime.com.

Chapter 3: Chapter opener: igor kisselev/Shutterstock; p. 44: © F. Poelking/ Age Fotostock; p. 46: (left) © Mandel Ngan/AFP/Getty Images; p. 46(right): © Paul Chiasson, The Canadian Press/AP Images; p. 47: © Olivia Arthur/Magnum Photos; p. 48: (left): © Adam Taylor / ©ABC / Courtesy Everett Collection; p. 48: (right) Photo by Kerry Hayes. Used by permission of Kinky Hair II Productions Incorporated; p. 48: Bottom: © Robert Laberge/Getty Images; p. 49: Sashabuzko/Dreamstime.com; p. 54: (top) © Tanushree Punwan/ Reuters/Corbis; p. 50: (bottom): © Gianni Muratore; p. 56: © Christine Pemberton/The ImageWorks p. 62: CP/Montreal Gazette/ Phil Carpenter.

Chapter 4: Chapter opener: CP/Montreal Gazette/Phil Carpenter; p. 66: © Steve Russell / GetStock.com; p. 69: Photo by Charles Robinson; p. 70: © Margot Granitsas Image Works; p. 71: © Jon Feingersh/Blend Images LLC; p. 77: © Carlos Osorio/AP Images; p. 75: © Bridget Clyde/ Stock Shot/ Alamy; p. 77: © David H. Wells/Image Works; p. 78: Jim West/ Alamy/ Getstock; p. 81: © Robert Brenner/PhotoEdit; p. 82: © Dave and Les Jacobs/Getty Images; p. 85: © A. Ramey/Photo Edit; p. 85: PhotoAlto/Sandro Di Carlo Darsa.

Chapter 5: Chapter opener: Tatianatatiana/Dreamstime; p. 91: (top): © Royalty-Free/CORBIS; p. 91: (bottom): Rick Hansen CP/ STF; p. 93: (top): © Bruce Dale/National Geogrphic Image Collection; p. 93: (bottom): © Jamstock/Dreamstime.com; p. 94: © Peter R. Hvizdak/Image Works; p. 95: (top): © THE CANADIAN PRESS/Graham Hughes; p. 95: (bottom): © China photos/ Getty Images; p. 96: © Vivian Moos/Corbis; p. 99: © © CBS/ Photofest; p. 99: (both): © Twentieth Century-Fox Film Corporation/Kobal Collection; p. 100: Norman Pogson/Alamy/Getstock; p. 105: © Chung Sung-Jun/Getty Images; p. 103: © Mike Goldwater/Alamy; p. 104: © Photo Japan/Alamy; p. 111: © Koichi Kamoshida/Getty Images; p. 113: The McGraw-Hill Companies, Inc./Christopher Kerrigan, photographer.

Chapter 6: Chapter opener: © McGraw-Hill Companies, Inc./Gary He, photographer; p. 116: ©Kumar Sriskandan/Alamy; p. 120: (top) © Roger Ball; (bottom): © William Campbell/ Sygma/Corbis; p. 121: Ken Woroner/History Channel/The Kobal Collection; p. 123: Katja Heinemann/Aurora Photos; p. 181: Getty Images/Photodisc; p. 184: Courtesy of Christine Magee; p. 186: © Frank Chmura/Alamy; p. 133: Tupungato/Dreamstime.com.

Chapter 7 opener: © Mike Greenslade/ Alamy; p. 192: Book cover reprinted with permission of Oxford University Press, UK; p. 139:

Left: Jackblue/Dreamstime.com; p. 139: Right: Photofusion Picture Library/Alamy; p. 144: © Imaginechina via AP Images; p. 146: (left) Karnow/Woodfin Camp & Associates; p. 146 (right): PhotoDisc/ Getty Images; p. 147: The commercial titled "Jeans" was done by Springer and Jacoby Werbung advertising agency for Against Child Labour (a UNICEF company) in Germany. Copywriter: Svend Keitel. Art Directpr: Claudia Todt. Creative Director: Timm Weber/ Bettina Olff. p. 150: © Stuart Franklin/Magnum Photos; p. 152: AP Photo/ Mindaugas Kulbis.

Chapter 8: Chapter opener: © Steve Russell/GetStock.com; p. 156: © Jgreeniaus / Dreamstime.com; p. 159: Goldenkb/Dreamstime. com/GetStock.com; p. 162: (top) © Tony Savino/The Image Works; p. 162: (bottom) © Enigma/ Alamy; p. 163: CP Photo/Le Journal de Montreal/Luc Belisle; p. 166: © Gaizka Iroz/ AFP/ Getty Images; p. 168: The Canadian Press/Sean Kilpatrick p. 169: Ministry of Education/Archives of Ontario; p. 171: Top: Vancouver Public Library, Special Collections, VPL 30625; p. 172: Bottom: Vancouver Public Library, Special Collections, VPL 6231.

Chapter 9: Chapter opener: © Thinkstock/Index Stock; p. 180: © Paul Baldesare/Alamy; p. 181: (top): © Craig Sjoden/ABC via Getty Images; p. 181 (bottom): Right: Harrison G. Pope, Jr. adapted from The Adonis Complex by Harrison G. Pope, Jr., Katherine Phillips, Roberto Olivardia. The Free Press, © 2000; p. 184: © Gideon Mendel/ Corbis; p. 184: (AP Photo/Mike Groll); p. 186: © Bob Daemmrich/ The Image Works; p. 189: © Lionel Bonaventure/AFP/Getty Images; p. 192: N. Levine 1988; Stockard 2002; Zeitzen 2008; p. 193: ©Terry Vine/Blend Images LLC; p. 247: Canadian Heritage Gallery;

Chapter 10: Chapter opener: © Lars A. Niki; p. 202: Book cover of Mix It Up: Popular Culture, Mass Media, and Society by David Grazian. © 2010 by W. W. Norton & Company, Inc. Used by permission of W. W. Norton & Company, Inc. Designer: Wes Youssi. Photo: Paul Bradbury/ Getty Images; p. 205: Brandchannel.com 2010; p. 142: © Gerald Herbert/AP Images; p. 209: © Jordan Althaus/© The CW/Courtesy of Everett Collection; p. 210: (top) © Kami/Arabianeye; (bottom) © Rubberball Productions; p. 216: (left): © Ben Rose/WireImage/Getty Images; p.150 (right) © RubberBall Productions; p. 152: © Noah Flanigan 2009.

Chapter 11: Chapter opener: © (AP Photo/Reed Saxon); p. 224: CP PHOTO/Toronto Star-Vince Talotta; p. 148: (left) © Lehtikuva/Jussi Nukari; (right) © John Smierciak/Chicago Tribune; p. 149: Courtesy of Mrs. Alexandra Milgram. © 1965 by Stanley Milgram. From the film Obedience, distributed by Penn State, Media Sales; p. 229: (top) © David McClain/Aurora Photos; (bottom) © Mohsen Shandiz/Corbis; p. 230: Paul Drinkwater/NBCU Photo Bank via AP Images; p. 234: © AP Images; p. 236: © Pinkcandy/Dreamstime.com.

Chapter 12: Chapter opener: © Forestpath/Dreamstime.com; p. 248: THE CANADIAN PRESS/Sean Kilpatrick; p. 249: Richard Wear/ DesignPics/Get Stock; p. 251: © ImagesBazaar/Alamy p. 252: © ImagesBazaar/Alamy; ,p.253: Jupiterimages/Getty Images; p. 261: © Arif Ali/AFP/Getty Images; p. 258: Cheryl Gerber for the New York Times/Redux Pictures; p. 259: © Waselchuk/New York Times Pictures; p. 269: © martin purmensky/iStockphoto.com.

Chapter 13: Chapter opener: © Jacob Silberberg/Panos Pictures; p. 270: Book cover of Toying with God: The World of Religious Games and Dolls by Nikki Bado-Fralick and Rebecca Sachs Norris, © 2010, reprinted with permission of Baylor University Press.; p. 272: Samrat35/ Dreamstime.com; 274: © John Birdsall/Image Works; p. 277: Kazuyoshi Nomachi/HAGA/Image Works; p. 280: © Robert Davies; p. 284: © Warner Bros Pictures/ Photofest © Warner Bros, Pictures.; p. 285: Tara Walton/Toronto Star; p. 286: © Yuriko Nagano; p. 288: © Dennis MacDonald/ Alamy.

name index

Lipset, S.M., 126
Lipson, K., 67
Liptak, A., 20
Liska, A.E., 236
Little Mosque on the Prairie, 210
Livernash, R., 362
Livingstone, D., 288
Ljunggren, D., 227
Loblaws Cos. Ltd., 117, 118
Lofland, L.H., 33, 187
Logos Christian Education
    program, 290
Lohan, L., 202
Lorber, J., 181
Loree, D.J., 173
Los Angeles Times, 204
Loving, M.J., 255
Loving, R., 255
Lowman, J., 37
Lucas, D.W., 90
Luciw, R., 194
Luckmann, T., 101
Luhmann, N., 15
Lukacs, G., 54
Luker, K., 196, 259
Lundy, C., 242
Lunman, K., 174
Luster, T., 256
Luther, M., 279
Luttinger, N., 21
Luxton, M., 16, 253
Lyall, S., 262
Lydecker, M., 330
Lynch, M., 329
Lyotard, J.F., 18

M

MacDonald, G.J., 282
Mack, M., 71
Mack, R., 99
Mackenzie, H., 116, 119
MacKinnon, C., 236
MacLeod, C., 207
MacMillan, A.B., 327
Madonna, 202
Maestretti, D., 283
Magee, C., 131
Maguire, B., 239
Mahbub ul Haq Human
    Development Centre, 302
Make Poverty History, 132
Makin, 237
Malthus, T.R., 319, 323
Man in Motion
    Foundation, 91–92
Mancal Group, 118
Mandela, N., 166, 349, 351
Mandell, N., 164, 237, 286
Mangham, C., 243
Manitoba Agriculture and
    Food, 258
Manitoba Human Rights
    Commission, 93
Manitoba Public Schools
    Act, 290

Mannix, F., 118
Mannix, R., 118
Manson, D.A., 239
Mansour, A., 163
Maracle, L., 168
Margolis, M., 149
Marino, D., 202
Mark, G., 110
Markusen, A., 339
Marr, P., 76
Marriott, M., 161
Marsden, L., 81
Marshall, D., 236
Marshall, G., 17
Marshall, K., 232
Martin, C.B., 195
Martin, D., 47
Martin, P., 174
Martineau, H., 9, 10
Marx, E., 21
Marx, K., 10–11, 12, 13, 14, 16,
    19, 22, 54, 72, 104, 105,
    116, 120–121, 122, 140,
    164, 186, 208, 252, 275,
    276, 295, 297, 306, 307,
    310, 320, 323, 327, 350,
    351, 354
Maryanski, A.R., 353
Masland, T., 118
Massmart, 55
Matrix Reloaded, The (film), 217
Matsushita, Y., 77
Matthews, B., 76
Matthews, D.R., 171, 265
Matthews, J., 289
Mayer, M., 110
Maynard, D., 332
McCabe, 85
McCloud, A.B., 280
McClung, N., 195
McDonald's, 350
McFalls, J.A., Jr., 326
McGill University, 203, 212
McGuire, M.B., 272
McIntosh, P., 161–162
McIntyre, L.J., 9
McKenna, B., 112
McKinlay, J.B., 330
McKinlay, S.M., 330
McKinney, L., 195
McLachlin, B., 188
McLean, E.A., 99
McLuhan, M., 202, 217
McNealy, S., 219
McNeil, D.G., Jr., 139
McPhail, M., 195
McPherson, B.J., 35
McTeer, M.A., 196, 197
Mead, G.H., 17–18, 19, 69,
    70–71, 72, 73, 74
Mead, M., 183, 186
Médecin sans Frontières, 151,
    152, 309
Media Awareness Network, 217
Medium, 210
Meichtry, S., 251
Meir, R., 364

Meissner, M., 130
Memecan, N., 148
Memmi, A., 123
Mendez, J.B., 107
Mensah, J., 131
Merrill, D.A., 351
Merton, R.K., 12–13, 15, 19, 96,
    106, 204, 205, 224, 232–233
Messner, M.A., 35
Messner, S.F., 236
Meston, C.M., 31, 32, 39
Meyer, M.W., 106
Meyerson, H., 112
Mia, I., 214
Michael, R., 40
Michaels, S., 40
Michels, R., 107, 109, 111, 351
Microfinance Information
    Exchange, 313
Microsoft, 296
Midgley, E., 174
Milan, A., 255, 264
Milgram, S., 225, 226–227, 285
Mill, J.S., 186
Miller, J., 235
Millet, K., 122
Mills, C.W., 5, 19, 121, 122,
    129, 206, 307
Miner, H., 44
Minnesota Center for Twin and
    Adoption Research, 68
Minton, H.L., 73
Missouri, M., 133
Mitchell, A., 289
Mitchell, K., 173
Miyata, K., 75
Mizruchi, M.S., 307
Moeller, S.D., 205
Moen, P., 194
Moffatt, S., 327
Mohai, P., 363
Mohanty, C.T., 16
Mojab, S., 248
Molotch, H., 20
Momigliana, A., 251
Monteiro, L.A., 332
Montag, H., 230
Moore, D., 202
Moore, K., 178
Moore, W.E., 78, 119, 122, 285,
    311, 348
Moran, T., 143
Morris, A., 351
Morris, B., 254
Morrison, D.E., 350
Morse, R., 20
Moss, K., 202
Mossman, 195
Mothers Against Drunk Driving
    (MADD), 239
Mothers of Supertwins, 265
MTV, 210, 216
MuchMusic, 217
Mueller, G.O., 241
Muir, T., 254
Mulroney, B., 304

Munsch, R., 182
Murdoch, R., 216
Murdock, G., 46, 250, 251
Murphy, E., 195
Murray, J., 181
Museveni, Y., 306
Muslim Canadian Congress, 180
Mydans, S., 207
MySpace, 75, 203

N

NAACP, 209
Nabalamba, A., 363
Naiman, J., 122
NASA, 204
Nash, M., 164
Nathanson, P., 212
National Advisory Commission
    on Criminal Justice, 238
National Center on Addiction
    and Substance Abuse, 235
National Council of Welfare, 133
National Geographic, 212, 335, 365
National Graduates Survey
    (NGS), 30
National Health and Social Life
    Survey (NHSLS), 40
National Indian Child Welfare
    Association, 169
National Institute of Child
    Health and Human
    Development, 40
National Post, 217, 248, 290
National Public Health Survey, 39
National Reconnaissance Office,
    106
National Security Agency
    (NSA), 106
Neilsen Company, 194, 205
Nell (film), 67
Nelson, A., 17, 39, 57, 60, 81,
    193, 194, 195, 196, 242
Nelson, E., 55, 203
Nelson, G., 290
Netting, N., 255
Network Center, 101
Neuwirth, R., 338
New Moon (film), 205
New Unionism Network, 111
New York Times, The, 263
Newman, W.M., 166
News Corporation of Australia,
    216
Nguyen, S.D., 171
Niebrugge, G., 17
Niebrugge-Brantley, J., 354
Nielsen, J.M., 182
Nike, 144, 145
Nolan, P., 48, 102, 103, 124, 333
Noonan, R.K., 351
Nordhaus, W.D., 125
Norris, D., 261
Norris, R.S., 270
NPD Group, 80
NVivo 7, 38

subject index

culture, 54, 56, 60
deviance, 232–33
disengagement theory, 80
dysfunctions, 15
education, 282–85
ethnocentrism, 58
expressiveness, 185
family, 252–53
gender relations, 184–85
Gulf of Mexico oil spill, 20
health and illness, 329–30
illicit drug use, 242
informal economy, 299
instrumentality, 185
Internet, 219, 359
labour migration, 365
latent functions, 15
manifest functions, 15
mass media, 204–5
multinational
    corporations, 143–44
race and discrimination, 164
research, 37
school, schooling, 76
social change, 353–54
social institutions, 99–100
social movements, 349–50
social norms, 225
social roles, 93
stratification, 119–20
television, 215
theory, 14–15
unions, 111
urban ecology, 335–37

G

Game stage (Mead), 17, 70–71
Gang imperialism, 238
Gangs, 97, 224
Gatekeeping, 206–7, 329
Gemeinschaft, 102, 105,
    109–10, 340
Gender
    and ageism, 82
    as ascribed status, 93
    body image, 181
    defined, 181
    interviewer characteristics, 32
    and nature-nurture
        debate, 183–84
    and occupational
        prestige, 125
    role of in cross-talk, 188
    as social construction, 181–84
    and social epidemiology, 328
    and social mobility, 131
    social movements, 351
    socialization and, 66, 74,
        76, 181–83
    and sociology, 21
    workforce
        participation, 190–94
Gender inequality
    in academia, 186–87
    and capitalism, 186, 311

division of labour, 181,
    185–86
earnings gap, 188–89,
    191, 193
and education of women, 185
and feminist perspective, 16
housework, 190, 193–94, 302
and human rights, 151
and poverty reduction, 147
and stratification, 122
suffrage movement, 195
women's movement, 194–95
work-life conflict, 193–94
Gender relations, 184–88
    conflict perspective, 185–86
    feminist perspectives, 186–87
    functionalist
        perspective, 184–85
    interactionist
        perspective, 187–88
Gender roles, 74
    and class, 182
    class and, 76
    cross-cultural
        perspective, 183–84
    media stereotypes, 35
    men's roles, 183
    women's roles, 182–83
    work-life conflict, 193–94
Gender socialization, 74–76
Gene therapy, 359
Generalized other, 18
Generational mobility, 130
Genetic engineering, 359–60
Genetically modified
    (GM) food, 359–60
Genocide, 165–66
Geophagy, 139
Gerontology, 80
Gesellschaft, 102, 105, 110, 340
Glass ceiling, 161, 191
Global economy
    global disconnect of
        developing nations, 214
    income inequality, 120
    and social inequality, 4, 21
Global feminism, 186
Global inequality
    colonialism, 140
    dependency theory, 140, 142
    foreign aid per capita, 146
    gross national income per
        capita, 141
    gross national product, 146
    income distribution by
        nation, 150
    modernization, 142
    neo-colonialism, 140
    poverty, 138
    stratification within
        nations, 148–50
    universal human
        rights, 151–52
    world systems analysis, 140,
        142, 190
Global warming, 21, 361
Globalization, 19, 21

communications technology, 47
cultural imperialism, 57–58
of culture, 46–48
defined, 19
and global inequality, 140–42
impact on developing
    nations, 296
impact on
    environment, 361–63
and labour unions, 126
and power, 300
and social change, 356–60
world consumption, 363
Goal displacement, 106
Government
    democracy, 303–4
    dictatorship, 303
    monarchy, 303
    oligarchy, 303
    totalitarianism, 303
Grandparenthood, 257–58
Great Britain, electronic
    surveillance, 227–28
Gross national product, 146
Groups
    charter groups, 13, 173
    coalitions, 97
    defined, 95
    entrance groups, 13
    and group identification, 11
    in-groups, 96–97
    out-groups, 96–97
    power, and social
        reality, 91–92
    primary group, 96
    reference groups, 97
    secondary group, 96
Guinea pig effect, 34
Gulf War Syndrome, 332

H

Habit training, 74
Hajj, 277–78
Hawthorne effect, 33–34, 108–9
Head tax, 164, 171
Health. *See also* illness
    and class, 327
    defined, 326
    determinants of, 327
    impact of class on, 129
    life expectancy, 321
    and poverty, 132, 147
    sexual orientation, 328–29
    and social assistance, 133–34
Health-care system, 332–33
Hegemony, 208
Heredity, influence of, 68–69
Heterosexist bias, 253
Hidden curriculum, 285
Hijab, 274
Hinduism, 273
HIV/AIDS, 147, 326, 331–32,
    343–44
    feminization of, 132, 324
Home-schooling, 289

Homophobia, 182
Homosexuality. *See* lesbian and
    gay relationships
Honour killings, 248
Horizontal mobility, 130
Horticultural society, 103
Human genome, 360
Human relations
    approach, 107–9
Human rights, 151–52
Human trafficking, 241
Hypothesis, 28

I

Id, 73
Ideal type, 10, 105
Identity theft, 219, 238
Ijime, 77
Illegal immigration, 174, 366
Illness
    "death control", 322
    determinants of health, 327
    labelling theory, 331–32
    medicalization of society, 328,
        330, 331
    and poverty, 129, 132
    sick role, 329
Immigrants
    assimilation, 166, 172
    as "other", 170–72
    and stratification, 170–73
    women, and poverty, 188–89
    women's health, 328
    workforce participation, 311
Immigration
    Canada, 158
    global immigration, 173–75
    illegal immigration, 174, 366
    labour migration, 365
    occupational
        mobility, 130, 148
    restrictive policies, 164
Imperialism, 47
Impression
    management, 71–72, 75
In vitro fertilization
    (IVF), 196, 264
Incest taboo, 254
Incidence, 326
Income, 116
Income inequality, 120. *See also*
    social inequality
    and class, 117–18, 125–26
    distribution of wealth, 148–50
    earnings gap, 188–89,
        191, 193
    global perspective, 143, 145–47,
        294
Independent variable, 28
Industrial Revolution, 104,
    139, 356
Industrial societies, 295
Industrial society, 103–4
Infant mortality rate, 129,
    321, 330

Role-taking (Mead), 70
Routine activities theory, 234
Russia, organized crime, 240
Rwanda, Tutsi genocide, 165

S

Sabotage, 356
Sample, sampling, 29–30
Sanctions, 52–53, 225
Sapir-Whorf hypothesis, 51
School, schooling
    as agent of socialization, 76–77
    bullying, 77–78
    as formal organizations, 287–88
    home-schooling, 289
    and social mobility, 131
    student subculture, 288
    teachers, 287–88
Science, 5
    Comte's hierarchy of, 9
Scientific management
    approach, 107–9
Scientific method
    conclusion development, 30
    control variable, 30
    data collection and
        analysis, 29–30, 37
    defined, 27
    defining the problem, 27–28
    hypothesis formulation,
        28–29
    reliability, 30
    review of literature, 28
    validity, 30
Secondary analysis, 34, 35
Secondary group, 96
Sects, 279, 281
Secularization, 270
Segmented audience, 214–16
Segregation, 166–67
Self
    face-work, 72
    looking-glass self, 70
    Mead's theory of, 17–18, 69,
        70–71
    psychological approaches to
        development, 73
Self-employment, 131
Self-image, 66–67
Self-injury, 26–27
Self-segregation, 166–67
Sensorimotor stage (Piaget), 73
Serial monogamy, 250
Settlement houses, 12
Sex, 181
Sex selection, 196–97, 265, 359
Sexism, 189
    in sociological research, 17
    women in politics, 304–6
Sexist bias, 253
Sexual behaviour
    reasons for, 31–32
    role of media in, 204
Sharia law, 280
Shia Muslims, 280

Significant others, 18
Singapore, social control
    campaigns, 227, 228
Slavery, 117, 118, 130, 164, 241
Slugging, 17
Social capital, 13
Social change
    in conflict perspective, 15–16
    conflict theory, 354
    defined, 348
    education as agent of, 284–85
    and the environment, 360–64
    evolutionary theory, 353
    feminist theories, 354–55
    functionalist theory, 353–54
    global perspective, 356–60
    interactionist theory, 355
    resistance to, forms
        of, 355–56
    and social reality, 91–92
Social compensation
    hypothesis, 75
Social constructionism, 364
    interactionist perspective, 17
Social constructionist
    perspective, 236
Social control, 225–29
    conformity, 224
    control theory, 229
    defined, 225
    education as agent of, 284
    formal methods, 227–28
    informal methods, 227
    law, and society, 228–29
Social enhancement
    hypothesis, 75
Social epidemiology, 326–29
    age, 328
    gender, 328
    health, 326
    incidence, 326
    morbidity rate, 326
    mortality rate, 326
    prevalence, 326
    race and ethnicity, 327
    sexual orientation, 328–29
    and social class, 327
Social inequality. See also
    income inequality
    defined, 21, 116
    and the global economy, 4
    significance of, 21–22, 119
Social institutions, 99–101
Social interaction, 90
    and sense of self, 73
Social media, 75, 78. See also
    Internet; mass media
Social mobility, 130–31
    developing nations, 148
    gender differences, 148, 150
    industrial nations, 148
Social movements
    defined, 349
    functionalist
        perspective, 349–50
    and gender, 351
    leadership, 351

new social movement, 351–53
relative deprivation, 350
resource mobilization, 351
Social networks
    as element of social
        structure, 98–99
    impact of, 212–13
    social capital of, 13
Social reality, 91–92
Social roles, 93–95
    defined, 93
    role conflict, 93–94
    role exit, 94–95
    role strain, 94
Social sciences, 5–7
Social stigma, 230–31
Social structure, 90
    agrarian society, 103
    elements of, 92–101
    global perspective, 101–5
    groups, 95–97
    horticultural society, 103
    industrial society, 103–4
    post-industrial society, 104–5
    postmodern society, 104–5
    pre-industrial society, 102
    social institutions, 99–101
    social networks, 98–99
    social roles, 93–95
    sociocultural
        evolution, 102–5
    statuses, 92–93
    virtual worlds, 99
Socialism, 297
Socialist feminism, 16, 186, 311
Socialization
    activity theory, 82
    agents of, 74–79
    Amish children, 74–76, 77
    anticipatory
        socialization, 78, 83
    childcare, 84–86
    conflict perspective, 72
    defined, 66
    degradation ceremony, 83
    disengagement theory, 80–82
    face-work, 72
    family as agent of, 74–76, 77,
        252
    feminist perspectives, 72–73
    functionalist perspective, 72
    groups and, 96
    habit training, 74
    heredity, influence of, 68–69
    impression management,
        71–72, 75
    isolation and, 67–68
    life course, 79–84
    looking-glass self, 70
    and mass media, 78, 204
    online social media, 75
    peer group, 77–78
    primate studies, 68
    psychological approaches, 73
    resocialization, 83–84
    role of, 67–69
    school, 76–77

self, stages of, 70–71
    and self-image, 66–67
    and social controls, 225–29
    social psychological
        perspectives, 69–72
    sociobiology, 69
    the state and, 79
    technology and, 78
    workplace, 78–79
Societal-reaction approach, 235
Society
    defined, 45
    McDonaldization of, 49
Sociobiology, 69
Sociocultural evolution, 102–5
Sociological imagination, 5, 18–22
Sociology
    approach, 18
    Chicago School, 17
    and common sense, 7–8
    defined, 5
    early developments, 9–11
    ethnography, 32–33
    as field of inquiry, 4–22
    major theoretical
        perspectives, 14–18, 19
    modern developments, 12–14
    and social sciences, 5–7
    sociological imagination,
        5, 18–22
    theory, 8–9
Squatter settlements, 338
State, the
    as agent of socialization, 79
    and labour unions, 107,
        110–12
Status group, 122
Statuses, 92–93, 94
    conferral of through mass
        media, 204
    educational bestowal of,
        285–86
    and stratification, 121–22
Stereotypes
    Asian Canadians, 170
    defined, 159
    gender roles, 35
    linguistic stereotypes, 51
    in mass media
        portrayals, 208–9
    media portrayals of women,
        35, 182–83, 211
    poverty, and the poor, 127–28
Stigma, 230–31
Stigmatization, 230
Stratification
    anti-colonial views of, 123
    Brazil, 149
    caste system, 117
    and class, 124–30
    closed system, 130
    Dahrendorf on, 121
    defined, 116
    and economic change, 311
    and educational
        achievement, 131
    intergroup relations, 165–67

Basketball's Great Dynasties
THE
LAKERS

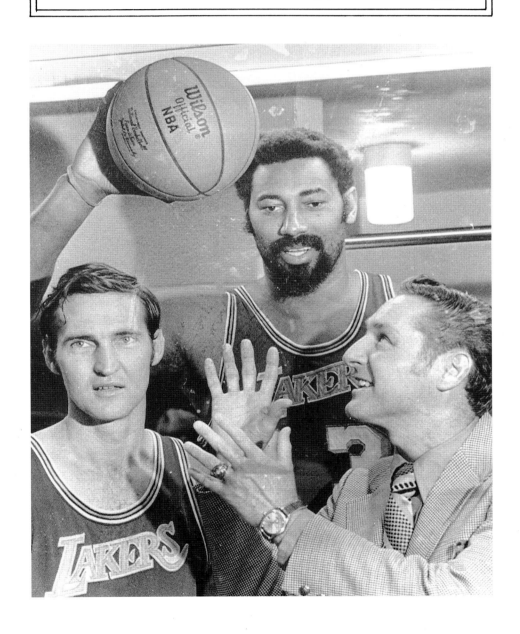

Basketball's Great Dynasties
THE
LAKERS

Jack Clary

SMITHMARK

This edition published in 1992
by SMITHMARK Publishers Inc.,
112 Madison Avenue
New York, New York 10016

SMITHMARK books are available for bulk
purchase for sales promotion and premium use. For
details write or telephone the Manager of Special
Sales, SMITHMARK Publishers Inc., 112 Madison
Avenue, New York, NY 10016. (212) 532-6600.

Produced by Brompton Books Corp.,
15 Sherwood Place
Greenwich, CT 06830

ISBN 0-8317-0673-2

Printed in Hong Kong

10 9 8 7 6 5 4 3 2 1

PICTURE CREDITS

All photographs courtesy UPI/Bettmann News-
photos except the following:

Allsport/Rick Stewart: page 74.
AP/Wide World Photo: pages 76, 77.
Malcolm Emmons: pages 50(both), 51(both), 52(top
    left), 53, 54(both), 55, 58(both), 59, 60(both), 63, 66
Nancy Hogue: pages 61(both), 62, 64(both), 65(both),
    67
Naismith Memorial Basketball Hall of Fame/The
    Edward J. and Gena G. Hickox Library: pages 14,
    15(top right).
Bruce Schwartzman: pages 69, 70, 72, 73(top left,
    right), 79

ACKNOWLEDGMENTS

The author must recognize the help he received from
a number of sources. Wayne Patterson, who directs
research at the Basketball Hall of Fame in Spring-
field, Massachusetts, was of immense assistance with
his great treasure trove of historical information.

In addition to material I gleaned during some 17
years of covering professional basketball while a
sportswriter and columnist in New York and Boston,
I also availed myself of a number of valuable research
tools, including Stew Thornley's fine book *The
History of the Lakers*, which provided immense detail
of the team's days in the Twin Cities; *The Fabulous
Lakers*, by Merv Harris; *The History of Professional
Basketball Since 1896*, by Glenn Dickey; *Showtime*,
by former Lakers coach Pat Riley; *Mr. Clutch: The
Jerry West Story*, Jerry's autobiography; and, from a
different perspective, *The Picture History of the Bos-
ton Celtics* by my former newspaper colleague,
George Sullivan.

I must also thank my editors at Brompton Books,
Jean Martin and Barbara Thrasher, designer Don
Longabucco, picture editor Sara Dunphy, and
indexer Elizabeth A. McCarthy.

Jack Clary
Stow, Massachusetts

Page 1: *The Los
Angeles Lakers' first
NBA championship
was engineered by,
from left: Jerry West,
Wilt Chamberlain
and coach Bill
Sharman.*

Page 2: *Kareem
Abdul-Jabbar, the
NBA's all-time
leading scorer, helped
the team to five NBA
titles in 14 seasons.*

Page 3: *Earvin
(Magic) Johnson
joined the team in
1979 and was the key
to the Lakers'
dominance of the
NBA during the
1980s.*

These pages: *Coach
Pat Riley (far left)
and owner Jerry Buss
(third from left)
guided the team to its
great title run in the
1980s.*

Contents

Preface

For more than three decades it has been "Showtime" in Los Angeles, where Elgin Baylor and Jerry West, Wilt Chamberlain and Kareem Abdul-Jabbar, and of course, Magic, have worked wonders. And before them in other joyous times were George Mikan, Jim Pollard, Vern Mikkelsen, Slater Martin and Whitey Skoog, and frosty nights in Minneapolis and St. Paul.

Professional basketball and the Lakers have formed a partnership that has commanded national attention for nearly a half century, because it was founded on excellence and has maintained that standard throughout the team's existence. Pro basketball's first dynasty belonged to the Lakers of Minnesota, and its most recent belonged to the Lakers of California. In be-

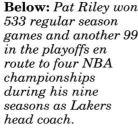

Below: *Pat Riley won 533 regular season games and another 99 in the playoffs en route to four NBA championships during his nine seasons as Lakers head coach.*

tween, the Lakers of both Minnesota and California were always among the elite of the National Basketball Association. No team in the history of the NBA or its parents, the Basketball Association of America and National Basketball League, ever reached as many championship finals as have the Lakers. That achievement proves that the Lakers possess the most telling quality by which great teams are judged: consistency. Considering that the longest gap between the Lakers' championship game appearances in nearly half a century is seven seasons, then they must be considered as one of the greatest franchises in the history of all professional sports.

The Lakers have always featured dominant players, beginning with George

Mikan, a bespectacled giant from DePaul University who was the most sought-after player when he graduated from college in 1946. He formed the backbone of the Lakers' first great dynasty when professional basketball was just beginning its growth in post-war America. Mikan's presence was the single greatest force in gaining serious public acceptance of the hoop sport as something other than a barnstorming exhibition or a loosely formed group of company-sponsored teams. He was more than just a big, gawky guy playing among small men. Rather, he was a talented big man who played with a grace never before seen in athletes his size. Not only could he dominate a game with his skills, but for the first time people began to realize that basketball was a game in which a player of Mikan's talent could inspire those on the court with him.

The Lakers won five championships with Mikan as center, and while he was the ack-nowledged star, he made teammates such as Vern Mikkelsen and Jim Pollard equally famous. Coach Johnny Kundla added speed and all-around play with two guards, Slater Martin and Whitey Skoog, who were intricate parts of his offense. As the Lakers began to dominate the NBA, the public began to understand that basketball played to its optimum meant more than just throwing the ball to the big guy and letting him shoot. Rather, the Lakers' game became one of great coordination between all five players, and a tremendous dominance of the pro game during the Mikan era.

When the Lakers moved to California in 1960, they entered into a tailor-made marriage; the sleek, fast team perfectly fit the glitzy Hollywood image of Los Angeles. This was a team with such great players as Elgin Baylor, the first offensive player in the NBA who truly was all but impossible to guard. He was complemented by Jerry West, the All-America guard from Cabin

Above: *NBA commissioner David Stern presents Magic Johnson with one of his three Most Valuable Player trophies.*

Creek, West Virginia, whose extraordinary basketball talent was matched by his Hollywood looks and entertainment skills.

It wasn't until the Lakers obtained Wilt Chamberlain, arguably the most talented player in the game's history, that the Los Angeles edition of the Lakers finally won an NBA championship 12 years after coming to the West Coast; and it wasn't until they got another great giant named Kareem Abdul-Jabbar, who had honed his skills as an All-America at UCLA, that they won another.

It was also no coincidence that their second dynasty began at this time as they had also added another player, Earvin Johnson. The 20-year-old lad's smile lit up all of southern California, as his skills rightly earned him the nickname "Magic." His tremendous basketball talent was matched by the great enthusiasm he displayed whenever he played.

Thus, Showtime at the Fabulous Forum with Magic and Kareem, and with a talented supporting cast, became an entertainment staple during the 1980s as the Lakers won five NBA titles and established themselves as one of the greatest teams in basketball history. That's exactly where they began – and where, undoubtedly, they will always stay.

Above: *George Mikan (99) was the NBA's first great center and led the Minneapolis Lakers to five championships.*

Right: *The Lakers celebrate breaking a title game drought against the arch-rival Celtics in 1985 at Boston Garden.*

Opposite: *Wilt Chamberlain (13) challenges Bill Russell of the Boston Celtics during the 1969 finals.*

1. Born in the Land of the Lakes

The Lakers have been a California sports institution for more than three decades, a familiar and comfortable part of a region that has always been a magnet for the stars and the star gazers. For most of this time, the Lakers have been hugely successful, and seem to be a perfect fit with the glitter and glamor of nearby Hollywood, where everything is made larger than life. Movie and television stars pay enormous sums to sit at courtside, where they often become as much a part of the attraction as the team and the games.

But there are many who rightly wonder what the "lake" in Lakers has to do with sunny, dry Southern California and the wonders of Hollywood. The answer, of course, is that the name has nothing to do with California. The Lakers were born a half continent away in the state of Minnesota, which proudly advertises itself as the "Land of 10,000 Lakes." And while the Lakers, in typical Hollywood fashion, have often seemed larger than life and sport, that success is only a continuation of an excellence that began on cold, snowy nights in the Twin Cities, and around the snow belt of the East and Midwest during the latter part of the 1940s and throughout the 1950s. At that time, Los Angeles had only the Rams of the National Football League (who transferred from Cleveland in 1946) and later the baseball Dodgers (who came from Brooklyn in 1958) as major league teams to call its own.

But in 1960, the Lakers were part of the National Basketball Association's East-Midwest concoction, itself an amalgam of the Basketball Association of America, formed after World War II, and the National Basketball League, which had existed since the late 1930s. Most of the BAA's owners were entrepreneurs who owned hockey teams and arenas in major cities east of the Mississippi River, and turned to basketball as a means to fill their buildings on what otherwise would be a "dark" night, and to take advantage of a burgeoning interest by Americans on expanding their entertainment tastes. Interest in college-level basketball had begun to spread, and new fans of the professional sport had developed from this audience. Large metropolitan areas such as New York City, Philadelphia and Chicago also had developed large groups of fans because the game had become very popular at the high school level.

Minnesotans were no different, and as a group were, then as now, a hearty breed who thrived on outdoor sports, particularly hunting and fishing. However, in the state's major metropolitan area, the twin cities of Minneapolis and St. Paul, sporting life took other forms. In the fall, it was built around the University of Minnesota's great

Below: *John Kundla was the Minneapolis Lakers' first coach, and guided the team to titles in three different leagues (NBL, BAA and NBA) during his first three seasons.*

football teams; in the winter it was built around a pair of professional hockey teams that played in the Central Hockey League, a minor league that fed the six teams of the National Hockey League; and in spring and summer it centered around twin entrants from each city in the American Association, a Class AAA baseball league that worked with such major league teams as the Brooklyn Dodgers, New York Giants and Boston Red Sox.

Until the time just after World War II, professional basketball was not part of the area's sports fabric. But it didn't take too long for the Twin Cities to become caught up in the explosion of post-war optimism, with new horizons being revealed by quicker air transportation; radio broadcasts, and then television, bringing sports events right into the home; a new leisure enjoyed by Americans now freed from the shackles of the Great Depression and the encumbrances of a world war; and a glut of college and pro players returning from the military. Entrepreneurs around the nation began expanding the hoop sport's boundaries, some by spreading out the National Basketball League, which had existed since 1937, and others by founding the BAA as a new competitor, and putting teams in most of the major cities east of the Mississippi.

The NBL had grown from an amalgamation of company-sponsored teams like the Goodyear Wingfoots and the Firestone Non-Skids from Akron, Ohio; the Chicago Gears, of the American Gear Company; the Fort Wayne Zollner Pistons of the Zollner

Piston Company; and the Anderson (Indiana) Packers, sponsored by the Duffey Packing Company, to spread itself from Syracuse to Denver, though most of its teams were located in medium-sized midwestern cities like Sheboygan, Oshkosh, Dayton, Fort Wayne, Toledo and Flint. The Twin Cities didn't experience this atmosphere until 1946 when Oshkosh defeated its Wisconsin rival, the Sheboygan Redskins at the Minneapolis Auditorium in an NBL game brought in to test the area as a potential franchise site. When more than 5,500 turned out for the game, Sid Hartman, a young Minnesota sportswriter, who was beginning a half-century career as one of the most influential persons in the area's sports world, rounded up his friend Ben

Left: *Arnie Ferrin, who as a freshman helped Utah to the 1944 NCAA title, was a fine "fourth man" for the Minneapolis Lakers' great front court of the late 1940s.*

Above: *Jim Pollard (seen here) teamed with George Mikan and Vern Mikkelsen to form an invincible front line in the Lakers' early years.*

Berger, who owned restaurants and theaters in the Twin Cities, and ice show promoter Morris Chalfen, and convinced them to purchase the defunct Detroit Gems NBL franchise for $15,000 and move it to Minneapolis.

Thus, the seeds for pro basketball were sown in the Twin Cities in the National Basketball League. Though by today's standards, the deal was like getting a franchise for nothing, in 1946 it was a lot of money — and the purchase price didn't include any players because the NBL already had dispersed the team's players throughout the league. But Hartman, Berger and Chalfen had a good plan, and the first part was hiring Max Winter, a former fight manager and saloon owner in Minneapolis, to run this new NBL franchise. Winter later formed the group that founded the Minnesota Vikings NFL team in the early 1960s, and he was president of that team for nearly 30 years.

The second part of the plan was to induce Coach Johnny Kundla to leave St. Thomas College and become head coach of the Lakers. Ironically, Kundla had been one of the officials in that Oshkosh-Sheboygan game that lighted the fires for professional basketball in the Twin Cities; a three-year Lakers contract lighted his fire, as well.

No one in the Lakers' management could have possibly known how fortunate they were to get Kundla, who was the driving force in helping the Lakers to become pro basketball's first great dynasty during the late 1940s and through the mid-1950s. He had been a schoolboy star in Minneapolis and helped the Minnesota Golden Gophers to the Big-10 title in 1937. After a brief stint in baseball's minor leagues, he became a championship high school coach in Minneapolis and played semi-pro basketball until serving a two-year stint in the Navy. He had completed just one season at St. Thomas when Hartman convinced him to join the Lakers.

Kundla's greatest strength as a coach was in recognizing the strengths of his players, and then utilizing them. For example, when he put together his great front line of George Mikan, Jim Pollard and Vern Mikkelsen, he realized that while all three could become great scorers, they would only get in each other's way if they vied for the ball on every play. So, he assigned Mikkelsen the role of setting screens and picks for the other two, and since he was also a superior rebounder, gave him a mandate to sweep the boards. Mikkelsen, in fact, became the game's first "power forward," and years later he admitted his greatest scoring nights came when he cleaned up the misses by Pollard and

Mikan during their off-nights.

Kundla also believed in a speed game, and sent his players flying down the court whenever possible. When the fast break was shut off, his half-court offense was almost as deadly as it worked to get the ball inside to the 6-foot, 11-inch tall Mikan. At all times, Kundla was a coach in total control. The result: He won six league championships during all or part of 12 seasons as the Lakers' head coach, and he compiled a record of 466 victories and 319 losses, plus a 70-38 record in the playoffs.

Kundla was a coach without players until shortly before the start of the 1947

NBL season, when the Lakers purchased two former Minneapolis schoolboy stars, Tony Jaros, with whom Kundla had played semi-pro basketball, and Don (Swede) Carlson from the Chicago Stags of the rival Basketball Association of America. Such was the innocence of those times that competing leagues engaged in commerce with each other even while competing for the same collegians.

Carlson was an unusual player. He was a fine playmaker and defensive specialist who had been the Stags' MVP the previous season, while helping them to the Western Division title and into the BAA's first

Opposite: *The Minneapolis Lakers were an aggressive, board-crashing team, as Jim Pollard (17) shows against the New York Knicks in 1953.*

Above: *Herm Schaefer also utilized coach John Kundla's speed game, seen here against the Knicks in a 1948 game.*

Right: *Vern Mikkelsen (right) was given the job of keeping opposing big men off George Mikan and Jim Pollard and rebounding their misses, making him the game's first "power forward."*

championship playoff. Although he was just 6-feet, 1 inch tall, he still played forward for the Lakers. Jaros was 6-feet, 3-inches tall, and he was such a fine athlete that he played triple-A baseball with the Minneapolis Millers in the spring and summer, and was a forward and guard with the Lakers during his four seasons with them.

Jaros and Carlson helped impart a distinctive hometown flavor to the Lakers,

contributed to additionally by three other Lakers players – Warren Ajax, Don Smith and Ken Exel, who also were former University of Minnesota players – a hallmark for the Lakers team in the Twin Cities, which had a dozen former Gophers on its roster during their 14 years.

But when the Lakers played their first NBL game on November 1, 1947, the team's star was from Oakland, California, and he was playing in Minneapolis thanks mainly to Hartman's power of persuasion. In between his sportswriting duties, Hartman landed the Lakers one of the great forwards in their history – in both Minneapolis and Los Angeles – when he talked Jim Pollard out of his long-held ambition to be a member of the 1948 U.S. Olympic team, and into signing a pro contract. Pollard, the star of Stanford's 1942 NCAA championship team, had played basketball in the Coast Guard during the war, and fended off many offers to turn pro while playing for an Amateur Athletic Union (AAU) team and waiting for the Olympic trials to begin. The 6-foot, 5-inch Pollard was the team's tallest starter when the season began, and he had such leaping ability that he became the first bona fide "dunker" in pro basketball, earning himself the nickname "Kangaroo Kid." For the next eight seasons, he was an All-Star forward en route to basketball's Hall of Fame. He was the team's second or third best scorer in seven of those eight seasons – no small feat, with Mikan and Mikkelsen on the team – and scored 6,522 points, an average of more than 13 per game during nearly 500 regular season games.

He was the star of that first game, scoring 10 points to help the Lakers to a 49-47 victory over the Oshkosh All-Stars on Carlson's field goal in the final 10 seconds. The Lakers were off and flying, but within two weeks of that victory, they would change the way that professional basketball was played for all time by signing the most dominating player of that time – George Mikan.

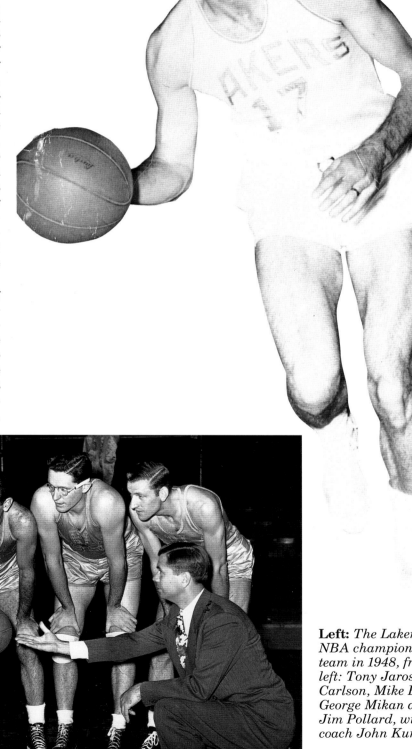

Left: *The Lakers' first NBA championship team in 1948, from left: Tony Jaros, Don Carlson, Mike Bloom, George Mikan and Jim Pollard, with coach John Kundla.*

Above: *During eight seasons, Jim Pollard was an All-Star four times, and later was elected to the Hall of Fame.*

2. George Mikan–Pro Basketball's First Unstoppable Force

The night before the Minneapolis Lakers began their National Basketball League existence, across the Mississippi River in St. Paul the newly formed St. Paul Saints had helped to kick off the new Basketball League of America in a loss to the Chicago Gears 59-49. Gears owner Maurice White had organized this new league, comprised mainly of cities in the Midwest and extending south to Houston and Atlanta. But the league's credibility was built on the Gears, which White had pulled from the NBL after winning that league's title in 1947.

The prime attraction was the Gears'

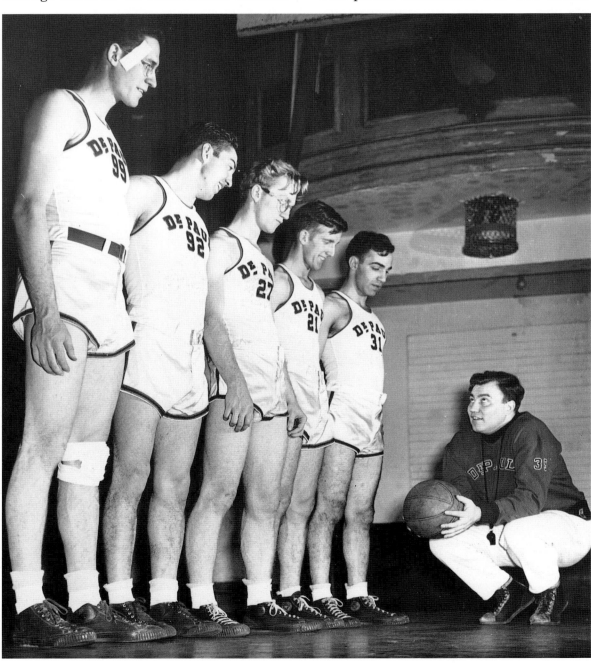

Right: *George Mikan (far left) was the star of DePaul's 1945 NIT champions, which were coached by the legendary Ray Meyer. Meyer spent hundreds of hours helping his gangly star master the fine points of playing center.*

Left: *George Mikan wasn't the only talented member of the family. Brother Ed (right) played for the NBA's Chicago Stags, often giving Mrs. Mikan some anxious moments when the two faced each other.*

center, George Mikan, an All-America from DePaul University in Chicago who had already developed into an awesome force while leading Chicago in its NBL title. The 6-foot, 11-inch Mikan had averaged 17 points a game. Few pro centers were as tall, none was as strong and no one seemed capable of coping with his wide sweeping hook shot. More than anything, he revolutionized the center position which heretofore had been mainly limited to rebounding because most of the taller players at that position were awkward and not gifted as shooters. But Mikan did both, and as a rebounder, he used both his height and strength to overpower opposing centers and forwards.

Of course, when Mikan began attracting attention, he in no way resembled someone once described as "the Superman of the Hardwood." Rather, he looked more like Clark Kent, scholarly and non-athletic with his glasses and a lean frame that belied his 245 pounds. Yet, he would prove to be both tough and durable, missing just two games during his nine seasons with the Lakers.

Mikan was not a naturally great player, and endured endless hours of tedious drills by his coach at DePaul, Ray Meyer, to sharpen his shooting, timing and quickness. In fact, he had been run off by Notre Dame coach George Keogan after being invited to work out with the Irish team during Christmas vacation of his freshman year at DePaul. He was badly limited because of a broken arch at the time, and didn't do well in this "tryout." Worse still, he left Notre Dame with Keogan's appraisal ringing in his ears: "Go back to DePaul. You'll make a better scholar than a basketball player."

Meyer forced Mikan to spend hour after hour skipping rope, shadow boxing, and even doing some ballet steps to improve his quickness and coordination because he simply was not endowed with the pure athletic skills which are the blessings of many great players. Meyer also forced him to learn to shoot his famous hook shot with both hands so defenses could not overload against him, and all of this paid off as he led all collegians in scoring in his junior and senior seasons. En route to their National Invitation Tournament title in New York in Mikan's junior year, DePaul defeated Rhode Island State 97-53 in the semifinals and Mikan matched the loser's point total. On defense, he also was partly responsible for the rulemakers legislating the goaltending rule, which prohibited knocking away a shot once it began its downward arc to the basket. (Bob Kurland, the 7-foot center at Oklahoma A&M at this time – and Mikan's foremost rival for recognition as college basketball's best center – also helped bring about the goal-tending rule.)

Naturally, Mikan was sought by many professional teams when he finished his college career. But George had a keen eye as to

Right: *George Mikan was acclaimed Greatest Basketball Player of the Half Century in 1950 by The Associated Press.*

Below: *The Laker's formidable front line of (from left) Tony Jaros, Jim Pollard, George Mikan, Mike Bloom and Don Carlson powered the team to three league titles from 1947-50.*

his exact worth (he always wore jersey number 99, he said, "because it was not quite a dollar"), and he signed with the Gears, who also had guaranteed him a job in the off-season, as soon as his senior season at DePaul had ended. It was just in time to participate in the Chicago World Professional Tournament, in which he was named Most Valuable Player despite the fact that his team finished third.

Back for the 1946-47 season with the Gears, Mikan missed nearly half the season in a salary dispute, yet averaged 17 points and led Chicago to the NBL title with a 20-points per game average in the playoffs. When the new Basketball League of America folded after just two weeks in 1947, the Gears tried to re-enter the National Basketball League but were unanimously rejected. The NBL then divided up the team's players in a dispersal draft, and the Lakers, because they held the franchise that had the league's worst record from the previous year, picked first and chose Mikan.

Mikan flew to Minneapolis for contract talks but could not reach a deal. However, the crafty Sid Hartman, who knew what a player of Mikan's magnitude would do for the Lakers franchise, deliberately got lost while driving Mikan to the airport, forcing

him to stay overnight. That was just enough time for talks to resume, and the following day, Mikan left for Chicago with a contract in hand.

That marked the beginning of one of the great dynasties in pro basketball history, as Mikan went on to lead the Lakers to six league championships during his seven full seasons. Mikan soon became a major force, once prompting New York's Madison Square Garden to bill an upcoming game between the Lakers and the hometown Knicks: "George Mikan versus Knicks".

While Max Winter and Coach Johnny Kundla surrounded him with other fine players, Mikan's presence, like that of Bill Russell in Boston and Kareem Abdul-Jabbar with a later edition of the Lakers, was the dominant force. He was a prolific scorer, and accumulated 11,351 points during his modest (by today's longevity standards) career, winning the league scoring title four straight times from 1947 to 1951, and the rebounding title twice after the NBA began keeping such statistics. When the Lakers jumped from the NBL into the Basketball Association of America (later to

be known as the NBA) in 1948-49, Mikan's second season, he helped the team to set a league scoring record in a 117-89 victory over the Providence Steamrollers. A few weeks later, he scored 47 points to tie another league mark, and broke it with a 48-point game shortly thereafter (Joe Fulks of Philadelphia then broke that mark later in the season with a 63-point game). Seven times that year he scored more than 40 – something that he did 47 times (he also broke 50 points four times) during his career.

Philadelphia Warriors coach Eddie Gottlieb tried to stop Mikan's scoring by fouling him before he shot the ball. Rules in those days awarded just one foul shot for a non-shooting violation, but when Mikan sank 80 percent of his foul shots that year, that tactic quickly disappeared. The rulemakers even had their shot when in 1951 they doubled the width of the foul lane to 12 feet while keeping the three-second rule, because Mikan had done so much of his scoring within the area just outside the old six-foot lane. A couple of years earlier, when the rule first was proposed, Lakers

Above: *George Mikan polishes his "image" before a 1949 game against the New York Knicks. The Madison Square Garden marquee didn't exaggerate, because Mikan often was a one-man force for the Lakers.*

Above: *George Mikan won the NBA's scoring title for four straight seasons (1947-51) and forced the rulemakers to widen the center lane because he was an almost unstoppable force in the narrower area.*

Other NBA teams adopted the same style – the Lakers and Pistons once played the NBA's lowest scoring game, a 19-18 Pistons victory in 1951. Fans became bored with this style of play, and it wasn't until four years later, with interest really on the wane, that Syracuse owner Danny Biasone proposed the 24-second clock. Basketball historians now agree this was the most important rule change the league adopted, doing much to promote competition and give the pro game its distinctive style.

But, back in 1947, Mikan's presence with the Lakers was a good news/bad news deal at first – good in the fact that it allowed Pollard to return to his natural forward position, where he began playing at a level that garnered a string of All-Star performances; bad because the Lakers lost four of their first five games with Mikan as center. He scored 16 points in his debut, a 56-41 loss to Sheboygan, and after the slump ended, helped the team to win 39 of its last 50 games and capture the NBL's Western Division title.

Mikan's force was obviously crucial to the Lakers' success, but he also had some talented helpers. In 1950, Kundla acquired three players who, with Mikan and Pollard, were the bulwark of his championship teams during the first half of the 1950s: forwards Vern Mikkelsen and Bob Harrison, and guard Slater Martin. Mikkelsen, a 6-foot, 7-inch native Minnesotan, was a territorial draft pick after playing center for Hamline University in St. Paul. He had already proven his worth against bigger teams and some great players, but his role at first was as backup to Mikan. It wasn't until the 1949 season, when Kundla installed what he called a "double pivot" with Mikkelsen at forward, that he emerged as the game's first power forward.

It wasn't an easy transition, Mikkelsen said later, because he had to learn to play facing the basket, and he developed a neat, two-handed, overhead set shot as one of his key weapons. "My function really wasn't to score," he said, "but to rebound and play defense." Still, he scored 10,063 points and averaged more than nine rebounds a game during his 10-season career.

Slater Martin was a 5-foot, 10-inch, 170-pound All-America guard from the University of Texas, where he once set a Southwest Conference record with 49 points in one game. He turned down a bid to play for the AAU powerhouse Phillips Oilers and joined the Lakers, where he ran the offense as a point guard. In addition to his fine shooting talent, he often guarded the opposition's best scoring guard. Bob Harrison was a tenacious, intelligent player from the University of Michigan who teamed with

general manager Max Winter declared that his team would never widen the lane in their building, and then threatened to sit Mikan out of any games on opposing courts that insisted on a widened lane. The new rule cost Mikan his first NBA scoring crown that season, but he still had a very respectable 24-point average.

He also was responsible for the NBA establishing its 24-second rule. During the latter part of Mikan's career, the Lakers had adopted a very deliberate style of offense in which they took the ball downcourt and then waited for Mikan to show up. With the mighty Mikan in the middle, the Lakers obviously dominated teams, and pressed their advantage by consuming huge amounts of time before taking a shot.

Martin in the back court until the team acquired Whitey Skoog in 1953. Skoog, from the University of Minnesota, added a deadly jump shot, and the three players allowed Kundla to maintain a solid back court in a game at all times.

One other interesting acquisition also came from the University of Minnesota when Bud Grant, a three-letter winner and an All-America end for the Gophers, joined the team in 1950. He also became a number one draft pick of the Philadelphia Eagles of the NFL, and played both sports before turning his attention to professional football in Canada. Later, of course, he returned to Minnesota and coached the Vikings, then owned by his former Lakers boss, Max Winter, to four Super Bowl appearances.

But Grant and the rest of the Lakers also learned that being a great team by no means granted immunity from the growing pains that afflicted pro basketball at that time. There was much more to the game than wins, points and great players. It was a feat just for the Lakers to survive the NBA's shaking out process that eventually solidified the league and the pro game. In fact, life in the NBA was primitive compared to that enjoyed by the players of today – even for a team like the Lakers that was well-managed, adequately financed and thrived on its heritage of excellence. The team had no full-time trainer until its final years in the Twin Cities, and Kundla himself taped ankles before games. If there was a serious injury, the public address announcer requested a doctor from the crowd. When the players arrived at their hotels on the road, the first thing they did was to take their uniforms from their bags and drape them above a radiator so they could dry. "You learned to live with that smell," Mikkelsen once said.

Sometimes getting there was more precarious. Train travel still was prevalent during the Lakers' dynasty years, and that meant cramped roomettes for big players, or even old fashioned upper berths in open sleeping cars, which were even more cramped and less private. Every team that played a Saturday night game in Rochester and was heading west afterward had to deal with the fact that there were no flights out of the city late at night, and the railroad train going westward came through the city at 10:22 – and was not scheduled to stop unless it had been requested. There were many times when the Lakers, scheduled to play in Minneapolis the next night, ran from Rochester's arena wearing their uniforms under their coats, carrying their street clothes, and sped to the railroad station lest the train come through and not

Above: *George Mikan is congratulated by his teammates after scoring a record-setting 48 points in a 1949 game, a feat he achieved four times that year.*

Left: *Slater Martin was one of the NBA's best guards ever, and he ran the Lakers' attack with great precision.*

stop. Then came an overnight ride to Chicago, followed by another train to Minneapolis, which usually arrived in mid-afternoon, just a few hours before the next tap-off. When the team played in Fort

Right: *George Mikan and Dolph Schayes (4) of the Syracuse Nats were the centerpieces of some rollicking playoff games during the early 1950s. Here, Mikan and Jim Pollard surround Schayes during a 1950 playoff game.*

Wayne and traveled by train, it had to make a special stop at a lone crossroads in the middle of Indiana, and the players then hoped a chartered bus would be there to meet them.

Air travel, which mostly consisted of two-engine planes, often wasn't much better. If there were severe head winds, four fuel stops during a 12-hour trip from Boston to Minneapolis were not unusual. In fact, an air trip almost proved disastrous to the entire team as late as January in 1960, the team's final season in Minneapolis, when commercial air travel was much more sophisticated. Owner Bob Short had purchased an old two-engine transport plane to alleviate some of the travel schedule problems. The Lakers had played the Hawks in St. Louis and were scheduled to use their plane that night to return to Minneapolis. But weather conditions were terrible, with a freezing drizzle that limited the ceiling to just 300 feet and visibility to less than three-quarters of a mile.

The co-pilot didn't want to take off with a traveling party that included the Lakers team, six adults and three children, but he was overruled by the pilot, Vern Ullman. The plane had not been airborne very long when the electrical system failed, knocking out radio communications, heat and the defrosting system, forcing the pilot to fly with cockpit windows open. When the compass went out, the pilot took the plane above the clouds and navigated toward the Twin Cities by using the north star and a magnetic compass. Five hours later, miles off course and with the fuel tanks all but dry, the plane was over the tiny hamlet of Carroll, in western Iowa, and Ullman was frantically searching for an airport. His visibility was severely hampered by blowing snow that frosted over the windshield but he followed a road out of the town, hoping it would lead to an airport. The road suddenly veered and the plane narrowly missed crashing into a grove of trees. Ullman reversed his course and followed the road back toward the lights of the town. But with no airport in sight, the pilots finally landed the plane safely in a cornfield. Everyone thankfully jumped from the plane into knee-deep snow, but a few weeks later, they were back on board, flying from city to city – and even over the Rockies en route to play two games in Los Angeles.

Still, none of these difficulties detracted from what those great George Mikan teams had accomplished; if anything, it underscored their achievements.

Above: *Jim Pollard (17) was a force by himself under the basket, seen here battling the Celtics' Bill Sharman who, years later, would lead the L.A. Lakers to their first world title.*

Left: *Sen. Hubert Humphrey (third from left) conducts a White House tour for his constituents – the 1949 NBA champion Minneapolis Lakers.*

3. Pro Basketball's First Dynasty

The Minneapolis Lakers of the Geroge Mikan era can claim one distinction accorded to no other NBA team: They won titles in three different leagues, and went outside and also defeated the fabulous Harlem Globetrotters in games billed as world professional championships. It was a glory run that was also tinged with all of the growing pains that the sport underwent during the first decade of its post-war expansion.

When the Lakers were born, pro basketball still consisted of a scattered number of leagues and teams, including the National Basketball League, of which the Lakers were a member, and the new Basketball Association of America. The championship series of those leagues was not the big deal the NBA finals are today, and in fact, winning the annual World Professional Basketball Championship in Chicago was considered a bigger plum than an NBL or a BAA title. The Lakers had even delayed their first NBL title series in 1947 to compete in that tournament, and they defeated Wilkes-Barre of the Eastern League, the Anderson Packers of the Midwest League and the independent New York Rens for the title. Two days later, they started the best-of-five NBL title series, and in four games they won the first of their six league titles.

But of all the "extra" league competitions, none was as big as a three-year series against the famed Harlem Globetrotters. The Globetrotters, of course, were renowned for their ability to mix superb basketball skills and comedy against any challenger, but they also had won world professional championship tournaments by playing serious basketball.

In 1948, spurred by some public rumbling that the Globetrotters should test their reputation against top-flight professional competition, a record Chicago Stadium crowd of 17,823 watched the Globetrotters play the Lakers as a preliminary to the Chicago Stags' BAA game. The Trotters had won 103 consecutive games, but after trailing 32-23 at halftime, they forgot about clowning and played serious basketball. The score was tied with a minute to play when Marques Haynes, the Globetrotters' great ballhandler, did his speciality – dribbled the ball and kept it away from the Lakers until the final seconds before feeding Elmer Robinson for a game-winning shot in the 61-59 victory.

The two met twice the following year, with more than 20,000 cramming Chicago Stadium to see the Trotters come from a 24-18 deficit in the second half – behind Goose Tatum, Nat (Sweetwater) Clifton and Haynes – to win 49-45, and added some comedy at the Lakers' expense in the fourth quarter. But a week later, the Lakers had the last laugh in a 68-53 victory before a record crowd in Minneapolis, and then

Below: *How tall was George Mikan? How about 6-feet, 10-inches or two photographers – and big enough to lead the NBA's rebounders for two seasons.*

Left: *Slater Martin led the Lakers in assists for six consecutive seasons (1950-56).*

Below: *Max Winter (center, between Carl Bennett of the Fort Wayne Pistons and Joseph Kimbrough of the Indianapolis Olympians) founded the Minneapolis Lakers, and later the NFL's Minnesota Vikings.*

dominated the Globetrotters in two more games in 1949.

All of this contributed to the Lakers' dominance of professional basketball for nearly a decade, and probably did more to call attention to the sport — as the great teams of the New York Yankees, Cleveland Browns and Montreal Canadiens did in the three other major pro sports — because they established a standard of excellence by which professional basketball was soon measured. A major step in this direction had occurred in 1948 when the Lakers, reluctantly at first, joined the Rochester Royals, Fort Wayne Pistons and Indianapolis Olympians to flee the NBL and enter the Basketball Association of America, which had franchises in most of the major cities east of the Mississippi River, and north of the Mason-Dixon Line. New league, new teams, new format — it really didn't matter as the Lakers continued their dominance, re-establishing their credentials with an opening game victory over the defending BAA champion Baltimore Bullets.

Still, they finished second to their old NBL rivals, the Royals, but Mikan totally

dominated the playoffs for the Lakers, and led them into the best-of seven BAA championship series against the Washington Capitols, coached by a future Lakers nemesis, Red Auerbach. Minneapolis jumped to a 3-0 series lead, and then clinched the 1949 BAA title in the sixth game with a 77-56 victory. Mikan scored 303 points in 10 playoff games and with his 1,698 for the regular season, scored more than 2,000 points for the first time in his career.

The final move to solidify pro basketball occurred before the start of the 1949-50 season when the BAA and seven existing NBL teams merged to form the National Basketball Association, at that time a three-division, 17-team league. The Lakers were in the Central Division with their old antagonists, the Rochester Royals, and the two tied for the division title at the end of the season. In a one-game playoff, Rochester led by six points with three minutes to play, but the Lakers tied the score and with three seconds left, Tony Jaros's set shot gave them a 78-76 victory.

It was relatively easy after that as the Lakers rolled into the NBA's first cham-

pionship final against the Syracuse Nats, and again won in six games. The clincher was a wild and woolly affair marred by several fights and the ejection of Nats player-coach Al Cervi before Minneapolis, behind Mikan's 40 points, plus 16 points and 10 assists by Jim Pollard, won 110-75.

The Lakers emerged from three different years in three different leagues with three different championships. Still, the Lakers of the Mikan dynasty could never shake the Rochester Royals. In the 1950-51 season, they again beat them out for the Western Division title – the NBA had by then pared down to a relatively svelte 11 teams. But with Mikan (who had won the scoring title with a 28.4 average) hobbled by a broken bone in his ankle, the Royals won the division playoff 3-1, and then defeated the New York Knicks for the NBA title – the only time during Mikan's career that he did not win a title.

However, he took one home in each of the next four seasons. In 1952, though Mikan, Pollard and Mikkelsen each scored over 1,000 points, the Lakers finished second to the Royals in the Western Division. When

the two met for the division title, the Royals jumped to a 1-0 lead in the best-of-five series, despite 47 points by Mikan. The Lakers won the next two and, looking down the barrel of another trip to Rochester where the Royals were all but unbeatable, Pollard put back a missed shot by Mikan in the game's closing seconds for an 82-80 division playoff title victory.

Against the Knicks for the NBA title, the Lakers got off to a 1-0 lead with an 83-79 overtime victory, setting the tone for a series that went seven games before the Lakers won the finale, 82-65. The two teams met again for the title in 1953, and this time the Knicks were preaching victory, and made their boasts look good by winning the first game in the Twin Cities, 96-88. In game two, the Lakers barely evened the series at home with a 73-71 win. The Knicks openly boasted that they would not have to return to Minnesota for any more games — and they were correct, because the Lakers swept the three games played in New York.

Those games were played in a small New York City armory because of Madison Square Garden's annual commitment to the circus, and that lessened the Knicks' home court advantage. The Lakers defense also did its part in game three as Whitey Skoog and Bob Harrison clamped on New York's top scorer, Ernie Vanderweghe, and Slater Martin held Dick McGuire to just two points as the Lakers, with Mikan scoring 20 and Pollard 19, won the game 90-75. In the fourth game, Mikan fouled out with two minues to play and the score tied, but Whitey Skoog was the last-minute hero for Minneapolis, scoring the Lakers' last four points in a 71-69 victory that really sealed their fifth title in six years.

Afterward, they celebrated in the famed Copacabana nightclub in New York City. Mikan declared this the sweetest of his four previous titles, and he vowed to play five more years. Little did any of them realize in their euphoria that night that their dynasty had only one more year to run, and Mikan himself would be long gone from the Lakers' basketball scene just five years hence.

When the 1953 season began, the Lakers were a more balanced team with the addition of former Ohio State All-America forward Dick Schnittker and top draft pick Clyde Lovellette, who was seen as Mikan's eventual successor. Schnittker originally belonged to the Washington Capitols, but became the Lakers' property after that team folded in 1952. Before he could join the Lakers, he was called into the service and didn't become available until the playoffs in 1953. Lovellette, a 6-foot, 10-inch center

Below: *George Mikan (left), chasing a loose ball with Harry Gallatin of the New York Knicks, caused the rulemakers to install the 24-second clock because he so dominated a game with his deliberate style of play.*

Left: *George Mikan, jousting with teammate Vern Mikkelsen (19) and Ed Macauley of the Celtics (22) for the ball, is third among the Lakers' all-time rebounders with a 13.4 average.*

Left: *The Minneapolis Lakers' 1953 NBA championship team surrounds owner Max Winter (center): (from left) Pep Saul, Whitey Skoog, Dick Schnittker, Jim Pollard, Jim Holstein, Lew Hitch, George Mikan, Slater Martin, Vern Mikkelsen, Bob Harrison and Assistant Coach Dave MacMillan.*

who had led Kansas to the NCAA championship in 1952 and had played another year of AAU competition, fulfilled his role and gave Mikan more rest so that he was fresh for a vigorous round-robin playoff series that eventually wound up in a seven-game NBA championship series against the Syracuse Nats.

Above: *Don Sunderlage (with ball) was among a group of "new faces" that began to change the Lakers after their five-season NBA title run ended in 1954.*

The Lakers won the first game and would have at least gone into overtime in the nationally televised second game had not Paul Seymour's wild fling from just beyond the halfcourt line gone into the basket in the final seconds for a Syracuse victory. The Nats dodged elimination in the sixth game when they scored the winning basket in the final seconds again. But in the seventh game, Pollard scored 27 points to gain the Lakers an 87-80 victory and their sixth title in seven years.

Pro basketball's first dynasty came to an abrupt end when Mikan retired just before the start of training camp for the 1954-55 season, ostensibly to pursue his law career. But when Max Winter sought to form a group to obtain a pro football franchise, Mikan purchased his Lakers stock and was named vice president and general manager. Mikan's foray into the front office was short-lived, because the following season he joined the Lakers for the last 37 games after the team had slipped into last place in the division. It was one last bit of Mikan magic: he not only raised attendance

figures (the team hadn't drawn 2,000 for any home game until he returned, as it went through its first losing season ever), but he also secured a second place finish after a one-game playoff victory over the St. Louis Hawks, with whom the Lakers were tied at the end of the regular season. The two teams immediately played each other in the first round of the playoffs, and though the Lakers outscored St. Louis by 56 points in the best-of-three series, the Hawks won 2-1, getting a 116-115 final game win on Al Ferrari's basket with 54 seconds to play.

Mikan had already been named Basketball Player of the Half Century by the Associated Press; and in his half season encore, he seemed to have answered the questions of those who claimed he could never succeed with the NBA's new 24-second rule. He retired for good as a player after the 1956 playoffs. It had been a great run for him and the Lakers for most of the decade in which they ruled the pro game.

But pro basketball in the Twin Cities would never be the same with George Mikan out of the starting lineup.

Above: *Kansas All-America Clyde Lovellette had a huge pair of shoes to fill after George Mikan retired in 1955.*

4. Westward Ho

Lakers fans in the Twin Cities couldn't know it at the time – and they wouldn't have believed it if they did – but when the Mikan era ended in 1956, their team had only four more seasons left in Minneapolis. The problems weren't always on the court; this was demonstrated when the team twice made the Western Conference finals against St. Louis, and the year before it left for Los Angeles, it had reached the NBA finals before being dispatched in four games by pro basketball's newest dynasty, the Boston Celtics.

Los Angeles, which has enjoyed three decades of great Lakers teams, never has had to endure the problems which forced the Minneapolis Lakers to move west. The team's difficulties began after their title years with a front office in disarray, lack of funds, some implausible personnel decisions, and a bit of bad luck. The ownership and cash problems were a constant threat and in 1957, a civic fund drive netted $200,000 to help buy out owner Ben Berger.

Instead of helping the situation, it only made matters worse because 117 investors then owned the team, and a 15-member board, headed by lawyer and trucking owner Bob Short (who had no great personal wealth) ran the team. Short was not able to resolve the financial problems that beset the team. To make matters worse, having so many bosses created internal chaos, short-circuiting any plans that might have helped the Lakers to survive the rebuilding process after the old championship team broke up.

Johnny Kundla also was tired of the coaching pressures, and became general manager in 1957, naming Mikan to succeed him as coach. George quickly discovered that he had been caught in a period of transition, with veteran players leaving, and a variety of old and young players coming and going. The team had no continuity, and when Mikan won only nine of his first 39 games, Short fired him and Kundla became both coach and general manager.

Right: *Some 50 Minneapolis businessmen raised $150,000 to keep the Lakers from moving to Kansas City in 1957. The group's chairman, Francis Ryan, presents the check to outgoing owner Ben Berger.*

Left: *Whitey Skoog goes after Richie Regan of the Rochester Royals in 1956 game action.*

Below: *Dick Schnittker challenges Syracuse's Bill Kenville during the 1954 NBA finals.*

Of course, all of this might have been solved before the season had the Lakers and Celtics been able to consummate a deal in which Boston reportedly had agreed to send former Kentucky stars Cliff Hagan, Frank Ramsey and Lou Tsioropoulos – all unavailable until 1958 because of military service – plus a number one draft pick to the Lakers for Vern Mikkelsen. Some in the Lakers' front office pushed it, but others who still coveted Mikkelsen dissuaded Berger. Later, the pro-trade forces said their strategy was to gain the first pick in the draft, with which they wanted to draft Bill Russell, the great center for the two-time NCAA champion University of San Francisco Dons. Russell had indicated that he wanted to succeed his idol, Mikan, as the team's center. Those who tried to engineer the Mikkelsen trade claimed that his loss easily could have meant the four more losses that would have given Minneapolis the worst record in the NBA.

Instead, they missed by three to the Rochester Royals and tied with St. Louis for the second worst record. Compounding the bad luck, they lost the right to pick second on a tie-breaker (St. Louis had a 7-5 edge in head-to-head competition against the Lakers that year), though Russell did his part to help them by demanding a $25,000

Above: *George Mikan (right) wasn't as successful coaching the Lakers as he was playing for them, and was relieved by his former coach John Kundla (left), halfway through the 1958 season.*

Opposite top and bottom: *Elgin Baylor (22), one of the game's greatest all-around players, rejuvenated the team as a rookie in 1958, helping them to their final Western Division title in Minneapolis.*

per year contract, scaring off both Rochester and St. Louis. Teams thought only in terms of offense back then, and Russell's reputation was mostly as a defensive player. The price tag was too much for the Royals for what they considered a "limited" player (how little they really knew!), and they decided to pick guard Sihugo Green from Duquesne. St. Louis owner Ben Kerner also felt the same way, nor did he want to break up the NBA's only all-white team because he had serious reservations about Russell being accepted by his fans. That left the Lakers next in line – except that Boston spoiled their chances by sending Ed Macauley and Cliff Hagan to the Hawks for their first round pick, which became Russell.

Had Russell come to the Lakers, a tremendous new dynasty might have been born, particularly had they also gotten Hagan, Ramsey and Tsioropoulos. (Hagan led the Hawks to an NBA title and is in the Hall of Fame, while the two other players became key members on the Celtics' title teams of the late 1960s and early 1960s). Instead, the Lakers settled for Jim Paxson, who lasted just one season. Ironically, instead of the Lakers getting Russell, he "got" them during the 1960s when Boston consistently thwarted the Lakers' NBA title hopes.

Another major factor contributing to the team's demise was the lack of a large enough arena in the Twin Cities to hold big crowds and alleviate a cash crunch. So the team became a traveling roadshow – even in Minneapolis where, for example, it played home games in an armory; in the Minneapolis Auditorium; in St. Paul, at Hamline College; and on neutral courts in four different states. Matters were so bad in the team's final season in Minneapolis that

star Elgin Baylor missed a home game because he went to the wrong arena – in Minneapolis!

The Lakers had drafted Baylor from the University of Seattle in 1958, though he still had a year's eligibility remaining because he had transferred from the College of Idaho. In a desperate move to save his franchise, Bob Short drafted him anyway and after months of negotiations, convinced him to sign. "If he hadn't," Short said later, "I would have been out of business because the club would have been bankrupt."

Now a member of the Hall of Fame, Baylor was a one-man scoring machine, one of the greatest offensive players around the basket in the game's history. His signature was his habit of twitching his head in every direction when he handled the ball. When he swooped to the basket, his tremendous quickness got him around defenders for twisting, driving layups; his great athletic ability allowed him to outleap taller opponents and score countless rebound baskets.

Baylor had his greatest seasons playing for the Lakers in Los Angeles, when he teamed with guard Jerry West to give the Lakers the most feared one-two scoring punch in the NBA during the first half of the 1960s. But even before he got to Los Angeles, he had made his mark. He was so important to Minneapolis that when he went into the army for six months of duty in Texas, Short moved his pre-season training camp to San Antonio so Baylor could participate. Midway through his rookie season in 1959, he scored 55 points in a game, the third highest in NBA history, and a year later he set the record with 64 points against the Boston Celtics.

In his rookie season, Baylor helped the Lakers to the NBA championship series, where the Celtics swept to their 4-0 victory; and in his second season, he had the Lakers on the brink of a second straight title series, being solely responsible for three victories against St. Louis, only to miss in the Western Conference finals.

When that series ended in St. Louis, so did the Lakers' residency in Minneapolis. Short had been threatening to move the team throughout the season, and had played "home" games away from the Twin Cities, including two in Los Angeles at the new Sports Arena adjacent to the Los Angeles Coliseum, to test the interest of West Coast fans. The league had already given him permission to move, and had threatened to take over the franchise if any home game brought less than $6,500 in gate receipts.

Finally, on April 28, 1960, the move became official, and Short noted, "When you

are in trouble, you have the choice of selling, taking bankruptcy, or operating your way out." Short chose the third option, and the move was approved by all NBA teams except the New York Knicks, which some said had hoped to stymie the move and force Short sell them Baylor to help their financial position. Still, because teams objected to paying added travel expenses, the Lakers had to pay part of each opponent's travel expenses to the West Coast, and each visitor played two games before leaving because the Lakers were the only NBA team on the West Coast until the Warriors transferred from Philadelphia to San Francisco after the 1962 season.

Short wasn't the only one wanting to put pro basketball in Los Angeles, but the NBA turned aside bids for the Los Angeles territory by radio executive Len Corbosiero and Harlem Globetrotters owner Abe Saperstein. Both had some chits, Corbosiero because he had introduced the pros to L.A. with an exhibition game between the Philadelphia Warriors and St. Louis Hawks in 1959 (drawing over 12,000 fans); Saperstein because his teams had always brought big crowds into sparsely settled NBA arenas as part of doubleheader programs that helped

Above: *Coach John Kundla's final Western Division champions, from left: back row, Kundla, Rod Hundley, Dick Garmaker, Vern Mikkelsen, Ed Fleming, Jim Krebs, Alex Ellis, Steve Hamilton; front row, Bob Leonard, Elgin Baylor and Larry Foust.*

Right: *Rookie Jerry West, leaping to block a shot by Boston's Bob Cousy, was a new star during the Lakers' first season in Los Angeles.*

the league survive during its first decade and a half. However, he was always a difficult negotiator, and those whom he had offended never forgot when it came time to consider his application for an NBA franchise.

But moving didn't mean that problems disappeared. Because the Lakers had to share the Sports Arena with UCLA and Southern Cal, many of the playing dates had already been gobbled up. So, they once more played many "home" games at different sites in the Los Angeles area. One playoff game was held at the old Shrine Auditorium and had to be played on the stage, where 6-foot, 11-inch center Ray Felix, in pursuit of a loose ball, fell into the orchestra pit.

As a result, crowds of about 3,000 were commonplace for the first half of the season, and about 5,000 for games until the playoffs. It wasn't until the final playoff game of the season that nearly 15,000 jammed the Sports Arena. Short had to purchase his own radio time, and hired Chick Hearn to broadcast the games, adding still another legend to the Lakers' family.

He also added a third legend when the club picked West Virginia All-America guard Jerry West in the first round of the 1960 draft, after Oscar Robertson had been selected by Cincinnati. West, good-naturedly dubbed "the Hick from Cabin Creek" in reference to his uniquely-named hometown in West Virginia, vied with Robertson, a teammate that year on the powerful U.S. gold medal Olympic basketball team, for recognition as the NBA's best guard during his career. West was a smooth, decisive player who fit Hollywood's image like a glove, with movie-star looks and a personality that was a promoter's dream. Yet his good looks and smooth manner belied a toughness that reflected his background in West Virginia, which was just about as far as you could get from Hollywood. His toughness also was reflected in the way in which he spearheaded the powerful Lakers' offense where his shooting talent – particularly his jump shot – was a deadly weapon.

Fred Schaus, West's coach at West Virginia whom Short hired to coach the Lakers in Los Angeles, once observed, "If you sat down to build a 6-foot, 3-inch basketball player, you would come up with a Jerry West. He had everything – a fine shooting touch, speed, quickness, all the physical assets, including a tremendous dedication to the game."

West, who played all of his 14 seasons from 1961 through 1974 with the Lakers, was one of the NBA's greatest clutch players ever, someone who wanted the ball when a game was on the line – and most

often made the decisive shot. Though so often frustrated by the Celtics, he drove Celtics coach Red Auerbach to desperation at times in trying to defense him. "You really can't stop West," Auerbach said. "You tried a number of ways – play him close, loose, deny him the ball. Still, he always found a way to get his 25 or 30 points."

West had some spectacular scoring seasons, including a 31-point average in 1965, followed by a 40.6 playoff average – though the Lakers were beaten by the Celtics. The following year he had a career-high 31.4 point average. Though he was the epitome of smooth and stylish play, West was never loath to take the ball inside against bigger and stronger players, and he paid a tough,

Above: *Two of the Lakers' brightest stars during their early seasons in Los Angeles: Jerry West (44) and Elgin Baylor (22).*

physical price – such as eight broken noses – from running a gauntlet of flying elbows under the boards.

Right: *Jerry West was an All-America from the University of West Virginia who became the Lakers' all-time top scorer with 25, 192 points.*

Below: *Rudy LaRusso (with ball) was a solid power forward for the Lakers during the 1960s.*

His playmaking often was overlooked because of his great scoring ability, yet he ran the powerful Lakers' attack that included such fine offensive players as Elgin Baylor, Wilt Chamberlain and Gail Goodrich. He led the Lakers in assists every season he played, finishing his career with 6,238, seventh best in NBA history, and is topped in the team's history only by Magic Johnson.

Baylor and West, teammates for all but Jerry's final season, were a fearsome scoring combination. During his career West scored 25,192 points, sixth best in the league's history, and Baylor was right behind him as seventh with 23,149 points. Baylor is second in all-time scoring average with 27.4, just ahead of West, who had a 27 points per game mark.

West and Baylor were the team's glamor twins when the Lakers began their Los Angeles residency. But the Lakers also brought along a group of other talented players from the Twin Cities who helped to make them immediately competitive and acceptable to a brand new audience that was not big on basketball savvy but knew all about success.

That group included forward Rudy LaRusso, a 6-foot, 8-inch, 220-pound power forward; guards Rod Hundley, Bob Leonard and Frank Selvy; centers Ray Felix and Jim Krebs; and forward Tom Hawkins.

Left: *With plays like this one Frank Selvy made against the St. Louis Hawks, the Lakers soon were renowned for their "prime time" up-tempo game in Los Angeles.*

Left: *Ray Felix was one of eight Lakers who made the move from Minneapolis to Los Angeles.*

These players formed a curious blend. Rudy LaRusso was a Dartmouth graduate, but no one who played against him ever put down Ivy League basketball: he was a tough, relentless player who gave no ground to anyone. He always guarded the opposition's top scoring forward, and his battles against the Celtics' Tom Heinsohn were memorable. Heinsohn always claimed that LaRusso was the toughest of all the forwards he ever faced.

Rod Hundley, on the other hand, had acquired the nickname "Hot Rod" as the star at West Virginia (he had preceded West there), and had been a number one draft pick of the Royals before coming to the Lakers in a trade for Clyde Lovellette. Hundley was a magician of sorts with the ball, a showy player who appealed to Hollywood's instincts for flash and dash. However, his best days were at Minneapolis, and after three years he was gone from the Lakers, and later became a popular broadcaster with Chick Hearn.

Frank Selvy was quiet, and his greatest claim to fame was being the first player ever to score 100 points in a college basketball game, while playing for Furman University in 1954. He was a steady player, and though he played for several teams before coming to Minneapolis, he probably had his most productive seasons with the Lakers until he retired after the 1964 season. Bob Leonard, nicknamed "Slick" because of his great ballhandling ability and knowledge of the game, played four seasons in Minneapolis and just one in Los Angeles, where he was the team's third guard behind Hundley and West. He later became a very successful coach with the Indiana Pacers of the

American Basketball Association and in the NBA.

The rest of the front court – Jim Krebs, Ray Felix and Tom Hawkins – was solid but never spectacular. Krebs and Felix, and later Leroy Ellis, who came to the team in 1962, split the center play while Hawkins, who also spent three seasons with the Cincinnati Royals before finishing his career in Los Angeles, was the third forward. But they merely were the spear carriers for the lavish production in which West and Baylor were the stars – and pro basketball had a slam-bang birth on the West Coast.

The only thing that really spoiled their fun was a team from the East Coast – the Boston Celtics.

5. Always a Bridesmaid

For all but two seasons of the 1960s, the Lakers were West and Baylor . . . Baylor and West. No matter what happened, Jerry West and Elgin Baylor were involved. But even their talented efforts weren't enough, as six times during the decade the team lost in the NBA championship finals to the Boston Celtics.

But while the Lakers' life was as frustrating as any team ever experienced in the history of the NBA, there is no denying that those two players were singularly responsible for establishing the popularity of the team – and the sport – in Los Angeles. In their first season playing together, 1960-61, West and Baylor were a force, even though

coach Fred Schaus did not start West for much of his rookie season. This was all the more incredible in that Schaus well knew what Jerry could do, having coached him to All-America status during three varsity seasons at West Virginia. Baylor averaged 35 points a game that year, West 19, and Schaus quickly learned that he needed both of them in the lineup at the same time. The result: In their second season, 1961-62, the two of them had 70 of the 119 points the club averaged in each game.

"I should have been a starter," West later said of his rookie season. "I was better than any of our other guards. I knew it and Fred should have known it . . . and he should

Below: *Jerry West goes up against the Celtics' great center Bill Russell – just one of the duels of great players from both teams that fueled this great rivalry during the 1960s.*

have realized that you learn more playing than sitting on the bench."

West and Baylor not only played well together but they also were roommates and close friends; and in time, each even could anticipate the other's moves, making them more dangerous.

Still, Baylor was the acknowledged star. When he scored his 15,000th point, the game was stopped and he was presented with the ball, amidst some other glitzy L.A. hoopla. When West scored his 15,000th point, while still a teammate of Elgin's, the game went on as if it was just another basket. West didn't like it, but he blamed the club. It was just a tribute to Elgin's stature as player and leader.

"One ball was enough for us," West said later. "Schaus taught a free-wheeling game, with the ball going to the top scorers so all of us could contribute."

But Baylor was always the unquestioned leader. After the Lakers once decided to wear blue blazers on the road, Bill Russell of Boston couldn't help but tease him. "I see you had a meeting to decide the color of the blazers and your choice of blue won out," Russell said, punctuating his observation with a screeching laugh and a wink.

"That's right," Baylor replied. "We voted on it, and it passed 1-0."

Baylor's first season in Los Angeles was as spectacular as the previous two in the Twin Cities. He averaged nearly 35 points a game, second in the NBA behind Wilt Chamberlain, and he was fourth in rebounds behind the NBA's three best at that time – Chamberlain, Russell and St. Louis' Bob Pettit – with 1,447, a stunning number for a non-center.

In that 1961-62 second season, Baylor and West put up some spectacular scoring numbers that were the norm for most of the dozen seasons they played together. Baylor got a career-high 63 in three overtimes against the Warriors, and 61 in a playoff game against the Celtics. West set a scoring record for NBA guards with 63 (and he was strapped with a severe cold) against the New York Knicks while only 2,766 watched in the Sports Arena. He had a 50-point night against the Royals at the same venue, and when the two teams met in Morgantown, West Virginia, in a homecoming of sorts for West, Jerry tallied 46. Even the fans in the Twin Cities got a peek at what they were missing when the club returned for the first time (Short brought them back

Below: *Another great rivalry matched Elgin Baylor (with ball) against the Celtics' Bob Cousy – or whoever else the Celtics used to try and stop him.*

Above: *A tribute to Elgin Baylor's all-around greatness is the fact that he became the Lakers' third all-time highest scorer with 23,149 points, and also their number two rebounder with a 13.5 average per game.*

of those wins because of illness. So West chipped in with 38 points and 15 rebounds in a 126-116 victory. In the final game of the 1960-61 season, against the Cincinnati Royals and Oscar Robertson, the Lakers trailed by one point in the final seconds when West stole the ball, passed it to Baylor, got a return pass and drove around Robertson to score the winning basket – his 22nd point of the game – in a 123-122 victory. Baylor had 38.

Rudy LaRusso, the rookie from Dartmouth, also made a huge contribution to the Lakers that season as the strong forward, averaging nearly 15 points, and he was second in rebounds with 781. Rod Hundley and Frank Selvy also broke double figures in scoring. But what plagued the Lakers then – as it had since Mikan retired and as it would until the final season of the decade when they signed Chamberlain – was the lack of a good center. It was the prime reason why they always were bridesmaids at the Celtics' NBA championship weddings.

Still, they made an artistic splash, though not a financial one for Bob Short, who was an absentee owner back in Minneapolis. As noted earlier, the crowds that he had hoped to attract didn't appear immediately because the team was playing at several sites and the Angelenos, famous for their "prove it to me" attitude, didn't turn on to the team until the playoffs, when the Lakers defeated Detroit in six games, winning the deciding game in the Shrine Auditorium (the Sports Arena was booked for another event) 137-120, as Baylor scored 35 points and West got 25.

For the third year in a row, they played St. Louis for the Western Conference title, and shocked the favored Hawks 122-118 in the opening game in St. Louis, as Baylor erupted for 44 points. Returning to Los Angeles tied at 1-1, and playing on another "home" court at Los Angeles State, they shocked St. Louis again, 118-102. But what many believe was a watershed for this team's existence was a heart-stopping 118-117 loss to the Hawks in the next game, during which the score was tied 20 times. West hit 10 of 19 field goals for 33 points but the Hawks' Bob Pettit pulled down 18 rebounds and scored 40 points. The Lakers didn't die easily, though, as back in St. Louis they took a 3-2 lead when Baylor scored 47 points and added 20 rebounds, and West had 24 points in a 122-112 victory.

Los Angeles then knew that it had a great basketball team, and more than 14,000 turned out in the Sports Arena, where the Hawks tied the series in a 114-113 overtime victory, despite another great performance by Baylor – 32 points, 21 re-

each season for as long as he owned the club for a regular season game), and West tallied 47 points against the Pistons.

It didn't take the Minneapolis fans long to realize what the Los Angeles fans had already found out the previous season – that West and Baylor gave the Lakers their best one-two punch since the Mikan era. For example, in West's rookie season, the Lakers beat Chamberlain's Philadelphia Warriors just twice, and Baylor missed one

bounds before fouling out in overtime. His loss was the difference in the game. The Lakers then jumped to a 12-1 lead in the seventh game but, despite 39 points by Baylor and 29 by West, they eventually lost the game – and the series – 105-103, as Baylor's final shot with three seconds to play just missed tying the game.

West had to carry much of the scoring load in his second season (1961-62), after Baylor left for army duty during the Cuban Missile Crisis, and was available only for weekend games and the playoffs. Still, the Lakers rolled to their first division title since 1954, and then rolled Detroit out of the playoffs. In the NBA finals against the defending champion Celtics, the teams split the first two games. In game three, a sold-out Sports Arena crowd watched West intercept an inbounds pass from Bob Cousy

to Sam Jones with three seconds to play and the score tied, and throw in the winning shot as the buzzer sounded, for a 117-115 victory. In game five Baylor's 61 points broke a 2-2 series tie, and all the Lakers had to do was win one more game to take the title from Boston.

That was like moving a mountain – and it almost happened. In the seventh and deciding game, the score was tied 100-100 on two baskets by Frank Selvy in the final minute, and after the Lakers regained possession with five seconds left on the clock, they set up their final play. Either Baylor or West figured to take the last shot, but Schaus set up screens by LaRusso and Baylor so that either West or Selvy would be free for the shot. Selvy inbounded the ball to Rod Hundley, who immediately looked for West, only to see him guarded by K. C.

Left: *The Lakers' Rudy LaRusso (35) and Tom Heinsohn of the Celtics (15) had some memorable battles against each other.*

Opposite: *"Hot Rod" Hundley lived up to his nickname with the Lakers in both Minneapolis and Los Angeles, and later became one of the team's play-by-play announcers.*

Left: *Rudy LaRusso displays some of his great defensive skills by stuffing a shot by the Hawks' great forward Bob Pettit.*

Left: *Tom Hawkins had two tours with the Lakers, coming with them from Minneapolis to Los Angeles, and later returning to finish his career with them in the late 1960s.*

Jones. He then tossed it back to Selvy, who was open nine feet from the basket with two seconds to play. Knowing the final seconds were ticking off, Selvy rushed his jump shot – one he usually made with ease – and the ball hit the rim, skipped across the basket, struck the back rim and fell off into Russell's hands.

"It was a fairly tough shot," Selvy said later. "I was on the baseline so far that I couldn't bank it in, but I thought it was going to be good. I would trade all my points for that one basket."

That one shot became an integral part of the Celtics' legend - the part in which they seemed to lead charmed lives in key games – and they outscored the Lakers 10-7 in the overtime to win the title 110-107.

The Lakers-Celtics rivalry was also becoming legend, as the two met in such highly emotional games as the 1963 finals. Cousy, the Celtics' great playmaker, was playing his final series. The Lakers had added Dick Barnett, whose famous "fall back" jump shot – he actually fell backward after releasing the ball – was always punctuated by his cry of , "Fall back, baby!". And they had added a pair of 6-foot, 11-inch front

Above and right:
The rebounding load fell primarily on Elgin Baylor (above) until the Lakers swung a deal to acquire center Darrell Imhoff (right), who played four seasons with the Lakers during the late 1960s.

courtmen, Gene Wiley and LeRoy Ellis, in an attempt to counter the up-front strength of St. Louis, Cincinnati and Boston. Combined with the holdovers from the previous season, Los Angeles won another Western Division title. They ousted St. Louis in the conference finals, but fell behind the Celtics 2-0 in the title round – until Baylor hit 38 and West, who had missed 24 games that year with a bad knee, tallied 42. Next they staved off elimination with a 126-119 win at Boston Garden as the Baylor-West combo tallied 75 points, and forced the sixth game in Los Angeles.

With a record crowd of 15,521 at the Sports Arena, and a national television audience watching, Cousy drove the Celtics to a nine-point lead with 11 minutes to play when he injured his ankle. He limped to the bench and the Lakers, behind Baylor and West, cut their deficit to one point with 4:43 to play. The euphoria of the Lakers' fans was interrupted when they saw Cousy limp back on to the floor, with his ankle frozen and strapped. Again, he took over play, and punctuated that final appearance in Celtics green by throwing the ball toward the ceiling of the Sports Arena as the clock ticked off the final three seconds in a 112-109 Boston victory.

The Lakers became a team in transition in 1965, when Short sold the team to millionaire Canadian entrepreneur Jack Kent Cooke for five million dollars. When Cooke had problems with the Los Angeles Coliseum Commission over terms of his lease at the Sports Arena, he began building The Forum at a cost of $16.25 million, and would move his team into it for the 1968 season.

In efforts to overcome some bad luck and find their footing, the Lakers underwent change during the mid-1960s. Center Jim Krebs was killed in an auto accident before the 1965 season, the effects of which lingered for that season because, while not the most talented player, he was a worker and a good offensive performer. The team obtained center Darrell Imhoff to replace him, and gained more defensive power. The Lakers added offense with guard Walt Hazzard, who had led UCLA to the national collegiate championship, and a year later added his teammate Gail Goodrich, giving them more firepower in the back court, but no defensive improvement. Expansion took forwards Bob Boozer and Jim King; LaRusso and Ellis were traded; and they added veterans Mel Counts and Tom Hawkins, along with rookies Archie Clark and Jerry Chambers. "We lost more than we gained from all of that," West noted later.

In the meantime, Baylor had become a fragile player, having injured his right knee during the 1965 playoffs, and having

Left: *Rookie guard Gail Goodrich had helped UCLA to win national championships in 1964 and 1965 before coming to the Lakers, where he added more firepower to an already potent offense.*

to undergo surgery. Interestingly, West then put on an incredible playoff scoring splurge with consecutive games of 49, 52, 44, 48 and 42 points. "I wouldn't have done that if Elgin hadn't been out," he said. "I wouldn't have had to." It took its toll, and the Celtics then zipped through the 1965 NBA finals in five games.

Then there was the case of the retiring coach – in 1966 Auerbach was finishing his final season as the Celtics' head coach and the team had dedicated the season to giving him a fond farewell. The Lakers had edged St. Louis in seven games, and when they met the Celtics in the first game of the finals, they overcame an 18-point Boston lead, as West scored nine of his 41 points in an overtime period to win 133-129. But the Celtics ripped off wins in the next three games before the Lakers returned home and got 32 points from West, 28 from Gail Goodrich and 26 from LaRusso, in a 123-115 victory. The sixth game was at Boston Garden and the Celtics were determined to give Auerbach his final victory and world championship at home. They jumped to a 10-0 lead, led by 16 at the half and were ahead by 13 with four minutes to play as the capacity

Above: *Walt Hazzard of the Lakers tries to drive around K.C. Jones of the Celtics in a 1966 playoff game.*

Above right: *Tom Hawkins is stopped on a necktie foul by Boston's Larry Siegfried in a 1968 playoff encounter.*

crowd in Boston Garden went wild, not only anticipating another title, but waiting eagerly for Auerbach to light his final "victory cigar."

Russell stuffed home a basket for a 10-point Celtics lead with 30 seconds to play, and despite two quick baskets by West that cut the lead to six points with 16 seconds left, Auerbach felt the game was won and lit up. This also was a signal for the thousands in the Garden to move toward the court for the post-game celebration. At that moment, the Celtics lost control of the game and the Lakers almost pulled off a miracle finish.

The crowd around the edge of the court became so unruly that the Celtics were forced to call timeout just to inbound the ball. Auerbach and his players also were overrun on the bench and had problems even seeing the game. Suddenly, the Celtics came unglued and turned the ball over four times in just 12 seconds. In a flash, the Lakers closed the gap to just two points on Ellis's basket with four seconds to play. That was a close as they came, but Auerbach admitted later, "I never came closer to disaster."

In 1967 the Lakers hired Bill van Breda Kolff, an ex-Marine and former NBA player who had been a successful coach at Princeton, where he helped Bill Bradley attain All-America honors. Schaus became general manager, and the Lakers, with their run-and-gun offense, faced a new life. Van Breda Kolff was a demanding coach who was not the least bit awed by his great players. When Baylor messed up a potential winning shot at the end of a game, he hounded him all the way to the locker room. "For 10 years you've been an All-Pro and you make a mistake a grade school kid wouldn't make," he told him.

"It was a different existence," West admitted. "Fred Schaus never gave us orders, he made suggestions. Van Breda Kolff wasn't the least bit awed by us. He brought new things and he put it to us, and wanted no backtalk. He challenged us to please him, and he made all of us pick up the pace."

Van Breda Kolff also was a much more emotional coach than Schaus, baiting his team and the officials with equal vigor. He was tagged with 60 technical fouls during his two years as head coach, and was kicked out of a 1968 playoff game against Boston, leaving Goodrich to finish as coach. "I don't think he had a flattering word to say about us all season," West remembered. "He always told us what we had to do to win every game in a basketball sense, and then he expected us to do it. That was a square deal as far as I was concerned."

It was enough for 52 victories in 1967-68, as the team made a great run in the second half of the season to finish second behind St. Louis. The Lakers beat Chicago in the first round of the playoffs, with West holding the

Bulls' Flynn Robinson to just four points in the deciding game after he had scored 41 in the previous game. They swept the San Francisco Warriors, but against the supposedly declining Celtics, then coached by Russell (who also played center) were swept out of another title shot in six games.

They had tied the series at two games apiece, and in the fifth game in Boston came from 19 points down to force an overtime on West's layup with 12 seconds to play. With a minute to play in the overtime, John Havlicek sank a 20-foot jumper for the winning points, and the Celtics capped their title domination in game six in Los Angeles with a 124-109 victory.

Van Breda Kolff knew precisely what was needed to halt the frustration against a team that had the game's best center.

He needed someone just as good.

Left: *Boston's great center Bill Russell, seen here batting Archie Clark's drive away from the basket, always proved to be the biggest impediment to the Lakers when they tried to unseat the Celtics. Russell led Boston past the Lakers six times in NBA title playoffs.*

6. Wilt…and a Title At Last

You didn't have to be a basketball genius in Los Angeles to figure out why the Lakers had come upon one frustrating year after another in their pursuit of an NBA championship. Plain and simple, they needed a dominating center.

And they got one who many still believe was the greatest in the game's history – Wilt Chamberlain.

From a perspective of more than two decades, Chamberlain's role in professional basketball can still light fires of controversy, even in Los Angeles where he has remained a legendary force. But for five years back in the late 1960s and early 1970s, there was no denying the importance of his role, nor the fact that he produced what

Lakers fans had sought since the team had arrived from Minnesota in 1960: a world championship.

Of course, it didn't come without some pain and suffering, and a lot of that was supplied by Chamberlain himself, who made those around him pay their own personal price for his services.

But there never has been any question that he was the most formidable player in the game's history – at least, when he put his mind to the task. At 7-feet, 1-inch (and many who faced him declared he was a few inches taller than that) and 275 pounds, Wilt was indeed a basketball superman. He was a superb athlete, who could run, jump and move with the sleekest NBA player. No

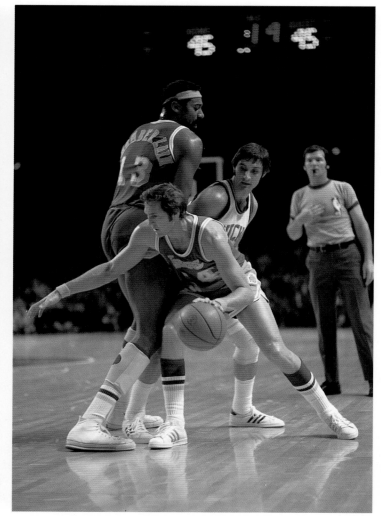

one in the league ever was stronger, and no one player could ever dominate a game so completely.

He had come to the Lakers from the Philadelphia 76ers prior to the 1968-69 season in a trade for Darrell Imhoff, Archie Clark, Jerry Chambers (who was then in military service, and never played for the 76ers) and a bundle of cash. He had already played for the Warriors in Philadelphia and San Francisco, and the 76ers, and though he had won seven scoring titles and five rebound crowns, had once scored 100 points in a game, and had led the 76ers to the NBA title in 1967, his ability to win "the big one" was still questioned.

In that sense, the marriage of Chamberlain to the Lakers was an ideal match. Still, Chamberlain really delivered what owner Jack Kent Cooke sought when he paid him an estimated three million dollars for five years: the Lakers won four Western Conference championships – and the long-sought NBA title – during Chamberlain's five Lakers seasons.

What is best remembered, though, was his consistent inability to get along with his coaches, first Bill van Breda Kolff, who was gone after a run-in with Chamberlain during the final minutes of the Lakers'

seventh-game loss to Boston in the 1969 NBA championship finals; then Joe Mullaney, who also lost a championship final during two years with Wilt; and Bill Sharman, a tough, determined man who brought championship credentials from his playing days with the Boston Celtics, and as a coach in both the American Basketball League and the American Basketball Association.

Sharman's most significant achievement, though, was convincing Chamberlain that his role in the team's overall scheme was vital to winning a championship. When Wilt finally listened, the Lakers got their long-sought title. It wasn't easy, though, because even in Chamberlain's first season with the Lakers, the atmosphere was strained. For the first time since moving to Los Angeles, the Lakers were not a happy team. Van Breda Kolff wanted Chamberlain to move around more

Left: *Elgin Baylor led the Lakers in scoring average six times and in rebounding average eight times during his career.*

Above: *When Wilt Chamberlain and coach Bill Sharman took over the team's fortunes, Baylor's productive seasons were cut down by injuries.*

on offense to open up the middle, to be able to set picks and to take the opposition's big men away from the basket. When he did his job, Chamberlain's presence in the middle enabled the Lakers to gamble more on defense – something they never did before – and took some of the rebounding load off Elgin Baylor. Jerry West also was more effective with his ball-hawking; and on offense, besides his scoring and passing, he got his team second and third shots off the offensive boards.

There were many other instances, though, when Chamberlain preferred to camp in a low post position, and actually blocked off the middle for the devastating drives by West, Baylor and Gail Goodrich that were so key in the Lakers' offense. When he played this way, he didn't get the ball out well to his wingmen flying down the court on a fast break, nor was he available to set screens for the outside shooters. When the ball came in to him, he played his own one-on-one game and the offensive came to a virtual stop. And of course, he was a poor foul shooter.

Even with all of this, the team's 55 victories were the most ever to that time, though West, who missed 21 games, still led the team in scoring with his 26-point average. Chamberlain chipped in with 20 points and an NBA-leading 20 rebounds. One night he scored 66 points against Phoenix, and took 42 rebounds against the Celtics.

But it was the Celtics who would really puncture the balloon. The Lakers rolled through the playoffs against San Francisco and Atlanta, holding the Hawks under 100

Above and right:
*Jerry West (**above**) and Gail Goodrich (**right**) were two of the highest scoring guards in Lakers history. They averaged nearly 43 points a game during the seven seasons they played together.*

Left: *Wilt Chamberlain and Kareem Abdul-Jabbar first played against each other when Wilt played for Los Angeles, but within a few years, Jabbar would take over his job.*

points three times. Then in the 1969 NBA finals they played Boston, a team they had beaten four of six times, including a 35-point victory in the final regular season encounter. Yet the old nightmare recurred.

The Lakers, with West scoring 53 points, still had to hold on to win the opening game, 120-118. In game two, West scored 41, Baylor had 32 and the Lakers took a 2-0 lead, 118-112. But in Boston, the Celtics evened the series, the second L.A. loss coming on Sam Jones's shot that hit the front rim and bounced in at the buzzer. Chamberlain

played one of his great games back in The Forum in a 117-104 victory, with West scoring 39 points, 28 in the second half, including 10 in a row. But Boston set up the showdown seventh game with a 99-90 win as West was hampered by a pulled hamstring and Chamberlain had vision problems after getting a finger in the eye in the previous game.

After the Lakers had gone up 2-0 in the series, Cooke had ordered several cases of victory champagne, and had transported the bubbly to Boston on both trips. Now,

Above: *Harold (Happy) Hairston shouldered much of the rebounding and scoring load after Elgin Baylor retired, and teamed in the front court with fellow New York City collegian Jim McMillian.*

Above right: *The NBA's two preeminent centers during the 1970s were Wilt Chamberlain and Kareem Abdul-Jabbar. Jabbar, who led the Milwaukee Bucks to the NBA title in 1971, became the Lakers' center in 1975, two years after Wilt retired.*

still confident that his team would win a title in the seventh game, he had the champagne iced down again. He also stashed thousands of victory balloons in The Forum's rafters, ready to spill down on the crowd the moment the game was won. The USC Marching Band was in the hallways of the arena, ready to come marching onto the court playing their school's famous fight song.

But in his final Celtics game, player-coach Bill Russell put Chamberlain back on his heels, and the Celtics controlled the entire game, gradually building up their lead to 103-94 with five and a half minutes to play. Then Chamberlain twisted his knee coming down with a rebound and took himself out of the game in favor of ex-Celtic Mel Counts. Counts picked up his teammates and with three minutes to play, the Lakers were within a point. But Don Nelson – an ex-Laker – put up a desperation shot that struck the basket, bounced several feet into the air, and fell through for a three-point lead.

At that point, Chamberlain motioned to van Breda Kolff that he wanted to return to the game, but the coach waved him off

because the team had rallied so well without him. And Chamberlain never moved from his seat for the rest of the game, finally won by Boston, 108-106. The balloons stayed in the rafters, the champagne remained corked, and the van Breda Kolff–Chamberlain feud is forever remembered for its culmination that night – the seventh time in 10 seasons that the Celtics had beaten the Lakers for the NBA championship.

Van Breda Kolff, who realized that he and Chamberlain could never co-exist and resigned two weeks after the playoffs, was replaced by Joe Mullaney, who had been a fine coach at Providence College for 15 years. He was a much quieter personality, and he calmed the stormy waters, allowing the Lakers to use their offensive talents as always, but stressing a team concept of defense that took some getting used to. He also teamed rookie Dick Garrett at guard with West, and put Keith Erickson at the other forward.

All of this worked well, and the team became more vibrant and exciting to watch. The season's first big matchup occurred early in the season when the Lakers and

Milwaukee Bucks – with the NBA's top draft pick, former UCLA All-America center Lew Alcindor – met for the first time. It was the classic battle of the new kid on the block versus the old gun fighter, and Old Wilt showed he was the boss by thoroughly outplaying the rookie in their first meeting.

That was just part of a seemingly smooth course to another Western Conference title when, on November 7, the unthinkable happened: Chamberlain's knee crumpled, and the once-indestructible Wilt hobbled to the sidelines, not to appear again until there were three games to play in the sea-son. Mullaney made three moves. First, he put Rick Roberson at center and the young-ster responded magnificently. Next, he sent Bill Hewitt to Detroit for Happy Hairston, and he added more power to the Lakers' front court. And last, but more importantly, he put most of the offensive burden on West, who responded by leading the NBA with a 31.2 scoring average.

When Chamberlain returned to the lineup to ready himself for the playoffs, the Lakers were a second-place team behind the Atlanta Hawks. But they swept through the 1970 conference playoffs, then faced the Eastern Conference's new power,

Below: *Wilt Chamberlain altered his game to stress rebounding and playmaking with the Lakers, yet he led the NBA in field goal percentage in three of his five years at L.A.*

Right: *Jerry West (44) thrived with Wilt Chamberlain (13) as his teammate because of Wilt's ability to block out and open lanes for his offense. West averaged nearly 26 points a game playing with him.*

the New York Knicks. The teams split the first two games in New York, and then a pair of overtime games in Los Angeles, the first fashioned on West's nearly court-length heave at the final gun to gain the extra period. In the fifth game at Madison Square Garden, the Lakers had a 13-point halftime lead, and Chamberlain already had 18 points and 12 rebounds. But in the second half, the Knicks scrambled all over the court, raising havoc with Los Angeles' smooth game. The New Yorkers held Wilt to just four points and seven rebounds in the last two quarters, shocking the Lakers, 107-100.

The Knicks, though, were handicapped by the absence of All-Pro center Willis Reed, whose hip injury kept him out of the sixth game. The Lakers gained an easy 135-113 victory, during which the unchallenged Chamberlain scored 45 points and collected 27 rebounds.

Playing in New York requires a certain amount of flair, and Reed provided it in the seventh game when, after being declared out of action, he suddenly limped onto the floor just before the tap-off. The crowd's reaction almost blew off Madison Square Garden's round roof and it was just the boost the Knicks needed, as they proceeded to blow away the Lakers, 113-99, for the NBA title.

The 1970-71 season began on a rocky note when Elgin Baylor played only two games, then sat out the season with bad knees. The Lakers also were hampered by some inconsistent play, and Coach Mullaney soon became frustrated when his easy-going manner of "suggesting" didn't work. He then determined that he would "demand" that his team follow his instructions – a complete change of coaching personality, guaranteed to doom any coach – and anyone who fell out of line sat on the bench. As luck had it, Chamberlain was the first to feel his lash when Mullaney benched him as a starter for a Christmas night game against the Celtics. Wilt had gone back to his native Philadelphia before the holidays during a three-day respite, and botched travel plans caused him to miss a mandatory practice session. That was cause enough in Mullaney's mind to enforce his new edict, and the team suddenly lurched into confusion.

Matters became worse later in the year, when West injured his knee and was lost for the rest of the season and for the playoffs, that included elimination by the eventual NBA champion Milwaukee Bucks – then led by Kareem Abdul-Jabbar.

Cooke was an ever-impatient owner, and he ordered Schaus to find another coach when Mullaney's regime seemed to fall apart. Into the picture for the 1971-72 season came Bill Sharman, who had just coached the Utah Stars to the American Basketball Association championship after the team had moved from Los Angeles. Sharman had been a collegiate star at Southern California before joining the Boston Celtics in the early 1950s. Along with assistant coach K. C. Jones, a former Celtics teammate, Sharman took some of the discipline and intensity they had learned under Red Auerbach in Boston, and integrated it into the Lakers' psyche. Gone were the informal practices under van Breda Kolff and Mullaney; in their place were nose-to-the-grindstone sessions in which Sharman scrapped any notions that the Lakers could win with a halfcourt offense. Instead, he believed an older team like the Lakers conserved more energy scoring quick baskets than battling for nearly 24 seconds to get a hard one.

The new coach had already sold Chamberlain on his philosophy by telling him not to worry about offense but to conserve his energy to play defense. Wilt, to his credit, was in the spirit of the team from the first day of training camp, and had one of the best all-around seasons of his career.

Sharman also brought other innovations. He was not a great "game" coach who made brilliant decisions on the bench, so he meticulously prepared his team for all eventualities against each opponent, lessening the "chance" factors. He also used film study, something only football teams did back then; and instituted shoot-arounds on the day of the game. It was all new to this team, which had little quality depth and could not sustain any long-term injuries to front line players. But no one dared to challenge Sharman, and everything paid off when the Lakers won their division with a record 69 victories.

The season didn't begin on such a high note, though, because Baylor retired after nine games rather than accept part-time status. He was replaced by Jim McMillian from Columbia, and the move really solidified the team, showing the other players that past achievements were second to present production. Still, the Lakers got off to a so-so 6-3 record, and endured back-to-back losses before beating Baltimore 110-106 on November 5, 1971. Then they caught fire and rolled off an NBA (and pro sports) record 33 consecutive victories. The streak was finally ended against Jabbar and the Milwaukee Bucks, 120-104, on January 9, 1972. The Lakers' final victory in the 33-game winning streak had been a 134-90 pasting of the Atlanta Hawks.

"I don't recall anyone getting excited until we hit 14 or 15 in a row," Sharman said later. "When we got to 18, we began feeling a little pressure but it was a good feeling. I never had to give them any pep talks because they had such great pride in what they were achieving."

Left: *Chamberlain and West led the Lakers on a 33-game winning spree from November 5, 1971 to January 9, 1972.*

These pages: *Jim McMillian* (**above**), *Happy Hairston* (**above right**) *and Wilt Chamberlain* (**opposite**) *combined for more than 47 points a game. Chamberlain and Hairston led the team's rebounders, and took the Lakers to the 1972 NBA title in five games over the New York Knicks.*

The 20th win, in overtime over Phoenix, tied the NBA record, and they set the new mark by beating Atlanta. The 33 consecutive victories included 16 on the road, and wins over 15 teams. This propelled the Lakers to 14 NBA season records, including most victories (69); most games scoring 100 or more points (81); and most home wins (36). The team also benefitted from great scoring seasons by Goodrich (25.9 point average) and West (25.8), plus a 14.8 mark by Chamberlain, who also led the NBA with over 19 rebounds per game.

They maintained the same pace in the playoffs, losing only two games in beating Chicago and the defending NBA champion Bucks, before a rematch with the New York Knicks. There were few moments of drama this time, though the Knicks shocked the Lakers with a 114-92 pasting in the opening game at The Forum with an awesome shooting display. The Lakers bounced back with a 114-92 victory in the second game as Wilt scored 23 points and grabbed 24 rebounds. He stayed hot in the opener at Madison Square Garden with 26 points in a 107-96 victory, to gain a 2-1 series lead.

Now desperate, the Knicks battled Los Angeles to the very end of the fourth game,

which was tied 99-99 with 11 second to play. West, in the midst of a scoring slump, swooshed a 20-footer from behind a massive pick set by Chamberlain. But Walt Frazier's basket just before the final buzzer sent the game into overtime.

There was no panic in this Lakers team. Instead, they settled down and McMillian sank three straight jump shots as Los Angeles danced off the court with a 116-111 victory.

It was only fitting that the championship be won in front of the long-suffering L.A. fans, and on May 7, 1972, they got their title with a 114-110 victory. Despite a chipped bone in his wrist, Chamberlain scored 24 points and grabbed 29 rebounds, while Goodrich had 25 points and West scored 23. "This is the most pleasant memory of my basketball career," Chamberlain said afterward. Several million Lakers fans in Los Angeles totally agreed.

It was the end of an era, as Wilt Chamberlain – one of basketball's most dominating players of all time – would retire after the 1972-73 season. As surely as he left his mark in Los Angeles, Chamberlain left his mark on the NBA record books as well.

7. A Little Bit of Magic

Below: *Magic Johnson added great playmaking when he joined the Lakers in 1979. The result: An NBA title in Magic's first season.*

Below right: *Johnson's skills were just what was needed to make Kareem Abdul-Jabbar more effective.*

It is often said that a bit of magic is what makes the glitter of Hollywood all so believable. And it was a bit of magic that made the Los Angeles Lakers of the 1980s so unbelievable.

The Lakers' "magic" belonged to a former Michigan State All-America player named Earvin Johnson, who had the very appropriate nickname, "Magic." While Wilt Chamberlain will always be remembered for helping the Los Angeles Lakers win their first NBA championship, he never will be held in the same esteem as Earvin "Magic" Johnson, who helped the Lakers become the NBA's dynasty of the 1980s.

Magic Johnson, a man made for the rollicking good times that seem to flow through Los Angeles and its entertainment community, came to the Lakers as a 20-year-old, replete with marvelous basketball skills, a personality that could brighten a hall as large as The Forum, and an ear-splitting grin that told everyone he was having a good time being one of the greatest players in the game's history. As only a sophomore, he had led his Spartans team to the 1979 NCAA national championship; he then gave up his two remaining years of eligibility after owner Jerry Buss flashed a mega-million dollar contract at him.

When Magic Johnson joined the Lakers in the fall of 1979, he also became a teammate of Kareem Abdul-Jabbar, Chamber-

lain's successor as the NBA's top center. Jabbar had come to the team in a 1975 trade with the Milwaukee Bucks that cost the Lakers guard Brian Winters, center Elmore Smith, and two high draft picks and prized rookies David Meyers of UCLA and Junior Bridgeman from the University of Louisville. Then-owner Jack Kent Cooke announced to all that with Jabbar as the center, his team would resume the brief championship run that Chamberlain had begun before his retirement in 1973, injuries, trades and other misfortunes had left Lakers fans wondering what had happened since that heady 1972 season.

Cooke tried to solve this sudden plunge with his bold move in getting Jabbar who, as Lew Alcindor in the late 1960s, had started UCLA's record-setting NCAA championship run. He also had led Milwaukee to the 1971 NBA title in just his second season, yet he was careful to put his own role into a clear perspective when he arrived in Los Angeles.

"One man can't do it by himself," he said. "Milwaukee won only one championship with me, and we had Oscar Robertson, a great playmaker and shooter, on that team. I know I'm going to help the Lakers, but it may not mean a championship."

He was absolutely correct, because the Lakers won only one division title during his next four seasons, and made it to the conference finals just once, losing to eventual NBA champion Portland in four games in 1977. Even with Bill Sharman and Jerry West as head coaches, the Lakers couldn't reincarnate the good times because the team lacked the continuity that would have come from a balanced combination of scorers, rebounders and playmakers.

Without question, Jabbar was the NBA's dominant player during the first half of his Lakers tenure, and he was a dominating force in the middle of the Lakers' offense and defense. He was the "go-to" scorer until Magic Johnson arrived and began to spread the ball to more shooters; and despite Jabbar's dislike for the physical pounding he had to take under the basket, his intimidating 7-foot, 2-inch size helped him become the NBA's all-time leading shot blocker (since such stats were begun in the 1973-74 season).

There was no denying his ability to score – he is the NBA's all-time champion – and his famed "sky hook" shot was impossible to stop because he actually was shooting the

Above left: *Kareem Abdul-Jabbar came to the Lakers in a blockbuster trade in 1976 and played for Jerry West.*

Above: *The expected championships did not arrive with Kareem, until West (seen above in 1977) moved to general manager and put together a well-balanced team.*

ball downward into the basket. He used it from any spot around the basket to help him lead the Lakers in scoring for all but his final three seasons, even in those when he played with such offensive stars as Magic Johnson, James Worthy, Jamaal Wilkes, Norm Nixon and Bob McAdoo.

Despite his extraordinary height, Jabbar was not the same rebounding force throughout his career that either Bill Russell or Wilt Chamberlain were, winning the NBA rebounding title just once, though he finished in the top five in each of his first eight seasons (Chamberlain was first in three of those years). For most of his Lakers seasons, Kareem really disliked the increased violence under the boards, and punctuated his displeasure by flattening Milwaukee's rookie center, Kent Benson, in the first game of the 1978 season after getting an elbow in the gut. The punch cost him a $5,000 fine and 21 days on the dis-

Below and opposite: Kermit Washington (below) added rebounding muscle to the Lakers in the mid-1970s, but the real force was Kareem Abdul-Jabbar (opposite), who led them in scoring during his first 11 seasons and was the top rebounder in eight of his first 10 seasons.

abled list because he broke his hand. Later that same season, while ostensibly acting as a peacemaker in a fight between his own teammate, Kermit Washington, and Houston's Kevin Kunnert, he wound up as part of a brawl in which $10,000 in fines were levied.

Jabbar was constantly compared to Russell and Chamberlain. Like both of them, he also was as complex a person as he was a talented performer. Russell, though, shut off everything when he played, and Chamberlain often turned his energies to playing whatever game fit his fancy at the moment. During his early seasons with the Lakers, Jabbar found it difficult to become part of the rough-and-tumble of the playing court, although he still managed to play on a par with the best.

Magic Johnson's appearance was the tonic that Jabbar needed to relax and enjoy his own talents and those of his teammates. Johnson was young, energetic and viewed life in an entirely different spectrum than did the moody Jabbar; and Magic's outlook became contagious. He was totally unawed by his older teammates and Jabbar's notoriety, and he made things happen. While Jabbar was the nominal leader and the team's captain, whose words carried great weight because they came at such rare intervals, the chemistry of the Lakers really improved with the addition of Magic Johnson. Hence, he became the team's day-by-day leader.

At 6-feet, 9-inches tall, Magic not only became the NBA's biggest point guard – though he had been a forward at Michigan State – but also one of its best, with the playmaking skills usually attributed to small, fast players. The team reacted well to his ability to move the ball around and keep everyone involved in the scoring, meaning that players weren't grousing about "not seeing the ball." That is one reason why he is the NBA's all-time assists leader. He also was a tremendous offensive force. He was lightning quick, and could flash into small openings near the basket for scooping layups. He developed a good outside game so that if a defense collapsed toward the middle and Jabbar, he popped in some longer range shots from outside.

NBA observers always declared that it was difficult to tell whether he was improving, because he always seemed to do just what he pleased. Whether he scored six points or 40 points, he could dominate a game to the same degree. He had the great ability to read the flow of a game and fit it into his personal game plan.

In 1979, when Jerry Buss became the Lakers' third owner, the acquisition of Magic Johnson became his first big coup.

Right: *Adrian Dantley averaged nearly 19 points a game during two seasons with the Lakers in the late 1970s.*

Far right: *Magic Johnson added both scoring and floor direction when he came to the Lakers in 1979.*

Jack Kent Cooke, who had been through a costly divorce settlement and wanted to devote his time to his 86 percent ownership of the Washington Redskins, sold the Lakers to Buss – as well as the Los Angeles Kings of the NHL, The Forum and his 13,000-acre ranch in the Sierra foothills – for $67.5 million, the biggest sale of sports property to that time.

Buss was the quintessential California success story. He left his Wyoming home at age 16 to hustle pool in Los Angeles, and yet still graduated from high school with honors. Before his 24th birthday, he had earned a doctorate in physical chemistry from the University of Southern California, and went to work for an aircraft company – but not for long, because he pooled his savings with a friend, Frank Mariani, to buy an apartment house. One building led to another and soon, the Buss-Mariani duo was running a $350 million real estate enterprise.

It wasn't long before he looked for more prestigious fields to conquer. He became a founder of the World Team Tennis League, owning the Los Angeles Strings, and signed Chris Evert and Ilie Nastase. He also bankrolled some other WTT franchises to keep the ill-fated venture alive at an eventual cost of about $2 million. When the league died, he sought out Cooke, and made the deal for the Lakers and his others sports properties.

Buss had a great feel for high-profile business, and he wasn't afraid to spend to make it all happen. He signed Magic Johnson to a 25-year contract for over $25 million, then reworked the deal so that Magic was paid $2.5 million for each of nine years, and then upped his annual wages to more than $3 million. He made courtside seats available at The Forum for several hundred dollars per game, knowing that some of Hollywood's most recognizable stars would fill them and add their own lustre to each event.

Buss got what he paid for when it came to Magic Johnson. Even as a rookie, he had the ability to raise the Lakers above problems, as he did when difficulties almost cost the team a second NBA championship in 1980. The Lakers started the 1979-80 season with Jack McKinney as head coach, but after nine games, he was severely injured in a bicycle accident and replaced by his assistant, Paul Westhead. Jerry Buss declared at the time that Westhead was only an interim head coach, and that McKinney could have his job back once he had recovered. But the team responded well to Westhead's coaching and to Johnson's talent. As McKinney recovered, so did the Lakers, and they were rolling toward the NBA finals when McKinney returned.

Buss deferred the coaching decision because he rightly did not wish to upset the chemistry that had been so successful to that point. Buss still maintained that McKinney would have the job at a future

ever, because the severity of Jabbar's sprain meant that he was definitely out of game six in Philadelphia. The best the Lakers hoped for was that the rest might allow him to get ready for a seventh and deciding game at the Friendly Forum. That was whistling in the dark, and the Lakers knew it.

But they really didn't know Magic Johnson very well.

The team was down to just seven regular players for game six because power forward Spencer Haywood had been suspended for disciplinary reasons after game two. Magic was the only one who could play center, meaning the Lakers were woefully undermanned to battle a Philadelphia front line of 7-foot, 1-inch Caldwell Jones and 6-foot, 11-inch Darryl Dawkins, as well as Bobby Jones, Julius Erving and Steve Mix.

"I looked at Caldwell and realized he's seven-one and he's got arms that make him

Left and below: The Lakers' UCLA Connection was never stronger than when Jamaal Wilkes (left) and Kareem Abdul-Jabbar (below) were teammates and helped the Lakers to NBA titles in 1980 and 1982.

date, but when the Lakers made it into the finals against the Philadelphia 76ers, he suddenly reversed himself and named Westhead as the full-time head coach. It was a decision the team really didn't need at that time, because it severely shook their concentration.

But this is where Magic's own particular "magic" was invaluable, as he not only was able to take the players' minds off that trauma, but he also would assume the awesome responsibility of replacing Jabbar in the crucial stages of a championship playoff, and make his teammates believe he could do the job.

The Lakers had taken a 3-2 lead in the series in Los Angeles, but Jabbar sprained his ankle so severely that he could not make the trip to Philadelphia for the sixth game against the 76ers. His loss was considered devastating because in the first four games he had averaged over 33 points and 13 rebounds. In the fifth game, the Lakers were holding a narrow lead when Jabbar twisted his ankle badly with 3:58 to play in the third quarter. When he hobbled back onto the court early in the fourth quarter, the crowd in The Forum went wild, and he proceeded to put on one of the most gutsy displays of his 20-year career. Seemingly unable to move, he drove himself to score 14 of his team's 27 fourth quarter points, finishing the game with 40, and helping L.A. to a 108-103 victory and their 3-2 lead.

The thrill of that victory was muted, how-

Opposite: *Jamaal Wilkes averaged more than 18 points a game during his eight seasons with the Lakers.*

Left: *Kareem Abdul-Jabbar was largely responsible for the Lakers' dominance of the NBA during the 1980s, and led them to five world titles.*

around nine-five," Magic said. "So I just decided to jump up and down at the opening tap-off, and then work on the rest of my game."

That included playing as a center, forward and guard for 47 of the 48 minutes of the game, during which he scored 42 points, hitting seven of 12 shots from the field in the first half alone, and 14 of 14 from the foul line. He had 15 rebounds, seven assists, three steals and a blocked shot.

More importantly, he seemed to elevate the play of those around him. Jamaal Wilkes played what many consider the best game of his career, with 37 points and 10 rebounds. Jim Chones had 11 points and 10 rebounds, and held the more ballyhooed Dawkins to just 14 points and four rebounds. Mark Landsberger, never considered a star, had 10 rebounds in 19 minutes, all of which helped to negate Philadelphia's alleged front-court advantage. Without the slower Jabbar, Magic Johnson ran the offense his way, and the Lakers ran the

76ers into the floor, while also outrebounding them 52-36.

The teams were tied 60-60 at the half, but the Lakers stormed to a 93-83 lead at the end of three quarters. Then the 76ers put on a big rush to close to within two points, at 97-95, with seven minutes to play. But the Lakers blew it open in the final five minutes, rushing from a 103-101 lead to an eight-point lead (111-103) with 2:22 to go, and finally to a 123-107 final.

"Everybody thought we were going to roll over," Johnson said afterward. "Everybody thought we were going to fade. We didn't. We fooled y'all."

While all of that set in motion the Era of Magic during the Reign of Kareem, what made it even more incredible was that, just three years after leading his high school team to the Michigan state title and a year after he had led his college team to the NCAA title, this 20-year-old rookie led his pro team to the NBA championship.

Talk about Magic!

8. The Magnificent Eighties

The Los Angeles Lakers clearly were the team of the 1980s.

General Manager Bill Sharman built the Lakers dynasty of the 1980s the same way in which he had seen Red Auerbach construct one while Sharman played for the Celtics. While the Celtics had Bill Russell as a dominating center, Sharman had Kareem Abdul-Jabbar. Whereas the Celtics had Bob Cousy to run the offense with his great passing, savvy and leadership, Sharman had Magic Johnson. While the Celtics had good shooters in Tom Heinsohn and guard Sam Jones, Sharman had James Worthy and Byron Scott. While Auerbach always had a power forward to defend against the opposition's top front-court scorer in Jim Loscutoff and Tom Sanders, Sharman had Michael Cooper. When Boston went to its bench for its "sixth man" and other role players, Sharman filled the Lakers' bench with such players as Kurt Rambis, Bob McAdoo, Mitch Kupchak, Mike McGee, Jamaal Wilkes, and A. C. Green.

He also knew what kind of coach was needed to make all of these parts work, and after Paul Westhead was released early in the 1982 season, he selected his assistant, Pat Riley, who had played for the Lakers after graduating from Kentucky, then had been part of its broadcasting team, before returning as an assistant coach in the late 1970s. As is the case with any fine coach, Riley was able to knit together the diverse personalities and supreme egos on his team, and make them play the style of basketball that he believed to be most effective. Like Bill van Breda Kolff before him, he was not awed by personal reputations, but unlike van Breda Kolff, he was not volcanic, and he ran a much tighter program.

While the media and public fawned over Kareem Abdul-Jabbar and Magic Johnson, they were just two players on the team to Coach Riley. He never referred to Johnson by his nickname, but always by his given name, Earvin, if only to show that he was above all the hype that surrounded this great young player. No one was immune

Right: *A familiar post-season scene in the Lakers' locker room during the 1980s: Accepting the NBA championship trophy.*

to his quick Irish temper, yet Riley was always willing to admit his own fallibility if he believed that it had cost his team a victory.

Every season he wrote letters to each player and laid down a theme for that year. For example, before they won the 1987 title, Riley had asked each for a career-best season; the following year, when they became the first team since the 1968-69 Celtics to repeat as NBA champs, he asked them to "begin a quest for greatness."

Riley and Sharman, and later Jerry West, when he became general manager, also enjoyed solid support from owner Jerry Buss, who provided everything the team needed. In return, he wanted nothing less than a champion. And during the 1980s, this is what he got:

The Lakers won five NBA titles, in 1980 and 1982 over the Philadelphia 76ers; in 1985 and 1987 over the Boston Celtics; and in 1988, over the Detroit Pistons. What he missed were NBA championships against the 76ers in 1983; against the Celtics in 1984; and against the Pistons in 1989. Thus, his team was in eight finals in 10 years — four in a row from 1982 to 1986 — and became the first team since the 1968-69 Celtics to win back-to-back NBA titles when they beat Boston and Detroit in 1987 and 1988.

They had started the run with that incredible victory over the 76ers in 1980, and the two teams met again in 1982. But for the second time, the Lakers beat Philadelphia in six games, clinching the title with a 114-104 victory in Philadelphia. This time, Jabbar and Johnson were on the court together and thoroughly frustrated a great 76ers team, featuring Julius "Dr. J" Erving, that was vying for the same dynasty status as the Lakers. The 76ers finally exacted their revenge the following season — sparked by the famed "Fo-Fo-Fo" prediction of center Moses Malone that his team would not lose a game in its three playoff rounds (they lost one in the conference finals to Milwaukee) — and zapped the Lakers in four straight games. The 76ers at this time were a great example of exactly how difficult it was to construct any dynasty because from 1977 through 1985 — nine seasons — they lost either in the Eastern Conference or NBA finals six of the seven times they made it that far. The seventh was their long-sought NBA title over the Lakers.

While the Sixers were struggling to find their championship niche, the Celtics, sparked by Larry Bird, Kevin McHale, center Robert Parish and guards Danny Ainge and Dennis Johnson, plus their usual deep bench, had returned from late-1970s oblivion. With this talented cast

they became the Lakers' biggest impediment, during the middle six years of the 1980s, to being called "team of the decade," because both clearly were the NBA's two best teams during this time. While the Lakers had won the NBA championship in 1980, the Celtics won it in 1981; while the Lakers won it in 1982, the Celtics took the title in 1984; while L.A. beat Boston for the crown in 1985, the Celtics won it against Houston in 1986 after the Lakers had lost to the Rockets in the Western Conference finals. The Lakers then came back to beat Boston for the crown in 1987.

Actually, the first championship meeting between the two, in 1984, came two years later than many NBA observers had predicted, because both teams compiled the NBA's best records in 1982. Pro basketball's newest personal rivalry featured Magic Johnson and Larry Bird. The rivalry had begun during the 1979 NCAA playoffs, when Magic's Michigan State Spartans had defeated Bird's Indiana State team for the collegiate title, and both players then entered the NBA as rookies. The rivalry even rubbed off on the fans, and this was evident in the closing minutes of the 76ers' clinching seventh-game victory at Boston Garden in the 1982 Eastern Conference finals. The Celtics fans, knowing their team would lose, began chanting at the Philly

Above: *Coach Pat Riley and Magic Johnson made the Lakers run during the 1980s — Riley with his coaching acumen and Johnson, who so capably directed his schemes.*

Above: *At 6-feet, 9-inches, Magic Johnson broke the mold of the small NBA point guard and became the NBA's all-time assists leader in 1991. He led the team in assists for nine straight seasons and averaged more than 11 per game during his career.*

players, "Beat L.A.! Beat L.A.!."

The right to be called "best" clearly drove this rivalry to a different level, and it showed when the two met in the finals in 1984 for the first time since 1969. The Lakers easily handled Boston in the opening game at Boston Garden, 115-109, and had all but sealed a 2-0 series advantage in the second game when a lazy inbounds pass from Johnson was intercepted by Gerald Henderson and turned into a tie-making basket that sent the game into overtime. The Celtics went on to win 124-121, but Magic redeemed himself in the third game with a record 21 assists as the Lakers won easily 137-104. But Boston tied the series 2-2 by winning the second overtime game of the series, 129-125, then took the lead 3-2, with a 121-103 victory back in non-air-conditioned Boston Garden, where the temperature registered over 100 degrees and totally zapped the Lakers. Los Angeles tied the series at The Forum in the sixth game, but the old Celtics jinx caught them for the third time in a seventh game as Boston won 111-103.

Though Johnson set a playoff assists record with 95, and averaged 18 points a game, he made crucial errors in key games – including seven turnovers in game seven – and came out a distant second to Bird in their individual battle.

This two-team war for supremacy continued in 1985, when both again posted the best records in the NBA, and then swept through the preliminary playoff rounds. Los Angeles had lost only two games, Boston just three, when the series opened with a roar – for Boston – at Boston Garden as the Celtics blew away the Lakers 148-114.

The frustration levels of Riley and Buss were already at the bursting point because of their team's inability to beat Boston, and this seemed to demolish any hopes they had of ending the Celtics' domination. But the Lakers were a much tougher team – mirroring their coach – than anyone had envisioned and they battled back with two straight wins for a 2-1 series lead. They beat the Celtics at their own physical game, matching them bang-for-bang and body-for-body. "Our fast break began with good, tough defense," forward Kurt Rambis said, "and that forces other teams out of their offense."

Jabbar helped to revive his team. He had 15 assists, and one of his famed sky hooks made him the NBA's all-time playoff scoring leader as the Lakers won those two games, 109-102 and 136-111, the latter an almost reverse carbon copy of the Celtics' first game blowout.

Boston tied the series 2-2 in the second game at The Forum on Dennis Johnson's basket with two seconds to play in a 107-105 victory. Riley found a way to stifle McHale midway through the fifth game after he had scored 16 points by switching Jabbar to guard him, and he made just three baskets the rest of the game as the Lakers took a 3-2 series lead with a 120-111 victory. Kurt Rambis, who did a fine job guarding Celtics center Robert Parish after Jabbar went to McHale, triggered the decisive 14-3 Lakers run after Worthy had blocked one of McHale's shots. The ball seemed headed out of bounds but Rambis dove after it, swatted it back into play while trampling some spectators, and the Lakers scored on that inspired play.

The Lakers finally delivered some long-awaited redemption to their fans – and they did it on the Celtics' hallowed parquet floor where so many hobgoblins of the past had devoured their title hopes and where Boston had never lost an NBA final. The Lakers' solid 111-100 victory brought them their third NBA title of the decade. Jabbar, chosen the series MVP, again led the way, scoring 18 of his 29 points in the second half. Worthy scored 28 points and not only led the Lakers' blistering fast break but also was an effective scorer from the perimeter. Michael Cooper's defense forced Bird into a very ordinary 12-for-29 shooting night.

Riley said later that the Lakers "had to win" in 1985 because they had lost in 1984 to a team that they felt was not as strong, and as a result of that defeat, his team had been mocked and humiliated.

"There comes a time when you have to plant your feet firmly, take a stand and kick some butt," Riley said after the win. "That's what we did. They can never mock us, or humiliate us, or disrespect us, which is what they did last year."

The so-called Celtics jinx was exorcised for good, and the Lakers began to make an undisputed claim as the "team of the decade" two years later when they beat Boston again for the title. The Celtics, who had beaten Houston in 1986 for the NBA crown, were hoping to become the first team since their ancestors of 1968-69 to repeat as champion.

Instead, they faced a Lakers team at its peak, after Riley, smarting from a 4-1 series thrashing by Houston in the 1986 Western Conference finals, reworked his fast break and watched his team, not even picked to win the conference title, race to the NBA's best record at 65-17. In so doing, Riley replaced Kurt Rambis at forward with young A. C. Green, and benefitted from an MVP contribution from Magic Johnson, who assumed more of the scoring burden and allowed Jabbar more rest, making him fresher for the playoffs.

To their talent the Lakers added a dash of luck, when they backed off a trade for Worthy at the last moment, and then in February, needing someone to balance their team, traded for 6-foot, 10-inch Mychal Thompson. The Celtics also were interested in Thompson but had no room, under the NBA salary cap, to get him. They paid in a different way, as Thompson helped to neutralize Boston's high-powered inside offense that featured Kevin McHale and Robert Parish.

Actually, the series was a battle of which inside game was best. Against the Celtics, who relied on a halfcourt offense, the Lakers' fierce fast break unleashed an offense that averaged 126 points in their three home games. In the opener, a 126-113

Below: *Pat Riley retired from the Lakers after the 1990 season and worked as a network television commentator – a job he once did for the Lakers – before signing a five-year contract as head coach of the New York Knicks.*

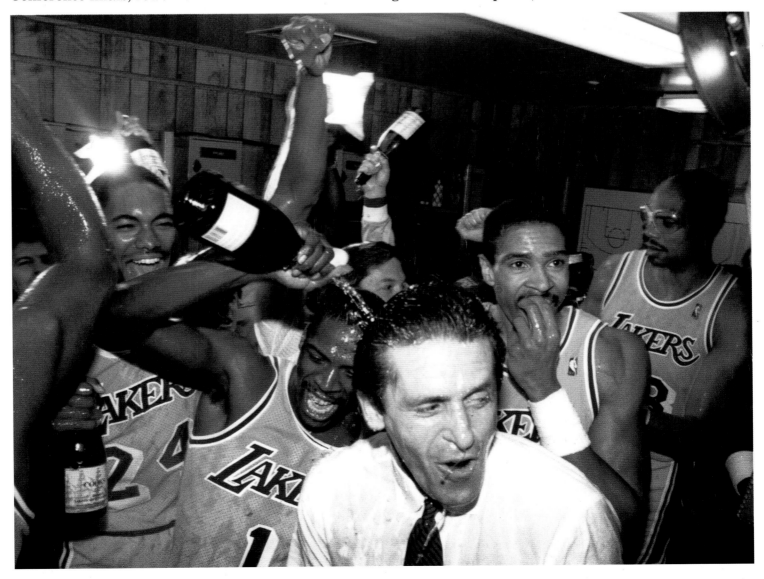

Right and far right: *Michael Cooper* **(right)** *and A.C. Green* **(far right)** *brought some long-range shooting skills and tough defense to the Lakers. Cooper always got the opposition's top scoring forward during his eight seasons with the team.*

blowout at The Forum, the Lakers scored 36 of their 55 baskets inside as Worthy (who was awesome in the three games in Los Angeles and all but disappeared in the three at Boston), scored 33 points and added 10 assists. The second game was an even bigger blowout, 141-122, as L.A. rolled to a 19-point halftime lead, 76-56, and had five players scoring 20 or more points against one of the NBA's best defensive teams.

The Celtics, with a 96-3 won-lost record at Boston Garden over two years, won the third game, but in game four the Lakers really won their title. They did it with a combination of tenacious defense, allowing Boston only Bird's three-point basket in the final three and a half minutes, and more than a bit of good fortune. The Celtics led by 16 points with five minutes left in the third quarter, but the Lakers crawled back into the game as their defense shut down the Celtics' inside offense and forced them to take bad shots from the outside. L.A. finally went ahead, 104-103, with less than four minutes to play, but Bird's three-pointer gave Boston a 106-104 lead.

Jabbar sank one of two fouls to close the gap to a point, but his missed second shot set up the most startling play of the series. The rebound bounced to the jumping McHale. Parish reached over and grabbed for it as Thompson shoved McHale out of the way (a "legal" shove, he said later) and the ball caromed off Kevin's hands and out of bounds with seven seconds to play.

Riley called time out and set up a play to

get the ball to Worthy driving to the basket. But when Magic got the ball inbounds, he couldn't find him and ignored Cooper who had come over. As McHale switched to cover him, he swooped to his right, across the key, and put a Jabbar-type sky hook that swished through with two seconds to play, for the winning points in a 107-106 victory.

Though trailing 3-1, the Celtics were not dead, and their inside game throttled the Lakers 123-108 in the fifth game, and did the same during the first half of the sixth game back at The Forum, as L.A. trailed 56-51 at the half. Thompson had replaced Jabbar after he picked up his fourth foul early in the third quarter, and the defensive pressure, as well as team quickness, instantly changed the Lakers. Thompson kept McHale from his favorite spot near the basket, and the Celtics missed five straight baskets before Worthy delivered the game's turn-around play. He knocked away a pass intended for McHale, dove on the floor to keep the ball from going out of bounds and then batted it to Magic Johnson, who sprinted downcourt for an easy basket to start a 10-0 run that gave the Lakers a 61-56 lead. They added an 8-2 burst for a nine-point lead en route to a 30-12 third quarter that sealed the win and the organization's 10th NBA title — their fifth in Los Angeles.

"I think we wore them down and they just couldn't keep up with us," said Magic, who scored 22 points and had 19 assists. "Our

This page: *James Worthy* (far left), *Mychal Thompson* (left) *and Kareem Abdul-Jabbar* (below) *were key players in the Lakers' defeat of the Celtics in the 1987 NBA finals. A trade for Thompson strengthened the team's front court, while Worthy's scoring broke open the clinching game.*

defense led to a rebound, and that led to the break. We forced them out, they only got one shot each trip down the court but never the shot they wanted."

Riley didn't waste much time after the game guaranteeing that the Lakers would win the NBA title the following season ("He must have sipped too much champagne," Magic Johnson said when he heard of Riley's boast). But there was method to his assumed madness, because he used the guarantee as a goal for the entire 1988 season. It was never easy; Jabbar's game had declined, and late in the year injuries to both Magic Johnson and Michael Cooper cut the team's efficiency, though they led the NBA with 62 victories.

It wasn't easy in the playoffs either, because the Lakers wound up playing three straight seven-game series as Utah and Dallas carried them to seven games in the Western Conference competition, and the Detroit Pistons dragged them to the final seconds of the seventh game of the NBA finals before they won the title. Detroit, young and very aggressive with their "bad boy" image fostered by center Bill Laimbeer and forward Ricky Mahorn, had eliminated the Celtics in the Eastern Conference finals, and used their rough-and-tumble style to take sleek teams like the Lakers out of their game.

It almost worked as Los Angeles, trailing 3-2, was just one game from elimination when they returned from Detroit to The Forum. The Lakers had never won a title

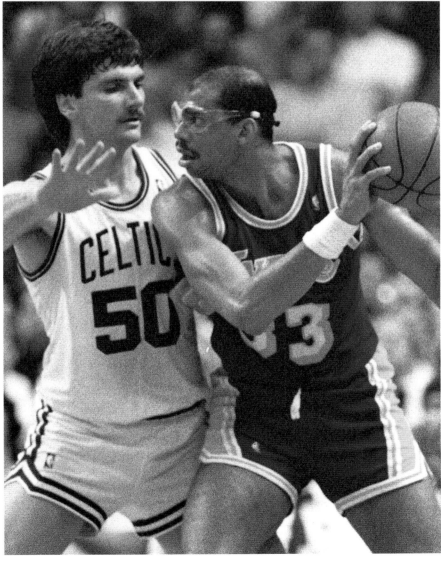

was no hesitation to go to Jabbar at that moment with the game – and a title – on the line. "Kareem is the best in those situations, whether he makes the shot or gets fouled," Magic said afterward.

Jabbar calmly sank two free throws that gave the Lakers their eventual 103-102 victory, thought they had to shut down one last Detroit surge with some good defense to preserve the win.

In the seventh game, despite the fact that Detroit controlled play for the first half, Worthy took over and brought the Lakers

Above: *The classic matchup of the 1980s: Magic Johnson vs. the Celtics' Larry Bird.*

when they trailed that deep into the finals, and it took some last-minute heroics for them to escape with a 103-102 victory and stave off elimination in the sixth game. Johnson, with his 22 points and 19 assists, and Worthy, with 25 points in the first three quarters, had kept the Lakers in the game. But after the Pistons' Isiah Thomas had scored his 43rd point and Joe Dumars sank two free throws, the Lakers trailed 102-99 with a minute to play. Byron Scott hit a jumper to close within a point, and the Lakers then dug into their well of experience and pride to close down Detroit on two subsequent offensive sets. Thomas missed an 18-foot jump shot with 26 seconds to play, and Worthy grabbed the rebound. Riley called time out, and set up two options: a pick-and-roll play between Johnson and Worthy, or the ball going to Jabbar inside. Detroit defensed the first and Jabbar was fouled by Laimbeer when he tried his sky hook.

Though he was not shooting well, there

their title. He scored 36 points, added 16 rebounds and 10 assists, and led a 36-21 third-quarter surge that eliminated the Pistons' 52-47 halftime advantage. At one point the Lakers led by 15 points, but Detroit battled back, and late in the game they trailed by just two points before the Lakers were able to hold on for a 108-105 victory. The Lakers had become the first team in two decades to win consecutive NBA titles!

The Lakers' greatest era in Los Angeles ended with that victory, and although they made it to the NBA finals in 1989 for the third straight year and seventh time in the decade, the inevitable pendulum that marks the time of every champion had swung away. Jabbar really was a part-time player (Mychal Thompson logged more minutes and points at center during the season); and with Magic Johnson and Byron Scott hobbled, the Lakers were eliminated in four straight by the Pistons.

Yet, it had been a grand run for a star-studded team in the purest Hollywood tradition, and Los Angeles loved every moment with their team of the decade!

Below: *Kareem Abdul-Jabbar, the best scoring center in NBA history, was the third link in the tradition of great Lakers' centers, following George Mikan and Wilt Chamberlain.*

9. New Faces of the Nineties

"The anchor has been lifted," Lakers coach Pat Riley announced dramatically when he convened his team for his final training camp in the fall of 1989.

The trade winds and the palm trees of Hawaii made the scene as serene as any travel agent ever envisioned, but for the Lakers, it was the beginning of a new era without Kareem Abdul-Jabbar, which meant that for the first time since 1976 – and for only the second time since Wilt Chamberlain came to LA in 1969 – the team had no dominating center.

That didn't bother Riley, who was beginning his final season as the team's head coach before heading for a network analyst's job (and ultimately the head coaching job of the New York Knicks), because he and the Lakers knew that during the pre-

vious two years with Jabbar in the lineup, the team was limited offensively. With him gone, the Lakers of 1990 were still favored to win an NBA title but unlike Lakers teams of the past that grew white-hot at times and ripped off winning streaks in bunches, this team had problems putting teams away. Its longest winning streak was nine games.

Yet, the one constant was Magic Johnson who, along with James Worthy, picked up the team's scoring load. The Lakers became his team and reflected his enthusiasm and joy for the game, something that had disappeared during the last two years of Jabbar's career.

On the court, Jabbar was replaced by Mychal Thompson, a better low post defensive player, and finally by their top draft pick, 21-year old Yugoslavian Vlade Divac. Divac, a 7-foot, 1-inch, 245-pound center, became the team's best shot blocker and seemed to rejuvenate the team with his vigorous play (he averaged about nine points and six rebounds during 20 minutes of play each game). As a result, the Lakers became more versatile offensively and stronger defensively.

They won 63 games, most in the Western Conference for the ninth straight season, six more than the previous season, and the third best in the team's history. In the playoffs they rolled past Houston in four games, and then were shocked by the Phoenix Suns who swept them out in just five games.

That was the first of two shock waves to sweep Los Angeles. The second came a short time later when Riley resigned for his network job. He was replaced by Mike Dunleavy, who had moved around the NBA for 11 seasons as a player, four of them with Milwaukee and coach Don Nelson for whom he also coached until the Lakers summoned him.

Dunleavy took much of Nelson's workaday approach to the game and the Lakers adopted a different, more deliberate style of play. This took some getting used to, and the team won just two of its first seven games before breaking out with some ves-

Below: *The Lakers' Magic Johnson goes for the lay-up over the Bulls' Scotty Pippen during action in the 1991 NBA finals. Johnson's sudden retirement in November 1991 after testing HIV positive stunned the basketball world.*

Left: *The Chicago Bulls' defense shut down L.A.'s offense during the 1991 NBA finals. Here Magic Johnson tries to pass the ball against defenders Michael Jordan and Horace Grant.*

tiges of their famed "Showtime" offense, winning 32 of their next 38 games, including 16 in a row at mid-season. Their 35-11 record was identical to the same point in the previous season, which they finished leading the league in victories. The 1991 team found a plus in free agent Sam Perkins and Divac became the full-time center, while Worthy quietly became the team's offensive leader.

All this wasn't quite enough, though, because the Portland Trail Blazers, who won 19 of their first 20 games, dethroned the Lakers as division champ for the first time since 1981. But the Lakers stunned the Blazers – and everyone else in the NBA – by ousting them in six games in the conference finals to play for their first NBA crown in the 1990s.

The finals weren't a happy experience, because the Chicago Bulls, led by Michael Jordan – the series was tabbed as the Michael vs. Magic show – dispatched them in five games after Los Angeles won the first game of the series on Perkins's three-point field goal with six seconds to play. But

the Bulls won the next four games, including three in a row (and one of those in overtime after LA had the lead with just three seconds to play) at the Fabulous Forum. Injuries to Worthy and Byron Scott sapped some of LA's offense, and the Bulls, led by Jordan and Scotty Pippen, clamped a ferocious defense underneath the basket, taking away the heart of the Lakers offense; eliminated Magic Johnson's passing lanes (he had fewer assists in the series than Jordan); and reduced LA to an outside jump-shooting team, the last option in their offensive schemes that was further hampered with the lightning-quick Bulls charging at the shooters and sticking hands in their faces as they tried to get off the shots. The result: the Lakers shot less than 50 percent for the entire series.

There were some who claimed the 1991 run was the beginning of another great decade for the Lakers, while others said it was an unexpected bonus from the giddy 1980s. Either way, it was Lakers basketball the way it will always be played – championship style to the very end.

Lakers Team Records

YEAR-BY-YEAR LAKERS STANDINGS

Year	Won	Lost	Pct.	Div. Fin.	Coach	Playoff Record	Playoff Finish
1947-48	43	17	.717	1	John Kundla	8-2	NBL Title
1948-49	45	15	.750	1	John Kundla	8-2	BAA Title
1949-50	51	17	.750	1(t)	John Kundla	10-2	NBA Title
1950-51	44	24	.647	1	John Kundla	3-4	Div. Finals
1951-52	40	26	.606	2	John Kundla	9-4	NBA Title
1952-53	48	22	.686	1	John Kundla	9-3	NBA Title
1953-54	46	26	.639	1	John Kundla	9-4	NBA Title
1954-55	40	32	.556	2	John Kundla	3-4	Div. Finals
1955-56	33	39	.458	2	John Kundla	1-2	1st Round
1956-57	34	38	.472	2	John Kundla	2-3	Div. Semis
1957-58	19	53	.264	4	George Mikan / John Kundla		DNQ
1958-59	33	39	.458	2	John Kundla	6-7	Div. Title
1959-60	25	50	.333	3	John Castellani / Jim Pollard	5-4	Div. Finals
1960-61*	36	43	.456	2	Fred Schaus	6-6	Div. Finals
1961-62	54	26	.675	1	Fred Schaus	7-6	Div. Title
1962-63	53	27	.663	1	Fred Schaus	6-7	Div. Title
1963-64	42	38	.525	3	Fred Schaus	2-3	Div. Semis
1964-65	49	31	.613	1	Fred Schaus	5-6	Div. Title
1965-66	45	35	.563	1	Fred Schaus	7-7	Div. Title
1966-67	36	45	.444	3	Fred Schaus	0-3	1st Round
1967-68	52	30	.634	2	Bill V.B.. Kolff	10-5	Div. Title
1968-69	55	27	.671	1	Bill V.B. Kolff	11-7	Div. Title
1969-70	46	36	.561	2	Joe Mullaney	11-7	Div. Title
1970-71	48	34	.585	1	Joe Mullaney	5-7	Conf. Semis
1971-72	69	13	.841	1	Bill Sharman	12-3	NBA Title
1972-73	60	22	.732	1	Bill Sharman	9-8	Conf. Title
1973-74	47	35	.573	1	Bill Sharman	1-4	1st Round
1974-75	30	52	.366	5	Bill Sharman		DNQ
1975-76	40	42	.488	4	Bill Sharman		DNQ
1976-77	53	29	.646	1	Jerry West	4-7	Conf. Semis
1977-78	45	37	.549	4	Jerry West	1-2	1st Round
1978-79	47	35	.573	3	Jerry West	3-5	1st Round
1979-80	60	22	.732	1	Jack McKinney / Paul Westhead	12-4	NBA Title
1980-81	54	28	.659	2	Paul Westhead	1-2	1st Round
1981-82	57	25	.695	1	Paul Westhead / Pat Riley	12-2	NBA Title
1982-83	58	24	.707	1	Pat Riley	8-7	Conf. Title
1983-84	54	28	.659	1	Pat Riley	14-7	Conf. Title
1984-85	62	20	.756	1	Pat Riley	15-4	NBA Title
1985-86	62	20	.756	1	Pat Riley	8-6	Conf. Semis
1986-87	65	17	.793	1	Pat Riley	15-3	NBA Title
1987-88	62	20	.756	1	Pat Riley	15-9	NBA Title
1988-89	57	25	.695	1	Pat Riley	11-4	Conf. Title
1989-90	63	19	.774	1	Pat Riley	4-5	Conf. Semis
1990-91	58	24	.707	2	Mike Dunleavy	12-7	Conf. Title

(t) Tie   *Began play in Los Angeles

Opposite: *Will the team of the 1980s become the team of the 1990s?*

ALL-TIME LAKERS CAREER LEADERS

GAMES PLAYED

Player	Years	No.
Kareem Abdul-Jabbar	1977-90	1093
Jerry West	1961-74	932
Earvin Johnson	1979-91	874
Michael Cooper	1978-90	873
Elgin Baylor	1959-72	846

REBOUNDS

Player	Years	No.
Elgin Baylor	1959-72	11,463
Kareem Abdul-Jabbar	1977-90	10,279
Earvin Johnson	1979-91	6,378
Vern Mikkelsen	1949-59	5,940
Rudy LaRusso	1959-67	5,571

POINTS

Player	Years	No.
Jerry West	1961-74	25,192
Kareem Abdul-Jabbar	1977-90	24,176
Elgin Baylor	1959-72	23,149
Earvin Johnson	1979-91	17,241
James Worthy	1982-91	13,211

ASSISTS

Player	Years	No.
Earvin Johnson	1979-91	9,920
Jerry West	1961-74	6,238
Norm Nixon	1977-83	3,846
Michael Cooper	1978-90	3,666
Elgin Baylor	1959-72	3,650

Index